National
Survey
of
State Laws

National Survey of State Laws

8th Edition by Richard A. Leiter

William S. Hein & Co., Inc.
Getzville, NY 2019

Publisher's Cataloging-in-Publication Data

Names: Leiter, Richard A., editor.

Title: National survey of state laws.

Description: 8th edition / by Richard A. Leiter. -- | Getzville, NY : William S. Hein & Co., Inc., 2019. | Revises the 7th edition (Getzville, New York : William S. Hein & Co., 2015). | Includes bibliographical references. | Contents: Business and consumer laws -- Criminal laws -- Education laws -- Employment laws -- Family laws -- General civil laws -- Real estate laws -- Tax laws -- Appendix.

Identifiers: ISBN: 978-0-8377-4104-8 | LCCN: 2019932585

Subjects: LCSH: Law--United States--States. | Commercial law--United States--States. | Consumer protection--Law and legislation--United States--States. | Criminal law--United States--States. | Educational law and legislation--United States--States. | Labor laws and legislation--United States--States. | Domestic relations--United States--States. | Civil law--United States--States. | Real property--United States--States. | Taxation--Law and legislation--United States--States.

Classification: LCC: KF386 .N38 2019 | DDC: 349.73--dc23

This volume is printed on acid-free paper by William S. Hein & Co., Inc.

DEDICATION

To Ian, Sammy, Little Sammy and
Emily Hope: Welcome to the family!

CONTENTS

PREFACE

National Survey of State Laws provides an overall view of some of the most-asked about and controversial legal topics in the United States. Presented in chart format, this reference allows users to make basic state-by-state comparisons of current state laws. The subjects featured fall into eight general legal categories:

Business and Consumer Laws
Criminal Laws
Education Laws
Employment Laws
Family Laws
General Civil Laws
Real Estate Laws
Tax Laws

The types of topics covered range from Abortion to the Right to Die, Gun Control to Prayer in Public Schools, Personal Income Tax to Right to Work, and Lemon Laws to Leases and Rental Agreements.

The information presented is culled from laws on the books as of December 1, 2018. However, the book has been revised continuously over the last two years and so while the most recent revisions were done by December 1, some chapters were revised at different points throughout this year.

Arrangement

National Survey of State Laws is divided by legal category into eight sections. Within each section each topic is arranged alphabetically and is presented in its own subsection, which begins with a general overview followed by a table that briefly summarizes each state's and the District of Columbia's statutes on particular aspects of law.

The salient points of each law appear at the top of each column. Beneath, brief statements provide the core points of the state statute. References to each state's statute or code section covering that law are also presented, enabling users who are interested in reading the original text to find it in the state's code of law. The appendix comprises a list of **Statutory Compilations Used in This Book** and provides the abbreviations and full names of each state code.

Acknowledgements

Since Hein took over publication of the book from Gale/Cengage in 2014 I've been grateful for Hein's patience as I've worked with Dan Rosati, Chris Czopp and Sheila Jarrett. The three of them have been extremely patient with me and my wife, Wendy, as we've updated the 7th edition to become the 8th edition. The patience is appreciated as our family has had quite a year: a marriage, two new grandchildren, two household moves and a new knee, not to mention me having to work for a living; and working this year involved one intense personnel matter, one happy resignation for greener pastures and hiring two new staff members, reorganizing a department, strategic planning and rethinking our collection development plan. (It's been quite busy.)

I need to also single out Wendy Leiter for special recognition. Since Hein became our publisher, she became the primary comprehensive copy editor and fact checker. She's a perfectionist without peer who, even though she was supposed to simply key in the updated information, was not content to key in anything that she didn't know was correct and ended up looking up every code section in the book! She deserves co-author credit.

The story about how the seventh edition came to be was a long time coming. It's a long story that involves the history of its genesis as a new title for Gale Research, its first foray into the law market, back when the company was independent and known as one of the premier publishers of reference works for libraries. After the first edition was published in 1993, the book went on to receive many flattering reviews and quickly became a standard reference work as attested to by its inclusion in Wilson Library Quarterly's list of "Field Tested Reference Resources" (in January 1995) and its recognition by the New York Public Library as one of the year's Outstanding Reference Resources in March 1994. The book's success surprised everyone, and the first edition ended up selling out of two printings, nearly unheard of, even for Gale.

Gale Research was subsequently bought/sold/acquired at least five times over the next fifteen years. First by Information Access, then Thomson, it then became a "Group" within the Thomson empire and finally Gale ended up as a division of Cengage Learning, a holding company with a few scattered divisions devoted to publishing. During that time, *National Survey of State Laws*, 4th edition, won the Andrews Bibliographical Award in 2003, and the company had grown so large and fractured that Gale's representatives who attended that year's AALL Annual Meeting for the first time didn't even know that they published the book and had never even heard of it. (When I visited their booth to share the glory (so to speak) they practically threw me out!) At some point Gale also sold the electronic rights to the book to Westlaw, by then a sister corporation, without telling me.

By 2008, Cengage Learning divided Gale into many pieces, one of which was a "legal" division, devoted to publishing in the law market. *National Survey of State Laws*, however, ended up in the catalog of business and education resources, which still primarily published books. The division of Gale that was exploring publications in the law market was focused on large ticket/digital "titles" such as Making of Modern Law. The Gale division that published NSSL decided to drop it, because, as the publisher of the business division said when I finally was able to talk to him face to face some four years later, "What is *this title* doing in my catalog? Why isn't Legal publishing it?" To make a long story short, after he consulted with the publisher in the legal division and hearing that NSSL didn't fit in the catalog with titles like MOML, I was able to get the rights to the book in the summer of 2013 and Hein agreed to take on the title.

So, I want to acknowledge several people who made this edition of the book possible. First, Mr. David Forman of Cengage Learning, who was the person who finally got the ball rolling within the Gale Cengage behemoth that allowed me to obtain the rights to the book and seek out another publisher. From the bottom of my heart, thank you David. Next I want to thank and acknowledge Kevin Marmion, former President (Emeritus?), (the big cheese) at Wm. S. Hein & Co. Inc., who agreed to take on NSSL, and early on even tried to buy the title from Gale Cengage with baffling, and even humorous, results. Thank you Kevin for being patient and good natured throughout the whole process. I am thrilled to have a publisher that's somewhat reminiscent of the publisher I originally signed on with; one in which you can actually talk to staff working on and marketing the book. Along those lines, thank you's go to Chris Czopp, Dan Rosati, Stephanie Ruesch, and Sheila Jarrett, each excellent representatives of the wonderful people, culture and professionalism that Hein exhibits in everything it does.

I also had a raft of research assistants working on this update and thank you to each and everyone of you for your hard work:

Lora Waeckerle
Amanda Wall
Tara Starzec
Megan Shupe
Sami Schmit
Lauren Nichols
Michael Faz
Taylor Hayes
Ryan Kirshenbaum
Jared Koch
Ken Yoho
Jenna (Woitaszewski) Christensen

Special acknowledgement is also due to Stefanie Pearlman who contributed the Animal Laws chapter.

I also would like to acknowledge the whole staff at the mighty Schmid Law Library, many of whom were forced to vicariously live through the agony and ecstasy of having the book dropped and then brought back to life. I wasn't happy when the book was dropped and was then ecstatic when Hein finally picked it up once and for all.

I continually acknowledge Cheryl Rae Nyberg, whose excellent book, *Subject Compilation of State Laws* was, is and continues to be of invaluable assistance to us in the compilation of each edition of this book. I am pleased to be sharing the same publisher with her, which allows us to provide cross references between the two works in the online editions.

It is with great joy that I acknowledge the strength of God's peace as the foundation for all things worth doing. To that peace, I humbly submit this work.

Editor's Note

Always consult an attorney before making decisions of any legal consequence. Never use a reference such as this, which is not meant to be an exposition of the law but a source for comparisons, as a definitive statement of the law.

Comments and suggestions regarding future editions of *National Survey of State Laws* are welcome and should be addressed to:

Editor, *National Survey of State Laws*
Richard Leiter
University of Nebraska
College of Law
402.472.5737
rleiter@unl.edu

I. BUSINESS AND CONSUMER LAWS

1. ANTITRUST

Antitrust violations are "crimes" committed by business entities that injure both competing businesses and the consumer by artificially inflating or fixing prices.

Antitrust laws came into national prominence in the late nineteenth century with the rise of the giant industrial monopolies. Two types of monopolies, horizontal and vertical, were felt to be particularly harmful to competition. In a horizontal monopoly, a single entity owns all or an unreasonable percentage of the firms competing in the same business, such as all the telephone or oil companies. In a vertical monopoly, a single entity owns all or an unreasonable percentage of all levels of business within a single industry, for example, all the forests, logging firms, mills, printing plants, and newspapers.

Through the exercise of its power to regulate interstate commerce, Congress has enacted the most sweeping of antitrust regulations in the Sherman Antitrust Act. Because of the great size of the businesses engaged in antitrust or anti-competitive practices as well, the federal government has taken the lead in enforcing against these types of unfair business practices.

Most antitrust statutes are enforced in two ways: the state attorney general can sue on behalf of the state in order to correct the unfair practice, either by obtaining an injunction prohibiting the offensive practice or by ordering fines or other redress to be paid or otherwise addressed to the consumers; the other way is by a private right of action, whereby consumers themselves or competing businesses sue to recover for damages or injuries suffered as a result of the offending behavior. Some states permit civil charge only; some permit civil and criminal charges.

Table 1: Antitrust

State	Code Section	Private Action?	Statutes of Limitations	Attorney Fees?
ALABAMA	6-5-60	Yes	Not specified	No
ALASKA	45.50.562 to 45.50.596	Yes; attorney general may also bring action	4 yrs.	Yes
ARIZONA	Uniform State Antitrust Act: 44-1401 to 44-1416	Yes; attorney general may also bring action	4 yrs. or within 1 yr. after the conclusion of state action	Yes
ARKANSAS	4-75-201 to 4-75-320	Yes; attorney general power to enforce	5 yrs.	Yes
CALIFORNIA	Bus. & Prof. §§ 16700 to 16770	Yes; attorney general may bring action on behalf of state	4 yrs.	Yes
COLORADO	Colorado Unfair Practices Act: 6-2-101 to 6-2-117; Colorado Antitrust Act of 1992: 6-4-101 to 6-4-122	Yes; attorney general may bring action on behalf of state	Civil actions: 4 yrs. or within 1 yr. after conclusion of action by state; Criminal actions: 6 yrs.	Yes
CONNECTICUT	Connecticut Antitrust Act, 35-24 to 35-46	Yes; attorney general also enforces	4 yrs. or within 1 yr. of conclusion of state action	Yes
DELAWARE	Delaware Antitrust Act: Tit. 6, §§ 2101 to 2114	Yes; attorney general also enforces	4 yrs. or within 1 yr. of conclusion of state action	Yes
DISTRICT OF COLUMBIA	28-4501 to 28-4518	Yes; corporation counsel (attorney general) power to enforce	4 yrs. or within 1 yr. of conclusion of District action	Yes
FEDERAL	15 USCA §§ 4; 15; 21	Yes, attorney general of respective district may bring action	4 yrs.	Yes; a person who is a foreign state may not recover an amount in excess of damages, the cost of the suit, including a reasonable attorneys fees
FLORIDA	Florida Antitrust Act of 1980: 542.15 to 542.36	Yes; attorney general also enforces	4 yrs. or within 1 yr. after conclusion of action by state	Yes
GEORGIA	Fair Business Practices Act: 10-1-390 to 10-1-408	Yes; attorney general power to enforce	2 yrs. or within 2 yrs. after conclusion of action by state	Yes
HAWAII	480-1 to 480-24	Yes; attorney general power to enforce	Four years or within 1 yr. after conclusion of action by state.	Yes
IDAHO	Idaho Competition Act: 48-101 to 48-118	Yes; attorney general also enforces	4 yrs. or within 1 yr. after conclusion of cause of action by state	Yes
ILLINOIS	Illinois Antitrust Act: 740 §§ 10/1 to 10/12	Yes; attorney general also enforces	4 yrs.	Yes

Table 1: Antitrust—Continued

State	Code Section	Private Action?	Statutes of Limitations	Attorney Fees?
INDIANA	24-1-1-1 to 24-1-3-5	Yes; attorney general power to enforce	Not specified	Yes; treble damages, cost of suit
IOWA	Iowa Competition Law: 553.1 to 553.19	Yes; attorney general power to enforce	4 yrs. or within 1 yr. after conclusion of cause of action by state	Yes for individual plaintiff but not for state
KANSAS	50-101 to 50-1,105	Yes; attorney general power to enforce	3 yrs.	Yes
KENTUCKY	Consumer Protection Act: 367.110 to 367.360	Yes; attorney general power to enforce	5 yrs. unless specified otherwise	No
LOUISIANA	51:121 to 51:152; Unfair Trade Practices and Consumer Protection Law: 51:1401 to 51:1428	Yes; attorney general also enforces	Not specified	Yes
MAINE	Tit. 10, §§ 1101 to 1110	Yes; attorney general power to enforce	Not specified	Yes
MARYLAND	Maryland Antitrust Act: Com. Law §§11-201 to 11-213	Yes; attorney general power to enforce	4 yrs. or within 1 yr. after conclusion of proceeding	Yes
MASSACHUSETTS	Massachusetts Antitrust Act: Ch. 93, §§ 1 to 114	Yes; attorney general also enforces	4 yrs. or within 1 yr. after conclusion of cause of action	Yes
MICHIGAN	Michigan Antitrust Reform Act: 445.771 to 445.788	Yes; attorney general also enforces	4 yrs. or within 1 yr. after conclusion of any state action	Yes
MINNESOTA	Minnesota Antitrust Law of 1971: 325D.49 to 325D.66	Yes; attorney general also enforces	4 yrs. or within 1 yr. after conclusion of cause of action	Yes
MISSISSIPPI	75-21-1 to 75-21-39; 75-24-19	Yes; attorney general power to enforce civil and criminal features of antitrust statutes	Not specified; within 3 yrs. of accrued cause of action; general provision, 15-1-49	Yes
MISSOURI	Missouri Antitrust Law: 416.011 to 416.161	Yes; attorney general also enforces	4 yrs. or within 1 yr. after conclusion of action	Yes
MONTANA	30-14-201 to 30-14-226	Yes; injured person or the attorney general power to enforce	Not specified	Yes
NEBRASKA	59-801 to 59-831	Yes; attorney general power to enforce	Not specified	Yes
NEVADA	Nevada Unfair Trade Practice Act: 598A.010 to 598A.280	Yes; attorney general power to enforce	4 yrs. or within 1 yr. after conclusion of any proceeding based on same matter	Yes
NEW HAMPSHIRE	356:1 to 356:14	Yes; attorney general power to enforce	4 yrs. or within 1 yr. after conclusion of any action	Yes

Table 1: Antitrust—Continued

State	Code Section	Private Action?	Statutes of Limitations	Attorney Fees?
NEW JERSEY	New Jersey Antitrust Act: 56:9-1 to 56:9-19	Yes; attorney general power to institute proceedings	4 yrs. or within 1 yr. of conclusion of state action	Yes; reasonable filing fees and cost of suit
NEW MEXICO	Antitrust Act: 57-1-1 to 57-1-19	Yes; attorney general power to enforce	Within 4 yrs. of accrued cause of action or plaintiff's discovery of cause of action; within 1 yr. after conclusion of action by state	Yes
NEW YORK	Gen. Bus. §§ 340 to 347	Yes; attorney general power to enforce; district attorney may prosecute with attorney general's authority in criminal proceedings	3 yrs. (suspended during pendency of federal action based in whole or in part on same matter)	Yes
NORTH CAROLINA	75-1 to 75-42	Yes	4 yrs. or 1 yr. after conclusion of any related cause of action	Yes
NORTH DAKOTA	Uniform State Antitrust Act: 51-08.1-01 to 51-08.1-12	Yes; attorney general power to enforce	4 yrs. or 1 yr. after conclusion of action by state	Yes
OHIO	1331:01 to 1331:99	Yes; attorney general power to enforce	4 yrs.	Yes; cost of suit and treble damages
OKLAHOMA	Oklahoma Antitrust Reform Act: Tit. 79, §§ 201 to 212	Yes; attorney general power to enforce	4 yrs.	Yes
OREGON	646.705 to 646.180	Yes; attorney general power to enforce	4 yrs. or within 1 yr. after conclusion of any proceeding based on the same matter	Yes; individual and state win reasonable attorney fees, expert's fee, and investigative fees
PENNSYLVANIA	Unfair Trade Practices and Consumer Protection Law: Tit. 73, §§ 201-1 to 201-93	Yes; attorney general power to enforce	Not specified	May be awarded at judicial discretion but no statutory right
RHODE ISLAND	Rhode Island Antitrust Act: 6-36-1 to 6-36-26	Yes, but private party plaintiff must notify attorney general of his complaint and file proof of service: attorney general power to enforce	4 yrs.	Yes; treble damages, reasonable costs and attorney fees
SOUTH CAROLINA	South Carolina Unfair Trade Practices Act: 39-5-10 to 39-5-180	Yes; attorney general power to enforce; however, 3 days before instituting legal proceedings, must give person chance to present reason why action should not be instituted	3 yrs.	Yes

Table 1: Antitrust—Continued

State	Code Section	Private Action?	Statutes of Limitations	Attorney Fees?
SOUTH DAKOTA	37-1-3.1 to 37-1-33	Yes; state's attorney power to enforce and must immediately notify the attorney general; the attorney general shall aid in prosecution	4 yrs. or 1 yr. after conclusion of civil or equitable action brought by state, whichever is later	Yes
TENNESSEE	47-25-101 to 47-25-112	Yes; attorney general and reporter power to institute criminal proceedings	Not specified	No
TEXAS	Texas Fair Enterprise and Antitrust Act of 1983: Bus. & Com. §§ 15.01 to 15.06	Yes; attorney general power to enforce	4 yrs. or 1 yr. after conclusion of action based on the same act	Yes
UTAH	Utah Antitrust Act: 76-10-3101 to 76-10-3118	Yes attorney general power to enforce	4 yrs. or 1 yr. after conclusion of action	Yes; and cost of suit
VERMONT	Tit. 9, §§ 2451 to 2466a	Yes	Not specified	Yes
VIRGINIA	Virginia Antitrust Act: 59.1-9.1 to 59.1-9.17	Yes; attorney general power to enforce	4 yrs. or 1 yr. after conclusion of action	Yes; cost of suit
WASHINGTON	19.86.010 to 19.86.920	Yes; attorney general power to enforce	4 yrs., except when attorney general brings action in whole or in part; in matter of private action, the private action's statute of limitations is suspended	Yes; cost of suit
WEST VIRGINIA	West Virginia Antitrust Act: 47-18-1 to 47-18-23	Yes; attorney general power to enforce	4 yrs., unless one civil action is brought, then any other is suspended during the first's pendency and 1 yr. after	Yes; filing fees, and reasonable expenses of discovery and document reproduction
WISCONSIN	133.01 to 133.18	Yes; dept. of justice or district attorney power to enforce	6 yrs. Statute begins running upon discovery of a cause of action by an aggrieved party; other actions have suspended statute of limitations during pendency of any civil or criminal action and for 1 yr. afterward	Yes; cost of suit
WYOMING	40-4-101 to 40-4-123	Yes; attorney general and county attorney power to enforce	Not specified	Not specified

2. ATTORNEYS

Note:

ABA = American Bar Association
AALS = American Association of Law Schools
MBE = Multistate Bar Examination
MCLE = Mandatory Continuing Legal Education
MEE = Multistate Essay Exam
MPT = Multistate Performance Test
MPRE = Multistate Professional Responsibility Examination
UBE = Uniform Bar Exam (MBE, MEE, and MPT)

Legal Education and Admission to the Bar

When the American Bar Association (ABA) was founded a little more than one hundred years ago, its first priority was to set standards for legal education. Its Section on Legal Education and Admission to the Bar immediately set out to accredit law schools and monitor the quality of the legal education each school provided. The purpose was to guard against widely varying levels of preparedness and education and, thus, professionalism, among attorneys.

What has become a near-universal requirement for becoming a lawyer is possession of a diploma from an ABA-accredited law school, which allows a law school graduate to take the bar examination in any state. Few states permit graduates of non-ABA accredited law schools to sit for their own bar exams, though California allows individuals who have not attended law school but have diligently and in good faith studied law for at least four years to sit for its bar exam. New York, Vermont and Washington also have conditions under which individuals who have not graduated from law school may sit for the bar exam. But by and large a law degree is necessary to take the bar exam, and in most cases it must be from an ABA-accredited school.

Many states allow reciprocity to attorneys already admitted to the bar in other states, while some place various restrictions upon attorneys admitted outside their jurisdictions, such as requiring attorneys admitted elsewhere to have actively been in practice for a certain number of years before s/he can be admitted without an examination. In general, reciprocity is permitted in two ways: accepting the Multistate Bar Examination score; or admitting on motion. States that do not permit attorneys from other jurisdictions to be admitted without examination require them to take a special or abbreviated exam. These states have a large number of attorneys and maintain that the requirement of the bar exam limits the numbers of attorneys coming into the state.

A recent change in bar exam testing is the addition of a new test called the Multistate Performance Test, designed to test reading, logical thinking and research and writing skills. As of the publication date more than half the states have adopted the new MPT.

The newest innovation in the bar exam testing is the introduction of the Uniform Bar Exam, which is a non-state specific exam administered and graded by the National Conference of Bar Examiners. More than half of the states have now adopted the UBE.

All but a handful of states now have MCLE requirements that range from a few hours per year to fifteen. Most of these states require that some of these credits be on the subject of professional ethics.

Table 2: Attorneys

State	Code Section	Education	Age
ALABAMA	S. Ct. Rule for Mandatory CLE 3; 34-3-1 to 34-3-2; Adm. to Bar Rules	Law school: graduation after at least 3 yrs. of 30 wks. each from ABA or AALS approved school or graduation after 4 yrs. of 30 wks. each from Birmingham School of Law, Jones Law Inst., or Miles College School of Law; Undergraduate: graduation from any accredited college or university	19
ALASKA	08.08.010 to 08.08.250; Alaska Bar Rules	Law school: ABA or AALS accredited law school or graduate of non-accredited school who has practiced in another jurisdiction for 5 of last 7 yrs.; one may register as law clerk to qualify as applicant without completing law school by presenting proof of bachelor's degree and completion of first year of law school; must have regular full-time employment with Alaska judge or attorney, tutor, and meet other specified study requirements	18
ARIZONA	Sup. Ct. Rules 31 to 40	Law school: ABA accredited or actively practiced 3 of last 5 yrs. in another state	
ARKANSAS	16-22-201 to 16-22-212; Ark. Rule for CLE 3; Adm. to Bar Rules	Law school: approved by ABA	21 unless graduate of accredited, recognized, or Class A law school
CALIFORNIA	Bus. & Prof. §§ 6060 to 6071	Law school: Graduate from law school accredited by examination committee full-time for 3 yrs. or part time for 4 yrs. or proof applicant has otherwise diligently and in good faith studied law for at least 4 yrs.; students at unaccredited law school must take preliminary bar exam at end of first year of law school; undergraduate: 2 yrs. or apparent intellectual ability equivalent to 2 yrs. of college work	18

Exam	Reciprocity	MCLE	Admitting Body	Residency
UBE; MPRE; MBE score from another jurisdiction accepted for 25 mos. if equal or better than national median; 2 day exam	Professors who have taught for 3 yrs. at accredited Alabama law schools and who are admitted in another state may apply for admission without exam; may be admitted without exam if actively practiced 5 out of 6 yrs. and passed exam of reciprocal state	12 hrs. each calendar year	Board of Bar Examiners	None
UBE; MPRE; UBE score may be transferred from elsewhere if scaled score is 280 or above and test was within last 5 yrs.; 2 day exam	May be admitted without exam if practiced 5 out of last 7 yrs. and passed exam in reciprocal state	No	Board of Governors	None required
UBE given twice per year; 2 day exam	Exam required by all applicants. Appearing ad hoc permitted, Rule 33(c)	15 hrs. per year, 3 must concern legal ethics	Supreme Court	None
MBE; MPT; essay; MPRE; may take MPRE unlimited number of times; 2 day exam	Exam required by all applicants	Resident: 12 hrs. annually, one must be ethics; Nonresident: must comply to requirements of their state and file annual certificate of completion	Courts of state; Board of Law Examiners	None
MBE; essay including performance test; MPRE Scaled Score 86; 2 day exam	Must: meet age and moral character requirements; be admitted before highest court in sister state or foreign country; have actively engaged in practice of law 4 of last 6 yrs.; may have to take attorney exam	25 hrs. every 36 mos., of which 4 hrs. must be legal ethics, 1 hr. must concern substance abuse, 1 hr. must concern elimination of bias	Supreme Court	None

Table 2: Attorneys—Continued

State	Code Section	Education	Age
COLORADO	13-93-101; CRCP Rules 203; 260	Law school: Class A: First professional degree from ABA-approved law school; Class B: ABA-approved or state-approved or common law English speaking nation, if portion of legal education from foreign jurisdiction, must graduate from ABA-approved school or, if graduate of state accredited school, then applicant must be admitted in state and have practiced law 3 of the last 5 yrs.	
CONNECTICUT	CT R. Super. Ct. Gen. §§ 2-1 to 2-83	Law school: graduate of school accredited by committee or Master of Laws from accredited school; must have passed professional responsibility exam or course	18
DELAWARE	Sup. Ct. Rules 52; 70; Mandatory CLE Rule 4; Board of Bar Examiners Rules 1 to 54	Law school: baccalaureate law degree or equivalent from ABA approved law school; Undergraduate: baccalaureate degree or equivalent or pass exam determined by board	21
DISTRICT OF COLUMBIA	D.C. Ct. App. Rule 46	Law school: ABA approved law school or if not, 26 semester hrs. at accredited school	
FLORIDA	Bar Rule 6-10.3; Rules of The S. Ct. Relating to Admissions to The Bar 1 to 5	Law school: graduate of ABA approved law school; Undergraduate: bachelor degree from regionally accredited school	18

Exam	Reciprocity	MCLE	Admitting Body	Residency
UBE Scaled Score 276; MPRE; 2 day exam	Class A applicant: admitted in another jurisdiction and actively practiced for 3 of the last 5 yrs. or UBE scaled score 276 within last 2 yrs.; Class B applicant: all others, must take UBE; all applicants must complete course on professionalism	45 units every 3 yrs., 7 units must be ethics	Supreme Court	
UBE; no limit to number of times; MPRE Scaled Score 80 or "C" or better in an ethics course	(1) Passed course or exam in professional responsibility; (2) Licensed to practice in a reciprocal state or territory of U.S. or in D.C. and (A) practiced at least 5 of 10 yrs. preceding application to CT Bar and is in good standing; or (B) if ever failed CT bar exam, practiced at least 5 of 10 yrs. preceding application in reciprocal state and is in good standing, providing 5 yrs. of practice occurred subsequent to last time applicant failed the CT bar exam	None	Superior Court	Must show intent to practice in state
MBE and essay; Rule 52 (6), MPRE Scaled Score 85; MPT; 2 ½ day exam	None; exam required of all applicants	24 hrs. every 2 yrs.; 4 must be legal ethics	Supreme Court on recommendation of board of 12 examiners	5 mos. clerkship in Delaware required for admission
UBE; MBE scores from other jurisdictions may be transferred; UBE scores from other jurisdictions may be transferred; MPT; 2 day exam	Active member in good standing of other jurisdiction for five years immediately preceding the application to DC; or J.D. or LL.B. from accredited school, admitted to any state or territory with at least 133 scaled score on MBE, and passed MPRE; must apply within 25 mos. of MBE	None	D.C. Court of Appeals	
MBE, essay, and MPRE Scaled Score 80; MBE scores not transferable; 2 day exam	None; exam required of all applicants	33 credit hrs. every 3 yrs., 5 must be in ethics, professionalism, or substance abuse	Supreme Court	

Table 2: Attorneys—Continued

State	Code Section	Education	Age
GEORGIA	15-19-30 to 15-19-34; State Bar Rules & Regs. 2-101; 8-104; Rules Governing Admission to Practice Law, Part B to D	Law school: Graduate of ABA approved school. Undergraduate: degree from accredited school or passed CLEP test	
HAWAII	Sup. Ct. Rules 1	Law school: graduate of ABA approved school or unaccredited and 5 of last 6 yrs. practice; LL.M. not satisfactory substitute for J.D. or LL.B.	
IDAHO	3-101; 3-408; Bar Commission Rules	Law school: graduate of ABA approved school; attorney applicants must be admitted to highest court of another state and practiced 5 of last 7 yrs.	18
ILLINOIS	S. Ct. Rules 701 to 719; 790 to 798	Law school: First law degree from ABA approved school; Undergraduate: must be graduate of 4 yr. high school or prep school and successfully completed at least 90 semester hrs. at college or university approved by Board of Law Examiners; in lieu of college or preliminary work, Board may accept satisfactory completion of program or curriculum of particular college or university	21
INDIANA	Rules for Admission to the Bar & the Discipline of Attys.	Law school: graduation from ABA approved school or approved list of Indiana Supreme Court or agency thereof; Indiana Supreme Ct. reserves the right to disapprove any school regardless of ABA approval; 2 hrs. in law school of legal ethics or professional responsibility	21

Exam	Reciprocity	MCLE	Admitting Body	Residency
MBE, essay, MPT, scaled score 270; MPRE scaled score 75; MBE scores not transferable; can take prior to graduation; 2 day exam	None; may be admitted without exam from states admitting GA attorneys without exam, must have practiced 5 of 7 yrs. immediately preceding application	12 hrs. minimum per year, including 1 hr. of professionalism	Board of Bar Examiners appointed by the Supreme Court	
MPT, MBE, essay, including legal ethics; MBE scores not transferable; MPRE Scaled Score 85; 2 day exam	Exam required of all; full-time faculty of U. of Hawaii Law School who meet citizenship and education requirements and admitted in another jurisdiction admitted for 3 yrs.; after 3 yrs. may be given permanent license	3 hrs. per year	Supreme Court	None
UBE; attorney applicants licensed for more than 5 yrs. need not take MBE; MPRE Scaled Score 85; 2 day exam	Applicants may transfer previous MBE score from another jurisdiction if taken within 37 mos. of date of exam; attys. licensed in WA and OR may be eligible for reciprocity in ID; all others must take exam; MBE portion not required if practiced 3 of last 5 yrs. preceding application	30 credit hrs. every 3 yrs., 3 must be in ethics or professional responsibility	Board of Commissioners of State Bar	
MPT, MBE, essay; MPRE scaled score 80; 2 day exam	Practiced in another jurisdiction 3 of the last yrs.; passed MPRE if licensed for fewer than 15 yrs.; may transfer previous UBE if all portions were taken in the same jurisdiction within the last 4 years.	20 credit hrs. every 2 yrs., at least 6 hrs. in professional responsibility	Board of Admissions appointed by Supreme Court	
MPT, essay, MBE; MPRE Scaled Score 80, 2 day exam	1 yr. conditional admission to members in good standing of another bar who are 21, residents of Indiana, of good moral character, and practiced for 5 of last 7 yrs.; may be received for 5 one-yr. periods after which admission shall be permanent	No less than 6 hrs. each calendar year and no less than 36 hrs. each 3-yr. educational period; 3 hrs. in professional responsibility each 3 yrs.; no more than 12 hrs. applied in non-legal subject matter	Supreme Court	

Table 2: Attorneys—Continued

State	Code Section	Education	Age
IOWA	602.10101 to 602.10141; Iowa Ct. R. 31.1 to 31.25; 41.3	Law school: LL.B. or J.D. from reputable law school	
KANSAS	Supreme Ct. Rules 701 to 723	Law school: degree from ABA accredited law school; Undergraduate: bachelor's degree from accredited college	
KENTUCKY	Supreme Ct. Rules 2.080 to 2.540; 3.645; 3.665(1); 3.685	Law school: graduate of ABA or AALS approved law school; if not ABA or AALS then must hold JD from law school in US accredited in jurisdiction of existence and which requires equivalent of 3 yr. course of study in KY; actively practiced law for 3 of 5 yrs., and meets all other KY requirements	
LOUISIANA	37:211 to 37:222; Sup. Ct. Rules 17; 18; 30 CLE Rule 3	Law school: ABA approved law school	18
MAINE	Tit. 4, §§ 801 to 811; Bar Rules 12; Bar Admission Rules 8 to 11A	Law school: ABA accredited; Undergraduate: at least 2 yrs. at accredited school if successfully completed 2/3 of ABA law school requirements plus 1 yr. in attorney's office in the state	
MARYLAND	Maryland Lawyers Act: Bus. Occup. & Prof. §§ 10-101 to 10-701; Bd. of Law Examiners Rules 1 to 7	Law school: J.D. or equivalent at school recognized by Board of Law Examiners; Undergraduate: adequate academic work to enter ABA approved school	18 to be admitted to bar but not to take exam
MASSACHUSETTS	Ch. 221, §§ 37 to 39; Supreme Judicial Court Rule 3:01	Law school: ABA approved or authorized foreign law school; Undergraduate: bachelor's degree	

Exam	Reciprocity	MCLE	Admitting Body	Residency
UBE; MPRE Scaled Score 80 good for 3 yrs.; 2 day exam	Member of any other U.S. bar who is resident may be admitted without exam if practiced 5 of last 7 yrs. with bona fide intent to practice in Iowa; certified UBE scaled score of 266 or above may be transferred	Minimum 15 hrs. during each calendar year and 3 ethics credits during every 2-yr. period	Supreme Court	Must show a bona fide intention to practice in Iowa
UBE, MBE scores may be transferred from another jurisdiction if within 13 mos. of current exam and if applicant passed entire bar exam of other jurisdiction in one sitting; MPRE scaled score 80; 2 day exam	May be admitted if the applicant has an active license in a jurisdiction that permits mutuality of admission without examination for Kansas bar members, has actively practiced for 5 of the last 7 years, and meets all moral and character fitness qualifications	At least 12 hrs. per year, 2 yrs. in professional responsibility, except: during first year of practice; retired or inactive; federal and state judges; others exempted for good cause	Supreme Court	
MBE, essays; written exam may cover 14 topics; must receive 75% or more; may take exam 3 times; must first pass MPRE before can sit for MBE; MPRE scaled score 75; 2 day exam	Citizen of U.S. admitted in D.C. or state and has practiced 5 of last 7 yrs. provided qualifications were equal or higher than those required for admission in Kentucky; an applicant who has received a 132 or above on the multistate exam in the last 3 yrs. needs only to take the essay portion	12 hrs. per yr., at least 2 hrs. of legal ethics or professional responsibility; hours accrue from July 1 to June 30, not on calendar yr.	Supreme Court	
Essay; MBE not used, but all applicants must pass MPRE with scaled score 80; may only take each subject examination twice; 3 day exam	None; exam required of all applicants	12.5 hrs. per year, including at least 1 hr. each legal ethics and professional responsibility.	Supreme Court appoints the Committee on Bar Admission	
UBE; MEE and/or MPT, essays; MPRE scaled score 80; 2 day exam	May be admitted if practiced at least 3 of last 5 years in another U.S. jurisdiction. And meets other qualifications; UBE scores within last 3 years may be transferred	11 hrs. including 1 hr. professional responsibility	Supreme Court creates Board of Bar Examiners	
Essay test; MBE; MPRE not required; must pass legal professionalism course offered by Bar Association; 2 day exam	If practiced at least 5 of the 7 yrs. preceding application and proof of good, moral character and intent to practice or teach and passes an examination	None	Court of Appeals and State Board of Law Examiners	
UBE; essay; MBE; MPRE scaled score 85; 2 day exam	Admitted elsewhere and satisfactory moral character and legal ability	None	Supreme Judicial Ct. appoints board of Bar Examiners	

Table 2: Attorneys—Continued

State	Code Section	Education	Age
MICHIGAN	600.901; 600.934; 600.937; 600.946; Board of Law Examiners Rules 1 to 8	Law school: reputable and qualified law school in U.S. or its territories; Undergraduate: at least 2 yrs. of study	18
MINNESOTA	481.01; Admission to the Bar Rules 1 to 19; St. Bd. of CLE Rule 9	Law school: J.D. or LL.B. from ABA approved school	18
MISSISSIPPI	73-3-2; Admission to the Bar Rules 1 to 14; Mandatory CLE Rule 3	Law school: 3 yr. law course of study at ABA approved school; Undergraduate: bachelor's degree or 3 yrs. of college work	21

Exam	Reciprocity	MCLE	Admitting Body	Residency
Essays; MBE, out-of-state MBE scores accepted if within preceding 3 yrs. and person meets all other requirements for admission and other state grants reciprocal right to elect to use score on MBE administered in Michigan; MPRE scaled score 85; 2 day exam	Practiced or taught 3 of last 5 yrs. and a graduate of ABA law school	None.	Supreme Court or any circuit court	Resident of one of states or D.C.
UBE, MBE; additional questions; MPRE scaled score 85 or higher; 2 day exam	Engaged in law 5 of last 7 yrs.; or may be admitted on motion if engaged in the practice of law for 5 of 7 yrs. preceding admission and a graduate of an ABA approved school and scored at least 145 on MBE; good moral character	45 hrs. every 3 yrs.. including at least 3 hrs. ethics or professional responsibility and 2 hrs. elimination of bias in the legal profession	Supreme Court	Must be resident or designate Clerk of Appellate Courts as agent for service of process or maintain office in state
MBE; MPT; additional subjects; MPRE scaled score 75; 2 day exam	Must have practiced at least 5 yrs. in a state that reciprocates with Mississippi; must meet other requirements for admission; may transfer MBE score if attained 20 mos. prior to MS exam	12 hrs. per year, at least 1 hr. legal ethics, professional responsibility, professionalism, malpractice prevention, substance abuse, or mental health (the "ethics/professionalism" hour); newly licensed after Aug. 1, 2015, must attend new lawyer program by conclusion of 2nd CLE yr.: 12 hrs. of CLE, including 6 hrs. basic skills; 6 hrs. ethics/professionalism; satisfies 2 yrs. CLE requirements; certain exceptions for new admittees previously licensed in another state	Supreme Court	

Table 2: Attorneys—Continued

State	Code Section	Education	Age
MISSOURI	484.020; Sup. Ct. Rules 8; 15	Law school: J.D. or LL.B. from ABA approved school	18
MONTANA	Board of Bar Examiners' Rules; Rules for Admission to the Bar; Rules for CLE, Rule 4	Law school: ABA accredited law school approved by Montana Supreme Court	21
NEBRASKA	7-101 to 7-116; Neb. Ct. R. §§ 3-101 to 3-129; 3-401.4	LL.B. or J.D. from approved law school	21
NEVADA	S. Ct. Rules 49 to 75; 77; 98; 210	Bachelor of Laws or equivalent from ABA approved school	Age of majority
NEW HAMPSHIRE	Sup. Ct. Rules 42; 53	Law school: graduate of 3-yr. full-time or 4-yr. part-time program from ABA approved school or foreign law school of common law country Undergraduate; 3 yrs. of work required for bachelor's degree	18

Exam	Reciprocity	MCLE	Admitting Body	Residency
UBE; MECT; MPRE scaled score 80; UBE score of at least 270 may be transferred if within 24 mos.; 2 day exam	Member of bar of another state and has practiced or taught for 5 of preceding 10 yrs. and graduate of ABA law school; may transfer UBE score of at least 260 taken within past 24 mos. and must take MECT	15 hrs. per yr., including at least 2 hrs. ethics, malpractice prevention, or professionalism; 2 hrs. of ethics required of all new admittees within 12 mos. of admission or reinstatement	Supreme Court	
UBE; MPRE scaled score 80; minimum UBE score of 266 to transfer in; must attend Montana Law Seminar given day after bar exam; 2 day exam	Certain attorney applicants may be admitted without examination or by abbreviated examination	15 hrs. per yr., including at least 2 hrs. ethics or professionalism	Supreme Court	
UBE; MPRE scaled score 85; 2 day exam	Licensed and in good standing in another state with equal educational qualifications and: have practiced 5 of last 7 yrs.; or UBE score of 270 and MPRE scaled score 85; or non-UBE score equivalent to passing UBE score and MPRE scaled score 85	10 hrs. per yr., including 2 hrs. professional responsibility	Supreme Court	
Essays; MPT; MBE; no transfer of MBE scores from another jurisdiction; MPRE scaled score 85; 2 1/2 day exam	Exam required of all. Law faculty members may be admitted if practiced for at least 5 yrs. and faculty for at least 2 yrs.	13 hrs. per year, including 2 hrs. ethics; 1 hr. substance abuse, addiction, and/or mental health issues	Supreme Court	
UBE; UBE scores may be transferred from another jurisdiction if passed within the past 3 yrs. or if in the past 3-5 yrs., applicant must have practiced for at least 2 yrs.; MPRE scaled score 79; completion of practical skills course within two years of admission to bar; 2 day exam	Can have admission on motion; special rules for VT and ME	12 hrs. per yr., including 2 hrs. legal ethics, professional responsibility, substance abuse, or attorney-client disputes	Supreme Court	

Table 2: Attorneys—Continued

State	Code Section	Education	Age
NEW JERSEY	Rules of General Application, Rule 1:23 to 1:27; 1:42	Law school: bachelor's degree or equivalent from ABA approved law school	18
NEW MEXICO	NMRA, Rules 15-101 to 15-406; 18-201 to 18-204	J.D. or LL.B. from ABA accredited law school or graduate from any law school who has been engaged in the practice of law 4 of the 6 yrs. preceding application	18
NEW YORK	Jud. §460 to 467; CPLR, Rules 9401 to 9407; NY Ct. Rules 520.1 to 520.17; 840.7; 1500.12; 1500.22; 6000.6; 6000.7	Law school: graduation from approved law school or 4 years of study in office of practicing attorney and at least 1 yr. in approved law school or approved study of law in foreign country	21
NORTH CAROLINA	84-24; Admission to Practice of Law Rules .0501 to .1005; State Bar Rules Ch. 1, Subch. D, .1518	Law school: LL.M., LL.B., J.D., or S.J.D.; degree from law school approved by Council of the North Carolina State Bar or law school approved by ABA at time degree received	18
NORTH DAKOTA	27-11-02; R. Continuing Legal Ed., Rule 3; Admission to Practice Rules 1 to 18	J.D. or equivalent from ABA approved or provisionally approved law school	18

Exam	Reciprocity	MCLE	Admitting Body	Residency
Essays; UBE; UBE scores may be transferred from another jurisdiction only by concurrent examination; MPRE scaled score 75 or grade of C in professional responsibility law school course; 2 days	May be admitted if applicant practiced law for 5 of last 7 years in another U.S. jurisdiction, completed course on NJ ethics and professionalism, and met all other application requirements	24 hrs. every 2 yrs., including 4 yrs. ethics or professionalism	Supreme Court	
Essays; UBE; transfer of UBE score accepted if score 260 or higher; MPRE scaled score 80; 2 day exam	None; all applicants must take exam except law faculty at the Univ. of NM may be admitted without exam	12 hrs. per year, including 2 hrs. legal ethics and professionalism	Supreme Court	
UBE; MBE; MBE transfer from another jurisdiction only on concurrent examination; MPRE scaled score 85; all applicants must complete 50 hrs. of pro bono service prior to filing application for admission; 2 day exam	May be admitted without exam from reciprocal states; must have practiced 5 of last 7 yrs.	New attorneys: 16 hrs. each during initial 2 yrs. of practice, including 3 hrs. ethics, 6 hrs. skills, 7 hrs. practice management; practicing attorneys: 24 hrs. every 2 yrs., including 4 hrs. ethics and professionalism	New York Court of Appeals	
Essays; MBE; UBE (Feb. 2019); MBE scores not transferable from another jurisdiction; MPRE scaled score 80 within 24 mos. before or 12 mos. after sitting for bar exam; 2 day exam	May be admitted from reciprocal states; must be in good standing, practiced or taught for 4 of last 6 yrs.; MPRE score of 80	12 hrs. per year, including 2 hrs. professional responsibility and/or professionalism; 1 additional hr. every 3 yrs. on substance abuse and debilitating mental conditions	General Court of Justice upon recommendation from Board of Law Examiners	
UBE; MPRE scaled score 85; UBE score 260 may be transferred from other jurisdiction or MBE of 150 in jurisdiction not using UBE if taken with essay or other written exam within 2 yrs. of exam; 2 day exam	Meets educational requirements; member of bar for at least 5 yrs. and practiced or taught for 4 of last 5 yrs.; 45 hrs. of CLE, including 3 hrs. ethics within last 42 mos.; or by transfer of exam scores: UBE score 260 in past 2 yrs.; or MBE 150 within 2 yrs. and admission to the bar in another state; and MPRE score 85 within 5 yrs.	45 hrs. per 3 yrs., including 3 hrs. ethics or professional responsibility	Supreme Court	

Table 2: Attorneys—Continued

State	Code Section	Education	Age
OHIO	Gov. Bar Rules 1 to 20	Law school: J.D. or equivalent from ABA approved law school; Undergraduate: bachelor's degree from accredited institution	21
OKLAHOMA	St. Admis. Rules 1 to 16; St. CLE Rule 3	Law school: graduate of law school accredited by ABA or Board of Bar Examiners	18
OREGON	9.220; Attorney Admission Rules 1.05 to 17.05; Minimum CLE Rule 3	Law school: J.D. or LL.B. from ABA approved law school	18
PENNSYLVANIA	St. Admis. Rules 103; 201 to 232; CLE Rule 105; CLE Bd. Reg. §§ 3; 4	Law school: LL.B. or J.D.; degree from ABA approved law school; Undergraduate: degree from accredited school or equivalent education	
RHODE ISLAND	S. Ct. Rules, Art. II, Rules 1 to 8; Art. IV, Rule 3; Art. IV, § 1.3.2	Law school: graduate of school approved and accredited by ABA and Board of Bar Examiners	21

Exam	Reciprocity	MCLE	Admitting Body	Residency
Essays; MPT; MBE; MBE scores from other jurisdictions not accepted; MPRE scaled score 85; 2½ day exam	Must have passed bar and been admitted in another state; engaged in practice of law for last 5 out of 10 yrs.; intend to practice in Ohio and have not failed Ohio bar exam	40 hrs. every 2 yrs., including 3 hrs. professional conduct: legal ethics; professionalism; alcoholism, substance abuse, or mental health issues; access to justice or fairness in courts	Supreme Court appoints bar examiners	
Essays; MBE; transfer MBE scores from another jurisdiction on concurrent exam only; MPRE scaled score 75; bar exam may be taken unlimited times; 2 day exam	Lawfully admitted and in good standing on active status in reciprocal state; continuous practice for 5 of last 7 yrs.; graduate of ABA approved law school; individual who has previously failed OK bar ineligible for admission on motion	12 hrs. per calendar yr., including 1 hr. legal ethics, professional responsibility, or malpractice	Supreme Court	
UBE; essays, combination of MEE and locally drafted; MPT; MBE; MBE scores from other jurisdictions not accepted; MPRE scaled score 85; 2 day exam	Passed bar; admitted; active, substantial, and continuous practice 5 of last 7 yrs. in reciprocal jurisdiction may be admitted without examination; all others must take exam	45 hrs. every 3 yrs., including 6 hrs. ethics incl. 1 hr. duty to report child or elder abuse; 3 hrs. access to justice every other reporting period. New admittees: 15 hrs., including 2 hrs. ethics and 10 hrs. practical skills from date of admission to 12/31 of next calendar yr.	Oregon State Bar under the direction of the S. Ct.	
6 essay questions; 1 performance question; MBE; MPRE scaled score 75; 2 day exam	Member in good standing of bar of reciprocal state; must have passed bar of other state or practiced 5 of past 7 yrs.; if ever failed Pa. bar, must take exam; MPRE score 75 or over; all others must take exam	12 hrs., including 2 hrs. ethics, professionalism, or substance abuse; new admittees must take 4 hr. Bridge the Gap program by first compliance deadline	Supreme Court	
Essays; MEE; MPT; MBE; transfer of MBE scores from another jurisdiction allowed; MPRE scaled score 80 good for 2 yrs.; no person who has failed a total of 5 bar exams, in RI or elsewhere, will again be permitted to take the RI bar exam, no exceptions; 2 day exam	If in practice or teaching 5 of last 10 yrs., applicant must take only essay portion of exam	10 hrs. each yr. with 2 hrs. in legal ethics	Supreme court	

Table 2: Attorneys—Continued

State	Code Section	Education	Age
SOUTH CAROLINA	40-5-10; 40-5-210 to 40-5-220; Appellate Ct. Rules 402; 408	Law school: graduate of law school approved by ABA or S.C. Supreme Court, or Council of Legal Education.	21
SOUTH DAKOTA	16-16-1 to 16-16-24	J.D. or L.L.B. from ABA accredited law school	18
TENNESSEE	S. Ct. Rules 6; 7; 21	Law school: graduate of ABA accredited law or board approved school; Undergraduate: bachelor's degree from regionally accredited school	18
TEXAS	Rules Governing Admission to the Bar, Rules I to XXII; St. Bar Rules Art. 12	J.D. or equivalent from approved law school	18
UTAH	Rules Governing Bar Admis. Rules 14-701 to 14-720; Mandatory CLE Rule 14-404	First Professional Degree from approved law school	21

Exam	Reciprocity	MCLE	Admitting Body	Residency
UBE; transfer of UBE scores accepted; MPRE Scaled Score of 77; 2 day exam	Admission on motion only for dean or tenured professor of University of South Carolina School of Law or Charleston School of Law, other requirements apply; exam required of all others	14 hrs. per yr., including 2 hrs. legal ethics/professional responsibility; 1 LEPR hr. every 3 yrs.; new admitted exempt from CLE 1st yr. of practice, 1st reporting yr. must take Essential Series in addition to regular reporting requirements	Supreme Court	
Essay question on Indian law; MEE; MPT; MBE; MBE scores from other jurisdictions accepted; MPRE scaled score 85, previous score within 28 mos. accepted; may take exam 3 times; 2 day exam	Graduate ABA approved law school; active in practice in reciprocal state for 5 yrs. immediately preceding application for admission without examination	No requirement	Supreme Court	Prior to admission, must be resident, maintain office in state or designate clerk of Supreme Court as agent for service of process
Essays; UBE; UBE scores from other jurisdictions accepted; MPRE scaled score 75; 2 day exam	Meets educational requirements; admitted in another state; has practiced at least 5 of last 7 yrs. immediately preceding admission; has passed equivalent exam	15 hrs. per calendar year, including 3 hrs. per year ethics and professionalism	State Board of Law Examiners supervised by Supreme Court	Citizen of Tennessee
Essays; Procedure and Evidence questions; MPT; MBE; MBE scores from other jurisdictions not accepted; MPRE scaled score 85; 2 1/2 day exam	Must have practiced 5 of last 7 yrs.; J.D. from approved law school; if valid active license from another jurisdiction, certain exceptions from law study requirement; cannot have failed Texas Bar Exam	15 hrs. per yr., including 3 hrs. legal ethics and professional responsibility	Supreme Court	
UBE; UBE score 270 or over accepted from another jurisdiction if within last 3 prior examinations from application; MPRE scaled score 86; 2 day exam	Must have passed MPRE and practiced 5 of past 7 yrs. or transfer of UBE score of 270 or higher; certain CLE requirements apply	24 hrs. each 2 yrs., including 3 hrs. ethics or professional responsibility, 1 hr. of which must be in area of professionalism and civility	Board of Bar Commissioners by delegation of Supreme Court	

Table 2: Attorneys—Continued

State	Code Section	Education	Age
VERMONT	CLE Rules § 4; R. Admis. to Bar §§ 1 to 15	Law school: Degree from approved law school, 3 mos. internship with Vt. attorney; or 4 yrs. study under supervision of VT attorney who has been admitted for at least 3 yrs.; Undergraduate: 3/4 work required for bachelor's degree at approved college	18
VIRGINIA	54.1-3925 to 54.1-3931; S. Ct. Rules 1A:1; Mandatory CLE Reg. 102	Law school: Graduate of ABA approved law school or 3 yrs. study under conditions prescribed by Board of Bar Examiners. Undergraduate: Bachelor's degree from 4 yr. accredited college or university	18
WASHINGTON	2.48.030; Admissions to Practice Rules 1 to 28	Law school: Graduate of approved law school or completion of law clerk program prescribed by Admission to Practice Rules; Undergraduate: not specified if law school graduate; if law office study, must have bachelor's degree from approved college or university	
WEST VIRGINIA	30-2-1; 30-2-2; Admission to Practice of Law Rules 1.0 to 10.5; State Bar Rules and Regs., Ch. 7	Law school: J.D. or LL.B. or equivalent from approved law school; Undergraduate: degree from accredited college or university	18

Exam	Reciprocity	MCLE	Admitting Body	Residency
Essay; UBE; UBE score may be transferred MBE; MBE score of or 135 greater may be transferred from another jurisdiction, concurrent exam only; MBE and essay must be passed at concurrent exam only; MPRE scaled score 80; 2 day exam	Must have practiced 5 of preceding 10 yrs. or less if less is required for VT attorneys in other state; special rules for ME and NH attys.	20 hrs. every 2 yrs., including at least 2 hrs. legal ethics	Supreme Court	
Essays; MBE, MPRE scaled score 85; 2 day exam	Must have practiced 3 of last 5 yrs. and admitted to bar of another jurisdiction for not less than 5 yrs.	12 hrs. per year, including at least 2 hrs. legal ethics or professionalism	Supreme Court	
UBE; UBE scores of 270 or higher transferrable from another jurisdiction for 40 mos. after date earned; MPRE scaled score 85, not more than 3 yrs. before or after UBE; also must pass Washington Law Component online test before admission; 2 day exam	Must be in good standing in another state and have practiced for at least 3 of 5 yrs. immediately preceding application	45 hrs. per 3 yrs., including 15 hrs. law and legal procedure and 6 hrs. legal ethics and professional responsibility; newly admitted lawyers exempt for calendar year of admission	Supreme Court; Board of Governors	
UBE; UBE score may be transferred; MPT; MEE; MBE; MBE score within past 13 mos. may be transferred from another jurisdiction if applicant passed entire bar exam in other jurisdiction; MPRE scaled score 80 within 25 mos. of passing WV bar exam	Must have practiced for 5 of last 7 yrs. and state of membership must be reciprocal with WV	24 hrs. every 2 fiscal yrs., including at least 3 hrs. in legal ethics, office management, substance abuse, or elimination of bias in the legal profession; new admitted must complete Bridge the Gap seminar within 6 mos. before or 12 mos. after admission	Supreme Court of Appeals	

Table 2: Attorneys—Continued

State	Code Section	Education	Age
WISCONSIN	S. Ct. Rules 40.01 to 40.15; 31.01 to 31.14	Law school: graduate of ABA accredited law school	Age of majority
WYOMING	5-2-118; 33-5-101 to 33-5-117; Rules for CLE, Rule 4; Admission to Practice Law Rules 201 to 305	J.D. from ABA accredited law school	Adult citizen of U.S.

Exam	Reciprocity	MCLE	Admitting Body	Residency
Essays; MBE; MBE scores from other jurisdictions may be transferred; MPRE not required; graduates of ABA approved law schools in WI admitted without exam by presenting certification showing satisfactory completion of law school and requirements relating to WI law; 2 day exam	Must have actively practiced for 3 of last 5 yrs. May be admitted without exam from reciprocal states	30 hrs. every 2 yrs., including 3 hrs. in legal ethics and professional responsibility	Supreme Court	
UBE; UBE scores 270 or over transferrable from another jurisdiction within past 3 yrs.; MPRE scaled score 85 not more than 3 yrs. prior or 1 mo. after successful UBE date; 2 day exam	Attorney from another state may be admitted without examination upon showing s/he has a J.D. or LL.B. from ABA approved law school; Is not now nor ever has been admitted to the practice of law in Wyoming or, if previously admitted, one whose membership was withdrawn; admitted to practice in other state by passing written exam as required by such other state; has not been denied on motion to practice in WY within last 2 yrs.; has not previously engaged in unauthorized practice of law; has practiced law for minimum of 300 hrs. per yr. for 5 of past 7 yrs. in reciprocal state; meets all other requirements prescribed by Board; member in good standing in all jurisdictions where admitted	15 hrs. per year, including 1 hr. legal ethics	Supreme Court	

3. DECEPTIVE TRADE PRACTICES

A deceptive trade practice is an activity in which an individual or business engages that is calculated to mislead or lure the public into purchasing a product or service. False advertising and odometer tampering are two of the most blatant examples of this commercial lying. Such activities are given special status as offenses against the citizenry in general and are therefore accorded by law special enforcement status.

Deceptive trade practices result in criminal prosecution in some states; in others, statutes provide for private enforcement, whereby a citizen is entitled to sue a business for violating deceptive trade practice laws and may be able to recover punitive damages and/or statutory fines. The attorney general of the state may also bring a lawsuit against an offending business enterprise.

Because a deceptive trade practice may affect individuals or businesses from more than one state, a number of states have adopted the standardized Uniform Deceptive Trade Practices Act (UDTPA). The Uniform Act does not add or detract from the law of any one state; rather, it is inclusive and tends to cover, in general terms, all the prohibitions and issues addressed in state law in this area. For example, the Uniform Act prohibits making deceptive representations in connection with commercial goods. This obviously covers odometer tampering, but it also addresses all forms of deception in the marketing or advertising of goods and services. Those states that have not adopted the UDTPA have laws similar to it.

There is little controversy among the states over what activity amounts to a deceptive trade practice. However, there is a great deal of variety concerning the remedies available for the violations and who may sue for those violations. There are two main purposes of the statutes providing for remedies for businesses engaging in unlawful activity: (1) injunctions or restraining orders forbidding the continued deceptive trade practice and (2) punishment via fines, damages, and imprisonment. But because businesses are generally in violation of deceptive trade practice laws, and because it is difficult to determine whom to punish in the violating business, fines are generally the most effective method of extracting restitution.

Table 3: Deceptive Trade Practices

State	Uniform Deceptive Trade Practices Act Adopted?	False Advertising Forbidden?	Who May Bring Suit	Remedies Available	Auto Odometer Tampering Forbidden?
ALABAMA	No, Deceptive Trade Practices Act: 8-19-1 to 8-19-15	Yes, 13A-9-42	Private parties; attorney general; district attorney, 8-19-8	Restraining orders, 8-19-8; actual damages or $100, whichever is greater, or in court's discretion up to three times actual damages, 8-19-10; continuous willful violation is Class A misdemeanor, 8-19-12; civil penalty up to $25,000 per violation of an order or injunction, 8-19-11; civil penalty not more than $2,000 per violation under 8-19-5 for knowingly engaging in practice declared unlawful, 8-19-11	Yes, 8-19-5(15)
ALASKA	No, Unfair Trade Practices and Consumer Protection: 45.50.471 to 45.50.561	Yes, 45.50.471(b)	Attorney general, 45.50.501; Private or class action suites, 45.50.531	Injunction; $500 or 3 times actual damages, whichever is greater; treble damages or equitable relief, 45.50.531	Yes, 45.50.471(b)(18)
ARIZONA	No	Yes, Class 1 misdemeanor; 44-1522; 44-1372.01; 44-6561; 13-2203	Attorney general; no language that indicates a consumer or private party may bring an action, 44-1524	Subpoena; injunction, civil damage, 44-1526 to 44-1528; if willfully violated: $10,000 civil penalty 44-1531 I; violating injunction: $25,000 penalty, 44-1532	Yes; class 1 misdemeanor, 44-1223

Table 3: Deceptive Trade Practices—Continued

State	Uniform Deceptive Trade Practices Act Adopted?	False Advertising Forbidden?	Who May Bring Suit	Remedies Available	Auto Odometer Tampering Forbidden?
ARKANSAS	No, 4-88-101 to 4-88-905	Yes, knowingly making a false representation, 4-88-107	Attorney general will bring claim; consumer, state agency, or private party files petition with attorney general, 4-88-111	Injunction and return any money for purchased good to consumer; suspend corporate charter or business permit; possible fine up to $10,000 per violation if violation of injunction willful; actual damages and reasonable attorney fees, 4-88-113; Class A misdemeanor if willful deceptive trade practice, 4-88-103	Yes, license may be denied, suspended or revoked for violation, 23-112-308(21)
CALIFORNIA	No, Unfair Practices Act: Bus. & Prof. §§ 17000 to 17101	Yes, Bus. & Prof. §§ 17500 to 17509	Attorney general; district attorney or other prosecuting attorney may bring suit for injunctive and civil penalties, Bus. & Prof. § 17535; Any individual may bring suit for injunction or restitution, Bus. & Prof. § 17203	Violation of provision misdemeanor punishable by imprisonment in county jail up to 6 mos. and/or fine up to $2,500, Bus. & Prof. § 17500	Yes, misdemeanor, Veh. §§ 28050 to 28053
COLORADO	Yes, Colorado Consumer Protection Act: 6-1-101 to 6-1-1121	Yes, 6-1-105	Attorney general; district attorney, 6-1-107; private citizens; class action, 6-1-111	Restraining order; injunctive relief, 6-1-109; 6-1-110; greater of amount of actual damages sustained, $500, or 3 times the amount of actual damages, if established by clear and convincing evidence that person engaged in bad faith conduct, plus costs of action and reasonable attorney fees, 6-1-113	Yes, 42-6-202

Table 3: Deceptive Trade Practices—Continued

State	Uniform Deceptive Trade Practices Act Adopted?	False Advertising Forbidden?	Who May Bring Suit	Remedies Available	Auto Odometer Tampering Forbidden?
CONNECTICUT	Yes, Conn. Unfair Trade Practices Act: 42-110a to 42-110q	Not generally; 42-110b describes "unfair or deceptive acts" in trade, defined in 42-110a(4) as including advertising	Commissioner of Consumer Protection; attorney general, 42-110d; private parties; class action, 42-110g	Restraining order; actual and punitive damages, costs, and reasonable attorney fees, 42-110k; 42-110m; civil penalties up to $5,000 for willful violation and $25,000 for violation of restraining order, 42-110o	Yes, class A misdemeanor, 14-106b
DELAWARE	Yes, Uniform Deceptive Trade Practices Act: Tit. 6, §§ 2531 to 2536	Yes, Tit. 6, § 2532	Attorney general, Tit. 6, § 2522; individual victim of deceptive trade practice, Tit. 6, § 2525	For violations of Tit. 6, §§ 2501 and 2502, fine up to $100, Tit. 6, § 2503; civil penalty fine up to $10,000 for each willful violation; restraining order; injunctive relief; treble damages; costs; attorney fees, Tit. 6, §§ 2522; 2533	Yes, Tit. 21, §6404
DISTRICT OF COLUMBIA	Yes, Consumer Protection Procedures Act: 28-3901 to 28-3913	Yes, 28-3904	Director of Department of Consumer and Regulatory Affairs; consumer, 28-3905	Appropriate civil penalties: injunction, actual and treble damages, attorney fees; consumer redress remedies; punitive damages, 28-3905	No

Table 3: Deceptive Trade Practices—Continued

State	Uniform Deceptive Trade Practices Act Adopted?	False Advertising Forbidden?	Who May Bring Suit	Remedies Available	Auto Odometer Tampering Forbidden?
FLORIDA	No, Florida Deceptive & Unfair Trade Practices Act: 501.201 to 501.213	Yes, 817.40; 817.41; 817.43 to 817.47	Enforcing authority for specific industry; consumer in private action, 501.207	False advertising: 2nd degree misdemeanor, 817.45; food: 2nd degree misdemeanor, 500.177; actual damages if in bad faith; injunction; declaratory judgment that act is violation, 501.207; damages vary based on industry where practice occurs; generally 2nd deg. misdemeanor; willful unfair trade practices in any industry may result in up to $10,000 civil penalty for each violation; reasonable attorney fees and costs, 501.2075	Yes, 3rd degree felony, 319.35; 501.976(12)
GEORGIA	Yes; Uniform Deceptive Trade Practices Act: 10-1-370 to 10-1-375; Fair Business Practices Act: 10-1-390 to 10-1-407	Yes, 10-1-393; 10-1-420; 10-1-421	Administrator; private party, 10-1-397; 10-1-399	Misdemeanor, 10-1-420; civil penalty $25,000, 10-1-405; enjoining practices, 10-1-423; exemplary damages for intentional violation, limited to actual damages if bona fide error, fine over $100 but less than $1,000 or prison for up to 20 days or both, 10-1-399 to 10-1-400; 10-1-421; exception for ignorance, 10-1-396	Yes, violator liable for three times actual damages or $1,500, whichever is greater, costs and attorney fees, 40-8-5
HAWAII	Yes, Uniform Deceptive Trade Practice Act: 481A	Yes, misdemeanor, 481A-3; 708-871	Consumer Protection Agency, 487; private parties, 481A-4	Injunction; costs to prevailing party; attorney fees, 481A-4	Yes, 486-77(1); 486-77(4)

Table 3: Deceptive Trade Practices—Continued

State	Uniform Deceptive Trade Practices Act Adopted?	False Advertising Forbidden?	Who May Bring Suit	Remedies Available	Auto Odometer Tampering Forbidden?
IDAHO	Yes, Idaho Consumer Protection Act: 48-601 to 48-619	Yes, 48-603	State, 48-606; private party, 48-606	Declaratory judgment; enjoining practices; specific performance; civil penalties up to $5,000; recover reasonable costs, investigative expenses, and attorney fees, 48-606; 48-607; in private action recover actual damages or $1,000 whichever is greater, costs, and attorney fees, 48-608	Yes, purchaser of vehicle could bring action and recover court costs and attorney fees, 49-1629; 49-1630
ILLINOIS	Yes, Uniform Deceptive Trade Practices Act: 815 §§ 510/1 to 510/7	Yes, 815 § 510/2	Any person likely to be damaged, 815 § 510/3	Injunctive relief, costs or attorney fees, 815 § 510/3	Yes, misdemeanor, 720 § 5/17-11
INDIANA	No, 24-5-0.5-1 to 24-5-0.5-12	Yes, 24-5-0.5-3	Consumer or consumer class; attorney general, 24-5-0.5-4	Actual damages; attorney fees; attorney general may seek injunction, costs and up to $15,000 for violating injunction, 24-5-0.5-8; penalty up to $500 for incurable deceptive act, 25-4-0.5-8	Yes, fine up to $1,500, 9-19-9-7
IOWA	No, 714.16	Yes, 714.16; 714H.3	Attorney general; consumer, 714.16; 714H.5	Temporary restraining order; preliminary injunction; permanent injunction; civil penalty not to exceed $40,000; up to $5,000 per day for violation of temporary restraining order, preliminary injunction or injunction; costs of court, investigation, reasonable attorney fees, 714.16	Yes, 321.71

Table 3: Deceptive Trade Practices—Continued

State	Uniform Deceptive Trade Practices Act Adopted?	False Advertising Forbidden?	Who May Bring Suit	Remedies Available	Auto Odometer Tampering Forbidden?
KANSAS	No, Kansas Consumer Protection Act: 50-623 to 50-643	Yes, 50-626	Attorney general or any other county or district attorney, 50-634; consumer, 50-634	Obtain declaratory or injunctive relief; reasonable expenses and investigation fees, 50-632; individual may receive attorney fees, 50-634; civil penalty up to $10,000 per violation; up to $20,000 per violation for supplier, 50-636	Yes, 50-648
KENTUCKY	No, Consumer Protection Act: 367-010 to 367-360	Yes, 367.170	Attorney general, consumer, 367.190; 367.220	Injunction, 367.190; restraining order; penalty for violation fine up to $25,000, civil penalty up to $2,000 per violation or up to $10,000 per violation if victim is 60 or over, 367.990; reasonable attorney fees; 367.220	Yes, license may be revoked; civil penalties of $5,000 per violation; class D felony, 190.270; 367.990
LOUISIANA	Yes, Unfair Trade Practices and Consumer Protection Law: 51:1401 to 51:1418	Yes, 51:411; 51:1405	Attorney general, 51:1407; individual who has suffered ascertainable loss, 51:1409	Actual damages; treble damages plus attorney fees and costs if willful; injunctive relief, 51:1407; additional relief as necessary to compensate, 51:1408; 51:1409	Yes; misdemeanor punishable by imprisonment up to 90 days and/or fine up to $500; 32:726.1
MAINE	Yes, Maine Unfair Trade Practices Act: Tit. 5, §§ 205-A to 214; Uniform Deceptive Trade Practices Act: Tit. 10, §§ 1211 to 1216	Yes, Tit. 10, § 1212	Attorney general, person likely to be damaged by practice, Tit. 10, § 1213; Tit. 5, §§ 209; 213	Injunction; attorney fees and costs; common law and other statutory remedies, Tit. 5, § 213; Tit. 10, § 1213	Yes, class C offense, Tit. 29-A, § 2106

Table 3: Deceptive Trade Practices—Continued

State	Uniform Deceptive Trade Practices Act Adopted?	False Advertising Forbidden?	Who May Bring Suit	Remedies Available	Auto Odometer Tampering Forbidden?
MARYLAND	No Consumer Protection Act: Com. Law §§ 13-101 to 13-501	Yes, Com. Law § 13-301	Consumer Protection Division; attorney general; consumer, Com. Law §§ 13-401 to 13-408	Fine up to $1,000 per violation; subsequent same violation $5,000; actual damages; possibly attorney fees, Com. Law §§ 13-401 to 13-411; misdemeanor punishable by imprisonment up to 12 months and/or fine up to $1,000 in addition to any civil penalties, Com. Law § 13-411	Yes, Transp. § 22-415
MASSACHUSETTS	Yes, Ch. 93A, §§ 1 to 11	Unlawful, Ch. 93A, § 2; Ch. 266, §§ 91 to 93	Attorney General, Ch. 93A, § 4; private party, Ch. 93A, § 9	Injunction; actual damages; double or treble damages, attorney fees and costs if willful violation, Ch. 93A, § 11	Yes; liable for three times actual damages or $1,500, whichever is greater; attorney fees, Ch. 266, § 141A; criminal penalty of imprisonment of 30 days to 2 yrs. and/or fine of $500 to $1,000, Ch. 266, § 141
MICHIGAN	No, Michigan Consumer Protection Act: 445.901 to 445.922	Yes, 445.903	Attorney general, 445.905; prosecuting attorney, 445.915; private citizen, 445.911; class action by attorney general, 445.910	Injunction; greater of actual damages or $250 plus attorney fees; persistent and knowing violation: fine up to $25,000; violation of injunction: fine of $5,000 per violation, 445.905; 445.911	Yes, greater of treble damages or $1,500; attorney fees and costs, 257.233a
MINNESOTA	Yes, Uniform Deceptive Trade Practices Act: 325D.43 to 325D.48	Yes, 325D.44	Attorney general, county attorney; any person likely to be damaged, 325D.45	Injunctive relief; court costs; attorney fees, 325D.45	Yes; gross misdemeanor, 325E.16; civil penalties of actual damages; costs; attorney fees; court has discretion to award greater of treble damages or $1,500, 325E.14

Table 3: Deceptive Trade Practices—Continued

State	Uniform Deceptive Trade Practices Act Adopted?	False Advertising Forbidden?	Who May Bring Suit	Remedies Available	Auto Odometer Tampering Forbidden?
MISSISSIPPI	Yes, 75-24-1 to 75-24-29	Yes, 75-24-5	Attorney general, 75-24-9; district attorney; county attorney, 75-24-21; injured consumer; no class actions, 75-24-15	Restoration of money or property; revocation of violator's business license, 75-24-11; injunction; civil penalty up to $10,000 for willful violations; attorney fees, 75-24-19; misdemeanor punished by fine up to $1,000, 75-24-20	Yes, 63-7-203; misdemeanor punishable by imprisonment up to 6 mos. and/or fine up to $500; 63-7-209
MISSOURI	No, 407.010 to 407.130	Yes, 407.020	Consumer; class action, 407.025; attorney general, 407.100	Class E felony, 407.020; false advertising: punitive damages; attorney fees; injunction, 407.025; restitution civil penalty not more than $1,000, 407.100	Yes, 407.511 to 407.558; greater of treble damages or $2,500; attorney fees, 407.546; injunction, 407.551; odometer fraud: 1st degree: class A misdemeanor, 407.516; 2nd degree: class D felony, 407.521; 3rd degree: class C misdemeanor, 407.526
MONTANA	No, Montana Unfair Trade Practices and Consumer Protection Act of 1973: 30-14-101 to 30-14-224	Yes, 30-14-103	County attorney; attorney general, 30-14-121; individuals; no class actions, 30-14-133; Dept. of Commerce, 30-14-111	Recovery of out-of-pocket losses, 30-14-132; greater of $500 or actual damages; treble damages; reasonable attorney fees; injunction, 30-14-133	Yes; imprisonment up to 10 yrs. and/or fine up to $5,000; motor vehicle dealer revocation of license, 30-14-133
NEBRASKA	Yes with modifications, 87-301 to 87-306	Yes, 87-302	Person likely to be damaged, 87-303; attorney general, 87-303.02	Criminal penalties for violating Act; costs; attorney fees; other common law and statutory remedies, 87-303; injunction; civil penalty up to $2,000 for each violation, 87-303.11	Yes, 60-190

Table 3: Deceptive Trade Practices—Continued

State	Uniform Deceptive Trade Practices Act Adopted?	False Advertising Forbidden?	Who May Bring Suit	Remedies Available	Auto Odometer Tampering Forbidden?
NEVADA	Revised Uniform Act adopted with significant variations, 598.0903 to 598.0999	Yes, 598.0915; 207.170 to 207.171	Attorney general; consumer advocate; consumer if he is victim of deceptive trade practice, 41.600; 509.0963; district attorney, 207.174	Injunction; return of money or property; penalty up to $10,000 for each violation; willful violation: misdemeanor, second offense: gross misdemeanor, third offense: felony; suspension of right to conduct business or dissolution of corporation possible, 598.0999; criminal and civil penalties, 207.174; 207.175; damages; attorney fees; costs, 41.600	Yes, 484D.310; knowing sale of vehicle with altered odometer: category B felony, 484D.335
NEW HAMPSHIRE	Yes, 358A:1- to 358-A:13	Yes, 358-A:2	Attorney general, consumer protection, 358-A:4; private action, 358-A:10; class action, 358-A:10-a	Misdemeanor penalty, 358-A:6; injunctive relief; equitable relief; attorney fees; greater of actual damages or $1,000; willful violation not less than double up to treble damages, 358-A:10; state civil penalties up to $10,000 per violation, 358-A:4	Yes; 1st offense: misdemeanor; 2nd offense class B felony, 262:17
NEW JERSEY	No, 56:8-1 to 56:8-20	Yes, 56:8-2	Attorney general; private party, 56:8-10; 56:8-11	Penalty as attorney general deems proper, 56:8-3.1; injunction; penalty up to $10,000 for 1st offense; $20,000 for subsequent offenses; attorney general may recover costs of suit in an action maintained by state, 56:8-13; senior citizens receive double amount or value, 56:8-11; 56:8-14	Yes; disorderly persons offense, 2C:21-8

Table 3: Deceptive Trade Practices—Continued

State	Uniform Deceptive Trade Practices Act Adopted?	False Advertising Forbidden?	Who May Bring Suit	Remedies Available	Auto Odometer Tampering Forbidden?
NEW MEXICO	Yes, Unfair Practices Act: 57-12-1 to 57-12-26	Yes, 57-15-1; 57-15-2	Attorney general, 57-12-8; any private person likely to be damaged, 57-12-10; district attorney, 57-15-5	Injunctive relief; greater of actual damages or $100; greater of $300 or treble damages; attorney fees and costs, 57-12-10; civil penalty up to $5,000 per violation, 57-12-11; false advertising civil penalty up to $500 per violation, 57-15-4	No specific provision for odometer tampering; willful misrepresentation of age and condition of motor vehicle: misdemeanor; treble damages, 57-12-6
NEW YORK	No, Consumer Protection From Deceptive Acts and Practices: Gen. Bus. §§ 349 to 350-F-1	Yes, Gen. Bus. §§ 350 to 350-A	Yes; Attorney general, Gen. Bus. § 350-D; private litigation for party injured, Gen. Bus. § 350-E	Treble damages up to $10,000 for willful violations; attorney fees, Gen. Bus. § 350-E	Yes; misdemeanor punishable by fine up to $500 per violation; fine up to $1,500 per violation if willful, Gen. Bus. § 392-E
NORTH CAROLINA	No; 75-1 to 75-42	Yes, 75-1.1; 75-29	Attorney general; person injured, 75-15.2; 75-16	Civil penalties: up to $5,000 per violation, 75-15.2; treble damages if injured, 75-16; attorney fees, 75-16.1	Yes, 20-343
NORTH DAKOTA	No, Unfair Trade Practices Law: 51-10-01 to 51-12-15	Yes, 51-12-01; 51-12-08	Attorney general; state's attorney, 51-10-05.1; 51-12-14; any person damaged, 51-10-06	False advertising: class B misdemeanor, 51-12-02; injunction, 51-10-06; 51-12-14	Yes; violation is class B misdemeanor; class C felony if prior conviction, 39-21-51
OHIO	Adopted with modifications, 4165.01 to 4165.04; overlaps with Uniform Consumer Sales Practice Act: 1345.01 to 1345.13	Yes, 1345.02; 4165.02	Attorney general, 1345.07; consumer, 1345.09; person likely to be damaged; person injured, 4165.03	Civil penalty up to $25,000 if practice found to be unfair or deceptive, 1345.07; injunction; actual damages; attorney fees, 4165.03; other remedies as available at common law and other statutes, 1345.09	Yes; 4549.42; greater of treble damages or $1,500; attorney fees; costs, 4549.46

Table 3: Deceptive Trade Practices—Continued

State	Uniform Deceptive Trade Practices Act Adopted?	False Advertising Forbidden?	Who May Bring Suit	Remedies Available	Auto Odometer Tampering Forbidden?
OKLAHOMA	Yes; Oklahoma Consumer Protection Act: Tit. 15, §§ 751 to 765	Yes; Tit. 15, § 753	Tit. 15, § 756.1 Attorney general; district attorney; consumer, Tit. 15, § 761.1	Declaratory judgment; restraining order; actual damages, revoke license; other appropriate relief, Tit. 15, § 756.1; actual damages; costs; attorney fees; civil penalty up to $10,000 per violation of injunction; up to $2,000 per violation if unconscionable, Tit. 15, § 761.1	Yes; Tit. 47, § 12-503; misdemeanor punishable by imprisonment up to 1 yr. and/or fine up to $10,000; greater of treble damages or $1,500; attorney fees; costs, Tit. 47, § 12-506
OREGON	Main provisions adopted with significant variations, 646.605 to 646.656	Yes, 646.608	State, 646.632; consumers, 646.638	Greater of actual damages or $200, whichever is greater; punitive and equitable relief; injunction; attorney fees, 646.638; additional orders as necessary to restore money or property to injured person or to insure cessation of unlawful trade practice, 646.636	Yes; class C felony; greater of $1,500 or treble damages; costs; reasonable attorney fees, 815.410;
PENNSYLVANIA	No, Unfair Trade Practices and Consumer Protection Law: Tit. 73, §§ 201-1 to 201-9	Yes; Tit. 73, §§ 201-2; 201-3	Private actions; attorney general; district attorney, Tit. 73, § 201-4; consumer-purchaser suffering ascertainable loss, Tit. 73, § 201-9	Greater of actual damages or $100; court may award treble damages but not less than $100, Tit. 73, § 207-9.2; civil penalty up to $1,000; $3,000 if victim is 60 or older, Tit. 73, § 201-8; suspend right to do business, Tit. 73, § 201.9; injunction; costs; attorney fees; any additional relief as deemed necessary or proper, Tit. 73, § 201-9.2	Yes, Tit. 75, § 7132; Greater of treble damages or $3,000; attorney fees, Tit. 75, § 7138; criminal penalties, Tit. 75, § 7139

Table 3: Deceptive Trade Practices—Continued

State	Uniform Deceptive Trade Practices Act Adopted?	False Advertising Forbidden?	Who May Bring Suit	Remedies Available	Auto Odometer Tampering Forbidden?
RHODE ISLAND	No, Unfair Trade Practice and Consumer Protection Act: 6-13.1-1 to 6-13.1-29	Yes, 6-13.1-1	Attorney general, 6-13.1-5; consumer with ascertainable loss, 6-13.1-5.2; class actions allowed, 6-13.11-5.2	Greater of actual damages or $200; punitive or equitable damages; injunction; attorney fees; costs, 6-13.1-5.2	Yes, 31-23.2-4; imprisonment up to 5 yrs. or fine up to $10,000 or $1.00 per mile mileage fraud; revocation of vehicle dealer's license, 31-23.2-3; 31-23.2-7
SOUTH CAROLINA	No, South Carolina Unfair Trade Practice Act: 39-5-10 to 39-5-560	Yes, 39-5-10; 39-5-20	Attorney general, 39-5-50; any person suffering ascertainable loss, 39-5-140; solicitor, county attorney or city attorney with prior approval by the attorney general, 39-5-130	Treble damages; actual damages; costs; attorney fees, 39-5-140; civil penalty up to $5,000 per violation, 39-5-110	No specific statute
SOUTH DAKOTA	No, 37-24-1 to 37-24-56	Yes, 37-24-6	Attorney general, 37-24-23; any individual, 37-24-31	Injunction, 37-24-23; civil penalty up to $2,000, 37-24-27; actual damages; additional orders or judgments as court deems necessary, 37-24-31; class 2 misdemeanor, 37-24-29; 37-24-6	Yes; 1st offense: class 1 misdemeanor; 2nd and subsequent violations: class 6 felony, 32-15-33
TENNESSEE	No, Tennessee Consumer Protection Act of 1977: 47-18-101 to 47-18-129	Yes, 47-18-104	Attorney general; any person with ascertainable loss; Div. of Consumer Affairs in Dept. of Commerce and Insurance, 47-18-106 to 47-18-109; 47-18-114	Injunctive relief; damages for injured customers; revocation of violator's license; civil penalty up to $1,000 per violation, up to $2,000 per violation of injunction; treble damages for willful violation; costs; attorney fees, 47-18-106; 47-18-108; 47-18-109; class B misdemeanor, 47-18-104, 39-14-127	Yes; class A misdemeanor, 47-18-104(16); 39-14-132

Table 3: Deceptive Trade Practices—Continued

State	Uniform Deceptive Trade Practices Act Adopted?	False Advertising Forbidden?	Who May Bring Suit	Remedies Available	Auto Odometer Tampering Forbidden?
TEXAS	No, Deceptive Trade Practices– Consumer Protection Act: Bus. & Com. §§ 17.41 to 17.63	Yes, Bus. & Com. § 17.46	Attorney general; consumers; consumer protection division, district attorney, Bus. & Com. §§ 17.47; 17.4 8	Injunction; restraining order; civil penalty up to $20,000 per violation; additional amount up to $250,000 if against consumer 65 or older; fine up to $10,000 per violation of injunction not to exceed $50,000, Bus. & Com. § 17.47; actual damages or restitution of property to consumer; treble damages if willful; costs; attorney fees; plus remedies available in other laws, Bus. & Com. §§ 17.43; 17.50	Yes, Bus. & Com. § 17.46(16)
UTAH	No, 13-11a-1 to 13-11a-6	Yes, 13-11a-3	State; consumer, 13-11a-4	Injunction; greater of $2,000 or actual damages; costs; attorney fees; corrective advertising; remedies are in addition to remedies available for same conduct under state or local law, 13-11a-4	Yes; offer for sale, sell, use, or install a device that causes the odometer to register miles other than true miles: class B misdemeanor, 41-1a-1310; tamper with odometer with intent to reduce true number of miles; knowingly sell or transfer vehicle with reduced miles; provide false odometer disclosure statement: third degree felony, 41-1a-1319

Table 3: Deceptive Trade Practices—Continued

State	Uniform Deceptive Trade Practices Act Adopted?	False Advertising Forbidden?	Who May Bring Suit	Remedies Available	Auto Odometer Tampering Forbidden?
VERMONT	No, Tit. 9, §§ 2453 to 2466a	Yes, Tit. 9, § 2453	Attorney general; state attorney, Tit. 9, § 2458; damaged consumer, Tit. 9, § 2461	Injunction; civil penalty up to $10,000 per violation, Tit. 9, § 2458; equitable relief; damages up to three times actual; attorney fees; exemplary damages, Tit. 9, § 2461; restitution of cash or goods, Tit. 9, § 2458	Yes; 1st offense: fine up to $1,000; up to $2,500 for each subsequent offense, Tit. 23, § 1704a
VIRGINIA	No, Virginia Consumer Protection Act: 59.1-196 to 59.1-207	Yes, 59.1-200	Attorney general; commonwealth attorney, 59.1-203; harmed individual, 59.1-204	Enjoin violations; greater of actual damages or $500, 59.1-204; fine up to $1,000 for willful violation; attorney fees; costs, 59.1-206	Yes; first offense: imprisonment in jail up to 1 yr. and/or fine up to $10,000; subsequent offenses: imprisonment 1-5 yrs. in state correctional facility and or fine up to $50,000, 46.2-112
WASHINGTON	No; 19.86.010 to 19.86.920	Yes; 19.86.020	Any injured person; attorney general, 19.86.090; 19.86.095	Civil penalties; injunction; treble damages not to exceed $10,000; costs; attorney fees; actual damages, 19.86.090	Yes; civil suit may recover costs and attorney fees, 46.37.540; 46.37.590
WEST VIRGINIA	No, West Virginia Consumer Credit and Protection Act: 46A-6-101 to 46A-8-102	Yes, 46A-6-102; 46A-6-104	Consumer with ascertainable loss, 46A-6-106	Greater of actual damages or $200; injunction; equitable relief, 46A-6-106	No specific provision against tampering
WISCONSIN	No, Wisconsin Consumer Act: 421 to 427	Yes, 423.301	Class actions; individuals; administrator, 426.110	Customer entitled to retain goods received without obligation to pay and recover any sums paid to merchant, 425.305; fine up to $2,000, 425.401; injunction; attorney fees, 426.110	Yes; imprisonment up to 12 mos. in county jail and/or fine up to $5,000, 347.415; 347.50

4. INTEREST RATES

Every state has very specific limits on the amount of interest that may be charged on consumer contracts, ranging anywhere from five to 25 percent. But because parties may always agree to interest rates that are above the legal limit, most consumer contracts include interest rates that are above that limit.

Thus few states have limits on what can be expressly agreed to in a contract. For example, Alaska limits express contract terms to five percent over the legal rate, while the District of Columbia has the highest stated ceiling, at 24 percent. A number of states allow the limit to be pegged to the rate set by the Federal Reserve Board; most of these states have limits of five percent above the Federal Reserve. Potentially, these may be much higher than the District of Columbia's 24 percent. Overall, it appears that the more rural the state, the lower the limits. Presumably, farmers are protected and are more secure with lower interest rates than citizens of generally urban states with larger economies.

Usury is an unconscionable and exorbitant rate or amount of interest which exceeds those permitted by law.

There is a great variety of statutory remedies for usury. A few states class usury as a crime and prescribe prison for violations of its usury laws. The majority of states provide for economic remedies such as forfeiture of all interest paid, recovery of double the usurious amount, payment of a fine, or making the contract unenforceable. Some states even specify that banks or savings and loans pay penalties. North Dakota has one of the more extreme usury penalties: it requires payment of all interest plus 25 percent of the principal.

For the most part there are myriad exceptions to the legal interest rate, which may be tied to the character of the lender, borrower, loan amount, the nature of the contract, or the matter that is the subject of the contract. Effectively, legal interest rates are no more than general guidelines for all transactions rather than the specific limits placed on them. There are so many exceptions in many states that it is often necessary to find a different rate for every conceivable situation.

Table 4: Interest Rates

State	Legal Maximum Rate of Interest	Usury Penalty	Judgments	Exceptions
ALABAMA	If agreed upon in writing, up to 8%, otherwise 6%, 8-8-1	Defense of usury may not be plead against holder of negotiable instrument, 8-8-12	Judgments for payment of money, other than costs, bear interest from date of entry at 7.5% per yr. if no contract; if based on contract, at contract rate; valid for judgments entered on or after September 1, 2011, 8-8-10	Loans over $2,000, 8-8-5; debts under National Housing Act or Veterans' Benefits acts, 8-8-6; industrial development boards and medical clinic boards, 11-54-97, 11-58-15; bonds issued by public or non-profit organizations, 8-8-7; public housing bonds, State Board of Education Securities, 24-1-32, 16-3-28; public hospital corporations, 22-21-6; warrants by cities and municipalities, 11-9-27; loans against life insurance policies, 27-15-8.1
ALASKA	Absent contract: 10.5%; express contract agreement: greater of 10% or 5% over annual rate charged by specified banks as of date of loan, 45.45.010	Double amount of usurious interest if action brought within 2 yrs., 45.45.030; if under contract at usurious rate, forfeiture of entire interest on debt, 45.45.040	If no contract, 3% above 12th Fed. Reserve Dist. discount rate on January 2 of year in which judgment is entered; if contract: contract rate; prejudgment interest accrues from earlier of day defendant is served or received notification that injury had occurred and suit might be brought, 09.30.070	Contract where principal amount exceeds $25,000, 45.45.010(b)
ARIZONA	10%; any rate may be agreed and contracted upon, 44-1201	Forfeit all interest, 44-1202; usurious payments deemed to be made toward principal; if payments exceed principal, judgment may be given in favor of debtor with interest at rate of 10%, 44-1203 to 44-1204	Lesser of 10% or 1% plus prime rate established by board of governors, 44-1201(b	Full exception for obligations insured or guaranteed by United States, 44-1206

Table 4: Interest Rates—Continued

State	Legal Maximum Rate of Interest	Usury Penalty	Judgments	Exceptions
ARKANSAS	6% default rate if none listed, 4-57-104; 17% maximum for all debts not governmental bonds or loans or loans by FDIC institutions, AR Const. amend. 89, § 3; General Assembly may from time to time fix rates for governmental loans, AR Const. amend. 89, § 8	General prohibition on usury, 4-57-105; statutory and constitutional provisions that provided specific remedy repealed with no current replacement	If contract, greater of 10% or contract rate; if no contract: 10%; rate can never exceed constitutional limit of 17%, 16-65-114	Credit cards, 4-107-307
CALIFORNIA	Loan/forbearance of any money, goods, or things in action, or accounts after demand: 7% or contract rate, CA Const. art. XV, § 1; contract rate shall not exceed 12%, Civ. § 1916-1	Any contract or agreement made for greater than 12% shall be null and void as to any stipulation to pay interest, Civ. § 1916-2; debtor may recover treble amount paid if action brought within 1 yr. of payment; willful violation is loan-sharking, a felony punishable by imprisonment in state prison up to 5 yrs. or county jail up to 1 yr., Civ. § 1916-3	Rate of interest on a judgment shall be set by legislature at not over 10%, variable and based upon interest rates charged by federal agencies and/or economic indicators; 7% if legislature does not set rate, CA Const. art. XV, § 1	Incorporated insurer, Ins. § 1100.1; licensed broker-deals, Corp. § 25211.5; indebtedness issued pursuant to corporate securities law, Corp. § 25116; licensed business and industrial development corporation, Fin. § 31410; state banks and national or foreign (other state) banks with office in state and acting as trustee, Fin. § 1556; bank holding companies, Fin. § 1287; state and federal savings and loans, Fin. § 7675
COLORADO	8%, 5-12-101; maximum rate under contract: 45%, 5-12-103; interest on consumer loan may not exceed 12% unless made by supervised lender, 5-2-201	Consumer loans: interest void and debtor granted right to recover interest payments, 5-5-201; knowingly exceeding 45% is class 6 felony, 18-15-104	8% if no rate specified in contract; rate on day of judgment if contract rate is variable, 5-12-102[4]	Savings and loans, 11-41-115; mortgages, 5-13-101; business and agricultural loans, 5-13-102); small business loans, 5-13-103

Table 4: Interest Rates—Continued

State	Legal Maximum Rate of Interest	Usury Penalty	Judgments	Exceptions
CONNECTICUT	12%, 37-4	Loan is not enforceable, 36a-573	8% unless agreement to contrary, 37-1	Loans before September 12, 1911; bank; savings and loan; credit union; certain mortgages; loan for motor vehicle; boat; loan for higher education, 37-9; pawnbroker and loan broker, 21-44; 10% for negligence actions arising after May 27, 1997, 37-3b
DELAWARE	Up to 5% over Federal Reserve discount rate; same maximum rate even if agreed upon in writing, Tit. 6, § 2301	Debtor not required to pay excess over legal rate; if whole debt is paid with interest over legal rate, debtor may recover 3 times amount of excess interest or $500, whichever is greater, if action brought within 1 yr., Tit. 6, § 2304(b)	Interest at 5% over Federal Reserve discount rate added to any final judgment for damages, commencing from date of injury, demand letter required prior to trial, Tit. 6, § 2301	No limit where loan exceeds $100,000 and is not secured by mortgage on borrower's personal residence, Tit. 6, § 2301(c); payment of interest owed on FHA loans cannot be defended on any ground other than usurious rate, Tit. 6, § 2301(b)
DISTRICT OF COLUMBIA	In absence of agreement: 6%, 28-3302; by contract in writing: up to 24%, 28-3301	Forfeiture of interest; usurious interest paid may be recovered, 28-3303 to 28-3304	4% allowed on judgments against the District of Columbia, its officers, or employees acting within scope of employment; where judgment is not against District of Columbia, its officers, or its employees acting within scope of employment or where interest is not fixed by contract: 70% of the rate set by the Secretary of Treasury, 28-3302; 26 USC 6621	Federally insured bank or savings and loan and on direct motor vehicle installment loans, 28-3308; 28-3601 to 28-3602; international banking facility loans or time deposits, 28-3301(g)

Table 4: Interest Rates—Continued

State	Legal Maximum Rate of Interest	Usury Penalty	Judgments	Exceptions
FLORIDA	Written contract: 18%; no limit on loans over $500,000 unless interest rate exceeds rate prescribed in § 687.071, currently 25%, 687.03; No written contract: average discount rate of Federal Reserve Bank of New York for preceding year plus 400 basis points, determined by the Chief Financial Officer and adjusted quarterly, 687.01; 55.03	All interest forfeited and repaid double, 687.04; criminal usury: credit at rate of 25-45% is misdemeanor punishable by imprisonment up to 60 days and/or $500 fine; over 45% is 3rd degree felony; keeping books/records for loan at 25% is 1st degree misdemeanor; if loan or forbearance is criminal, debt is not enforceable, 687.071	Judgment must bear on its face the rate of interest payable and accrues on judgment until paid; interest rate established at time judgment is obtained and is adjusted annually on January 1 with rate set by Chief Financial Officer until paid, 55.03	If specifically licensed in business making loans, 516.031; sale of motor vehicles, 520.01 to 520.014
GEORGIA	No written contract or rate not specified: 7%; written contract: Loan up to $3,000: 16%; over $3,000: any rate of interest, with varying terms regarding acceleration and payment mechanics for contracts over $250,000, 7-4-2; in no event can more than 5% per MONTH be charged, 7-4-18	Forfeiture of entire interest, 7-4-10; criminal misdemeanor, 7-4-18	Prime rate determined by Federal Reserve System plus 3% or rate of interest specified in written contract, 7-4-12(b)	Small industrial loans, 7-3-14; bank fees and other charges of financial institutions not considered interest, 7-4-18(d)

Table 4: Interest Rates—Continued

State	Legal Maximum Rate of Interest	Usury Penalty	Judgments	Exceptions
HAWAII	No written contract: 10%; obligations of the state limited to lower of 10% or prime rate for each calendar quarter, 478-2; written contract: 12% or 24% if creditor is financial institution regulated under Ch. 412 (other than trust company or credit union), 478-4	Creditor may recover principal only and debtor recovers costs; if interest has been paid, judgment shall be for principal less amount of interest paid, 478-5; imprisonment up to 1 yr. and/or $250 fine, 478-6	10% on any judgment in any civil suit, 478-3	Certain real property transactions secured by a variety of liens described in § 478-8; payment of any claim under § 431:13-108, Reimbursement for accident and health or sickness insurance benefits; credit sales subject to Ch. 476 or interest rate does not exceed 18%; indebtedness secured by time share interest and interest rate does not exceed 18%; loan from employee benefit plan or employees' retirement system of State of Hawaii; mortgage loan made by financial institution pursuant to § 412:2-108, Alternative mortgage loans rules, 478-8
IDAHO	12% unless express written contract fixing different rate, 28-22-104	Plaintiff may recover amount of actual injury, 6-807; 6-1602	5% plus annual average yield on U.S. Treasury securities as determined by Idaho state treasurer, 28-22-104	
ILLINOIS	9%, but relevant amount is limit as of the time the contract is made, 815 § 205/4	Recipient subject to suit for double all interest, charges, and attorney fees and court costs, 815 § 205/6	9%, or 6% when judgment debtor is unit of local government, school district, or community college, 735 § 5/2-1303; 735 § 5/12-109	Loan under Consumer Installment Loan Act, 205 § 670/1; short-term loans, 815 § 205/4.1a; installment loans, 815 § 205/4a; 205 § 670/15; pawnbrokers, 205 § 510/2; reverse mortgage loan, 205 § 305/46

Table 4: Interest Rates—Continued

State	Legal Maximum Rate of Interest	Usury Penalty	Judgments	Exceptions
INDIANA	Unsupervised consumer loan: 25%, 24-4.5-3-201; supervised loan: finance charge may not exceed greater of total of 36% on unpaid principal up to $2,000 plus 21% on unpaid principal $2,000 to $4,000 plus 15% on unpaid principal over $4,000, or 25% on unpaid balance of principal, 24-4.5-3-508	Class A misdemeanor for supervised lender to knowingly charge in excess of 24-4.5-3-508 for consumer loan, 24-4.5-5-301; consumer has right to refund of amount paid in excess of statute and up to 3 times the amount in court's discretion, 24-4.5-5-202	At contract rate not exceeding 8%, or 8% if there is no contract between the parties, beginning from the date of verdict or the finding of the court, 24-4.6-1-101; 6% beginning 45 days after judgment if against the state, 34-54-8-5	Supervised loan is a consumer loan in which rate of loan finance charge exceeds 25%, 24-4.5-3-501
IOWA	5% unless agreed in writing to pay interest at rate not to exceed 2% above monthly average 10-yr. constant maturity rate of U.S. government notes, 535.2(1); 535.2(3)	Plaintiff may have judgment only for principal debt without interest or costs; forfeiture of 8% by the year of principal remaining unpaid at time of judgment, 535.5	10% unless rate up to § 535.2 amount is expressed in contract, 535.3; 668.13	Loan for real property, business or agricultural loans, 535.2(2)
KANSAS	10% when no other rate of interest is agreed upon, 16-201; written contract: 15% unless otherwise specifically authorized by law, 16-207(a)	Forfeit all interest in excess of maximum rate; forfeit sum equal to amt. of excess interest that may be set up as defense or counterclaim in any action to enforce collection; borrower shall also recover reasonable attorney fee, 16-207(d)	4% above federal discount rate as of July 1 preceding judgment; limited actions: 12%, 16-204; judgment on contract: contract rate controls up to legal maximum rate, 16-205	Business and agricultural loans; note secured by real estate mortgage; qualified plan loans, 16-207
KENTUCKY	8% absent agreement otherwise; parties may agree to a rate not to exceed 4% above discount rate of Fed. Reserve Bank or 19% whichever is less for principal amount up to $15,000; over $15,000: any rate, 360.010	Borrower may recover twice interest paid, provided action is commenced within 2 yrs. of time usurious action occurred, 360.020	12%; if written contract, at contract rate, 360.040	Banks, 360.010(2); credit unions, 286.6-465; small loans, 286.4-530
LOUISIANA	12%, 9:3500	Entire interest forfeited, 9:3501	Rate set forth by commissioner of financial institutions, 13:4202; state agencies: 6%, 13:5112	Secured by mortgage, 9:3504; borrowing for commercial/business purposes, 9:3509

Table 4: Interest Rates—Continued

State	Legal Maximum Rate of Interest	Usury Penalty	Judgments	Exceptions
MAINE	6% unless otherwise agreed upon in writing, Tit. 9-B, § 432	Civil penalty up to $5,000; actual damages or $250, whichever is greater, plus attorney fees and costs of action, Tit. 9-A, § 120	Before judgment: U.S. Treasury Bill rate plus 6% unless contracted, then contract rate, Tit. 14, § 1602-B; after judgment: U.S. Treasury rate plus 6% unless contracted, then contract rate, Tit. 14, § 1602-C	Pawnbrokers, Tit. 30-A, § 3963; secured transactions, Tit. 11, § 9-1201; consumer credit, Tit. 9-A, § 2-201
MARYLAND	6%, MD Const. art. III, § 57; 8% if written agreement, Com. Law § 12-103	Forfeit triple interest and charges collected or $500, whichever is greater, Com. Law § 12-114	10%; money judgment may carry contract rate until originally scheduled maturity date, Cts. & Jud. Proc. § 11-106; 11-107; 11- 301	Mortgage secured loans, Com. Law § 12-103; unsecured loans secured by other than savings, Com. Law § 12-103; installment loans not secured by real property, Com. Law § 12-103; open-end retail accounts, Com. Law §12-506; installment sales contract for motor vehicles and other consumer goods, Com. Law § 12-609 to 12-610
MASSACHUSETTS	6% unless contract, Ch. 107, § 3	Over 20%: criminal usury; usurious loan may be voided by supreme judicial or superior court in equity upon petition by person to whom loan was made, Ch. 271, § 49	12% from date of commencement of action, Ch. 231, § 6B; if written contract, at contract rate up to 12%, Ch. 231, § 6C; costs, expenses, and interest for insubstantial, frivolous or bad faith claims or defense, Ch. 231, § 6F	Small loans, Ch. 140, § 96; open-end credit transaction, Ch. 140, § 114B; life insurance policy loans, Ch. 175, § 142
MICHIGAN	5%; written agreement: 7%, 438.31; preempted for certain home loans by Molosky v. Washington Mutual, 664 F.3d 109 (6th Cir. 2011)	Barred from recovery of any interest, official fees, delinquency or collection charge, attorney fees or costs; borrower entitled to recover attorney fees and costs, 438.32	Rate of interest equal to 1% plus the avg. interest paid at auctions of 5–yr. U.S. treasury notes during the 6 mos. immediately preceding July 1 and January 1, as certified by state treasurer and compounded annually; written instrument: contract interest rate if legal at time executed, 600.6013	Small loans, 493.1; credit union loans, 490.422(d); certain foreign loans, 493.18; depository institution; regulated lender, 445.1854

Table 4: Interest Rates—Continued

State	Legal Maximum Rate of Interest	Usury Penalty	Judgments	Exceptions
MINNESOTA	6%; written contract: 8% up to $100,000; over $100,000: no limitation on interest rate, 334.01	Contract void, 47.20; 334.03; borrower may recover full interest and premiums with costs, 334.02; usurious interest by banks, savings and loans and credit unions results in forfeitures of all interest; payor may recover twice interest paid, 48.196	Judgment up to $50,000: interest rate based on secondary market yield of 1-yr. U.S. Treasury bills, determined on or before December 20 of prior year by state court administrator; over $50,000 (other than against the state): 10%, 549.09	Depository institutions, 48.195; credit unions, 52.14; dealers under Securities Exchange Act, 334.19; mortgage loans, 47.204; business and agricultural loans, 334.011; plans subject to provisions of Employee Retirement Income Security Act of 1974, 334.01; loans secured by savings accounts, 334.012
MISSISSIPPI	8%, 75-17-1[1]; written contract: 10% or 5% above discount rate, 75-17-1[2]	Misdemeanor punishable by fine $100 to $1,000; forfeit all interest and other charges and borrower may recover; if rate exceeds maximum by 100%, forfeit all principal and interest or other charges paid, and borrower may recover, 75-67-119	Interest at annual rate set by judge; written contract: contract rate, 75-17-7	Residential real property loan, 75-17-1; mobile homes, 75-17-23; partnership, joint venture, religious society, unincorporated assoc. or domestic or foreign corp., 75-17-1 [3]

Table 4: Interest Rates—Continued

State	Legal Maximum Rate of Interest	Usury Penalty	Judgments	Exceptions
MISSOURI	When no other rate agreed upon: 9%, 408.020; contract rate not to exceed 10% except when market rate is higher, 408.030	Excess interest over legal rate applied to principal or debtor may recover, 408.050; 408.060; debtor may recover twice amount of interest paid, costs of suit, and attorney fees, 408.030	9% or higher rate lawfully stipulated, 408.040	Loans to corporation, general partnership, limited partnership, or limited liability company; business loans of $5,000 or more; real estate loan other than residential real estate loan and loans less than $5,000 secured by real estate used for agricultural activity loans of $5,000 or more secured solely by stock, bonds, bills of exchange, CDs, or other commercial paper pledged as collateral, 408.035
MONTANA	10%, 31-1-106; written agreement: 15% or rate up to 6 percentage pts. above prime rate published in by federal reserve system, 31-1-107	Forfeiture of 2 times interest received, 31-1-108	10% or contract rate, 25-9-205	Regulated lenders; finance operation that finances transactions between merchants, 31-1-112
NEBRASKA	6%, 45-102; written contract: 16%, 45-101.03; any contract seeking to prevent debtor from paying obligation in full in same amt. originally contracted plus interest not in excess of max. legal rate is also usury, 45-109	Only principal recoverable; 45-105; contracts usurious under § 45-109: principal plus interest not exceeding legal contract rate, 45-110	Interest fixed at 2% above bond equivalent yield of avg. accepted auction price for 1st auction of each annual quarter of 26-wk. U.S. Treasury bills in effect on date of judgment; agreed-upon rate of oral or written contract; rate specifically provided by law, 45-103	Loans by Department of Banking, loan to any corporation; principal over $25,000; loan guaranteed by state/federal government on securities, open credit accounts; savings and loans; business or agricultural purpose loans; installment contract for goods and services; loan to any corporation, partnership or trust, 45-101.04

Table 4: Interest Rates—Continued

State	Legal Maximum Rate of Interest	Usury Penalty	Judgments	Exceptions
NEVADA	No limit for what parties may contract; otherwise prime rate of Nevada's largest bank plus 2%, 99.040; 99-050		Contract rate or prime rate at largest bank in Nevada plus 2%, 17.130	Licensee may lend at any interest rate, 677.730
NEW HAMPSHIRE	10% unless differently stipulated in writing, 336:1		Determined by state treasurer as the prevailing discount rate of interest on 26–week U.S. treasury bills at the last auction preceding September in each year, plus 2% points rounded to the nearest tenth, 336:1	Educational institutions, 195-F:15; public utility, 374-C:14; pawnbrokers and small loans, 399-A:3; home mortgage loan, 399-A:2; consumer credit, 358-K:1
NEW JERSEY	6%: written contract: 16%; over $50,000: no limit, 31:1-1	Only principal may be recovered, 31:1-3; usury is criminal offense punishable by fine up to $250,000, 2C:21-19	Tort actions: pre-judgment interest at 0.25%, 4:42-11; contract actions: no pre-judgment interest, 59:13-8	Savings and loans; banks; Department of Housing and Urban Affairs and other organizations authorized by the Emergency Home Finance Act of 1970; state or federal government or quasi-governmental organizations, 31:1-1
NEW MEXICO	15% in absence of contract fixed rate, 56-8-3	Forfeit all interest; borrower may recover 2 times amount paid, 56-8-13	8¾%; written contract: contract rate; judgment for tortious conduct: 15%, 56-8-4	Corporations and limited partnerships, 56-8-9; 56-8-21; pawn brokers, 56-12-13
NEW YORK	16%, Banking §14-a, incorporated into Gen. Oblig. § 5-501(1))	Usurious notes void, Gen. Oblig. (§5-511(1)); borrower may recover any amount over legal rate, Gen. Oblig. §5-513; if bank, savings and loan, or trust company, interest forfeited and recovery of 2 times interest paid, Gen. Oblig. §5-511(1)	9%, C.P.L.R. §§ 5003; 5004	Loans insured by federal housing commission; loan over $250,000 except secured by real estate; loans over $2,500,000, Gen. Oblig. § 5-501; debit balance on customer accounts with a broker or dealer, Gen. Oblig. § 5-525

Table 4: Interest Rates—Continued

State	Legal Maximum Rate of Interest	Usury Penalty	Judgments	Exceptions
NORTH CAROLINA	8%, 24-1; written contract: greater of 16% or latest non-competitive rate for 6-mo. U.S. Treasury bills as of the 15th day of the month plus 6%, rounded to nearest .5% for loans up to $25,000; over $25,000: any rate is for loans up to $25,000; over $25,000: any rate, 24-1.1	Forfeiture of all interest; party paying may recover double interest paid, 24-2	8%, 24-1; written contract: contract rate, 24-5	Home loans secured by mortgage or first deed of trust, 24-1.1A; savings and loan associations, 24-1.4; loans to corporations, 24-9; equity lines of credit, 24-1.2A
NORTH DAKOTA	6%, 47-14-05; written contract: up to 5.5% higher than average interest on 6-mo. U.S. treasury bills for 6 mos. immediately preaching month in which transaction occurs, as computed and declared on last day of each mo. by state banking commissioner; maximum allowable interest rate ceiling must be at least 7%, 47-14-09	Forfeit all interest and 25% of principal, 47-14-10; class B misdemeanor, 47-14-11; 2 times amt. interest pd. may be recovered, 47-14-10	Contract rate, otherwise prime rate published in Wall Street Journal plus 3%, 28-20-34	Loans to corporations; agency funded by state/federal government; amount over $35,000; loans to partnerships/limited partnerships, 47-14-09
OHIO	8%, 1343.01	Excess interest applied to principal, 1343.04	Contract rate if specified, 1343.02; otherwise federal short-term rate determined by tax commissioner each October 15, plus 3%, 1343.03; 5703.47(B)	Loan amount exceeds $100,000; broker/dealer registered; secured by mortgage or deed of trust; business loan, 1343.01
OKLAHOMA	6%; written contract: any rate as may be authorized by law, Tit. 15, § 266	Forfeiture of entire interest; may recover 2 times any interest amt. pd. over legal rate, OK Const. art. XIV, § 3; if a bank is guilty of loaning at usurious rate, cancellation of bank charter and liquidation of assets of bank, Tit. 15, § 272	At contract rate or prime rate listed in 1st ed. of Wall Street Journal for each yr. plus 2%, Tit. 12, § 727.1	Pawnshops, Tit. 59, § 1510; small loans and retail installment, Tit. 14A, § 3-201

Table 4: Interest Rates—Continued

State	Legal Maximum Rate of Interest	Usury Penalty	Judgments	Exceptions
OREGON	9% unless otherwise agreed, 82.010	Forfeit interest on loan but borrower must repay the principal, 82.010	9% written contract: contract rate, 82.010	Business or agricultural loan; loan under $50,000, 82.010; financial institution or trust company as defined under § 706.008; consumer finance license defined under Ch. 725; pawnbroker licensed under Ch. 726; lender approved under the National Housing Act, loans secured with real property; loan secured through U.S. government, securities or commercial paper; broker-dealers registered under the Securities Exchange Act of 1934, 82.025
PENNSYLVANIA	6%, Tit. 41, §§ 201; 202	Borrower not required to pay amount over legal rate and may recover 3 times amount in excess; attorney fees may be awarded; intentional violation is 3rd degree misdemeanor, Tit. 41, §§ 501 to 507	Interest at lawful rate, Tit. 42, § 8101	Federal Housing Administration, Veteran's Administration or other department/agency of U.S. government; Tit. 41, §§ 301; 302; business loan; unsecured loan; noncollaterialized loan in excess of $35,000; obligation to pay a sum of money in an original bona fide principal amount more than $50,000, Tit. 41, § 301

Table 4: Interest Rates—Continued

State	Legal Maximum Rate of Interest	Usury Penalty	Judgments	Exceptions
RHODE ISLAND	12% unless different rate expressly stipulated, 6-26-1; otherwise, 21%, 6-26-2	Contract shall be void; knowing violation is criminal usury punishable by imprisonment up to 5 yrs., 6-26-3; borrower may recover 2 times amount of usurious interest paid, 6-26-4	12% unless otherwise already agreed upon rate, 6-26-1; 9-21-10	Licensed pawnbroker, 6-26-2; 19-26-18; commercial loans over $1,000,000, not secured by mortgage on personal residence; credit card transactions, 6-26-2; revolving or open-end credit plan; 6-27-4; finance charge for retail sales, 6-27-4
SOUTH CAROLINA	8.75%, 34-31-20		Prime rate published in Wall Street Journal plus 4%, 34-31-20	See South Carolina Consumer Protection Code, 37-1-101, et seq.
SOUTH DAKOTA	Absent agreement, 12%, 54-3-4; various official state interest rates: Category A-4.5%; Category B-10%; Category C-12%; Category D-1% per month or fraction thereof; Category E-4%; Category F-15%; Category G-5/6% per month or fraction thereof, 54-3-16	Penalties repealed July 1982; punishable as misdemeanor for pawnbrokers, 37-16-1	10%, 54-3-5.1; interest on inverse condemnation actions: Category A-4.5%	Real estate mortgages; Uniform Credit Code security agreements; revolving charge accounts, 54-11-); regulated lenders, 54-3-13
TENNESSEE	10%, 47-14-103	Contract unenforceable; if found unconscionable, lender must refund charges, fees, and commission fees and successful plaintiff may recover reasonable attorney fees, 47-14-117; willful collection is class A misdemeanor, 47-14-112	2% less than formula rate published by commissioner of financial institutions; written contract: contract rate, 47-14-121	Installment loans, 45-2-1106; loans under $1,000, 47-14-104; savings and loans, 45-3-705; single payment loans, 47-14-104; special formula rate used for transactions with state or state subdivision, 47-14-103(2)

Table 4: Interest Rates—Continued

State	Legal Maximum Rate of Interest	Usury Penalty	Judgments	Exceptions
TEXAS	When not specified, 6%, Fin. § 302.002	The greater of 3 times the amount computed by subtracting amount of interest allowed by law from the total amount of interest contracted for, charged, or received; or $2,000 or 20% of the amount of principal, whichever is less, Fin. §§ 305.001 to 305.003; creditor who is liable is also liable for reasonable attorney fees, Fin. § 305.005; each offense is misdemeanor punishable by fine up to $1,000, Fin. 305.008	If contract rate, then lesser of the contract rate or 18% Fin. § 304.002	Small loans, Fin. § 342.004; secondary mortgage loans, Fin. § 342.006
UTAH	10%; written contract: contract rate, 15-1-1	3rd degree felony, 76-6-520	Federal postjudgment interest rate as of Jan. 1 of each year plus 2%; written contract: contract rate and judgment must conform to contract, 15-1-4	Pawnbrokers (11-6-4)
VERMONT	12%, Tit. 9, § 41a	Forfeit all interest, all expenses of collection, and reasonable attorney fee; first offense: imprisonment up to 6 mos. and/or fine up to $500; subsequent offenses: imprisonment up to 1 yr. and/or fine up to $1,000, Tit. 9, § 50	12%, Tit. 12, § 2903	Retail installment contract, Tit. 9, §§ 41a 2405); municipal bonds, Tit. 24, § 1761; loan secured for recreational vehicle, aircraft, water craft, or farm equipment, Tit. 9 § 41a)

Table 4: Interest Rates—Continued

State	Legal Maximum Rate of Interest	Usury Penalty	Judgments	Exceptions
VIRGINIA	6% or contract rate, 6.2-301	Borrower may recover total amount paid and 2 times any amount paid immediately preceding date of filing; court costs; and reasonable attorney fees, 6.2-305	6% or at contract rate, whichever is higher, 6.2-302	Open-end credit, 6.2-433; private college/university; state or national bank; savings and loan; credit unions; secured by mortgage or deed of trust; installment credit plan, pension plans; industrial loan associations; stock option financing programs; pledged securities; insured or guaranteed by certain government agencies, 6.2-309 to 6.2329
WASHINGTON	12%, 19.52.010(1); written contract: contract rate if not over higher of 12% or 4% above equivalent coupon issue yield of average bill rate for 26-wk. U.S. treasury bills, 19.52.020	Borrower entitled to costs; attorney fees; and 2 times excess amount paid, 19.52.030(1)	Written contract: contract rate if specified in judgment; unpaid child support, 4.56.110	Broker dealers, 19.52.110; retail installment contract or transaction, 19.52.100; 19.52.130; sales contract providing for deferred payment, 19.52.120; financing of mobile homes, 19.52.160
WEST VIRGINIA	6%; written contract: contract rate up to 8%, 47-6-5	Forfeit all interest; debtor may recover 4 times all interest agreed to be paid with $100 minimum, 47-6-6; supervised lender: misdemeanor, 46A-5-103; court may award reasonable attorney fees, 46A-5-104	7–11%, 56-6-31; 46A-3-111	Life insurer, 33-13-8; consumer credit sales, 46A-3-101; installment sale for business purposes; loans for business purposes, 47-6-11

Table 4: Interest Rates—Continued

State	Legal Maximum Rate of Interest	Usury Penalty	Judgments	Exceptions
WISCONSIN	5% unless otherwise agreed in writing, 138.04	Imprisonment up to 6 mos. and/or fine $25 to $500, 138.06(2); interest not recoverable for usurious contract except for "bottomry and respondent bonds and contracts," 138.06(1)	1% plus prime rate, 815.05(8)	State-chartered financial institutions, 138.041; residential mortgage loans, 138.052(7); loans to corporations, 138.05(5); installment contract on auto, 218.0142
WYOMING	7% absent agreement otherwise or provision of law, 40-14-106		10% ; written contract: contract rate; late child support or maintenance which becomes a judgment shall not bear interest, 1-2-102(c)	Extensions of credit to government or governmental agencies; credit sales, loans or leases for agricultural purposes, 40-14-121

5. LEMON LAWS

Everyone has heard of someone who has bought a new car that was a "lemon." The car had either one major defect that could not be repaired or numerous minor defects that were always in need of repair.

Prior to the 1970s, when consumer advocacy hit its peak and numerous laws were enacted to protect the buyers of lemons, the only recourse the purchaser had was his or her warranty. As long as the manufacturer and dealer exercised their best efforts to fix the car while it was under warranty, the owner was stuck with the lemon. After the warranty period expired, the owner paid for the repairs.

"Lemon laws," or new car warranty laws, were enacted to place limits on what the consumer must endure should he or she purchase a lemon. Under the terms of the lemon laws, if the car cannot be fixed, the consumer must be compensated, either with a new car or with a cash refund. States are split among those that leave the decision of the specific remedy up to the consumer, manufacturer, or seller. All states now have lemon laws. In many states, the consumer has at least one year from the date of purchase to make a claim under the law. Most states allow the consumer two years or 24,000 miles, whichever comes first, to make a claim.

Table 5: Lemon Laws

State	Code Section	Title of Act	Definition of Defects	Time Limit for Manufacturer Repair	Remedies
ALABAMA	8-20A-1 to 8-20A-6	Motor Vehicle Lemon Law Rights	Nonconformity to any applicable express warranties which significantly impairs the use, value or safety of motor vehicle	24 mos. following delivery of vehicle or 24,000 miles, whichever comes first	Consumer's option: replace with comparable new car or accept return of car and refund consumer full contract price and nonrefundable portions of extended warranties and services, all collateral charges, all finance charges incurred after first reported nonconformity and incidental damages including cost of alternative transportation for time without vehicle; all this minus allowance for consumer's use of nonconforming vehicle
ALASKA	45.45.300 to 45.45.360	Motor Vehicle Warranties	Nonconformity to applicable express warranties	Term of express warranty or within 1 yr. from date of delivery to original owner, whichever is first	At owner's option, replacement of vehicle with new, comparable one or refund full purchase price less a reasonable allowance for use of motor vehicle
ARIZONA	44-1261 to 44-1267	Motor Vehicle Warranties	Nonconformity to applicable express warranties of any defect/condition which substantially impairs use and value of motor vehicle	Time period of express warranty or the period of 2 yrs. or 24,000 miles, whichever is earlier	Replacement with new motor vehicle or refund to consumer of full purchase price including all collateral charges, less a reasonable allowance for consumer's use of vehicle

Table 5: Lemon Laws—Continued

State	Code Section	Title of Act	Definition of Defects	Time Limit for Manufacturer Repair	Remedies
ARKANSAS	4-90-401 to 4-90-417	New Motor Vehicle Quality Assurance Act	Nonconformity to applicable manufacturer's express warranty or implied warranty of any defect/condition that substantially impairs use, market value, or safety of motor vehicle	24 mos. following delivery of vehicle or 24,000 miles, whichever comes later	Consumer's option: replace with new motor vehicle acceptable to consumer or repurchase motor vehicle and return full purchase plus collateral and reasonably incurred incidental charges; less reasonable offset for use and physical damage
CALIFORNIA	Civ. § 1793.22	Tanner Consumer Protection Act	Nonconformity to applicable express warranties which substantially impairs the use, value, or safety of motor vehicle	18 mos. from date of delivery to buyer or 18,000 miles, whichever occurs first	Replace the goods or reimburse buyer in an amount equal to the purchase price paid by the buyer, less the amount directly attributable to the use by the buyer prior to the discovery of the nonconformity
COLORADO	42-10-101 to 42-10-107	Motor Vehicle Warranties	Nonconformity to express warranties which substantially impairs use and market value of motor vehicle	Warranty period or within 1 yr. following date of original delivery of vehicle to consumer, whichever is the earlier date	Manufacturer's option: replace with comparable vehicle or accept return of vehicle from consumer and refund full purchase price, including sales tax, fees and similar governmental charges, less a reasonable allowance for consumer's use

Table 5: Lemon Laws—Continued

State	Code Section	Title of Act	Definition of Defects	Time Limit for Manufacturer Repair	Remedies
CONNECTICUT	42-179	New Automobile Warranties	Nonconformity to applicable express warranties which substantially impairs the use, safety, or value of motor vehicle	Repair defects covered by written warranties within 2 yrs. following original delivery or first 24,000 miles, whichever is first	Replace vehicle with new vehicle acceptable to consumer or refund (upon accepting return of vehicle) the (1) full contract price including but not limited to charges for undercoating, dealer prep, transportation, and installed options; (2) all collateral charges, including but not limited to sales tax, license and regulation fees, and similar government charges; (3) all finance charges after he first reports conformity and during any subsequent period vehicle is out of service due to repair; (4) all incidental damages, less a reasonable allowance for consumer's use
DELAWARE	Tit. 6, §§ 5001 to 5009	Automobile Warranties	Nonconformity to any applicable express warranty which substantially impairs the use, value, or safety of motor vehicle	Term of warranty or during period of 1 yr. following date of original delivery to consumer, whichever is earlier	Consumer's option: replace with comparable new automobile acceptable to consumer or repurchase and refund full purchase, including all credits and allowances for any trade-in vehicle

Table 5: Lemon Laws—Continued

State	Code Section	Title of Act	Definition of Defects	Time Limit for Manufacturer Repair	Remedies
DISTRICT OF COLUMBIA	50-501 to 50-510	Automobile Consumer Protection Act of 1984	Nonconformity to all warranties which results in significant impairment of vehicle. "Significantly impair" means to render the motor vehicle unreliable or unsafe for normal operation or to reduce its resale value below the average resale value for comparable motor vehicles	First 18,000 miles of operation or during period of 2 yrs. following date of delivery to original purchaser, whichever is earlier	Consumer's option: replace with comparable vehicle or accept return and refund full purchase price, including all sales tax, license fees, registration fees, and any similar governmental charges; less reasonable allowance for use
FLORIDA	681.10 to 681.118	Motor Vehicle Warranty Enforcement Act	Nonconformity to warranties which substantially impair the use, value, or safety of motor vehicle	24 mos.	Consumer's unconditional option: replace with vehicle acceptable to consumer or repurchase vehicle and refund to consumer full purchase price, including all reasonably incurred collateral and incidental charges, less reasonable offset for use
GEORGIA	Georgia Lemon Law: 10-1-780 10-1-798	Georgia Lemon Law	Nonconformity to applicable express warranties which means a defect, a serious safety defect, or a condition, any of which substantially impair the use, value, or safety of motor vehicle	Within 24 mos. following purchase of vehicle or 24,000 miles following delivery of vehicle to original consumer, whichever occurs first	Consumer's option: replace with identical or reasonably equivalent vehicle including payment of all collateral charges which consumer/lessor will incur a second time, less reasonable offset for use or repurchase and refund purchase price plus all collateral charges and incidental costs, less reasonable offset for use

Table 5: Lemon Laws—Continued

State	Code Section	Title of Act	Definition of Defects	Time Limit for Manufacturer Repair	Remedies
HAWAII	481I-1 to 481I-4	Motor Vehicle Express Warranty Enforcement (Lemon Law)	Nonconformity to all applicable express warranties that substantially impairs the use, market value, or safety of motor vehicle	Express warranty period, 2 yrs. after original delivery or first 24,000 miles, whichever occurs first	Replace with comparable vehicle or accept return and refund the full purchase price including, but not limited to charges for undercoating, dealer preparation, transportation, installed options, and all collateral charges, and less a reasonable allowance for consumer's use of vehicle
IDAHO	48-901 to 48-913	New Motor Vehicle Warranties	Nonconformity to applicable express warranties which impairs use or market value of vehicle	2 yr. period following date of original delivery of vehicle to buyer or first 24,000 miles or period of express warranty, whichever is earlier	Consumer's option: replace with comparable new vehicle or accept return and refund full purchase price including all collateral charges, less a reasonable allowance for buyer's use of vehicle
ILLINOIS	815 §§ 380/1 to 380/8	New Vehicle Buyer Protection Act	Nonconformity to applicable express warranties which substantially impair the use, market value, or safety of motor vehicle	Within statutory warranty period: the period of 1 yr. or 12,000 miles, whichever occurs first after date of delivery of a new vehicle to consumer	Replace with new vehicle of like model line, if available, or otherwise a comparable motor vehicle or accept return and refund consumer full purchase price of new vehicle, including all collateral charges, less a reasonable allowance for consumer use of vehicle

Table 5: Lemon Laws—Continued

State	Code Section	Title of Act	Definition of Defects	Time Limit for Manufacturer Repair	Remedies
INDIANA	24-5-13-1 to 24-5-13-24	Indiana Motor Vehicle Protection Act of 1988	Nonconformity to applicable express warranties which significantly impairs the use, market value or safety of motor vehicle or renders vehicle nonconforming to terms of applicable manufacturer's warranty	If reported within term of protection: 18 mos. after date of delivery to buyer or 18,000 miles whichever occurs first	Consumer's option: Replace with vehicle of comparable value, including reimbursement to buyer of any fees of transferring registration or sales tax incurred as result of replacement or refund full contract price of vehicle, including all credits and allowances for any trade-in vehicle and less reasonable allowance for use
IOWA	322G.1 to 322G.15	Defective Motor Vehicles (Lemon Law)	Nonconformity to all applicable express warranties	Term of manufacturer's written warranty or during period of 2 yrs. following date of original delivery of a motor vehicle to consumer or first 24,000 miles, whichever is first	Replace with identical or reasonably equivalent vehicle, including collateral and incidental charges less reasonable offset for use, or refund full purchase or lease price including all collateral and reasonably incurred incidental charges, less a reasonable offset for consumer's use
KANSAS	50-645 to 50-646	Lemon Law	Nonconformity to applicable warranties which significantly impairs the use or value of motor vehicle	1 yr. from date of original delivery of vehicle to consumer or term of any warranties, whichever is earlier	Replace with comparable vehicle under warranty or accept return and refund full purchase price including all collateral charges, less a reasonable allowance for consumer's use

Table 5: Lemon Laws—Continued

State	Code Section	Title of Act	Definition of Defects	Time Limit for Manufacturer Repair	Remedies
KENTUCKY	367.840 to 367.846	Defective New Cars	Nonconformity to applicable express warranties which significantly impairs the use, value, or safety of the motor vehicle	First 12 mos. following date of delivery or first 12,000 miles, whichever is first	Consumer's option: replace vehicle with comparable motor vehicle or accept return and refund full purchase price including amount paid for vehicle, finance charge, all sales tax, license fee, registration fee, any similar governmental charges, plus all collateral charges, less reasonable offset for use
LOUISIANA	51:1941 to 51:1948	Louisiana Lemon Law	Nonconformity to applicable express warranties which substantially impairs the use, market value, or both, of a motor vehicle	Term of warranty or during period of 1 yr. following date of original delivery, whichever is earlier	Manufacturer's option: Replace with comparable new motor vehicle or accept return and refund full purchase price plus any amounts paid by the consumer at the point of sale and all collateral costs, less a reasonable allowance for use
MAINE	Tit. 10, §§ 1161 to 1169	Maine Lemon Law	Nonconformity to all express warranties which substantially impairs use, safety, or value of vehicle	Term of express warranties within a period of 3 yrs. following date of original delivery to consumer, or during first 18,000 miles, whichever is earlier date	Buyer's option: replace with comparable new vehicle or accept return of vehicle and refund full purchase price (or in case of lease, payments made so far) including any paid financing charges, all collateral charges, and reasonable costs incurred by the consumer for towing and storage of the vehicle and alternative transportation, less reasonable allowance for use

Table 5: Lemon Laws—Continued

State	Code Section	Title of Act	Definition of Defects	Time Limit for Manufacturer Repair	Remedies
MARYLAND	Com. Law §§ 14-1501 to 14-1504	Automotive Warranty Enforcement Act	Nonconformity to all applicable express warranties which substantially affects use and market value of vehicle	Warranty period equal to or greater than first 15,000 miles or first 15 mos. following date of original delivery of vehicle to consumer	Consumer's option: replace with comparable motor vehicle acceptable to customer or accept return and refund full purchase price including all excise tax license fees, registration fees, and any similar governmental charges, less reasonable allowance for consumer's use (not to exceed 15% of purchase price) and for damage not attributable to normal wear
MASSACHUSETTS	Ch. 90, § 7N 1/2	Not specified	Nonconformity to applicable express warranties or implied warranty which significantly affects use, market value, or safety of vehicle	Term of protection: 1 yr. or 15,000 miles of use from date of original delivery, whoever comes first	Manufacturer's option: replace with vehicle acceptable to consumer or accept return and refund full contract price including all credits and allowances for any trade-in vehicle, less a reasonable allowance for use

Table 5: Lemon Laws—Continued

State	Code Section	Title of Act	Definition of Defects	Time Limit for Manufacturer Repair	Remedies
MICHIGAN	257.1401 to 257.1410	New Motor Vehicles Warranties	Nonconformity to manufacturer's express warranties that significantly affects use or value of vehicle	Term of manufacturer's express warranty or 1 yr. from date of delivery of new motor vehicle to original consumer, whichever is earlier	Consumer's option: replace with a comparable replacement vehicle currently in production and acceptable to consumer or accept return of vehicle and refund full purchase price including cost of any options or other modifications installed or made by or for the manufacturer, towing costs and reasonable costs for a comparable rental vehicle, less a reasonable allowance for consumer's use of vehicle and less an amount equal to any appraised damage that is not attributable to normal wear and tear. Consumer has right to demand refund. If vehicle was leased, consumer has right to refund of the lease price or may agree to accept comparable replacement vehicle in lieu of refund for the lease price paid. If consumer agrees to accept replacement vehicle, lease agreement shall not be altered except with respect to the identification of the vehicle

Table 5: Lemon Laws—Continued

State	Code Section	Title of Act	Definition of Defects	Time Limit for Manufacturer Repair	Remedies
MINNESOTA	325F.665	Not specified	Nonconformity to all applicable express warranties which substantially affects the use or market value of vehicle	During term of applicable express warranty or during period of 2 yrs. following date of original delivery of vehicle to consumer, whichever is earlier	Consumer's option: replace with comparable vehicle or accept return and refund to consumer full purchase price including cost of any options or other modifications made/installed/arranged by manufacturer (or agents or dealer) within 30 days of original delivery, and all other charges, less a reasonable allowance for consumer use of vehicle
MISSISSIPPI	63-17-151 to 63-17-165	Motor Vehicle Warranty Enforcement Act	Nonconformity to all applicable express warranties which impairs the use, market value, or safety of vehicle	Term of express warranties or during period of 1 yr. following date of original delivery of motor vehicle to consumer, whichever period expires earlier	Consumer's option: replace with comparable vehicle acceptable to consumer or accept return and refund full purchase price, including all reasonably incurred collateral charges, less a reasonable allowance for consumer's use
MISSOURI	407.560 to 407.579	New Motor Vehicle Warranties, Nonconformity (Lemon Law)	Nonconformity to all applicable express warranties which impairs the use, market value, or safety of vehicle	Term of express warranties or during 1 yr. following date of original delivery to consumer, whichever expires earlier	Manufacturer's option: replace with comparable new vehicle acceptable to consumer or take title from consumer and refund full purchase price, including all reasonably incurred collateral charges, less reasonable allowance for use

Table 5: Lemon Laws—Continued

State	Code Section	Title of Act	Definition of Defects	Time Limit for Manufacturer Repair	Remedies
MONTANA	61-4-501 to 61-4-533	Not specified	Nonconformity to all applicable express warranties which substantially affects the use, market value, or safety of vehicle	Warranty period within 2 yrs. after date of original delivery to consumer or during first 18,000 miles of operation, whichever is earlier; however, if consumer notifies manufacturer in writing of nonconformity within warranty, manufacturer must fix regardless of expiration of warranty	Replace with new vehicle of same model and style and of equal value unless for reasons of lack of availability such replacement is impossible, in which case it shall be replaced with vehicle of comparable market value or accept return and refund full purchase price plus reasonable collateral and incidental damages, less a reasonable allowance for consumer's use of vehicle
NEBRASKA	60-2701 to 60-2709	Not specified	Nonconformity to all applicable express warranties which substantially affects the use and market value of vehicle	Term of such express warranties or during period of 1 yr. following date of original delivery of new vehicle to consumer, whichever is earlier	Replace with comparable vehicle or accept return and refund full purchase price including all sales tax, license fees, registration fees, and any similar government charges, less a reasonable allowance for consumer's use
NEVADA	597.600 to 597.688	Not specified	Nonconformity to all applicable express warranties which substantially impairs the use and market value of vehicle	Before expiration of manufacturer's express warranties or no later than 1 yr. after date of delivery to original buyer, whichever is earlier	Replace with comparable vehicle of same model having same features; if vehicle cannot be delivered within reasonable time, then a comparable vehicle substantially similar to replaced vehicle or accept return and refund full purchase price including all sales tax, license fees, registration fees, and other similar governmental charges, less a reasonable allowance for consumer's use

Table 5: Lemon Laws—Continued

State	Code Section	Title of Act	Definition of Defects	Time Limit for Manufacturer Repair	Remedies
NEW HAMPSHIRE	357-D:1 to 357-D:12	Not specified	Nonconformity to all applicable express warranties or implied warranties which substantially impairs the use, safety, or market value of vehicle	Term of express/implied warranty or within 1 yr. following date of original delivery, whichever is earlier	Consumer's option: within 30 days after an order by new motor vehicle arbitration board, replace with new comparable vehicle with all options and accessories or accept return and refund to consumer full purchase price and all credits and allowances for trade-in/down payment, license fees, finance charges, credit charges, registration fees and other similar charges and incidental and consequential damages less a reasonable allowance for use. Other provisions for leased vehicles, 357-D:3(IX)
NEW JERSEY	56:12-29 to 56:12-49	Not specified	Nonconformity to express warranties which substantially impairs the use, market value, or safety of vehicle	Term of warranty or during period of 1 yr. following date of original delivery to consumer, or 12,000 miles of operation, whichever is earlier	Consumer's option: accept return and refund full purchase price including any stated credit/allowance for consumer's used motor vehicle, cost of any options/other modifications arranged, installed/ made by manufacturer within 30 days after date of original delivery and sales tax, license and registration fees, finance charges and other incidental fees less a reasonable allowance for use

Table 5: Lemon Laws—Continued

State	Code Section	Title of Act	Definition of Defects	Time Limit for Manufacturer Repair	Remedies
NEW MEXICO	57-16A-1 to 57-16A-9	Motor Vehicle Quality Assurance Act	Nonconformity to all applicable express warranties which substantially impairs the use or market value of vehicle	Term of express warranties or 1 yr. following date of original delivery, whichever is earlier	Replace with comparable vehicle or accept return and refund full purchase price including all collateral charges, less a reasonable allowance for consumer's use of vehicle
NEW YORK	Gen. Bus. § 198-a	New Car Lemon Law	Nonconformity to all express warranties that substantially impairs the value of the motor vehicle	First 18,000 miles or during period of 2 yrs. following date of original delivery, whichever is earlier reporting of nonconformity by consumers	Consumer's option: replace vehicle with comparable motor vehicle or accept return and refund full purchase price, or if applicable, the lease price and any trade-in allowance plus fees and charges less reasonable allowance for consumer's use in excess of first 12,000 miles pursuant to mileage deduction formula and a reasonable allowance for any damage not attributable to normal wear and improvements; vehicle must be sold and registered in New York
NORTH CAROLINA	20-351 to 20-351.11	New Motor Vehicles Warranties Act	Nonconformity to all applicable express warranties which substantially impairs the value of vehicle	For period of 1 yr. or term of express warranties, whichever is greater, following date of original delivery of vehicle to consumer; express warranties for a new motor vehicle shall remain in effect at least 1 yr. or 12,000 miles; can occur no later than 24 mos. or 24,000 miles following original delivery	Consumer's option: replace with comparable new vehicle or accept return and refund full contract price, all collateral charges, all finance charges incurred since reporting nonconformity, and any incidental damages and monetary consequential damages, less reasonable allowance for consumer's use

Table 5: Lemon Laws—Continued

State	Code Section	Title of Act	Definition of Defects	Time Limit for Manufacturer Repair	Remedies
NORTH DAKOTA	51-07-16 to 51-07-22	Not specified	Nonconformity to all applicable express warranties which substantially impairs the use and market value of vehicle	Term of express warranties or during period of 1 yr. following date of original delivery to consumer, whichever is earlier	Replace with comparable vehicle or accept return and refund full purchase price, including all collateral charges, less reasonable allowance for consumer's use not exceeding 10¢ per mile driven or 10% of purchase price, whichever is less
OHIO	1345.71 to 1345.78	Nonconforming New Motor Vehicles Law	Nonconformity to express warranty of the manufacturer or distributor which substantially impairs the use, value, or safety of a motor vehicle	1 yr. following date of original delivery or during first 18,000 miles, whichever is earlier	Consumer's option: replace with new vehicle acceptable to consumer or accept return of vehicle from consumer and refund full purchase price, all collateral charges, all finance charges, and all incidental damages
OKLAHOMA	Tit. 15, § 901	Not specified	Nonconformity to any applicable express warranties which substantially impairs the use and market value of vehicle	Term of express warranties or during 1 yr. following date of original delivery to consumer, whichever is earlier	Replace with new or comparable vehicle or accept return and refund full purchase price including all taxes, license, registration fees, and all similar governmental fees, excluding interest, less a reasonable allowance for consumer's use
OREGON	646A.400 to 646A.418	Enforcement of Express Warranties on New Motor Vehicles	Nonconformity to applicable manufacturer's express warranties which substantially impairs the use, market value, or safety of vehicle	During period of 2 yrs. following date of original delivery of motor vehicle to consumer or during period ending on date on which mileage reaches 24,000 miles, whichever is earlier	Replace with new motor vehicle or accept return and refund full purchase/lease price paid, including taxes, license and registration fees, and any similar collateral charges, excluding interest, less a reasonable allowance for consumer's use of vehicle

Table 5: Lemon Laws—Continued

State	Code Section	Title of Act	Definition of Defects	Time Limit for Manufacturer Repair	Remedies
PENNSYLVANIA	Tit. 73, §§ 1951 to 1963	Automobile Lemon Law	Nonconformity to warranties which substantially impairs the use, market value, or safety of vehicle	1 yr. following date of actual delivery to consumer, within first 12,000 miles of use or during time of the warranty, whichever may first occur	Purchaser's option: replace with comparable vehicle of equal value or accept return and refund full purchase price, including all collateral charges, less a reasonable allowance for purchaser's use not exceeding 10¢ per mile or 10% of purchase price, whichever is less
RHODE ISLAND	31-5.2-1 to 31-5.2-14	Consumer Enforcement of Motor Vehicle Warranties	Nonconformity to applicable express warranties or implied warranties that substantially impairs use, value, or safety of vehicle	Term of protection equals 1 yr. or 15,000 miles from date of original delivery, whichever comes first	Consumer's option: replace with comparable new vehicle in good working condition or accept return and refund full contract price of vehicle including all credits and allowances for any trade-in vehicle, less a reasonable allowance for use
SOUTH CAROLINA	56-28-10 to 56-28-110	Not specified	Nonconformity to all applicable express warranties which substantially impairs the use, safety, or market value of vehicle	Within 1 yr. of purchase or first 12,000 miles of operation, whichever occurs first and if it is reported during terms of express warranty	Manufacturer's option: replace with comparable vehicle or accept return and refund full purchase price as delivered including applicable finance charges, sales taxes, license fees, registration fees, and any other similar governmental charges, less a reasonable allowance for consumer's use of vehicle

Table 5: Lemon Laws—Continued

State	Code Section	Title of Act	Definition of Defects	Time Limit for Manufacturer Repair	Remedies
SOUTH DAKOTA	32-6D-1 to 32-6D-11	Not specified	Nonconformity to any express warranty which significantly impairs the use, value, or safety of vehicle	Reported within lemon law rights pd.—1 yr. after date of original delivery of vehicle or first 12,000 miles whichever occurs earlier; however, obligation to repair does not extend beyond period of 2 yrs. following delivery or 24,000 miles whichever occurs first	Consumer's option: replace with comparable new vehicle and refund all collateral charges, including excise tax, license and registration fees and similar government charges, or accept return and refund full contract price including all undercoating, transportation, dealer prep, installed options, collateral charges, finance charges and any incidental damages
TENNESSEE	55-24-101 to 55-24-112	Motor Vehicle Warranties	Nonconformity to all applicable express warranties that substantially impairs the motor vehicle	Term of applicable warranties or 1 yr. following date of original delivery of vehicle to consumer, whichever comes first	Replace with comparable vehicle or accept return and refund full purchase price (cost paid by consumer including all collateral charges, less a reasonable allowance for use)
TEXAS	Occ. §§ 2301.601 to 2301.613	Warranties: Rights of Vehicle Owners	Nonconformity to all applicable express warranties which creates a serious safety hazard or substantially impairs the use or market value of the motor vehicle	Term of such express warranties within 1 yr. of purchase or first 12,000 miles whichever occurs first	Replace with comparable motor vehicle or accept return and refund full purchase price less a reasonable allowance for owner's use and any other allowances or refunds payable to owner
UTAH	13-20-1 to 13-20-8	New Motor Vehicles Warranties Act	Nonconformity to all applicable express warranties which substantially impairs the use, safety, or market value of vehicle	Term of express warranties or 1 yr. following date of original delivery of vehicle to consumer, whichever is earlier	Replace with comparable new vehicle or accept return and refund full purchase price, including all collateral charges, less a reasonable allowance for consumer's use

Table 5: Lemon Laws—Continued

State	Code Section	Title of Act	Definition of Defects	Time Limit for Manufacturer Repair	Remedies
VERMONT	Tit. 9, §§ 4170 to 4181	New Motor Vehicle Arbitration	Nonconformity to applicable manufacturer's express warranties which substantially impairs the use, safety, or market value of vehicle	Term of warranty	Consumer's option: replace with new vehicle from same manufacturer of comparable worth to the same make and model with all the options and accessories and with appropriate adjustments being allowed for any model year differences or accept return and refund full purchase price as indicated in purchase contract and all credits and allowances for any trade-in or down payment, licensing fees, finance charges, credit charges, registration fees and any similar charges, and incidental and consequential damages, less reasonable allowance for use
VIRGINIA	59.1-207.9 to 59.1-207.16:1	Virginia Motor Vehicle Warranty Enforcement Act	Nonconformity to all warranties which significantly impairs the use, safety, or market value of vehicle	Manufacturer's warranty period or lemon law rights period ending 18 mos. after date of original delivery to consumer of new motor vehicle	Replace with comparable vehicle acceptable to consumer or accept return and refund full purchase price, including all collateral charges, and incidental damages, less a reasonable allowance for consumer's use of vehicle up to first notice of nonconformity given

Table 5: Lemon Laws—Continued

State	Code Section	Title of Act	Definition of Defects	Time Limit for Manufacturer Repair	Remedies
WASHINGTON	19.118.005 to 19.118.904	Motor Vehicle Warranties	Nonconformity to the Warranty which substantially impairs the use, value, or safety of the vehicle	Term of the warranty period (period ending 2 yrs. after date of original delivery or first 24,000 miles, whichever is first) or period of coverage of applicable manufacturer's written warranty, whichever is less	Consumer's option: replace with identical or reasonably equivalent vehicle including any service contract, undercoating, rustproofing, and factory or dealer installed options. Manufacturer responsible for sales tax, license and registration fees. Compensation for reasonable offset for use to be paid by consumer to manufacturer; or repurchase vehicle, manufacturer shall refund to consumer the purchase price, all collateral charges and incidental costs, less a reasonable offset for use
WEST VIRGINIA	46A-6A-1 to 46A-6A-9	Consumer Protection - New Motor Vehicle Warranties	Nonconformity to all applicable express warranties which substantially impairs the use or market value of vehicle	Term of express warranties or during 1 yr. following date of original delivery of vehicle to consumer, whichever is later	Repair or replace with comparable new vehicle which does conform to the warranties
WISCONSIN	218.0171	Not specified	Nonconformity to applicable express warranties which substantially impairs the use, safety, or market value of vehicle	Term of warranty or 1 yr. after first delivery of motor vehicle to consumer, whichever is sooner	Consumer's option: accept return and replace with comparable new vehicle and refund any collateral costs or accept return and refund full purchase price plus any sales tax, finance charge, amount paid by the consumer at point of sale, and collateral costs, less a reasonable allowance for use

Table 5: Lemon Laws—Continued

State	Code Section	Title of Act	Definition of Defects	Time Limit for Manufacturer Repair	Remedies
WYOMING	40-17-101	Not specified	Nonconformity to applicable express warranties which substantially impairs the use or market value of vehicle	1 yr. following original delivery of vehicle to consumer; if reports within 1 yr., the repairs shall be made even if the 1 yr. period has expired	Replace with new or comparable vehicle of same type and similarly equipped or accept return and refund full purchase price including all collateral charges less a reasonable allowance for consumer's use

II. CRIMINAL LAWS

6. CAPITAL PUNISHMENT

The acceptance of capital punishment, or the death penalty, as a sentence for heinous criminal acts has been hotly debated across the nation over the last few decades. On the books in most states, the death penalty has been challenged by many, originally on grounds that it violated the constitutional prohibition against cruel and unusual punishment, and later on the procedural grounds that there were not enough due process protections for defendants accused of capital crimes. In general, it was held that since the sentence was so severe, the law must impose the strictest standards of proof to sentence a defendant to death. Consequently, many states have gone through periods in which the death penalty was held as legal, then illegal, then revised and held as legal, then illegal again, and then further revised and held as legal once more. This shifting status often brought unbalanced—unjust—sentencing. For instance, in many of these states one of two defendants accused of identical unrelated crimes committed within weeks of each other drew the death sentence while the other did not, merely because the statute under which they were sentenced was ruled unconstitutional in the intervening time.

The Supreme Court has since handed down explicit guidelines defining the legal imposition of the death penalty, allowing states a new opportunity to legislate a legal death penalty statute that is less likely to be ruled unconstitutional in the future. This does not mean that the process is not still open to attack. As of this writing, new cases on the death penalty are currently wending their way through the courts to the Supreme Court.

Thirty-eight states currently have death penalty statutes on the books. In a few states, the statute remains on the books though it has been declared unconstitutional. In some of these cases, the state legislature can either revise or rewrite the death penalty statute if it chooses to make it the law. In the case of Nebraska, the death penalty was repealed by legislative action and vetoed by the governor. The veto was overridden on May 27, 2015 and the governor and attorney general have vowed to "appeal" the vote or sue for judicial intervention to bring the death penalty back. There has even been talk of a grassroots group attempting to bring the death penalty back by voter initiative.

There are twelve states that authorize the death penalty for non-homicide crimes. Of note is California, often known for its radical politics, which lists treason as a capital crime. Other common non-homicide capital offenses are kidnapping, hijacking, and other serious crimes that involve hostage-taking or placing a victim in extreme danger.

In the last five years, the method of execution has become the most controversial element of death penalty statutes. Five states, Alabama, Georgia, Kentucky, New York, and Ohio, have changed their method of execution from electrocution to lethal injection. Georgia, however, is an interesting case. In the fifth edition of this book it was noted that Georgia had switched from lethal injection to electrocution. Three years in the sixth edition they switched back to lethal injection. Changes like this are an excellent example of the passionate thinking about this very grave aspect of penal law.

Some states have very complicated criminal statutes; therefore, the following tables may contain less information on some states if nothing explicit can be determined from the state statute alone. Occasionally it is necessary to consult lists or sentencing guidelines that are not part of the code to determine these rules.

Table 6: Capital Punishment

State	Code Section	Allowed?	Effect of Incapacity	Minimum Age
ALABAMA	13A-5-39 to 13A-5-59; 15-18-82; 15-18-82.1	Yes	Mitigating circumstance if defendant under influence of extreme mental or emotional disturbance; forbid execution of "insane" person	No minimum age, but age is a mitigating circumstance
ALASKA	12.55.015	Not authorized		
ARIZONA	13-751; 13-752; 13-757	Yes, for 1st degree murder with mitigating factors	Considered mitigating circumstance	18
ARKANSAS	5-4-601 to 5-4-618; 5-51-201	Yes, capital murder and treason	No defendant with mental retardation at the time of committing murder shall be sentenced to death	"The youth of the defendant at the time of the commission of the capital murder" shall be a mitigating circumstance. 5-4-605 (4)
CALIFORNIA	Penal §§ 37; 190 to 190.5; 3600 to 3706	Yes, if crime is 1st degree murder with enumerated special circumstances	If defendant found insane at any time prior to execution, the execution is suspended. Upon recovery, execution is rescheduled	18

Non- homicidal	Capital Homicide	Method of Execution
None	Homicide during the commission of kidnapping; robbery; rape/sodomy; burglary; sexual abuse; arson; hijacking; murder of police officer or public official while on duty or when related to or caused by or is related to his official position, act, or capacity; murder for pecuniary or other valuable consideration; two or more persons murdered in same act/course of conduct; victim less than 14 years old; murder under life sentence; murder during arson or by means of explosives; murder by defendant who has previously been convicted of murder within 20 years; murder of witness in civil or criminal trial when murder is caused by or related to the testimony; murder during act of unlawfully assuming control of any aircraft; murder when deadly weapon is fired outside of a dwelling when victim is in dwelling; murder by deadly weapon used from or within a vehicle	Lethal injection, unless defendant requests electrocution
None	Previous capital convictions or homicides; previous conviction of a "serious offense"; previous felonies with use or threat of violence; knowingly created grave risk of death to persons in addition to victim; procured commission of offense by payment; especially heinous, cruel or depraved manner; adult person and victim under 15 or over 70; victim on duty peace officer and defendant knew or should have known; in custody of state dept. of corrections, law enforcement agency or jail at time of homicide	Lethal injection. If defendant is convicted for crime committed prior to November 23, 1992, he or she shall choose between lethal gas or lethal injection
Treason	Homicide committed by a person incarcerated for felony conviction; committed by person unlawfully at liberty after being imprisoned for felony conviction; use of threat or violence in commission of felony; knowingly created grave risk of death to person other than victim or caused the death of more than one person in the same criminal episode; committed in order to prevent arrest or escape custody; committed for pecuniary gain; committed for purposes of disrupting/hindering lawful exercise of any government or political function; especially cruel or depraved manner by use of torture or methods evidencing the defendant's pleasure in committing the murder; committed by means of destructive explosive, bomb, similar device	Lethal injection or electrocution if lethal injection held unconstitutional
Treason	Murder committed for financial gain; previously convicted of first/second degree murder; multiple murders in same proceeding; bomb, explosives, grave risk; for purposes of avoiding lawful arrest or attempt to escape lawful custody; murder intentional and involved the infliction of torture; intentional killing of peace officer, federal law officer/agent, fireman in performance of duties, and defendant should have known or knew official status of victim; victim was a juror in any court of record in local, state, or federal system in any state and the murder was intentionally carried out in retaliation or prevention of the victim's official duties; the murder was intentional and perpetrated by means of a firearm being discharged from a motor vehicle intentionally at another outside the vehicle with intent to kill; witness of crime intentionally killed to prevent retaliatory testimony at criminal proceeding; retaliation against judge or former judge of this state or any other state, prosecutor, etc.; state officials or officials of any local government of this state or any other state for reasons relating to their office; lying in wait; especially cruel, atrocious, heinous; racial; committed along with robbery, kidnapping, rape, sodomy, oral copulation, burglary, performance of a lewd act upon a child under the age of 14; arson, train wrecking; carjacking; intentionally poisoned; mayhem; rape by instrument; member of a street gang murdering to further activities of the gang	Lethal gas or lethal injection, but if defendant fails to choose, lethal injection

Table 6: Capital Punishment—Continued

State	Code Section	Allowed?	Effect of Incapacity	Minimum Age
COLORADO	18-3-101 to 18-3-107; 18-3-301 to 18-3-306; 18-1.3-1201 to 18-1.3-1207	Yes for Class 1 felonies	Mitigating factor; suspend sentence; if "mentally retarded" then sentenced to life in prison	18
CONNECTICUT	53a-46a; 53a-54b; 54-100	Yes, capital felony, if committed prior to April 25, 2012. Death penalty repealed for crimes committed after that date	No death sentence	18
DELAWARE	Tit. 11, §§ 636; 4209	Yes	Exempt from execution while incapacitated; life imprisonment if clear and convincing evidence of serious intellectual developmental disorder at time of crime	18
DISTRICT OF COLUMBIA	22-2104; 22-2104.1	No		

Non- homicidal	Capital Homicide	Method of Execution
First degree kidnapping if victim has been injured, but defendant will not be sentenced to death if victim is liberated alive prior to the conviction of kidnapper. Treason	Murder committed by person imprisoned for Class 1, 2 or 3 felony; previous crime of violence; intentionally killed peace officer/former peace officer, judge, firefighter, elected official, federal officer he knew or should have known to be engaged in official duties or retaliation for past official duties; kidnapped person intentionally killed; agreement to kill; explosives or incendiary device; pecuniary gain; heinous or cruel; hate crime; victim was under 12; defendant killed 1 or more persons in the same episode; defendant killed victim knowing she was pregnant	Lethal injection
None	Murder committed in commission of felony; 2 or more prior felonies involving infliction of serious bodily injury; knowingly created grave risk of death to other persons; murder of a police officer, chief inspector in criminal justice, constable performing criminal law duties, special police; especially heinous, cruel, depraved manner; committed for pecuniary gain; murder committed by a kidnapper of kidnap victim either during abduction or before victim can be returned to safety; seller of illegal narcotic if purchaser dies as a result of use of narcotic; murder of person under 16; during commission of 1st degree sex assault; murder of 2 or more persons at the same time or in the course of a single transaction; murder committed by one who was under sentence of life imprisonment at time of murder	Lethal injection by a continuous intravenous injection of a substance or substances sufficient to cause death
None	Murder committed while in or escaped from custody/confinement; committed for purposes of avoiding/preventing arrest or for effecting escape from custody; committed against law enforcement officer, corrections employee, fireman engaged in duties; committed against judge, attorney general, other state officer (former or present) during or because of exercise of official duty; hostage/ransom; witness to crime to avoid testimony; paid for it/pecuniary gain; convicted of prior felony using or threat of violence; rape, sodomy, unlawful sexual intercourse, arson, kidnapping, burglary; multiple victims; outrageously or wantonly vile, horrible or inhumane treatment involving torture, depravity of mind or use of explosive device or poison; agent or employee of another person; defendant serving life sentence; victim was pregnant, handicapped, severely disabled or 62 years of age or older; child 14 years or younger and murderer was 4 years older; present or past nongovernment informant or provided information and killed in retaliation; murder was premeditated and result of substantial planning; or murder committed for purpose of interfering with victim's exercise of a constitutional right protected by the first amendment or because of the victim's race, religion, national origin, or disability	Lethal injection. If lethal injection held unconstitutional: hanging

Table 6: Capital Punishment—Continued

State	Code Section	Allowed?	Effect of Incapacity	Minimum Age
FLORIDA	775.082; 782.04; 921.141; 921.142; 922.052 to 922.15	Yes	Exempt from execution if insane or pregnant for duration of condition	Age of defendant at the time of the crime shall be a mitigating circumstance
GEORGIA	17-10-30 to 17-10-44	Yes	Suspend sentence; shall not be executed; if pregnant, time period after no longer pregnant	
HAWAII	706-656	No		

Non- homicidal	Capital Homicide	Method of Execution
May apply to capital drug trafficking; may apply to sexual battery	Capital felony committed by person serving sentence of imprisonment or under community control; previous capital felony or felony using or threat of violence; knowingly created great risk of death to many persons; the capital felony was committed while defendant was engaged in, was an accomplice, in commission of or attempt to commit or flight after committing or attempt to commit any robbery, sexual battery, aggravated child abuse, aggravated abuse of a disabled or elderly person, aggravated stalking, carjacking, arson, burglary, kidnapping, aircraft piracy, unlawful throwing, placing, or discharging of a destructive device or bombings; capital felony for purposes of avoiding lawful arrest or effecting escape from custody; capital felony for pecuniary gain; capital felony to hinder lawful exercise of governmental function or enforcement of laws; capital felony especially heinous, atrocious or cruel; premeditated homicide; victim of capital felony was public official or law enforcement officer engaged in official duties; victim of capital murder was less than 12 years old; criminal felony committed by a criminal street gang member	Lethal injection, unless person sentenced to death elects for electrocution; if either or both found to be unconstitutional, then by any constitutional method
Aircraft hijacking or treason in any case	Murder, rape, armed robbery, kidnapping committed by person with prior record of conviction for capital felony; murder, rape, armed robbery, kidnapping committed while engaged in commission of other capital felony; knowingly created grave risk of death to multiple persons in public place by use of weapon/device; murder committed for financial gain; judicial officer, district attorney or solicitor (or formers) because of exercise of duties; committed as agent of another; outrageously or wantonly vile, horrible or inhuman; against peace officer, corrections officer, fireman while performing duties; offender escaped from lawful custody/confinement; committed while avoiding lawful arrest; committed during aggravated sexual assault or child molestation	Lethal injection

Table 6: Capital Punishment—Continued

State	Code Section	Allowed?	Effect of Incapacity	Minimum Age
IDAHO	18-207; 18-4001 to 18-4004; 18-4504 to 18-4505; 19-2515 to 19-2524; 19-2701 to 19-2720	Yes	If pregnant, death sentence is suspended until no longer pregnant. If defendant is found to be "mentally retarded," then no death penalty. Idaho has no insanity defense, however mental illness is consideration in sentencing	
ILLINOIS	720 §§ 5/9-1; 5/10-2; 5/30-1; 725 § 5/119-5; 730 § 5/5-5-3	Yes	Mitigating factor	18

Non- homicidal	Capital Homicide	Method of Execution
Kidnapping in the 1st degree unless prior to imposition of sentence victim is liberated unharmed	At least one aggravating circumstance: (a) defendant was previously convicted of another murder; (b) at the time murder was committed, defendant also committed another murder; (c) defendant knowingly created a great risk of death to many persons; (d) murder was committed for remuneration or the promise of remuneration or defendant employed another to commit the murder for remuneration or promise of remuneration; (e) murder was especially heinous, atrocious or cruel, manifesting exceptional depravity; (f) by the murder, or circumstances surrounding its commission, the defendant exhibited utter disregard for human life; (g) murder was committed in perpetration of, or attempt to perpetrate, arson, rape, robbery, burglary, kidnapping or mayhem and defendant killed, intended to kill, or acted with reckless indifference to human life; (h) murder was committed in perpetration of, or attempt to perpetrate, an infamous crime against nature, lewd and lascivious conduct with a minor, sexual abuse of a child under sixteen (16) years of age, ritualized abuse of a child, sexual exploitation of a child, sexual battery of a minor child sixteen (16) or seventeen (17) years of age, or forcible sexual penetration by use of a foreign object, and the defendant killed, intended a killing, or acted with reckless indifference to human life; (i) defendant, by conduct before, during or after the commission of murder at hand, exhibited propensity to commit murder probably constituting continuing threat to society; (j) murder was committed against former or present peace officer, executive officer, officer of the court, judicial officer or prosecuting attorney because of exercise of official duty or because of victim's former or present official status; (k) murder was committed against witness or potential witness in criminal or civil legal proceeding because of such proceeding	Lethal injection
Treason	First degree murder committed upon a peace officer or fireman in the performance of his duties; an employee of the Department of Corrections in the performance of his duties; an inmate in a correctional facility or otherwise was present in the facility with the approval of the prison administration; murder involves more than one victim; committed during hijacking of airplane, train, ship, bus, or other public conveyance; committed for financial gain; committed during robbery, stalking, burglary, arson, kidnapping, drug conspiracy, sexual assault; victim was under 12; murder of witness in order to prevent victim from testifying against defendant; while defendant was incarcerated and was committing any other offense punishable under IL law as a felony; victim was an emergency medical technician; murder involving torture; committed by using firearm in motor vehicle with victim outside of vehicle; victim over 60; victim disabled; victim was teacher murdered at school; victim under order of protection from defendant; in connection with or as a result of the offense of terrorism	Lethal injection. If lethal injection held illegal or unconstitutional: electrocution

Table 6: Capital Punishment—Continued

State	Code Section	Allowed?	Effect of Incapacity	Minimum Age
INDIANA	35-38-6-1 to 35-38-6-10; 35-50-2-3; 35-50-2-9	Yes	Hearing to determine whether defendant has ability to understand proceedings; if ability lacking, court can delay or continue trial; may not impose death sentence if determined mentally retarded. If defendant is pregnant, sentence is suspended until no longer pregnant	18
IOWA	902.1	No		
KANSAS	21-5209; 21-5402 to 21-5402; 21-6617 to 21-6619; 21-6622 to 21-6625; 22-4001	Yes	Mental disease or defect no defense unless as a result defendant lacked culpable mental state. If convicted defendant is determined at hearing to have intellectual disability, court shall sentence as otherwise provided by law, no death or life imprisonment without parole or mandatory term of imprisonment	18

Non- homicidal	Capital Homicide	Method of Execution
None	Intentional murder while committing/attempting to commit arson, burglary, child molesting, criminal deviate conduct, kidnapping, rape, robbery, carjacking, criminal gang activity dealing in cocaine or narcotic drug; unlawful detonation of explosive with intent to injure; lying in wait; hiring or hired to kill; victim was law enforcement officer, etc.; another conviction of murder; under sentence of life imprisonment and time; victim dismembered; victim less than 12 years old; victim was witness against defendant; has committed another murder at any time regardless of whether convicted; committed murder by firing into an inhabited dwelling or from a vehicle; victim of murder was pregnant and murder resulted in intentional killing of a viable fetus; victim was burned, mutilated or tortured while victim was still alive	Lethal injection
None	Capital murder is the intentional and premeditated killing of any person in the commission of kidnapping or aggravated kidnapping when committed with intent to hold person for ransom; intentional and premeditated killing of any person pursuant contract or agreement or being a party to the contract or agreement pursuant to which such person is killed; intentional and premeditated killing of any person by inmate or prisoner of state or community correctional institution; intentional and premeditated killing of victim of one of the following crimes: rape, criminal sodomy or aggravated criminal sodomy or any attempt thereof; intentional and premeditated killing of a law enforcement officer; intentional and premeditated killing of more than one person as part of the same act or in two or more acts connected together or constituting parts of common scheme or course of conduct; or intentional and premeditated killing of a child under the age of 14 in the commission of kidnapping or aggravated kidnapping when the kidnapping or aggravated kidnapping was committed with intent to commit a sex offense upon the child or with intent that the child commit or submit to a sex offense. Aggravating circumstances: defendant previously convicted of a felony in which the defendant inflicted great bodily harm, disfigurement, dismemberment or death on another; defendant knowingly or purposely killed or created a great risk of death to more than one person; defendant committed the crime for defendant's self or another for purpose of receiving money or any other thing of monetary value; defendant authorized or employed another person to commit the crime; defendant committed crime in order to avoid or prevent lawful arrest or prosecution; defendant committed crime in an especially heinous, atrocious or cruel manner--a finding that the victim was aware his or her fate or had conscious pain and suffering as a result of the physical trauma that resulted in the victim's death is not necessary to find that the manner in which the defendant killed the victim was especially heinous, atrocious or cruel; defendant committed the crime while serving a sentence of imprisonment on conviction of a felony; victim was killed while engaging in, or because of the victim's performance or prospective performance of, the victim's duties as a witness in a criminal proceeding	Lethal injection

Table 6: Capital Punishment—Continued

State	Code Section	Allowed?	Effect of Incapacity	Minimum Age
KENTUCKY	431.220; 431.240; 509.040; 532.025; 640.040	Yes	Execution suspended if person is insane or pregnant with child until restored to sanity or delivered of child	16
LOUISIANA	14:30; 14:113; 15:567 to 15:570	Yes	If woman defendant is found to be pregnant, execution is stayed until 90-120 days from end of pregnancy; a person may not be executed while suffering from mental illness	No minimum age
MAINE	Tit. 17A, §§ 1152; 1251	No		
MARYLAND	Art. 27 §§ 71-79 Repealed	No		
MASSACHUSETTS	Ch. 279, §§ 57-71	No; statutes still on books, but *Commonwealth v. Colon-Cruz*, 393 Mass. 150, 470 N.E.2d 116 (1984) said state statute violates state constitution	Suspend sentence if insane or pregnant	No minimum age
MICHIGAN	Const. 1963, art. 4, § 46	No		
MINNESOTA	609.10; Laws 1911, ch. 387	No		
MISSISSIPPI	97-3-21; 97-7-67; 97-25-55; 99-19-51; 99-19-57; 99-19-101 to 99-19-107	Yes; if death penalty found unconstitutional, then life imprisonment without parole	Suspend sentence if insane or pregnant	Age may be a mitigating factor in a separate sentencing hearing

Non- homicidal	Capital Homicide	Method of Execution
Kidnapping if victim not released alive or dies later or caused by kidnapping	Prior capital offense conviction; substantial history of serious assaultive criminal convictions while committing arson, robbery, burglary, rape, sodomy; knowingly created great risk of death to more than 1 person in a public place; for remuneration; intentional and resulted in multiple deaths; intentional and victim state or local official or police officer in performance of duties; victim had protective order against defendant	Lethal injection; if received death penalty prior to March 31, 1998, choice between electrocution or lethal injection, lethal injection is default method
Treason	Murder committed during commission of aggravated rape, forcible rape; aggravated kidnapping; aggravated burglary; aggravated arson; drive-by shooting; aggravated escape; armed robbery or simple robbery or first degree robbery victim was fireman or police officer engaged in lawful duties; previous conviction of murder and other serious crimes; knowingly created a risk of death or great bodily harm to more than 1 person; for remuneration; especially heinous, atrocious or cruel; victim under age of 12 years or over 65 years; distribution, etc. of a controlled dangerous substance; victim was witness against defendant	Lethal injection
None	Victim was police officer, special police officer, state or federal law enforcement officer, officer or employee of the department of corrections, sheriff's department, fireman, etc. acting in official duty; while defendant incarcerated; victim was judge, prosecuting attorney, juror or witness in official duty; previous murder conviction or of an offense in any federal state or territorial jurisdiction of the U.S. which is the same or necessarily includes the elements of an offense of murder in 1st degree; for hire; to avoid arrest, while escaping; involved torture or infliction of extreme pain; course of conduct-killing or serious injury to more than one person; explosive device; while rape, rape of a child, assault on a child, indecent assault and battery on a child under 14 years old, assault with intent to rape, assault on a 16-year-old with intent to rape; assault and battery, kidnapping, kidnapping for ransom; breaking and entering with intent to commit a felony, armed assault in a dwelling, confining or putting in fear or harming for purpose of stealing from depositories; murder occurred while in defendant in possession of a sawed-off shotgun or machine gun; robbery, arson, etc.	Electrocution or at election of prisoner, lethal injection
Treason; aircraft piracy	Murder committed while under sentence of imprisonment; previous conviction of another capital offense or felony involving violence; knowingly created great risk of death to many persons; while committing/attempting to commit robbery, rape, arson, burglary, kidnapping, aircraft piracy; sexual battery, unnatural intercourse with child under 12 years, nonconsensual unnatural intercourse with mankind, battery of child, unlawful detonation of explosives; avoiding/preventing arrest or escape from custody; for pecuniary gain; disrupt/hinder lawful exercise or enforcement of laws; heinous, atrocious or cruelty	Lethal injection

Table 6: Capital Punishment—Continued

State	Code Section	Allowed?	Effect of Incapacity	Minimum Age
MISSOURI	546.720; 546.800 et seq.; 552.060; 565.020; 565.032	Yes	Sentence is suspended until certified as free of mental disease or defect. If defendant is found to be pregnant, sentence is suspended and case is sent to governor, who, after defendant is found to be no longer pregnant, may commute sentence to life in prison, or set new execution date	16
MONTANA	45-5-102; 46-18-220; 46-18-303; 46-19-103; 46-19-201 to 46-19-204	Yes	If defendant is found to be mentally unfit, sentence is suspended, but if fitness is regained, execution must be carried out unless so much time has elapsed that it would be unjust; if pregnant, suspended	18
NEBRASKA	28-105 to 28-105.02; 28-303; 29-2523 to 29-2524; 83-964	Yes. [However, in the 2015 Legislature, the death penalty was repealed by legislative action and vetoed by the governor. On May 27, 2015, the repeal was over-ridden. Later that year, the governor, in a somewhat unusual move and largely using his own money, worked to get Referendum 426 which proposed to reinstate the death penalty on the November 2016 ballot. On November 8, 2016, the referendum passed.]	If woman convict is found to be pregnant, execution is suspended until she is no longer pregnant; if convict is determined to be mentally incompetent, execution is suspended until competency is restored; not against any person with mental retardation	18 at time of crime

Non- homicidal	Capital Homicide	Method of Execution
None	Murder committed by one with prior conviction for murder in 1st degree or multiple assaultive convictions; while committing or attempting to commit another homicide; knowingly created great risk of death to more than 1 person; for monetary value; victim was judicial or former judicial officer, present or former prosecuting attorney or assistant prosecuting attorney, assistant circuit attorney, peace officer, elected official during or because of the exercise of official business/duty; for hire; outrageously or wantonly vile, horrible or inhuman; while escaping, avoiding, or awaiting arrest; engaged in rape, sodomy, burglary, robbery, kidnapping or any felony offense; victim was witness or potential witness; victim was employee of correctional system in course of duty; victim was an inmate of correctional facility/institution; hijacking; to conceal or prevent prosecution of a felony offense; to prevent victim from initiating/aiding prosecution; murder was commission of a crime which is part of a pattern of criminal street gang activity	Lethal gas or lethal injection
Aggravated assault or aggravated kidnapping while incarcerated at state prison by person previously convicted for murder or persistent felony offender	Murder committed while currently serving sentence of imprisonment; previous murder conviction; committed by torture; lying in wait or ambush; part of scheme or operation which would result in death of more than 1 person; victim was peace officer performing duty; aggravated kidnapping; while incarcerated at state prison by person previously convicted of murder or persistent felony offender; while committing sexual assault, sexual intercourse without consent, deviate sexual conduct or incest and victim less than 18 years	Lethal injection
None	Previous felony conviction involving of violence; multiple victims; for hire, pecuniary gain; defendant hired another to commit murder for defendant; law enforcement official or public servant with custody of defendant; committed to hinder lawful exercise of governmental function or enforcement of laws; to conceal crime or identity of person committing crime; offender should have known victim was public servant; especially heinous, atrocious, cruel; created great risk of death to at least several persons	Lethal injection

Table 6: Capital Punishment—Continued

State	Code Section	Allowed?	Effect of Incapacity	Minimum Age
NEVADA	176.025; 176.355; 176.455 to 176.475; 200.030 to 200.035	Yes	Suspend sentence when defendant is found insane or pregnant	18 at time of crime
NEW HAMPSHIRE	630:1 to 630:6	Yes	Exempt from execution if pregnant. Defendant's mental health is a mitigating factor	18
NEW JERSEY	2C:11-3; 2C:11-3b	No		
NEW MEXICO	202-12-42; 31-18-14	No		
NEW YORK	Correct. § 656 to 658; Crim. Proc. § 400.27; Penal § 60.06	Yes; for 1st degree murder	Suspend sentence if insane; if mentally retarded, life sentence without parole or term of imprisonment for class A-I felony of murder in the first degree; stay execution to extent necessary if pregnant	18 at time of crime

Non- homicidal	Capital Homicide	Method of Execution
None	First degree murder and murder of multiple victims (random, no motive); involved torture; peace officer or fireman engaged in official duties; for remuneration; avoid lawful arrest or effect escape from custody; connection with robbery, sexual assault, arson, burglary, kidnapping; knowingly created great risk of death to more than one person other than the victim; previous murder/felony convictions involving use/threat of violence; offender serving sentence; victim was less than 14 years old; murder committed because of victim's race, religion, or ethnic background	Lethal injection
None	Capital murder: victim is law enforcement or judicial officer acting in line of duty or as consequence of or in retaliation for actions in line of duty; while kidnapping or attempting to kidnap; for pecuniary gain or hiring person to cause death; committed by person already sentenced to life imprisonment without parole for another murder; in connection with aggravated felonious sexual assault; in connection with offense of controlled substances acts; in connection with burglary. Aggravating factors: defendant purposely killed victim; purposely inflicted serious bodily injury that resulted in death; created grave risk of death to person other than participant in offense and resulted in death of victim; convicted of another offense resulting in death of person for which sentence of life imprisonment or death was authorized by law; previously convicted of 2 or more offenses punishable by at least 1 yr. imprisonment involving serious bodily injury or distribution of controlled substance; in commission of murder, created grave risk of death to one or more additional victims; committed offense after substantial planning and premeditation; victim particularly vulnerable due to old age, youth, or infirmity; especially heinous, cruel, or depraved manner; pecuniary gain; committed for purpose of avoiding arrest or escaping lawful custody	Lethal injection, or hanging if lethal injection becomes impractical to carry out
Espionage is recognized as a crime triable by court martial with a possible sentence of death § 20-12-42		
None	Victim was public officer in official duty; victim was employee of state correctional institution in official duty; defendant was under sentence for a minimum of 15 year or had escaped from confinement or custody; committed an act of terrorism; convicted of 2 class A felonies or class B violent felonies committed on different occasions in 10 year period prior to murder; victim killed to prevent being a witness; for pecuniary gain; multiple victims; defendant acted in an especially cruel or wanton manner; victim killed in furtherance of an act of terrorism	Lethal injection

Table 6: Capital Punishment—Continued

State	Code Section	Allowed?	Effect of Incapacity	Minimum Age
NORTH CAROLINA	14-17; 15A-1001 to 15A-1008; 15A-2000 to 15A-2005; 15-187	Yes	No defendant may be tried, convicted, sentenced, or punished if determined to be mentally incapacitated. Proceedings will commence if capacity regained. No defendant who is mentally retarded shall be sentenced to death	18 at time of crime
NORTH DAKOTA	12.1-32-01	No		
OHIO	2929.02 to 2929.06; 2949.22 to 2949.31	Yes	Suspend sentence if insane or pregnant	18
OKLAHOMA	Tit. 21, §§ 701.10 to 705; Tit. 22, §§ 1005 to 1014	Yes	Suspend sentence if insane or pregnant	
OREGON	137.080 to 137.090; 137.473; 161.295 to 161.370.; 163.105, 163.150	Yes	Prohibits death penalty	
PENNSYLVANIA	Tit. 18, § 1102; Tit. 42, § 9711; Tit. 61, § 4304	Yes		18
RHODE ISLAND	11-23-2	No		

Non- homicidal	Capital Homicide	Method of Execution
None	Capital felony committed by person lawfully incarcerated; previous capital felony convictions; previous felony conviction involving use/threat of violence; avoid lawful arrest or escape from custody; in connection with homicide, rape or sex offense, robbery, arson, burglary, kidnapping or aircraft piracy or bombing; for pecuniary gain; hinder lawful exercise of governmental function or enforcement of laws; victim was law enforcement officer, employee of Corrections Department jailer, fireman, judge or justice, prosecutor, juror or witness while engaged in duties or former; especially heinous, atrocious, or cruel; great risk of death to more than one person; in connection with other crimes of violence against other person(s)	Lethal injection
None	Assassination of public official; for hire; escape detection, apprehension, trial or punishment for another offense; committed while a prisoner in detention facility; prior murder convictions or multiple victims now; victim was peace officer; rape, kidnapping, aggravated arson, aggravated robbery, aggravated burglary; witness of crime to prevent testimony or retaliation for testimony	Lethal injection
None	Previous felony conviction involving use/threat of violence; knowingly created great risk of death to more than one person; for remuneration or employed another for remuneration; especially heinous, atrocious or cruel; avoiding lawful arrest or prosecution; committed while serving sentence for felony; probability of defendant being continuing threat to society; victim was a peace officer or guard	Lethal injection or electrocution if lethal injection held to be unconstitutional or firing squad if both of above found to be unconstitutional
None	In determining aggravating circumstances, court shall consider any evidence received during proceeding; presentence report; any other relevant evidence court deems trustworthy and reliable	Lethal injection
None	Murder of fireman, peace officer, public servant killed in performance of duties; victim was a judge of any court in unified judicial system, attorney general of Pennsylvania, deputy attorney general, district attorney/assistant district attorney, member of a general assembly, governor, lieutenant governor, auditor general, state treasurer, state law enforcement official, local law enforcement official, federal law enforcement official or person employed to assist or assisting any law enforcement official in performance of his/her duties; in defendant paid or was paid to perform the murder; the victim was a hostage being held for ransom; during an aircraft hijacking; victim was prosecution witness to prevent testimony; during perpetration of a felony; knowingly created grave risk of death to another in addition to victim; torture; significant history of felony convictions involving use/threat of violence; previous life sentence or death; defendant convicted of voluntary manslaughter either before or at time of killing; defendant committed the killing or was accomplice in killing; committed during perpetration of a felony under the Controlled Substance, Drug, Device & Cosmetic Act; victim was or had been in competition with defendant in the sale, manufacture, distribution or delivery of any controlled substance, counterfeit controlled substance, etc.; victim was under 12; victim was known to defendant to be in her third trimester of pregnancy; at the time of killing, victim was or had been a non-governmental informant; defendant was under court order restricting defendant's behavior toward the victim	Lethal injection

Table 6: Capital Punishment—Continued

State	Code Section	Allowed?	Effect of Incapacity	Minimum Age
SOUTH CAROLINA	16-3-10 to 16-3-28; 24-3-530; 44-23-410 to 460	Yes	A female who is pregnant may not be executed until 9 months after she is no longer pregnant; defendant's capacity to appreciate conduct is a mitigating circumstance	Under 18 at time of crime is a mitigating circumstance
SOUTH DAKOTA	22-16-4; 23A-27A-1 to 23A-27A-44	Yes	Sentence suspended during period of mental incompetency or while defendant is pregnant. In event of pregnancy, execution may be carried out not less than 30 days nor more than 90 days from date of new warrant from the governor appointing the execution; life sentence without parole if mentally retarded at time of crime and was mentally retarded before age 18	18
TENNESSEE	39-13-201 to 39-13-208; 37-1-102; 40-23-114	Yes	Prohibited for defendant with "intellectual disability:" Significantly subaverage general intellectual functioning as evidenced by a functional intelligence quotient (I.Q.) of seventy (70) or below; Deficits in adaptive behavior; and, the intellectual disability must have been manifested during the developmental period, or by eighteen (18) years of age	18
TEXAS	Crim. Proc. §§ 37.071; 43.14; Penal §§ 8.07; 12.31; 19.03	Yes	Jury shall be instructed, "[w]hether, taking into consideration all of the evidence, including the circumstances of the offense, the defendant's character and background, and the personal moral culpability of the defendant, there is a sufficient mitigating circumstance or circumstances to warrant that a sentence of life imprisonment without parole rather than a death sentence be imposed."	18

Non-homicidal	Capital Homicide	Method of Execution
None	Murder in connection with any criminal sexual conduct, kidnapping, burglary, armed robbery, larceny with use of deadly weapon, poison, drug trafficking, physical torture during commission of a drug trafficking felony; prior murder conviction; dismemberment of a person; knowingly created great risk of death to multiple persons in public place; for money or monetary value; judicial officer, solicitor, or other officer of the court (or formers) because of exercise of duties; agent/employee of another; law enforcement officer, peace officer, correction employees, fireman (or formers) related to duty; family members of above-mentioned; multiple victims; victim is a child 11 or under; killing of a witness	Electrocution or lethal injection, at the election of the defendant, but if lethal injection is held unconstitutional, then electrocution; if election is waived, then lethal injection
	Prior felony convictions, class A/B felony/serious assaultive criminal convictions; knowingly created great risk of death to others; for the benefit of the defendant or another; for the purpose of receiving money or any other thing of monetary value; for remuneration or as agent/employee of another; members of criminal justice system (judge, attorneys) related to their exercise of duties; outrageously or wantonly vile, horrible or inhuman; law officer, corrections employee, fireman while engaged in performance of official duties; offender escaped from lawful custody/confinement; avoiding lawful arrest of himself or another; in connection with distributing, manufacturing or dispensing illegal substances; testimony regarding impact of crime on victim's family; if victim is less than 13 years old	Lethal injection
	Offender over 18, victim under 12; previous felony convictions; great risk of death to multiple persons other than victim; employed or done for remuneration; especially heinous, atrocious or cruel; avoiding lawful arrest of defendant or another; in connection with any first degree murder, arson, rape, robbery, burglary, theft, kidnapping, aircraft piracy, bombing; committed while in lawful custody/confinement or escape from; committed against law enforcement officer, corrections person, firefighter engaged in duties, also judge, attorney general, district attorney, etc. (and formers) due to performance of duties; against elected official; "mass" murderer; mutilation of victim's body; victim was 70 or older or victim was particularly vulnerable due to disability; committed in course of terrorism; murder of pregnant woman; random murder without reason	Lethal injection unless offense committed prior to January 1 1999, then may elect for electrocution
	Victim is peace officer or fireman in official duty; while committing/attempting to commit kidnapping, burglary, robbery, aggravated sexual assault or arson; obstruction; retaliation; for remuneration or employs another; while escaping; incarcerated and victim is employee or inmate; murder more than one person during same criminal transaction or scheme or course of conduct; victim under 6 years	Lethal injection

Table 6: Capital Punishment—Continued

State	Code Section	Allowed?	Effect of Incapacity	Minimum Age
UTAH	76-3-206 to 76-3-207.5; 76-5-202; 77-15A-101 to 77-15A-106; 77-18-5.5; 77-19-201 to 77-29-206	Yes	No person who is incompetent to proceed shall be tried. Mentally retarded defendant is not subject to death penalty. If convicted defendant is found incompetent or pregnant, sentence is suspended until competency returns or person is no longer pregnant, at which time sentence is reimposed and to be carried out within 30-60 days	
VERMONT	Tit. 13, §§ 3401; 7101 to 7107	None for murder. Statute has not been amended to conform to Supreme Court's decision in *Furman v. Georgia*, 408 U.S. 238 (1972); hence is unconstitutional		
VIRGINIA	18.2-10; 18.2-17; 18.2-31; 19.2-167 to 19.2-182; 53.1-233, 19.2-264.2 to 19.2-264.5	Yes	Cannot stand trial for criminal offense if insane	16
WASHINGTON	9.82.01; 10.95.010 to 10.95.080; 10.95.180	Yes	Mitigating factor; exempt from execution of mentally retarded	18
WEST VIRGINIA	61-11-2	No		
WISCONSIN	939.50(3)(a); 940.01	No		

Non- homicidal	Capital Homicide	Method of Execution
	Offender confined in jail or other correctional facility; multiple murders; knowingly creates great risk of death to person other than victim; in connection with aggravated robbery, robbery, rape, rape of child, object rape, object rape of child, forcible sodomy, sodomy upon child, sexual abuse of child, child abuse of child under 14, aggravated sex assault, aggravated arson, arson, burglary, kidnapping; avoiding lawful arrest; pecuniary or other personal gain; contracted; previously convicted of murder or felony involving use/threat of violence; purpose of preventing witness from testifying in criminal procedure or person from offering evidence or hindering lawful governmental function or enforcement of laws; official or candidate for public office, homicide based on/related to official position; firefighter, peace officer, law officer or anyone involved in criminal justice system; bombs; in connection with unlawful control of aircraft, train, other public conveyance; poison; hostage/ransom; homicide especially heinous, atrocious, cruel or depraved manner	Lethal injection for any defendant sentenced to death after May 3, 2004; defendants sentenced prior to that time may have right to choose firing squad. If lethal injection is found unconstitutional either on its face or as applied, then method of execution is firing squad
Treason.	None. Maximum penalty for homicide is life in prison without parole	Electrocution
	Capital offenses include willful, deliberate, premeditated killing: In connection with abduction for extortion of money or pecuniary benefit; for hire; committed while confined to state correctional facility; armed robbery; rape, sodomy; law officer for purposes of interfering with official duties; multiple murders; victim in commission of abduction, intended to extort money or for pecuniary benefit; controlled substance; outrageously or wantonly vile, horrible or inhuman; continuing serious threat to society; willful killing of a pregnant woman by person who knows woman is pregnant; any person under 14 by a person 21 and older; act of terrorism	Electrocution or by lethal injection
Treason	Law enforcement officer, corrections officer or firefighter in performance of official duties; offender escaped from confinement; offender in custody as consequence of felony conviction; agreement for money or value; contracted; obtain, maintain or advance position in organization; during course of or as a result of shooting from or near a motor vehicle used as a transport; victim was member or former member of criminal justice system (judge, attorney, juror, parole officer, etc.) related to their official duties; committed to conceal crime or identity of person committing crime; multiple victims; in connection with robbery, rape, burglary, kidnapping, arson; victim was news reporter and committed to obstruct investigation, research or reporting activities; victim had court order against defendant; victim and defendant were of same household and within 5 years harassment or criminal assault had occurred 3 or more times	Lethal injection or hanging at election of defendant

Table 6: Capital Punishment—Continued

State	Code Section	Allowed?	Effect of Incapacity	Minimum Age
WYOMING	6-2-101 to 6-2-109; 7-13-901 to 7-13-904	Yes	Suspend sentence if mentally incapacitated or pregnant	16

Non- homicidal	Capital Homicide	Method of Execution
None	While under sentence, on parole/probation, after escaping detention or released on bail; previous conviction for murder in first degree or felony using violence; knowingly created great risk of death to 2 or more persons; while committing/attempting to commit aircraft piracy or unlawful discharge of bomb; while escaping or avoiding arrest; for pecuniary gain; was especially atrocious or cruel; court official in exercise of official duty; victim is less than 17 years or older than 65 years; victim especially vulnerable due to significant mental or physical disability; poses substantial and continuing threat or likely to commit acts again; while committing/attempting to commit robbery, sexual assault, arson, burglary, kidnapping	Lethal injection or lethal gas if injection ruled unconstitutional

7. COMPUTER CRIMES

The body of laws governing crimes on the internet are some of the most rapidly changing of all state laws. Controversial issues such as online pornography, the copying and posting of copyrighted information from an authorized site on the internet to another site, and privacy of communication and access to materials on the internet are hotly debated, and no clear method for dealing with them has yet been devised. In addition, recent efforts to regulate the world of the internet have taken place largely at the federal level. As of this writing, major federal legislation has just been enacted that covers many activities on the internet. The regulations enforcing its various provisions have not yet been written, and much of the act is not yet effective. Accordingly, there is still much speculation about what the law means.

On the state level, the one thing upon which there is much unanimity is that theft of information or money in electronic form is much the same as theft in any other form. State laws on computer crime, therefore, focus on theft of information or money through the use of a computer or an online computer service.

Virtually every state requires that one have the requisite mental state before they may be convicted of a computer crime. One must willfully, knowingly, or purposely access computer-based data and intend to steal, destroy or alter computer-based information, steal services, passwords, or otherwise interfere with hardware or software, etc. It is not enough for purposes of these laws to accidently or unintentionally wander into areas on the internet where valuable or secure information may reside. If one enters such an area using computers or computer technology, to be found guilty of a crime, it must be with the intent to steal, destroy, or defraud.

A handful of states do not explicitly ban access to certain computer files. In most states, mere access can be prosecuted as a crime. Many states have the additional requirement that damage sustained by the victim of the crime be of a certain amount before the crime becomes a felony. In very few states, there is either no misdemeanor provision at all or no money amount distinguishing one from the other.

One new development that is only beginning is legislation regarding the use of computers in acts of terrorism. Only Connecticut mentions terrorism by name, but many imply it in language that makes it a crime to use computers to disrupt government services or public utilities. It is anticipated that in the next few years, there will be a growing number of states first defining certain computer crimes as terrorism and then enhancing the penalties for committing such crimes. In the meantime, this chapter at least can be used as a guidepost to identify the specific laws in question, even if the specific provisions change in the details.

Table 7: Computer Crimes

State	Code Section	Mental State Required for Prosecution	Misdemeanor
ALABAMA	13A-8-112	Knowingly, without authority or exceeds authorization	Access; alter, damage, delete, or destroy programs or data; disclose, use, control, or take programs, data, or supporting documentation; introduce a virus; disrupt or deny use by authorized user; prevent user from exiting a system in order to compel continued communication with system; obtain confidential or private information; give a password or other confidential information to another person without consent: class A misdemeanor
ALASKA	11.46.740	Knowingly, without reasonable grounds	None
ARIZONA	13-2316 to 13-2316.02	Intentionally, knowingly, recklessly	None
ARKANSAS	5-41-101 to 5-41-206	Intentionally, purposefully, without authorization	Computer trespass: class C misdemeanor; computer trespass as second or subsequent violation or causes damage less than $500: class B misdemeanor; computer trespass that causes damage of $500 to $2,500, unlawful computerized communications, unlawful act regarding a computer, unlawful interference with access to computers, unlawful use or access to computers, unlawful use of encryption if concealing a class C, D, or unclassified felony, computer password disclosure: class A misdemeanor
CALIFORNIA	Penal § 502	Knowingly, without permission	Access plus scheme to defraud or wrongfully control money, property, or data; take or copy data; add, alter, or delete data; disrupt or deny computer services to authorized user; disrupt or deny government computer services to authorized user; add, alter, or delete public safety infrastructure data or programs; disrupt or deny public safety infrastructure system computer services to authorized user; introduce virus; introduce virus into public safety infrastructure system

Felony	Attempt Proscribed?	Civil Action?
Commit offense with intent to commit unlawful act or obtain a benefit: class C felony; violation results in damage of $2,500 or more, or intent to obtain benefit, commit unlawful act, or defraud or harm and causes impairment of governmental services, or relates to access to criminal justice information system: class B felony; violation results in damage of $100,000 or more, or if caused physical injury to any person not involved in act: class A felony	No	No
Obtain or change information about a person; install or use keystroke logger: class C felony	No	No
Access system or obtain confidential information, unlawfully possess 5 or fewer access devices, unauthorized release of proprietary information: class 6 felony; computer tampering which causes substantial emotional distress and serves no legitimate purpose, unlawfully possess of 5 to 100 access devices: class 5 felony; tamper with programs or data, introduce a virus, disrupt a computer or system, unlawfully possess 100 or more access devices, unauthorized release of proprietary information related to critical infrastructure resource: class 4 felony; access plus scheme to defraud: class 3 felony; tamper with critical infrastructure resource: class 2 felony	No	No
Computer fraud, computer trespass that causes damage of $2,500 or more, unlawful use of encryption if concealing a class A, B, or Y felony, unlawful act involving electronic mail, computer password disclosure plus scheme to defraud: class D felony; unlawful act regarding a computer plus scheme to defraud or damage of $500 or more or causes interruption of public service, unlawful use, access, or interference with access to computers plus scheme to defraud: class C felony	No	Yes
Access plus scheme to defraud or wrongfully control money, property, or data; take or copy data; add, alter, or delete data; disrupt or deny computer services to authorized user; disrupt or deny government computer services to authorized user; add, alter, or delete public safety infrastructure data or programs; disrupt or deny public safety infrastructure system computer services to authorized user	No	Yes

Table 7: Computer Crimes—Continued

State	Code Section	Mental State Required for Prosecution	Misdemeanor
COLORADO	18-5.5-101 to 18-5.5-102	Knowingly, without authorization	Computer crime: access, alter, damage, introduce virus; damage of $50 to $300: class 3 misdemeanor; damage of $300 to $750: class 2 misdemeanor; damage of $750 to $2,000, or automated circumvention of electronic limitations on number of event tickets: class 1 misdemeanor
CONNECTICUT	53a-250 to 53a-261; 53a-301	Knowingly, without authorization	Unauthorized access to computer systems; theft of computer services; interruption of computer services; misuse of computer system information; destruction of computer equipment and total damage exceeds $500: class A misdemeanor; same computer crimes and total damage up to $500: class B misdemeanor
DELAWARE	Tit. 11, §§ 931 to 941	Knowingly, intentionally, recklessly, negligently	Unauthorized access; theft or interruption of computer services; misuse of computer system information or destruction of computer equipment; sending commercial email after being asked to stop and damages $1,500 or less: class A misdemeanor
DISTRICT OF COLUMBIA	None		
FLORIDA	Florida Computer Crimes Act: 815.01 to 815.07	Willfully, knowingly, and without authorization	Modify equipment or supplies used in a computer: 1st degree misdemeanor

Felony	Attempt Proscribed?	Civil Action?
Computer crime: damage of $2,000 to $5,000: class 6 felony; damage of $5,000 to $20,000: class 5 felony; damage of $20,000 to $100,000: class 4 felony; damage of $100,000 to $1 million: class 3 felony; damage of $1 million or more: class 2 felony	No	No
Same offenses listed above and damage over $10,000: class B felony; damage over $5,000: class C felony; damage over $1,000 or reckless conduct creates risk of physical injury: class D felony ; computer crime in furtherance of terrorist purposes: class B felony, mandatory 5 yr. imprisonment if directed against public agency charged with protection of public safety	No	Yes
Same offenses as above and damages over $1,500 or risk of serious physical injury to another person: class G felony; same offenses and damage over $1,000 or risk of injury to another person: class F felony; same offenses and damages over $5,000: class E felony; same offenses and damages over $10,000: class D felony	No	Yes
Offense against intellectual property: introduce virus, destroy data or programs, disclose or take data or programs that is a trade secret; offense against users of computers: access, disrupt or deny access to authorized user, destroy or damage equipment or supplies used in a computer, introduce virus, engage in surveillance by acing inherent feature of computer, plus damage of $5,000 or more or attempt to defraud or impair governmental operation or interrupt public or private transit: 3rd degree felony; offense against intellectual property plus scheme to defraud: 2nd degree felony; offense against users of computers plus endanger human life or disrupt direct administration of medical care: 1st degree felony	No	Yes

Table 7: Computer Crimes—Continued

State	Code Section	Mental State Required for Prosecution	Misdemeanor
GEORGIA	Georgia Computer Systems Protection Act: 16-9-90 to 16-9-109.1 Note: Section does not specifically classify crimes listed as either felony or misdemeanor. Offenses listed in misdemeanor or felony columns are based on the levels of punishments imposed rather than by explicit classification.	Knowingly, intentionally	Traffic in passwords
HAWAII	708-890 to 708-895.7	Intentionally, knowingly	
IDAHO	18-2201 to 18-2202	Knowingly	Use, access, or attempt to access

Felony	Attempt Proscribed?	Civil Action?
Computer theft; trespass, including modification, destruction, interfering with use; invasion of privacy; forgery	Yes	Yes
Computer Fraud: 1st degree: knowingly access computer, computer system, or computer network with the intent to commit the offense of theft in the 1st degree: class A felony; 2nd degree: same action with the intent to commit the offense of theft in the 2nd degree: class B felony; 3rd degree: knowingly access computer, computer system, or computer network with the intent to commit the offense of theft in the 3rd or 4th degree: class C felony; Computer Damage: 1st degree: Intentional damage or attempt to damage computer, computer system, or computer network that controls critical infrastructure and results or would result in damage to computer or infrastructure: class A felony; 2nd degree: cause transmission of program, information, code, or command and knowingly causes damage; intentionally accesses computer, system, or network without authorization and knowingly causes at least $5,000 damage, modification or impairment of medical examination, diagnosis, treatment or care or impairment or disruption of government operations: class B felony; 3rd degree: knowingly access computer, system, or network without authorization and thereby recklessly cause damage: class C felony; Unauthorized Access: 1st degree: knowingly access and obtain information for purpose of financial gain; committed in furtherance of any other crime; value of information over $20,000; or information requires protection against unauthorized disclosure by statute or rules of court: class A felony; 2nd degree: knowingly accesses a computer, system, or network without authorization and thereby obtain information: class B felony; 3rd degree: access computer, system, or network without authorization: class C felony	No	No
Access or attempt to access with purpose to scheme, defraud or obtain property, money or services; alter, damage, or destroy computer, computer system, computer network or software/ data/ documentation	Yes	No

Table 7: Computer Crimes—Continued

State	Code Section	Mental State Required for Prosecution	Misdemeanor
ILLINOIS	720 §§ 5/17-50 to 5/17-55	Knowingly, without authorization	Access, falsify or forge email transmission, distribute software to falsify routing information: class B misdemeanor; access and obtain data or services, unlawful use of encryption: class A misdemeanor
INDIANA	35-43-2-3	Knowingly; intentionally	Unauthorized access: class A misdemeanor
IOWA	702.1A; 702.14; 714.1 to 714.2; 716.6B	Knowingly	Unauthorized access data containing confidential record, operational or support data of public utility, water district, rural municipal utility, or public airport: aggravated misdemeanor; data copied, altered, or deleted: serious misdemeanor; any unauthorized access not aggravated or serious misdemeanor: simple misdemeanor; Theft penalties: theft of data or services value $500 to $1,000: aggravated misdemeanor; value $200 to $500: serious misdemeanor; value less than $200: simple misdemeanor
KANSAS	21-5839	Knowingly, without authorization, exceed authorization	Access, disclose password: class A nonperson misdemeanor
KENTUCKY	434.840 to 434.860	Knowingly; intentionally	Unlawful access 4th degree: unauthorized access resulting in no damage: class B misdemeanor; unlawful access 3rd degree: loss or damage less than $300: class A misdemeanor

Felony	Attempt Proscribed?	Civil Action?
Access plus scheme to defraud, access to obtain control over money, property, or services up to $1,000 plus scheme to defraud, access and obtain data or services second or subsequent offense, alter or delete program or data, introduce virus: class 4 felony; obtain or damage computer, program, or data, plus scheme to defraud, access to obtain control over money, property, or services of $1,000 to $50,000 plus scheme to defraud, alter or delete program or data second or subsequent offense and/or disrupt government or public utility, introduce virus second or subsequent offense: class 3 felony; access to obtain control over money, property, or services of $50,000 or more plus scheme to defraud, alter or delete program or data and create danger of harm or death: class 2 felony	Yes	Yes
Disrupt or deny services to authorized user; destroy, damage, or contaminate computer: level 6 felony; if loss is at least $5,000 or committed to defraud or obtain property or interrupts or impairs government operation or public services: level 5 felony; endangers human life: level 4 felony	No	No
Theft penalties: theft of data or services value over $10,000: class C felony; value $1,000 to $10,000: class D felony	No	Yes
Alter or damage computer or system, use computer or system in scheme to defraud or obtain money, property, or services: severity level 8 nonperson felony; same offenses plus loss over $100,000: level 5 nonperson felony	Yes	No
Unlawful access 2nd degree: unauthorized access resulting in loss or damage $300 or more: class D felony; unlawful access 1st degree: unauthorized access with purpose of scheme to defraud; obtain money, property, or services by false or fraudulent pretenses; misuse of computer information: class C felony	Yes	No

Table 7: Computer Crimes—Continued

State	Code Section	Mental State Required for Prosecution	Misdemeanor
LOUISIANA	14:73.1 to 14:73.10 Note: Section does not specifically classify crimes listed as either felony or misdemeanor. Offenses listed in misdemeanor or felony columns are based on the levels of punishments imposed rather than by explicit classification.	Intentionally	Alter, damage or destroy hard/software valued under $500; interfere with use of another valued under $500
MAINE	Tit. 17-A, §§ 431 to 437	Intentionally; knowingly	Unauthorized access
MARYLAND	Crim. Law § 7-302	Intentionally; willfully	Unauthorized access; copy or possess all or part of database: misdemeanor punishable by imprisonment up to 3 yrs. and/or fine up to $1,000; access, copy or possess with intent to cause malfunction or interrupt operation or intent to alter, damage or destroy data, network, software, system, database or service; unauthorized possession, identification, publicizing, or distribution of access code with loss under $10,000: misdemeanor punishable by imprisonment up to 5 yrs. and/or fine up to $5,000; commit any act above with intent to interrupt or impair functioning of state government or anything related to electricity or natural gas service owned by private or public utility with loss under $50,000: misdemeanor punishable by imprisonment up to 5 yrs. and/or fine up to $25,000
MASSACHUSETTS	Ch. 266, §§ 33A; 120F; Ch. 274, § 1	Intentionally	Unauthorized access: imprisonment in house of correction up to 30 days and/or fine up to $1,000; obtain commercial computer services by fraud or misrepresentation; unauthorized charging to account of another; tampering with facility of equipment: imprisonment in house of correction up to 2 1/2 yrs. and/or fine up to $3,000

Felony	Attempt Proscribed?	Civil Action?
Alter, damage or destroy hard/software valued over $500; interfere with use of another valued over $500; computer fraud	No	No
Copy, alter, damage, or destroy hard/software; introduce virus	No	No
Access, copy or possess with intent to cause malfunction or interrupt operation or intent to alter, damage or destroy data, network, software, system, database or service; unauthorized possession, identification, publicizing, or distribution of access code with loss $10,000 or more: felony punishable by imprisonment up to 10 yrs. and/or fine up to $10,000; commit any act above with intent to interrupt or impair functioning of state government or anything related to electricity or natural gas service owned by private or public utility with loss of $50,000 or more: felony punishable by imprisonment up to 10 yrs. and/or fine up to $25,000	Yes	No
None	Yes	No

Table 7: Computer Crimes—Continued

State	Code Section	Mental State Required for Prosecution	Misdemeanor
MICHIGAN	752.791 to 752.797	Intentionally	Unauthorized access with intent to defraud or obtain money or property by false pretense: Loss/damage $200 or less: imprisonment up to 93 days and/or fine up to $500 or 3x loss; $200 to $1,000 or 1 prior conviction: imprisonment up to 1 yr. and/or fine up to $2,000 or 3x loss; use of computer to commit other crime: misdemeanor punishable by imprisonment for up to 1 yr. and/or fine up to $5,000 if underlying crime is misdemeanor or felony with maximum sentence up to 1 yr.
MINNESOTA	609.87 to 609.8913	Intentionally	Misdemeanor: Computer damage; computer theft with loss under $500; unauthorized computer access: imprisonment up to 90 days and/or fine up to $1,000; gross misdemeanor: unauthorized computer access with access to personal data; in manner that risks public health or safety; in manner that compromises security of data; 2nd or subsequent unauthorized access misdemeanor conviction within 5 yrs.: imprisonment up to 1 yr. and/or fine up to $3,000
MISSISSIPPI	97-45-1 to 97-45-33 Note: Section does not specifically classify crimes listed as either felony or misdemeanor. Offenses listed in misdemeanor or felony columns are based on the levels of punishments imposed rather than by explicit classification	Intentionally	Computer fraud: access with intent to defraud, obtain money, property, or services, delete or alter programs or data, introduce virus; offense against computer users: deny access to authorized user, unauthorized use of passwords or other means of access; tampering with computer equipment: modify or destroy computer equipment; offense against intellectual property: destroy, modify, disclose, or use intellectual property: loss less than $1,000: imprisonment up to 6 months and/or fine up to $1,000
MISSOURI	537.525; 569.095 to 569.099	Knowingly, without authorization	Tampering with computer data: modify, destroy, or disclose program, data, supporting documentation, or password, access and intentionally examine information about another person, receive, retain, or disclose data obtained in this way; tampering with computer equipment: modify, damage, or destroy computer equipment; tampering with computer users: access or deny access to authorized user: class A misdemeanor

Felony	Attempt Proscribed?	Civil Action?
Unauthorized access with intent to defraud or obtain money or property by false pretense: Loss/damage $1,000 to $20,000 or 2 prior convictions: imprisonment up to 5 yrs. and/or fine up to $10,000 or 3x loss; $20,000 or more or 3 prior convictions: imprisonment up to 10 yrs. and/or fine up to 3x loss; unauthorized access to acquire, damage, delete, or destroy; or attach or create opportunity for unknowing insertion to acquire, damage, delete, or destroy: imprisonment up to 15 yrs. and/or fine up to $10,000; with prior conviction: imprisonment up to 10 yrs. and/or fine up to $50,000; use of computer to commit other crime: felony if underlying crime is misdemeanor or felony with maximum sentence of more than 1 yr.	No	No
Computer damage; computer theft: loss $500 to $2,500: imprisonment up to 5 yrs. and/or fine up to $10,000; loss over $2,500: imprisonment up to 10 yrs. and/or fine up to $50,000; unauthorized computer access in manner that creates grave risk of death of a person; 2nd or subsequent unauthorized access gross misdemeanor conviction: imprisonment up to 10 yrs. and/or fine up to $20,000	Yes	No
Computer fraud, offense against computer users: loss of $1,000 or more: imprisonment up to 3 yrs. and/or fine up to $2,000; loss of $1,000 to $5,000: imprisonment up to 5 yrs. and/or fine up to $10,000; loss of $5,000 to $25,000: imprisonment up to 10 yrs. and/or fine up to $10,000; loss of $25,000 or more: imprisonment up to 20 yrs. and/or fine up to $10,000	No	No
Tampering with computer data, equipment, or users: loss of $750 or more and/or scheme to defraud: class E felony; tampering with computer equipment: loss of $25,000 or more: class D felony	No	Yes

Table 7: Computer Crimes—Continued

State	Code Section	Mental State Required for Prosecution	Misdemeanor
MONTANA	45-2-101; 45-6-310 to 45-6-311	Knowingly, purposefully	Any of the following, causing damages less than $1,500: access; access plus scheme to defraud; alter, damage or destroy hard/software
NEBRASKA	Computer Crimes Act: 28-1341 to 28-1348	Intentionally, without authority	Access that creates risk to public health and safety, deprive or obtain property or services of $500 to $1,500, harm or disrupt operations of $500 to $1,500, obtain confidential public information second or subsequent offense: class I misdemeanor; access that compromises data security, deprive or obtain property or services of less than $500, harm or disrupt operations of less than $500, obtain confidential public information, access without authorization second or subsequent offense: class II misdemeanor; access without authorization: class V misdemeanor
NEVADA	205.473 to 205.513	Knowingly, willfully	Unauthorized access; interference with or denial of access or use: gross misdemeanor
NEW HAMPSHIRE	638:16 to 638:19	Knowingly	Computer crime is a misdemeanor if damage is $1,000 or less
NEW JERSEY	2C:20-23 to 2C:20-39 Note: Section does not specifically classify crimes listed as either felony or misdemeanor. Offenses listed in misdemeanor or felony columns are based on the levels of punishments imposed rather than by explicit classification.	Purposely, knowingly	Computer criminal activity: includes unauthorized access; access with intent to defraud; alter, damage, or destroy hard/software; damages up to $5,000
NEW MEXICO	30-45-1 to 30-45-7	Knowingly, willfully	Unauthorized access; access plus scheme to defraud; alteration, damage, or destruction of hard/software; disclosure, copying, or display of computer information with damage less than $250: petty misdemeanor; $250 to $500: misdemeanor

Felony	Attempt Proscribed?	Civil Action?
Any of the following, causing damages greater than $1,500: access; access plus scheme to defraud; alter, damage or destroy hard/software	No	No
Deprive or obtain property or services of $5,000 or more, harm or disrupt operations of $5,000 or more: class III felony; access that creates grave risk of death, deprive or obtain property or services of $1,500 to $5,000, harm or disrupt operations of $1,500 to $5,000: class IV felony	No	No
Unauthorized access with intent to defraud or obtain property; damage in excess of $500; or interrupts/impairs public service or utility: class C felony; interference with or denial of access with intent to defraud or obtain property: class C felony; forgery by creation, alteration, or deletion of data: class D felony	Yes	No
Computer crime with damages over $1,500: class A felony; computer crime with damages $1,000 to $1,500 or offender's conduct creates risk of physical injury: class B felony	No	No
Computer criminal activity: includes unauthorized access; access with intent to defraud; alter, damage, or destroy hard/software; damages over $5,000	No	No
Unauthorized access; access plus scheme to defraud; alteration, damage, or destruction of hard/software; disclosure, copying, or display of computer information with damage $500 to $2,500: 4th degree felony; $2,500 to $20,000: 3rd degree felony; $20,000 or more: 2nd degree felony	No	No

Table 7: Computer Crimes—Continued

State	Code Section	Mental State Required for Prosecution	Misdemeanor
NEW YORK	Penal §§ 156.00 to 156.50	Knowingly; intentionally	Unauthorized use of computer: class A misdemeanor; computer tampering in 4th degree: class A misdemeanor; unlawful duplication of computer-related material in 2nd degree: class B misdemeanor
NORTH CAROLINA	14-453 to 14-458.2	Willfully	Unlawful access for purposes other than to scheme, defraud, or obtain property; altering, damaging, or destroying computer software, programs, or data; computer trespass with less than $2,500 damage: class 1 misdemeanor; computer trespass with no damage: class 3 misdemeanor
NORTH DAKOTA	12.1-06.1-08	Intentionally	Computer crime: class A misdemeanor
OHIO	2913.01; 2913.041	Knowingly	Unauthorized use of computer property: 4th degree misdemeanor; unauthorized use with intent to defraud or obtain property or services: 1st degree misdemeanor
OKLAHOMA	Oklahoma Computer Crimes Act: Tit. 21, §§ 1951 to 1959	Willfully	Unauthorized access or attempt to access computer, system, network, or other property; willful use to annoy, abuse, threaten, or harass another person
OREGON	164.125; 164.377	Knowingly	Unauthorized access: class A misdemeanor; theft of services: loss up to $100: class C misdemeanor; $100 to $1,000: class A misdemeanor
PENNSYLVANIA	Tit. 18, §§ 7601 to 7661	Intentionally and knowingly	Unlawful transmission of email: 3rd degree misdemeanor punishable by fine up to $2,500; damage $2,500 or more and caused by reckless disregard for consequences: 1st degree misdemeanor punishable by fine up to $10,000
RHODE ISLAND	11-52-1 to 11-52-8	Purposefully, intentionally, knowingly	Theft of data or services valued under $500; cyberstalking; online impersonation
SOUTH CAROLINA	16-16-10 to 16-16-40	Willfully, knowingly, maliciously	Computer crime in 2nd degree: class A misdemeanor; computer crime in 3rd degree: class B misdemeanor
SOUTH DAKOTA	43-43B-1 to 43-43B-8	Knowingly	Obtaining use, altering or destroying system, access and disclosure without consent where value up to $1,000: class 1 misdemeanor; obtaining use, altering or destroying system as part of deception where value up to $1,000: class 1 misdemeanor

Felony	Attempt Proscribed?	Civil Action?
Computer tampering in 3rd degree: class E felony; computer tampering in 2nd degree: class D felony; computer tampering in 1st degree: class C felony; criminal possession or unlawful duplication of computer-related material: class E felony; computer trespass: class E felony	Yes	No
Computer trespass with damage of $2,500 or more: class I felony; denying access to government computer services: class H felony; unlawful access with purpose to scheme, defraud, or obtain property; damage computer, system, network, or parts with damage over $1,000: class G felony; unauthorized access to any government computer: class F felony	No	Yes
Computer fraud: class C felony	Yes	Yes
Unauthorized of computer property with intent to defraud or obtain property or services with loss of $1,000 to $7,000: 5th degree felony; $7,500 to $15,000: 4th degree felony $150,000 or more: 3rd degree felony; enhanced penalties if victim is elderly or disabled	Yes	No
Unauthorized access plus scheme to defraud; alter, damage, or destroy hard/software; exceed limits of authorization and damage, destroy, or steal computer; disrupt services or deny access or other services to authorized user; provide or assist in providing means of accessing computer system, or network	Yes	Yes
Access plus scheme to defraud; alter, damage, or destroy hard/software; theft of data or intimate image: class C felony; theft of services loss $1,000 to $10,000: class C felony; over $10,000: class B felony	Yes	No
Unlawful use, destruction, damage, or alteration of computer or related system or services; disruption of service, theft, unlawful duplication, trespass; distribution of virus or password or other confidential information: 3rd degree felony; unlawful transmission of email with damages of $2,500 or more and caused by malicious act: 3rd degree felony punishable by fine up to $15,000	No	No
Access of computer for fraudulent purposes; intentional access, alteration, damage, or destruction; computer theft with a value over $500; use if false information and tampering with computer source documents; online impersonation second or subsequent offense	No	Yes
Computer crime in 1st degree: class E felony; 2nd or subsequent convictions of computer crime in 2nd degree: class F felony	No	No
Obtaining use, altering or destroying system, access and disclosure without consent where value involved is more than $1,000: class 6 felony; obtaining use, altering or destroying system as part of deception with value more than $1,000: class 4 felony	Yes	No

Table 7: Computer Crimes—Continued

State	Code Section	Mental State Required for Prosecution	Misdemeanor
TENNESSEE	39-14-601 to 39-14-606; 39-14-105	Knowingly, directly or indirectly	Unauthorized access: class C misdemeanor; introducing virus: class B misdemeanor; hacking into any computer system: class A misdemeanor; theft of property or services: falsify or forge e-mail transmission, access with intent to obtain money, property, or services, cause false computer output, or fraudulently create or alter financial instrument or financial transfer, damage or destroy computer, make unauthorized copy of computer data or program, receive, use, or conceal proceeds from a violation: class A misdemeanor
TEXAS	Penal §§ 33.01 to 33.07	Knowingly, intentionally	Breach of computer security, electronic data tampering, unlawful decryption: loss less than $100: class C misdemeanor; $100 to $750: class B misdemeanor; $750 to $2,500: class A misdemeanor
UTAH	Utah Computer Crimes Act: 76-6-701 to 76-6-705	Intentionally, knowingly, without authorization	Access, damage or interfere with data, engage in denial of service attack: loss up to $500 or information not confidential: class B misdemeanor; $500 to $1,500: class A misdemeanor; dissemination of identifying information with intent to harass: adult's information: class B misdemeanor; minor's information or 2nd or subsequent offense: class A misdemeanor
VERMONT	Tit. 13, §§ 1; 4101 to 4107 Note: Section does not specifically classify crimes listed as either felony or misdemeanor. Offenses listed in misdemeanor or felony columns are based on the levels of punishments imposed rather than by explicit classification.	Knowingly, intentionally	Unauthorized access: imprisonment up to 6 mos. and/or fine up to $500; unauthorized access for fraudulent purposes with damages up to $500: imprisonment up to 1 yr. and/or fine up to $500; 2nd or subsequent offense: imprisonment up to 2 yrs. and/or fine up to $1,000; alter, damage, interfere with operation, steal, or destroy with damages up to $500: 1st offense: imprisonment up to 1 yr. and/or fine up to $5,000; 2nd or subsequent offense: imprisonment up to 2 yrs. and/or fine up to $10,000

Felony	Attempt Proscribed?	Civil Action?
Theft of property or services: $1,000 to $2,500: class E felony; $2,500 to $10,000: class D felony; $10,000 to $60,000: class C felony; $60,000 to $250,000: class B felony; $250,000 or more: class A felony	Yes	Yes
Breach of computer security, electronic data tampering, unlawful decryption: loss of $2,500 to $30,000: state jail felony; $30,000 to $150,000: 3rd degree felony; $150,000 to $300,000: 2nd degree felony; $300,000 or more: 1st degree felony; enhancements for serious bodily injury or death, access to government or critical infrastructure system	No	No
Access, damage or interfere with data, engage in denial of service attack: loss $1,500 to $5,000, property obtained is license or entitlement, damage is to license or entitlement of another, information obtained is confidential or, breach security system: 3rd degree felony; $5,000 or more: 2nd degree felony; dissemination of identifying information with intent to harass: 2nd dissemination of minor's information; 3rd or subsequent dissemination of adult's information: 3rd degree felony; interfere or interrupt critical infrastructure: 3rd degree felony	Yes	No
Unauthorized access for fraudulent purposes with damages over $500: imprisonment up to 10 yrs. and/or fine up to $10,000; alter, damage, interfere with operation, steal, or destroy with damages over $500: imprisonment up to 10 yrs. and/or fine up to $25,000	No	Yes

Table 7: Computer Crimes—Continued

State	Code Section	Mental State Required for Prosecution	Misdemeanor
VIRGINIA	Virginia Computer Crimes Act: 18.2-152.1 to 18.2-152.15	Intentionally	Computer trespass: class 3 misdemeanor; damages $2,500 or more: class 1 misdemeanor; computer fraud with value of property or services less than $200: class 1 misdemeanor; computer invasion of privacy; theft of computer services; personal trespass by computer done unlawfully but not maliciously; computer harassment: class 1 misdemeanor
WASHINGTON	Washington Cybercrime Act: 9A.90.010 to 9A.90.110	Intentionally, knowingly, maliciously, without authorization	2nd degree computer trespass; spoofing; 2nd degree electronic tampering; gross misdemeanor
WEST VIRGINIA	West Virginia Computer Crime and Abuse Act: 61-3C-1 to 61-3C-21	Knowingly, willfully	Unauthorized access to computer services; unauthorized possession of computer data or programs having value under $5,000; disruption or denial of computer services; unauthorized possession of computer information; disclosure of computer security info; obtaining confidential public info.; computer invasion of privacy; obscene, anonymous, harassing and threatening communications
WISCONSIN	943.70; 939.32	Willfully, knowingly, without authorization	Offense against computer data and programs: class A misdemeanor; offenses against computers, computer equipment or supplies: class A misdemeanor
WYOMING	6-3-501 to 6-3-506	Knowingly	Crime against computer equipment and supplies; computer trespass with loss up to $10,000

Felony	Attempt Proscribed?	Civil Action?
Computer fraud with value of property or services obtained $200 or more: class 5 felony; computer trespass with damages $2,500 or more caused by malicious act or affecting government or public utility, class 6 felony; personal trespass by computer done maliciously: class 3 felony	No	Yes
1st degree computer trespass; 1st degree electronic tampering; electronic data service interference; electronic data theft: class C felony	No	No
Computer fraud and access to legislature computer; unauthorized possession of computer data or programs having value of $5,000 or more; alteration, destruction, etc. of computer equipment; soliciting, etc. a minor via computer	Yes	Yes
Offense against computer data and programs with intent to defraud or obtain property: class I felony; damage over $2,500: class F felony; damage over $2,500, impairment of government operations or public utility; creates risk of death or great bodily harm; offense against computers, computer equipment or supplies if creates risk of death or great bodily harm: class F felony; offense against computers, computer equipment or supplies with intent to defraud or obtain property: class I felony; damage over $2,500: class H felony; creates risk of death or great bodily harm: class F felony	Yes	Aggrieved party may sue for injunctive relief
Crime against intellectual property; crime against computer equipment and supplies with intent to scheme, defraud, or obtain property; crime against users with value over $750; computer trespass with loss of $10,000 or more	No	No

8. CRIMINAL STATUTES OF LIMITATIONS

A statute of limitations is a law which forbids prosecutors from charging someone with a crime that was committed more than a specified number of years ago. The general purpose of statutes of limitations is to make sure convictions occur only upon evidence (physical or eyewitness) that has not deteriorated with time. After the period of the statute has run, the criminal is essentially free.

Statutes of limitations generally require the criminal to remain in the state, gainfully employed and visible, seeming to necessitate that the criminal remain "catchable." If the authorities fail to discover a criminal living in the open within a specified amount of time, society has determined that at that point the criminal should be able to live free from the possibility of prosecution. It appears that this notion is born out of a sense of mercy more than pragmatics: if the criminal is a fugitive, out of the state in which the crime was committed or otherwise living in hiding, this tolls, or suspends, the statute. (Once the criminal reenters the state, the statute resumes running.) However, if the criminal were living an open, public, so-called "reformed" life, after a reasonable period of time, he is allowed to be free from capture.

Not all crimes are governed by statutes of limitations. Murder, for example, has none. Sex offenses with minors, crimes of violence, kidnapping, arson, and forgery have no statutes of limitations in a number of states. In Arizona and California crimes involving public money or public records have no statutes of limitations. In Colorado, Illinois, Nebraska and Rhode Island, treason has none. A handful of states have recently added terrorism to the list of crimes in those states with no statute of limitations, while one state has recently added terrorism to the list of crimes, but with an 8 year statute of limitations.

Many states have adopted systems that classify felonies by category. Therefore, in order to effectively compare statutes of limitations provisions, it is necessary to determine which crimes in that state fit into particular classes. For example, Missouri lists murder or Class A felonies as crimes with no statutes of limitations. Each crime must then be looked up in that state's statutes to determine its classification.

Table 8: Criminal Statutes of Limitations

State	Code Section	Felonies	Misdemeanors	Acts During Which Statute Does Not Run
ALABAMA	15-3-1 to 15-3-8	Arson, forgery, any capital offense, counterfeiting, attempted or actual use or threat of violence, felony with serious physical injury/death, any sex offense with person under 16, drug trafficking: none; conversion of state or county revenue: 6 yrs.; unlawfully taking or using temporarily the property of another: 30 days; other felonies: 3 yrs.	12 mos.	Prosecution commences upon indictment, issuing warrant or binding over of defendant
ALASKA	12.10.010 to 12.10.040	Murder, attempt or conspiracy to commit murder, felony sexual abuse of minor, certain sexual assaults, kidnapping, child pornography, sex trafficking of victim under 20, human trafficking: none; certain violent felonies: 10 yrs.; all others: 5 yrs.; any offense that includes fraud or breach of fiduciary obligation or official misconduct in public office: extension 1 yr. after discovery of offense, max. 3 yr. extension	5 yrs.	If hiding outside the state: max. 3 yr. extension when prosecution against accused for the same conduct is pending in this state
ARIZONA	13-107	Homicide, any conspiracy to commit homicide resulting in death, violent sexual assault, misuse of public money, falsifying public records, attempt to commit any of these: none; class 2-6 felonies: 7 yrs.	1 yr.; petty offenses: 6 mos.	Absent from state or no reasonably ascertainable residence in state; identity not known

Table 8: Criminal Statutes of Limitations—Continued

State	Code Section	Felonies	Misdemeanors	Acts During Which Statute Does Not Run
ARKANSAS	5-1-109	Murder, rape of minor, sexual indecency, assault, or incest against minor, sexual misconduct with child, including explicit conduct or performance, transporting minor for or direction or promotion of conduct, or computer exploitation: none. 3rd or 4th deg. sexual assault, 1st deg. endangering welfare of minor, permitting abuse of minor, computer child pornography: until victim turns 28 if minor at time of violation and not previously reported; arson: 10 yrs.; class Y or A felony: 6 yrs., no limitation if rape and DNA evidence identifies offender; class B, C, D, or unclassified felony: 3 yrs.; felonious conduct in public office: 5 yrs. after discovery or leaving office, 10 yrs. max. extension; certain offenses against minors if limitation period has not expired since victim turned 18: statutory period starts at age of majority	1 yr.	Continually absent from state or has no reasonably ascertainable home or work within state: max. 3 yr. extension when prosecution against accused for same conduct is pending in this state
CALIFORNIA	Pen. §§ 799 to 805	Murder, other offenses punishable by death or life imprisonment, certain offenses involving substantial sexual conduct, embezzlement of public funds: none; child pornography, sex offenses: 10 yrs. after committed or victim turns 18; offenses punishable by 8 or more yrs. imprisonment: 6 yrs.; elder abuse or child neglect: 5 yrs.; false or fraudulent insurance claims: 4 yrs.; offenses punishable by imprisonment: 3 yrs.	1 yr.; misdemeanor violation committed on minor under 14: 3 yrs.; sexual exploitation by physician or therapist: 2 yrs.	Not in state, max. 3 yr. extension; statutory periods do not begin until offense is or should have been discovered

Table 8: Criminal Statutes of Limitations—Continued

State	Code Section	Felonies	Misdemeanors	Acts During Which Statute Does Not Run
COLORADO	16-5-401	Murder, kidnapping, treason, forgery regardless of penalty provided, any sex offense against a child, conspiracy or solicitation to commit any of these offenses: none; fleeing of vehicular homicide, fleeing scene of accident that resulted in death of person: 5 yrs.; if both vehicle homicide and leaving scene that resulted in death occur as part of same criminal episode: 10 yrs.; misdemeanor against child under 15: 3 yrs. 6 mos.; other felonies: 3 yrs.; 3 yr. extension for bribery and abuse of office	18 mos.; class I and II traffic offenses: 1 yr.; petty offenses: 6 mos.; 3rd degree sexual assault: 5 yrs.	Absent from state: 5 yrs. max. extension
CONNECTICUT	54-193 to 54-193B	Murder or capital Class A felony, intentionally acting during proceeding to convict an innocent person: none; if imprisonment penalty is more than 1 yr.: 5 yrs.; any other: 1 yr.; sexual abuse, exploitation, or assault: 30 yrs. after victim reaches majority or 5 yrs. from date of notification by victim, whichever is earlier; when DNA available for sexual assault offenses: none if DNA evidence establishes the identity of the person who committed the offense and the victim notified police within 5 yrs. of offense	1 yr.	Fleeing or residing outside state
DELAWARE	Tit. 11, § 205(a); 205(b); 205(c); 205(e); 205(h); 205(i)	Murder, attempt to commit murder, class A felony, attempt to commit class A felony, any sexual offense where victim was under 18: none; others: 5 yrs. unless forensic DNA evidence, then 10 yrs.; any offense which includes forgery, fraud, breach of fiduciary duty, theft or misapplication of property, misconduct in public office: additional 3 yrs.	Class A: 3 yrs.; others: 2 yrs.	Fleeing or hiding from justice action commenced
DISTRICT OF COLUMBIA	23-113	Murder of police officer, 1st or 2nd degree terrorism, 1st or 2nd degree murder: none; 1st or 2nd degree sexual abuse: 15 yrs.; other sexual crimes against minor, sexual abuse of a patient or ward: 10 yrs.; other felonies in 1st and 2nd degree: 6 yrs.; all other crimes: 3 yrs.; if offense includes official misconduct, fraud or breach of fiduciary trust: max. 9 yrs.	3 yrs.; if offense includes official misconduct, fraud, or breach of fiduciary trust: max. 6 yrs.	Fleeing from justice: if victim is minor, statute runs after victim reaches majority; if victim is ward or patient: when freed from care; if victim is subject to human trafficking: when freed

Table 8: Criminal Statutes of Limitations—Continued

State	Code Section	Felonies	Misdemeanors	Acts During Which Statute Does Not Run
FLORIDA	775.15	Felony that resulted in death, perjury in official proceeding that relates to prosecution of capitol felony, capital or life felony: none sexual battering offenses, lewd or lascivious offenses, battery, kidnapping, burglary, robbery, aggravated child abuse: none if DNA evidence establishes identity; 1st degree felony: 4 yrs.; felony resulting in injury to person where felony arises from use of destructive device: 10 years; 2nd degree felony for abuse or neglect of aged or disabled adult: 5 yrs.; others: 3 yrs.; insurance fraud, violation of securities transaction: 5 yrs.; violation of environmental control: 5 yrs. after date of discovery; any offense which fraud or breach of fiduciary obligation is a material element: 3 yrs.; misconduct in public office: within 2 yrs. of leaving office or any greater limit; video voyeurism: 1 yr. extension after discovery; sexual offenses under age 18: begins running at age 18 or when violation is reported, whichever is earlier.	Other 1st degree misdemeanors: 2 yrs.; 2nd degree and noncriminal violations: 1 yr.	Continually absent from state, no reasonably ascertainable work or abode in state: maximum extension 3 yrs.
GEORGIA	17-3-1 to 17-3-3	Murder: none; forcible rape, victim of felony is 65 or older: 15 yrs.; crimes punishable by death or life imprisonment, felonies committed against minor: 7 yrs.; others: 4 yrs.; crimes against victims under 14: 18 yrs.; for victims under 16 yrs. of age of offenses such as rape, sodomy, incest, and child molestation: statute will run upon the victim turning 16 or when the violation is reported, whichever occurs earlier; none if crime committed after July 1, 2012; if DNA evidence establishes identity of accused in armed robbery, kidnapping, rape, aggravated child molestation, aggravated sodomy, aggravated sexual battery: none	2 yrs.	Nonresident; when person or crime is unknown; accused is current government officer or employee charged with theft by conversion of public property, accused is guardian or trustee and crime charged is theft by conversion of property of ward or beneficiary

Table 8: Criminal Statutes of Limitations—Continued

State	Code Section	Felonies	Misdemeanors	Acts During Which Statute Does Not Run
HAWAII	701-108	Murder, 1st or 2nd degree murder, attempted murder, 1st or 2nd degree attempted murder, criminal conspiracy or solicitation to commit murder in any degree, continuous sexual assault of minor under 14: none; manslaughter where death not caused by motor vehicle: 10 yrs.; class A felony: 6 yrs.; others: 3 yrs.; if fraud or breach of fiduciary obligation is element: 2-6 yrs. extension after discovery; if based on misconduct in public office: 2-3 yrs. extension upon discovery; felony with DNA evidence test: 10 yr. extension	Misdemeanor or parking violation: 2 yrs.; petty misdemeanor: 1 yr.	Continuously absent from state or no reasonably ascertainable residence or work within the state while prosecution is pending: maximum extension 4 yrs.; prosecution pending in this state for same conduct
IDAHO	19-401 to 19-406	Murder, voluntary manslaughter, rape, sexual abuse of child or lewd conduct with child, acts of terrorism: none; failure to report neglect of a child: 4 yrs.; sexual exploitation by medical care provider: 2 yrs.; other felonies: 5 yrs.	1 yr.	Absent from state

Table 8: Criminal Statutes of Limitations—Continued

State	Code Section	Felonies	Misdemeanors	Acts During Which Statute Does Not Run
ILLINOIS	720 §§ 5/3-5 to 5/3-7	1st or 2nd degree murder, attempt to commit first degree murder, criminal solicitation to commit murder, involuntary manslaughter, reckless homicide, treason, arson, forgery, child pornography under 720 § 11/20.1(a) or 11/20.1B(a): none; theft over $100,000: 7 yrs. from last act committed; extended limitations when: victim of theft a minor or under legal disability, then during minority or legal disability or within 1 yr. of termination; misconduct in public office: within 1 yr. of discovery, max 3 yr. extension; incestual sexual conduct or penetration of a minor: 1 yr. after victim turns 18; child pornography, indecent solicitation or juvenile pimping of a child, sexual abuse of a minor: within 1 yr. of victim turning 18, min. 3 yrs. from time of offense; sexual conduct or penetration in professional of fiduciary relationship: 1 yr. after discovery by victim; hazardous waste violations: 5 yrs. after discovery; criminal sexual assault, aggravated criminal sexual abuse: 10 yrs. if reported within 3 yrs., if victim is minor: none; failure by required reporter under Abused and Neglected Child Reporting Act to report sexual assault or sexual abuse of minor: 20 yrs. after victim turns 18; any offense involving sexual conduct or penetration where DNA profile of offender entered in database within 10 yrs., victim reported within 3 yrs. (unless given longer under statute) or victim died within 2 yrs.: none	18 mos.; misdemeanor sexual abuse: 10 yrs. after victim turns 18	Nonresident prosecution pending; defendant is a public officer and the offense is theft of public funds; material witness is placed on active military duty

Table 8: Criminal Statutes of Limitations—Continued

State	Code Section	Felonies	Misdemeanors	Acts During Which Statute Does Not Run
INDIANA	35-41-4-2	Murder, class A or level 1 or 2 felony: none; forgery of instrument for payment: 5 yrs.; misuse of funeral trust or escrow account funds: 5 yrs. after death of purchaser; child molesting if offender is at least 16 and victim not more than 2 yrs. younger: 5 yrs.; child molesting, vicarious sexual gratification, child solicitation or seduction, incest: until victim turns 31; class B, C, D or level 3, 4, 5 felony: 5 yrs., 1 yr. extension if DNA evidence identifying offender is or should have been discovered; others: 5 yrs.	2 yrs.	Nonresident, absent from state, conceals self or evidence of crime; prosecution considered timely if defendant pleads guilty at any time; public official and offense is theft of public funds
IOWA	802.1 to 802.10	1st and 2nd degree murder: none; 1st, 2nd, 3rd degree sex abuse and victim under 18: within 10 yrs. after victim turns 18; other 1st, 2nd, 3rd degree sex abuse: 10 yrs. or within 3 yrs. after identity determined through DNA profile, whichever is later; incest with person under 18: within 10 yrs. after victim turns 18; sexual exploitation by counselor or therapist: 10 yrs., unless victim under 18 yrs., then 10 yrs. after victim turns 18; fraud or breach of fiduciary duty: extension up to 3 yrs.; others: 3 yrs.	Serious misdemeanor: 3 yrs.; simple misdemeanor or violation of ordinances: 1 yr.	Outside state or nonresident; public official is in office and offense arises from misconduct
KANSAS	21-5107	Murder, rape, aggravated criminal sodomy, terrorism, illegal use of weapons of mass destruction: none; if victim is Kansas public employees retirement system: 10 yrs.; sexually violent crimes: 10 yrs. or 1 yr. after identity established by DNA testing, whichever is later, if victim is minor: 10 yrs. after victim turns 18; arson: 5 yrs.; others: 2 yrs.	5 yrs.	Absent from state or concealed within state; concealed crime, prosecution pending
KENTUCKY	500.05	Felony: none	1 yr., if victim is under 18: 5 yrs. after victim turns 18	

Table 8: Criminal Statutes of Limitations—Continued

State	Code Section	Felonies	Misdemeanors	Acts During Which Statute Does Not Run
LOUISIANA	Crim. Proc. Art. 571 to 577	Crimes with punishment of death or life imprisonment, forcible rape: none; felony punishable by hard labor: 6 yrs.; felony not necessarily punishable by hard labor: 4 yrs.; aggravated sexual battery, human trafficking, carnal knowledge, indecent behavior or molestation of juvenile, child pornography, crime against nature, incest: 30 yrs. or within 3 yrs. after identity determined by DNA profile, whichever is later	Punishment of fine or forfeiture: 6 mos.; fine and/or prison: 2 yrs.	Avoiding detection, fleeing, outside state, absent residence in state; lacks mental capacity to proceed at trial
MAINE	Tit. 17-A, § 8	Murder, 1st or 2nd degree criminal homicide, incest, rape, or gross sexual assault if victim is under 16 yrs. of age: none; class A, B, C crime involving gross sexual assault: 6 yrs.; class A, B, C crime: 6 yrs.; class D, E crime: 3 yrs.; if breach of fiduciary obligation: 1 yr., max. extension 5 yrs.; official misconduct: 2 yrs., max. extension 5 yrs.		Absent from state or prosecution pending in state: maximum 5 yrs. extension
MARYLAND	Cts. & Jud. Proc. §§ 5-106; 5-107; 5-117	No general statute of limitations for felonies, may be limitation periods in statutes for individual offenses; murder: none; manslaughter or homicide by vehicle, welfare or Medicare fraud, tax-related offense, sex discrimination in paying wages, compensation in connection with adoption, unauthorized practice of medicine, charitable solicitation offense, illegal sale of firearms, computer crimes, offenses by nursing home administrators, offense relating to environmental protection: 3 yrs.; criminal offense under state election laws, conflict of interest laws, criminal misfeasance by officer of the state or conspiracy thereof, violation of fisheries provisions, abuse or neglect of vulnerable adult, violation of insurance article, sexual abuse of minor student by person of authority: 2 yrs.; assault, libel, or slander: 1 yr.; sexual abuse that occurred while victim was minor: within 7 yrs. of date victim turns 18	Misdemeanor punishable by imprisonment: none; other misdemeanors: 1 yr.; vehicle violations of unlawfully using a driver's license or fraudulently using false name when applying for driver's license: 2 yrs.; Sabbath breaking, drunkenness, or selling alcoholic beverages after hours or to a minor in Allegany County: 30 days	

Table 8: Criminal Statutes of Limitations—Continued

State	Code Section	Felonies	Misdemeanors	Acts During Which Statute Does Not Run
MASSACHUSETTS	Ch. 2, § 63	Murder: none; robbery, intent to rob or murder with dangerous weapon: 10 yrs.; rape, assault with intent to rape, rape/abuse/assault of child: 15 yrs.; others: 6 yrs.; indecent assault on child, on mentally retarded person, rape/abuse/assault of child, kidnapping of minor, sexual offenses such as drugging for sex, enticing for marriage, inducing minor into prostitution, lewd and lascivious behavior or acts, dissemination of harmful matter to minors, exhibiting nudity, or crime against nature: period commences when victim reaches 16 or violation is reported, whichever is earlier	6 yrs.	Offender not usually and publicly resident of state
MICHIGAN	767.24	Murder, conspiracy to commit murder, solicitation to commit murder, 1st degree criminal sexual conduct, violation of Michigan Anti-Terrorism Act: none; kidnapping, extortion, attempted murder, manslaughter, 1st degree home invasion, false pretenses involving real property forgery: 10 yrs.; if DNA evidence obtained: none until offender identified, then 10 yrs. after identification or when victim turns 21, whichever is later; other: 6 yrs.	6 yrs.	Not resident, did not usually and publicly reside
MINNESOTA	628.26	Murder: none; bribery, medical assistance fraud, theft: 6 yrs., value of stolen property/services over $35,000: 5 yrs.; familial sexual abuse, criminal sexual conduct: 9 yrs., if victim is minor: within 3 yrs. after victim turns 18, if DNA evidence collected and capable of testing: any time after offense is reported; arson, environmental offenses: 5 yrs.; all others: 3 yrs.	3 yrs.	Not inhabitant of or usually resident within state

Table 8: Criminal Statutes of Limitations—Continued

State	Code Section	Felonies	Misdemeanors	Acts During Which Statute Does Not Run
MISSISSIPPI	99-1-5 to 99-1-9	Murder, manslaughter, aggravated assault, aggravated domestic violence, kidnapping, arson, burglary, forgery, counterfeiting, robbery, larceny, rape, embezzlement, obtaining money or property under false pretenses or by fraud, felonious abuse or battery of child, touching or handling child for lustful purposes, sexual battery of child, exploitation of children, promoting prostitution when the person involved is minor, any human trafficking offense: none; larceny of timber; 6 years; conspiracy, felonious assistance-program fraud, felonious abuse of vulnerable persons: 5 years; all others: 2 yrs., 1 yr. extension if indictment is lost, destroyed, quashed, or abated, or judgment arrested or reversed	2 yrs.	Absent from state, fleeing, hiding
MISSOURI	556.036; 556.037	1st degree or forcible rape, 1st degree or forcible sodomy, attempted 1st degree or forcible rape or sodomy, murder or class A felony: none; 1st degree, class B or 2nd degree arson, knowingly burning or exploding: 5 yrs.; others: 3 yrs.; unlawful sexual offenses against a minor: 30 yrs. after victim turns 18 if fraud or breach of fiduciary duty is material element of offense: 1-3 yrs. after discovery; intentional fraudulent claim of child support: 1-3 yrs. after discovery; official misconduct: 2-3 yrs. after offense or public employment	1 yr.; infractions: 6 mos.	Absent from state: maximum 3 yr. extension; hiding from justice, prosecution pending for same conduct, lacks mental fitness

Table 8: Criminal Statutes of Limitations—Continued

State	Code Section	Felonies	Misdemeanors	Acts During Which Statute Does Not Run
MONTANA	45-1-205; 45-1-206	Deliberate, mitigated, or negligent homicide: none; sexual assault, sexual intercourse without consent, incest: 10 yrs. or within 20 yrs. after victim turns 18; indecent exposure, deviate sexual conduct, sexual or ritual abuse of child if victim is under 18: within 5 yrs. of victim turning 18, 1 yr. extension if DNA identifies suspect; theft involving breach of fiduciary obligation: within 1 yr. of discovery or if involving minor, within 1 yr. of termination of minority; unlawful use of computer: within 1 yr. of discovery of offense; reckless driving: 3 yrs.	Misdemeanor sexual assault, sexual intercourse without consent, indecent exposure, incest, sexual or ritual abuse of children: 1 yr. or within 5 yrs. after victim turns 18 if minor at time of offense; fish, wildlife, or outfitter activity laws: within 3 yrs. after offense committed; others: 1 yr.	When offender is not usually and publicly resident of state or beyond jurisdiction of state; prosecution pending for same conduct
NEBRASKA	29-110	Murder, treason, arson, forgery, 1st or 2nd deg. sexual assault, 1st, 2nd, or 3rd deg. sexual assault of child: none; kidnapping, false imprisonment, child abuse, pandering, debauching minor, child pornography when victim is under 16 at time of offense: later of 7 yrs. or within 7 yrs. after victim turns 16; knowing, intentional abuse, neglect, or exploitation of vulnerable or senior adult: 6 yrs.; violation of Nebraska Securities Act, criminal impersonation, identity theft, identity fraud, public assistance violation over $500: 5 yrs.; others: 3 yrs.	18 mos.; if fine less than $100 or jail time less than 3 mos.: 1 yr.	Fleeing justice
NEVADA	171.080 to 171.100	Murder, terrorism: none; sexual assault: 20 yrs., none if written report filed during period of limitation; theft, robbery, arson, burglary, forgery: 4 yrs.; sex trafficking: 4 yrs., none if written report filed within period of limitation; sexual abuse of child: by time victim reaches 36, or 43 if person "does not discover or reasonably should not have discovered" s/he was victim; felony against minor: 4 yrs. after discovery; others: 3 yrs.; kidnapping, attempted murder: 5 yr. extension after reporting	Gross misdemeanor: 2 yrs.; others: 1 yr.	Prosecution commences when indictment is presented

Table 8: Criminal Statutes of Limitations—Continued

State	Code Section	Felonies	Misdemeanors	Acts During Which Statute Does Not Run
NEW HAMPSHIRE	625:8	Murder, assist or conceal murder, falsify evidence: none; class A or B felony or unemployment compensation offense: 6 yrs.; offense of hunting game or fur-bearing animals or violation of off-highway recreational vehicles: 3 yrs.; theft, breach of fiduciary duty: 1 yr. after discovery; official misconduct: within 2 yrs. of offense; sexual assault and related offenses when victim is under 18: within 22 yrs. of victim's 18th birthday; motor vehicle accident resulting in death: 6 mos.	1 yr.; violations: 3 mos.	Absent from state, no residence or work in state; prosecution pending for same conduct
NEW JERSEY	2C:1-6	Murder, manslaughter, sexual assault, terrorism: none; official misconduct, bribery and related offenses: 7 yrs.; others: 5 yrs.; sexual assault, criminal sexual contact, and endangering welfare of children if victim is under 18: later of 5 yrs. after victim attains 18 or 2 yrs. after discovery	Petty offense or disorderly persons offense: 1 yr.	Fleeing justice; prosecution pending for same conduct; if DNA evidence available: time starts running when state is in possession
NEW MEXICO	30-1-8 to 30-1-9.2	Capital or 1st degree felony: none; 2nd degree: 6 yrs.; 3rd and 4th degree, identity theft, tax fraud or evasion: 5 yrs.; others: 3 yrs.; child abuse, criminal sexual penetration, or criminal sexual contact of minor: until victim reaches 18 or offense is reported, whichever occurs first	2 yrs.; petty: 1 yr.	Fleeing justice or not usually or publicly resident of state; enumerated procedural defects; when DNA evidence is available and suspect has not been identified for criminal sexual penetration, time starts running when DNA profile is matched with suspect
NEW YORK	Crim. Proc. § 30.10	Murder, class A felony, 1st. deg. rape, 1st. deg. aggravated sexual abuse, 1st deg. sexual conduct against child: none; terrorism: 8 yrs., none if creates foreseeable risk of death or serious injury; 2nd deg. sexual conduct against child: 5 yrs.; others: 5 yrs.; violation of collection, treatment, disposal of refuse and solid waste: 4 yrs.; larceny committed in violation of fiduciary duty: within 1 yr. of discovery of offense; official misconduct: 5 yrs.; sexual offense against minor: period of limitation begins when child turns 18 or offense is reported, whichever is earlier	2 yrs.; petty offenses: 1 yr.; tax law misdemeanor: 3 yrs. (N.Y.C. Admin. Code)	Absent from state or whereabouts unknown, extension up to 5 yrs.

Table 8: Criminal Statutes of Limitations—Continued

State	Code Section	Felonies	Misdemeanors	Acts During Which Statute Does Not Run
NORTH CAROLINA	15-1	None	Malicious misdemeanor: none; all others: 2 yrs.	
NORTH DAKOTA	29-04-01 to 29-04-04	Murder: none; gross sexual imposition by force, threat of death or serious injury, or kidnapping; human trafficking: 7 yrs.; sexual abuse of minor under 18: 10 yrs. or within 3 yrs. of reporting offense, 3 yr. extension if suspect is identified after time has expired by DNA or fingerprint obtained at time of offense; theft: later of within 3 yrs. of commission of last act, discovery of stolen property, or discovery of loss	Misdemeanor theft: later of within 2 yrs. of commission of last act, discovery of stolen property, or discovery of loss; all others: 2 yrs.	Absent from state
OHIO	2901.13	Murder or aggravated murder: none; rape, sexual battery, attempt or complicity to commit rape or sexual battery: 25 yrs.; manslaughter, kidnapping, unlawful sexual conduct with a minor, compelling prostitution, arson, robbery, burglary, aggravated riot, felonious or aggravated assault of a peace officer, felonious assault, or conspiracy or attempt to commit any of the above: 20 yrs.; physical wound or neglect of a child under 18 or of disabled child under 20: period of limitation begins when victim reaches 20 or agency or peace officer is notified	2 yrs.; minor misdemeanor: 6 mos.	Absent from state or conceals identity or whereabouts or undiscovered corpus delicti; prosecution pending for same conduct

Table 8: Criminal Statutes of Limitations—Continued

State	Code Section	Felonies	Misdemeanors	Acts During Which Statute Does Not Run
OKLAHOMA	Tit. 22, §§ 151 to 153	Murder: none, 1st deg. solicitation for murder, bribery, embezzlement of public money or other assets, falsification of public records, conspiracy to defraud the state or other subdivision, arson, use of deadly weapon to commit or attempt felony: 7 yrs. after discovery, if school district: 5 yrs.; violation of state income tax laws, identity theft: 5 yrs., rape or forcible sodomy, lewd or indecent proposals or acts against children, crimes involving minors in pornography, sodomy: 12 yrs., if victim is minor: by victim's 45th birthday; none if DNA establishes identity but must be started within 3 yrs. from date identity is established; criminal conspiracy, embezzlement, criminal state income tax violations, false or bogus check: 5 yrs.; criminal fraud or workers' compensation fraud: 3 to 7 yrs.; accessory after the fact: same limitation as that of felony to which person was accessory; all others: 3 yrs.	3 yrs.	Absent from state or not resident of state

Table 8: Criminal Statutes of Limitations—Continued

State	Code Section	Felonies	Misdemeanors	Acts During Which Statute Does Not Run
OREGON	131.125; 131.145; 131.155	Aggravated murder, murder or attempt, conspiracy or solicitation to commit, or any degree of manslaughter: none; 1st deg. rape, 1st deg. sodomy, 1st deg. unlawful sexual penetration, 1st deg. sexual abuse: 12 yrs., if victim under 18: until victim reaches 30; arson, felony strangulation, 1st deg. criminal mistreatment, 2nd or 3rd deg. rape, 2nd or 3rd deg. sodomy, 2nd deg. unlawful sexual penetration, 2nd deg. sexual abuse, using child in display of sexual conduct, 1st deg. encouraging child sexual abuse, incest, promoting prostitution, compelling prostitution, luring a minor: 6 yrs., if victim under 18, until victim reaches 30 or within 12 yrs. after offense reported, whichever occurs first; any of 1st deg. theft, 1st deg. aggravated theft, extortion, 1st, 2nd, or 3rd deg. robbery, 1st deg. forgery, fraudulent use of credit card, identity theft: 6 yrs. if victim 65 or older, all others: 3 yrs.	3rd deg. sexual abuse, providing or exhibiting obscene materials to minors, misdemeanor strangulation: 4 yrs., if victim under 18: earlier of 4 yrs. or when victim turns 22; all other misdemeanors: 2 yrs.; violations: 6 mos.	Absent from state; hiding within state; not resident of state; max. extension 3 yrs.
PENNSYLVANIA	Tit. 42, §§ 5551 to 5554	Murder, voluntary manslaughter, conspiracy or solicitation to commit murder and murder results, felony connected with 1st or 2nd deg. murder, vehicular homicide, aggravated assault of police officer: none; major offenses or conspiracy or solicitation to commit major offense: 5 yrs.; fraud or breach of fiduciary duty: 1 yr. after discovery, max. extension 3 yrs.; official misconduct: anytime during employment and up to 5 yrs. after, max. extension 8 yrs.; sexual offense committed against minor: any time up to later of period of limitation or date minor reaches 50, period of limitation starts when minor reaches age 18; major sexual offenses: 12 years; human trafficking of adult: 10 yrs.; labor servitude of minor: 10 yrs. after victim turns 18; all others: 2 yrs.; any sexual offense: 1 yr. extension after DNA establishes identity	2 yrs.; summary offenses: 30 days; misdemeanor sexual offense: 1 yr. extension after DNA establishes identity	Absent from state; no ascertainable residence or place of work within state; prosecution pending for same conduct; victim of abuse or neglect under 18

Table 8: Criminal Statutes of Limitations—Continued

State	Code Section	Felonies	Misdemeanors	Acts During Which Statute Does Not Run
RHODE ISLAND	12-12-17; 12-12-18	Treason against state, homicide, arson, burglary, counterfeiting, forgery, robbery, rape, sexual assault, child molestation, bigamy, manufacturing, selling, distributing or possession of controlled substance, or conspiracy to any of the above, crime punishable by life imprisonment: none; larceny, embezzlement, bribery, extortion, racketeering, antitrust violation, or conspiracy to any of the above: 10 yrs.; violations of refuse or hazardous waste disposal or water pollution: 7 yrs.; others: 3 yrs.	3 yrs.	Stolen, lost, destroyed information: extends limitation period 1 yr.
SOUTH CAROLINA	No statute of limitations for any criminal prosecution			
SOUTH DAKOTA	23A-42-1 to 23A-42-5	Murder, class A, B, or C felony: none; all other public offenses: 7 yrs.	7 yrs.	Absent from state
TENNESSEE	40-2-101 to 40-2-106	Any crime punishable by death or life imprisonment: none; class A felony: 15 yrs.; class B felony, arson: 8 yrs.; defrauding state, evading or defeating any tax, fraudulent return, willfully failing to pay tax or make return at time required by law : 6 yrs.; class C or D felony: 4 yrs.; class E felony: 2 yrs.; others: 3 yrs.; offense committed against a child: 4 yrs. after offense is committed, or when child reaches majority, whichever occurs later except aggravated rape, child pornography: 25 yrs. after 18th birthday; sex trafficking: 15 yrs. after 18th birthday; promoting prostitution: 10 yrs. after 18th birthday	Criminal impersonation through use of fraudulently obtained driver license: later of 3 yrs. or 1 yr. after expiration of license; gaming: 6 mos.; others: 12 mos.	Concealing fact of crime, absent from state

Table 8: Criminal Statutes of Limitations—Continued

State	Code Section	Felonies	Misdemeanors	Acts During Which Statute Does Not Run
TEXAS	Crim. Proc. Art. 12.01 to 12.07	Murder, manslaughter, certain sexual assaults, sexual assaults with DNA evidence, continuous sexual abuse of child, indecency with child, leaving scene of accident, compelling prostitution: none; thefts involving fiduciaries or officials forgery, sexual assault, 1st degree injury to elderly, arson, human trafficking: 10 yrs.; misapplication of fiduciary property, money laundering, Medicaid fraud, bigamy, credit card abuse, securing execution of document by deception under Tax § 162, false statement to obtain property or credit, fraudulent use or possession of identifying information, exploitation of child, elderly, or disabled individual: 7 yrs.; other theft, burglary, robbery, and certain sexual assaults, abandoning a child, insurance fraud, injury to elderly or disabled individual not punishable as 1st deg. felony: 5 yrs.; others: 3 yrs.; if victim is under 17: trafficking, injury to child, compelling prostitution: 10 yrs. after victim's 18th birthday; sexual performance by a child, aggravated kidnapping: 20 yrs. after victim's 18th birthday; criminal attempt, criminal conspiracy or organized activity, criminal solicitation: same limitation as felony solicited	2 yrs.	Absent from state, pendency of indictment, information complaint

Table 8: Criminal Statutes of Limitations—Continued

State	Code Section	Felonies	Misdemeanors	Acts During Which Statute Does Not Run
UTAH	76-1-301 to 76-1-306	Capital felony, aggravated murder, murder, manslaughter, child abuse homicide, aggravated kidnapping, child kidnapping, rape, rape of child, object rape, object rape of child, forcible sodomy, sodomy on child, sexual abuse of child, aggravated sexual abuse of child, aggravated sexual abuse, any predicate offense to murder or aggravating offense to aggravated murder, aggravated human trafficking or aggravated human smuggling, aggravated exploitation of prostitution involving child: none; forcible sexual abuse or incest: 8 yrs. if reported within 4 yrs. after commission; other felony or negligent homicide: 4 yrs.; fraud or breach of fiduciary obligation, official misconduct: 3 yrs. max. extension; violent felony: none if identity of perpetrator unknown but DNA evidence is collected and would identify the person at a later date, 1 yr. after identification made if statute has run; misuse of public monies, falsification or alteration of public records, bribery: 2 yrs. after facts reported to prosecutor	2 yrs.; infractions: 1 yr.	Absent from state
VERMONT	Tit. 13, §§ 4501 to 4511	Arson causing death, kidnapping, murder, aggravated sexual assault, human trafficking, aggravated sexual assault of child, sexual assault, aggravated human trafficking: none; manslaughter, lewd and lascivious conduct, sexual abuse of vulnerable adult, grand larceny, robbery, burglary, embezzlement, forgery, bribery offenses, false claims fraud, felony tax offenses: 6 yrs.; arson: 11 yrs.; lewd and lascivious conduct with child, sexual exploitation of minor, manslaughter against child under 18: 40 yrs.; all others: 3 yrs.	3 yrs.	Prosecution commences when arrest is made, citation issued, indictment or information presented

Table 8: Criminal Statutes of Limitations—Continued

State	Code Section	Felonies	Misdemeanors	Acts During Which Statute Does Not Run
VIRGINIA	19.2-8	Murder, manslaughter: none; cruelty to animals: 5 yrs. except for agricultural animals: 1 yr.; making false presentation under VA Unemployment Compensation Act to receive benefits, attempt to evade or failure to pay taxes, violation of laws re: discharge, dumping, or emission of toxic substance, violation of rules of VA Real Estate Board, illegal sales of wild birds, animals, or freshwater fish: 3 yrs.; malfeasance in office, Building Code violations: 2 yrs.; violation of Campaign Finance Disclosure Act: within 1 yr. of discovery, max. 3 yrs. after offense	Petit larceny: 5 yrs.; attempt to produce abortion: 2 yrs.; others: 1 yr.	Fleeing justice or concealing self to avoid arrest
WASHINGTON	9A.04.080	Murder, arson causing death, homicide by abuse, vehicular homicide, vehicular assault causing death, hit-and-run injury/accident causing death: none; public official misconduct, arson if no death, any felony committed by public officer: 10 yrs.; 1st and 2nd deg. rape: 3 yrs. or 10 yrs. if reported within 1 yr.; indecent liberties, attempted murder, trafficking: 3 yrs.; against minor: 1st or 2nd deg. rape, 1st or 2nd deg. rape of child, 2nd or 3rd deg. child molestation, indecent liberties, incest, sexual exploitation of minor: until 30th birthday; committing, promoting, or promoting travel for commercial sexual abuse of minor: later of 10 yrs. or 30th birthday if victim under 18; leading organized crime or criminal profiteering, theft, trafficking of stolen property: 6 yrs.; class C felony: 5 yrs.; bigamy and all other felonies: 3 yrs.; sexual offenses: 1 yr. extension after DNA identifies suspect	Gross misdemeanors: 2 yrs.; misdemeanor: 1 yr.	Not publicly a resident
WEST VIRGINIA	61-11-9	None	Petty larceny or perjury: 3 yrs.; others: 1 yr.	Stolen, lost, destroyed indictment

Table 8: Criminal Statutes of Limitations—Continued

State	Code Section	Felonies	Misdemeanors	Acts During Which Statute Does Not Run
WISCONSIN	939.74	1st or 2nd deg. intentional homicide, felony murder, 1st deg. reckless homicide, 1st deg. sexual assault, sexual assault of a child, engaging in repeated acts of sexual assault of the same child, attempt to commit 1st or 2nd deg. intentional homicide, sexual assault, and sexual assault of a child: none; intentional or recklessly causing of bodily harm, failing to prevent bodily harm, mental harm, enticement causing bodily or mental harm, or giving or selling a controlled substance to a child: before victim turns 26; sexual assault, physical abuse causing, sexual exploitation, incest, enticement of, or solicitation for prostitution of a child: before victim turns 45; if DNA evidence collected and can identify offender, within 1 yr. of identification if collected before time limitation expired; recklessly causing death of human being or unborn child: 15 yrs.; 2nd and 3rd deg. sexual assault: 10 yrs.; theft: 1 yr. after discovery, max. 5 yr. extension; others: 6 yrs.	Misdemeanors or adultery: 3 yrs.	Not publicly a resident; if victim is unable to seek issuance of a complaint, that time period excluded due to threats, etc.; prosecution pending for same act
WYOMING	No statute of limitations for any criminal prosecution			

9. DRUNK DRIVING

Penalties for drunk driving continue to become tougher over the years as the cost of this dangerous behavior rises. Reckless alcohol consumption among young people has also risen markedly, and it has been met with sharp intolerance. There are often lower legal limits for minor drivers and longer driver's license suspensions.

Drunk driving, driving while intoxicated (DWI), or driving under the influence (DUI), is typically determined by the alcohol content found in the driver's blood. Blood alcohol content (BAC) may be determined in two ways: through breath analysis or urinalysis. All states have now lowered the legal limit of blood alcohol content to 0.08 percent. Several states have also set a separate limit at 0.02 or 0.04 percent for commercial vehicle or public school bus drivers.

Penalties for drunk driving are severe in most states. Virtually every state suspends the driver's license on a first offense, and the length of suspension increases sharply with each successive offense. There is, however, a great deal of variation in the lengths of suspension of driving privileges among the states. A recent development is the introduction of Ignition Interlocking Device (IID) as an option for drivers convicted of driving while under the influence. All but twelve states now offer offenders a way to avoid virtually any penalties, at least for the first offense, by agreeing to the installation of IID in their car.

Another recent development is the addition of enhancements for driving while legally intoxicated with a minor on board. Several states have added enhancements if there is a "minor" in the car, while other states specify children under 14 or 16 years old.

Table 9: Drunk Driving

State	Code Section	BAC Legal Limit	Rehabilitation Required?
ALABAMA	32-5A-191; 32-5A-304	.08% BAC; under 21 or school bus or day care driver on duty: .02%	Yes; DUI court referral program approved by state; driver's license not reissued without proof of completion of program
ALASKA	28.35.030; 28.15.181	.08% BAC as determined by test taken within 4 hrs. of offense	Yes, must satisfy screening, evaluation, referral, and program requirements of agency authorized by state to provide rehabilitative treatment; while in prison or as a condition of parole a court may order the administration of drugs intended to prevent the consumption of alcoholic beverages
ARIZONA	28-1381 to 28-1390; 28-3319	.08% BAC within 2 hrs. of driving or being in actual physical control of vehicle; commercial vehicle drivers: .04% BAC	Yes; court ordered treatment programs must be completed and may reduce the penalties for license suspension, IID use, and time of incarceration.
ARKANSAS	5-65-103 to 5-65-123	.08% BAC as determined by test	Alcohol education program prescribed and approved by the Office of Alcohol and Drug Abuse Prevention
CALIFORNIA	Veh. §§ 13352; 13386; 23152 to 23217	.08% BAC at time of driving as determined by chemical test within 3 hrs. of driving, rebuttably presumed that percentage at time of driving was equal to or more than at time of test; commercial vehicle driver or passenger-for-hire driver: .04% BAC	Yes: must participate in a driving-under-the-influence program in driver's county of residence or employment

Driver's License Suspension/ Ignition Interlock Device	Other Penalties
90 day suspension or IID for 6 mos.; 90 days and 2 yr. IID if offender refuses to provide BAC or child under 14 was passenger or person other than driver was injured; 2nd offense within 5 yrs.: 1 yr. suspension or 2 yrs. IID after minimum 45 day suspension; 3rd offense: 3 yr. suspension or 3 yrs. IID after minimum 180 day suspension; 4th or subsequent offense: 5 yr. suspension or 5 yrs. IID after minimum 1 yr. suspension	Imprisonment up to 1 yr. and/or fine $600 to $2,100; 2nd offense within 5 yrs.: Imprisonment 5 days to 1 yr. or community service 30 days to 1 yr. and fine $1,100 to $5,100; 3rd offense: Imprisonment 60 days to 1 yr. and fine $2,100 to $10,100; 4th or subsequent offense: class C felony, imprisonment 1 yr. 1 day to 10 yrs. and fine $4,100 to $10,100; sentence for any offense doubled if offender over 21 and transporting minor under 14 at time of offense or BAC is .15% or higher.
Suspension at least 90 days and 6 mos. IID; 2nd offense: Suspension at least 1 yr. and 1 yr. IID; 3rd offense: Suspension at least 3 yrs. and 18 mos. IID; 4th offense: Suspension at last 5 yrs. and 24 mos. IID; 5th offense: suspension at least 5 yrs. and 30 mos. IID; 6th offense: suspension at least 5 yrs. and 36 mos. IID	Imprisonment at least 72 hrs. at community residential center or electronic monitoring at private residence and at least $1,500 fine, must perform 24 hrs. community service while imprisoned; 2nd offense: imprisonment at least 20 days at community residential center or electronic monitoring at private residence and at least $3,000 fine, must perform 160 hrs. community service while imprisoned; 3rd offense: imprisonment at least 60 days and at least $4,000 fine; 4th offense: imprisonment at least 120 days and minimum $5,000 fine; 5th offense: imprisonment at least 240 days and at least $6,000 fine; 6th & subsequent offenses: imprisonment at least 360 days and at least $7,000 fine;
Automatic 30 day suspension plus additional 60 days of restricted driving only to work/school, plus: 1st offense: IID for 12 mos., which may be deferred if offender successfully completes an alcohol education program for a minimum of 16 hrs. and other requirements met, IID for 18 mos. if BAC is .20 or more; 2nd offense within 84 months : 12 mos. suspension; IID for 12 to 24 mos. depending on BAC	Imprisonment at least 10 consecutive days and at least $1,250 fine; 2nd and subsequent offenses within 84 mos.: imprisonment at least 90 days and at least $3,000 fine
6 mos. suspension or IID unless waived by court; 2nd offense: 24 mos. suspension or IID; 3rd offense: 30 mos. suspension or IID; 4th and subsequent offenses: 4 yr. revocation, not eligible for IID	Imprisonment 1 day to 1 yr. and fine $150 to $1,000, court can order community service in lieu of jail; 2nd offense: imprisonment 7 days to 1 yr. or at least 30 days community service and fine $400 to $3,000; 3rd offense: imprisonment 90 days to 1 yr. or at least 90 days community service and fine $900 to $5,000; 4th offense: imprisonment 1 to 6 yrs. at least 1 yr. community service and fine $900 to $5,000; 5th or subsequent offense: imprisonment 2 to 10 yrs. or at least 2 yrs. community service and fine $900 to $5,000
6 mos. suspension, or if probation granted, could be 90 days with exception of traveling to work and rehab program; court may require IID; 2nd offense: 2 yrs., suspension, after 12 mos. a restricted license may be granted upon enrollment in an 18 or 30 month licensed program; 3rd offense: 3 yrs. suspension, after 24 mos. a restricted license may be granted upon completion of an 18 or 30 month authorized program; 4th offense: 4 yrs., after 24 mos. a restricted license may be granted upon completion of an 18 or 30 month authorized program; IID required on all restricted licenses after 1st offense	Imprisonment up to 6 mos. and fine $390 to $1,000; 2nd offense within 10 yrs.: imprisonment 90 days to 1 yr. and fine $390 to $1,000; 3rd offense within 10 yrs.: imprisonment 120 days to 1 yr. and $390 to $1,000 and designation as habitual traffic offender for 3 yrs.; 4th within 10 yrs.: imprisonment 180 days to 1 yr. and fine $390 to $1,000 and designation as habitual traffic offender for 3 yrs.; penalties increase if violations include bodily injury.

Table 9: Drunk Driving—Continued

State	Code Section	BAC Legal Limit	Rehabilitation Required?
COLORADO	42-2-129; 42-2-132; 42-4-1301; 42-4-1307	.08% BAC at the time of driving or within 2 hrs. after driving; under age 21: .02% BAC within 2 hrs. of driving; between .05% and .08% BAC, presumption is that driver was impaired; driving while ability impaired" or "DWAI" means driving a motor vehicle or vehicle when a person has consumed alcohol or one or more drugs, or a combination of both alcohol and one or more drugs, that affects the person to the slightest degree so that the person is less able than the person ordinarily would have been, either mentally or physically, or both mentally and physically, to exercise clear judgment, sufficient physical control, or due care in the safe operation of a vehicle.	Yes, alcohol and drug driving safety programs in each judicial district provide presentence alcohol and drug evaluations and recommend treatment
CONNECTICUT	14-227a to 14-227l	.08% BAC at time of offense; commercial vehicle driver: .04%; under age 21: .02%	Court may order participation in alcohol education and treatment program in addition to any fine or sentence
DELAWARE	Tit. 21, §§ 4177 to 4177M	.08% BAC as shown by test taken within 4 hrs. of offense; evidence of .05-.08% BAC raises no presumption of intoxication but may be used as factor in intoxication determination; under age 21: .02% BAC within 4 hrs. of driving	Yes – minimum 3 mo. program required; many treatment programs available which may determine the length of sentence, including the required duration of IID use; program may require period of sobriety which may be measured by periodic tests and/or transdermal continuous alcohol monitoring device

Driver's License Suspension/ Ignition Interlock Device	Other Penalties
1st and 2nd offenses: 1 year; 3rd or subsequent: license will be revoked indefinitely; may be reinstated after 2 yrs. if offender completes drug and alcohol program and completes motor vehicle testing; in all cases, offender will be required to use an IID for a minimum of 1 yr. as a condition of bond or probation at offender's own expense.	Imprisonment 5 days to 1 yr., 10 days to 1 yr. if BAC is .20 or higher, fine $600 to $1,000 and 48-96 hrs. useful public service; 2nd offense: imprisonment 10 days to 1 yr., fine $600 to $1,500, 48-120 hrs. useful public service, and 2 yrs. probation; 3rd offense: imprisonment 60 days to 1 yr., fine $600 to $1,500, 48-120 hrs. of useful public service and 2 yrs. probation; felony offense: imprisonment 90 days to 2 yrs., 48-120 hrs. useful public service, and 2 yrs. probation
Suspension 45 days and 1 yr. IID; 2nd offense within 10 yrs.: suspension 45 days and 3 yrs. IID; if offender under 21, driving restricted to work, school, or treatment for 1 yr. after suspension; 3rd and subsequent offense within 10 yrs.: licensed revoked permanently; after 2 yrs., offender may request hearing for reversal or reduction of revocation and must show good cause; if revocation reversed or reduced, offender must have IID for life but may request hearing to remove IID after 15 yrs.	Imprisonment up to 6 mos. with minimum 48 hours consecutive, or probation including 100 hrs. community service, and fine $500 to $1,000; 2nd offense within 10 yrs.: imprisonment up to 2 yrs. with minimum 120 days consecutive, probation including 100 hrs. community service and fine $1,000 to $4,000; 3rd and subsequent offense within 10 yrs.: imprisonment up to 3 yrs. with minimum of 1 yr. consecutive, probation including 100 hrs. community service, and fine $2,000 to $8,000
BAC .08-.15%: 12 month revocation; .15 -.19%: 18 month revocation; .20% or greater or chemical test was refused: 24 month revocation; 2nd offense: BAC .08-.15%: 18 mo. revocation; .15-.19%: 24 mo. revocation; .20% or greater or chemical test was refused: 30 mo. revocation; 3rd offense: BAC .08-.15%: 24 mo. revocation; .15-.19%: 30 mo. revocation; .20% or greater or chemical test was refused: 36 mo. revocation; 4th or subsequent offense: 60 mo. revocation regardless of BAC; IID: 1st offense: may apply for IID restricted permit 1-3 mos. after revocation; time of application and duration of IID use will be determined based on treatment program elected; 2nd and subsequent offenses or offender who refused a chemical test: may apply for IID restricted permit after 12 mos.; duration of IID use will be determined based on treatment program elected.	Imprisonment up to 12 mos. and/or fine $500 to $1,500; 2nd offense within 10 yrs.: imprisonment 60 days to 18 mos. and fine $750 to $2,500; 3rd offense: class G felony, punishable by 1 to 2 yrs. imprisonment and fine up to $5,000; 4th offense: class E felony, punishable by 2 to 5 yrs. imprisonment and fine up to $7,000; 5th offense: class E felony, punishable by imprisonment 3 to 5 yrs. and fine up to $10,000; 6th offense: class E felony, punishable by imprisonment 4 to 8 yrs. and fine up to $10,000; 7th and subsequent offense: class C felony, punishable by imprisonment 5 to 15 yrs. and fine up to $15,000; additional penalties when offense is committed with passenger under 17

Table 9: Drunk Driving—Continued

State	Code Section	BAC Legal Limit	Rehabilitation Required?
DISTRICT OF COLUMBIA	50-1403.01; 50-2201.05a; 50-2206.11 to 50-2206.18	.08% BAC; .10% alcohol in urine (less than .03% BAC or .04% in urine is evidence of intoxication but no presumption of intoxication; greater than .05% BAC or .06% in urine constitutes prima facie case of intoxication); under age 21: no measurable amount of alcohol for blood, breath, or urine	Yes, can request person enter diversion program
FLORIDA	316.193, 322.28	.08% BAC; .08% in breath	Yes, required attendance at licensed substance abuse course, including psychological evaluation
GEORGIA	40-5-62; 40-5-63; 40-5-67; 40-6-391	.08% BAC within 3 hrs. of driving or being in actual physical control; commercial motor vehicle driver: .04% BAC; under age 21: .02% BAC within 3 hrs. of driving	Yes – treatment is required in addition to other penalties for every offense; license reinstated upon completion of clinical evaluation and DUI Alcohol or Drug Use Risk Reduction Program approved by Department of Human Resources and pays fee of $210 or $200.
HAWAII	291E-3; 291E-61; 291E-61.5; 291E-64	.08% BAC or breath within 3 hrs. after the time of the alleged violation; no presumption for .05-.08% BAC, but may be used in intoxication determination; under age 21: any measurable amount of alcohol	14 hrs. minimum alcohol abuse rehab program including education and counseling or comparable program approved by court; subsequent offense: may be required pending evaluation by substance abuse counselor
IDAHO	18-8001 to 18-8011	.08% BAC; under age 21: .02-.08% BAC; .20% BAC is considered excessive; commercial truck driver: .04% BAC	Alcoholic evaluation at own expense at approved facility; if necessary, an appropriate alcoholic treatment must be completed in addition to the rest of the sentence

Driver's License Suspension/ Ignition Interlock Device	Other Penalties
IID for 6 mos.; 2nd offense: IID for 1 yr.; 3rd offense: IID for 2 yrs.; if 3 or more offenses in 5 yrs., revocation without ability to be reinstated	Imprisonment up to 180 days, 10 day mandatory minimum if BAC .20-.25%, 15 day mandatory minimum if .25-.30%, 20 day mandatory minimum if .30% or higher, and $1,000 fine; 2nd offense: imprisonment 10 days to 1 yr., 15 day mandatory minimum if .20-.25%, 20 day mandatory minimum if .25-.30%, 25 day mandatory minimum if .30% or higher, and fine $2,500 to $5,000; 3rd offense: 15 days to 1 yr., 20 mandatory minimum if .20-.25%, 25 day mandatory minimum if .25-.30%, 30 day mandatory minimum if .30% or higher, and fine $2,500 to $10,000; 4th and subsequent offense: additional 30-day mandatory minimum term of incarceration shall be imposed for each additional violation; commercial drivers subject to additional 5 day mandatory minimum term of incarceration; if minor in vehicle, imprisonment minimum 5 days per minor, 10 days per minor if minors not restrained with age-appropriate child passenger safety retrains, and fine $500 to $1,000 per minor
Revocation 180 days to 1 yr. followed by 6 mos. mandatory IID; 2nd offense within 5 yrs.: revocation 5 yrs. followed by 1 yr. mandatory IID; 3rd offense within 10 yrs.: revocation 10 yrs. followed by 2 yrs. mandatory IID	Imprisonment up to 6 mos. and fine $500 to $1,000; up to 9 mos. and $1,000 to $2,000 if BAC .15% or higher or accompanied by minor; 2nd offense: imprisonment up to 9 mos. and fine $1,000 to $2,000; up to 12 mos. and fine $2,000 to $4,000 if .15% or higher or accompanied by minor; 3rd offense within 10 yrs.: 3rd degree felony, punishable by imprisonment up to 5 yrs. and $5,000 fine; 3rd offense after 10 yrs.: imprisonment up to 12 mos. and fine $2,000 to $5,000; 4th and subsequent offense: 3rd degree felony, punishable by imprisonment up to 5 yrs. and $2,000 fine
1 yr. revocation, may apply for reinstatement after 120 days if completed DUI Alcohol or Drug Use Risk Reduction Program and pays restoration fee; 2nd offense within 5 yrs.: 3 yr. revocation; 3rd offense within 5 yrs.: 5 yr. revocation and considered habitual violator	Imprisonment 10 days to 12 mos., probation 12 mos. less any time served, minimum 40 hrs. community service, fine $300 to $1,000; 2nd offense within 5 yrs.: imprisonment 90 days to 12 mos., probation 12 mos. less any time served, minimum 30 days community service, fine $600 to $1,000; 3rd offense within 10 yrs.: imprisonment mandatory 15 days to 120 mos., probation 12 mos. less any time served, minimum 30 days community service, fine $1,000 to $5,000; 4th or subsequent offense within 10 yrs.: imprisonment 1 to 5 yrs., probation 5 yrs. less any time served, 60 days community service, fine $1,000 to $5,000; guilty of separate crime of child endangerment if minor present in vehicle
1st offense or more than 5 yrs. since previous conviction: Revocation 1 yr. and IID during revocation on any vehicle operated by person; subsequent offense within 5 yrs.: revocation 18 mos. to 2 yrs.; IID during revocation on any vehicle operated by person	Imprisonment 48 hrs. to 5 days and/or 72 hrs. community service and/or fine $150 to $1,000; 2nd offense within 5 yrs.: imprisonment 5 to 14 days, 48 hrs. consecutively, or 240 hrs. community service and fine $500 to $1,500; 3rd offense within 5 yrs.: imprisonment 10 to 30 days, 48 hrs. consecutively, and fine $500 to $2,500; 3rd and subsequent offense within 10 yrs.: habitual offender, class C felony, punishable by imprisonment or probation 5 yrs., mandatory 10 days imprisonment, at least 48 hrs. served consecutively
30 days mandatory suspension, 60-150 days restricted privileges; 2nd offense within 10 yrs.: 1 yr. mandatory suspension after release from confinement followed by at least 1 yr. IID; 3rd offense within 10 yrs.: suspension mandatory 1 yr. to 5 yrs. followed by at least 1 yr. IID 10	Imprisonment up to 6 mos. and/or fine up to $1,000; 2nd offense within 10 yrs.: imprisonment 10 days to 1 yr., 1st 48 hrs. consecutively, and fine up to $2,000; 3rd offense within 10 yrs.: felony, punishable by imprisonment mandatory 30 days up to 5 yrs. and fine up to $5,000; separate penalties for minors under 21 with BAC less than .08% and excessive BAC, over .20%

Table 9: Drunk Driving—Continued

State	Code Section	BAC Legal Limit	Rehabilitation Required?
ILLINOIS	625 §§ 5/11-501 to 5/11-507	.08% BAC; less than .05% at test: presumed not to be under the influence of alcohol; .05%-.08% at test: no presumption of guilt but take it with other evidence; .08% at test: guilty; under age 21: 0.00% BAC	Professional evaluation to determine if there is abuse problem and extent; defendant pays cost; program must be approved/licensed by Dept. of Alcohol and Substance Abuse
INDIANA	9-30-5-1 to 9-30-5-18; 9-30-10-4	.08 to .15% BAC: class C misdemeanor; BAC .15% or more: class A misdemeanor; under age 21: BAC .02-.08%: class C infraction	If second or subsequent offense, must receive assessment of degree of alcohol abuse and if appropriate order to successfully complete an alcohol treatment or deterrent program.
IOWA	321J.2 to 321J.25	.08% BAC; under age 21: .02% BAC within 2 hrs. after driving or in physical control of motor vehicle presumed to be alcohol concentration at time of driving	May be ordered to attend a course for drinking drivers; BAC over .20% or 2nd offense: must undergo substance abuse evaluation prior to sentencing; 3rd offense or if evaluation recommends treatment: may be assigned to facility by director of corrections dept. Note that any portion of sentence for 2nd, 3rd, or subsequent offense may be served as inpatient treatment for alcoholism or drug addiction or dependency

Driver's License Suspension/ Ignition Interlock Device	Other Penalties
Driving privileges revoked for indefinite period; IID required on all vehicles owned by person who has been convicted of a second or subsequent offense	Class A misdemeanor, if transporting someone under 16, imprisonment 6 mos., 25 days community service, fine at least $1,000; if BAC .16% or more, mandatory minimum 100 hrs. community service and $500 fine; 2nd offense: mandatory min. of either 5 days imprisonment or 240 hrs. community service in addition to any other criminal or administrative sanction; BAC .16% or more, additional mandatory minimum 2 days imprisonment and mandatory minimum fine $1,250; aggravated driving under influence of alcohol: class 4 felony; 3rd offense: class 2 felony; BAC .16% or over, mandatory minimum 90 days imprisonment and mandatory minimum fine $2,500 in addition to any other criminal or administrative sanction; if transporting someone under 16: mandatory $25,000 fine and 25 days community service in program benefiting children in additional to any other criminal or administrative sanction; 4th offense: class 2 felony, no probation or conditional discharge; BAC .16% or more, mandatory minimum $5,000 fine; if transporting someone under 16, additional mandatory $25,000 fine and 25 days of community service in program benefiting children; 5th offense: class 1 felony no probation or conditional discharge; BAC .16% or more, mandatory minimum $5,000 fine; if transporting someone under 16, additional mandatory $25,000 fine and 25 days of community service in program benefiting children; 6th or subsequent offense: class X felony no probation or conditional discharge; BAC .16% or more, mandatory minimum $5,000 fine; if transporting someone under 16, additional mandatory $25,000 fine and 25 days of community service in program benefiting children
If no previous conviction in last ten years may suspend for not more than 2 years; if previous conviction more than five years but less than ten years before; may suspend for not more than two years, court may stay the execution of part of the suspension and grant the person specialized driving privileges for a period of time equal to the length of the stay; if previous conviction less than five years, may suspend for not more than two years, court may stay the execution of part of the suspension and grant the person specialized driving privileges for a period of time equal to the length of the stay, possibly with IID; any probationary periods include equipping motor vehicle with IID	Class C misdemeanor; 2nd offense within five years: level 6 felony, punishable by 5 days imprisonment or 180 hours of community restitution or service; 3rd offense within 5 yrs.: imprisonment at least 10 days or at least 360 hrs. community restitution or service; transported at least 1 person less than 18 yrs. of age: level 6 felony
Minimum 180 days to 1 yr.; 2nd offense: 1 yr.; 3rd or subsequent offense: 6 yrs.	Imprisonment 48 hrs. to 1 yr. and fine $1,250; 2nd offense: imprisonment 7 days to 2 yrs. and fine $1,875 to $6,250; 3rd offense: imprisonment 30 days to 5 yrs. and fine of $3,125 max of $9,375

Table 9: Drunk Driving—Continued

State	Code Section	BAC Legal Limit	Rehabilitation Required?
KANSAS	8-1001 to 8-1025; 8-1567 to 8-1567a	.08% BAC within 2 hrs. of operating vehicle; if BAC is less than .08%, this may be considered with other evidence of intoxication; under age 21: .02% BAC	Must enroll in alcohol and drug safety action education or treatment program; 2nd offense: must complete a treatment program for alcohol and drug abuse; 3rd offense: must complete treatment program for alcohol and drug abuse
KENTUCKY	189A.010 to 189A.345	.08% BAC within 2 hrs. of driving; .05-.08% not considered a presumption of intoxication but considered with other evidence of intoxication; under age 21: .02% BAC within 2 hrs. of driving	Must attend alcohol or substance abuse education or treatment program: 1st offense: 90 days; 2nd offense: 1 yr.; 3rd or subsequent offense: 1 yr., may be inpatient program
LOUISIANA	14:98 to 14:98.7; 32:414	.08% BAC	Court approved substance abuse program and court approved driver improvement program is a min. condition for all probation, parole, or suspension of sentence
MAINE	Tit. 29A, § 2411	.08% BAC	Yes, for 2nd and subsequent offense, defendant may be required to participate in a Weekend Intervention Program or residential treatment program administered by the Office of Substance Abuse
MARYLAND	Transp. 16-205; 16-212; 21-902 to 212-902.4	.08% BAC	Driver Improvement Program and Alcohol Education Program required

Driver's License Suspension/ Ignition Interlock Device	Other Penalties
Suspension 30 days, 1 yr. and 1 yr. IID; 2nd offense: suspension 1 yr. and 1 yr. IID; 3rd offense: suspension 1 yr. and 2 yrs. IID; 4th offense: suspension 1 yr. and 3 yrs. IID; 5th or subsequent offense: suspension 1 yr. and 10 yrs. IID; all revocations are reinstated at the above time periods only upon completion of alcohol and drug safety program; BAC .15% or higher: 1st offense: suspension 1 yr. and 1 yr. IID; 2nd offense: suspension 1 yr. and 2 yrs. IID; 3rd offense: suspension 1 yr. and 3 yrs. IID; 4th offense: suspension 1 yr. and 4 yrs. IID; 5th or subsequent offense: suspension 1 yr. and 10 yrs. IID; refusal to take test: 1st offense: suspension 1 yr. and 2 yrs. IID; 2nd offense: suspension 1 yr. and 3 yrs. IID; 3rd offense: suspension 1 yr. and 4 yrs. IID; 4th offense: suspension 1 yr. and 5 yrs. IID; 5th or subsequent offense: suspension 1 yr. and 10 yrs. IID	Class B, nonperson misdemeanor, punishable by imprisonment 48 hrs. to 6 mos. and fine $750 to $1,000; 2nd offense: class A, nonperson misdemeanor, punishable by imprisonment 90 days to 1 yr. and fine $1,250 to $1,750; 3rd offense: class A nonperson misdemeanor, nonperson felony if within past 10 yrs., punishable by imprisonment 90 days to 1 yr. and fine $1,750 to $2,500; 4th or subsequent offense: nonperson felony, punishable by imprisonment 90 days to 1 yr. and fine $2,500; if transporting child under 14, punishment enhanced by 1 mo. imprisonment which must be served consecutively and shall not exceed maximum sentence allowable by law
30 to 120 days; 2nd offense within 10 yrs.: 12-18 mos.; 3rd offense within 10 yrs.: 24-36 mos.; 4th offense within 10 yrs.: 60 mos., if person is under 18 yrs. of age, license revoked until he or she reaches 18 or the above relevant penalty, whichever is the longer revocation; not eligible for reinstatement until completion of alcohol or substance abuse education or treatment program; may petition to reduce applicable minimum period of revocation by half, but not less 12 mos., if using IID	Imprisonment 48 hrs. to 30 days jail and/or 2 to 30 days community labor and fine $200 to $500; 2nd offense within 10 yrs.: imprisonment 7 days to 6 mos., possible 10 days to 6 mos. community labor in addition to jail term, and fine $350 to $500; 3rd offense within 10 yrs.: imprisonment 30 days to 12 mos. and possible 10 days to 1 yr. community labor in addition to jail term and fine $500 to $1,000; 4th and subsequent offense within 10 yrs.: class D felony. Note: all prior convictions include other states
90 days; can be restricted if necessary, $100 reinstatement fee; 2nd offense: 1 yr., $200 reinstatement fee; 3rd or subsequent offense: 2 yrs., $300 reinstatement fee; may be ordered to install IID as condition of probation	Imprisonment 10 days to 6 mos., possible suspension by attending program with minimal jail time or community service and fine $300 to $1,000; 2nd offense: imprisonment 30 days to 6 mos., possible suspension by attending program with minimal jail time or community service and fine $750 to $1,000; 3rd offense: imprisonment 1 to 5 yrs. and $2,000 fine; 4th offense: imprisonment 10 to 30 yrs. at hard labor and $5,000 fine; prior convictions include other states
150 days; 2nd offense: 3 yrs.; 3rd offense: 6 yrs.; 4th offense: 8 yrs.	Fine not less than $500; $600 if person failed to submit to test; imprisonment if aggravated violation; 2nd offense: imprisonment not less than 7 days and fine not less than $700; $900 if failed to submit to test; 3rd offense: imprisonment not less than 30 days and fine not less than $1,100; $1,400 if failed to submit to test; 4th offense: imprisonment not less than 6 mos. and fine not less than $2,100; $2,500 if failed to submit to test
Up to 60 days; 2nd offense: 120 days; up to 1 yr. if prior conviction within 5 yrs.; may order use of IID for 3 yrs. as condition of probation	"Under the influence": 1st offense: imprisonment up to 1 yr. and fine up to $500; "while intoxicated": 1 offense: imprisonment up to 1 yr. and/or fine up to $1,000; 2nd offense: imprisonment up to 2 yrs. and/or fine up to $2,000; 3rd and subsequent offense: imprisonment at least 3 yrs. and/or fine at least $3,000; offenses including bodily injury or death or fleeing/evading police involve stiffer penalties

Table 9: Drunk Driving—Continued

State	Code Section	BAC Legal Limit	Rehabilitation Required?
MASSACHUSETTS	Ch. 90, §§ 24 to 24 1/2	.08% BAC; <.05%, presumption is not under the influence; .05-.08% BAC, no presumption; under age 21: .02%	Appropriate to defendant with his/her consent as a condition of probation upon written finding that appropriate and adequate treatment is available to defendant and defendant would benefit and safety of public would not be endangered; minimum 14 days in residential alcohol treatment program at defendant's cost
MICHIGAN	257.625 to 257.625o	.08% BAC, .10% eff. 10/1/2021; under age 21: .02%	Screening and assessment to determine the likely benefit from rehabilitation; court may order person to participate and successfully complete one or more alcohol or drug education or treatment programs
MINNESOTA	169A.01 to 169A.78; 171.306	.08% BAC within 2 hrs. of driving; commercial motor vehicle driver: .04% BAC within 2 hrs. of driving; under age 21: any amount	Must submit to level of care recommended in mandatory chemical use assessment, at driver's expense
MISSISSIPPI	63-11-23; 63-11-30; 63-11-31	.08% BAC; under age 21 .02% or more; commercial motor vehicle driver: .04% BAC	Required alcohol safety education program
MISSOURI	302.525; 302.505; 478.007; 577.010, 577.012	.08% BAC; under age 21: .02% BAC or more	Yes, court shall order participation and successful completion of alcohol or drug-related traffic offender education or rehab program which meets standards established by Dept. of Public Safety and Dept. of Mental Health and professional assessment
MONTANA	61-5- 205; 61-5-208; 61-8-406; 61-8-410; 61-8-722	.08% BAC; under age 21: .02% BAC or more; commercial motor vehicle driver: .04% BAC	Defendant shall complete alcohol information course at alcohol treatment program approved by Dept. of Corrections & Human Services which may include alcohol or drug treatment or both if considered necessary by counselor conducting program

Driver's License Suspension/ Ignition Interlock Device	Other Penalties
1 yr.; 2nd offense: 2 yrs.; 3rd offense: 8 yrs.; 4th offense: 10 yrs.; can apply for new license on grounds of hardship and registrar's discretion: 1st offense: within 3 mos.; 2nd offense: within 6 mos.; 3rd offense: within 2 yrs.; 4th offense: within 5 yrs.; 5th offense: revoked for life; for all offenses, IID for 2 yrs. required before license reinstated	Imprisonment up to 2½ yrs. and or fine $500 to $5,000, jail time may be ordered by court to be served only on weekends, evenings, and holidays; 2nd offense within 10 yrs.: imprisonment 60 days to 2½ yrs. and fine $600 to $10,000; 3rd offense within 10 yrs.: imprisonment 180 days to 2½ yrs. and fine $1,000 to $15,000, or same fine and 2½ to 5 years in state prison; 4th offense within 10 yrs.: imprisonment 2-2½ yrs. and fine $1,500 to $25,000, or same fine and 2-2½ yrs. in state prison; 5th or subsequent offense: imprisonment 2½ yrs. and fine $2,000 to $50,000, or same fine and 2½-5 yrs. in state prison
6 mos.; 2nd or subsequent offense within 7 yrs.: 1 yr., injuries or death-causing accidents heighten restrictions; court may order IID as condition of probation	Imprisonment up to 93 days and/or fine $100 to $500 and costs of prosecution and up to 360 hours community service; 2nd offense within 7 yrs.: imprisonment 5 days to 1 yr. and 30 to 90 days community service, fine $200 to $1,000; 3rd offense: felony, punishable by imprisonment 1 to 5 yrs. or probation with imprisonment in county jail 30 days to 1 yr. and 60 to 180 days community service; injuries or death-causing accident heightens penalties of all offenses
30 days; 2nd offense within 10 yrs.: at least 1 yr.; 3rd offense within 10 yrs.: at least 3 yrs.; 4th and subsequent offenses: at least 4 yrs.; 5th and subsequent offenses: at least 6 yrs.; license may be reinstated under IID program	Misdemeanor; 2nd offense within 10 yrs.: gross misdemeanor, punishable by at least 30 days jail or 8 hrs. community service for each jail day served less than 30; 3rd offense within 10 yrs.: gross misdemeanor, punishable by at least 90 days jail or intensive supervision; 4th offense: 180 days jail or intensive supervision or up to 150 days home detention; 5th or subsequent offense: 1 yr. jail or intensive supervision; judge can instead require person as condition of probation to drive with IID
120 days; 2nd offense: 1 yr.; 3rd offense: full period of sentence, then IID for 3 yrs.; 4th or subsequent offense: full period of sentence, then IID for 10 yrs.; under age 21: 1st: 120 days; 2nd: 1 yr.; 3rd offense in 5 yrs.: 2 yrs. or until reach age 21	Imprisonment up to 48 yrs. and/or fine $250 to $1,000; 2nd offense within 5 yrs.: imprisonment 5 days to 1 yr. and fine $600 to $1,500 and 10 days to 1 yr. community service; 3rd offense within 5 yrs.: felony; imprisonment 1-5 yrs. and fine $2,000 to $5,000; 4th or subsequent offense: felony, punishable by imprisonment 2-10 yrs. and fine $3,000 to $10,000; under age 21: 1st offense: $250 fine; 2nd offense within 5 yrs.: fine up to $500; 3rd or subsequent offense within 5 yrs.: fine up to $1,000
30 days followed by 60 days restricted license, may include use of IID; 2nd or subsequent offense: 1 yr. with IID for at least 6 mos. following reinstatement	Class B misdemeanor; 2nd offense within 10 yrs.: Prior offender, class A misdemeanor; 3rd offense within 10 yrs.: persistent offender, class D felony, punishable by minimum 48 consecutive hrs. in jail or 10 days community service before sentence or parole; after 10 yrs. with no other alcohol-related offenses on record, can apply for expungement
6 mos.; subsequent offense: 1 yr.; completion of alcohol information course or treatment must be completed before revocation ends	Imprisonment up to 10 days and fine $300 to $1,000; 2nd offense: imprisonment 5 to 30 days and fine $600 to $1,000; 3rd offense: imprisonment 10 days to 6 mos. and fine $1,000 to $5,000, except for initial 5 to 10 days in jail, rest of jail time can be home address

Table 9: Drunk Driving—Continued

State	Code Section	BAC Legal Limit	Rehabilitation Required?
NEBRASKA	28-105; 28-106; 60-6,196 to 60-6,211.11;	.08% BAC; under age 21: .02% BAC	Presentence evaluation in alcohol assessment, paid for by person convicted; judge may order program based on results of assessment
NEVADA	484C.110 to 484C.640	.08% BAC within 2 hrs. after driving or being in actual physical control of vehicle	Must pay for and complete educational course on alcohol and substance abuse; 2nd offense within 7 yrs.: court may order to undergo program of treatment for alcoholism or drug abuse; for 1st and 2nd violation: person may apply to undergo 1 yr. program for alcoholism and drug abuse if he or she is classified by counselor or physician as drug abuser or alcoholic; may also apply for program of treatment as conditional suspension of sentence
NEW HAMPSHIRE	265-A:2 to 265-A:42	.08% BAC; under age 21: .02% or more	Yes, Impaired Driver Intervention Program; must successfully complete to get license back; must be approved by the commissioner of the Department of Health and Human Services and the commissioner of Safety
NEW JERSEY	39:4-50; 39:4-50.14; 39:4-50.17	.08% BAC; under age 21: .01% or more	Screening, evaluation, referral program, and fee requirements of Div. of Alcoholism's Intoxicated Driving Programs Unit and 12-48 hrs. in 2 consecutive days in Intoxicated Driver Resource Center and a program of alcohol education and highway safety as proscribed by director of Div. of Motor Vehicles
NEW MEXICO	66-5-29; 66-5-501 to 66-5-504; 66-8-102; 66-8-112	.08% BAC within 3 hrs. of driving; under age 21: .02% BAC; commercial motor vehicle driver: .04% within 3 hrs. of driving	May be required by court to enroll in screening program to determine level of abuse and recommendation of treatment, if necessary; must complete any recommended treatment program required by court; 1st offense: must attend driver rehab program for alcohol or drugs, a "DWI school," and any other rehab programs the court finds necessary; upon 2nd or 3rd conviction, person required to complete not less than 28 day inpatient, residential, or in-custody substance abuse treatment program; not less than 90 day outpatient treatment program; or any other substance abuse treatment program, all of which must be approved by the court

Driver's License Suspension/ Ignition Interlock Device	Other Penalties
6 mos., if judge orders suspension of sentence or probation, 60 days from time of order, alternative to immobilization is use of IID; 2nd offense within 12 yrs.: suspension for 45 days and 1 yr. IID; 3rd or subsequent offense within 12 yrs.: 15 yrs., if probation or suspended sentence, license must be revoked for at least 2 yrs., then may have IID	Imprisonment 7 to 60 days and $500 fine; 2nd offense within 12 yrs.: imprisonment 30 days to 6 mos. and $500 fine; 3rd offense within 12 yrs.: imprisonment 90 days to 1 yr. and $1,000 fine; 4th and subsequent offense: imprisonment up to 5 yrs. and/or up to $10,000 fine
Revoked if BAC is greater than .08%; may apply for restricted license if person meets certain conditions and pays for IID	Imprisonment 2 days to 6 mos. or 48 to 96 hrs. community service and fine $400 to $1,000; 2nd offense within 7 yrs.: imprisonment 10 days to 6 mos., 100 to 200 hrs. community service and fine $750 to $1,000; 3rd or subsequent offense within 7 yrs.: category B felony, punishable by imprisonment 1 to 6 yrs. and fine $2,000 to $5,000; civil penalty of $35 paid to court in addition to any penalty
9 mos. to 2 yrs.; 2nd offense: 3 yrs.; 3rd offense: indefinite, minimum 5 yrs.; 4th or subsequent offense: indefinite, minimum 7 yrs.; reinstatement may be subject to IID for 12 mos. to 2 yrs.	Fine at least $500; 2nd offense within 2 yrs.: imprisonment at least 60 days and $750 fine; 2nd offense between 2 and 10 yrs.: imprisonment at least 17 days and $750 fine; 3rd offense: imprisonment 180 days and full substance disorder evaluation and $750 fine; enhanced penalties for transporting person under 16, speeding 30 mph over limit, or accident resulting in serious bodily injury
3 mos. to 1 yr.; 2nd offense: 2 yrs.; 3rd offense: 10 yrs.; if driver is under 17, period of revocation begins at 17th birthday; IID required for 2nd or subsequent offense; if underage and BAC .01-.08%, suspension 30 to 90 days beginning on day eligible to obtain license and community service 15 to 30 days	Imprisonment up to 30 days, 12 to 48 hrs. in Intoxicated Driver Resource Center, fine $250 to $400; 2nd offense: imprisonment 48 hrs. to 90 days, 30 days community service, fine $500 to $1,000; 3rd offense: imprisonment 180 days, up to 90 days can be exchanged for community service, and $1,000 fine; underage for drinking and found DWI are subject to stiffer penalties
1 yr.; 2nd offense: 2 yrs.; 3rd offense: 3 yrs.; 4th or subsequent offense: for remainder of offender's life subject to 5 yr. review; may apply for IID license	Imprisonment 24 hrs. to 90 days and fine up to $500, if sentence suspended or in part deferred, probation up to 1 yr.; 2nd offense: imprisonment 96 hrs. to 364 days and fine $50 to $1,000; probation may be 1 to 5 yrs. if sentence suspended or in part deferred and at least 48 hrs. community service; 3rd offense: imprisonment 30 to 364 days and/or fine $750 to $1,000 and at least 96 hrs. community service; 4th offense: 4th degree felony, punishable by 18 mos. imprisonment, 6 mos. may not be suspended; 5th offense: 4th degree felony, punishable by 2 yrs. imprisonment., 1 yr. may not be suspended; 6th offense: 3rd degree felony, punishable by 30 mos. imprisonment, 18 mos. may not be suspended; 7th or subsequent offense: 3rd degree felony, punishable by 3 yrs. imprisonment, 2 yrs. may not be suspended

Table 9: Drunk Driving—Continued

State	Code Section	BAC Legal Limit	Rehabilitation Required?
NEW YORK	Veh. & Traf. 1192 to 1199	.08% BAC; commercial motor vehicle drivers: .04%; under age 21: .02%	Court may require attendance at single session of "victims impact program"
NORTH CAROLINA	20-138.1 to 20-138.5; 20-17; 20-17.6; 20-17.8; 20-179	.08% BAC at any relevant time after the driving; commercial motor vehicle driver: .04%; under age 21: no amount of alcohol	Assessment may be required for alcoholism and substance abuse and appropriate treatment if necessary in program approved by Dept. of Human Resources; if placed on probation then must obtain substance abuse assessment and education or treatment for restoration of driver's license as condition of probation
NORTH DAKOTA	39-06.1-10; 39-08-01	.08% BAC within 2 hrs. of driving	Order for addiction evaluation by appropriate licensed addiction treatment program with appropriate treatment if necessary
OHIO	4510.02; 4510.021; 4511.19; 4511.99; 5119.38	.08% BAC; under 21: .02% BAC	Driver's Intervention Program as 1 yr. alternative to jail sentence; rehab may be required in sentences; 4th or subsequent offense: required attendance at alcohol and drug addiction program
OKLAHOMA	Tit. 47, §§ 6-205.1; 11-902	.08% BAC within 2 hrs. after arrest	Participate in assessment and evaluation; 2nd offense: shall follow all recommendation s made in assessment and evaluation for treatment at defendant's expense; 3rd offense: follow all recommendations made in assessment and evaluation for treatment and 240 hrs. community service and use of IID
OREGON	161.605; 161.615; 809.428; 813.010 to 813.616	.08% BAC; under 21: any amount	Mandatory complete exam by court approved agency/organization to determine whether individual has a problem condition involving alcohol or controlled substances; complete a treatment program if exam shows it necessary; if none necessary, then complete alcohol and drug information program.

Driver's License Suspension/ Ignition Interlock Device	Other Penalties
90 days; 2nd offense within 5 yrs.: 6 mos.; 3rd offense within 10 yrs.: 6 mos.; in addition to other punishments, may impose a term of probation or conditional discharge provided an IID is installed for a period of no less than one year	Imprisonment up to 15 days and/or fine $300 to $500; 2nd offense within 5 yrs.: imprisonment up to 30 days and/or fine $500 to $750; 3rd or subsequent offense within 10 yrs.: imprisonment up to 180 days and/or fine $750 to $1,500
License may be revoked; IID required for reinstatement; if BAC 0.15% or higher or 2nd or subsequent offense in 7 yrs.: 1 yr. if original revocation was 1 yr.; 3 yrs. if original revocation was 4 yrs.; 7 yrs. if original revocation was permanent	Court assesses the following levels of penalties based upon a list of grossly aggravating, aggravating and mitigating factors: level 5: 24 hrs. jail, 24 hrs. community service, and $200 fine; level 4: 48 hrs. jail, 48 hrs. community service, and $500 fine; level 3: 72 hrs. jail, 72 hrs. community service, and $1,000; level 2: up to $2,000 fine, 7 days to 12 mos. jail; level 1: up to $4,000 fine, 30 days to 24 mos. jail. Level 1 and 2 reserved for grossly aggravating factors only, such as prior convictions, serious injury, driving with child under 16 yrs. old
90 days; 2nd offense within 5 yrs.: 1 yr.; 3rd offense within 5 yrs.: 2 yrs.; increased suspension periods for BAC of .18%; may issue temporary restricted license that takes effect after 30 days of suspension with IID if was 1st offense; may not if it is 2nd or subsequent offense; except may be issued if participating in 24/7 sobriety program and offender has not committed offense for period of 1 yr. before date of filing application	Class B misdemeanor, $500 fine; 2nd offense within 5 yrs.: class B misdemeanor, punishable by imprisonment at least 10 days, $1,500 fine, at least 12 mos. participation in 24/7 sobriety program; 3rd offense within 5 yrs.: class A misdemeanor, punishable by imprisonment 120 days, $2,000 fine, at least 1 yr. supervised probation, participation in 24/7 sobriety program; 4th or subsequent offense, punishable by imprisonment at least 1 yr. and 1 day; $2,000 fine, order for additional evaluation, at least 2 yrs. supervised probation, participation in 24/7 sobriety program
6 mos. to 3 yrs.; 2nd offense within 6 yrs.: 1 to 5 yrs.; 3rd offense within 6 yrs.: 2- to 0 yrs.; 4th offense within 6 yrs.: min. 3 yrs. to permanent.	Imprisonment 3 days to 6 mos. and fine $375 to $1,075, class 5 license suspension; 2nd offense: imprisonment 10 days to 6 mos. and fine $525 to $1,625, class 4 license suspension; 3rd offense: imprisonment 30 days to 1 yr. and fine $850 to $2,750, class 3 license suspension; 4th or subsequent offense: imprisonment 60 days to 1 yr. and fine $1,350 to $10,500, class 2 license suspension
1 yr.; 2nd offense within 5 yrs.: 24 mos., may be modified with at least 24 mos. IID; 3rd offense within 5 yrs.: 48 mos., may be modified with at least 48 mos. IID	Imprisonment 10 days to 1 yr. and fine up to $1,000; 2nd offense within 10 yrs.: felony, punishable by imprisonment 1 to 5 yrs. and fine up to $2,500; 3rd offense within 10 yrs.: felony, punishable by imprisonment 1 to 7 yrs. and fine up to $5,000; 4th or subsequent offense: felony, punishable by imprisonment 1 to 10 yrs. and fine up to $5,000
1 yr.; 2nd or subsequent offense within 5 yrs.: 3 yrs.	Class A misdemeanor, punishable by imprisonment up to 364 days and minimum $1,000 fine, fees for programs; 2nd offense: imprisonment up to 1 yr. and minimum $1,500 fine, fees for programs; 3rd or subsequent offense: imprisonment up to 1 yr. and minimum $2,000 fine, fees for programs; 4th or subsequent offense: class C felony, punishable by imprisonment up to 5 yrs.

Table 9: Drunk Driving—Continued

State	Code Section	BAC Legal Limit	Rehabilitation Required?
PENNSYLVANIA	Tit. 75, §§ 1532; 3802 to 3817	.08% BAC within 2 hrs. of driving or actual physical control of vehicle; under 21: .02% BAC within 2 hrs. of driving or actual physical control of any vehicle; commercial or school vehicle driver: .04% BAC within 2 hrs. of driving or actual physical control of vehicle	Evaluation to determine extent of person's involvement with alcohol or controlled substances using Court Reporting Network instruments (may order treatment if necessary) and mandatory attendance in approved alcohol highway safety school; may require as part of sentencing or condition of parole, probation or Accelerated Rehabilitative Disposition or other preliminary disposition, that the person successfully complete a prescribed program of individual or group intervention or supervised inpatient or outpatient treatment; if after evaluation and further examination and hearing it is determined that a defendant is an alcohol abuser who represents a serious threat, may order defendant committed for treatment at a facility or institution;
RHODE ISLAND	31-27-2 to 31-27-3.1	.08% BAC	Attendance required at special course on DWI or under the influence of controlled substance and/or alcoholic or drug treatment for individual
SOUTH CAROLINA	56-5-2930 to 56-5-2995	"Under influence of intoxicating substances—liquor or drugs"; .08% BAC	Evaluation and successful completion of Alcohol and Drug Safety Action Program certified by South Carolina Commission on Alcohol and Drug Abuse prior to reinstatement of license
SOUTH DAKOTA	22-6-1; 22-6-2; 32-23-1 to 32-23-23	.08% BAC or "under the influence"; under age 21: .02% BAC	Required if .17% BAC; court-ordered evaluation to determine if addicted to alcohol
TENNESSEE	40-2-101; 55-10-401 to 55-10-424	"Under the influence" .08% BAC; commercial motor vehicle driver: .04% BAC	2nd or subsequent offense: as condition of probation, may be ordered to participate in a substance abuse treatment program, which includes after care recommended by treatment program, licensed or certified by the department of mental health and substance abuse services, which includes certified drug or DUI court

Driver's License Suspension/ Ignition Interlock Device	Other Penalties
1 mo. as condition of participation in Accelerated Rehabilitative Disposition program, to 12 mos.; 2nd conviction within 10 yrs.: IID may be granted for duration of restricted license period	Misdemeanor, punishable by up to 6 mos. probation and $300 fine; 2nd offense: imprisonment 5 days to 6 mos. and fine $300 to $2,500; 3rd or subsequent offense: misdemeanor in 2nd degree, punishable by imprisonment 10 days to 2 yrs. and fine $500 to $5,000; sentencing and fines higher for minors and commercial drivers, and judge may impose up to 150 hrs. community service in addition to above penalties
Suspension at least 30 days and IID 3 mos. to 1 yr.; 2nd offense: suspension at least 45 days and IID 6 mos. to 2 yrs.; suspension at least 60 days and IID 1 to 4 yrs.	Imprisonment up to 1 yr. and/or 10 to 60 hrs. community service and fine $100 to $300; 2nd offense within 5 yrs.: imprisonment 10 days to 1 yr. and $400 fine; 3rd or subsequent offense within 5 yrs.: imprisonment 1 to 3 yrs. and $400 fine, may have car seized and sold by State of Rhode Island with proceeds going to general fund; anyone convicted under this section pays highway assessment fine of $500; different penalties for those under 18
1st: 6 mos., may obtain IID license for remainder of suspension, if remained rid less than 3 mos., IID for 3 mos.; 2nd offense: 2 yrs. IID; 3rd offense: 3 yrs. IID; 4th or subsequent offense: IID for life	Imprisonment 48 hrs. to 30 days or 48 hrs. public service and $400 fine; 2nd offense: imprisonment 5 days to 1 yr. or minimum 30 days public service and fine $2,000 to $5,100; 3rd offense with 10 yrs.: imprisonment 60 days to 3 yrs. and fine $3,800 to $6,300; 4th and subsequent offense: imprisonment 1 to 5 yrs.
Minimum 30 days to 1 yr.; 2nd offense: minimum 1 yr.; 3rd offense: minimum 1 yr.; 4th offense: minimum 2 yrs.; 5th or subsequent offense: minimum 3 yrs.; 6th or subsequent offense with at least 5 convictions within 25 yrs.: minimum 3 yrs.; supervision may include IID	Class 1 misdemeanor, punishable by imprisonment 1 yr. and/ or $2,000; 2nd offense within 5 yrs.: imprisonment 3 days to 1 yr. and/or $2,000 fine; 3rd offense within 5 yrs.: class 6 felony, punishable by imprisonment 10 days to 2 yrs. and/or $4,000 fine; 4th offense: class 5 felony, punishable by imprisonment 5 yrs. and may impose $10,000 fine; 5th or subsequent offense: class 4 felony, punishable by 20 days to 10 yrs. and may impose $20,000 fine
1 yr.; 2nd offense: 2 yrs.; 3rd offense: 6 yrs.; 4th or subsequent offense: 8 yrs.; may apply for restricted license with IID	Imprisonment 48 hrs. to 11 mos. 29 days and fine $350 to $1,500, as condition of probation, remove litter during daylight hours from public roadways and property for a period of 24 hours in 3 shifts of 8 consecutive hours each; 2nd offense within 10 yrs.: imprisonment 45 days to 11 mos. 29 days and fine $600 to $3,500; 3rd or subsequent offense: imprisonment 120 days to 11 mos. 29 days and fine $1,100 to $10,000; 4th or subsequent offense: class E felony, punishable by imprisonment 150 days to 2 yrs. and fine $3,000 to $15,000; enhanced penalties for multiple offenders within 10 yrs., serious bodily injury, or minor offenders

Table 9: Drunk Driving—Continued

State	Code Section	BAC Legal Limit	Rehabilitation Required?
TEXAS	Penal §§ 12.21; 12.22; 12.34; 42.12; 49.01; 49.04, 49.09; Transp. § 521.246	Intoxicated: "not having normal use of menial or physical faculties by reason of introduction of alcohol . . ." or .08% BAC	Judge may suspend sentence and place defendant on community supervision; provided that in felony case, minimum period of community supervision is same as minimum term of imprisonment
UTAH	41-6A-501 to 41-6A-530	.08% BAC at time of test	Assessment and educational series at a licensed alcohol dependency rehab facility; court may order treatment if person has problem; 2nd offense: same as above, treatment at court's discretion; 3rd or subsequent offense: same as above, treatment at alcohol rehab facility is mandatory
VERMONT	Title 23, §§ 1201 to 1220B	.08% BAC; under 21: .02% BAC; school bus driver: .02% BAC; commercial motor vehicle driver: .04% BAC	Alcohol assessment screening-therapy program or driver rehab if necessary at court's discretion; 2nd offense: completion or substantial progress in completing therapy program; no license suspended or revoked may be reinstated even with IID except in 1st suspension after successful completion of Alcohol and Driving Ed. Program, and assessment for further treatment; in 2nd offense, suspension after completion of alcohol and driving rehabilitation program and completion or substantial progress in completing a therapy program; in 3rd or subsequent offense, same as 2nd offense requirements; may also apply for reinstatement after three years of total abstinence where the license has been suspended for life; eligible only once for reinstatement after suspension for life
VIRGINIA	18.2-266 to 18.2-273; 46.2-391	.08% BAC; under age 21: .02% BAC	Alcohol Safety Action Program certified by commission on the VA Alcohol Safety Action Program (VASP) for 1st or 2nd offense at court's discretion

Driver's License Suspension/ Ignition Interlock Device	Other Penalties
Judge may order suspension subject to IID	Class B misdemeanor, punishable by imprisonment 72 hrs. to 180 days and $2,000 fine; 2nd offense within 10 yrs.: class A misdemeanor, punishable by imprisonment 30 days to 1 yr. and $4,000 fine; court may order community supervision
120 days; 2nd offense within 10 yrs.: 2 yrs.; suspension may be shortened upon completion of 24-7 sobriety program	Class B misdemeanor, punishable by 48 hrs. jail and at least 48 hrs. compensatory-service work program or 48 hrs. electronic monitoring and fine at least $700, class A misdemeanor if bodily injury involved or child under 16 is passenger; 2nd offense within 6 yrs.: imprisonment at least 240 hrs. or at least 240 hrs. community service and at least $800 fine; 3rd or subsequent offense within 10 yrs.: 3rd degree felony, punishable by imprisonment 1,500 hrs. and at least $1,500 fine
May operate under terms of IID after 30 days of 90-day period unless offense involved a collision resulting in serious bodily injury or death to another; 2nd offense: may operate under terms of IID after 90 days of 18 month period unless offense involved a collision resulting in serious bodily injury or death to another; 3rd offense: may operate under terms of IID after one year of lifetime suspension unless offense involved a collision resulting in serious bodily injury or death to another	Imprisonment up to 2 yrs. and/or fine up to $750; 2nd offense: imprisonment 48 hrs. to 2 yrs. and fine up to $1,500; 3rd offense: imprisonment up to 5 yrs., 400 hrs. community service, and fine up to $2,500; 4th or subsequent offense: imprisonment up to 10 yrs. and fine up to $5,000; serious injury or death carries harsher penalties
1 yr.; 2nd offense within 10 yrs.: 3 yrs.; 3rd offense within 10 yrs.: revoked indefinitely; may petition for restoration after 5 yrs. from date of last conviction and court may, in its discretion, restore on condition of IID for period of at least 6 mos. prior to evaluation, court must order evaluation of person and include assessment of degree of alcohol abuse and appropriate treatment	1st offense for person under age 21: .02 to .08% BAC: mandatory fine of $500 and mandatory min. of 50 hours of community service; 1st offense: mandatory minimum fine of $250; 2nd offense w/in 5 years: imprisonment 1 mo. to 1 yr. and mandatory minimum fine of $500; 2nd offense w/in 5 to 10 years: class 7 felony, punishable by imprisonment not less than 1 mo. and mandatory min. fine of $500; 2nd offense within 5 to 10 yrs.: imprisonment minimum of 1 mo. and $500 fine; 3rd offense within 10 yrs.: class 6 felony, punishable by imprisonment minimum 90 days and mandatory minimum fine $1,000; 4th or subsequent offense within 10 yrs.: imprisonment mandatory minimum 1 yr. and mandatory minimum $1,000 fine

Table 9: Drunk Driving—Continued

State	Code Section	BAC Legal Limit	Rehabilitation Required?
WASHINGTON	9.94A.603; 46.61.502 to 46.61.524; 46.20.720	.08% BAC within 2 hrs. of driving; under age 21: .02% BAC within 2 hrs. of driving	A diagnostic evaluation and treatment recommendation by alcoholism agency approved by Dept. of Social & Health Services and completion of alcohol information course; when sentenced under 9.94A.603, court shall order alcohol dependency treatment
WEST VIRGINIA	17C-5-2 to 17C-5-10; 17C-5A-2 to 17C-5A-4	.08% BAC; under	Yes, an approved educational and treatment program; may be deferred upon condition of participation in motor vehicle alcohol test and lock program; for reissue of license, must participate in treatment program that includes treatment of alcoholism, alcohol and drug abuse, psychological counseling, education courses on the dangers of alcohol and drugs as they related to driving;
WISCONSIN	340.01; 343.30 to 343.307; 346.63 to 346.65	.08% BAC; under age 21: 0.0% BAC; commercial motor vehicle driver: .00% BAC	Assessment by approved public treatment facility for examining person's use of alcohol or drugs and for developing a driver safety plan for the person
WYOMING	31-5-233; 31-5-234; 31-7-127; 31-7-128; 31-7-401; 31-7-402	.08% BAC within 2 hrs. of driving or being in physical control of vehicle; .05-.08% no presumption but may be used as evidence; under age 21: .02% BAC	Person convicted shall be ordered to/shall receive substance abuse assessment at or before sentencing; judge may suspend part or all of discretionary portion of imprisonment sentence and place on probation on condition of completion of alcohol education or treatment program

Driver's License Suspension/ Ignition Interlock Device	Other Penalties
90 days; 2nd offense within 3 yrs.: 2 yrs. and subject to vehicle seizure and forfeiture; 3rd or subsequent offense: 3 yrs.; may substitute IID for sobriety program monitoring; may order that for period of suspension, revocation, or denial of driving privileges, use of IID; IID use 1st offense: 1 yr.; 2nd offense: 5 yrs.; 3rd or subsequent offense: 10 yrs.; longer suspension period for higher BAC: over .15%	1st offense with no prior offenses in 7 yrs.: Imprisonment up to 364 days and fine $350 to $5,000; 2nd offense within 7 yrs.: imprisonment 30 to 364 days and electronic home monitoring and fine $500 to $5,000; 3rd or 4th offense within 7 yrs.: imprisonment 90 to 364 days, 6 mo. period of 24/7 sobriety program monitoring, 120 days electronic home monitoring and fine $1,000 to $5,000
6 mos. or 15 days with an additional 120 days in Motor Vehicle Test and Lock Program; may apply for reissuance after 90 days; prior revocation w/in ten yrs.: 10 yrs.; may apply for reissuance once one-half the time has elapsed and has successfully completed treatment program; prior revocation more than once within 10 yrs.: life; may not be reissued until at least 10 yrs. have elapsed and has successfully completed the program; Motor Vehicle Alcohol Test and Lock Program for all whose licenses have been revoked	Imprisonment up to 6 mos. and fine $100 to $500; 2nd offense: imprisonment 6 mos. to 1 yr. and fine $1,000 to $3,000; 3rd offense: felony, punishable by imprisonment 1 to 3 yrs. and fine $3,000 to $5,000; bodily injury, death, or .02-.10% BAC for minors results in harsher penalties
6-9 mos.; 2nd offense within 5 yrs.: 1 yr. to 18 mos., court may order motor vehicle to be seized; 3rd or subsequent offense within 10 yrs.: 2 to 3 yrs.; may apply for occupational license with IID	$150 to $300 fine; 2nd offense within 5 yrs.: imprisonment 5 days to 6 mos. and fine $350 to $1,100; 3rd offense within 10 yrs.: imprisonment 30 days to 1 yr. and fine $60 to $2,000; 4th offense within 10 yrs.: imprisonment 60 days to 1 yr. and fine $600 to $2,000; 5th offense within 10 yrs.: imprisonment 6 mos. to 5 yrs. and fine $600 to $2,000; may do community service in lieu of all or part of fine
90 days; 2nd offense within 10 yrs.: 1 yr., vehicle registration also suspended by the state; 3rd or subsequent offense within 10 yrs.: 3 yrs.; if served at least 45 days of suspension, may apply for IID restricted license	Misdemeanor, punishable by imprisonment up to 6 mos. and/or fine up to $750; 2nd offense within 10 yrs.: imprisonment 7 days to 6 mos. and fine $200 to $750; 3rd or subsequent offense within 10 yrs.: imprisonment 30 days to 6 mos. and fine $750 to $3,000; 4th or subsequent offense within 10 yrs.: felony, punishable by imprisonment up to 7 yrs. and/or fine up to $10,000; harsher penalties for serious bodily injury

10. GUN CONTROL

The state laws controlling the purchase of firearms are varied and constantly changing. The laws reviewed here are current, but there is still a great amount of legislation pending before state governments designed primarily to make the legal purchase of guns more difficult. Each state has some form of restriction on the buying of guns, though rural states tend to be less restrictive in controlling guns than highly urban states due to the greater numbers of hunters and sportsmen in their populations. Nonetheless, in most states convicted felons and minors cannot purchase guns; in some, aliens and individuals with mental disabilities cannot. Machine guns, automatic weapons, sawed-off shotguns, and guns with silencers are banned in many.

One of the more controversial restrictions applied to the purchase of guns is a waiting period, in which a certain amount of time must pass between the time an individual purchases a gun and is able to take possession of the gun. With the rise in gun-related crimes, a number of states already have instituted waiting periods to discourage rash actions.

A relatively new development is the passage in some states of laws that permit people to carry weapons openly or, in many cases, people may carry them concealed, with or without permits. The numbers of states that today ban either ripen or concealed carry of handguns are now the overwhelming minority, and the chart below makes the United States sound like the Hollywood versions of the old Wild West, in which everyone carried a gun. At the same time, as laws have been enacted that allow people to carry weapons, there has been a growing number of laws passed that restrict where guns may be carried. In the last edition of this book, laws concentrated mostly on restrictions of possession of guns near or on school grounds. today's laws cover many types of public places, including liquor stores, churches, and government buildings, to name a few.

_____

*This chapter was updated by Jared Koch, Juris Doctor Candidate, Class of 2018, University of Nebraska College of Law.

Table 10: Gun Control

State	Code Section	Illegal Arms	Waiting Period	Who May Not Possess	Possession in Public Areas	Concealed or Open Carry Permitted?
ALABAMA	13A-11-61.2; 13A-11-63 to 13A-11-66; 13A-11-72; 13A-11-73; 16-1-24.3	Short-barreled rifle; short-barreled shotgun	None	Convicted of committing or attempting to commit crime of violence; person subject to a protection order for domestic abuse; minor; drug addict or habitual drunkard; person of unsound mind	1 yr. expulsion of students determined to have brought to school or have in their possession a firearm in a school building, on school grounds, on school buses, or at other school-sponsored function. No person shall knowingly with intent to do bodily harm possess a deadly weapon on the premises of a public school; school security personnel and school resource officers are exempt; law enforcement officers also exempt. A person may not knowingly possess or carry a firearm inside a police station; inside or on the premises of a prison or jail; inside an inpatient mental health facility; inside a courthouse; law enforcement officers exempt	Concealed carry allowed with permit. Open carry permitted, except for in vehicle.

Table 10: Gun Control—Continued

State	Code Section	Illegal Arms	Waiting Period	Who May Not Possess	Possession in Public Areas	Concealed or Open Carry Permitted?
ALASKA	11.61.190 to 11.61.220; 18.65.700; 18.65.800	Device made or adapted to muffle the report of firearm; firearm capable of shooting more than one shot automatically without manual reloading, by a single function of trigger; rifle with barrel less than 16 inches; shotgun with barrel less than 18 inches or firearm made from a rifle or shotgun which, as modified, has an overall length of less than 26 inches; possession, sale, transfer, or manufacture of above firearms is illegal	None	Convicted felon or adjudicated a delinquent minor for conduct constituting a felony if committed by an adult	May not possess a firearm on the grounds of a school without the permission of the chief administrative officer; on the grounds of a child care facility; person 21 years of age or older may possess an unloaded firearm in rural area for purpose of entering hunting area and school board has accepted this exemption; student may possess a deadly weapon, other than a firearm, if obtains permission of the chief administrative officer	Concealed carry and open carry allowed without permit; residents may obtain a concealed carry permit for reciprocity with other states

Table 10: Gun Control—Continued

State	Code Section	Illegal Arms	Waiting Period	Who May Not Possess	Possession in Public Areas	Concealed or Open Carry Permitted?
ARIZONA	13-3101 to 13-3102; 13-3112	A firearm that is capable of shooting more than one shot automatically, without manual reloading, by a single function of the trigger; a rifle with a barrel length of less than sixteen inches, or shotgun with a barrel length of less than eighteen inches, or any firearm that is made from a rifle or shotgun and that, as modified, has an overall length of less than twenty-six inches	None	A person who has been found to constitute a danger to self or to others; who has a persistent, acute, or grave disability pursuant to court order; who has been convicted of a felony; who at the time of possession is serving a term of imprisonment; who is at the time of possession serving a term of probation pursuant to a conviction for a domestic violence offense; who is an undocumented alien or nonimmigrant alien; who has been found incompetent; who is found guilty except insane	Prohibited in any public establishment after a reasonable request by the operator of the establishment to remove the weapon and place it in the custody of the operator of the establishment for temporary storage; in any election polling place on the day of any election; on school grounds; exception for law enforcement officials	Concealed carry and open carry allowed without permit; residents may obtain a concealed carry permit for reciprocity with other states.
ARKANSAS	5-73-103 to 5-73-104; 5-73-119; 5-73-120; 5-73-122; 5-73-306 to 5-37-312	Machine gun; sawed-off shotgun or rifle; firearm specially made or adapted for silent discharge	None	Convicted felon; adjudicated mentally ill; committed involuntarily to any mental institution	Prohibited on school property; school bus; publicly owned buildings; police station; prison or jail; courthouse; inside the passenger terminal of an airport; church or place of worship; exception for law enforcement officials	Concealed carry allowed with permit. Open carry permitted on personal property; if carrying a weapon on a journey, except in airport terminal; when hunting game.

Table 10: Gun Control—Continued

State	Code Section	Illegal Arms	Waiting Period	Who May Not Possess	Possession in Public Areas	Concealed or Open Carry Permitted?
CALIFORNIA	Penal §§ 626.9; 16000 to 17800; 23500 to 33690	Cane gun; wallet gun; any firearm not immediately recognized as such; short-barreled shotgun or rifle, i.e., barrel of less than 18 inches for shotgun, less than 16 inches for rifle, or less than 26 inches designed to fire a fixed shotgun shell or cartridge; zip gun; any bullet with explosive agent; multi-burst trigger activator; any unconventional pistol; any undetectable firearm; centerfire rifles that can fire a .50 BMG cartridge	10 days	Any person convicted of a felony; addicted to the use of any narcotic drug; convicted of certain misdemeanors; prohibited from firearm possession as a condition of probation; adjudged or alleged to have committed certain juvenile offenses; prohibited from firearm possession by temporary restraining order or injunction	Open carry prohibited in public place or public street; exception for law enforcement officer; established target range; licensed hunter engaged in hunter or in training a dog; within gun show; within school zone with written permission of school authority	Concealed carry allowed with permit. Open carry generally prohibited.
COLORADO	18-12-102 to 18-12-303	machine gun; short shotgun; short rifle	None	Minor (under 18); felons; persons convicted for attempt or conspiracy to commit a felony	Prohibited on school grounds; seminary; in chambers, galleries, or offices of the general assembly; exception for concealed weapon with permit; exception for law enforcement officers	Concealed carry of handguns allowed with permit; no permit required in private vehicle. Open carry allowed without permit except where restricted by municipalities

Table 10: Gun Control—Continued

State	Code Section	Illegal Arms	Waiting Period	Who May Not Possess	Possession in Public Areas	Concealed or Open Carry Permitted?
CONNECTICUT	29-27 to 38p; 53a-211 to 53a-217	Sawed-off shotgun with barrel less than 18 inches or overall length of less than 26 inches	None	Persons convicted of a felony; convicted for the commission of a serious juvenile offense; discharged from custody within the preceding 20 years after having been found not guilty by reason of mental disease or defect; subject to a restraining order due to the use, attempted use, or threatened use of physical force against another person; confined to a hospital for persons with psychiatric disabilities	Prohibited on school grounds; exception for approved school officials and law enforcement officials	Concealed and open carry allowed with permit
DELAWARE	Tit. 11, §§ 1441; 1444; 1445; 1448; 1457	Sawed-off shotgun; machine gun; any other firearm or weapon which is adaptable for use as a machine gun	None	Any person convicted of a felony or crime of violence involving physical injury to another; committed for a mental disorder; convicted for unlawful use, possession or sale of illegal substance; who, as a juvenile, has been adjudicated as delinquent for conduct if such conduct would be a felony if committed by an adult; any juvenile; subject to a family court protection from abuse order; convicted of a misdemeanor crime of domestic violence	Prohibited on school property; in school owned vehicles; exception for school-authorized instruction	Concealed carry allowed with permit. Open carry generally permitted

Table 10: Gun Control—Continued

State	Code Section	Illegal Arms	Waiting Period	Who May Not Possess	Possession in Public Areas	Concealed or Open Carry Permitted?
DISTRICT OF COLUMBIA	22-4501 to 22-4517	Machine gun; sawed-off shotgun; imitation pistol	10 days	A person convicted of a crime punishable by imprisonment for a term exceeding one year; fugitive from justice; addicted to any controlled substance; subject to a restraining order or order requiring the person to relinquish possession of any firearms; convicted of an intrafamily offense within the past 5 years	Prohibited within 1000 feet of day care center; school or university; public swimming pool, playground, video arcade, youth center, or public library; in and around public housing	Concealed or open carry of pistol allowed with permit.
FLORIDA	790.001 to 790.338	Short-barreled rifle or shotgun; machine gun; exception for antique firearms	3 days, excluding weekends and legal holidays	A person convicted of a felony; found to have committed a delinquent act that would be a felony if committed by an adult; subject to a restraining order for committing acts of domestic violence, stalking, or cyberstalking; violent career criminal	3rd degree felony; may carry in case of firearms program, class, or function approved in advance; may carry in a case to career center having firearms training range; may carry in vehicle pursuant to 790.25(5) except school districts may adopt written and published policies that waive this exception. 790.115, 810.095	Concealed carry allowed with permit; open carry not permitted. Firearm in vehicle must be concealed and securely eased or otherwise not readily accessible for immediate use

Table 10: Gun Control—Continued

State	Code Section	Illegal Arms	Waiting Period	Who May Not Possess	Possession in Public Areas	Concealed or Open Carry Permitted?
GEORGIA	16-11-120 to 16-11-173	Sawed-off shotgun; sawed-off rifle; machine gun; dangerous weapon	None	Convicted felon; a person under the age of 18	Prohibited in a government building as a non license holder; courthouse; jail or prison; place of worship, unless authorized; state mental health facility; on premises of a nuclear power facility; within 150 feet of any polling place when elections are being conducted	Concealed carry allowed without permit if enclosed in a case and unloaded. Open carry allowed without permit in home, vehicle, or own place of business; otherwise allowed with permit
HAWAII	134-1 to 134-34	Assault pistols; automatic firearms; rifles with barrel lengths less than sixteen inches; shotguns with barrel lengths less than eighteen inches; cannons	No shorter than 14 days	A person who is a fugitive from justice; prohibited from possessing firearms under federal law; under indictment for or convicted of a felony, crime of violence, or illegal sale of any drug; under treatment for drug abuse; acquitted of a crime on the grounds of mental disease, disorder, or defect; diagnosed as having a significant behavioral, emotional, or mental disorders	Prohibited on public highways, except for with permit in vehicle	Concealed and open carry allowed with permit. Permits only issued in exceptional cases
IDAHO	18-3301 to 18-3325	Any type of weapon which will or may be converted to expel a projectile by explosive or other propellant, the barrel of which has a bore of more than .700 inches in diameter, except rifled and unrifled shotguns	None	Convicted felon; person in penal institution; under 18 without consent or accompaniment of parent or guardian (except sawed-off gun/rifle or automatic weapon)	Prohibited on school property. Concealed carry prohibited in courthouse; juvenile detention facility or jail; exception for law enforcement officers	Concealed carry allowed with permit; no permit needed for firearm that is not loaded and concealed in motor vehicle. Open carry generally permitted

Table 10: Gun Control—Continued

State	Code Section	Illegal Arms	Waiting Period	Who May Not Possess	Possession in Public Areas	Concealed or Open Carry Permitted?
ILLINOIS	720 §§ 5/24-1 to 5/24-10; 430 § 66/10	Machine gun; rifle with barrel less than 16 inches; shotgun with barrel less than 18 inches or any weapon made from rifle or shotgun and as modified has overall length less than 26 inches	72 hours for handgun; 24 hours for rifle or shotgun	A person who is a narcotic addict; a patient in a mental institution within the past 5 years; a person with an intellectual disability; convicted of a felony; confined in a penal institution; a gang member	Prohibited on the premises of any school	Concealed carry allowed with permit. Open carry prohibited; exception for shooting ranges, authorized parades, hunting
INDIANA	33-23-15-2; 35-47-1-1 to 35-47-4-7; 35-47-5-8 to 35-47-5-11; 35-47-9-2 to 35-47-10-10	Machine gun	None	A person convicted of a serious violent felony; convicted of domestic battery; convicted for resisting law enforcement within past five years; alcohol or drug abuser; has a propensity for violent or emotionally unstable conduct; convicted for any crime involving an inability to safely handle a handgun; has an adjudication as a delinquent child for an act that would be a felony if committed by an adult; involuntarily committed to a mental institution; found to be mentally incompetent	Prohibited in or on school property; on a school bus; exception if firearm is locked in trunk, kept in glove compartment, or stored out of plain sight in locked motor vehicle	Concealed and open carry allowed with permit

Table 10: Gun Control—Continued

State	Code Section	Illegal Arms	Waiting Period	Who May Not Possess	Possession in Public Areas	Concealed or Open Carry Permitted?
IOWA	724.1 to 724.31	Machine guns; short-barreled rifle or shotgun; any weapon other than shotgun or muzzle-loading rifle, cannon, pistol, revolver, or musket, which fires or can be made to fire a projectile by the explosion of a propellant charge which has a barrel of more than six-tenths of an inch in diameter	3 days for handgun permit required for purchase	Any person addicted to the use of alcohol; probable cause exists to believe that the person is likely to use a weapon unlawfully or in such other manner as would endanger the person's self or others; convicted of a felony; adjudicated delinquent on the basis of conduct that would constitute a felony if committed by an adult; convicted of any serious or aggravated misdemeanor within past three years; prohibited by federal law from possessing a firearm	Prohibited in, on, or within 1000 feet of school property; exception for law enforcement officers and persons specifically authorized by the school	Open or concealed carry allowed with permit
KANSAS	21-6301 to 21-6304; 21-6309; 75-7c03	Shotgun with barrel less than 18 inches; automatic weapons	No	Any person addicted to and an unlawful user of a controlled substance; mentally ill person subject to involuntary commitment; felon	Prohibited on any school property; within any building located within the capitol complex; within or on the grounds of the governor's residence; within any other state-owned or leased building if so designated by the secretary of administration; within any county courthouse; exception for law enforcement officers	Concealed carry allowed with permit. Open carry allowed without permit

Table 10: Gun Control—Continued

State	Code Section	Illegal Arms	Waiting Period	Who May Not Possess	Possession in Public Areas	Concealed or Open Carry Permitted?
KENTUCKY	527.010 to 527.210; 237.060 to 237.110	Armor-piercing or "black talon" ammunition; defaced firearm	None	Persons convicted of a felony; barred by federal law from purchase of firearms; adjudicated mentally defective and committed to mental institutions	Prohibited on school property; exception for firearm contained within and not removed from vehicle; exception for law enforcement officers	Concealed carry allowed with permit. Open carry allowed without permit
LOUISIANA	14:95.1 to 14:95.10; 40:1379.3; 40:1751 to 40:1812	Machine and sub-machine guns; those with serial or identification number removed or altered; armor-piercing ammunition	None	Convicted of certain felonies (murder, manslaughter, aggravated battery, violating uniform controlled substances law, etc.); convicted of crime of violence (felony burglary, felony illegal use of weapons) or crime defined as sex offense or domestic abuse	Prohibited on school property; exception for law enforcement officers, school officials, any person with the written permission of the principal, students carrying a firearm to or from a class for which it is required, students possessing a firearm in his dormitory room or while going to or from his vehicle. Prohibited within 1000 feet of any parade or demonstration; on the premises of an alcohol beverage outlet. Law enforcement officers shall not carry in a courtroom while attending as a party to a proceeding	Concealed carry allowed with permit. Open carry generally permitted

Table 10: Gun Control—Continued

State	Code Section	Illegal Arms	Waiting Period	Who May Not Possess	Possession in Public Areas	Concealed or Open Carry Permitted?
MAINE	Tit. 12 § 11212; Tit. 15 § 393; Tit. 17A §§ 1051 to 1058; Tit. 20A § 6552; Tit. 25 §§ 2001 to 2003	Machine gun; armor-piercing ammunition	None	Any person convicted of a crime punishable by imprisonment for a term of one year or more; adjudicated to have engaged in conduct as a juvenile that, if committed by an adult, would have been a disqualifying conviction; is subject to a restraining order; committed involuntarily to a hospital; fugitive from justice; unlawful user of or is addicted to any controlled substance; an alien who is illegally or unlawfully in the United States; has been dishonorably discharged from the United States Armed Forces; has renounced that person's citizenship of the United States	Prohibited on school property; exception for law enforcement officials and persons in possession which is authorized by a written policy adopted by the school board. Prohibited in a courthouse	Concealed carry allowed with permit. Open carry generally permitted. Only concealed carry is allowed in vehicles with permit.

Table 10: Gun Control—Continued

State	Code Section	Illegal Arms	Waiting Period	Who May Not Possess	Possession in Public Areas	Concealed or Open Carry Permitted?
MARYLAND	Pub. Safety §§ 5-102 to 5-406; Crim. Law §§ 4-101 to 4-407	Short-barreled rifle or shotgun; restricted firearm ammunition; assault weapons	7 days; application for handgun qualification license required and approved or denied within 30 days	A person who is a fugitive from justice; is a habitual drunkard; is addicted to a controlled dangerous substance or is a habitual user; suffers from a mental disorder and has a history of violent behavior against the person or another; has been found incompetent to stand trial; has been found not criminally responsible; has been voluntarily admitted for more than 30 consecutive days to a mental health facility; has been involuntarily committed to a mental health facility; is under the protection of a guardian appointed by a court; against whom an order for protection has been issued; if under the age of 30 years at the time of possession, has been adjudicated delinquent by a juvenile court for an act that would be a disqualifying crime if committed by an adult; convicted of a crime of violence; guilty of a felony	Prohibited on school property; exception for law enforcement officers, persons engaged in organized shooting activity for educational purposes, and persons engaged in a historical demonstration using a weapon for educational purposes with written invitation from the school principal. Prohibited at a demonstration in a public place	Concealed and open carry allowed with permit

Table 10: Gun Control—Continued

State	Code Section	Illegal Arms	Waiting Period	Who May Not Possess	Possession in Public Areas	Concealed or Open Carry Permitted?
MASSACHUSETTS	Ch. 269, §§ 10 to 10h; Ch. 140, §§ 121 to 131p	Machine guns or sawed-off shotgun, unless with permit	None	Alien; convicted felon; convicted of unlawful use, possession, or sale of drugs or habitual drunkenness; confined in mental hospital or institution for mental illness; currently under order to surrender firearms license or ID card	Prohibited in any building or on the grounds of a school	Concealed and open carry allowed with permit
MICHIGAN	750.222 to 750.239; 28.422	Machine gun; automatic weapons; armor-piercing ammunition; short-barreled shotgun or rifle; semiautomatic firearm conversion devices	None	A person convicted of a felony; adjudged insane and not restored to sanity by court order; under an order of involuntary commitment; adjudged legally incapacitated; illegal alien or not a Michigan resident	Prohibited in a financial institution; church or other house of religious worship; a court; a theatre; a sports arena; a day care center; a hospital; an establishment licensed under the Michigan liquor control act; weapon free school zone; exception for law enforcement officers	Concealed carry allowed with permit. Open carry allowed without permit, but permit required to open carry in vehicle

Table 10: Gun Control—Continued

State	Code Section	Illegal Arms	Waiting Period	Who May Not Possess	Possession in Public Areas	Concealed or Open Carry Permitted?
MINNESOTA	609.66 to 609.67; 624.71 to 624.719	Machine gun or machine gun conversion kit; short-barreled shotgun; spring gun; swivel guns, set guns	5 business days for handgun or assault weapon from day dealer delivers transfer report to police chief or sheriff. Does not apply to private sales or if purchaser has transferee or carry permit.	A person convicted of a crime of violence; committed by a judicial determination that the person is mentally ill; convicted of a misdemeanor or gross misdemeanor related to controlled substances; committed to a treatment facility for chemical dependency; charged with committing a crime of violence and placed in a pretrial diversion program by the court before disposition; convicted of assaulting a family or household member and was found to have used a firearm during commission of the assault; convicted of a crime punishable by imprisonment for a term exceeding one year; subject to an order for protection	Prohibited on school property; exception for law enforcement officers and firearm safety or marksmanship courses. Rifles and shotguns prohibited on government property	Concealed and open carry allowed with permit

Table 10: Gun Control—Continued

State	Code Section	Illegal Arms	Waiting Period	Who May Not Possess	Possession in Public Areas	Concealed or Open Carry Permitted?
MISSISSIPPI	45-9-101; 97-37-1 to 97-37-17	Rifle with a barrel of less than 16 inches in length; shotgun with a barrel of less than 18 inches in length; machine gun; fully automatic firearm or deadly weapon	None	Convicted felons (unless they have certificates of rehabilitation); intoxicated persons	Prohibited on school property; school bus; exception for BB gun, air rifle, or air pistol; exception for non-student storing firearm in vehicle; exception for educational or school-sanctioned ceremonial purposes. Prohibited in police station; prison or jail; courthouse; courtroom (except concealed carry by judge); any polling place; any meeting place of the governing body of any governmental entity; any meeting of the Legislature or a committee thereof; any portion of an establishment primarily devoted to dispensing alcoholic beverages; inside the passenger terminal of any airport, unless encased for shipment; any church or other place of worship; any place where the carrying of firearms is prohibited by federal law	Concealed and open carry allowed with permit; concealed carry prohibited in any place where a written notice is clearly posted by the owner of the premises

Table 10: Gun Control—Continued

State	Code Section	Illegal Arms	Waiting Period	Who May Not Possess	Possession in Public Areas	Concealed or Open Carry Permitted?
MISSOURI	21.750; 571.010 to 571.500	Machine gun; short-barreled rifle/shotgun; gas gun; explosive weapon; bullet which explodes upon impact; defaced firearm	None	Any person convicted of dangerous felony; fugitive from justice, habitually intoxicated or drugged condition, or mentally incompetent	Prohibited in any church or place of worship; any election precinct on any election day; any government building; any school; any school bus; exception for law enforcement officers. Concealed carry prohibited in any police station; prison or jail; courthouse; any establishment licensed to dispense intoxicating liquor for consumption on the premises; child care facility; gated area of an amusement park; sports arena or stadium with seating capacity of 5000 or more; hospital accessible by the public	Concealed carry allowed with permit. Open carry generally permitted; persons with concealed carry permit can open carry in jurisdictions where open carry prohibited
MONTANA	45-3-111; 45-8-301 to 45-8-361	Sawed-off rifle or shotgun; machine gun; a weapon of a caliber greater than .60 which fires fixed ammunition other than a shotgun or shotgun ammunition	None	Convicted felon; adjudicated mental incompetents; illegal aliens	Prohibited in a school building; government building; bank; a room in which alcoholic beverages are sold, dispensed, and consumed under a license	Concealed carry allowed with permit. Open carry generally permitted.

Table 10: Gun Control—Continued

State	Code Section	Illegal Arms	Waiting Period	Who May Not Possess	Possession in Public Areas	Concealed or Open Carry Permitted?
NEBRASKA	28-1201 to 28-1212.04; 69-2428	Machine gun; short rifle or short shotgun; defaced firearm; stolen firearm	None	Any person convicted of a felony; fugitive from justice; subject of a current and validly issued domestic violence protection order and is knowingly violating such order; defaced firearm	Prohibited in a school; on school grounds; in a school-owned vehicle	Concealed carry allowed with permit. Open carry generally permitted
NEVADA	202.253 to 202.369; 503.165	Metal penetrating bullets; short-barreled rifle or shotgun; machine gun or silencer; firearm with altered serial number; spring pistol or rifle	Up to 120 days —for concealed weapons permit only	A person convicted of a misdemeanor crime of domestic violence; convicted of a violence; a fugitive from justice; an unlawful user of, or addicted to, any controlled substance; otherwise prohibited by federal law from having a firearm in his or her possession; adjudicated as mentally ill or committed to any health facility; entered a plea of guilty but mentally ill in any court; found guilty but mentally ill in any court; acquitted by reason of insanity in any court; illegally or unlawfully in the United States	Prohibited in private or public school; child care facility; exception for law enforcement officers; exception for persons with written permission from school principal or person designated by child care facility	Concealed carry allowed with permit, except in a public building that has metal detector at entrance. Open carry generally permitted, except in vehicle on public highway or any other way open to the public
NEW HAMPSHIRE	159:1 to 159:26; 193-D:1	Teflon coated, armor piercing, or exploding bullet; spring gun; gun with changed, altered removed, or obliterated maker, model, manufacturer's number, or other identifying marks	None	Career criminals; convicted felons	Prohibited on school property; school buses; courtroom; courthouse	Concealed or open carry allowed with permit

Table 10: Gun Control—Continued

State	Code Section	Illegal Arms	Waiting Period	Who May Not Possess	Possession in Public Areas	Concealed or Open Carry Permitted?
NEW JERSEY	2C:39-1 to 2C:39-16; 2C:58-1 to 2C:58-19	Sawed-off shotguns; defaced firearms; body armor penetrating bullets	Handguns: At least 7 days from application for permit; processing permit application may take up to 30 days for residents, 45 days for non-residents	Convicted of aggravated assault, arson, burglary, escape, extortion, homicide, kidnapping, robbery, aggravated sexual assault, sexual assault, bias intimidation, endangering the welfare of a child, stalking, domestic violence, or certain weapons-related offenses; committed for mental disorder unless satisfactory proof he no longer suffers from a disorder which interferes or handicaps him in handling a firearm; convicted of unlawful use, possession, or sale of controlled dangerous substance or drug dependent; convicted of a disorderly persons offense of domestic violence or who is subject to a court order prohibiting the possession of firearms or whose firearm has been seized pursuant to New Jersey's domestic violence law	Prohibited in buildings or on grounds of educational institutions; except with written authorization of governing officer of the institution	Concealed and open carry allowed with permit
NEW MEXICO	29-19-9; 30-7-1 to 30-7-16	Exploding bullets	None	Convicted felon	Prohibited on school or university premises; licensed liquor establishments; exception for law enforcement officers; exception for school-approved programs	Concealed carry allowed with permit; open carry generally permitted

Table 10: Gun Control—Continued

State	Code Section	Illegal Arms	Waiting Period	Who May Not Possess	Possession in Public Areas	Concealed or Open Carry Permitted?
NEW YORK	Penal §§ 265.00 to 265.45; 400.00	Imitation pistol; armor piercing ammunition; machine gun; defaced firearm; assault weapon; three or more firearms	None	Any person convicted of a felony; not a citizen of the United States	Prohibited on school grounds; exception with written authorization of educational institution	Concealed carry license issued for limited purposes. Open carry generally prohibited

Table 10: Gun Control—Continued

State	Code Section	Illegal Arms	Waiting Period	Who May Not Possess	Possession in Public Areas	Concealed or Open Carry Permitted?
NORTH CAROLINA	14-402 to 14-415.27	Machine gun; submachine gun; or other like weapons; unlicensed pistol or crossbow	None	Any person not a citizen or permanent resident of the United States; suffers from a physical or mental infirmity; ineligible to own, possess, or receive a firearm under state or federal law; under indictment or against whom a finding of probable cause exists for a felony; adjudicated guilty in any court of a felony, except a felony that pertains to antitrust violations, unfair trade practices, or restraints of trade, or the person's firearm rights have been restored; fugitive from justice; an unlawful user of or addicted to a controlled substance; adjudicated to be lacking mental capacity or mentally ill, except if the individual's rights have been restored; dishonorably discharged from the Armed Forces of the United States; adjudicated guilty of a crime of violence; is free on bond pending trial, appeal, or sentencing for a crime which would disqualify him from obtaining a concealed handgun permit; convicted of an impaired driving offense within three years prior to date of application for permit	Possession: class I felony; discharging: class F felony; BB gun, stun gun, air rifle, or pistol: misdemeanor; class I misdemeanor instead of felony if person is not student or school employee; person is not student attending school-sponsored activity; firearm is unloaded and locked in motor vehicle; does not apply to weapon used solely for school-sanctioned purposes or program; home schools; those used for hunting purposes on specific properties; certain law enforcement officers; firefighters; armed armored car service guard; volunteer school safety resource officer. 4-269.2(b)	Concealed carry allowed with permit; open carry generally permitted

Table 10: Gun Control—Continued

State	Code Section	Illegal Arms	Waiting Period	Who May Not Possess	Possession in Public Areas	Concealed or Open Carry Permitted?
NORTH DAKOTA	62.1-02-01 to 62.1-05-02	Short-barreled rifle or shotgun; machine gun; fully automatic rifle; silencer; federally licensed firearm or dangerous weapon not in compliance with National Firearms Act	None	A person convicted of a felony offense involving violence or intimidation; diagnosed and confined or committed to a hospital or other institution as a mentally deficient person	Prohibited in an establishment which sells alcoholic beverages for consumption; athletic or sporting event; a school; a church; a publicly owned or operated building; government building; exception for law enforcement officers	Concealed carry allowed with permit. Open carry generally permitted if unloaded
OHIO	2923.11 to 2923.25	Automatic or sawed-off firearm; zip-gun; rocket launcher; firearm muffler or suppressor	None	Fugitive from justice; under indictment or convicted of felony of violence or adjudged juvenile delinquent for commission of such felony; under indictment or convicted of illegal possession, use, sale of drugs; drug dependent or chronic alcoholic; mentally incompetent; under 18 except for hunting or marksmanship and under adult supervision; serving sentence at a detention center	Prohibited in any room in which any person is consuming beer or intoxicating liquor in a liquor permit premises; school safety zone; courthouse. Concealed carry prohibited in police station; place of worship, unless the place of worship permits otherwise; a child day-care center; a commercial aircraft; government facility	Concealed carry allowed with permit. Open carry generally permitted; firearm in vehicle must be unloaded, secured on rack or holder, and inaccessible without leaving vehicle

Table 10: Gun Control—Continued

State	Code Section	Illegal Arms	Waiting Period	Who May Not Possess	Possession in Public Areas	Concealed or Open Carry Permitted?
OKLAHOMA	Tit. 21, §§ 1272 to 1290.26	Sawed-off shotgun or rifle; armor penetrating ammunition	None	Any person convicted of a felony; adjudicated delinquent; mentally incompetent or deficient or otherwise mentally or emotionally unbalanced or disturbed	Prohibited in any establishment where liquor is consumed; government building; courthouse; prison or jail; public or private school; sports arena during a professional sporting event, unless allowed by the event holder; any place where gambling is authorized by law, unless allowed by the property owner	Concealed and open carry allowed with permit. No permit needed when hunting; during competition or firearm class; participation in or preparation for military function or police function; during practice or performance for entertainment purposes; for lawful self-defense. No permit needed to transport firearm in vehicle if unloaded and in a case designed for carrying firearms
OREGON	166.180 to 166.490	Machine gun; short-barreled rifle/shotgun; silencer; armor piercing ammunition	None	Convicted felon; juvenile felony offender (within 4 yrs. of discharge); committed to Oregon Health Authority or mentally ill; subject to order prohibiting purchase or possession of firearms; inmates of institutions	Prohibited in public building; court facility; school; exception for law enforcement officers	Concealed carry allowed with permit. Open carry generally allowed

Table 10: Gun Control—Continued

State	Code Section	Illegal Arms	Waiting Period	Who May Not Possess	Possession in Public Areas	Concealed or Open Carry Permitted?
PENNSYLVANIA	Tit. 18, §§ 908; 912; 913; 6101 to 6127	Machine gun; sawed-off shotgun with a barrel less than 18 inches; firearm specially made or adopted for concealment or silent discharge; stun gun; firearm with altered manufacturer's number	None	Any person convicted of felony or enumerated offenses in § 6105; fugitive from justice; convicted of a controlled substance offense; convicted of driving under the influence of alcohol or a controlled substance; adjudicated as an incompetent or involuntarily committed to a mental institution; illegally or unlawfully in the United States; subject to an active protection from abuse order; adjudicated delinquent; prohibited from possessing or acquiring a firearm under federal law	Prohibited on school property; exception for lawful supervised school activity or course. Prohibited in court facility; exception for law enforcement officials.	Concealed carry allowed with permit. Open carry generally allowed without permit, but permit needed to open carry in Philadelphia or in vehicle
RHODE ISLAND	11-47-1 to 11-47-63	Sawed-off shotgun or rifle; machine gun; silencer; armor piercing bullets; defaced firearm	7 days	Illegal alien; adjudicated mentally incompetent and under treatment or confinement; habitual drunkard or drug addict adjudicated or in treatment; convicted of crime of violence; fugitive from justice; minor under 18, except for hunting or permit for rifle range or camp training and under adult supervision, ROTC, target shooting, or parade activities	Prohibited on school grounds; exception for firearm instruction or safety courses, government-sponsored military-related programs such as ROTC, interscholastic shooting or marksmanship events, military history and firearms collection courses or programs, and the use of blank guns in theatrical or athletic events; prohibition does not apply to colleges or universities	Concealed or open carry allowed with permit.

Table 10: Gun Control—Continued

State	Code Section	Illegal Arms	Waiting Period	Who May Not Possess	Possession in Public Areas	Concealed or Open Carry Permitted?
SOUTH CAROLINA	16-23-10 to 16-23-530; 23-31-215	Machine gun; sawed-off shotgun/rifle, military firearm; teflon-coated ammunition; defaced firearm; tear-gas gun	None	Any person convicted of crime of violence; member of subversive organization; under 18 with military exception; adjudicated to be unfit to possess firearm; fugitive from justice; habitual drunkard or drug addict; mentally incompetent	Prohibited on school property; does not apply to guard; law enforcement officer; member of armed forces; student of military science.	Concealed carry allowed with permit. Open carry prohibited; exceptions for law enforcement officers, members of the military, licensed hunters, a person in the business of manufacturing or dealing in firearms, on personal property
SOUTH DAKOTA	13-32-7; 22-1-2; 22-14-5 to 22-14-28; 23-7-1 to 23-7-51	Silencer; machine gun; short shotgun; altered manufacturer's serial number	None	Any person convicted of a crime of violence; convicted of a controlled substances felony; convicted of any misdemeanor crime involving an act of domestic violence within one year	Prohibited in county courthouse; elementary or secondary school premises; exception for law enforcement officers	Concealed carry allowed with permit. Open carry generally permitted

Table 10: Gun Control—Continued

State	Code Section	Illegal Arms	Waiting Period	Who May Not Possess	Possession in Public Areas	Concealed or Open Carry Permitted?
TENNESSEE	39-17-1301 to 39-17-1364	Machine gun; short-barreled rifle or shotgun; silencer; explosive weapon; device designed, made or adapted for delivering or shooting an explosive weapon; hoax device	None	Any person convicted of a felony involving the use or attempted use of force, violence or a deadly weapon; convicted of a felony drug offense; convicted of a misdemeanor crime of domestic violence; subject to an order of protection; prohibited from possessing a firearm under federal law	Prohibited in any public or private school building; school bus; school grounds; public recreational areas; exception for law enforcement officers; pupils enrolled in a course requiring carrying of firearms. Prohibited in an establishment for consumption of liquor if under the influence of alcohol or a controlled substance	Concealed or open carry allowed with permit.
TEXAS	Penal Code §§ 46.01 to 46.15; Gov't Code § 411.172	Machine gun; short-barreled firearm; silencer; armor-piercing ammunition; zip gun; explosive weapon	None	Convicted felon within 5 yrs. of release or parole; sale, rental, lease, or gift to minor under 18 without parental consent; confined in penal institution	Prohibited on school premises; premises of a polling place on the day of an election or while early voting is in progress; premises of any government court, unless pursuant to written authorization of the court; premises of a racetrack; secured area of an airport; within 1000 feet of designated place of execution on a day that a sentence of death is to be imposed	Concealed or open carry allowed with permit

Table 10: Gun Control—Continued

State	Code Section	Illegal Arms	Waiting Period	Who May Not Possess	Possession in Public Areas	Concealed or Open Carry Permitted?
UTAH	53-5-701 to 53-5-712; 76-10-500 to 76-10-532	Defaced pistol or revolver	None	Any person convicted of a violent felony; on probation or parole for a felony; on parole from a juvenile detention center; within the last 7 years adjudicated delinquent for an offense which if committed by an adult would have been a violent felony; illegally or unlawfully in the United States; on probation for a conviction for possessing a controlled substance; an unlawful user of a controlled substance; found not guilty by reason of insanity for a felony offense; found mentally incompetent to stand trial for a felony offense; adjudicated as mentally defective or committed to a mental institution; renounced citizenship	Prohibited on a public street; in a posted prohibited area; airport secure areas; house of worship or private residence after notice has been given; exception for shooting competitions and hunting; law enforcement officials. Prohibited on or about school premises; exception with approvable by school administrator; in connection with approved activity	Concealed carry allowed with permit. Open carry generally permitted
VERMONT	Tit. 13, §§ 4001 to 4016	Silencer; "zip" gun; slung shot; drone equipped with a dangerous or deadly weapon	None	Any person convicted of a violent crime	Prohibited in a school bus; in school building or on school property; in a courthouse	Concealed or open carry allowed without permit

Table 10: Gun Control—Continued

State	Code Section	Illegal Arms	Waiting Period	Who May Not Possess	Possession in Public Areas	Concealed or Open Carry Permitted?
VIRGINIA	18.2-279 to 18.2-311.2	Sawed-off shotgun/rifle; machine gun if for "offensive or aggressive" purpose; silencer	None	Any person convicted of a felony; adjudicated delinquent at the age of 14 or older of murder, kidnapping, robbery, or rape; any person under the age of 29 adjudicated delinquent of an offense which would be a felony if committed by an adult; not a citizen of the United States; not lawfully admitted for permanent residence; acquitted by reason of insanity; adjudicated legally incompetent or mentally incapacitated; involuntarily admitted or ordered to outpatient treatment; subject to a protective order; convicted of a drug offense	Prohibited on school property; place of religious worship; in courthouse; airport terminal. Semi-automatic weapons and shotguns prohibited on public street; public park; any other place open to the public in the cities of Alexandria, Chesapeake, Fairfax, Falls Church, Newport News, Norfolk, Richmond, or Virginia Beach, or in the counties of Arlington, Fairfax, Henrico, Loudon, or Prince William; exception for law enforcement officers	Concealed carry allowed with permit. Open carry generally allowed with permit; firearm in vehicle must be secured in a container or compartment within vehicle

Table 10: Gun Control—Continued

State	Code Section	Illegal Arms	Waiting Period	Who May Not Possess	Possession in Public Areas	Concealed or Open Carry Permitted?
WASHINGTON	9.41.010 to 9.41.810	Machine gun, short-barreled shotgun or rifle; defaced firearm	None, but law allows 5 days to complete background check	Aliens unless legal permanent resident or "alien firearms license"; convicted of serious offense; convicted or found not guilty by reason of insanity of any felony other than a "serious offense" or certain crimes committed against a member of family or household; under 18, except as provided (hunter's safety course, hunting, trapping, etc.); committed by court to institution for treatment of mental illness; free on bond for a serious offense	Prohibited on school premises; exception for student or employee of private military academy on academy property; law enforcement officers; firearms or air gun competition; firearms secured within a vehicle; firearms safety course. Prohibited in a jail; courthouse; public mental health facility; secure area of airport; exception for law enforcement officers	Concealed carry allowed with permit. Open carry allowed to protect self or another against unlawful force; otherwise prohibited

Table 10: Gun Control—Continued

State	Code Section	Illegal Arms	Waiting Period	Who May Not Possess	Possession in Public Areas	Concealed or Open Carry Permitted?
WEST VIRGINIA	61-7-1 to 61-7-15	Machine gun; submachine gun or other fully automatic weapon	None	Any person convicted of a crime punishable by imprisonment for more than one year; habitually addicted to alcohol; unlawful user of controlled substance; adjudicated mentally incompetent or involuntarily committed to a mental institution; illegally or unlawfully in the United States; dishonorably discharged from the armed forces; subject to a domestic violence protective order; convicted of a misdemeanor offense of assault or battery; convicted of a felony crime of violence; convicted of a felony controlled substance offense	Prohibited on school premises; exception for law enforcement officers; unloaded firearm in motor vehicle; specifically authorized by the school principal; authorized programs or raffles which include the display of unloaded firearms; the official mascots of West Virginia University (the Mountaineer) or Parkersburg South High School (the Patriot) acting in his or her official capacity	Concealed carry allowed with permit. Open carry generally permitted
WISCONSIN	175.35; 941.20 to 941.298; 948.605	Machine gun or other fully-automatic weapon; short-barreled rifle/ shotgun; silencer	48 hrs.; extended to 3 working days if history of felony charge	Any person convicted of a felony; adjudicated delinquent that if committed by an adult would be a felony; found not guilty of a felony by reason of mental disease or defect; committed for treatment and subject to an order not to possess a firearm; subject to an injunction; subject to an order not to possess a firearm	Prohibited in any building owned or leased by the state or a political subdivision; gun-free school zones; exception for law enforcement officials	Concealed carry allowed with permit. Open carry generally allowed

Table 10: Gun Control—Continued

State	Code Section	Illegal Arms	Waiting Period	Who May Not Possess	Possession in Public Areas	Concealed or Open Carry Permitted?
WYOMING	6-8-101 to 6-8-406; 21-4-305; 23-3-112;	Fully-automatic weapon in state game fields or forests	None	Convicted of any felony, in any state; adjudicated mentally incompetent; committed to mental institution	Prohibited in law enforcement facilities; prison or jail; courtroom (except judge); meeting of governmental entity or legislature; school, college, or professional athletic event not related to firearms; establishment licensed to dispense alcohol for consumption on the premises; place of worship; school facility; where prohibited by federal law	Concealed carry allowed with permit, but no permit necessary if person meets requirements for permit. Open carry generally permitted

11. HELMET AND SELECTED SAFETY LAWS FOR MOTORCYCLISTS AND BICYCLISTS

Statistics demonstrate that the most serious injuries to motorcycle or bicycle riders are head injuries, and that the use of helmets and other safety gear can prevent many serious injuries. With increasing frequency, states have created statutes to improve the safety of vehicle operators, passengers, and the public. This is true concerning smaller vehicles like motorcycles and bicycles, which are increasing in popularity and importance, as they are generally more environmentally friendly and less expensive than bulkier options.

Like many legal compromises, motorcycle and bicycle safety laws require a balance between individual liberties and regulated precautions. In this realm, however, the compromises that states have considered appropriate are far from uniform. Indeed, state laws on such issues are diverse and inconsistent. Consequently, anyone involved with or interested in these vehicles should have knowledge of at least the laws of the state in which he or she resides. Because of this, a state-by-state comparison is desirable for guidance.

The history of motorcycle helmet laws in particular has been quite dramatic. To increase helmet use, in 1967 the federal government forced states to enact helmet laws by conditioning certain federal funding on their enactment. In the face of losing such large benefits, states toed the line, and almost every state enacted a helmet law covering all riders by the early 1970s. Not long thereafter, however, states' lobbying efforts convinced the federal legislature to abandon financial penalties if states refused to comply. Thus, by 1980 most states totally repealed their helmet laws or severely narrowed them by restricting only young riders. Since then, enjoying complete individual freedom, states have chosen many options, ranging from the three states that have no helmet law at all to the twenty-six whose helmet law covers all riders. The remaining states do something in between, generally requiring helmets for younger riders (and some for those with instructional permits). A few statutes even consider proof of medical insurance and/or completing safety courses. Eye protection, generally through glasses, visors, and/or windshields, is another common safety requirement placed on motorcyclists by statute, being utilized by about two-thirds of states.

Regarding bicycle helmets, no state has a universal restriction, most likely due to the limited speeds as compared to motorcycles. In fact, the majority of states have no bicycle helmet law at all. Nevertheless, almost half of the states have laws that require younger riders to wear helmets, ranging from eleven and younger to seventeen and younger. Two states even restrict children less than one year old from being a passenger on a bicycle.

Perhaps not surprisingly, in recent decades states have enacted laws requiring certain lights, reflectors, and/or reflective gear to be used by bicyclists at night. All states require front lamps and rear lamps or reflectors. In addition, about one-third require reflective material on the bicycle's sides. Six even require pedal reflectors, though most of these allow other reflective gear, such as ankle bands, to substitute. Increasing technological advances, especially in batteries and lamps, have made requiring bicycle visibility equipment more practical.

In addition to motorcycle- and bicycle-related state statutory requirements, it is also important to remember that many localities have ordinances that call for different or greater safety precautions than those required by state law, though oftentimes state law trumps local law or local law cannot be considered valid if it is inconsistent with state law.

Table 11: Helmet and Selected Safety Laws for Motorcyclists and Bicyclists

State	Code Section	Motorcycle Helmet Required	Motorcycle Vision Protection Required	Bicycle Helmet Required	Bicycle Helmet Required
ALABAMA	32-5A-245 motorcycle helmet; 32-5A-283 bicycle helmet; 32-5A-265 bicycle visibility	All operators and passengers		15 and younger	Equipped at night with a white front lamp, visible for 500 feet, and a red rear reflector, visible from 100 to 600 ft.
ALASKA	28.35.245 motorcycle helmet; Admin. Code Tit. 13, § 04.350 motorcycle vision protection; Admin. Code Tit. 13, §§ 04.320; 04.335 bicycle visibility	Operators 17 and younger and those with instructional permits; passengers of all ages	Eye protection device, windscreen, or windshield		Between ½ hour after sunset and ½ hour before sunrise and when conditions render persons or vehicles not clearly discernible at 1,000 ft., equipped with a white front lamp, visible for 500 ft., a red rear reflector, and reflective material visible from both sides of the bicycle
ARIZONA	28-964 motorcycle helmet/vision protection; 28-817 bicycle visibility	Operators and passengers 17 and younger	Protective glasses, goggles, a transparent face shield, or a windshield		Equipped at night with a white front lamp, visible for 500 ft., and a red rear reflector, visible from 50 to 300 ft.
ARKANSAS	27-20-104 motorcycle helmet/vision protection; 27-36-204; 27-36-220 bicycle visibility	Operators and passenger 20 and younger	Protective glasses, goggles, or a transparent face shield		Every bicycle shall be equipped with a white lamp on front visible for 500 ft. and red lamp visible for 500 ft. or reflector visible at night for 350 ft. on the rear

Table 11: Helmet and Selected Safety Laws for Motorcyclists and Bicyclists—Continued

State	Code Section	Motorcycle Helmet Required	Motorcycle Vision Protection Required	Bicycle Helmet Required	Bicycle Helmet Required
CALIFORNIA	Veh. § 27803 motorcycle helmet; Veh. § 21212 bicycle helmet; Veh. § 21201 bicycle visibility	All operators and passengers		17 and younger	Equipped during darkness with a white front lamp or lamp on the bicyclist visible for 300 ft. from the front and sides, a red rear reflector or solid or flashing red light with built-in reflector visible for 500 ft., a white or yellow reflector on each pedal, visible from the front and rear for 200 ft., and either reflectorized tires or white or yellow side reflectors on the forward sides and white or red side reflectors on the rear sides
COLORADO	42-4-232 motorcycle vision protection; 42-4-221 bicycle visibility		Goggles or eyeglasses with lenses made of safety glass or plastic or helmet containing eye protection made of safety glass or plastic	Under 18	Between sunset and sunrise and when conditions render persons and vehicles not clearly discernible at 1,000 ft., equipped with a white front lamp visible for 500 feet, a red rear reflector visible for 600 ft., and either reflective material visible from both sides for 600 ft., or a lamp visible for 500 ft.
CONNECTICUT	14-289g motorcycle helmet; 14-289d motorcycle vision protection; 14-286d bicycle helmet; 14-288 bicycle visibility	Operators and passengers 17 and younger	A vision-protecting device, including but not limited to goggles, glasses, face shields, windshields and wind screens	15 and younger	Between ½ hour after sunset and ½ hour before sunrise, where there is precipitation, and when conditions render persons and vehicles not clearly discernible at 500 ft., equipped with a white front lamp visible for 500 ft., a rear reflector visible for 600 ft. and reflective material visible from both sides for 600 ft.

Table 11: Helmet and Selected Safety Laws for Motorcyclists and Bicyclists—Continued

State	Code Section	Motorcycle Helmet Required	Motorcycle Vision Protection Required	Bicycle Helmet Required	Bicycle Helmet Required
DELAWARE	Tit. 21, § 4185(b) motorcycle helmet/vision protection; Tit. 21, § 4198K bicycle helmet; Tit. 21, § 4198F bicycle visibility	All operators and passengers must have a helmet in his or her possession; operators and passengers 18 and younger must wear one	Eye protection approved by the Secretary of Safety and Homeland Security	17 and younger	Equipped at night with a white front lamp, visible for 500 ft., a red rear reflector visible for 600 ft., and either reflective material visible from both sides for 600 ft. or a lamp visible from both sides for 500 ft.
DISTRICT OF COLUMBIA	D.C. Mun. Regs. Tit. 18, § 2215 motorcycle helmet/vision protection; 50-1605 bicycle helmet; D.C. Mun. Regs. Tit. 18, § 1204 bicycle visibility	All operators and passengers	Wind screen, windshield, goggles, face shield, or spectacles with safety glass lenses	16 and younger	Equipped at night with a steady or flashing white front lamp or lamp on the bicyclist's arm or leg visible at 500 ft., and either a red rear reflector visible from 50 to 300 ft. or a steady or flashing red rear lamp visible for 500 ft.
FLORIDA	316.211 motorcycle helmet/vision protection; 316.2065 bicycle helmet/bicycle visibility	All operators and passengers, except any person over 21 who can show proof of a medical insurance policy with at least $10,000 in medical benefits	Eye protection device approved by the U.S. Dept. of Transportation	15 and younger	Equipped between sunset and sunrise with a white front lamp visible for 500 ft. and a red rear lamp and a red rear reflector, each visible for 600 ft.
GEORGIA	40-6-315 motorcycle helmet/vision protection; 40-6-296 bicycle helmet/visibility	All operators and passengers	Windshield or eye protection device of a type approved by the Commissioner of Public Safety	15 and younger when riding on a highway, sidewalk, or path under the jurisdiction of the state	Equipped at night with a white front lamp visible for 300 ft., and a red rear reflector visible for 300 ft.

Table 11: Helmet and Selected Safety Laws for Motorcyclists and Bicyclists—Continued

State	Code Section	Motorcycle Helmet Required	Motorcycle Vision Protection Required	Bicycle Helmet Required	Bicycle Helmet Required
HAWAII	286-81 motorcycle helmet/vision protection; 291C-150 bicycle helmet; 291C-147 bicycle visibility	Operators and passengers 17 and younger	Windscreen, windshield, safety glasses, goggles, or a face shield	15 and younger	Between ½ hour after sunset and ½ hour before sunrise, equipped with a white front lamp or lamp on the bicyclist's left arm or leg visible for 500 ft., a rear red reflector visible for 600 ft. and either reflective material, visible from both sides for 600 ft., or a lamp visible from both sides for 500 ft.
IDAHO	49-666 motorcycle helmet; 49-723 bicycle visibility	Operators and passengers 17 and younger			Between sunset and sunrise and when there is not sufficient light to render clearly discernible persons and vehicles at 500 ft., equipped with a front lamp or lamp on the operator visible for 500 ft., and a clearly visible rear reflector
ILLINOIS	625 § 5/11-1404 motorcycle vision protection; 625 § 5/11-1507 bicycle visibility		Glasses, goggles, or a transparent shield		Equipped at night with a white front lamp visible for 500 ft. and a red rear reflector visible from 100 to 600 ft.; a red rear lamp visible for 500 ft. may be used in addition to reflector
INDIANA	9-19-7-1 motorcycle helmet; 9-21-11-9 bicycle visibility	Operators and passengers 17 and younger	Glasses, goggles, or a transparent shield to be worn by operators and passengers 17 and younger		Between ½ hour after sunset and ½ hour before sunrise, equipped with a white front lamp, visible for 500 ft., and either a red rear lamp or a red rear reflector visible for 500 ft.

Table 11: Helmet and Selected Safety Laws for Motorcyclists and Bicyclists—Continued

State	Code Section	Motorcycle Helmet Required	Motorcycle Vision Protection Required	Bicycle Helmet Required	Bicycle Helmet Required
IOWA	321.397 bicycle visibility				Between sunset and sunrise and when conditions render persons and vehicles not clearly discernible at 500 ft., equipped with a white front lamp visible for 300 ft. and either a red rear lamp or a red rear reflector visible for 300 ft.
KANSAS	8-1598 motorcycle helmet/vision protection; 8-1592 bicycle visibility	Operators and passengers 17 and younger	Windscreen with a minimum height of 10 ins. measured above the center of the handlebars, or an eye-protective device consisting of protective glasses, goggles, or a transparent face shield which is shatter proof and impact resistant		Equipped at night with white front lamp visible for 500 ft. and a red rear reflector visible from 100 to 600 ft.
KENTUCKY	189.285 motorcycle helmet/vision protection; 601 Ky. Admin. Regs. 14:020 bicycle visibility	Operators and passengers 20 and younger; operators who have held a valid motorcycle license for less than 1 yr.	Eye-protective device		Equipped with a red rear reflector visible for 100 ft.; between ½ hr. after sunset and ½ hr. before sunrise and when conditions render visibility equally as low, equipped with a front lamp which clearly reveals substantial objects at least 50 ft. ahead and which is visible for 500 ft., and with a red light or flashing red light, visible for 500 ft.
LOUISIANA	32:190 motorcycle helmet/vision protection; 32:199 bicycle helmet; 32:329 bicycle visibility	All operators and passengers	All helmets must have a visor	11 and younger	Equipped at night with a white front lamp visible for 500 ft. and a red rear reflector and two side reflectors visible from 100 to 600 ft.

Table 11: Helmet and Selected Safety Laws for Motorcyclists and Bicyclists—Continued

State	Code Section	Motorcycle Helmet Required	Motorcycle Vision Protection Required	Bicycle Helmet Required	Bicycle Helmet Required
MAINE	Tit. 29, § 2083; Tit. 29, § 2323 bicycle helmet/visibility	Operators with a learner's permit or within one year of successfully completing a driving test, as well as their passengers; passengers 17 and younger		15 and younger	Equipped at night with a white front lamp visible for 200 ft., a red or amber rear reflector visible for 200 ft. and reflector material on the pedals unless the bicyclist wears reflective material on the feet or ankles
MARYLAND	Transp. § 21-1306 motorcycle helmet/vision protection; Transp. § 21-1207.1 bicycle helmet/visibility	All operators and passengers	Windscreen or eye-protective device	15 and younger on public property	When conditions render persons and vehicles not clearly discernible at 1,000 ft., equipped with a white front lamp visible for 500 ft. and either a red rear reflector visible from 100 to 600 ft. or a rear red or flashing amber lamp visible for 500 ft.
MASSACHUSETTS	Ch. 90, § 7 motorcycle helmet/vision protection; Ch. 85, § 11B bicycle helmet/visibility	All operators and passengers	Windshield, windscreen, eye glasses, goggles, or a protective face shield	16 and younger; may not transport children less than 1 yr. old	Between ½ hour after sunset and ½ before sunrise, equipped with a white front lamp visible for 500 ft. either a red rear lamp or red rear reflector visible for 600 ft. reflectors either on each pedal or around each ankle visible for 600 ft. and reflectors or reflective material on the bicycle sides or the bicyclist's sides visible for 600 ft.; allows generator-powered lamps which emit light only when the bicycle is moving

Table 11: Helmet and Selected Safety Laws for Motorcyclists and Bicyclists—Continued

State	Code Section	Motorcycle Helmet Required	Motorcycle Vision Protection Required	Bicycle Helmet Required	Bicycle Helmet Required
MICHIGAN	257.658 motorcycle helmet; 257.662 bicycle visibility	All operators and passengers 20 and under; all operators 21 and over unless such operator has had a motorcycle endorsement or driver's license for 2 or more yrs. or has passed approved motorcycle safety course and carries insurance with $20,000 or more in medical benefits. All passengers 21 and over unless they or the operator have insurance that will provide the passenger with $20,000 or more in medical benefits			Between ½ hour after sunset and ½ hour before sunrise, equipped with a white front lamp visible for 500 ft. and a rear red reflector visible from 100 to 600 ft.
MINNESOTA	169.974 motorcycle helmet/vision protection; 169.222 bicycle visibility	Operators and passengers 17 and younger; operators during a 1 yr. instructional permit	Eye-protective device		Equipped at night with a white front lamp visible for 500 ft. red rear reflector visible from 100 to 600 ft.; when there is not sufficient light to render persons and vehicles on the highway clearly discernible at 500 ft., equipped with reflective surfaces on each side of each pedal visible for 600 ft.
MISSISSIPPI	63-7-64 motorcycle helmet; 63-7-11; 63-7-13 bicycle visibility	All operators and passengers			Between sunset and sunrise and when there is not sufficient light to clearly discern persons at 500 feet, equipped with a white front lamp visible for 500 ft. and either a rear reflex mirror reflector or a rear red lamp visible for 500 ft.

Table 11: Helmet and Selected Safety Laws for Motorcyclists and Bicyclists—Continued

State	Code Section	Motorcycle Helmet Required	Motorcycle Vision Protection Required	Bicycle Helmet Required	Bicycle Helmet Required
MISSOURI	302.020 motorcycle helmet; 307.185 bicycle visibility	All operators and passengers			Between ½ hour after sunset and ½ hour before sunrise, equipped with a white front lamp visible for 500 ft. either a red rear reflector or a red rear lamp visible for 600 ft., reflective material and/or lights on any part of the bicyclist's pedals, crank arms, shoes or lower leg, visible at 200 ft. and reflective material and/or lights on each side of the bicycle or bicyclist, visible at 300 ft.
MONTANA	61-9-417 motorcycle helmet; 61-8-607 bicycle visibility	Operators and passengers 17 and younger			Equipped at night with a white front lamp visible for 500 ft., a colorless front reflector, colorless or amber pedal reflectors, a red rear reflector, and either tires with retroflective sidewalls or tires with reflectors mounted on wheel spokes; colorless or amber on the front and amber or red on the rear; additionally, red rear reflector visible for 500 ft. may be used
NEBRASKA	60-6.279 motorcycle helmet; 60-6.318 bicycle visibility	All operators and passengers			Equipped at night with a front lamp visible for 500 ft., and a red rear reflector, visible from 100 to 600 ft.
NEVADA	486.231 motorcycle helmet/vision protection; 484B.783 bicycle visibility	All operators and passengers	All operators and passengers: windscreen, protective glasses, goggles, or face shields		Equipped at night with a white front lamp visible for 500 ft., a red rear reflector visible from 50 to 300 ft. and either side reflective material visible for 600 ft., or side lamps visible for 500 ft.

Table 11: Helmet and Selected Safety Laws for Motorcyclists and Bicyclists—Continued

State	Code Section	Motorcycle Helmet Required	Motorcycle Vision Protection Required	Bicycle Helmet Required	Bicycle Helmet Required
NEW HAMPSHIRE	265:123 motorcycle vision protection; 265:144 bicycle helmet; 266:86 to 266:87 bicycle visibility	All operators and passengers 17 and under	Windshield or screen which protects the operator's eyes and face when sitting erect, or eyeglasses, goggles, or a protective face shield	15 and younger	Equipped during darkness with a white front lamp, visible for 300 ft., a red rear reflector visible for 300 ft.; and either pedal clips or reflectorized leg bands/equipment on the lower exterior of the bicyclist's legs or shoes
NEW JERSEY	39:3-76.7 motorcycle helmet; 39:4-10.1 bicycle helmet; 39:4-10 bicycle visibility	All operators and passengers; helmets must be reflectorized on both sides	Goggles or face shield to be worn by operator	16 and younger	Equipped at night with a white front lamp visible for 500 ft., and a red rear lamp visible for 500 ft.
NEW MEXICO	66-7-356 motorcycle helmet; 66-7-355 motorcycle vision protection; 66-3-707 bicycle visibility	Operators and passengers 17 and younger	Windshield or protective device which may be a faceshield attached to a safety helmet, goggles, or safety eyeglasses		Equipped at night with a white front lamp visible for 500 ft., a red rear reflector visible from 50 to 300 ft., a read rear lamp visible for 500 ft. may be used in addition to reflector
NEW YORK	Veh. & Traf. § 381 motorcycle helmet/ vision protection; Veh. & Traf. § 1238 bicycle helmet; Veh. & Traf. § 1236 bicycle visibility	All operators and passengers	Goggles or a face shield	13 and younger; may not transport children less than 1 yr. old	Between ½ hour after sunset and ½ hour before sunrise, equipped with a white front lamp visible for 500 ft., and red rear light visible for 300 ft., one of which must be visible for 200 ft. to each side
NORTH CAROLINA	20-140.4 motorcycle helmet; 20-171.9 bicycle helmet; 20-129 bicycle visibility	All operators and passengers		15 and younger	Equipped at night with a front lamp visible for 300 ft., and either a rear reflex mirror or a red rear lamp visible for 200 ft.
NORTH DAKOTA	39-10.2-06 motorcycle helmet; 39-10.1-07 bicycle visibility	Operators 17 and younger, as well as all passengers, regardless of age			Equipped at night with a white front lamp visible for 500 ft. and an approved red rear reflector

Table 11: Helmet and Selected Safety Laws for Motorcyclists and Bicyclists—Continued

State	Code Section	Motorcycle Helmet Required	Motorcycle Vision Protection Required	Bicycle Helmet Required	Bicycle Helmet Required
OHIO	4511.53 motorcycle helmet/vision protection; 4511.56 bicycle visibility	Operators and passengers 17 and younger, as well as their passengers; operators during their first year of licensure, as well as their passengers	Safety glasses or other protective eye device		Between sunset and sunrise and when conditions cannot render discernible persons, vehicles, and substantial objects at 1,000 ft., equipped with a white front lamp, visible for 500 ft. to the front and 300 ft. to the sides (allows a generator-powered lamp that emits light only when the bicycle is moving), a red rear reflector, visible from 100 to 600 ft., a red rear lamp (flashing or steady) visible for 500 ft., which may substitute for the red rear reflector if the red rear lamp is visible from 100 to 600 ft.; disallows additional red lamps and red reflectors on the front of the bicycle and white lamps and white reflectors on the rear
OKLAHOMA	Tit. 47, § 12-609 motorcycle helmet/ vision protection; Tit. 47, §§ 12-702– 706 bicycle visibility	Operators and passengers 17 and younger	Windshield, goggles, or other protective eyewear		Equipped with a red rear reflector visible for 600 ft. and a lamp, visible from both sides for 1,000 ft.; between ½ after sunset and ½ before sunrise and when conditions render persons and vehicles not clearly discernible at 1,000 ft., equipped with a white front lamp visible for 1,000 ft., a red rear lamp visible for 1,000 ft., and reflective material visible from both sides for 600 ft.

Table 11: Helmet and Selected Safety Laws for Motorcyclists and Bicyclists—Continued

State	Code Section	Motorcycle Helmet Required	Motorcycle Vision Protection Required	Bicycle Helmet Required	Bicycle Helmet Required
OREGON	814.269 motorcycle helmet; 814.486 bicycle helmet; 815.280 bicycle visibility	All operators and passengers		15 and younger	Equipped during limited visibility conditions with a white front lamp visible for 500 ft. and either a red rear reflector or red rear lamp visible for 600 ft.
PENNSYLVANIA	Tit. 75, § 3525 motorcycle helmet/vision protection; Tit. 75, § 3510 bicycle helmet; Tit. 75, § 3507 bicycle visibility	Operators and passengers 20 and younger; operators during their first two yrs. of licensure unless they have completed a safety course approved by the department or the Motorcycle Safety Foundation	Approved eye-protective device	11 and younger	Equipped between sunset and sunrise with a white front lamp or lamp on the bicyclist visible for 500 ft., a red rear reflector visible for 500 ft. and an amber reflector on each side
RHODE ISLAND	31-10.1-4; 31-10.1-6 motorcycle helmet/vision protection; 31-19-2.1 bicycle helmet; R.I. Gen. Laws § 31-19-10 (bicycle visibility)	Operators 20 and younger and those during their first year of licensure; all passengers	Eye protection approved by administrator of Dept. of Vehicles	15 and younger	Equipped at night with a white front lamp visible for 500 ft. and a red rear reflector visible for 600 ft.
SOUTH CAROLINA	56-5-3660 motorcycle helmet; 56-5-3670; 56-5-3680 motorcycle vision protection; 56-5-3470 bicycle visibility	Operators and passengers 20 and younger; helmets must be reflectorized on both sides	Operators 20 and younger must use a windscreen, goggles or a face shield		Equipped at night with a white front lamp visible for 500 ft. and a red rear reflector visible from 50 to 300 ft.; red rear lamp visible for 500 ft. may be used in addition to reflector
SOUTH DAKOTA	32-20-4 motorcycle helmet; 32-20-4.1 motorcycle vision protection; 32-17-4; 32-17-25 bicycle visibility	Operators and passengers 17 and younger	Windscreen or eye protection device		Between ½ after sunset and ½ before sunrise and when conditions render persons and vehicles not clearly discernible at 200 ft., equipped with a front lamp visible for 300 ft. and either a red or yellow rear reflex mirror or a red or yellow rear lamp visible for 200 ft.

Table 11: Helmet and Selected Safety Laws for Motorcyclists and Bicyclists—Continued

State	Code Section	Motorcycle Helmet Required	Motorcycle Vision Protection Required	Bicycle Helmet Required	Bicycle Helmet Required
TENNESSEE	55-9-302 motorcycle helmet; 55-9-304 motorcycle vision protection; 55-52-105 bicycle helmet; 55-8-177 bicycle visibility	All operators and passengers	Windshield, safety goggles, face shield, or glasses containing impact resistant lenses	15 and younger	Equipped at night with a white front lamp visible for 500 ft. and a red rear reflector or lamp visible for 500 ft.
TEXAS	Transp. § 661.003 motorcycle helmet; Transp. § 551.104 bicycle visibility	All operators and passengers, unless they are at least 21 and can either show proof of successfully completing a motorcycle operator training and safety course or show proof of a medical insurance policy with benefits for injuries incurred as the result of riding on or operating a motorcycle			Equipped at night with a white front lamp visible for 500 ft. and either a red rear reflector visible from 50 to 300 ft. or a red rear lamp visible for 500 ft.
UTAH	41-6a-1505 motorcycle helmet; 41-6a-1114 bicycle visibility	Operators and passengers 17 and younger			Between ½ hour after sunset and ½ hour before sunrise and when conditions render persons and vehicles not clearly discernible at 1,000 ft., equipped with a white front lamp visible for 500 ft., either a red rear reflector visible for 500 ft. or a red bicycle taillight emitting a flashing or non-flashing light visible for 500 ft. and either reflective material visible from both sides for 500 ft. or a lamp, visible from both side for 500 ft.

Table 11: Helmet and Selected Safety Laws for Motorcyclists and Bicyclists—Continued

State	Code Section	Motorcycle Helmet Required	Motorcycle Vision Protection Required	Bicycle Helmet Required	Bicycle Helmet Required
VERMONT	Tit. 23, § 1256 motorcycle helmet; Tit. 23, § 1257 motorcycle vision protection; Tit. 23, § 1141 bicycle visibility	All operators and passengers; helmets must be reflectorized in part	Windshield, windscreen, eye glasses, goggles, or protective face shield that has colorless lenses during insufficient lighting or unfavorable atmospheric conditions		Equipped 1/2 hr. after sunset to 1/2 hr. before sunrise with a white front lamp visible for 500 ft. and a red rear reflector and/or flashing or steady red lamp visible for 300 ft.; lamps may be worn on operator's person
VIRGINIA	46.2-910 motorcycle helmet/vision protection; 46.2-1015 bicycle visibility	All operators and passengers	Windshield, face shield, safety glasses, or goggles		Equipped between sunrise and sunset with a white front lamp visible for 500 ft., a red rear reflector visible for 600 ft., and a red rear lamp visible for 500 ft.
WASHINGTON	46.37.530 motorcycle helmet/ vision protection; 46.37.020 bicycle visibility	All operators and passengers; may not transport children 4 and younger	Windshield, glasses, goggles, or face shield		Between ½ after sunset and ½ hour before sunrise and when conditions render persons and vehicles not clearly discernible at 1,000 ft., equipped with a white front light visible for 500 ft. and a red rear reflector visible for 600 ft.
WEST VIRGINIA	17C-15-44 motorcycle helmet/ vision protection; 17C-11A-4 bicycle helmet; 17C-11-7 bicycle visibility	All operators and passengers	Face shield, goggles, or safety, shatter-resistant eyeglasses	14 and younger	Equipped at night with a white front lamp visible for 500 ft. and a red rear reflector, visible from 50 to 300 ft.
WISCONSIN	347.485 motorcycle helmet/vision protection; 347.489 bicycle visibility	Operators and passengers 17 and younger; operators with an instructional permit	Windshield, protective face shield attached to the headgear, glasses, goggles		Equipped during darkness with a white front lamp visible for 500 ft. and a red rear reflector with at least 2 in. of surface area and visible from 50 to 500 ft. or a steady or flashing red rear lamp visible for 500 ft.

Table 11: Helmet and Selected Safety Laws for Motorcyclists and Bicyclists—Continued

State	Code Section	Motorcycle Helmet Required	Motorcycle Vision Protection Required	Bicycle Helmet Required	Bicycle Helmet Required
WYOMING	31-5-115 motorcycle helmet; 31-5-706 bicycle visibility	All minor operators and passengers 17 and younger			Equipped at night with a white front lamp visible for 500 ft. and a red rear reflector visible for 600 ft.; a red rear lamp visible for 500 ft. may be used in addition to the reflector

12. ILLEGAL DRUGS

Even though the laws regarding marijuana possession and use have take a sharp turn toward acceptance and even legalization nationwide, the laws surrounding heroine and cocaine remain very tough. In fact, the sixth (2008) edition of this book included marijuana in this chapter on "illegal drugs." The laws have changed so dramatically in the last seven years that it has earned it's own chapter!

Drug laws are among the most complex criminal laws on the books. Often certain offenses are given class designations whereby any number of specific criminal offenses are grouped into various classes and sentences prescribed according to mandated terms, called "sentencing guidelines." Sentencing guidelines set absolute minimum and maximum sentences for specific crimes and take much of the discretion for setting sentences away from judges. Sentencing guidelines have become very controversial lately as legislatures attempt to assert more control over punishments imposed on criminals. From year to year, punishments, it seems, vary often enough not to put them on the books.

One recent trend in drug legislation is the growing incorporation of special enhancements directed at selling to or from minors. Several states have recently amended these particular laws by incorporating mandatory sentencing to adults selling to minors. While such laws have been common, some of the new amendments are becoming more specific by including language such as that found in California. That state's new laws note particularly that enhancements attach when the seller is over 18 and the buyer is a minor 4 years younger. The intent of the legislation to protect minors from influence by corrupt adults is easy to see. The specific age and number of years difference between the parties is less clear.

In most cases in the following tables, reference to the code sections give a picture of the potential punishments for the violation of a specific crime. Since the class schedules among illegal drugs overlap and because the penalties are often extremely involved and difficult to summarize, reference is often made only to the class designation. In these cases, however, it is still possible to draw comparisons among states by studying the degrees assigned to the violation. In addition, quick reference to the individual state code listed should provide easy access to more detailed information.

Table 12a: Illegal Drugs: Cocaine

State	Code Section	Possession	Sale	Trafficking
ALABAMA	13A-5-9; 13A-12-210 to 13A-12-212; 13A-12-215; 13A-12-231(2); 13A-12-250; 13A-12-270; 20-2-1	Class D felony; 8-28g is evidence of possession with intent to distribute: class B felony	Class A felony; sale to minor: class A felony, no probation; sale within 3 mi. of school or public housing project: additional 5 yr. penalty; subsequent offense: offenses subject to the Habitual Felony Offender Act; unlawful distribution of controlled substance: class B felony	Sale and trafficking are the same; anything over 28g is considered trafficking; 28-500g: mandatory 3 yrs. and $50,000 fine; 500g to 1 kilo: min. 5 yrs. and $100,000 fine; 1-10 kilos: minimum 15 yrs. and $250,000 fine; over 10 kilos: mandatory life without parole
ALASKA	11.71.010 to 11.71.900	Possessing any amount: class C felony; within 500 ft. of school, youth center or on school bus: Class B felony	Delivering to one under 19 and at least 3 yrs. younger: unclassified felony; manufacture or delivery of 2.5g or more: Class B felony; manufacture or delivery of less than 2.5g: class C felony; repeat or habitual offender: harsher penalties	"Continuing criminal enterprise": unclassified felony
ARIZONA	13-3401; 13-3408 to 13-3422; Uniform Controlled Substances Act: 36-2501 to 36-2552	Class 4 felony, but for one not previously convicted of felony, court can make it Class 1 misdemeanor; Fine of not less than $2,000 or 3 times the value of substance, whichever is greater	Class 3 felony; Fine of greater of 3 times value of drugs or $2,000; Selling to minors: class 2 felony and fine of $2,000 or 3 times value, whatever is greater; in drug-free school zone: add 1 yr. to sentence and fine for selling to minors	Class 2 felony (transport/import); Class 2 felony (manufacture)
ARKANSAS	5-4-501; 5-64-402 to 5-64-423; 5-64-440 to 5-64-446	Less than 2g: class C felony; 2-10g: class B felony; 10-200g: class A felony; possession or 2-10g on or within 1,000 ft. of school, park, or public safe place: enhanced sentence of additional 10 yrs.; harsher penalties for repeat offenders—imprisonment 3 yrs. to life; violation by public official or law enforcement officer: enhanced penalties of imprisonment up to 10 yrs. and at least $10,000 fine	Class Y felony: depending on amount, imprisonment 10 to 40 yrs. or life and fines between $25,000 and $250,000; subsequent offense: double penalties; enhanced sentence of additional 10 yrs. within 1,000 ft. of school, park, or public place	A person engages in trafficking cocaine if he or she possesses, possesses with the purpose to deliver, delivers, or manufactures 200g or more

Table 12a: Illegal Drugs: Cocaine—Continued

State	Code Section	Possession	Sale	Trafficking
CALIFORNIA	Health & Safety §§ 11000 to 11356.5	State prison and fine up to $70; if probation granted, there are additional requirements	State prison 2-4 yrs.; Possession for sale of "cocaine base": state prison 3-5 yrs.; Sale to minors: state prison 3, 5, or 7 yrs.; Sale to day care, preschool, or school children: 5, 7, or 9 yrs.; Anyone over 18 who sells to a minor or uses a minor in the sale process is punishable in state prison for 3, 6, or 9 yrs.; Sale within 1,000 ft. of school: additional 3, 4, or 5 yrs.; If sale occurred upon the grounds of a child day care, school, church, synagogue, or youth center, punishment is automatically enhanced by one year; Anyone over 18 yrs. who sells to a minor at least 4 years younger as a full and separate enhancement shall be punished by imprisonment in state prison for 3, 4 or 5 yrs. Sale on many public areas punishable by state prison for 5, 7, or 9 yrs. if seller 5 yrs. older than minor	Transport/import 3-5 yrs.; County to noncontiguous county: 3, 6, or 9 yrs.
COLORADO	18-18-101 to 18-18-405	Level 4 felony; 2 or more prior convictions within 10 yrs.: up to triple penalties; 3 or more convictions within 10 yrs.: up to 4 times maximum penalty	Over 225g: level 1 felony; 14-225g: level 2 felony; 4-14g: level 3 felony; less than 4g: level 4 felony	
CONNECTICUT	21a-240; 21a-243; 21a-278; 21a-279	Any quantity: class A misdemeanor	1/2 ounce or more: 5 yrs. to life; sale to minor under 18 and at least 2 yrs. junior: additional mandatory 2 yrs.; possession with intent to sell or distribute within 1500 ft. of school or public safe place: additional mandatory 3 yrs.	

Table 12a: Illegal Drugs: Cocaine—Continued

State	Code Section	Possession	Sale	Trafficking
DELAWARE	Tit. 16, §§4701; 4751A to 4756; 4763	Class B felony: Over 25g; 20-25g with aggravating factor; 10-15g with 2 or more aggravating factors; class C felony: over 20g; 10-15g with aggravating factor; over 5g with 2 aggravating factors; class D felony: 15-20g; over 5g with 1 aggravating factor; class B misdemeanor: under 5g; class A misdemeanor: under 5g with aggravating factor Aggravating factors: Offense committed within protected school zone, park, recreational area, or place of worship or in a vehicle; crime involved person under age of 18, either as accomplice or intended recipient and defendant adult more than 4 yrs. older than minor; defendant attempted to prevent arrest or detention with use of force or violence or tried to flee in vehicle while officer attempted to arrest to detain defendant	Class B felony: manufacture, delivery, or possession with intent to deliver 20-25g; 10-15g with aggravating factor; class C felony: manufacture, delivery, or possession with intent to deliver 10-15g; any amount with aggravating factor; class D felony: manufacture, delivery, or possession with intent to deliver any amount	
DISTRICT OF COLUMBIA	48-901.02 to 48-906.03	Misdemeanor punishable by imprisonment up to 180 days and/or fine up to $1,000; subsequent offense: up to double penalties; if 1st drug conviction, judge may defer adjudication of guilt and sentence offender to probation up to 1 yr. after which charges will be dismissed and record sealed if probation requirements are satisfied	Sale, manufacture, distribute: imprisonment up to 30 yrs. and/or fine of at least $7,500; subsequent offense: up to double penalties; within drug-free zone or to minors: up to double penalties	

Table 12a: Illegal Drugs: Cocaine—Continued

State	Code Section	Possession	Sale	Trafficking
FLORIDA	775.082 to 775.084; 893.01 to 893.03; 893.13 to 893.135	3rd degree felony; possession of 28g is trafficking: 1st degree felony	2nd degree felony; if sale to person under 18 or within 1,000 ft. of a school, church, public housing facility, assisted living facility or child care facility: 1st degree felony	All sentencing is to be done pursuant to sentencing guidelines: 28-200g: mandatory imprisonment 3 yrs. and $50,000 fine; 200-400g: mandatory imprisonment 7 yrs. and $100,000 fine; 400g to 150kg: mandatory imprisonment 15 yrs. and $250,000 fine; over 150kg: 1st degree felony with life imprisonment
GEORGIA	16-13-20 to 16-13-26; 16-13-31	Less than 1g: 1-3 yrs.; 1-4g: 1-8 yrs.; 4-28g: 1-15 yrs.; over 28g is trafficking	Felony: 5 to 30 yrs.; subsequent offense: 10 to 40 yrs. or life imprisonment	28-200g: mandatory imprisonment 10 yrs. and $200,000 fine; 200-400g: mandatory imprisonment 15 yrs. and $300,000 fine; over 400g: mandatory imprisonment 25 yrs. and $1,000,000 fine
HAWAII	329-16; 706-640; 712-1240 to 1249.7	1/8 to 1 oz.: class B felony punishable by imprisonment up to 10 yrs. and fine up to $25,000; 1 oz. or more: class A felony punishable by imprisonment up to 20 yrs. with no probation or suspended sentence and fine up to $50,000; subsequent offense: class A or B felony based on quantity	Any amount: class B felony; 1/8 oz. or more, or any amount to a minor: class A felony; distribution or intent to distribute any amount within 750 ft. of school, public park, or public housing project: class A felony; knowingly employing, using, enticing or coercing person under 18 to facilitate illegal distribution: class B felony except class A felony if offense occurs in, on, or near school, school vehicle or public park	
IDAHO	37-2701 to 37-2703; 37-2706 to 37-2707; 37-2732 to 37-2739b	Felony punishable by imprisonment up to 7 yrs. and/or fine up to $15,000; subsequent offense: double penalties; possession of 28g or more is trafficking	Felony punishable up to life imprisonment and fine up to $25,000; subsequent offense: double penalties; distribution or possession with intent to distribute on same premises as child under 18: additional penalty of imprisonment up to 5 yrs. and/or $5,000 fine	28-200g: mandatory 3 yrs. imprisonment and minimum $10,000 fine; 200-400g: mandatory 5 yrs. imprisonment and minimum $15,000 fine; over 400g: mandatory 10 yrs. imprisonment and minimum $25,000 fine; Maximum imprisonment: life; maximum fine: $100,000

Table 12a: Illegal Drugs: Cocaine—Continued

State	Code Section	Possession	Sale	Trafficking
ILLINOIS	Uniform Controlled Substances Act: 720 §§ 570/201 to 570/603	1-15g: class 1 felony punishable by $250,000 fine; 15-100g: class 1 felony punishable by mandatory imprisonment 4 to 15 yrs.; 100-400g: mandatory imprisonment 6 to30 yrs.; 400-900g: mandatory 8 to 40 yrs.; over 900g: mandatory 10 to 50 yrs.; Fines for any offense involving 100g. or more: greater of $200,000 or street value; 2nd or subsequent offense: up to double penalties	15-100 g: 6 to 30 yrs.; 100-400g: 9 to 40 yrs.; 400-900g: 12 to 50 yrs.; over 900g: 15 to 60 yrs.; Sale to minors: double penalties; Within 1,000 ft. of truck stop or safety rest: double penalties; Within 1,000 ft. of school: Class Y felony	Trafficking: double penalties
INDIANA	35-48-1-7; 35-48-2-1;35-48-2-5; 35-48-2-6.; 35-48-4-1 to 35-48-4-17	Level 6 felony: 1-5g; level 5 felony: 5-10g (or 1-5g with enhancing circumstance); level 4 felony: 10-28g (or 5-10g with enhancing circumstances); level 3 felony: 28g or more (or 10-28g with enhancing circumstance)	Level 5 felony: any amount; level 4 felony: 1-5g; level 3 felony: 5-10g (or 1-5g with enhancing circumstances); level 2 felony: 10g or more (or 5-10g with enhancing circumstance)	
IOWA	124.101; 124.206; 124.401 to 124.416	First offense any amount: Misdemeanor; subsequent offenses: class D felony	Up to 100g: Class C felony, punishable by imprisonment up to 10 yrs. and fine $1,000 to $50,000; 100-500g: class B felony, up to 25 yrs. and fine $5,000 to $100,000; over 500g: class B felony, up to 50 yrs. and fine up to $1,000,000; within 1,000 ft. of school: additional 5 yrs.; adult distributes to minor: class B felony, minimum 5 yrs., minimum 10 yrs. if with 1,000 ft. of school	
KANSAS	65-4101 to 65-4140; 21-5705	Level 5 felony	Level 4 felony: 3.5g or less; level 3 felony: 3.5-100g; level 2 felony: 100g-1kg; level 1 felony: more than 1kg; severity increased one level if within 1000 feet of any school property	

Table 12a: Illegal Drugs: Cocaine—Continued

State	Code Section	Possession	Sale	Trafficking
KENTUCKY	218A.010 to 218A.14151; 218A.991 to 218A.994A	Class D felony; subsequent offense: class C felony	Class C felony; subsequent offense: class B felony; selling to minor: class C felony 1st offense; subsequent offense: class B felony	First offense: Class C felony; subsequent offense: class B felony; within 1,000 yds. of school: higher penalties
LOUISIANA	40:961 to 40:971.2; 40:981 to 40:982	Under 2g: imprisoned with or without hard labor up to 2 yrs. and fine up to $5,000; 2-28g: imprisoned with or without hard labor 1-5 yrs. and fine up to $5,000; over 28g treated as possession with intent to distribute	Distribute or possess with intent to distribute: 28g or less: imprisoned with or without hard labor for 1-10 yrs. and fine up to $50,000; more than 28g: imprisoned 1-20 yrs. at hard labor and fined up to $50,000; distribute to child under 12: minimum 15 yrs. with no parole, probation, or suspension; drug-free zone: imprisonment for 1.5 times longest term without benefit of parole, probation, or suspension and maximum fine; sale adult to minor under at 18 and 3 yrs. junior: imprisoned at hard labor 1.5 times maximum term or twice fine amount	Production or manufacturing cocaine base: imprisonment at hard labor without parole or suspension 10 to 30 yrs., first 10 yrs. without benefit of parole, probation, or suspension of sentence and up to $500,000 fine
MAINE	Tit. 17-a, §§ 1101 to 1118	Class D crime; over 14g: class B crime and creates presumption of trafficking; permissible inference of evidence of unlawful furnishing: over 7g of cocaine or over 2g of cocaine base: class C crime	Class C crime; over 14g cocaine or 4g cocaine base: class B crime; use of motor vehicle to facilitate unlawful furnishing: suspension of driver's license for up to 5 yrs.; sale to minor or within 1,000 ft. of school: enhanced penalties	14g or more: Class B crime; 112g or more or 32g cocaine base or more; within 1,000 ft. of school or safe zone; enlists or uses person under 18: class A crime

Table 12a: Illegal Drugs: Cocaine—Continued

State	Code Section	Possession	Sale	Trafficking
MARYLAND	Crim. Law §§ 5-601 to 5-628	Misdemeanor, punishable by imprisonment of 1 yr. and fine up to $5,000; 2nd conviction: 18 months and $5,000 fine; subsequent conviction: 2 yrs. and $5,000 fine; bringing 28g into state: felony, up to 25 yrs. and/or fine up to $50,000	Felony, punishable by imprisonment up to 20 yrs. and/or fine up to $15,000; second offense: up to 20 yrs. and $15,000 fine; third offense; up to 25 yrs. and fine up to $25,000; fourth offense: up to 40 yrs. and fine up to $25,000; possessing or distributing 448g or more cocaine or 50g or more cocaine base: mandatory 5 yrs. and fine up to $100,000; sale to minors or near school property: stricter penalties; hire or use minor to manufacture, deliver, or distribute: felony, up to 20 yrs. and or fine up to $20,000; within 1,000 ft. of school: up to 20 yrs. and up to $20,000 fine; subsequent violations: 5 to 40 yrs. and/or $40,000 fine	If "drug kingpin": Imprisonment 20 to 40 yrs. and/or fine up to $1,000,000
MASSACHUSETTS	Ch. 94C, §§ 1; 31 to 48	Imprisonment up to 1 yr. and/or fine up to $1,000; subsequent offense: up to 2 yrs. and/or fine up to $2,000; over 14g is trafficking	Imprisonment 2½ to 10 yrs. and/or fine $1,000 to $10,000; subsequent offense: up to 15 yrs. and $2,500 to $25,000; distributing to minor: 3 to 15 yrs. and fine $1000 to $25,000; within 300 ft. of school: 2.5 to 15 yrs. and fine $1,000 to $10,000; using minor to distribute: 5 to 15 yrs. and fine $1,000 to $100,000	18-36g: Imprisonment mandatory 2 to 15 yrs. and possible fine $2,500 to $25,000; 36-100g: mandatory 3.5 to 20 yrs. and possible fine $5,000 to $50,000; 100-200g: 8 to 20 yrs. and fine $10,000 to $100,000; over 200g: mandatory 12 to 20 yrs. and possible fine $50,000 to $500,000
MICHIGAN	333.7214; 333.7401 to 333.7461	Felony: Less than 50g: Imprisonment up to 4 yrs. and/or fine up to $25,000; 50-450g: up to 20 yrs. and/or up to $250,000; 450-1,000g: up to 30 yrs. and/or up to $500,000; 1,000g or more: up to life imprisonment and/or up to $1,000,000	Felony: Less than 50g: Imprisonment up to 20 yrs. and/or fine up to $25,000; 50-450g: up to 20 yrs. and/or up to $250,000; 450-1,000g: up to 30 yrs. and/or up to $500,000; 1,000g or more: up to life imprisonment and/or up to $1,000,000; sale to minor or near school property: enhanced penalties	

Table 12a: Illegal Drugs: Cocaine—Continued

State	Code Section	Possession	Sale	Trafficking
MINNESOTA	152.01 to 152.029	Any amount: Imprisonment up to 5 yrs. and/or fine up to $10,000, with intent to distribute: up to 15 yrs. and/or fine up to $100,000; 3-6g: up to 20 yrs. and/or fine up to $250,000; 6-50g: up to 25 yrs. and/or fine up to $500,000; 50g or more: up to 30 yrs. and fine up to $1,000,000; subsequent offense: depends on level of prior offense; 6 mos. to 40 yrs. and/or fine up to $1,000,000	Any amount: Imprisonment up to 20 yrs. and/or fine up to $250,000; 3-17g: up to 25 yrs. and/or fine up to $500,000; over 17g: up to 30 yrs. and fine up to $1,000,000; subsequent offense: depends on level of prior offense; 1 to 40 yrs. and/or fine up to $1,000,000; sale to minor, any amount: up to 25 yrs. and/or fine up to $500,000	Importing more than 17g into state: up to 35 yrs. and fine up to $1,250,000
MISSISSIPPI	41-29-101 to 41-29-105; 41-29-115; 41-29-139 to 41-29-152	Less than 0.1g: misdemeanor, punishable by imprisonment up to 1 yr. and/or fine up to $1,000; 0.1-2g: felony, up to 3 yrs. and/or fine up to $50,000; 2-10g: felony, up to 8 yrs. and/or fine up to $250,000; 10-30g: felony, 3-20 yrs. and/or fine up to $500,000; 30g or more: trafficking	Less than 2g: Imprisonment up to 8 yrs. and/or fine up to $50,000; 2-10g: 3 to 20 yrs. and/or up to $250,000; 10-30g: 5 to 30 yrs. and/or up to $500,000; sale to minor under 21, near school or safe zone property or subsequent offense: up to double penalties	30g or more: Trafficking, punishable by imprisonment 10 to 40 yrs. and fine $5,000 to $1,000,000, not eligible for probation or parole; 200g or more: aggravated trafficking, 25 yrs. to life imprisonment and $5,000 to $1,000,000
MISSOURI	195.010 to 195.017; 579.015 to 579.086	Class D felony; Subsequent offense: subject to prior & persistent offenders statute	Class C felony; subsequent offense: subject to prior & persistent offenders; distribution to minor under 17 at least 2 yrs. junior: class B felony; within 2,000 ft. of school: class A felony	2nd degree trafficking: Possesses, buys, or attempts to buy: 150-450g: class B felony; more than 450g: class A felony; 8-24g cocaine base: class B felony; over 24g: class A felony; 1st degree trafficking: deliver or attempt to deliver: 150-450g: class A felony; 450g or more: class A felony, no probation or parole; 2-6g cocaine base: class A felony; over 6g: class A felony, no probation or parole

Table 12a: Illegal Drugs: Cocaine—Continued

State	Code Section	Possession	Sale	Trafficking
MONTANA	45-9-101 to 45-9-109; 50-32-101; 50-32-222	Imprisonment up to 5 yrs. and fine up to $5,000; Criminal possession with intent to sell: up to 20 yrs. and fine up to $50,000	Imprisonment 2 yrs. to life and fine up to $50,000, up to 40 yrs. if sale to minor; 2nd and subsequent offenses: offense: up to life and fine up to $50,000; offense of criminal sale of dangerous drugs on or near school property: 3 yrs. to life and fine up to $50,000	Criminal production/ manufacture: 5 yrs. to life and fine up to $50,000; 2nd offense: 20 yrs. to life and fine up to $50,000; 3rd offense: 40 yrs. to life and fine up to $50,000
NEBRASKA	28-401 to 28-462	Class IV felony	10-28g: Class1 D felony; 28-140g: Class 1C felony; over 140g: Class 1B felony (Crack or cocaine); Class III felony anyone 18 or older who knowingly sells to a minor in, on, or within 1,000 ft. of the real property of a private/ public school. From elementary through university or youth centers: Shall be punished by the next higher penalty classification greater than Class B felony	
NEVADA	453.011; 453.316 to 453.348; NAC 453.520	1st and 2nd offense: Category E felony, punishable by imprisonment 1 to 4 yrs. and fine up to $5,000; 3rd offense: category D felony, 1 to 4 yrs. and fine up to $20,000	1st offense: Category D felony, punishable by imprisonment 1 to 4 yrs. and fine up to $5,000; 2nd offense: class C felony, 1 to 5 yrs. and fine up to $10,000; 3rd offense: category B felony, 3 to 16 yrs. and fine up to $20,000 for each offense; on school property, activity sponsored by school, or on school bus: enhanced penalties, up to 1 to 20 additional years; sell to minor: category A felony, life with possibility of parole after 5 yrs. served, or definite term of 15 yrs. with eligibility for parole after 5 yrs. served, and fine up to $20,000	28-100g: Category C felony, punishable by 1 to 5 yrs. and up to $100,000 fine; over 400g: category A felony: life with possibility of parole after 5 yrs. served, or definite term of 15 yrs. with eligibility for parole after 5 yrs. served, and fine up to $250,000

Table 12a: Illegal Drugs: Cocaine—Continued

State	Code Section	Possession	Sale	Trafficking
NEW HAMPSHIRE	318-B:1; 318-B:26	Class B felony, punishable by imprisonment up to 7 yrs. and/or fine up to $25,000; subsequent offense: class A felony, up to 15 yrs. and/or fine up to $50,000	Under .5oz. (less than 1 oz. of crack): imprisonment up to 7 yrs. and/or $100,000; .5 to 5 oz. (1-5 oz. of crack): up to 20 yrs. and/or $300,000; 5 oz. and over: up to 30 yrs. and/or $500,000; subsequent offense: under .5 oz. (less than 1 oz. of crack): up to 15 yrs. and/or $200,000; .5 to 5 oz. (1-5 oz. of crack): up to 40 yrs. and/or $500,000; 5 oz. and over: maximum life and/or $500,000; within 1,000 ft. of school: double penalties	
NEW JERSEY	24:21-1 to 24:21-6; 24:21-29; 2C:35-2 to 2C:35-10; 2C:43-6	Crime of 3rd degree, punishable by imprisonment up to 3 to 5 yrs. and/or fine up to $35,000; possess on or within 1,000 ft. of school: 100 hrs. community service if not imprisoned	.5 oz. or less: crime of 3rd degree, punishable by imprisonment 3 to 5 yrs. and fine up to $75,000; .5 oz. to 5 oz.: crime of 2nd degree, 5-10 yrs. and fine up to $150,000; over 5 oz.: crime of 1st degree, 10 to 20 yrs. and fine up to $500,000; selling within 1,000 feet of school: enhanced penalties; subsequent offense; sell to minor or pregnant woman: up to double penalties	Leader of narcotics trafficking network: life imprisonment, eligible for parole after 25 yrs., and fine up to $750,000 or 5 times street value of substance, whichever is greater
NEW MEXICO	30-31-1 to 30-31-41	4th degree felony, punishable by imprisonment up to 18 mos. and fine up to $5,000	2nd degree felony, punishable by imprisonment 9 to 15 yrs.; subsequent offense: 1st degree felony, 18 yrs. to life; sell to minor: 1st offense: 2nd degree felony, 9 to 15 yrs.; subsequent offense: 1st degree felony, 18 yrs. to life	2nd degree felony, punishable by imprisonment 9 to 15 yrs.; subsequent offense: 1st degree felony, punishable by 18 yrs. to life
NEW YORK	Penal §§ 220 to 220.78; Pub. Health §§ 3306, 3307	Knowingly possessing any amount: class A misdemeanor; over 500 mg: class D felony; 1/8 oz. or more: class C felony; 1/2 oz. or more: class B felony; 4 oz. or more: class A-II felony; 8 oz. or more: class A-I felony	Class B felony in general, then: 1/2 oz. or more: class A-II felony; 2 oz. or more: Class A-I felony; on school grounds or sale to someone under 21: class B felony	

Table 12a: Illegal Drugs: Cocaine—Continued

State	Code Section	Possession	Sale	Trafficking
NORTH CAROLINA	90-86 to 90-89	Class I felony	Class G felony; Selling of controlled substance to person under 16 or pregnant female or within 300 ft. of school property: Class E felony	28-200g: Class G felony, punishable by imprisonment 35 to 42 mos. and at least $50,000 fine; 200-400g: class F felony, 70 to 93 mos. and at least $100,000 fine; 400g or more: class D felony: 175 to 222 mos. and at least $250,000 fine
NORTH DAKOTA	19-03.1-01 to 19-03.1-28	Class C felony; within 1,000 ft. of school: class B felony	Class B felony, punishable by imprisonment at least 1 yr.; 2nd offense, at least 3 yrs.; 3rd offense, 10 yrs.; over 500g cocaine or 5g crack: class B felony; sale within 1,000 ft. of school or to a minor, at least 4 yrs.; subsequent offense selling to minor, 8 yrs.; solicits, hires, or uses minor: class B felony; subsequent offense, at least 3 yrs.	

Table 12a: Illegal Drugs: Cocaine—Continued

State	Code Section	Possession	Sale	Trafficking
OHIO	2925.01 to 2925.11	Under 5g: 5th degree felony, punishable by imprisonment 6 to 12 mos. and/or fine up to $2,500; 5-10g: 4th degree felony, 6 to 18 mos. and/or fine up to $5,000; 10-20g: 3rd degree felony, 9 to 36 mos. and/or fine up to $10,000; 20-27g: 2nd degree felony, 2 to 8 yrs. and/or fine up to $15,000; 27-100g: 1st degree felony, 11 yrs. and/or fine up to $20,000; over 100g, 1st degree felony, 11 yrs. and/or fine up to $20,000; in addition to above penalties, suspension of driver's license for 6 mos. to 5 yrs.; if defendant charged with 4th degree felony can prove possession solely for personal use, judge may reduce penalties to those for 5th degree felony or misdemeanor	No specific provision for "sale": trafficking is defined as "intended for sale or resale by offender or another person" 2925.03(A)(2)	Under 5g: 5th degree felony, 4th degree felony if in vicinity of school or juvenile; 5-10g: 4th degree felony, 3rd degree felony if in vicinity of school or juvenile; 10-20g: 3rd degree felony, 2nd degree felony if in vicinity of school or juvenile; 20-27g: 2nd degree felony, 1st degree if in vicinity of school or juvenile; 27-100g: 1st degree felony; 100g or more: 1st degree felony, maximum prison sentence imposed
OKLAHOMA	Tit. 63, §§ 2-101; 2-206; 2-401 to 2-415	Felony, punishable by imprisonment up to 5 yrs. and fine up to $5,000; second offense: up to 10 yrs. and fine up to $10,000; subsequent offense: felony, 4 to 15 yrs. and fine up to $10,000; within 1,000 ft. of school or in presence of child under 12: up to double penalties; subsequent offense: up to triple penalties	Felony, punishable by imprisonment up to 7 yrs. and fine up to $100,000; second offense: up to 14 yrs.; subsequent offense: up to 20 yrs.; within 1,000 ft. of school: up to double penalties; subsequent offense: up to triple penalties; using or soliciting use of services of person under 18, or in presence of child under 12: 2 to 10 yrs.; second offense: 4 to 20 yrs.; subsequent offense: 10 yrs. to life	28-300g: Prison term and fine $25,000 to $100,000; 300g or more: prison term and fine $100,000 to $500,000

Table 12a: Illegal Drugs: Cocaine—Continued

State	Code Section	Possession	Sale	Trafficking
OREGON	475.752; 475.876 to 475.934	Class A misdemeanor; class C felony if person possesses 2g or more, has a prior felony conviction, has 2 or more prior convictions for unlawful possession, or the possession is a commercial drug offense	Class B felony; 10g or more: commercial drug offense if greater than $300 cash, firearm, packaging materials, customer list, stolen property, or using public lands; sale to minor under 18 or within 1,000 ft. of school: class A felony	Class A or B felony; delivery and manufacture of 10g or more: category 8 crime
PENNSYLVANIA	Tit. 35, §§ 780-101 to 780-104; 780-113; 780-114 to 780-115	Misdemeanor, punishable by imprisonment up to 1 yr. and/or fine up to $5,000; subsequent offense: up to 3 yrs. and/or fine up to $25,000	Felony, punishable by imprisonment up to 15 yrs. and/or fine up to $250,000, or higher fine if necessary to recover drug profit; subsequent offense or sale to minor: double penalties; delivery or possession with intent to deliver within 1,000 ft. of school or within 250 ft. of recreation center or playground or on school bus: imprisonment 2 to 4 yrs.	
RHODE ISLAND	21-28-4.01 to 21-28-4.22	Nolo contendere pleas: 100 hrs. community service and drug education program; Up to 1 oz.: 3 yrs. and/or $500 to $5,000; 1 oz.-1kg: 10 to 50 yrs. and/or $10,000-$50,000; over 1kg: 20 yrs. to life and $25,000 to $1,000,000	Person not drug dependent: Life imprisonment and/or fine $10,000 to $500,000; drug dependent: 30 yrs. and/or fine $3,000 to $100,000; over 1 oz.-1kg: 10 to 50 yrs. and fine $10,000 to $500,000; over 1kg: up to life imprisonment and fine up to $1,000,000; within 300 yds. of school: double penalties; sale to minor and 3 yrs. junior: minimum 15 yrs. and fine up to $500,000; 2nd offense: double penalties; 3rd and subsequent offenses: triple penalties	

Table 12a: Illegal Drugs: Cocaine—Continued

State	Code Section	Possession	Sale	Trafficking
SOUTH CAROLINA	44-53-110 to 44-53-474	Misdemeanor, punishable by imprisonment up to 3 yrs. and/or fine up to $5,000; subsequent offense: felony, up to 5 yrs. and/or fine up to $7,500; 3rd offense: felony, up to 10 yrs. and/or fine up to $12,500; possession of over 10 grams is prima facie evidence of intent to sell/distribute	Any amount: felony, punishable by imprisonment up to 15 yrs. and/or fine up to $25,000; subsequent offense: felony, 5 to 30 yrs. and/or fine up to $50,000; 3rd offense: 15 to 30 yrs. and/or fine up to $50,000; distributee or possess with intent to distribute within 1/2 mi. radius of school or public park: felony, up to 10 yrs. and/or fine up to $10,000 but misdemeanor, up to 1 yrs. and/or fine up to $1,000 if violation involves only the purchase of controlled substance; sale to minor under 18: up to 20 yrs. with no probation and/or fine up to $30,000	10-28g: Imprisonment 3 to 10 yrs. without parole or suspension and $25,000 fine; 2nd offense: 5 to 30 yrs. without parole or suspension and $50,000 fine; subsequent offense: mandatory minimum 25 to 30 yrs. without parole or suspension and $50,000 fine; 28-100g: 7 to 25 yrs. without parole or suspension and fine up to $50,000; 2nd offense: 7 to 30 yrs. and $50,000 fine; subsequent offense: mandatory minimum 25 yrs. to 30 yrs. and $50,000 fine; 100-200g: mandatory minimum 25 yrs. without parole or suspension and $50,000 fine; 200-400g: mandatory 25 yrs. without parole or suspension and $100,000 fine; 400g or more: mandatory minimum 25 yrs. to 30 yrs. without parole or suspension and $200,000 fine
SOUTH DAKOTA	22-42-1 to 22-42-22; 34-20B-1 to 34-20B-16	Class 5 felony	Class 4 felony, punishable by mandatory imprisonment 1 yr. without suspension; fine up to $10,000 for any conviction; sale to minor: class 2 felony, mandatory 5 yrs.; subsequent offense: mandatory 10 yrs. without suspension; sale to minor: mandatory 15 yrs. without suspension; sale within drug-free zone: class 4 felony, minimum 5 yrs.	

Table 12a: Illegal Drugs: Cocaine—Continued

State	Code Section	Possession	Sale	Trafficking
TENNESSEE	39-17-401 to 39-17-418.	Possession or casual exchange of less than .5 oz.: Class A misdemeanor except felony if adult to minor and adult is 2 yrs. the minor's senior; subsequent offense: If 2 or more prior convictions: class E felony; less than .5g: class C felony, may be fined up to $100,000, class B felony if injury or death occurrence or defendant was in possession of deadly weapon.	Less than .5g: Class C felony and fine up to $100,000; .5g or more: class B felony and fine up to $100,000; 26g or more: class B felony and fine up to $200,000; 300g or more: class A felony and fine up to $500,000; sale to minor under 18 or in drug-free school zone: one class higher than amount required; minimum penalty amounts: 1st drug felony: $2,000; 2nd: $2,500; 3rd: $3,000	
TEXAS	Health & Safety §§ 481.032; 481.101 to 141	Less than 1g: state jail felony; 1-4g: 3rd degree felony; 4-200g: 2nd degree felony; 200-400g: 1st degree felony; 40g and over: imprisonment 10 to 99 yrs. or life in Texas Department of Criminal Justice institution and/or $100,000 fine	Less than 1g: state jail felony; 1-4g: 2nd degree felony; 4-200g: 1st degree felony; 200-400g: Texas Dept. of Criminal Justice institution for 10 to 99 yrs. or life and/or $100,000 fine; 400g and over: Texas Dept. of Criminal Justice institution for 15 to 99 yrs. or life. and/or $250,000 fine; delivery to minor under 17 who is enrolled in school: 2nd degree felony; within drug-free zone: stricter penalties	
UTAH	58-37-1 to 58-37-4.2; 58-37-8	Class A misdemeanor for first or second conviction; subsequent conviction: 3rd degree felony	2nd degree felony; subsequent offense: 1st degree felony; within 1,000 ft. of school or sale to a minor: 1 degree higher than provided except 1st degree felony is 5 yrs. mandatory imprisonment	

Table 12a: Illegal Drugs: Cocaine—Continued

State	Code Section	Possession	Sale	Trafficking
VERMONT	Tit. 18 §§4231	Up to 2.5g: Imprisonment up to 1 yr. and/or fine up to $2,000; 2.5g to 1 oz.: up to 5 yrs. and/or fine up to $100,000; 1 oz. to 1 lb.: up to 10 yrs. and/or fine up to $250,000; subsequent offense: double penalties	Dispensing: Imprisonment up to 3 yrs. and/or fine up to $75,000; Sale: up to 5 yrs. and/or fine up to $100,000; sale or delivery of 2.5g-1 oz.: up to 10 yrs. and/or fine up to $250,000; 1 oz. or more: up to 20 yrs. and/or fine up to $1,000,000; subsequent offense: double penalties; sale to minor or on school grounds: up to 5 to 10 yrs. and/or fine up to $25,000	Permissive inference: 150g or more cocaine or 60g crack cocaine with intent to sell or dispense: imprisonment up to 30 yrs. and/or fine up to $1,000,000
VIRGINIA	54.1-3448; 18.2-247 to 18.2-255.2	Class 5 felony	Imprisonment 5 to 40 yrs. and fine up to $500,000; if defendant proves he gave drug not for profit, not to an inmate, or not for recipient to become addicted, then class 5 felony; 100g or more: 5 yrs. to life and fine up to $500,000; over 5kg: "drug kingpin," mandatory 20 yrs. to life; subsequent offense: 5 yrs. to life and fine up to $500,000; sale within 1,000 ft. of school or park: felony, 1 to 5 yrs. and fine up to $100,000; sale to minor under 18 and 3 yrs. junior: felony, 10 to 50 yrs. and up to $100,000 fine	Transporting 1 oz. or more: felony, 5 to 40 yrs. (3 yr. mandatory minimum) and fine up to $1,000,000; 2nd or subsequent offense: mandatory 10 yrs. to be served consecutively with any other sentence
WASHINGTON	69.50.101, et seq.	Up to 5 yrs. and/or $10,000; Subsequent offense: double penalties	Class B felony; 1) up to 10 yrs. and/or $25,000 (less than 2kg) or 2) $100,000 and $50 for each gram in excess (over 2kg) Subsequent offense: up to double penalties; Sale within 1,000 ft. of school: double penalties; Sale to minor: Class C felony	

Table 12a: Illegal Drugs: Cocaine—Continued

State	Code Section	Possession	Sale	Trafficking
WEST VIRGINIA	60A-1-101 to 60A-2-204; 60A-4-401 to 60A-4-413	Misdemeanor, punishable by imprisonment 90 days to 6 mos. and/or fine up to $1,000; subsequent offense: double penalties	Felony, punishable by imprisonment 1 to 15 yrs. and/or fine up to $25,000; subsequent offense: double penalties; sale to minor or within 1,000 ft. of school: mandatory 2 yrs.	Transport into state with intent to deliver: felony, 1 to 15 yrs. and/or fine up to $25,000
WISCONSIN	961.41 to 961.50	Possession or attempt to possess: Imprisonment in county jail up to 1 yr. and/or fine up to $5,000; subsequent offense: class I felony; within 1,000 ft. of school or public park: 100 hrs. community service	Less than 1g.: class G felony; 1-5g: class F felony; 5-15g: class E felony; 15-40g class D felony; 40g or more: class C felony; distribution to minor under 17 and at 3 yrs. junior or intent to distribute within 1,000 ft. of school or park: maximum prison term increased by 5 yrs.; knowingly hire or use person under 17: class F felony	
WYOMING	35-7-1001 to 35-7-1057	Less than 3g of cocaine or less than .5g crack: misdemeanor, punishable by imprisonment fine up to up to 1 yr. and/or $1,000; over 3g cocaine or over .5g crack: felony, up to 7 yrs. and/or fine up to $15,000; subsequent offense: up to 5 yrs. and/or fine up to $5,000	Imprisonment up to 10 yrs. and/or fine up to $10,000; subsequent offense or sale to minor or within drug-free zone: double penalties	

Table 12b: Illegal Drugs: Heroin

State	Code Section	Possession	Sale	Trafficking
ALABAMA	20-2-1; 20-2-23(b)(2)(j); 13A-5-9; 13A-12-210 to 13A-12-212; 13A-12-231(3); 13A-12-250; 13A-12-270	Unlawful possession: class D felony, 13A-12-212; unlawful possession with intent to distribute: class B felony, 13A-12-211	4-14g: mandatory imprisonment 3 yrs. and $50,000 fine; 14-28g: 10 yrs. and $100,000; 28-56g: 25 yrs. and $500,000; 56g or more: life without parole; sale to minor: class A felony; unlawful distribution of controlled substance: class B felony; subsequent offense: subject to Habitual Felony Offender Act; 2-4g is evidence of possession with intent to distribute	Class A felony: 4-14g: imprisonment minimum 3 yrs. and $50,000 fine; 14-28g: minimum 10 yrs. and $100,000; 28-56g: minimum 25 yrs. and $500,000; over 56g: life without parole
ALASKA	11.71.010 to 11.71.040; 11.71.140	Possession of any amount: class C felony punishable by imprisonment up to 5 yrs. and fine up to $50,000; possession of any amount within 500 ft. of school, youth center, or on school bus: class B felony	Sale to anyone under 19 at least 3 yrs. younger than seller: unclassified felony; sale of heroin in general: class A felony; harsher penalties for repeat or habitual offenders	Participation in "continuing criminal enterprise": unclassified felony
ARIZONA	13-3401; 13-3408 to 13-3422; 36-2501 to 36-2552	Class 4 felony and mandatory fine greater of not less than $2,000 or 3 times value determined by court of drugs in addition to any other penalties	Class 3 felony; sale to minor: class 2 felony; drug-free school zone: add 1 yr. to sentence; in all cases: mandatory fine greater of not less than $2,000 or 3 times value determined by court of drugs in addition to any other penalties	Transport/import: class 2 felony; possess materials to manufacture: class 3 felony; manufacture: class 2 felony; in all cases: mandatory fine greater of not less than $2,000 or 3 times value determined by court of drugs in addition to any other penalties
ARKANSAS	5-64-402 to 5-64-446	Less than 2g: class D felony; 2-28g: class C felony; 28-200g: class B felony; possession of 2-28g on or within 1,000 ft. of school, park, or public safe place: enhanced sentence of 10 yrs.; repeat offenders: harsher penalties 3 yrs. to life; violations by public officials or law enforcement officers: enhanced penalties, up to 10 yrs. and $10,000 fine	2-28g: class B felony; 28-200g: class A felony; delivery to minor under 18 and at least 3 yrs. junior: double penalties; possession of any amount with purpose to deliver or actual delivery, manufacture, or traffic within 1,000 ft. of school, park, or public place: enhanced sentence of 10 yrs.	Delivery or manufacture of 200g or more: class Y felony

Table 12b: Illegal Drugs: Heroin—Continued

State	Code Section	Possession	Sale	Trafficking
CALIFORNIA	Health & Safety §§ 11000 to 11033; 11054; 11350 to 11356.5	Imprisonment up to 1 yr. in county jail and fine up to $70; if probation granted: additional requirements	Imprisonment in state prison 2 to 4 yrs.; possession/purchasing for sale: imprisonment in state prison 3 to 5 yrs.; sale to minors: imprisonment in state prison 3, 5, or 7 yrs.; sale to day care, preschool, or school children: imprisonment state prison 5, 7, or 9 yrs.; over 18 selling to minor or using minor in sale process: imprisonment in state prison for 3, 6, or 9 yrs.; sale within 1,000 ft. of school: additional 3, 4, or 5 yrs.; enhanced penalties for sale on grounds of day care, school, church, synagogue or youth center, seller over 18 and buyer a minor at least 4 yrs. younger	Transport/import: Imprisonment 3 to 5 yrs.; county to non-contiguous county: imprisonment 3, 6, or 9 yrs.
COLORADO	18-18-101 to 18-18-203; 18-18-413.5; 18-18-405	Level 4 drug felony; 2 or more prior convictions within 10 yr. period: up to triple penalties; 3 or more convictions within 10 yr. period: up to 4 times maximum penalty	Less than 2g: level 4 drug felony; 2-7g: level 3 drug felony; 7-112g: level 2 drug felony; over 112g: level 1 drug felony; sell or distribute any amount to minor and 2 yrs. junior: level 1 felony	

Table 12b: Illegal Drugs: Heroin—Continued

State	Code Section	Possession	Sale	Trafficking
CONNECTICUT	21a-240; 21a-243; 21a-278 to 21a-283a	Imprisonment up to 7 yrs. and/or fine up to $50,000; 2nd offense: imprisonment up to 15 yrs. and/or fine up to $100,000; subsequent offense: imprisonment up to 25 yrs. and/or fine up to $250,000; additional 2 yrs. imprisonment if within 1,500 ft. of school	Imprisonment up to 15 yrs. and/or fine up to $50,000; 2nd offense: imprisonment up to 30 yrs. and/or fine up to $100,000; subsequent offense: imprisonment up to 30 yrs. and/or fine up to $250,000; sale by non-drug dependent person: imprisonment mandatory min. 5 yrs. to 20 yrs.; 2nd offense: imprisonment mandatory min. 10 yrs. to 5 yrs.; sale of 1 oz. or more: mandatory min. 5 yrs. to 20 yrs.; 2nd offense: max. life sentence; enhanced penalties within 1500' of school or public safe place, sale to minor at least 2 yrs. jr.; court may suspend mandatory min. sentence if person is under 18 or lacks mental capacity	
DELAWARE	Tit. 16, §§ 4701; 4714; ; 4751A to 4769	Under 1g: class B misdemeanor; class A misdemeanor with aggravating factor; 2-3g: class E felony; 3-4g or over 1g with aggravating factor (if applicable, can be subject to First Offenders Controlled Substances Diversion Program): class D felony; over 4g or 2-3g with aggravating factor or over 1g with 2 aggravating factor: class C felony; over 5g or 4-5g with aggravating factor or 2-3g with 2 aggravating factors: class B felony. See trafficking column for aggravating factors	Manufacture, deliver, or possess with intent to deliver any amount: class D felony; 2-3g or any amount with aggravating factor: class C felony, mandatory 6 yrs. if not addicted; 4-5g or 2-3g with aggravating factor: class B felony; where death is involved as result: class B felony; enhanced penalties with aggravating factors	Aggravating factors for possession or sale: offense committed within a protected school zone, park, recreation area, or place of worship; offense occurred in a vehicle; crime involved person under 18, either as accomplice or intended recipient of heroin and defendant was adult more than 4 yrs. older; defendant, during or immediately following crime, attempted to prevent arrest or detention with use of force or violence or tried to flee in vehicle from arrest or detention

Table 12b: Illegal Drugs: Heroin—Continued

State	Code Section	Possession	Sale	Trafficking
DISTRICT OF COLUMBIA	48-901.02 to 48-902.04; 48-904.01 to 48-904.10	Misdemeanor punishable by imprisonment up to 180 days and/or fine up to $1,000; subsequent offense: up to double penalties; if 1st drug conviction, judge may defer adjudication of guilt and sentence offender to probation up to 1 yr. after which charges will be dismissed and record sealed if probation requirements are satisfied	Sale, manufacture, distribution: crime punishable by imprisonment up to 30 yrs. and/or fine $75,000 to $500,000; subsequent offense: double penalties; within drug-free zone or sale to minors: up to double penalties	
FLORIDA	775.082 to 775.31; 893.01 to 893.21	3rd degree felony; possession of 4g (trafficking): 1st degree felony	2nd degree felony; sale of over 10g or to minor under 18: 1st degree felony; more severe penalties near school	All sentencing to be done pursuant to sentencing guidelines: 4-14g: imprisonment 3 yrs. and $50,000 fine; 14-28g: 15 yrs. and $100,000; 28g-30kg: 25 yrs. and $500,000; over 30kg: life imprisonment
GEORGIA	16-13-20 to 16-13-56	Less than 2g: Imprisonment 1 to 3 yrs.; 2-4g: 1 to 8 yrs.; 4-28g: 1 to 15 yrs.	Felony: Imprisonment 5 to 30 yrs.; subsequent offense: imprisonment 10 to 40 yrs. or life; hire, solicit, engage, or use person under 17 to manufacture, distribute, or dispense: felony punishable by imprisonment 5 to 20 yrs. and/or fine up to $20,000	4-14g: Imprisonment mandatory 5 yrs. and $50,000 fine; 14-28g: mandatory 10 yrs. and $100,000; over 28g: mandatory 25 yrs. and $500,000
HAWAII	329-14; 329-41 to 329-43; 712-1240 to 712-1243; 712-1249.6; 712-1249.7 to 712-1256	Any amount: class C felony; 1/8-1 oz.: class B felony; 1 oz. or more: class A felony; subsequent offense: class A or B felony based on quantity	Any amount: Class B felony; 1/8 oz. or more, or any amt. to a minor or within 750 ft. of school, public park, or public housing project: class A felony; knowingly employ, persuade, entice, or coerce person under 18 to facilitate illegal distribution: class B felony; offense occurs on or near school property, school vehicles, or public parks: class A felony	

Table 12b: Illegal Drugs: Heroin—Continued

State	Code Section	Possession	Sale	Trafficking
IDAHO	37-2701 to 37-2705; 37-2732 to 37-2739B	Felony, punishable by imprisonment up to 7 yrs. and/or $15,000 fine; subsequent offense: double penalties; possession of 2g or more is considered trafficking	Felony. punishable by imprisonment up to life and $25,000 fine; subsequent offense: double penalties; distribute or possess with intent to distribute on same premises where child under 18 and at least 3 yrs. younger is present: additional prison term up to 5 yrs. and/or $5,000 fine	2-7g: mandatory imprisonment 3 yrs. and min. $10,000 fine; 7-28g: mandatory 10 yrs. and mini. $15,000; 28g and over: mandatory 15 yrs. and min. $25,000; max. sentence is life imprisonment and $100,000 fine; 2nd trafficking conviction: double penalties
ILLINOIS	720 §§ 570/201 to 570/205; 570/401 to 570/414	Up to 15g: class 4 felony, punishable by imprisonment 1 to 3 yrs. and fine up to $25,000; 15-100g: class 1 felony, 4 to 15 yrs. and fine up to $200,000; 100-400g: 6 to 30 yrs.; 400-900g: 8 to 40 yrs.; over 900g: 10 to 50 yrs.; fines for any offense involving 100g or more: greater of $200,000 or street value	1 to 15g: class 1 felony, punishable by imprisonment 4 to 15 yrs. and fine up to $250,000, class X felony if within 1,000 ft. of school; 15-100 g: 6 to 30 yrs.; 100-400g: 9 to 40 yrs.; 400-900g: 12 to 50 yrs.; over 900g: 15 to 60 yrs.; fines for class X felony offenses: greater of $500,000 or street value; within 1,000 ft. of truck stop or safety rest or deliver to person under 18: double penalties; using or employing minor to deliver: up to 3x max. sentence	Double penalties
INDIANA	35-48-4-1 to 35-48-4-17; 35-48-1-2 to 35-48-2-6	Any amount: Level 6 felony; 5-10g or less than 5g with enhancing circumstance: level 5 felony; 10-28g or 5-10g if enhanced: level 4 felony; 28g or more or 10-28g if enhanced: level 3 felony; enhancing circumstances: prior conviction; possession of firearm; on school bus; within 500 ft. of school property or public park; manufactured drug; committed offense knowingly in physical presence of child under 18	Any amount: Level 5 felony; 3-7g: level 4 felony; 7-12g or 2-7g with enhancing circumstance: level 3 felony; 12g or more or 7-12g with enhancing circumstance: level 2 felony; enhancing circumstances: prior conviction; possession of firearm; on school bus; within 500 ft. of school property or public park; delivered to person under 18 at least 3 yrs. junior; manufactured drug; committed offense knowingly in presence of child under 18	

Table 12b: Illegal Drugs: Heroin—Continued

State	Code Section	Possession	Sale	Trafficking
IOWA	124.101 to 124.206; 124.401 to 124.416	1st offense: serious misdemeanor; 2nd offense: aggravated misdemeanor; subsequent offenses: class D felony; within 1,000 feet of school, recreation area, or on school bus: 100 hrs. community service	Less than 100g: Class C felony, punishable by imprisonment up to 10 yrs. and fine $1,000 to $50,000; 100g to 1 kg: class B felony, up to 25 yrs. and $5,000 to $100,000; over 1kg: class B felony, up to 50 yrs. and up to $1,000,000; subsequent offense: triple penalties; within 1,000 feet of school or recreation area: additional 5 yrs.; adult distributing to minor: class B felony, imprisonment minimum 5 yrs. or 10 yrs. if within 1,000 ft. of school or recreation area or on school bus	
KANSAS	21-5701 to 21-5717; 65-4101	Level 5 felony	Less than 1g: level 4 felony; 1-3.5g: level 3 felony; 3.5-100g; level 2 felony; more than 100g: level 1 felony; severity of offense increased one level if the controlled substance was distributed on or within 1000 ft. of school property	
KENTUCKY	218A.010 to 218A.14151; 218A.991 to 218A.994	Class D felony; subsequent offense: class C felony	Class C felony; subsequent offense: class B felony; selling to minor: 1st offense: class C felony; subsequent offense: class B felony; penalty increased one level if committed while in possession of firearm	First offense: class D felony; subsequent offense: class C felony; within 1,000 yds. of school: higher penalty; penalty increased one level if committed while in possession of firearm

Table 12b: Illegal Drugs: Heroin—Continued

State	Code Section	Possession	Sale	Trafficking
LOUISIANA	40:961 to 40:971.2; 40:981 to 40:982	Under 2g: imprisonment with or without hard labor 2-4 yrs.; 2-28g: imprisonment at hard labor 2 to 10 yrs. and up to $5,000 fine	Any amount: Imprisonment at hard labor 5-40 years and fine up to $50,000; Child Endangerment Law: distribute or possess with intent to distribute to child under 12: min. mandatory 10 yrs. without benefit of parole, probation, or suspension of sentence; sell or distribute in drug-free zone: max. fine and 1.5 times longest term of imprisonment without benefit of parole, probation, or suspension; sell or distribute by person over 18 to minor at least 3 yrs. younger: imprisonment at hard labor 5-30 yrs.; if seller is 25 or older: 10-30 yrs.; distribution to a student: 1.5 times max. term and/or double fine	
MAINE	Tit. 17A, §§ 1101 to 1118	Under 2g: class C crime, punishable by imprisonment up to 5 yrs. and/or $5,000 fine; 2g creates presumption of trafficking	1-2g: class B crime, punishable by imprisonment up to 5 yrs. and/or $5,000 fine; more serious penalties for sale to minor or within 1,000 ft. of school	Possession of 2g or more: class B crime, punishable by imprisonment up to 10 yrs. and/or fine up to $20,000; aggravated if greater than 6g or within 1,000 ft. of school or safe zone or if person enlists, solicits, or conspires with person under 18 or person possesses a firearm at time of offense: class A crime, punishable by imprisonment up to 30 yrs. and/or fine up to $50,000

Table 12b: Illegal Drugs: Heroin—Continued

State	Code Section	Possession	Sale	Trafficking
MARYLAND	Crim. Law §§ 5-601 to 5-628	Misdemeanor, punishable by imprisonment up to 4 yrs. and/or fine up to $25,000; over 28g: mandatory 5 yrs. imprisonment and fine up to $100,000; bringing 4g into state: felony, punishable by imprisonment up to 25 yrs. and/or fine up to $50,000; subsequent offense: double penalties	Felony, punishable by imprisonment up to 20 yrs. and/or fine up to $15,000; over 28g: mandatory 5 yrs. and fine up to $100,000; 2nd offense: imprisonment up to 20 yrs. and/or fine up to $15,000; 3rd offense: up to 25 yrs. and /or fine up to $25,000; 4th and subsequent offense: up to 40 yrs. and/or fine up to $25,000; within 1,000 ft. of school: up to 20 yrs. and/or up to $20,000; subsequent violations: 5 to 40 yrs. and/or $40,000	If "drug kingpin": Imprisonment 20 to 40 yrs. and/or fine up to $1,000,000
MASSACHUSETTS	Ch. 94C, §§ 1; 31 to 48	Imprisonment up to 2 yrs. and/or fine up to $2,000; subsequent offense: imprisonment 2.5 to 5 yrs. or 2.5 yrs. and $5,000 fine; greater than 14g considered trafficking	Imprisonment 2.5 to 10 yrs. and/or $1,000 to $10,000 fine; subsequent offense: imprisonment 3.5 to 15 yrs. and/or $2,500 to $25,000 fine; 3rd offense: imprisonment not less than 40 yrs.; sale to minors or near school property: stricter penalties; causes, induces, or abets minor under 18: felony, punishable by mandatory imprisonment 5 to 15 yrs. imprisonment and/or $1,000 to $100,000 fine	18-36g: Imprisonment 3.5 to 30 yrs. and/or $5,000 to $50,000 fine; 36-100g: imprisonment 5 to 30 years and/or $5,000 to $50,000 fine; 100-200g: imprisonment 8 to 30 yrs. and/or $10,000 to $100,000 fine; over 200g: imprisonment 12 to 30 yrs. and/or $50,000 to $500,000 fine

Table 12b: Illegal Drugs: Heroin—Continued

State	Code Section	Possession	Sale	Trafficking
MICHIGAN	333.7212; 333.7401 to 333.7461	Felony: Less than 50g: Imprisonment up to 4 yrs. and/or fine up to $25,000; 50-450g: imprisonment up to 20 yrs. and/or fine up to $250,000; 450-1,000g: imprisonment up to 30 yrs. and/or fine up to $500,000; 1,000g or more: up to life imprisonment and/or fine up to $1,000,000; 2nd or subsequent offense: double penalties	Felony: Less than 50g: Imprisonment up to 20 yrs. and/or fine up to $25,000; 50-450g: imprisonment up to 20 yrs. and/or fine up to $250,000; 450-1,000g: imprisonment up to 30 yrs. and/or fine up to $500,000; 1,000g or more: up to life imprisonment and/or fine up to $1,000,000; sale to minor or near school property: enhanced penalties; 2nd or subsequent offense: double penalties; additional penalties if subsequent offense of selling to minor or near school	
MINNESOTA	152.01 to 152.029	Any amount: Imprisonment up to 5 yrs. and/or fine up to $10,000; with intent to distribute: imprisonment up to 15 yrs. and/or fine up to $100,000; 3-6g: imprisonment up to 20 yrs. and/or fine up to $250,000; 6-25g: imprisonment up to 25 yrs. and/or fine up to $500,000; 25g or more: imprisonment up to 30 yrs. and/or fine up to $1,000,000	Any amount: Imprisonment up to 20 yrs. and/or fine up to $250,000; 3-10g: imprisonment up to 25 yrs. and/or fine up to $500,000; over 10g: imprisonment up to 30 yrs. and fine up to $1,000,000; over 100g: imprisonment up to 40 yrs. and/or fine up to $1,000,000; sale to minor, any amount: imprisonment up to 25 yrs. and/or fine up to $500,000	

Table 12b: Illegal Drugs: Heroin—Continued

State	Code Section	Possession	Sale	Trafficking
MISSISSIPPI	41-29-101 to 41-29-105; 41-29-113; 41-29-139 to 41-29-152	Less than 0.1g: misdemeanor, punishable by imprisonment up to 1 yr. and/or fine up to $1,000; 0.1-2g: felony, imprisonment up to 3 yrs. and/or fine up to $50,000; 2-10g: felony, imprisonment up to 8 yrs. and/or fine up to $250,000; 10-30g: felony, imprisonment 3 to 20 yrs. and/or fine up to $500,000; 30g or more considered trafficking	Less than 2g: Imprisonment up to 8 yrs. and/or fine up to $50,000; 2-10g: imprisonment 3 to 20 yrs. and/or fine up to $250,000; 10-30g: imprisonment 5 to 30 yrs. and/or fine up to $500,000; sale to minor under 21, near school or safe zone property or subsequent offense: up to double penalties	30g or more: Trafficking, punishable by imprisonment 10 to 40 yrs. and fine $5,000 to $1,000,000, not eligible for probation or parole; 200g or more: aggravated trafficking, imprisonment 25 yrs. to life and fine $5,000 to $1,000,000
MISSOURI	195.010 to 195.017; 579.015 to 579.086	Class D felony	Class C felony; distribution to minor under 17 at least 2 yrs. junior: class B felony; within 2,000 ft. of school: class A felony	Distributing, delivering, manufacturing, producing, or attempts to do so: 1st degree trafficking, 30-90g: class B felony; 90g or more: class A felony; possessing, purchasing, attempting to purchase, or bringing into state: 2nd degree trafficking: 30-90g: class C felony; 90g or more: class B felony
MONTANA	45-9-101 to 45-9-109; 50-32-101; 50-32-222	Imprisonment 5 yrs. and/or fine up to $5,000	Imprisonment up to 25 yrs. and fine up to $50,000, sale to minor: imprisonment up to 40 yrs. and fine up to $50,000; 2nd and subsequent offense: up to life imprisonment and fine up to $50,000; offense of criminal sale of dangerous drugs on or near school property: imprisonment 3 yrs. to life and fine up to $50,000	Criminal production/ manufacture: imprisonment up to 25 yrs. and/or fine up to $50,000

Table 12b: Illegal Drugs: Heroin—Continued

State	Code Section	Possession	Sale	Trafficking
NEBRASKA	28-401 to 28-416	Class IV felony	10-28g: Class 1D felony; 28-140g: class 1C felony; 140g or more: class 1B felony; sale to minor, within 1,000 ft. of school, university, playground, public youth center, public swimming pool, or video arcade; using or employing minor to deliver: harsher penalties	
NEVADA	453.011; 453.316 to 453.348; NAC 453.510	Category E felony, 1st and 2nd offenses punishable by imprisonment 1 to 4 yrs. and fine up to $5,000; 3rd offense: 1 to 4 yrs. and fine up to $20,000	1st offense: category D felony, punishable by imprisonment 1 to 4 yrs. and fine up to $5,000; 2nd offense: category C felony, 1 to 5 yrs. and fine up to $10,000; 3rd offense: category B felony 3 to 16 yrs. and fine up to $20,000 fine for each offense; selling on school property, school activity or on school bus: harsher penalties up to 1 to 20 additional yrs.; sell to minor under 18: category A felony, 2nd or subsequent offense punishable by life imprisonment with possibility of parole after minimum 5 yrs. served, or definite term of 15 yrs. with eligibility for parole beginning after minimum 5 yrs. served; fine up to $20,000	4-14g: category B felony, punishable by imprisonment 1 to 6 yrs. and fine up to $50,000; 14-28g: category B felony, 2 to 15 yrs. and fine up to $100,000; 28g or more: category A felony, life imprisonment with possibility of parole after minimum 10 yrs. served or definite term of 25 yrs. with eligibility of parole after minimum up yrs. served; fine up to $500,000; double penalties for sale near school

Table 12b: Illegal Drugs: Heroin—Continued

State	Code Section	Possession	Sale	Trafficking
NEW HAMPSHIRE	318-B:1; 318-B:26	Class B felony, punishable by imprisonment up to 7 yrs. and/or fine up to $25,000; subsequent offense: class A felony, up to 15 yrs. and/or fine up to $50,000	Under 1g: Imprisonment up to 7 yrs. and/or fine up to $100,000; 1-5g: imprisonment up to 20 yrs. and/or fine up to $300,000; 5g and over: up to life imprisonment and/or fine up to $500,000; subsequent offense: under 1g: imprisonment up to 15 yrs. and/or fine up to $200,000; 1-5g: imprisonment up to 40 yrs. and/or fine up to $500,000; dispense or possess with intent to sell within 1,000 ft. of school: double penalties	
NEW JERSEY	24:21-1 to 24:21-5; 24:21-29; 2C:35-2 to 2C:35-10; 2C:43-6	Crime of 3rd degree, punishable by imprisonment up to 3 to 5 yrs. and/or fine up to $35,000; possess on or within 1,000 ft. of school: 100 hrs. community service if not imprisoned	.5 oz. or less: crime of 3rd degree; .5 oz. to 5 oz.: crime of 2nd degree; over 5 oz.: crime of 1st degree; selling within 1,000 feet of school: enhanced penalties; subsequent offense; sell to minor or pregnant woman: up to double penalties	Leader of narcotics trafficking network: life imprisonment, eligible for parole after 25 yrs., and fine up to $750,000 or 5 times street value of substance, whichever is greater
NEW MEXICO	30-31-1 to 30-31-41	4th degree felony, punishable by imprisonment up to 18 mos. and fine up to $5,000	2nd degree felony, punishable by imprisonment 9 to 15 yrs.; subsequent offense: 1st degree felony, imprisonment 18 yrs. to life; sell to minor: 1st offense: 2nd degree felony, imprisonment 9 to 15 yrs.; subsequent offense: 1st degree felony, imprisonment 18 yrs. to life	2nd degree felony, punishable by imprisonment 9 to 15 yrs.; subsequent offense: 1st degree felony, punishable by imprisonment 18 yrs. to life; trafficking within a drug-free school zone: 1st degree felony
NEW YORK	Penal §§ 220 to 220.78; Pub. Health §§ 3306-3307	Knowingly possessing any amount: class A misdemeanor; over 500 mg: class D felony; 1/8 oz. or more: class C felony; 1/2 oz. or more: class B felony; 4 oz. or more: class A-II felony; 8 oz. or more: class A-I felony	Class B felony in general, then: 1/2 oz. or more: class A-II felony; 2 oz. or more: Class A-I felony; on school grounds or sale to someone under 21: class B felony	

Table 12b: Illegal Drugs: Heroin—Continued

State	Code Section	Possession	Sale	Trafficking
NORTH CAROLINA	90-86 to 90-99	Class I felony	Class G felony; sale of controlled substance to person under 16 or to pregnant female: class D felony; sale to person 13 or younger: class C felony; 21 or over selling on or within 300 ft. of public park or school: class E felony; 28g or more considered trafficking	4-14g: Class F felony, punishable by imprisonment 70 to 93 mos. and fine not less than $50,000; 14-28g: class E felony, 90 to 120 mos. and not less than $100,000; 28g and over: class C felony, 225 to 282 mos. and not less than $500,000
NORTH DAKOTA	19-03.1-01 to 19-03.1-28	Ingestion: Class A misdemeanor; exposure to child or vulnerable adult: class C felony, if injury occurs: class B felony, if death: class A felony; within 1,000 ft. of school: class B felony	Class A felony, punishable by mandatory 1 yr. imprisonment; sale within 1,000 ft. of school or to a minor: mandatory 4 yrs. imprisonment; solicits, hires, or uses minor: class B felony	
OHIO	2925.01 to 2925.11	Under 5g: 5th degree felony, punishable by imprisonment 6 to 12 mos. and/or fine up to $2,500; 5-10g: 4th degree felony, 6 escalating penalties for greater amounts up to over 100g: 1st degree felony, punishable by imprisonment 11 yrs. and/or fine up to $20,000; in addition to other penalties, suspension of driver's license for 6 mos. to 5 yrs.; if defendant charged with 4th degree felony can prove possession solely for personal use, judge may reduce penalties to those for 5th degree felony or misdemeanor	No specific provision for "sale"	Trafficking defined as "intended for sale or resale by offender or another person, 2925.03(A)(2); under 1g: 5th degree felony, 4th degree felony if in vicinity of school or juvenile; escalating penalties for greater amounts up to 250g or more: 1st degree felony, max. prison sentence imposed

Table 12b: Illegal Drugs: Heroin—Continued

State	Code Section	Possession	Sale	Trafficking
OKLAHOMA	Tit. 63, §§ 2-101; 2-204; 2-401 to 2-413	Felony, punishable by imprisonment up to 5 yrs. and fine up to $5,000; 2nd offense: up to 10 yrs. and fine up to $10,000; subsequent offense: 4-15 yrs. and fine up to $10,000; within 1,000 ft. of school or in presence of child under 12: up to double penalties; subsequent offense: up to triple penalties	Felony, punishable by imprisonment 7 yrs. to life and fine up to $100,000; 2nd offense: up to 14 yrs.; subsequent offense: up to 20 yrs.; within 1,000 ft. of school or in presence of child under 12: up to double penalties; subsequent offense: up to triple penalties; using or soliciting use of services of person under 18: double penalties	10-28g: prison term and fine $25,000 to $50,000; 28g or more: prison term and fine $50,000 to $500,000
OREGON	475.752; 475.848 to 475.930	Class A misdemeanor; class B felony if person has a prior felony conviction, 2 or more prior convictions for unlawful possession, possession is a commercial drug offense, or person possesses at least 1g	3-5g: Class A felony; commercial drug offense if greater than $300 cash, use of firearm, packaging materials, customer list, stolen property, or using public lands; over 5g: category 6 crime; sale to minor under 18 or within 1,000 ft. of school: class A felony	Class A felony; delivery and manufacture of over 5g: category 8 crime
PENNSYLVANIA	Tit. 35, §§ 780-101 to 780-104; 780-113; 780-114 to 780-115	Misdemeanor, punishable by imprisonment up to 1 yr. and/or fine up to $5,000; subsequent offense: up to 3 yrs. and/or fine up to $25,000	Felony, punishable by imprisonment up to 15 yrs. and/or fine up to $250,000, or higher fine if necessary to recover drug profit; subsequent offense or sale to minor: double penalties; delivery or possession with intent to deliver within 1,000 ft. of school or within 250 ft. of recreation center or playground or on school bus: imprisonment 2 to 4 yrs.	

Table 12b: Illegal Drugs: Heroin—Continued

State	Code Section	Possession	Sale	Trafficking
RHODE ISLAND	21-28-4.01 to 21-28-4.22	Imprisonment 3 yrs. and/or fine $500 to $5,000; nolo contendere plea: 100 hrs. of community service and drug education program; 1 oz. to 1kg: imprisonment up to 50 yrs. and/or fine up to $500,000; over 1kg: up to life imprisonment and fine up to $1,000,000	Person not drug dependent: Life imprisonment and/or fine $10,000 to $500,000; drug dependent: imprisonment 30 yrs. and/or fine $3,000 to $100,000; over 1 oz.-1kg: imprisonment 10 to 50 yrs. and fine $10,000 to $500,000; over 1kg: 20 yrs. to life imprisonment and fine $25,000 to $1,000,000; within 300 yds. of school: double penalties; sale to minor and 3 yrs. junior: minimum 15 yrs. imprisonment and fine up to $500,000; 2nd offense: double penalties; 3rd and subsequent offenses: triple penalties	
SOUTH CAROLINA	44-53-110 to 44-53-474	Misdemeanor, punishable by imprisonment up to 2 yrs. and/or fine up to $5,000; subsequent offense: felony, imprisonment up to 5 yrs. and/or up to $5,000 fine; 3rd offense: felony, imprisonment up to 5 yrs. and/or fine up to $10,000; possession of more than 2 grains of heroin is prima facie evidence of intent to sell/distribute	Any amount: felony, punishable by imprisonment up to 15 yrs. and/or fine up to $25,000; subsequent offense: felony, imprisonment 5 to 30 yrs. and/or fine up to $50,000; 3rd offense: imprisonment 15 to 30 yrs. and/or fine up to $50,000; distributee or possess with intent to distribute within 1/2 mi. radius of school or public park: felony, imprisonment up to 10 yrs. and/or fine up to $10,000 but misdemeanor, imprisonment up to 1 yrs. and/or fine up to $1,000 if violation involves only the purchase of controlled substance; sale to minor under 18: up to 20 yrs. with no probation and/or fine up to $30,000	4-14g: Imprisonment 7 to 25 yrs. without parole or suspension and $50,000 fine; subsequent offense: mandatory minimum 25 yrs. imprisonment without parole or suspension and $100,000 fine ; 14-28g: mandatory 25 yrs. imprisonment without parole or suspension and $200,000 fine; over 28g: mandatory 25 to 40 yrs. imprisonment without parole or suspension and $200,000 fine

Table 12b: Illegal Drugs: Heroin—Continued

State	Code Section	Possession	Sale	Trafficking
SOUTH DAKOTA	22-42-1 to 22-42-22; 34-20B-1 to 34-20B-13	Class 5 felony	Class 4 felony, punishable by mandatory imprisonment 1 yr. without suspension; fine up to $10,000 for any conviction; sale to minor: class 2 felony, mandatory 5 yrs.; subsequent offense: mandatory 10 yrs. without suspension; sale to minor: mandatory 15 yrs. without suspension; sale within drug-free zone: class 4 felony, minimum 5 yrs.	
TENNESSEE	39-17-401 to 39-17-418	Possession or casual exchange of less than .5 oz.: Class A misdemeanor except felony if adult to minor and adult is 2 yrs. the minor's senior; subsequent offense: if two or more prior convictions: class E felony; less than .5g: class C felony, may be fined up to $100,000, class B felony if injury or death occurrence or defendant was in possession of deadly weapon.	Class B felony and fine up to $100,000; over 15g: class B felony and fine up to $200,000; over 150g: class A felony and fine up to $500,000; sale to minor under 18 or in drug-free school zone: one class higher than amount required; minimum penalty amounts: 1st drug felony: $2,000; 2nd: $2,500; 3rd: $3,000	
TEXAS	Health & Safety §§ 481.032; 481.101 to 141	Less than 1g: state jail felony; 1-4g: 3rd degree felony; 4-200g: 2nd degree felony; 200-400g: 1st degree felony; 40g and over: imprisonment 10 to 99 yrs. or life in Texas Department of Criminal Justice institution and/or $100,000 fine	Less than 1g: state jail felony; 1-4g: 2nd degree felony; 4-200g: 1st degree felony; 200-400g: Texas Dept. of Criminal Justice institution for 10 to 99 yrs. or life and/or $100,000 fine; 400g and over: Texas Dept. of Criminal Justice institution for 15-99 yrs. or life and/or $250,000 fine; delivery to minor under 17 who is enrolled in school: 2nd degree felony; within drug-free zone: stricter penalties	

Table 12b: Illegal Drugs: Heroin—Continued

State	Code Section	Possession	Sale	Trafficking
UTAH	58-37-1 to 58-37-4.2; 58-37-8	3rd degree felony; subsequent offense: 1 degree greater penalty than provided	2nd degree felony; subsequent offense: 1st degree felony; within 1,000 ft. of school or sale to a minor: 1 degree higher than provided except 1st degree felony is 5 yrs. mandatory imprisonment	
VERMONT	Tit. 18, §4233	Up to 200mg: Imprisonment up to 1 yr. and/or fine up to $2,000; 200mg-1g: up to 5 yrs. and/or fine up to $100,000; 1-2g: up to 10 yrs. and/or fine up to $250,000; 2g and over: up to 20 yrs. and/or fine up to $1,000,000; subsequent offense: up to double penalties	Delivery: Imprisonment up to 3 yrs. and/or fine up to $75,000; Sale: up to 5 yrs. and/or fine up to $100,000; Sale or delivery: over 200mg: up to 10 yrs. and/or fine up to $250,000; over 1g: up to 20 yrs. and/or fine up to $1,000,000; subsequent offense: double penalties; sale to minors at least 3 yrs. union: up to 5 yrs.; sale on school grounds: up to 10 yrs.	Permissive inference: 3.5g or more with intent to sell or dispense: imprisonment up to 30 yrs. and/or fine up to $1,000,000; knowingly transporting more than 1g: up to 10 yrs. and/or fine up to $100,000
VIRGINIA	54.1-3445; 18.2-247 to 18.2-255.2	Class 5 felony	Imprisonment 5 to 40 yrs. and fine up to $500,000; if defendant proves he gave drug not for profit, not to an inmate, or not for recipient to become addicted, then class 5 felony; over 100g: felony, imprisonment 5 yrs. to life and fine up to $1,000,000; over 1kg: "drug kingpin," mandatory imprisonment 20 yrs. to life; subsequent offense: imprisonment 5 yrs. to life and fine up to $500,000; sale within 1,000 ft. of school or park: felony, imprisonment 1 to 5 yrs. and fine up to $100,000; sale to minor under 18 and 3 yrs. junior: felony, imprisonment 10 to 50 yrs. and up to $100,000 fine	Transporting 1 oz. or more: felony, imprisonment 5 to 40 yrs. 3 yrs. mandatory and fine up to $1,000,000; 2nd or subsequent offense: mandatory 10 yrs. to be served consecutively with any other sentence

Table 12b: Illegal Drugs: Heroin—Continued

State	Code Section	Possession	Sale	Trafficking
WASHINGTON	69.50.204; 69.50.401 to 69.50.440	Class C felony: Imprisonment up to 5 yrs. and/or fine up to $10,000; subsequent offense: double penalties	Less than 2kg: class B felony, punishable by imprisonment up to 10 yrs. and/or fine up to $25,000; 2kg or more: class B felony, imprisonment up to 10 yrs. and/or fine up to $100,000 plus $50 for each gram over 2kg; sale to minors: class C felony; sale within 1,000 ft. of school: double penalties	
WEST VIRGINIA	60A-1-101 to 60A-2-204; 60A-4-401 to 60A-4-413	Misdemeanor, punishable by imprisonment 90 days to 6 mos. and/or fine up to $1,000; subsequent offense: double penalties	Felony, punishable by imprisonment 1 to 15 yrs. and/or fine up to $25,000; subsequent offense: double penalties; sale to minor or within 1,000 ft. of school: imprisonment mandatory 2 yrs.	Transport into state with intent to deliver: felony, punishable by imprisonment 1 to 15 yrs. and/or fine up to $25,000
WISCONSIN	961.41 to 961.50	Class I felony; within 1,000 ft. of school or public park: 100 hrs. community service	Less than 3g: class F felony; 3-10g: class E felony; 10-50g: class D felony; over 50g: class C felony; distribution to minor under 17 and at 3 yrs. junior or intent to distribute within 1,000 ft. of school or park: maximum prison term increased by 5 yrs.; knowingly hire or use person under 17: class F felony	

13. MARIJUANA LAWS

In the 1960s, many things in our culture changed. Hair styles and lifestyles changed permanently and profoundly. Even in the midst of all the radical-ness and new-age-ness and optimism of the Age of Aquarius, there were few of us survivors who even dared to imagine that one day you'd be able to walk into a store and legally buy marijuana!

The present laws are a testament to many baby boomers that dreams really do come true, slowly but surely. It should be pointed out that for many years before Prohibition was overturned, doctors prescribed alcohol for a variety of common maladies, including anxiety and stress. My grandfather was pharmacist in those days and I have a stack of old prescriptions from his store in Pismo Beach, California, that prescribe, for example, "two ounces of whiskey before evening meals," or, my personal favorite, "two ounces of whiskey, as needed."

To date, more than half the states now have laws which allow use of marijuana for a variety of medical reasons and fifteen others have decriminalized personal possession of small amounts to minor misdemeanors or infractions. Seven states have actually legalized recreational use of marijuana.

Legalization optimists will certainly see these developments as evidence that the nations marijuana laws will soon go the way of Prohibition laws. The fact is that the laws are changing rapidly and the chances are that this chapter will need to be updated by the time it gets into print.

_____

*This chapter was updated by Ashley Rae Fischer, Juris Doctor Candidate, Class of 2018, University of Nebraska Law.

Table 13: Marijuana Laws

State	Code Section	Summary	Personal Possession Limits/Penalties
ALABAMA	20-2-1 to 20-2-3; 20-2-23; 13A-5-6, 13A-5-11, 13A-12-210 to 215	Decriminalized: No; Medical: Yes, but extremely limited; Recreational: No	Possession for personal use: Less than 1kg (2.2 lbs.): Class A misdemeanor, punishable by imprisonment up to 1 yr. and $6,000 fine; possession of any amount over 1kg or a subsequent offense under 1kg: class C felony, punishable by 1 to 10 yrs. imprisonment and $15,000 fine
ALASKA	11.71.010 to 11.71.900; 12.55.035; 12.55.125, 12.55.135; 17.37.10 to 17.37.80	Decriminalized: Yes; Medical: Yes; Recreational: Yes	Adults 21+ may legally possess no more than 1 oz. of usable marijuana in public or up to 4 oz. in residence and may cultivate or transport no more than 6 marijuana plants, of which no more than 3 may be mature; use or display of 1 to 4 oz. of marijuana in public: class B misdemeanor, punishable by imprisonment up to 90 days and/or fine up to $2,000; possessing greater than 4 oz. in public: class C felony, punishable by imprisonment up to 5 yrs. and/or fine up to $50,000.
ARIZONA	13-702; 13-3401; 13-3405; 36-2501 to 36-2553; 36-2801 to 36-2819	Decriminalized: No; Medical: Yes; Recreational: No;	Possession ≤2 lbs.: Class 6 felony, punishable by imprisonment 4 mos. to 2 yrs. and $750 fine or fine to exhaust proceeds of offense; 2-4 lbs.: class 5 felony, punishable by imprisonment 6 mos. to 2.5 yrs. and $750 fine or fine to exhaust proceeds of offense; ≥4 lbs.: class 4 felony, punishable by imprisonment 1 to 3.75 yrs. and at least $750 fine or fine to exhaust proceeds of offense
ARKANSAS	5-64-101 to 5-64-446	Medical: Yes; Recreational: No	Qualified patient or registered caregiver may possess less than 2.5 oz.; medical marijuana usage may be asserted as affirmative defense

Medical Requirements/Limits	Sale Limits/Penalties	Miscellaneous
Alabama's Controlled Substances Therapeutic Research Program allows for medical research and experimentation with regard to the use of cannabis under strictly controlled circumstances	Sale of any amount: Class B felony, punishable by imprisonment 2 to 20 yrs. and $30,000 fine; sale to minor: class A felony, punishable by imprisonment 10 yrs. to life with no suspension or probation and fine up to $60,000; sale within 3 mi. of a school or a public housing project: additional felony, punishable by additional 5 yrs. imprisonment. Marijuana conviction will result in a 6-month driver's license suspension.	6 mos. driver's license suspension for any conviction
Patients with qualifying medical condition or their caregiver may legally possess ≤1 oz. of usable marijuana in public or up to 4 oz. in residence; patients must have a preexisting relationship with the recommending doctor; caregiver must be 21+ and never convicted of a felony controlled substance offense; State Licensed Dispensaries: No; Home Cultivation: Yes; patients or their primary caregivers may possess no more than 6 marijuana plants, of which no more than 3 may be mature in an enclosed, locked location. ID Card Reciprocity: No.	Adults 21+ may gift up to 1 oz. and up to 6 immature plants to other adults 21+, however, they cannot be compensated for these transactions; selling less than 1 oz.: misdemeanor, punishable by imprisonment up to 1 yr. and/or $10,000 fine; selling 1 oz. or more: felony, punishable by imprisonment up to 5 yrs. and/or $50,000 fine; selling to minor under 19 who is 3 yrs. or more seller's junior: felony, punishable by imprisonment up to 10 yrs. and/or $100,000 fine	If minor under 18 is convicted of a marijuana offense, he or she must perform 96 hrs. community work and minor's driver's license or permit shall be revoked for 6 mos.; additional 6 mos. if community work is not completed
Patients with qualifying medical condition or their caregiver may legally possess ≤2.5 oz. of usable marijuana; patients must have preexisting relationship with recommending doctor; caregiver must be 21 or older and never convicted of felony controlled substance offense; State Licensed Dispensaries: Yes; state-licensed nonprofit dispensaries may produce and dispense marijuana to authorized patients on a not-for-profit basis; patients limited to 2.5 oz. per 14 days; Home Cultivation: Yes, but limited; if patient's residence is further than 25 miles from state-licensed dispensary, he or she may cultivate up to 12 marijuana plants in an enclosed, locked facility; ID Card Reciprocity: Yes for patients with conditions that qualify under Arizona law and who have been diagnosed by licensed person with authority to prescribe drugs to humans in the state of the person's residence; ID cards serve only as affirmative and do not allow out-of-state residents to obtain marijuana from state licensed dispensaries	Sale, or possessing for sale: ≤2 lbs.: Class 4 felony, punishable by imprisonment 1 to 3.75 yrs. and fine $750 or amt. to exhaust proceeds of drug offense; 2-4 lbs.: class 3 felony, punishable by imprisonment 2 to 8.75 yrs. and fine $750 or amt. to exhaust proceeds of drug offense; over 4 lbs.: class 2 felony, punishable by imprisonment 2 to 12.5 yrs. and fine $7,570 or amt. to exhaust proceeds of drug offense; sale within drug-free school zone: add 1 yr. to sentence and $2,000 fine; enhanced penalties for employing minor in commission of drug offense, prior offense, or committing drug offense in school zone	
Patients and caregivers must obtain registry card from Dept. of Health and provide physician certification within 30 days of application; under 18 must provide parent or guardian consent, parent or guardian must register as designated caregiver, and patient's physician must explain effects of marijuana usage to patient and parent or legal guardian	State dispensaries and cultivation facilities regulated by Medical Marijuana Commission	6 mos. driver's license suspension for any conviction, 277-16-915(b)(1)(A)

Table 13: Marijuana Laws—Continued

State	Code Section	Summary	Personal Possession Limits/Penalties
CALIFORNIA	Health & Safety §§ 11357 to 11362.9	Medical: Yes; Recreational: Yes	Individuals 21 and over may possess sup to 28.5g of marijuana or up to 8g of concentrated cannabis; personal cultivation of up to 6 marijuana plants and possession not marijuana produced is also permitted; plants and amount of marijuana produced by plants over 28.5g must be kept in private residence in locked space not visible from public place; use of marijuana products outside of licensed area or in any area where use of tobacco products is prohibited is not permissible; if person is under 18, possession of up to 28.5g of marijuana or up to 4g. of concentrated cannabis: infraction punishable by 4 hrs. drug counseling and 10 hrs. community service, more severe penalty for subsequent offenses; possession of over 28.5g: infraction punishable by 8 hrs. of drug education and up to 40 hrs. of community service, more severe penalty for subsequent offenses; if 18-21: infraction and subject to fine up to $100; persons 18 and over who possess over 28.5g of marijuana: imprisonment up to 6 mos. and/or fine up to $500; possession by anyone 18 or older of up to 28.5g of marijuana or up to 4g of concentrated cannabis on grounds of any K-12 school during open hours: misdemeanor punishable by fine up to $250, imprisonment in county jail for up to 10 days and/or fine up to $500 for subsequence offenses; if person is under 18: possession of up to 28.5g of marijuana or up to 4g of concentrated cannabis on grounds of any K-12 school during open hours: infraction punishable by 4 hrs. drug counseling and 10 hrs. community service; various penalties for smoking in public or other regulated or prohibited spaces

Medical Requirements/Limits	Sale Limits/Penalties	Miscellaneous
Patients with qualifying medical condition or their caregiver may legally possess 8 oz. or more and 6 mature plants, or 12 immature plants; individual cities and counties allowed to enact higher, but not lower, limits than the state standard; defense can also be raised for more as the California Supreme Court has affirmed that a patient may possess up to whatever amount is necessary for their personal medical use as determined by their doctor; patients must have a preexisting relationship with the recommending doctor; caregiver must be 18+ and never convicted of a felony controlled substance offense; State Licensed Dispensaries: Yes, although regulations regarding licensing and licensing are not expected until 2017, paying the state sales tax and/or city specific taxes; Home Cultivation: Yes, at least 6 mature plants or 12 immature plants, but counties may allow for more; ID Card Reciprocity: No	Commercial sale of up to 28.5g of marijuana or up to 8g of concentrated cannabis to persons 21 or older permissible with license and subject to 15% state excise tax in addition to any state or local sales tax; selling marijuana without a license: civil penalties up to 4 times amount of license fee; unlawful transportation for sale of less than 28.5g of marijuana: infraction punishable by fine up to $100; more than 28.5g: imprisonment for up to 6 mos. and/or fine up to $500	Recreational and medical use of marijuana regulated by Bureau of Marijuana Control; cultivation subject to cultivation tax of $9.25/oz. for marijuana flowers and $2.75/oz. for marijuana leaves

Table 13: Marijuana Laws—Continued

State	Code Section	Summary	Personal Possession Limits/Penalties
COLORADO	CO Const. art. XVIII, §§ 14 and 16; 12-43.3-101 to 12-43.3-1102; 12-43.4-101 to 12-43.4-1101; 18-1.3-501; 18-1.3-401.5; 25-1.5-105 to 25-1.5-106	Decriminalized: Yes; Medical: Yes; Recreational: Yes	Adults 21+ may legally purchase, possess and transport no more than 1 oz. of usable marijuana in public and may cultivate or transport no more than 6 marijuana plants, of which no more than 3 may be mature; possession of less than 2 oz. is a drug petty offense, punishable by fine up to $100; over 2 oz. to 6 oz.: level 2 drug misdemeanor, punishable imprisonment up to 3 mos. and $250 fine; over 6 oz. to 12 oz.: level 1 drug misdemeanor punishable by imprisonment up to 18 mos. and $5,000 fine; over 12 oz.: level 4 drug felony, punishable by imprisonment up to 1 yr. and $100,000 fine
CONNECTICUT	21A-240 to 21A-283a; 21A-408 to 21A-408q	Decriminalized: Yes; Medical: Yes; Recreational: No	Possession less than 5 oz.: civil penalty, punishable by $150 fine; subsequent offenses: fine $200 and $500; .5 oz. to 4 oz.: imprisonment up to 1 yr. and $1,000 fine; subsequent offenses: imprisonment 5 yrs. and $3,000 fine; possession over 4 oz.: imprisonment up to 5 yrs. and/or fine up to $2,000; subsequent offenses: imprisonment up to 10 yrs. and/or fine up to $5,000

Medical Requirements/Limits	Sale Limits/Penalties	Miscellaneous
Patients with a qualifying medical condition or their caregiver may legally possess up to 2 oz. of usable marijuana; patients must have preexisting relationship with recommending doctor; caregiver must be 18 or over; State Licensed Dispensaries: Yes; Home Cultivation: Yes; patients or primary caregivers may possess up to 6 marijuana plants, of which no more than 3 may be mature in an enclosed, locked location; ID Card Reciprocity: No	Transfer of less than 1 oz. by persons 21 or over for no remuneration: no penalty; sale of marijuana to a person over 21: under 4 oz.: level 1 drug misdemeanor, punishable by imprisonment up to 18 mos. and $5,000 fine; over 4 oz. to up to 12 oz.: level 4 drug felony, punishable up to 1 yr. imprisonment and $100,000 fine; over 12 oz. to up to 5 lbs.: level, 3 drug felony, punishable by a maximum of 4 yrs. imprisonment and $500,000 fine; more than 5 lbs. to less than 50 lbs. is a level 2 drug felony, punishable by a maximum of 8 yrs. imprisonment and $750,000 fine; more than 50 lbs.: level 1 drug felony punishable by a maximum of 32 yrs. imprisonment and fine up to $1 million; Sale of marijuana to a person under 21: up to 1 oz. is a level 4 drug felony punishable by a maximum of 1 yr. imprisonment and $100,000 fine; over 1 oz. to less than 6 oz. is a level 3 drug felony punishable by a maximum of 4 yrs. imprisonment and $500,000 fine; over 6 oz. to up to 2.5 lbs. is a level 2 drug felony, punishable imprisonment up to 8 yrs. and $750,000 fine; over 2.5 lbs.: level 1 drug felony, punishable by imprisonment up to 32 yrs. and fine up to $1 million	Non-residents 21+ may purchase up to .25 oz. at a time from licensed retail store; non-resident may visit more than 1 store a day and face no penalty, so long as they do not exceed the 1 oz. possession limit; Colorado allows marijuana stores to operate from 8AM to midnight; cities can implement more restrictive hours; possession on federal land not protected and punishable by 1st offense: imprisonment up to 1 yr. and $1,000 fine; 2nd offense: imprisonment mandatory 15 days to 2 yrs.; 3rd or subsequent offense: imprisonment 90 days to 3 yrs. and $5,000 fine
Patients with qualifying medical condition or caregiver may legally possess a 1 mo. supply, currently set by the Dept. of Consumer Protection at up to 2.5 oz., unless patient's physician determines greater amount is necessary; patient must have preexisting relationship with recommending doctor; caregiver must be 18 or over; State Licensed Dispensaries: Yes; Home Cultivation: No; ID Card Reciprocity: No.	Less than 1kg: imprisonment up to 7 yrs. and $25,000 fine; subsequent offenses: imprisonment up to 15 yrs. and $100,000 fine; court may prescribe alternative sentence of imprisonment up to 3 yrs., with probation at any time; over 1kg: imprisonment 5 to 20 yrs.; subsequent offenses: imprisonment 10 to 20 yrs.; court may exception to mandatory minimum sentence if defendant under 18 or mentally impaired; if sale within 1,500 ft. of school or day care center: additional mandatory 3 yrs. imprisonment; sale to minor or person 2 yrs. junior: additional mandatory 2 yrs. imprisonment; using person under 18 to assist in sale: additional 3 yrs. imprisonment	

Table 13: Marijuana Laws—Continued

State	Code Section	Summary	Personal Possession Limits/Penalties
DELAWARE	Tit. 16, §§ 4701 to 4722; 4752 to 4769; 4901A to 4927A	Decriminalized: Yes; Medical: Yes; Recreational: No	Possession up to 1 oz. by a person over age 21:civil penalty of $100 and forfeit marijuana; if person is between 18 and 21: unclassified misdemeanor; under 18: class B misdemeanor.
DISTRICT OF COLUMBIA	7-1671 .01 to 7-1671.13; 9-04.01 to 9-04.10; 48-911.01	Decriminalized: Yes; Medical: Yes; Recreational: Yes	Adults may legally possess up to 2 oz. and cultivate no more than 6 plants in their primary residence, with 3 or fewer mature at any one time; transfer or gift without payment up to 1 oz. to another person 21+ is also permitted; possession of more than 2 oz.: misdemeanor, punishable by imprisonment up to 180 days and fine up to $1,000, first time offenders eligible for probation in lieu of imprisonment or fine
FLORIDA	775.082; 893.13; 893.135; FL Const. art. X, § 29	Medical: Yes; Recreational: No	Under 20g: 1st degree misdemeanor, punishable by imprisonment up to 1 yr. and $5,000 fine; over 20g: felony, punishable by imprisonment up to 5 yrs. and $5,000 fine

Medical Requirements/Limits	Sale Limits/Penalties	Miscellaneous
Patients with qualifying medical condition or caregiver may legally possess up to 6 oz. of usable marijuana; patient must have preexisting relationship with recommending doctor; caregivers must be 21 or over with no violent or drug felony conviction; State Licensed Dispensaries: Yes; Registered "compassion centers" must operate on a not for profit basis, may not dispense more than 3 oz. of marijuana to a single patient in any 14-day period, and may not employ anyone under 21; Home Cultivation: No; ID Card Reciprocity: Yes; Delaware allows access to medical marijuana for visiting patients diagnosed with a debilitating medical condition, possess a valid ID card or equivalent issued in another state; not a resident of Delaware or resident for less than 30 days	Manufacturing, distributing, or possessing with intent to distribute: less than 5 lbs.: class E felony, punishable by imprisonment up to 5 yrs. and fine up to $10,000; 5-100 lbs.: class B felony, punishable by imprisonment 2 to 25 yrs. and fine up to $25,000; 100-500 lbs.: felony, punishable by imprisonment mandatory minimum 4 yrs. and fine up to $50,000; over 500 lbs.: felony, punishable by imprisonment mandatory minimum 8 yrs. and fine up to $100,000; distributing to minor under 21: class E felony, punishable by imprisonment up to 5 yrs. and fine up to $10,000; under 16: mandatory 6 mos. imprisonment; under 14: mandatory 1 yr. imprisonment; using minor to distribute drugs: felony, punishable by imprisonment up to 10 yrs. and fine up to $250,000; within 300 ft. of park, recreation area, church, synagogue, or other place of worship: felony, punishable by imprisonment up to 15 yrs. and fine up to $250,000	
Patients with qualifying medical condition or caregiver may legally possess up to 2 oz. per 30-day period; patient must have preexisting relationship with recommending doctor; caregiver must be 18 or over with no conviction for possession or sale of controlled substance; State Licensed Dispensaries: Yes; Home Cultivation: No; ID Card Reciprocity: No.	Adults may cultivate with no penalty in their primary residence up to 6 plants, no more than 3 mature at any one time; not-for-profit transactions involving small amounts also permitted; distribution, manufacture, or possession with intent to distribute: imprisonment up to 5 yrs. and/or fine up to $50,000; sale up to .5 lb.: imprisonment up to 180 days and/or fine up to $1,000; distribution to minor by person over 21: double penalties; enlist minor to distribute: imprisonment up to 10 yrs. and fine up to $10,000; 2nd offense: imprisonment up to 20 yrs. and up to $20,000; within 1,000 ft. of school, recreation center, or in and around public housing: double penalties; subsequent offenses: double penalties	
Medical use of marijuana permissible for patients with qualifying debilitative conditions and registered caregivers; state controlled marijuana dispensaries and cultivation facilities established and regulated by Dept. of Health	Sale of up to 20g without compensation: misdemeanor, punishable by imprisonment up to 1 yr. and $10,000 fine; up to 25 lbs.: felony, punishable by imprisonment up to 5 yrs. and $5,000 fine; 25-2,000 lbs.: felony, punishable by imprisonment 3 to 15 yrs. and $25,000 fine; 2,000 to 10,000 lbs.: felony, punishable by imprisonment 7 to 30 yrs. and $50,000 fine; 10,000 lbs. or more: felony, punishable by 15 to 30 yrs. and $200,000 fine; sale within 1,000 ft. of school: felony, punishable by imprisonment up to 15 yrs. and $15,000 fine	2 yrs. driver's license suspension for any conviction

Table 13: Marijuana Laws—Continued

State	Code Section	Summary	Personal Possession Limits/Penalties
GEORGIA	16-13-2; 16-13-30 to 16-13-56	Decriminalized: No; Medical: No; Recreational: No	Up to 1 oz.: misdemeanor, punishable by imprisonment up to 1 yr. and/or $1,000 fine; over 1 oz.: felony, punishable by imprisonment 1 to 10 yrs.
HAWAII	329-14 to 329-50; 706-640 to 706-648; 712-1240 to 712-1257	Decriminalized: No; Medical: Yes; Recreational: No	Less than 1 oz.: Petty misdemeanor, punishable by imprisonment up to 30 days and/or $1,000 fine; 1 oz. to 1 lb.: misdemeanor, punishable by imprisonment up to 1 yr. and/or $2,000 fine
IDAHO	37-2701 to 37-2751	Decriminalized: No; Medical: No; Recreational: No	Up to 3oz: misdemeanor, punishable by imprisonment up to 1 yr. and/or fine up to $1,000; 3 oz. to 1 lb.: felony, punishable by imprisonment up to 5 yrs. and/or fine up to $10,000; using or being under the influence on public property or private property open to public: misdemeanor, punishable by imprisonment up to 6 mos. and/or fine up to $1,000; subsequent offenses within 5 yrs.: punishable by imprisonment 120 days to 1 yr. if offender refuses to complete treatment

Medical Requirements/Limits	Sale Limits/Penalties	Miscellaneous
	Sale or delivery of up to 10 lbs.: felony, punishable by imprisonment 1 to 10 yrs.; 10-2,000 lbs.: imprisonment 5 to 30 yrs. and/or up to $100,000 fine; 2,000-10,000 lbs.: imprisonment 7 to 30 yrs. and/or fine up to $250,000; over 10,000 lbs.: imprisonment 15 to 30 yrs. and fine up to $1,000,000; sale or delivery within 1,000 ft. of school grounds, park, housing project, or drug free zone: felony punishable by imprisonment up to 20 yrs. and/or one up to $20,000; 2nd or subsequent offense: imprisonment minimum 5 yrs. to 40 yrs. and/or fine up to $40,000	Driver's license suspension: 1st offense in 5 yrs.: at least 180 days; restoration fee up to $210; 2nd offense in 5 yrs.: at least 3 yrs., after 1 yr. may apply for reinstatement for fee up to $310; 3rd of subsequent offense in 5 yrs.: at least 5 yrs., may apply for reinstatement after 2 yrs. if certain conditions met and fee up to $410
Patients with qualifying medical condition or their caregiver may legally possess up to 4 oz. of usable marijuana or 7 marijuana plants; patients must have preexisting relationship with recommending doctor; caregiver must be 18 or older; State Licensed Dispensaries: Yes; Home Cultivation: Yes, patients may cultivate up to 7 marijuana plants, mature or immature; ID Card Reciprocity: No.	Sale less than 1oz.: misdemeanor, punishable by imprisonment up to 1 yrs. and/or $2,000 fine; 1 oz. to 1 lb.: class C felony, punishable by imprisonment up to 5 yrs. and/or $10,000 fine; 1-5 lbs.: class B felony, punishable by imprisonment up to 10 yrs. and $25,000 fine; 5 lbs. or more: class A felony, punishable by imprisonment up to 20 yrs. and $50,000 fine; within 750 ft. of school or park or on or within 10 ft. of parked school vehicle: class C felony, punishable by imprisonment up to 5 yrs. and/or $10,000 fine; using minor under 18 to assist in distribution: class B felony, punishable by imprisonment up to 10 yrs. and/or $25,000 fine, double penalties if in school or other prohibited areas	Commercial driver's license may be suspended if convicted of the unlawful transportation, possession, or use of marijuana while on duty
	Sale or delivery up to 1 lb. or up to 25 plants: felony, punishable by imprisonment up to 5 yrs. and/or fine up to $15,000; deliver or import into state more than 1 lb. or more than 25 plants: considered trafficking: felony punishable by imprisonment 5 to 15 yrs. and fine up to $50,000; subsequent offense: double penalties; deliver by person 18 or older to minor at least 3 yrs. his or her junior: double penalties; delivery on premises where person under 18 is present: felony punishable by imprisonment up to 5 yrs. and/or fine up to $5,000	

Table 13: Marijuana Laws—Continued

State	Code Section	Summary	Personal Possession Limits/Penalties
ILLINOIS	410 §§ 130/1 to 130/999; 720 §§ 550/1 to 550/19; 570/100 to 570/414	Decriminalized: No; Medical: Yes; Recreational: No	Possession of less than 2.5g: class C misdemeanor, punishable by imprisonment up to 30 days; 2.5-10g: class B misdemeanor, punishable by imprisonment up to 1 yr.; 2nd or subsequent offense: 10-30g: class 4 felony, punishable by imprisonment 1 to 3 yrs. and $25,000 fine; possession 30-500g: class 4 felony, punishable by imprisonment 1 to 3 yrs. and $25,000 fine; 2nd or subsequent offense: class 3 felony, punishable by imprisonment 2 to 5 yrs. and $25,000 fine; possession of 500-2,000g: class 3 felony, punishable by imprisonment 2 to 5 yrs. and $25,000 fine; 2,000-5,000g: class 2 felony, punishable by imprisonment 3 to 7 yrs. and $25,000 fine; over 5,000g: class 1 felony, punishable by 4 to 20 yrs. and $25,000 fine
INDIANA	35-48-1-19 to 3-48-4-17	Decriminalized: No; Medical: No; Recreational: No	Up to 30g: class A misdemeanor, punishable by imprisonment up to 1 yr. and $5,000 fine; over 30g: class D felony, punishable by imprisonment 6 mos. to 3 yrs. and $10,000 fine
IOWA	124.101 to 124.212; 124.401 to 124.416	Decriminalized: No; Medical: No; Recreational: No	Any amount: misdemeanor, punishable imprisonment up to 6 mos. and/or $1,000 fine; 2nd offense: misdemeanor, punishable by imprisonment up to 1 yr. and/or fine $315 to $1,875; 3rd offense: aggravated misdemeanor, punishable by imprisonment up to 2 yrs. and/or fine $625 to $6,250; within 1,000 ft. of school or park: 100 hrs. of community service added to penalty
KANSAS	65-4101 to 65-4140; 21-5706, 21-6805	Decriminalized: No; Medical: No; Recreational: No	Any amount: class A misdemeanor, punishable by imprisonment up to 1 yr. and $2,500 fine; subsequent offense: felony, punishable by imprisonment 10 to 42 mos. and fine up to $100,000

Medical Requirements/Limits	Sale Limits/Penalties	Miscellaneous
Patients with qualifying medical condition or their caregivers may legally possess up to 2.5 oz. per 14-day period; patient must have preexisting relation with recommending doctor; caregiver must be 18 or older; State Licensed Dispensaries: Yes; Home Cultivation: No; ID Card Reciprocity: No	Selling or possessing with the intent to sell, up to 2.5g: class B misdemeanor, punishable by imprisonment up to 6 mos.; 2.5-10g: class A misdemeanor, punishable imprisonment up to 1 yr.; 10-30 g: class 4 felony, punishable by imprisonment 1 to 3 yrs. and $25,000 fine; 30-500g: class 3 felony, punishable by imprisonment 2 to 5 yrs. and $50,000 fine; 500-2,000g: class 2 felony, punishable by imprisonment 3 to 7 yrs. and $100,000 fine; 2,000-5,000g: class 1 felony, punishable by imprisonment 4 to 20 yrs. and $150,000 fine; over 5,000g: class X felony, punishable by imprisonment 6 to 30 yrs. and $200,000 fine; employing or using person under 18: up to 3x penalties; subsequent offenses, delivery to pregnant woman or delivery within 1,000 ft. of school or safe place: up to 2x penalties	
	Sale 30g or less: class A misdemeanor, punishable by imprisonment up to 1 yr. and $5,000 fine; 30g to 10 lbs.: class D felony, punishable by imprisonment 6 mos. to 3 yrs. and $10,000 fine; over 10 lbs. or within 1,000 ft. of school (any amount) or other specified areas: felony, punishable by imprisonment 2 to 8 yrs. and $10,000 fine; sale of any amt. to minor: class D felony, punishable by imprisonment 7 mos. to 3 yrs. and $10,000 fine	6 mos. to 2 yrs. driver's license suspension for any conviction
	Distribution up to 50kg: class D felony, punishable by imprisonment up to 5 yrs. and fine $750 to $7,500; 50-100kg: class C felony, punishable by imprisonment up to 10 yrs. and fine $1,000 to $50,000; 100-1,000kg: class B felony, punishable by imprisonment up to 25 yrs. and fine $5,000 to $100,000; if person over 18 solicits minor under 18 to assist in sale: class C felony, punishable by imprisonment up to 10 yrs. and fine $1,000 to $50,000; if person over 18 distributes to minor under 18: class B felony, punishable by imprisonment 5 to 25 yrs. and fine $5,000 to $100,000; if within 1,000 ft. of school or park: mandatory minimum 10 yrs.	180 days driver's license suspension for any conviction
	Any amount: felony, punishable by imprisonment 14 to 51 mos. and fine up to $300,000; within 1,000 ft. of school zone: felony, punishable by imprisonment 46 to 83 mos. and fine up to $300,000	

Table 13: Marijuana Laws—Continued

State	Code Section	Summary	Personal Possession Limits/Penalties
KENTUCKY	218A.010 to 218A.140; 218A.1411; 218A.1421 to 218A.1423; 532.060	Decriminalized: No; Medical: No; Recreational: No	Less than 8 oz: class B misdemeanor, punishable by imprisonment up to 45 days and $250 fine; over 8 oz. prima facie evidence of intent to sell
LOUISIANA	40:961 to 40:996.6	Decriminalized: No; Medical: No; Recreational: No	Less than 60 lbs.: imprisonment up to 6 mos. and/or fine up to $500; 2nd offense: imprisonment up to 5 yrs. and/or fine $250 to $2,500; 3rd and subsequent offense: imprisonment up to 20 yrs. and/or fine up to $5,000; 60-2,000 lbs.: felony, punishable by imprisonment 5 to 30 yrs. and fine $100,000 to $400,000; 10,000 lbs. or more: felony, punishable by imprisonment 25 to 40 yrs.; possession, distribution, or cultivation within 2,000 ft. of drug free zone: 1.5x maximum sentence allowed for underlying offense

Medical Requirements/Limits	Sale Limits/Penalties	Miscellaneous
	Less than 8 oz: class A misdemeanor, punishable by imprisonment up to 1 yr. and $500 fine; 2nd or subsequent offense: class D felony, punishable by imprisonment 1 to 5 yrs. and $10,000 fine; 8 oz. to 5 lbs.: class D felony, punishable by imprisonment 1 to 5 yrs. and fine $1,000 to $10,000; 2nd or subsequent offense: class C felony, punishable by imprisonment 5 to 10 yrs. and $10,000 fine; over 5 lbs.: class C felony, punishable by imprisonment 5 to 10 yrs. and fine $1,000 to $10,000; 2nd or subsequent offense: class B felony, punishable by imprisonment 10 to 20 yrs.; within 1,000 ft. of school or park: felony, punishable by imprisonment 1 to 5 yrs. and fine $1,000 to $10,000	
	Sale, distribution or cultivation of any amount: imprisonment 5 to 30 yrs. and fine up to $450,000; subsequent offense: imprisonment 10 to 60 yrs. and fine up to $100,000; prior offenses include any drug conviction regardless of location; if seller is 18+ and sells to minor under 18 at least 3 yrs. junior: imprisonment up to 45 yrs.; subsequent offense: imprisonment up to 90 yrs.; distribution to elementary, middle, or high school student and/or soliciting minor to distribute: imprisonment maximum term of 45 yrs. and fine up to $75,000; subsequent offense: imprisonment up to 90 yrs. and $150,000 fine	19 and older: driver's license suspension 30 days to 1 yr. for any conviction

Table 13: Marijuana Laws—Continued

State	Code Section	Summary	Personal Possession Limits/Penalties
MAINE	Marijuana Legalization Act: Tit. 7, 2441 to 2454; Tit. 17A, §§ 1101 to 1118; Tit. 22, §§ 2383; 2421 to 2430; Tit. 36, § 1817	Decriminalized: Yes; Medical: Yes; Recreational: Yes	Person 21 or older may use, possess or transport up to 2.5 oz. of marijuana, up to 6 flowering marijuana plants, 12 immature plants, and unlimited seedlings, and may transfer up to 2.5 oz. of prepared marijuana and up to 6 immature plants or seedlings to another person 21 or older; plants or seedlings must have legible tag including name and Maine driver's license number or Maine identification number; marijuana may be consumed in nonpublic place including rivage residence but not consumed where use of tobacco is also limited or prohibited or in licensed retail marijuana establishment; consuming marijuana in non-private place: civil fine up to $100
MARYLAND	Crim. Law §§ 5-601 to 5-628; Health-Gen. §§ 13-3301 to 13-3316	Decriminalized: Yes; Medical: Yes; Recreational: No	Up to 10g: civil infraction, punishable by $100 fine; subsequent offense: $250 fine; 10g - 50 lbs.: misdemeanor, punishable by imprisonment up to 1 yr. and $1,000 fine

Medical Requirements/Limits	Sale Limits/Penalties	Miscellaneous
Patients with qualifying medical condition or caregiver may legally possess up to 2.5 oz. of usable marijuana and 6 marijuana plants; patient must have preexisting relationship with recommending doctor; caregiver must be 21+ and no drug conviction; State Licensed Dispensaries: Yes; Home Cultivation: Yes; cultivation for medical use is not considered cultivation for personal use; patient or primary caregiver may possess no more than 6 mature marijuana plants in an enclosed, locked location; ID Card Reciprocity: Yes; qualifying out-of-state patient with valid ID card or equivalent may engage in conduct authorized for the registered patient for 30 days without having to obtain a Maine ID card	Person 21 or older may purchase up to 2.5 oz. of prepared marijuana and accessories from licensed marijuana retail establishment and may purchase up to 12 immature plants or seedlings from licensed retail marijuana cultivation facility; licensed retail marijuana establishment may only sell marijuana, marijuana products, or other non-consumable related items; licensed retail marijuana establishments prohibited from selling or giving away other consumable items that do not contain marijuana, e.g., cigarettes, alcohol, sodas, and candy; cost of retail marijuana license between $250 and $2,500 with $10 to $250 one-time application fee; penalty for licensee violation of any state licensing provisions: revocation of license or fine $500 to $10,000; trafficking 1-20 lbs.: class C felony, punishable by imprisonment up to 5 yrs. and $5,000 fine; 20 lbs. or more: class B felony, punishable by imprisonment up to 10 yrs. and $20,000 fine; sale to minor or within 1,000 ft. of school or school bus: felony, punishable by imprisonment up to 5 yrs. and $5,000 fine	Magazine with primary focus of marijuana or marijuana businesses may only be sold at licensed marijuana retail establishment where persons 21 or older are present; sales tax on marijuana or marijuana products: 10%; regulation and control of licensing, taxing, selling, and possession managed by Dept. of Agriculture, Conservation and Forestry
Patients with qualifying medical condition or caregiver may legally possess up to 30-day supply of marijuana, amt. determined by Commission; patient must have preexisting relationship with recommending doctor; caregiver must be 18 or older; State Licensed Dispensaries: Yes; Home Cultivation: No; ID Card Reciprocity: No.	Possession with intent to distribute less than 50 lbs.: felony, punishable by imprisonment up to 5 yrs. and $15,000 fine; subsequent offense: imprisonment minimum 2 yrs.; more than 50 lbs. (acts in proceeding 90 days can be aggregated): imprisonment mandatory minimum 5 yrs.; within 1,000 ft. of school or in school vehicle: felony, punishable by imprisonment up to 20 yrs. and $20,000 fine; subsequent violation: additional 5 to 40 yrs. imprisonment and $40,000 fine; using or soliciting minor to distribute in school vehicle or within 1,000 ft. of school: felony, punishable by imprisonment up to 20 yrs. and $20,000 fine; subsequent violation: additional 5 to 40 yrs. imprisonment and $40,000 fine; using or soliciting minor to distribute, deliver, or manufacture marijuana: felony, punishable by imprisonment up to 20 yrs. and $20,000 fine	Edible forms of marijuana are not permitted; offenses involving the use of marijuana in public carries a civil fine of up to $500

Table 13: Marijuana Laws—Continued

State	Code Section	Summary	Personal Possession Limits/Penalties
MASSACHUSETTS	Ch. 94C, §§ 1 to 49; 1-1 to 1-17	Decriminalized: Yes; Medical: Yes; Recreational: Yes	Person 21 or older may not be prosecuted for possessing, using, or purchasing up to 1 oz. of marijuana, or for possessing up to 10 oz. of marijuana in primary residence, or for cultivating up to 6 marijuana plants; if more than 1 oz. kept inside primary residence, it must be secured by lock, penalty of $100 fine and forfeiture of excess marijuana if not; smoking or consuming marijuana in public area other than licensed marijuana establishment: fine up to $100; may not possess "open container" of marijuana in passenger are or any other readily accessible area of motor vehicle; fine for violation: up to $500
MICHIGAN	333.7401 to 333.7461; 333.26421 to 333.26430	Decriminalized: No; Medical: Yes; Recreational: No	Possession any amount: Misdemeanor, punishable by imprisonment up to 1 yr. and/or $2,000 fine; use: misdemeanor, punishable by imprisonment up to 90 days and/or $100 fine; possession in park: misdemeanor or felony at judge's discretion, punishable by imprisonment up to 2 yrs. and/or $2,000 fine
MINNESOTA	152.021 to 152.029; 152.21 to 152.37	Decriminalized: No; Medical: Yes; Recreational: No	Up to 42.5g: Misdemeanor, punishable by fine up to $200; 42g to 10kg: felony, punishable by imprisonment up to 5 yrs. and/or fine up to $5,000; 10-50kg: imprisonment up to 20 yrs. and/or fine up to $250,000; 50-100kg: imprisonment up to 25 yrs. and/or fine up to $500,000; more than 100kg: imprisonment up to 30 yrs. and/or fine up to $1,000,000; more than 1.4g inside one's vehicle, not in trunk: misdemeanor, punishable by imprisonment up to 90 days and/or fine up to $1,000

Medical Requirements/Limits	Sale Limits/Penalties	Miscellaneous
Patients with qualifying medical condition or caregiver may legally possess 60-day supply, typically 10 oz. but doctor can certify more is needed; medical users exempt from 10 oz. personal possession limit; patient must have preexisting relationship with recommending doctor; caregiver must be 21+ and registered with health dept.; State Licensed Dispensaries: Yes; Home Cultivation: Yes, but only to patients whose access to dispensaries is limited by financial hardship, physical incapacity to access reasonable transportation, or lack of dispensaries reasonably close or that will deliver to patient; ID Card Reciprocity: No	Any licensed establishment may sell marijuana to person 20 or older in compliance with regulations established by Cannabis Control Commission; any sale of marijuana by licensed marijuana establishment to individual subject to Massachusetts state sales tax and 3.75% excise tax	Person 21 or older may not be arrested or prosecuted for possessing marijuana-related accessories or transferring accessories to another person 21 or older
Patients with qualifying medical condition or caregiver may legally possess up to 2.5 oz. of usable marijuana and 12 marijuana plants; patient must have preexisting relationship with recommending doctor; caregiver must be 21 or older with no felony convictions within 10 yrs. and no drug convictions; State Licensed Dispensaries: No, but several cities have enacted ordinances recognizing, licensing, and regulating dispensaries; Home Cultivation: Yes, no more than 12 plants in an enclosed locked facility; ID Card Reciprocity: Yes; other state, district, territory, commonwealth, or insular possession of the U.S. must offer reciprocity to have reciprocity in Michigan.	Sale without compensation: Misdemeanor, punishable by imprisonment up to 1 yr. and/or $1,000 fine; less than 5kg: felony, punishable by imprisonment up to 4 yrs. and/or $20,000 fine; 5-45kg: felony, punishable by imprisonment up to 7 yrs. and/or $500,000 fine; 45kg or more: felony, punishable by imprisonment up to 15 yrs. and/or $10,000,000 fine; sale to minor or near school property: up to double penalties	Marijuana must be in case in a trunk while it is transported, or if no trunk, in case not readily accessible from inside vehicle; 6 mos. driver's license suspension any conviction
Patients with qualifying medical condition or caregiver may legally possess 30-day supply; patient must have preexisting relationship with recommending doctor; caregiver must be 21 or older with no disqualifying drug conviction; State Licensed Dispensaries: Yes; Home Cultivation: No; ID Card Reciprocity: No; only non-smokable forms of marijuana is legal; permissible forms include liquids such as oils, pills, or vaporization that does not entail use of dried leaves	Up to 42.5g without compensation: misdemeanor, punishable by fine up to $200; less than 5kg: felony, punishable by imprisonment up to 5 yrs. and/or fine up to $10,000; 5-25kg, imprisonment up to 20 yrs. and/or fine up to $250,000; 25-50kg: imprisonment up to 25 yrs. and/or fine up to $500,000; more than 50kg: imprisonment up to 30 yrs. and/or fine up to $1,000,000; importing 50kg or more: felony, punishable by imprisonment up to 35 yrs. and/or fine up to $1,250,000; sale to minor: felony, punishable by imprisonment up to 20 yrs. and/or fine up to $250,000; within school zone or other specified area: felony, punishable by imprisonment up to 15 yrs. and/or fine up to $100,000	Possession while driving motor vehicle: 30 days driver's license suspension

Table 13: Marijuana Laws—Continued

State	Code Section	Summary	Personal Possession Limits/Penalties
MISSISSIPPI	41-29-101 to 41-29-191	Decriminalized: Yes; Medical: No; Recreational: No	Up to 30g: Civil infraction, punishable by fine $100 to $250; 2nd offense: imprisonment 5 to 60 days and/or fine up to $250; 3rd offense: imprisonment 5 days to 6 mos. and/or fine up to $500; 30-250g: felony, punishable by imprisonment up to 3 yrs. and/or fine up to $3,000; 250-500g: imprisonment 2 to 8 yrs. and/or fine up to $50,000; 500g. to 5kg: imprisonment 6 to 24 yrs. and/or fine up to $500,000; 5kg or more: imprisonment 10 to 30 yrs. and/or fine up to $1,000,000; if in any part of vehicle except trunk: misdemeanor, punishable by additional penalty of imprisonment up to 90 days and fine up to $1,000
MISSOURI	195.010 to 195.375	Decriminalized: No: Medical: No; Recreational: NO	Less than 35g: class A misdemeanor, punishable by imprisonment up to 1 yr. and fine up to $1,000; 35g to 30kg: class C felony, punishable by imprisonment up to 7 yrs. and fine up to $5,000
MONTANA	45-9-101; 45-9-102; 45-9-109; 45-9-201 to 45-9-208; Montana Medical Marijuana Act: 50-46-301 to 50-46-345	Decriminalized: No; Medical: Yes; Recreational: No	Up to 60g: Misdemeanor, punishable by imprisonment up to 6 mos. and fine $100 to $500; 2nd offense: imprisonment up to 3 yrs. and/or fine up to $1,000; over 60g: felony, punishable by imprisonment up to 5 yrs. and/or fine up to $50,000

Medical Requirements/Limits	Sale Limits/Penalties	Miscellaneous
	Up to 30g: imprisonment up to 3 yrs. and/or fine up to $3,000; 30g to 1kg: imprisonment up to 20 yrs. and/or fine up to $30,000; over 1kg: imprisonment 10 to 40 yrs. and fine $500,000 to $1,000,000; sale to minor or within 1,500 ft. of school, church, or other designated area: felony with double penalties; subsequent convictions: double 1st offense penalties	6 mos. driver's license suspension for any conviction
	Up to 5g: class C felony, punishable by imprisonment up to 7 yrs. and fine up to $5,000; 5g to 30kg: class B felony, punishable by imprisonment 5 to 15 yrs. and fine $5,000 to $20,000; 30-100kg: class A felony, punishable by imprisonment 10 yrs. to life and fine $5,000 to $20,000; 100kg or more: class A felony, punishable by imprisonment 10 yrs. to life with no probation or parole and fine $5,000 to $20,000; within 2,000 ft. of school or 1,000 ft. of public housing: imprisonment 10 yrs. to life and fine $5,000 to $20,000	
Patients with qualifying medical condition or caregiver may legally possess up to 1 oz.; patient must have preexisting relationship with recommending doctor; caregiver must be 21 or older and cannot accept monetary compensation for services; State Licensed Dispensaries: No; Home Cultivation: Yes; patients may cultivate up to 12 seedlings and 4 mature plants; ID Card Reciprocity: No	Distribute any amount, with or without compensation: imprisonment minimum 2 yrs. to life and/or fine up to $50,000; any amount to minor with or without compensation: imprisonment minimum 4 yrs. and fine up to $50,000; increased penalties for repeat offenses; within 1,000 ft. of school grounds: felony, punishable by imprisonment minimum 3 yrs. to life and fine up to $50,000	Anyone convicted of drug offense characterized as a misdemeanor must attend drug information course; imprisonment for drug felonies may be eligible for suspended or deferred imposition under conditions including: commitment to drug treatment facility up to 1 yr.; community service in drug education or treatment facility up to 2,000 hrs.; driver's license suspension: 1st offense: 6 mos.; 2nd offense: 1 yr.; subsequent offense: 3 yrs.

Table 13: Marijuana Laws—Continued

State	Code Section	Summary	Personal Possession Limits/Penalties
NEBRASKA	28-401 to 28-418	Decriminalized: Yes; Medical: No; Recreational: No	Less than 1 oz.: infraction, punishable by fine up to $300 and drug education course; 2nd offense: misdemeanor, punishable by imprisonment 5 days and/or $400 fine; 3rd and subsequent offense: misdemeanor, punishable by imprisonment 7 days and/or $500 fine; 1 oz. to 1 lb.: misdemeanor, punishable by imprisonment 3 mos. and/or $500 fine; over 1 lb.: felony, punishable by imprisonment 5 yrs. and/or $10,000 fine
NEVADA	193.130; 193.140; 453.011 to 453.348; 453A.010 to 453A.810	Medical: Yes; Recreational: Yes	Individuals 21 or older may possess up to 1 oz. of marijuana or up to 1/8 oz. concentrated marijuana and may cultivate up to 6 marijuana plants in private residence with limit of 12 plants per household; private cultivation must be in locked or secured room or greenhouse not accessible to public; violation of cultivation rules: misdemeanor, punishable by fine up to $600, escalated penalties for subsequent offenses; person under 21 who is not licensed medical marijuana user entering licensed marijuana establishment: misdemeanor, punishable by fine up to $500

Medical Requirements/Limits	Sale Limits/Penalties	Miscellaneous
	Any amount: felony, punishable by imprisonment 1 to 20 yrs. and fine up to $25,000; sale to minor: felony, punishable by 3 to 20 yrs. and fine up to $50,000; within 1,000 of school or 100 to 1,000 ft. of other designated area: imprisonment 3 to 50 yrs. and fine up to $50,000	
Patients with qualifying medical condition or caregiver may legally possess up to 2.5 oz. every 14 days; patient must have preexisting relationship with recommending doctor; caregiver must be 18+; State Licensed Dispensaries: Yes; Home Cultivation: Yes; patients may cultivate up to 12 mature plants; may be limited if the patient lives within 25 miles of operating dispensary; amount cannot be limited if the patient is cultivating a specific strain that is not carried at the dispensary; ID Card Reciprocity: No.	Licensed establishments may sell up to 1 oz. of marijuana or up to 1/8 oz. of concentrated marijuana to persons 21 or older; individuals may not smoke or consume marijuana products inside licensed marijuana establishment; establishments must pay state excise tax of 15% of fair market value at wholesale of the marijuana	Establishments seeking to obtain license to sell marijuana and marijuana products must pay one-time license fee of $5,000; cost of initial issuance of license for establishment seeking to sell marijuana and marijuana products may not exceed $20,000; minor convicted of any marijuana offense: 90 days to 2 yrs. driver's license suspension

Table 13: Marijuana Laws—Continued

State	Code Section	Summary	Personal Possession Limits/Penalties
NEW HAMPSHIRE	126-X:1 to 126-X:11; 318-B:1 to 318-B:30	Decriminalized: No; Medical: Yes; Recreational: No	Any amount: class A misdemeanor, punishable by imprisonment 1 yr. and/or fine up to $2,000
NEW JERSEY	2C:35-2 to 2C:35-31; 24:21-1 to 24:21-5; 24:61-1 to 24:61-16	Decriminalized: No; Medical: Yes; Recreational: No	Up to 50g: disorderly person offense, punishable by imprisonment up to 6 mos. and fine up to $1,000; more than 50g: felony, punishable by imprisonment up to 18 mos. and fine up to $25,000; possession within 1,000 ft. of school adds 100 hrs. of community service to sentence

Medical Requirements/Limits	Sale Limits/Penalties	Miscellaneous
Patients with qualifying medical condition or caregiver may legally possess up to 2 oz. of marijuana; patient must have preexisting relationship with recommending doctor; Caregivers: No; State Licensed Dispensaries: Yes; Home Cultivation: No; ID Card Reciprocity: Yes; out-of-state patients with valid medical marijuana card from another state will be allowed to bring their cannabis into New Hampshire and use it in the state; must have documentation from their physician of qualifying condition	Less than 1 oz.: felony, punishable by imprisonment 3 yrs. and/or fine up to $25,000; 1 oz. to 5 lbs.: felony, punishable by imprisonment 7 yrs. and/or fine up to $100,000; 5 lbs. or more: felony, punishable by imprisonment 20 yrs. and/or fine up to $300,000; subsequent offense: imprisonment up to 40 yrs. and/or fine up to $500,000; sale within 1,000 ft. of school zone: felony with double penalties	Under 21: 90 days to 1 yr. driver's license suspension; under 18 and convicted of sale or possessions to sell: revocation or denial of driver's license or privilege to drive for 1 to 5 yrs.; in case of denial of application for license, period imposed begins on date person is eligible by age for issuance of license Persons under 21 yrs. of age will face a driver's license suspension for 90 days to 1 yr. Any person under 18 yrs. of age who is convicted of the sale or possession with intent to sell shall be subject to revocation or denial of a driver's license or privilege to drive for 1 to 5 yrs.; in case of denial of an application for a license under this section, the period imposed shall begin on the date the person is eligible by age for the issuance of a license
Patients with qualifying medical condition or caregiver may legally possess up to 2 oz. of marijuana per month; patient must have preexisting relationship with recommending doctor; caregiver must be 18 or older with no felony drug conviction; State Licensed Dispensaries: Yes; Home Cultivation: No; ID Card Reciprocity: No.	Sale or distribution less than 1 oz.: felony, punishable by imprisonment up to 18 mos. and fine up to $25,000; 1 oz. to 5 lbs.: imprisonment 3 to 5 yrs. and fine up to $25,000; 5-25 lbs.: imprisonment 5 to 10 yrs. and fine up to $150,000; 25 lbs. or more: imprisonment 10 to 20 yrs. and fine up to $300,000; sale within 1,000 ft. of school property or school bus: felony, punishable by imprisonment 3 to 5 yrs. and fine up to $150,00; 1/2 or 1/3 of sentence if less than 1 oz.; less than 1 oz. within 500 ft. of certain public property: felony, punishable by imprisonment 3 to 5 yrs. and fine up to $25,000; more than 1 oz.: felony, punishable by imprisonment 5 to 10 yrs. and fine up to $150,000; sale to minor or pregnant woman: felony with double penalties	Possible 6 mos. to 2 yrs. driver's license suspension any conviction; if under 17, suspension begins at 17th birthday

Table 13: Marijuana Laws—Continued

State	Code Section	Summary	Personal Possession Limits/Penalties
NEW MEXICO	26-2B-1 through 26-2B-7; 30-31-1 to 30-31-41	Decriminalized: No; Medical: Yes; Recreational: No	Up to 1 oz.: petty misdemeanor, punishable by imprisonment up to 15 days and/or fine $50 to $100; subsequent offense: imprisonment up to 1 yr. and/or fine $100 to $1,000; 1-8 oz.: misdemeanor, punishable by imprisonment up to 1 yr. and fine $100 to $1,000; over 8 oz.: 4th degree felony, punishable by imprisonment 1.5 yrs. and fine up to $5,000
NEW YORK	Penal §§ 220 to 220.78; Pub. Health §§ 3306; 3307; 3360 to 3369	Decriminalized: Yes; Medical: Yes; Recreational: No	Up to 25g: $100 fine; 2nd offense within 3 yrs.: $200 fine; 3rd or subsequent offense within 3 yrs.: imprisonment up to 15 days and/or $250 fine; 25g to 2 oz.: class B misdemeanor, punishable by imprisonment up to 3 mos.; 2-8 oz.: class A misdemeanor, punishable by imprisonment up to 1 yr.; 16 oz. to 10 lbs.: class D felony, punishable by imprisonment up to 7 yrs.; over 10 lbs.: class C felony, punishable by imprisonment up to 15 yrs.; marijuana open to public view or burnt in public: class B misdemeanor, punishable by imprisonment up to 90 days and $250 fine
NORTH CAROLINA	15A-1340.17; 90-86 to 90-113.8	Decriminalized: No; Medical: No; Recreational: No	Up to 5 oz.: class 3 misdemeanor, punishable by fine up to $200; .5-1.5 oz.: class 1 misdemeanor, punishable by imprisonment 1 to 45 days and discretionary fine for 1st offense and max. fine $1,000; 1.5 oz. to 10 lbs.: class I felony, punishable by imprisonment 3 to 8 mos. and discretionary fine for 1st offense

Medical Requirements/Limits	Sale Limits/Penalties	Miscellaneous
Patients with qualifying medical condition or caregiver may legally possess up to 6 oz. of marijuana or more if authorized by their physician; patient must have preexisting relationship with recommending doctor; caregiver must be 18 or older ; State Licensed Dispensaries: Yes; Home Cultivation: Yes, patient may cultivate up to 16 plants, with no more than 4 mature; ID Card Reciprocity: No.	Less than 100 lbs.: 4th degree felony, punishable by imprisonment 1.5 yrs. and fine up to $5,000; subsequent offense: 3rd degree felony, punishable by imprisonment up to 3 yrs. and fine up to $5,000; more than 100 lbs.: 3rd degree felony, punishable by imprisonment up to 3 yrs. and/or fine up to $5,000; subsequent offense: 2nd degree felony, punishable by imprisonment up to 9 yrs. and/or fine up to $10,000; distribution to minor under 18: 3rd degree felony, punishable by imprisonment up to 3 yrs. and/or fine up to $5,000; subsequent offense: 2nd degree felony, punishable by imprisonment up to 9 yrs. and/or fine up to $10,000; within drug-free school zone: 1st degree, punishable by imprisonment 18 yrs. and $15,000 fine	15 or older: driver's license license may be revoked
Patients with qualifying medical condition or caregiver may legally possess a 30-day supply, amt. determined by health commissioner or patient's doctor; patient must have preexisting relationship with recommending doctor; caregiver must be 21 or older; State Licensed Dispensaries: Yes, but no more than 5; Home Cultivation: No; ID Card Reciprocity: No; NY law does not allow the smoking of marijuana; approved forms include liquids, oil (which may be vaporized), administration via inhaler, and capsules for oral consumption		Youthful offender or other juvenile adjudication in connection with any crime in violation of Federal Controlled Substances Act: mandatory 6 mos. driver's license suspension
	Delivery of under 5g for no compensation considered possession; possession with intent to distribute less than 10 lbs.: 1st offense: class I felony, punishable by imprisonment 3 to 8 mos. and discretionary fine; sale less than 10 lbs.: 1st offense: class H felony, punishable by imprisonment 4 to 8 mos. and discretionary fine; 10-50 lbs.: class H felony, punishable by imprisonment 25 to 30 mos. and at least $5,000 fine; 50-2,000 lbs.: class G felony, punishable by imprisonment 35 to 42 mos. and at least $25,000 fine; 2,000-10,000 lbs.: class F felony, punishable by imprisonment 70 to 80 mos. and at least $50,000 fine; 10,000 lbs. or more: class d felony, punishable by imprisonment 175 to 219 mos. and at least $200,000 fine; sale or delivery to minor or pregnant woman of any age: felony, punishable by imprisonment up to 92 mos. and fine to be set by court; sale or delivery in or within 1,000 ft. of school, child care center, or park: 1st offense: class E felony, punishable by imprisonment 15 to 31 mos. and discretionary fine	

Table 13: Marijuana Laws—Continued

State	Code Section	Summary	Personal Possession Limits/Penalties
NORTH DAKOTA	12.1-32-01 to 12.1-32-16;-03.1-01 to 19-03.1-46; North Dakota Compassionate Care Act: 19-24-01 to 19-24-13	Decriminalized: No; Medical: Yes; Recreational: No	Less than .5 oz.: class B misdemeanor, punishable by imprisonment up to 30 days and/or fine up to $1,500; .5-1 oz.: class A misdemeanor, punishable by imprisonment up to 1 yr. and/or fine up to $3,000; 1 oz. to 500g: class C felony, punishable by imprisonment up to 5 yrs. and/or fine up to $5,000; 500g or more: class B felony, punishable by imprisonment up to 10 yrs. and fine up to $20,000; 1st conviction can be removed from record after 2 yrs. if no further criminal violations; possession

Medical Requirements/Limits	Sale Limits/Penalties	Miscellaneous
2925.01 to 2925.45; 3719.01 to 3719.99; Medical Marijuana: 3796.01 to 3796.30;	Decriminalized: No; Medical: Yes; Recreational: No	Less than 100g: minor misdemeanor, punishable by $150 file; 100-200g: misdemeanor, punishable by imprisonment 30 days and fine up to $250; 2020-1,000g: 5th degree felony, punishable by imprisonment 6 to 12 mos. and fine up to $2,500; 1,000-5,000g.: 3rd degree felony, punishable by imprisonment 1 to 5 yrs. and/or fine $5,000 to $10,000; 5,000-20,000g: 3rd degree felony, punishable by imprisonment 1 to 5 yrs. and/or fine $5,000 to $10,000; 20,000-40,000g: 2nd degree felony, punishable by imprisonment 5 to 8 yrs. and fine up to $15,000; over 40,000g: 2nd degree felony, punishable by mandatory imprisonment 8 yrs. and fine up to $15,000

Table 13: Marijuana Laws—Continued

State	Code Section	Summary	Personal Possession Limits/Penalties
OHIO	2925.01 to 2925.45; 3719.01 to 3719.99; Medical Marijuana: 3796.01 to 3796.30	Decriminalized: No; Medical: Yes; Recreational: No	Less than 100g: minor misdemeanor, punishable by $150 file; 100-200g: misdemeanor, punishable by imprisonment 30 days and fine up to $250; 201-1,000g: 5th degree felony, punishable by imprisonment 6 to 12 mos. and fine up to $2,500; 1,000-5,000g: 3rd degree felony, punishable by imprisonment 1 to 5 yrs. and/or fine $5,000 to $10,000; 5,000-20,000g: 3rd degree felony, punishable by imprisonment 1 to 5 yrs. and/or fine $5,000 to $10,000; 20,000-40,000g: 2nd degree felony, punishable by imprisonment 5 to 8 yrs. and fine up to $15,000; over 40,000g: 2nd degree felony, punishable by mandatory imprisonment 8 yrs. and fine up to $15,000
OKLAHOMA	Tit. 63, §§ 2-101;2-201 to 2-212; 2-401 to 2-413; 2-801 to 805	Decriminalized: No; Medical: No; Recreational: No	Any amount: violation, punishable by imprisonment up to 1 yr.; subsequent offense: felony, punishable by imprisonment 2 to 10 yrs.
OREGON	153.005 to 153.121; 161.605 to 161.685; 475.525 to 475.565; Control and Regulation of Marijuana Act: 475B.005 to 475B.395; Oregon Medical Marijuana Act: 475B.400 to 475B.525; 475B.550 to 475B.800	Medical: Yes; Recreational: Yes	Persons over 21 may possess up to 8 oz. of useable marijuana in their home and up to 1 oz. outside the home, as well as grow up to 4 plant per residence, out of public view; may not be sold or smoked in public; Possession of up to 2 times allowable amount: class B violation; 2 to 4 times allowable amount: class B misdemeanor; over 4 times allowable amount: class A misdemeanor

Medical Requirements/Limits	Sale Limits/Penalties	Miscellaneous
The Ohio General Assembly passed medical marijuana legislation effective September 8, 2016, and established a medical marijuana control program in the Dept. of Commerce and State Bd. of Pharmacy. The Commerce Dept. shall provide for licensure of cultivators, processors, and testing laboratories; the Pharmacy Bd. shall provide for licensure of retail dispensaries and registration of patients and their caregivers; the Medical Marijuana Control Program will be administered by both, and they were charged with drafting and adopting all relevant rules and regulations by September 8, 2017, 3796.02 to 3796.04; patients must apply and register with board of pharmacy; patient must have bona fide relationship with recommending physician; qualified, registered patient or caregiver may possess up to 90 day supply of medical marijuana and marijuana paraphernalia; only non-smokable forms of marijuana are legal, including oils, tinctures, pills, or vaporization; registered patient prohibited from operating vehicles while under influence of medical marijuana; State Licensed Dispensaries: Yes; Home Cultivation: No; ID Card Reciprocity: Bd. of Pharmacy will negotiate with other states with similar requirements	Gift of up to 20g: 1st offense: minor misdemeanor, punishable by fine up to $150; 2nd offense: misdemeanor, punishable by imprisonment 60 days and fine up to $4,500; sale <200g: felony, punishable by imprisonment 12 mos. and fine up to $2,500; 200-1,000g: 4th degree felony, punishable by imprisonment 6 to 18 mos. and variable fine; 1,000-5,000g: 3rd degree felony, punishable by imprisonment 1 to 5 yrs. and variable fine; 5,000-20,000g: 3rd degree felony, punishable by imprisonment 1 to 5 yrs. and variable fine; 20,000-40,000g: 2nd degree felony, punishable by imprisonment 5 to 8 yrs. and variable fine; over 40,000g: 2nd degree felony, punishable by imprisonment mandatory 8 yrs.; sale to minor or within 1,000 ft. of school: stricter penalties	6 mos. to 5 yrs. driver's license suspension any conviction
	Sale less than 25 lbs.: felony, punishable by imprisonment 2 yrs. to life and $20,000 fine; 25-1,000 lbs.: felony, punishable by imprisonment 4 yrs. to life and fine $25,000 to $100,000; 1,000 lbs. or more: felony, punishable by imprisonment 4 yrs. to life and fine $100,000 to $500,000; sale to minor: felony with double penalties; sale within 2,000 ft. of school, public park, or public housing: felony with double penalties	6 mos. to 3 yrs. driver's license suspension for any conviction
Patients with qualifying medical condition or caregiver may legally possess up to 24 oz. of marijuana; patient must have preexisting relationship with recommending doctor; caregiver must be 18 or older; State Licensed Dispensaries: Yes; Home Cultivation: Yes; patient may cultivate up to 18 seedlings and 6 mature plants; ID Card Reciprocity: No	Medical dispensaries can sell up to ¼ oz. of marijuana to a person over 21 per day, and must use a mechanism to ensure compliance with this	Conviction for possession of ≥1 oz., delivery, or cultivation: automatic 6 mos. driver's license suspension absent compelling reason not to suspend

Table 13: Marijuana Laws—Continued

State	Code Section	Summary	Personal Possession Limits/Penalties
PENNSYLVANIA	Tit. 35, §§ 780-101 to 780-144; Medical Marijuana Act: Tit. 35, §§ 10231.101 to 10231.2110	Decriminalized: No; Medical: Yes; Recreational: No	Up to 30g: Misdemeanor, punishable by imprisonment up to 30 days and/or fine up to $500; Over 30g: misdemeanor, punishable by imprisonment up to 1yr. and/or fine up to $5,000; 2nd or subsequent offense: double penalties

Medical Requirements/Limits	Sale Limits/Penalties	Miscellaneous
Patient must be certified by physician and obtain identification card from Dept. of Health; patient may have up to 2 caregivers; caregiver may only act as such for up to 5 patients; patient or caregiver may possess up to a 30-day supply; only non-smokable forms of marijuana are legal, including oils, tinctures, liquid, pills, topical forms,or vaporization and may not be incorporated into edible form unless necessary to aid ingestion by patient; unused medical marijuana must be kept in original packaging; patient or caregiver must be in possession of valid ID whenever in possession of medical marijuana; possession of more than legally permitted amount: 3rd degree misdemeanor; State Licensed Dispensaries: Yes; may not dispense more than a 30-day supply of medical marijuana until patient has exhausted all but a 7-day supply; Home Cultivation: No; ID Card Reciprocity: No	General: Distribution of less than 30g no compensation: misdemeanor, punishable by imprisonment up to 30 days and/or fine up to $500; sale: 2-10 lbs.: felony, punishable by imprisonment minimum 1 yr. and fine up to $5,000; less than 1,000 lbs.: felony, punishable by imprisonment up to 3 yrs. and up to $25,000 fine; if previous drug conviction, mandatory 3 yrs. and mandatory $25,000; over 1,000 lbs.: felony, punishable by imprisonment up to 10 yrs. and fine up to $100,000; delivery within 1,000 ft. of school or 250 ft. of playground: imprisonment 2 to 4 yrs.; subsequent offenses or sale to minor under 18 by person over 21: double penalties	General: 6 mos. driver's license suspension for any conviction; 2nd offense: 1 yr.; subsequent offense: 2 yrs.

Table 13: Marijuana Laws—Continued

State	Code Section	Summary	Personal Possession Limits/Penalties
RHODE ISLAND	21-28-1.01 to 21-28-2.08; 21-28-4.01 to 21-28-4.22; 21-28-6.1 to 21-28-6.14	Decriminalized: Yes; Medical: Yes; Recreational: No	Up to 1 oz. by individual 18 or older: civil infraction, punishable by $150 fine; if under 18: notify parent or guardian; minor required to complete drug awareness and education program; 3rd possession within 18 mos.: criminal charges; 1 oz. to 1kg: misdemeanor, punishable by imprisonment up to 1 yr. and/or fine up to $500
SOUTH CAROLINA	44-53-110 to 44-53-590	Decriminalized: No; Medical: No; Recreational: No	≤1 oz.: misdemeanor, punishable by imprisonment 30 days and/or fine $100 to $200; subsequent conviction: misdemeanor, punishable by imprisonment up to 1 yr. and or fine $200 to $1,000

Medical Requirements/Limits	Sale Limits/Penalties	Miscellaneous
Patients with qualifying medical condition or caregiver may legally possess up to 2.5 oz. of usable marijuana and 12 marijuana plants; patient must have preexisting relationship with recommending doctor; caregiver must be 21 or older; patient with debilitating medical condition, with ID card or equivalent, may engage in medical use of marijuana; out-of-state residents may assist with medical use of marijuana by patient with a debilitating medical condition; two or more cardholders can cooperatively cultivate marijuana subject to the following limits: for non-residential locations, no more than 10 oz. usable marijuana, 48 mature plants, and 24 seedlings; for residential locations, no more than 10 oz. usable marijuana, 24 mature plants, and 12 seedlings; State Licensed Dispensaries: Yes; Home Cultivation: Yes; patient may cultivate up to 12 mature plants and 12 seedlings in an indoor facility; ID Card Reciprocity: Yes	Sale or cultivation of under 1kg: felony, punishable by imprisonment up to 30 yrs. and/or fine up to $100,000; 1-5kg: imprisonment 10 to 50 yrs. and/or fine up to $500,000; >5kg: imprisonment 20 yrs. to life and/or fine up to $100,000; delivery to minor at least 3 yrs. junior: additional penalty of imprisonment 2 to 5 yrs. and fine up to $10,000; sale within 300 yds. of school, public park, or playground: double penalties; probation sentences: offender must undergo drug abuse evaluation, attend drug education course, and perform 100 hrs. community service	
	Sale: less than 10 lbs.: felony, punishable by imprisonment 5 yrs. and fine up to $5,000; 10-100 lbs.: felony, punishable by imprisonment 1 to 10 yrs. without suspension or probation and $10,000 fine; 2nd offense: felony, punishable by imprisonment 5 to 20 yrs. without suspension or probation and $25,000 fine; 3rd or subsequent offense: felony, punishable by imprisonment mandatory 25 yrs. without suspension or probation and $25,000 fine; 100-2,000 lbs.: felony, punishable by imprisonment mandatory 25 yrs. without suspension or probation and $25,000 fine; 2,000-10,000 lbs.: felony, punishable by imprisonment mandatory 25 yrs. without suspension or probation and $50,000 fine; over 10,000 lbs.: felony, punishable by imprisonment mandatory 25 yrs. without suspension or parole and $200,000 fine; sale to minor or within .5 mile radius of school, playground, or public park: felony, punishable by imprisonment 10 yrs. and fine up to $10,000	

Table 13: Marijuana Laws—Continued

State	Code Section	Summary	Personal Possession Limits/Penalties
SOUTH DAKOTA	22-42-6 to 22-42-21; 34-20B-1 to 34-20B-114	Decriminalized: No; Medical: No; Recreational: No	≤2 oz.: Class 1 misdemeanor, punishable by imprisonment 1 yr. and/or $2,000 fine; 2 oz. to .5 lb.: class 6 felony, punishable by imprisonment 2 yrs. and/or $4,000 fine; .5-1 lb.: class 5 felony, punishable by imprisonment 5 yrs. fine up to $10,000; 1-10 lbs.: class 4 felony, punishable by imprisonment 10 yrs. and fine up to $20,000; over 10 lbs.: class 3 felony, punishable by imprisonment 15 yrs. and fine up to $30,000
TENNESSEE	39-17-401 to 39-17-454	Decriminalized: No; Medical: No; Recreational: No	≤.5 oz.: Class A misdemeanor, punishable by imprisonment up to 1 yr. and fine up to $2,500, minimum fine 1st offense: $250; 2nd offense: $500; 3rd offense: class E felony, punishable by imprisonment 1 to 6 yrs. and mandatory minimum $1,000 fine
TEXAS	Health & Safety §§ 481.001 to 481.032; 481.120 to 481.141	Decriminalized: No; Medical: No; Recreational: No	≤2 oz.: Class B misdemeanor, punishable by imprisonment up to 180 days and/or fine up to $2,000; 2-4 oz.: class A misdemeanor, punishable by imprisonment up to 1 yr. and/or fine up to $4,000; 4oz. to 5 lbs.: state jail felony, punishable by imprisonment 180 days to 2 yrs. and fine up to $10,000; 5-50 lbs.: 3rd degree felony, punishable by imprisonment 2 to 10 yrs. and fine up to $10,000; 50-2,000 lbs.: 2nd degree felony, punishable by imprisonment 2 to 20 yrs. and fine up to $10,000; over 2,000 lbs: felony, punishable by imprisonment 5 to 99 yrs. and fine up to $50,000

Medical Requirements/Limits	Sale Limits/Penalties	Miscellaneous
	Less than .5 oz.: Class 1 misdemeanor, punishable by imprisonment 15 days to 1 yr. and/or fine up to $2,000; .5-1 oz.: class 6 felony, punishable by imprisonment 2 yrs. and fine up to $4,000; 1-8 oz.: class 5 felony, punishable by imprisonment 5 yrs. and fine up to $10,000; .5-1 lb.: class 4 felony, punishable by imprisonment 10 yrs. and fine up to $20,000; over 1 lb.: class 3 felony, punishable by imprisonment 15 yrs. and fine up to $30,000; sale or distribution to minor: felony, punishable by imprisonment up to 25 yrs. and fine up to $50,000; sale within 1,000 ft. of school or 500 ft. of other designated drug free areas: felony, punishable by imprisonment up to 5 yrs. and $10,000 fine	
	.5 oz. to 10 lbs.: Class E felony, punishable by imprisonment 1 to 6 yrs. and fine up to $5,000; 10-70 lbs.: class D felony, punishable by imprisonment 2 to 12 yrs. and fine up to $5,000; 70-300 lbs.: class B felony, punishable by imprisonment 8 to 30 yrs. and fine up to $200,000; over 300 lbs.: class A felony, punishable by imprisonment 15 to 60 yrs. and fine up to $500,000; 1st time felony conviction: minimum $2,000 fine; 2nd felony conviction: minimum $3,000 fine; 3rd and subsequent felony convictions: minimum $5,000 fine and punished 1 grade higher; sale to minor or sale within 1,000 ft. of school: unclassified felony, penalty enhanced one sentencing grade	
	Sale or delivery with no compensation: ≤7g: Class B misdemeanor, punishable by imprisonment up to 180 days and/or fine up to $2,000; with compensation: class A misdemeanor punishable by imprisonment up to 1 yr. and/or fine up to $4,000; 7g to 5 lbs.: state jail felony, punishable by imprisonment 180 days to 2 yrs. and fine up to $10,000; 5-50lbs: 3rd degree felony, punishable by imprisonment 2 to 10 yrs. and fine up to $10,000; 50-2,000 lbs.: 2nd degree felony, punishable by imprisonment 2 to 20 yrs. and fine up to $10,000; over 2,000 lbs: felony, punishable by imprisonment 10 yrs. to life and fine up to $100,000; sale to minor: 2nd degree felony, punishable by imprisonment 2 to 20 yrs. and fine up to $10,000	180 days driver's license suspension for any conviction

Table 13: Marijuana Laws—Continued

State	Code Section	Summary	Personal Possession Limits/Penalties
UTAH	58-37-1 to 58-37-21; 76-3-203; 76-3-301	Decriminalized: No; Medical: No; Recreational: No	Less than 1 oz.: Class B misdemeanor, punishable by imprisonment 6 mos. and fine up to $1,000; 2nd offense: class A misdemeanor; 3rd or subsequent offense: 3rd degree felony; 1 oz. to 1 lb.: class A misdemeanor, punishable by imprisonment 1 yr. and fine up to $2,500; 1-100 lbs.: 3rd degree felony, punishable by imprisonment 5 yrs. and fine up to $5,000; over 100 lbs.: 2nd degree felony, punishable by imprisonment 1-15 yrs. and fine up to $10,000 Possession of less than 1 oz. is a Class B misdemeanor punishable by 6 mos. imprisonment and a maximum fine of $1,000; A 2nd conviction is a class A misdemeanor; 3rd or subsequent conviction is a 3rd degree felony. Possession of 1 oz.-1 lb. is a Class A misdemeanor punishable by 1 yr. imprisonment and a maximum fine of $2,500; 1 lb.-100 lbs. is a 3rd Degree felony punishable by 5 yrs. imprisonment and a maximum fine of $5,000; Over 100 lbs. is a 2nd Degree felony punishable by 1-15 yrs. imprisonment and a maximum fine of $10,000
VERMONT	Tit. 18, §§ 4230; 4471 to 4474m	Decriminalized: Yes; Medical: Yes; Recreational: No	≤1 oz. by person 21+: Civil infraction, punishable by fine up to $200; 2nd offense: fine up to $300; 3rd or subsequent offense: fine up to $500; 1-2 oz.: misdemeanor, punishable by imprisonment up to 6 mos. and/or fine up to $500; 2nd conviction: misdemeanor punishable by imprisonment up to 2 yrs. and/or fine up to $2,000; 2 oz. to 1 lb.: felony, punishable by imprisonment up to 3 yrs. and/or fine up to $3,000; 1-10 lbs.: felony, punishable by imprisonment up to 5 yrs. and fine up to $100,000; over 10 lbs.: felony, punishable by imprisonment up to 15 yrs. and/or fine up to $500,000; consuming marijuana while driving: civil fine up to $500; municipalities may impose higher penalties on public use

Medical Requirements/Limits	Sale Limits/Penalties	Miscellaneous
	Any amount: 2nd degree felony, punishable by imprisonment 5 yrs. and fine up to $5,000; sale in presence of minor or within 1,000 ft. of school or other designated drug-free public area: stricter penalties The sale of any amount is a 2nd Degree felony punishable by 5 yrs. imprisonment and a maximum fine of $5,000. The sale in the presence of a minor or within 1,000 ft. of a school and other designated drug-free public areas— stricter penalties	6 mos. driver's license suspension for any conviction
Patients with qualifying medical condition or caregiver may legally possess up to 2 oz. of marijuana and 2 mature marijuana plants and 7 immature marijuana plants; patient must have preexisting relationship with recommending doctor; caregiver must be 21+ with no drug conviction; State Licensed Dispensaries: Yes; Home Cultivation: Yes, patients may cultivate up to 7 plants of which no more than 2 may be mature; ID Card Reciprocity: No.	Less than .5 oz.: misdemeanor punishable by imprisonment up to 2 yrs. and/or fine up to $10,000; .5 oz. to 1 lb.: felony, punishable by 5 yrs. and/or fine up to $100,000; 1-50 lbs.: felony, punishable by imprisonment up to 15 yrs. and/or fine up to $500,000; over 50 lbs. presumed to be trafficking, punishable by imprisonment up to 30 yrs. and/or fine up to $1,000,000; sale to minor: felony, punishable by imprisonment up to 5 yrs. and/or fine up to $25,000	Persons 16 to 21 who possess up to 1 oz. must attend Diversion Program's Youth Substance Abuse Safety Program; failure to complete results in: $300 civil fine and 90 days driver's license suspension; 2nd offense: $600 civil fine and 180 days driver's license suspension; 3rd offense: misdemeanor, punishable by imprisonment up to 30 days and/or fine up to $600

Table 13: Marijuana Laws—Continued

State	Code Section	Summary	Personal Possession Limits/Penalties
VIRGINIA	54.1-3445; 18.2-247 to 18.2-264	Decriminalized: No; Medical: No; Recreational: No	Class I misdemeanor, punishable by imprisonment up to 30 days and/or fine up to $500; 2nd or subsequent offense: imprisonment up to 12 mos. and/or fine up to $2,500; possession of less than .5 oz. presumed possession for personal use
WASHINGTON	69.50.101 to 69.50.608; 69.51A - 69.51A.901	Decriminalized: Yes; Medical: Yes; Recreational: Yes	Adults 21+ may possess up to 1 oz. of cannabis, 16 oz. if infused in product in sold form and 72 oz. if infused in product in liquid form for personal use with no criminal or civil penalties imposed; public consumption subject to civil infraction and fine; possession 1 oz. to 40g: misdemeanor, punishable by imprisonment 24 hrs. to 90 days and fine up to $1,000; additional mandatory fine, 1st offense: $250; 2nd or subsequent offense $500; over 40g: class C felony, punishable by imprisonment up to 5 yrs. and/or fine up to $10,000; additional mandatory fine, 1st offense: $1,000; 2nd or subsequent offense: $2,000
WEST VIRGINIA	60A-1-101 to 60A-2-213; 60A-4-401 et seq.	Decriminalized: No Medical: No Recreational: No	Possession in any amount is a misdemeanor punishable by 90 days to 6 mos. imprisonment and a $1,000 fine. If 1st offense and under 15 grams, offender may be granted conditional discharge with probation in lieu of jail.

Medical Requirements/Limits	Sale Limits/Penalties	Miscellaneous
	Distributing .5 oz. to 5 lbs.: Class 5 felony, punishable by imprisonment 1 to 10 yrs. and $2,500 fine; 5 lbs. to 100kg: felony, punishable by imprisonment 5 to 30 yrs.; over 100kg: imprisonment 20 yrs. to life; 3rd sale or intent to distribute conviction: imprisonment mandatory 5 yrs.; gifting to inmate in state or local correctional facility: class 4 felony, punishable by imprisonment 2 to 10 yrs. and fine up to $100,000; distributing to minor or using minor at least 3 yrs. junior to assist in sale: <1 oz.: felony, punishable by imprisonment 2 to 5 yrs. and fine up to $100,000; >1 oz.: imprisonment 5 to 50 yrs. and fine up to $100,000; >.5 oz. within 1,000 ft. of school or school bus stop: felony, punishable by imprisonment 1 to 5 yrs. and fine up to $100,000; if person proves he sold marijuana as accommodation to another and not with intent to profit: class 1 misdemeanor, punishable by imprisonment up to 1 yr. and fine up to $2,500	6 mos. driver's license suspension for any conviction
Patients with qualifying medical condition or caregiver may legally possess up to 2 oz. of marijuana per month; patient must have preexisting relationship with recommending doctor; caregiver must be 18 or older; State Licensed Dispensaries: No, but some cities have regulated dispensaries; Home Cultivation: Yes, patients may cultivate up to 15 plants; ID Card Reciprocity: No.	Any amount: Class C felony, punishable by imprisonment up to 5 yrs. and/or fine up to $10,000, with additional mandatory fine, 1st offense: $1,000; 2nd offense: $2,000; sale to minor under 18 and at least 3 yrs. junior: class B felony, punishable by imprisonment up to 10 yrs. and/or fine up to $10,000; cultivation, sale, delivery, or possession with intent to sell within 1,000 ft. of school, public park, public housing designated as drug free zone: double penalties; 2nd or subsequent offenses: double penalties	Juveniles 13 to 21 driving privileges revoked for any conviction: 1st offense: 1 yr. or until person is 17, whichever is longer; 2nd or subsequent offense: 2 yrs. or until person is 18, whichever is longer
	Sale of any amount is a felony punishable 1 to 5 yrs. imprisonment and a fine of not more than $15,000. Sale or distribution to a minor or within 1,000 ft. of a school: mandatory minimum of 2 yrs. imprisonment.	Mandatory driver's license revocation of 180 days for any felony offense when a motor vehicle is used in its commission, including the sale, delivery, or manufacture of marijuana.

Table 13: Marijuana Laws—Continued

State	Code Section	Summary	Personal Possession Limits/Penalties
WISCONSIN	961.41 to 961.50	Decriminalized: No; Medical: No; Recreational: No	Misdemeanor, punishable by imprisonment up to 6 mos. and/or fine up to $1,000; 2nd and subsequent offense: class I felony, punishable by imprisonment up to 3.5 yrs. and/or fine up to $10,000
WYOMING	35-7-1001 to 35-7-1057	Decriminalized: No; Medical: No; Recreational: No	Being under the influence: misdemeanor, punishable by imprisonment up to 90 days and fine up to $100; possession ≤3 oz.: misdemeanor, punishable by imprisonment up to 1 yr. and fine up to $1,000; over 3 oz.: felony, punishable by imprisonment up to 5 yrs. and fine up to $10,000; 3rd or subsequent offense: imprisonment up to 5 yrs. and fine up to $5,000; possession within 500 ft. of school: additional $500 fine

Medical Requirements/Limits	Sale Limits/Penalties	Miscellaneous
	≤200g: Class I felony, punishable by imprisonment up to 3.5 yrs. and/or fine up to $10,000; 200-1,000g: class H felony, punishable by imprisonment up to 6 yrs. and/or fine up to $10,000; 1,000-2,000g: class G felony, punishable by imprisonment up to 10 yrs. and/or fine up to $25,000; 2,500-10,000g: class F felony, punishable by imprisonment up to 12.5 yrs. and/or fine up to $25,000; over 10,000g: class E felony, punishable by imprisonment up to 15 yrs. and/or fine up to $50,000; subsequent offenders: enhanced penalties	6 mos. to 5 yrs. driver's license suspension for any conviction
	Any amount: Felony, punishable by imprisonment up to 10 yrs. and fine up to $10,000	Under 19: 1st offense: 90 days driver's license suspension for any conviction; 2nd drug or alcohol offense within 12 mos.: 6 mos. suspension

14. PROHIBITED CONSENSUAL SEXUAL ACTIVITY

The laws covered by this chapter concern state legislation intended to control the private sexual practices of citizens. A related issue, that of exposure of a sexual partner to AIDS, is also covered here; therefore, it covers situations where the sex act is not fully consensual, such as whether the victim of a sexual crime can compel testing of the perpetrator. In any case, knowingly exposing another to the AIDS virus may be a crime whether the sexual activity is a crime or not.

For centuries, public norms in western culture generated virtually no controversy with respect to the laws governing sexual conduct. This does not mean that there was no "illegal" sexual conduct. It only means that there was general disapproval of it, even while such practices were being engaged in on a regular basis by certain segments of society. However, as gay men and women have become more visible and vocal about their orientations and practices, and more demanding that their contact be accepted as "normal" in the "general" conscience of society, the old laws are beginning to be called into question. The boldest challenge to these laws has been a Supreme Court case decided in the mid-1980s in which a person was arrested for violating Georgia's statute prohibiting sodomy. The challenge was based on the principle that consensual sex between two adults was a private matter which the state had no authority to regulate. In that case, the defendant lost, and the Supreme Court held that the state has sufficient interest in preventing sodomy to warrant the enactment of laws banning the behavior.

However, in 2003 the Supreme Court decided a similar case from Texas. In that case, decided by a mere 5–4 majority, the Court decided that its earlier decision was in error and declared all laws that prohibit private same-sex sexual conduct to be unconstitutional.

Even though the laws have been overturned as unconstitutional, many states have left them "on the books," either as a hollow protest against the decision of the Court or as a matter of mere legislative inertia. These statutes are still recorded in the following charts for historical purposes only.

This chapter also includes references to statutes in which exposure of another to the HIV/AIDS virus or other sexually transmitted disease (STD) has been made a crime. Intentional exposure of another to an STD is a felony in many states. In addition, many states give the victim of a sexual offense the right to require a convicted perpetrator to submit to a test for STD. Mandatory testing has always been controversial and resisted by libertarians, but in criminal cases involving sex offenses, there is less resistance to the idea of forcing people to be tested.

The final area covered in this chapter involves categories of crimes that are used to prohibit various kinds of sexual activity. The statutes listed in the column headed "Other Crimes Relating to Consensual Sexual Acts" range from explicit bans on prostitution, lewd public acts, and indecent exposure, to loitering and disorderly conduct. Although some of the offenses listed, such as loitering, can be applied to activity that is non-sexual in nature, these statutes are frequently used to disrupt or prohibit sexual activity or even to discourage non-married couples from living together. These laws illustrate the difficulties which law enforcement officers and officials have in trying to regulate intimate, private behavior. The laws are very general and often vague and may be applied to numerous activities deemed offensive by the person charged with enforcing public order.

Table 14: Prohibited Consensual Sexual Activity

State	Sodomy: Applicability to:	Sodomy: Penalty	Exposing Another to/ Compelled Testing for AIDS/HIV	Other Crimes Relating to Consensual Sex Acts
ALABAMA	All persons	Sodomy 2nd degree: offender over 16 and victim over 12 but under 16; victim mentally incapable of consent; Class B felony, 13A-6-64; Sodomy 1st degree: offender over 16 and victim under 12; victim physically or mentally incapable of consent; Class A felony, 13A-6-63	Victim of sexual offense may request offender be tested, 22-11A-17(c)	Sexual misconduct: class A misdemeanor (consent is not defense), 13A-6-65 (a)(3); Loitering: violation, 13A-11-9; Indecent exposure: class A misdemeanor, 13A-6-68; Public lewdness: class C misdemeanor, 13A-12-130
ALASKA			Upon receipt of a petition by the victim, the court shall order testing if probable cause is found that a crime involving sexual penetration took place. 18.15.300	Indecent exposure 2nd degree: class B misdemeanor; class A misdemeanor if act occurs within observation of a person under 16, 11.41.460; Indecent exposure 1st degree: in view of person under 16 and offender masturbates or has previous conviction: class C felony, 11.41.458; (a)(7) Disorderly conduct: class B misdemeanor, 11.61.110
ARIZONA			Allows for order for HIV test if defendant charged with sexual offense, 13-1415	Indecent exposure: class 1 misdemeanor; class 6 felony if to person under 15, 13-1402; Public sexual indecency: class 1 misdemeanor; class 5 felony if to a minor, 13-1403; Adultery: class 3 misdemeanor, 13-1408; Loitering: class 3 misdemeanor, 13-2905
ARKANSAS	Animal	Bestiality: Class A misdemeanor, 5-14-122	Knowingly exposing another person to HIV: class A felony, 5-14-123; Testing for HIV-Sexual offenses: Court may order testing of accused; mandatory if victim requests and defendant is convicted, 16-82-101	Sexual indecency with a child: class D felony, 5-14-110; Public sexual indecency: class A misdemeanor, 5-14-111;Indecent exposure: class A misdemeanor, 5-14-112;Loitering: class C misdemeanor, 5-71-213

Table 14: Prohibited Consensual Sexual Activity—Continued

State	Sodomy: Applicability to:	Sodomy: Penalty	Exposing Another to/ Compelled Testing for AIDS/HIV	Other Crimes Relating to Consensual Sex Acts
CALIFORNIA	Both sexes	If one person is under 18: imprisonment up to 1 yr; one person over 21 and the other under 16: felony; one person under 14 and the other more than 10 yrs. older: imprisonment 3, 6, or 8 yrs.; one person incapable of resisting: imprisonment 3, 6, or 8 yrs., Penal § 286	Testing for HIV required if convicted of certain sexual offenses or if probable cause is found of transfer of bodily fluids capable of transferring HIV in certain situations, Penal § 1202.1	Incest: imprisonment in state prison, Penal § 285; Lewd & lascivious acts: if one person is under 14: felony; if one person is 14 or 15 and the other is at least 10 yrs. older: public offense, Penal § 288;Oral copulation: If one person is under 18: imprisonment up to 1 yr; one person over 21 and the other under 16: felony; one person under 14 and the other more than 10 yrs. older: imprisonment 3, 6, or 8 yrs.; one person incapable of resisting: imprisonment 3, 6, or 8 yrs., Penal § 288a;Intercourse or sodomy with a child 10 or under: felony, imprisonment 25 yrs. to life; oral copulation by one over 18 on child 10 or under: felony, 15 yrs. to life, Penal § 288.7; Lewd or obscene conduct; indecent exposure; obscene exhibitions: misdemeanor, Penal § 314; Public nuisance: misdemeanor, Penal § 372; Disorderly conduct: misdemeanor, Penal §647
COLORADO			Testing mandatory if bound over for trial for any sexual offense involving penetration, 18-3-415	Disorderly conduct: Class 1 petty offense, 1888-9-106; Public indecency: Class 1 petty offense, 18-7-301; Indecent exposure: Class 3 misdemeanor, 18-7-302
CONNECTICUT			A court may order HIV/ AIDS testing of a person accused of a crime involving a sexual act, 54-102a	Sexual intercourse with relative within any degree of kindred: Class D felony, 53a-72a; Prostitution: Class A misdemeanor, 53a-82; Breach of peace: Class B misdemeanor, 53a-181; Public disturbance: infraction, 53a-181a; Disorderly conduct: Class C misdemeanor, 53a-182; Obstructing free passage: Class C misdemeanor, 53a-182a; Public indecency: Class B misdemeanor, 53a-186

Table 14: Prohibited Consensual Sexual Activity—Continued

State	Sodomy: Applicability to:	Sodomy: Penalty	Exposing Another to/ Compelled Testing for AIDS/HIV	Other Crimes Relating to Consensual Sex Acts
DELAWARE			Upon request by the victim, the court shall order HIV testing of a defendant arrested and charged with an offense in § 1076 if this title, Tit. 10, § 1077	Indecent exposure in 2nd degree: unclassified misdemeanor, Tit. 11, § 764; Indecent exposure in 1st degree: Class A misdemeanor, Tit. 11, § 765; Disorderly conduct: unclassified misdemeanor, Tit. 11, § 1301; Loitering: violation, Tit. 11, § 1321; Lewdness: Class B misdemeanor, Tit. 11, § 1341; Prostitution: Class B misdemeanor, Tit. 11, § 1342
DISTRICT OF COLUMBIA			Upon request of a victim, the court shall order an HIV test from an individual convicted of an offense as defined by § 22-3901, 22-3902	Lewd, indecent, or obscene acts: misdemeanor; imprisonment up to 90 days and/or fine up to $500, imprisonment, 22-1312;Engaging in or soliciting for purposes of prostitution: Imprisonment up to 90 days and/or fine up to $500; 2nd offense: imprisonment up to 180 days and/or fine up to $1,000; 3rd and subsequent offenses: imprisonment up to 2 yrs. and/or fine up to $12,500, 22-2701; Certain obscene activities: Imprisonment up to 180 days and/or fine up to $1,000, 22-2201
FLORIDA	Both sexes	Unnatural and lascivious act: misdemeanor of the 2nd degree, 800.02	Criminal transmission of HIV: 3rd degree felony; only applies to list of enumerated sexual offenses; court may order test if defendant commits an offense of enumerated list. 384.24 Unlawful for person with sexually transmitted disease, when such person knows he or she is infected, to have sexual intercourse with another unless other person told of disease and consents: 1st degree misdemeanor, 775.0877	Prostitution, lewd, indecent act: misdemeanor in 2nd degree, 796.07; Lewd and lascivious behavior: 2nd degree misdemeanor, 798.02; Exposure of sex organs: 1st degree misdemeanor, 800.03; Living in open adultery: 2nd degree misdemeanor, 809.01; Breach of peace: 2nd degree misdemeanor, 877.03

Table 14: Prohibited Consensual Sexual Activity—Continued

State	Sodomy: Applicability to:	Sodomy: Penalty	Exposing Another to/ Compelled Testing for AIDS/HIV	Other Crimes Relating to Consensual Sex Acts
GEORGIA	Both sexes; Note: This section has been held unconstitutional in *Powell v. State*, 510 S.E. 2d 18 (1998)	Sodomy: imprisonment 1 to 20 yrs.; aggravated sodomy: imprisonment for life or 25 yrs. followed by probation for life, 16-6-2	Reckless conduct by HIV infected person: felony, 16-5-60; HIV test required for AIDS-transmitting crimes (sodomy; aggravated sodomy; solicitation of sodomy), 17-10-15	Public indecency: misdemeanor, 16-6-8 ; Solicitation of sodomy: misdemeanor; if solicited person under 18 years old: felony, 16-6-15 ; Masturbation for hire: misdemeanor, 16-6-16 ; Fornication: misdemeanor, 16-6-18 ; Adultery: misdemeanor, 16-6-19 ; Disorderly conduct: misdemeanor, 16-11-39
HAWAII			Upon request of the victim, the court shall order an HIV test of the charged person after a probable cause determination, 325-16.5	Indecent exposure: petty misdemeanor, 707-734; Open lewdness: petty misdemeanor; 712-1217
IDAHO	Both sexes or with an animal	Crime against nature: felony punishable by imprisonment not less than 5 yrs., 18-6605	Transfer of body fluid which may contain the HIV virus: felony, 39-608	Participation in, or production or presentation of, obscene live conduct in public place: misdemeanor, 18-4104; Public display/exhibit/depiction of offensive sexual material: misdemeanor, 18-4105; Adultery: fine of not less than $100, or imprisonment in the county jail for not less than 3 mos., or imprisonment in the state penitentiary for a period not exceeding 3 yrs., or in the county jail for a period not exceeding 1 yr., or by fine not exceeding $1,000, 18-6601
ILLINOIS			HIV testing may be requested by victim of sexual assault crime upon preliminary hearing or indictment, 720 § 5/11-1.10; Criminal transmission of HIV: Class 2 felony, 720 § 5/12-16.2	Public indecency: Class A misdemeanor, 720 § 5/11-30; Adultery: Class A misdemeanor, 720 § 5/11-35; Fornication: Class B misdemeanor, 720 § 5/11-40
INDIANA			HIV testing required if convicted of sex crime or offense related to controlled substances, 35-38-1-9.5	Public indecency-indecent exposure: Class A misdemeanor, 35-45-4-1; Public nudity: Class C misdemeanor, 35-45-4-1.5
IOWA			Victim may request HIV testing of defendant charged with or convicted of sexual assault, 915.42	Indecent exposure: serious misdemeanor, 709.9

Table 14: Prohibited Consensual Sexual Activity—Continued

State	Sodomy: Applicability to:	Sodomy: Penalty	Exposing Another to/ Compelled Testing for AIDS/HIV	Other Crimes Relating to Consensual Sex Acts
KANSAS	Same sex, between person or animal, or with person under 16 years of age	Criminal sodomy: Class B nonperson misdemeanor if person is over 16 yrs. old; If between 14 and 16 yrs. old, Level 3 person felony; 21-5504	In a crime where transmission of fluids may have taken place, the court shall order infectious disease testing of an arrested and charged person, upon: request of the victim or district attorney or if the defendant has indicated to an officer that he/she is infected, 65-6009	Adultery: Class C misdemeanor, 21-5511; Lewd and lascivious behavior: Class B nonperson misdemeanor if in presence of persons 16 and over; Level 9 person felony if in presence of persons under 16, 21-5513
KENTUCKY	Same sex. Note: This section has been held unconstitutional in *Kentucky v. Wasson*, 842 S.W. 2d 487 (1992)	Sodomy in the 4th degree: Class A misdemeanor, 510.100	Upon conviction of sexual activity crime, court shall order HIV testing of defendant, 510.320	Indecent exposure: Class B misdemeanor, 510.150
LOUISIANA	Both sexes or with an animal	Unnatural carnal copulation: imprisonment with or without hard labor up to 5 yrs. and/or fine up to $2,000; with person under 18, imprisonment 15-50 yrs. and/or fine up to $50,000; with person under 14, imprisonment 25-50 yrs. and/or fine up to $75,000, 14:89	Intentional exposure to AIDS virus: imprisonment with or without hard labor up to 10 yrs. and/or fine up to $5,000; against police officer: imprisonment with or without hard labor up to 11 yrs. and/or fine up to $6,000, 14:43.5; Court shall order HIV test of person convicted of sexual offense, 15:535	Prostitution 1st offense: imprisonment up to 6 mos. and/or fine up to $500; 2nd offense: imprisonment up to 2 yrs. and/or fine up to $2,000; 3rd and subsequent offenses: imprisonment 2 to 4 yrs. and fine $500 to $4,000, 14:82; Marriage or sexual intercourse with blood relative: ascendant and descendant, or between brother and sister: imprisonment at hard labor up to 15 yrs.; between uncle and niece, or aunt and nephew: imprisonment with or without hard labor up to 5 yrs. and/or fine up to $1,000, 14:89; Sexual acts prohibited in public: imprisonment minimum 10 days to 1 yr., at least of 10 days must be served without probation, parole or suspension of sentence and fine up to $1,000, 14:106.2; Obscenity (indecent exposure): imprisonment with or without hard labor 6 mos. to 3 yrs. and/ or fine of $1,000 to $2,500, 14:106

Table 14: Prohibited Consensual Sexual Activity—Continued

State	Sodomy: Applicability to:	Sodomy: Penalty	Exposing Another to/ Compelled Testing for AIDS/HIV	Other Crimes Relating to Consensual Sex Acts
MAINE			Victim may petition court to order HIV test of convicted sexual offender, Tit. 5, § 19203-F	Indecent conduct: Class E crime, Tit. 17-A, § 854
MARYLAND			Exposure of other individuals by individual with HIV virus: misdemeanor, Health-Gen. § 18-601.1; Victim may request HIV testing upon conviction of crime involving a prohibited exposure, Crim. Proc. § 11-112	Indecent exposure: misdemeanor, Crim. Law § 11-107
MASSACHUSETTS	Both sexes or with an animal	Crime against nature: imprisonment up to 20 years, Ch. 272, § 34		Open and gross lewdness and lascivious behavior: felony; imprisonment up to 3 years or fine up to $300, 272 § 16; Resorting to restaurants or taverns for immoral purposes: imprisonment up to 1 yr. and/ or fine $25 to $500, 272 § 26; Dissemination or possession of obscene matter: imprisonment up to 5 years in state prison or up to 2.5 yrs. in jail or house of correction and/or fine $1,000 to $10,000 for 1st offense, $5,000 to $20,000 for 2nd offense, $10,000 to $30,000 for 3rd and subsequent offenses, 272 § 29; Unnatural and lascivious acts: felony, imprisonment up to 5 yrs. in state prison or up to 2.5 yrs. in jail or house of correction or fine $100 to $1,000, 272 § 35; Disorderliness in public conveyances; disturbance of travelers: misdemeanor, 272 § 43; Indecent exposure: imprisonment up to 6 mos. in jail or house of correction and/ or fine up to $200, 272 § 53

Table 14: Prohibited Consensual Sexual Activity—Continued

State	Sodomy: Applicability to:	Sodomy: Penalty	Exposing Another to/ Compelled Testing for AIDS/HIV	Other Crimes Relating to Consensual Sex Acts
MICHIGAN	Both sexes or with any animal	Crime against nature or sodomy: felony; not more than 15 years, 750.158	If a defendant is bound over on a violation involving sexual penetration or exposure to bodily fluids, the court shall order testing. If a person is arrested and charged with prostitution-related violations, the court may order testing, 333.5129	Disorderly conduct: misdemeanor, 750.168; Lewd and lascivious cohabitation and gross lewdness: misdemeanor, 750.335; Indecent exposure: misdemeanor, 750.335a; Gross indecency between male persons: felony, 750.338; Gross indecency between female persons: felony, 750.338a; Soliciting and accosting: misdemeanor, 750.448
MINNESOTA	Both sexes	609.293 Sodomy: misdemeanor. Note: Recognized as unconstitutional in *In Re Proposed Petition to Recall Hatch*, 628 N.W. 2d 125 (2001)	609.2241 Knowing transfer of communicable disease: if crime involved sexual penetration with another person without having first informed the other person that the person has a communicable disease; if crime involved transfer of blood, sperm ... except for medical research; if crime involved sharing of nonsterile needles; penalty is as provided under attempt, assault, and murder statutes 611A.19 Victim may request HIV test of convicted sexual offender	617.23 Indecent exposure: misdemeanor
MISSISSIPPI	Both sexes or with a beast	Unnatural intercourse: imprisonment up to 10 yrs., 97-29-59	Any person convicted of sex offense after 7/1/94 shall be tested for HIV, 99-19-203	Indecent exposure (public): misdemeanor; imprisonment up to 6 mos. and/or fine up to $500, 97-29-31; Disturbance by abusive language or indecent exposure (private property): misdemeanor, 97-35-11; Disturbance of public peace: misdemeanor, 97-35-15

Table 14: Prohibited Consensual Sexual Activity—Continued

State	Sodomy: Applicability to:	Sodomy: Penalty	Exposing Another to/ Compelled Testing for AIDS/HIV	Other Crimes Relating to Consensual Sex Acts
MISSOURI	Animal	Unlawful sex with an animal: Class A misdemeanor, 566.111	Knowingly infected with HIV-prohibited acts, create risk of transmittal: class A or B felony, 191.677; Any person convicted of or who pleads guilty to sex offense in Chap. 556 shall be ordered by court to undergo HIV test, 191.663; Court may order testing when it has reasonable grounds to believe an individual is infected with HIV and there is clear and convincing evidence that individual will present health threat to others if infected, 191.674	Sexual misconduct in 1st degree: Class B misdemeanor, 566.093; Sexual misconduct in 2nd degree: Class C misdemeanor, 566.095
MONTANA	Both sexes	Deviate sexual conduct: felony; imprisonment up to 10 years and/or fine up to $50,000. Note: This statute is held unconstitutional by *Gryczan v. State*, 942 P.2d 112 (Mont. 1997), 45-8-218	Exposure of another to sexually transmitted disease: misdemeanor, 50-18-112; Any person convicted of sexual offense must be tested for HIV if victim requests, 46-18-256	Indecent exposure: imprisonment up to 6 mos. and/ or fine up to $500, 45-5-504; Obscenity: imprisonment up to 6 mos. and/or fine $500 to $1,000, 45-8-201
NEBRASKA			If victim of sexual assault or sex offense involving sexual contact or penetration requests, court shall order HIV testing of convicted offender, 29-2290	Public indecency: Class II misdemeanor, 28-806
NEVADA	Both sexes	Commission of certain sexual acts in public: Category D felony (applies only to sodomy in public), 201.190	Intentional transmission of HIV: Category B felony, 201.205; As soon as practical after a person is arrested for a crime in which the victim alleges sexual penetration, the arrestee will be tested for HIV, 441A.320	Open or gross lewdness: gross misdemeanor 1st offense; subsequent offense category D felony, 201.210; Indecent exposure: gross misdemeanor 1st offense; subsequent offense category D felony, 201.220; Engage in lewdness in public/ prostitution: misdemeanor, 207.030
NEW HAMPSHIRE			Any person convicted of offense under this chapter shall be administered an HIV test, 632-A:10-b	Indecent exposure: misdemeanor, 645:1; Adultery: class B misdemeanor, 647:3

319

Table 14: Prohibited Consensual Sexual Activity—Continued

State	Sodomy: Applicability to:	Sodomy: Penalty	Exposing Another to/ Compelled Testing for AIDS/HIV	Other Crimes Relating to Consensual Sex Acts
NEW JERSEY			Upon request of victim, any person convicted of sexual assault or aggravated sexual assault shall be HIV tested, 2C:43-2.2	Lewdness: misdemeanor, 2C:14-4; Public communication of obscenity: crime of 4th degree, 2C:34-4
NEW MEXICO			Court may order test for sexually transmitted diseases when it determines from the facts of the case that there was a transmission or likelihood of transmission of bodily fluids from the offender to the victim of the criminal offense, 24-1-9.1	Indecent exposure: misdemeanor, 30-9-14; Indecent dancing: petty misdemeanor, 30-9-14.1; Indecent waitering: petty misdemeanor, 30-9-14.2
NEW YORK			Upon request of victim of felony offense enumerated in any section of Penal § 130, the court must order the convicted person to be tested for HIV, Crim. Proc. § 390.15	Disorderly conduct: violation, Penal § 240.20; Loitering: violation, Penal § 240.35; Public lewdness: Class B misdemeanor, Penal § 245.00; Exposure of a person: violation, Penal § 245.01
NORTH CAROLINA	Both sexes or beast	Crime against nature: Class I felony, 14-177	Upon indictment or finding probable cause on an offense involving nonconsensual vaginal, anal, or oral intercourse or intercourse with a child under 12, or under G.S.14-202.1 with a child under 16, a victim may request testing; If the court finds probable cause that a significant risk of transmission exists, the court shall order testing, 15A-615	Indecent exposure: Class 2 misdemeanor, 14-190.9
NORTH DAKOTA			HIV transfer of body fluid: Class A felony (affirmative defense-transferred by consensual sex) 12.1-20-17; If victim petitions court may order defendant charged with sex offense under Chap. 12.1-20 to be HIV tested, 23-07.7-01	Fornication: Class A misdemeanor, 12.1-20-08; Adultery: Class A misdemeanor, 12.1-20-09; Indecent exposure: Class A misdemeanor, 12.1-20-12.1; Disorderly conduct: Class B misdemeanor, 12.1-31-01

Table 14: Prohibited Consensual Sexual Activity—Continued

State	Sodomy: Applicability to:	Sodomy: Penalty	Exposing Another to/ Compelled Testing for AIDS/HIV	Other Crimes Relating to Consensual Sex Acts
OHIO			If person charged with violation of division (B) of section § 2903.11 or §§ 2907.02; 2907.03; 2907.04; 2907.05; 2907.12; 2907.24; 2907.25; or 2907.241, the court shall order the accused to submit to HIV testing upon request of the victim or prosecuting attorney, 2907.27	Disorderly conduct: misdemeanor, 2917.11; Public indecency: 4th degree misdemeanor, 2907.09
OKLAHOMA	Both sexes or a beast	Crime against nature: felony; 10 years, Tit. 21, § 886	Knowingly engaging in conduct reasonably likely to transfer HIV virus: felony; imprisonment up to 5 yrs., Tit. 21, § 1192.1	Indecent exposure: felony; imprisonment up to 10 years and fine up to $20,000, Tit. 21, § 1021; Prostitution, lewdness, or assignation: misdemeanor, Tit. 21, § 1029
OREGON			Upon request of victim of crime involving transmission of bodily fluids, court shall order HIV testing of convicted offender or person charged with such offense after determining probable cause, 135.139	Public indecency: Class A misdemeanor, 163.465
PENNSYLVANIA			Upon request of the victim, a test shall be conducted if defendant is convicted of Tit. 18, §§ 3121 to 3123, 3128, 4302, or 6301; Tit. 35, § 521.11a	Disorderly conduct: summary offense, Tit. 18, § 5503; Indecent exposure: misdemeanor 2nd degree, Tit. 18, § 3127; Open lewdness: misdemeanor 3rd degree, Tit. 18, § 5901
RHODE ISLAND	With a beast	Crime against nature with beast: felony; imprisonment 7 to 20 yrs., 11-10-1	Exposing another person to sexually transmitted diseases: misdemeanor; imprisonment up to 3 mos. or $100 fine, 23-11-1; Any person convicted of possession of a hypodermic needle associated with intravenous drug use shall take an HIV test, 21-28-4.20; Upon request of the victim, any person convicted of committing a sexual offense involving sexual penetration shall be tested for STDs, including HIV/AIDS, 11-37-17	Disorderly conduct: imprisonment up to 6 months and/or fine up to $500, 11-45-1; Indecent exposure-disorderly conduct: imprisonment up to 1 yr. and/or fine up to $1,000, 11-45-2

Table 14: Prohibited Consensual Sexual Activity—Continued

State	Sodomy: Applicability to:	Sodomy: Penalty	Exposing Another to/ Compelled Testing for AIDS/HIV	Other Crimes Relating to Consensual Sex Acts
SOUTH CAROLINA	Both sexes or beast	Buggery or sodomy: felony; imprisonment 5 years and/or fine not less than $500, 16-15-120	Knowingly exposing others to AIDS virus: felony; imprisonment up to 10 years or fine up to $5,000, 44-29-145; Court shall order HIV testing of offender if victim requests and there is probable cause that the offender committed the offense and that bodily fluids were transmitted, 16-3-740	Prostitution: lewdness, assignation, and prostitution generally: misdemeanor, 16-15-90; Indecent exposure: misdemeanor, 16-15-130; Exposure of private parts: misdemeanor, 16-15-365
SOUTH DAKOTA	With a beast	Bestiality: Class 6 felony, 22-22-42	Victim or law enforcement officer where exchange of body fluids has occurred may petition court to order HIV testing of defendant, 23A-35B-3; Intentional exposure to HIV infection: Class 3 felony, 22-18-31	Public indecency: Class 2 misdemeanor, 22-24-1.1; Indecent exposure: Class 1 misdemeanor, 22-24-1.2
TENNESSEE	Same sex	(Former statute ruled unconstitutional in 1996)	Exposure of others by infected person: Class C misdemeanor (sexually transmitted disease) 68-10-107; When a person is initially arrested for allegedly violating §§ 39-13-502; 39-13-503; 39-13-506; or 39-13-522, that person shall undergo HIV testing immediately, 39-13-521; Aggravated prostitution. Committing prostitution with knowledge that such person is infected with HIV/ AIDS: Class C felony, 39-13-516	Indecent exposure: Class B misdemeanor, 39-13-511; Prostitution and patronizing prostitution: Class B misdemeanor, 39-13-512; 39-13-514; Promoting prostitution: Class E felony, 39-13-515
TEXAS	Same sex	Homosexual conduct: Class C misdemeanor. Note: Found unconstitutional by *Laurence v. Texas*, 539 U.S. 558 (2003) Penal § 21.06	Upon indictment for felony sex offense or upon request of victim of alleged sex offense, court may order HIV testing of offender, Crim. Proc. § 21.31	Public lewdness: Class A misdemeanor, Penal § 21.07; Indecent exposure: Class B misdemeanor, Penal § 21.08; Disorderly conduct: Class C misdemeanor, Penal § 42.01

Table 14: Prohibited Consensual Sexual Activity—Continued

State	Sodomy: Applicability to:	Sodomy: Penalty	Exposing Another to/ Compelled Testing for AIDS/HIV	Other Crimes Relating to Consensual Sex Acts
UTAH	Both sexes	Sodomy: Class B misdemeanor, 76-5-403	At victim's request, person convicted of sex offense or attempted sex offense must be HIV tested, 76-5-502	Disorderly conduct: Class C misdemeanor if offense continues after a request to desist, otherwise it is an infraction, 76-9-102; Lewdness: Class B misdemeanor, 76-9-702; Patronizing a prostitute or engaging in prostitution: Class B misdemeanor, 76-10-1303; 76-10-1304
VERMONT			A person diagnosed and reported as being infected must submit to regular testing and treatment, Tit. 18, § 1091a; Upon conviction of a criminal offense involving a sexual act with risk of transmission and request of the victim, the court shall order a test for AIDS and other STDs, Tit. 13, § 3256	Lewd and lascivious conduct: felony; imprisonment up to 5 yrs. and/or fine up to $300, or both, Tit. 13, § 2601; Prohibited acts: Occupy, reside in or permit building to be used for the purpose of prostitution, lewdness, or assignation; promote, aid, abet, or engage in prostitution, lewdness, or assignation: imprisonment up to 1 yr. or fine up to $100 for 1st offense; imprisonment up to 3 yrs. for subsequent offenses, Tit. 13, § 2632
VIRGINIA	Both sexes or any brute animal	Crime against nature: Class 6 felony, 18.2-361	Testing for HIV may be requested following arrest for crime involving sexual assault or §§ 18.2-361, 18.2-366, 18.2-370, and 18.2-370.1. 18.2-62	Fornication: Class 4 misdemeanor, 18.2-344; Prostitution: Class 1 misdemeanor, 18.2-346; Incest: Class 5 or class 3 felony 18.2-361; Indecent exposure: Class 1 misdemeanor, 18.2-387
WASHINGTON			All persons convicted of sexual offense under § 9A.44, offenses relating to prostitution under § 9A.88 or drug offenses using hypodermic needles under § 69.50 shall be HIV tested as soon as possible after sentencing, 70.24.340	Indecent exposure: misdemeanor, 9A.88.010; Prostitution: misdemeanor, 9A.88.030; Patronizing a prostitute: misdemeanor, 9A.88.110
WEST VIRGINIA			Upon conviction of sexual offense, HIV testing of convicted mandatorily ordered by the court, 16-3C-2	Indecent exposure: misdemeanor, 61-8-9

Table 14: Prohibited Consensual Sexual Activity—Continued

State	Sodomy: Applicability to:	Sodomy: Penalty	Exposing Another to/ Compelled Testing for AIDS/HIV	Other Crimes Relating to Consensual Sex Acts
WISCONSIN			In a criminal action for sex assault, the district attorney or victim may request the court order the defendant to be HIV tested, 968.38	Disorderly conduct: Class B misdemeanor, 947.01; Vagrancy: Class C misdemeanor, 947.02;Public fornication: Class A misdemeanor, 944:15; Adultery: Class I felony, 944,16; Sexual gratification: Class A misdemeanor, 944.17; Lewd and lascivious behavior: Class A misdemeanor, 944.20
WYOMING				Prostitution: misdemeanor, 6-4-101; Soliciting an act of prostitution: misdemeanor, 6-4-102; Public indecency: misdemeanor, 6-4-201

15. SEAT BELT LAWS

This 50-state-survey explores the differences between states for seat belt laws, including child restraint system laws. Most states require all drivers and passengers to be restrained by a seat belt (at least in the front seat) or child restraint system. Many seat belt laws cover only adults or older children, which makes sense when read with the child restraint laws that typically have coverage for children not covered by the seat belt laws.

One of the largest variances within the states was whether the seat belt law was a primary or secondary enforcement law. Primary enforcement indicates that a law enforcement officer may stop a car and issue a ticket even if there are no other traffic infractions. In contrast, secondary enforcement requires that there be another citable infraction before a seat belt ticket can be issued. The majority of states have primary enforcement laws with only 15 states having secondary enforcement. Interestingly, some states have more of a hybrid enforcement scheme that allow primary enforcement for the front seat, but secondary enforcement for the back seat.

Children restraint system laws also showed significant variances throughout the states. While many states had thorough laws specifying the age, weight, and height requirement and specific type of seat (rear-facing, forward facing, booster, seat belt), several states had much broader laws that only indicated children of a certain age should be secured by a child restraint system. These states often deferred to manufacturer instructions to ensure children were in the appropriate seat for their age, weight, and height. A concern with this method is that it provides less notice for individuals and law enforcement regarding what type of seat the law requires.

The fine information provided in the survey is the base fines before court costs. This was another area where states varied significantly. Some states have identical fines for seat belt and child restraint system laws. Many have a higher fine for violating a child restraint system law. This coincides with the purpose of the child restraint laws: to provide for the safety of children when riding in vehicles. Surprisingly a couple states have lower fines for child restraint law violations (see Michigan, West Virginia). The majority of states have the same fine regardless of the number of times the law has been violated. Other states have a tiered fine system that provide a lower fine for the first offense and a higher fine for the second, third, or subsequent offense. Some of the fines for a second or subsequent offense are as high as $500-$1,000.

An outlier in reviewing these laws is New Hampshire, which does not have a general seat belt law. Children under the age of 18 are covered under the child restraint system laws.

---

*This survey was compiled by Amanda Wall, UNL College of Law, JD 2019.

Table 15: Seat Belt Laws

State	Code Section	Seat/Seat Belt/Child Restraint	Enforcement	Can Passenger be Ticketed	Fine
ALABAMA	32-5B-4; 32-5B-5; 32-5-222	Under 1 or under 20 lbs: rear-facing infant only or convertible seat; under 40 lbs: convertible or other forward-facing seat; under 6: booster seat; 6-15: seat belt; over 15: seat belt in front seat	Primary		Child restraint violation: $25, $15 going to Pub. Health Dept. child restraint voucher program for families of limited income; fine dismissed on proof of purchase of restraint; seat belt violation: $25
ALASKA	28.05.095; 28.05.099	Under 1 or less than 20 lbs.: rear-facing child restraint device; 1-4 and over 20 lbs.: child restraint device meeting USDT standards and used in accordance with manufacturer instructions; 4-8 yrs., 20-65 lbs., and height under 57 in.: booster seat; 4-8 and over 65 lbs. or 57 in.: seat belt; 8-16 under 65 lbs. and under 57 in.: seat belt or appropriate child restraint device at discretion of driver; over 16: seat belt in all seats	Primary		Child restraint violation: $50; seat belt violation: $15
ARIZONA	28-907; 28-909	Under 5: child restraint system; 5-8 and under 4'9" in all vehicles with equipment required for vehicles manufactured 1972 and after and designed for under 10 passengers: child restraint system; 8-16: seat belt in all seats; under 16: seat belt in all seats; everyone: seat belt in front seat	Secondary		Child restraint violation: $50; seat belt violation: $10 for each violation
ARKANSAS	27-34-103; 27-34-104	Under 6 and less than 60 lbs.: child passenger safety seat; 6-16 or 60 lbs.: properly secured seat belt in all seats; over 16: seat belt in front seat	Primary		Child restraint violation: $25 to $100, no more than minimum fine upon proof of acquisition of approved child passenger safety seat; seat belt violation: $25

Table 15: Seat Belt Laws—Continued

State	Code Section	Seat/Seat Belt/Child Restraint	Enforcement	Can Passenger be Ticketed	Fine
CALIFORNIA	Veh. §§ 27315; 27360; 27360.5; 27363	Under 2 or under 40 lbs. or 40 in.: rear-facing child restraint system; 2-7 or over 40 lbs. or 40 in.: child restraint system, under 8 and over 4'9" may wear seat belt; all in rear seat; 8-16: child restraint system or seat belt in all seats; 16 and over: seat belt in all seats	Primary; driver not responsible for proper restraint of child up to age 16 if parent or guardian of child is passenger in vehicle	If passenger is over 16, both driver and passenger are ticketed	Child restraint violation: $100; seat belt violation: $20
COLORADO	42-4-236; 42-4-237; 42-24-1701	Under 1 and under 20 lbs.: rear-facing in rear seat; 1-4 and 20 to 40 lbs.: rear or forward-facing restraint system; 4-8: properly restrained in child restraint system; 8-16: seat belt in all seats; 16 and older: seat belt in front seat	Secondary		Child restraint violation: $81; seat belt violation: $71
CONNECTICUT	14-100a; 53a-36; 53a-42	Under 2 or under 30 lbs.: rear-facing child restraint system equipped with 5-point harness; 2-5 or 30-40 lbs.: rear- or forward-facing child restraint system equipped with 5-point harness; 5-8 or 40-60 lbs.: rear- or forward-facing child restraint system equipped with 5-point harness or booster seat secured by seat safety belt; 8-16: seat belt in all seats; everyone: seat belt in front seat, all seats if driver is under 18	Primary	Yes	Child restraint violation: 1st violation: $50 and completion of car seat safety course; 2nd violation: fine up to $199 and completion of class; 3rd violation: class A misdemeanor punishable by imprisonment up to 1 yr. and/or fine up to $2,000; seat belt violation: if the operator is over 18: $50; under 18: $75

Table 15: Seat Belt Laws—Continued

State	Code Section	Seat/Seat Belt/Child Restraint	Enforcement	Can Passenger be Ticketed	Fine
DELAWARE	Tit. 21, §§ 4802; 4803	Under 7 and under 65 lbs.: child safety seat or booster seat, positioned according to manufacturer's instructions and appropriate for child's height and weight; 8-16 or over 65 lbs.: may wear seat belt; child under 12 and under 65 in. may not occupy front passenger seat of any vehicle equipped with passenger-side airbag that is not deliberately disabled unless vehicle has no rear seat or rear seat is occupied with children under 12 and shorter than 65 in.; 16 and over: seat belt in all seats	Primary; failure to wear seat belt by more than 1 person in same vehicle at same time is treated as a single civil violation	No	Child restraint violation: $25; seat belt violation: $25
FLORIDA	316.18; 316.613; 316.614	Under 4: separate carrier or integrated child seat; 4-6: separate carrier, integrated child seat, or booster; 6-18: seat belt in all seats; everyone: seat belt in all seats	Primary	Yes, if over 18 and in front seat	Child restraint violation: $60; seat belt violation: $30
GEORGIA	40-8-76.1; 40-8-76	Under 8: restraining system appropriate for child's height and weight in rear seat unless vehicle has no rear seat or rear seat is occupied with other children; if under 8 and over 4' 9": may use seat belt; over 8: seat belt in all seats	Primary		Child restraint violation: 1st offense: $50; 2nd offense: $100; seat belt violation $15
HAWAII	291-11.5; 291-11.6	Under 4: child passenger restraint system; 4-8: child safety seat or booster seat; if over 4' 9" or over 40 lbs.: may use seat belt in back seat; 8 and over: seat belt in all seats	Primary		Child restraint violation: $100; seat belt violation: $45 per violation

Table 15: Seat Belt Laws—Continued

State	Code Section	Seat/Seat Belt/Child Restraint	Enforcement	Can Passenger be Ticketed	Fine
IDAHO	49-672; Id. R. Infr., Rule 9(b)(2); 49-673	Under 7: properly secured in child safety restraint that meets requirements of federal motor vehicle safety standard no. 213; 7 and over: seat belt in all seats	Secondary	Any occupant over 18 may be cited	Child restraint violation: $84; seat belt violation: $10
ILLINOIS	625 § 5/12-603.1; 625 §§ 25/4; 25/6	Under 8 and under 40 lbs.: child restraint system; 8-16 or over 40 lbs.: seat belt in back seat; 16 and over: seat belt in all seats	Primary; law enforcement officer may not search or inspect motor vehicle, contents, driver, or passenger solely because of violation of this seat belt law		Child restraint violation: 1st offense: $75; 2nd offense: $200; seat belt violation: $25
INDIANA	9-19-10-2; 9-19-10-3.1; 9-19-10-8; 9-19-11-2; 34-28-5-4(d)	Under 8: must be secured in child restraint system according to manufacturer's instructions; 8 and over: seat belt required in all seats	Primary; vehicle, contents, driver, or passenger may not be inspected, searched, or detained solely because of violation of this seat belt law.	Passengers over 16 will be ticketed	Child restraint violation: Class D infraction: $25; seat belt violation: Class D infraction: $25
IOWA	321.445; 805.8A(14)(c); 321.446; 805.8A(14)(c)	Under 1 or under 20 lbs.: rear-facing child restraint system; 1-6: child restraint system; 6-18: child restraint system or seat belt; 18 and over: seat belt in front seat	Primary	Yes; driver and front seat passengers may be charged separately; driver will not be charged for passenger infraction if passenger is over 14	Child restraint violation: $100; seat belt violation: $50
KANSAS	8-1344; 8-1345(a); 8-2503; 8-2504	Under 4: child restraint system; 4-7 and under 4' 9" or 80 lbs.: child restraint system; 8-14 or over 4' 9" or 80 lbs.: may use seat belt; 14 and over: seat belt in all seats	Primary; secondary for back seat violation		Child restraint violation: $60; seat belt violation: 18 or older: $30; 14-17: $60

Table 15: Seat Belt Laws—Continued

State	Code Section	Seat/Seat Belt/Child Restraint	Enforcement	Can Passenger be Ticketed	Fine
KENTUCKY	189.125; 189.990(25); 189.125(6); 189.990(26)	40 inches tall or less: child restraint system; under 8 and 40 to 57 in.: child booster seat; over 57 in.: may use seat belt without booster seat; 8 and over: seat belt in all seats	Primary		Child restraint violation: $50; booster seat violation: $30; seat belt violation: $25
LOUISIANA	32:295; 32:295.1	Under 1 or under 20 lbs.: rear-facing child safety seat; 1-4 or 20-40 lbs.: forward-facing child safety seat; 4-6 or 40-60 lbs.: child booster seat; 6-13 or over 60 lbs.: booster seat or seat belt; if child fits more than 1 category, more protective category applies; 13 and over: seat belt in all seats	Primary offense if failure to secure child in seat at all; secondary for failure to secure in age or size appropriate restraint		Child restraint violation: 1st offense: $100; 2nd offense: $200; 3rd and subsequent offenses: $500; seat belt violation: 1st offense: $50; 2nd offense: $75
MAINE	Tit. 29-A, § 2081	Under 40 lbs.: child safety seat 40-80 lbs.: child restraint system; 8-18: seat belt can be used; under 12 or under 100 lbs.: rear seat when possible ; 18 and over: seat belt in all seats	Primary	Passengers over 18	Child restraint violation: 1st offense: $50; 2nd offense: $125; 3rd and subsequent offenses: $250; seat belt violation: 1st offense: $50; 2nd offense: $125; 3rd and subsequent offenses: $250
MARYLAND	Transp. § 22-412.2; Transp. § 22-412.3	Under 8 or under 4' 9": child safety seat; 8-16: child safety seat or seat belt; 16 and over: seat belt in all seats	Primary		Child restraint violation: $50; seat belt violation: $50
MASSACHUSETTS	Ch. 90, § 7AA; Ch. 90, § 13A.	Under 8: child passenger restraint; if over 57" tall, may use seat belt; 8-13: seat belt; 13 and over: seat belt in all seats	Secondary	Passengers over 16	Child restraint violation: $25; seat belt violation: $25 per violation
MICHIGAN	257.710d; 257.710e	Under 4: child restraint system and in rear seat unless vehicle has no rear seat or all are occupied with children under 4; 4-8 and under 4' 9": child restraint system; 8-15: may use seat belt; 16 and over: seat belt in front seat	Primary		Child restraint violation: $10; seat belt violation: $25

Table 15: Seat Belt Laws—Continued

State	Code Section	Seat/Seat Belt/Child Restraint	Enforcement	Can Passenger be Ticketed	Fine
MINNESOTA	169.685(5); 169.686	Under 8 and under 4' 9": child restraint system; 8 and over: seat belt in all seats	Primary	Passengers 15 and older; driver ticketed for passenger under 15	Child restraint violation: $50; seat belt violation: driver or passenger under age of 15: $25; passengers 15 and older: $15
MISSISSIPPI	63-2-1; 63-2-7	Under 4: child passenger restraint device or system; 4-6 and under 4' 9" or under 65 lbs.: booster seat; 7 and over: seat belt in all seats	Primary	No	Child restraint violation: $25; seat belt violation: $25
MISSOURI	307.178; 307.179	Under 4: appropriate child passenger restraint system; under 40 lbs. regardless of age: appropriate child passenger restraint system; 4-7, under 4' 9" and under 80 lbs.: appropriate child passenger restraint system; 4' 9" or 80 lbs.: may use booster seat or seat belt as appropriate; 16 and over: seat belt in all seats	Secondary	Passengers over 16	Child restraint violation: $50; violation of 4' 9" or 80 lb. requirement: $10; seat belt violation: $10
MONTANA	61-9-420; 61-9-424; 61-13-103; 61-13-104	Under 6 and under 60 lbs.: child safety restraint; 6 and over: seat belt in all seats	Secondary unless passenger under 6 years old		Child restraint violation: $100; seat belt violation: $20
NEBRASKA	60-6,267; 60-6,268(1); 60-6,270 to 60-6,272	Current until 12/31/2018: Under 6: child passenger restraint system; 6-18: seat belt in all seats; Effective 1/1/2019 (LB42): Under 2: rear-facing child passenger restraint system until child outgrows manufacturer's maximum allowable height or weight; 2-8: correctly installed child passenger restraint system in rear seats unless all rear seats are occupied by children under 8; 8-18: booster seat or seat belt; 18 and over: seat belt in front seat	Secondary; primary if person under 18 is riding in or on any portion of vehicle not designed or intended for the use of passengers when vehicle is in motion	Yes	Child restraint violation: $25; seat belt violation: $25

331

Table 15: Seat Belt Laws—Continued

State	Code Section	Seat/Seat Belt/Child Restraint	Enforcement	Can Passenger be Ticketed	Fine
NEVADA	484B.157; 484D.495	Under 6 or under 60 lbs.: child restraint system; 6 and over or over 60 lbs.: seat belt in all seats	Secondary	Passenger over 18	1st offense: $100-$500 fine or 10-50 hrs. community service; 2nd offense: $500-$1,000 fine or 50-100 hrs. community service; 3rd or subsequent offense: 30-180 day driver's license suspension; seat belt violation: $25
NEW HAMPSHIRE	265:107-a	Under 7: child restraint system unless over 57 in.; 7-18: must wear seat belt			Child restraint violation: 1st offense: $50; 2nd offense: $100
NEW JERSEY	39:3-76.2a; 39:3-76.2d; 39:3-76.2f; 39:3-76.2j	Under 2 and under 30 lbs.: rear facing child passenger restraint system equipped with five-point harness; under 4 and under 40 lbs.: rear facing child passenger restraint system equipped with 5-point harness until child outgrows manufacturer's top height or weight recommendation or forward facing child passenger restraint system; 4-8 and under 57 in.: forward facing child passenger restraint system with 5-point harness until child outgrows manufacturer's top height or weight recommendation or secured in booster seat in rear seat of vehicle; 8 and over: seat belt in all seats	Primary		Child restraint violation: $50 to $75; seat belt violation: $20
NEW MEXICO	66-7-369; 66-7-372; 66-7-373(D); 66-8-116	Under 1: rear facing child passenger restraint device in rear seat; 1-4 or under 40 lbs.: child passenger restraint; 5-6 or under 60 lbs.: appropriate child passenger restraint device or child booster seat; 7-12: child passenger restraint device or seat belt; 18 and over: seat belt in all seats	Primary; each child under shall be properly secured in a child passenger restraint device or by a safety belt		Child restraint violation: $25; seat belt violation: $25

Table 15: Seat Belt Laws—Continued

State	Code Section	Seat/Seat Belt/Child Restraint	Enforcement	Can Passenger be Ticketed	Fine
NEW YORK	Veh. & Traf. § 1229-c	Current until 11/1/2019: Under 4: permanently affixed appropriate child restraint system; if over 40 lbs., seat may be one used in conjunction with combination lap and shoulder seat belts; 4-8: appropriate child restraint system or seat belt; 8-16: seat belt; restrictions same for front and back seats Effective 11/1/2019: All of above and: Under 2: rear facing child restraint system unless child exceeds manufacturer's maximum height or weight recommendation; 16 and over: seat belt in front seat	Primary		Child restraint violation: $25 to $100; seat belt violation: $50
NORTH CAROLINA	20-135.2A; 20-137.1	Under 8 and under 80 lbs.: weight-appropriate child passenger restraint system; 8-16: child passenger restraint system or seat belt; 16 and over: seat belt in all seats	Primary; secondary for the rear seat	Yes	Child restraint violation: $25; seat belt violation: driver and front seat passengers: $25; rear seat occupants: $10
NORTH DAKOTA	39-06.1-06; 39-21-41.2; 39-21-41.4; 39-21-41.5	Under 8: child restraint system, if over 57 in. may use seat belt; 8-18: seat belt in all seats; 18 and over: seat belt use in front seat	Secondary		Child restraint violation: $25; seat belt violation: $20
OHIO	4511.81; 4513.263	Under 4 and under 80 lbs.: child restraint system; 4-8 and less than 4' 9": properly installed booster seat; 8-15: seat belt in all seats; 15 and over: seat belt in front seat	Secondary	Yes	Child restraint violation: $25 to $75; seat belt violation:driver: $30; front seat passenger: $10

Table 15: Seat Belt Laws—Continued

State	Code Section	Seat/Seat Belt/Child Restraint	Enforcement	Can Passenger be Ticketed	Fine
OKLAHOMA	Tit. 47, § 12-417; Tit. 47, § 11-1112	Under 2 or until child reaches manufacturer's maximum height or weight recommendation: rear facing child passenger restraint system; under 4: child passenger restraint system; 4-7 and under 4' 9": child passenger restraint system or booster seat; 8 yrs. or 4' 9": seat belt; 8 and over: seat belt in front seat	Primary		Child restraint violation: $50; seat belt violation: $20
OREGON	811.210	Under 2: rear facing child safety system; over 40 lbs. and less than 4' 9": booster seat; over 8 or 4' 9": seat belt in all seats	Primary		Child restraint violation: Class D violation; $110; seat belt violation: Class D violation; $110
PENNSYLVANIA	Tit. 75, § 4581	Under 2: rear facing child passenger restraint system; 2-4: child passenger restraint system; 4-7: booster seat; under 18: seat belt in all seats; 18 and over: seat belt in front seat	Secondary § 4581(b)		Child restraint violation: $75; seat belt violation: $10
RHODE ISLAND	31-22-22; 31-41.1-4	Under 2 or less than 30 lbs.: rear-facing car seat; over 2 or over height and weight recommendation of rear-facing seat: forward-facing car seat with harness up to maximum allowed by manufacturer; under 8, under 57", and under 80 lbs: child restraint system in rear seat, over 57" or 80 lbs. may use seat belt; 8 and over: seat belt in all seats	Primary		Child restraint violation: $85; seat belt violation: $40

Table 15: Seat Belt Laws—Continued

State	Code Section	Seat/Seat Belt/Child Restraint	Enforcement	Can Passenger be Ticketed	Fine
SOUTH CAROLINA	56-5-6410; 56-5-6520; 56-5-6540	Under 2: properly secured in rear-facing child passenger restraint system in rear passenger seat; 2-4 or under 2 and has outgrown rear-facing seat: forward-facing child passenger restraint system with harness in rear passenger seat; 4-8 and has outgrown harness child passenger restraint system: belt-positioning booster seat in rear passenger seat; 8 or 57" tall: may use adult seat belt; 8 and over: seat belt in all seats	Primary	Passengers over 17	Child restraint violation: $150; seat belt violation: $25
SOUTH DAKOTA	32-37-1; 32-37-1.1; 32-37-1.3; 32-38-1; 32-38-5	Under 5: properly secured in child passenger restraint system; if 40 lbs., may use seat belt; driver's responsibility to ensure children 5-18 wear seat belts in all seats; 18 and over: seat belt in front seat	Secondary		Child restraint violation: $25; seat belt violation: $20
TENNESSEE	55-9-602; 55-9-603	Under 1 or under 20 lbs.: rear-facing child restraint system; 1-3 and over 20 lbs.: forward-facing child restraint system; 4-8 and less than 4' 9": booster seat; 9-12 or over 4' 9": seat belt; all in rear seat if available; 13-15: seat belt in all seats; 16 and over: seat belt in front seat	Primary; driver not liable for any passenger over 16		Child restraint violation: $50; seat belt violation: 1st offense: $30; 2nd and subsequent offense: $30
TEXAS	Transp. § 545.412; Transp. § 545.413	Under 8: secured by child safety seat unless taller than 4' 9"; 8 and over: seat belt in all seats	Primary	Passengers 15 and over	Child restraint violation: $25 to $250; seat belt violation: $25 to 50
UTAH	41-6a-1803	Under 8: child restraint device; if over 57", may use seat belt; 8-16: seat belt; driver responsible for securing all passengers under 16; 16 and over: seat belt in all seats	Primary	Passengers over 16	Child restraint violation: $45; seat belt violation: $45

Table 15: Seat Belt Laws—Continued

State	Code Section	Seat/Seat Belt/Child Restraint	Enforcement	Can Passenger be Ticketed	Fine
VERMONT	Tit. 23, § 1259	Under 1 and under 20 lbs.: rear-facing child passenger restraining system not in front of an active air bag; 1-8 and over 20 lbs.: child passenger restraining system; 8-17: child passenger restraining system or seat belt; 18 and over: seat belt in all seats	Secondary		Child restraint violation: 1st offense: $25; 2nd offense: $50; 3rd and subsequent offense: $100; seat belt violation: 1st offense: $25; 2nd offense: $50, 3rd and subsequent offense: $100
VIRGINIA	46.2-1094; 46.2-1095	Under 8: child restraint device; rear-facing devices in back seat when available; 9-17: seat belt in all seats; 18 and over: seat belt in front seat	Secondary	Passenger over 18	Child restraint violation: 1st offense: $50; 2nd and subsequent offense: $500; seat belt violation: $25
WASHINGTON	46.61.687; 46.61.688	Under 8 or under 4' 9": child restraint system; 8-15 or over 4' 9": seat belt; under 13 in rear seat when available; driver responsible for securing all passengers under 16; 16 and over: seat belt in all seats	Primary	Yes	Child restraint violation: up to $250; seat belt violation: up to $250
WEST VIRGINIA	17C-15-46; 17C-15-49	Under 8: child passenger safety device system; if over 4' 9", may use seat belt; 8-18 or over 4'9": seat belt in all seats; 18 and over: seat belt in front seat	Primary		Child restraint violation: $10-20; seat belt violation: $25
WISCONSIN	347.48; 347.50; 814.65	Under 1 or under 20 lbs.: rear-facing child safety restraint system in rear seat if available; 1-3 and 20-40 lbs.: forward-facing child safety restraint system in rear seat if available; 4-8, 40-80 lbs., and up to 57": child safety restraint system or booster seat; if over 80 lbs. and 57", may use seat belt; 8 and over: seat belt in all seats			Child restraint violation: $30 to $75; seat belt violation: $15

Table 15: Seat Belt Laws—Continued

State	Code Section	Seat/Seat Belt/Child Restraint	Enforcement	Can Passenger be Ticketed	Fine
WYOMING	31-5-1303; 31-5-1304; 31-5-1402	Under 9: child restraint system in rear seat when available; driver responsible for securing all passengers under 12; 9 and over: seat belt in all seats	Secondary	Yes	Child restraint violation: 1st offense: up to $50; 2nd and subsequent offenses: up to $100; seat belt violation: driver: up to $25; passenger: up to $10

16. THEFT OF IDENTITY

With modern technology and the attendant changes to the ways we live come new hazards and new crimes. One of the crimes to emerge with new virulence in this high-tech age is that of theft of identity. However, it should be made clear that this is a crime that is as old as history itself. From Jacob stealing Esau's birthright, to Jean Valjean becoming the Mayor, Monsieur Madeleine, to illegal immigrants to the United States fleeing despots of Central America, there have been many different reasons for appropriating another's identity. The computer age has simply made the act very easy, lucrative and possible in proportions and in volumes never before imagined.

As the name of the crime suggests, this crime occurs whenever someone appropriates another's identity or portion of it and uses it to appropriate the victim's money, credit or other thing of value. These crimes are particularly susceptible to abuse in an electronic environment because of the relative anonymity of online or telephone transactions. With nothing more than a credit card number, social security number or bank number, an unscrupulous person may be able to steal a victim's money or defraud unsuspecting banks or credit card companies by applying for and obtaining credit cards or credit lines.

But money is not the only goal of identity thieves. People may simply want a driver's license, passport, academic credentials or a credit history. With such things, people can enter or reside in the country illegally, or simply start lives over again.

The occurrence of these sorts of crimes is growing steadily. Relatively scarce a half century ago, official estimates now place the occurrence of identity theft at nearly a million a year. In response to the growing concern and attendant losses to businesses and victims, every state has now enacted legislation to protect the public.

It should be noted that in all states, theft by whatever means is a crime. The purpose of these statutes is to especially punish people who steal parts of a person's personal identity such as private financial or other personal information. In many cases, these statutes act as enhancements to existing laws. For example, in some states, people found guilty of theft under the Theft of Identity Statute will be automatically guilty of a felony, regardless of the amount stolen. All states have an established dollar amount, usually $1,000, above which a theft is a felony. However, in a state without the statute, a person stealing the same amount of money using the same method may only be guilty of a misdemeanor.

There is considerable variation among the states on the particular provisions of the statutes. For example, about five states have included provisions that make "trafficking" in identities or identity information illegal and state that possession of five or more identities creates a presumption that the person is guilty of trafficking. Some states have also included provisions that list various aggravating factors that will further enhance these crimes. For example, Florida provides for greater penalties if the crime is committed with public records, and Illinois and a few other states enhances penalties if the crime is perpetrated against an elderly person, or if the victim is a minor.

Table 16: Theft of Identity

State	Code Section	Crime/Penalties	Who May Prosecute
ALABAMA	13-A-5-6; The Consumer Identity Protection Act: 13A-8-190 to 13A-8-201	Class B felony punishable by imprisonment 2 to 20 yrs. and restitution, including lost wages and attorney fees; court may order restitution for financial loss to any other person or entity suffering loss from the violation; persons convicted must pay $25 per day and medical expenses for time spent in county or municipal jails or state prison facility	Any prosecuting authority
ALASKA	11.46.565; 11.46.570	2nd degree criminal impersonation: class A misdemeanor; 1st degree: class B felony	
ARIZONA	13-2001 to 13-2010; 13-2101 to 13-2110; 44-1373	Taking identity of another: class 4 felony; criminal impersonation: class 6 felony; aggravated taking of identity of another: class 3 felony; trafficking in the identity of another person or entity: class 2 felony	Any prosecuting authority
ARKANSAS	5-37-227	Financial identity fraud: class C felony, class B if victim is elderly or disabled; non-financial identity fraud: class D felony, class C if victim is elderly or disabled person; restitution may be ordered	Any prosecuting authority
CALIFORNIA	Penal §§ 530.5, to 530.8; Civil § 1798.93	Criminal offense punishable by imprisonment in county jail up to 1 yr. and/or fine or imprisonment pursuant to Penal § 1170(h)	Any prosecuting authority
COLORADO	18-1.3-603; 18-5-901 to 18-5-905	Identity theft: class 4 felony; criminal possession of 1 financial device: class 1 misdemeanor; 2 or more: class 6 felony; 4 or more, at least 2 to different persons: class 5 felony; criminal possession of 1 or more identity document issued to same person: class 1 misdemeanor; 2 or more, at least 2 to different persons: class 6 felony; possession of identity theft tools: class 5 felony	
CONNECTICUT	52-571h; 53a-129a to 53a-129e	Identity theft 1st degree: class B felony; 2nd degree: class C felony; 3rd degree: class D felony; trafficking in personal identity information: class D felony; court may award other remedies provided by law, including, but not limited to, the costs of providing not less than 2 yrs. of commercially available identity theft monitoring and protection for victim	Any prosecuting authority
DELAWARE	Tit. 11, §§ 828; 854; 907	Criminal impersonation: class A misdemeanor; Idensity theft: class D felony; full restitution to victim, including lost wages and reasonable attorney fees	Any prosecuting authority

Exemptions	Civil Action	Civil Remedies	Miscellaneous
Criminal statute does not apply to minors seeking to obtain privileges denied to minors	Civil action allowed	Greater of $5,000 per incident or 3 times actual damages; attorney fees and court costs	Statutes create the related crimes of 'trafficking in Stolen Identities'– a class B felony, and 'obstructing justice using a false identity' – a class C felony
Criminal statute does not apply to minors seeking to obtain privileges denied to minors		Civil action allowed	Violation also constitutes unfair or deceptive practice under the Deceptive Trade Practices Act, §4-88-101 to 4-88-804
	Civil action allowed against those who make mistaken claim against victim of identity theft	Judgment against claimant providing declaration that victim is not obligated on claim; any security or other interest is void and unenforceable; injunction to stop attempts to collect; actual damages, attorney fees and costs; equitable relief that court deems appropriate; possible civil penalty up to $30,000	Deptartment of Justice database of identity theft victims; other assistance available to victims
	Civil action allowed	Greater of $1,000 or treble damages; costs and reasonable attorney fees if plaintiff prevails	
			Person who possesses credit card or other document of another for purpose of identity theft is guilty of possession of burglar's tools, a class F felony

Table 16: Theft of Identity—Continued

State	Code Section	Crime/Penalties	Who May Prosecute
DISTRICT OF COLUMBIA	22-3227.01 to 22-3227.08; 22-3571.01	Identity theft 2nd degree: imprisonment up to 180 days and/or fine as set forth in 22-3571.01 if property or amount of financial injury has some value or if victim is falsely accused or arrested for committing crime because of use without permission of victim's identifying information; 1st degree: imprisonment up to 10 yrs. and/or fine as set forth in 22-3571.01, two times value of property or two times amount of financial injury, whichever greatest if property or amount of financial injury is $1,000 or more	
FLORIDA	817.568; 817.569; 817.5685	Identity theft: 3rd degree felony; restitution may be ordered, including attorney fees; grading may be increased to 2nd or 1st degree felony if loss more than $5,000 or multiple victims; unlawful possession of personal identification information of another: 1st degree misdemeanor; if more than 5 IDs: 3rd degree felony	Any prosecuting attorney
GEORGIA	16-9-120 to 16-9-132	Identity theft: criminal offense punishable by imprisonment 1-10 yrs. and/or fine up to $100,000; restitution may be ordered; 2nd or subsequent offense: imprisonment 3-15 yrs. and/or fine up to $250,000; aggravated identity fraud: imprisonment 1-15 yrs. and/or fine up to $250,000; sentence runs consecutively to any other sentence	Attorney General and prosecuting attorneys
HAWAII	708-839.55; 708-839.6 to 708-839.8	Identity theft 1st degree: class A felony; 2nd degree: class B felony; 3rd degree: class C felony; unauthorized possession of confidential personal information: class C felony	Any prosecuting attorney
IDAHO	8-3126; 8-3128	Identity theft: misdemeanor punishable by imprisonment in county jail up to 1 yr. and/or fine up to $1,000; if loss exceeds $300: felony punishable by imprisonment up to 5 yrs. and/or fine up to $50,000	Any prosecuting authority
ILLINOIS	720 §§ 5/16-30 to 5/16-37	Identity theft with loss not exceeding $300: class 4 felony; previous conviction for identity theft or several other theft and fraud related crimes: class 3 felony; loss $300 to $2,000: class 3 felony; loss $2,000 to $10,000: class 2 felony; loss $10,000 to $100,000: class 1 felony; loss over $100,000: class X felony; penalties greater in certain other instances and for aggravated identity theft when victim is 60 or older or disabled, or identity theft occurs in furtherance of activities of an organized gang	Any prosecuting authority
INDIANA	35-43-5-3.5	Level 6 felony; if more than 100 victims, amount of fraud or harm is at least $50,000, or victim is under 18 and accused's child, dependent, or ward: level 5 felony	Any prosecuting authority

Exemptions	Civil Action	Civil Remedies	Miscellaneous
	Civil action allowed		If public records used to commit offense, the offense is reclassified to next higher degree
Criminal statute does not apply to minors seeking to obtain privileges denied to minors or to those who lawfully obtain credit information for a bona fide commercial transaction or who exercise rights of a creditor in good faith			
Affirmative defense if person had reasonable belief that possession was authorized by law or by consent of another person			
	Civil action allowed	May recover court costs, attorney fees, lost wages, and actual damages; if no actual damage, victim will receive $2,000	A defense to aggravated identity theft does not exist merely because accused reasonably believed victim to be younger than 60
Criminal statute does not apply to minors seeking to obtain privileges denied to minors			Not a defense that no person was harmed or defrauded

Table 16: Theft of Identity—Continued

State	Code Section	Crime/Penalties	Who May Prosecute
IOWA	715A.8; 714.16B	Loss up to $1,000: aggravated misdemeanor; $1,000 to $10,000: class D felony; greater than $10,000: class C felony	Any prosecuting authority
KANSAS	21-6107; 21-6604(b)(1)	Identity theft: severity level 8 nonperson felony; if loss is more than $100,000: level 5 nonperson felony; identity fraud: severity level 8 nonperson felony	Any prosecuting authority
KENTUCKY	15.231; 411.210; 514.160; 514.170; 532.034	Identity theft: class D felony; restitution shall be ordered to victim for financial loss, including costs to correct credit history or in connection with any civil proceeding to satisfy obligation of victim, lost wages and attorney fees; may include restitution to financial institution that suffers direct financial loss; trafficking in stolen identities: class C felony	Attorney General has concurrent jurisdiction with Commonwealth attorneys and county attorneys
LOUISIANA	14:67.16; 14:73.10	Loss $1,000 or more: imprisonment with or without hard labor up to 10 yrs. and/or fine up to $10,000; loss $500 to $1,000: imprisonment with or without hard labor up to 5 years and/or fine up to $5,000; loss $300 to $500: imprisonment with or without hard labor up to 3 year and/or fine up to $3,000; loss less than $300: imprisonment with or without hard labor up to 6 mos. and/or fine up to $500; 2 or more previous convictions: imprisonment with or without hard labor up to 10 yrs., and/or fine up to $20,000; escalated penalties if victim is under 17 or over 60; perpetrator may be ordered to make full restitution to victim and any other person who suffers financial loss	Any prosecuting authority
MAINE	Tit. 17-A, § 905-A	Misuse of identification: class D crime	
MARYLAND	Crim. Law §§ 8-301; 8-305	Value $100 to $1,500: misdemeanor punishable by imprisonment up to 1 yr. and/or fine up to $500; $1,500 to $25,000: felony punishable by imprisonment up to 5 yrs. and/or fine up to $10,000; $25,000 to $100,000: felony punishable by imprisonment up to 10 yrs. and/or fine up to $15,000; $100,000 or more: felony punishable by imprisonment up to 20 yrs. and/or fine up to $25,000; intent to manufacture, distribute or dispense stolen identification: felony punishable by imprisonment up to 10 yrs. and/or fine up to $25,000	Attorney general or state's attorney

Exemptions	Civil Action	Civil Remedies	Miscellaneous
	Civil action allowed	Greater of $5,000 or 3 times actual damages; attorney fees and court costs; cost of repairing credit history and rating; cost incurred for bringing civil or administrative proceeding to satisfy a debt, lien, judgment, or other obligation of the victim	The value of property or services stolen will be its highest value by any reasonable standard
		Pay restitution including attorney fees and costs incurred to repair victim's credit history or rating or satisfy any debt, lien, or obligation incurred by victim because of theft	
Criminal statute does not apply to minors seeking to obtain privileges denied to minors; does not apply to credit or debit card fraud under 434.550 to 434.730	Civil action allowed	Compensatory and punitive damages; reasonable costs and attorney fees if plaintiff prevails	Theft of Identity or trafficking in stolen identities by business that has violated section 514.160 or 514.170 more than once is violation of Consumer Protection Act
Criminal statute does not apply to minors seeking to obtain privileges denied to minors			Online impersonation punishable by imprisonment 10 days to 6 mos. and/or fine $250 to $1000; if offender is under 17, disposition of matter governed by Title VII of Children's Code; provisions do not apply to any person employed by a social networking website, interactive computer service provider, telecommunications service provider, cable operator, internet service provider, or law enforcement officer or agency
Good faith belief of legitimate use is affirmative defense			
			Identity theft passport may be obtained by victim to help protect from consequences of actions of person who stole identity

Table 16: Theft of Identity—Continued

State	Code Section	Crime/Penalties	Who May Prosecute
MASSACHUSETTS	Ch. 266, § 37E	Criminal offense punishable by imprisonment up to 2.5 yrs. and/or fine up to $5,000; perpetrator shall be ordered to make restitution for costs to correct credit history and costs of civil/ administrative proceeding to satisfy debt or other obligation resulting from crime, including lost wages and attorney fees	Any prosecuting authority
MICHIGAN	Identity Theft Protection Act: 445.61 to 445.79c	Felony punishable by imprisonment up to 5 yrs. and/or $25,000 fine; 2nd violation: imprisonment up to 10 yrs. and/or $50,000 fine; 3rd violation: imprisonment up to 15 yrs. and/or $75,000 fine	
MINNESOTA	609.527	Criminal offense: Sngle victim with loss $250 or less: imprisonment up to 90 days and/or fine up to $1,000; single victim with loss $250 to $500: imprisonment up to 1 yr. and/or fine up to $3,000; 2 to 3 victims or total loss $500 to $2,500: imprisonment up to 5 yrs. and/or fine up to $10,000; 4 to 7 victims or loss over $2,500: imprisonment up to 10 yrs. and/or fine up to $20,000; over 8 victims or loss over $35,000: imprisonment up to 20 yrs. and/or fine up to $100,000; victim of crime has rights to restitution	Any prosecuting authority
MISSISSIPPI	97-19-85; 97-45-19; 97-45-23; 97-45-33	Fraudulent use of identity, social security number, credit card or debit card number or other identifying information to gain something of value: felony offense punishable by imprisonment up to 5 yrs. and/or fine up to $5,000; identity theft: felony punishable by imprisonment 2 to 15 yrs. and/or up to $10,000 fine; if loss less than $250: misdemeanor punishable by imprisonment up to 6 mos. and/or fine up to $1,000	Attorney general or his designee; district attorney
MISSOURI	570.223; 570.224; 557.021	No value: class B misdemeanor; Up to $750: class A misdemeanor; $750 to $25,000: class D felony; $25,000 to $75,000: class C felony; $75,000 or more: class B felony; court may order restitution for costs and attorney fees to clear credit history or rating and in connection with any civil or administrative proceeding to satisfy any debt, lien, or other obligation; trafficking in stolen identities: class B felony	Any prosecuting authority
MONTANA	45-6-332	Loss less than $1,500: fine up to $500; 2nd offense: imprisonment up to 6 mos. and/or fine up to $500; 3rd or subsequent offense: imprisonment 5 days to 1 yr. and fine up to $500; escalated penalty if victim is under 18; $1,500 to $5,000: imprisonment in state prison up to 10 yrs. and/or fine up to $5,000; 2nd offense: imprisonment up to 5 yrs. and/or fine up to $1,500; 3rd or subsequent offense: imprisonment 2 to 5 yrs. and fine up to $5,000; escalated penalty if victim is under 18	Any prosecuting authority

Exemptions	Civil Action	Civil Remedies	Miscellaneous
			Online impersonation punishable by imprisonment 10 days to 1 yr. and/or or fine $250 to $1,000
Criminal statute does not apply to: minors seeking to obtain privileges denied to minors; identification or information obtained in the course of a bona fide consumer or commercial transaction; good faith exercise of security interest or right of offset by a creditor or financial institution	Civil action allowed	$5000 for each incident, or 3 times actual damages, whichever is greater; enjoin and restrain future acts; reasonable attorney fees to plaintiff	

Table 16: Theft of Identity—Continued

State	Code Section	Crime/Penalties	Who May Prosecute
NEBRASKA	28-639 to 28-640; 29-2280	Loss up to $500: class II misdemeanor; 2nd offense: class I misdemeanor; 3rd or subsequent offense: class IV felony; $500 to $1,500: class I misdemeanor; 2nd or subsequent offense: class IV felony; $1,500 to $5,000: class IV felony; 2nd or subsequent offense: class III felony; $5,000 or more: class IIA felony; 2nd or subsequent offense: class II felony	County attorney of any county in which any part of identity fraud occurred
NEVADA	205.463 to 205.465	Category B felony punishable by imprisonment 1 to 20 yrs. and possible fine up to $100,000; court may order restitution for costs and attorney fees to repair credit history or rating and to satisfy any debt, lien, or other obligation incurred by victim	
NEW HAMPSHIRE	638:25 to 638:27	Identity fraud: class A felony; penalty includes order to make restitution for economic loss sustained by victim	Any prosecuting authority
NEW JERSEY	2C:21-17; 2C:21-17.1; 2C:21-17.4	Loss up to $500 and 1 victim: crime of 4th degree; 2nd or subsequent conviction: crime of 3rd degree; $500 to $75,000 or 2 to 5 victims: crime of 3rd degree; $75,000 or more or 5 or more victims: crime of 2nd degree; court may order restitution for costs to clear credit history or rating and in connection with any civil or administrative proceeding to satisfy any debt, lien, or other obligation	
NEW MEXICO	30-16-24.1	Identity theft: 4th degree felony; identity theft by electronic fraud: 4th degree felony; any penalty includes order for restitution to victim of any financial loss, including costs and attorney fees in to clear credit history or rating and in connection with any civil or administrative proceeding to satisfy any debt, lien, or other obligation	
NEW YORK	Penal 60.27; 190.77 to 190.84	Identity theft 3rd degree: class A misdemeanor; 2nd degree: class E misdemeanor; 1st degree: class D felony; aggravated identity theft: class D felony; restitution or reparation for actual out-of-pocket loss caused and any cost or loss incurred due to any adverse action taken against victim	
NORTH CAROLINA	1-539.2C; 14-113.20 to 14-113.25	Identity theft: class G felony; if victim suffers arrest, detention, or conviction as a result of the offense: class F felony; restitution may be ordered, including actual losses, lost wages, attorney fees, and other costs; trafficking in stolen identities: class E felony	Attorney General may investigate but shall refer all cases to district attorney of county in which crime occurred

Exemptions	Civil Action	Civil Remedies	Miscellaneous
Criminal statute does not apply to those who lawfully obtain credit information for a bona fide commercial transaction or in good faith exercise rights of a creditor or lawfully comply when required by any warrant, levy, court order or other decree or directive	Civil action allowed	Victim may seek damages, enjoin/restrain perpetrator from future acts of theft; prevailing party may recover court costs and attorney fees	Identity fraud: class I misdemeanor; 2nd or subsequent conviction: class IV felony
Criminal statute does not apply to minors attempting to obtain privileges denied to minors	Civil action allowed		
Does not apply to minors attempting to obtain privileges denied to minors			
Criminal statute does not apply to those who lawfully obtain credit information for a bona fide commercial transaction or in good faith exercise rights of a creditor or lawfully comply when required by any warrant, levy, court order or other decree or directive	Civil action allowed	Civil damages $500 to $5,000 or 3 times actual damages per incident of identity theft; victim may enjoin identity thief from future acts of theft; court may award reasonable attorney fees to tprevailing party	

Table 16: Theft of Identity—Continued

State	Code Section	Crime/Penalties	Who May Prosecute
NORTH DAKOTA	12.1-23-11; 32-03-52	Identity theft to obtain anything of value: class C felony; loss over $1,000: class B felony; 2nd or subsequence offense: class A felony; theft to interfere with contract or service or obtain or continue employment: class A misdemeanor; 2nd or subsequent offense: class C felony	Any prosecuting authority
OHIO	2913.49	Identity fraud: 5th degree felony; loss $1,000 to $7,500: 4th degree felony; loss $7,500 to $150,000: 3rd degree felony; loss $150,000 or more: 2nd degree felony; if victim is elderly or disabled adult, active duty member or spouse: offense is 1 degree higher	
OKLAHOMA	Tit. 21, § 1533.1	Identity theft: felony punishable by imprisonment 1 to 5 yrs. and/or or fine up to $100,000; restitution may be ordered; intent to lend, sell or otherwise offer use of personal identifying information: misdemeanor punishable by imprisonment in county jail up to 1 yr. and/or fine up to $100,000	Any prosecuting authority
OREGON	137.717; 165.800; 165.803	Identity theft: class C felony; aggravated identity theft: class B felony; presumptive sentence of imprisonment up to 24 mos.; longer sentence if perpetrator has previous convictions for identity theft, forgery, credit card fraud, or computer crime	Any prosecuting authority
PENNSYLVANIA	Tit. 18, §§ 1107.1; 4120	Loss less than $2,000: 1st degree misdemeanor; $2,000 or more: 3rd degree felony; if 3rd or subsequent offense of any value: 2nd degree felony; if committed in furtherance of criminal conspiracy: 3rd degree felony; if victim 60 or older, care-dependent person, or under 18: offense 1 degree higher; court may order restitution for costs to clear credit history or rating and in connection with any civil or administrative proceeding to satisfy any debt, lien, or other obligation	Attorney General has authority to investigate and prosecute if crime occurs in more than one county or in another state
RHODE ISLAND	11-49.1-1 to 11-49.1-5	Identity fraud: Felony punishable by mprisonment up to 3 yrs. and/or fine up to $5,000; 2nd conviction: imprisonment 3 to 5 yrs. and/or fine up to $10,000; 3rd or subsequent conviction: imprisonment 5 to 10 yrs. and/or minimum $15,000 fine	Any prosecuting authority
SOUTH CAROLINA	Personal Financial Security Act: 16-13-510 to 16-13-530	Identity fraud or financial identity fraud: automatic felony punishable by imprisonment up to 10 yrs. and/ or fine in the discretion of the court; court may order restitution for victim	Any prosecuting authority
SOUTH DAKOTA	22-6-1.1; 22-40-8	Identity theft: class 6 felony punishable by imprisonment up to 1 yr.	Any prosecuting authority

Exemptions	Civil Action	Civil Remedies	Miscellaneous
		Identity theft use of Social Security number: any equitable relief court deems appropriate and greater of actual or liquidated damages up to $10,000; court may award costs and attorney fees	
	Civil action allowed		
	Civil action allowed for damages		
Criminal statute does not apply to minors seeking to obtain privileges denied to minors			
Criminal statute does not apply to minors seeking to obtain privileges denied to minors			Any property used as a means of violating identity theft laws will be seized and forfeited to the state: proceeds 20% to Attorney General earmarked for identity theft investigation and 80% to other state/local law enforcement agencies
Criminal statute does not apply to those who lawfully obtain credit information for a bona fide commercial transaction or in good faith exercise rights of a creditor or lawful good faith compliance			Financial identity fraud enabling unlawfully present alien to live or work in the United States: 1st offense: misdemeanor punishable by 30 days imprisonment or $100 fine; 2nd offense: felony punishable by imprisonment up to 5 yrs. or $500 fine

Table 16: Theft of Identity—Continued

State	Code Section	Crime/Penalties	Who May Prosecute
TENNESSEE	39-14-150; Identity Theft Deterrence Act: 47-18-2101 to 47-18-2110	Identity theft: class D felony; identity theft trafficking: class C felony; restitution will be awarded state for reasonable attorney fees, costs, and expenses of investigation and prosecution	Attorney General may bring action to restrain or enjoin perpetrator from further identity theft acts, or to request freeze of perpetrator's assets, or for other appropriate or necessary measures; otherwise any prosecuting authority may prosecute
TEXAS	Penal § 32.51	Fraudulent use or possession up to 5 items: state jail felony; 5 to 10 items: 3rd degree felony; 10 to 50 items: 2nd degree felony; 50 or more items: 1st degree felony; offense increased 1 category if victim is elderly or thief used information with intent to facilitate offense; restitution may be ordered for lost income or other expenses, other than attorney fees	
UTAH	76-6-1101 to 76-6-1105	Loss up to $5,000: 3rd degree felony; loss $5,000 or more: 2nd degree felony; multiple violations may be aggregated into single offense; unlawful possession of another's identification documents: class A misdemeanor; 3rd degree felony if multiple documents; restitution shall be ordered or stated in record why not ordered, including costs and attorney fees in to clear credit history or rating and in connection with any civil or administrative proceeding to satisfy any debt, lien, or other obligation	Attorney general must investigate violations in addition to other law enforcement agencies
VERMONT	Tit. 13, § 2030	Identity theft: criminal offense punishable by imprisonment up to 3 yrs. and/or fine up to $5,000; 2nd and subsequent offense: imprisonment up to 10 yrs. and/or fine up to $10,000	
VIRGINIA	18.2-186.3	Loss up to $200: class 1 misdemeanor; 2nd violation or loss more than $200: class 6 felony; if violation results in arrest and detention of person whose identification documents or information were used to avoid summons, arrest, prosecution, or to impede a criminal investigation: class 5 felony; in addition to other punishment, court shall order perpetrator to make restitution to victim as the court deems appropriate, including victim's expenses in correcting credit report or other records	Any prosecuting authority

Exemptions	Civil Action	Civil Remedies	Miscellaneous
	Civil action allowed	Court may award 3 times actual damages and other relief as is necessary and proper; victim may enjoin perpetrator from further actions in violation of identity theft laws; victim may be awarded attorney fees and costs; civil penalty shall be awarded equal to the greatest of: $10,000, $5,000 per each day victim's identity is assumed, or 10 times the amount obtained or attempted to be obtained; victim shall receive restitution for all ascertainable loss, plus interest on the loss	If injunction obtained by Attorney General Is violated: civil penalty up to $5,000 per violation, plus contempt sanctions and award of attorney fees and costs to state for additional filings; violation of identity theft laws is a violation of Tennessee Consumer Protection Act of 1977
			Any violation of identity theft laws is also a violation of the Utah Consumer Sales Practices Act
			Attorney General may assist victim to obtain information necessary to correct victim's credit report or other records, if such assistance is requested

Table 16: Theft of Identity—Continued

State	Code Section	Crime/Penalties	Who May Prosecute
WASHINGTON	9.35.001 to 9.35.900	Loss up to $1,500: 2nd degree identity theft, class C felony; loss over $1,500 or victim is a senior or vulnerable person: 1st degree identity theft, class B felony	Any prosecuting authority
WEST VIRGINIA	61-3-54	Felony punishable by imprisonment up to 5 yrs. and/or fine up to $1,000	
WISCONSIN	943.201; 943.203	Class H felony	
WYOMING	1-1-128; 6-3-901	Loss less than $1,000: misdemeanor punishable by imprisonment up to 6 mos. and/or fine up to $750; $1,000 or more: felony punishable by imprisonment up to 10 yrs. and/or fine up to $10,000; court may order restitution to victim for costs incurred, including attorney fees, costs to clear credit history, costs of civil/administrative proceeding to satisfy debt, lien, or other obligation resulting from crime	Any prosecuting authority

Exemptions	Civil Action	Civil Remedies	Miscellaneous
Criminal statute does not apply to: efforts by financial institutions to test security procedures or to maintain confidentiality of customer information; investigations of employee misconduct or negligence; or efforts to recover personal information of the financial institution obtained by another person in any manner described above; criminal statute does not apply to minors seeking to obtain privileges denied to minors	Civil action allowed	Civil damages equal to the greater of $1,000 or actual damages, including costs to repair victim's credit record and reasonable attorney fees	Criminal statute does not apply to financial information repository efforts to test security procedures, investigation of employee misconduct or negligence, or to recover stolen information and does not apply to minors seeking to obtain privileges denied to minors
Criminal statute does not apply to minors seeking to obtain privileges denied to minors			
	Civil action allowed	Victim may enjoin or restrain perpetrator from further violations of identity theft law; victim may recover damages subject to setoff against judgment ordered under criminal law; prevailing party may recover court costs and attorney fees	

III. EDUCATION LAWS

17. COMPULSORY EDUCATION

Public schools are a relatively new concept in Western culture. Not until the nineteenth century did states officially begin to take responsibility for educating children. Before that time education was a private matter, either handled by parents, churches, or communities that joined together and paid a teacher to educate their children.

Some early state constitutions and territory charters specifically stated that the government was responsible for the training of children in morals and the overall knowledge necessary for them to become responsible citizens. Often this responsibility was acted upon merely by subsidizing the building of schools; minimum requirements for the type of education or the number of years of education that were required of students were not set.

Today education is a responsibility that local, state, and federal governments take seriously. The teaching of morality has given way to standard academic focuses, and compulsory education laws, requiring public school attendance of all children generally between the ages of six or seven and sixteen, have been enacted. However, these rules frequently exempt children with permanent or temporary mental or physical disabilities, and a few states exempt students who live more than two miles from a public transportation route. Alternatives to state-run schools, including private and parochial schools and home schools, are also available.

Table 17: Compulsory Education

State	Code Section	Age Requirements	Exceptions
ALABAMA	16-1-11 to 16-1-11.4; 16-28-1 to 16-28-24	Between 6 and 17; may opt out until age 7	Students may attend church school, private (including home) school or be privately tutored by certified instructor. Exceptions to attendance include child whose physical or mental condition prevents attendance; child with lack of transportation who would be compelled to walk over 2 mi. to attend public school; child legally and regularly employed; child who has completed the course of study of the public schools of the state through high school.
ALASKA	14.30.010 to 14.30.047	Between 7 and 16	Enrollment in private, religious, federal government school; enrolled in approved correspondence study; homeschooled by parent or guardian; alternate educational experience approved by the school board; child has physical or mental condition preventing attendance; in custody of court of law enforcement officer; temporarily ill or injured; over 2 miles from school with no transportation; has completed 12th grade; suspended or expelled
ARIZONA	15-801 to 15-808	Between 6 and 16 or 10th grade	Private, charter, or home school or parent/guardian sign a contract to participate in an Arizona empowerment scholarship account pursuant to § 15-2402; physical or mental condition makes attendance impractical; completed 10th grade; over 14 and employed at a lawful wage-earning occupation with consent of parent or guardian; enrolled in vocational or other state-approved education program; suspended or expelled; reasons for non-attendance satisfactory to the school principal or the school principal's designee
ARKANSAS	6-15-501 to 6-15-509; 6-18-201 to 16-18-231	Between 5 and 17	May attend private, parochial, or home school; child has received a high school diploma; parent may elect to withhold child from kindergarten; any child over 16 enrolled in post-secondary vocational institution or college or specific adult education programs upon certain conditions
CALIFORNIA	Educ. §§ 48200 to 48208; 48400; 48293; 51745 to 51749	Between 6 and 18; unless otherwise exempted, persons 16 to 18 not attending full-time school must attend special continuation education classes	Private school; private tutor with state credential; children holding work permits (subject to compulsory part-time classes); child of 15 may take a leave of absence for supervised travel, study, training, or work not available to the student under another education option if certain conditions are met; illegal aliens
COLORADO	22-33-104 to 22-33-110	Between 7 and 17	Child attends independent or parochial school that provides basic academic education or is instructed at home; is absent due to physical/mental/emotional disability; is lawfully employed; in custody of court or law enforcement authority; graduated 12th grade; is suspended or expelled
CONNECTICUT	10-184 to 10-185	Between 5 and 18; can delay start until 6 or 7	Child receiving equivalent instruction elsewhere; high school graduate; start of school may be delayed until 6 or 7; parent may allow student to withdraw at age 17

Home School Provisions	Penalties on Parents for Noncompliance
Exempt from regulation except reporting enrollment of children of mandatory school age	Misdemeanor: Fine up to $100 and possibly up to 90 days hard labor for the county
Children homeschooled by their parent or guardian are exempt from the compulsory attendance law. No registration or curriculum requirements are placed on home schools not funded with public dollars.	Knowing noncompliance is violation with fine up to $300; every 5 days of noncompliance is separate violation
Homeschooling is regulated by county. Parent/guardian must file affidavit of intent to homeschool with county school superintendent. All Arizona students must receive instruction in reading, grammar, mathematics, social studies, and science. Homeschooled children must be allowed to participate in interscholastic athletics for the school district in which he or she resides.	Class 3 misdemeanor; failure to provide affidavit of intent to provide instruction in a homeschool: petty offense
Parent/guardian must provide written notice of intent to homeschool to superintendent each year, including core curriculum, schedule of instruction and qualifications of parent/teacher. Also must sign waiver acknowledging State of Arkansas is not liable for the education of their children during time they are homeschooled. Testing and other regulations apply: see 16-15-504	Penalty as set by law, 6-18-201
No specific statutes. Options: (1) establish private school based in home and file private school affidavit and meet other private school requirements; (2) if parent/guardian has teaching credential for grades and subjects taught, child qualifies under private tutor exemption; (3) public or charter school independent study program	Guilty of an infraction; 1st conviction: fine up to $100; 2nd conviction: fine up to $250; 3rd or subsequent convictions: fine up to $500; in lieu of any fines, court may order person placed in parent education and counseling program
Parents not subject to "Colorado Education Licensing Act of 1991"; parents must give written notice every year and children shall be evaluated at grades 3, 5, 7, 9 and 11. Other curriculum and testing regulations apply: see 22-33-104.5	The board of education of each school district shall adopt and implement policies and procedures to work with children who are habitually truant. District may initiate court proceeding as last resort to compel child and child's parent to comply
If parents wish to educate their child in their home, they must show equivalency to local school board as described in 10-184	Fine up to $25 per day: each day is distinct offense; exception for parents of child destitute of clothing

Table 17: Compulsory Education—Continued

State	Code Section	Age Requirements	Exceptions
DELAWARE	Tit. 14, §§ 2702 to 2705; 2729	Between 5 and 16; may delay start 1 yr.	Private or home school attendance; by parents' request with written documentation of physician or psychiatrist; if granted by local school authorities as being in the best interests of the child
DISTRICT OF COLUMBIA	38-201 to 38-209	Between 5 and 18 in "an educational institution"	High school graduate; flexible hours if 17 and lawfully employed
FLORIDA	1002.41 to 1002.455; 1003.21 to 1003.27	Between 6 and 16	Certificate of exemption granted by the district school superintendent; private school, tutoring, or home school program
GEORGIA	20-2-690 to 20-2-701	Between 6 and 16	Private school or home study; high school diploma
HAWAII	302A-1132 to 302A-1134	Between 5 and 18	Child is physically or mentally unable to attend; child is at least 15 and suitably employed and excused by school representative or judge; permission after investigation by the family court; child has graduated high school; child is enrolled in an appropriate alternative educational program
IDAHO	33-201 to 33-208	Between 7 and 16	Kindergarten is not mandatory; child's physical/mental/emotional condition does not permit attendance
ILLINOIS	105 §§ 5/26-1 to 5/26-16	Between 6 and 17	Child attending private or parochial school; child is physically/mentally unable to attend school; child is excused by county superintendent; child 12 to 14 attending confirmation classes; pregnant female with complications to pregnancy; child is necessarily and lawfully employed; excused for temporary cause by principal or teacher
INDIANA	20-33-2-1 to 20-33-2-47	Between 7 and 16 if an exit interview requirement is met; otherwise 18	Child provided with instruction equivalent to public education or in nonaccredited, nonpublic school; child is physically/mentally unfit for attendance
IOWA	299.1 to 299.24; 299A.1 to 299A.12	Between 6 and 16	Accredited private college preparatory school; completed requirements for graduation from accredited school or GED; sufficient reason by court of record or judge; while attending religious services or receiving religious instruction; physical/mental conditions do not permit attendance

Home School Provisions	Penalties on Parents for Noncompliance
Must submit enrollment and attendance information to Dept. of Education. Children must receive regular and thorough instruction in the subjects prescribed for the public schools of the State in a manner suitable to children of the same age and stage of advancement	1st offense: imprisonment up to 10 days and/or $25 to $300 fine; 2nd offense: imprisonment up to 20 days and/or $50 to $500 fine; 3rd and subsequent offenses: imprisonments up to 30 days and/pr $230 to $1,150 fine; court may order unpaid community service as alternative sentence
Home schooling is regulated by the District of Columbia Municipal Regulations: see 5 DCMR §§ 5200 to 5299	Misdemeanor: Imprisonment up to 5 days and/or fine not less than $100 per offense. Court may impose community service as alternative sentence. One offense is the equivalent of missing 2 full days or 4 half days in one month; failure to enroll child is also offense
Notify superintendent of schools, maintain a portfolio of records and materials, and evaluate education annually, including a national student achievement test or other method of evaluation	Non-enrollment: superintendent may begin criminal prosecution; refusing to have child attend regularly is second degree misdemeanor
Must teach at least reading, language arts, math, social studies, and science; parents must give annual notice; parent must teach only his or her children or hire a private tutor who holds at least a high school diploma or a GED equivalency diploma; subject to standardized testing; must provide annual progress assessment report; minimum 180 days of instruction per year and at least 4.5 hours of instruction per day	Misdemeanor: imprisonment up to 30 days and/or fine up to $100; court may order community service as alternative sentence; each day's absence is separate offense after guardian has been notified
Parents must file notification of intent to home school with principal of assigned school and must keep record of planned curriculum	Petty misdemeanor
Under Idaho statutes, parents and guardians are granted the freedom and responsibility to determine the method of education to be pursued for each child. No registration, reporting, or compulsory testing requirements for home educated students exist. Parents must instruct in accordance with 33-202	Proceedings brought under provisions of the Juvenile Corrections Act
No specific statutes, but according to *People v. Levisen*, 90 N.E.2d 213 (1950), a home school is considered a private school and in compliance with compulsory attendance if it meets the exemption condition of 105 § 5/26-1: Any child attending a private or a parochial school where children are taught the branches of education taught to children of corresponding age and grade in the public schools, and where the instruction of the child in the branches of education is in the English language.	Class C misdemeanor: imprisonment up to 30 days and/or fine up to $500
Notice to superintendent of school if requested and must provide instruction equivalent to that given in the public schools	Class B misdemeanor
Must provide competent private instruction and meet attendance requirements set by school district; file report to school district including outline of course of study; evaluate and report results to school district annually	Violation is public offense. 1st offense: simple misdemeanor punishable by imprisonment up to 10 days or fine up to $100; 2nd offense: serious misdemeanor punishable by imprisonment up to 20 days and/or fine up to $500; 3rd or subsequent offenses: serious misdemeanor punishable by imprisonment up to 30 days and/or fine up to $1,000; court may order unpaid community service in lieu of fine or imprisonment for any offense.

Table 17: Compulsory Education—Continued

State	Code Section	Age Requirements	Exceptions
KANSAS	72-3115 to 72-3135	Between 7 and 18; until only 16 with parental consent	Private, denominational, or parochial school taught by competent instructor (substantially equivalent period of time); exceptional students may have different requirements; high school diploma or GED; attending Kansas academy of math and science
KENTUCKY	159.010 to 159.180; 159.990	Between 6 and 16; local boards may require to age 18	Graduate from approved 4 year high school; enrolled in private, parochial, or church school; child less than 7 years old and in regular attendance in a private kindergarten-nursery school; physical/mental condition prevents it; enrolled in program for exceptional children
LOUISIANA	17:221 to 17:236.2	Between 7 and 18	High school graduate; mentally/physically/emotionally incapacitated to perform school duties; children temporarily excused from school (personal or relative's illness, death, religion); withdrawal by student with written consent of parent, guardian, or tutor
MAINE	Tit. 20-A, §§ 5001-A; 5053-A	Between 7 and 17	Graduates early; 15 years old or finished 9th grade with permission from parent, approved by principal for suitable program of work and study, permission from school board and written agreement that parent and board will annually meet until 17th birthday to review educational needs; matriculated and attending post-secondary, degree-granting institution full-time; equivalent instruction from private school or other approved manner; enrolled in online learning program
MARYLAND	Educ. § 7-301	Between 5 and 16	Receiving other regular, thorough instruction in studies usually taught in public schools to children of same age group; mental/emotional/physical condition which makes his instruction detrimental to his progress or whose presence presents danger of serious physical harm to others; attends alternative education program; is severely ill; is married
MASSACHUSETTS	Ch. 76, §§ 1 to 21	Established by Board of Education, minimum age no higher than 6: see 603 CMR 8.02	Physical/mental condition does not permit; granted an employment permit by the superintendent of schools when such superintendent determines that the welfare of such child will be better served through the granting of such permit; otherwise instructed in a manner approved in advance by the superintendent or the school committee.
MICHIGAN	380.1561 to 380.1599	Between 6 and 18	Enrolled in approved non-public school; under age 9 and lives 2.5 miles or more from school with no transportation provided; attending confirmation or other religious instruction; high school graduate; home schooled in organized educational program

Home School Provisions	Penalties on Parents for Noncompliance
Home school falls under non-accredited private school. Must meet statutory requirement of competent instructor and instruction time substantially equivalent to public school and must register with state board of education.	Secretary of Social & Rehabilitative Services investigates matter; determination made as to criminal prosecution or county attorney can make petition alleging child in need of care
Considered non-accredited private school; must notify director of pupil personnel of intent to home school; must maintain academic records and attendance	1st offense: $100 fine; 2nd offense: $250 fine; subsequent: Class B misdemeanor
Parent must apply to Board of Elementary and Secondary Education for approval of home study; must make renewal application each year; must sustain curriculum of quality at least equal to that offered by public schools; competency-based education exams (may be administered by local school board upon parental request)	Fine up to $250 and/or imprisoned up to 30 days with minimum probation of 40 hours community service and/or family counseling or parenting sessions for violating compulsory attendance age requirements or if child is not regularly attending assigned classes or is habitually tardy; all other violations fine up to $15 for each offense; each day violated is separate offense
Initially file notice of intent to provide home instruction to school officials of the administrative unit in which student resides and to commissioner within 10 calendar days of beginning home instruction; annually file subsequent year letter along with assessment results	Civil violation punishable by fine up to $250, may be suspended if court orders other disposition, including community service or counseling
Home schooling is governed by the Code of Maryland Regulations. The home instruction program shall provide regular, thorough instruction in the studies usually taught in the public schools to children of the same age; include instruction in English, mathematics, science, social studies, art, music, health, and physical education; and take place on a regular basis during the school year and be of sufficient duration to implement the instruction program. Other regulations apply: see COMAR 13A.10.01	Misdemeanor. 1st offense: imprisonment up to 10 days and/or fine up to $50 per day of unlawful absence. Subsequent offense: imprisonment up to 30 days and/or fine up to $100 per day of unlawful absence.
Approval falls to superintendent or school committee that may use same standard of evaluation as for private schools: school committees shall approve a private school when satisfied that the instruction in all the studies required by law equals in thoroughness and efficiency, and in the progress made therein, that in the public schools in the same town. See Care & Protection of Charles, 504 N.E. 2d 592 (1987).	Fine up to $20 fine for any absence over 7 days or 14 half-days in a period of 6 mos.
Education program subjects: reading, spelling, math, science, literature, civics, writing, English grammar; registering of home school with department of education is voluntary, but if registered, parent/teacher must have bachelor's degree or teaching certificate unless religious objection	Warrant issued, hearing and determination made; misdemeanor: imprisonment 2 to 90 days and/or fine of $5 to $50

Table 17: Compulsory Education—Continued

State	Code Section	Age Requirements	Exceptions
MINNESOTA	120A.22 to 120A.38	Between 7 and 17	High school graduate; approval by school board for reasons including physical/mental health prevents it, child has completed graduation requirements, religious instruction.
MISSISSIPPI	37-13-91	Between 6 and 17	Child is physically/mentally/emotionally incapable of attendance; enrolled in special or remedial type education; educated in legitimate home instruction program
MISSOURI	167.031 to 167.061	Between 7 and 17	Determined mentally/physically incapacitated; child is 14 to 17 and legally and desirably employed
MONTANA	20-5-102 to 20-5-111	Between 7 and the later of attaining 16 or finishing 8th grade	Enrolled in another district or state; supervised correspondence or home study; determined by district judge or board of trustees that attendance is not in best interest of child or school; enrolled in nonpublic or home school
NEBRASKA	79-201 to 79-210; 79-1601 to 79-1607; 43-2007	Between 6 and 18, or only 16 upon release provided by local public school	Child has graduated high school; may apply to superintendent if child 14 to 16 is employed and has completed 8th grade and earnings are necessary for his support or dependents; child is physically/mentally incapacitated; illness or severe weather conditions make attendance impossible; child is at least 16 and has been withdrawn pursuant to 79-202; attends private or denominational school
NEVADA	392.040 to 392.125; 392.700 to 392.705	Between 7 and 18	Private or home school; physical/mental condition preventing attendance; completion of 12 grades; permission to take GED; residence too far from nearest school; 15-18 and completed 8th grade and entered proper employment or apprenticeship
NEW HAMPSHIRE	193:1 to 193:18; Ch. 193-A	Between 6 and 18	Physically or mentally unable to attend school; home schooled; completed requirements for graduation; in the best welfare of the child; 16 or over and has waiver from superintendent for alternative learning plan
NEW JERSEY	18A:38-25 to 18A:38-31	Between 6 and 16	Mental or physical condition such that student cannot benefit from instruction in school; attending day school or elsewhere providing equivalent instruction to that provided in the public schools for children of similar grades and attainments

Home School Provisions	Penalties on Parents for Noncompliance
Writing, reading, literature and fine arts, math, science, social studies including history, geography, and government, and health and physical education; instruction, textbooks, and materials must be in English; child must be assessed each year with standardized achievement test; superintendent can make on-site visits to evaluate	Petty misdemeanor; any fines to benefit the school district where the offense occurred
Parent must file a "certificate of enrollment" with local school attendance officer by September 15 of each year, and education must be a "legitimate home instruction program"	Guilty of contributing to the neglect of a child and punished according to §97-5-39: misdemeanor punishable by imprisonment up to 1 yr. and/or fine up to $1,000
Primary purpose is provision of private or religious-based instruction; no more than 4 pupils may be unrelated by consanguinity to the 3rd degree; no tuition charged; parents must keep written records, samples of child's academic work, portfolio of samples of child's work, and evaluation of progress; minimum hours of instruction in reading, language arts, math, social studies, science	Class C misdemeanor; upon conviction each successive school day is separate violation; penalty may be mitigated by enrolling and showing child is attending school
Give annual notice to county superintendent; To qualify its students for exemption from compulsory enrollment under 20-5-102, a nonpublic or home school: (1) shall maintain records on pupil attendance and disease immunization and make the records available to the county superintendent of schools on request; (2) shall provide at least the minimum aggregate hours of pupil instruction in accordance with 20-1-301 and 20-1-302; (3) must be housed in a building that complies with applicable local health and safety regulations; (4) shall provide an organized course of study that includes instruction in the subjects required of public schools as a basic instructional program pursuant to 20-7-111; and (5) in the case of home schools, shall notify the county superintendent of schools of the county in which the home school is located in each school fiscal year of the student's attendance at the school.	Fine up to $100, ordered to perform 20 hrs. community service, give bond of $100 and follow district's truancy plan
Home school valid if it complies with 79-1601 through 79-1607; subject to and governed by the provisions of the general school laws of the state so far as the same apply to grades, qualifications, and certification of teachers and promotion of pupils; adequate supplies and equipment, course of study substantially same as given in the public schools where children would have attended	Class III misdemeanor
Must file notice of intent with superintendent. Parent must prepare education plan of equivalent instruction of the kind and amount approved by the state board of education. Must be allowed to participate in public school extracurricular activities.	Misdemeanor
Instruction in science, math, language, government, history, health, reading, writing and spelling, history of U.S. and New Hampshire constitution and exposure to and appreciation of art and music; notification and evaluation required; home schooled children shall have access to curricular courses and programs offered by school district where child resides	Compel child to attend school and guilty of violation; any fines collected shall be used by district; penalty amounts are left up to the districts
Must receive equivalent instruction to that provided in public schools	Parent deemed disorderly person: 1st offense punishable by fine up to $25; subsequent offenses punishable by fine up to $100 at court's discretion

Table 17: Compulsory Education—Continued

State	Code Section	Age Requirements	Exceptions
NEW MEXICO	22-1-2(E); 22-1-2.1; 22-12-1 to 12-22-9; 22-8-2M	Between 5 and 18	Graduated or GED; parent may give written, signed permission for the school-age person to leave school in case of hardship approved by the local superintendent.;
NEW YORK	Educ. §§ 3201 to 3234	Between 6 and 16. Some local differences exist	Mental/physical condition endangers child or others; completed 4 year high school program; full-time employment certificate; may also be allowed to attend part-time with employment; alternatives to public school: non-public or home instruction
NORTH CAROLINA	115C-378 to 115C-380; 115C-547 to 115C-565	Between 7 and 16	Approved by state board of education (mental or physical inability to attend, immediate demands of the farm or home, etc.)
NORTH DAKOTA	15.1-20-01 to 15.1-20-4; 15.1-23	Between 7 and 16	Approved non-public school or home educated; completed high school; child necessary to support family; disability rendering attendance or participation impractical
OHIO	3321.01 to 3321.13	Between 6 and 18	Child received high school diploma; lawfully employed (if over 14 for necessary work); physical/mental condition does not permit attendance; child being instructed at home
OKLAHOMA	Tit. 70, § 10-105	Between 5 and 18	Mental/physical disability prevents attendance; child is 16 and has permission of school and parents; emergency
OREGON	339.010 to 339.095; 339.990	Between 6 and 18	Child has completed 12th grade; attending private school; proof of equivalent knowledge of subjects through 12th grade; children taught by parent or private teacher; over 16 and lawfully employed; child is emancipated
PENNSYLVANIA	Tit. 24, §§ 13-1326 to 13-1339	Between 8 and 17	High school graduate; 15 and enrolled in trade/business school with district approval; home schooled; private or religious school; 16 and gainfully/lawfully employed; mentally or physically unable to attend; 15 with permit engaged in farming or domestic service, 14 if completed highest elementary grade; resides over 2 miles from school with no free roundtrip transportation, exceptions apply
RHODE ISLAND	16-19-1 to 16-19-10	Between 6 and 18	Private school, homeschooled, or accepted into accredited post-secondary program; physical/mental condition renders attendance inexpedient or impractical; excluded from school by virtue of general law or regulation; 16 with waiver and alternative learning plan

Home School Provisions	Penalties on Parents for Noncompliance
Means of meeting compulsory education requirement; instructor must possess at least high school diploma or equivalent; must notify state annually of intent to home school; must maintain records of immunization or waiver of requirement	Petty misdemeanor: 1st offense punishable by fine $25 to $100 or community service; 2nd and subsequent offenses punishable by imprisonment up to 6 mos. and/or fine up to $500
Instruction given to a minor must be at least substantially equivalent to the instruction that would be received by minors of like age and attainments in the public school where child resides; must file annual instruction plans and assessments	1st offense: imprisonment up to 10 days or fine up to $10. Subsequent offense: imprisonment up to 30 days and/or fine up to $50
Maintain such minimum curriculum standards as are required of public schools; must be recognized by Office of Non-Public Schools and meet requirements of Article 39 of Chapter 115C (standardized testing, high school competency, health and safety standards notice)	Class 1 misdemeanor
Must file annual statement of intent with superintendent of local district; parent must possess high school diploma or GED or be monitored by school district; parent must maintain academic records and assess progress annually; instruction must include subjects taught in public school. See 15.1-23 for additional regulations	First offense: infraction. Subsequent offense: class B misdemeanor
Home schooling is governed by the Ohio Administrative Code Chapter 3301-34. Regulations include: annual notification of intent to superintendent of local school district; instruction must include language reading, writing, spelling, geography, history, civics, math, science, health, physical education, fine arts, and safety unless instruction would conflict with religious beliefs	File complaint; required to give $500 bond conditioned that child will attend school; violation: fine up to $500 or 70 hrs. community service; upon refusal to pay fine, imprisonment 10 to 30 days
Instruction must be in good faith and equivalent to that given by the state, Op. Atty. Gen. 73-129 (Feb. 13, 1973); minimum 180 days of instruction per year	Misdemeanor; 1st offense: $25 to $50 and/or imprisonment up to 5 days; 2nd offense: $50 to $100 and/or imprisonment up to 10 days; subsequent: $100 to $250 and/or imprisonment up to 15 days
Must file notification of intent to homeschool; child must be examined at grades 3, 5, 8, and 10 in accordance with requirements of 339.030	Class C violation
Must file notarized notice of intent including outline of educational objectives; maintain portfolio of records and materials; standardized testing at grades 3, 5, and 8. See Tit. 24, § 13-1327.1 for additional regulations	First offense: fine up to $300 and court costs; second offense: fine up to $500 and court costs; subsequent offense: fine up to $700 and court costs. Court may order community service or a course/program designed to improve school attendance in lieu of or in addition to any other sentence
Must file letter of intent with local school district; keep attendance records and provide substantially period of attendance as public school; instruction must be thorough and efficient and must include reading, writing, geography, arithmetic, English, civics and history of U.S. and Rhode Island, health, and physical education	Fine up to $50 for each absent day; if total days in one school year exceed 30, imprisonment up to 6 mos. and/or fine up to $500

Table 17: Compulsory Education—Continued

State	Code Section	Age Requirements	Exceptions
SOUTH CAROLINA	59-65-10 to 59-65-90	Between 5 and 17	High school graduate or GED; private, parochial or home school; physically or mentally unable to attend school; completed 8th grade and employment necessary to family; 16 and determined to be disruptive to educational program but must be employed until 17
SOUTH DAKOTA	13-27-1 to 13-27-51	Between 6 and 18	Child achieved 8th grade and fits into a religious exemption; competent instruction received from another source; illness in the family; over 16 and completes GED
TENNESSEE	49-6-3001 to 49-6-3051	Between 6 and 17 inclusive	HS graduate or GED; physical/mental condition renders child incapacitated to perform school duties; 17 and conduct detrimental to good order and benefit of other students; non-public school; home schooled and 17
TEXAS	Educ. §§ 25.085 to 25.0952	Between 6 and 18	High school graduate or GED; private or parochial school that includes course in good citizenship; special education out of resident district; physical or mental condition makes attendance infeasible; expelled; 17 and studying for GED with parental permission or court ordered; 17 and homeless or residence established away from parents; 16 and studying for GED if in Job Corps training program or recommended by public agency supervising child; enrolled in Texas Academy of Leadership in Humanities or Texas Academy of Math and Sciences or Texas Academy of International Studies
UTAH	53A-11-101 to 53A-11-106	Between 6 and 18	16 and completed 8th grade, partial release to attend trade school; completed work required for high school graduation or demonstrated master of skills and competencies in § 53A-15-102(1); physical or mental condition renders attendance inexpedient and impracticable; employed and has opportunities for education in connection with job; 16 and determined unable to profit from school; home schooled
VERMONT	Tit. 16, §§ 166b; 1121 to 1127	Between 6 and 16, or 10th grade; if over 16 and enrolled, must complete term unless meets exceptions	Child physically/mentally unable to attend; child has completed 10th grade; child is excused by superintendent; enrolled in and attending a postsecondary school

Home School Provisions	Penalties on Parents for Noncompliance
Home schools may elect to: (1) follow provisions of 59-65-40,including: parent must have high school diploma or equivalent and pass test or have bachelor's degree; instruct 4.5 hrs./ day and 180 days/yr.; curriculum must include reading, writing, math, social studies, science and must be approved by school district; maintain records; access to library; participate in statewide testing; or (2) operate under auspices of South Carolina Association of Independent Home Schools; or (3) operate under auspices of a home school association of greater than 50 members that meets the requirements of 59-65-47. Options 2 and 3 exempt home school from any further requirements of 59-65-40.	Imprisonment up to 30 days or fine up to $50; each absence is separate offense; court may suspend any conviction in its discretion
May not instruct over 22 children; instructor need not be certified; department of education may investigate and determine if instruction is being provided; national standardized testing in grades 2, 4, 8, and 11; instruction time must be equivalent to public school; curriculum must include basic skills of language arts and mathematics	Class 2 misdemeanor; each subsequent offense is Class 1 misdemeanor
Must file annual notification of intent to local director of schools; instructor must have at least high school diploma or GED; maintain attendance records and instruct at least 4 hrs. per day; standardized testing at grades 5, 7, and 9; exceptions for affiliation with church-related schools	After notice and failure to comply, judge may fine up to $50 or 5 hours community service
Home school is private school if children are taught in a bona fide manner from curriculum designed to meet basic education goals (*Texas Educ. Agency v. Leeper* 893 S.W. 2d 432 (1994)); must include a course on good citizenship	Warn parent in writing; on noncompliance, file complaint against parents for offense of class C misdemeanor; each day constitutes separate offense
Must file notice of intention to home school with local district and agree to teach subjects required by Utah department of education and for same length of time required in public schools. Students may dual enroll in public school and participate in extracurricular activities.	Class B misdemeanor
Must file annual enrollment notice with department of education; annual progress assessments in each subject area of the minimum course of study by licensed teacher assessment, parent/instructor report with portfolio of sample work, or standardized testing administered by licensed teacher who is not parent/guardian	Fine up to $1,000

Table 17: Compulsory Education—Continued

State	Code Section	Age Requirements	Exceptions
VIRGINIA	22.1-254 to 22.1-269.1	Between 5 and 18	Private, denominational, parochial or home school or taught by qualified tutor; high school diploma or GED; upon recommendation of court; under 10 and living over 2 miles from school and no transportation within 1 mile; 10 to 17 living over 2.5 miles from school and no transportation within 1.5 miles; conscientiously opposed to attendance at school because of bona fide religious training or belief
WASHINGTON	28A.225.010; 28A.225.090	Between 8 and 18	Private or home school; physically/mentally incapable of attending; 16 or older and legally employed with parental permission or emancipated; has met high school graduation requirements or GED
WEST VIRGINIA	18-8-1 to 18-1-11	Between 6 and 16	Private, parochial, home, or other approved school; physical/mental incapacity; conditions rendering attendance impossible or hazardous; high school diploma or GED; work permit granted for students who have completed 8th grade; serious illness or death in family; destitution in the home
WISCONSIN	118.15 to 118.60	Between 6 and 18	Graduated from high school; physical/mental condition renders incapable; private or home school; 16 or over and attending technical school leading to high school graduation
WYOMING	21-4-101 to 21-4-107	Between 7 and 16 (or completion of 10th grade)	Attendance detrimental to mental/physical health of child or other children; attendance would be undue hardship; home-schooled or private school; suspended or expelled

Home School Provisions	Penalties on Parents for Noncompliance
Must file notification of intent; parent/teacher must hold high school diploma, be certified teacher, use approved correspondence course, or provide evidence of adequate education; annual evaluation or standardized testing required	Class 3 misdemeanor
Planned and supervised instruction and educational activities, including occupational education, science, math, language, social studies, history, health, writing, reading, spelling, and art and music appreciation; parent must have 45 college level credit hours or complete course in home-based instruction or be supervised by credentialed person, or be deemed sufficiently qualified by superintendent	$25 for each day of unexcused absence and/or community service
Must file notification of intent; keep attendance and progress records; parent/instructor must have high school diploma or GED; must have outlined plan of instruction; annual assessment by standardized testing, report of progress with portfolio of work samples, or alternative assessment agreed upon by parent and superintendent	First offense: fine $50 to $100 plus costs or parent must attend school with child all day for as many days as court decides. Subsequent offense: fine $50 to $100 and required to attend school with child all day for as many days as court decides or imprisonment 5 to 20 days. In all cases, sentence may be delayed for 60 school days, if child attends school all 60 of those days, sentence may be suspended.
Must meet requirements for a private school such as at least 875 hrs. of instruction each year; instruction in reading, language arts, math, social studies, science, and health; performance monitored on regular basis	First offense: imprisonment up to 30 days and/or fine up to $500. Subsequent offense: imprisonment up to 90 days and/or fine up to $1,000. Community service may be imposed instead of other sentence. If child's disobedience can be shown, action shall be dismissed
Must annually submit curriculum to local school board; curriculum must meet requirements of basic academic educational program, including reading, writing, math, civics, history, literature, and science	Misdemeanor: imprisonment up to 10 days and/or $5 to $25

18. CORPORAL PUNISHMENT IN PUBLIC SCHOOLS

In 1977, the U.S. Supreme Court ruled in *Ingraham v. Wright* that schools may use corporal punishment despite parental objection. Prior to that ruling, there were few, if any, state statutes regulating the use of physical means of discipline in schools. After the decision, states began to address the issue. At present, only three states (including the District of Columbia) have no statutes covering corporal punishment. In the last 20 years, some 26 states have revised their laws to expressly prohibit the practice.

The following chart covers only state statutes regarding corporal punishment. It should be noted that there are also local rules that authorize the use of corporal punishment or that require parental consent before corporal punishment can be imposed upon a child. Local school districts, and even individual schools, often have their own policies and procedures for handling disciplinary problems.

This issue has become very controversial lately. With heightened public awareness of child abuse and increased sensitivity to the emotional well-being of children, many schools and teachers are loath to impose any physical discipline whatsoever upon students for fear of emotionally scarring them or being accused of child abuse themselves.

Table 18: Corporal Punishment in Public Schools

State	Code Section	Punishment Allowed	Circumstances Allowable
ALABAMA	16-1-24.1; 16-28A-1	Local school boards to adopt code for conduct and discipline of student. Teachers are given authority and responsibility to use appropriate means of discipline up to and including corporal punishment in accordance with local code	
ALASKA	11.81.430		When use of force is consistent with the welfare of the students and if authorized by school regulations adopted by the school board
ARIZONA	15-843	Procedures for disciplining pupils, including the use of corporal punishment, are decided and allowed by governing board of local school district; use of corporal punishment is to be consistent with state board of education guidelines	
ARKANSAS	6-18-503; 6-18-505	Use of corporal punishment allowed when authorized by school district and administered in accord with district's written student discipline policy.	"In order to maintain discipline and order within public schools."
CALIFORNIA	Educ. §§ 49000; 49001	Corporal punishment prohibited.	Reasonable and necessary force may be used for safety § 49001
COLORADO	18-1-703; 22-32-109(2)(a)	18-1-703 A teacher or other person entrusted with the care and supervision of a minor, may use reasonable and appropriate physical force upon the minor when reasonably necessary and appropriate to maintain discipline or promote the welfare of the minor. 22-32-109(2)(a) Reasonable and appropriate physical intervention or force may be used in dealing with disruptive students consistent with the local school district conduct and discipline code	
CONNECTICUT	53a-18(6)	Corporal punishment prohibited.	Reasonable physical force to protect from physical injury, obtain possession of dangerous instrument or controlled substance, protect property from physical damage, or restrain or remove minor to maintain order
DELAWARE	Tit. 14, § 702	Corporal punishment prohibited.	To quell disturbance, obtain possession of weapon, self-defense or defense of others, protection of property, to prevent student from harming self, protect bodily safety of others, or to maintain order and control
DISTRICT OF COLUMBIA	No statutory provisions		

Table 18: Corporal Punishment in Public Schools—Continued

State	Code Section	Punishment Allowed	Circumstances Allowable
FLORIDA	1003.32	Corporal punishment allowed, subject to prescribed procedures. Each local school board has authority to prohibit or allow corporal punishment and must include procedures for corporal punishment or alternative method of control or punishment in the district's written discipline policy. Districts allowing corporal punishment must review that policy every 3 yrs.	Must have approval in principle by the principal before it is used; presence of another informed adult; and that an explanation is provided to parents
GEORGIA	20-2-730 to 20-2-732	Corporal punishment allowed; policies are set by local school boards	It may not be excessive or unduly severe or be used as a first line of punishment; it must be administered in the presence of a school official; a written explanation must be provided to parent on request; and it may not be administered if a physician certifies that the child's mental or emotional stability could be affected
HAWAII	302A-1141	Physical punishment may not be used, but a teacher may use reasonable force to restrain a student in attendance from hurting himself or any other person or property with other teacher present and out of other students' presence	
IDAHO	33-1224	A teacher shall have the power to adopt any reasonable rule or regulation consistent with school board policies to control and maintain discipline in the classroom. Note: While the statute does not specifically address corporal punishment, the Idaho State Department lists a corporal punishment sample in its School Safety/Discipline Manual (Sample Policy 547)	
ILLINOIS	105 § 5/24-24	Corporal punishment prohibited.	
INDIANA	20-33-8-8 to 20-33-8-12	Teachers may take any disciplinary action necessary to promote orderly student conduct. Governing board of school corporation must establish and make available written discipline rules	
IOWA	280.21	Infliction of corporal punishment not allowed. Physical contact not considered corporal punishment if "reasonable and necessary under the circumstances."	
KANSAS	No statutory provisions		

Table 18: Corporal Punishment in Public Schools—Continued

State	Code Section	Punishment Allowed	Circumstances Allowable
KENTUCKY	158.148; 158.444; 160.290	Local school boards set disciplinary rules in accordance with statewide guidelines. Statutes do not speak directly of corporal punishment, but the Kentucky Board of Education is required to maintain a data collection system of incidents including corporal punishments	
LOUISIANA	17:223; 17:416; 17:416.1	Each parish and city school board shall have discretion in the use of corporal punishment; each board shall adopt rules and regulations to implement and control any form of corporal punishment in the schools in its district	Each teacher may take disciplinary action to correct a student who disrupts normal classroom activities, who is disrespectful to a teacher, who willfully disobeys a teacher, who uses abusive or foul language directed at a teacher or another student, who engages in bullying, who violates school rules, or who interferes with an orderly education process
MAINE	Tit. 17-A, § 106	Corporal punishment prohibited. Reasonable degree of nondeadly force permitted to control disturbing behavior or to remove person from scene of disturbance	
MARYLAND	Educ. § 7-306	Corporal punishment may not be administered to discipline student	
MASSACHUSETTS	Ch. 71, § 37G	Corporal punishment prohibited. Teacher or other authorized person may use reasonable force to protect themselves, pupils, or other persons from an assault by a pupil	
MICHIGAN	380.1312	Corporal punishment prohibited. Reasonable force may be used in defense of self or others, to prevent pupil from harming self or others, to quell disturbance that threatens physical injury to any person, to obtain possession of weapon or dangerous object, to protect property	
MINNESOTA	121A.58	Corporal punishment prohibited	
MISSISSIPPI	37-11-57	Corporal punishment administered in a reasonable manner, or any reasonable action to maintain control and discipline of students taken by a public school teacher or other authorized employee does not constitute negligence or child abuse	Reasonable physical force as necessary to maintain order
MISSOURI	160.261	"Spanking" approved and not considered child abuse when administered in reasonable manner and in accordance with written policy of discipline approved by board; where unreasonableness is alleged, initial investigation to be by school and not division of family services	

Table 18: Corporal Punishment in Public Schools—Continued

State	Code Section	Punishment Allowed	Circumstances Allowable
MONTANA	20-4-302	No school district employee may inflict corporal punishment on a pupil	Physical pain resulting from a physical restraint which is reasonable and necessary is not corporal punishment (to quell a disturbance, provide self-protection, protect others from physical injury, obtain possession of a weapon, protect property from serious harm, maintain orderly conduct.)
NEBRASKA	79-295	Corporal punishment prohibited	
NEVADA	392.4633	Corporal punishment prohibited	Reasonable and necessary force for: quell disturbance; obtain possession of weapon; self-defense; to escort disruptive student
NEW HAMPSHIRE	627:6	Corporal punishment prohibited	
NEW JERSEY	18A:6-1	Corporal punishment prohibited	Reasonable force may be used to quell a disturbance, obtain possession of weapons, etc., for self-defense or for protection of person or property and not considered corporal punishment
NEW MEXICO	22-5-4.3	Corporal punishment prohibited	
NEW YORK	No statutory provisions	Corporal punishment is prohibited by the New York Code of Rules and Regulations, 8 NYCRR 19.5	
NORTH CAROLINA	115C-288; 115C-390.1 to 115C-390.4	Corporal punishment permitted except on a student whose parent or guardian has stated in writing is shall not be used	
NORTH DAKOTA	15.1-19-02	Corporal punishment prohibited	
OHIO	3319.41	Corporal punishment prohibited	Board may not prohibit use of reasonable force to quell a disturbance, threatening physical injury; gain possession of weapon; or protect property
OKLAHOMA	Tit. 21, § 30-844; Tit. 70, § 24-100.4	Boards to adopt policy for the control and discipline of students, including, but not limited to, spanking, switching or paddling	
OREGON	339.25	Infliction of corporal punishment is not authorized	
PENNSYLVANIA	Tit 18, § 509	Allows if necessary to maintain reasonable discipline	
RHODE ISLAND	No statutory provisions	No statutory provision, but § 3.6 of the Rhode Island Board of Regents for Elementary and Secondary Education Physical Restraint Regulations states that corporal punishment shall not be used in public education programs	
SOUTH CAROLINA	59-63-260	Boards may provide corporal punishment for any pupil that it deems just and proper	

Table 18: Corporal Punishment in Public Schools—Continued

State	Code Section	Punishment Allowed	Circumstances Allowable
SOUTH DAKOTA	13-32-2; 22-18-5	Allowed if reasonable and necessary for discipline of child	
TENNESSEE	49-6-4103; 49-6-4104	Any teacher or school principal may use corporal punishment in a reasonable manner against any pupil for good cause in order to maintain discipline and order within the public schools. Each local board of education shall adopt rules and regulations it deems necessary to implement and control any form of corporal punishment in the schools in its district	
TEXAS	Educ. 37.0011	Local boards may adopt policies allowing corporal punishment, but parent or guardian may in writing prohibit the use on their child	
UTAH	53A-11-802	Corporal punishment prohibited	Use of reasonable and necessary physical restraint or force for self-defense or other appropriate circumstances listed in statute
VERMONT	Tit. 16, § 1161a	Corporal punishment prohibited, but reasonable and necessary force may be used to quell a disturbance, obtain possession of weapon, in self-defense, or protection of persons or property	
VIRGINIA	22.1-279.1	Corporal punishment prohibited, but "incidental, minor or reasonable physical contact or other actions" permitted to maintain order and control; reasonable and necessary force permitted to quell a disturbance or remove a child to prevent harm, in self-defense, to obtain possession of weapon or other dangerous object	
WASHINGTON	28A.150.300	Corporal punishment is prohibited	
WEST VIRGINIA	18A-5-1	Corporal punishment is prohibited	
WISCONSIN	118.31	Corporal punishment prohibited	Reasonable and necessary force allowed for safety or defense of self or others, to quell disturbance, remove weapon or other dangerous object and other circumstances listed in statute
WYOMING	21-4-308	Local board may adopt rules for reasonable forms of punishment and disciplinary measures. Teachers and other authorized persons may impose reasonable forms of punishment and disciplinary measures for insubordination, disobedience, and other misconduct and are immune from liability in the exercise of reasonable corporal discipline of a student as authorized by board policy	

19. PRAYER IN PUBLIC SCHOOLS

Although the United States Supreme Court ruled prayer in public schools unconstitutional in 1962, many individual states have not taken action to conform with the Court's edict. Until the early 1960s, there were no laws on the subject of prayer in schools, though some states' supreme courts have addressed the practice under their own state constitutions. After the Supreme Court struck down the practice—without reference to any specific legal precedent or established legal theory—many states responded by drafting laws authorizing prayers and moments of silence designed to avoid the Supreme Court's definition of impermissible activity. Twenty-nine states have enacted such laws. For example, Delaware authorizes a brief period of silence up to two minutes of silence "to be used according to the dictates of the individual conscience of each student"; other states' statutes authorize "brief times" of one, two, or five minutes of "silent prayer," "silent reflection," or "silent meditation." The law in this area, though settled, is still controversial.

There are strong efforts afoot to reintroduce prayer in public schools, particularly by individuals who maintain that the current crisis in public education (low test scores, violence in the classrooms, drug and alcohol abuse) began when prayer was made illegal, and, conversely, strong efforts to fight the reintroduction, particularly by proponents of the theory of the separation of church and state.

The prevailing theme in the proposals to reintroduce prayer in public schools is one of voluntariness. Such efforts, however, are doomed as long as peer pressure in the classroom is equated with state action; that is, as states cannot encourage a particular religious practice, peer pressure exerted upon nonparticipants in a "voluntary" program is considered coercive.

Table 19: Prayer in Public Schools

State	Code Section	Provisions
ALABAMA	16-1-20; 16-1-20.3; 16-1-20.5	Period of silence up to 1 min.; student-initiated voluntary prayer permitted; students have right to pray or engage in religious activities to same extent that students may engage in nonreligious activities
ALASKA	No statutory provisions	
ARIZONA	15-342	Local boards may require a period of silence up to 1 min. at beginning of school day
ARKANSAS	6-10-115	Mandatory 1 min. period of silence at beginning of the school day
CALIFORNIA	No statutory provisions	
COLORADO	No statutory provisions	
CONNECTICUT	10-16a	Opportunity for voluntary silent meditation at the start of each day
DELAWARE	Tit. 14, § 4101-A	Period of silence up to 2 min. to be used according to dictates of individual student's conscience; 1st Amendment to Constitution read to students on 1st day of school
DISTRICT OF COLUMBIA	No statutory provisions	
FLORIDA	1003.45(2)	School board may provide period up to 2 min. at beginning of school day or school week for the purpose of silent prayer or meditation
GEORGIA	20-2-1050 to 20-2-1051	Period of quiet reflection up to 60 sec. at beginning of school day; participation by students not required; student-initiated voluntary prayer permitted
HAWAII	No statutory provisions	
IDAHO	No statutory provisions	
ILLINOIS	105 §§ 20/0.01 to 20/5: Silent Reflection and Student Prayer Act	Brief period of silence which shall not be conducted as a religious exercise but as opportunity for silent prayer or silent reflection; student-initiated voluntary prayer permitted
INDIANA	20-30-5-4.5	Daily moment of silence in each classroom or on school grounds
IOWA	No statutory provisions	
KANSAS	72-9929	In each classroom, teacher in charge may observe brief period of silence at beginning of school day for purpose of prayer or silent reflection
KENTUCKY	158.175	Local school board may authorize voluntary recitation of Lord's prayer and Pledge of Allegiance in elementary schools, in line with policy to teach country's history and as affirmation of freedom of religion in this country; teacher in charge in any classroom may authorize moment of silence up to 1 min. at start of day
LOUISIANA	17:2115 to 17:2115.3	Voluntary brief time of silent meditation or prayer at start of day; student-initiated prayer permitted no official prayer to be adopted
MAINE	Tit. 20-A, § 4805	School board may require brief period of silence at start of day for reflection or meditation
MARYLAND	Educ. § 7-104	Principals and teachers may require participation in daily 1 min. meditation at start of day; student or teacher may read the holy scriptures or pray during meditation period
MASSACHUSETTS	Ch. 71, §§ 1A ; 1B	Up to 1 min. period of silence observed daily at start of day; child may participate in voluntary prayer at start of day with approval of child's parents

Table 19: Prayer in Public Schools—Continued

State	Code Section	Provisions
MICHIGAN	380.1565	School board may provide opportunity each school day for students to participate in voluntary time of silent meditation; state board to develop guidelines
MINNESOTA	121A.10	A moment of silence may be observed
MISSISSIPPI	37-13-4.1; 37-13-8	School board may authorize up to 60 sec. moment of quiet reflection at start of day; student-initiated voluntary prayer permitted on school property
MISSOURI	No statutory provisions	
MONTANA	20-7-112	Any teacher, principal, or superintendent may open the school day with a prayer
NEBRASKA	No statutory provisions	
NEVADA	388.075	Period of silence at start of each school day for voluntary individual meditation, prayer, or reflection
NEW HAMPSHIRE	189:1-b; 194.15-a	Period up to 5 min. available to exercise freedom of assembly and participate voluntarily in free exercise of religion; no teacher supervision; no prescribed form or content of prayer; school district may authorize voluntary recitation of Lord's Prayer in public elementary schools as an affirmation of the freedom of religion in this country
NEW JERSEY	18A:36-4	Voluntary period of silence up to 1 min. at start of day, to be used solely at the discretion of the individual student for quiet and private contemplation or introspection
NEW MEXICO	22-27-3	Students in public schools may voluntarily engage in student initiated moments of silent meditation
NEW YORK	Educ. § 3029-a	Brief period of silent meditation which may be opportunity for silent meditation on a religious theme or silent reflection
NORTH CAROLINA	115C-47(29)	A period of silence not to exceed one minute in duration shall be observed and silence maintained
NORTH DAKOTA	15.1-19-03.1	Period of silence up to 1 min. at beginning of school day for meditation or prayer
OHIO	3313.601	Reasonable periods of time for programs or meditation upon a moral, philosophical, or patriotic theme
OKLAHOMA	Tit. 70, §§ 11-101.1 to 11-101.2	The board of education of each school district shall permit those students and teachers who wish to do so to participate in voluntary prayer
OREGON	No statutory provisions	
PENNSYLVANIA	Tit. 24, § 15-1516.1	Brief period of silent prayer or meditation which is not a religious exercise but an opportunity for prayer or reflection as child is disposed
RHODE ISLAND	16-12-3.1	Period of silence up to 1 min. for meditation; silence to be maintained
SOUTH CAROLINA	59-1-443	Mandatory minute of silence at the beginning of each school day
SOUTH DAKOTA	No statutory provisions	
TENNESSEE	49-6-1004	Mandatory period of silence of approximately 1 min.; voluntary student participation in or initiation of prayer permitted
TEXAS	Educ. § 25.901	Student has absolute right to individually, voluntarily, and silently pray or meditate in a nondisruptive manner
UTAH	53A-11-901.5	Teacher may provide for the observance of a period of silence

Table 19: Prayer in Public Schools—Continued

State	Code Section	Provisions
VERMONT	No statutory provisions	
VIRGINIA	22.1-203; 22-1.203.1	School may establish the daily observance of 1 min. of silence; students may engage in voluntary student-initiated prayer
WASHINGTON	No statutory provisions to 28A.195.020	Private schools recognized as having right to prayer in classes and assemblies
WEST VIRGINIA	Const. art. III, § 15a (ruled unconstitutional 1985)	Designated brief time for students to exercise their right to personal and private contemplation, meditation, or prayer
WISCONSIN	No statutory provisions	
WYOMING	No statutory provisions	

20. PRIVACY OF SCHOOL RECORDS

The question of privacy has long been a cornerstone of the American constitutional and democratic experiment. The matter of individual privacy has been intricately entangled with the right of individuals to freedom of conscience and speech, within limits.

The right to privacy has been interpreted to mean freedom from government intrusion, such as unwarranted surveillance and searches of cars, residences and persons. The matter has become complicated today with the advent of modern personal technology, social media and the internet because not only are people much more willing to give personal information to online services, but also the services, software and the devices themselves are constantly collecting, storing and curating the information for use by themselves and others.

Modern educational practices now often involve requiring large numbers of standardized tests for students, and many utilize online coursework. In this context, there is wide opportunity for schools, school districts, testing services and others to not only track test score but also to monitor more generally individual students' progress, preferences and performance.

The question of the right of privacy and, specifically, who should have access to student records has divided parents and students from school teachers and administrators. There are strong arguments on both sides. School teachers and administrators believe, traditionally, that they should be able to deal with the children they teach in utter confidence—especially when it comes to evaluation of ability, behavior, and psychological factors. School administrators may have critical opinions and evaluations to make and pass on to colleagues in order to effectively deal with a particular student's potential for success or failure in school. Release of these opinions to the family or the student may actually have a detrimental effect on the student and/or the teacher or the school's ability to help the student.

On the other hand, students and parents have a deep interest in knowing how they or their child are evaluated—to know what school administrators are saying about the child and what impact those opinions are having on his or her progress in school. Parents may worry that negative evaluations or assessments may be off-base, inaccurate, or the result of an objective evaluation that misses personal situations and emotions. In addition, negative evaluations may be the result of physical or psychological handicaps or deficiencies in ability that need special attention and may be helped if parents or students are made aware of them. Parents have a responsibility for the quality of education that their children receive as well as a right to participate in decisions that affect class placement and particular courses and subjects taught.

This dynamic between the parents' right to have input into their child's education and the school's responsibility to professionally teach and discipline its students is what has driven the development of certain privacy rules. There is also a new dynamic that is becoming a factor in education and, specifically, access to records: over the last thirty years, the growing disillusionment with our traditional education system, which insisted on certain standards of performance for all students, has given way to the belief that each child has different learning curves and behavioral norms that need to be respected. As a result, standards of education and behavior are no longer standard and regular but adjust to the needs, wants, and potential of each student and his or her family. In order to monitor the attention that individual children are getting, laws have guaranteed parents access to student records.

As a result of this tension there is growing awareness of the potential for turning the data collected through the processes of teaching and testing into valuable commercial information. California has passed new legislation that will become the law in 2016, so is not reflected in the chart below, that will specifically [forbid] companies from selling or otherwise using such information for commercial purposes. President Obama in his 2015 State of the Union pledged to make such data not only easier to collect, but easier for parents to access. Simultaneously, he also pledged to make it more onerous for entities that collect the information to use it for commercial purposes, and specifically referred to the new California statute as an example of the kind of protection he has in mind. Over the next few years, it is expected that many laws at the state and federal levels will ensue to protect student records from exploitation.

Another area concerning school records that is becoming an issue encompasses child abuse, neglect, and personal health. With today's broader definition of abuse, a family's religious convictions or practices, cultural heritage, social orientation, or lack of awareness may qualify. In an extreme example, state authorities took custody of minor children because their parents failed to keep their children's dental appointments! There may be a need for parents to monitor school records in order to see that educators are not misinterpreting and misconstruing various family customs, practices, and behavior or undermining certain training being done at home.

The Family Educational Records Protection Act (FERPA) was originally passed in 1976 and has been amended many times since. Its purpose is to guarantee parents free access to student school records. Under provisions of the Act, the Secretary of Education has the authority to withhold all federal funding to institutions that do not make school records available to a student's parents. There are exceptions to this rule, such as authorizing the transfer of transcripts when a student changes schools or applies for admission elsewhere, for researchers doing studies of educational techniques and practices when such research can be conducted confidentially and anonymously, for state or federal officials conducting audits of public assistance programs, or in the course of normal business. Many states now rely on FERPA to protect student privacy and insure parental access. A few states have gone beyond the protections of the federal act.

Table 20: Privacy of School Records

State	Code Section	Who Has Access	Penalties
ALABAMA	36-12-40	Parent of minor child may inspect regulation and circulation records of any school that pertain to child	
ALASKA	25.20.130	Both custodial and non-custodial parent	
ARIZONA	15-141	Governed by FERPA; Dept. of Juvenile Corrections has access to any pupil referred	Injunctive or special relief by Superior Court
ARKANSAS	6-20-510	Records regarding handicapped students or foster children are to be kept confidential by respective school districts and Dept. of Education	
CALIFORNIA	Educ. §§ 49073 to 49079.7	FERPA implemented; school districts determine release of directory information; parents/pupils have access; release with written consent or by court order; no release to private profit making entities; no release if pupil is homeless or by pupil request	Misdemeanor if private school or college uses information for anything other than academic or professional goals
COLORADO	22-2-111, 24-72-204	Unless contrary to federal, state or judicial law, law enforcement officers have access without parental consent; student records confidential except when requested by governor or committee of the general assembly	
CONNECTICUT	10-154a	Communication relating to alcohol or drugs between the nurse and student need not be disclosed to parent	
DELAWARE	Tit. 14, § 4111	Confidential; parent/guardian may inspect records in accordance with Dept. of Educ. rules; records may be released with written consent	
DISTRICT OF COLUMBIA	38-607	Student's health file confidential and subject to inspection, disclosure, and use only under applicable district and federal law	
FEDERAL	20 U.S.C. § 1232g Family Educational Records Protection Act	Parents and specifically authorized state or federal officials for purposes of auditing public assistance programs; right transfers to student at age 18; researchers for purposes of gathering data to improve educational testing or educational curriculum (provided privacy is protected), authorized school administrators or other educational institutions as authorized by student or parents for purposes of application for admission to an educational institution or for employment	Withdrawal of all federal funding
FLORIDA	1002.21 to 1002.225	FERPA mostly implemented; parents and pupils have access; right transfers to pupil at age 18 or when attending post-secondary educational institution	Injunctive relief and attorney fees and court costs may be awarded

Table 20: Privacy of School Records—Continued

State	Code Section	Who Has Access	Penalties
GEORGIA	20-2-720	Both parents (custodial and non-custodial parent absent court order or terminated parental rights)	
HAWAII	302A-1137	Authorized police officers have access to attendance records or student	
IDAHO	32-717A	Custodial and non-custodial parent	
ILLINOIS	105 §§ 10/1 to 10/10	Inspection allowed by students and parents but restricted to third parties. Exceptions listed in 105 ILCS 10/6 (1-9). Information communicated in confidence by a student or parents to school personnel is not available. All rights and privileges become student's exclusively at age 18	Damages, injunctive relief, and other remedies available
INDIANA	20-33-7-1 to 20-33-7-3	Custodial and noncustodial parent, unless court order limiting noncustodial parent	A school complying with FERPA is immune from civil liability
IOWA	22.7	Student's personal information in records is confidential	
KANSAS	72-6310	Governed by FERPA	
KENTUCKY	164.283, KY Rules of Evid. 506	Parents of any student under age 21. Counselor-student communications are privileged. All student academic records are confidential with exemptions cited in 164.283 (3)-(10)	
LOUISIANA	9:351	Custodial and non-custodial parent has right to inspect child's records	
MAINE	Tit. 20-A, § 6001	Governed by FERPA	
MARYLAND	4-313	Student, guardian, or elected/appointed official who supervises student may inspect record	
MASSACHUSETTS	Ch. 71, §§ 34A; 34G	Student (transcript), parent, guardian, student over 18 may inspect	
MICHIGAN	600.2165	In legal proceedings, counselors, teachers, and school employees may not disclose information or records of student's behavior received in confidence without consent. If student is 18 years of age or younger, consent may be given by parent or legal guardian	
MINNESOTA	13.02 to 13.32	Records are private except for directory information and shall be released only pursuant to valid court order. Minor may request information to be withheld from parent or guardian if in best interest of minor	Willful violation by political subdivision: exemplary damages of not less than $1,000 and not more than $15,000 for each violation; injunctive relief
MISSISSIPPI	37-15-3	Governed by FERPA; records not available to the general public	

Table 20: Privacy of School Records—Continued

State	Code Section	Who Has Access	Penalties
MISSOURI	167.020	School districts may report or disclose education records to law enforcement and juvenile justice authorities if the disclosure concerns ability to effectively serve; prior to adjudication the student whose records are released must comply with FERPA	
MONTANA	10.55.909	Governed by FERPA	
NEBRASKA	84-712.05 to 84-712.09	Records withheld from public unless disclosed in court or administrative proceeding or for routine directory information.	Violation by official: subject to removal or impeachment and class III misdemeanor
NEVADA	49.290 to 49.291; 125C.005	Both custodial and non-custodial parent; communication between counselor-pupil or teacher-pupil is privileged.	
NEW HAMPSHIRE	91-A:5	Exempted from public access.	
NEW JERSEY	18A:36-19	Parent/guardian or pupil with reasonable protection of privacy rights. State board of education establishes rules.	
NEW MEXICO	40-4-9.1 (J) (4) (c)	Both custodial and non-custodial parent.	
NEW YORK	Educ. § 3222	Parent applies for schooling record for complying minor.	
NORTH CAROLINA	8-53.4; 115C-174.13; 115C-402	Not subject to public inspection; minimum competency test scores of students not public and available consistent with FERPA; counselor communication privileged. May be obtained by parent or student upon request.	
NORTH DAKOTA	15.1-24-04	Any record of student's medical treatment is confidential and may not be released without written consent of student; if student is under 14, written consent of student's parent/guardian is required.	
OHIO	149.41; 3319.321	No release without student's consent if over 18; if 18 or under, consent of parent or guardian is necessary. Directory information may be released. Rights of school district to renew or select student records are restricted.	
OKLAHOMA	Tit. 51, § 24A.16; Tit. 70, § 6-115	Confidential except for directory information; teacher may not reveal student-obtained information unless required by contract or released to a parent or guardian of such child on request. May be released for program evaluation and program effectiveness. May be released to student or parent upon request	Misdemeanor for teacher to reveal information regarding any child except as required in performance of contractual duties or requested by parents; misdemeanor for any violation by public official, punishable by imprisonment up to 1 yr. and/or fine up to $500

Table 20: Privacy of School Records—Continued

State	Code Section	Who Has Access	Penalties
OREGON	336.187; 326.565	Consistent with state and federal law regarding record custody and disclosure; may be transferred by request when student transfers schools or is placed in a state institution; disclosure allowed to law enforcement and/or child protective services and/or health professionals in "health or safety emergency"	
PENNSYLVANIA	Tit. 23, § 5336; Tit. 24, § 1409	Both parents; child's school health record transferred to other PA school or to parent/guardian; court may deny access to records when domestic violence is present in family	
RHODE ISLAND	16-38-5; 16-71-3	No release without student, parent, or legal guardian consent except to the extent authorized by FERPA	Misdemeanor to circulate a questionnaire "so framed as to ask intimate questions about themselves or families, thus trespassing upon the pupils' constitutional rights and invading the privacy of the home" without approval of local school commissioner and department of education; can be fined $100
SOUTH CAROLINA	30-1-10 to 30-4-40	Records of school district considered public records and dealt with according to Title 30	Removal or destruction of records: misdemeanor punishable by $500 to $5,000 fine; failure to deliver: misdemeanor punishable by fine up to $500
SOUTH DAKOTA	19-19-508.1; 25-5-7.3	Primary residential parent may access; school counselor or communications privileged except in cases of child abuse or if waived	
TENNESSEE	10-7-504	School records confidential except when compelled under legal process or released for safety of person or property; outsiders are authorized access to pupil records for research and statistical purposes; pupil or guardian may give consent for others to have access	
TEXAS	Educ. § 26.004	Parent has access to all written records concerning the parent's child	
UTAH	53A-3-402.1	Custodial and non-custodial parents have equal access to records unless school has copy or actual knowledge of court order restricting non-custodial parent	
VERMONT	Tit. 1, § 317(c)(11)	Records are exempt from public inspection and copying unless request is made pursuant to FERPA (P.L. 93-380)	
VIRGINIA	22.1-287 to 22.1-289	Available to parents and student only unless parent/guardian consents to release	

Table 20: Privacy of School Records—Continued

State	Code Section	Who Has Access	Penalties
WASHINGTON	28A.605.030	Parent or guardian has right to review all educational records; school may not release records without written consent of student's parent or guardian	
WEST VIRGINIA	48-9-601	Custodial and non-custodial parents have equal access to child's educational records absent a court order to the contrary	
WISCONSIN	118.125; 118.126	All records confidential. Pupil, parents, courts and school officials (under certain circumstances), and persons designated by parents or pupil may receive a copy upon request; behavioral records must be destroyed 1 yr. after student is no longer enrolled unless student permits by written consent; any student's record related to physical health that is not pupil health record to be treated as health patient record under 146.81 to 146.84; school personnel engaging in alcohol/drug abuse program to keep confidential information received from pupil about own or another pupil's use unless pupil consents, serious danger exists to anyone's health or safety, or required to report under child abuse and neglect laws, 48.981	
WYOMING	16-4-203	Student, parent, or legal guardian may consent to release	Violation of privacy records laws may result in fine up to $750

IV. EMPLOYMENT LAW

21. RESTRICTIVE COVENANTS IN EMPLOYMENT

There are many times when a business may wish to share information about a new product or service with people outside the business entity in order to obtain feedback or publicity, or the business may be concerned about employees sharing information about new products or services with people outside the business and losing a competitive advantage in the marketplace. In such situations, a business may require an employee or outsider to sign a non-disclosure agreement (NDA) that typically requires the employee not to disclose the product, service or procedure that they have seen. The logic behind these agreements is easy to see because businesses rely on their ideas for their success, and if they leak outside the business, they made lose an important advantage in the marketplace, even if the idea is patented or trademarked.

It is exciting for journalists or members of focus groups to get exclusive looks at new products and services before they are made public, and it gives people the opportunity to give feedback so that the final product may be made better. Controversy only arises regarding NDAs when they are considered too long in duration or require unreasonable penalties if violated. There are also issues when the subject of the NDA is against common sense or public policy.

NDAs are fairly common and have their roots in common law when there aren't statutes that specifically authorize their legality.   Another form of agreement that businesses may require employees to sign is called a Non-Compete Clause or Non-compete Agreement (NCA). NCAs may be very important to some businesses because a successful business is comprised of many valuable tools: client lists, supplier lists, manufacturing processes, etc. A business, especially one that employs specialized people to conduct its business, may require that if an employee leaves a business for any number of reasons, s/he may not compete with the former business for a period of time. The length of time that an NCA may bind an employee varies among states; frequently the term must be "reasonable". The length of time may also be influenced by the nature of the work that the employee is doing. For example, a partner in a specialized medical or law practice may be prevented for a period of years from leaving and starting his or her own practice because the original partnership may fear losing clients or patients.

Finally, there has been recent controversy regarding NDAs signed between two private parties concerning private, possibly illegal, immoral, or embarrassing behavior or information. States have approached such agreements with caution. Many states have no specific statutes about these kinds of agreements and rely exclusively on the common law of contracts that requires contracts to be reasonable and negotiated between two equal parties. The subject of such agreements must also be a reasonable topic for agreement.

Table 21: Restrictive Covenants in Employment

State	Non-compete Agreement (NCA) Enforceable by State Statute?	NCA Limitations	Non-disclosure Agreement (NDA) Enforceable under State Statute?
ALABAMA	Contracts restraining exercise of lawful profession, trade or business are statutorily void; exceptions exist, 8-1-190	Enforceable restrictive covenants: contract limiting ability to hire employee of party to the contract who is uniquely essential to the management, organization, or service of the business; agreement between 2 or more parties to limit commercial dealings to each other; seller of goodwill of business may enter into general and/or geographical NCA with seller; employee of a commercial entity may agree to NCA re current customers for like business, subject to reasonable time constraints, 18 mos. or as long as post-separation consideration is paid; upon dissolution of a commercial entity, parties may enter into geographical NCA, 8-1-190	Yes; protectable interests include trade secrets and confidential information, 8-1-190; 8-1-191
ALASKA	Not addressed by state statute; permissible under common law using Restatement (Second) of Contracts	Factors to be considered include presence of time and space limitations; whether: employee is sole contact with customer; employee possesses trade secrets or confidential information; covenant eliminates competition that would be unfair to employer; covenant is designed to restrain employee's skill and experience; benefit and detriment to employer and employee is proportional; covenant bars employee's only means of support; employee's talent to be suppressed was developed during employment; prohibited employment is incidental to the former employment, *Data Mgmt. Inc. v. Greene*, 757 P.2d 62, 65 (Alaska 1988) (citing Restatement (Second) of Contracts § 184(2) (1981); *Raimonde v. Van Vlerah*, 42 Ohio St. 2d 21, 325 N.E.2d 544 (1975))	Not addressed by state statute; enforceable under common law
ARIZONA	Not addressed by state statute; permissible under common law using Restatement (Second) of Contracts	NCA must be: ancillary to valid employment contract; not unreasonable in scope; not made in bad faith or contrary to public policy; designed to protect legitimate interest, *Lassen v. Benton*, 86 Ariz. 323, 328, 346 P.2d 137, 140 (1959); *Mattison v. Johnston*, 730 P.2d 286, 288 (Ariz. Ct. App. 1986)	Not addressed by state statute; enforceable under common law; see NCA limitations
ARKANSAS	Statutorily enforceable; certain conditions must be met, 4-75-101	Covenant must: be ancillary to employment relationship or part of otherwise enforceable employment agreement; employer must have protectable business interest; covenant must be limited in time and scope not greater than necessary to defend protectable business interest. Reasonableness factors include: nature of protectable business interest; geographical scope and feasibility of such scope; whether covenant is limited to specific group of individuals associated with the business; and the nature of business; employment alone is sufficient consideration for an NCA; 2 yr. covenant presumed reasonable, 4-75-101	Not addressed by state statute; enforceable under common law

NDA Limitations	Trade Secrets Code Section	Significant Deviations from Uniform Trade Secrets Act	Employment-related Settlement Agreement Non-disclosure Enforceable?	Settlement Agreement Non-disclosure Limitations
N/A	8-27-1 to 8-27-6	Information must be used in trade or business, not publicly or known or generally known in trade or business of person asserting information is trade secret; misappropriation not defined; espionage not contained in definition of improper means; exemplary damages min. recoverable amt.: $1,000; violation may be class C felony; 2 yr. statute of limitations.; no severability or attorney fees provision	N/A	N/A
Enforceable as long as reasonable, *Recreational Data Servs., Inc. v. Trimble Navigation Ltd.*, 2017 WL 2951450 (Alaska Mar. 24, 2017); *Reeves v. Alyeska Pipeline Serv. Co.*, 56 P.3d 660, 666 (Alaska 2002)	45.50.910 to 45.50.945	Recovery of damages limited to actual lost and unjust enrichment; no provision for attorney fees; 3 yr. statute of limitations; Act does not apply to actions brought by the attorney general under the Alaska Unfair Trade Practices and Consumer Protection Act or the Alaska Restraint of Trade Act; no severability provision; no attorney fees provision	N/A	N/A
Same restrictions as NCA	44-401 to 44-407	3 yr. statute of limitations; no severability provision	N/A	N/A
N/A	4-75-601 to 4-75-607	Damages provision does not specify exemplary damages for willful and malicious misappropriation; 3 yr. statute of limitations; no severability provision	N/A	N/A

Table 21: Restrictive Covenants in Employment—Continued

State	Non-compete Agreement (NCA) Enforceable by State Statute?	NCA Limitations	Non-disclosure Agreement (NDA) Enforceable under State Statute?
CALIFORNIA	Every contract restraining anyone from engaging in lawful profession, trade, or business is statutorily void; exceptions exist, Bus. & Prof. § 16600	Enforceable covenants: seller of business may create geographical NCA with buyer, Bus. & Prof. § 16601; partners in partnership may enter into geographical NCA so long as partnership continues business, Bus. & Prof § 16602; LLC members may enter into geographical NCA so long as LLC business continues, Bus. & Prof. § 16602.5	Not addressed by state statute; enforceable under common law
COLORADO	Statutorily void; exceptions exist, 8-2-113	NCA enforceable if for: contract for purchase and sale of business or business assets; contract for protection of trade secret; contractual provision providing for recovery of expense of educating and training employee who has served employer for under 2 yrs.; executive and management personnel and officers and employees who constitute professional staff to executive and management personnel, 8-2-113	Yes; statute limiting ability to enter into restrictive covenants does not apply to contracts protecting trade secrets, 8-2-113
CONNECTICUT	Not addressed by state statutes; permissible under common law	NCA must be reasonable in: length of time; geographical scope; fairness to employer; restraint on employee's ability to work; extent of public interest interference. *Robert S. Weiss & Associates, Inc. v. Wiederlight*, 208 Conn. 525, 529, n. 2, 546 A.2d 216 (1988); *Scott v. General Iron & Welding Co.*, 171 Conn. 132, 137, 368 A.2d 111 (1976)	Not addressed by state statute; enforceable under common law; see NCA limitations
DELAWARE	Not addressed by state statutes; permissible under common law	NCA must meet the requirements of general contract law; be geographically and temporally reasonable in duration; advance a legitimate economic interest of the employer; satisfy balancing of equities, *All Pro Maids, Inc. v. Layton*, 2004 WL 1878784, at *5 (Del. Ch. Aug. 9, 2004); *Delaware Exp. Shuttle, Inc. v. Older*, 2002 WL 31458243, at *11 (Del. Ch. Oct. 23, 2002)	Not addressed by state statute; enforceable under common law

NDA Limitations	Trade Secrets Code Section	Significant Deviations from Uniform Trade Secrets Act	Employment-related Settlement Agreement Non-disclosure Enforceable?	Settlement Agreement Non-disclosure Limitations
N/A	Civ. §§ 3426 to 3426.11	Excludes reverse engineering from definition of "improper means"; adds LLC to definition of person; specifies that recoverable amounts for attorney fees include certain expert witness fees; 3 yr statute of limitations	Certain settlement NDAs allowed	Settlement NDA not allowed for certain cases of elder abuse or dependent adult abuse, and felony sex offense cases, Civ. Proc. § 1002
N/A	7-74-101 to 7-74-110	Does not define the word "person"; expands definition of "trade secret" to include any scientific or technical information, design, process, procedure, improvement, confidential business or financial information, list of names/addresses/phone numbers owner of "trade secret" must have taken measures to protect; injunctive relief provision does not include language permitting continuance of injunction for reasonable period to eliminate commercial advantage derived from misappropriation; damages provision includes language permitting reasonable royalties; 3 yr. statute of limitations	N/A	N/A
Same restrictions as NCA	35-50 to 35-58	Adds LLC to definition of "person"; adds drawings, cost data and customer lists to definition of "trade secret"; attorney fees provision does not permit fees for willful and malicious misappropriation; no exceptional circumstances language in the injunctive relief provision; 3 yr .statute of limitations; no severability provision	N/A	N/A
N/A	Tit. 6, §§ 2001 to 2009	"Person" includes statutory trust; 3 yr. statute of limitations; no severability provision	N/A	N/A

Table 21: Restrictive Covenants in Employment—Continued

State	Non-compete Agreement (NCA) Enforceable by State Statute?	NCA Limitations	Non-disclosure Agreement (NDA) Enforceable under State Statute?
DISTRICT OF COLUMBIA	Contracts that restrain trade are statutorily illegal, 28-4502	NCA must be reasonable; not be larger or more extensive than required for necessary protection of business interest; not go against public policy, *Godfrey v. Roessle*, 5 App. D.C. 299, 303–04 (1895); *Deutsch v. Barsky*, 795 A.2d 669, 674 (D.C. 2002)	Not addressed by state statute; enforceable under common law
FLORIDA	Statutorily enforceable, so long as certain conditions are met; 542.335	Enforceable so long as contract is reasonable in time, area, and line of business; must be in writing; person seeking enforcement must prove existence of one or more legitimate business interests (including trade secrets, other valuable business secrets, substantial customer or prospective customer relationships, customer, patient or client goodwill); covenant presumed reasonable if less than 5 yrs. and presumed unreasonable if more than 10 yrs., 542.335	Yes; prohibition of restraints on trade does not apply to activity or conduct permitted under common law, 542.20
GEORGIA	General Assembly has enforcement power over competition agreements between employers and employees, Ga. Const. art. III, § VI, ¶ V(c)(2); contracts restraining trade statutorily unenforceable, 13-8-2; certain restrictive covenants are statutorily enforceable, 13-8-50	Restrictive covenants in employment contracts enforceable if they are: reasonable in time, geographical area and scope; serve legitimate purpose of protecting legitimate business interests; create environment favorable to attracting commercial enterprises to Georgia and keeping existing businesses in state, 13-8-50; restrictions on competition enforceable on employees who: customarily and regularly solicit customers or prospective customers; customarily and regularly engage in making sales or obtaining orders or contracts; perform management duties, direct work of 2 or more employees, or have hiring and firing authority or influence, 13-8-53	Yes; prohibition of restraints on trade does not apply to agreements to maintain confidential information or trade secrets, 13-8-53(e)

NDA Limitations	Trade Secrets Code Section	Significant Deviations from Uniform Trade Secrets Act	Employment-related Settlement Agreement Non-disclosure Enforceable?	Settlement Agreement Non-disclosure Limitations
Upheld as long as reasonable and not more extensive than necessary to protect business interest, *Deutsch v. Barsky*, 795 A.2d 669, 674–75 (D.C.2002)	36-401 to 36-410	3 yr. statute of limitations; no severability provision	N/A	N/A
Same restrictions as NCA	688.001 to 668-009	No severability provision; 3 yr. statute of limitations	Settlement NDA not allowed as it relates to public hazard or information that may be useful to public in protecting themselves from public hazard, 69.081(4)	Any part of a contract that conceals or purports to conceal a public hazard or any information which may be useful to members of the public in protecting themselves from a public hazard is void, Florida Sunshine in Litigation Act, 69.081
Same restrictions as NCA; additional condition that the NDA may only be for period information remains confidential or a trade secret, 13-8-53(e)	10-1-760 to 10-1-767	Excludes reverse engineering from the definition of improper means; trade secret expressly includes technical or nontechnical data, drawing, financial data or plans, product plans, and lists of actual or potential customers or suppliers; injunction may be continued where trade secret ceases to exist due to fault of enjoined party or others by improper means; contract not required to obtain damages or injunctive relief; damages may be measured in terms of reasonable royalty if neither damages nor unjust enrichment are proved by preponderance of evidence; 5 yr. statute of limitations; no severability provision	N/A	N/A

Table 21: Restrictive Covenants in Employment—Continued

State	Non-compete Agreement (NCA) Enforceable by State Statute?	NCA Limitations	Non-disclosure Agreement (NDA) Enforceable under State Statute?
HAWAII	Contracts restraining trade statutorily illegal; exceptions exist, 480-4(a)	Enforceable restrictive covenants: agreement by seller of business not to compete in connection with sale of the business for reasonable time and geographical scope; agreement between partners not to compete with partnership, so long as the time and geographical area are reasonable; agreement of lessee to be restricted in use of leased premises to certain business; agreement by employee not to use employer's trade secrets in competition with employer during employment or thereafter, or after termination, for time reasonably necessary to protect employer without imposing undue hardship on employee, 480-4(c)	Yes; prohibition of restraints on trade does not apply to agreements not to use trade secrets in competition within time reasonably necessary to protect employer, 480-4(c)(4)
IDAHO	Certain NCAs statutorily enforceable, 44-2701	Key employee or independent contractor may enter into NCA protecting employer's legitimate business interest if: reasonable as to time, geographical area, and type of employment or line of business; NCA does not impose greater restraint than reasonably necessary to protect employer's legitimate business interest, 44-2701; restriction presumed reasonable if 18 mos. or less, and if geographical area is limited to where the services are provided or where employee has significant presence or influence, 44-2704	Yes; key employees or independent contractors may enter into written agreements that protect legitimate business interests of their employers, 44-2701
ILLINOIS	Certain NCAs statutorily prohibited under Illinois Freedom to Work Act, 820 § 90/1	Any covenant not to compete between an employer and a low wage employee statutorily illegal and void, 829 § 90/10; covenant not to compete is agreement between employer and a low wage employee restricting employee from doing any work for specified period of time or geographical area, or work for another employer in similar capacity as for the employer included as party to the agreement; low wage employee is employee earning greater of federal, state, or local hourly minimum wage or $13 per hr. 829 § 90/5	Not addressed by state statute; enforceable under common law

NDA Limitations	Trade Secrets Code Section	Significant Deviations from Uniform Trade Secrets Act	Employment-related Settlement Agreement Non-disclosure Enforceable?	Settlement Agreement Non-disclosure Limitations
N/A	482B-1 to 482B-9	Injunctive relief: alleged wrongful user bears the burden of proof of exceptional circumstances; 3 yr. statute of limitations	N/A	N/A
Same restrictions as NCA	48-801 to 48-807	Defines computer program; trade secrets subject to disclosure by public agency; 3 yr. statute of limitations; no severability provision	N/A	N/A
N/A	765 §§ 1065/1 to 1065/9	Excludes reverse engineering from the definition of improper means; trade secret includes technical or nontechnical data, drawing, financial data, and list of actual or potential customers or suppliers; trade secret must be sufficiently secret to derive economic value from not being generally known to others who can obtain economic value; injunction may be continued to deter willful and malicious misappropriation, or where the trade secret ceases to exist by improper means; court may condition future use of trade secret upon payment of reasonable royalty if unreasonable to prohibit future use due to overriding public interest; court may award damages caused by misappropriation measured in terms of a reasonable royalty if damages or unjust enrichment cannot be proven by preponderance of evidence	N/A	N/A

Table 21: Restrictive Covenants in Employment—Continued

State	Non-compete Agreement (NCA) Enforceable by State Statute?	NCA Limitations	Non-disclosure Agreement (NDA) Enforceable under State Statute?
INDIANA	Not addressed by state statute; permissible under common law	NCA is enforceable if: reasonable with respect to necessity of the breadth of the protection of covenantee; reasonable with respect to the restriction on covenantor; reasonably in public's interest; determinations based on facts and circumstances, considering legitimate interests of covenantee and protections granted by covenant in terms of time, space, and type of conduct to be protected, *Licocci v. Cardinal Associates, Inc.*, 445 N.E.2d 556, 561 (Ind. 1983)	Not addressed by state statute; enforceable under common law to protect trade secret defined by Indiana Uniform Trade Secrets Act
IOWA	Not addressed by state statute; permissible under common law	Courts perform 3-part balancing test: whether restriction is reasonably necessary for protection of employer's business interest; whether restriction is unreasonably restrictive of employee's rights; whether restriction is prejudicial to public's interest, *Baker v. Starkey*, 259 Iowa 480, 493, 144 N.W.2d 889, 897 (1966)	Not addressed by state statute; enforceable under common law
KANSAS	Not addressed by state statute; permissible under common law	NCA enforceable if: ancillary to employment contract; reasonable under the circumstances; not adverse to public welfare; protecting legitimate business interest; sole purpose not to avoid ordinary competition, *Weber v. Tillman*, 913 P.2d 84, 89 (Kan. 1996)	Not addressed by state statute; enforceable under common law
KENTUCKY	Not addressed by state statute; permissible under common law	NCA enforceable if reasonable in scope and purpose; reasonableness is determined by: nature of the business and employment; scope of restrictions with respect to character, duration and territorial extent, *Hall v. Willard & Woolsey P.S.C.*, 471 S.W.2d 316, 317 (Ky. Ct. App. 1971)	Not addressed by state statute; enforceable under common law

NDA Limitations	Trade Secrets Code Section	Significant Deviations from Uniform Trade Secrets Act	Employment-related Settlement Agreement Non-disclosure Enforceable?	Settlement Agreement Non-disclosure Limitations
Protectable trade secrets have 4 general characteristics: information; deriving independent economic value; not generally known or readily ascertainable by proper means by others who can obtain economic value from disclosure or use; subject of reasonable efforts reasonable to maintain secrecy, *Burk v. Heritage Food Service Equipment, Inc.*, 737 N.E.2d 803, 813-14 (Ind. Ct. App. 2000)	24-2-3-1 to 24-2-3-8	Adds limited liability corporation to the definition of person; 3 yr. statute of limitations; no Effect on Other Law provision, but Short Title states that the Indiana Uniform Trade Secrets Act displaces conflicting state law on misappropriation of trade secrets, except contract and criminal law, which is stricter than the Uniform rule that provides exception for contract, civil and criminal remedies; no severability provision	Statements made during settlement negotiations performed by a mediator not public unless parties agree	Confidential statements made to mediator regarding settlement presumed confidential unless parties agree otherwise, 4-21.5-3.5-18
NDA must be: reasonably necessary for the protection of employer's business; not unreasonably restrictive of employee's rights; not prejudicial to the public interest, *Revere Transducers, Inc. v. Deere & Co.*, 595 N.W.2d 751, 762 (Iowa 1999)	550.1 to 550.8	Defines the word knowledge; Act specifies that implied or express consent of owner of trade secret is complete defense for person disclosing trade secret; 3 yr. statute of limitations; no provision regarding effect on other law and severability	N/A	N/A
N/A, *Puritan-Bennett Corp. v. Richter*, 679 P.2d 206, 212 (Kan. 1984)	60-3320 to 660-3330	3 yr. statute of limitations	N/A	N/A
N/A	365.880 to 365.900	Adds data to definition of trade secrets; 3 yr. statute of limitations	N/A	N/A

Table 21: Restrictive Covenants in Employment—Continued

State	Non-compete Agreement (NCA) Enforceable by State Statute?	NCA Limitations	Non-disclosure Agreement (NDA) Enforceable under State Statute?
LOUISIANA	Agreements restraining exercise of lawful profession, trade or business statutorily null and void; exceptions exist, 23:921	Exceptions general prohibition on restrictive covenants: choice of forum and law clauses in employment contracts null and void unless expressly, knowingly, and voluntarily agreed to and ratified by employee after occurrence of incident subject to the civil action; seller of business may agree with buyer to refrain from carrying on similar business within specified area for up to 2 yrs., so long as buyer carries on business; employee may agree with employer to refrain from carrying on similar business within specified area for up to 2 yrs., so long as employer carries on business; independent contractor may agree with person for whom contractor is performing services to refrain from carrying on similar business for up to 2 yrs.; upon dissolution of partnership, the partners may agree to refrain from carrying on similar business within specified area for up to 2 yrs.; LLC members may agree to refrain from carrying on similar business within specified area for up to 2 yrs., 23:921	Not addressed by state statute; enforceable under common law
MAINE	Not addressed by state statute; permissible under common law	Durational and geographical limitations are required, *Bernier v. Merrill Air Eng'rs*, 2001 ME 17, P17, 770 A.2d 97, 102 (2001) (citing *Revere Transducers, Inc. v. Deere & Co.*, 595 N.W.2d 751, 104 (Iowa 1999)	Not addressed by state statute; enforceable under common law

NDA Limitations	Trade Secrets Code Section	Significant Deviations from Uniform Trade Secrets Act	Employment-related Settlement Agreement Non-disclosure Enforceable?	Settlement Agreement Non-disclosure Limitations
When no NDA, trade secrets are protected where confidential relationship exists, *Engineered Mech. Servs., Inc. v. Langlois*, 464 So. 2d 329, 334 (La. Ct. App. 1984)	51:1431 to 51:1439	Exceptional circumstances not required for injunction to condition future use upon payment of reasonable royalty; court simply must determine that it would be unreasonable to prohibit future use; damages provision lacks UTSA clause permitting measurement of damages in form of reasonable royalty; no exemplary damages for willful and malicious misappropriation; 3 yr. statute of limitations; no severability clause	Settlement NDA not allowed if agreement has purpose or effect of concealing public hazard, information relating to public hazard, or information which may be useful to members of the public in protecting themselves from injury	CCP Art. 1426(D)
To determine if information is trade secret under Maine UTSA, the following factors must be applied: value of the information to competitors; amount of effort or money expended in developing information; extent of measures taken to guard secrecy of the information; ease or difficulty for others to acquire or duplicate information; degree to which third parties have placed information in public domain or rendered information readily ascertainable, *Spottiswoode v. Levine*, 1999 ME 79, P16, 730 A.2d 166, 172	Tit. 10, §§ 1541 to 1548	Misappropriation may be restrained or enjoined; injunctive relief provision applies to all forms of injunctive relief, including temporary restraining orders, preliminary injunctions and permanent injunctions; Maine UTSA does not affect duty of any person to disclose information where expressly required by law or provisions of the Maine Tort Claims Act; 4 yr. statute of limitations	N/A	N/A

Table 21: Restrictive Covenants in Employment—Continued

State	Non-compete Agreement (NCA) Enforceable by State Statute?	NCA Limitations	Non-disclosure Agreement (NDA) Enforceable under State Statute?
MARYLAND	Not addressed by state statute; permissible under common law	NCA enforceable if: supported by adequate consideration; ancillary to employment contract; confined within limits not wider in area and duration than reasonably necessary to protect employer's business; restrictions do not impose undue hardship on employee; restrictions do not disregard interests of public, *Becker v. Bailey*, 299 A.2d 835, 837-38 (Md. 1973)	Not addressed by state statute; enforceable under common law
MASSACHUSETTS	Not addressed by state statute; permissible under common law using Restatement (Second) of Contracts	NCA enforceable if: necessary to protect legitimate business interest; reasonably limited in time and space; not injurious to public's interest, *Boulanger v. Dunkin' Donuts Inc.*, 815 N.E.2d 572, 576-77 (Mass. 2004) (citing *All Stainless, Inc. v. Colby*, 364 Mass. 773, 778, 308 N.E.2d 481 (1974)); Restatement of Contracts §§ 515-16	Not addressed by state statute; enforceable under common law
MICHIGAN	Certain NCAs statutorily prohibited under Michigan Antitrust Reform Act, 445.774a	NCA enforceable if: restriction protects employer's reasonable competitive business interests; restriction expressly prohibits employee from engaging in employment or line of business after termination of employment; restriction is reasonable as to duration, area and type of employment	Yes; employer can obtain agreement to protect employer's reasonable competitive business interest, 445.774a
MINNESOTA	Not addressed by state statute; permissible under common law	Covenant enforceable if: for just and honest purpose; for protection of legitimate interest of employer; reasonable as between parties; not injurious to public, *Bennett v. Storz Broad. Co.*, 134 N.W.2d 892, 898 (Minn. 1965)	Not addressed by state statute; enforceable under common law; see NCA limitations

NDA Limitations	Trade Secrets Code Section	Significant Deviations from Uniform Trade Secrets Act	Employment-related Settlement Agreement Non-disclosure Enforceable?	Settlement Agreement Non-disclosure Limitations
Courts recognize duty not to disclose proprietary information even where there is no contractual duty	Com. Law §§ 11-1201 to 11-1209	3-yr. statute of limitations; Maryland UTSA does not limit any common law or statutory defense or immunity by state personnel; no severability provision	N/A	N/A
NDA should identify the processes or information sought to be protected, *Dynamics Research Corp. v. Analytic Sciences Corp.*, 9 Mass. App. Ct. 254, 277, 400 N.E.2d 1274 (1980)	USTA has not been adopted in Mass; trade secrets protected under statutory and common law; state statute protects trade secrets from bring embezzled, stolen, carried away, concealed, copied, intentionally converted by fraud or deception, Ch. 93, § 42; Ch. 266, § 30	N/A	N/A	N/A
NDA must be reasonable in: duration; geographical area; type of employment or line of business	445.1901 to 445.1910	Narrows scope of definition of person by excluding: business trust; estate; trust; joint venture; no exemplary damages for willful or malicious misappropriation; 3 yr. statute of limitations; no severability provision	N/A	N/A
Same restrictions as NCA	325C.01 to 325C.08	Adds to definition of trade secret by specifying that if employee or other person has reason to know that owner of trade secret intends or expects secrecy, existence of trade secret is not negated merely because employee or other person acquired it without express notice of it; 3 yr. statute of limitations; no severability provision	N/A	N/A

Table 21: Restrictive Covenants in Employment—Continued

State	Non-compete Agreement (NCA) Enforceable by State Statute?	NCA Limitations	Non-disclosure Agreement (NDA) Enforceable under State Statute?
MISSISSIPPI	Not addressed by state statutes; permissible under common law citing Corbin on Contracts (1962) and A.L.R.	NCA enforceable if reasonable in duration and geographical scope, *Redd Pest Control Company v. Heatherly*, 248 Miss. 34, 157 So.2d 133 (1963) (citing 6A, Corbin on Contracts (1962); 41 A.L.R.2d 15; 43 A.L.R.2d 94)	Not addressed by state statute; enforceable under common law
MISSOURI	Contracts restraining trade statutorily unlawful, 416.031; narrow exceptions exist for trade secrets and customer contacts	Restrictive covenants in employment agreements only enforceable if necessary to protect trade secret or customer contacts, *Schmersahl, Treloar & Co., P.C. v. McHugh*, 28 S.W.3d 345, 349 (Mo.App.2000); covenant must be: necessary to protect legitimate interest of employer; narrowly tailored in terms of area and time; not protecting mere competition by former employee, *Healthcare Servs. of the Ozarks, Inc. v. Copeland*, 198 S.W.3d 604, 610 (Mo. 2006)	Not addressed by state statute; enforceable under common law
MONTANA	Contracts restraining the exercise of a lawful profession, trade or business statutorily void; exceptions exist, 28-2-703; other restrictions established under common law	Exceptions general prohibition on restrictive covenants: person who sells goodwill of business may agree with buyer to refrain from carrying on similar business within designated geographical area; (2) partners may agree upon dissolution that one or more may not carry on similar business within designated geographical area., 28-2-703-05; NCA must also: be reasonable in time and place; be based on good consideration; afford reasonable protection and not impose unreasonable burden on employer, employee or public, *State Medical Oxygen and Supply, Inc. v. Am. Medical Oxygen Co.*, 782 P.2d 1272, 1275 (Mont. 1989) (citing *O'Neill v. Ferraro*, 182 Mont. 214, 218-19, 596 P.2d 197, 199 (1979)	Not addressed by state statute; enforceable under common law

NDA Limitations	Trade Secrets Code Section	Significant Deviations from Uniform Trade Secrets Act	Employment-related Settlement Agreement Non-disclosure Enforceable?	Settlement Agreement Non-disclosure Limitations
N/A	75-26-1 to 75-26-19	3-.yr statute of limitations	N/A	N/A
N/A	417.450 to 417.467	No exemplary damages for willful and malicious misappropriation; punitive damages with no cap allowed if misappropriation is outrageous because of evil motive or reckless indifference to rights of others; no attorney fees provision; 5 yr. statute of limitations; Act does not affect discovery of any matters discoverable in litigation, except litigation that alleges misappropriation of trade secrets as a cause of action	N/A	N/A
Similar restrictions as NCA. *Access Organics, Inc. v. Hernandez*, 341 Mont. 73, 175 P.3d 899 (Mont. 2008)	30-14-401 to 30-14-409	Exemplary damages not capped at twice the amount of ordinary damages; 3 yr. statute of limitations.; no severability provision	N/A	N/A

Table 21: Restrictive Covenants in Employment—Continued

State	Non-compete Agreement (NCA) Enforceable by State Statute?	NCA Limitations	Non-disclosure Agreement (NDA) Enforceable under State Statute?
NEBRASKA	Not addressed by state statutes; permissible under common law	Covenant enforceable if: restriction is not injurious to public; restriction is no greater than reasonably necessary to protect legitimate interest of employer; restriction is not unduly harsh and oppressive on employee, *Polly v. Ray D. Hilderman & Co.*, 225 Neb. 662, 665, 407 N.W.2d 751, 754 (1987) (citing *American Sec. Servs. v. Vodra*, 222 Neb. 480, 486, 385 N.W.2d 73, 78 (1986)	Not addressed by state statute; enforceable under common law

NDA Limitations	Trade Secrets Code Section	Significant Deviations from Uniform Trade Secrets Act	Employment-related Settlement Agreement Non-disclosure Enforceable?	Settlement Agreement Non-disclosure Limitations
Employer may contractually protect: secrets which have been communicated to employee during course of employment; confidential information communicated be employer to employee, but not involving trade secrets, such as information on unique business method; employee's special influence over employer's customers, obtained during course of employment; contacts developed during employment; employer business's development of goodwill, *Gaver v. Schneider's O.K. Tire Co.*, 289 Neb. 491, 503-4, 856 N.W.2d 121, 130-31 (2014) (citing 54A Am. Jur. 2d Monopolies and Restraints of Trade § 906 at 208 (2009)	87.501 to 87.507	Adds limited liability corporation to definition of person; removes UTSA's allowance for exemplary damages for willful and malicious misappropriation; no provision regarding applicability of other law	N/A	N/A

Table 21: Restrictive Covenants in Employment—Continued

State	Non-compete Agreement (NCA) Enforceable by State Statute?	NCA Limitations	Non-disclosure Agreement (NDA) Enforceable under State Statute?
NEVADA	Agreements preventing any person from obtaining employment elsewhere in Nevada statutorily illegal; certain restrictive covenants are enforceable, 613.200	Restrictive covenants enforceable if prohibiting employee from disclosing trade secrets, business methods, list of customers, secret formulas or processes or confidential information learned during course of employment, if agreement is supported by valuable consideration and otherwise reasonable in scope and duration	Yes; employer can enter into agreement with employee prohibiting employee from disclosing trade secrets, business methods, customer lists, secret formulas or processes or confidential information learned in course of business, 613.200(4)
NEW HAMPSHIRE	Statutorily enforceable if certain conditions are met, 275:70	NCAs required by employer as condition of employment must be provided to potential employee prior to acceptance; agreements regarding other provisions of employment, nondisclosure, trade secrets, intellectual property remain enforceable	Yes; any provision of employment, confidentiality, nondisclosure, trade secret, intellectual property assignment or other type of employment agreement is enforceable, 275:70

NDA Limitations	Trade Secrets Code Section	Significant Deviations from Uniform Trade Secrets Act	Employment-related Settlement Agreement Non-disclosure Enforceable?	Settlement Agreement Non-disclosure Limitations
NDA must be supported by valuable consideration; reasonable in scope and duration, 613.200(4)	600A.010 to 600A.100	Definition of improper means includes willful breach or inducement of breach of duty to maintain secrecy and duty imposed by common law, statute, contract, license, protective order or other court or administrative order; defines owner of trade secret; definition of trade secret expanded to include product, system, design, prototype, procedure, computer programming instruction or code; definition excludes certain information that manufacturer or pharmaceutical sales representative is required to report; Act contains a clause specifying that the owner of a trade secret is presumed to make a reasonable effort to maintain secrecy if the words "Confidential" or "Private" or other indication of secrecy is placed on any medium that describes or includes any portion of the trade secret. The presumption may be rebutted by clear and convincing evidence that the owner did not make reasonable efforts. Act contains provision describing criteria and criminal penalties for theft of trade secrets; Act contains provision specifying rules for when trade secret posed online remains trade secret; 3 yr. statute of limitations; no severability provision	Certain settlement NDAs unlawful	Settlement NDAs not allowed when settling claim brought against present or former state employee, officer, immune contractor and state legislator, 41.0375
The agreement must not: be greater than necessary to protect employer's legitimate interests; impose undue hardship on the employee; be harmful to public interest. *ACAS Acquisitions (Precitech) Inc. v. Hobert*, 923 A.2d 1076 (N.H. 2007)	350-B:1 to 350-B:9	No severability provision; 3 yr. statute of limitations	N/A	N/A

Table 21: Restrictive Covenants in Employment—Continued

State	Non-compete Agreement (NCA) Enforceable by State Statute?	NCA Limitations	Non-disclosure Agreement (NDA) Enforceable under State Statute?
NEW JERSEY	Not addressed by state statutes; permissible under common law	NCA enforceable if it: simply protects legitimate interests of employer; imposes no undue hardship on employee; is not injurious to the public, *Solari Indus. v. Malady*, 264 A.2d 53, 56 (N.J. 1970); *Karlin v. Weinberg*, 77 N.J. 408, 422, 390 A.2d 1161 (1978)	Not addressed by state statutes; enforceable under common law
NEW MEXICO	Not addressed by state statutes; permissible under common law	NCA must be reasonable in time and space, taking into account nature of business, location, parties involved, purchase price and main object of restriction, *Bowen v. Carlsbad Ins. & Real Estate, Inc.*,724 P.2d 223, 225 (N.M. 1986 (citing *Gann v. Morris*, 122 Ariz. 517, 518, 596 P.2d 43, 44 (App.1979))	Not addressed by state statutes; enforceable under common law
NEW YORK	Not addressed by state statute; permissible under common law using Restatement (Second) of Contracts	Covenant enforceable if: geographically and temporally reasonable; necessary to protect legitimate interest of employer; not harmful to general public; not unreasonably burdensome on employee, *BDO Seidman v. Hirshberg*, 690 N.Y.S.2d 854, 856-57 (1999) (citing Restatement (Second) of Contracts § 188; *Reed, Roberts Assocs. v. Strauman*, 40 N.Y.2d 303, 307, 386 N.Y.S.2d 677, 353 N.E.2d 590 (1976))	Not addressed by state statutes; enforceable under common law

NDA Limitations	Trade Secrets Code Section	Significant Deviations from Uniform Trade Secrets Act	Employment-related Settlement Agreement Non-disclosure Enforceable?	Settlement Agreement Non-disclosure Limitations
Same restrictions as NCA, *Raven v. Klein & Co., Inc.,* 195 N.J. Super. 209, 213 (1984)	56:15-1 to 56:15-9	Definition of improper means expanded to include limitation of use or disclosure of trade secret, access unauthorized or exceeding scope of authorization, or other means violating rights under state law; defines proper means and reverse engineering; definition of trade secret includes business data compilation, design, diagram, invention, plan, procedure, and prototype; Act contains provision specifying that person who misappropriates trade secret cannot use as a defense the existence at time of misappropriation of proper means to acquire trade secret; attorney fees provision provides definition of bad faith; 3 yr. statute of limitations; provision detailing Act's effect on other law specifies that N.J. Tort Claims Act supersedes any action for misappropriation of trade secret brought against public entity or employee; no severability provision	N/A	N/A
N/A	57-3A-1 to 57-3A-7	3 yr. statute of limitations; no severability provision; no provision describing Act's effect on other law	N/A	N/A
NDA enforceable where: employee's services are unique or extraordinary; covenant is reasonable, *Reed, Roberts Assocs., Inc. v. Strauman,* 386 N.Y.S.2d 677, 680 (1976)	USTA not adopted in New York; trade secrets governed by common law	N/A	Settlement NDA's not allowed; not for in-court settlements	Unless another rule applies for good cause, courts will not seal court records; courts must consider interests of the public in determination, Comp. Codes R. & Regs,. tit. 22, § 216.1 (1986 & Supp. 1992)

Table 21: Restrictive Covenants in Employment—Continued

State	Non-compete Agreement (NCA) Enforceable by State Statute?	NCA Limitations	Non-disclosure Agreement (NDA) Enforceable under State Statute?
NORTH CAROLINA	Restraints on trade statutorily prohibited, 75-1; contracts limiting right to do business must be in writing, 75-4; certain restraints permitted under common law	NCAs must: be in writing; geographically and temporally reasonable; be part of employment contract; be based on consideration; not go against public policy; be designed to protect the employer's legitimate business interest, *A.E.P. Indus., Inc. v. McClure*, 308 N.C. 393, 402-3, 302 S.E.2d 754, 760 (1983); *Scott v. Gillis*, 197 N.C. 223, 148 S.E. 315 (1929)	Not addressed by state statutes; enforceable under common law
NORTH DAKOTA	Contracts restraining exercise of lawful profession, trade or business statutorily void; exceptions exist 9-08-06	Exceptions to general prohibition on restrictive covenants: person who sells goodwill of business may agree with buyer to refrain from carrying on similar business within a specified geographical area while buyer carries on business; partners upon dissolution may agree to refrain from carrying on similar business within the same city as the partnership business, 9-08-06	Not addressed by state statutes; enforceable under common law

NDA Limitations	Trade Secrets Code Section	Significant Deviations from Uniform Trade Secrets Act	Employment-related Settlement Agreement Non-disclosure Enforceable?	Settlement Agreement Non-disclosure Limitations
Same restrictions as NCA	66-152 to 66-162	No definition of improper means; definition of misappropriation expressly excludes activities relating to trade secrets arrived at by independent development, reverse engineering, or obtained from another person with a right to disclose the secret; Act: specifies existence of trade secret is not negated merely because information comprising trade secret has also been developed, used or owned by more than one person or licensed to others; permits court to grant preliminary injunctions; expands injunctions provision to include situations of good faith acquisition of trade secret; bars damages in circumstances where defendant knew or had reason to know the information was trade secret; permits punitive damages for willful and malicious misappropriation, but does not contain a provision permitting exemplary damages; contains provision regarding burden of proof for misappropriation; 3 yr. statute of limitations; no severability provision	Certain settlement NDAs unlawful	No government agency or representative to enter into settlement if terms provide conditions are to be confidential, except for medical malpractice actions against hospitals, 132-1.3
N/A	47-25.1-01 to 47-25.1-08	Adds limited liability corporation to the definition of person; 3 yr. statute of limitations; no severability provision	N/A	N/A

Table 21: Restrictive Covenants in Employment—Continued

State	Non-compete Agreement (NCA) Enforceable by State Statute?	NCA Limitations	Non-disclosure Agreement (NDA) Enforceable under State Statute?
OHIO	Contracts in form of a trust, defined as a combination of capital, skill or acts by 2 or more people to create or carry out restrictions in trade or commerce, are statutorily illegal and void, 1331.04. Certain common law restrictions and exceptions exist	NCA enforceable if reasonable, considering: absence or presence of limitations as to time and space; if employee represents sole contact with customer; if employee is possessed with confidential information or trade secrets; if covenant seeks to eliminate competition which would be unfair to the employer or merely seeks to eliminate ordinary competition; if covenant seeks to stifle inherent skill and experience of employee; if benefit to employer is disproportional to the detriment to employee; if covenant operates as a bar to employee's sole means of support; if employee's talent which employer seeks to suppress was actually developed during period of employment; if forbidden employment is merely incidental to main employment, *Raimonde v. Van Vlerah*, 42 Ohio St.2d 21, 325 N.E.2d 544 (1975); *Imperial Home Decor Grp. v. Murray*, 75 F. Supp. 2d 753, 755 (N.D. Ohio 1999)	Not addressed by state statutes; enforceable under common law
OKLAHOMA	Statutorily enforceable if certain conditions are met, Tit. 15, § 219A	Person making NCA with employer allowed to engage in same business as long as former employee does not directly solicit sale of goods, services or combination of goods and services from established customers of former employer, Tit. 15, § 219A	Not addressed by state statutes; enforceable under common law
OREGON	Statutorily voidable; not enforceable by court unless certain conditions are met, 653.295	NCA generally void unless:employer discloses to employee at least 2 wks. before first day or NCA is agreed to upon subsequent bona fide advancement of employee by employer; employee must be person and employer must have a protectable interest; annual income of employee exceeds median family income for 4-person family; terms cannot exceed 18 mos. from termination, 653.295	Yes; right to protect trade secrets or proprietary information by injunction or other lawful means not restricted by statute prohibiting NCAs, 653.295(5)

NDA Limitations	Trade Secrets Code Section	Significant Deviations from Uniform Trade Secrets Act	Employment-related Settlement Agreement Non-disclosure Enforceable?	Settlement Agreement Non-disclosure Limitations
All restrictive covenants in employment contracts must be reasonable; see NCA limitations for factors that contribute to reasonableness	1333.61 to 1333.69	Definition of person taken from a different state statute but definition is similar to the Uniform act; definition of trade secret expanded to include scientific or technical information, design, procedure, improvement, business information or plans, financial information, listing of names, addresses or phone numbers; damages in form of reasonable royalty must be equitable under the circumstances considering loss to complainant or benefit to misappropriator; court may award punitive damages for willful and malicious misappropriation exemplary or punitive damages may not exceed 3 times amount awarded for ordinary damages; 4 yr. statute of limitations.; no severability provision	N/A	N/A
N/A	Tit. 78, §§ 85 to 94	3 yr. statute of limitations; no severability provision	N/A	N/A
NDA must be: restricted with respect to time or place; supported by valuable consideration; reasonable and not an interference with public interest, *N. Pac. Lumber Co. v. Moore*, 551 P.2d 431, 434 (Or. 1976)	646.461 to 646.475	Reverse engineering and independent development alone are not considered improper means; definition of trade secret includes drawings, cost data, and customer lists; temporary, preliminary, and permanent injunctions permitted; Act does not affect defense, immunity, or limitation of liability afforded public bodies, officers, employees, or agents; public bodies, officers, employees, or agents immune from trade secret misappropriation claims based on disclosure or release of information in obedience to or good faith reliance on any order of disclosure permitted by law; 3 yr. statute of limitations; no severability provision	Certain settlement NDAs allowed	Public body, officer, employee, or agent cannot enter into settlement that makes terms confidential, 17.095(1)

Table 21: Restrictive Covenants in Employment—Continued

State	Non-compete Agreement (NCA) Enforceable by State Statute?	NCA Limitations	Non-disclosure Agreement (NDA) Enforceable under State Statute?
PENNSYLVANIA	Not addressed by state statutes; permissible under common law	Covenant enforceable if: incident to employment relationship between parties; restrictions reasonably necessary for protection of employer; restrictions reasonably limited in duration and geographical area, *Sidco Paper Co. v. Aaron*, 465 Pa. 586, 591, 351 A.2d 250 (1976)	Not addressed by state statutes; enforceable under common law
RHODE ISLAND	Not addressed by state statute; permissible under common law using Restatement (Second) of Contracts	NCA enforceable if: reasonable; not extending beyond what is apparently necessary for protection of those it favors; restriction ancillary to otherwise valid transaction or relationship; restriction supported by adequate consideration; restriction designed to protect legitimate interest, *Durapin, Inc. v. Am. Prods., Inc.*, 559 A.2d 1051, 1053 (R.I. 1989); Restatement (Second) of Contracts § 187.	Not addressed by state statutes; enforceable under common law

NDA Limitations	Trade Secrets Code Section	Significant Deviations from Uniform Trade Secrets Act	Employment-related Settlement Agreement Non-disclosure Enforceable?	Settlement Agreement Non-disclosure Limitations
N/A	Tit. 12, §§ 5301 to 5308	Definition of trade secret includes drawings, customer lists, and items with potential value; definitions section includes willful and malicious; 3 yr. statute of limitations; no severability provision	N/A	N/A
N/A	6-41-1 to 6-41-11	3 yr. statute of limitations	N/A	N/A

Table 21: Restrictive Covenants in Employment—Continued

State	Non-compete Agreement (NCA) Enforceable by State Statute?	NCA Limitations	Non-disclosure Agreement (NDA) Enforceable under State Statute?
SOUTH CAROLINA	Not addressed by state statutes; permissible under common law	NCA enforceable if: narrowly drawn to protect legitimate interests of employer; reasonably limited in time and place with respect to its operation; not unduly harsh and oppressive in curtailing legitimate efforts of employee to earn livelihood; reasonable from public policy standpoint; supported by valuable consideration, *Rental Uniform Serv. of Florence, Inc. v. Dudley*, 278 S.C. 674, 675-76, 301 S.E.2d 142 (1983)	Confidentiality agreements used to protect trade secrets generally enforceable under state statute, 39-8-30(D); 39-8-60(H)

NDA Limitations	Trade Secrets Code Section	Significant Deviations from Uniform Trade Secrets Act	Employment-related Settlement Agreement Non-disclosure Enforceable?	Settlement Agreement Non-disclosure Limitations
N/A	39-8-10 to 39-8-130	Definition of improper means expanded to include duties imposed by common law, statute, contract, license, court or administrative order; definition of trade secret includes products, systems, prototypes, procedures or codes and specifies that trade secret may consist of simple fact, item or procedure or series which collectively can make substantial difference in efficiency of process or production of product, or may be basis of marketing or commercial strategy; trade secret is protectable and enforceable until disclosed or discovered by proper means; employees have duty to refrain from using or disclosing trade secret without employer's permission independently of and in addition to any written contract of employment or other agreement; civil action permitted to recover damages incurred as result of misappropriation, wrongful disclosure or use of trade secrets; contractual duties to keep trade secrets not considered void or against public policy for lack of durational or geographical limitation; reasonable time for injunction to take into account avg. rate of business growth that would have been gained from non-misappropriated use of trade secret; to determine need for preservation of secrecy, court to first determine whether substantial need exists by person seeking discovery; court may not order direct access to databases containing trade secrets unless information cannot be obtained through other means; court may condition production of trade secret on posting of appropriate bond; person receiving information regarding trade secrets subject to S.C. law	N/A	N/A

Table 21: Restrictive Covenants in Employment—Continued

State	Non-compete Agreement (NCA) Enforceable by State Statute?	NCA Limitations	Non-disclosure Agreement (NDA) Enforceable under State Statute?
SOUTH DAKOTA	Contracts restraining exercise of lawful profession, trade or business statutorily void; exceptions exist, 53-9-8	Exceptions to the general prohibition on restrictive covenants: person who sells goodwill of business may agree with buyer to refrain from carrying on similar business within specified geographical area as long as buyer carries on similar business within area; upon dissolution, partners may agree to refrain from carrying on similar business within same municipality as partnership business; employee may agree with employer not to engage directly or indirectly in same business for up to 2 yrs. from date of termination of agreement and not to solicit existing customers within a specified geographical area for up to 2 yrs., so long as employer continues to carry on similar business 53-9-8-11	No state statute; enforceable under common law
TENNESSEE	Not addressed by state statutes; permissible under common law using Restatement of the Law, Contracts and C.J.S. Contracts	NCA enforceable if: reasonable; time and territorial limits are no greater than necessary to protect business interests of employer; reasonableness is determined using the following: consideration supporting the agreement; threatened danger to employer in absence of agreement; economic hardship imposed on employee; whether covenant is harmful to public interest, *Allright Auto Parks, Inc. v. Berry*, 219 Tenn. 280, 409 S.W.2d 361, 363 (1966); *Hasty v. Rent–A–Driver, Inc.*, 671 S.W.2d 471, 472-73 (Tenn.1984); Restatement of the Law, Contracts, § 514; 17 C.J.S. Contracts §§ 238-258	No state statute; enforceable under common law; TUTSA specifies contractual duty to maintain secrecy or limit use of trade secret not deemed void merely for lack of temporal or geographical limitation, 47-25-1708(b)(1)

NDA Limitations	Trade Secrets Code Section	Significant Deviations from Uniform Trade Secrets Act	Employment-related Settlement Agreement Non-disclosure Enforceable?	Settlement Agreement Non-disclosure Limitations
NDAs must: be used to protect employer's trade secret or confidential information; not impose undue hardship on employee;not be injurious to public, *1st Am. Sys., Inc. v. Rezatto*, 311 N.W.2d 51, 59 (S.D. 1981)	37-29-1 to 37-29-11	Definition of person includes limited liability companies; no severability provision	N/A	N/A
N/A	47-25-1701 to 47-25-1709	Trade secret includes technical, nontechnical or financial data, and plan; court may issue injunction to eliminate commercial advantage that would otherwise be derived from misappropriation, to deter willful and malicious misappropriation, or where trade secret ceases to exist due to fault of enjoined party or others by improper means; 3 yr. statute of limitations; Act to be applied separately to any claim against each other person who receives trade secret from another person who has misappropriated it; no severability provision	N/A	N/A

Table 21: Restrictive Covenants in Employment—Continued

State	Non-compete Agreement (NCA) Enforceable by State Statute?	NCA Limitations	Non-disclosure Agreement (NDA) Enforceable under State Statute?
TEXAS	Statutorily enforceable if conditions are met, Bus. & Com. § 15.50	NCA enforceable if: ancillary to or part of otherwise enforceable agreement at time agreement is made; limitations as to time, geographical area, and scope of activity to be restrained; limitations imposed are reasonable and do not impose greater restraint than necessary to protect goodwill or other business interest of promisee, Bus. & Com. § 15.50	Not addressed by state statute; enforceable under common law to protect trade secret defined by the Texas Uniform Trade Secrets Act
UTAH	Statutorily enforceable if certain conditions are met, 34-51-201	Post-employment restrictive covenants can only exist for 1 yr. from day employee is no longer employed	Not addressed by state statute; enforceable under common law
VERMONT	Not addressed by state statutes; permissible under common law using A.L.R.	NCA enforceable if: not contrary to public policy; necessary for protection of employer; not unnecessarily restrictive of rights of employee; due regard is given to subject matter of contract and circumstances and conditions under which it is to be performed, *Vt. Elec. Supply Co. v. Andrus*, 315 A.2d 456, 458 (Vt. 1974) (citing *Dyar Sales & Machinery Co. v. Bleiler*, 106 Vt. 425, 434, 175 A. 27 (1934); 9 A.L.R. 1468 Note (b), 1	Not addressed by state statute; enforceable under common law relying on Restatement (Second) of Contracts

NDA Limitations	Trade Secrets Code Section	Significant Deviations from Uniform Trade Secrets Act	Employment-related Settlement Agreement Non-disclosure Enforceable?	Settlement Agreement Non-disclosure Limitations
N/A	Civ. Prac. & Rem. §§ 134A.001 to 134A.008	Definitions added for: claimant; clear and convincing; owner; proper means; reverse engineering; willful and malicious; no definition of person; improper means expanded to include limitation of use or prohibition of discovery of trade secret; trade secret includes all forms and types of information, including business, scientific, technical, economic, or engineering, prototypes, plans, program devices, codes, procedures and financial data; injunction may only be ordered where if it does not prohibit person from using general knowledge, skill and experience acquired during employment; presumption in favor of granting protective orders and presumption that party is allowed to participate and assist counsel in preparation of party's case; court may limit or exclude party and representative's access to alleged trade secret if other countervailing interests overcome presumption; Act specifies factors to balance when determining whether countervailing interests exist; Act supersedes the Tex. R. Civ. Proc. but does not affect disclosure of public information by governmental body	Tex. open records law states that settlement agreements are court records presumed to be open to the public	Texas open records law does not apply to monetary consideration in settlements but does apply to records that have probable adverse effect upon general public health or safety, administration of public office, or operation of government, Tex. R. Civ. P. 76a(2)(b)
N/A	13-24-1 to 13-24-9	3 yr. statute of limitations; no severability provision	N/A	N/A
NDA must: not be contrary to public policy; be necessary to protect employer; not be unnecessarily restrictive on employee's rights, *Vt. Elec. Supply Co. v. Andrus*, 132 Vt. 195, 198, 315 A.2d 456, 458 (1974)	Tit. 9, §§ 4601 to 4609	No definition of person; attorney fees may be awarded when there is a substantially prevailing party; fees must be reasonable; no exemplary damages for willful or malicious misappropriation; court may award punitive damages; no statute of limitations provision; no severability provision	N/A	N/A

Table 21: Restrictive Covenants in Employment—Continued

State	Non-compete Agreement (NCA) Enforceable by State Statute?	NCA Limitations	Non-disclosure Agreement (NDA) Enforceable under State Statute?
VIRGINIA	Not addressed by state statutes; permissible under common law	NCA enforceable if restraint is reasonable and is: no greater than necessary to protect employer's legitimate business interest; not unduly harsh and oppressive in curtailing employee's legitimate efforts to earn a livelihood; of sound public policy, *Roanoke Eng. Sales v. Rosenbaum*, 223 Va. 548, 552, 290 S.E.2d 882, 884 (1982))	Not addressed by state statutes; permissible under common law
WASHINGTON	Not addressed by state statute; permissible under common law using Restatement (Second) of Contracts	NCA enforceable when validly formed and are reasonable; reasonableness factors: whether restraint is necessary for protection of the business or goodwill; whether restraint on employee is greater than reasonably necessary to secure such protection to employer's business or goodwill; degree of injury to public, *Perry v. Moran*, 748 P.2d 224, 228 (Wash. 1987) (citing *Racine v. Bender*, 141 Wash. 606, 612, 252 P. 115 (1927)	Not addressed by state statutes; permissible under common law citing 9 A. L. R. 1467, 1468
WEST VIRGINIA	Contracts in restraint of trade or commerce statutorily unlawful, 47–18–3(a); common law establishes certain exceptions, citing A.L.R.	NCA enforceable if: supported by consideration; ancillary to a lawful contract; reasonable; consistent with public interest, *Reddy v. Cmty. Health Found. of Man*, 298 S.E.2d 906, 910-11 (W. Va. 1982); 62 A.L.R.3d 1014 (1975)	Not addressed by state statute; enforceable under common law relying on Restatement (Second) of Contracts

NDA Limitations	Trade Secrets Code Section	Significant Deviations from Uniform Trade Secrets Act	Employment-related Settlement Agreement Non-disclosure Enforceable?	Settlement Agreement Non-disclosure Limitations
Same restrictions as NCA, *Nortec Commc'ns, Inc. v. Lee-Llacer*, 548 F. Supp. 2d 226, 230 (E.D. Va. 2008) (citing *Foti v. Cook*, 220 Va. 800, 806, 263 S.E.2d 430 (1980))	59.1-336 to 59.1-343	Improper means includes use of computer or computer network without authority; reasonable royalty may be imposed if complainant cannot prove a greater amount of damages by other methods of measurement; court may award punitive damages up to $350,000; attorney fees provision does not include award of attorneys fees when motion to terminate injunction is made or resisted in bad faith; 3 yr. statute of limitations; no severability provision	N/A	N/A
NDAs enforceable when validly formed, reasonable and there is sufficient consideration; reasonableness factors: whether restraint is necessary for protection of the business or goodwill; whether restraint on employee is greater than reasonably necessary to secure such protection to employer's business or goodwill, *Racine v. Bender*, 141 Wash. 606, 612, 252 P. 115 (1927)	19.108.010 to 19.108.930	Court may award reasonable royalty if it determines it would be unreasonable to prohibit future use; no severability provision; 3 yr. statute of limitations	Certain settlement NDAs allowed	Settlement NDAs enforceable only when confidentiality is in public's best interest; members of public have right to information necessary to understand nature, source, and extent of risk associated with a public hazard, 4.24.611(2)
NDA must be reasonable, specifically with respect to time or geographical scop, *Reddy v. Comm. Health Found. of Man*, 171 W.Va. 368, 298 S.E.2d 906, 911 (1982)	47-22-1 to 47-22-10	3 yr. statute of limitations; damages in the form of unjust enrichment are those not taken into account in computing actual loss	N/A	N/A

Table 21: Restrictive Covenants in Employment—Continued

State	Non-compete Agreement (NCA) Enforceable by State Statute?	NCA Limitations	Non-disclosure Agreement (NDA) Enforceable under State Statute?
WISCONSIN	Statutorily enforceable if certain conditions are met, 103.465	NCA enforceable only if restriction: has specified territory and time; is reasonably necessary to protect employee, 103.465	Courts treat NDAs as restrictive covenants under 103.465
WYOMING	Not addressed by state statutes; permissible under common law using Restatement (Second) of Contracts); any agreement must be in writing, 1-23-105	NCA enforceable if: in writing; part of contract of employment; based on reasonable consideration; reasonable in length of time and geographic limitations; not against public policy, *Hopper v. All Pet Animal Clinic, Inc.*, 861 P.2d 531, 540 (Wyo. 1993); Restatement (Second) of Contracts § 186-188	Not addressed by state statute; enforceable under common law relying on Restatement (Second) of Contracts

NDA Limitations	Trade Secrets Code Section	Significant Deviations from Uniform Trade Secrets Act	Employment-related Settlement Agreement Non-disclosure Enforceable?	Settlement Agreement Non-disclosure Limitations
Enforceable if reasonably necessary for protection of employer, 103.465	134.9	Adds a definition of readily accessible; to be granted injunctive relief, complainant must include description of alleged trade secret with enough detail to inform individual to be enjoined of the nature of the complaint, possibly including written disclosure of trade secret; to be granted damages in form of a reasonable royalty, complainant must not be able to prove amount of damages; no attorney fee provision; no statute of limitations; no severability provision	N/A	N/A
NDA must not: be greater than necessary to protect employer; impose undue hardship on employee; be injurious to the public, *Hopper v. All Pet Animal Clinic, Inc.*, 861 P.2d 531, 539–40 (Wyo.1993) (citing *Dutch Maid Bakeries v. Schleicher*, 58 Wyo. 374, 131 P.2d 630, 634-35 (1942)	40-24-101 to 40-24-110	4 yr. statute of limitations; no severability provision	N/A	N/A

22. LEGAL HOLIDAYS

The diversity of our country is reflected in the various holidays recognized by the individual states. While many holidays, including New Year's Day, Memorial Day, and Labor Day, are considered legal holidays in all states, others, such as Good Friday and Robert E. Lee's Birthday, are recognized in only a handful, while a few are particular to only one state, for example Alaska Day and Pioneer Day.

The recognition of civil rights leader Martin Luther King, Jr.'s birthday has sparked a great deal of controversy. In some of the states where it is recognized, it is not a paid holiday for state employees.

Due to the myriad local holidays in the states, only the major holidays are featured below for comparison.

Table 22: Legal Holidays

State	Code Section	Holidays
ALABAMA	1-3-8	New Year's Day; Martin Luther King, Jr.'s and Robert E. Lee's Birthday; George Washington's and Thomas Jefferson's Birthday; Mardi Gras (Mobile & Baldwin Counties only); Confederate Memorial Day; National Memorial Day; Jefferson Davis' Birthday; 4th of July; Labor Day; Columbus Day, Fraternal Day, and American Indian Heritage Day; Veterans Day; Thanksgiving Day; Christmas Day; Sundays
ALASKA	44.12.010	New Year's Day; Martin Luther King, Jr.&'s Birthday; Presidents Day; Seward's Day; Memorial Day; Independence Day; Labor Day; Alaska Day; Veterans Day; Thanksgiving Day; Christmas Day; Sundays
ARIZONA	1-301	New Year's Day; Martin Luther King, Jr./Civil Rights Day; Lincoln/Washington Presidents Day; Mother's Day; Memorial Day; Father's Day; Independence Day; American Family Day; Labor Day; Constitution Commemoration Day; Columbus Day; Veterans Day; Thanksgiving Day; Christmas Day; Sundays
ARKANSAS	1-5-101	New Year's Day; Martin Luther King, Jr.'s Birthday; George Washington's Birthday and Daisy Gatson Bates Day; Memorial Day; Independence Day; Labor Day; Veterans Day; Thanksgiving Day; Christmas Eve; Christmas Day
CALIFORNIA	Gov. § 6700; 19853	New Year's Day; Martin Luther King, Jr. Day; Lincoln Day; Presidents Day; Cesar Chavez Day; Good Friday (12 noon to 3 pm); Memorial Day; Independence Day; Labor Day; Admission Day; Native American Day; Columbus Day; Veterans Day; Thanksgiving Day; Christmas Day; Sundays
COLORADO	24-11-101; 24-11-112	New Year's Day; Martin Luther King, Jr.'s Birthday; Washington-Lincoln Day; Cesar Chavez Day; Memorial Day; Independence Day; Labor Day; Columbus Day; Veterans Day; Thanksgiving Day; Christmas Day
CONNECTICUT	1-4	New Year's Day; Martin Luther King, Jr. Day; Lincoln Day; Washington's Birthday; Memorial Day; Independence Day; Labor Day; Columbus Day; Veterans Day; Thanksgiving Day; Christmas Day
DELAWARE	Tit. 1, § 501	New Year's Day; Martin Luther King, Jr. Day; Good Friday; Memorial Day; Independence Day; Labor Day; Veterans Day; Thanksgiving Day; Friday after Thanksgiving; Christmas Day; Day of biennial general elections; Saturdays
DISTRICT OF COLUMBIA	28-2701	New Year's Day; Martin Luther King, Jr.'s Birthday; Washington's Birthday; DC Emancipation Day; Memorial Day; Independence Day; Labor Day; Columbus Day; Veterans Day; Thanksgiving Day; Christmas Day; Presidential inauguration day
FEDERAL	5 USCA § 6103	New Year's Day; Martin Luther King, Jr.'s Birthday; Washington's Birthday; Memorial Day; Independence Day; Labor Day; Columbus Day; Veterans Day; Thanksgiving Day; Christmas Day
FLORIDA	110.117; 683.01	New Year's Day; Martin Luther King, Jr.'s Birthday; Robert E. Lee's Birthday; Lincoln's Birthday; Susan B. Anthony's Birthday; Washington's Birthday; Shrove Tuesday (certain counties only); Good Friday; Pascua Florida Day; Confederate Memorial Day; Memorial Day; Jefferson Davis Birthday; Flag Day; Independence Day; Labor Day; Columbus Day; Farmers'; Day; General Election Day; Veterans Day; Thanksgiving Day; Friday after Thanksgiving; Christmas Day; Sundays
GEORGIA	1-4-1	New Year's Day; Martin Luther King, Jr.'s Birthday; Washington's Birthday (observed at Christmas); Confederate Memorial Day; Memorial Day; Independence Day; Labor Day; Columbus Day; Veterans Day; Thanksgiving Day; Friday after Thanksgiving; Christmas Day

Table 22: Legal Holidays—Continued

State	Code Section	Holidays
HAWAII	8-1	New Year's Day; Martin Luther King, Jr. Day; Presidents Day; Prince Jonah Kuhio Kalanianaole Day; Good Friday; Memorial Day; King Kamehameha Day; Independence Day; Statehood Day; Labor Day; Veterans Day; Thanksgiving Day; Christmas Day; all election days, except primary and special election days, in the county wherein the election is held
IDAHO	73-108	New Year's Day; Martin Luther King, Jr. Day and Idaho Human Rights Day; Washington's Birthday; Memorial Day; Independence Day; Labor Day; Columbus Day; Veterans Day; Thanksgiving Day; Christmas Day; Sundays
ILLINOIS	205 § 630/17	New Year's Day; Martin Luther King, Jr.'s Birthday; Lincoln's Birthday; Presidents Day; Casimir Pulaski's Birthday; Good Friday; Memorial Day; Independence Day; Labor Day; Columbus Day; Veterans Day; Thanksgiving Day; Christmas Day
INDIANA	1-1-9-1; 1-1-9-2	New Year's Day; Martin Luther King, Jr.'s Birthday; Abraham Lincoln's Birthday; George Washington's Birthday; Good Friday; Memorial Day; Independence Day; Labor Day; Columbus Day; election day; Veterans Day; Thanksgiving Day; Christmas Day; Sundays
IOWA	1C.1; 1C.2	New Year's Day; Dr. Martin Luther King, Jr.'s Birthday; Lincoln's Birthday; Washington's Birthday; Memorial Day; Independence Day; Labor Day; Veterans Day; Thanksgiving Day; Christmas Day
KANSAS	35-107	New Year's Day; Martin Luther King, Jr. Day; President's Day; Memorial Day; Independence Day; Labor Day; Columbus Day; Veterans Day; Thanksgiving Day; Christmas Day
KENTUCKY	2.110	New Year's Day; Martin Luther King, Jr.'s Birthday; Robert E. Lee Day; Franklin D. Roosevelt Day; Lincoln's Birthday; Washington's Birthday; Memorial Day; Confederate Memorial Day and Jefferson Davis Day; Independence Day; Labor Day; Columbus Day; Veterans Day; Thanksgiving Day; Christmas Day
LOUISIANA	1:55	New Year's Day; Battle of New Orleans; Martin Luther King, Jr.'s Birthday; Robert E. Lee's Birthday; Washington's Birthday; Good Friday; Confederate Memorial Day; National Memorial Day; Independence Day; Huey P. Long Day; Labor Day; Columbus Day; All Saints Day; Veterans Day; Thanksgiving Day; Christmas Day; general election day in even numbered years; certain paid holidays vary from year to year at governor's discretion; Sundays
MAINE	Tit. 4, § 1051; Tit. 20-A, § 4802	New Year's Day; Martin Luther King, Jr. Day; Washington's Birthday; Patriots Day; Memorial Day; Independence Day; Labor Day; Columbus Day; Veterans Day; Thanksgiving Day; Christmas Day; Sundays
MARYLAND	Gen. Provis. § 1-111	New Year's Day; Martin Luther King, Jr.'s Birthday; Lincoln's Birthday; Washington's Birthday; Maryland Day; Good Friday; Memorial Day; Independence Day; Labor Day; Defenders Day; Columbus Day; statewide general election day; Veterans Day; Thanksgiving Day; Friday after Thanksgiving for American Indian Heritage Day; Christmas Day
MASSACHUSETTS	Ch. 4, § 7	New Year's Day; Martin Luther King, Jr.'s Birthday; President's Day; Patriots Day; Memorial Day; Independence Day; Labor Day; Columbus Day; Veterans Day; Thanksgiving Day; Christmas Day
MICHIGAN	435.101	New Year's Day; Martin Luther King, Jr. Day; Lincoln's Birthday; Washington's Birthday; Memorial Day; Independence Day; Labor Day; Columbus Day; Veterans Day; Thanksgiving Day; Christmas Day
MINNESOTA	645.44	New Year's Day; Martin Luther King, Jr.'s Birthday; Washington's and Lincoln's Birthday; Memorial Day; Independence Day; Labor Day; Columbus Day; Veterans Day; Thanksgiving Day; Friday after Thanksgiving; Christmas Day

Table 22: Legal Holidays—Continued

State	Code Section	Holidays
MISSISSIPPI	3-3-7	New Year's Day; Robert E. Lee's and Martin Luther King, Jr.'s Birthday; Washington's Birthday; Confederate Memorial Day; National Memorial Day and Jefferson Davis Birthday; Independence Day; Labor Day; Veterans Day; Thanksgiving Day; Christmas Day
MISSOURI	9.010	New Year's Day; Martin Luther King, Jr.'s Birthday; Lincoln's Birthday; Washington's Birthday; Truman Day; Memorial Day; Independence Day; Labor Day; Columbus Day; Veterans Day; Thanksgiving Day; Christmas Day
MONTANA	1-1-216	New Year's Day; Martin Luther King, Jr.'s Birthday; Lincoln's and Washington's Birthday; Memorial Day; Independence Day; Labor Day; Columbus Day; state general election day; Veterans' Day; Thanksgiving Day; Christmas Day; Sundays
NEBRASKA	25-2221	New Year's Day; Martin Luther King, Jr.'s Birthday; Presidents Day; Arbor Day; Memorial Day; Independence Day; Labor Day; Columbus Day; Veterans Day; Thanksgiving day; Friday after Thanksgiving; Christmas Day
NEVADA	236.015	New Year's Day; Martin Luther King, Jr.'s Birthday; Washington's Birthday; Memorial Day; Independence Day; Labor Day; Nevada Day; Veterans Day; Thanksgiving Day; Friday after Thanksgiving (Family Day); Christmas Day
NEW HAMPSHIRE	288:1; 288:2	New Year's Day; Martin Luther King, Jr. Civil Rights Day; Washington's Birthday; Memorial Day; Independence Day; Labor Day; Columbus Day; day of biennial election; Veterans Day; Thanksgiving Day; Christmas Day;
NEW JERSEY	36:1-1; 36:1-1.2	New Year's Day; Martin Luther King, Jr.'s Birthday; Lincoln's Birthday; Washington's Birthday; Good Friday; Memorial Day; Independence Day; Labor Day; Columbus Day; Veterans Day; Thanksgiving Day; Christmas Day; any general election day
NEW MEXICO	12-5-2	New Year's Day; Martin Luther King, Jr.'s Birthday; Washington's and Lincoln's birthday, President's Day; Memorial Day; Independence Day; Labor Day; Columbus Day; Veterans Day; Thanksgiving Day; Christmas Day
NEW YORK	Gen. Constr. § 24; 25	New Year's Day; Martin Luther King, Jr. Day; Lincoln's Birthday; Washington's Birthday; Memorial Day; Flag Day; Independence Day; Labor Day; Columbus Day; Veterans Day; Thanksgiving Day; Christmas Day; any general election day
NORTH CAROLINA	103-4	New Year's Day; Martin Luther King, Jr.'s Birthday; Robert E. Lee's Birthday; Washington's Birthday; Greek Independence Day; Good Friday; Anniversary of signing of Halifax Resolves; Confederate Memorial Day; Anniversary of Mecklenburg Declaration of Independence; Memorial Day; Independence Day; Labor Day; First Responders Day; Columbus Day; Yom Kippur; the Tuesday after the first Monday in November in general election years; Veterans Day; Thanksgiving Day; Christmas Day
NORTH DAKOTA	1-03-01; 1-03-01.1	New Year's Day; Martin Luther King, Jr. Day; Washington's Birthday; Good Friday; Memorial Day; Independence Day; Labor Day; Veterans Day; Thanksgiving Day; Christmas Day
OHIO	1.14	New Year's Day; Martin Luther King, Jr. Day; Washington-Lincoln Day; Memorial Day; Independence Day; Labor Day; Columbus Day; Veterans Day; Thanksgiving Day; Christmas Day
OKLAHOMA	Tit. 25, §§ 82.1, 82.2	New Year's Day; Martin Luther King, Jr.'s Birthday; Presidents Day; Memorial Day; Independence Day; Labor Day; Veterans Day; Thanksgiving Day; Friday after Thanksgiving; Christmas Day; Saturday; Sundays
OREGON	187.010; 187.020	New Year's Day; Martin Luther King, Jr.'s Birthday; Presidents Day; Memorial Day; Independence Day; Labor Day; Veterans Day; Thanksgiving Day; Christmas Day; Sundays

Table 22: Legal Holidays—Continued

State	Code Section	Holidays
PENNSYLVANIA	Tit. 44, § 11	New Year's Day; Martin Luther King, Jr. Day; Presidents Day; Good Friday; Memorial Day; Flag Day; Independence Day; Labor Day; Columbus Day; election day; Veterans Day; Thanksgiving Day; Christmas Day
RHODE ISLAND	25-1-1	New Year's Day; Martin Luther King, Jr.'s Birthday; Washington's Birthday; Rhode Island Independence Day; Memorial Day; Independence Day; Victory Day; Labor Day; Columbus Day; election day; Veterans Day; Thanksgiving Day; Christmas Day
SOUTH CAROLINA	53-5-10	New Year's Day; Martin Luther King, Jr. Day; Washington's Birthday/Presidents Day; Confederate Memorial Day; National Memorial Day; Independence Day; Labor Day; Veterans Day; Thanksgiving Day; Friday after Thanksgiving; Christmas Eve; Christmas Day; day after Christmas
SOUTH DAKOTA	1-5-1	New Year's Day; Martin Luther King, Jr. Day; Lincoln's and Washington's Birthday; Memorial Day; Independence Day; Labor Day; Native American Day; Veterans Day; Thanksgiving Day; Christmas Day
TENNESSEE	15-1-101	New Year's Day; Martin Luther King, Jr. Day; Washington Day; Good Friday; Memorial Day; Independence Day; Labor Day; Columbus Day; Veterans Day; Thanksgiving Day; Christmas Day; county, state, or national election days
TEXAS	Gov't § 662.003	New Year's Day; Martin Luther King, Jr. Day; Confederate Heroes Day; Presidents Day; Texas Independence Day; San Jacinto Day; Memorial Day; Emancipation Day; Independence Day; Lyndon Baines Johnson Day; Labor Day; Veterans Day; Thanksgiving Day; Friday after Thanksgiving; Christmas Eve; Christmas Day; day after Christmas
UTAH	63G-1-301	New Year's Day; Martin Luther King, Jr. Day; Washington and Lincoln Day; Memorial Day; Independence Day; Pioneer Day; Labor Day; Columbus Day; Veterans Day; Thanksgiving Day; Christmas Day; Sundays
VERMONT	Tit. 1, § 371	New Year's Day; Martin Luther King, Jr.'s Birthday; Lincoln's Birthday; Washington's Birthday; Town Meeting Day; Memorial Day; Independence Day; Bennington Battle Day; Labor Day; Columbus Day; Veterans Day; Thanksgiving Day; Christmas Day
VIRGINIA	2.2-3300	New Year's Day; Lee-Jackson Day; Martin Luther King, Jr. Day; Washington's Birthday; Memorial Day; Independence Day; Labor Day; Columbus and Yorktown Victory Day; Veterans Day; Thanksgiving Day; Friday after Thanksgiving; Christmas Day
WASHINGTON	1.16.050	New Year's Day; Martin Luther King, Jr.'s Birthday; Presidents Day; Memorial Day; Independence Day; Labor Day; Veterans Day; Thanksgiving Day; Native American Heritage Day (Friday after Thanksgiving); Christmas Day; Sundays
WEST VIRGINIA	2-2-1	New Year's Day; Martin Luther King, Jr.'s Birthday; Presidents Day; Memorial Day; West Virginia Day; Independence Day; Labor Day; Columbus Day; Veterans Day; Thanksgiving Day; Lincoln's Day (day after Thanksgiving); Christmas Day; general, primary, or special election days
WISCONSIN	995.20	New Year's Day; Martin Luther King, Jr.'s Birthday; Presidents Day; Good Friday (11am-3pm observed for purpose of worship); Memorial Day; Juneteenth Day; Independence Day; Labor Day; Columbus Day; Veterans Day; Thanksgiving Day; Christmas Day; partisan primary and November general election days
WYOMING	8-4-101	New Year's Day; Martin Luther King, Jr.'s Birthday and Wyoming Equality Day; Washington's and Lincoln's Birthday; Memorial Day; Independence Day; Labor Day; Veterans Day; Thanksgiving Day; Christmas Day

23. MINIMUM WAGE

As part of the Fair Labor Standards Act, the federal government established a minimum wage, the least dollar amount that may be paid hourly workers in both the private and public sectors. This rate is currently $7.25 per hour, and all covered nonexempt workers in all 50 states are guaranteed this wage, and if their state minimum wage is higher than the federal, the higher rate will apply.

While the national minimum wage covers more than 130 million American workers, there are certain exempt professions and situations. Domestic workers are not covered in some situations; fishermen, employees of certain small newspapers, babysitters, and agricultural seasonal workers in small family farms are some of the common exemptions from the federal minimum wage law. Others who are exempt include those in seasonal employment, such as at amusement parks or seasonal recreation centers, and in "exempt" occupations, such as managers, salesmen, or administrators who are not paid on an hourly basis. These exempt workers are sometimes covered by state minimum wage laws, in which case the state minimum wage applies even if it is lower than the federal rate.

Subminimum wages are hourly rates below the established minimum wage that may be paid for a limited time to learners, apprentices, messengers, student workers, and those employed in occupations not ordinarily given to full-time workers. The subminimum wage permits businesses to be able to continue to hire certain types of workers in certain nontraditional, "convenience" occupations.

In the last few years there has been a great deal of activity among states to raise their minimum wage and some of the raises have been substantial. In order to alleviate the burden on employers, statutes have generally raised the minimum wage gradually over a span of several years. For example in the District of Columbia the minimum wage is presently $13.25, but will be raised each year by a certain amount until it reaches $15 by July 1, 2020. The new law also ensures that the minimum wage will continue to rise with inflation by tying it to the CPI, or the federal minimum wage plus $1, whichever is greater. Only two states have taken no action at all, in which case the federal law applies. Perhaps those states have determined the market is the best regulator of wages. That is, if the offered wage is too low, the employer will get either no applicants or those with no experience and few skills. Generally, the higher the wage, the better the applicant pool, however circumstances occur in which workers may be taken advantage of either out of desperation or ignorance. This is precisely why the minimum wage exists.

Table 23: Minimum Wage

State	Code Section	Minimum Wage Per Hour	Subminimum Wage Per Hour
ALABAMA	No statutory provisions		
ALASKA	23.10.065; 23.10.070; 23.10.071	2018: $9.84 thereafter adjusted annually for inflation; wage is never to be lower than $1 less than federal rate; public school bus drivers to be paid double minimum wage	Dept. of Labor Commissioner to set rate of statutory minimum for learners and/or apprentices; individuals whose earning capacity is impaired due to physical or mental defect, age, or injury; individuals in work therapy in residential drug or alcohol treatment programs designed to extend more than 120 days; tipped employees: employers to pay workers full state minimum wage before tips
ARIZONA	23-363	2018: $10.50; min. wage increased annually until reaching $12 by 1/1/20, thereafter increased on each January 1 based on increase in cost of living	Tipped Employees—up to $3/hr. less than minimum wage as long as weekly tips plus direct wage is at least minimum wage; 2018 tipped employees direct min. wage: $7.50
ARKANSAS	11-4-201 to11-4-219	2018: $8.50	85% min. wage for any full time student; tipped employees: if tips plus direct wage do not equal state min. wage, employer must make up difference; 2018 tipped employees direct min. wage: $2.63/hr.; director may provide by regulation for the employment in any occupation of individuals whose earning capacity is impaired by age or physical or mental deficiency or injury at wages lower than the min. wage rate; notice and public hearing required
CALIFORNIA	Labor §§ 1182; 1182.4; 1182.11; 1182.12	2018: $11 if over 25 employees; $10.50 if 25 or fewer employees, increasing annually to $15 by 1/1/23, thereafter annually based on lesser of 3.5% or rate of change in the averages of the most recent 7/1 to 6/30 period over the preceding 7/1 to 6/30 period for the US CPI-W	85% for student employee, camp counselor or program counselor; tipped employees: employers to pay workers full state min. wage before tips
COLORADO	8-6-101 to 8-6-119; Const. art. 18, § 15	2018: $10.20, increasing annually by $.90 each January 1 until reaching $12 by 1/1/20, thereafter annually for cost of living increases; Dept. of Labor director may set minimum wages for specific industries	85% of minimum wage to unemancipated minors or persons with a physical disability; tipped employees: if tips plus direct wage do not equal state min. wage, employer must make up difference; no more than $3.02/hr. in tip income may be used to offset min. wage of tip employees; 2018 tipped employees direct min. wage: $7.18

Table 23: Minimum Wage—Continued

State	Code Section	Minimum Wage Per Hour	Subminimum Wage Per Hour
CONNECTICUT	31-58; 31-60	2018: $10.10 or ½ of 1% rounded to the nearest whole cent more than the highest federal min. wage, whichever is greater	Rates for learners, beginners, and persons under 18 not less than 85% of min. wage for first 200 hrs. of employment; tipped employees: if tips plus direct wage do not equal the state min. wage, employer must make up difference; tipped employees min. wage may be offset as gratuities by 36.8% of current min. wage; 18.5% for bartenders; 2018 tipped employees direct min. wage: $6.38; $8.23 (bartenders)
DELAWARE	Tit. 19, §§ 902(a); 905; 906	2018: $8.25; $8.75 (eff. 10/1/18); $9.25 (eff. 10/1/19) or equal to the federal min. wage if greater than state min. wage	Dept. of Labor may lower min. wage rate for individuals whose earning capacity is impaired by age, physical or mental defect or injury, and for learners and apprentices after public hearing and reasonable notice; tipped employees; if tips plus direct wage do not equal state min. wage, employer must make up difference; 2018 tipped employees direct min. wage: $2.23
DISTRICT OF COLUMBIA	32-1003; 32-1004	2018: $13.25, increasing annually until reaching $15 by 7/1/20, and each July 1 thereafter in proportion to any annual average increase in the CPI or, in all cases, federal min. wage plus $1, whichever is greater	Specific rates established by wage orders for various categories of employees; tipped employees: if tips plus direct wage do not equal district min. wage, employer must make up difference; 2018 tipped employees direct min. wage: $3.89, increasing to $5 by 7/1/20, and each July 1 thereafter in proportion to any annual average increase in the CPI
FEDERAL	Fair Labor Standards Act (FLSA): 29 USC §§ 203(m); 206	2018: $7.25; applies to all employees covered by FLSA in 50 states, territories, and possessions; standard applies to employees,not specifically exempt who are: engaged in interstate commerce; engaged in production of goods for commerce; or employed in an enterprise engaged in commerce or production of goods for commerce	$4.25 for up to 90 days of training for persons under 20; tipped employees: if tips plus direct wage do not equal federal min. wage, employer must make up difference; 2018 tipped employees direct min. wage: $2.13
FLORIDA	448.110	2018: $8.25; increased annually based upon cost of living formula	Tipped employees: if tips plus direct wage do not equal state min. wage, employer must make up difference; 2018 tipped employees direct min. wage: $5.23
GEORGIA	34-4-3; 34-4-4	2018: $5.15, except if an act of Congress mandates a higher amount; certain exceptions apply.	Rate set by Commissioner
HAWAII	387-2; 387- 9	2018: $10.10	Rate set by director; tipped employees: if tips plus direct wage do not equal state min. wage, employer must make up difference; 2018 tipped employees direct min. wage: $9.35

Table 23: Minimum Wage—Continued

State	Code Section	Minimum Wage Per Hour	Subminimum Wage Per Hour
IDAHO	44-1502; 44-1505; 44-1506	2018: $7.25; amount to conform to and track with federal min. wage	$4.25 for first 90 days for workers under 20 or workers with disabilities if employer issued special certificate; rate set by Director for apprentices or learners; tipped employees: if tips plus direct wage do not equal state min. wage, employer must make up difference; 2018 tipped employees direct min. wage $3.35/hr.
ILLINOIS	820 §§ 105/4; 105/6; 105/5	2018: $8.25	70% of minimum wage for up to 6 mos. for learners; workers with disabilities if employer issued special certificate; student workers for length of time receiving course credit; minors may receive $.50 less than min. wage; tipped employees: if tips plus direct wage do not equal state min. wage, employer must make up difference; no allowance for gratuities as part of hourly wage rate may exceed 40% of applicable min. wage rate for tipped employees; 2018 tipped employees direct min. wage: $4.95
INDIANA	22-2-2-4	2018: $7.25; to increase by same amount as federal min. wage increases	$4.25 for first 90 days for workers under 20; tipped employees: if tips plus direct wage do not equal state min. wage, employer must make up difference; 2018 tipped employees direct min. wage: $2.13
IOWA	91D.1(1)	2018: $7.25; to increase by same amount as federal min. wage increases	$6.35 for first 90 calendar days of employment; tipped employees: if tips plus direct wage do not equal state min. wage, employer must make up difference; 2018 tipped employees direct min. wage: $4.35
KANSAS	44-1203; 44-1207	2018: $7.25; to increase by same amount as federal min. wage increases	80% of min. wage for learners and apprentices; 90% after 2 mos.; full min. wage after 3 mos.; 85% for handicapped and patient laborers with permit from Sec. of Human Resources; tipped employees: if weekly tips plus direct wage do not equal state min. wage, employer must make up difference; 2018 tipped employees direct min. wage: $2.13/hr.
KENTUCKY	337.275; 337.010	2018: $7.25; to increase by same amount as federal min. wage increases	Lower min. wage may be paid to learners, students, workers with disabilities as certified by Commissioner of Labor; ; tipped employees: if weekly tips plus direct wage do not equal state min. wage, employer must make up difference; 2018 tipped employees direct min. wage: $2.13/hr.
LOUISIANA	No statutory provisions	No local governmental subdivision shall establish a minimum wage rate, 23:642	

Table 23: Minimum Wage—Continued

State	Code Section	Minimum Wage Per Hour	Subminimum Wage Per Hour
MAINE	Tit. 26, §§ 664; 666	2018: $10, increasing annually until reaching $12 by 1/1/2020, and each January 1 thereafter by amount of any increase in cost of living based on CPI-W	Director may issue special certificate for lower wages for individuals with disabilities due to age; Director may issue special certificate for lower wages for individuals with disabilities due to age; tipped employees: if tips plus direct wage do not equal state min. wage, employer must make up difference; tip credit may not exceed 50% of the min. hourly wage established; 2018 tipped employees direct wage: $5
MARYLAND	Lab. & Empl. §§ 3-413; 410; 414	2018: $10.10; employers must pay employees the greater of the federal min. wage or the state min. wage	80% of min. wage for learners and apprentices; 85% of min. wage for first 6 mos. for employees under 20; director may issue special certificate for individuals with disabilities for lower wage rates; tipped employees: if weekly tips plus direct wage do not equal state min. wage, employer must make up difference; 2018 tipped employees direct min. wage: $3.63/hr.
MASSACHUSETTS	Ch. 151, §§ 1 to 22	2018: $11; rate to increase by $1 each January 1 until reaching $15 on 1/1/23; in no case shall the min. wage rate be less than $.50 higher than the effective federal min. rate	Scale of rates for specified occupations; tipped employees: if weekly tips plus direct wage do not equal state min. wage, employer must make up difference; 2018 tipped employees direct min. wage: $3.75; rate to increase by $.60 each January 1 until reaching $6.75 on 1/1/23
MICHIGAN	408.414; 408.414b; 408.414c	2018: $9.25; rate to be adjusted every January by an amount reflecting avg. annual percentage change in the CPI for most recent 5-yr. period for which data is available	$4.25 first 90 days if worker is under 20 yrs. of age; director may set a lower wage for apprentices, learners, and individuals with physical or mental disabilities who are unable to meet normal production standards; if worker is less than 18, 85% of minimum wage; tipped employees: if tips plus direct wage do not equal state min. wage, employer must make up difference; tipped employees direct wage for is 38% of the min. wage rate; 2018 tipped employees direct min. wage: $3.52
MINNESOTA	177.24; 177.28	2018: $9.65 large employers (gross revenues over $500,000); $7.87 small employers; increased annually by the lesser of 2.5% or the percentage increase in the rate of inflation	$7.87 training wage first 90 days if worker under 20; Dept. of Industry & Labor authorized to set rate for disabled workers commensurate with ability; tipped employees: no tip credit against min. wage; employer must pay full state min. wage plus any tips earned
MISSISSIPPI	No statutory provisions establishing min. wage; public employees: 17-1-51; 25-3-40	Public employees: same as min. wage established under Fair Labor Standards Act as funds are available; no local govt. authorized to establish mandatory min. living wage rate	

Table 23: Minimum Wage—Continued

State	Code Section	Minimum Wage Per Hour	Subminimum Wage Per Hour
MISSOURI	290.500 to 290.530	2018: $7.85; increased annually based upon cost of living formula	Training wage up to first 6 mos. for workers under 20: no less than $.90 below min. wage; director may set lower wage for disabled workers tipped employees: if tips plus direct wage do not equal state min. wage, employer must make up difference; direct wage half of min. wage; 2018 tipped employees direct min. wage: $3.925
MONTANA	39-3-401 to 39-3-409	2018: $8.30; min. wage greater of federal or current state min. wage and subject to cost of living adjustment based on Consumer Price Index; $4 for small employer (annual gross sales $110,000 or less)	Special provisions for certain exempt workers; tipped employees: no tip credit against min. wage; employer must pay full state min. wage plus any tips earned, small employer exception applies
NEBRASKA	48-1203; 48-1203.01	2018: $9	Training wage at least 75% of federal min. wage for first 90 days if under 20; additional 90 day period may be added under certain conditions if employee is still under 20; tipped employees: if tips plus direct wage do not equal state min. wage, employer must make up difference; 2018 tipped employees direct min. wage: $2.13
NEVADA	Const. art 15, § 16	2018: $7.25 if employer offers/makes available health benefits; $8.25 if no health benefits offered/made available; Increased annually based upon cost of living formula	Tipped employees: employer must pay full state min. wage before tips
NEW HAMPSHIRE	279:21, 279:22, 279:22(a)	$7.25; minimum wage shall be no lower than federal minimum wage	75% of statutory minimum for learners and apprentices for up to 6 mos.; commissioner may set wages for disabled employees; tipped employees: if tips plus direct wage do not equal state min. wage, employer must make up difference; direct min. wage per hour is 45% of state min. wage; 2018 tipped employees direct min. wage: $3.26
NEW JERSEY	34:11-56a4; 34:11-56a17; Const. art 1, ¶ 23	2018: $8.60; increased annually based upon cost of living formula	85% of minimum wage for certain workers, such as learners, apprentices, and disabled, with special certificate from commissioner; tipped employees: tipped employees: if weekly tips plus direct wage do not equal state min. wage, employer must make up difference; 2018 tipped employees direct min. wage: $2.13
NEW MEXICO	50-4-22(A); 50-4-23	2018: $7.50	Commissioner may issue certificates not less than 50% of min. wage for individuals mentally or physically handicapped; tipped employees: employers to pay workers same as federal tipped min. wage; 2018 tipped employees direct min. wage: $2.13

Table 23: Minimum Wage—Continued

State	Code Section	Minimum Wage Per Hour	Subminimum Wage Per Hour
NEW YORK	Lab. § 652(1)	2018: $10.40; increasing annually until reaching $12.50 on 12/31/20; higher rates for New York City, or greater if federal law is set higher	With approval of Labor Dept., disabled persons may be paid less than min. wage; tipped employees: if tips plus direct wage do not equal state min. wage, employer must make up difference; 2018 tipped employees direct wage: $2.90 (food servers); $1.75 (service employees); different rates for New York City
NORTH CAROLINA	95-25.3	2018: $7.25; to increase by same amount as federal min. wage increases	90% of the statutory minimum for learners and apprentices; commissioner may establish rate at least 85% of min. wage for those unemployed for at least 15 wks. or in seasonal, recreational or food establishments; tipped employees: if weekly tips plus direct wage do not equal state min. wage, employer must make up difference; 2018 tipped employees direct min. wage: $2.13
NORTH DAKOTA	34-06-03 to 34-06-22	2018: $7.25; Commissioner of Labor may adopt standards for min. wage rates for each occupation in the state	85% of min. wage for student learners enrolled in vocational school with cCommissioner approval; Commissioner may issue permits to individuals to earn less than min. wage set for that occupation if physically or mentally impaired, or a learner or apprentice in that occupation; tipped employees: if tips plus direct wage do not equal state min. wage, employer must make up difference; 2018 tipped employees direct min. wage: $4.86
OHIO	4111.02; 4111.06	2018: $8.30; employers who gross less than $305,000 shall pay employees no less than federal min. wage	Director of commerce may approve less than minimum for workers with physical or mental disabilities; tipped employees: if tips plus direct wage do not equal state min. wage, employer must make up difference; 2018 tipped employees direct min. wage: $4.15
OKLAHOMA	Oklahoma Minimum Wage Act: Tit. 40, §§ 197.1 to 197.17	2018: $7.25; min. wage never to be less than federal min. wage; min. wage rate for employers with fewer than 10 full-time employees and gross annual sales up to $100,000: $2; exempt employees also must be paid at least $2	Commissioner of Labor sets amount for learners apprentices, and individuals whose earning capacity is impaired by age or physical or mental deficiency or injury; in 2015, tipped employees direct min. wage $3.825/hr; *exception for employers with fewer than 10 full-time employees who have gross annual sales of $100,000 or less, $2/hr.; tipped employees: if tips plus direct wage do not equal state min. wage, employer must make up difference; 2018 tipped employees direct min. wage: $2.13
OREGON	653.025; 653.070	2018: $10.75, increasing annually until reaching $13.50 on 7/1/22, thereafter annually based on cost of living formula	75% of min. wage for student learners; tipped employees: employer must pay full state min. wage before tips

Table 23: Minimum Wage—Continued

State	Code Section	Minimum Wage Per Hour	Subminimum Wage Per Hour
PENNSYLVANIA	Tit. 43, §§ 333.104	2018: $7.25, to increase by same amount as federal min. wage increases	Learners and/or apprentices; 85% of the statutory minimum for individuals whose earning capacity is impaired by physical or mental deficiency or injury may be paid less if employer issued special certificate; tipped employees: if tips plus direct wage do not equal state min. wage, employer must make up difference; 2018 tipped employees direct min. wage $2.83
RHODE ISLAND	28-12-3 to 28-12-10	2018: $10.10, increasing to $10.50 by 1/1/19	90% of min. wage for any full time student under 19; 75% for 14 and 15 year olds working less than 24 hours in a week; individuals whose earning capacity is impaired by physical or mental disabilities may be paid less if employer issued special certificate; tipped employees: if tips plus direct wage do not equal state min. wage, employer must make up difference; 2018 tipped employees direct min. wage: $3.89
SOUTH CAROLINA	6-1-130	No local governmental subdivision shall establish a minimum wage rate greater than federal min. rate	
SOUTH DAKOTA	60-11-3 to 60-11-5	2018: $8.85, adjusted annually based on cost of living formula	Apprentices, learners, and individuals with mental or physical deficiencies may be paid less if employer issued special certificate; individuals under 20 may be paid opportunity wage; Tipped Employees – Employer may pay a direct wage of less than the state min. wage, if that amount combined with the tips received at least equals the state min. wage.; tipped employees: if tips plus direct wage do not equal state min. wage, employer must make up difference; direct min. wage for tipped employees may not be less than 50% of state min. wage; 2018 tipped employees direct min. wage $4.325
TENNESSEE	No statutory provisions		
TEXAS	Lab. §§ 62.051 to 62.057	2018: $7.25; to increase by same amount as federal min. wage increases	Min. wage rate based on productive capacity for individuals whose productive capacity is impaired, or individuals who receive services from the Dept. of Mental Health & Mental Retardation; tipped employees: if tips plus direct wage do not equal state min. wage, employer must make up difference; 2018 tipped employees direct min. wage: $2.13

Table 23: Minimum Wage—Continued

State	Code Section	Minimum Wage Per Hour	Subminimum Wage Per Hour
UTAH	34-40-103; 34-40-104; 34-23-301	2018: $7.25 to increase by same amount as federal min. wage increases	$4.25 for first 90 days for minors; commissioner sets rate for individuals whose capacity is impaired by age, physical or mental deficiencies, or injury; tipped employees: if tips plus direct wage do not equal state min. wage, employer must make up difference; 2018 tipped employees direct min. wage: $2.13
VERMONT	Tit. 21, §§ 384(a); 385	2018: $10.50 increasing annually by 5% or the CPI-U, whichever is smaller	Wage board determines rate for learners, apprentices, or handicapped persons; tipped employees: if tips plus direct wage do not equal state min. wage, employer must make up difference; rate must be at least one-half of min. wage; 2018 tipped employees direct min. wage: $5.25
VIRGINIA	40.1-28.09; 40.1-28.10	2018: $7.25; to increase by same amount as federal min. wage increases	Tipped employees: if weekly tips plus direct wage do not equal state min. wage, employer must make up difference; 2018 tipped employees direct min. wage: $2.13
WASHINGTON	49.46.020; 49.46.060	2018: $11.50, increasing to $13.50 by 1/1/2020; thereafter increased annually based upon cost of living formula	Director may issue special certificate for lower wages for learners, apprentices, messengers, and individuals whose earning capacity is impaired by age or physical or mental deficiency or injury; tipped employees: employer must pay full state min. wage before tips
WEST VIRGINIA	21-5C-2	2018: $8.75; when federal min. wage is equal to or greater than the state min. wage, state min. wage will increase by the same amount	$6.40 for first 90 days if under 20; tipped employees: if tips plus direct wage do not equal state min. wage, employer must make up difference; 2018 tipped employees direct min. wage: $2.62
WISCONSIN	104.01 to 104.12	2018: $7.25 (eff. 7/24/2009)	$5.90 "opportunity" wage for first 90 days if under 20; Dept. of Workforce Development to set rates for student learners or handicapped employees; tipped employees: if tips plus direct wage do not equal state min. wage, employer must make up difference; 2018 tipped employees direct min. wage: $2.33 ($2.13 to employees under 20 for first 90 days)
WYOMING	27-4-202	2018: $5.15	$4.25 for first 90 days if under 20; tipped employees: if tips plus direct wage do not equal state min. wage, employer must make up difference; 2018 tipped employees direct min. wage: $2.13

24. RIGHT TO WORK

As labor unions began to organize and to bargain with employers on behalf of its members, many troublesome issues started to arise. For instance, if a union negotiated a contract with a company, did the contract cover only union members or those employees who refused to join the union too? Could the union insist that the employer refuse to hire nonunion members? If a member violated some union policy, could the union insist that the employer fire the employee?

To say that the union had the power to decide who worked and who did not meant that the employer was deprived of a fundamental right in running his business. Conversely, if an employer who hired and fired whom he pleased, it meant that, potentially, the union contract could be undermined simply by hiring nonunion employees.

Over the years an intricate system of rules, regulations, and laws has evolved to manage the many thorny issues that have arisen in the context of union contracts, including the protection of the rights of nonunion employees to work for unionized employers. These "right to work" laws generally forbid both unions and employers from denying a nonunion employee a job solely on account of his union status. About twenty states are currently "right to work" states. Fewer than twenty states and the District of Columbia have no statutory provision, apparently allowing the union to bargain with the employer for the right to insist upon union membership as a condition for employment.

Table 24: Right to Work

State	Code Section	Policy	Prohibited Activity	Penalties
ALABAMA	25-7-30 to 25-7-36	The right of persons to work shall not be denied or abridged on account of membership or nonmembership in any labor union or labor organization	Any agreement/combination between employer and labor union or organization denying nonmembers right to work is prohibited; labor organizations cannot require membership, abstention, or payment of union dues	Harmed person may recover such damages sustained by reason of denial or deprivation of employment
ALASKA	No statutory provisions			
ARIZONA	23-1302 to 23-1307; Ariz. Const. art. XXV	No person shall be denied opportunity to work because of nonmembership in a union	Threatened or actual interference with person, his family, or property to force him to join union, strike against his will, or leave job; conspiracy to induce persons to refuse to work with nonmembers; agreements which exclude person from employment because of nonmembership in union	Any act/agreement in violation of article is illegal and void; damages; injunctive relief
ARKANSAS	Ark. Const. amend. 34; 11-3-301 to 11-3-304	Freedom of organized labor to bargain collectively and unorganized labor to bargain individually	Union affiliation or non-affiliation not to be condition of employment; contracts to exclude persons from employment	Persons violating chapter guilty of a misdemeanor; $100 to $5,000 fine
CALIFORNIA	No statutory provisions			
COLORADO	Labor Peace Act: 8-3-101 to 8-3-123	Labor Peace Act unique by stating policy favoring both rights of workers to be employed and unions to represent employees; Colorado not considered a right to work state		
CONNECTICUT	No statutory provisions			
DELAWARE	No statutory provisions			
DISTRICT OF COLUMBIA	No statutory provisions			
FLORIDA	Fla. Const. art. I, § 6	The right of persons to work shall not be denied or abridged by membership or nonmembership in any labor union or organization	Public employees do not have right to strike; right of employees to bargain collectively through a labor union shall not be denied or abridged	

Table 24: Right to Work—Continued

State	Code Section	Policy	Prohibited Activity	Penalties
GEORGIA	34-6-21 to 34-6-28	No person shall be required as a condition of employment to be or remain a member of a labor organization or to resign or to refrain from membership with a labor organization	Membership in or payment to labor organization as condition of employment; contracts requiring membership in or payment to labor organization as contrary to public policy; deduction from wages of fees for labor organization without individual's order or request	Injunctive relief; costs and reasonable attorney fees; actual damages; misdemeanor punished as provided in §17-10-3
HAWAII	377-1 to 377-18	Hawaii is not a right to work state; employees may be required to join union under collective bargaining agreement	Employees who belong to religious body historically conscientiously opposed to union membership not required to join or support any labor organization as condition of employment	
IDAHO	44-2001 to 44-2213	The right to work shall not be subject to undue restraint or coercion, infringed upon or restrained in any way based on membership, affiliation, or financial support of a labor organization	Freedom of choice guaranteed, discrimination prohibited; deductions from wages unless signed written authorization by employee; coercion and intimidation of employee, his family, or property	Any agreement null and void and of no legal effect; misdemeanor punishable by imprisonment up to 90 days and/or fine up to $1,000; injunctive relief; may recover any and all damages including costs & attorney fees
ILLINOIS	No statutory provisions			
INDIANA	22-6-6-1 to 22-6-6-13	None stated	A person may not require an individual to become or remain a member of a labor organization; pay dues, fees, assessments, or other charges of any kind or amount to a labor organization; or pay to a charity or third party an amount that is equivalent to or a pro rata part of dues, fees, assessments, or other charges required of members of a labor organization; as a condition of employment or continuation of employment	Knowing or intentional violation is class A misdemeanor; any agreement that violates is void

Table 24: Right to Work—Continued

State	Code Section	Policy	Prohibited Activity	Penalties
IOWA	731.1 to 731.9	No person shall be deprived of the right to work at a chosen occupation because of membership, affiliation, withdrawal/expulsion, or refusal to join any labor union	Refusal to employ because of membership in a labor organization; contracts to exclude; union dues as prerequisite to employment; deducting dues from pay unless signed written authorization from employee	Any contract contravening policy is illegal and void; guilty of a serious misdemeanor; injunction
KANSAS	44-831; Kan. Const. art. XV, § 12	There is a cause of action if there is a constitutional violation. No person shall be denied opportunity to obtain or retain employment because of membership or nonmembership in any labor organization	Agreements to exclude persons from employment or continuance of employment based on membership or nonmembership in any labor organization	Damages; attorney fees
KENTUCKY	336.130; 336.990	Employees free from restraint or coercion to negotiate terms of their employment	No employee required to join, remain member of labor union, or pay dues or other similar charges to labor organization, charity, or third party in lieu of dues	Fine $100 to $1,000 per violation by employee or labor organization; may also be guilty of class A misdemeanor; aggrieved may obtain injunctive relief plus costs and attorney fees
LOUISIANA	23:981 to 23:987	All persons shall have the right to form, join, and assist labor organizations or to refrain from such activities without fear of penalty or reprisals.	Cannot be required to become or remain member of labor organization or pay dues or fees as condition of employment; agreements between labor organization and employer	Such agreements are unlawful, null and void, and of no legal effect; misdemeanor; imprisonment up to 90 days and fine up to $1,000; injunctive relief; recover any and all damages
MAINE	No statutory provisions			
MARYLAND	No statutory provisions			
MASSACHUSETTS	Ch. 149, §§ 19 to 24J	No person shall, by intimidation or force, prevent or seek to prevent a person from entering into or continuing in the employment of any person	No person shall, himself or by his agent, coerce or compel a person into a written or oral agreement not to join or become a member of a labor organization as a condition of his securing employment or continuing the employment of such person	Legal and equitable relief

Table 24: Right to Work—Continued

State	Code Section	Policy	Prohibited Activity	Penalties
MICHIGAN	Private: 423.1 to 423.30; public: 423.209 to 423.217	Employees may organize together or form, join, or assist in labor organization or refrain from any or all of the activities identified in § 423.8(a)	A person shall not be forced, intimidated, or threatened into becoming a member of a labor organization or otherwise affiliate with or financially support a labor organization, refrain from engaging in employment, or refrain from joining or otherwise financially supporting a labor organization, pay to any charitable organization or third party an amount in lieu of, equivalent to, or any portion of dues, fees, assessments or other charges or expenses required of members of or employees represented by a labor organization	Damages and/or injunctive relief, costs, and reasonable attorney fees; civil fine $500
MINNESOTA	No statutory provisions			
MISSISSIPPI	71-1-47; 71-1-53; Miss. Const. art. VII, § 198A	The right to work shall not be denied or abridged because of membership or nonmembership in a labor union or organization	Agreement or combination between employer and labor organization to make membership condition of employment or where union or organization acquires an employment monopoly; requirement to become or remain member; requirement to abstain or refrain from membership; requirement to pay dues	Misdemeanor; $25 to $250 fine
MISSOURI	Const. art. 1, § 29; 290.590, passed by legislature and signed by governor, to be effective on approval as ballot initiative on Nov. 6, 2018	Employees have right to organize but shall not be compelled to do so	No employee required to join, remain member of labor union, or pay dues or other similar charges to labor organization, charity, or third party in lieu of dues	Class C misdemeanor; injured party entitled to actual damages, costs, and attorney fees
MONTANA	No statutory provisions			
NEBRASKA	28-106; 48-217; 48-219; Neb. Const. art. XV, § 13	No person shall be denied employment because of membership, affiliation, resignation, or expulsion in or from a labor organization or because of refusal to join or pay fees	Contracts between employer and labor organization to exclude because of membership or nonmembership	Class IV misdemeanor; $100 to $500 fine

Table 24: Right to Work—Continued

State	Code Section	Policy	Prohibited Activity	Penalties
NEVADA	613.230 to 613.300	No person shall be denied the opportunity to obtain or retain employment because of nonmembership in a labor organization	Agreements prohibiting employment because of nonmembership in labor organization; strike or picketing to force or induce employer to make agreement; compelling person to join labor organization, strike, or leave employment; conspiracy to cause discharge or denial of employment or to induce refusal of work on basis of membership	Any act in violation shall be illegal and void; liable for damages; injunctive relief
NEW HAMPSHIRE	No statutory provisions			
NEW JERSEY	No statutory provisions, but state courts have upheld closed-shop and union-shop agreements, *F. F. East Co. v. United Oysterman's Union,* 21 A.2d 799			
NEW MEXICO	No statutory provisions			
NEW YORK	No statutory provisions			
NORTH CAROLINA	95-78 to 95-84	The right to live includes the right to work. The right to work shall not be denied or abridged on account of membership or nonmembership in any labor union or organization	Agreement or combination between employer and labor organization where nonmembers are denied right to work or where membership is made condition of employment or where organization acquires employment monopoly; non-membership status as condition of employment; payment of dues as condition of employment	Any damages sustained
NORTH DAKOTA	34-01-14	The right of a person to work shall not be abridged or denied on account of membership or nonmembership in any labor union or organization	All contracts in negation or abrogation of right to work are invalid; "agency shop" dues "check off" of nonmember of union as condition of employment or continuance	Contracts declared invalid, void, and unenforceable

Table 24: Right to Work—Continued

State	Code Section	Policy	Prohibited Activity	Penalties
OHIO	4113.02 Not considered a right to work state	None stated	Any agreement between employer and employee in which either party agrees to join, quit, or remain a part of a labor organization as a condition of employment is "contrary to public policy and void."	Contract void
OKLAHOMA	51-101 to 51-113; OK Const. art. 23, § 1A	No person shall be discharged from or denied employment as a member of any paid fire department in any municipality by reason of membership or non in, or the payment or nonpayment of any dues, fees or other charges to an organization for collective bargaining	Person shall not be required as condition of employment or continuance to resign or refrain from voluntary membership, affiliation, or financial support of a labor organization; become a member; pay dues, fees, or charges; pay to any third party in lieu of payments regularly required of members to labor organization; or be recommended, approved, referred, or cleared by or through a labor organization	
OREGON	No statutory provisions			
PENNSYLVANIA	No statutory provisions			
RHODE ISLAND	No statutory provisions			
SOUTH CAROLINA	41-7-10 to 41-7-130	The denial of the right to work because of membership or nonmembership in a labor organization is against public policy	Agreements between employer and labor organization denying nonmembers right to work or requiring union membership; requirement of membership or to refrain from membership or payment of dues as condition of employment; deduction of dues from wages without authorization; contracts declared to be unlawful by §§ 41-7-20 or 41-7-30; 41-7-40	Misdemeanor; imprisoned for 10 to 30 days and/or fine $10 to $1,000 ; damages, costs, and attorney fees
SOUTH DAKOTA	22-6-2; 60-8-3 to 60-8-8; 60-10-10; S. Dak. Const. art. VI, § 2	The right of persons to work shall not be denied or abridged on account of membership or nonmembership in a labor union or organization	Any agreement relating to employment denying free exercise of right to work; any coercion to enter into such agreement; coercion of employee to join union; interference with right to work by use of force or violence	Class 2 misdemeanor; 30 days imprisonment in county jail and/or $500 fine

Table 24: Right to Work—Continued

State	Code Section	Policy	Prohibited Activity	Penalties
TENNESSEE	40-35-111; 50-1-201 to 50-1-207	It is unlawful to deny employment because of affiliation or nonaffiliation with a labor union	Contracts for exclusion from employment because of affiliation or nonaffiliation with labor union; exclusion from employment for payment or failure to pay union dues.	Class A misdemeanor; imprisoned up to 11 months and 29 days and/or fine up to $2,500
TEXAS	Lab. § 101.001 to 101.004	No person shall be denied employment on account of membership or nonmembership in a labor union	Any contract which requires membership or nonmembership; denial of right to work and bargain freely with employer, individually or collectively	Contract is void
UTAH	34-34-1 to 34-34-17	The right of persons to work shall not be denied or abridged on account of membership or nonmembership in a labor union, labor organization, or any other type of association	Agreement, understanding, or practice denying right to work based on membership in labor organization; compelling person to join or not join organization; employer cannot require union membership, abstinence from membership, or payment of dues or fees	Injunctive relief; any and all damages; injunction; misdemeanor.
VERMONT	No statutory provisions			
VIRGINIA	40.1-58 to 40.1-69	The right to work shall not be abridged or denied on account of membership or nonmembership in a labor union or organization	Agreements between labor organization to deny nonmembers right to work or where membership is made condition of employment or where union acquires monopoly; requirement of membership, nonmembership, or payment of dues as condition of employment	Damages sustained; agreements in violation are illegal and contrary to public policy; illegal conduct contrary to public policy; misdemeanor; injunctive relief
WASHINGTON	No statutory provisions			
WEST VIRGINIA	21-5G-1 to 21-5G-7	None stated	No employee required to join, remain member of labor union, or pay dues or other similar charges to labor organization, charity, or third party in lieu of dues	Misdemeanor and may be liable for fine $500 to $5,000
WISCONSIN	111.04	Employer may not require employees to join or refrain from joining, or pay dues or the equivalent to a union		

Table 24: Right to Work—Continued

State	Code Section	Policy	Prohibited Activity	Penalties
WYOMING	27-7-108 to 27-7-115	No person is required to become a member of a labor organization or abstain therefrom as a condition of employment	Requirement of membership or nonmembership or payment of dues as a condition of employment; requirement of connection with or approval from labor union	Misdemeanor; damages sustained; injunctive relief; imprisonment in county jail up to 6 mos. and/or fine up to $1,000

25. WHISTLEBLOWER STATUTES

Whistleblower statutes protect employees when they find themselves in the difficult position of discovering their employer violating a law or in some way breaching the public trust. If the employer is warned of the problem but takes no action, or asks the employee to keep the situation confidential, the employee may be personally participating in a crime and may be exposed to a certain amount of personal liability. Sometimes, the right thing to do is to report the employer to the authorities (or, "blow the whistle"), but the employee may risk losing his job or position within the company. In this situation, the employee may be torn between a legal or ethical duty and perceived loyalty to his employer. "Whistleblower" issues arise in various circumstances, such as when an employee discovers that his employer that is a government contractor is overbilling the government, or when a public or private employer is discovered cutting corners on safety matters in violation of rules and regulations under state occupational health and safety acts. Other situations may involve employer practices of job discrimination, abuse of adult or juvenile patients in a health care facility, or medical malpractice.

In these situations, if an employee exposes an unsafe, illegal or unethical practice to the authorities, the employee may be the subject of punitive or retaliatory action, such as dismissal, transfer to an undesirable job assignment, demotion, etc. Whistleblower statutes may prohibit dismissal or other retaliatory action against the employee. They may also provide for enhanced monetary awards to employees who "blow the whistle" on an unscrupulous employer.

State whistleblower statutes vary in a number of respects. Some states only provide explicit protection of public employees or those working for government contractors. Statutes also vary with respect to whom is protected or on whom the whistle may be blown. Some states extend protection to other co-workers who assist the whistleblower; some explicitly protect an employee who blows the whistle on fellow employees or another person or business entity with a business relationship with the employer.

Most states limit remedies that an employee may recover to actual damages, such as back pay or fringe benefits. In some cases, however, the employee is given a money award tied to the illegal or unethical activity exposed. In South Carolina, if the employee's report or complaint results in a savings of public funds, s/he may recover 25% of the estimated net savings in the first year after corrective action is undertaken, up to $2,000.

It should be noted that in addition to state statutes, there are a number of federal whistleblower provisions which protect employees in much the same way. In fact, one state, Illinois, has recently taken the unusual step of repealing its whistleblower statute, apparently in deference to the federal law. There is some sound logic in this; if the state and federal laws are roughly equivalent the state can save valuable administrative resources in the repeal because it is no longer under an obligation to enforce its own law. Many federal laws include much harsher penalties for employers and greater rewards for employees who risk careers and livelihoods by reporting activity that is damaging to the public trust.

Table 25: Whistleblower Statutes

State	Code Section	Prohibited Activity	Public or Private Employees?
ALABAMA	25-5-11.1; 25-8-57	Termination for filing written notice of violation of safety rule under 25-5-11 (c)(4); termination for filing action against employer to recover workers' compensation	Both
ALABAMA	36-25-24; The State Employees Protection Act: 36-26A-1 to 36-26A-7	Cannot discharge, demote, transfer, or otherwise discipline regarding compensation, terms, conditions, or privileges	Public
ALASKA	Alaska Whistleblower Act: 39.90.100 to 39.90.150	Cannot discharge, threaten, disqualify, or otherwise discriminate for actual or expected reports to public body or for participating in court action, investigation, hearing, or inquiry held by public body on matter of public concern	Public
ALASKA	18.60.088; 18.60.089; 18.60.91; 18.60.095	Cannot discharge or discriminate if employee or representative files complaint, institutes proceeding, or testifies regarding violation of safety or health standard that threatens physical harm or imminent danger	Private
ARIZONA	38-531 to 38-534	Employee who has control over personnel actions cannot take reprisal against another employee for disclosure of information to public body on violation of any law or mismanagement, waste of funds, or abuse of authority	Public
ARIZONA	23-425; 23-418; 23-418.01	Cannot discharge or discriminate if employee files complaint, institutes proceeding, or testifies regarding violation of health or safety statutes	Both
ARKANSAS	16-123-107, 16-123-108	Cannot discriminate if employee in good faith opposed act or practice made unlawful or testified or participated in proceeding regarding violation of Arkansas Civil Rights Act	Both
CALIFORNIA	Labor §§ 1102.5 to 1105	Cannot prevent or retaliate against employee for disclosing information to government, law enforcement agency, person with authority over the employee or authority to investigate or correct violation, or for testifying before public body conducting investigation, hearing, or inquiry if employee has reasonable cause to believe violation exists	Both

Opportunity for Employer to Correct?	Remedies	Penalties
Yes; employer may not retaliate against employee or individual who tries to remedy violations of child labor chapter	Cannot discharge, discipline, threaten, harass, blacklist, or in any other manner discriminate if employee disclosed information, refused to obey illegal order, or revealed any violation of statute	
	Civil action within 2 yrs. of violation: court can award back pay, front pay, and compensatory damages	
	Civil action for punitive damages as well as other appropriately found relief: municipality not liable if it adopts ordinance that provides similar protections	Civil penalty: fine up to $10,000
Yes	May file complaint with commissioner of health and safety within 30 days of violation to get reinstatement, back pay, and other appropriate relief	Willful violation: fine up to $70,000; serious violation: fine up to $7,000; citation: fine up to $7,000
	Civil action: may recover attorney fees, costs, back pay, general and special damages, and full reinstatement or injunctive relief; may make complaint to appropriate independent personnel board, school district governing board, or community college governing board of discharged for disclosing; excludes state university or boards of regents which have rule or provision for protecting employees at time personnel action is taken; employee can appeal final administrative decision or get trial de novo in superior court	Civil penalty: fine up to $5,000
	May file a complaint with commissioner within 30 days of violation for reinstatement, back pay, and other appropriate relief	Willful or repeated violation: fine $5,000 to $70,000 for each violation; additional $25,000 fine against employer assessed penalty under 23-418 for each employee who suffers permanent injury or death
	File civil action within 1 yr. of violation to enjoin further violations, recover compensatory and punitive damages and court and attorney fees	
	Can recover damages for injury suffered; possibility of temporary injunctive relief	Misdemeanor--individual: imprisonment in county jail up to 1 yr. and/or fine up to $1,000; corporate: fine up to $5,000; if employer is corporation or limited liability company: civil penalty of fine up to $10,000 per violation of § 1102.5

Table 25: Whistleblower Statutes—Continued

State	Code Section	Prohibited Activity	Public or Private Employees?
COLORADO	24-50.5-101 to 24-50.5-107	Cannot initiate or administer any disciplinary action if employee disclosed information on actions of state agencies that are not in the public interest, unless employee knows information is false or discloses with disregard for truth, or disclosed information on records closed to public inspection or discloses information which is confidential under any other law	Public
COLORADO	24-114-101 to 24-114-103	Cannot initiate or administer any disciplinary action if employee discloses information unless employee knows information is false, or information confidential under laws	Private
CONNECTICUT	4-61dd; 31-51m	Cannot discharge, discipline, or otherwise penalize because employee or representative reports violation or suspected violation or is requested by public body to participate in an investigation, hearing, or inquiry, or if public employee reports to public body concerning unethical practices, mismanagement, or abuse of authority, unless employee knows such report is false	Both
DELAWARE	Delaware Whistleblowers' Protection Act: Tit. 19, § 1701 to 1708	Cannot discharge, threaten, or otherwise discriminate against employee for actual or expected report to public body unless employee knows that report is false, or for participating in investigation, hearing, or inquiry held by public body, or for refusing to commit or assist in commission of violation, or for reporting to supervisor	Both
DELAWARE	Tit. 29, § 5115	Cannot discharge, threaten, or otherwise discriminate because employee reported violation or suspected violation of law or regulation to an elected official a unless employee knows report is false	Public
DISTRICT OF COLUMBIA	1-615.51 to 1-615.59	Cannot discharge, suspend, demote, or take other retaliatory action if employee in good faith discloses information of gross mismanagement, gross misuse or waste of funds, abuse of authority, or violates a law, rule, or regulation	Public

Opportunity for Employer to Correct?	Remedies	Penalties
Employee must make good faith effort to provide supervisor or appointing authority or member of general assembly with information to be disclosed prior to disclosing	Employee in state personnel system: may file written complaint with state personnel board within 10 days to get reinstatement, back pay, restore lost service credit, records expunged, and any other additional relief as found appropriate by the board; if no complaint filed or complaint was denied: employee can bring civil suit to recover damages, court costs, and other relief	
Employee must make good faith effort to provide supervisor or appointing authority or member of general assembly with information to be disclosed prior to disclosing	Can bring civil action; court can give damages, court costs and other appropriate relief	
	Employee may bring civil action within 90 days of final administrative decision or violation for reinstatement, back pay, reinstatement of benefits, court and attorney fees; public employees: transmit facts and information to auditors of public accounts; file claim within 30 days of incident with employee review board or in accordance with collective bargaining contract	
Burden of proof on employee to show that primary basis for discharge, threats, or discrimination alleged to be in violation was that employee undertook act protected under § 1703		
	Civil action: file within 90 days of alleged violation for injunctive relief and/or actual damages	
	File civil action for injunction, reinstatement to same position, full fringe benefits, and seniority rights, back pay and interest on back pay, compensatory damages, reasonable attorney fees and court costs within 3 yrs. after violation or 1 yr. after employee first becomes aware of it; if disclosure assists in securing right to recover, actual recovery, or prevention of loss of more than $100,000 in public funds, the Mayor may pay reward between $5,000 and $50,000 to the disclosure	

Table 25: Whistleblower Statutes—Continued

State	Code Section	Prohibited Activity	Public or Private Employees?
FLORIDA	112.3187	Cannot dismiss, discipline, or take other adverse personnel action against employee for disclosing information of any violation or suspected violation of law or regulation or act by independent contractor which creates substantial and specific danger to the public's health, safety, and welfare or act of gross management malfeasance, gross public waste of funds or gross neglect of duty unless information is known by employee to be false	Both
GEORGIA	45-1-4	Cannot enforce any policy preventing disclosure of violation, retaliate against employee for making complaint or disclosing information, unless information was disclosed with knowledge that it was false or with willful disregard for its truth or falsity	Public
HAWAII	Whistleblowers' Protection Act: 378-61 to 378-70	Cannot discharge, threaten, or otherwise discriminate because employee or representative reports or is about to report to public body a violation or suspected violation of law or rule or is requested by public body to participate in a hearing, investigation, inquiry, or court action, unless employee knows report is false	Both
IDAHO	Idaho Protection of Public Employees Act: 6-2101 to 6-2109	Cannot take adverse action against employee for communicating in good faith the existence of any waste of public funds, property or manpower or violation or suspected violation, including participating in an investigation, hearing, court proceeding, inquiry or other form of administrative review, or where employee refused or objected to directive employee reasonably believed was violation; employer cannot implement rules or policies that unreasonably restrict employee's ability to document a violation	Public
ILLINOIS	20 § 415/19c.1	Cannot discipline for disclosing information that person reasonably believes shows a violation of any rule or law or mismanagement, waste of funds, abuse of authority, or specific and substantial danger to public health or safety	Public
ILLINOIS	Whistleblower Act: 740 §§ 174/10 to 174/40	Cannot retaliate against employee for disclosing information to government or law enforcement agency or as part of a court, hearing or other proceeding if the employee has reasonable cause to believe that the information discloses a violation; employer may not make, adopt, or enforce any rule, regulation, or policy preventing such disclosure.	Both

Opportunity for Employer to Correct?	Remedies	Penalties
It is an affirmative defense that adverse action was based on grounds other than, and would have been taken absent, employee's exercise of rights protected by § 112.3187	State employee: file complaint alleging prohibited personnel action with appropriate authority within 60 days after action; upon termination of investigation, employee may pursue available administrative remedy or bring civil action within 180 days after receipt notice of termination; local public employee: file complaint with appropriate local government authority within 60 days after violation; may bring civil action within 180 days after final decision of local authority, or 180 days after violation if no administrative procedure local government authority exists by ordinance or contract; any other person: file civil action after exhausting administrative remedies,, within 180 days after violation; all actions for reinstatement, back and full benefits, lost wages, reasonable costs, injunction	
	File civil action in superior court within earlier of 1 yr. of discovering retaliation or 3 yrs. after retaliation for an injunction, reinstatement of same or equivalent position, full fringe benefits and seniority rights, lost wages and benefits, any other allowable compensatory damages, reasonable attorney fees, court costs, and expenses	
	File civil action within 2 yrs. after violation; remedies include: reinstatement, back pay, full reinstatement of benefits and seniority rights, actual damages and any other appropriate relief, court costs and attorney fees	Civil penalty: $500 to $5,000 fine per violation
	File civil action within 180 days of violation for injunction and/or actual damages, including injunction, reinstatement, full fringe benefits and seniority rights, lost wages/benefits, reasonable court costs and attorney fees	Civil penalty fine: up to $500
		Class B misdemeanor
	Civil action for reinstatement with same seniority status, back pay with interest, and compensation for any damages, including litigation costs, expert witness fees and reasonable attorney fees	Civil penalty: class A misdemeanor

Table 25: Whistleblower Statutes—Continued

State	Code Section	Prohibited Activity	Public or Private Employees?
INDIANA	4-15-10-4; 36-1-8-8 (public); 22-5-3-3 (private)	Cannot dismiss, withhold salary increases or employment-related benefits, transfer or reassign, deny promotion or demote if employee reports violation of federal law or regulation, state law or rule, violates ordinance of a political subdivision or misuse of public funds	Both
IOWA	70A.28; 70A.29	Cannot discharge, deny appointment or promotion if employee discloses information s/he reasonably believe evidences a violation of law or rule, mismanagement, gross abuse of funds, abuse of authority, or substantial and specific danger to public health or safety, unless disclosure prohibited by statute	Public
KANSAS	Kansas Whistleblower Act: 75-2973	Supervisor or appointing authority of state agency cannot prohibit employee from discussing agency's operation or any other matters of public concern with any member of the legislature or auditing agency, reporting violation of state or federal law, rules or regulations, or require employee to give notice to the supervisor or appointing authority prior to making any such report	Public
KENTUCKY	61.101 to 61.103	Cannot retaliate or threaten to use authority or influence in any manner against employee who in good faith reports an actual or suspected violation, mismanagement, fraud, waste, abuse of authority or substantial and specific danger to public health or safety	Public
KENTUCKY	338.121; 338.991	Cannot discharge or discriminate if employee or representative files complaint, institutes proceeding or testifies regarding violation of any occupational safety or health statute that threatens physical harm and imminent danger	Both
LOUISIANA	23:967	Cannot make reprisal against employee who, after advising employer of the violation, in good faith discloses or threatens to disclose a workplace act or practice that violates state law, provides information, testifies, or objects to or refuses to participate in an employment act or practice in violation of law	Both
LOUISIANA	30:2027	Cannot retaliate against an employee who discloses or threatens to disclose a violation of environmental law, rule, or regulation or provides information to or testifies before an investigation hearing	Both
LOUISIANA	42:1169	Cannot discipline or make reprisal against an employee who reports a violation or act of impropriety within a government entity or related to scope and/or duties of public employment or public office within state government	Public

Opportunity for Employer to Correct?	Remedies	Penalties
	Report to supervisor or appointing authority or state ethics commission if supervisor or appointing authority involved with violation; if no good faith effort made by reportee, submit a written report to any concerned person, agency, or organization; can also seek legal remedy	Class A infraction or misdemeanor
	If employer is not head of a state department/agency or serving in supervisory capacity within the executive branch of state government, employee can enforce through civil action, and employer is liable for affirmative relief, including reinstatement, back pay, or any other equitable relief including attorney fees and costs	Simple misdemeanor
	Permanent classified employee: appeal to state civil service board, any court of law, or administrative hearing within 90 days of alleged disciplinary action; unclassified employee: file civil action for injunction and/or actual damage within 90 days of alleged violation; employee may recover court costs including reasonable attorney and witness fees	Violator may be suspended on leave without pay up to 30 days; if willful or repeated violation, may require resignation or disqualification for appointment to or employment as state officer or employee for up to 2 yrs.
	File civil action within 90 days after violation for appropriate injunctive relief and/or punitive damages	
	File complaint with commissioner after reasonable time after violation occurred for reinstatement, back pay, and other appropriate relief	Civil penalty: fine up to $10,000 per violation; if willful or repeated violation: $5,000 to $70,000 fine per violation
Employee must advise employer of violation of law	Civil action to recover damages, attorney fees, and court costs	
	Civil action for triple damages, court costs, attorney fees and all other civil and criminal remedies	
	If employee is suspended, demoted, or dismissed, then report to board of ethics for elected officials or commission on ethics for public employees; remedies: reinstatement, back pay and benefits	

Table 25: Whistleblower Statutes—Continued

State	Code Section	Prohibited Activity	Public or Private Employees?
MAINE	Whistleblowers' Protection Act: Tit. 26, § 831 to 840	Cannot discharge, threaten, or otherwise discriminate if employee reports a violation of a law or rule of the state, political subdivision or US, a condition or practice that would put at risk the health or safety of that employee or is requested to participate in an investigation, hearing, or inquiry or refuses to carry out a directive that violates the act, or deviates from applicable patient standard of care	Both
MARYLAND	State Fin. & Proc. §§ 11-301 to 11-306	May not take or refuse to take any personnel action as reprisal against employee because employer discloses abuse of authority, gross mismanagement or waste of money, violation and specific danger to public health or violation of law or objects, or refuses to participate in violation of law	State Contractor Employees' Whistleblower Protection
MARYLAND	State Pers. & Pens. §§ 5-301 to 5-314	Cannot take or refuse to take any personnel action as reprisal if applicant or employee discloses abuse of authority, gross mismanagement or waste of money, violation of law or substantial and specific danger to public health or safety and seeks a remedy	Public
MASSACHUSETTS	Ch. 149, § 185	Cannot discharge, suspend, demote, or take other retaliatory action if employee discloses or threatens to disclose violation, provides information or testifies, or objects or refuses to participate in violation of law, rule or risk to public health, safety, or environment	Public
MICHIGAN	Whistleblowers' Protection Act: 15.361 to 15.369	Cannot discharge, threaten, or otherwise discriminate if employee or representative of employee reports or is about to report violation of law, regulation, or rule or because employee testifies in hearing or a court action unless employee knows disclosure is false	Both

Opportunity for Employer to Correct?	Remedies	Penalties
Employee must first report violation to a supervisor and give employer a reasonable opportunity to correct unless employee has specific reason to believe that reports to employer won't result in correction	Arbitration before Maine Human Rights Commission	Violator liable for civil fine of $10 day of willful violation which shall not be suspended
	File civil action within 1 yr. or alleged violation; available remedies: injunction; reinstatement; removal of any adverse personnel record; reinstatement of full fringe benefits and seniority rights; compensation for lost wages, benefits, and other remuneration; damages, costs and reasonable attorney fees	
	Can submit a complaint to the secretary within 6 mos. of first knowledge of violation; if violation found, secretary can remove detrimental information from complainant's personnel record, reinstatement, promotion or end of suspension, back pay, leave or seniority and attorney's and court fees	
Employee must bring violation to attention of supervisor and afford supervisor the opportunity to correct unless employee is certain supervisor knew of violation and situation is an emergency, employee reasonably fears physical harm resulting from disclosure, or disclosure is evidence of a crime	File civil action within 2 yrs. of incident; court can give all civil law tort remedies including temporary restraining order, preliminary/ permanent injunction, reinstatement, reinstate full benefits and seniority rights, three times back pay and benefits, court and attorney fees	
	File civil action within 90 days if violation for injunction and/or actual damages, including attorney fees. Court may award: reinstatement, back pay, reinstate benefits and seniority rights, and court costs	Civil fine up to $500

Table 25: Whistleblower Statutes—Continued

State	Code Section	Prohibited Activity	Public or Private Employees?
MINNESOTA	181.931 to 181.937	Cannot discharge or otherwise make reprisals against employee because employee in good faith reports a violation or is requested to participate in an investigation, hearing, or inquiry; refuses to perform an action that employee has reason to believe is in violation and employee informs employer that refusal is for that reason; employee in good faith reports a situation in which quality of health care services violates legal or ethical standard and potentially places public at risk of harm; public employee communicates findings of scientific or technical study that employee in good faith believes to be truthful and accurate, including reports to governmental body or law enforcement official; employee in classified service of state government communicates information employee believes to be truthful and accurate to a legislator, legislative auditor or constitutional officer, unless employee knows disclosure is false, made in reckless disregard of the truth or disclosed information is confidential under common law	Both
MISSISSIPPI	25-9-171 to 25-9-177	Cannot dismiss or otherwise adversely affect compensation or employment status if employee testifies or provides information to investigative body	Public
MISSOURI	287.780	Shall not discharge or discriminate against employee for exercising right to file workers' compensation	Both
MISSOURI	105.055	Cannot prohibit a public employee from or take any disciplinary action against a public employee for the disclosure of any alleged prohibited activity under investigation, or for the disclosure of information which the employee reasonably believes evidences a violation of any law, rule or regulation; or mismanagement, a gross waste of funds or abuse of authority, violation of policy, waste of public resources, alteration of technical findings or communication of scientific opinion, breaches of professional ethical canons, or a substantial and specific danger to public health or safety, if the disclosure is not specifically prohibited by law	Public
MONTANA	39-2-901 to 39-2-915	Cannot discharge or otherwise terminate employee in retaliation if employee refuses to violate constitutional provision, statute or administrative rule regarding public health, safety, or welfare or reports a violation of the same	Both

Opportunity for Employer to Correct?	Remedies	Penalties
	Civil action to recover all damages, costs, and attorney fees as well as injunctive relief	Civil penalty: $25 per day per injured employee up to $750 per injured employee
May not recover damage or other remedies unless prohibited action is direct result of providing information to state legislative body	Civil action for back pay and reinstatement, injunctive relief, compensatory damages, court costs and attorney fees	Each member of any agency's governing board or authority or executive director may be individually liable for civil fine up to $10,000 per violation
	Civil action for damages	
No prior notice required	Administrative appeal, if disciplinary action taken, with administrative hearing commission within 30 days of action; commission can modify and/or reverse disciplinary action and order appropriate relief; file civil action for damages within 1 yr. of alleged violation; court may award actual damages and attorneys fees	State personnel advisory board can recommend that violator be suspended without pay for maximum 30 days; if willful or repeated violation, recommend forfeiture and disqualification of appointment or state employment for a maximum of 2 yrs.
	Must first exhaust internal procedures for appealing discharge; after 90 days or exhaustion, whichever comes first, can file action for up to 4 yrs. back pay and fringe benefits, less interim earnings; punitive damages if employer engaged in fraud or malice in discharging	

Table 25: Whistleblower Statutes—Continued

State	Code Section	Prohibited Activity	Public or Private Employees?
NEBRASKA	81-2701 to 81-2711	Person with authority to take personnel action cannot dismiss, or take other personnel action if employee discloses information or testifies before public counsel or other officials	Public
NEBRASKA	48-1114	Cannot discriminate against any individual because he or she opposed any practice made an unlawful employment practice by the Nebraska Fair Employment Practice Act, federal or state law, or testified, assisted, or participated in any manner in an investigation, proceeding, or hearing	Public
NEVADA	281.611 to 281.671	Cannot directly or indirectly intimidate, threaten, coerce, command, or influence another state officer or employee or prevent disclosure of violation of state law or regulation, abuse of authority, substantial and specific danger to public health or safety or gross waste of public money	Public
NEVADA	618.445	Cannot discharge or discriminate if employee files complaint, institutes , proceeding, or testifies regarding violation of health and safety statutes	Both
NEW HAMPSHIRE	98-E:1 to 98-E:4	Cannot interfere in any way with employee's right to publicly discuss and give opinions as an individual on all matters concerning the state and its policies, unless disclosure threatens need of employer to protect legitimate confidential and privileged records or communication	Public
NEW HAMPSHIRE	Whistleblowers' Protection Act: 275-E:1 to 275-E:9	Cannot discharge, threaten, or otherwise discriminate if employee reports violation of any state, federal or political subdivision law or rule, or testifies as to violation or refuses to execute directive which would result in violation	Both
NEW JERSEY	34:19-1 to 34:19-14	Cannot discharge or take other retaliatory action if employee discloses or threatens to disclose activity, policy, or practice, testify, object to or refuse to participate if action violates law, rule is fraudulent or criminal or incompatible with clear mandate concerning public health, safety, welfare, or protection of the environment	Both
NEW MEXICO	10-16C-1 to 10-16c-6	Cannot take retaliatory action because public employee communicates to employer or third party unlawful or improper act, provides information to or testifies before a public body as part of an investigation hearing or inquiry or objects to or refuses to participate in an activity, policy, or practice that constitutes an unlawful or improper act	Public
NEW MEXICO	50-9-25	Cannot discharge or discriminate if employee files complaint, testifies, exercises a right or institutes a proceeding related to the New Mexico Occupational Health and Safety Act	Both

Opportunity for Employer to Correct?	Remedies	Penalties
	If incident occurs or is about to occur, employee contacts public counsel who sends finding to personnel appeals board or director/chief operations officer of agency, who, after a hearing, can stay or reverse personnel action, grant back pay or other appropriate relief and reasonable attorney fees, or employee can maintain an action under Administrative Procedures Act for damages, reinstatement, back pay or other relief including attorney fees	
		Class III misdemeanor
	File written appeal with dept. of personnel within 2 years of disclosing; hearing officer can order person to desist and refrain from such action	
	File complaint within 30 days of violation, after first notifying employer and division, for a reinstatement, back pay and lost work benefits	
	May seek injunctive relief and/or maintain a civil action to recover damages; court may award damages, costs, and reasonable attorney fees	Guilty of violation if willfully and knowingly violating any provision
Must first bring allegation to supervisor and allow for a reasonable opportunity to correct unless employee has specific reason to believe notice would not result in prompt remedy of violation	Reasonable effort to remedy incident though in-house grievance procedure, employee can get hearing with labor commissioner or designee who can reinstate, order back pay, fringe benefits, and seniority rights as well as injunctive relief	Failure to comply with rules is a violation for each day of noncompliance
Must bring violation to attention of a supervisor and afford a reasonable opportunity to correct, unless violation is known to supervisor or employee reasonably fears physical harm as a result of disclosure and situation is an emergency in nature	File civil action within 1 yr. of incident for injunction, reinstatement, reinstate full benefits and seniority rights, back pay and benefits, reasonable court and attorney fees, punitive damages	Civil fine up to $10,000 for 1st violation; up to $20,000 for each subsequent violation
	Actual damages; reinstatement with same seniority status; 2 times amount of back pay with interest; compensation for special damages, litigation cost, and reasonable attorney fees; civil action must be filed with 2 yrs. from the date on which retaliatory action occurred	
	File complaint within 30 days of incident for reinstatement or rehiring with back pay	

Table 25: Whistleblower Statutes—Continued

State	Code Section	Prohibited Activity	Public or Private Employees?
NEW YORK	Civ. Serv. § 75-b	Shall not dismiss or take other disciplinary action against public employee because employee discloses to a governmental body information regarding violation of law, rule, or regulation and violation presents substantial or specific danger to public health or safety, or which employee believes constitutes an improper governmental action	Public
NEW YORK	Labor § 740	Cannot discharge, suspend, demote or take other adverse employment action if employee discloses or threatens to disclose, provides information or testifies, or objects to or refuses to participate in an action that violates law, rule, or regulation or presents a substantial and specific danger to public health or safety	Both
NORTH CAROLINA	126-84 to 126-88	Cannot discharge, threaten or otherwise discriminate if employee or representative reports or is about to report violation of state or federal law, rule or regulation, fraud, misappropriation of state resources or substantial and specific danger to public health and safety	Public
NORTH CAROLINA	95-240 to 95-245	Cannot discriminate or take other retaliatory action if employee in good faith files claim, initiates action, testifies, or provides information on worker's compensation, OSHA, and wages or hours	Both
NORTH DAKOTA	34-11.1-04; 34-11.1-07; 34-11.1-08	Cannot dismiss or otherwise discriminate if employee reports in writing a violation of federal or state laws, agency rules or misuse of public resources	Public
OHIO	124.341	Cannot take any disciplinary action against public employee for reporting violation of law or misuse of public resources	Public
OHIO	4113.52	Cannot take any disciplinary or retaliatory action; if employee reports violation of state or federal statute, ordinance, or regulation of a political subdivision	Both
OKLAHOMA	Tit. 74, § 840-2.5	Public employee cannot prohibit or take disciplinary action if employee discloses public information, reports violation of law, rule, or policy, mismanagement, gross waste of public funds, abuse of authority, or substantial and specific danger to public health and safety	Public

Opportunity for Employer to Correct?	Remedies	Penalties
Must first provide appointing authority or designee the information to be disclosed and provide reasonable time to take appropriate action unless imminent or serious danger to public health or safety	Reinstate with back pay; dismiss disciplinary action	
Must first report violation to supervisor and allow reasonable opportunity to correct	File civil action within 1 yr. of incident for injunction, reinstatement, full fringe benefits and seniority rights, back pay, and reasonable attorney fees and court costs	
	File within 1 yr. of incident for damages, injunction or other appropriate relief; remedies include reinstatement, back pay, full fringe benefits and seniority rights, costs, and reasonable attorney fees; if court finds willful violation, 3 times actual damages plus costs and reasonable attorney fees	
If after investigation there is reasonable cause to believe allegation is true, Commissioner shall attempt to eliminate alleged violation by informal methods before civil action is filed	File complaint with Commission of Labor within 180 days of incident; if not resolved or Commissioner does not file action on behalf of employee, employee may request right to sue letter and file civil action within 90 days of its issuance for injunction, reinstatement, full fringe benefits and seniority rights, back pay and benefits and reasonable attorney fees; if court finds willful violation, 3 times damages	
	All available legal remedies	Violation is a class B misdemeanor
	File appeal with state personnel board of review within 30 days after notice of action	
Must notify and file a report; employer has 24 hours to correct	Can file a civil action for injunction, reinstatement, back pay, full fringe benefits and seniority rights, court and attorney fees. If employer deliberately violates statute, court can award interest on back pay	
	File appeal with Oklahoma Merit Protection Commission within 60 days of disciplinary action for corrective action	Suspension without pay, demotion, discharge, or 6 mo. probation; if knowing or willful violation, violator's position and hold person ineligible for appointment or employment for 1-5 yrs.

Table 25: Whistleblower Statutes—Continued

State	Code Section	Prohibited Activity	Public or Private Employees?
OKLAHOMA	Tit. 40, § 401 to 424	Cannot discharge, discriminate, or take adverse personnel action if employee files a complaint, institutes a proceeding, or testifies regarding a violation of Occupational Safety and Health Act which causes or is likely to cause death or serious physical harm	Public
OREGON	659A.199	Cannot discharge or otherwise retaliate against employee for reporting information that employee believes is in violation of state or federal law, rule, or regulation	Private
OREGON	Whistleblower Law: 659A.200 to 659A.224	Public employer cannot discriminate, dismiss, or take other disciplinary action if employee responds to official request to disclose or threatens to disclose violation of federal or state law, rule or regulation, mismanagement, gross waste of funds, abuse of authority, or substantial and specific danger to public health and safety or the fact that a recipient of state funds is subject to a felony or misdemeanor or warrant for arrest	Public
OREGON	654.062	Cannot bar, discharge, or otherwise discriminate if employee or prospective employee or representative opposes, makes a complaint, institutes a proceeding or testifies about a violation of law, regulation or standard pertaining to safety and health	Both
PENNSYLVANIA	Whistleblower Law: Tit. 43 §§ 1421 to 1428	Cannot discharge, threaten, or otherwise retaliate or discriminate if employee responds to official request or in good faith reports wrongdoing or waste by public body or other employer	Both
RHODE ISLAND	RI Whistleblowers' Protection Act: 28-50-1 to 28-50-9	Cannot discharge, threaten, or otherwise discriminate if employee or representative reports to a public body a violation of law, regulation or rule or because employee responds to an official request	Both
SOUTH CAROLINA	8-27-10 to 8-27-60	Cannot dismiss, suspend, demote, or decrease compensation if employee files a report for violation of law, substantial abuse, misuse, or loss of substantial public funds or resources	Public
SOUTH CAROLINA	41-15-510; 41-15-520	Cannot discharge or discriminate if employee files complaint, institutes a proceeding or testifies regarding statutes, rules, or regulations regarding occupational safety and health	Both
SOUTH DAKOTA	20-13-26	Cannot retaliate against an employee for filing a charge, testifying, or assisting in the enforcement of the Human Rights Act	Both

Opportunity for Employer to Correct?	Remedies	Penalties
Yes	File complaint with commissioner	Misdemeanor
	Common law remedies; reinstate and back pay	
	Right to appeal to Employment Relations Board within 30 days of action for reinstatement and back pay	Class A misdemeanor
	File complaint with commissioner of the Bureau of Labor & Industries within 30 days of violation for reinstatement and back pay as well as other appropriate relief; may also file civil action	
	File a civil action for injunction and/or damages within 180 days after disciplinary action; court may award reinstatement, back pay, full fringe benefits and seniority rights, actual damages and reasonable attorney fees	Fine up to $10,000; if violation was with intent to discourage disclosure of criminal activity, court may order person's suspension from public service for up to 7 years, unless person holds an elected public office
	File civil action within 3 yrs. of violation for injunction and/or actual damages including reinstatement, back pay, full fringe benefits and seniority rights, and attorney fees	
	If employee report results in saving of public funds, employee will be rewarded 25% of estimated net savings from 1st year implementation or up to $2,000; employee must pursue all available grievance or other administrative remedies before filing nonjury civil action for reinstatement, back pay, actual damages up to maximum $15,000, reasonable attorney fees up to $10,000 for trial and $5,000 for appeal	
	File complaint with commission of labor within 30 days of violation for reinstatement, back pay and other appropriate relief	

Table 25: Whistleblower Statutes—Continued

State	Code Section	Prohibited Activity	Public or Private Employees?
SOUTH DAKOTA	60-11-17.1 to 60-11-20; 60-12-21	Cannot discharge, discriminate, or engage in any economic or other reprisal if employee reports violation of wage rules or makes any other complaint or testimony; can not threaten to terminate or take other retaliatory action if employee reports or is about to report sex discrimination in wages	Private
TENNESSEE	8-50-116	Shall not discharge, demote, suspend, reassign, transfer, discipline, threaten, or discriminate against a state employee because employee reports violation of federal law, rule, or regulation; fraud; misappropriation of resource; danger to the health or safety of public or employees; gross mismanagement; gross waste; gross abuse of authority	Public
TENNESSEE	50-1-304	Cannot discharge or terminate if employee refuses to participate in or refuses to remain silent about violation of criminal or civil code, US laws, or neglect to protect public health, safety or welfare	Public
TENNESSEE	50-3-106; 50-3-409	Cannot discharge or discriminate if employee files a complaint, institutes a proceeding, or testifies regarding a violation of any statute or regarding occupational safety and health	Both
TEXAS	Lab. § 21.055	Cannot retaliate or discriminate against a person who opposes a discriminatory practice, makes or files a charge, files a complaint, or testifies or participates in any manner	Both
TEXAS	Gov't §§ 554.001 to 554.010	Cannot suspend, terminate, or take other adverse personnel action if employee reports a violation of law by employer or other employee	Public
UTAH	UT Protection of Public Employees Act: 67-21-1 to 67-21-10	Cannot take adverse action because employee communicates violation of law or rule, waste or misuse of public funds, property, or manpower, or gross management, abuse of authority, or unethical conduct as it relates to a state government job	Public
VERMONT	Tit. 3, §§ 973 to 978	Cannot engage in retaliatory action against state employee because employee: refuses to comply with an illegal order or reports to public body that government violated the law or engaged in waste, fraud, abuse of authority; threat to health of employees, public, or persons under care of the state; assists or participates in proceeding	Public
VERMONT	Tit. 21, § 231	Cannot discharge or discriminate if employee files complaint, institutes proceeding or testifies regarding violation of occupational, health and safety code	Both

Opportunity for Employer to Correct?	Remedies	Penalties
	Department of Labor and Regulation shall upon request of employee take an assignment in trust for wages or any claim for liquidated damages and may bring any legal action necessary to collect the claim	
	File complaint within 1 yr. of occurrence for actual damages, injunctive relief, or other remedies; if willful violation, court may award up to 3 times actual damages plus costs and attorney fees	
	May sue employer for retaliatory discharge, damages, and reasonable attorney fees and costs	
	File complaint with Commission of Labor within 30 days of violation for reinstatement, back pay, and other appropriate relief	
	Must report to appropriate law enforcement authority, then exhaust grievance or appeal process before suing no later than 90th day after violation, for injunction, actual damages, court costs and reasonable attorney fees; remedies may also include reinstatement, back pay, full fringe benefits, seniority rights, and set maximum on compensatory damages	Supervisor taking adverse personnel action may be fined up to $15,000
	File civil action within 180 days of violation for injunction or actual damages and court and attorney fees; court may award reinstatement, back pay, full fringe benefits and seniority rights	Violator subject to civil fine up to $500
Confidential information not protected	Reinstatement to same position, seniority, and work location; back pay, lost wages, benefits, and other remuneration; compensatory damages; interest on back pay; injunctive relief and reasonable cost and attorney fees; if violation willful, intentional, and egregious violation, an amount up to the amount of back pay in addition to actual back pay	
	File a complaint with commission within 30 days of violation for reinstatement with back pay as well as other relief	

Table 25: Whistleblower Statutes—Continued

State	Code Section	Prohibited Activity	Public or Private Employees?
VIRGINIA	40.1-51.2:1; 51.2:2	Cannot discharge or discriminate if employee files, testifies, or otherwise acts to exercise rights under safety and health statute	Private
WASHINGTON	42.40.010 to 42.41.902 ; 49.60.210; 49.60.230; 49.60.250(6)	Cannot discharge or otherwise retaliate against employee for disclosing information of improper government action, identifying rules warranting review, or providing information unless disclosing is prohibited by law, or opposing discriminatory practice	Both
WEST VIRGINIA	Whistleblower Law: 6C-1-1 to 6C-1-8	Cannot discharge, threaten, or otherwise discriminate or retaliate if employee or representative reports or testifies as to a violation of law, regulation, or of code of conduct or ethics designed to protect public from employer waste	Public
WEST VIRGINIA	21-3A-13	Cannot discharge or discriminate if employee files complaint, institutes proceeding, or testifies regarding violation of the occupational safety and health act	Public
WISCONSIN	230.80 to 230.89	Cannot initiate, administer, or threaten to take retaliatory action if employee discloses violation of state or federal law, rule, or regulation, mismanagement or abuse of authority, substantial waste of public funds or a danger to public health or safety	Public
WYOMING	27-11-109(e)	Cannot discharge or discriminate if employee files notice of complaint, institutes proceeding or testifies as to violation of the occupational health and safety statutes	Both
WYOMING	9-11-103	Cannot discharge, discipline, or retaliate if employee reports violation of law, rule, regulation, fraud, waste, gross mismanagement of state governmental agency, or danger to health or safety or refuses to participate in investigation or to carry out directive beyond scope of employment that might result in serious injury or death	Public

Opportunity for Employer to Correct?	Remedies	Penalties
Yes in conciliation after complaint filed and investigation indicates a violation	File complaint with commissioner within 60 days of violation for reinstatement and back pay; if commissioner refuses to issue charge, employee can file in circuit court for appropriate relief	
	File complaint with Human Rights Commission within 2 yrs. of act of discrimination; in addition to any other remedy, judge may require restoration of benefits, back pay, and any increases with interest; Local government violation: file complaint with local government within 30 days of violation, then can request hearing to get reinstatement, back pay, injunctive relief, and costs and attorney fees	Retaliator subject to fine up to $5,000 and up to 30-day suspension without pay
	File civil action within 180 days of violation for reinstatement, back pay, full fringe benefits and seniority rights, actual damages, court and attorney fees	Civil fine up to $500; if violation committed with intent to discourage disclosure and violator holds public office by election or appointment: suspension up to 6 months
	File complaint with commissioner within 30 days for reinstatement, back pay, and other appropriate relief	
Commission will conduct conciliation after complaint filed and investigation indicates a violation	File complaint with state employment relation commission within 60 days of retaliation; commission can award reinstatement, back pay, expungement of adverse material on employee's file, and attorney fees	If respondent fails to comply with commission order, 10 to $100 fine for every day of failure
Employee must act in good faith and within the scope of duties of employment; employee must first bring to attention of supervisor and allow reasonable opportunity to correct	After exhausting administrative remedies, bring civil action within 90 days after violation or date of final administrative determination; for reinstatement, back wages, benefits, and reasonable attorney fees	

V. FAMILY LAWS

26. ABORTION

The laws governing abortion are the most controversial in the United States today. The disunity among states regarding these laws, particularly those that define a legal abortion, reflects society's conflicting views toward abortion.

Abortion laws, as treated here, contain three main parts: a definition of an illegal abortion, a definition of a legal abortion, and a section dealing with consent and/or notice. There are also sections dealing with the penalties for violating the laws, residency requirements, waiting periods, and abortionists' licensing requirements. These sections are impossible to compare. Because the Supreme Court through inconsistent rulings has caused the laws regulating abortion to be so unsettled, many state legislatures are not enacting any legislation pending the outcome of various lawsuits and federal legislation. Therefore, waiting periods, spousal notification, and other particulars mentioned below are *not* separately treated because the Court has virtually preempted the states' power to legislate in these areas. However, these sections are ancillary to those questions regarding the legality of the act itself.

Illegal Abortion

In no state is unrestricted abortion legal; indeed, virtually all states begin with the presumption that abortion is a crime, though all state statutes do have definitions of legal abortions. About twenty states define an illegal abortion in terms of the definition of a legal abortion; for example, Hawaii defines an illegal abortion as failure to meet the criterion of a legal abortion. (The definition of a legal abortion, in Hawaii, is simply the destruction of a nonviable fetus.) About fifteen states, however, predominately in the East and the South, do define illegal abortions without reference to legal instances of abortion. A few of these, interestingly, include in their definitions the provision that if the mother dies, *then* the abortion is illegal. Of these states, only some have specific statutes defining an illegal abortion; others merely define a legal abortion and impose penalties for their violation. The remaining states have definitions that specifically mention the limits of when an abortion is acceptable. For example, West Virginia defines an illegal abortion as any activity "with intent to destroy an unborn child or produce abortion [or] if mother dies unless to save the mother."

Legal Abortion

Legal abortion is universally defined in terms of the mother's convenience or health. Though few definitions mention the life or health of the fetus, many refer to its "viability" as a standard for when an abortion may be performed with impunity, and without further attempt to define the term. These definitions are objective in that specific time parameters are set, outside of which an abortion cannot legally be done, absent exigent circumstances. The most unrestrictive of all definitions occur in Hawaii and Alaska, where a legal abortion is an abortion on "any nonviable fetus." Interestingly, the definition of an illegal abortion in these two states is equally open; they say essentially that any act knowingly found to be contrary to the legal definition is illegal. After viability has been established, most states give additional instances when abortion may be legal: to save the life of the mother or if there are severe defects present in the fetus.

Partial Birth Abortion

The procedure called "partial birth abortion" has lately become the subject of numerous state statutes in the wake of the controversial vetoing by President Clinton of a federal bill that would have banned the procedure. The term means an abortion in which the person performing the abortion deliberately and intentionally delivers a living fetus or a substantial portion thereof into the vagina for the purpose of performing a procedure the person knows will kill the fetus, performs the procedure, kills the fetus and completes the delivery. In the last two years, twenty-one states have enacted legislation banning or limiting the practice of this procedure. Recently, the Supreme Court held that Nebraska's attempt to ban partial-birth abortion was unconstitutional.

State of the Statutes

Prior to 1973 and the *Roe v. Wade* decision by the Supreme Court (410 U.S. 113 (1973)), the regulation of abortion was left to the states. In *Roe v. Wade*, the Supreme Court decided that the Constitution protected a woman's right to abortion, a novel right said to be found in the unstated right to privacy, from state regulation during the first trimester of pregnancy. However, the Court also held that the states have an "important and legitimate interest in protecting the potentiality of human life." The abortion controversy has revolved around the states' consequent attempts to protect unborn life. The Supreme Court's patchwork of opinions following *Roe* has left abortion a highly unsettled area of law. Many statutes reflect state attempts at balancing a woman's right to choose an abortion with the state's compelling interest in protecting fetal life.

The statutes in this chapter are as they currently appear in the state codes. Interestingly enough, some of the statutes may be unconstitutional if challenged, based on prior Supreme Court rulings. Following are the general areas of abortion legislation and the Supreme Court's treatment of each:

• *Parental Consent.* States may require a minor seeking an abortion to obtain the consent of a parent or guardian as long as there is an adequate judicial bypass procedure.

• *Informed Consent.* A state may require a physician to provide a woman with such information such as alternatives to abortion, sources of financial aid, development of the child, and the gestational age of the child. Prior to 1992, informed consent provisions were unconstitutional.

• *Spousal Consent.* A state may not require a married woman to obtain her husband's consent before undergoing an abortion.

• *Abortion Method.* A state may not require the physician performing the abortion to use the technique providing for the best opportunity for the unborn child to survive the abortion.

• *Second Physician.* A state may not require that a second physician attend the abortion to take immediate control of the care of a child born alive in an abortion unless the provision has an exception for a situation when the health of the mother was endangered.

• *Waiting Period.* A twenty-four hour waiting period does not constitute an undue burden on a woman's decision to abort and, therefore, is constitutional. Prior to 1992, waiting period requirements were unconstitutional.

• *Parental Notice.* A state may require that one parent be notified of a minor's abortion, but not two.

• *Fetal Remains.* States may not require that the remains of the unborn child are disposed of in a "humane and sanitary" manner as it may suggest a mandate for some sort of "decent burial."

Table 26: Abortion

State	Code Section	Statutory Definition of Illegal Abortion	Statutory Definition of Legal Abortion
ALABAMA	13A-13-7; 26-21-1 to 26-22-5; Women's Right to Know Act: 26-23A-1 to 26-23A-13, for mental health of women, provisions ensure she has complete information prior to receiving abortion; Alabama Pain-Capable Unborn Child Protection Act: 26-23B-1 to 26-23B-9, asserting authority to protect life of unborn child; Federal Abortion Mandate Opt Out Act: 26-23C-1 to 26-23C-4, opt out provisions do not apply when life of mother may be endangered	Willfully administers by drug, substance, instrument which induces abortion or miscarriage. Partial Birth Abortion: any physician who performs a partial birth abortion within this state and thereby kills a human fetus, except to save life of the mother, shall be guilty of a class C felony and upon conviction shall be punished as prescribed by law.	Necessary purpose to preserve life, health of mother or where fetus is not viable; Termination of Ectopic Pregnancy: term "abortion" shall not be construed to apply to ectopic pregnancy
ALASKA	11.41.150; 11.41.160; 18.16.010–18.16.090	Knowingly doesn't meet standards for legal abortion. Partial Birth Abortion: unlawful unless to save life of mother when no other medical procedure would suffice; murder/manslaughter of unborn child	Terminate pregnancy of nonviable fetus
ARIZONA	13-3603 to 13-3605; 36-2151 to 36-2164	By drug, instrument with intent to procure miscarriage (unless necessary to save mother's life). Partial Birth Abortion: Felony unless to save the life of the mother if no other medical procedure would save the mother's life Use of any means to terminate the clinically diagnosable pregnancy of a woman with knowledge that the termination by those means will cause, with reasonable likelihood, the death of the unborn child.	Necessary to preserve life of mother

Penalty	Consent	Residency	License
Reckless inducement of abortion: Imprisonment up to 12 mos. and fine $100 to $1,000; abortion of viable fetus: class A felony; violation of regulations concerning abortion procedures: class C felony	Written consent of parent or guardian to perform abortion on unemancipated minor or judicial waiver of consent		Abortion of viable fetus must be performed by physician, in a hospital, with concurrence of 2nd licensed physician as to viability
Imprisonment up to 5 yrs. and/or fine up to $1,000; partial birth abortion: class C felony; murder of unborn child: unclassified felony; manslaughter of unborn child: class A felony	Patient; one parent or guardian if unmarried, unemancipated patient less than 18, except in medical emergency or judicial waiver of consent	30 days before procedure	Physician licensed by State Medical Board; hospital or other facility approved by Dept. of Health and Social Services or hospital operated by federal government
Imprisonment 2 to 5 years	Written consent of one parent or legal guardian if unmarried or unemancipated patient is under 18, except by court order or medical emergency		

Table 26: Abortion—Continued

State	Code Section	Statutory Definition of Illegal Abortion	Statutory Definition of Legal Abortion
ARKANSAS	5-61-101 to 5-61-102; 20-9-302; 20-16-601 to 20-16-602; 20-16-701 to 20-16-707; 20-16-801 to 20-16-810; 20-16-1703	Intentional termination of pregnancy with intent other than to increase probability of live birth or to remove dead or dying fetus, when fetus is viable. Viable fetus defined as one which can live outside the womb; fetus is presumed nonviable prior to end of 25th week of pregnancy. Partial Birth Abortion: class D felony unless to save the woman's life when no other form of abortion would suffice for that purpose	Abortion of viable fetus permitted when necessary to preserve life of mother, or where pregnancy is result of rape or of incest of minor; written certification by licensed physician required
CALIFORNIA	Health & Safety §§ 123418 to 123468	Performed by unauthorized person; performed on fetus judged viable by physician and continuation of pregnancy posed no risk to life or health of pregnant woman	Any medical treatment intended to induce the termination of a pregnancy except for the purpose of producing a live birth
COLORADO	12-37.5-102 to 12.37.5-108; 18-3.5-101 to 18-3.5-110		Intentional ending of pregnancy by licensed physician using accepted medical procedures and as required, with appropriate consent; continuation of pregnancy likely to result in death or permanent physical or mental impairment of mother, or child born with grave mental or physical retardation, or within first 16 weeks of pregnancy and pregnancy result of sexual assault or incest. court declared unconstitutional, but not repealed
CONNECTICUT	19a-600 to 19a-602	No abortion may be performed after viability of fetus	Pregnant woman's sole decision to terminate pregnancy before viability; after viability, only to preserve life or health of pregnant woman
DELAWARE	Tit. 11, § 654; Tit. 24, § 1766; 1780-1795	By drugs or act done with intent to cause termination of pregnancy	Continuation of pregnancy would result in death or injury to mother; mental and/or physical retardation of child or pregnancy result of rape or incest or unlawful sexual intercourse, but must be performed within first 20 wks.
DISTRICT OF COLUMBIA	22-101, repealed D.C. Law 15-154 (Act 15-255)		

Penalty	Consent	Residency	License
Class D felony	If minor or incompetent, written notice to parent or guardian required at least 48 hrs. before procedure, except by court order, medical emergency, upon declaration of child abuse, neglect, incest, parents' whereabouts unknown, or parent and minor have not been in contact for at least 1 yr.; informed consent of mother required		Physicians must be licensed to practice medicine in state or class D felony
In case of unemancipated minor: misdemeanor, punishable by imprisonment in county jail up to 30 days and/or fine up to $1,000	In case of unemancipated minor, written consent of minor and one parent or legal guardian, or by order of petition to Juvenile Court or in a medical emergency requiring immediate medical attention		Health care provider authorized to perform abortion pursuant to Bus. & Prof. § 2253
Class 4 felony, class 2 felony if woman dies; if caused upon sudden heat of passion; upon reckless operation of vehicle; under circumstances manifesting extreme indifference to value of human life; caused recklessly during commission of or flight from violent crime: class 5 felony	Mother; mother and father, if married; mother and parent/guardian if under 18 years unless necessary to save mother's life or avoid serious injury; if married, mother and her husband; no parental consent necessary if minor declares she is victim of abuse		Licensed physician using accepted medical procedures in a hospital licensed by Dept. of Public Health and Environment
	Minors under 16 must be provided with information and counseling and then sign and date standard form, except in case of medical emergency		
Class C felony, punishable by imprisonment 2 to 10 yrs. and fine up to $5,000	24 hr. waiting period following written consent and full explanation of procedure; if unmarried and under 18 or mentally ill or incompetent, consent of parent	120 days before procedure unless employed in state or patient of state-licensed M.D. prior to conception or medical emergency	Licensed physician, nationally accredited hospital; approval of hospital abortion review board

Table 26: Abortion—Continued

State	Code Section	Statutory Definition of Illegal Abortion	Statutory Definition of Legal Abortion
FLORIDA	390.011 to 390.025; 797.02; 797.03	Termination of pregnancy during last trimester which does not meet requirements of legal abortion; Partial Birth Abortion: prohibited except when necessary to save the life of the mother when her life is physically endangered and no other medical procedure would suffice for that purpose; any person advertising, distributing, or selling any substance, drug, or preparation or instrument or device for the purpose of causing or inducing or procuring a miscarriage is guilty of a misdemeanor in the 1st degree; any person assisting in an abortion without a license or in unaccredited facility or on woman in 3rd trimester is guilty of 2nd degree misdemeanor	Regulated only in last trimester; necessary to save life or preserve health of mother and requires 2 physicians' certifications of medical necessity unless one physician certifies need for emergency medical abortion and no 2nd physician available; must be performed in accredited hospital
GEORGIA	15-11-110 to 15-11-680; 16-12-140 to 16-12-144; 31-98-2	By administering medicine, drugs, or substance or using instrument with intent to procure miscarriage or abortion. Partial Birth Abortion: unlawful except to save the mother's life when that life is physically endangered and no other medical procedure will suffice to save her life	After 1st trimester, must be performed in licensed hospital or health facility; after 2nd trimester, physician and 2 consulting physicians must certify it is necessary to preserve life or health of mother
HAWAII	453-16	Termination of viable fetus	Operation to terminate pregnancy of nonviable fetus; woman has right to terminate pregnancy if necessary to protect her life or health

Penalty	Consent	Residency	License
2nd degree misdemeanor, punishable by imprisonment up to 60 days; 1st degree misdemeanor, punishable by imprisonment up to 1 yr.; death of mother: 2nd degree felony	Voluntary written consent of mother or of the court-appointed guardian of a mentally incompetent woman, except in a medical emergency		Validly licensed hospital or medical facility; third trimester in hospital only
Imprisonment 1 to 10 years; partial birth abortion: imprisonment up to 5 yrs. and/or $5,000 fine	Except in medical emergency, written, informed consent of parent or guardian of unemancipated minor under the age of 18; parent must have 24-hour notice before scheduled abortion unless waived or minor obtains judicial approval that minor is either mature enough to decide without parent's consent or parent's consent is not in best interests of the minor		1st trimester: licensed physician; 2nd trimester: licensed physician and licensed hospital or health facility or ambulatory surgical center
Imprisonment up to 5 yrs. and/or fine up to $1,000			Licensed M.D. or osteopath; performed in licensed hospital, clinic, or physician's office

Table 26: Abortion—Continued

State	Code Section	Statutory Definition of Illegal Abortion	Statutory Definition of Legal Abortion
IDAHO	Pain-Capable Unborn Child Protection Act: 18-501 to 510; 18-601 to 18-616; Note: Planned Parenthood v. Wasden, 376 F.3d 908, 926 (9th Cir. 2004), cert. denied, 544 U.S. 948 (2005), called into question several provisions of Idaho statutes. As of 2013, no existing laws have been repealed, and there is pending legislation to address federal court's concerns	Provides, supplies, administers drugs or substances to woman, or uses instrument with intent to produce abortion; Partial Birth Abortion: unlawful except when necessary to save the life of the mother when it is physically endangered	In 1st and 2nd trimesters: consultation between licensed M.D. and mother and determination by M.D. that abortion is appropriate considering various mental, physical, and family factors including circumstances of pregnancy, such as rape or incest; 3rd trimester: must be necessary to preserve life of mother or fetus and M.D. must consult another corroborating physician.
ILLINOIS	Illinois Abortion Law of 1975: 720 §§ 510/1 to 510/15; Partial-Birth Abortion Ban Act: 720 §§ 513/1 to 513/99; Parental Notice of Abortion Act: 750 §§ 70/1 to 70/99	Use of any instrument, drug, or any other device to terminate pregnancy of a woman known to be pregnant with an intention other than to increase the probability of a live birth, to preserve the life or health of the child after live birth, or to remove a dead fetus	If fetus nonviable and abortion not necessary to preserve mother's health, physician must certify nonviability; if fetus is viable, abortion must be medically necessary to preserve life or health of mother; physician must certify this necessity
INDIANA	16-34-1-1 to 16-34-2-7	Any abortion not as provided for in 1st or 2nd trimester; Partial Birth Abortion: person may not lawfully or knowingly perform a partial birth abortion unless physician reasonably believes it is necessary to save the life of the mother and that no other medical procedure is sufficient	During 1st trimester with mother's consent and based on physician's professional and medical judgment; after 1st trimester but before viability, permissible with mother's consent and if performed in hospital or surgical center; after viability, procedure necessary to prevent impairment of life or health of mother and performed in hospital with premature birth care unit and with 2nd physician present
IOWA	707.7 to 707.10	Feticide: Intentional termination of human pregnancy after end of 2nd trimester; Abortion: termination of a human pregnancy with the intent other than to produce a live birth or remove a dead fetus	Necessary to preserve life or health of mother or fetus; after end of second trimester with every reasonable effort made to preserve life of viable fetus; Partial Birth Abortion if to save life of mother

Penalty	Consent	Residency	License
Not licensed: felony, punishable by imprisonment 2 to 5 yrs. and or fine up to $5,000; licensed: professional discipline and fine of not less than $1,000; 2nd violation: license or certification suspended for not less than 6 mos. and fine of not less than $2,500; subsequent violations: license or certification revoked and fine not less than $5,000; accomplice or accessory to illegal abortion or mother who knowingly submits to or terminates own pregnancy otherwise than by live birth: felony, punishable by imprisonment 1 to 5 yrs. and/or fine up to $5,000; hospital, nurse, or other health care personnel not in violation if providing services in good faith upon directions of physician	Mother must give "informed consent" after information about development of fetus, adoption and other services, risks, etc.; abortion on minor requires written consent of parent unless minor is emancipated, has been given right to self-consent by court, or court finds abortion without consent of parent is in best interest of the minor or where medical emergency exists with no time to obtain consent; medical emergency exception for minors unconstitutionally narrow as is rest of parental consent law at 18-609A despite severability provision. *Planned Parenthood of Idaho v. Wasden*, 376 F.3d 908, 926 (9th Cir. 2004), cert. denied, 544 U.S. 948 (2005)		1st trimester: licensed physician in hospital or properly staffed clinic or physician's office with arrangements with nearby acute care hospital for complications or emergencies; 2nd and 3rd trimesters: licensed physician; licensed hospital and in the "best medical interest" of pregnant woman
Class 2 felony: Imprisonment 3 to 7 yrs. and If fetus could have survived with or without support and physician does not use method to keep it alive: Class 3 felony; any person who knowingly performs partial-birth abortion and thereby kills human fetus or infant: class 4 felony	Written informed consent by minor and actual or constructive notice must be given to adult family member 48 hrs. prior to abortion procedure on an unmarried woman younger than 18; exceptions for medical emergency or judicial notice		Licensed physician
Knowingly or intentionally performing abortion not expressly provided for in statute: level 5 felony; failure to meet consent requirements: class A misdemeanor	Written consent of mother or 1 parent or guardian if unemancipated minor under 18; court can waive parental consent requirement; consent requirement not applicable in emergency		1st trimester: licensed physician; 2nd trimester, before viability: same as 1st and licensed hospital; after viability: same as 2nd and physician must certify reasons for procedure to hospital regarding reasons for procedure
Partial Birth Abortion: Class C felony if not to save life of mother; feticide: class C felony; attempted abortion after 2nd trimester: class D felony; no license: class C felony			Licensed physician

Table 26: Abortion—Continued

State	Code Section	Statutory Definition of Illegal Abortion	Statutory Definition of Legal Abortion
KANSAS	65-6701 to 65-6739; 65-67a.01	To perform or induce abortion when fetus is viable, that is, in attending physician's best medical judgment, fetus is capable of sustained survival outside the uterus without extraordinary medical means	As long as fetus is not viable and mother's informed consent obtained; abortion of viable fetus permitted if 2nd physician certifies that abortion is necessary to preserve life of mother or fetus has severe, life-threatening deformity or abnormality
KENTUCKY	311.710 to 311.830; 311.990	Abortion after viability unlawful except to preserve life or health of woman; abortionist shall take all reasonable steps to preserve the life and health of the child; Partial Birth Abortion unlawful except to preserve life or health of woman	1st trimester: Physician determines abortion is necessary or accepts referral and describes in writing except in case of medical emergency; voluntary and informed consent required; after viability, only to save life of mother and steps must be taken to preserve life and health of child
LOUISIANA	14:87 to 14:88; 40:1299.30 to 40.1299.35.19	Deliberate termination of human pregnancy after fertilization of a female ovum, after viability by any person, even the woman herself, with intent other than to produce live birth, remove ectopic pregnancy, or remove dead fetus; Partial Birth Abortion: unlawful except when necessary to save life of a woman endangered by physical disorder, physical illness, or physical injury when no other medical procedure would suffice	Licensed physician shall determine if child is viable and shall first perform or cause to be performed an ultrasound examination pursuant to the provisions of Subsection D of this Section. The physician shall enter such findings and determination of viability in the medical record of the pregnant woman, along with photographs or prints of the ultrasound evidencing the findings; in order to preserve the health of the woman, must make judgment of advisability or necessity of abortion, shall certify medical reasons for viability abortion, and procedure must be performed in licensed hospital; 2nd physician must be in attendance for the abortion of a viable fetus

Penalty	Consent	Residency	License
Abortion on pain-capable unborn child except to save life or prevent substantial and irreversible impairment to mother: class A nonperson misdemeanor; 2nd or subsequent violation: severity level 10, person felony	Informed consent of all women before abortion, not applicable in emergency; notice must be given to 1 parent or guardian of unemancipated minor; court can waive parental notice requirement on finding minor sufficiently mature or notice not to be in minor's best interest		Licensed physician; 2nd physician not financially associated with 1st physician to certify abortion of viable fetus to preserve life of mother
Physician did not believe it necessary, did not receive written referral; violating notice to spouse provisions; violating any regulations on abortions after viability; use of saline method of abortion after first trimester: class D felony; non-licensed physician: class D felony; performing abortion on viable fetus except to preserve life and health of mother: class C felony; violating woman's consent provisions; aborting with reckless disregard of whether mother is minor: class A misdemeanor	Written informed consent of mother with 24-hour waiting period; of 1 parent or guardian if mother under 18 and unemancipated, except when medical emergency; court may waive parental consent; doctor must notify spouse if possible prior to abortion, if not possible, within 30 days of abortion [notification of spouse has been held unconstitutional by the attorney general. OAG 82-97.]		1st trimester: licensed physician; after 1st trimester: licensed physician in licensed hospital unless medical emergency
Crime of abortion: imprisonment at hard labor 1 to 10 yrs. and $10,000 to 100,000 fine; violation of 40:1299.30 to 40:1299.35.19: imprisonment up to 2 yrs. or fine up to $1,000; a person who kills a viable child during labor shall be sentenced to life imprisonment at hard labor, except when the death of the child results from an express act to save the life of the child or the mother	Written informed consent of woman 24 hours prior to abortion; if unemancipated minor, signed consent of parent or guardian or court, except in medical emergency or if judicial consent		Licensed physician with admitting privileges to hospital within 30 miles of location where abortion takes place; after viability must be in licensed hospital

Table 26: Abortion—Continued

State	Code Section	Statutory Definition of Illegal Abortion	Statutory Definition of Legal Abortion
MAINE	Tit. 22, §§ 1591 to 1599-A	Intentional interruption of a pregnancy by the application of external agents, whether chemical or physical, or the ingestion of chemical agents with an intention other than to produce a live birth or to remove a dead fetus	Before viability by physician; after viability, only when necessary to preserve life or health of mother
MARYLAND	Health-Gen. §§ 20-207 to 20-214; Crim. Law § 2-103	Performed after viability unless to protect life or health of mother or if fetus is suffering from genetic defect or serious deformity or abnormality	Performed before fetus is viable or at any time where termination procedure is necessary to protect life, health of woman or fetus is affected by serious genetic defect or abnormality; procedure must be least intrusive and not inconsistent with established medical practice
MASSACHUSETTS	Ch. 112, §§ 12K to 12U	Failure to meet standards for legal abortion; violation of procedural standards such as informed consent, medical procedure required, etc.; knowing destruction of the life of an unborn child or the intentional expulsion or removal of an unborn child from the womb other than for the principal purpose of live birth or removing a dead fetus	Under 24 wks., abortion may be performed only by physician and only if in physician's best judgment the abortion is necessary under the circumstances; after 24 weeks physician must provide written statement that: 1) necessary to save life of mother; 2) continuation will impose substantial risk of grave physical or mental impairment; no procedure can be used which destroys or injures fetus unless in physician's opinion other available procedures would be greater risk to mother or future pregnancies and all reasonable steps must be taken to preserve life, health of aborted child
MICHIGAN	333.17016; 750.14; 750.15; 722.901 to 722.908	Drug, substance, instrument, or device employed with intent to terminate pregnancy for a purpose other than to increase probability of a live birth, to preserve the health of the child, or to remove a dead fetus; Partial Birth Abortion: unlawful except to save the life of a mother endangered by physical illness, physical injury, or physical disorder when no other medical procedure will suffice	After viability, when necessary to preserve life of mother

Penalty	Consent	Residency	License
Physician fails to perform any required action: class D crime, punishable by fine up to $1,000 for each violation; not taking reasonable steps to preserve life of live born child: subject to homicide, manslaughter and/ or malpractice liability	Informed written consent by minor and consent of 1 parent or guardian required for persons under 18 except in emergencies or if judicial consent is obtained; informed written consent of all women required; all minors required to undergo counseling		Licensed physician
Physician not liable if decision to abort made in good faith and in best medical judgment; prosecution for murder or manslaughter if intended death, serious injury, wanton or reckless disregard that actions might seriously injure fetus	Physician may not perform an abortion on an unmarried minor unless physician first gives notice to parent or guardian, unless minor does not live with parent or guardian and reasonable efforts to give notice are unsuccessful or if in physician's judgment notice to parent or guardian may lead to physical or emotional abuse, or the minor is mature and capable of informed consent or notice would not be in the best interest of minor		Licensed physician
Imprisonment 1 to 5 yrs.; if conduct also violates other criminal laws, those penalties may apply as well	Written informed consent within 24 hrs. before procedure except in emergencies; if mother less than 18 and unmarried; consent of both parents or guardians or court if convinced of mother's maturity or that procedure is in mother's best interest, except in medical emergency		Licensed physician except in medical emergency; after 13th week, must be performed in licensed hospital
Felony: Imprisonment up to 4 yrs. and/or fine up to $2,000; if mother dies: manslaughter, punishable by imprisonment up to 15 yrs. and/or fine up to $7,500; violation of parental consent requirement: misdemeanor; selling or advertising for sale any drugs expressly for use of females for purpose of procuring an abortion: misdemeanor	No abortion may be performed on minor without her consent and that of one parent or guardian except in medical emergency; court may waive parental consent if minor is mature and well-informed so as to be able to make the decision, or waiver is in minor's best interest	Requirements apply even if minor is not resident	

Table 26: Abortion—Continued

State	Code Section	Statutory Definition of Illegal Abortion	Statutory Definition of Legal Abortion
MINNESOTA	145.411 to 145.424; 617.20 to 617.22	Failure to meet standards of legal abortion; sale or manufacture of drug, substance, or instrument intended for unlawful use in miscarriage or abortion procedure; act, procedure, or use of any instrument, medicine, or drug which is supplied, prescribed for, or administered to a pregnant woman which results in the termination of pregnancy	Before viability, by a trained physician; after viability, second half of gestation, must be performed in hospital and necessary to preserve life, health of mother and procedure used will reasonably assure live birth; after 20th wk., 2nd physician must be immediately accessible for any resulting live birth
MISSISSIPPI	41-41-31 to 41-41-73; 41-75-1 to 41-75-29; 97-3-3 to 97-3-5	Willfully or knowingly by means of instrument, medicine, drug, or any other substance causing any pregnant woman to abort or miscarry; Partial Birth Abortion: prohibited unless necessary to save mother's life if no other medical procedure would suffice	Necessary to preserve mother's life; pregnancy result of rape
MISSOURI	188.010 to 188.230	Intentional destruction of the life of an embryo or fetus in the womb or intentional termination of pregnancy with intention other than live birth or removal of dead unborn child; abortion for purpose of providing fetal organs or tissue for transplant or other purpose; use of public facilities, employees or funds for abortion, except where necessary to save mother's life	After viability, necessary to preserve life, health of mother; method used must be one most likely to preserve life, health of fetus unless greater risk to mother

Penalty	Consent	Residency	License
Sale or manufacture of drug, substance, or instrument intended for unlawful use in miscarriage or abortion procedure; perform illegal abortion: felony	Informed consent of mother		Licensed physician; licensed abortion facility or hospital if after first trimester
Felony, punishable by imprisonment 1 to 10 years; if mother dies, murder; if physician or nurse convicted, license will be revoked; selling, giving away, possessing or in any manner anything causing unlawful abortion: misdemeanor, punishable by imprisonment up to 3 mos. and fine $25 to $200; allowing child born live to die: felony, punishable by imprisonment 1 to 10 yrs. and fine $25,000 to $50,000; Partial Birth Abortion: felony, punishable by imprisonment up to 2 yrs. and/ or fine up to $25,000	Written informed consent of the mother at least 24 hrs. before the abortion, except in emergency; unmarried woman under 18 must have written consent of both parents, with exceptions for medical emergency or judicial waiver		Licensed physician; prior advice of two licensed physicians required in writing
Take life of child aborted alive: 2nd degree murder; anyone not a physician attempting to perform abortion; physician without privileges at hospital offering OB/Gyn care: class B felony; committing or assisting in unlawful abortion: class A misdemeanor and possible revocation of license; failure to maintain confidentiality: misdemeanor; abortion of viable unborn child: class C felony, punishable by imprisonment up to 1 yr. and fine $10,000 to $50,000 and possible suspension or revocation of license	Prior, informed, written consent of mother 72 hrs. before abortion; if mother is less than 18 and unemancipated, informed written consent of one parent or guardian or court order		Licensed physician only; must be performed in hospital after 16 wks.; after viability, licensed physician must certify abortion necessary including medical indicators and method to be utilized with reasoning for decision; second physician must be in attendance to aid fetus; at 20 wks., physician required to determine whether fetus is viable, using ordinary skill and care and testing

Table 26: Abortion—Continued

State	Code Section	Statutory Definition of Illegal Abortion	Statutory Definition of Legal Abortion
MONTANA	50-20-101 to 50-20-511	Use or prescribe of any instrument, medicine, drug, or other substance or device to intentionally terminate the pregnancy of a woman known to be pregnant, with an intention other than to increase the probability of a live birth, to preserve the life or health of the child, or to remove a dead fetus; Partial Birth Abortion: unlawful except to save the life of mother when endangered by physical disorder, illness, or injury when no other medical procedure would save the woman's life	After viability, necessary to preserve life or health of mother; procedure utilized must not negligently or intentionally endanger life of fetus unless to preserve mother's life
NEBRASKA	28-325 to 28-346; Pain-Capable Unborn Child Protection Act: 28-3,102 to 28-3,111; 71-6901 et seq.; 38-2021; 71-6901 to 71-6911	Use of any instrument, medicine, drug, or any other substance, device, or means with intent to terminate the clinically diagnosable pregnancy of a woman with knowledge that those means will with reasonable likelihood cause the death of the unborn child; not an abortion if done with intent to save life or preserve health of unborn child, remove dead unborn child, or remove ectopic pregnancy; Partial Birth Abortion: unlawful except to save the life of the mother whose life is endangered by physical disorder, illness, or injury, including life-endangering physical condition cause by or arising from pregnancy itself	If mother's life is endangered
NEVADA	442.240 to 442.270	Termination of a human pregnancy with an intention other than to produce the birth of an infant capable of sustained survival by natural or artificial support or to remove a dead fetus	Only within first 24 wks. unless necessary to preserve life, health of mother

Penalty	Consent	Residency	License
Violation of infant protection; violation of abortion practices by physician: felony, punishable by imprisonment up to 5 yrs. and/or fine up to $1,000; violation of consent provisions or of inducing woman to have abortion: misdemeanor, imprisonment up to 6 mos. and/or fine up to $500; no penalties may be placed on the mother; illegal partial birth abortion: felony, 5 to 10 yrs. and/or fine up to $50,000 and permanent revocation of physician's license	Informed consent of mother 24 hrs. prior to procedure, signed by mother and her physician except when physician certifies necessity to preserve mother's life or that delay will create serious risk of substantial irreversible impairment of major bodily function; if under 18 and unmarried, written notice of a parent or guardian except in case of medical emergency or where notice is judicially waived		Licensed physician or physician's assistant; after first 3 months in licensed hospital; after viability, physician must certify in writing necessity of procedure including grounds for decision plus two other physicians must confirm decision except when necessary to preserve mother's life
Physician performing abortion in violation of any standards: class III misdemeanor:	Unemancipated minor under 18 must get written notarized consent of pregnant woman and parent or legal guardian; if victim of sexual abuse, neglect, or child abuse, by parent or legal guardian		Licensed physician
Violation of notice or consent statutes: misdemeanor; failure to take steps to preserve life of infant: physician liable for malpractice and wrongful death	Informed written consent of mother, certified by in writing physician; physician must also certify mother's marital status and age; if mother under 18, unemancipated and unmarried, actual notice to parent or guardian required before procedure unless immediately necessary to protect life or health of minor; if actual notice is unsuccessful, then physician must delay abortion until notifying parent by certified mail; court may authorize abortion if mature or in minor's best interest		Licensed physician who must exercise "best clinical judgment"; licensed hospital after 24th wk. and records of mother must contain facts upon which physician based decision that continued pregnancy would endanger life, health of mother

Table 26: Abortion—Continued

State	Code Section	Statutory Definition of Illegal Abortion	Statutory Definition of Legal Abortion
NEW HAMPSHIRE	132:32 to 132.36; Partial Birth Abortion Ban Act: 329:32 to 329:42; 630:1	Abortion: Intentional use of prescription, any instrument, medicine, drug, or any other substance or device to terminate the pregnancy of a female known to be pregnant with an intention other than to increase the probability of live birth, to preserve the life or health of the child after live birth, or to remove an ectopic pregnancy or the products from a spontaneous miscarriage; Partial Birth Abortion: illegal unless the life of the mother is endangered by a physical disorder, illness, or injury including a life-endangering physical condition caused by or arising from the pregnancy itself	Death of fetus specifically not homicide
NEW JERSEY	Partial-Birth Abortion Ban Act of 1997: 2A:65A-1 to 2A:65A-7; Parental Notification for Abortion Act: 9:17A-1.1 to 9:17A-1.12	Partial Birth Abortion prohibited unless necessary to save life of mother	
NEW MEXICO	30-5-1 to 10-5-3; 30-5A-1 to 30-5A-5	By administering medical drug or other substance or means whereby an untimely termination of pregnancy is produced with intent to destroy fetus and not a justified medical termination; Partial Birth Abortion: unlawful except to save the life of woman or to prevent great bodily harm to woman	Continuation likely to result in death or impairment of mother's mental or physical health or fetus likely to have grave physical or mental defect; or pregnancy result of rape or incest; partial birth abortion: prohibited except to save mother from death or great bodily harm and no other procedure will suffice
NEW YORK	Penal §§ 125.05; 125.20; 125.40-60; Pub. Health § 4164	Failure to meet standards for legal abortion; causes mother to die; not within first 24 wks.; administering or taking drugs or any other manner with intent to cause a miscarriage	Within first 24 wks. or necessary to preserve mother's life; if mother performs abortion it must be on the advice of physician within the first 24 wks. or to preserve her own life
NORTH CAROLINA	14-44 to 14-46; 90-21.6 to 90-21.10	Willfully administer to mother; prescribe, advise, procure substance or instrument with intent to destroy child or procure miscarriage	First 20 wks., of pregnancy no medical requirements regarding mother or fetus; after 20 wks., must be substantial risk that would threaten life or health of mother

Penalty	Consent	Residency	License
Illegal Partial Birth Abortion: class B felony, punishable by imprisonment 1 to 10 yrs. and/or $10,000 to $100,000 fine; abortion without consent: misdemeanor and grounds for civil action	If unemancipated minor or incompetent: Written notice to parent or guardian at least 48 hrs. before pending abortion by personal delivery or certified mail unless there is medical emergency or persons entitled to notice certify in writing that they have been notified, or court decides minor is mature and capable of giving informed consent		Physician and documented referral from another unaffiliated physician must both determine that life of mother is endangered
Partial Birth Abortion: Knowing performance by licensed physician or other health care professional: immediate revocation of professional license and subject to $25,000 fine for each incident; failure to give parental notice: fine $1,000 to $5,000	In case of unemancipated minor, written notice must be given to parent 48 hrs. before procedure at parent's last known address by personal delivery by physician or certified mail, unless medical emergency or waiver by court		
Criminal abortion: 4th degree felony; abortion resulting in woman's death: 2nd degree felony; Partial Birth Abortion: 4th degree felony, punishable by imprisonment up to 18 mos. and fine up to $5,000; mother may not be prosecuted	Mother must request procedure; if under 18, the procedure must be requested by her and parent or guardian		Licensed physician; licensed hospital; written certification of hospital board required, committee of 2 licensed physicians and alternates who decide questions of medical justification of specific case
Not justifiable abortional act and after 24 wks.: Class E or D felony; woman dies from act,: class B felony; self-abortion or issuing abortion articles: class B or A misdemeanor			Licensed physician; after 12th wk., must be in hospital on in-patient basis; after 20th wk., 2nd M.D. must be present to handle medical care of any live birth
Class H felony, punishable by imprisonment up to 10 yrs. and/or fine; class I felony: imprisonment up to 5 years and/or fine; failure to obtain parental consent: class 1misdemeanor	Unemancipated minor: written consent of mother plus written consent of parent or guardian, exception for medical emergency or judicial waiver		Licensed physician, licensed hospital or clinic

Table 26: Abortion—Continued

State	Code Section	Statutory Definition of Illegal Abortion	Statutory Definition of Legal Abortion
NORTH DAKOTA	Abortion Control Act: 14-02.1-01 to 14-02.1-12	Non-licensed person performs abortion; if licensed physician but doesn't conform to standards for legal abortion	During 1st 12 wks., no restrictions; after viability, necessary to preserve life or health of mother; must be in hospital
OHIO	2919.11 to 2919:18	Failure to obtain informed consent; taking life of fetus born alive or failing to provide reasonable medical attention to same; after viability, purposeful termination of a human pregnancy by any person, including the mother herself, with the intention other than to produce a live birth or remove a dead fetus	Performed or induced by a physician who determines in good faith that the fetus is not viable or to prevent the death or serious bodily injury of the pregnant woman
OKLAHOMA	Tit. 63, §§ 1-730 to 1-741; Tit. 21, §§ 684; 714; 861	Non-licensed person performs abortion; failure to meet standards for legal abortion; taking life of viable fetus unless necessary to preserve life or health of mother or failure to provide medical aid to fetus; purposeful termination of a human pregnancy with intent other than to produce a live birth or remove a dead fetus; Partial Birth Abortion: illegal except when necessary to save the mother when her life is endangered by a physical disorder, illness, or injury	After viability, necessary to preserve life, health of mother; if abortion is self-induced, must be under supervision of physician; after viability, physician required to aid fetus, except in medical emergency

Penalty	Consent	Residency	License
Physician: Class A misdemeanor; anyone not physician who performs abortion: class B felony; if physician does not take proper care to preserve life of unborn or born viable fetus: class C felony; all other violations of N.D. Abortion Control Act: class A misdemeanor	Informed consent of mother as certified by physician at least 24 hrs. before procedure; before viability, if mother is unemancipated minor physician must inform both parents or guardian at least 24 hrs. before minor's consent, exception for emergency or judicial waiver; after viability, husband's written consent, unless separated, or consent of a parent or guardian if mother is less than 18 years and unmarried, unless procedure is necessary to preserve life, health of mother; court can authorize abortion on minor without parental consent		Physician using medical standards applicable; licensed hospital required after first 12 wks. of pregnancy as well as physician must certify facts and have 2 physicians concur with his medical judgment for abortion, unless medical emergency
Violators guilty of unlawful abortion: 1st degree misdemeanor; 2nd violation: 4th degree felony; purposely terminating child born alive or failing to take measures to save its life: guilty of abortion manslaughter, 1st degree felony	Informed consent of mother; if mother is unemancipated minor, parental informed consent also required with 24 hrs. actual notice; court may authorize minor to consent without parental notification; other family members over 21 may issue consent if minor in danger of physical, sexual, or emotional abuse from parent; constructive notice of at least 48 hrs. by both certified and ordinary mail allowed if parents or family members cannot be reached with reasonable effort		Licensed physician
Person who administers or uses drugs or any other instrument to procure miscarriage unless to save life of mother: imprisonment 2 to 5 yrs.; person not licensed physician performing abortion: imprisonment 1 to 3 years in state penitentiary; anyone aborting viable fetus not to prevent mother's death or health impairment: homicide; quick child or mother dies: 1st degree manslaughter; Partial Birth Abortion: imprisonment up to 2 yrs. and/or $10,000 fine			Licensed physician; approved hospital required after first trimester; physician must certify necessity of procedure after viability, including factors considered

Table 26: Abortion—Continued

State	Code Section	Statutory Definition of Illegal Abortion	Statutory Definition of Legal Abortion
OREGON	435.435 to 435.996		
PENNSYLVANIA	Tit. 18, §§ 3201 to 3220	Failure to obtain informed consent of woman; failure to meet standards for legal abortion; using any means to cause the death of an unborn child but not meaning use of intrauterine device or the birth control pill; solely for the reason of the child's sex; without making diagnosis of gestational age; use of public funds, facilities, or officials	Physician must find, in his clinical judgment, that abortion must be necessary or that a referring physician has sent a written signed statement saying so; after viability, necessary to preserve life of mother or prevent serious risk of substantial and irreversible impairment of bodily function; viability defined as when physician, based on facts of particular case, finds reasonable likelihood of fetus' sustained survival outside the mother's body.
RHODE ISLAND	11-9-18; 23-4.7-1 to 23-4.8- 5; 23-4.12-1 to 23-4.12-6	Failure to obtain informed consent unless necessary to preserve life of mother; failure to provide for any fetus born alive; administering to pregnant woman medicine, drug, instrument, etc. with intent to terminate pregnancy; Partial Birth Abortion is unlawful except to save the life of a woman endangered by physical injury when no other medical procedure would suffice,	

Penalty	Consent	Residency	License
			No physician is required to give advice with respect to or participate in any abortion if refusal is based on election not to do so and physician so advises patient; no hospital employee or member of medical staff is required to participate in abortions if individual notifies hospital of such election
Failing to adequately care for viable fetus; physician violating medical consultation provisions; finding abortion necessary; violation of 2nd physician requirement: 3rd degree felony and license may be revoked; person inducing abortion in violation of consent standards: 1st offense: summary offense; 2nd and subsequent offenses: 3rd degree misdemeanor; violation of informed consent or spousal notification provisions: guilty of unprofessional conduct, license may be revoked; violation of gestational age determination requirement: 3 mos. suspension of license and if falsification of records, 3rd degree misdemeanor; civil penalties: physician who violates rule regarding medical consultation and judgment or informed consent liable to patient for any damages: $5,000 in punitive damages and reasonable attorney fees	Except for medical emergency, physician must give information to mother at least 24 hours before abortion; if mother under 18 years and not emancipated, both mother's and one parent or guardian's informed consent required; court may authorize physician to perform abortion; if the woman is married, she must provide signed statement that she has notified her spouse of the abortion		Licensed physician; licensed hospital or facility; hospital only after 24 wks. with 2nd physician to aid fetus
Physician who violates consent provisions guilty of unprofessional conduct; failure to provide medical care for infant born alive: imprisonment up to 5 yrs. and/or fine up to $5,000; charge of manslaughter if baby dies; Partial Birth Abortion: felony for abortionist, mother may not be charged	Informed written consent after required disclosures unless emergency; if mother under 18 and unemancipated, parental consent of at least one parent required; court may waive; if married, husband must be notified if reasonably possible by physician or in written statement by woman unless separated or emergency		

Table 26: Abortion—Continued

State	Code Section	Statutory Definition of Illegal Abortion	Statutory Definition of Legal Abortion
SOUTH CAROLINA	44-41-10 to 44-41-85	Failure to meet standards for legal abortion; self-abortion that does not meet standards for legal abortion; use of instrument, medicine, drug, or other substance or device with intent to terminate pregnancy for reasons other than to increase probability of a live birth, preserve child's life or health, or to remove a dead fetus; Partial Birth abortion: illegal except when performed to save life of mother endangered by physical disorder, illness, or injury when no other medical procedure would suffice.	1st trimester with mother's consent; 2nd trimester with consent in hospital; 3rd trimester, necessary to preserve life or health of mother; if basis is mental health must be so certified in writing by two consulting physicians, one of whom is consulting psychiatrist
SOUTH DAKOTA	22-17-5 to 22-17-6; 34-23A-1 to 34-23A-45	Failure to meet standards for legal abortion; failure of physician to obtain informed consent; Partial Birth Abortion is unlawful except in order to save the life of the mother when it is endangered by physical disorder, illness, or injury and no other medical procedure would suffice; abortion due to sec of fetus	Wks. 1 to 24: in M.D.'s medical judgment; after 24th wk., necessary to preserve life or health of mother
TENNESSEE	37-10-301 to 37-10-307; 39-15-201 to 39-15-209	Failure to meet standards for legal abortion including residency requirement; attempted criminal abortion; coerced or compelled abortion; administering to pregnant woman medicine, drug, or any substance or instrument with intent to destroy such child; Partial Birth Abortion: no person shall knowingly perform a partial birth abortion except when necessary to save the life of the mother if endangered by a physical disorder, illness, or injury	1st trimester with woman's consent upon advice of her physician; after 1st trimester and before viability, same, but in a hospital.; after viability, necessary to preserve life or health of mother

Penalty	Consent	Residency	License
Person unlawfully inducing abortion: felony, punishable by imprisonment 2 to 5 yrs. and/or fine up to $5,000; mother soliciting abortion or self-aborting unlawfully: imprisonment up to 2 yrs. and/or fine up to $1,000; abortion intentionally performed without conforming to consent standards for minors or others: misdemeanor, punishable by imprisonment up to 3 yrs. and/or $2,000 to $10,000 fine; 3rd or subsequent offense: imprisonment 60 days to 3 yrs.; physician performing: felony, punishable by imprisonment no less than 5 yrs. and up to $5,000 fine	Mother's written consent required; if mother married and in 3rd trimester, husband's consent is required; if mother under 17 years and unmarried, consent of 1 parent or guardian required, except in medical emergency of if pregnancy is result of incest: court may order minor's right to abortion without parental consent; spousal, parental or legal guardian's consent for incompetent woman		1st trimester on advice of licensed physician; 2nd trimester must be performed by licensed physician in licensed hospital; 3rd trimester, second physician's written recommendation required, facts and reasons supporting recommendations must be certified by both physicians
Violating informed consent statutes: class 2 misdemeanor; any unauthorized abortion: class 6 felony; intentional killing of fetus by causing injury to mother: class 4 felony; perform sex-selective abortion: class 6 felony	Voluntary written informed consent of mother 24 hrs. before procedure; if mother unmarried minor, 48-hr. notice to parent or guardian also required; parental consent exempted with medical emergency, or judicial waiver		First 12 wks., licensed physician, solely medical judgment; after 24 wks., licensed physician and hospital for medical necessity only
Impermissible abortion: class C felony; mother attempting to procure a miscarriage: class E felony; physician fails to use due care to preserve life of baby born alive or violation of 48-hr. waiting period: class E felony; abortion on non-Tennessee resident: class C felony; coercion to obtain abortion: class A misdemeanor; physician performs abortion on minor violating consent statute: misdemeanor	Informed, written consent of mother; 48-hr. waiting period between physician giving mother information and consent; after viability, same as 1st trimester except physician must certify in writing to the hospital that procedure was necessary; if mother is minor, consent by at least 1 parent required; minor may petition court for waiver, no consent necessary if emergency	Mother must produce evidence to physician that she is bona fide resident prior to procedure except in medical emergency; physician must still give information to mother	1st trimester: licensed physician upon his medical advice and woman's consent; after 1st trimester to viability; licensed physician, licensed hospital; after viability: only to preserve life of mother

Table 26: Abortion—Continued

State	Code Section	Statutory Definition of Illegal Abortion	Statutory Definition of Legal Abortion
TEXAS	Civ. Stat. § 4512.5; Health & Safety §§ 171.004 to 171.064	Destroys the vitality or life of child which otherwise would have been born alive in birth or before; operating a facility without license, failure to meet Board of Health standards, or failure to make reports to Department of Health; cannot abort unborn child 20 wks. or more except if done to avert woman's death or serious risk or substantial and irreversible physical impairment of major bodily function, other than psychological function	Before 20 wks. or if done to prevent woman's death or serious risk of physical impairment
UTAH	76-7-301 to 76-7-324	Failure to meet standards for legal abortion; coercing someone to have abortion; intentional termination of human pregnancy including all procedures undertaken to kill alive, unborn child or produce a miscarriage; Saline Abortion: after viability has been determined, no person may knowingly perform a saline abortion procedure, unless all other available abortion procedures would pose a risk a risk to the life or health of the pregnant woman, or, when due to a serious medical emergency, time does not permit; Partial Birth Abortion: prohibited unless it is necessary to save the life of a mother whose life is endangered by a physical disorder, illness, or injury	Before viability; after viability, necessary to save mother's life or health, if woman was raped or incest committed, or child has grave and lethal defects
VERMONT	Statute repealed effective March 24, 2014		
VIRGINIA	18.2-71 to 18.276.2	Failure to meet standards for legal abortion; cause or administer drug or other means to woman with intent to destroy unborn child or produce abortion or miscarriage; Partial Birth Abortion: a physician shall not knowingly perform a partial birth abortion that is not necessary to save the life of a mother	1st trimester, no restrictions; 2nd trimester, in licensed hospital; 3rd trimester, continuation of pregnancy likely to result in death, physical or mental impairment of mother

Penalty	Consent	Residency	License
Abortion of viable fetus: imprisonment 5 yrs. to life; operating facility without license: class A misdemeanor: fine $100 to $500 per day; failure to report as legally required: class A misdemeanor; violating informed consent requirement: misdemeanor, punishable by fine up to $10,000 and administrative penalty	Voluntary and informed consent of the woman		Licensed physician; 16 wks. or more, ambulatory surgical center or hospital licensed to perform abortion unless necessary to protect life or health of mother; 20 wks. or more: must certify in writing medical indications supporting physician's judgment; private hospital or facility is not required to make its facilities available for an abortion unless physician determines mother's life is immediately endangered
Failure to meet standards, coercion, person performing unauthorized abortion not using medical skills to save unborn child, experimentation or buying or selling unborn child: 3rd degree felony; Physician not giving informed consent: unprofessional conduct; license may be revoked or suspended	Informed consent of mother required. M.D. must provide mother with information regarding abortion at least 72 hrs. before procedure except in medical emergency; in case of minor, written consent of parent or right by court order, or if done to prevent minor's death or serious health issues		
Class 4 felony: imprisonment 2 to 10 years and/or fine up to $100,000; encourage or promote performance of abortion: class 3 misdemeanor	Informed, written consent of mother; if incompetent, written permission from parent or guardian must be obtained except in case of medical emergency or spontaneous miscarriage		Any time, licensed physician; 2nd and 3rd trimesters, licensed hospital; 3rd trimester, attending physician and two consulting physicians certify medical necessity; if necessary to save mother's life or substantial and irremediable impairment of mental or physical health of the mother, no condition applies except licensed physician; life support for the child must be on hand and used if necessary

Table 26: Abortion—Continued

State	Code Section	Statutory Definition of Illegal Abortion	Statutory Definition of Legal Abortion
WASHINGTON	Reproductive Privacy Act: 9.02.100 to 9.02.902	Any medical treatment intended to induce the termination of a pregnancy except for the purpose of producing a live birth	Reproductive Privacy Act: "The state may not deny or interfere with a woman's right to choose to have an abortion prior to viability of the fetus or to protect her life or health." State may regulate as is medically necessary to protect the life, health of mother and consistent with established medical practice and in keeping with the least restrictive on the woman's right to have an abortion
WEST VIRGINIA	16-2F-1-9; 33-42-8; 61-2-8;	Administer substance or use means with intent to destroy unborn child or produce abortion unless in good faith to save woman or child; Partial Birth Abortion: abortion in which the person performing the abortion partially vaginally delivers a living fetus before killing the fetus and completing the delivery	Necessary to save life of mother or fetus; performed by physician
WISCONSIN	48.375; 253.10; 940.04	Intentionally destroys life of unborn child; causes death of mother during procedure; mother intentionally destroys unborn child or consents to same; mother intentionally destroys life of unborn quick child or consents to same	Necessary to save life of mother or advised by two other physicians as necessary
WYOMING	35-6-101 to 35-6-118	Any procedure after viability that is not necessary; Physician who intentionally terminates viability of unborn fetus during legal abortion; use of other than accepted medical procedures; other than licensed physician, including mother on self, performs act, procedure, prescription administered to produce premature expulsion, removal, or termination of fetus except when continuation of pregnancy threatens fetus's viability; using public funds for abortion other than those resulting from incest or sexual assault	After viability, necessary to preserve health, life of mother according to appropriate medical judgment

Penalty	Consent	Residency	License
Unauthorized abortion performed: class C felony			Licensed physician
Performing illegal abortion: felony, punishable by imprisonment 3 to 10 yrs.; if mother dies: murder; violation of minor notification requirements: misdemeanor, punishable by imprisonment in county jail up to 30 days and/or $500 to $1,000 fine: Partial Birth Abortion: felony, punishable by imprisonment up to 2 yrs. and/ or $10,000 to $50,000 fine	24 hrs. actual notice or 48 hrs. constructive notice to parent or guardian of minor under 18 who has not graduated from high school; minor can petition court for waiver of notification or it may be waived by another physician not associated with attending physician; no consent necessary if emergency		
Person other than mother intentionally destroys life of unborn child: class H felony, punishable by imprisonment up to 6 yrs. and/or fine up to $10,000; intentionally destroy life of unborn quick child or death of mother: class E felony, punishable by imprisonment up to 15 yrs. and/or fine up to $50,000	Informed written consent of unemancipated minor as well as informed, written consent of parent, guardian, or other adult family member unless the pregnancy is a result of sexual assault or incest or a physician believes the minor to be suicidal; court may waive; no consent necessary in medical emergency		Licensed physician; licensed maternity hospital except in medical emergency
Physician aborting viable fetus; use of other than accepted medical procedures; person other than physician performing abortion: felony, punishable by imprisonment up to 14 years	Unemancipated minor's written consent and one of minor's parents must have written notification 48 hrs. before abortion; physician must have minor's and one parent's consent or court order; minor can petition court to waive parental consent; consent not required in an emergency		Licensed physician

515

27. ADOPTION

There is great variety among states regarding adoption laws, perhaps due to the very personal nature of these laws. A long legal tradition did not surround family law, and as state governments began to take responsibility for regulating family relationships, they tended to develop very unique and regional variations on aspects of family law, including adoption. These variations spawned difficult legal conflicts as modern families grew more mobile, and these conflicts gave rise to the desire to standardize laws among the states into Model Acts and Uniform Laws. Although the need for adoption standardization is strong to date, only eight states have adopted the Uniform Adoption Act.

Any adult may adopt any other person with only minor logical restrictions. A married person must apply for adoption jointly with his or her spouse, for example, and, if the child in certain states is over the age of ten, twelve, or fourteen, the state will require his or her consent as well (except in Louisiana and Wisconsin, where the child's consent is not required). "Objective" standards, like Hawaii's requirement of a "proper" adopter, or Illinois's "reputable" one, and Virginia's "natural" one, also are present, as are specific requirements, for example, that the adopter be at least ten years older than the adoptee. Sometimes the adoptee must be a minor. In Florida homosexuals are specifically excluded in the language of the statute from adopting; however, this statute was struck down by a Florida court of appeals in the case, *Florida Dept. of Children and Families v. Adoption of XXG*, 45 So. 3d 79 (2010), and the language in the statute has still not been amended to reflect this! It is also unclear whether in other states terms such as "proper," "reputable," or "natural" refer to a prospective parent's sexual orientation.

In general, family laws are changing as society's value system changes and is scrutinized. In the area of adoption, there is a growing trend to recognize the rights and opinions of children at younger ages, and to recognize the rights of non-traditional individuals. Indeed, same-sex couples are recognized as adoptive parents in a number of states. Also, some states appear headed in the direction of "open" adoption, whereby any individual may adopt any other individual for any reason.

Federal Law

Federal law has preempted the entire scope of the laws of adoption regarding Native Americans, provoking controversy over a non-Native American family's ability to adopt a Native American. In 1991, when a member of the Aleut tribe had a baby out of wedlock, a non-Native couple living in Vancouver, British Columbia, adopted the child. The tribe sued for custody of the child and won the right to intervene in the adoption by claiming that they had a vital interest in preserving the child's Indian heritage. The California court upheld the tribe's right to intervene, but in the child's interest let her remain with her adoptive parents because she had been living with them for nearly two years.

Table 27: Adoption

State	Code Section	Uniform Act?	Who May Be Adopted	Age That Consent of Child Is Required
ALABAMA	26-10A-1 to 26-10A-38	No	Any minor; any adult under following conditions: permanently disabled; determined to have intellectual disability; consents to adoption and is related or stepchild; consents to be adopted by a husband and wife	14 and older unless adoptee does not have mental capacity to give consent
ALASKA	25.23.010 to 25.23.240	Yes	Any person	10 and older unless court dispenses with minor's consent in minor's best interest.
ARIZONA	8-101 to 8-145; 14-8101	No	Any child under 18 or foreign born person under age 21 who is not illegal alien and is present within the state; any adult person 21 and younger who is a stepchild, niece, cousin, nephew, or grandchild of the adopting person; an adult who was placed in the care of the adopting parent as a foster child as a juvenile and maintained familiar relationship for more than 5 yrs.	12 and older in open court
ARKANSAS	9-9-201 to 9-9-508	Yes	Any person	12 and older unless court dispenses with minor's consent in minor's best interest
CALIFORNIA	Fam. §§ 8500 to 9340	N	Any unmarried minor child; any married minor or adult	12 and older
COLORADO	14-1-101; 19-5-200.2 to 19-5-304	No	Any child under 18; 18-21 may be adopted as child upon court approval; any adult	12 and older
CONNECTICUT	45a-724 to 45a-765	No	Any person; spouse, if any, of adopted adult must consent	12 and older
DELAWARE	Tit. 13, §§ 901 to 965	No	Any person	14 and older, unless court waives consent in best interest of child

Who May Adopt	Adoptive Home Residency Prior to Decree?	State Agency/Court	Statute of Limitations to Challenge
Any adult person or husband and wife jointly; no rule or regulation of Department of Human Resources shall prevent adoption by single person solely because of a certain age or by a person because he or she works outside the home	60 days, unless waived by court when good cause is shown	Dept. of Human Resources/Probate Ct.	1 yr., except for grounds that minor was kidnapped
Husband and wife together; unmarried adult, including father or mother of person to be adopted; married person without other spouse joining, if other spouse is not person to be adopted and other person is parent of adoptee and consents to adoption, or consent is excused by court because other spouse is unreasonably withholding consent, or spouses are legally separated	Yes, but no specified length of time required	Health & Social Services/Superior Ct.	1 yr.
Any adult resident of the state is eligible to adopt; husband and wife may jointly adopt children; adults may adopt adult relatives; nonresident adult if child is dependent, was placed in applicant's home and dept. recommends adoption after review; preference is given to married man and woman over single adult if all factors equal	No	Dept. of Child Safety/Superior Ct., Juvenile Division	1 yr.
Husband and wife together, unmarried adult, unmarried parent of child, single married parent of child if other parent consents, they are legally separated or excused by court	6 mos.; not required if minor is in custody of Dept. of Health & Human Services and must reside outside of home to receive medically necessary care	Human Services/Probate Ct.	1 yr.
Any adult; any married couple if both parties consent or consent excused by court; adults must be 10 yrs. older than child unless stepparent, sister, brother, aunt, uncle, or first cousin and court approves	No	State Dept. of Social Services/Superior Ct.	On any grounds except fraud: 1 yr.; fraud: 3 yrs., or 90 days after discovery of fraud, whichever is earlier
Any person over 21 or minor with court approval; married person or civil union partner must petition jointly with spouse/partner unless such spouse is natural parent of or has previously adopted child or is legally separated	No	Social Services/Juvenile Ct.	Jurisdictional or procedural defect: 91 days; in stepparent adoption, fraud upon court or party: 1 yr.
Any person 18 or older, as long as adoptee is younger; married persons must join in adoption unless court finds sufficient reason for nonjoinder	No	Children and Youth Services/Probate Ct.	Not specified
Unmarried person; divorced or legally separated person; husband and wife who are living together; must be legal resident of Delaware and over 21	6 mos.	Dept. of Services for Children, Youth & Families/Family Ct.	6 mos.

Table 27: Adoption—Continued

State	Code Section	Uniform Act?	Who May Be Adopted	Age That Consent of Child Is Required
DISTRICT OF COLUMBIA	16-301 to 16-315	No	Any person	14 and older
FEDERAL	25 U.S.C. §§ 1901 to 1963	Indian Child Welfare Act of 1978		
FLORIDA	Florida Adoption Act: 63.012 to 63.236	No	Any person	12 and older unless court dispenses with consent in best interest of child
GEORGIA	19-8-1 to 19-8-26	No	Any child 10 yrs. younger than petitioner; any adult who gives written consent.	14 and older
HAWAII	578-1 to 578-17	No	Any person; adult adoptee must give consent	10 and older, unless court dispenses with consent in best interest of child; if married adult, spouse must consent
IDAHO	16-1501 to 16-1515	No	Any child, with consent of living parents if child is under 18; any adult where the person adopting has sustained relation of parent.	12 and older unless adoptee lacks mental capacity to consent; consent of spouse required if adoptee is married
ILLINOIS	750 §§ 50/1 to 50/24	No	Any child; any adult if he or she has resided in home of persons intending to adopt at any time for more than 2 continuous yrs. or adoptee is a relative	14 and older, unless waived by the court
INDIANA	31-19-1-1 to 31-19-29-6	No	Any person	14 and older; consent of spouse, if any, is required

Who May Adopt	Adoptive Home Residency Prior to Decree?	State Agency/Court	Statute of Limitations to Challenge
Any person, provided spouse, if any, joins in petition unless spouse is natural parent of adoptee and consents thereto	6 mos.	Mayor or licensed agency/ Superior Ct. of D.C.	1 yr.
Placement preferences		Indian Tribe exclusive jurisdiction/Tribal Ct.	2 yrs., unless otherwise permitted under state law
Unmarried adult; husband and wife jointly, unless other spouse is child's parent and consents or failure to join or consent is excused by court for good cause or in best interest of child; married person cannot adopt his or her spouse	90 days	Dept. of Health & Rehabilitative Services/ Circuit Ct.	1 yr.
Any adult at least 25 or married and living with spouse and bona fide resident for 6 mos. prior to filing petition; must be 10 yrs. older than adoptive child; must be financially, physically, and mentally able to have permanent custody; if married, both spouses must consent unless one spouse is child's parent	No	Dept. of Human Services/ Superior Ct. in county or juvenile courts	6 mos.
Any proper adult person, not married, or married to legal parent of minor, or husband and wife jointly.	No	Human Services/Family Ct.	1 yr.
Any adult resident of Idaho for at least 6 consecutive mos. prior to filing who is either 15 yrs. older than child or 25 yrs. of age or older; except spouse of natural parent or person adopting adult who has shown a substantial relationship as a parent has been maintained in excess of 1 yr. may adopt without above age restriction. No married person can adopt without consent of spouse.	No	Dept. of Health & Welfare/Magistrate's Division or District Ct.	6 mos. except for fraud
Any reputable person under no legal disability of legal age who has resided continually in Illinois for at least 6 mos., or 90 days for armed forces; residency requirement waived in adoption of relative or if child placed by an agency; if petitioner is married, husband or wife must join in petition unless separated over 1 yr.; minor may petition by leave of court upon good cause shown	6 mos. unless waived by court	Dept. of Children and Family Services/Circuit Ct.	1 yr. after entry of order
Any resident of state; if petitioner is married, spouse must join or consent if such spouse is natural or adoptive parent of the child; nonresidents of state may adopt hard to place child as defined in 31-19-2-3	Period of supervision within sole discretion of court hearing adoption petition	Public Welfare/Probate Ct. (in counties with one)	6 mos. after entry or decree or 1 yr. after adoptive parents obtain custody, whichever is later

Table 27: Adoption—Continued

State	Code Section	Uniform Act?	Who May Be Adopted	Age That Consent of Child Is Required
IOWA	600.1 to 600.25	No	Any natural person	14 and older
KANSAS	Kansas Adoption and Relinquishment Act: 59-2111 to 59-2144	No	Any person; adult with consent of spouse if married, or legal guardian if disabled	14 and older and of sound intellect
KENTUCKY	199.470 to 199.590; 405.390	No	Any person	12 and older, unless waived by court
LOUISIANA	Ch.C. Art. 1167 to 1279.7	No	Any child or adult; special procedures exist to adopt adult	Not required
MAINE	Tit. 18A, §§ 9-101 to 9-404	No	Any person, minor or adult; only a minor can be placed under guardianship	14 and older
MARYLAND	Fam. Law §§ 1-201; 5-301 to 5-4c-07	No	Any person	10 and older if the natural parents' rights have been terminated
MASSACHUSETTS	Ch. 210, §§ 1 to 14	No	Any person younger than adopter; special requirements for child under age 14	12 and older
MICHIGAN	Michigan Adoption Code: 710.21 to 710.70	No	Any person	14 and older
MINNESOTA	259.20 to 259.89	No	Any person	14 and older
MISSISSIPPI	93-17-1 to 93-17-307	No	Any person	14 and older
MISSOURI	453.010 to 453.170	No	Any person	14 and older

Who May Adopt	Adoptive Home Residency Prior to Decree?	State Agency/Court	Statute of Limitations to Challenge
Unmarried adult; husband and wife together; husband or wife separately under certain circumstances, 600.4	180 days; may be shortened for good cause	Human Services/Juvenile Ct.	Not specified
Any adult, or husband and wife jointly, except one spouse cannot adopt without consent of other	Not required	Dept. of Children and Families/District Ct.	Not specified
Any person over 18 who is a resident of or who has resided in Kentucky for 12 mos. immediately preceding filing; husband and wife must petition jointly unless one spouse is natural parent and court does not object	Unless placed by cabinet or agency, 90 days prior to filing adoption petition	Cabinet for Families and Children/Circuit Ct.	1 yr.; if ethnological ancestry difference: 5 yrs.
Any single person 18 or older or a married couple jointly	6 mos. if agency; 1 yr. if private	Dept. of Social Services/ Juvenile Ct.	30 days; 6 mos. from discovery if for fraud or duress, but no later than 1 yr. from decree, or 2 yrs. if perpetrated by adoptive parent
Unmarried person; husband and wife jointly; resident or nonresident	1 yr. may be required at discretion of court	Human Services/Probate Ct.	Not specified
Any adult; court cannot deny petition just because petitioner is single; married persons must act jointly unless legally separated, one spouse is natural parent of adoptee, or spouse is incompetent	180 days, or shorter if allowed by court	Social Services Administration/Equity Ct. unless child is under jurisdiction of Juvenile Ct.	1 yr.
Any person of full age; if married, spouse must join unless excused or in process of divorce; adoptee must be younger than petitioner; certain exceptions apply, Ch. 210, § 1	6 mos. if adoptee is under 14 unless requirement waived	Social Services/ Probate Ct.	120 days for appeal; may only be made by parent
Any person; if married, spouse must join or consent, unless excused	6 mos. unless waived by court	Family Independence Agency/Family Division of Circuit Ct.	21 days from entry of order or denial of petition for rehearing
Any person who has resided in the state for more than 1 yr., unless length of residence is reduced to 30 days in child's best interest or waived altogether if child is related or has had significant contact	3 mos.; may be waived by court	Human Services/Juvenile Ct.	Not specified
Any unmarried adult or husband and wife jointly; must be Mississippi resident for consecutive mos. before filing	6 mos.; waiting period may be shortened if child resided in adoptive home prior to entry of interlocutory decree or is stepchild of petitioner	Dept. of Human Services/ Chancery Ct.	6 mos. from date of final decree
If spouse does not join married petitioner, court may order joinder; if spouse does not comply, judge may dismiss petition;	6 mos., unless adopted by foster parent; may be waived by court in certain circumstances	Social Services, Div. of Family Services/Juvenile Div. of Circuit Ct.	1 yr.

Table 27: Adoption—Continued

State	Code Section	Uniform Act?	Who May Be Adopted	Age That Consent of Child Is Required
MONTANA	42-1-101 to 42-7-106	Yes	Any person	12 and older, unless child does not have mental capacity to consent
NEBRASKA	43-101 to 43-166	No	Any child; any adult child	14 and older
NEVADA	127.003 to 127.420	No	Any person; consent of spouse required for adult persons	14 and older
NEW HAMPSHIRE	170-B:1 to 170-B:31	No	Any person	14 and older, unless excused by court; consent by spouse, if any, of adoptee necessary unless excused by good cause
NEW JERSEY	9:3-37 to 9:3-56 (minor); 2A:22-1 to 2A:22-3 (adult)	No	Any person	10 and older to be given consideration
NEW MEXICO	32A-5-1 to 32A-5-45 (minor); 40-14-1 to 40-14-15 (adult)	Yes	Any person; any adult with consent	14 yrs. and older, unless lacking mental capacity
NEW YORK	Dom. Rel. §§ 109 to 117	Yes	Any person	14 yrs. and older, unless excused
NORTH CAROLINA	48-1-100 to 48-10-105	No	Any person; any adult with consent; spouses may not adopt each other	12 and older

Who May Adopt	Adoptive Home Residency Prior to Decree?	State Agency/Court	Statute of Limitations to Challenge
Unmarried person at least 18 yrs. old; husband and wife jointly or separately when one spouse is a parent of the child, legally separated, judicially incompetent	6 mos., unless waived by court	Dept. of Public Health and Family Services/ District or Tribal Ct.	Not specified
Any adult person may adopt minor child; adult child may be adopted by spouse of such child's parent; husband and wife must jointly adopt child, unless one is parent of child	6 mos. except in adoptions of adult child	Dept. of Social Services/ County Ct.	2 yrs.
Minor: Any adult who is 10 yrs. older than adoptee, unless related or child of spouse and court approves; if petitioner is married, spouse must join or consent if capable; petitioner must have resided in state for 6 mos. preceding adoption. Adult: Any adult may adopt younger adult except spouse	6 mos.	Human Resources, Division of Child and Family Services/District Ct.	Not specified
Any adult 18 or older; spouse must join unless excused, spouse assents and is parent of adoptee or adoptee is over 18, or couple is legally separated	6 mos.	Dept. of Health and Human Services/Probate Ct.	1 yr.
Any person 18 or older and 10 yrs. older than adoptee; if petitioner is married, spouse must consent or join; court may waive any of these requirements for good cause.	6 mos.	Dept. of Children and Families/Superior Ct., Chancery Division, Family Dept.	Not specified
Any resident individual approved by the court as a suitable adoptive parent; if petitioner is married, spouse must join unless natural parent of adoptee, legally separated, or excused from joining by court; nonresidents may adopt if adoptee is resident or was born in state, is less than 6 mos. old, and was placed by agency licensed in state	Up to 60 days if less than 1 yr. old when placed; 120 days if more than 1 yr. old when placed; may be waived	Children, Youth and Families Dept./District Ct., Children's Court Division	1 yr. except where Indian Child Welfare Act of 1978 prevails
Any unmarried person; adult married couple together; any two unmarried adult intimate partners together; adult married person legally separated pursuant to a decree or for at least 3 yrs. prior to filing; adult or minor married couple together may adopt child or either born in or out of wedlock; adult or minor spouse may adopt such child of other spouse	3 mos.; may be waived by judge	As defined by social services law/Family Ct.	Not specified
Any adult person over 18; husband and wife jointly, unless one spouse has been declared incompetent or requirement is waived; only one unmarried person may file; petitioner must have resided in state for 6 mos. preceding filing of petition; residency requirement waived under certain circumstances	At least 90 days unless waived by Court	Health and Human Services/Superior Ct.	6 mos.

Table 27: Adoption—Continued

State	Code Section	Uniform Act?	Who May Be Adopted	Age That Consent of Child Is Required
NORTH DAKOTA	14-15-01 to 14-15.1-08	Yes	Any person	10 and older unless waived by the court
OHIO	3107.01 to 3107.99	Yes	Any child; adults if totally or permanently disabled, intellectually disabled, child of petitioner or had kinship, childcare, or stepparent relationship with petitioner as child and consents to adoption	12 and older
OKLAHOMA	Tit.10, §§ 7501-1.1 to 7510-3.3	No, but some sections incorporated	Any person; any adult with consent	12 and older.
OREGON	109.304 to 109.410	No	Any person; any adult with consent	14 and older
PENNSYLVANIA	Tit. 23, §§ 2101 to 2938	No	Any person	12 and older
RHODE ISLAND	15-7-2 to 15-7-26	No	Any person	14 and older
SOUTH CAROLINA	63-9-10 to 63-9-2290	No	Any child present in state; any adult with spouse's consent, if any	14 and older, unless lacking mental capacity or not in child's best interest
SOUTH DAKOTA	25-6-1 to 25-6-25	No	Any person	12 and older
TENNESSEE	36-1-101 to 36-1-305	No	Any person	14 and older
TEXAS	Fam. §§ 162.001 to 162.602	No	Any person	12 and older

Who May Adopt	Adoptive Home Residency Prior to Decree?	State Agency/Court	Statute of Limitations to Challenge
Unmarried adult or parent of child to be adopted; husband and wife jointly unless legally separated, petitioner is stepparent, or excused	6 mos.	Human Services/District Ct.	1 yr.
Unmarried adult; unmarried minor parent of adoptee; husband and wife, at least one of whom is adult, together, unless legally separated or otherwise excused	6 mos.	Human Services/Probate Ct.	1 yr.
Husband and wife if both over 21 or either husband or wife if other spouse is parent or relative of child; unmarried person 21 or older; married person 21 or older who is legally separated from spouse	6 mos., discretionary	Department of Human Services/District Ct.	1 yr.
Any person; petitioner, child, one parent or person consenting must be resident of Oregon for 6 mos.; if petitioner is married, spouse must join; compliance with Indian Child Welfare Act required if applicable.	Not required	Dept. of Human Services/Circuit Ct.	1 yr.
Any person	Not required, but may do temporary placement	Pennsylvania Adoption Cooperative Exchange (PACE) in Dept. of Public Welfare/Common Pleas Ct.	Not specified
Any person residing in state may adopt any younger person; if petitioner is married, spouse must join, requirement may be waived if it can be shown adoption would be in child's best interest; nonresident may petition under certain circumstances	6 mos., but court may waive for good cause	Child Welfare Services Dept. for Children and their Families/Family Ct. (children); Probate Ct. (adults)	180 days
Any South Carolina resident may petition court to adopt child; nonresidents may apply in exceptional circumstances.; any adult person may adopt any other adult person	90 days	State Dept. of Social Services/Family Ct.	Relief may be granted after duty of decree only for extrinsic fraud
Any adult person may adopt any child at least 10 yrs. younger; any adult may adopt another adult with consent; spousal consent required	6 mos.	Social Services/Circuit Ct.	2 yrs., except for fraud
Any person over 18 who has been Tennessee resident for 6 mos.; residency requirement may be waived under certain circumstances; spouse must join if competent, unless natural parent of child to be adopted	6 mos. unless waived by court	Children's Services/Chancery or Circuit Ct.	1 yr.
Any adult; if petitioner is married, spouse must join unless one is parent of child; if adult adoption, petitioner must be resident of state	6 mos., may be waived	Human Services/District Ct. or county court with family law jurisdiction	6 mos.

Table 27: Adoption—Continued

State	Code Section	Uniform Act?	Who May Be Adopted	Age That Consent of Child Is Required
UTAH	Utah Adoption Act: 78B-6-101 to 78B-6-146	No	Any child 10 yrs. younger than petitioner; any adult	12 and older unless lacking mental capacity
VERMONT	Tit.15A, §§1-101 to 8-101	No	Any person; if adult, with consent and consent of spouse, if any	14 and older
VIRGINIA	63.2-1200 to 63.2-1253	No	Any child; adult under certain conditions	14 and older
WASHINGTON	26.33.010 to 26.33.903	No	Any person	14 and older
WEST VIRGINIA	48-22-101 to 48-22-903	No	Any person; adults with consent	12 and older
WISCONSIN	48.46; 48.81 to 48.979; 882.01 to 882.04	No	Any child present in state at filing or any adult	No child's consent required; however, minors 14 and older must attend hearing unless court orders otherwise
WYOMING	1-22-101 to 1-22-203	No	Any person within state at filing; adult must consent and be adopted by relative	14 and older

Who May Adopt	Adoptive Home Residency Prior to Decree?	State Agency/Court	Statute of Limitations to Challenge
Any adult; if married, spouse must consent if able; single person who is "cohabitating" and involved in a sexual relationship without being married may not adopt	6 mos.; 1 yr. for adoptive stepparents	Child and Family Services/District or Juvenile Ct.	Cannot be contested after entry of final adoption decree by party to proceeding; no person may contest after 1 yr.
Any person; if petitioner is married, spouse must consent if able, unless legally separated; parent and partner may adopt if in best interest of the child	180 days	Social & Rehabilitation Services/Probate Ct.	Not specified
Any natural person may petition to adopt minor child; if petitioner is married, spouse must join; any natural person may adopt another adult under certain conditions, 63.2-1243	6 mos.; may be waived by court	Public Welfare or Social Services/Circuit Ct.	6 mos.
Any legally competent person 18 or over	Not required	Social & Health Services/Superior Ct.	1 yr.
Any unmarried person; married person with spouse's consent; husband and wife jointly; petitioner to adopt adult must be resident of state Any person not married; any married person with spouse's consent; husband and wife jointly; adult petitioner must be resident of stat	6 mos.	Department of Human Services/Circuit Ct.	6 mos.
Unmarried adult; husband and wife jointly; spouse of minor's parent may adopt minor; must be Wisconsin residents and of same religion as adoptee's natural parents if practicable and requested by birth parent; any resident adult may adopt any other adult with consent and consent of petitioner's spouse, if any	6 mos.	Department of Health & Social Services/Circuit Ct.	Adoptive parent may not move court for relief from order granting adoption; petition for termination of parental rights and appeal to ct. of appeals only remedies for adoptive parent who wishes to end parental relationship with adopted child; birth parent has 30 days from entry of judgment to move to withdraw consent to termination of parental rights, 48.46
Any adult person who has resided in state during 60 days immediately preceding filing of petition and who is determined by court to be fit and competent to be a parent	6 mos.	Department of Family Services/District Ct.	Not specified

28. ANNULMENT AND PROHIBITED MARRIAGE

Annulment

Annulment differs from divorce in that it addresses defects in a marital relationship occurring at the time of the formation of that relationship. Thus, if a marriage is illegally formed, when it is annulled the parties regain their legal rights and responsibilities as they existed before the marriage occurred. By contrast, a divorce deals with problems in a marital relationship arising after the marriage is formed. Traditionally, after a divorce the parties have continuing legal status as ex-spouses involving division of property, custody of children, and alimony.

Annulments are becoming similar to divorces in that with annulments courts may now divide marital property, order the payment of spousal support or alimony, or decree nearly anything that would be common upon a decree of divorce. Unlike with divorce, however, certain rights or entitlements such as worker's compensation benefits or alimony from a previous marriage that may have ended upon marriage will be restarted upon annulment, because the decree legally makes the marriage nonexistent.

Grounds for annulments and prohibited marriages are varied. Insanity, fraud, force, duress, impotency, being underage, and polygamy are all leading grounds for annulment. There are also a few more creative grounds. Delaware and Colorado, for instance, has an annulment provision considering if the act were done as "Jest or Dare." A couple of states will also make a marriage void or voidable if a party is found to have AIDS or venereal disease.

Prohibited Marriage

Many states prohibit marriage between parties more closely related than second cousins, though in some states first cousins may marry. In three states that prohibit marriages of first cousins, an exception is made for elderly parties: in Arizona and Indiana if parties are over 65 and one is sterile, or in Wisconsin if the woman is over 55 and one party is sterile. Only in Rhode Island do special exceptions exist for a particular religious group: Jews are permitted to marry according to religious law exclusive of state rules.

An issue which has lately caused a great deal of controversy is same-sex marriages. Until 1993, same-sex marriages were specifically banned in only about seven states. Since then there has been a remarkable amount of activity on this topic. For example, in that year the Supreme Court of Hawaii ruled that the state's prohibition of same-sex marriages was a violation of the equal protection clause of the U.S. Constitution because it discriminated on the basis of sex. The court then sent the case back to the trial court to gather additional evidence regarding the state's "compelling interest" in banning same-sex marriages.

Immediately, fearful that they would be compelled under the constitutional principles of full faith and credit to honor Hawaiian same-sex marriages, many states reacted by passing legislation specifically banning the practice. However, voters in Hawaii approved a constitutional amendment giving the legislature the authority to limit marriage to persons of the opposite sex, and, for a time, did so. In November of 2013, however, the legislature met in special session and passed legislation that allowed same-sex marriage. In 2000, the Vermont Supreme Court ruled that same-sex couples are entitled to all of the benefits of marriage.

To date, several dozen states have enacted specific legislation, passed referenda and statutes specifically banning or approving same-sex marriage have been challenged in state and federal courts, with mixed results. Included in the mix are several state constitutional amendments and legislative actions that are very similar to the federal Defense of Marriage Act (DOMA), signed by President Clinton in September 1996.

On the last day of the 2015 term, the Supreme Court released one of its most potent rulings, *Obergefell v. Hodges*, 576 U.S. __, 135 S. Ct. 2584 (2015), which found that the Constitution of the United States guarantees same-sex couples a fundamental right to marriage, thus voiding all state prohibitions to same-sex marriage. In the chapter below, we have included an asterisk to designate each code section that contains a specific same-sex prohibition. Many states may not revise their statutes to reflect the Supreme Court's ruling, out of spite, protest or simple legislative inertia. The chart below will be updated to reflect such changes as they happen. For the time being, state statutes that still contain language that prohibits same sex marriage will be marked with an asterisk, even though Obergefell clearly makes such statutes unconstitutional.

Table 28: Annulment and Prohibited Marriage

State	Code Section	Grounds for Annulment	Limitation	Legitimacy of Children	Prohibited Marriages
ALABAMA	13A-13-1; 13A-13-3; 30-1-4 to 30-1-6; 30-1-19*; AL Const. art. I, § 36.03*	Under 16, or 16-18 without parental consent; bigamy; incest			Bigamous; incestuous; same sex*
ALASKA	25.05.01 to 25.05.171; 25.05.013*; 25.20.050; 25.24.020; 25.24.030; AK Const. art. 1, § 25*	Under 14, or 14-18 without court or parental consent; insufficient understanding for consent; consent was obtained by force or fraud; failure to consummate; either party of unsound mind; bigamy; incest	Cannot be brought after party freely cohabits with the other after age of consent if underage, or coming to reason if of unsound mind, or knowledge of fraud if fraud is involved	Children legitimate if parents subsequently marry, if acknowledged in writing by father and mother, or by adjudication of paternity by court	Either party has living spouse at time; parties related closer than fourth degree of consanguinity; same sex*
ARIZONA	25-101*; 25-102; 25-122; 25-125*; 25-301 to 25-302; 25-1401; AZ Const. art. 30, § 1*	Under 16 without consent of court; under 18 without prenatal consent; superior courts may dissolve and adjudge marriage null and void when cause alleged constitutes impediment rendering it void		Every child is legitimate child of its natural parents	Between parents and children, grandparents and grandchildren, brothers and sisters, (half and whole), aunt and nephew, uncle and niece, first cousins unless both are over 65 or one is not able to reproduce; same sex*
ARKANSAS	9-11-101 to 9-11-109*; 9-11-208*; 9-11-209; 9-12-101 to 9-12-202; 9-12-311; AR Const. Amend. 83, § 1*	Under 16 for female, 17 for male, 16/17 to 18 without parental consent, exceptions for pregnancy or couple has child; incapable of consent due to age or understanding; incapable for physical causes; if consent obtained by fraud or force; incest			Incest; same sex*

Table 28: Annulment and Prohibited Marriage—Continued

State	Code Section	Grounds for Annulment	Limitation	Legitimacy of Children	Prohibited Marriages
CALIFORNIA	Fam. §§ 2200; 2201; 2210; 2211	Party did not have capability to consent; another living spouse; unsound mind, unless party freely cohabitated with spouse after coming to reason; consent obtained by force or fraud, unless party freely cohabitated with spouse afterward; physically incapable of entering marriage state	Age of consent: Underage party within 4 yrs. of reaching age of consent or by parent before party has reached age; fraud: within 4 yrs. of discovery of fraud by injured party; husband/ wife living, either party during life or by former spouse; unsound mind, any time before death; consent by force, within 4 yrs. of marriage by injured party; physical incapability, within 4 yrs. by injured party		Ancestor and descendant of any degree, brother and sister (half-blood included), uncle and niece, aunt and nephew; bigamy and polygamy
COLORADO	14-2-110; 14-2-104*; 14-10-111	Consent lacking due to mental incapacity, alcohol, drugs; underage without parental consent; jest or dare; duress; fraudulent act; physical incapacity to consummate; bigamy	Lacking capacity due to mental infirmity, influence of alcohol, drugs, or fraud duress; jest or dare: 6 mos. after knowledge of described condition; lack of physical capacity to consummate the marriage: 1 yr. after the knowledge of condition; underage without consent of parents or guardian: 24 mos. from date of marriage; prohibited marriages: declaration of invalidity must be brought prior to death of either party or priority settlement or closing of estate	Children of invalid marriage are legitimate	Prior marriage still valid; between ancestor and descendant, whole- or half-blood brother and sister, whole- or half-blood uncle and niece or aunt and nephew, except where permitted by aboriginal cultures; marriage void by law of place where marriage was contracted; same sex*

Table 28: Annulment and Prohibited Marriage—Continued

State	Code Section	Grounds for Annulment	Limitation	Legitimacy of Children	Prohibited Marriages
CONNECTICUT	46b-20a; 46b-21; 46b-30; 46b-40; 46b-48; 46b-60	Underage; bigamy; spouse convicted of offense against chastity	Offense against chastity: petitioner must file within 4 mos. of conviction	Children of void marriage are legitimate	No person may marry parent, grandparent, child, grandchild, sibling, parent's sibling, sibling's child, stepparent, or stepchild
DELAWARE	Tit. 13, §§ 101 to 105; 1301; 1506	Lack of capacity to consent at time of solemnization because of mental infirmity or incapacity, or because of influence of alcohol, drugs, or other incapacitating substances; physical incapacity to consummate; underage without consent of parents; fraud; duress; jest or dare; bigamy; polygamy	Lack of capacity, fraud, duress, jest or dare: within 90 days of obtaining knowledge; inability to consummate: 1 yr. after knowledge obtained; underage: within 1 yr. of marriage; prohibited: any time before death of either party or prior to settlement of estate; may also be sought by appropriate state official or by child of either party	Children born of annulled, void, or voidable marriages are legitimate	Between person and ancestor, descendant, brother, sister, uncle, aunt, niece, nephew, first cousin; person on parole except with court permission
DISTRICT OF COLUMBIA	16-904; 16-907 to 16-909; 46-401 to 46-405	Unable to consent because of mental incapacity; consent by force, fraud or coercion; matrimonial incapacity without knowledge of spouse; insanity, unless voluntary cohabitation after discovery of insanity; underage; bigamy		A child born in or out of wedlock or adopted is legitimate child of father and mother and legitimate relative of parents' relatives by blood or adoption	Between ancestor and descendant, uncle and niece, aunt and nephew, brother and sister and corresponding in-law relationships; marriage in foreign state to avoid law; bigamy
FLORIDA	741.21 to 741.212*; 826.01 to 826.04; FL Const. art I, § 27*	No statutory provisions		No statute governing legitimacy of children	No marriage between persons related by lineal consanguinity, sister, aunt, niece, brother, uncle, nephew; common law marriages after 1967; bigamy: same sex*

Table 28: Annulment and Prohibited Marriage—Continued

State	Code Section	Grounds for Annulment	Limitation	Legitimacy of Children	Prohibited Marriages
GEORGIA	19-3-2 to 19-3-7, 19-3-3.1*; 19-4-1; GA Const. art. I, § 4, ¶ I*	Unable, unwilling, or fraudulently induced to contract; unsound, underage without parental consent; drunkenness at time of marriage to induce consent	No annulment granted where children are born or are to be born of marriage; valid if after removal of impediment, cohabitation with free and voluntary consent and ratification of marriage; unwilling or fraudulently induced: valid if subsequent cohabitation and consent freely given	Issue of void marriage legitimate, if children born before annulment	Related by blood or marriage, father and daughter or stepdaughter, mother and son or stepson, whole- or half-blood brother and sister, grandparent and grandchild, aunt and nephew, uncle and niece; bigamous; same sex*
HAWAII	580-21 to 580-29; 572-1; 572-2	Underage, unless freely cohabitates after reaching legal age; bigamous; lacking mental capacity to consent; consent obtained by force, duress, fraud and no subsequent cohabitation; party afflicted with loathsome disease unknown to party seeking annulment; incestuous	For spouse still living: any time during either party's lifetime; underage: until they attain legal age and freely cohabit; cannot be brought by party who was of legal age at time of marriage; physical incapacity: within 2 yrs. of marriage; lack of mental capacity: until mental capacity attained and parties freely cohabit; declarations or confessions not sufficient; courts require other satisfactory evidence of facts	Children of annulled or prohibited marriages are legitimate	Between ancestor and descendant, any degree, whole- or half-blood brother and sister, uncle and niece, aunt and nephew, aunt and niece, uncle and nephew, legitimate or illegitimate; bigamous

Table 28: Annulment and Prohibited Marriage—Continued

State	Code Section	Grounds for Annulment	Limitation	Legitimacy of Children	Prohibited Marriages
IDAHO	32-201 to 32-207; 32-209*; 32-501 to 32-503	Underage without parental consent, unless freely cohabits after reaching age of consent, former spouse living and marriage still in force; unsound mind, unless cohabits after coming to reason; force or fraud, unless cohabits freely afterward; physical incapacity and physical incapacity continues and appears to be incurable	Underage: by parent, any time before majority reached; by minor, within 4 yrs. of reaching age of consent; spouse living: any time during life; unsound mind: by injured party, relative, or guardian any time before death; fraud: within 4 yrs. of discovery; force: within 4 yrs. of marriage unless freely cohabits; incapacity to consummate: 4 yrs. from marriage	Not affected by annulment unless grounds is fraud, that woman was pregnant with another man's child, children must be begotten before annulment judgment	Incestuous: between ancestor and descendant of any degree, whole-and half-blood brother and sister, uncle and niece or nephew, aunt and nephew or niece, first cousins; polygamous marriages; same sex*
ILLINOIS	750 §§ 5/212 to 5/214; 5/301 to 5/303	Underage without parental consent or judicial approval; lack of capacity to consent due to mental incapacity or infirmity, alcohol, drugs, force, duress, fraud; physically incapable of consummating and other party did not know; prohibited marriage	Underage: any time prior to reaching age of consent;; lack of capacity to consent: 90 days after knowledge of lack; inability to consummate: 1 year after knowledge; all petitions for annulment must be brought before death of either party, except in case of bigamous marriage: not to exceed 3 yrs. following death of 1st party	Children born or adopted of prohibited or annulled marriage are legitimate	Former marriage undissolved; between ancestor and descendant, brother and sister half or whole blood, uncle and niece, aunt and nephew, half or whole first cousins unless no chance of reproduction or both parties over 50 yrs.; common law marriages,

Table 28: Annulment and Prohibited Marriage—Continued

State	Code Section	Grounds for Annulment	Limitation	Legitimacy of Children	Prohibited Marriages
INDIANA	31-11-1-1* to 31-11-2-3; 31-11-8-1 to 31-11-10-4; 31-13-1-1 to 31-13-1-3; 31-13-2-1	Underage without parental consent or judicial approval; mentally incompetent to consent; fraud; unsound mind; married in another state with intent to evade marriage laws of Indiana		Children of incestuous marriage are legitimate; child conceived before marriage is annulled is legitimate	More closely related than second cousin, unless first cousins both 65 or older at marriage and married after September 1, 1977; common law after 1957; same sex*
IOWA	595.2*; 595.19; 598.29 to 598.31	Underage without parental or judicial consent; prohibited; impotency; prior marriage undissolved; lacking capacity to consent	Underage: until reaching age of majority; marriage valid if parties live and cohabit together after death or divorce of former spouse	Children born outside of wedlock become legitimate by subsequent marriage of parents; children born of prohibited or annulled marriage are legitimate unless court finds otherwise upon proof	Undissolved prior marriage; between descendant and ancestor, brother and sister, aunt and nephew, uncle and niece, first cousins, same sex*
KANSAS	23-2501* to 23-2503; 23-2702; KS Const. art. XV, § 16*	Induced by fraud; void; mistake of fact; lack of knowledge of a material fact or any other reason justifying rescission of contract of marriage			Incestuous: between ancestor and descendant, whole- and half-blood brother and sister, uncle and niece, aunt and nephew, first cousins; same sex*
KENTUCKY	391.100; 402.005*; 402.010 to 402.030; 402.020*; 402.040*; 402.045*; 402.070; 403.120; KY Const., § 233A*	Capacity lacking due to force, fraud, drugs, or alcohol; mental incapacity; physical incapacity to consummate and other party did not know; underage without consent or judicial approval; prohibited	Underage: before cohabitation after reaching age 18; no consent or physical incapacity: within 90 days of knowledge; prohibited: up to 1 yr. after discovery, but only lack of capacity claim may be sought after death of either party	Children born of unlawful or void marriages are legitimate	Any kin closer than whole- or half-blood second cousin; with person mentally disabled; living spouse; underage; solemnized before one without authority unless parties believed he had authority; same sex*; between more than 2 persons

Table 28: Annulment and Prohibited Marriage—Continued

State	Code Section	Grounds for Annulment	Limitation	Legitimacy of Children	Prohibited Marriages
LOUISIANA	Civ. Code Art. 86* to 96; 89*	Null without marriage ceremony, by procuration, or in violation of an impediment; consent not freely given		Child of marriage contracted in good faith is legitimate	Prior undissolved marriage; ancestors and descendants, collaterals within the fourth degree; may marry within fourth degree if related by adoption and judicial authorization contracted by procuration; same sex*
MAINE	Tit. 19-A, §§ 652; 701 to 753	Incapacitated person; polygamous marriage; underage without consent or court approval			Between ancestor and descendant, brother and sister, aunt and nephew, uncle and niece, first cousins unless cousins obtain physician's certificate of genetic counseling prior to marriage; marriage with incapacitated person; marriage out of state to evade law; polygamous
MARYLAND	Fam. §§ 2-201 to 2-301; 5-202			Children of annulled or void marriages are legitimate	Parties within 3 degrees of lineal consanguinity or within 1st degree of collateral consanguinity or other degrees of affinity; underage without parental consent or woman to be married is pregnant or has given birth; under 15

Table 28: Annulment and Prohibited Marriage—Continued

State	Code Section	Grounds for Annulment	Limitation	Legitimacy of Children	Prohibited Marriages
MASSACHUSETTS	Ch. 207, §§ 1 to 17	Invalid marriage		Issue of relationship in consanguinity or affinity is illegitimate; issue of marriage void for prior marriage of insanity, or nonage of parties is legitimate; issue of marriage void by reason of prior marriage is legitimate if born or begotten before second marriage declared void	Polygamous; marriage between ancestors or descendants, brother and sister, aunt and nephew, uncle and niece, first cousins; provisions continue even after dissolution, by death or divorce unless divorce given because original marriage unlawful or void; under 18 without parental consent
MICHIGAN	551.1*; 551.271*; 551.272*; 552.1 to 552.4; 552.29 to 552.39; MI Const. art I, § 25*	Underage; mental incapacity; physical incapacity to consummate; force or fraud	Underage: unless they freely cohabit upon reaching majority, cannot be brought by other party who was of age at time of marriage; incapacity: 2 years from marriage; mental incapacity: unless upon restoration of reason, they freely cohabit; force or fraud: unless there is voluntary cohabitation prior to commencement of suit	Issue of marriage void for incapacity to contract or bigamy entered into in good faith are legitimate issue of party capable of contracting	Bigamous; same sex*; marriage between ancestors or descendants, brother and sister (blood or affinity), aunt and nephew, uncle and niece, first cousins

Table 28: Annulment and Prohibited Marriage—Continued

State	Code Section	Grounds for Annulment	Limitation	Legitimacy of Children	Prohibited Marriages
MINNESOTA	517.01 to 517.03; 518.01 to 518.055	Underage without parental or court consent unless cohabits freely after attaining age of consent; lacking capacity to consent due to mental issues, alcohol, drugs, force, or fraud; physical incapacity to consummate and other party did not know it at the time	Lacking capacity to consent: 90 days after obtaining knowledge of condition and before freely cohabited after restoration to reason; lacking physical capacity: 1 yr. after obtaining knowledge of condition; underage: before reaching proper age; no annulment action may be brought after death of either party		Previously undissolved marriage; between ancestor and descendant, or between siblings, whether whole- or half-blood or by adoption, aunt and nephew, uncle and niece, first cousins, all family restrictions for whole or half blood, except for those permitted by established custom of aboriginal cultures; developmentally disabled with guardian or conservator of human services must have permission to marry
MISSISSIPPI	93-1-1 to 93-1-5; 93-7-1– to 93-7-5; MS Const. art. XIV, § 263a*	Underage without parental permission unless followed by cohabitation; incurable impotency, adjudicated mental illness or incompetency; incapable of consent from lack of understanding, force, fraud, unless ratified; pregnant by another man and husband did not know, unless ratified	Mental incapacity, lack of consent, pregnancy: within 6 months of ground for annulment is or should be discovered	Void or annulled marriage's issue is legitimate; issue of incestuous marriage is not	Bigamous; incestuous, between ancestor and descendant, brother and sister, aunt and nephew, uncle and niece, first cousins by blood, daughter or son-in-law to father or mother-in-law; same sex*; marrying out of state in attempt to evade Miss. marriage laws

Table 28: Annulment and Prohibited Marriage—Continued

State	Code Section	Grounds for Annulment	Limitation	Legitimacy of Children	Prohibited Marriages
MISSOURI	451.020; 451.022*; 451.030; 451.040; 451.090; 474.080; MO Const. art. I, § 33*			Issue of all marriages deemed null in law, or dissolved by divorce, are legitimate	Between ancestor and descendant, brother and sister, uncle and niece, aunt and nephew, first cousins; between persons lacking capacity to enter into marriage contract; bigamous; common law marriages, same sex*; underage unless parental consent, no license to any person under 15 without good cause shown
MONTANA	40-1-103*, 40-1-401*; 40-1-402; MT Const. art. XIII, § 7*	Incapacity to consent due to mental issues, alcohol, duress, fraud, or force; incapacity to consummate and other party did not know; under 16 or 16-17 without parental consent or judicial approval; prohibited marriage	Mental infirmity, alcohol, drugs: within 1 yr. after knowledge; force, duress, fraud: 2 yrs. after knowledge; physical incapacity: party must not know at time of marriage and must bring within 4 yrs.; underage: until age of majority; prohibited: any time prior to death of parties; declaration of invalidity may not be sought after death of either party	Children born of invalid or prohibited marriages are legitimate	Previous marriage undissolved; between ancestor and descendant, brother and sister, first cousins, uncle and niece, aunt and nephew; same sex*

Table 28: Annulment and Prohibited Marriage—Continued

State	Code Section	Grounds for Annulment	Limitation	Legitimacy of Children	Prohibited Marriages
NEBRASKA	42-103; 42-118; 42-374; 42-375; 42-377; NE Const. art. I, 29*	Underage without parental permission or if couple separates and no subsequent cohabitation; force or fraud; impotency at time of marriage; previous marriage undissolved	May not be decreed annulled if marriage is voidable and parties freely cohabited after ground for annulment was terminated or became known to innocent party	Children born to annulled marriages shall be legitimate unless otherwise decreed by court	Marriage void when previous marriage undissolved; either party at marriage is mentally incompetent to enter marriage relation; between ancestor and descendant, whole- or half-blood brother and sister, first cousins of whole blood, uncle and niece, aunt and nephew, applies to children and relatives born in our out of wedlock; no person with venereal disease may marry; same sex*
NEVADA	122.010; 122.020*; 125.290 to 125.350; 125.410; NV Const. art. I, § 21*	Underage without parental consent or court approval; lack of understanding to consent; insanity; fraud; where grounds to void the contract in equity	Underage unless freely cohabit after reaching age: within 1 yr. after 18; fraud: may not annul if after discovery parties voluntarily cohabit; insanity: may not annul if freely cohabit after restored to sound mind	Issue of all marriages deemed null are legitimate	Previous marriage undissolved; not nearer in kin than second cousins; common law marriages; same sex*
NEW HAMPSHIRE	457:1-a; 457:2; 457:8; 458:1; 458:23	Underage until confirming marriage upon reaching age	Underage: no cause if marriage confirmed after arrival at age of consent	Children of void or voidable marriages are legitimate	Between ancestor and descendant, brother and sister, uncle and niece or nephew, aunt and nephew or niece, cousins; previous marriage undissolved; proxy marriages legitimacy

Table 28: Annulment and Prohibited Marriage—Continued

State	Code Section	Grounds for Annulment	Limitation	Legitimacy of Children	Prohibited Marriages
NEW JERSEY	2A:34-1; 2A:34-20; 37:1-1; 37:1-10	Previous marriage, civil union, or domestic partnership undissolved; incest; impotency if unknown and unratified; lack of consent due to alcohol, understanding capacity, drugs, duress, fraud and did not later ratify marriage; underage unless marriage confirmed after reaching age; any cause allowable under general equity jurisdiction of Superior Ct.	Underage: unless confirmed after age of consent; incestuous: during lifetime of parties	Children of void or voidable marriages are legitimate	Between ancestor and descendant, brother and sister, uncle and niece, aunt and nephew of whole or half blood; underage without parental consent; common law after 12/1/1939
NEW MEXICO	40-1-6; 40-1-7; 40-1-9	Underage	Underage: any time until age of majority by minor party, marriage valid if parties cohabit until they reach majority	Children are legitimate if marriage declared void	Between ancestor and descendant, whole- or half-blood brother and sister, uncle and niece, aunt and nephew, legitimate or illegitimate; underage without parental consent or court approval

Table 28: Annulment and Prohibited Marriage—Continued

State	Code Section	Grounds for Annulment	Limitation	Legitimacy of Children	Prohibited Marriages
NEW YORK	Dom. Rel. §§ 5 to 7; 24; 140	Undissolved previous marriage; underage; incurable mental illness for 5 yrs. or more; physical incapacity; consent by force, duress or fraud; incapable of consent for want of understanding	Undissolved: any time during lifetime of parties; underage: until legal age of consent, no voluntary cohabitation after reaching majority, cannot be brought by party of age at time of marriage, underage not absolute right to annulment, decided by court discretion; mental incapacity: any time during which incapacity continues, unless freely cohabits after restored to sound mind; physical incapacity: within 5 yrs. of marriage if unknown at marriage or did not know it was incurable; force, duress, fraud: within civil statute of limitations and during lifetime of guilty party unless voluntary cohabitation after discovery	Children of void or voidable marriages are legitimate	Between ancestor and descendant, whole- or half-blood brother and sister, uncle and niece, aunt and nephew, previous marriage undissolved
NORTH CAROLINA	50-11.1; 51-1*; 51-1.2* to 51-3; NC Const. art. XIV, § 6*	Underage without parental consent or judicial approval; previously undissolved marriage; impotent; lack of consent due to lack of will or understanding; belief that female is pregnant followed by separation and no birth	Underage: no marriage declared void if girl is pregnant or has given birth unless child is dead, or if cohabitation after 16 ; no marriage followed by cohabitation and birth of issue voidable after death of either party, except for bigamy	Children born of voidable or bigamous marriage are legitimate	Bigamy; between double first cousins or nearer in kin than first cousin; same sex*

Table 28: Annulment and Prohibited Marriage—Continued

State	Code Section	Grounds for Annulment	Limitation	Legitimacy of Children	Prohibited Marriages
NORTH DAKOTA	14-03-01* to 14-03-03; 14-03-06*; 14-03-08*; 14-04-01 to 14-04-03; ND Const. art. XI, § 28*	Under 16; 16-18 without parental consent, unless freely cohabited after reaching age of consent; previous marriage undissolved, with exception of former spouse absent and believed dead for period of 5 yrs. preceding 2nd marriage; unsound mind, fraud, or force, unless ratified; physically incapable and capacity continues and appears incurable; incestuous	Previous marriage undissolved: any time during life of parties; underage: by underage party within 4 yrs. after reaching age of consent or parent before party reaches age of consent; unsound mind: any time before death of either party, unless freely cohabited after coming to reason; fraud: any time before the death of either party unless freely cohabited; force or physically incapable: 4 yrs. of the marriage unless freely cohabited after full knowledge; incestuous: any time	Issue of void or voidable marriages are legitimate	Under 16; between ancestor and descendant, brother and sister, uncle and niece, aunt and nephew, first cousins, whether whole or half blood, legitimate or illegitimate; bigamous; same sex*
OHIO	3101.01*; 3105.31; 3105.32; 3111.01; OH Const. art. XV, § 11*	Underage without parental consent or judicial approval; previous marriage undissolved; mental incompetence; consent obtained by fraud or force; never consummated	Underage: Within 2 yrs. of reaching age of consent unless voluntary cohabitation after coming of age; previous marriage undissolved: any time during life of parties; mental: any time before death unless cohabitation after restoration of competency; fraud: within 2 yrs. of discovering fraud unless voluntary cohabitation; force: 2 yrs. after marriage unless voluntary cohabitation; no consummation: 2 yrs. from marriage	Uniform Parentage Act states "parent and child relationship" extends equally to all children and all parents, regardless of marital status of parents, 3111.01	Male under 18 or female under 16 without parental consent; between persons nearer in kin than second cousins; previous marriage undissolved; same sex*

Table 28: Annulment and Prohibited Marriage—Continued

State	Code Section	Grounds for Annulment	Limitation	Legitimacy of Children	Prohibited Marriages
OKLAHOMA	Tit. 43, §§ 2 to 3.1*; 128; OK Const. art. II, § 35*	Incapable of contracting due to lack of age or understanding unless cohabitation after incapacity ceases		Issue of annulled marriage are legitimate	Between ancestor and descendant, stepparent and stepchild, uncle and niece, aunt and nephew, brother and sister, first cousins, but will recognize marriage of first cousins married in state where legal; same sex*
OREGON	106.010*; 106.020 to 106.030; 106.190; 107.015; OR Const. art. XV, § 5a*	Incapable of consent for age or lack of understanding; consent obtained by force or fraud and not otherwise ratified		Issue of prohibited marriage is legitimate	Previous marriage undissolved; between whole- or half-blood first cousins or nearer in kin unless parties are first cousins by adoption only; same sex*
PENNSYLVANIA	Tit. 23, §§ 1102*; 1103; 1304; 1702 to 1704*; 3303 to 3309; 5102	Under 16 unless court approval; under 18 without parental consent or court approval; common law marriage of minors under 18; previous marriage undissolved; within consanguinity lines prohibited; lacked capacity by insanity or serious mental disorder or did not intend to consent; under influence of alcohol or drugs; naturally and incurably impotent not known to other party prior to marriage; fraud, duress, coercion, or force	All: No voluntary cohabitation after removal of impediment, before death of either party, not product of collusion; underage: if not subsequently ratified upon reaching age or under the influence: within 60 days of marriage; incestuous: before death; fraud/duress/coercion/force: no subsequent voluntary cohabitation after knowledge or release	All children irrespective of marital status of parents	Between ancestor and descendant, aunt and nephew, brother and sister, uncle and niece, first cousins; bigamous; one party is of unsound mind; induced by fraud or duress; impotence; common law after 2004

Table 28: Annulment and Prohibited Marriage—Continued

State	Code Section	Grounds for Annulment	Limitation	Legitimacy of Children	Prohibited Marriages
RHODE ISLAND	15-1-1 to 15-1-9; 15-5-1	No statutory provision for annulment; a marriage may be declared void during a divorce proceeding		Issue of marriage declared void marriage are legitimate	Bigamy; mental incompetence at time of marriage; incest between ancestor and descendant, stepparent and stepchild, brother and sister, uncle and niece, aunt and nephew; special exceptions for Jewish marriages allowed by Jewish religious law
SOUTH CAROLINA	20-1-10; 20-1-15*; 20-1-50; 20-1-80; 20-1-90; 20-1-250; 20-1-530; S.C. Const. art. XVII, § 15*	Under 16; 16-17 without parental consent or judicial approval; no consummation by cohabitation		Parties entering bigamous marriage in good faith have legitimate children	Underage; mentally incompetent; between ancestor and descendant, spouse of ancestor or descendant, brother and sister, uncle and niece, aunt and nephew; bigamy; same sex*
SOUTH DAKOTA	25-1-1* to 25-1-9; 25-1-38*; 25-3-1 to 25-3-12; 25-8-57; SD Const. art. XXI, § 9*	Underage without parental consent; previous marriage undissolved; either party of unsound mind; consent by fraud or force; physical incapacity	Underage: before freely cohabiting after reaching age of consent, by minor: within 4 yrs. of reaching age of consent, by parent: until child reaches age of consent; previous marriage undissolved: any time during life of party; unsound mind: any time during life of party unless freely cohabiting after coming to reason; force or fraud: within 4 yrs. of discovery unless willful cohabitation; physical incapacity: 4 yrs. after marriage	Children are legitimate when marriage is annulled for reasons of mental illness or previously undissolved marriage; any child born in wedlock or within 10 mos. after dissolution of marriage, even if declared void, is presumed legitimate	Under 16; between ancestor and descendant, whole- or half-blood brother and sister, uncle and niece, aunt and nephew, whole- or half-blood cousins, including those created in adoption, stepparent and stepchild; bigamy; same sex*

Table 28: Annulment and Prohibited Marriage—Continued

State	Code Section	Grounds for Annulment	Limitation	Legitimacy of Children	Prohibited Marriages
TENNESSEE	36-3-101 to 36-3-113*; 36-4-125; Tenn. Const. art. XI, § 18*	Underage without parental consent; previous marriage undissolved		Annulment shall not affect the legitimacy of children	Between ancestor and descendant, brother and sister, uncle and niece, aunt and nephew; bigamous; mentally deficient or mentally ill; same sex*
TEXAS	Fam. §§ 1.102; 2.001*; 6.102 to 6.111; 6.201 to 6.206; 6.204*; Tex. Const. art. I, § 32*	Underage without parental consent or court order, unless ratified by cohabitation; under influence of alcohol and drugs; mental or physical impotency; fraud, duress, or force; mental incompetence; concealed divorce which occurred within 30 days preceding marriage; marriage took place within 72 hours after marriage license; previous marriage undissolved, most recent marriage presumed valid until valid prior marriage proven	Underage: must be must be filed within 90 days of marriage and before minor's 18th birthday; impotency: permanently impotent and petitioner did not know; fraud/duress/ force: no voluntary cohabitation after release; mental incapacity: no knowledge of incapacity; concealed divorce: before 1st anniversary of marriage; in all instances, no voluntary cohabitation after knowledge and before death of either party	Rebuttable presumption that child is legitimate	Between ancestor and descendant, brother and sister, whole or half blood or by adoption, aunt and nephew, uncle and niece; bigamous, becomes valid after dissolution of 1st marriage if parties live together and present themselves as married; either party under 16 unless court order; either party current or former stepchild of the other party; same sex*
UTAH	30-1-1 to 30-1-3; 17.0 to 17.4	When marriage prohibited or grounds existing at common law	Court may refuse annulment based on underage if determined in best interest of children	Previous undissolved marriage: if contracted in good faith; issue of later marriages are legitimate	Between ancestor and descendant, whole- and half-blood brother and sister, uncle and niece, aunt and nephew, first cousins or if both 65 or older, or 55 or older and one found by court to be unable to reproduce, or between relations within but not including fifth degree of consanguinity; previous marriage undissolved; underage

Table 28: Annulment and Prohibited Marriage—Continued

State	Code Section	Grounds for Annulment	Limitation	Legitimacy of Children	Prohibited Marriages
VERMONT	Tit. 15, §§ 1a to 4; 8; 511 to 520	Under 16; lack of mental capacity; physically incapable of marriage state; consent obtained by force or fraud	Underage: until parties obtain legal age and cohabit; cannot be brought by party of age at time of marriage; mental incapacity: any time during life of either party or after death of the mentally incapacitated party unless voluntary cohabitation after being restored to reason; physical incapacity: 2 yrs. from marriage; consent by force or fraud: any time unless parties before commencement of action voluntarily cohabit	Children of annulled marriage are legitimate	Between ancestor and descendant, siblings, aunt and niece or nephew, uncle and niece or nephew, prohibitions apply even after divorce has dissolved relationship unless marriage was void or unlawful; previous marriage undissolved
VIRGINIA	20-31.1; 20-38.1; 20-43; 20-45.1; 20-45.2*; 20-48; 20-89.1	Underage unless emancipated; lack of capacity to consent because of mental incapacity or infirmity; natural or incurable impotency; fraud or duress; convicted felon without other party's knowledge; wife pregnant by another man or husband fathered child with another woman born within 10 mos. after marriage without other's knowledge; either had been prostitute without other's knowledge	All actions must be brought within 2 yrs. of marriage; no annulment allowed for fraud, duress, mental incapacity, felony, pregnancy or fathering if parties cohabited after knowledge	Children of prohibited marriages are legitimate	Previous marriage undissolved; between ancestor and descendant; whole- or half-blood brother and sister, uncle and niece, or aunt and nephew; bigamous; parties under 18; same sex*

Table 28: Annulment and Prohibited Marriage—Continued

State	Code Section	Grounds for Annulment	Limitation	Legitimacy of Children	Prohibited Marriages
WASHINGTON	26.04.010, 26.04.020; 26.04.130; 26.04.210; 26.09.040	Underage without parental consent; under 17 without waiver of superior ct. judge; incapable of consent due to lack of age or understanding; consent gained by fraud, duress, or force, voidable by party laboring under disability or upon whom force or fraud was imposed; incapable of consent because of alcohol or incapacitating substances	All: during lifetime of both parties unless ratified by freely cohabiting after attaining age, capacity, or discovery of fraud	Children born during marriage later voided are born and remain legitimate	Previous marriage undissolved; between persons closer in kin than whole- or half-blood second cousins
WEST VIRGINIA	42-1-7; 48-1-101; 48-2-104*; 48-2-302 to 48-2-303; 48-2-602; 48-2-603*; 48-3-103; 48-3-105;	Underage without parental consent, court approval also required under 16; previous marriage undissolved; within line of prohibited consanguinity; mentally incompetent; sexually transmitted disease, provided not then cured; impotency; convicted of felony prior to marriage without knowledge of other party; wife with child of another man	Underage: cannot be brought by party who was of age; incapable of consent: cannot be brought by party who could consent; fraud, force, or coercion: cannot be brought by guilty party or injured party if they had knowledge; child by other man or felony: cannot be brought by other party if cohabiting after knowledge	Children of annulled or prohibited marriage are legitimate	Between ancestor and descendant, brother and sister, half-brother and half-sister, aunt and nephew, uncle and niece, first cousins, double cousins, unless relationship created solely by adoption; out of state marriage entered into to avoid state law; same sex*

Table 28: Annulment and Prohibited Marriage—Continued

State	Code Section	Grounds for Annulment	Limitation	Legitimacy of Children	Prohibited Marriages
WISCONSIN	765.001 to 765.31; 767.313; 767.803; W.S.A. Const. art. XIII, § 3*	Underage without parental consent or court approval, lack capacity to consent due to lack of age, mental infirmity, alcohol, drugs, force, duress, or fraud; lack capacity to consummate; marriage prohibited by state law	Underage: within 1 yr. of marriage, by parent if party under 18; mental infirmity, alcohol, drugs, force, duress, fraud, no capacity to consummate: within 1 yr. of knowledge; where marriage prohibited by law, 10 yrs.; bigamy, no limit	Issue of void marriage is legitimate	Previous marriage undissolved; either party incapable of consent; between persons no closer in kin than whole- or half-blood 2nd cousins, or 1st cousins if woman is 55 or one party is sterile; marriage out of state to avoid state law; same sex*
WYOMING	14-2-504; 20-1-101*; 20-1-113; 20-2-101	Underage without parental consent, court approval also required under 16 ; physical or mental incapacity; consent by fraud or duress with no subsequent voluntary cohabitation;	Underage: until couple cohabits upon reaching age of consent, cannot be brought by party who was of age at time; physical incapacity, can be brought only by party not physically incapacitated: until 2 yrs. after marriage; mental incapacity: until free cohabitation after restoration of capacity	Legitimacy rebuttably presumed	Previous marriage undissolved; party mentally incompetent; between ancestor and descendant, brother and sister, uncle and niece, aunt and nephew, first cousins, whether either party is illegitimate; same sex*

29. CHILD ABUSE

If child abuse is not the most serious crime facing our society today, it is certainly one of the most heart-wrenching. There are many attempts underway to remedy the underlying causes of child abuse, but until it is eliminated states have unanimously responded with laws specifically designed to identify and punish child abusers.

Child abuse is an insidious type of crime where for many reasons the victims are unable to or are fearful of confronting or reporting the perpetrator to authorities. Therefore, the laws surrounding abusive activity contain an element not found in many other criminal statutes. Under the laws of many states, third parties with knowledge of or reasonable cause to believe that abuse has occurred, are under a legal obligation to report the situation to the authorities.

The reporting provision is the most controversial and the most problematic of this area of the law. In our society, many relationships are held in particularly high regard and communications in those relationships are given special protection. For example, the law seeks to encourage communication between patient and doctor, client and attorney, and congregant and clergy, and protects the content of any communication between them from discovery by third parties by providing a "privilege," or a rule, that prohibits the doctor, lawyer or clergy from revealing the content of any communications that take place within that particular professional relationship. There are also certain occasions, not covered by the privilege, where parties may presume their relationship to be confidential, such as between parent and teacher. Under the child abuse laws for some of these relationships, the professional in such relationships must now report any known or suspected abusive behavior to the proper authorities.

Virtually every state requires doctors, teachers, day care providers and law enforcement officers to report child abuse, but there is less uniformity among the states with regard to lawyers, clergy, therapists, or counselors. A few states require commercial photographic film processors to report to the proper authorities evidence of abusive activity. Some states are very specific in stating exactly who may be protected by the privilege, but some are noticeably vague. This is because the privilege itself is considered so important that a general abrogation of the privilege may be generally detrimental to the important relationships involved. For example, some states require health care professionals to report incidences of abuse, while others list as many as 20 to 29 professions, including dentists, chiropractors, nurses, hospital personnel and Christian Science practitioners.

The loss or abuse of privilege is not the only controversial or problematic provision of these laws. In many states, the definitions of what constitutes abuse is so broad as to cover a number of different circumstances, including some that may not be abusive at all. Coupled with the fact that in many states one need only have a reasonable suspicion that abuse has occurred in order to report it to the authorities, the laws have left many people fearful that innocent behavior may be misinterpreted by well-meaning, or worse, ill-meaning, private citizens.

The agency to whom suspected abuse is reported is often a state child protection office that is not hindered by the same constitutional restrictions to which traditional law enforcement agencies are subject. These agencies are sometimes allowed to take custody of children prior to actually proving that abuse has occurred. This is done in order to protect the child in question from potential abuse when the agent believes that there is a strong likelihood that the child will be, or continue to be harmed. Some critics of these laws fear the potential of extreme invasions into relationships between parent and child on the basis of very little evidence. Indeed, there have been cases where significant charges of child abuse have been made against individuals and severe action taken against them, such as children taken away from parents, day care centers closed down, only to have the charges later dismissed as lacking any concrete evidence whatsoever. For these reasons most states have passed laws that impose penalties not only for failure to report suspected abuse, but also for false reporting.

In the last decade, state laws have changed in two significant ways. Several more states have added enticing or forcing children into sexually exploitive activity to the definition of child abuse. Obviously, this new definition results from increased attention being given to child pornography. Another change is the addition of prenatal child abuse to the state statutes of South Dakota, Wisconsin, and, arguably, Texas. These provisions raise some difficult questions, to the modern mind at least, about the definition of a "child" in the eyes of the law. It is very likely that these laws may find their way into the courts for further definition.

Table 29: Child Abuse

State	Code Section	What Constitutes Abuse	Mandatory Reporting Required By
ALABAMA	26-14-1 to 26-15-14	Harm or threatened harm to a child's health or welfare through nonaccidental physical or mental injury or sexual abuse/exploitation, including enticement/coercion of a child to engage in or assist any other person to engage in any sexually explicit conduct or simulation	All hospitals, clinics, sanitariums, doctors, physicians, surgeons, medical examiners, coroners, dentists, osteopaths, optometrists, chiropractors, podiatrists, physical therapists, nurses, public and private K-12 employees, school teachers, and officials, peace officers, law enforcement officials, pharmacists, social workers, day care workers or employees, mental health professionals, employees of public and private institutions of post-secondary and higher education, members of the clergy unless privileged communication, or anyone else called on to render aid or medical assistance to any child
ALASKA	47.17.010 to 47.17.290	Physical injury or neglect, mental injury (injury to emotional well-being or intellectual or psychological capacity of child as evidenced by an observable and substantial impairment on child's ability to function); sexual abuse/exploitation, maltreatment, including any visual depictions of a child engaged in sexual conduct	Practitioners of healing arts; school teachers and administrative staff members of public and private schools; social workers; peace officers and officers of the Dept. of Corrections; child care providers; administrative officers of institutions; paid employees of domestic violence and sexual assault programs and counseling or crisis intervention programs; paid employees of organization providing drug or alcohol treatment; child fatality review teams
ARIZONA	8-201; 13-3620	Infliction or allowing of physical injury, impairment of bodily function or disfigurement, serious emotional damage diagnosed by a doctor or psychologist, and as evidenced by severe anxiety, depression, withdrawal, or aggressive behavior caused by acts or omissions of individual having care and custody of child	Physician; physician's assistant; optometrist; dentist; osteopath; chiropractor; podiatrist; behavioral health professional; nurse; psychologist; counselor; social worker; peace officer; child welfare investigator; child protective services worker; member of the clergy, priest, Christian Science practitioner unless a confidential communication or confession; parent; stepparent; guardian of the minor; school personnel; domestic violence victim advocate; any person responsible for the minor's care or treatment

Basis of Report of Abuse/Neglect	To Whom Reported	Penalty for Failure to Report or False Reporting	Means of Reporting	Retaliation
When a child is known or suspected to be victim of abuse or neglect	A law enforcement official, who shall subsequently inform the Department of Human Resources	Knowingly fail to report: misdemeanor with up to 6 months jail or $500; public or private employer that takes retaliatory action against an employee solely for reporting: class C misdemeanor	Immediate oral report by telephone or direct communication followed by a written report to a duly constituted authority, meaning any person or entity authorized by the Department of Human Resources to receive reports	
Have reasonable cause to suspect that child has suffered harm as a result of abuse or neglect	Dept. of Health and Social Services	Class A misdemeanor	Immediately report to the nearest Department of Health and Social Services office, or to a peace officer if the office cannot be reasonably contacted	
Have reasonable belief minor victim of physical injury, abuse, reportable offense or neglect with the intent to cause or allow the death of an infant	To peace officer or child protective services of the department of economic security	Class 1 misdemeanor except class 6 felony if failure involves a "reportable" offense	Immediately report by telephone or electronically	

Table 29: Child Abuse—Continued

State	Code Section	What Constitutes Abuse	Mandatory Reporting Required By
ARKANSAS	Child Maltreatment Act: 12-18-101 to 12-18-1202	Extreme or repeated cruelty; conduct creating a realistic and serious threat of death, disfigurement, or bodily organ impairment; injury to intellectual, emotional, and psychological development evidenced by observable and substantial impairment of ability to function within a normal range; injury at variance with history given; non accidental physical injury; physical injury without justifiable cause; giving, or permitting consumption or use of controlled substances; sexual abuse or exploitation; reasonable and moderate physical discipline not considered abuse	Child care or foster care worker; coroner; day care center worker; dentist; dental hygienist; domestic abuse advocate; domestic violence shelter employee or volunteer; Department of Human Services employee; Division of Youth Services contractor; foster parent; judge; law enforcement official; licensed nurse; medical personnel; mental health professional or paraprofessional; osteopath; peace officer; physician; prosecuting attorney; resident intern; school counselor or official; social worker; surgeon; teacher; court-appointed special advocate program staff or volunteer; juvenile intake or probation officer; clergy member unless confidential communication; child advocacy or safety center employee; attorney ad litem; sexual abuse advocate; rape crisis advocate or volunteer; child abuse advocate or volunteer; victim or witness coordinator; victim assistance professional; Crimes Against Children Division of the Department of Arkansas State Police employee; reproductive health care facility employee or volunteer

Basis of Report of Abuse/Neglect	To Whom Reported	Penalty for Failure to Report or False Reporting	Means of Reporting	Retaliation
Reasonable cause to suspect child maltreatment has occurred, or a child has died as a result of child maltreatment, or observes a child being subjected to conditions that would reasonably result in child maltreatment	Department of Human Services Child Abuse Hotline	Knowing failure to notify by a mandated reporter: class A misdemeanor; reckless failure to report: class C misdemeanor; purposeful false report: class A misdemeanor for the first offense, class D felony for subsequent offense; unlawful restriction of reporting: class A misdemeanor; civil liability for failure to report: proximately caused damages	Immediately notify the Child Abuse Hotline	

Table 29: Child Abuse—Continued

State	Code Section	What Constitutes Abuse	Mandatory Reporting Required By
CALIFORNIA	Child Abuse and Neglect Reporting Act: Penal § 11164 to 11174.3	Physical injury or death inflicted by other than accidental means; sexual abuse as defined in 11165.1; neglect as defined in 11165.2; willful harming or injuring of a child or endangering the person or health of a child as defined in 11165.3; unlawful corporal punishment or injury as defined in 11165.4	Teacher; instructional aide; teacher's aide or teacher's assistant employed by public or private school; classified employee of public school; administrative officer or supervisor of child welfare and attendance, or a certificated pupil personnel employee of public or private school; administrator of public or private day camp; administrator or employee of public or private youth center, youth recreation program, or youth organization; administrator or employee of public or private organization whose duties require direct contact and supervision of children; employee of a county office of education or State Department of Education whose duties bring the employee into contact with children on a regular basis; licensee, administrator, or employee of a licensed community care or child day care facility; Head Start program teacher; licensing worker or licensing evaluator employed by a licensing agency; public assistance worker; employee of a child care institution; social worker, probation officer, or parole officer; employee of a school district police or security department; administrator, presenter, or counselor in child abuse prevention program in a school; district attorney investigator, inspector, or local child support agency caseworker, unless working with attorney appointed to represent a minor; peace officer; non-volunteer firefighter; physician, surgeon, psychiatrist, psychologist, dentist, resident, intern, podiatrist, chiropractor, licensed nurse, dental hygienist, optometrist, marriage and family therapist, clinical social worker, professional clinical counselor, or any other person who is currently licensed under Division 2 of the Bus. & Prof. Code; emergency medical technician, paramedic, or other person certified pursuant to Division 2.5 of the Health and Safety Code; psychological assistant; marriage and family therapist trainee; unlicensed marriage and family therapist intern; state or county public health employee who treats a minor for any condition; coroner; medical examiner or other person who performs autopsies; commercial film and photographic print or image processor; child visitation monitor; animal control officer or humane society officer; clergy member or custodian of records of a clergy member; employee police, county sheriff's, county probation, or county welfare department; employee or volunteer of a Court Appointed Special Advocate program; custodial office; person providing services to a minor under § 12300 or 12300.1 of the Welf. & Inst. Code; alcohol and drug counselor; clinical counselor trainee or intern; employee or administrator any postsecondary institution, whose duties bring them into contact with children; athletic coach, administrator, or director employed by any K-12 school; commercial computer technician or his or her employer; any athletic coach or staff at postsecondary institution

Basis of Report of Abuse/Neglect	To Whom Reported	Penalty for Failure to Report or False Reporting	Means of Reporting	Retaliation
Knows, observes, or reasonably suspects child abuse or neglect	Any police or sheriff's department or the county welfare department	Failure to report: misdemeanor; imprisonment in county jail up to 6 mos. and/or fine up to $1,000	Make initial report by telephone as soon as practicable, followed by written report within 36 hrs.; intentional concealing failure to report: continuing offense until offense is discovered	

Table 29: Child Abuse—Continued

State	Code Section	What Constitutes Abuse	Mandatory Reporting Required By
COLORADO	Child Protection Act of 1987: 19-3-301 to 19-3-315	Act or omission that threatens the health or welfare of a child, including unjustified injury or death; a child is subjected to unlawful sexual behavior; where child is in need of food, clothing, shelter that a prudent parent has failed to provide; subjected to emotional abuse; the presence of a child where controlled substances are found; child tests positive for controlled substance at birth	Physician or surgeon, including a physician in training; child health associate; medical examiner or coroner; dentist; osteopath; optometrist; chiropractor; podiatrist; registered nurse or licensed practical nurse; hospital personnel engaged in the admission, care, or treatment of patients; Christian science practitioner; public or private school official or employee; social worker; mental health professional; dental hygienist; psychologist; physical therapist; veterinarian; peace officer; pharmacist; commercial film and photographic print processor; firefighter; victim's advocate; licensed professional counselors; licensed marriage and family therapists; registered psychotherapists; clergy member; registered dietitian; state department of human services worker; juvenile parole and probation officers; child and family investigators; state bureau of animal protection officers and agents; animal control officers; child protection ombudsman; WIC educator; coach or staff of private sports program; registered psychologist, therapist, or counselor candidate; emergency medical service providers
CONNECTICUT	17a-100 to 17a-131a; 46b-120	Physical injury not by accidental means; injuries at variance with the history given of them; in a condition that is the result of maltreatment, including malnutrition, sexual molestation or exploitation, deprivation of necessities, emotional maltreatment, cruel punishment	Licensed physician or surgeon; resident physician or intern; registered nurse; licensed practical nurse; medical examiner; dentist; dental hygienist; psychologist; school employee; social worker; police officer; juvenile or adult probation or parole officer; clergy member; pharmacist; physical therapist; optometrist; chiropractor; podiatrist; mental health professional; physician assistant; licensed or certified emergency medical services provider; licensed or certified alcohol and drug counselor; licensed marital and family therapist; sexual assault or domestic violence counselor; licensed professional counselor; licensed foster parent; person paid to care for a child in any facility, child day care center, group day care home or family day care home licensed by the state; Department of Children and Families employee; Department of Public Health employee; Office of Early Childhood employee responsible for licensing child day care centers, group day care homes, family day care homes or youth camps; the Child Advocate; any Office of the Child Advocate employee; family relations counselor, family relations counselor trainee or family services supervisor employed by the Judicial Department
DELAWARE	Tit. 16, §§ 901 to 914	Physical injury through unjustified force; emotional abuse; sexual abuse; mal- or mistreatment; exploitation; torture	Persons in healing arts (medicine, dentistry, psychologist); social worker; school employee; medical examiner; health care institution; Medical Society of Delaware; law enforcement agency

Basis of Report of Abuse/Neglect	To Whom Reported	Penalty for Failure to Report or False Reporting	Means of Reporting	Retaliation
Reasonable cause to know or suspect that a child has been subjected to abuse or neglect, or who has observed abuse or neglect	County department, local law enforcement agency, or through the child abuse reporting hotline system	Willful violation: Class 3 misdemeanor plus liability for proximately caused damages	Immediately report to county department, local law enforcement agency, or child abuse reporting hotline, followed promptly by a written report prepared by those persons required to report	
Reasonable cause to suspect or believe that any child has been abused, neglected, or placed in imminent risk of serious harm	Commissioner of Children and Families or a law enforcement agency	False report: jail up to 1 year and/or fine up to $2,000	Oral report made as soon as practicable, but within 12 hrs., by telephone or in person, followed by written report submitted within 48 hrs. of oral report	Retaliation against mandated reporters prohibited
Knows or reasonably suspects child abuse or neglect	Dept of Services for Children, Youth, & Their Families	Civil penalty up to $10,000 for 1st violation; up to $50,000 for any subsequent violation	Immediate oral report	

Table 29: Child Abuse—Continued

State	Code Section	What Constitutes Abuse	Mandatory Reporting Required By
DISTRICT OF COLUMBIA	4-1301.02 to 4-1301.09a; 16-2301(23)	Infliction of physical or mental injury; sexual abuse or exploitation; negligent treatment or maltreatment; does not include reasonable and moderate discipline by a parent, guardian, or custodian	Child and Family Services Agency employees, agents, and contractors; every physician; psychologist; medical examiner; dentist; chiropractor; registered nurse; licensed practical nurse; person involved in the care and treatment of patients; law-enforcement officer; humane or animal cruelty officer; school official teacher; athletic coach; Department of Parks and Recreation employee; public housing resident manager; social service worker; day care worker; human trafficking counselor; domestic violence counselor; mental health professional; such persons not required to report when employed by a lawyer in a matter in which the suspicion arises solely in the course of that representation
FLORIDA	39.01(2); 39.201 to 39.206	Willful or threatened acts or omissions resulting in physical, mental, or sexual injury or harm, causing or likely to cause impairment of physical, mental, or emotional health	Physician; osteopathic physician; medical examiner; chiropractic physician; nurse; hospital personnel engaged in the admission, examination, care, or treatment of persons; health or mental health professional; practitioner who relies solely on spiritual means for healing; school teacher or other school official or personnel; social worker; day care center worker; professional child care, foster care, residential, or institutional worker; law enforcement officer; judge.
GEORGIA	19-7-5	Physical injury or death inflicted on a child by other than accidental means including neglect, sexual abuse/exploitation	Licensed physicians licensed; physician assistants; interns; residents; hospital or medical personnel; dentists; licensed psychologists and interns; registered professional nurses; licensed practical nurses; nurse's aides; professional counselors; social workers; marriage and family therapists; school teachers, administrators, guidance counselors, visiting teachers, social workers, or psychologists; child welfare agency person; child-counseling personnel; child service organization personnel; law enforcement personnel; reproductive health care facility or pregnancy resource center personnel and volunteers
HAWAII	350-1 to 350-5	Acts or omissions that have resulted in harm to child's physical or psychological health or welfare (or substantial risk of being harmed); specific injuries listed in 350-1	Any licensed, registered professional of the healing arts or any other health-related occupation; school employees; law enforcement employees; child care providers; medical examiners/coroners; employees of public or private social, medical or mental health services agency, recreational/sports employees

Basis of Report of Abuse/Neglect	To Whom Reported	Penalty for Failure to Report or False Reporting	Means of Reporting	Retaliation
Knows or has reasonable cause to suspect a child is in immediate danger of being mentally or physically abused or neglected	Police Dept. or Child and Family Services Agency	Willful failure to report: imprisonment up to 180 days and/or fine up to $1,000	Immediately in writing	
One who knows or has reasonable cause to suspect neglect, abuse, or abandonment	Department of Children and Family Services	Knowing and willful failure: 3rd degree felony; by any academic institution in Florida if abuse on the property: fine up to $1 million for each failure	Immediately to Department's central abuse hotline	
Reasonable cause to believe a child has been abused	Child welfare agency providing protective services as designated by Department of Human Resources (or in absence of such, to police authority or district attorney)	Misdemeanor	Oral report within 24 hrs. followed by written report if requested	
Reason to believe that child abuse or neglect has occurred or may occur in reasonably foreseeable future	Department of Human Services or police department	Petty misdemeanor	Immediate oral report, followed by written report	

Table 29: Child Abuse—Continued

State	Code Section	What Constitutes Abuse	Mandatory Reporting Required By
IDAHO	Child Protective Act: 16-1601 to 16-1643	Conduct or omission resulting in injury, malnutrition, failure to thrive, or death that is not justifiably explained or where the history given is in variance to the condition, sexual conduct or exploitation harming or threatening the health or welfare of the child, or causing mental injury	Physician; nurse; resident; intern; coroner; school teacher; day care personnel; social worker; or other person
ILLINOIS	Abused and Neglected Child Reporting Act: 325 §§ 5/1 to 5/11.8	Inflicting or causing, allowing, or creating a substantial risk of physical injury, other than by accident, that causes death, disfigurement, impairment of physical or emotional health, or loss or impairment of any bodily function; committing or allowing to be committed any sex offense; torture, excessive corporal punishment, female genital mutilation; giving child access to controlled substances; involuntary servitude or trafficking	Physician; resident; intern; hospital; hospital administrator and personnel engaged in examination, care, and treatment; surgeon; dentist; dental hygienist; osteopath; chiropractor; podiatrist; physician assistant; substance abuse treatment personnel; funeral home director or employee; coroner; medical examiner; emergency medical technician; acupuncturist; crisis line or hotline personnel; certified and non-certified school personnel; higher educational institution personnel; assigned educational advocate; school board member; Chicago Board of Education member; member of governing body of a private school; truant officers; social worker; social services administrator; domestic violence program personnel; registered nurse; licensed practical nurse; genetic counselor; respiratory care practitioner; advanced practice nurse; home health aide; nursery school or child day care center director or staff; recreational or athletic program or facility personnel; early intervention provider; law enforcement officer; licensed professional counselor; licensed clinical professional counselor; registered psychologists and assistants; psychiatrist; Department field personnel; supervisor or administrator of general assistance under the Illinois Public Aid Code; probation officer; animal control officer; any foster parent, homemaker, or child care worker; clergy

Basis of Report of Abuse/Neglect	To Whom Reported	Penalty for Failure to Report or False Reporting	Means of Reporting	Retaliation
Observation of or reason to believe that a child has been abused, neglected or abandoned, or subject to conditions or circumstances which would reasonably result in abuse, abandonment, or neglect	Department of Health and Welfare or law enforcement agency	Failure to report: Misdemeanor; report in bad faith: misdemeanor; liable for actual damages or statutory damages of $2,500, whichever is greater, plus attorney fees and costs of suit; if acting with malice or oppression, court may award treble actual damages or treble statutory damages, whichever is greater	Within 24 hrs.	
Reasonable cause to believe a child may be abused or neglected	Department of Children and Family Services; may notify person in charge of institution or designated agent that a report has been made	Failure to report: Class A misdemeanor; if physician: referred to state medical disciplinary board; if dentist: referred to Dept. of Professional Regulation; false report: offense of disorderly conduct; second offense is class 4 felony	Immediately	

Table 29: Child Abuse—Continued

State	Code Section	What Constitutes Abuse	Mandatory Reporting Required By
INDIANA	31-9-2-14; 31-33-5-1 to 31-33-5-4; 31-33-22-1 to 31-33-22-5; 31-34-1-1 to 31-34-1-16	Mental or physical condition seriously impaired or endangered as a result of neglect or injury; sex offense; child is missing; child is allowed to participate in obscene performance; there is a rebuttable presumption of endangerment when a child resides on a property where a controlled substance is manufactured	Health care provider; any member of medical or other private or public institution, school, facility or agency; any other individuals
IOWA	232.68 to 232.77	Any nonaccidental physical injury or mental injury to child's intellectual or psychological capacity as evidenced by substantial and observable impairment in child's ability to function within normal range; commission of sexual offense; an illegal drug present in child's body; cohabitation with person on sex offender registry; manufacture of meth or possession of meth ingredients in presence of child; bestiality in presence of child; allowing prostitution; failure in care of child to provide food, shelter, or clothing necessary for child's health and welfare	Any health practitioner; social workers; health care facility employee; psychologist; school employee; day care center employee; substance abuse program employee; human services institution employee; peace officer; juvenile detention or shelter care employee; mental health professional; counselor; foster care facility operator or employee; any other person may make a report
KANSAS	38-2201 to 38-2288	Infliction of mental, physical, or emotional injury causing deterioration of child including maltreatment, or exploitation to the extent the child's health or emotional well-being is endangered; includes sexual abuse	Person licensed to practice healing arts; dentistry; optometry; postgraduate trainees in state board approved programs; licensed professional or practical nurses; chief administrative officers of medical care facilities; persons licensed to provide mental health services; teachers or employees of educational institution; persons licensed to provide child care services; firefighters, EMT personnel; law enforcement officers; juvenile intake and assessment workers; court services officers; community corrections officers; case managers; mediators; any person employed or volunteering for an organization providing social services to pregnant teens

Basis of Report of Abuse/Neglect	To Whom Reported	Penalty for Failure to Report or False Reporting	Means of Reporting	Retaliation
Reason to believe child is victim of child abuse or neglect	Division of Family and Children; child abuse hotline or local law enforcement agency; the individual in charge of the institution	Intentionally and knowing false report: class A misdemeanor and liable to person accused for actual damages and possible punitive damages; Level 6 felony if the false reporter has previous unrelated conviction of making a knowing false report; knowingly fails to make a report: class B misdemeanor	Immediate oral report	
Reasonably believes a child has suffered abuse	State Department of Human Services	Knowingly and willfully fails to report: simple misdemeanor and civilly liable for proximately caused damages; knowing false report: simple misdemeanor	Oral report within 24 hrs.; written report within 48 hrs. or oral report	Employer is prohibited from taking retaliatory action for a good faith report
Reasonably suspects child has been harmed as a result of physical, mental, or emotional abuse or neglect or sexual abuse	Secretary of the Department of Social and Rehabilitation Services or law enforcement agency	Willful and knowing failure to report or prevention or interference with reporting: class B misdemeanor. False report: class B misdemeanor	Immediate oral report, followed by a written report if requested	Retaliation is prohibited; violation is class B misdemeanor

Table 29: Child Abuse—Continued

State	Code Section	What Constitutes Abuse	Mandatory Reporting Required By
KENTUCKY	600.010 to 600.990	Inflicting, allowing, or creating physical or emotional injury by other than accidental means; parental incapacity to meet the immediate or ongoing needs of the child; repeatedly failing or refusing to provide essential parental care; commit or allow sexual abuse, exploitation, prostitution, abandonment, or exploitation	Physician; osteopathic physician; nurse; teacher; school personnel; social worker; coroner; medical examiner; child-caring personnel; resident; intern; chiropractor; dentist; optometrist; emergency medical technician; paramedic; health professional; mental health professional; peace officer; any organization or agency for any of the above
LOUISIANA	14:403; Children's Code Art. 603; 609	Acts seriously endangering the physical, mental, or emotional health of child, including infliction or allowing infliction or attempted infliction of physical or mental injury; exploitation by overwork; sexual abuse or involvement in pornography; coerced abortion upon a child	Health practitioner; mental health or social service practitioner; teacher or child care provider; police officer or law enforcement; commercial film and photographic print processor; mediators; clergy; appointed parenting coordinator; court appointed special advocate volunteers; youth activity provider; athletic coach
MAINE	Tit. 22, §§ 4001 to 4019	Threat to child's health or welfare by physical, mental, or emotional injury or impairment, sexual abuse/exploitation, deprivation of essential needs	When acting in a professional capacity: allopathic or osteopathic physician, resident, intern, emergency medical services, medical examiner, physician's assistant, dentist, dental hygienist, dental assistant, chiropractor, podiatrist, registered or licensed practical nurse, teacher, guidance counselor, school official, Court Appointed Special Advocate volunteers, homemaker, home health aide, medical or social service worker, psychologist, child care personnel, mental health professional, law enforcement, state or municipal fire inspector, municipal code enforcement officer, commercial film and photographic print processor, clergy unless during confidential communications, chair of a professional licensing board, humane agent employed by the Dept. of Agriculture, Conservation & Forestry, sexual assault counselor, family or domestic violence victim advocate, school bus driver or attendant; any person who has assumed responsibility for care or custody of child regardless of compensation; any person affiliated with a church or religious institution serving in an administrative capacity or in a position of trust regardless of compensation

Basis of Report of Abuse/Neglect	To Whom Reported	Penalty for Failure to Report or False Reporting	Means of Reporting	Retaliation
Knows or has reasonable cause to believe that child is dependent, neglected, or abused	Local law enforcement or Kentucky state police, commonwealth's attorney, cabinet or representative	Intentional violation: class B misdemeanor for 1st offense; 2nd offense: class A misdemeanor; 3rd offense: class D misdemeanor	Immediate oral or written report; written report within 48 hrs. of original report	
Cause to believe that a child's physical or mental health or welfare is endangered as a result of abuse or neglect	Department of Children and Family Services or state child protection reporting hotline	Knowingly and willfully fails to report or makes a false report: imprisonment up to 6 mos. and/or fine up to $500	Immediately	
Knows or has reasonable cause to suspect a child has been or is likely to be abused or neglected	Department of Human Services or district attorney's office	Civil violation with fine of not more than $500	Immediately, followed by a written report within 48 hrs. if requested by the Department	No discrimination in any way by an employer for a good faith report or participation in an investigation

Table 29: Child Abuse—Continued

State	Code Section	What Constitutes Abuse	Mandatory Reporting Required By
MARYLAND	Fam. Law § 5-701 to 5-715	Physical or mental injury of a child under circumstances that indicate the child's health or welfare is harmed or at substantial risk of being harmed; sexual abuse	All health practitioners; police officers; educators; human service workers; any other person, if notification does not violate privilege or confidentiality
MASSACHUSETTS	Ch. 119, §§ 21; 51A	Physical or emotional abuse or injury causing harm to child's health or welfare including sexual abuse/neglect, malnutrition and physical dependence upon addictive drug at birth, sexual exploitation, being a human trafficking victim	Physician; medical intern; hospital personnel engaged in the examination, care or treatment of persons; medical examiner; psychologist; emergency medical technician; dentist; nurse; chiropractor; podiatrist; optometrist; osteopath, licensed allied mental health and human services professional; drug and alcoholism counselor; psychiatrist; clinical social worker; public or private school teacher; educational administrator; guidance or family counselor; child care worker; child care facility employee; residential child care services funded by the commonwealth or licensed under chapter 15D; voucher management agencies; family child care systems; child care food programs; department of early education and care licensor; school attendance officer; probation officer; clerk-magistrate of a district court; parole officer; social worker; foster parent; firefighter; police officer; priest; rabbi; clergy member; ordained or licensed minister; leader of any church or religious body; accredited Christian Science practitioner; person employed by a church or religious body with regular interaction with children; person charge of a medical or other institution, school or facility; the child advocate

Basis of Report of Abuse/Neglect	To Whom Reported	Penalty for Failure to Report or False Reporting	Means of Reporting	Retaliation
Reason to believe a child has been subjected to abuse or neglect	Social Services Administration of the department or appropriate law enforcement agency	Prevention or interference with making a report: misdemeanor punishable by imprisonment up to 5 yrs. and/or fine up to $10,000	Immediate oral report, followed by written report 48 hrs. after abuse is reasonably suspected; must send copy of report to the local State's Attorney	
Reasonable cause to believe a child is suffering from physical or emotional injury causing harm or substantial risk of harm to child's health and welfare	Department of Children and Families	Failure to report or false report: fine up to $1,000; knowing or will failure to report: imprisonment up to 2.5 yrs. and/or fine up to $5,000; upon finding of guilt, the appropriate professional licensing authority shall be notified by the court	Immediate oral report followed by detailed written report within 48 hrs.	No retaliation by an employer against an employee who files a good faith report or participates in an investigation; retaliation penalty is liability for treble damages, costs, and attorney fees

Table 29: Child Abuse—Continued

State	Code Section	What Constitutes Abuse	Mandatory Reporting Required By
MICHIGAN	Child Protection Law: 722.621 to 722.638	Harm or threatened harm to child's health or welfare that occurs through nonaccidental physical or mental injury, sexual abuse/exploitation, or maltreatment	Physician; dentist; physician's assistant; registered dental hygienist; medical examiner; nurse; licensed emergency medical care provider; audiologist; psychologist; marriage and family therapist; licensed professional counselor; social worker; licensed master's or bachelor's social worker; registered social service technician; social service technician; court employee in professional capacity; school administrator; school counselor or teacher; law enforcement officer; member of the clergy; regulated child care provider; Family Independence Agency employee; employee of entity that would be prohibited from reporting in the absence of state mandate or court order due to federal funding, regulations, or contacts
MINNESOTA	626.556	Physical or mental injury inflicted on child other than by accidental means or which can't be reasonably explained; any aversive or deprivation procedures; sexual abuse, neglect-failure to protect a child from conditions which endanger the child's health; discipline which is not reasonable	Professional and professional's delegate in healing arts, social services, hospital administration, psychological treatment, child care, education, law enforcement, clergy (for information received while engaged in ministerial duties); any other person may report
MISSISSIPPI	43-21-105; 43-21-353	Sexual abuse or exploitation, emotional abuse, mental injury, nonaccidental physical injury, maltreatment	Attorney; physician; dentist; intern; resident; nurse; psychologist; social worker; family protection specialist; child caregiver; minister; law enforcement officer; school employee; or any other person

Basis of Report of Abuse/Neglect	To Whom Reported	Penalty for Failure to Report or False Reporting	Means of Reporting	Retaliation
Reasonable cause to suspect child abuse or neglect; pregnancy under 12 or venereal disease in child over 1 mo. but under 12 yrs. is reasonable cause to suspect abuse	State Family Independence Agency	Failure to report: civilly liable for proximately caused damages; knowing failure to report: misdemeanor punishable up to 93 days in jail and/or fine up to $500; intentionally making false report: if abuse would be misdemeanor or not a crime if true: misdemeanor punishable by 93 days in jail and/or fine up to $100; if abuse would be felony if report were true: felony punishable by lesser of the penalty for the abuse falsely reported, or imprisonment for up to 4 yrs. and/or fine up to $2,000	Immediate oral report followed by written report within 72 hrs.	No reporter shall be penalized for making report or cooperating in an investigation
Knows or has reason to believe a child is being neglected or physically or sexually abused or has been in preceding 3 yrs.	Local welfare agency, police department, county sheriff, or agency responsible for investigating the report	Failure to report: misdemeanor; failure to report 2 or more children not related to perpetrator abused by same perpetrator within preceding 10 yrs.: gross misdemeanor; failure by parent, guardian or caretaker: gross misdemeanor if child suffers harm; if a child dies, felony and imprisonment up to 2 yrs. and/or fine up to $4,000; knowing or reckless false report: person civilly liable for actual damages suffered, punitive damages, and attorney fees and costs	Within 24 hrs.	Employer is prohibited from retaliating against a reporter or child that is subject of the report; there is a rebuttable presumption that adverse action within 90 days is retaliation; retaliation punishable by actual damages and up to $10,000 in additional penalty
Reasonable cause to suspect that a child is neglected or abused	Department of Human Services	Willful violation: imprisonment up to 1 yr. and/or fine up to $5,000	Immediate oral report followed as soon as possible by written report	

Table 29: Child Abuse—Continued

State	Code Section	What Constitutes Abuse	Mandatory Reporting Required By
MISSOURI	210.110 to 210.165	Any physical injury, sexual or emotional abuse inflicted on child other than by accidental means by caregiver; spanking in a reasonable manner not included	Physician; medical examiner; dentist; chiropractor; coroner; optometrist; nurse; hospital or clinic personnel; any other health practitioner; psychologist; social worker; mental health professional; day care center worker; juvenile officer; probation or parole officer; teacher; school official; law enforcement officer; minister; podiatrist; resident; intern; person with responsibility for the care of children
MONTANA	41-3-101 to 41-3-208	Harm or substantial risk of harm to child's health and welfare; abandonment including acts or omissions of person responsible for child's welfare; exposing child to criminal distribution of dangerous drugs; sexual abuse; does not include self-defense, defense of others, or action taken to prevent self-harm of child	Physician; resident; intern; nurse; osteopath; chiropractor; podiatrist; medical examiner; member of hospital staff; coroner; dentist; optometrist; mental health professional; religious healers; school teachers and officials; social workers; day care/child care workers; foster care worker; clergy (unless privileged communication); law enforcement officer; guardian ad litem or court appointed advocate
NEBRASKA	28-710 to 28-717	Knowingly, intentionally or negligently causing or permitting a child to be: placed in a situation endangering life or physical or mental health, cruelly confined or punished, deprived of necessaries, child under 6 yrs. left unattended in vehicle, or sexually abused or exploited	Physician; medical institution; nurse; school employee; social worker; any other person
NEVADA	432B.010 to 432B.320	Physical or mental injury of a nonaccidental nature; sexual abuse or exploitation; negligent treatment or maltreatment such that child's health or welfare is harmed; excessive corporal punishment; nonmedical remedial treatment recognized and permitted in lieu of medical treatment is not abuse	Person providing licensed or certified services pursuant to State statutes; any personnel of a medical facility licensed pursuant to Ch. 449; coroner; clergy, Christian Science practitioner, religious healer unless learned during a confession; employee of a licensed or endorsed school person who maintains or is employed by an agency or service advising persons on abuse or neglect of a child; employee or volunteer at a youth shelter; employees of entities providing organized activities for children; any other person may report

Basis of Report of Abuse/Neglect	To Whom Reported	Penalty for Failure to Report or False Reporting	Means of Reporting	Retaliation
Reasonable cause to suspect that a child has been or may be subjected to abuse or neglect or observes such conditions or circumstances that would reasonably result in abuse or neglect	Missouri Department of Social Services, Children's Division	Class A misdemeanor	Immediate oral report	Sanctions or adverse employment action is prohibited
Know or have reasonable cause to suspect that a child is abused or neglected	Department of Public Health and Human Services	Guilty of misdemeanor and civilly liable for proximately caused damages	Prompt	
Reasonable cause to believe that a child has been subjected to abuse or neglect or observes child being subjected to conditions and circumstances which would reasonably result in abuse or neglect	Department of Health and Human Services or law enforcement agency; state-wide toll-free number to report abuse or neglect	Willful failure: class III misdemeanor	Immediate oral report followed by written report	
Know or have reason to believe a child has been abused or neglected	Law enforcement agency or local office of Division of Child and Family Services of the Department of Human Resources; a toll-free telephone number for reporting	Knowing or willful violation: misdemeanor for first offense; gross demeanor for any subsequent violation	Oral report within 24 hrs.	

Table 29: Child Abuse—Continued

State	Code Section	What Constitutes Abuse	Mandatory Reporting Required By
NEW HAMPSHIRE	Child Protection Act: 169-C:1 to 169-C:40	Sexual abuse; intentional physical injury; psychological injury such that child exhibits symptoms of emotional problems generally recognized to result from consistent mistreatment or neglect; or physical injury by other than nonaccidental means	Physician; surgeon; medical examiner; psychiatrist; optometrist; resident; intern; osteopath; psychologist; therapist; nurse, dentist, chiropractor; hospital personnel; Christian Science practitioner; school teacher or official; social worker; day care worker; foster or child care worker; law enforcement official; priest; minister; rabbi; any other person
NEW JERSEY	9:6-8.9 to 9:6-8.20	Physical injury by other than accidental means; causing substantial risk of death or serious disfigurement or protracted impairment of physical or emotional health; sexual abuse or acts of sexual abuse; willful abandonment; willful isolation of ordinary social contact to indicate emotional or social deprivation; inappropriate placement in institution; neglect by not supplying adequate care, necessaries or supervision	Any person
NEW MEXICO	32A-4-1 to 32A-4-34	Physical, emotional or psychological abuse including sexual abuse, exploitation, torture, confinement, cruel punishment, placing a child in a situation that may endanger the child's life breath	Any person, including licensed physicians, residents, or interns; law enforcement officer; presiding judge; registered nurse; visiting nurse; school teacher; school official; social worker in professional capacity; clergy if information is not privileged

Basis of Report of Abuse/Neglect	To Whom Reported	Penalty for Failure to Report or False Reporting	Means of Reporting	Retaliation
Having reason to suspect that a child has been abused or neglected	Department of Health and Human Services	Knowing violation: misdemeanor	Immediate oral report, followed by a written report within 48 hrs. of the oral report if requested	
Having reasonable cause to believe that a child has been subjected to child abuse or acts of child abuse	Child Protection and Permanency	Knowing violation: disorderly person	Immediate	Discharge from employment or any manner of discrimination with respect to employment gives the reporter a cause of action resulting in reinstatement with back pay or other legal or equitable relief
Knows or has reasonable suspicion that child is abused or neglected	Law enforcement agency or department office in county where child resides or tribal law enforcement or social services for Indian child	Misdemeanor punishable by imprisonment up to 1 yr. and/or fine up to $1,000		

Table 29: Child Abuse—Continued

State	Code Section	What Constitutes Abuse	Mandatory Reporting Required By
NEW YORK	Soc. Serv. §§ 411 to 428	Injury by other than accidental means causing death, disfigurement, impairment of physical or emotional health; deliberate indifference causing such injury; creating substantial risk of such injury; sexual abuse, permitting sexual criminal behavior	Physician; registered physician assistant; surgeon; medical examiner; coroner; dentist; dental hygienist; osteopath; optometrist; chiropractor; podiatrist; resident; intern; psychologist; registered nurse; social worker; emergency medical technician; licensed creative arts therapist; licensed marriage and family therapist; licensed mental health counselor; licensed psychoanalyst; licensed behavior analyst; certified behavior analyst assistant; hospital personnel; Christian Science practitioner; school personnel required to hold a teaching, administrative, or coaching license or certificate; social services worker; director of a children's camp; day care center worker; school-age child care worker; family day care; child care or foster care worker; mental health professional; substance abuse counselor; alcoholism counselor; all persons credentialed by the office of alcoholism and substance abuse services; peace officer; police officer; district attorney; investigator employed in the office of a district attorney; or other law enforcement personnel; any person may report
NORTH CAROLINA	7B-101 to 7B-311	Inflicts or allows to be inflicted or creates a substantial risk of injury other than by accidental means; commits, permits, or encourages any type of sexual abuse; creates or allows serious emotional damage to juvenile; uses inappropriate devices or procedures to modify behavior; encourages, directs, or approves of delinquent acts involving moral turpitude; commits or allows trafficking servitude	Any person or institution
NORTH DAKOTA	14-09-22; 50-25.1-01 to 50-25.1-19	Inflict or allow bodily or mental injury or sexual abuse	Physician; nurse; dentist; optometrist; dental hygienist; medical examiner or coroner; medical or mental health professional; religious practitioner of the healing arts; school teacher or administrator; school officer; juvenile court personnel; probation officer; division of juvenile services employee; clergy as long as not derived from spiritual advisor capacity any person may report

Basis of Report of Abuse/Neglect	To Whom Reported	Penalty for Failure to Report or False Reporting	Means of Reporting	Retaliation
Reasonable cause to suspect that a child is abused or maltreated or knows from personal knowledge of parent or guardian, facts, conditions, or circumstances which, if correct, would render the child abused or maltreated	Statewide central register of child abuse or local child protective services	Civil liability for proximately caused damages	Immediate oral report followed by written report within 48 hrs. of oral report	Retaliatory personnel action against the reporter is prohibited
Cause to suspect that juvenile is abused, neglected, or dependent, or has died as the result of maltreatment	Director of Department of Social Services in county where juvenile resides	Knowing or wanton failure: Class 1 misdemeanor		
Having knowledge or reasonable cause to suspect that a child is abused or neglected or has died as a result of abuse or neglect, including images discovered on a computer	Dept. of Human Services or its designee	Willful failure to report: infraction; Willful false report: class B misdemeanor and liable for all civil damages including exemplary damages; if false report made to law enforcement officer: class A misdemeanor	Immediate oral or written report; written report within 48 hrs. of an oral report if requested	Retaliation following a good faith report is prohibited and is a class B misdemeanor; employer liable for all civil damages; there is a rebuttable presumption that adverse action within 90 days of a report is retaliation

Table 29: Child Abuse—Continued

State	Code Section	What Constitutes Abuse	Mandatory Reporting Required By
OHIO	2151.031; 2151.421; 2151.99; 2921.14	Victim of sexual activity as defined in ch. 2907; endangered as defined in 2919.22; exhibits evidence of physical or mental injury or death by other than accidental means; suffering physical or mental injury that harms or threatens the child's health or welfare; subjected to out-of-home care child abuse	Attorney; physician; hospital intern or resident; dentist; podiatrist; practitioner of limited branch of medicine specified in § 4731.15; registered nurse; licensed practical nurse; visiting nurse; other health care professional; licensed psychologist; licensed school psychologist; marriage and family therapist; speech pathologist or audiologist; coroner; day care administrator or employee; child day camp administrator or employee; child care agency administrator or employee; school teacher or employee; social worker; professional counselor; county humane society agent; person other than cleric rendering spiritual treatment through prayer; county department of job and family services professional employee working with children or families; county board of developmental disabilities member or superintendent; contracted investigative agent for county board; respite care facility employee; home health agency employee; homemaker services entity employee; assessor pursuant to ch. 3107 or 5103; third party employed by a public children services agency; agency person may report
OKLAHOMA	Tit. 10A, §§ 1-1-105; 1-2-101	Harm or threatened harm to child's health, safety, or welfare including but not limited to nonaccidental physical or mental injury sexual abuse or exploitation	Every person; physician; surgeon; other health care professional

Basis of Report of Abuse/Neglect	To Whom Reported	Penalty for Failure to Report or False Reporting	Means of Reporting	Retaliation
Knows or reasonably suspects child has suffered or faces threat of suffering any physical or mental wound, injury, disability, or condition that reasonably indicates abuse or neglect	The Public Children's Services Agency or municipal or county peace officer in county where child resides	Guilty of making a false report or failure to report religious leader's abuse by church member or failure to report when child under reporter's control, supervision: misdemeanor of the first degree. Failure to report: misdemeanor of 4th degree	By telephone or in person followed by a written report if requested	
Having reason to believe that child is a victim of abuse or neglect	Department of Human Services; statewide hotline available	Knowing and willful failure to report: misdemeanor; knowledge of prolonged (at least 6 mos.) or ongoing abuse with knowing and willful failure to report: felony		Retaliation against good faith reporters is prohibited, punishable by liability for damages, costs, and attorney fees

Table 29: Child Abuse—Continued

State	Code Section	What Constitutes Abuse	Mandatory Reporting Required By
OREGON	419B.005 to 419B.100	Any assault of a child and any physical injury to a child caused by other than accidental means (including injuries at variance with explanation given for injury); rape; sexual abuse or exploitation; allowing child to engage in prostitution; negligent treatment; failure to provide adequate care; buying or selling child as described in 163.537; threatening harm to child's health or welfare; any mental injury which includes only observable and substantial impairment to child's ability to function; permitting a child to enter or remain in a place where methamphetamines are being manufactured; unlawful exposure to controlled substance that substantially risks child's health or safety; reasonable discipline is not abuse	Any public or private official, except no requirement for psychiatrist, psychologist, clergy, attorney or guardian ad litem to report privileged communication; attorney not required to report information detrimental to client
PENNSYLVANIA	Tit. 23, § 6303 to 6319	Act which causes nonaccidental serious physical injury, mental injury, sexual abuse or exploitation, serious physical neglect constituting prolonged or repeated lack of supervision or failure to provide essentials of life	Generally, a person who comes into contact with children in the course of their employment; licensed physician; osteopath, medical examiner; optometrist; podiatrist; intern; licensed registered or practical nurse; coroner; dentist; chiropractor; hospital personnel; Christian Science practitioner; clergy, school teacher, nurse or administrator; social services worker; day care or child center worker; mental health professional; peace officer; law enforcement official; funeral director; foster care worker
RHODE ISLAND	40-11-1 to 40-11-17	Child whose physical or mental health or welfare is harmed or threatened with harm including excessive corporal punishment, sexual abuse/exploitation, neglect, or abandonment, failure to provide necessaries and a minimum degree of care	Any person

Basis of Report of Abuse/Neglect	To Whom Reported	Penalty for Failure to Report or False Reporting	Means of Reporting	Retaliation
Have reasonable cause to believe that child has suffered abuse	Local office of Dept. of Human Services, designee, or county law enforcement where reporter resides	Failure to report or false report: class A violation, must be prosecuted within 18 mos.; false report with intent to influence custody, parenting time, visitation or child support decision is considered a false report	Immediate oral report by telephone or otherwise	
Reasonable cause to suspect (within their respective training) that child is abused	Department of Public Welfare of the Commonwealth	Willful failure to report: 3rd degree misdemeanor; subsequent violations: 2nd degree misdemeanor	Immediately by telephone, followed by a written report within 48 hrs. of the oral report	Any good faith reporter that is discharged or discriminated against has a cause of action, punished by appropriate relief, including reinstatement with back pay
Reasonable cause to know or suspect that a child has been abused or neglected or been the victim of sexual abuse or died as a result	Department of Children, Youth, and Families	Failure to report: Misdemeanor imprisonment up to 1 yr. and/or fine up to $500 and civilly liable for proximately caused damages; false report: imprisonment for up to 1 yr. and/or fine up to $1,000	Report within 24 hrs.	

Table 29: Child Abuse—Continued

State	Code Section	What Constitutes Abuse	Mandatory Reporting Required By
SOUTH CAROLINA	64-7-10 to 63-7-450	Inflict or allow physical or mental injury, including excessive corporal punishment; commits or allows a sexual offense; failure to supply with necessaries; abandonment; encourages, condones, approves of delinquent acts; any of the above such that a child that joins the household subsequently is at substantial risk of abuse or neglect	Physician; nurse; dentist; optometrist; medical examiner or coroner; county medical examiner or coroner's office employee; other medical or emergency medical services; mental health or allied health professional; clergy including Christian Science practitioner or religious healer; school teacher, counselor, principal, assistant principal, or attendance officer; social or public assistance worker; substance abuse treatment staff; childcare worker; foster parent; police or law enforcement officer; juvenile justice worker; undertaker; funeral home director or employee; film processor; computer technician; judge, CASA volunteer

Basis of Report of Abuse/Neglect	To Whom Reported	Penalty for Failure to Report or False Reporting	Means of Reporting	Retaliation
Having reason to believe that a child's physical or mental health or welfare has been or may be adversely affected by abuse or neglect	County Department of Social Services or law enforcement agency in county where child resides or is found	Failure to report: misdemeanor, imprisonment up to 6 mos. and/or fine up to $500; false report: subject to civil action for actual & punitive damages, costs and attorney fees; knowingly false report: misdemeanor; imprisonment up to 90 days and/or fine up to $5,000; department may file civil action to recover investigation costs following a bad faith report	Oral report by telephone or otherwise	

Table 29: Child Abuse—Continued

State	Code Section	What Constitutes Abuse	Mandatory Reporting Required By
SOUTH DAKOTA	26-8A-1 to 26-8A-34	Child whose parent, guardian, or custodian has abandoned the child or has subjected the child to mistreatment or abuse; who lacks proper parental care; whose environment is injurious to the child's welfare; whose parent, guardian, or custodian fails or refuses to provide necessaries; who is homeless, without proper care, or not domiciled with the child's parent, guardian, or custodian through no fault of the child's parent, guardian, or custodian; who is threatened with substantial harm; who has sustained emotional harm or mental injury evidenced by an observable and substantial impairment in child's ability to function; who is subject to sexual abuse, molestation, or exploitation; who was subject to prenatal exposure to alcohol, marijuana, or any drug abuse; whose parent, guardian, or custodian knowingly exposes the child to an environment that is being used for the manufacture, use, or distribution of methamphetamines or other unlawfully manufactured drug or substance	Physician; osteopath; dentist; chiropractor; nurse; optometrist; mental health professional; psychologist; religious healing practitioner; social worker; parole or court services officer; law enforcement officer; teacher; school counselor or official; licensed or registered child care provider; coroner; chemical dependency counselor; domestic abuse shelter worker; podiatrist; hospital intern or resident; child advocacy or welfare services provider, employee, or volunteer; any safety sensitive position defined in § 23-3-6412; any other person may report

Basis of Report of Abuse/Neglect	To Whom Reported	Penalty for Failure to Report or False Reporting	Means of Reporting	Retaliation
Have reasonable cause to suspect a child has been abused or neglected	State's attorney in county where child resides or is present, department of social services or to law enforcement officer	Intentional failure to report: class 1 misdemeanor	Immediate oral report by telephone or otherwise	

Table 29: Child Abuse—Continued

State	Code Section	What Constitutes Abuse	Mandatory Reporting Required By
TENNESSEE	37-1-102; 37-1-401 to 37-1-414; 37-1-602	Any wound, injury, disability, or physical or mental condition caused by brutality, abuse, or neglect; also includes sexual abuse	Any person
TEXAS	Family 261.001 to 261.410	Causing or permitting mental or emotional injury impairing child's growth, development, or psychological functioning; physical injury resulting in substantial harm, or which is at variance with explanation given; sexual conduct harmful to a child's mental, emotional or physical welfare; causing or permitting the filming or photographing of pornographic depictions; use of a controlled substance that results in physical, mental, or emotional injury; knowingly causing or permitting trafficking of a child	Professionals, defined as individuals licensed or certified by the state or employed by a licensed or certified facility that has direct contact with children in the normal course of their duties, including teachers, nurses, doctors, day-care employees, employees of a clinic or health care facility that provides reproductive services, juvenile probation officers, and juvenile detention or correctional officers; any other person
UTAH	62A-4a-401 to 62A-4A-415	Non-accidental or threatened harm, sexual abuse or exploitation	Any person licensed under Tit. 58, Ch. 67, Utah Medical Practice Act or Ch. 316, Nurse Practice Act; clergy with consent of the person making confession

Basis of Report of Abuse/Neglect	To Whom Reported	Penalty for Failure to Report or False Reporting	Means of Reporting	Retaliation
Having knowledge or being called on to render aid to any child suffering from or sustaining a wound or injury which is of such a nature as to reasonably indicate or which on the basis of available information reasonably appears to have been caused by brutality, abuse or neglect	Department of Children's Services; judge having juvenile jurisdiction over the child; sheriff of the county where child resides; chief law enforcement official of the municipality where child resides	Knowing failure to report: class A misdemeanor punishable by fine up to $2,500; knowing and malicious false report: class E felony	Report by telephone or otherwise	
Having cause to believe that a child's physical or mental health or welfare has been or may be adversely affected by abuse or neglect	Texas Dept. of Family & Protective Services or any state or local law enforcement agency, state agency in charge of facility in which abuse occurred or Texas Youth Commission if report based on child's information. Abuse involving person responsible for child's care must be reported to Texas Dept. of Family & Protective Services	Knowing failure to report: class A misdemeanor, except it is a state jail felony if it is shown at trial that the child had an intellectual disability and resided in a state supported living center, or that the actor intended to conceal the abuse; knowing false report: state jail felony, but if previously convicted, then 3rd degree felony, also liable for civil penalty of $1,000	Professionals must report within 48 hrs. of the fist suspicion of abuse	Employer may not suspend, terminate, or otherwise discriminate against a good faith reporter or employee cooperating with an investigation of abuse; may sue for injunctive relief, damages, or both
Reason to believe that a child has been subjected to abuse or observe a child being subjected to conditions or circumstances which would reasonably result in abuse or who attends birth or cares for child with fetal alcohol or drug dependency	Nearest peace officer, law enforcement agency, or office of the division	Willful failure to report: Class B misdemeanor (must be commenced within 4 yrs. from date of knowledge of abuse and failure to report)	Immediate report followed by written report within 48 hrs. if requested	

Table 29: Child Abuse—Continued

State	Code Section	What Constitutes Abuse	Mandatory Reporting Required By
VERMONT	Tit. 33, § 4911 to 4923	Child whose physical health, psychological growth and development or welfare is harmed or is at substantial risk of harm by the acts or omissions of persons responsible for child; includes sexual abuse, abandonment, emotional maltreatment, failure to supply necessaries	Physician; surgeon; osteopath; chiropractor; licensed, certified or registered physician assistant; resident physician; intern; hospital administrator; registered nurse; licensed practical nurse; medical examiner; emergency medical personnel; dentist; psychologist; pharmacist; health care provider; child care worker; school superintendent; headmaster of independent school; teacher; student teacher; any school employee; mental health professional; social worker; probation officer; Agency of Human Services employee, contractor, or grantee; police officer; camp owner, administrator, or counselor; clergy; any other concerned persons may report
VIRGINIA	63.2-100; 63.2-1501 to 63.2-1530	To create, inflict or threaten to create or inflict or allow to be created or inflicted upon a child a physical or mental injury by other than accidental means or create a substantial risk of death or impairment; neglect; abandonment; sexual abuse/exploitation	Any person licensed to practice medicine or healing arts; hospital resident or intern; nurses; social worker; probation officer; child care worker; school employee; teacher; mental health professional; law enforcement officer; mediator; any employee of facility which takes care of children; court appointed special advocate; persons trained by Department to recognize and report abuse; employees of public assistance agencies; athletic coach; youth day camp or program workers; non-attorney employed by higher education institution gathering information in course of providing legal representation
WASHINGTON	26.44.010. to 26.44.900	The injury, sexual abuse/exploitation or negligent treatment of a child, under circumstances which indicate that such child's health, welfare, or safety is harmed	All practitioners; coroners; law enforcement officer; school personnel; nurse; social services counselor; psychologist; department of early learning employee; pharmacist; child care providers; juvenile probation officer; health and social services department employee; responsible living skills program staff; HOPE center staff; state family and children's ombudsmen; supervisor in profit or nonprofit organization who reasonably believes supervisee is abusing; any adult who believes a child residing with them has suffered severe abuse; corrections officers whose beliefs are based on observations of offenders with child
WEST VIRGINIA	49-6A-1 to 49-6A-11; 49-1-3	Physical, mental, or emotional injury; sexual abuse or exploitation; sale or attempted sale of child; domestic violence; excessive corporal punishment	Medical, dental, or mental health professional; religious healer; Christian Science practitioner; school teacher or personnel; social services worker; child care worker; foster care worker; Division of Juvenile Services employee; magistrate; youth camp worker; children's organized activities employee, coach or volunteer; commercial film or photographic print processor; EMT; peace or law enforcement official; circuit court judge; family court judge; clergy; humane officer

Basis of Report of Abuse/Neglect	To Whom Reported	Penalty for Failure to Report or False Reporting	Means of Reporting	Retaliation
Reasonable cause to believe that a child has been abused or neglected	Commissioner for Children and Families or Department of Children and Families	Failure to report: Fine up to $500. Failure to report with intent to conceal: imprisonment up to 6 mos. and/or fine up to $1,000	Within 24 hrs.	Retaliation against a good faith reporter is prohibited; civil cause of action for compensatory and punitive damages available
Have reason to suspect that a child is abused or neglected including certain indicators of fetal alcohol or drug dependency or exposure	Department of Social Services toll-free child abuse or neglect hotline; department of public welfare or social services in county where child resides	Failure to report within 24 hours of first suspicion of child abuse: fine up to $500; subsequent failures: fine of at least $1,000; in case of sexual abuse: Class 1 misdemeanor; false report by person over 14: Class 1 misdemeanor for first defense; subsequent offense: Class 6 felony		
Reasonable cause to believe that a child has suffered abuse or neglect	State Department of Social and Health Services or proper law enforcement agency	Misdemeanor	Within 48 hrs. of having reasonable cause; written report if requested	
Reasonable cause to suspect that a child is abused or neglected or observes a child subjected to conditions likely to result in abuse or neglect	Department of Health and Human Resources; if serious physical abuse or sexual abuse, report also to State Police and any law enforcement with jurisdiction	Failure to report: Misdemeanor punishable by imprisonment in county jail up to 30 days and/or fine up to $1,000	Immediately by telephone, followed by written report within 48 hrs. if requested	

Table 29: Child Abuse—Continued

State	Code Section	What Constitutes Abuse	Mandatory Reporting Required By
WISCONSIN	48.02; 48.981	Physical injury inflicted on child other than by accidental means, sexual abuse/exploitation, emotional damage, (harm to child's psychological or intellectual functioning which is exhibited by anxiety, depression, or other outward behavior) or neglect (failure to provide necessaries of life); on unborn child, habitual lack of self control by expectant mother in use of alcohol and controlled drugs; permitting or encouraging prostitution; manufacturing meth in child's presence, premises of child's home, or where meth can be seen, smelled, heard by child	Physician; coroner; medical examiner; nurse; dentist; chiropractor; optometrist; acupuncturist; other medical or mental health professional; social worker; marriage or family therapist; counselor; public assistance worker; school employee, teacher, administrator, or counselor; mediator; child care or day care center worker; dietitian; physical or occupational therapists; EMT; clergy; audiologist; speech-language pathologists; police or law enforcement officer; attorney; first responder; court appointed special advocate; member of treatment staff or alcohol or drug abuse counselor; any person may report
WYOMING	14-3-201 to 14-3-216	The inflicting or causing of physical or mental injury, harm or imminent danger to the physical or mental health or welfare of a child other than by accidental means including abandonment, excessive/unreasonable corporal punishment, malnutrition, intentional or unintentional neglect or the commission of a sexual offense. Imminent danger includes driving under influence	Any person; member/staff of medical (public or private) institution; school; agency; or facility must also notify person in charge

Basis of Report of Abuse/Neglect	To Whom Reported	Penalty for Failure to Report or False Reporting	Means of Reporting	Retaliation
Reasonable cause to suspect that a child has been abused or neglected or has been threatened with abuse or neglect or that abuse or neglect will occur	The county department (or licensed child welfare agency under contract with the county department); sheriff or police department	Imprisonment up to 6 mos. and/or fine up to $1,000	By telephone or personally	No good faith reporter may be discharged, disciplined, or otherwise discriminated against in regard to employment
Knowledge or reasonable cause to believe or suspect that a child has been abused or neglected or who observes any child being subjected to conditions or circumstances which would reasonably result in abuse or neglect	Child protective agency or local law enforcement agency	Knowing and intentional false report: Misdemeanor punishable by imprisonment up to 6 mos. and/or fine up to $750		Any employer, public or private, who discharges, suspends, disciplines or penalizes an employee solely for making a report of neglect or abuse is guilty of a misdemeanor punishable by imprisonment up to 6 mos. and/or fine up to $750

30. CHILD CUSTODY

Because of the importance of the laws regarding child custody, all fifty states and the District of Columbia have adopted the Uniform Child Custody Act.

Prior to the twentieth century, it was standard that the father would take sole custody of the children upon divorce. In the twentieth century, however, it became common practice to award custody of children "of tender years" to the mother. It is now most common to award custody to both parents at the same time, in an arrangement known as "joint custody," under which custody of the children is divided into legal and physical custody, with both parents sharing responsibility for the children simultaneously. However, joint custody does not necessarily mean equal custody. Rather, it merely means custody co-exists between parents with the physical arrangements coordinated in the best interests of the children. All but five states recognize the joint custody arrangement in child custody matters. Eight states, apparently feeling the need to remove the children from the pressures of having to make difficult and emotional decisions, do not consider the wishes of the children when awarding custody. However, it is safe to say that judges will never completely ignore children's wishes in considering custody matters, just as they will not make them bear the brunt of the responsibility for a decision when answering the objections of a parent. In the majority of states listed as not taking into account the child's wishes, the statute also reads that the decision regarding placement of the child must be based on what is in the "best interests" of the child.

A relatively new provision in the law of child custody is allowing grandparents visitation rights. Unheard of until the late 1990s, today all states except two specifically allow grandparents to petition for visitation of unmarried minor children.

Table 30: Child Custody

State	Code Section	Year Uniform Child Custody Act Adopted	Joint Custody?	Grandparent Visitation?	Child's Wishes Considered?
ALABAMA	30-3-1 to 30-3-200; 30-3B-101 to 30-3B-405	UCCJA: 1980; UCCJEA: 2000	Yes; 30-3-150	Grandparents may petition for visitation; 30-3-4.2	Yes
ALASKA	25.20.060 to 25.20.140; 25.24.150; 25.30.300 to 25.30.910	UCCJA: 1977; UCCJEA: 1998	Yes, "shared"; 25.20.060	Yes; 25.20.065	Yes
ARIZONA	25-401 to 25-415; 25-1001 to 25-1067	UCCJA: 1996; UCCJEA: 2001	No, parenting time based on "best interest of children"; 25-403	Yes; 25-409	Yes
ARKANSAS	9-13-101 to 9-13-407; 9-19 101 to 9-19-401	UCCJA: 1979; UCCJEA: 1999	Yes; 9-13-101	Yes; 9-13-103	No
CALIFORNIA	Fam. §§ 3000 to 3204; 3400 to 3465	UCCJA: 1973; UCCJEA: 2000	Yes; presumption; Fam. § 3080	Yes; Fam. §§ 3100(a); 3102 to 3104	Yes
COLORADO	14-10-123; 14-13-101 to 14-13-403; 19-1-117	UCCJA: 1973; UCCJEA: 2000	No; Colorado uses term "parental responsibility" which can be joint or primary for both residence and decision making; 14-10-103; 14-10-124	Yes; 19-1-117	Yes
CONNECTICUT	46b-56 to 46b-62	UCCJA: 1978; UCCJEA: 2000	Yes; 46b-56a	Yes; 46b-59	Yes
DELAWARE	Tit. 13, §§ 721 to 733; 1901 to 1943	UCCJA: 1976; UCCJEA: 2002	Yes; Tit. 1, 3 §§ 727; 728	Yes; Tit. 13, § 728	Yes
DISTRICT OF COLUMBIA	16-911; 16-914; 16-4601.01 to 16-4604.02	UCCJA: 1983; UCCJEA: 2001	Yes; 16-911(a)(5)	No	Yes
FLORIDA	61.13; 61.501 to 61.542	UCCJA: 1977; UCCJEA: 2002	Yes; shared 61.13(2)(b)2	Grandparents may file petition; court will decide based on child's best interest and other criteria; 725.001	Yes
GEORGIA	19-9-1 to 19-9-104	UCCJA: 1978; UCCJEA: 2001	Yes; 19-9-3(a)(5)	Yes; 19-9-3(d)	Yes
HAWAII	571-46 to 571-46.3; 583A-101 to 583A-317	UCCJA: 1973; UCCJEA: 2003	Yes; 571-46.1	Yes; 571-46.3	Yes

Table 30: Child Custody—Continued

State	Code Section	Year Uniform Child Custody Act Adopted	Joint Custody?	Grandparent Visitation?	Child's Wishes Considered?
IDAHO	32-11-101 to 32-11-405; 32-717; 32-717B; 32-719	UCCJA: 1977; UCCJEA: 2000	Yes; 32-717B	Yes; 32-719	Yes
ILLINOIS	750 §§ 5/601 to 5/611; 36/101 to 36/403	UCCJA: 1979; UCCJEA: 1999	Yes; 750 § 5/602.1	Yes; 750 §§ 5/607	Yes
INDIANA	31-17-1-1 to 31-17-7-2; 31-21-1-1 to 31-21-7-3	UCCJA: 1977; UCCJEA: 2007	Yes; 31-17-2-13 to 31-17-2-15	Yes; 31-17-5-1 to 31-17-5-10	Yes
IOWA	598.41; 598B.101 to 598B.402; 600C.1	UCCJA: 1977; UCCJEA: 2999	Yes; 598.41(2)	Yes; 600C.1	Yes
KANSAS	60-23-3203; 23-3206; 23-3301; 38-1336 to 38-1377	UCCJA: 1978; UCCJEA: 2000	Yes; 23-3206	Yes; 23-3301	Yes
KENTUCKY	403.270; 403.800 to 403.880; 405.021	UCCJA: 1980; UCCJEA: 2004	Yes; 403.270(5)	Yes; 405.021	Yes
LOUISIANA	9:331 to 9:334; 9:355.12; 13:1801 to 13:1842; Civ. Code Art. 131	UCCJA: 1978; UCCJEA: 2007	Yes; 9:335; Civ. Code Art. 131	Yes; 9:334	Yes
MAINE	Tit. 19-A, §§ 1651 to 1654; 1731 to 1783; 1801 to 1805	UCCJA: 1979; UCCJEA: 2000	Yes; Tit. 19-A, § 1651	Yes; Tit. 19-A §§ 1801 to 1805	Yes
MARYLAND	Fam. §§ 5-203; 9-102; 9.5-101 to 9.5-318	Precursor to UCCJA: 1957; UCCJEA: 2004	Yes; Fam. § 5-203(d)(2)	Yes; Fam. § 9-102	No; Fam. § 9-103 Child 16 yrs. old may petition for change of custody
MASSACHUSETTS	Ch. 208, §§ 28; 31; Ch. 209C §§ 10; Ch. 119, § 39D	UCCJA: 1983; UCCJEA: not yet adopted	Yes; Ch. 208, § 31; Ch. 209C § 10	Yes; Ch. 119, § 39D	No
MICHIGAN	722.21 to 722.31	UCCJA: 1976; UCCJEA: 2002	Yes; 722.26a	Yes; 722.27b	Yes
MINNESOTA	257C.08; 518.17; 518.155; 518.175; 518D.101 to 518D.317	UCCJA: 1977; UCCJEA: 2000	Yes; 518.17	Yes; 257C.08; 518.1752	Yes
MISSISSIPPI	93-5-23; 93-5-24; 93-16-1; 93-24-1 to 93-24-75	UCCJA: 1982; UCCJEA: 2004	Yes; 93-5-24	Yes; 93-16-1 to 93-16-7	No
MISSOURI	452.375; 452.402; 452.700 to 452.930	UCCJA: 1978; UCCJEA: 2009	Yes; 452.375	Yes; 452.402	Yes
MONTANA	40-4-211 to 40-4-221; 40-7-101 to 40-7-317; 40-9-102	UCCJA: 1977; UCCJEA: 1999	Yes; parenting plan; child's best interest; 40-4-212	Yes; 40-9-102	Yes

Table 30: Child Custody—Continued

State	Code Section	Year Uniform Child Custody Act Adopted	Joint Custody?	Grandparent Visitation?	Child's Wishes Considered?
NEBRASKA	42-364; 43-1226 to 43-1266; 43-1802;	UCCJA: 1979; UCCJEA 2004	Yes; 42-364(5)	Yes; 43-1802	Yes
NEVADA	125.465; 125.480; 125A.005 to 125A.605; 125C.050	UCCJA: 1979; UCCJEA: 2003	Yes; 125C.0015	Yes; 125C.050	Yes
NEW HAMPSHIRE	458-A:1 to 458-A:40; 461-A:1 to 461-1:24	UCCJA: 1979; UCCJEA: 2010	Yes; parenting plan; child's best interest; 461-A:6	Yes; 461-A:13	Yes
NEW JERSEY	2A:34-53 to 2A:34-95; 9:2-1 to 9:2-12.1	UCCJA: 1979; UCCJEA: 2004	Yes; 9: 2-4(a)	Yes; 9-2-7.1	Yes
NEW MEXICO	40-4-9; 40-4-9.1; 40-9-2 to 40-9-4; 40-10A-101 to 40-10A-403	UCCJA: 1981; UCCJEA: 2001	Yes; 40-4-9.1	Yes; 40-9-2 to 40-9-4	Yes
NEW YORK	Dom. Rel. §§ 75 to 78-A; 240	UCCJA: 1977; UCCJEA: 2002	Yes; Dom. Rel. § 240	Yes; Dom. Rel. § 240(1)	Yes
NORTH CAROLINA	50-11.2; 50-13.2; 50A-101 to 50A-317	UCCJA: 1979; UCCJEA: 1999	Yes; 50-13.2	Yes; 50-13.2(b1)	Yes
NORTH DAKOTA	14-09-05.1; 14-09-06.2; 14-14.1-01 to 14-14.1-37	UCCJA: 1969; UCCJEA: 1999	No; parental responsibility; parenting plan; best interest of child; 14-09-00.1; 41-09.30 to 14-09.33	Yes; 14-09-05.1 Yes	Yes
OHIO	3105.21; 3109.04; 3109.051; 3127.01 to 3127.53	UCCJA: 1977; UCCJEA: 2005	Yes; 3109.04(A)	No; 3109.051	Yes
OKLAHOMA	Tit. 43 §§ 109; 112; 551-101 to 551-402	UCCJA:1980; UCCJEA: 1998	Yes; Tit. 43, §112	Yes; Tit. 43 § 109.4	Yes
OREGON	107.105; 107.169; 109.119; 109.701 to 109.834	UCCJA: 1973; UCCJEA: 1999	Yes; 107.105(a); 107.169	Yes; 109.119	No
PENNSYLVANIA	Tit. 23, §§ 5301; 5324; 5328; 5401 to 5482	UCCJA: 1980; UCCJEA: 2004	Yes, "shared"; Tit. 23, § 5323	Yes; Tit. 23, §§ 5324(3); 5328(c)	Yes
RHODE ISLAND	15-5-16; 15-5-24.1 to 15-5-24.3; 15-14.1-1 to 15-14.42	UCCJA: 1978; UCCJEA: 2003	No	Yes; 15-5-24.1 to 24.3	No
SOUTH CAROLINA	20-3-160; 63-3-530; 63-15-30 to 63-15-394	UCCJA: 1981; UCCJEA: 2008	Yes; 63-15-240(A)(3)	Yes; 63-3-530(A)(33)	Yes; 63-15-30
SOUTH DAKOTA	25-4-45; 25-4-52; 25-5-7.1; 26-5B-101 to 26-5B-405	UCCJA: 1978; UCCJEA: 2005	Yes; 25-5-7.1	Yes; 25-4-52	Yes

Table 30: Child Custody—Continued

State	Code Section	Year Uniform Child Custody Act Adopted	Joint Custody?	Grandparent Visitation?	Child's Wishes Considered?
TENNESSEE	36-6-101; 36-6-106; 36-6-201 to 16-6-243; 36-6-306; 36-6-307	UCCJA: 1979; UCCJEA: 1999	Yes; 36-6-101(a)	Yes; 36-6-306; 36-6-307	Yes
TEXAS	Fam. §§ 153.001 to 152.317; 153.001 to 153.709	UCCJA: 1983; UCCJEA: 2000	Yes; Joint Managing Conservator; Fam. § 153.003	Yes; Fam. § 153.433	Yes
UTAH	30-3-5; 30-3-10 to 30-3-40; 30-5-2; 78B-13-101	UCCJA: 1980; UCCJEA: 2000	Yes; 30-3-10.1 to 30-3-10.4	Yes; 30-5-2	Yes
VERMONT	Tit. 15, §§ 665; 1011; 1061 to 1096	UCCJA: 1979; UCCJEA: 2011	Yes; Tit. 15, § 665(a)	Yes; Tit. 15, § 1011	No
VIRGINIA	16.1.241; 20-107.2; 20-124.1; 20-124.2; 20-146.1 to 20-146.38	UCCJA: 1979; UCCJEA: 2001	Yes; 20-124.1; 20-124.2(B)	Yes; 16.1-241; 20-124.1	Yes
WASHINGTON	26.09.050; 26.09.240; 26.10.100; 26.27.011 to 26.27.941	UCCJA: 1979; UCCJEA: 2001	No	Yes; 26.09.240	Yes
WEST VIRGINIA	48-9-101; 48-9-207; 48-10-101 to 48-10-1201; 48-20-101 to 48-20-404	UCCJA: 1981; UCCJEA: 2001	Yes; 48-9-207	Yes; 48-10-101 to 48-10-404	Yes
WISCONSIN	767.41; 767.43; 767.44; 822.01 to 822.47	UCCJA: 1975; UCCJEA: 2006	Yes; 767.41(1)(b)	Yes; 767.43; 767.44	Yes
WYOMING	20-2-201; 20-5-201 to 20-5-502; 20-7-101	UCCJA: 1973; UCCJEA: 2005	Yes; 20-2-201(d)	Yes; 20-7-101	Yes

31. CHILD SUPPORT GUIDELINES

Modern child support orders, at their essence, provide for the care of children.

Under the English common law, fathers had a moral obligation to support their children. The Elizabethan Poor Law of 1601 codified this obligation and called for the imprisonment of fathers who failed to do so. Coinciding with the industrial revolution, American and English courts began awarding custody of children to mothers. Eventually, courts began to pair maternal custody awards with judgments for the necessities of children, and by the 1970s, every American state had enacted criminal or civil remedies for nonsupport.

Yet, prior to the federal Family Support Act of 1988 (FSA), state courts varied widely in their approaches to calculating and ordering child support. The FSA compelled states to adopt uniform child support guidelines by withholding federal welfare funding from noncompliant states. Today, every state has adopted some form of guidelines.

However, the codification of guidelines is by no means uniform. A plurality of state legislatures have enacted child support guidelines under state law, with a minority of state legislatures delegating this responsibility to state high courts, and an even slimmer minority tasking this responsibility to state agencies. Some states blend all three.

And despite the FSA, states still vary in their approach to calculating child support for noncustodial parents. Currently, three models are used. Forty states along with the District of Columbia have adopted the Income Shares Model, which considers the income of both parents to calculate child support. Eight states have adopted the Obligor Income Model, which only considers the income of noncustodial parents. And three states have adopted the Melson Formula, a modified version of the Income Shares Model, named after its creator, Judge Edward F. Melson, Jr. of the Delaware Family Court. The Melson Formula accounts for basic parental requirements, but it also restricts economic advancement of parents until the basic poverty needs of their children have been met. While all states regard guideline-determined calculations as presumptive child-support awards, some states differ on the burden of proof required to deviate from these calculations. Most states treat guideline-determined calculations as rebuttable presumptions, but five states have raised this burden.

Beyond variations in child support models, states also differ in their adoptions of policy considerations regarding child support. For example, some states prioritize the necessity to support children above parental needs. This policy is often codified via a minimum support guidelines, which either presume or mandate support for children, even if ordered support renders parental income below the Federal Poverty Guidelines. In states with mandatory or presumptive minimum support, parental obligations range from $14 per month in North Dakota to $100 per month in a sextuplet of states.

Furthermore, many states encourage modification of child support when parental income changes. This policy is reflected in judicial presumptions that favor modification when new calculations of child support (accounting for new parental income) substantially vary from original support orders. All states that recognize these presumptions require a minimum variation of at least ten percent, while a handful of states raise this threshold to twenty percent.

This state survey does not attempt to address all the unique disparities of child support guidelines across the states. Instead, it attempts to provide an overview of core commonalities and a flavor for noteworthy nuances.

_____

*This chapter was authored by David Pontier, J.D. Candidate, 2017, University of Nebraska at Lincoln College of Law.

Table 31: Child Support Guidelines

State	Code Section	Method of Calculating Support	Standard Applied to Deviate from Guidelines	Presumptive Monthly Minimum Support Obligation?	Does Newly Calculated Support Discrepancy Create Presumption of Modification?
ALABAMA	Ala. R. Jud. Admin. 32	Income Shares Model, R. 32(C)(1) to 32(C)(2)	Rebuttable presumption, R. 32(A)	No	Yes, if greater than 10%, R. 32(A)(3)(c)
ALASKA	Alaska R. Civ. P. 90.3	Obligor Income Model, R. 90.3	Clear and convincing evidence, R. 90.3(c)(1)	Yes: $50, R. 90.3(c)(3)	Yes, if greater than 15%, R. 90.3(h)(1)
ARIZONA	25-320; Arizona Child Support Guidelines: 25-320, Appendix	Income Shares Model	Rebuttable presumption	No	Yes, if at least 15%
ARKANSAS	Ark. Sup. Ct. Admin. Order 10	Obligor Income Model, 10(III)	Rebuttable presumption, 10(I)	No	No
CALIFORNIA	Fam. §§ 4050 to 4076	Income Shares Model, Fam. § 4055	Rebuttable presumption, Fam. §§ 4052.5(b); 4057	No	No
COLORADO	14-10-115	Income Shares Model, 14-10-115(7)(a)(I)	Rebuttable presumption, 14-10-115(8)(e)	Yes: $50, 14-10-115(7)(a)(II)(B)	No
CONNECTICUT	46B-215; Conn. Agencies Regs. §§ 46b-215a-1 to 46b-215a-6	Income Shares Model, 46b-215a-2c(c)(3)	Rebuttable presumption, 46b-215a-5c(a)	No	No
DELAWARE	Del. Fam. Ct. Civ. R. 500 to 508	Melson Formula, R. 503	Rebuttable presumption, R. 500	Yes: $100, R. 506(a)	No
DISTRICT OF COLUMBIA	16-916.01	Income Shares Model with more extensive formula deviations, 16-916.01(f)(1)	Rebuttable presumption, 16-916.01(p)	Yes: $75, 16-916.01(g)(3)(A)	Yes, if at least 15%, 16-916.01(r)(4)(A)
FLORIDA	61.30	Income Shares Model, 61.30(9)	Rebuttable presumption, 61.30(1)(a)	Yes: percentage of obligor's income, 61.30(6)(a)	No
GEORGIA	19-6-15	Income Shares Model, 19-6-15(b)	Rebuttable presumption, 19-6-15(c)(1)	Yes: $100, 19-6-15(i)(2)(B)(vi)	No
HAWAII	576D-7; Hawaii Child Support Guidelines	Melson Formula, Guideline II(A)	Exceptional circumstances, Guideline II(B)(2)(a)(i)	Yes: $77, Guideline V(M)	Yes, if at least 10%, Guideline III(C)(2)
IDAHO	32-706; Idaho Child Support Guidelines	Income Shares Model, ICSG § 10(a)	Rebuttable presumption, 32-706(5)	Yes: $50, ICSG § 4(d)	No

Table 31: Child Support Guidelines—Continued

State	Code Section	Method of Calculating Support	Standard Applied to Deviate from Guidelines	Presumptive Monthly Minimum Support Obligation?	Does Newly Calculated Support Discrepancy Create Presumption of Modification?
ILLINOIS	750 §§ 5/505 to 5/510	Obligor Income Model, 750 § 505(a)(1)	Rebuttable presumption, 750 § 505(a)(2)	Yes: percentage of obligor's income, 750 § 505(a)(1)	Yes, if at least 20%, 750 § 510(a)(2)(A)
INDIANA	Indiana Child Support Rules and Guidelines	Income Shares Model, Guideline 3	Rebuttable presumption, Rule 2	No	No
IOWA	598.21 to 598.48; Child Support Guidelines: Iowa Ct. R. Ch. 9	Income Shares Model, R. 9.14	Rebuttable presumption, R. 9.4	Yes: noncustodial parent must provide health insurance, but according to income, only if at no cost to add children or at reasonable cost determined by table in R. 9.12(4)	Yes, if at least 10%, 598.21C(2)(a)
KANSAS	20-165; Kan. Child Support Guidelines, S. Ct. Admin. Order No. 287	Income Shares Model, Guideline II.C	Rebuttable presumption, Guideline I	No	Yes, if at least 10%, Guideline V.B.1
KENTUCKY	403.210 to 403.250	Income Shares Model, 403.212(3)	Rebuttable presumption, 403.211(2)	Yes: $60, 403.212(4)	Yes, if at least 15%, 403.213(2)
LOUISIANA	9:315	Income Shares Model, 9:315.2	Rebuttable presumption, 9:315.1	Yes: $100, 9:315.14	No
MAINE	Tit. 19-A, §§ 2001 to 2012	Income Shares Model, Tit. 19-A, § 2006	Rebuttable presumption, Tit. 19-A, § 2005	Yes: percentage of obligor's income, Tit. 19-1, § 2006(5)(C)	Yes, if greater than 15%, Tit. 19-A, § 2009(3)
MARYLAND	Fam. §§ 12-101 to 12-204	Income Shares Model, Fam. § 12-204	Rebuttable presumption, Fam. § 12-202(a)(2)(i)	Yes: $20, Fam. § 12-204(e)	No
MASSACHUSETTS	Ch. 208, § 28; Mass. Child Support Guidelines	Income Shares Model, Guideline II(D)	Rebuttable presumption, Guidelines Preamble	Yes: $80, Guideline II(C)	No
MICHIGAN	552.605; Michigan Child Support Formula Manual	Income Shares Model, 2017 MCSF § 3.01	Rebuttable presumption; 2017 MCSF § 1.01(B)	Yes: percentage of obligor's income, 2017 MCSF § 3.02(C)	No
MINNESOTA	518A.26 to 518A.79	Income Shares Model, 518A.34	Rebuttable presumption, 518A.35(1)(a)	Yes: $50, 518A.42(2)	Yes, if at least 20%, 518A.39(2)(b)(1)

Table 31: Child Support Guidelines—Continued

State	Code Section	Method of Calculating Support	Standard Applied to Deviate from Guidelines	Presumptive Monthly Minimum Support Obligation?	Does Newly Calculated Support Discrepancy Create Presumption of Modification?
MISSISSIPPI	43-19-101 to 43-19-103	Obligor Income Model, 43-19-101(1)	Rebuttable presumption, 43-19-101(1)	Yes, percentage of obligor's income, 43-19-101(1)	No
MISSOURI	452.340 to 452.370; Mo. R. Civ. P. Rule 88; Mo. R. Civ. P. Form 14; Mo. R. Civ. P. Child Support Schedule	Income Shares Model, Form 14, Line 5	Rebuttable presumption, Rule 88.01(b)	Yes: $50, Child Support Schedule	Yes, if at least 20%, 452.370(1)
MONTANA	40-4-204 to 40-4-210; Child Support Guidelines: Mont. Admin. R. 37.62.101 to 37.62.148	Melson Formula, Child Support Guidelines Rule 11	Clear and Convincing, 40-4-204(3)(a)	Yes: percentage of obligor's income, Child Support Guidelines Rule 15	No
NEBRASKA	42-364.16; Neb. Ct. R. 4-201 to 4-222	Income Shares Model, Rule 4-207	Rebuttable presumption, Rule 4-203	Yes: $50, Rule 4-209	Yes, if at least 10%, Rule 4-217
NEVADA	125B	Obligor Income Model, 125B.070	Rebuttable presumption, 125B.080(5)	Yes: $100, 125B.080(4)	Yes, if at least 20%, 125B.145(4)
NEW HAMPSHIRE	458-C:1 to 458-C:9	Income Shares Model, 458-C:3	Rebuttable presumption, 458-C.4(II)	Yes: $50, 458-C:2(V)	No
NEW JERSEY	N.J. R. Prac. App. 9	Income Shares Model, App. 9-A(4)	Rebuttable presumption, App. 9-A(5)	Yes: $5/wk., App. 9A(2)(a)	No
NEW MEXICO	40-4-11	Income Shares Model, 40-4-11.1(K)	Rebuttable presumption, 40-4-11.1(A)	No	Yes, if greater than 20%, 40-4-11.4(A)
NEW YORK	Dom. Rel. §§ 236; 240	Income Shares Model, Dom. Rel. § 240(1-b)(b)(1)	Rebuttable presumption, Dom. Rel. § 240(1-b)(f)	Yes: $25, Dom. Rel. § 240(1-b)(d)	Yes, if at least 15%, Dom. Rel. § 236(9)(b)(2)(ii)(B)
NORTH CAROLINA	50-13.4; N.C. Child Support Guidelines, AOC-162-A (Rev. 1/15)	Income shares Model, Guidelines: Basic Child Support Obligation	Rebuttable presumption, 50-13.4(c)	Yes: $50, Guidelines: Self-Support Reserve	Yes, if at least 15%, Guidelines: Modification
NORTH DAKOTA	14-09-09.7; Admin. Code § 75-02-04.1	Obligor Income Model, Admin. §75-02-04.1-05	Rebuttable presumption, 14-09-09.7(4)	Yes: $14, Admin. § 75-02-04.1-10	No

Table 31: Child Support Guidelines—Continued

State	Code Section	Method of Calculating Support	Standard Applied to Deviate from Guidelines	Presumptive Monthly Minimum Support Obligation?	Does Newly Calculated Support Discrepancy Create Presumption of Modification?
OHIO	3119	Income Shares Model, 3119.022	Rebuttable presumption, 3119.03	Yes: $50, 3119.06	Yes, if greater than 10%, 3119.79(A)
OKLAHOMA	Tit. 43, §§ 115 to 120	Income Shares Model, Tit. 43, § 118D(A)	Rebuttable presumption, Tit. 43, § 118(A)	Yes: $50, Tit. 43, § 119(A)	No
OREGON	25.010 to 25.990; Admin. R. 137-050-0700 to 137-050-0765	Income Shares Model, Rule 137-050-0710	Rebuttable presumption, 25.280	Yes: $100, Rule 137-050-0755	No
PENNSYLVANIA	Tit. 23, § 4322; R. Civ. P. §§ 1910.16 to 1910.21	Income Shares Model, Rule 1910.16-2	Rebuttable presumption, Tit. 23, § 4322(b)	No	No
RHODE ISLAND	15-5-16.2; R.I. Fam. Ct. Admin. Order 2012-05	Income Shares Model, Order 2012-05: II	Rebuttable presumption, Order 2012-05: II	Yes: $20, Order 2012-05:III	No
TENNESSEE	36-5-101; Comp. R. & Regs. 1240-2-4	Income Shares Model, Rule 1240-2-4	Rebuttable presumption, 36-5-101(e)(1)(A)	Yes: $100, Rule 1240-2-4-.03(6)(A)(4)	Yes, if at least 15%, Rule 1240-2-4-.05
TEXAS	Fam. §§ 154.121 to 154.133; 156.401	Obligor Income Model, Fam. § 154.125	Rebuttable presumption, Fam. § 154.122	No	No
UTAH	78B-12-101 to 78B-12-403	Income Shares Model, 78B-12-205	Rebuttable presumption, 78B-12-210	Yes: $30, 78B-12-302	Yes, if at least 10%, 78B-12-210(8)(b)(ii)(A)
VERMONT	Tit. 15, §§ 650 to 670; Admin. Code 12-3-400:1001	Income Shares Model, Tit. 15, § 656	Rebuttable presumption, Tit. 15, § 655	No	Yes, if greater than 10%, Tit. 15, § 660(b)
VIRGINIA	20-108	Income Shares Model, 20-108.2	Rebuttable presumption, 20-108.1(B)	Yes: $68, 20-108.2(B)	No
WASHINGTON	26.19	Income Shares Model, 26.19.080	Rebuttable presumption, 26.19.035	Yes: $50, 26.19.065	No
WEST VIRGINIA	48-11-105; 48-13-101 to 48-13-804	Income Shares Model, 48-13-201`	Rebuttable presumption, 48-13-203	Yes: $50, 48-13-302	Yes, if greater than 15%, 48-11-105(b)
WISCONSIN	49.22; 767.511; Admin. Code. DCF 150.01 to 150.05	Income Shares Model, DCF 150.03(1)	Conclusive presumption with statutory exceptions, 767.511(1j)	Yes: percentage of obligor's income, DCF 150, App. C	No
WYOMING	20-2-301 to 20-2-316	Income Shares Model, 20-2-304(a)	Rebuttable presumption, 20-2-304(a)	Yes: $50, 20-2-304(b)	Yes, if at least 20%, 20-2-311(a)

32. DOMESTIC VIOLENCE

The Violence Against Women Act of 1994 was enacted to end domestic violence against women. However, following its enactment, it became clear to states that one of leading causes of domestic violence was the laissez-faire response by law enforcement officials to domestic violence calls. In response, some states enacted mandatory arrest statutes which require law enforcement officers to arrest an individual after a report of domestic violence. Presently, all state statutes allow law enforcement officials to arrest individuals without a court issued warrant under certain circumstances, and all states and the District of Columbia include domestic violence calls as grounds for a warrantless arrest.

Currently, 32 states require law enforcement officials to either arrest an individual for domestic violence in all cases or in the case that a court order has been violated. In contrast, around 20 states permit law enforcement officials to use their discretion to arrest an individual if there is probable or reasonable cause. Six states statutorily prefer arrest in all domestic violence situations but do not require it. For example, in Massachusetts, arresting an individual is preferred in a response to a domestic violence call where mandatory arrest criteria is not met.

Further, some state laws contemplate whether law enforcement should arrest more than one individual after a domestic violence report. Today, 20 states explicitly address mutual arrests, while the other 30 states are silent on the issue. Although outside the scope of this survey, the question remains whether mutual arrest is impliedly allowed in the states that make no mention of mutual arrests in the statute. Of the 20 states that address mutual arrests, most provide that mutual arrest is allowed and the arrests are in the officer's discretion. Many provide that officers should determine if one person is the primary aggressor. If an officer determines that only one person is the primary aggressor, then only the primary aggressor should be arrested. While no state expressly bans mutual arrest, some states discourage mutual arrests.

In addition to mandatory arrest statutes, most states enacted mandatory reporting statutes for health professionals. These statutes require the health professional to report specific injuries or wounds to law enforcement. These laws are generally applicable to any age, but other statutory provisions linked to mandatory reporting requirements for health professionals cover special groups such as children and the elderly. Three states, Alabama, New Mexico, and Wyoming, have no mandatory reporting requirements for health professionals in this context.

Mandatory reporting statutes fall into three general categories: 1) states that require reporting of injuries caused by certain types of weapons; 2) states that require reporting for injuries caused in furtherance of a criminal offense; and 3) states that require reporting for any evidence of domestic violence. The most common statutes require health professionals to report injuries caused by gunshot and/or knife wounds. In order to fall under the mandatory umbrella of the most common of these statues, the injury must be severe and in furtherance of a felony offense. However, a minority of states require health professionals to report injuries that are thought to be caused by domestic violence without an independent criminal offense.

Table 32: Domestic Violence

State	Code Section	Mandatory or Discretionary	Arrest of More Than One Person	Mandatory Reporting: Health Care	Type of Injury
ALABAMA	Arrest: 15-10-3(8)	Discretionary		No	
ALASKA	Arrest: 18.65.530(A); 18.65.530(B) Mandatory Reporting: 08.64.369	Mandatory	Yes; officer discretion	Yes	Burns, gunshot wounds, non-accidental wounds from dangerous object, and any injury that may result in death
ARIZONA	Arrest: 13-3601(B) Mandatory Reporting: 13-3806	Mandatory if physical injury or dangerous weapon; discretionary for all other cases	Yes; officer discretion	Yes	Gunshot or knife wounds or other injuries from a fight or other illegal conduct
ARKANSAS	Arrest: 16-81-113(a)(1)(A); 16-81-113 (a)(2)(A) Mandatory Reporting: 12-12-602	Preferred arrest		Yes	Burns, gunshot or knife wounds or other intentionally inflicted wounds
CALIFORNIA	Arrest: Penal § 13701(B) Mandatory Reporting: Penal §§ 11160; 11161	Preferred arrest; mandatory if in violation of court order	Yes, but discouraged	Yes	Suspected injuries from assaultive or abusive conduct
COLORADO	Arrest: 18-6-803.6 Mandatory Reporting: 12-36-135	Mandatory	Yes; officer discretion	Yes	Gunshot wound or other injury resulting from a criminal offense
CONNECTICUT	Arrest: 46b-38b(a) Mandatory Reporting: 19a-490f	Mandatory	Yes; officer discretion	Yes	Gunshot or knife wounds
DELAWARE	Arrest: Tit. 11, §§ 1046(c); 1904(A)(4) Mandatory Reporting: Tit. 24, § 1762; Tit. 16 § 6601B	Mandatory if in violation of court order; discretionary for all other cases		Yes	Burns, gunshot or knife wounds, and poisonings
DISTRICT OF COLUMBIA	Arrest: 16-1031(a) Mandatory Reporting: 7-2601	Mandatory		Yes	Gunshot wounds or injuries from other dangerous weapons
FLORIDA	Arrest: 741.29(3)-(4) Mandatory Reporting: 790.24; 877.155	Discretionary	Yes, but discouraged	Yes	Gunshot or knife wounds, burns, or other life threatening injuries
GEORGIA	Arrest: 17-4-20(a); 17-4-20.1(a); 17-4-20.1(b) Mandatory Reporting: 31-7-9	Discretionary	Yes, but discouraged	Yes	Intentionally inflicted injuries

Table 32: Domestic Violence—Continued

State	Code Section	Mandatory or Discretionary	Arrest of More Than One Person	Mandatory Reporting: Health Care	Type of Injury
HAWAII	Arrest: 709-906(2) Mandatory Reporting: 453-14	Discretionary		Yes	Gunshot or knife injuries or any injury that may result in death
IDAHO	Arrest: 19-603(6) Mandatory Reporting: 39-1390	Discretionary		Yes	Gunshot wound or other injury resulting from a criminal offense
ILLINOIS	Arrest: 725 § 5/112A-30 Mandatory Reporting: 20 § 2630/3.2	Discretionary		Yes	Gunshot wound or other injury resulting from a criminal offense
INDIANA	Arrest: 35-33-1-1(A)(5)(B) Mandatory Reporting: 35-47-7-1; 35-47-3	Discretionary		Yes	Burns, gunshot or knife wounds, non-accidental wounds from dangerous objects
IOWA	Arrest: 236.12(2)(a); 236.12(2)(b) Mandatory Reporting: 147.111; 147.113A	Mandatory if physical injury or with dangerous weapon; discretionary for all other cases		Yes	Burns, gunshot wounds, non-accidental wounds from dangerous objects, or other injuries resulting from a criminal act
KANSAS	Arrest: 22-2307(b)(1) Mandatory Reporting: 21-6319	Mandatory		Yes	Gunshot or knife injuries
KENTUCKY	Arrest: 403.760(2); 431.005(2)(a) Mandatory Reporting: 209A.030	Mandatory if in violation of court order; discretionary for all other cases		Yes	Suspected abuse or neglect
LOUISIANA	Arrest: 46-2140(A)-(B) Mandatory Reporting: 12:20:44 AM	Mandatory	Yes; primary aggressor preferred	Yes	Gunshot wounds
MAINE	Arrest: Tit. 19-A, § 4012(5) Mandatory Reporting: Tit. 17, § 512	Mandatory		Yes	Gunshot wounds
MARYLAND	Arrest: Cts. & Jud. Proc. § 3-1508(b) & Crim. Proc. § 2-204 Mandatory Reporting: Health-Gen. § 20-703	Mandatory if in violation of court order; discretionary for all other cases	Yes; primary aggressor preferred	Yes	Gunshot wounds

Table 32: Domestic Violence—Continued

State	Code Section	Mandatory or Discretionary	Arrest of More Than One Person	Mandatory Reporting: Health Care	Type of Injury
MASSACHUSETTS	Arrest: Ch. 209(a), § 6(7) Mandatory Reporting: Ch. 112, §12A	Preferred arrest; mandatory if in violation of court order		Yes	Burns, gunshot wounds, non-accidental wounds from dangerous objects
MICHIGAN	Arrest: 764.15a Mandatory Reporting: 750.411	Discretionary		Yes	Gunshot or knife wounds or other injuries from violent conduct
MINNESOTA	Arrest: 518B.01(14); 629.341(1) Mandatory Reporting: 626.52	Mandatory if in violation of court order; discretionary for all other cases		Yes	Burns; gunshot wounds; non-accidental wounds from dangerous objects
MISSISSIPPI	Arrest: 99-3-7(3) Mandatory Reporting: 45-9-31	Mandatory	Yes; officer discretion	Yes	Gunshot or knife injuries
MISSOURI	Arrest: 455.085.1; 455.085.3 Mandatory Reporting: 578.35	Mandatory if in violation of court order; discretionary for all other cases	Yes; primary aggressor preferred	Yes	Gunshot wounds
MONTANA	Arrest: 46-6-311(2)(a); 46-6-311(b) Mandatory Reporting: 37-2-302	Preferred arrest	Yes; primary aggressor preferred	Yes	Gunshot or knife injuries
NEBRASKA	Arrest: 29-404.02(1)(c); 42-928 Mandatory Reporting: 28-902	Mandatory if in violation of court order; discretionary for all other cases	Yes; officer discretion	Yes	Injuries resulting from criminal offense
NEVADA	Arrest: 171.137 Mandatory Reporting: 629.041; 629.045	Mandatory	Yes; primary aggressor preferred	Yes	Gunshot or knife wounds; burns
NEW HAMPSHIRE	Arrest: 594:10(1)(B); 173-B:9 Mandatory Reporting: 631:06:00	Mandatory if in violation of court order; discretionary for all other cases		Yes	Gunshot wound or other injury resulting from a criminal offense
NEW JERSEY	Arrest: 2c:25-21 Mandatory Reporting: 2C:58-8	Mandatory arrest if physical injury, use of a dangerous weapon or violation of a court order	Maybe	Yes	Gunshot wounds or injuries from explosives or other dangerous weapons
NEW MEXICO	Arrest: 31-1-7(A); 40-13-6(c)	Mandatory if in violation of court order; discretionary for all other cases		No	

Table 32: Domestic Violence—Continued

State	Code Section	Mandatory or Discretionary	Arrest of More Than One Person	Mandatory Reporting: Health Care	Type of Injury
NEW YORK	Arrest: Crim. Proc. § 140.10 Mandatory Reporting: Penal §§ 265.25; 265.26	Mandatory if person committed felony against person in the same household or in violation of a court order; discretionary in all other cases		Yes	Burns, gunshot or knife wounds, non-accidental wounds from dangerous objects
NORTH CAROLINA	Arrest: 15a-401; 50B-4.1 Mandatory Reporting: 90-21.20	Mandatory if in violation of court order; discretionary for all other cases		Yes	Gunshot or knife injuries; poisoning; other injury from a criminal act of violence
NORTH DAKOTA	Arrest: 14-07.1-10 Mandatory Reporting: 43-17-41	Preferred arrest		Yes	Gunshot or knife injuries or sexual offenses
OHIO	Arrest: 2935.032(A)(1)(a); 2935.03(B)(3)(d) Mandatory Reporting: 2921.22	Mandatory	Yes; primary aggressor preferred	Yes	Gunshot or knife injuries; burns; other injury from a criminal act of violence
OKLAHOMA	Arrest: Tit. 22, §§196(6); 196(8) Mandatory Reporting: 22-58	Discretionary		Yes, but only by request of victim	Any criminally injurious conduct
OREGON	Arrest: 133.055 Mandatory Reporting: 146.750; 146.740	Mandatory		Yes	Injuries from non-accidental means
PENNSYLVANIA	Arrest: Tit. 18, § 2711(a); Tit. 23, § 6113 Mandatory Reporting: Tit. 18, § 5106	Mandatory if in violation of court order; discretionary for all other cases		Yes, but only by request of victim	Wounds from dangerous weapons or any intentional act resulting in serious bodily injury
RHODE ISLAND	Arrest: 12-29-3(b) to 12-29-3(c) Mandatory Reporting: 23-28.2-24; 11-47-48	Mandatory	Yes; officer discretion	Yes	Burns or gunshot wounds
SOUTH CAROLINA	Arrest: 16-25-70 Mandatory Reporting: 16-3-1072	Mandatory if physical injury; discretionary for all others	Yes; primary aggressor preferred	Yes	Gunshot wounds
SOUTH DAKOTA	Arrest: 23a-3-2.1 Mandatory Reporting: 23-13-10	Mandatory		Yes	Gunshot wounds

Table 32: Domestic Violence—Continued

State	Code Section	Mandatory or Discretionary	Arrest of More Than One Person	Mandatory Reporting: Health Care	Type of Injury
TENNESSEE	Arrest: 36-3-619(a); 36-3-619(b) Mandatory Reporting: 38-1-101; 36-3-621(C)(1)	Preferred arrest	Yes; primary aggressor preferred	Yes	Gunshot or knife injuries, poisoning, suffocation or other injury from a criminal act of violence
TEXAS	Arrest: Civ. Proc., Art. 14.03 Mandatory Reporting: Health & Safety § 161.041	Mandatory if in violation of court order; discretionary for all other cases		Yes	Gunshot wounds
UTAH	Arrest: 77-36-2.2(2); 77-36-(3) Mandatory Reporting: 26-23a-2	Mandatory	Yes; primary aggressor preferred	Yes	Injuries from gunshot, knife, explosives, deadly weapons or any other injury resulting from a criminal act
VERMONT	Arrest: VRCP Rule 3 Mandatory Reporting: 13 § 4012	Discretionary		Yes	Gunshot wounds
VIRGINIA	Arrest: 19.2-81.3 Mandatory Reporting: 54.1-2967	Discretionary		Yes	Gunshot or knife wounds
WASHINGTON	Arrest: 10.31.100(1); 10.31.100(2) Mandatory Reporting: 70.41.440	Mandatory	Yes; primary aggressor preferred	Yes	Gunshot wounds
WEST VIRGINIA	Arrest: 48-27-1001; 48-27-1002(a); 48-27-1002(b) Mandatory Reporting: 61-2-27; 61-2-27a	Mandatory if in violation of court order; discretionary for all other cases		Yes	Burns, gunshot or knife wounds, non-accidental wounds from dangerous objects
WISCONSIN	Arrest: 968.075(2) Mandatory Reporting: 255.4	Mandatory		Yes	Burns, gunshot wounds, or any injuries from a criminal act
WYOMING	Arrest: 7-20-102	Discretionary	No		

33. GROUNDS FOR DIVORCE

The bond of marriage and the nuclear family unit were thought to be sacred unions to be preserved at all costs. Divorce was a stigma, and a "bad" marriage was a thing to be endured for the sake of the family and, in particular, the children. However, the last 50 years have seen a remarkable shift in emphasis in the area of divorce.

Originally, in order to obtain a divorce, the pleading party had to show fault on the other side of the marriage, proving that the spouse had committed some act or activity believed ruinous to the marital relationship, such as adultery, cruelty, or desertion. The other party could then counter by proving fault in the pleading spouse or that the alleged activity did not occur. Fault was important not only in obtaining the divorce, but also in factoring property divisions and alimony.

No-fault divorce is the relatively recent invention of legislators who deemed it necessary in order to allow women to free themselves from destructive marriages. Under no-fault divorce, a party does not need to prove any fault; all that is required is to claim that there exists irretrievable breakdown or irreconcilable differences between the spouses or desertion. The pleading party in a divorce action merely needs to claim that she or he is so unhappy that leaving home (or "constructive desertion") or dissolving the marriage is the only solution.

All states have adopted no-fault divorce, either as the only grounds for divorce or as an additional ground. As a practical matter, however, the other grounds are seldom used owing to the difficulty of proving things like adultery, mental cruelty, and the like. These are only used in situations where proof of fault will affect the court's decisions with regard to the distribution of property, alimony, or child custody. Thus, only about 10 percent of divorces actually go to trial today.

In the accompanying table, the No-Fault column lists the particular type of no-fault statute that exists in the state. If there are no items listed under Grounds, then no-fault is the only ground for divorce in that state. If grounds are listed, no-fault is simply an additional available ground.

Table 33: Grounds for Divorce

State	Code Section	Residency	Waiting Period
ALABAMA	30-2-1 to 30-2-12	At least one party must have resided in state for at least 6 months prior to filing	30 days from date of the filing of the summons and complaint
ALASKA	25.24.050 to 25.24.080; 25.24.200 to 25.24.260	Plaintiff must be resident for any amount of time	
ARIZONA	Uniform Marriage and Divorce Act §§25-311 et seq.	One party must be resident for 90 days prior to filing	60 days
ARKANSAS	9-12-301 to 9-12-325; 9-11-808	One party resident 60 days before filing and 3 full months before final judgment. Covenant marriage: one or both spouses domiciled in state and asserted ground committed or occurred in state or while matrimonial domicile was in state. If not, party filing must have been domiciled in state prior to time cause of action accrued and at time action is filed	30 days or until 90 days residence
CALIFORNIA	Fam. §§ 2310 to 2348	One party must have been resident 6 months and for 3 months in county where action is filed	60 days, court may extend for good cause; if reasonable possibility of reconciliation, court shall continue proceeding for up to 30 days
COLORADO	Uniform Dissolution of Marriage Act: 14-10-101 to 14-10-133	One spouse domiciliary for 90 days preceding commencement of action	Decree may be entered 90 days after service of process or appearance of respondent, if one party denies marriage is irretrievably broken, court may continue matter for 30-60 days
CONNECTICUT	46b-40; 46b-44; 46b-67	Resident for 12 months before filing or 1 party domiciliary at time of marriage and returned with intent to stay or the cause for dissolution occurred after either moved to the state	90 days

No Fault	Defenses	Grounds
Incompatible temperaments; irretrievable breakdown; separation (2 yrs.)	Condonation (not if parties connived to commit adultery), collusion	Physically incapacitated from entering into marriage state; adultery; 1 yr. voluntary abandonment; imprisonment 2 yrs. of 7+ year sentence; crime against nature before or after marriage; alcohol/drug addiction after marriage; complete incompatibility of temperaments; insanity, must be in mental hospital for 5 successive years; irretrievable breakdown; wife pregnant at time of marriage without husband's knowledge; actual or reasonable apprehension of violence; wife lived in state separate from husband for 2 yrs. with no support
Dissolution: incompatibility of temperament	For adultery: procurement, connivance, express or implied forgiveness, dual guilt, or waiting over 2 yrs. to bring action. Procurement or express forgiveness is defense to any other ground.	Failure to consummate; adultery; conviction of felony; willful desertion for 1 yr.; cruelty or violence; habitual drunkenness or drug addiction; incurable mental illness (18 mos. institution prior to action)
Irretrievable breakdown; separation	One party denies marriage is irretrievably broken	Irretrievable breakdown except for covenant marriage: adultery, conviction of felony, abandonment for one year; physical, sexual, or emotional abuse or domestic violence; living apart for 2 yrs., or 1 yr. after legal separation; drug/alcohol abuse; both spouses agree.
Separation of 18 months	Collusion, consent or equal guilt in adultery	General grounds: impotence; conviction of felony or infamous crime; habitual drunk for 1 yr.; cruel and barbarous treatment as to endanger life; offers indignities making condition intolerable; adultery; separated for 18 continuous months; separated for 3 yrs. because one party committed for incurable insanity; spouse legally obligated to support other had ability and willfully fails to do so. Covenant marriage: adultery; felony conviction and sentenced to death or prison; physical or sexual abuse of spouse or child; 2 yr. legal separation, or 3 yrs. if children; habitual drunk for 1 yr.; cruel and barbarous treatment so as to endanger life or others; offers indignities making condition intolerable
Irreconcilable differences; permanent legal incapacity to make decisions		Irreconcilable differences; permanent legal incapacity to make decisions
Irretrievable breakdown	Lack of jurisdiction	
Irretrievable breakdown; separation (lived apart for at least 18 mos. prior to complaint)		Adultery; cruelty or violence; willful desertion for 1 yr.; drug/alcohol addiction; insanity; unexplained absence for at least 7 yrs.; conviction of infamous crime; fraudulent contract; legal confinement for mental illness 5 out of last 6 yrs.

Table 33: Grounds for Divorce—Continued

State	Code Section	Residency	Waiting Period
DELAWARE	Delaware Divorce & Annulment Act: Tit. 13, §§ 1501 to 1523	Action brought where either party is a resident for 6 months or longer	Decree final when entered subject to right of appeal within 30 days
DISTRICT OF COLUMBIA	16-901 to 16-925	One party bona fide resident for 6 months	30 days after docketing of decree or judgment subject to right of appeal
FLORIDA	61.021; 61.052; 61.19	Petitioner must have residence in Florida 6 months before filing suit	20 days after petition file
GEORGIA	19-5-1 to 19-5-17	One party resident for 6 months before action	Decree in effect immediately except for irretrievable breakdown, in which case court may not grant divorce in less than 30 days from service on respondent
HAWAII	580-1; 580-41 to 580-56	One party domiciled or physically present 6 months before filing.	Court fixes time after decree that it is final but not over 1 month
IDAHO	32-601 to 32-805	Plaintiff must be resident for 6 full weeks before commencing action	Decree entered immediately on determination of issues (for adultery, within 2 yrs., for felony conviction, before the end of sentence or 1 yr. after pardon)
ILLINOIS	Ch. 750 §§ 5/401 to 5/413; 5/451 to 5/457	One spouse must be resident of Illinois for 90 days before commencing action	Final when entered subject to right of appeal
INDIANA	31-15-2-2 to 31-15-2-18	One party at filing must be resident for 6 months	Final hearing no sooner than 60 days after filing; continue matter for 45 days if possibility for reconciliation; after 45, judge may enter decree upon request; if no request after 90 days, matter is dismissed
IOWA	598.1 to 598.19	Unless respondent is a resident and given personal service, petitioner must have been resident for last year	90 days after service of original notice (time may be shortened by court in emergency)
KANSAS	23-2701 to 23-2718	One party must have been resident for 60 days before filing	Hearing not for 60 days after filing (unless emergency)
KENTUCKY	403.010 to 403.260	One party must be resident of state and have been for 180 days before filing	Final when entered (parties have to have lived apart for 60 days prior to decree)
LOUISIANA	Civ. Code Art. 102 to 104		Must live separate and apart for 180 days or 365 days if minor children after filing or service of petition

No Fault	Defenses	Grounds
Irretrievable breakdown; voluntary separation	Defenses of condonation; connivance, recrimination, insanity and lapse of time are preserved only for a marriage that is separated and the separation caused by misconduct; respondent's failure of jurisdictional/ residential requirements	Separation caused respondent's misconduct, mental illness or incompatibility
Voluntary separation (6 months) or separation for 1 yr. without cohabitation		
Irretrievable breakdown; mental incapacity of one or the parties		Mental incapacity of one party for preceding period of at least 3 yrs.
Irretrievable breakdown	For adultery, desertion, cruelty, or intoxication: collusion, both parties guilty, subsequent voluntary condonation and cohabitation, consent	Adultery; cruelty or violence; willful and continued desertion for at least 1 yr.; drug/alcohol addiction; impotency; mental incapacity or insanity; pregnant at time of marriage by man other than husband; conviction of crime for which the sentence is 2 yrs. or more; force, duress, or fraud in obtaining marriage; irreconcilable differences; intermarriage within prohibited degrees of consanguinity or affinity
Irretrievable breakdown; separation for at least 2 yrs. or under decree of separation	Recrimination no defense	Irretrievable breakdown; separation for at least 2 yrs. or under decree of separation
Separation (5 yrs.); irreconcilable differences	Collusion; condonation; recrimination or limitation and lapse of time	Adultery; extreme cruelty or violence; willful neglect or desertion; habitual intemperance; insanity; conviction of felony; irreconcilable differences
Irretrievable breakdown; separation (2 yrs.). Note: Under certain conditions, parties may file joint petition for simplified dissolution	Collusion	Adultery; cruelty or violence; willful desertion for 1 yr.; drug/ alcohol addiction for 2 yrs.; impotency; unexplained absence; conviction of crime; venereal disease; 2 yr. separation by irreconcilable differences; undissolved prior marriage, attempted murder of spouse
Irretrievable breakdown		Impotency; insanity for at least 2 yrs.; conviction of felony
Irretrievable breakdown		Irretrievable breakdown
Incompatibility		Insanity (mental illness/incapacity); incompatibility; failure to perform material marital duty/obligation
Irretrievable breakdown		
Separation for at least 6 mos.	Reconciliation	Adultery; conviction of felony

Table 33: Grounds for Divorce—Continued

State	Code Section	Residency	Waiting Period
MAINE	Tit. 19-A, §§ 901 to 908	Parties must reside there and have been married there or resided there when cause of action accrued, or plaintiff resides there in good faith in state 6 months prior to action, or defendant is a resident	Court may make it final immediately, but otherwise it is subject to an appeal period
MARYLAND	Fam. Law § 7-101 to 7-107	If grounds occurred outside the state, one party must have resided in state 1 yr. before filing	Upon meeting requirements, absolute divorce granted
MASSACHUSETTS	208 §§ 1 to 55	Parties must have lived together in the commonwealth unless plaintiff lived there 1 yr. before filing or cause occurred in the commonwealth and plaintiff filed when living there	30 days after initial approval under certain conditions, or hearing 6 months after complaint filed if those conditions not met
MICHIGAN	552.1 to 552.104	One party must have resided in Michigan for 180 days before filing and one party has resided in county where complaint is filed for 10 days immediately preceding filing except in certain situations	
MINNESOTA	518.06 to 518.195	One party must have resided in state or been a domiciliary for 180 days before filing	Decree entered immediately upon finding irretrievable breakdown, subject to appeal
MISSISSIPPI	93-5-1 to 93-5-34	One party actual, bona fide resident for 6 months before suit	Final decree entered immediately but may be revoked at any time by granting court upon joint request of parties
MISSOURI	452.300 to 452.430	Either party must be a resident for 90 days	Final when entered, subject to appeal. Court's order of distribution of marital property is not subject to modification
MONTANA	40-4-101 to 40-4-136	One party must be domiciled in Montana for 90 days	Decree is final, subject to appeal
NEBRASKA	42-341 to 422-381	Marriage solemnized in the state and one party resides in-state since marriage or one party has resided in-state (making it a permanent home) for 1 yr. before filing	No suit for divorce heard until 60 days after service of process
NEVADA	125.010, to 125.185	Unless grounds accrued in county where action brought, one party must have been a resident at least 6 weeks before filing	Decree is final when entered
NEW HAMPSHIRE	458:4 to 458:15	Both parties domiciled or plaintiff was domiciled and defendant was personally served or plaintiff domiciled in state at least 1 yr. before action	No special provision
NEW JERSEY	2A:34-1 to 2A:34-22	Either party a bona fide resident of New Jersey at time cause of action arose and until commencement of action except 1 yr. before action for adultery	Decree immediately final, pending any appeal

No Fault	Defenses	Grounds
Irreconcilable differences	Recrimination is comparative not absolute defense; sometimes condonation in court's discretion	Adultery; cruelty or violence; utter desertion for 3 consecutive yrs.; drug/alcohol addiction; impotence; nonsupport; irreconcilable differences; judicial determination of incapacity and appt. of guardian
Separation (2 yrs. or voluntary for 12 months); limited divorce for cruelty, vicious conduct; separation; desertion	Recrimination or condonation is factor but not absolute bar	Adultery; desertion for 12 mos. without interruption; insanity (confined for 3 yrs.); conviction of crime (sentenced for at least 3 yrs. and served at least 12 months); cruelty, excessively vicious conduct; voluntary separation grounds for limited divorce
Irretrievable breakdown	No defense	Adultery; utter desertion for 1 yr.; cruelty; drug/alcohol addiction; impotency; nonsupport; conviction of crime (sentenced for at least 5 yrs.); absence (raises presumption of death)
Irretrievable breakdown		Breakdown of marriage relationship
Irretrievable breakdown	All abolished by § 5l8.06	
Irreconcilable differences (only if uncontested)	Recrimination not absolute bar; collusion (adultery)	Adultery; cruelty or violence; willful desertion; drug/alcohol addiction; natural impotency; incurable insanity for 3 yrs.; pregnant at time of marriage; conviction of crime; prior marriage undissolved; in line of consanguinity
Irretrievable breakdown	Abolished by § 452.310	Irretrievable breakdown
Irretrievable breakdown; separation (180 days); serious marital discord	Abolished by § 40-4-105	Irretrievable breakdown; separation (180 days); serious marital discord
Irretrievable breakdown		Irretrievable breakdown
Separation(1 yr. without cohabitation); incompatibility		Insanity (for 2 yrs. prior); lived apart without cohabitation for 1 yr.; incompatibility
Irreconcilable differences; separation (absent 2 yrs.)	Common law defenses: condonation, connivance, recrimination, insanity a factor, but not defense	Adultery; cruelty or violence; drug/alcohol addiction; impotency; nonsupport; unexplained absence (for 2 yrs.); conviction of crime (with imprisonment for more than 1 yr.); joining religious group believing the relation of husband and wife unlawful and refusal to cohabit for 6 mos.; refusal to cohabit for 2 yrs.
Separation (18 months); irreconcilable differences	Abolished by § 2A:34-7	Adultery; cruelty or violence; desertion from 12 mos.; drug/alcohol addiction; insanity/mental illness (confined for 24 mos.); conviction of crime (imprisonment for at least 18 mos.); deviant sexual behavior without plaintiff's consent

Table 33: Grounds for Divorce—Continued

State	Code Section	Residency	Waiting Period
NEW MEXICO	40-4-1 to 40-4-20	New Mexico domicile required plus 6 months residency of either party	No special provision
NEW YORK	Dom. Rel. §§ 170; 171; 202; 230; 231	Were married in state or reside in state as husband and wife and either party has been resident 1 yr. before commencing suit; cause occurred in New York and both parties are resident at commencement of suit; either has been resident for 2 yrs.	
NORTH CAROLINA	50.2 to 50.22	Either party a bona fide resident for 6 months before bringing action	Decree final immediately
NORTH DAKOTA	14-05-01 to 14-05-29	Plaintiff resident for 6 months before commencement of action or entry of divorce decree	Decree must specify time when parties may remarry
OHIO	3105.01 to 3105.16; 3105.61 to 3105.65	Plaintiff must have been resident 6 months	Decree immediately final, but court may order conciliation period for up to 90 days
OKLAHOMA	Tit. 43, §§ 101 to 140	One party must have been resident in good faith for 6 months before filing	Final immediately unless appealed, but neither may marry for 6 months (if so guilty of bigamy) nor cohabit for 30 days (if so guilty of adultery)
OREGON	107 .005 to 107.452	One party resident for 6 months prior unless marriage solemnized in state, either is resident at time of filing, dissolution based on void marriage	Decree final immediately; no trial until 90 days after service (unless emergency)
PENNSYLVANIA	Tit. 23, §§ 3101 to 3333; Pa. R. Civ. P. 1920.1-1920.92	Bona fide residency by one party at least 6 months before filing	Immediately final, subject to appeal
RHODE ISLAND	15-5-1 to 15-5-29	One party resident 1 yr.; if based on defendant's residency, he must be personally serviced with process	Final decree entered any time within 30 days or 3 months from decision date
SOUTH CAROLINA	20-3-10 to 20-3-440	One party resident 1 yr.; if both residents when action commenced, then only 3 month requirement	Decree cannot be entered until 3 months after filing unless divorce sought on grounds of separation or desertion

No Fault	Defenses	Grounds
Separation (permanent); incompatibility		Adultery; cruelty or violence; desertion/abandonment; incompatibility
Separation (1 yr. or more)	Adultery: Offense committed with plaintiff's connivance; offense forgiven (shown affirmatively, by voluntary cohabitation, or by no action commenced within 5 yrs. of discovery of offense); plaintiff also guilty of adultery; defendant may set up misconduct of plaintiff as justification	Adultery; cruel and inhuman treatment; abandonment (for 1 or more years); imprisonment of defendant for 3 or more consecutive yrs.; lived apart for 1 or more yrs.
Separation (one year)		Adultery; divorce from bed and board; cruelty or violence; desertion (abandonment); drug/alcohol addiction; incurable insanity (confined/separated for 3 consecutive yrs.). Offers indignities that renders other spouse's condition/life intolerable/burdensome; maliciously turns other out of doors
Irreconcilable differences	Condonation; lapse of time	Adultery; cruelty or violence; willful desertion or neglect; drug/alcohol addiction; insanity for period of 5 yrs.; conviction of felony. Irreconcilable differences
Separation (1 yr.); incompatibility (unless denied by other party)	Res judicata and recrimination not defenses	Adultery; cruelty or violence; desertion; alcohol addiction; imprisonment; prior marriage undissolved; fraudulent contract; other party procures a divorce out of state; gross neglect of duty
Incompatibility		Adultery; cruelty or violence; abandonment/desertion (1 yr.); alcohol addiction; impotency; insanity (for 5 yrs. prior); pregnant at time of marriage (not by husband); conviction of felony; fraudulent contract; procuring divorce out of state not releasing one party; gross neglect of duty
Irremedial breakdown; separation for 1 yr.	Abolished by § 107.036	When either party was incapable of making contract or consenting for want of legal age or sufficient understanding. Doctrines of fault and in pari delicto abolished by § 107.036
Irretrievable breakdown; separation (2 yrs.)	Existing common-law defense, to all grounds but irretrievably broken marriage	Adultery; cruelty or violence; desertion for 1 or more yrs.; insanity (confined for 18 mos.); bigamy; conviction of crime (sentenced to prison for 2 or more yrs. also; indignities makes life intolerable and burdensome; irretrievable breakdown and 90 days passed since action was filed and mutual consent)
Irretrievable breakdown; separation (for at least 3 yrs.)	Collusion	Adultery; cruelty or violence; desertion for 5 yrs.; drug/alcohol addiction; impotency; nonsupport; any other gross/repugnant behavior (refusal and neglect)
Separation (for 1 yr. continuously)	Collusion	Adultery; cruelty or violence; desertion for 1 yr.; drug/alcohol addiction; lived apart without cohabitation for 1 year

Table 33: Grounds for Divorce—Continued

State	Code Section	Residency	Waiting Period
SOUTH DAKOTA	25-4-2 to 25-4-83	Plaintiff, at time action is commenced, must be a resident	Action for divorce not heard for 60 days from completed service of plaintiff's summons. (Court can continue for 30 day if reconciliation possible)
TENNESSEE	36-4-101 to 36-4-135	No residency required if acts committed while plaintiff was resident; or if grounds arose out of state and plaintiff or defendant has resided in state 6 months preceding filing (1 yr. prior for military personnel or spouse)	Hearing 60 days from filing of complaint, 90 days if children under 18
TEXAS	Fam. §§ 6.001 to 6.008; 6.301 to 6.711	One party domiciliary for preceding 6 months and resident of county for preceding 90 days	60 days from when suit was filed. Neither party may remarry before 31st day after decree signed (may be waived by court)
UTAH	30-3-1 to 30-3-40	One party bona fide resident 3 months before commencing action	Decree becomes absolute on day signed by court. Hearing 90 days from filing of complaint
VERMONT	Tit. 15, §§ 551 to 563; 591 to 637	6 months before commencing action and 1 yr. before final hearing. 2 yrs. before commencing action for grounds of insanity	
VIRGINIA	20-91 to 20-124	One party resident and domiciled 6 months before suit. 20-97	Decree immediate on determination of issues. Remarriage prohibited during appeal
WASHINGTON	26.09.030; 26.09.150	Plaintiff must be a resident or a member of armed forces stationed in state.	90 days must elapse from point of filing petition; decree is final subject to right of appeal.
WEST VIRGINIA	48-5-101 to 48-5-707	If cause is adultery, one party must be resident at time action brought; if defendant is nonresident and service cannot be effected within the state, the plaintiff must have been a resident for 1 yr. prior to commencement of action. If ground other than adultery, one party must be resident at time the cause arose or since then has become a resident and lived in state 1 yr. before action; if parties married in West Virginia, then only one must be resident upon filing—no specified length of time	

No Fault	Defenses	Grounds
Irreconcilable differences	Connivance; collusion; condonation; limitation or lapse of time	Adultery; extreme cruelty; willful desertion or neglect; habitual intemperance; conviction of felony; irreconcilable differences
Separation of 2 yrs. with no minor children; irreconcilable difference	For adultery, defense if complainant guilt of like act, or had sex with spouse after adultery with knowledge; or husband solicited wife for prostitution or exposed her to lewd society that ensnared her to adultery	Adultery; cruelty or violence including attempted murder of the other; desertion for 1 yr. or absent state for 2 yrs.; drug/alcohol addiction; impotency; pregnant at time of marriage by another man, without knowledge of husband; offers indignities that renders other spouse's condition/life intolerable, conviction of infamous crime or felony; previous marriage unresolved; also irreconcilable differences; lived separately without cohabitation for 2 continuous years and there are no minor children; abandonment or refusing/ neglecting to provide when having the ability to do so
Separation (3 yrs.); marriage is insupportable due to discord	Defense of recrimination abolished; condonation is defense only when reasonable expectation of reconciliation; defense of adultery abolished	Adultery; cruelty or violence; abandonment/desertion (1 yr.); insanity (confined for at least 3 yrs.); conviction of felony and imprisonment at least 1 yr. (unless spouse testifies against convicted spouse)
Separation (3 yrs.); irreconcilable differences		Adultery; cruelty or violence; desertion (1 yr.); alcohol addiction; impotency; nonsupport; incurable insanity; conviction of felony; also irreconcilable differences and lived separately under decree of separation for 3 consecutive years
Separation (6 months	Recrimination and condonation not defenses	Adultery; intolerable severity; desertion (7 yrs.); nonsupport; incurable insanity (confined for 5 yrs.); conviction of crime with imprisonment over 3 yrs.; living apart for 6 consecutive months and resumption of marital relations not reasonably probable
Separation (1 yr.)	Adultery, buggery, or sodomy: cohabitation after knowledge, act occurred more than 5 yrs. before suit for divorce, or party procured or connived act	Adultery or sodomy or buggery committed outside the marriage; subsequent conviction of felony and confined for more than one year without cohabitation following confinement; cruelty, caused fear of bodily hurt or willfully deserted 1 yr. from the date of such act; lived separate lives without cohabitation and without interruption for one year
Irretrievable breakdown.		Irretrievable breakdown
Separation (1 yr.) ; irreconcilable differences	Condonation; connivance; plaintiff's own misconduct; offense occurred more than 3 yrs. prior to divorce action; collusion is not a bar; adultery: voluntary cohabitation after knowledge or offense occurred more than 3 yrs. prior; no divorce granted if plaintiff guilty of uncondoned adultery within 3 yrs., unless grounds separation or irreconcilable differences	Adultery; cruelty or violence; drug/alcohol addiction; insanity (confined for 3 yrs. prior to complaint); conviction of crime subsequent to the marriage; neglect or abuse of child; abandonment or desertion for 6 mos.; irreconcilable differences if other party admits; also lived apart without cohabitation and without interruption for one year

Table 33: Grounds for Divorce—Continued

State	Code Section	Residency	Waiting Period
WISCONSIN	767.301 to 767.395	Either party bona fide resident at least 6 months	Judgment effective immediately. No trial until 120 days after service of summons or filing of joint petition (court can order immediate hearing for health and safety of party or child)
WYOMING	20-2-101 to 20-2-116	Plaintiff must have resided 60 days before filing, unless marriage took place in Wyoming and plaintiff has lived there continuously	Final decree upon issue of determination but never issued less than 20 days from when complaint filed

No Fault	Defenses	Grounds
Irretrievable breakdown; separation 12 months.	If both parties do not agree the marriage is irretrievably broken and have not lived apart for 12 months, court may suggest counseling and set for rehearing in 30-60 days; other defenses abolished.	Irretrievable breakdown; separation 12 months
Irreconcilable differences		Insanity (confined for at least 2 years preceding commencement of action)

34. MARITAL PROPERTY

Marital property is generally considered to be all property acquired by a couple during their marriage or earned by either spouse during their marriage. It is all property owned by the marital estate. Generally, gifts or inheritances to either spouse along with any money or property earned prior to the marriage are the separate property of that spouse unless it is somehow "converted" into marital property.

There are two general categories that define marital property: community property and not community property. Nine states recognize community property. In these states, all property or income acquired by either spouse during marriage is considered equally owned by both spouses for purposes of the division of the property upon death or divorce or for purposes of business transacted by either spouse. This property ownership scheme has its roots in Spanish Law. Consequently, community property laws are found generally in those states that were originally possessions of or which in some way owe some of their legal heritage to colonial Spain.

If a state is not a community property state, various rules and schemes apply to define the nature of marital property. For example, there are a number of legal options from which a couple may choose when they decide to acquire property together. They may choose joint tenancy, tenancy by the entirety, or tenancy-in-common. In most states, the character of the property in question is determined by the nature of the property itself, the nature of the event giving rise to the need for the particular characterization of property ownership, and the manner, agreement, and instrument by which it was acquired. If the event giving rise to the need

for the characterization is divorce, a set of rules will apply to each portion of the marital property, depending on how it was acquired and what kind of property it is: bank account, primary home, automobile, etc.

Upon an individual's death, property will be distributed subject to the individual's legal will or trust, the rules of marital property, and/or intestate succession. A very old common law scheme of division of marital property is known as "dower and curtesy." Dower was a way that a woman, who traditionally was not given the opportunity to own property while married, was given a share of her husband's estate upon his death. Dower generally preserved a percentage share of the value of the estate. Curtesy is essentially the same system in reverse, giving the husband a percentage share of his wife's estate. However, dower and curtesy has generally become obsolete in the modern world. Laws of descent and distribution, divorce and property distribution, and use of joint tenancies, tenancies-in-common, and tenancies by the entirety have largely made it unnecessary to be concerned with the surviving spouse being left with no part of the marital property.

A growing number of states have adopted the Uniform Disposition of Community Property Rights at Death Act (UDCPRDA). This protects couples that move from a community property state into one where community property is not recognized, from drastic changes in the character and disposition of their property upon the death of a spouse. This is an important consideration in today's highly mobile society.

Table 34: Marital Property

State	Community Property?	Dower and Curtesy?
ALABAMA	No	Dower and curtesy abolished, 43-8-57
ALASKA	Yes, Community Property Act: 34.77.010 to 34.77.995	No dower and curtesy rights, 13.35, repealed 1963; Comp. L. 1933 § 4601, as amended SLA 1935, Ch. 37, p. 91
ARIZONA	Yes, 25-211	Dower and curtesy abolished, 1-201
ARKANSAS	No, but 28-12-101 to 28-12-120 Uniform Disposition of Community Property Rights at Death Act (UDCPRDA) adopted	Dower allowed; common law curtesy abolished; statutory allowance called curtesy provided, 28-11-301 to 28-11-307
CALIFORNIA	Yes, Fam. § 751; 770	No estate by dower or curtesy, Prob. § 6412
COLORADO	No, but 15-20-101 to 15-20-111 Uniform Disposition of Community Property Rights at Death Act (UDCPRDA) adopted	Curtesy and dower abolished, 15-11-112
CONNECTICUT	No, but 45a-458 to 45a-467 Uniform Disposition of Community Property Rights at Death Act (UDCPRDA) adopted	No dower or curtesy when marriage occurred after April 20, 1877, 46b-36
DELAWARE	No	Dower and curtesy abolished, Tit. 12, § 511
DISTRICT OF COLUMBIA	No	Dower and curtesy abolished, 19-102
FLORIDA	No, but 732.216 to 732.219 Uniform Disposition of Community Property Rights at Death Act (UDCPRDA) adopted	Dower and curtesy abolished, 732.111; Statutory right to elective share of surviving spouse recognized, 732.201 to 732.2155
GEORGIA	No	Dower and curtesy abolished, 53-1-3
HAWAII	510-21 to 510-30 No, but Uniform Disposition of Community Property Rights at Death Act (UDCPRDA) adopted	Statutory right to elective share of surviving spouse recognized, 560:2-201 to 560:2-214
IDAHO	32-906 Yes	Curtesy and dower abolished, 32-914
ILLINOIS	No	Dower and curtesy abolished as of 1/1/1972, 755 § 5/2-9
INDIANA	No	Dower and curtesy abolished, 29-1-2-11
IOWA	No	Curtesy abolished, 633.238; dower abolished, 633.211
KANSAS	No	Dower and curtesy abolished, 59-505
KENTUCKY	No, but 391.210 to 391.260 Uniform Disposition of Community Property Rights at Death Act (UDCPRDA) adopted	Yes, with exceptions, 392.010 to 392.140
LOUISIANA	Civ. Code Art. 2334 to 2345 Yes, with considerable exceptions	Unknown to the law of Louisiana
MAINE	No	Dower and curtesy abolished, Tit. 18-A, § 2-113
MARYLAND	No	Dower and curtesy abolished, Est. & Trusts § 3-202
MASSACHUSETTS	No	Dower & curtesy abolished, Ch. 190B, § 2-112
MICHIGAN	No, but 557.261 to 557.271 Uniform Disposition of Community Property Rights at Death Act (UDCPRDA) adopted	Dower; 558.1 to 558.92; No curtesy or dower allowed in community property, 557.214
MINNESOTA	No	Provides for actions based on dower and curtesy or interest in lieu of same, 519.101
MISSISSIPPI	No	Dower and curtesy abolished, 93-3-5

628

Table 34: Marital Property—Continued

State	Community Property?	Dower and Curtesy?
MISSOURI	No	Dower and curtesy abolished, 474.110
MONTANA	No, but 72-9-101 to 72-9-120 Uniform Disposition of Community Property Rights at Death Act (UDCPRDA) adopted	Dower and curtesy abolished, 72-2-122
NEBRASKA	No, unless contrary can be proved, 42-603	Dower and curtesy abolished, 30-104
NEVADA	Yes, 123.130; 123.220; 123.230	Dower and curtesy abolished, 123.020
NEW HAMPSHIRE	No	Dower and curtesy abolished, 560:3
NEW JERSEY	No	Dower and curtesy abolished as to all property obtained after May 28, 1980, 3B:28-2; some rights exist re property obtained before that date, 3B:28-1 to 3B:28-19
NEW MEXICO	Yes, 40-3-6 to 40-3-17	Dower and curtesy abolished, 45-2-112
NEW YORK	No, but Est. Powers & Trusts §§ 6-6.1 to 6-6.7 Uniform Disposition of Community Property Rights at Death Act (UDCPRDA) adopted.	Certain dower rights for widow of marriage before September 1, 1930, Real Prop. §§ 190; 190b; Curtesy abolished except certain rights remain for widower of woman who died on or before August 31, 1930, Real Prop. § 189
NORTH CAROLINA	No, however 31C-1 to 31C-12 Uniform Disposition of Community Property Rights at Death Act adopted	Dower and curtesy abolished, 29-4
NORTH DAKOTA	No	Dower and curtesy abolished, 14-07-09
OHIO	No	Dower, 2103.02 to 2103.09; Curtesy abolished, husband has dower interest, 2103.09
OKLAHOMA	Community property repealed, Tit. 43, § 215	Dower and curtesy abolished, Tit. 84, § 214
OREGON	Community property repealed effective April 11, 1949, 108.520, but 112.705 to 112.775 Uniform Disposition of Community Property Rights at Death Act (UDCPRDA) adopted.	Dower and curtesy abolished for surviving spouse of person who dies after July 1, 1970, 112.685 to 112.695
PENNSYLVANIA	No. *Willcox v. Penn Mut. Life Ins. Co.*, 357 Pa. 581, 55 A.2d 521 (1947) State Supreme Court held community property law (Tit. 48, §§ 201 et seq.) invalid under state constitution	Share of spouse's estate which is allotted to surviving spouse by rules of intestate succession or by election against will is in lieu and full satisfaction of dower or curtesy at common law, Tit. 20, § 2105
RHODE ISLAND	No	Dower and curtesy abolished, 33-25-1
SOUTH CAROLINA	No	Dower barred for divorced wife, 20-3-190
SOUTH DAKOTA	No	Dower and curtesy abolished, 29A-2-112
TENNESSEE	No	Dower and curtesy, unless vested, abolished as of April 1, 1977, 31-2-102
TEXAS	Yes, Fam. §§ 3.001 to 3.104; Prob. §§ 38; 45	Does not exist
UTAH	No	No dower and curtesy rights, 757-2-112
VERMONT	No	Dower and curtesy rights abolished, Tit. 14, § 302
VIRGINIA	No, but 64.2-315 to 64.2-324 Uniform Disposition of Community Property Rights at Death Act (UDCPRDA) adopted	Dower and curtesy abolished, 64.2-301
WASHINGTON	Yes, 26.16.030	Dower and curtesy abolished, 11.04.060
WEST VIRGINIA	No	Dower and curtesy abolished, 43-1-1

Table 34: Marital Property—Continued

State	Community Property?	Dower and Curtesy?
WISCONSIN	Adopted Uniform Marital Property Act with variations on January 1, 1986, 766.31	No dower or curtesy rights exist
WYOMING	No, but 2-7-720 Uniform Disposition of Community Property Rights at Death Act (UDCPRDA) adopted	Dower and curtesy abolished, 2-4-101(b)

35. MARRIAGE AGE REQUIREMENTS

The laws regulating marriage are quite uniform. The right to marry is considered very personal, and once the "age of majority," or when one can marry without the permission of a parent or guardian, is reached, it is the couple's sole decision whether or not to marry. However, below this age, parental consent is required (though states do not require the consent of a parent or guardian who is not present in the country or who has abandoned his or her child). The age of majority is now universally eighteen, except in Mississippi, where the parties need to be twenty-one.

While only two states, California and Massachusetts, have no statutory minimum age under which marriage licenses will not be issued, many states with a minimum age requirement do permit marriages between minors under that age. Virtually all states allowing the marrying of minors require court approval in addition to parental consent. A growing number of states now require counseling for minors seeking to marry. Provisions for underage marriages exist in order to permit pregnant minor females and/or minor couples to marry, and prevailing code language still clearly reflects that bias. Ohio has the most explicit rule on this issue. In that state, the juvenile court is authorized to grant official consent to the marriage of underage persons, and the probate court issues the license. According to Ohio statutes, the probate court may delay issuing the license until the court is convinced that the female is pregnant and will carry the child to term or may even delay issuance of the license until the baby is born.

Table 35: Marriage Age Requirements

State	Code Section	Minimum Legal Age With Parental Consent	Minimum Legal Age Without Parental Consent	Comments
ALABAMA	30-1-4; 30-1-5	Male: 16; Female: 16	Male: 18; Female: 18	Marriage under 16 is voidable, not void. Marriage between 16 and 18 without parental consent is not grounds for annulment.
ALASKA	25.05.171	Male: 16; Female: 16	Male: 18; Female: 18	Superior court judge may grant permission for person over 14 at hearing with parents and minor.
ARIZONA	25-102	Male: 16; Female: 16	Male: 18; Female: 18	Minors under 16 may be allowed to marry with parental consent and approval of superior court judge.
ARKANSAS	9-11-102 to 9-11-105	Male: 17; Female: 16	Male: 18; Female: 18	Minors under minimum age may obtain license in case of pregnancy or birth of child, with parental consent and judicial order.
CALIFORNIA	Fam. §§ 300 to 303	Male: No age limit; Female: No age limit	Male: 18; Female: 18	Minors under 18 need parental consent and a court order obtained on the showing the court requires
COLORADO	14-2-106; 14-2-108	Male: 16; Female: 16	Male: 18; Female: 18	Minors under 16 may be allowed to marry with parental consent and/or approval of juvenile court judge (if parents not living together).
CONNECTICUT	46b-30	Male: 16; Female: 16	Male: 18; Female: 18	Minors under 16 may be allowed to marry with parental consent and consent of probate judge.
DELAWARE	Tit. 13, § 123	Male: 18; Female: 18	Male: 18; Female: 18	Minors under minimum age may obtain license in case of pregnancy or birth of child with medical certification.
DISTRICT OF COLUMBIA	46-403; 46-411	Male: 16; Female: 16	Male: 18; Female: 18	Parental consent not required if minor was previously married.
FLORIDA	741.0405	Male: 16; Female: 16	Male: 18; Female: 18	Parental consent not required if minor was previously married or parents are deceased. Under age 18, a county judge has discretion whether or not to give license if the couple has a child or is expecting one (upon sworn affidavits that they are the parents).
GEORGIA	19-3-2; 19-3-37	Male: 16; Female: 16	Male: 18; Female: 18	Parents must appear before judge to consent to marriage.
HAWAII	572-1(2); 572-2	Male: 16; Female: 16	Male: 18; Female: 18	In certain circumstances, 15 year olds may obtain license, but never under 15.
IDAHO	32-202	Male: 16; Female: 16	Male: 18; Female: 18	Minors under age 16 may obtain license with parental consent and order of the court.

Table 35: Marriage Age Requirements—Continued

State	Code Section	Minimum Legal Age With Parental Consent	Minimum Legal Age Without Parental Consent	Comments
ILLINOIS	750 §§ 5/203; 5/208	Male: 16; Female: 16	Male: 18; Female: 18	If no parents to consent, judicial consent with finding that parties are capable of marriage. No provisions for marriage under age 16.
INDIANA	31-11-1-4 to 31-11-1-6	Male: 17; Female: 17	Male: 18; Female: 18	Minors ages 15-17 may obtain license in case of pregnancy, birth of child and with approval of judge of superior or county court.
IOWA	595.2	Male: 16; Female: 16	Male: 18; Female: 18	Minors 16-17 may obtain license without parental consent with approval of court if both parents dead or incompetent or marriage in parties' best interest.
KANSAS	23-2505	Male: 16; Female: 16	Male: 18; Female: 18	Clerk or judge may issue for person 15 years old if in best interest of the person.
KENTUCKY	402.02	Male: 16; Female: 16	Male: 18; Female: 18	Minors under age 18 may obtain license without parental consent in case of pregnancy or birth of child and with permission of district court judge.
LOUISIANA	Ch. C. Art. 1543 to 1550	Male: 16; Female: 16	Male: 18; Female: 18	Minor under 16 must obtain both parental consent and authorization of court.
MAINE	Tit. 19-A, § 652	Male: 16; Female: 16	Male: 18; Female: 18	Minors under 16 may be allowed to marry with parental consent and approval of court.
MARYLAND	Fam. § 2-301	Male: 16; Female: 16	Male: 18; Female: 18	Minors under 15 yrs. old may not marry. Minors 15 yrs. old may obtain license in case of pregnancy or birth of child with parental consent.
MASSACHUSETTS	Ch. 207, §§ 7; 24; 25	Male: not specified; Female: not specified	Male: 18; Female: 18	No statutory provision for minimum age with consent. Common law prevails. If parent deserted or incapable of consent, not necessary to obtain consent.
MICHIGAN	551.51; 551.103; 551.201	Male: 16; Female: 16; (consent of 1 of the parents required of both sexes)	Male: 18; Female: 18	
MINNESOTA	517.02	Male: 16; Female: 16	Male: 18; Female: 18	

Table 35: Marriage Age Requirements—Continued

State	Code Section	Minimum Legal Age With Parental Consent	Minimum Legal Age Without Parental Consent	Comments
MISSISSIPPI	93-1-5	Male: 17; Female: 15	Male: 21; Female: 21	Minors under minimum age may obtain license with parental consent and approval of court. Minor females age 15 yrs. and older and males 17 yrs. and older but under 21 may obtain license with parental consent and court order.
MISSOURI	451.09	Male: 15; Female: 15	Male: 18; Female: 18	Minors under 15 may obtain license under special circumstances and for good cause.
MONTANA	40-1-202; 40-1-213	Male: 16; Female: 16	Male: 18; Female: 18	Minors age 16 or 17 must participate in marriage counseling and must show capable of marriage.
NEBRASKA	42-102; 42-105	Male: 17; Female: 17	Male: 18; Female: 18	
NEVADA	122.020; 122.025	Male: 16; Female: 16	Male: 18; Female: 18	Minors under 16 may obtain license by parental consent and approval of court in extraordinary circumstances.
NEW HAMPSHIRE	457:4 to 457:6	Male: 14; Female: 13	Male: 18; Female: 18	Any marriage contracted by persons under 18 may, in discretion of superior court, be annulled at suit of the party who at the time of marriage was under 18. The parent or guardian can also annul, unless the parties confirm marriage upon reaching age of consent (18 years).
NEW JERSEY	37:1-6	Male: 16; Female: 16 (unless parents of unsound mind)	Male: 18; Female: 18	Minors under 16 may obtain license by parental consent and approval of court. If male under 18 yrs. old and has been arrested on charge of sexual intercourse with single female who thereby became pregnant, consent not required.
NEW MEXICO	40-1-6	Male: 16; Female: 16	Male: 18; Female: 18	Minors under 16 may only obtain license by order of children's court or family division of district court. Courts may authorize marriage in settlement of action to compel support, and establish parentage, or in case of pregnancy.
NEW YORK	Dom. Rel. §§ 7; 15; 15a	Male: 16; Female: 16	Male: 18; Female: 18	Minors under 16 must have approval of parents and court. Minors 16 and 17 must have only parental consent. No license to minors under 14.

Table 35: Marriage Age Requirements—Continued

State	Code Section	Minimum Legal Age With Parental Consent	Minimum Legal Age Without Parental Consent	Comments
NORTH CAROLINA	51-2, 51-2.1	Male: 16; Female: 16 (One or both parents' consent unless minor has certificate of emancipation)	Male: 18; Female: 18	Minors 14-15 may obtain license with court order in case of pregnancy or birth of child.
NORTH DAKOTA	14-03-02	Male: 16; Female: 16	Male: 18; Female: 18	No license issued to persons under 16.
OHIO	3101.01 to 3101.05	Male: 18; Female: 16	Male: 18; Female: 18	Parties under minimum age may marry with consent of juvenile court where female is pregnant and intends to have the child.
OKLAHOMA	Tit. 43, § 3	Male: 16; Female: 16	Male: 18; Female: 18	Minors under 16 may obtain license in case of pregnancy or birth of child with parental consent and court authorization.
OREGON	106.010, 106.060	Male: 17; Female: 17	Male: 18; Female: 18	If parent is out of state and either party is a resident, parental consent not required.
PENNSYLVANIA	Tit. 23, §§ 1304(1) to 1304(2); 1304(b)(1) to 1304(b)(2)	Male: 16; Female: 16	Male: 18; Female: 18	Minors under 16 may obtain license with parental consent and approval of court if in best interest of applicant.
RHODE ISLAND	15-2-11	Male: 16; Female: 16	Male: 18; Female: 18	Younger parties may obtain license in special circumstances.
SOUTH CAROLINA	20-1-250; 20-1-300	Male: 16; Female: 16	Male: 18; Female: 18	Younger parties may obtain license in case of pregnancy or birth of child (with proof of pregnancy from doctor) and with consent of one of the parents of the female.
SOUTH DAKOTA	25-1-9	Male: 16; Female: 16; (consent of 1 parent)	Male: 18; Female: 18	
TENNESSEE	36-3-104 to 36-3-107	Male: 16; Female: 16; (3 day waiting period except for certain circumstances where waived)	Male: 18; Female: 18	Minors under 16 may obtain license in special circumstances.
TEXAS	Fam. §§ 2.101; 2.102; 2.103	Male: 16; Female: 16; (consent must be given during 30-day period immediately preceding the date of application for license)	Male: 18; Female: 18	Minors under 18 can petition court in his own name for permission to marry

Table 35: Marriage Age Requirements—Continued

State	Code Section	Minimum Legal Age With Parental Consent	Minimum Legal Age Without Parental Consent	Comments
UTAH	30-1-2; 30-1-9; 30-1-30; 30-1-31	Male: 16; Female: 16	Male: 18; Female: 18	Exceptions may be made for persons who are 15 yrs. old with court approval. A minor who is 15 yrs. old and his or her parent must petition to the court for permission for the minor to marry.
VERMONT	Tit. 18, § 5142	Male: 16; Female: 16	Male: 18; Female: 18	
VIRGINIA	20-48		Male: 18; Female: 18 unless emancipated	
WASHINGTON	26.04.010	Male: 17; Female: 17	Male: 18; Female: 18	Minors under 17 may obtain license in special circumstances.
WEST VIRGINIA	48-2-301	Male: 16; Female: 16	Male: 18; Female: 18	Minors under 16 may obtain license with parental consent and court order.
WISCONSIN	765.02	Male: 16; Female: 16	Male: 18; Female: 18	
WYOMING	20-1-102	Male: 16; Female: 16	Male: 18; Female: 18	Minors under 16 may obtain license in special circumstances.

36. PROTECTIVE ORDERS

Protective orders are typically used in domestic disputes to ban one party from contact with another or from interfering with an order of the court with respect to child visitation or custody rights. They are also frequently used in cases of spousal abuse to keep the violent party from coming into contact with the victim. Protective orders are usually temporary measures that the court uses in order to remedy suspected destructive activity while the parties gather and present evidence showing that a more permanent remedy is required. Protective orders may sometimes be granted ex parte, that is without the presence of the party being effected, but only when there is substantial evidence that the party applying for the order is under an imminent threat of injury or when there is good evidence that an order of the court will be violated.

Protective orders have a wide range of temporary duration. Typically, they last for one year with extensions possible under certain particular circumstances. Nine states allow imposition of protective orders for up to three years, and New Mexico limits them to just six months. Ohio has enacted a law that sets the duration of a protective order at five years, the longest of any state. Violations of protective orders also vary widely. Although most states impose a maximum one year sentence and a $1,000 fine, three states require mandatory jail time for violating a protective order.

Virtually all states require transmission of protective orders to local law enforcement agencies. Ten states require transmission within 24 hours. A few states have set up state-wide registries or information systems that keep track of protective orders that are presently in effect. Utilization of technology, such as the internet and wide area networks, permit easy access to statewide registries. In Iowa, for example, it is required to get certified copies of protective orders into the hands of law enforcement agencies within six hours of issuance.

Table 36: Protective Orders

State	Code Section	Activity Addressed by Order	Duration
ALABAMA	30-5-1 to 30-5-11	Enjoining contacts of abuse; harassing communication; excluding party from dwelling, school or place of employment; regarding minors: award temporary custody and establish visitations as well as temporary support; enjoin defendant from interfering; direct law enforcement to accompany plaintiff to residences to protect from abuse; protects against direct and indirect communication; may order possession and use of an automobile and other essential personal effects, regardless of ownership	Temporary ex parte order remains in effect until final protection order is entered; final protection order is permanent, subject to appellate review, unless otherwise specified or modified by subsequent court order
ALASKA	11.56.740; 13.26.850 to 13.26.209; 18.65.530; 18.65.850 to 18.65.870; 18.66.100-18.66.180	Enjoining contacts of domestic violence or stalking or sexual assault; communication or entering a propelled vehicle occupied by or possessed by party; excluding party from dwelling, school, or place of employment, or any specified place frequented by petitioner; award temporary custody; prohibit respondent from using or possessing weapons; request peace officer accompany petitioner; award custody; prohibit respondent from consuming controlled substances; pay costs	Until further order of court for threats and acts of domestic violence; 1 yr. for other acts; protective order for stalking and sexual assault: 6 mos. unless otherwise dissolved; ex part protective order expires after 20 days
ARIZONA	13-3602	Enjoined from committing acts of domestic violence; excluded from dwelling, place of employment, school or other place of reasonable cause of harm; participation in domestic violence counseling; prohibition from possession of a firearm; restrained from contacting plaintiff or other designated persons; grant exclusive care or control of any involved animals	1 yr.; a modified order expires 1 yr. after service and the initial order and petition
ARKANSAS	9-15-201 to 9-15-217	Exclude from dwelling, place of business or employment, school or other location of victim; award temporary support and custody; establish visitation; enforce costs; prevent direct or indirect contact; prevent direct care, custody, or control of any pet in household	Minimum 90 days, maximum 10 yrs.; temporary order effective until date of hearing

Penalty for a Violation of Order	Who May Apply for Order	Fees Waived?	Transmission to Law Enforcement	Civil Liability
Willful violation: Class A misdemeanor, jail up to 1 yr. and/or fine up to $2,000; 2nd conviction: 30 days unsuspended jail sentence plus 1/3 incarceration costs and fine; 3rd or subsequent: 120 days unsuspended jail sentence plus 1/3 incarceration costs and fine;	Parent, legal guardian, legal custodian, or the State Department of Human Resources may petition for relief on behalf of a minor or any person prevented by physical or mental incapacity from seeking a protection order; any person on behalf of themselves pro se or through an attorney	No court costs shall be assessed for filing, issuance, registration, or service of a protective order or petition order or for a witness subpoena under this chapter; costs may be assessed against the defendant at the discretion of the court	Copy issued to law enforcement officials with jurisdiction to enforce the order or agreement	Civil contempt
Automatic arrest; class A misdemeanor punishable by imprisonment up to 1 yr. and fine up to $10,000	Adult or minor through parent or guardian, guardian ad litem, or attorney	No filing or service fees may be charged	Copy of order transmitted to appropriate local law enforcement agency and entered in central registry of protective orders under 18.65.540; law enforcement agencies shall inform peace officers	A person may not bring a civil action for damages against the state, its officers, agents, or employees, or law enforcement agency, its officers, agents, or employees for any failure to comply with the provisions of protective order chapter
Arrest and prosecution for the crime of interfering with judicial proceeding and any other crime committed in disobeying the order	Any person; parent, legal guardian or custodian for minor; third party for person temporarily or permanently unable to request an order	No filing or process service fees may be charged	Copies sent to sheriff's office in county in which court is located within 24 hrs. after acceptance of service or return of affidavit	Civil contempt
Class A misdemeanor: maximum penalty imprisonment 1 yr. in county jail and/or fine up to $1,000; 2nd offense within 5 yrs. is class D felony	Family or household member or on behalf of family or household member who is minor or adjudicated incompetent, or an employee or volunteer of a domestic violence shelter or program on behalf of a minor, including a married minor	Yes	Copy issued to law enforcement officer with jurisdiction to accompany petitioner in possession of dwelling or otherwise assist in service of order	Civil contempt

Table 36: Protective Orders—Continued

State	Code Section	Activity Addressed by Order	Duration
CALIFORNIA	Fam. §§ 6221 to 6389; Penal § 273.6	Enjoining contact and specific behavior, including telephoning, harassing, assaulting, stalking, falsely personating; excluding from dwelling; fraudulent activities regarding insurance beneficiaries; possessing or attempting to possess firearm; regarding minor child: custody; visitation; payment of child support; participation in counseling.	Emergency order: earlier of the close of 5th business day after issue or 7 calendar days; others: up to 5 yrs.; may be extended; 3 yrs. if failure to state expiration date on order
COLORADO	13-14-100.2 to 13-14-110; 14-10-108; 19-1-113 to 19-1-114	Enjoin contact; exclude party from dwelling or dwelling of another, place of employment or place of education; regarding minor child: temporary custody; Emergency order: restrain from threatening, molesting, injuring, or contacting another or minor children of either; excluding from dwelling, if minor child, temporary custody; specify arrangement for possession and care of animal; prohibit possession of firearm or ammunition	Emergency: maximum close of business on 3rd day following issue, unless continued
CONNECTICUT	46b-15 to 46b-19	Regarding minor children: temporary custody, visitation; enjoin contact; exclude from dwelling of family or of applicant; threatening, harassing assaulting, molesting sexual assault; enjoining from injuring or threatening to injure animal owned by applicant	1 yr. unless extended ex part order re temporary care and custody of child; temporary order until hearing for custody which shall not be more than 5 days from issuance of order or less than 3 days from return of service, whichever is later
DELAWARE	Tit. 10, § 1041 to 1048	Enjoin contact; exclude from dwelling; regarding minor children: temporary custody, visitations, support; prohibit use/possession of firearms or disposal of property; award monetary compensation to petitioner; counseling; restrain from committing acts of domestic violence	Ex parte order: maximum 30 days. General order: maximum 1 yr. unless extended except may restrain from contact or committing acts of domestic violence up to 2 yrs. unless extended
DISTRICT OF COLUMBIA	7-1906 to 7-1910; 16-1001 to 16-1006	Enjoin contact; order counseling or psychiatric or medical treatment; exclude from dwelling and possession of other personal property; regarding minor children: temporary custody, visitations award court costs and attorney fees to petitioner; prohibits firearm possession; directs care, custody, or control of owned domestic animals	Provisional protective order up to 45 days, may extend up to an additional 45 days; temporary protective order: maximum 14 days, effective until hearing held for provisional protection order; general protective order: maximum 1 yr. unless extended

Penalty for a Violation of Order	Who May Apply for Order	Fees Waived?	Transmission to Law Enforcement	Civil Liability
Misdemeanor punishable by imprisonment up to 1 yr. and/or fine up to $1,000; with physical injury: imprisonment 30 days to 1 yr. and/or fine up to $2,000; subsequent conviction within 7 yrs.: imprisonment 6 mos. to 1 yr. and/or fine up to $2,000	Spouse; cohabitant; fiance/ fiancee; parent of one's child; blood relations	No filing fee	Must submit proof of service to Dept. of Justice within 1 business day of service; immediate notification by electronic submission of any modification, extension, or termination	
Class 2 misdemeanor; class 1 misdemeanor if prior conviction or other restraining order	Court may authorize mandatory protection order	May not assess cost in cases where relief is sought by victim of domestic abuse or violence, stalking, sexual assault, or abuse	Law enforcement agency with jurisdiction to enforce the order; court electronically transfers copy of order to central registry of protection orders	
Criminal trespass: in 1st degree, for entering or remaining in dwelling. Maximum penalty up to 1 yr. in jail and/or fine up to $2,000	Family or household member subjected to a continuous threat of physical pain or injury; person in a dating relationship who is subjected to continuous threat of physical injury		Yes; immediately; appropriate law enforcement agency within 48 hrs. of issuance if employed in another town	Contempt of court
Class A misdemeanor and imprisonment and/or fine	Member of a protected class on behalf of self and their minor child or an infirm adult; Division of Child Protective Services on behalf of minor child or impaired adult by Division of Adult Protective Services		Order entered into Delaware Justice Information system on or before the next business day; copy sent to Delaware law enforcement agency where petitioner resides and/or where abuse received	Contempt
Criminal contempt: misdemeanor: Imprisonment up to 180 days and/or fine up to $1,000	Minor 16 or older may file on own behalf or parent, guardian, or other appropriate adult, or any adult may file on own behalf	Sliding scale based on ability to pay; cannot be denied services because of inability to pay	Metropolitan police department	Contempt

Table 36: Protective Orders—Continued

State	Code Section	Activity Addressed by Order	Duration
FLORIDA	741.30; 741.31	Exclude from dwelling; enjoin contact; regarding minor children: grant temporary custody visitations, temporary support; counseling; batterers' intervention program; restrain from committing any acts of domestic violence	Ex parte temporary: maximum 15 days; general protective order: maximum 1 yr., can reapply but maximum 1 additional yr. each time; injunction restraining respondent from committing any acts of domestic violence is effective until modified or dissolved
GEORGIA	16-5-94; 16-5-95; 19-13-1 to 19-13-6	Enjoin contact; exclude from dwelling; regarding minor children: grant temporary custody, visitations, support and attorney fees, counseling; provide suitable alternate housing for petitioner and minor children; provide for possession of personal property	Any order granted under this code shall remain in effect for up to one year §19-3-4(c)
HAWAII	586-1 to 586-11	Enjoin contact; exclude from dwelling and petitioner's work; regarding minor children: grant temporary visitation, counseling	Temporary restraining order: maximum 180 days; extended protective order may be for "such further fixed reasonable period as the court deems appropriate." § 586.5.5

Penalty for a Violation of Order	Who May Apply for Order	Fees Waived?	Transmission to Law Enforcement	Civil Liability
Criminal contempt: misdemeanor in 1st degree; imprisonment up to 1 yr.	Any family or household member who is a victim of domestic violence or one who has reasonable cause to believe he or she is about to become victim	Yes	Within 24 hrs. of issuance; clerk of court gives to sheriff or law enforcement agency of county where respondent resides and to sheriff with jurisdiction over petitioner	Civil contempt
Misdemeanor	Person who is not minor on behalf of self or a minor		Sheriff of the county where order was entered	Contempt
Violation of temporary restraining order: Misdemeanor: required counseling and if 1st conviction, mandatory minimum jail 48 hours and fine of $150 to $500; 2nd conviction: mandatory minimum 30 days jail and fine of $250 to $1,000, otherwise mandatory minimum 48 hours; court may waive if 2nd was for nondomestic abuse and 1st conviction was for domestic abuse. Violation of protective order: 1st conviction, mandatory minimum jail 48 hours and up to $150 fine if non-domestic and $150 to $500 if domestic abuse; 2nd conviction domestic, mandatory minimum 30 days and $250 to $1,000 fine; subsequent violations: after 2nd conviction for violation of same order, mandatory minimum 30 days jail and fine of $250 to $1,000	Any family or household member on behalf of self, a minor member or one who is incapacitated or physically unable to file petition, or any state agency on behalf of minor, incapacitated or unable member		Within 24 hours to county police department by county clerk	

Table 36: Protective Orders—Continued

State	Code Section	Activity Addressed by Order	Duration
IDAHO	39-6301 to 39-6317	Enjoin contact; exclude from dwelling; regarding minor children: grant temporary custody; pay court cost's and attorney fees; counseling or treatment services; restrain from committing acts of domestic violence; directly or indirectly communicating; restrained from coming within 1,500 ft. or other distance from petitioner, or petitioner's residence, school, or place of employment or any other specified place frequented by petitioner	Ex parte temporary protective order: maximum 14 days, can be reissued
ILLINOIS	750 § 60/201 to 60/227.1	Prohibits contact; entering or remaining present at petitioner's dwelling; school, place of employment, or other specified places at times when petitioner is present; counseling; or rehabilitative programs; regarding minor children: grant temporary custody, visitations, support; possession of personal property, including animals residing in household; prohibition from firearm possession; prohibition of access to records	Emergency: minimum 14 to maximum 21 days; interim: up to 30 days; plenary: maximum 2 yrs.; all orders can be extended
INDIANA	34-26-5-1 to 34-26-5-20	Enjoin contact; exclude from dwelling, school, place of employment, or specified place frequented by petitioner; regarding minor children: support, custody, maintenance, counseling; refrain from disturbing peace of petitioner; refrain from damaging petitioner's property; order possession of property, including automobile, regardless of ownership; pay rent or mortgage payments, reimburse petitioner for costs related to domestic or family violence, including medical expenses, counseling, shelter, and repair or replacement of damaged property; pay attorney fees; prohibition from firearm possession	Effective for 2 yrs. unless otherwise ordered
IOWA	236.1 to 236.20	Counseling; enjoin contact; exclude from dwelling, school, or place of employment; regarding minor children: temporary custody, visitations, support, maintenance; prohibit possession of firearms and offensive weapons	Emergency: maximum 72 hrs.; temporary order only issued and effective before protective order hearing; general: maximum 1 year.

Penalty for a Violation of Order	Who May Apply for Order	Fees Waived?	Transmission to Law Enforcement	Civil Liability
Misdemeanor: imprisonment up to 1 yr. and fine up to $5,000	Family or household member, even if person has left dwelling to avoid abuse; custodial or noncustodial parent or guardian may file for minor	Yes, court may order respondent to reimburse petitioner court fees	On or before next judicial day to appropriate law enforcement agency by clerk	
If knowing violation: class A misdemeanor; if violating order concerning minors: class 4 felony; if willful violation: contempt of court; may include jail, restitution, fines, attorney fees and costs, or community service. Court encouraged to follow these guidelines: 1st violation: minimum 24 hrs. jail; 2nd or subsequent violation: minimum 48 hrs. jail	A person who has been abused by a family or household member, or by any person on behalf of minor child or adult who cannot file due to age, health, disability, or inaccessibility	Yes; no fees for filing petitions or certifying orders.	Certified copy filed with sheriff or other law enforcement official same day order is issued	Contempt of court
Imprisonment and/or fine	Person who has been victim of domestic violence or, if minor, parent, guardian, or other representative may file on their behalf	Yes, but may collect from party against whom the order is sought if court finds issue meritorious	Transmit by end of the same business day a copy to each law enforcement agency designated by petitioner; some orders must be entered into Indiana Data and Communication System (IDACS)	
Misdemeanor: minimum jail confinement of 7 days and possible fine	Person seeking relief from domestic abuse on behalf of self or unemancipated minor	Yes	Certified copy to county sheriff within 6 hrs. of filing of the order, then county sheriff's dispatcher shall notify all law enforcement agencies having jurisdiction over matter	Contempt

Table 36: Protective Orders—Continued

State	Code Section	Activity Addressed by Order	Duration
KANSAS	60-3101 to 60-3112	Enjoin contact; exclude from dwelling; regarding minors: temporary custody, visitations, support, counseling; provide suitable alternate housing; attorney fees	Emergency: until 5PM on first day that court resumes business; may then seek temporary court order; temporary order until hearing but may be extended; support order: maximum 1 yr., may be extended for 1 yr. maximum; general: maximum 1 yr., may be extended for 1 yr. maximum
KENTUCKY	403.715 to 403.785; 209.100; 209.110	Enjoin contact; exclude from dwelling; regarding minors: temporary custody, support, counseling; restrain from disposing of or damaging property; going to or within specified distance of specifically described residence, school, or place of employment; approaching within specified distance not to exceed 500 ft.	General: maximum 3 yrs.; may be reissued for 3 yrs.. with unlimited reissues
LOUISIANA	46:2131 to 46:2142	Enjoin contact; exclude from dwelling, school, place of employment; regarding minors: temporary custody; awarding use of property, such as automobile jointly owned; prohibit disposing of property mutually owned; refrain from interfering with employment; grant possession of mutually owned pets	Maximum 18 mos.; may be extended
MAINE	Tit.. 15, § 321; Tit. 19A § 4001 to 4014	Enjoin direct or indirect contact; exclude from dwelling, school, or place of employment; support regarding minors: temporary custody, visitations; counseling, court costs and attorney's fee; prohibition from possession of a firearm or dangerous weapon; order termination of a life insurance policy; care and custody of any animal in household	Temporary: remains in effect pending service of final order; general: maximum 2 yrs., may be extended

Penalty for a Violation of Order	Who May Apply for Order	Fees Waived?	Transmission to Law Enforcement	Civil Liability
Violation of enjoining contact: assault, battery, or domestic battery; violation of exclusion from dwelling: criminal trespass. Violation of protective order: class A person misdemeanor; assault: class C person misdemeanor; battery: class B person misdemeanor punishable by imprisonment 48 hrs. to 6 mos. and $200 to $500 fine; 2nd conviction in 5 yrs.: class A person misdemeanor punishable by imprisonment 90 days to 1 yr. and $500 to $1,000 fine; 3rd or subsequent conviction in 5 yrs.: person felony punishable by imprisonment 90 days to 1 yr. and $1,000 to $7,500 fine	Intimate partner or household member under § 60-3102 or parent of or adult residing with a minor child on behalf of minor child	Yes	Copy to police department of petitioner's residential city or to sheriff of the petitioner's residential county if no residential city	Contempt of court
Class A misdemeanor; substantial violation under § 403.761 may have GPS monitoring	Family member or unmarried couple member who is a resident or has fled to this state to escape domestic violation and abuse on behalf of self or minor family member	Yes	Copy to appropriate law enforcement agency within 24 hrs.; copy to appropriate agency for entry of domestic violation records into Law Information Network of Kentucky	Contempt of court
Imprisonment up to 6 mos. and/or fine up to $500	Any person; adult household member, parent or district attorney on behalf of minor or incompetent	Paid by perpetrator	Copy of Uniform Abuse Protection Order to chief law enforcement official of parish where protected persons reside, by end of next business day after filing; Louisiana Protective Order Registry no later than next business day.	Contempt of court
Class D crime	Any abused family or household member; if minor, person responsible for the child or representative of Dept. of Human Services	Yes	For temporary emergency or interim relief; copy to law enforcement agency as soon as possible; general: copy to law enforcement agency most likely to enforce order	

Table 36: Protective Orders—Continued

State	Code Section	Activity Addressed by Order	Duration
MARYLAND	Fam. Law §§ 4-501 to 4-530	Enjoin contact; exclude from dwelling, place of employment, temporary residence, or school; regarding minors: temporary custody, counseling, visitations, maintenance; award possession of any pet	Temporary: 7 days, may be extended to maximum 6 mos.; general: maximum 1 yr. or 2 yrs. if act of abuse was committed within 1 yr. of prior final protective order
MASSACHUSETTS	Ch. 208, § 34C; Ch. 209A, §§ 1 to 11	Enjoin contact; exclude from dwelling and workplace; regarding minors: temporary custody, support; suspend firearms license; monetary compensation; court may recommend batterer's treatment program; alcohol limitations	Maximum 1 yr., may be extended
MICHIGAN	600.2950 to 600.2950m	Enjoin contact or threatening; exclude from premises, school and placement of employment or engaging in contact that impairs petitioner's employment or educational relationship or environment; prohibit appearing in sight of petitioner; regarding minors: exclude from minor children; enjoin possession of firearms; deny access to information	Minimum 182 days unless modified
MINNESOTA	518B.01	Enjoin contact; exclude from dwelling and reasonable area surrounding; place of employment; regarding minors: temporary custody, visitation, support; domestic abuse counseling or educational program; restitution; continue payment of joint insurance coverage; issue property limitations; direct possession of pet or companion animal owned	General: maximum 1 yr., may be extended; ex parte order: maximum 1 yr.; up to 50 yrs. if respondent has violated an order for protection on 2 or more occasions
MISSISSIPPI	93-21-1 to 93-21-33	Enjoin contact; exclude from dwelling; place of work; prohibit disposing of property mutually owned; regarding minors: temporary custody, visitations, support; restitution for monetary losses suffered as a result of abuse; ordered counseling or professional medical treatment	Temporary: maximum 30 days; provisions not to be effective beyond 180 days; general: such period as court deems appropriate

Penalty for a Violation of Order	Who May Apply for Order	Fees Waived?	Transmission to Law Enforcement	Civil Liability
Criminal prosecution, imprisonment, or fine.	Person eligible for relief; on behalf of minor or vulnerable adult: state's attorney; dept. of social services; law enforcement officer; person related by blood, marriage or adoption, or adult who resides in the home	Yes	Copy to appropriate law enforcement agency immediately; copy to Domestic Violence Central Repository	Contempt
Imprisonment up to 2.5 yrs. and/or fine up to $5,000 and order appropriate treatment; additional $25 fine for deposit into General Fund: if retaliation: imprisonment at least 60 days and $1,000 to $10,000 fine	Person suffering from abuse from an adult or minor family or household member	Yes	Copy to appropriate law enforcement agency as soon as is practicable	Contempt
Criminal contempt: jail up to 93 days and fine up to $500	Household member, spouse/ex-spouse, parent of child, member of dating relationship		Copy entered into law enforcement information network by law enforcement agency designated by court in order	Yes, contempt for false statements made in court
Misdemeanor: minimum 3 days jail and counseling; gross misdemeanor if convicted under certain laws within 10 yrs.: minimum 10 days and counseling; court may order 5 yrs. imprisonment and/or $10,000 fine if repeat violation likely or if possessing dangerous weapon	Any family or household member; guardian; regarding minors: reputable adult 25 or older as determined by the court, or minor on minor's own behalf if court determines minor has sufficient maturity; family or household member; guardian	Yes; respondent may be directed to pay them	Copy within 24 hrs. to local law enforcement agency with jurisdiction over the residence of the applicant	Contempt
Misdemeanor: maximum 6 mos. jail and/or fine up to $1,000; or contempt of court	Any person; any parent, adult household member, or next friend on behalf of minor or incompetent	Yes, if court finds that abuse has been committed, abuser may be assessed fines.	Order entered into Mississippi Protection Order Registry and copy provided to sheriff's dept. in county of court of issuance	Contempt

Table 36: Protective Orders—Continued

State	Code Section	Activity Addressed by Order	Duration
MISSOURI	455.005 to 455.549	Enjoin contact; exclude from dwelling; regarding minors: temporary custody, visitation, support; counseling; order temporary possession of property, including automobiles; pay for cost of medical treatment and services that result from injuries from domestic violence; court costs	Full order: min. 180 days to 1 yr., may be renewed for same amount of time
MONTANA	40-4-121 to 40-4-125; 40-15-101 to 40-15-408; temporary order during dissolution of marriage only; 45-5-626	Enjoin contact; exclude from dwelling, school, and employment of petitioner and up to 1,500 ft. of those places or any specified place or named family member; counseling; regarding minors: enjoin contact; prohibit respondent from removing child from jurisdiction of court; prohibition from possession of a firearm; during dissolution, includes temporary maintenance and support; limiting use of property	Temporary: maximum 20 days; during dissolution: maximum 1 yr., may be modified
NEBRASKA	28-311.09; 42-901 to 42-940; 43-2934	Enjoin contact; exclude from dwelling or any other place specified by court; regarding minors; temporary custody; visitation; parenting time; prohibit possession of firearm	Maximum: 1 yr. unless modified
NEVADA	33.017 to 33.440	Enjoin contact; exclude from dwelling, school, or place of employment, or any specified place frequented by applicant; regarding minors: temporary custody, visitations; assignment of income for support; enjoin from injuring animal owned by adverse party and specify possession of animal	Temporary order: maximum 30 days or until hearing; extended: 1 yr.
NEW HAMPSHIRE	173B:1 to 173B:26	Enjoin contact; exclude from dwelling, school, place of employment, or any specified place frequented regularly by plaintiff or by any family or household member; regarding minors: temporary custody, visitations, support; counseling; relinquishment of weapons and firearms; awarding possession of property including automobile; court costs and attorney fees	Maximum: 1 yr., may be extended up to 5 yrs. for each extension
NEW JERSEY	2C:25-17 to 2C:25-35; 2C:29-9	Enjoin contact; exclude from dwelling, school, employment; regarding minors: visitation, support, custody, counseling: prohibit from possession of a firearm; reimburse petitioner's related expenses	

Penalty for a Violation of Order	Who May Apply for Order	Fees Waived?	Transmission to Law Enforcement	Civil Liability
Class A misdemeanor except class D felony if convicted of same within 5 yrs.	Any person who has been subject to abuse by present or former family or household member, or who has been the victim of stalking	Yes	Copy to local law enforcement agency in jurisdiction where petitioner resides; copy for entry into Missouri uniform law enforcement system	
Imprisonment up to 6 mos. and/or fine up to $500; 2nd conviction: imprisonment 24 hrs. to 6 mos. and/or fine $200 to $500; 3rd or subsequent offense: imprisonment 10 days to 2 yrs. and fine $500 to $2,000	Person in reasonable apprehension of bodily injury by partner of family member or victim of one of enumerated offenses committed by partner or family member or victim of assault, aggravated assault, assault on minor or there offenses or is partner or family member of victim of deliberate or mitigated deliberate homicide; regarding minors: parent, guardian ad litem or other representative	No cost to file	Copy mailed to the appropriate law enforcement agency within 24 hrs. of receiving proof of service	
Class IV felony if violator has prior conviction for violating an order	Any victim of domestic abuse or harassment	Yes, in good faith	Copy to local police department or local law enforcement agent and local sheriff's office	
Misdemeanor or maximum penalty prescribed by law; violation of possession of firearm: gross misdemeanor	Spouse; former spouse; blood or marital relative; parent of one's child; dating relation; minor	Court assesses against respondent at final disposition and can reduce or waive them	Copy by end of next business day to appropriate law enforcement agency with jurisdiction over residence, school, child care facility, or place of employment	Contempt
Criminal contempt; knowingly violation: class A misdemeanor; subsequent violations will result in enhanced penalties	Any person; a minor petitioner need not be accompanied by a parent or guardian	Yes	Copy within 24 hrs. to local law enforcement agency having jurisdiction to enforce the order	Contempt
Contempt: crime in 4th degree; if 2nd or subsequent domestic violation contempt offense: jail minimum 30 days	Any person claiming to be a victim of domestic violence who is 18 or older or an emancipated minor		Copy to appropriate chiefs of police, members of state police, and other law enforcement agencies	Contempt

Table 36: Protective Orders—Continued

State	Code Section	Activity Addressed by Order	Duration
NEW MEXICO	31-19-1; 40-13-2 to 40-13-12	Enjoin contact; exclude from dwelling; regarding minors: visitation, support; restrain from disposing of property; order to reimburse protected party for related expenses; counseling	Emergency: 72 hrs. or next judicial day, whichever is later; maximum: 6 mos., may be extended for 6 mos.
NEW YORK	Dom. Rel. § 240; Family Court Act §§ 822; 828; 841 to 847	Enjoin contact; exclude from dwelling, school, place of employment, and any other specific location designated by court; regarding minors: visitation; custody; counseling; reimburse reasonable expenses; refrain from harming companion animal; prohibition against firearms § 842-a	Not to exceed 2 yrs. or 5 yrs. if aggravated or previous violation § 842
NORTH CAROLINA	50B-1 to 50B-9; 50C-1	Enjoin contact; exclude from dwelling; provide suitable alternative housing; provide possession of personal property, including custody of pet; regarding minors: temporary custody, visitations, support, counseling; prohibit possession of a firearm; court costs and attorney fees	1 yr.; may be renewed for an additional two yrs. for good cause
NORTH DAKOTA	14-07.1 to 14-07.20	Enjoin contact; exclude from dwelling; regarding minors: temporary custody, visitations, support, counseling; surrender of firearm; court costs and attorney fees; awarding use of personal property, including motor vehicle	Emergency: 72 hrs. unless continued by court; temporary: maximum 30 days
OHIO	3113.31	Enjoin contact; exclude from dwelling, school, place of employment; regarding minors: temporarily allocate parental rights, visitations, support, counseling for respondent or petitioner, or domestic violence victim, or any combination	Maximum 5 yrs., may be renewed; or upon court action for divorce

Penalty for a Violation of Order	Who May Apply for Order	Fees Waived?	Transmission to Law Enforcement	Civil Liability
Misdemeanor: imprisonment up to 1 yr. and/or fine up to $1,000; 2nd or subsequent offense: jail minimum 72 consecutive hrs.	Any victim of domestic abuse	Yes	Copy to local law enforcement agency	Contempt
Jail up to 6 mos.; forfeiture of bail § 846-a	Any person in relation to the respondent of spouse, or former spouse; parent, child; member of the same family or household; authorized entity; peace officer; police officer; court § 822		Copy to sheriff's office or police department in county or city in which petitioner resides	Contempt § 846
Class A1 misdemeanor; violation concurrent with felonious conduct: charged with higher felony; 4th subsequent: class H felony; violation of gun prohibition: class H felony	Any aggrieved party; a minor may be represented by a person who resides with or has custody	Yes	Copy to police department of city of victim's residence or sheriff of county police department where victim resides and to minor's school	Contempt
Class A misdemeanor; 2nd or subsequent: class C felony	Any family or household member or any other person where court finds relationship is sufficient to warrant issuance of domestic violation protective order	Yes	Copy transmitted by close of business day to local law enforcement agency with jurisdiction over victim's residence	Contempt
1st degree misdemeanor; violation with certain other crimes: 5th degree felony; violation concurrent with another felony: 3rd degree felony	Person; parent or adult household member on behalf of other family or household member	Yes	Copy to all law enforcement agencies with jurisdiction	Contempt

Table 36: Protective Orders—Continued

State	Code Section	Activity Addressed by Order	Duration
OKLAHOMA	Tit. 22, §§ 60.1 to 60.20	Any terms and conditions the court believes reasonably necessary to cease abuse, stalking, harassment; counseling; exclusive possession of any animal owned	Emergency temporary: until close of business on next day after order is issued; general: 3 yrs. max until modified or extended; 5 yrs. for any issued on or after Nov. 1, 2012
OREGON	107.700 to 107.735; 135.247	Enjoin contact; exclude from dwelling and restrained from entering a reasonable surrounding area or any other premises; regarding minors: temporary custody; visitations; counseling; support; limit alcohol intake preceding parenting time; provide safety for any service, therapy, or companion animal	Temporary: 1 year; restraining order: effective until expires or terminated by court
PENNSYLVANIA	Tit. 23, §§ 6101 to 6122	Enjoin contact; exclude from dwelling, school, business or place of employment, or defendant provide suitable alternate housing; regarding minors: temporary custody, visitations, support; relinquish weapons; pay reasonable losses suffered as a result of abuse	Emergency: expires at end of next business day; general: maximum 3 yrs.; may be extended for another term; no limit to number of extensions
RHODE ISLAND	12-29-1.2; 15-15-1 to 15-15.1-9	Enjoin contact; exclude from dwelling; regarding minors: temporary custody, support; prohibition against firearms	Temporary: maximum 21 days, may be extended; general: maximum 3 yrs., may be extended; support payments: maximum 90 days

Penalty for a Violation of Order	Who May Apply for Order	Fees Waived?	Transmission to Law Enforcement	Civil Liability
Misdemeanor: imprisonment up to 1 yr. and or fine up to $1,000; if causes physical injury or impairment, imprisonment 20 days to 1 yr. and/ or fine up to $5,000; if minor child convicted, counseling and community service hours; 2nd or subsequent conviction: felony punishable by imprisonment 1 to 3 yrs. and/or fine $2,000 to $10,000; 2nd or subsequent with injury: felony punishable by imprisonment 1 to 5 yrs. and/or fine $3,000 to $10,000	Victim or any adult or emancipated minor household member on behalf of any other family or household member who is a minor or incompetent; any minor who is 16 or 17	Yes, filing fee; court will assess fees against defendant at hearing. If petition for order was frivolous then fees may be assessed to plaintiff	Within 24 hrs. of return of service, court will send copies to all appropriate law enforcement agencies designated by petitioner	
Contempt: fine up to $500 or 1% annual income, whichever is greater	Any person who has been the victim of abuse within preceding 180 days	Yes	Copy to county sheriff, and entered into Law Enforcement Data System	Contempt
Indirect criminal contempt: Imprisonment up to 6 mos. or probation and $300 to $1,000 fine and fees and costs; if minor convicted: alleged delinquent act	Adult or emancipated minor; any parent, adult household member, or guardian ad litem on behalf of minor; guardian of person for adult incompetent	Fees and costs assessed to defendant when order granted	Copy to statewide registry of protection orders within 24 hrs. of entry of order; copy to police dept. with proper jurisdiction and copy to county registry of protection order	Contempt of court
If defendant has actual notice of protective order: misdemeanor punishable by imprisonment up to 1 yr. and/or fine up to $1,000	Any victim of domestic abuse	Yes	Copy forwarded immediately to law enforcement agency designated by petitioner; filed in Restraining Order No-Contact Order System (R.O.N.C.O.)	Contempt of court

Table 36: Protective Orders—Continued

State	Code Section	Activity Addressed by Order	Duration
SOUTH CAROLINA	20-4-10 to 20-4-160	Enjoin contact or attempt to communicate; exclude from dwelling, place of employment or education, or other location; regarding minors: temporary custody, visitations, support; prohibit disposal of personal property mutually owned; court costs and attorney fees	Minimum 6 mos., maximum 1 yr., may be extended.
SOUTH DAKOTA	25-10-1 to 25-10-13	Enjoin contact; exclude from dwelling; regarding minors: temporary custody, visitations, support; counseling; temporary only: enjoin contact and exclude from dwelling	Temporary: 30 days unless good cause is shown to continue; protective order: fixed period of time not to exceed 5 yrs.
TENNESSEE	36-3-601 to 36-3-625	Enjoin contact; exclude from dwelling or provide suitable alternate housing; regarding minors: temporary custody, visitations, support; counseling; direct custody of any animal owned; costs of breaching lease or rental agreement as result of domestic abuse or protective order; temporary prohibited possession of firearms	Protective order effective for 1 yr. or court of divorce action modifies or dissolves it, may be extended up to 5 yrs.; 2nd or subsequent: extension up to 10 yrs.
TEXAS	Fam. §§ 81.001 to 88.008	Enjoin contact; exclude from dwelling, business or place of employment, child-care facility or school; regarding minors: enjoin contact, temporary custody, support; counseling; reasonable court costs and attorney fees; prohibition against firearms; prohibit disposing of property or removing pet, companion, or assistance animal from possession of protected person	Temporary: maximum 20 days, may be extended; general: maximum 2 yrs.; order is valid until superseded
UTAH	78B-7-101 to 78B-7-407	Enjoin contact; exclude from dwelling, school, or place of employment; regarding minors: temporary custody, visitations; prohibit from purchasing, using, or possessing a firearm upon finding that it may pose a threat to petitioner	Ex parte: maximum 20 days unless modified
VERMONT	Tit. 15, §§ 1101 to 1160	Enjoin contact; exclude from residence or other locations; regarding minors: temporary custody, support (maximum 3 mos.); custody of pet	A fixed period at the expiration of which time the court may extend order

Penalty for a Violation of Order	Who May Apply for Order	Fees Waived?	Transmission to Law Enforcement	Civil Liability
Imprisonment 30 days or fine up to $200; if contempt of court: imprisonment up to 1 yr. and/or fine up to $1,500; if violation by entering or remaining on grounds of domestic violence shelter in which protected person resides or the shelter's administrative offices: misdemeanor punishable by imprisonment up to 3 yrs. and fine up to $3,000	Any household member on behalf of self or minor household members	Yes	Copy to local law enforcement agencies with jurisdiction over area where petitioner resides	Contempt of court
If knows of order: class 1 misdemeanor if assault occurs or 3rd violation in 5 years: class 6 felony	Any family or household member		Copy to local law enforcement agency having jurisdiction over area where petitioner resides within 24 hrs.	Contempt of court
Criminal contempt	Any victim or emancipated minor; if filed by an unemancipated minor, then parent or guardian signature needed or nonprofit caseworker if not against parent or guardian		Copy to local law enforcement agency with jurisdiction over area where petitioner resides	Contempt of court
Temporary: imprisonment up to 6 mos. and/or fine up to $500; general: imprisonment up to 1 yr. and/or fine up to $4,000; if family violence occurs, can be prosecuted for misdemeanor or felony punishable by imprisonment up to 2 yrs.	Any victim; adult member of family or dating relationship; prosecuting attorney; Dept. of Family and Protective Services; any adult to protect a child	Yes; fees paid by respondent	Copy to chief of police where protected resides and to department of public safety and to school	Contempt of court
Class A misdemeanor subject to enhancement provisions of § 77-36-1.1	Any cohabitant who has been subjected to abuse or domestic violence or to whom there is a substantial likelihood of abuse or domestic violence	Yes	Electronically copy by end of next business day to local law enforcement agencies designated by petitioner and copy to statewide domestic violations network	Contempt of court
Criminal contempt: imprisonment up to 6 mos. and/or fine up to $1,000	Any family or household member on behalf of self or their children	Yes	Copy to Dept. of Public Safety relief from abuse database	

Table 36: Protective Orders—Continued

State	Code Section	Activity Addressed by Order	Duration
VIRGINIA	16.1-253 to 16.1-253.4	Enjoin contact; exclude from dwelling or provide suitable alternative housing; regarding minors: visitations; use of motor vehicle	Emergency: 72 hrs. after issuance
WASHINGTON	26.50.01 to 26.50.903	Enjoin contact; exclude from dwelling, employment, school and day care; regarding minors: temporary custody; counseling; electronic monitoring; court costs and attorney fees; order possession of essential effects and use of vehicle	Restraining order to protect minors: maximum 1 yr., may be extended; ex parte temporary order: maximum 14 or 24 days, may be reissued
WEST VIRGINIA	48-27-101 to 48-27-1105	Enjoin contact; exclude from dwelling, business, school, or place of employment of petitioner or household or family members; prohibit disposal of personal property; order possession of any animal owned; counseling; regarding minors: temporary custody, visitations, support; prohibition from possession of a firearm; reimburse for reasonable expenses	Emergency order: effective until modified; final order: 90-180 days; may be extended
WISCONSIN	813.12; 813.122	Enjoin contact; exclude from dwelling; regarding minors: reasonable visitation; surrender of firearms, unless respondent is a peace officer	Temporary: Until hearing; Child abuse injunction: maximum 2 yrs. or until child victim is 18, whichever is first; domestic abuse injunction: 4 yrs.
WYOMING	6-4-404; 35-21-101 to 35-21-112	Enjoin contact; exclude from dwelling; regarding minors: refrain from removing child of petitioner; temporary custody; visitation; support; counseling; restrain disposal of property; order payment of any medical costs incurred as result of abuse	Protective order: maximum 1 yr.; extensions up to 1 yr. each

Penalty for a Violation of Order	Who May Apply for Order	Fees Waived?	Transmission to Law Enforcement	Civil Liability
Contempt of court and Class 1 misdemeanor; violation with assault and battery or furtively entering home: Class 6 felony, no suspension and another order maximum 2 yrs.	Any person or the court.	Yes	Copy to primary law-enforcement agency	Contempt of court
Contempt of court: gross misdemeanor; if assault less than 1st or 2nd degree occurs: class C felony; if reckless or substantial risk of death or serious injury: class C felony; if at least 2 prior protective order violations: class C felony	Any person 16 yrs. and older, under 16 must seek relief by parent, guardian, guardian ad litem, or next friend; any person 13 and older may seek relief against respondent 16 or older; Dept. of Social and Health Services may seek on behalf of and with consent of any vulnerable adult	Yes	Entered into statewide judicial information system within 1 judicial day; copy on or before next judicial day to appropriate law enforcement agency	Contempt of court
Misdemeanor: imprisonment 1 day to 1 yr. and $250 to $2,000 fine; 2nd or subsequent offense: misdemeanor punishable by imprisonment 3 mos. to 1 yr. and $500 to $3,000 fine	Person or adult family or household member on behalf of minor or incapacitated; person who reported or was witness to domestic violence	Yes	Copy within 24 hrs. to any law enforcement agency having jurisdiction including city police, county sheriff's office or local office of the West Virginia State Police	Contempt
Knowing violation of child abuse restraining orders: imprisonment up to 9 mos. and/or fine up to $1,000; domestic abuse order or restraining order for individuals at risk: imprisonment up to 9 mos. and/or fine up to $10,000	Any person adjudicated incompetent		Copy to law enforcement agency with jurisdiction within 24 hrs.; made available to other agencies through a verification system	
If willful violation: misdemeanor: imprisonment up to 6 mos. and/or $750 fine	Any victim of domestic abuse	Yes	Copy to county sheriff who notifies local law enforcement agency in petitioner's county	Yes

VI. GENERAL CIVIL LAWS

37. ANIMAL WELFARE

Traditionally, animals have been treated as property, not as beings or persons capable of ownership of property or of possessing the right to be free of abuse or harm. Of course, in the past, domestic animals were primarily used for food or transportation, and hence were a valuable economic tool. Farm and working animals were the only animals that were protected in some measure against abuse, but only insofar as treatment affected the economic value of the animal. Since companion animals did not even have the economic value, the law did not specifically recognize them as warranting particular consideration. In this context, the law primarily protected the owners of domesticated farm animals and beasts of burden from economic loss as a result of injury or theft of the animals.

In modern times, domesticated animals have achieved enhanced roles in the lives of their owners. Companion animals have become family members, and some owners, faced with the possibility that their beloved pets may outlive them and face one-way tickets to the pound, have tried to make provisions for their pets in their wills. So-called "pet trusts" have evolved over the last century and are becoming recognized by more and more states. In addition, the law has also come to recognize a basic "right" of certain animals to be free from harm.

Animal law is a rapidly growing area of the law. Law schools are teaching courses in animal law and states are strengthening penalties for crimes against animals. Several states are placing a greater emphasis on the protection of companion animals. As such, this chapter is devoted largely to the discussion of companion animals; specifically, it will discuss honorary or "pet" trusts, animal abuse, and animal fighting.

Despite the traditional status of animals as property, a majority of the states now allow people to leave money for the care of animals through an honorary or "pet" trust. Perhaps being led by provisions in the Uniform Probate Code and/or the Uniform Trust Code's provision for pet trusts, many states have passed laws permitting this type of trust.

Also covered in this chapter is a section on animal abuse. States tend to vary on the animals that they protect. As such, when the statute provides a definition for the word "animal," that definition is provided in this section. Although most states define animal abuse or cruelty to animals in a similar fashion, they are still fairly divided on the appropriate penalties for persons committing crimes against animals.

In some states, these offenses are misdemeanors and in others they are felonies. Some states are increasing penalties for crimes against dogs and/or cats or for people committing torture against an animal. Most states require misdemeanor offenses to be enhanced into felonies when an individual is a repeat offender. Several also provide for restitution to the owner, anger management classes, and/or mental health evaluations as a condition of probation or a part of punishment. Since these enhancements and provisions are not particularly unique to animal issues, they are not discussed in this chapter. Abandonment and neglect (failure to provide adequate food, shelter, water, etc.) are included in this section, but crimes such as bestiality are not. As the punishment, not the description of the offense, is what tends to vary the most between the states, descriptions will only be provided when they are unique, they are necessary to distinguish two or more statutes by the same state, or when different actions provide different punishments.

Finally, this chapter will discuss animal fighting. Most states prohibit animal fighting in some form. Some only prohibit cockfighting and/or dogfighting. In states with a specific statute against dogfighting, the punishment is typically higher than punishments for other type of animal fighting. Although these statutes typically provide a very long list of prohibited activities (such as owning or training an animal for the purpose of an exhibition of fighting, allowing property to be used for a fight, judging or accepting admission fees for a fight, etc.), the description of each offense will be summarized in the same fashion as in the section on cruelty to animals above.

As this chapter will focus on companion animals, crimes involving wildlife or farm animals, such as bear wrestling, bull fighting, greased pig contests, horse tail docking and dyed chicks are not covered (with the exception of cockfighting). Also not discussed are traditional exceptions to the statutes, such as for veterinarians, scientific experimentation, hunting, and other historically permitted purposes. Statutes defining proper ways to transport animals, unless unique or defined within a cruelty statute, are also not included in this section. Additional protections provided to service animals for the disabled or for police/fire assistance are also excluded.

_____

*This chapter was compiled by Stefanie Pearlman, Professor of Law Library, Schmid Law Library, University of Nebraska, College of Law.

Table 37: Animal Welfare

State	Pet Trusts	Animal Abuse
ALABAMA	Trust may be created for the care of animal alive during settlor's lifetime; trust terminates upon the death of animal or death of last surviving animal alive during settlor's lifetime, 19-3B-408	Cruelty to animals: class A misdemeanor punishable by imprisonment up to 1 yr. and/or fine up to $3,000, 13A-11-14; aggravated cruelty: class C felony, 13A-11-14.1; 1st degree cruelty to dog or cat: class C felony; 2nd degree: class A misdemeanor, 13A-11-241
ALASKA	Trust for care of designated domestic or pet animal is valid and terminates when living animal is not covered by the trust, 13.12.907	Cruelty to animals: class C felony if offense includes the infliction of severe and prolonged pain or suffering or animal is killed or injured by use of a decompression chamber, or if pet or livestock is intentionally killed or injured by use of poison; class A misdemeanor to cause death or severe and prolonged suffering with criminal negligence, to kill or injure an animal with intent to threaten, terrorize or intimidate another person, or to engage or film or cause another to engage in sexual conduct with an animal, 11.61.140
ARIZONA	Trust for the care of designated domestic or pet animal allowed and terminates when living animal is not covered by the trust, 14-2907	Cruelty to animals: class 1 misdemeanor; class 6 felony if offense involves cruel neglect/abandonment that results in serious physical injury or intentional or knowing infliction of cruel mistreatment, 13-2910
ARKANSAS	Trust may be created for the care of animal(s) alive during settlor's lifetime and terminates upon death of last surviving animal, 28-73-408	Animal: any living vertebrate, except humans and fish, 5-62-102; cruelty to animals: unclassified misdemeanor punishable by imprisonment up to 1 yr. and/or fine up to $1,000, 5-62-103; aggravated cruelty to dog, cat, or horse: class D felony, 5-62-104
CALIFORNIA	Trust for the care of animal is a trust for lawful non charitable purpose and terminates when no animal living at time of settlor's death is alive; trusts are to be used only for benefit of animal, unless otherwise stated in the trust instrument, Prob. § 15212	Poisoning animal without consent of owner: misdemeanor, some exceptions apply, Penal § 597; cruelty to animals: felony punishable by imprisonment and/or fine up to $20,000; or misdemeanor punishable by imprisonment up to 1 yr. in county jail and/or or fine up to $20,000, Penal § 597; failure to care for animals: misdemeanor, Penal §§ 597f; 597.1; attaching live animals to power propelled devices to be pursued by dogs: misdemeanor, Penal § 597h; willful abandonment of any animal: misdemeanor, Penal § 597s; improper confinement of an animal: misdemeanor, Penal § 597t; leaving animal in motor vehicle that results in great bodily harm punishable by imprisonment up to 6 mos. and/or fine up to $500, Penal § 597.7; killing dog or cat for its pelt, or dealing in these pelts: misdemeanor, Penal § 598a
COLORADO	A trust for care of designated domestic or pet animals or their offspring in gestation is valid and terminates when no living animal is covered under the trust, unless the trust instrument provides for an earlier termination, 15-11-901	Animal: any living dumb creature, 18-9-201(2); cruelty to animals: class 1 misdemeanor; aggravated cruelty to animals: class 6 felony, 18-9-202
CONNECTICUT	Trust may be created for the care of animal alive during the settlor's lifetime and terminates at the death of last surviving animal, 45a-489a	Cruelty to animals punishable by imprisonment up to 1 yr. and/or fine up to $1,000; 2nd or subsequent offense or if person maliciously and intentionally maims, mutilates, tortures, wounds or kills an animal: class D felony, 53-247

Animal Fighting

Dogfighting, including presence as spectator: class C felony, 3-1-29; keeping cockpit or fighting cocks in any public place is punishable by $20 to $50 fine, 13A-12-4; hog and canine fighting: class A misdemeanor, 13A-12-6

Animal fighting: class C felony; attending exhibition: class B misdemeanor, 11.61.145

Animal fighting: class 5 felony, 13-2910.01; presence at an animal fight is a class 6 felony, 13-2910.02; cockfighting: class 5 felony, 13-2910.03; presence at a cockfight: class 1 misdemeanor, 13-2910.04

1st degree unlawful animal fighting: class D felony; 2nd degree unlawful dogfighting, including purchasing ticket, presence at, or witnessing as public spectacle: class A misdemeanor, 5-2-120

Fighting animals or cockfighting: misdemeanor; dogs excluded, Penal § 597b; spectator at an animal fight, dogs excluded: misdemeanor, Penal § 597c; manufacture, buy, sell, barter, exchange or possess cockfighting implements: misdemeanor, Penal § 597i; owning, training, keeping or possessing bird or other animal with the intent to use it in fighting: misdemeanor, Penal § 597j; use of certain burs on animals: misdemeanor, Penal § 597k; fighting dogs: felony punishable by imprisonment of 16 mos. or 2 to 3 yrs. and/or fine up to $50,000; spectator at fight: guilty of an offense punishable by jail up to 1 yr. and/or fine up to $5,000, Penal § 597.5

Animal fighting, including presence as spectator: class 5 felony, 18-9-204

Animal fighting, including being present as a spectator: class D felony, 53-247

Table 37: Animal Welfare—Continued

State	Pet Trusts	Animal Abuse
DELAWARE	Trust for the care of one or more specific animals living at settlor's death is valid and terminates upon death of all animals living at settlor's death and covered by terms of the trust, Tit. 12, § 3555	Cruelty to animals: class A misdemeanor; if offense involves cruelly or unnecessarily killing animal or killing or seriously injuring animal while under false pretenses to a shelter, vet clinic or other facility: class F felony; animals do not include fish, crustacean or mollusk, Tit. 11, § 1325; trade in cat or dog flesh: class A misdemeanor; trade in dog or cat hair, with certain exceptions: class B misdemeanor, Tit. 11, § 1325A
DISTRICT OF COLUMBIA	Trust may be created for care of animal(s) alive during settlor's lifetime and terminates upon death of last surviving animal, 19-1304.08	Cruelty to animals or unnecessarily failing to provide certain necessities: punishable by imprisonment up to 180 days and/or fine up to $250; if intent to commit serious bodily injury or death or manifestation of extreme indifference to animal life resulting in serious bodily injury/death of the animal: felony punishable by imprisonment up to 5 yrs. and/or a fine up to $25,000; additional cruelties applicable to owners or persons having custody of animals, 22-1001
FLORIDA	Trust may be created for the care of an animal alive during settlor's lifetime and terminates upon the death of last surviving animal alive during settlor's lifetime and covered by the trust, 736.0408	Animals include every living dumb creature, 828.02; cruelty to animals: 1st degree misdemeanor; 3rd degree felony if violator intentionally commits act which results in cruel death or excessive or repeated infliction of unnecessary pain or suffering, 828.12; confinement without sufficient food, water, or exercise and abandonment 1st degree misdemeanor, 828.13; killing dog or cat with sole intent of selling or giving away its pelt, engaging in business of buying or selling dog or cat pelts, or selling, buying, or having a dog or cat killed for its pelt : 3rd degree felony, 828.123; selling pelt of a dog or cat or garment made with the fur of a dog or cat: 1st degree misdemeanor, 828.1231
GEORGIA	Trust for care of animal(s) alive during the settlor's lifetime may be created and terminates upon death of last surviving animal, 53-12-28	Cruelty to animals: misdemeanor; if person knowingly and maliciously causes death or physical harm to animal by rendering body part useless or serious disfigurement of animal: aggravated cruelty punishable by imprisonment of 1-5 yrs. and/or fine up to $15,000; animals do not include fish or pests that may be exterminated or removed from businesses, etc., 16-12-4
HAWAII	Trust for care of 1 or more designated domestic or pet animals is valid and terminates when no living animal is covered by the trust, 560:7-501	Animals: every living creature, except humans, 711-1100; 1st degree cruelty to animals, including torture, mutilation or poisoning of a pet or equine animal or killing pet belonging to another without permission: class C felony, 711-1108.5; 2nd degree cruelty to animal, including deprivation of necessary sustenance, inhumane confinement and unsupervised tethering: misdemeanor, 711-1109
IDAHO		Animal: any vertebrate member of animal kingdom, except man, 25-3502; poisoning animal belonging to another punishable by imprisonment up to 3 yrs. or county jail up to 1 yr. and a fine $100 to $5,000, 25-3503; cruelty to animals punishable by jail up to 6 mos. and/or fine $100 to $5,000, 25-3504; abandonment of animal without care: misdemeanor, 25-3511

Animal Fighting
Fighting animals or fowl: class E felony; gambling on outcome of fight or knowing presence at or before fight: class F felony, Tit. 11, § 1326
Engaging in animal fighting, including stealing an animal to participate in fight and knowing presence at a fight: felony punishable by fine set by 22-3571.01 and/or imprisonment up to 5 yrs., 22-1006.01; keeping or using a place for fighting punishable by imprisonment up to 180 days and/or fine up to $250, 22-1009; neglect of sick, infirm or disabled animals is offense punishable by imprisonment up to 180 days and/or fine up to $250, 22-1001
Fighting or baiting animals, including attendance at fight or baiting of animals: 3rd degree felony, 828.122
Dogfighting: felony punishable by imprisonment 1 to 5 yrs. and/or mandatory fine of $5,000; person who is knowingly present as a spectator is guilty of a misdemeanor of a high and aggravated nature, 16-12-37
Fighting or baiting animals: misdemeanor; class C felony if 10 or more animals involved at any 1 instance, 711-1109; 1st degree fighting dogs, including knowingly holding fight and recklessly allowing fight on person's property: class B felony, 711-1109.3; 2nd degree fighting dogs, including wagering or attendance at fight or possessing device to train or prepare dog to fight: class C felony, 711-1109.35
Participating in cockfight: misdemeanor; If gambling or controlled substances are present: felony, 25-3506; participating in dogfight: felony; spectator at dogfight: misdemeanor, 25-3507

Table 37: Animal Welfare—Continued

State	Pet Trusts	Animal Abuse
ILLINOIS	Trust allowed for one or more designated domestic or pet animal and terminates when no living animal is covered by the trust, 760 § 5/15.2	Animal: every living creature, domestic or wild, but not man, 510 § 70/2.01; companion animal: animal kept as pet, including, but not limited to felines, equines, and canines, 510 § 70/2.01a; cruel treatment or abandonment of an animal: class A misdemeanor, 510 § 70/3.01; intentionally cause a companion animal serious injury or death: class 4 felony, 510 § 70/3.02; animal torture: class 3 felony, 510 § 70/3.03; creating, selling, marketing, or possessing a depiction of animal cruelty: class A misdemeanor, 510 § 70/3.03-1; poison dog or other domestic animal: class A misdemeanor, 510 § 70/6; confine animal in motor vehicle in health threatening manner: class C misdemeanor, 510 § 70/7.1
INDIANA	Trust may be created to provide for the care of animal(s) alive during the settlor's lifetime and terminates upon the death of the last surviving animal, 30-4-2-18	Animal: not including a human being, 35-46-3-3; beating a vertebrate animal: class A misdemeanor; knowingly or intentionally torture or mutilate a vertebrate animal: level 6 felony, 35-46-3-12; abandonment/neglect: class A misdemeanor, 35-46-3-7; killing vertebrate animal to threaten family or household member: level 6 felony, 35-46-3-12.5
IOWA	Trust for care of animal living at time of settlor's death is valid and terminates when no living animal is covered by its terms, 633a.2105	Animal: nonhuman vertebrate, not including livestock, any game or fur-bearing animal, fish, reptile or amphibian (unless owned), or any nongame species declared to be a nuisance, 717B.1; animal torture: aggravated misdemeanor, 717B.3A; animal abuse: aggravated misdemeanor, 717B.2; animal neglect: simple misdemeanor, serious misdemeanor if offense is intentional and serious injury or death results, 717B.3; abandonment of cats and dogs: simple misdemeanor, 717B.8
KANSAS	Trust may be created for the care of animal(s) alive during settlor's life and terminates upon the death of the last surviving animal, 58a-408	Animal: every living vertebrate, except humans, 21-6411; cruelty to animals: nonperson felony punishable by imprisonment of 30 days to 1 yr. and a fine $500 to $5,000; 1st offense of lesser cruelty to animals, including abandonment, neglect, and knowingly but not maliciously killing an animal: class A nonperson misdemeanor; 2nd and subsequent convictions of such cruelty are nonperson felonies punishable by imprisonment of 5 days to 1 yr. and fine of $500 to $2,500, 21-6412
KENTUCKY	Trust may be created for the care of animal(s) alive during settlor's life and terminates upon the death of the last surviving animal, 386B.4-080	2nd degree cruelty to animals: class A misdemeanor, 525.130; torture of dog or cat: class A misdemeanor for 1st offense: class D felony for each subsequent offense; Class D felony at 1st offense if dog or cat suffers serious physical injury or death as a result of the torture, 525.135
LOUISIANA	Trust may be created to provide for the care of one or more animals and terminates upon the death of the last surviving animal, 9:2263	Simple cruelty, including intentional or criminally negligent abandonment and mistreatment, is punishable by imprisonment up to 6 mos. and/or fine up to $1,000 on 1st offense; 2nd and subsequent convictions carry much stiffer penalties; aggravated cruelty, including torture, maiming or other mistreatment causing unnecessary physical pain, suffering, or death, is punishable by imprisonment of 1-10 yrs. (with or without hard labor) and/or fine $5,000 to $25,000, 14:102.1

Animal Fighting
Most aspects of dogfighting: class 4 felony; if dog participates in fight and person under 18 yrs. is present, illegal wagering is involved, or fight is in furtherance of street gang activity: class 3 felony; soliciting minors to violate this section: class 4 felony; adult who brings person under 13 yrs. to dogfight: class 3 felony, 720 § 5/48-1; animal fighting, excluding dogs, including being present as spectator: class 4 felony, 510 § 70/4.01
Purchase or possession of animal for fighting: level 6 felony, 35-46-3-8; possession of animal fighting paraphernalia: class B misdemeanor, 35-46-3-8.5; promoting, staging, or using animal in a fight: level 6 felony, 35-46-3-9; 35-46-3-9.5; attending fighting contest: class A misdemeanor, 35-46-3-10
Animal fighting: class D felony; spectators of fight: aggravated misdemeanor, 717D.2; 717D.4
Dogfighting: severity level 10 nonperson felony; attending dogfight: class B nonperson misdemeanor, 21-6414; if convicted under 21-6414: class B misdemeanor to own/keep dog within 5 yrs. of conviction, 21-6415; cockfighting: class 10 nonperson felony; attending cockfight class B nonperson misdemeanor, 21-6417
Causing four-legged animal to fight for pleasure or profit: class D felony, 525.125; participate in animal fight other than provided in 525.125, including being a spectator: class A misdemeanor, 525.130
Dogfighting, including presence as a spectator is punishable by imprisonment 1 to 10 yrs. and/or a fine between $1,000 and $25,000, or both, 14:102.19; hog and canine fighting is punishable by imprisonment up to 6 mos. and/or fine up to $1,000, 14:102.5; cockfighting is punishable by imprisonment up to 6 mos. and/or fine up to $1,000, 14:102.23; attendance at cockfight is punishable by imprisonment up to 6 mos. and fine up to $500, 14:102.24

Table 37: Animal Welfare—Continued

State	Pet Trusts	Animal Abuse
MAINE	Trust may be created to provide for care of animal(s) alive during settlor's lifetime and terminates upon death of last surviving animal, Tit. 18-B, § 408	Cruelty to animals, including veterinarian killing/attempting to kill animal in manner that does not conform to certain national standards, killing or torturing animal to frighten or intimidate a person, abandoning or poisoning animal, or killing another's cat or dog: class D crimes; aggravated cruelty to animals if person causes extreme physical pain, death, or physical torture to an animal: aggravated cruelty to animals, punishable by fine $1,000 to $10,000 in addition to other sentencing provisions, Tit. 17, § 1031; shooting at bird for a target for amusement or test of marksmanship: class D crime, Tit. 17, § 1032
MARYLAND	Trust may be created for care of animal(s) alive during settlor's lifetime and terminates at the death of the last surviving animal, Est. & Trusts § 14.5-407	Animal: any living creature, except humans, Crim. Law § 10-601; abuse of animals, including overwork and failure to provide necessary food and shelter: misdemeanor offense punishable by imprisonment up to 90 days and/or fine up to $1,000, Crim. Law § 10-604; aggravated cruelty to animals, including intentional mutilation, torture, cruel beating or cruel killing: felony, punishable by imprisonment of up to 3 yrs. and/or fine up to $5,000, Crim. Law § 10-606; abandonment of domestic animal: misdemeanor, punishable by a fine up to $100, Crim. Law § 10-612; poisoning/giving ground glass to a dog: misdemeanor, punishable by fine up to $100, Criminal Law § 10-618; leaving dog outside and unattended with restraint: misdemeanor, punishable by imprisonment pup to 90 days and/or a fine up to $1,000, Crim. Law § 10-623
MASSACHUSETTS	Trust for care of animal(s) alive during settlor's lifetime is valid and terminates upon the death of the last surviving animal, unless the trust instrument provides for an earlier termination. Ch. 203E, § 408	Cruelty to animals is punishable by imprisonment up to 7 yrs. in state prison or up to 2.5 yrs. in house of correction and/or fine up to $5,000, Ch. 272, § 77; devocalization of a dog or cat is punishable by not more imprisonment up to 5 yrs. in state prison or up to 2.5 yrs. in house of correction and/or fine up to $2,500; certain exceptions apply, Ch. 262 §801/2; non-veterinarian who crops ears of a dog is subject to fine up to $250, Ch. 272, § 80A; exhibiting dog with cropped/cut ear is punishable by a fine up to $250, Ch. 272, § 80B; taking animal without owner's consent for exhibition, mutilation, or experimentation is punishable by fine of $100 to the maximum fine allowed by the charge of larceny of an item of the same value as the animal, Ch. 272, § 80C; failure to report striking and injuring or killing dog or cat with motor vehicle is punishable by fine up to $50, Ch. 272, § 80H; leasing or renting dog is punishable by a minimum fine of $100, Ch. 272, § 80I; removing certain identification from dog of another is punishable by a fine of up to $100, Ch. 272, § 85A

Animal Fighting

Animal fighting: class C crime, punishable by mandatory fine of not less than $500 in addition to other penalties; viewing animal fight: class D crime, Tit. 17, § 1033

Attending a dogfight or cockfight: misdemeanor, punishable by imprisonment up to 1 yr. and/or fine of up to $2,500, Crim. Law § 10-605; aggravated cruelty to animals-dogfight: felony, punishable by imprisonment up to 3 yrs. and/or a fine up to $5,000, Crim. Law § 10-607; aggravated cruelty to animals-cockfight, including possession with intent to use of an implement of cockfighting: felony, punishable by imprisonment up to 3 yrs. and/or a fine of up to $5,000, Crim. Law § 10-608

Animal fighting (including dog and bird) is punishable by imprisonment up to 5 yrs. in state prison or up to 1 yr. in jail or house of correction and/or fine up to $1,000, Ch. 272, § 94; aiding or being present at such an exhibit is punishable by imprisonment up to 5 yrs. in state prison or 2.5 yrs. in house of correction and/or fine up to $1,000, Ch. 272, § 95

Table 37: Animal Welfare—Continued

State	Pet Trusts	Animal Abuse
MICHIGAN	Trust for the care of designated domestic or pet animal is valid and terminates when no living animal is covered by the trust, 700.2722	Animal: any vertebrate other than a human being; failure to provide adequate care, abandonment, overwork, negligently allowing a sick or hurt animal to suffer, and certain types of tethering involving 3 or fewer animals: misdemeanors, punishable by imprisonment up to 93 days, fine up to $1,000, and/or up to 200 hrs. community service for 1 animal; penalties increase for 2 or 3 animals; if more than 4 animals: felony with escalating penalties with number of animals involved, 750.50; knowingly inflicting pain, including killing, torturing, and poisoning: felony, punishable by imprisonment up to 4 yrs., fine up to $5,000 for a single animal and $2,500 for each additional animal not to exceed $20,000, and/or up to 500 hours of community service; does not apply to lawful killing of livestock, hunting, trapping, fishing, pest control or animal research, 750.50b
MINNESOTA	Trust may be created to provide for care of animal(s) alive during settlor's lifetime and terminates upon death of last surviving animal; may not be enforced for more than 90 yrs., 501C.0408	Animal: any living creature, except members of the human race, 343.20; cruelty to animals, including torture, deprivation of certain necessities, abandonment and improper caging for public display: misdemeanor; intentional violation with resulting bodily harm to pet or companion animal punishable by imprisonment up to 1 yr. and/or fine up to $3,000; if death or great bodily harm results, imprisonment up to 2 yrs. and/or fine up to $5,000; penalties continue to escalate with severity of abuse and subsequent violations, including additional punishment if the purpose of the actions was to intimidate, threaten or terrorize a person, 343.21; unjustifiably poisoning animal: gross misdemeanor, 343.27
MISSISSIPPI	Trust may be created to provide for care of animal(s) alive during settlor's lifetime and terminates upon death of last surviving animal, 91-8-408	Intentional or criminally negligent cruelty to living creatures other than cats or dogs: misdemeanor, 97-41-1; confinement of any living creature other than dog or cat without sufficient food and water: misdemeanor, 97-41-7 Neglect or failure to provide creature other than cat or dog with necessary sustenance, food, or drink: misdemeanor, 97-41-9; simple cruelty to a dog or cat, including intentional or negligent wounding, deprivation of adequate shelter, food or water, and cruel confinement or carrying: misdemeanor, punishable by imprisonment up to 6 mos. and/or fine up to $1,000; aggravated cruelty to a dog or cat, including malicious intentional torture, burning, starving, and mutilation: misdemeanor, punishable by imprisonment up to 6 mos. and/or fine up to $2,500 with more severe penalties for subsequent convictions, 97-41-16 Mississippi Dog and Cat Pet Protection Law of 2011; willful and unlawful poisoning of certain animals, including horses, deer, dogs, cats and chickens, is punishable by imprisonment up to 3 yrs. in penitentiary or up to 1 yr. in county jail and/or fine up to $500, 97-41-17

Animal Fighting
Participating in animal fighting or baiting, or use of animal as target to be shot at as a test of skill in marksmanship: felony, punishable by imprisonment up to 4 yrs., fine $5,000 to $50,000, and/or 500 to 1,000 hours of community service; being present at such an activity: felony, punishable by imprisonment up to 4 yrs., fine $1,000 to $5,000, and/or 250 to 500 hours of community service; persons convicted under this section shall not own or possess an animal of the same species for 5 yrs.; several penalties also provided for owners of animals trained to fight that attack other persons, 750.49
Cockfighting, dogfighting or violent pitting of one pet or companion animal against another: felony; purchasing admission or gaining admission to such activity: gross misdemeanor, 343.31
Fighting animals or tormenting or torturing the same: misdemeanor, does not apply to dogs, 97-41-11; dogfighting: felony, punishable by imprisonment 1 to 5 yrs. and/or fine $1,000 to $5,000; intentional presence at dogfight or preparations for dogfight: felony, punishable by imprisonment up to 1 yr. and/or fine $500 to $5,000, 97-41-19

Table 37: Animal Welfare—Continued

State	Pet Trusts	Animal Abuse
MISSOURI	Trusts may be created to provide for the care of animal(s) alive during the settlor's lifetime and terminate upon the death of the last surviving animal, 456.4-408	Animal: any living vertebrate, except a human being, 578.005; animal neglect or abandonment: class C misdemeanor, 578.009; knowing failure by an owner or custodian to provide adequate control of animal for 12 or more hrs.: class C misdemeanor, punishable by a fine up to $200 for 1st offense, 578.011; animal abuse: class A misdemeanor, 578.012; attaching live animal to machine or device propelled by any power to be pursued by a dog or dogs: class A misdemeanor, 578.027; removing electronic or radio transmitting collar from dog without owner's consent: class A misdemeanor, 578.028; releasing lawfully confined animal without consent of owner/custodian: class B misdemeanor, 578.029
MONTANA	Trust for the care of a domestic or pet animal is valid and terminates when no living animal is covered by the trust, 72-2-1017	Animal cruelty: failure to provide necessities, abandonment, torture and promoting or participating in race over 2 mi. long, punishable by imprisonment in county jail up to 1 yr. and/or fine up to $1,000, 45-8-211; aggravated animal cruelty: killing or inflicting cruelty to animal in order to terrify, torture, or mutilate, or cruelty to collection, kennel or herd of 10 or more animals, punishable by imprisonment up to 2 yrs. and/or fine up to $2,500, 45-8-217
NEBRASKA	Trust may be created for care of animal(s) alive during settlor's lifetime and terminates upon the death of the last surviving animal, 30-3834	Animal: any vertebrate member of the animal kingdom, not including uncaptured, wild creatures or livestock, 28-1008; abandonment or cruel neglect of an animal: class I misdemeanor; class 4 felony if it results in serious injury, illness or death; cruel mistreatment: class I misdemeanor; class IV felony if mistreatment involves knowing or intentional torture, repeated beating, or mutilation, 28-1009
NEVADA	Trust may be created to provide for care of animal(s) alive during settlor's lifetime and terminates upon death of last surviving animal covered by terms of the trust, 163.0075	Animal: every living creature, except humans, 574.050; overdriving, torturing, injuring, abandoning, improperly tethering or penning, or failure to provide proper sustenance to animal: misdemeanor, punishable by imprisonment 2 days to 6 mos. in jail and fine $200 to $1,000 and 48 to 120 hrs. community service; willfully and maliciously torturing, maiming, mutilating, or killing animal kept for companionship or pleasure, or any dog or cat: category D felony if done to threaten or terrorize person: category C felony, 574.100; mistreatment of dog owned by another person that is used in an event in which skill, breeding or stamina of the dog is judged or examined: class D felony, if mistreatment results in death: class C felony, 574.107; abandonment of disabled animal: misdemeanor, 574.110; willfully put in public place any substance that might injure an animal: misdemeanor, 547.160; leave cat or dog unattended in motor vehicle during periods of extreme heat or cold: misdemeanor, 574.195
NEW HAMPSHIRE	Trust may be created for the care of animal(s) alive during settlor's lifetime and terminates upon death of last surviving animal, 564-B:4-408	Animal: domestic animal, household pet, or wild animal in captivity; Cruelty to animals, including negligence and abandonment: misdemeanor for 1st offense, class B felony for 2nd and subsequent offenses; purposefully beating, whipping, torturing, or mutilating: class B felony, 655:8; confining animal in motor vehicle when so hot or cold that it would cause serious harm: misdemeanor, 644:8-AA; transporting dog in back of pickup without observing specific safety conditions: violation, 644.8-F

Animal Fighting
Dogfighting: class E felony; spectator at dogfight: class A misdemeanor, 578.025; connection with or interest in management or lending property to fighting or baiting of any creature except dogs: class A misdemeanor, 578.050; bait or fight animals, permit, promote, advertise, stage, or collect admission fee for such baiting/fight between 2 or more animals: class D felony; attend baiting/fight, sell or transport animal bred to fight, possess, manufacture, or trade in cockfighting implements: class A misdemeanor, 578.173
Causing animals to fight, including owning, training, allowing, or participating in any way: felony, punishable by imprisonment 1 to 5 yrs. and/or fine up to $5,000, 45-8-210
Dogfighting, cockfighting, bearbaiting, or pitting an animal against another: class IIIA felony; knowing, willing presence at such exhibition: class IIIA felony, 28-1005
Knowing participation in or connection with baiting or fighting any bird or animal: category E felony, 574.060; promoting, instigating, aiding or furthering fight between animals in exhibition or for amusement or gain: gross misdemeanor; if involving dog: category E felony; witnessing fight or involved with use of implements related to cock or other bird fighting: gross misdemeanor; if violator is not natural person: additional penalty of fine up to $10,000, 574.070
Keeping, breeding, or training any bird, dog, or other animal with intent to use it or offspring to fight or establishing or promoting said fight: class B felony; intentional presence at fight: class B felony, 644:8-A

Table 37: Animal Welfare—Continued

State	Pet Trusts	Animal Abuse
NEW JERSEY	Trust for care of domesticated animal is valid and terminates upon death of last surviving animal, 3B:31-24	Animal: entire brute creation, 4:22-15; knowingly, purposefully, or recklessly tormenting, torturing, maiming, or needlessly mutilating living animal: crime of the 4th degree; if animal dies or suffers serious bodily injury: crime of the 3rd degree; other related offenses to animals: disorderly persons offenses, punishable by imprisonment up to 6 mos. and/or fine $250 to $1,000 and community service up to 30 days, 4:22-17; carrying live animal in cruel or inhumane manner: disorderly persons offense, 4:22-18; abandoning disabled or sick animal: disorderly persons offense; abandoning domesticated animal: disorderly persons offense subjected to the maximum $1,000 penalty, 4:22-20; hit, run over, or injure cat, dog, horse, or cattle with motor vehicle and fail to report: petty disorderly persons offense, 4:22-25.1; 4:22-25.2; Selling the hair or fur of a domestic cat or dog: crime of the fourth degree, 4:22-25.3; selling, bartering or offering to sell flesh of domestic dog or cat for human consumption: disorderly persons offense, punishable by imprisonment up to 30 days and fine not less than $100, 4:22-25.4; civil penalties for acts constituting cruelty are listed at 4:22-26
NEW MEXICO	Trust for care of designated domestic or pet animal is valid and terminates when no living animal is covered by the trust, 46-12-123	Insects and reptiles not included in definition of animals; cruelty to animals: misdemeanor; extreme cruelty to animals involving intentional or malicious torture, mutilation, injury, poisoning of an animal or malicious killing of animal: 4th degree felony, 30-18-1

Animal Fighting
Involvement with a fight or baiting involving living animal: crime of the third degree, 4:22-24
Dogfighting, including attendance as a spectator: 4th degree felony; cockfighting: petty misdemeanor, 30-18-9

Table 37: Animal Welfare—Continued

State	Pet Trusts	Animal Abuse
NEW YORK	Trust for the care of designated domestic/pet animal valid and terminates when no living animal is covered by the trust, Est. Powers & Trusts § 7-8.1	Animal: every living creature, except humans, Agric. & Mkts. § 350; any act of cruelty or failing to provide proper sustenance: class A misdemeanor, Agric. & Mkts. § 353; aggravated cruelty to animals, including intentionally killing or causing serious physical injury to companion animal: felony, punishable by imprisonment up to 2 yrs., Agric. & Mkts. § 353-a; failure to provide appropriate shelter for dogs left outdoors: violation, punishable by fine $50 to $100; does not affect protections under other provisions article, Agric. & Mkts. § 353-b; confining companion animal in motor vehicle in extreme heat or cold without ventilation: violation, punishable by fine $50 to $100, Agric. & Mkts. § 353-d; abandoning animal or leaving it to die in public or allowing disabled animal to lie in public place more than 3 hrs. after receiving notice that it is disabled: misdemeanor punishable by imprisonment up to 1 yr. and/or fine up to $1,000, Agric. & Mkts. § 355; carrying animal in cruel manner: misdemeanor, punishable by imprisonment up to 1 yr. and/or fine up to $1,000, Agric. & Mkts. § 359; interference with certain animals used for racing, breeding or certain other competitions: felony, Agric. & Mkts. § 361; throwing substance injurious to animals in public place: misdemeanor, punishable by imprisonment up to 1 yr. and/or fine up to $1,000, Agric. & Mkts. § 362; clipping or cutting ear of dog without anesthetic or by someone other than licensed veterinarian: misdemeanor, punishable by imprisonment up to 1 yr. and/or fine up to $1,000, Agric. & Mkts. § 365; removing, seizing or transporting dog for research purposes without consent of owner: misdemeanor punishable by imprisonment up to 6 mos. and/or fine up to $500, Agric. & Mkts 366-a; market or trade in domesticated dog or cat fur, hair, flesh or skin: civil penalties up to $1,000 for individual or up to $5,000 for corporation; subsequent violation punishable by civil penalty up to $25,000, Agric. & Mkts 379
NORTH CAROLINA	Trust for the care of one or more designated domestic or pet animals alive at the time of creation of the trust is valid and terminates at the death of the last surviving animal, 36C-4-408	Intentional cruelty to animals: class 1 misdemeanor; maliciously killing an animal by intentional deprivation of necessary sustenance or malicious torture, mutilation, poisoning or killing any animal: class H felony, 14-361; instigating or promoting cruelty to animals: class 1 misdemeanor, 14-360; abandonment of animal: class 2 misdemeanor, 14-361.1; maliciously restraining dog using chain or wire grossly in excess of size necessary to restrain: class 1 misdemeanor, 14-362.3; carrying any animal in cruel or inhuman manner: class 1 misdemeanor, 14-363
NORTH DAKOTA	Trust may be created for the care of animal(s) alive during settlor's lifetime and terminates upon the death of last surviving animal, 59-12-08	Willful neglect of an animal: class A misdemeanor, 36-21.2-01; willful engagement in animal abuse: class A misdemeanor, 36-21.2-02; animal cruelty, including intentionally breakage animal's bones, causing prolonged impairment of animal's health, mutilation, torture: class C felony, 36-21.2-03; leaving animal in unattended vehicle without ensuring its health and safety: infraction, 36-21.2-12

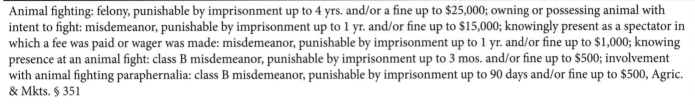

Animal Fighting
Animal fighting: felony, punishable by imprisonment up to 4 yrs. and/or a fine up to $25,000; owning or possessing animal with intent to fight: misdemeanor, punishable by imprisonment up to 1 yr. and/or fine up to $15,000; knowingly present as a spectator in which a fee was paid or wager was made: misdemeanor, punishable by imprisonment up to 1 yr. and/or fine up to $1,000; knowing presence at an animal fight: class B misdemeanor, punishable by imprisonment up to 3 mos. and/or fine up to $500; involvement with animal fighting paraphernalia: class B misdemeanor, punishable by imprisonment up to 90 days and/or fine up to $500, Agric. & Mkts. § 351
Involvement in cockfighting, including presence as a spectator: class I felony, 14-362; involvement in fighting or baiting between animals other than cocks or dogs, including presence as a spectator: class 2 misdemeanor, 14-362.1; involvement in dogfighting or baiting, including presence as a spectator: class H felony, 14-362.2
Involvement in cockfighting, dogfighting, bearbaiting, bear fighting, kangaroo boxing, and similar activities: class C felony; spectator at such event: class A misdemeanor, 36-21.1-07

Table 37: Animal Welfare—Continued

State	Pet Trusts	Animal Abuse
OHIO	Trust may be created for the care of animal(s) alive during settlor's lifetime and terminates upon death of last surviving animal, 5804.08	Abandonment of domestic animals: 2nd degree misdemeanor, 959.01, 959.99; killing or injuring a horse, mare, foal, filly, jack, mule, sheep, goat, cow, steer, bull, heifer, ass, ox, swine, dog, cat, or other domestic animal that is property of another without owner's consent: 2nd degree misdemeanor; if value of the animal or its injuries is $300 or more: 1st degree misdemeanor. 959.02; 959.99; administering poison to domestic animal without owner's consent; 4th degree misdemeanor, 959.03; 959.99; cruelty to animals, including torture, needless mutilation or killing, and lack of access to shelter from weather that would cause suffering: 2nd degree misdemeanor, 959.13; 959.99; cruelty against a companion animal: 1st degree misdemeanor; if custodian or caretaker of companion animal negligently neglects, needlessly kills, or deprives companion animal of necessary sustenance or care: 2nd degree misdemeanor; if that person is kennel owner, manager, or employee: 1st degree misdemeanor; dog kennel owner, manager, or employee knowingly deprives companion animal of necessary substance or care, needlessly kills or commits cruelty: 5th degree felony, 959.131; 959.99
OKLAHOMA	Trust for care of designated domestic or pet animal(s) is valid and terminates when no living animal is covered by the trust, unless trust instrument provides for earlier termination, Tit. 60, § 199	Animal: any mammal, bird, fish, reptile, or invertebrate, including wild and domesticated species, other than humans, Tit. 21, § 1680.1; cruelty to animals, including willful deprivation of necessities, torture, and mutilation: felony, punishable by imprisonment in State Penitentiary up to 5 yrs. or in county jail up to 1 yr. or fine up to $5,000, Tit. 21, § 1685; abandonment of a domestic animal in any public place: misdemeanor, punishable by imprisonment in county jail up to 1 yr. and/or fine $100 to $500, Tit. 21, §§ 1691; 1692; poisoning animal belonging to another: felony, punishable by imprisonment in the State Penitentiary up to 3 yrs. or in county jail for up to 1 yr. and/or fine up to $250, Tit. 21, § 1681; use of live animal as lure or bait in training greyhound: misdemeanor, punishable by fine up to $250, Tit. 21, § 1685.1; carrying animal in inhuman manner so as to cause torture: misdemeanor, punishable by imprisonment in county jail up to 1 yr. and/or fine $100 to $500, Tit. 21, § 1688; unjustifiably administering poison to any animal: misdemeanor, Tit. 21, §§ 1689; 1692

Animal Fighting
Animal fighting, including cockfighting, bearbaiting, or pitting an animal against another: 4th degree misdemeanor; person purchasing ticket of admission or witnessing such event is an aider or abettor, 959.15; 959.99; dogfighting, including paying to be spectator: 4th degree felony, 959.16; 959.99
Instigating fights between animals, except dogs: misdemeanor, Tit. 21, § 1682; keeping places for fighting animals, except dogs: misdemeanor, Tit. 21, § 1683; instigating cockfight: felony, punishable by imprisonment in state penitentiary 1 to 10 yrs. and/ or fine $2,000 to $20,000, Tit. 21, §§ 1692.2; 1692.8; keeping place, equipment, or facilities for cockfighting: felony, punishable by imprisonment in state penitentiary 1 to 10 yrs. and/or fine $2,000 to $20,000, Tit. 21, §§ 1692.3; 1692.8; servicing or facilitating a cockfight: felony, punishable by imprisonment in state penitentiary 1 to 10 yrs. and/or fine $2,000 to $20,000, Tit. 21, §§ 1692.4; 1692.8; owning, possessing, keeping or training a bird for fighting: felony, punishable by imprisonment in state penitentiary 1 to 10 yrs. and/or fine $2,000 to $20,000, Tit. 21, §§ 1692.5; 1692.8; spectator knowingly present at cockfight or place where preparations are being made for cockfight: misdemeanor, punishable by imprisonment in county jail up to 1 yr. and/or fine up to $500, Tit. 21, §§ 1692.6; 1692.8; instigating or encouraging dogfight: felony, punishable by imprisonment in state penitentiary 1 to 10 yrs. and/ or fine $2,000 to $25,000, Tit. 21, §§ 1694; 1699.1; keeping a place, equipment or facilities for a dogfight, felony, punishable by imprisonment in state penitentiary 1 to 10 yrs. and/or fine $2,000 to $25,000, Tit. 21, §§ 1695; 1699.1; servicing or facilitating dogfight is a felony, punishable by imprisonment in state penitentiary 1 to 10 yrs. and/or fine $2,000 to $25,000, Tit. 21 §§ 1696; 1699.1; owning, possessing, keeping, or training any dog for fighting: felony, punishable by imprisonment in state penitentiary 1 to 10 yrs. and/or fine $2,000 to $25,000, Tit. 21, §§ 1697; 1699.1; spectator knowingly present at dogfight or place where preparations are being made for a dogfight: misdemeanor, punishable by imprisonment in county jail up to 1 yr. or fine up to $500, Tit. 21, §§ 1698, 1699.1

Table 37: Animal Welfare—Continued

State	Pet Trusts	Animal Abuse
OREGON	Trust may be created for the care of animal(s) alive during settlor's lifetime and terminates upon death of last surviving animal, 130.185	Animal: any nonhuman mammal, bird, reptile, amphibian, or fish; domestic animal: any animal, except livestock, owned or possessed by a person, 167.310; 2nd degree animal abuse, including intentional, knowing, or reckless infliction of injury to animal, 167.315; 1st degree animal abuse, including intentional, knowing, or reckless serious physical injury or death: class A misdemeanor; if knowingly committed in presence of minor child: class C felony, 167.320; 1st degree aggravated animal abuse, including malicious killing or intentional torture of animal: class C felony, 167.322; 2nd degree animal neglect: class B misdemeanor, 167.32; 1st degree animal neglect, neglect resulting in serious physical injury or death: class A misdemeanor; class C felony if offense involves 10 or more animals or knowingly committed in presence of minor child, 167.330; possession of domestic animals by violator of certain animal-related offenses: class C misdemeanor, 167.332; abandonment of domestic of equine animal: class B misdemeanor, 167.340; obtain previously abused, neglected, or abandoned animal and knowingly allow person from whom animal was forfeited to possess it: class C misdemeanor, 167.349; possession of 10 or more sexually intact dogs 8 mos. or older and fail to follow guidelines: class B misdemeanor, 167.376; commerce in fur of domestic cats or dogs: class A misdemeanor, 167.390
PENNSYLVANIA	Trust may be created for the care of animal(s) alive during settlor's lifetime and terminates upon death of last surviving animal, Tit. 20, § 7738	Intentional, knowing, or reckless abuse of animal causing bodily injury; placing animal at risk of injury: 2nd degree misdemeanor, Tit. 18, § 5532; torturing or causing serious bodily injury or death to animal: 3rd degree felony, Tit. 18, § 5534
RHODE ISLAND	Trust may be created to provide for care of animal(s) alive during settlor's lifetime and terminates upon death of last surviving animal, 4-23-1	Animal: any living creature, except humans, 4-1-1; overwork, mistreatment, or failure to feed animals is punishable by imprisonment up to 11 mos. and/or fine $50 to $500, 4-1-2; unnecessary cruelty is punishable by imprisonment up to 11 mos. and/or fine $50 to $500, 4-1-3; abandonment of infirm animals is punishable by imprisonment up to 11 mos. and/or fine $50 to $500, 4-1-4; malicious injury to or killing animals, including dismemberment or malicious killing, wounding, or poisoning animals and is punishable by imprisonment up to 2 yrs. or fine up to $1,000, and 10 hrs. of community service, 4-1-5; keeping or using live bird for purpose of target to be shot at for amusement or skill in marksmanship is punishable by imprisonment up to 10 days and/or fine up to $20, 4-1-16; abandonment of animal without providing for its care is punishable by imprisonment up to 11 mos. and/or fine $50 to $500; if abandonment results in death, it is punishable by imprisonment up to 2 yrs. or fine up to $1,000, and 10 hrs. community service, 4-1-26; possessing animal after being forbidden by a judge to do so after violation of a law in this chapter: misdemeanor, punishable by imprisonment up to 1 yr. and/or fine up to $1,000, 4-1-40; any person or corporation that requires devocalization or declawing as a requirement for property occupancy shall be fined up to $1,000, 4-1-41

Animal Fighting
Involvement in animal fighting, including birds, reptiles, amphibians, fish, or nonhuman mammals except dogs or fighting birds: class C felony, 167.355; dogfighting, including owning a fighting dog, promoting a dogfight, accepting admission costs, or permitting property to be used for a dogfight: class C felony, 167.365; participation in dogfighting, including knowingly attending: class C felony, 167.370; possessing dogfighting paraphernalia with intent to use: class C felony, 167.372; cockfighting, including owning fighting bird, promoting fight, accepting admission costs, permitting property to be used for fight, or being involved with creation or sale of implements: class C felony, 167.428; participation in a cockfight, including knowing attendance: class C felony, 167.431
Animal fighting, including spectators: 3rd degree felony, Tit. 18, § 5543
Animal fighting: fight between any bird, dog, or animal with any other bird, dog or animal, punishable by imprisonment up to 2 yrs. and/or fine up to $1,000, 4-1-9; possession or training of fighting animals is punishable by imprisonment up to 2 yrs. and/or fine up to $1,000, 4-1-10; intentional attendance at bird or animal fight is punishable by imprisonment up to 2 yrs. and/or fine up to $1,500, 4-1-11

Table 37: Animal Welfare—Continued

State	Pet Trusts	Animal Abuse
SOUTH CAROLINA	Trust may be created for care of animal(s) alive or in gestation during the settlor's lifetime, whether alive or not at time the trust is created, and terminates at death of the last surviving animal, 62-7-408	Animals: all living vertebrate creatures, except homo sapiens, 47-1-10; ill-treatment of animals: misdemeanor, punishable by imprisonment up to 60 days and/or fine $100 to $500; torture, torment, needless mutilation, cruel killing, or infliction of excessive or repeated unnecessary pain or suffering on any animal or causing these acts to be done: felony, punishable by imprisonment 180 days to 5 yrs. and fine of $5,000; section exempts fowl, 47-1-40; cruelly working or carrying an animal: misdemeanor, punishable by imprisonment up to 60 days and/or fine $100 to $500, 47-1-50; abandonment of animals: misdemeanor, punishable by imprisonment up to 30 days and/or fine $200 to $500; hunting dogs that are positively identifiable in accordance with 47-3-510 or 47-3-530 are exempt from this section, 47-1-70; importing or exporting dog or cat under 8 wks. of age without being accompanied by its dam: misdemeanor, punishable by imprisonment up to 30 days and/or fine of $200 to $500, 47-1-200
SOUTH DAKOTA	Trust for care of designated animal is valid and terminates when no living animal is covered by the trust, 55-1-21	Animal: any mammal, bird, reptile, amphibian, or fish, except humans; mistreatment: causing or permitting continuation of unjustifiable physical pain or suffering of animal; cruelty: intentional, willful, and malicious infliction of gross physical abuse on animal that causes prolonged pain, serious physical injury, or results in death; neglect: failure to provide food, water, protection from the elements, adequate sanitation, adequate facilities or care considered to be standard or accepted for a specific animal's health and well-being, 40-1-1; neglect, abandonment, or mistreatment of animal: class 1 misdemeanor, 40-1-.2.3; cruelty to animal: class 6 felony; allowing fatally injured or diseased animal to suffer needlessly or abandoning it to die: class 1 misdemeanor, 40-1-12; failure to euthanize animal injured or diseased past recovery within 12 hrs. of notice by certain officials to euthanize the animal: class 1 misdemeanor, 40-1-13; poisoning animal of another: class 1 misdemeanor, 40-1-20; intentionally kill or injure any animal of any age or value belonging to another: class 1 misdemeanor, 40-1-21
TENNESSEE	Trust may be created to provide for care of animal(s) alive during settlor's lifetime and terminates upon death of last surviving animal; the trust may not be enforced for more than 90 yrs., 35-15-408	Animal: domesticated living creature or a wild creature previously captured, 39-14-201; cruelty to animals, including torture, abandonment, unreasonable failure to provide certain necessities, and tethering a dog in a manner that causes bodily injury: class A misdemeanor; knowingly interfere with certain permitted agricultural practices: class B misdemeanor; excludes law enforcement officer with probable cause, 39-14-202; aggravated cruelty to animals, intentionally killing or causing serious physical injury to companion animal with aggravated cruelty and no justifiable purpose: class E felony, 39-14-212; intentionally removing certain identification from dog to prevent its owner from locating it: class B misdemeanor, punishable only by fine; if the dog is lost or killed as a result: class A misdemeanor, punishable only by fine, 39-14-213

Animal Fighting
Animal: any live vertebrate creature, domestic or wild, 16-27-20; animal fighting: felony, punishable by imprisonment 5 yrs. and/or $5,000 fine, 16-27-30; knowingly present during preparations for fighting or baiting, or knowingly present when a fighting or baiting is taking place or about to take place: misdemeanor, punishable by imprisonment 6 mos. and/or $500 fine, 16-27-40
Own, possess, keep, or train any animal with intent to engage animal in fight with another animal: class 6 felony; cause animal to fight with another animal or cause any animal to injure another animal for amusement or gain: class 6 felony; permit prohibited activity to be done on any premises under person's control, or aid or abet prohibited activity: class 6 felony; spectator at animal fight: class 1 misdemeanor, 40-1-10.1
Owning any bull, bear, dog, cock, or other animal for the purpose of fighting, baiting, or injuring another animal for amusement, sport, or gain or cause such animals to fight, bait, or injure another, or to permit such acts on his property: class A misdemeanor; offense involving any other animal: class E felony; knowing spectator at a dogfight: class B misdemeanor; knowing spectator at any other animal fight: class C misdemeanor, 39-14-203

Table 37: Animal Welfare—Continued

State	Pet Trusts	Animal Abuse
TEXAS	Trust may be created to provide for the care of animal(s) alive during the settlor's lifetime and terminates upon the death of the last surviving animal, Prop. § 112.037	Animal: domesticated living creature, including any stray or feral cat or dog, and wild living creature previously captured; does not include uncaptured wild creature or livestock; livestock: cattle, sheep, swine, goats, ratites, or poultry commonly raised for human consumption, horse, pony, mule, donkey, or hinny, hoofstock or fowl raised under agricultural practices, Penal §§ 42.09; 42.092; intentionally, knowingly or recklessly torture, cruelly kill, poison, or cause serious bodily injury, trip a horse: 3rd degree felony; use a live animal or livestock as a lure in dog racing or training for dog racing: state jail felony; fail to provide certain necessities, unreasonably abandon, cruelly transport or confine, cause bodily injury to an animal without owner's consent, seriously overwork an animal or livestock: class A misdemeanor, Penal §§ 42.09; 42.092
UTAH	Trust for the care of designated domestic or pet animal is valid and terminates when no living animal is covered by the trust, 75-2-1001; trust may be created as provided in 75-2-1001 to provide for care of pet or animal, 75-7-408	Animal: live, nonhuman vertebrate creature, certain exceptions apply, 76-9-301(b); cruelty to animals, including failure to provide certain necessities, abandonment and injuring an animal: class B misdemeanor if committed intentionally or knowingly; if committed recklessly or with criminal negligence: class C misdemeanor; aggravated cruelty to an animal including torturing, poisoning, or killing animal without having legal privilege to do so: class A misdemeanor if committed intentionally or knowingly; class B misdemeanor if committed recklessly; class C misdemeanor If committed with criminal negligence, 76-9-301; intentionally or knowingly torture companion animal: 3rd degree felony, 76-9-301
VERMONT	Trust may be created for the care of animal(s) alive during settlor's lifetime and terminates upon death of last surviving animal, Tit. 14A, § 408	Animals: all living, sentient creatures, except humans, Tit. 13, § 351; cruelty to animals includes inhumanely tethering animal, intentionally killing animal belonging to another, depriving animal of certain necessities, and using an animal as live bait or lure; officials from pounds, humane societies, or other such agencies prohibited from selling or conveying animal in his or her care for purpose of research or vivisection Tit. 13, §§ 352; 365; 386. These offenses are punishable by imprisonment up to 1 yr. and/or fine up to $2,000; civil citation may be issued in lieu of criminal citation or arrest for a first offense inhumane tethering or deprivation of necessities, Tit. 13, § 353; aggravated cruelty to animals includes killing an animal by intentionally causing it undue pain or suffering or intentionally, maliciously, and without just cause torturing, mutilating, or cruelly beating an animal, tit. 13, § 352a; offense is punishable by imprisonment up to 3 yrs. and/or fine up to $5,000. Tit. 13, § 353; concealing a domestic animal owned by another is punishable by imprisonment up to 1 yr. and/or fine up to $2,000, Tit. 13, § 361; exposing poison to the land with the intent that it be taken by an animal is punishable by imprisonment up to 1 yr. and/or fine up to $2,000, Tit. 13, § 362; selling or giving away dogs, puppies, cats, or kittens on the side of a highway, under certain conditions, is punishable by fine up to $250, Tit. 13, § 366

Animal Fighting
Cause animal to fight with another if either is not a dog: state jail felony, Penal § 42.092; knowingly cause dogs to fight, to participate in earnings or operation of facility used for dogfighting, or use or permit use of any property for dogfighting: state jail felony; own or train dog with intent for it to be used in a dogfight, for person to knowingly attend dogfight as a spectator, or to own or possess dogfighting equipment with intent for it to be used to train dog for dogfighting or in furtherance of dogfighting: class A misdemeanor, Penal § 42.10; knowingly cause cockfight or participate in earnings of cockfight: state jail felony; use one's property for a cockfight, own or train a cock for a fight, or be intentionally involved with cockfighting paraphernalia: class A misdemeanor; attend cockfight as spectator: class C misdemeanor, Penal § 42.105
Dogfighting: 3rd degree felony, punishable by fine up to $25,000; intentionally present as a spectator: class B misdemeanor, 76-9-301.1; animal fighting with another like animal for amusement or gain: class B misdemeanor if committed intentionally or knowingly; if committed recklessly or with criminal negligence: class C misdemeanor; does not apply to dogs, 76-9-301(2)(d); causing any animal to fight with a different kind of animal or creature for amusement or gain: class B misdemeanor if committed intentionally or knowingly; if committed recklessly or with criminal negligence: class C misdemeanor, 76-9-301(2)(e); knowingly be spectator during preparations for animal fight or during fight, regardless if entrance fee has been charged: class B misdemeanor, 76-9-301.5
Animal fighting, including acting as a judge or spectator, is punishable by imprisonment up to 5 yrs. and/or fine up to $5,000, Tit. 13, §§ 352(5); 352(6); 353; 364

Table 37: Animal Welfare—Continued

State	Pet Trusts	Animal Abuse
VIRGINIA	Trust may be created for the care of animal(s) alive during settlor's lifetime and terminates upon death of last surviving animal; trust funds may be applied to outstanding expenses of the trust and for burial or post-death expenditures for animal beneficiaries as provided by the trust, 64.2-726	Animal: any nonhuman vertebrate species, including fish, except fish captured, killed or disposed of in a reasonable or customary manner, 3.2-6500; cruelty to animals, including torture, abandonment, mutilation, deprivation of certain necessities, and carrying an animal in an inhumane manner: class 1 misdemeanor; killing domestic dog or cat for its hide, fur or pelt: class 1 misdemeanor; commit certain acts of cruelty that cause the death or euthanasia of dog or cat that is companion animal: class 6 felony, 3.2-6570; failure to provide certain necessities to companion animals: class 4 misdemeanor; applies to owners, pounds, shelters, pet shops, groomers, and other like places, 3.2-6503; abandoning or dumping any animal: class 3 misdemeanor, 3.2-6504; import or export for sale any dog or cat under 8 wks. of age without its dam: class 1 misdemeanor, 3.2-6508; failure of dealer or pet shop to provide adequate care for animals: class 3 misdemeanor, 3.2-6511; failure of boarding establishment or groomer to provide certain levels of care: class 1 misdemeanor, 3.2-6518; sale or trade of any companion animal by person who has been convicted of certain offenses against animals: class 1 misdemeanor, 3.2-6570.1
WASHINGTON	Trust for care of animal(s) is valid; animals may be individually identified or identified in such other matter that they can be identified; unless otherwise provided in the trust instrument or this chapter, trusts terminate when no animal covered by the trust is living, 11.118.005 to 11.118.110	Animal: any nonhuman mammal, bird, reptile, or amphibian, 16.52.011; every creature, alive or dead, other than a human being, 16.52.205; willfully transporting or confining any domestic animal(s) in a manner that jeopardizes its safety: misdemeanor, 16.52.080; cutting more than one-half of the ear(s) of a domestic animal, including dogs: misdemeanor, punishable by fine up to $20, 16.52.095; poisoning animals under circumstances that do not constitute 1st degree animal cruelty: gross misdemeanor, 16.52.190; 1st degree animal cruelty, including intentionally inflicting substantial pain, causing physical injury, or killing animal by means causing undue suffering or force minor to do same; acting with criminal negligence to starve, dehydrate, or suffocate animal and as a result cause suffering or death: class C felony, 16.52.205; 2nd degree animal cruelty, including inflicting unnecessary suffering or pain upon animal in circumstances not amounting to 1st degree animal cruelty, abandonment or deprivation of necessities: gross misdemeanor, 16.52.207; use or trap domestic dog or cat as bait, prey or targets in training other animals to track, fight or hunt: 1st or 2nd degree animal cruelty, 16.52.300; failure by dog breeder to meet certain conditions: gross misdemeanor, 16.52.310 Using hook with intent to pierce flesh or mouth of a bird or animal: gross misdemeanor, 16.52.365

Animal Fighting
Most animal fighting offenses are class 1 misdemeanors; class 6 felony if dog is one of the animals; device or substance is used to enhance fight; money or anything of value is wagered or paid for admission; animal is possessed, owned, trained, or transported with intent of it fighting; person allows minor to attend fight or be involved in certain aspects of fight, 3.2-6571
Animal fighting, including attending fight as knowing spectator: class C felony; animals defined as dogs or male chickens for purposes of this section, 16.52.117

Table 37: Animal Welfare—Continued

State	Pet Trusts	Animal Abuse
WEST VIRGINIA	Trust may be created for the care of animal(s) alive during settlor's lifetime and terminates upon death of last surviving animal, 44D-4-408	Cruelty to animals, including abandonment, failure to provide certain necessities, cruelly chaining an animal, and leaving an animal unattended and confined in a motor vehicle when physical injury/death is likely to result: misdemeanor, punishable by imprisonment in jail up to 6 mos. and/or fine $300 to $2,000, 61-8-19(a); torture, mutilation, or malicious killing of an animal: felony, punishable by imprisonment 1 to 5 yrs. and fine $1,000 to $5,000, 61-8-19(b); excludes livestock, poultry, gaming fowl, or wildlife kept in private or licensed game farm, 61-8-19(f); possessing animal within certain time period after conviction under this section: misdemeanor, punishable by fine up to $2,000 and forfeiture of animal, 61-8-19(i); keeping or using live birds to be shot at for amusement or test of skill in marksmanship: misdemeanor punishable by imprisonment up to 1 mo. and/or fine up to $50, 61-8-20
WISCONSIN	Trust may be created to provide for animal(s) alive during the settlor's lifetime and terminates upon the death of last surviving animal, 701.0408	Animals: as every living warm-blooded creature (except humans), reptile, or amphibian, 951.01; It is an offense to treat any animal, regardless of ownership, in a cruel manner, 951.02; no person may kill animal by decompression, 951.025; dognapping or catnapping includes removing a dog or cat from one place to another without the owner's consent, 951.03; offense to lead an animal from a motor vehicle or trailer or semi trailer drawn by a motor vehicle, 951.04; no person may transport any animal in or upon any vehicle in a cruel manner, 951.05; offense to expose any domestic animal owned by another to any known poisonous substance or certain controlled substances for the purpose of harming the animal, 951.07; no person may use certain devices that are attached upon an animal for any performance, 951.06; unlawful to shoot at animals that are caged or staked or otherwise confined in an artificial enclosure or to instigate, promote, participate in the earnings of, abet as a spectator, or intentionally maintain or allow such a place to be used for such a shooting; does not apply to captive wild birds or farm raised deer, 951.09; owners/persons responsible for animals must provide a sufficient supply of food and water, 951.13; owners/persons responsible for animals must provide proper shelter and sanitation, both indoors and outdoors, 951.14; no person may abandon any animal; 951.15; any person who intentionally or negligently violates § 951.02 and mutilation, disfigurement or death results, it is a class I felony, 951.18
WYOMING	Trust may be created for the care of animal(s) alive during settlor's lifetime and terminates upon death of last surviving animal, 4-10-409	Cruelty to animals, including torture, injury, mutilation, carrying animal in risky manner, failure to provide proper food or shelter, abandonment: misdemeanor, punishable by imprisonment up to 6 mos. and/or fine up to $750, 6-3-203(e); if offender knowingly and with intent to cause death, injury or undue suffering, cruelly beats, tortures, torments, injures, or mutilates an animal resulting in death or euthanasia of the animal: felony, punishable by imprisonment up to 2 yrs. and/or fine up to $5,000, 6-3-203(n); household pet cruelty, including keeping any domesticated animal, excluding livestock, in manner that results in chronic or repeated serious physical harm or keeping household pet confined in conditions that constitute public health hazard: misdemeanor, 6-3-203(p)

Animal Fighting
Participation in animal fighting venture: misdemeanor, punishable by imprisonment in county jail up to 1 yr. and/or fine $100 to $1,000; if animal involved is wild animal, game animal, certain fur-bearing animals, wildlife not indigenous to West Virginia, canine, feline, porcine, bovine, or equine species whether wild or domesticated: felony, punishable by imprisonment in state correctional facility for 1 to 5 yrs. and/or fine $1,000 to $5,000, 61-8-19a; Knowing attendance at animal fighting venture as provided above: misdemeanor, punishable by imprisonment in county or regional jail up to 1 yr. and/or fine $100 to $1,000, 61-8-19b
Animal fighting, including a fight between an animal and a person, excluding rodeos and bloodless bullfights: Class I felony. Spectator at fight or possess or train any animal within 5 yrs. of conviction under this section: Class A misdemeanor, 951.08; 951.18
Cruelty to animals, including knowingly being present at exhibition of fighting fowls or dogs, 6-3-203(g); aggravated cruelty to animals, including owning, possessing, keeping or training fowls or dogs with intent to allow dog or fowl to engage in exhibition of fighting with another dog or fowl, or allowing any dog or fowl to fight with another dog or fowl, promoting or allowing activity to take place on own premises, 6-3-203(c) Offenses under these sections are misdemeanors, punishable by imprisonment up to 6 mos. and/or fine up to $750, 6-3-203(e); offenses are felonies, punishable by imprisonment up to 2 yrs. and/or fine up to $5,000, if offender knowingly and with intent to cause death, injury or undue suffering, cruelly beats, tortures, torments, injures, or mutilates animal resulting in death or euthanasia of animal, 6-3-203(n)

38. BULLYING

Bullying has been the topic of many news segments and the subject of many community discussions. It has probably been a part of human society since the beginning of our existence and has always been a painful thing to endure and a painful thing to watch. Much has been written about why bullies bully as well as the effect that crowds and mobs have on bullies and bullying, and none of it is good. Bullying is a reminder of just how cruel and nasty we humans can be to one another

There are two forms of bullying, one physical and one non-physical, or psychological. Physical bullying is behavior that runs afoul of traditional manners and rules of standard civility, and sometimes criminal laws. Non-physical bullying is difficult to define. Teasing, calling people offensive names, insulting them, or spreading rumors about them are all forms of bullying. Some of these actions can also stray into the jurisdiction of criminal laws. Social media has created a dangerous and fertile environment in which this tendency toward cruelly can fester and grow.

Victims of bullying, if it has risen to the level of criminal behavior, may report the conduct to police or other appropriate authorities. However, much behavior that is considered bullying today is verbal or digital communication, and that can be difficult to characterize as criminal because it involves thoughts, opinions, and ideas that, no matter how distasteful, may be protected by free speech principles.

Most people who are accused of bullying are minors, making enforcement particularly difficult because fines or prison terms are not easy penalties to levy upon juveniles. As a result, legislatures are reluctant to enact direct criminal penalties for bullying. Nearly every state has passed legislation that condemns bullying, but they do so indirectly, often requiring school districts and/or schools to adopt policies to punish bullies.

Because many of the high profile incidences of bullying are so tragic, many legislators feel compelled to enact laws to prohibit such behavior and punish the wrongdoers. Passing the laws described below, while not exactly criminalizing the behavior, at least give the legislators grounds to claim that they have addressed the problem.

*This Chapter was updated and created by Gregg Moran, JD Candidate, Class of 2017, University of Nebraska College of Law and Jenna Woitaszewski, JD Candidate 2018, University of Nebraska College of Law.

Table 38: Bullying

State	Code Section	Criminalized Specifically	State Policy	Cyber Recognized Specifically	Hazing
ALABAMA	13A-11-8; 16-1-23; Student Harassment Prevention Act: 16-28B-1 to 16-28B-9	No; hazing: class C misdemeanor, 16-1-23; harassment: class C misdemeanor, 13A-11-8	Dept. of Education is to develop, and each local school board adopt, policies to management and prevent harassment of students by students in grades K-12	No; definition of harassment in 16-28B-3 includes electronic acts; electronic communication is included in definition of harassing communications under 13A-11-8	Class C misdemeanor, 16-1-23
ALASKA	14.33.200 to 14.33.250	No; definition of 2nd degree harassment in 11.61.120(a)(7) includes repeated electronic communication that insults or intimidates person under 18	Each school district must adopt policy prohibiting harassment, intimidation, or bullying of any student	No; definition of 2nd degree harassment in 11.61.120(a)(7) includes repeated electronic communication that insults or intimidates person under 18	No
ARIZONA	15-341(A)(36); 15-2301	No; harassment under 13-2921 includes communication or act that harasses another person and is class 1 misdemeanor	Governing board of each school district to make and enforce anti-bullying policy; schools themselves to create and enforce anti-hazing policies	No; harassment in 13-2921 includes electronic communication in manner that harasses	Every public education institution must adopt and enforce anti-hazing policy, 15-2301

Table 38: Bullying—Continued

State	Code Section	Criminalized Specifically	State Policy	Cyber Recognized Specifically	Hazing
ARKANSAS	5-71-217; 6-5-201 to 6-5-202; 6-18-514	Cyberbullying: class B misdemeanor; of school employee: class A misdemeanor; hazing: class B misdemeanor	Bd. of Directors of every public school required to adopt policies to prevent bullying. Every public school student in state has right to receive education in environment free from substantial intimidation, harassment, or threat of harm by another student, 6-18-514; safe school committee created under 6-15-1301 charged with creating model policies and procedures to ensure productive learning environment	Class B misdemeanor; if victim is school employee: class A misdemeanor, 5-71-217	Class B misdemeanor and required expulsion, 6-5-202
CALIFORNIA	Safe Place to Learn Act: Educ. §§ 234 to 234.5; Educ. §§ 32260 to 32283.5; 48900; 48900.9	No; Penal § 646.9 (stalking) vaguely addresses bully-like actions	State policy to ensure all location educational agencies continue to work to reduce discrimination, harassment, violence, intimidation, and bullying, Educ. § 234(b); each school district responsible for development of school safety plans; each schoolsite council responsible for developing plan for that school, Educ. § 32282; Dept. of Justice and State Dept. of Educ. to provide training in prevention of bullying, Educ. §§ 32283; 32283.5	Cyber sexual bullying is grounds for suspension or expulsion, Educ. § 48900	If no serious bodily injury: misdemeanor; if injury or death: felony, Penal § 245.6; grounds for school suspension or expulsion, Educ. § 48900

Table 38: Bullying—Continued

State	Code Section	Criminalized Specifically	State Policy	Cyber Recognized Specifically	Hazing
COLORADO	22-32-109.1; School Bullying Education & Prevention Program: 22-93-101 to 22-93-106	No; harassment: class 3 misdemeanor; if based on race, religion, or origin: class 1 misdemeanor, 18-9-124	School boards required to adopt safe school plans, 22-32-109.1(2)	No; bullying definition includes electronic act or gesture, 22-32-109.1(1)(b)	Class 3 misdemeanor, 18-9-124
CONNECTICUT	10-222d to 10-222n; 53-23a	No; 1st deg. harassment: class C misdemeanor and includes intent to annoy by communication, 53a-182b	Local school board to develop and implement safe school climate plan, 10-222d; annual training required of school employees in prevention, identification and response to bullying, 10-222j	Cyberbullying defined as any act of bullying through use of internet, interactive and digital technologies, cellular mobile telephone or other mobile electronic devices or any electronic communications, 10-222d; harassment sent electronically included in 53a-182b	No student organization or member may engage in hazing; penalty to organization of fine up to $1,500 and at least 1 yr. suspension of organization from institution; penalty to member of fine up to $1,000; both in addition to any criminal or civil remedy, 53-23a
DELAWARE	Tit. 11, 1311; Tit. 14, § 4112D; Anti-Hazing Law: Tit. 14, §§ 9301 to 9304; Admin. Code Tit. 14, § 624	No; harassment: class A misdemeanor and includes taunts and challenges, Tit. 11, § 1311	Each school district and charter school must prohibit bullying and develop a policy including specific components listed in Tit. 14, § 4112D(b); each educational institution is required to adopt a written anti-hazing policy, Tit. 14, § 9304	Each school district required to prohibit cyberbullying and treat incidents of cyberbullying in same manner as incidents of bullying, Admin. C. Tit. 14, § 624	Class B misdemeanor, Tit. 14, § 9303

Table 38: Bullying—Continued

State	Code Section	Criminalized Specifically	State Policy	Cyber Recognized Specifically	Hazing
DISTRICT OF COLUMBIA	2-1535.01 to 2-1535.09; 38-2602	No	Each agency, educational institution, and grantee is required to adopt bullying prevention policy; each agency has control over content if it contains provisions in the statute, including expected code of conduct, consequences, procedures for reporting and investigation, 2-1535.03	No; definition of bullying includes electronic communication, 2-1535.01; cyberbullying is required survey topic in annual School Climate Survey, 38-2602(b)(27)	No
FLORIDA	748.048; 1006.135; 1006.147; 1006.63	No; definition of stalking includes conduct aimed at substantial emotional distress, 784.048	Each school district required to adopt policy prohibiting bullying and harassment of K-12 student or employee; policy to be in substantial conformity with Dept. of Educ. model policy, 1006.147; each district must also adopt policy prohibiting hazing and establishing consequences, 1006.135; districts to adopt rules	Defined as form of bullying, 1006.147(3)(b); definition of cyberstalking includes electronic communication serving no legitimate purpose, directed at specific person and causing substantial emotional distress, 748.048	1st deg. misdemeanor; if serious bodily injury or death: 3rd deg. felony, 1006.63
GEORGIA	16-5-61; 16-11-39.1; 20-2-751.4	No; harassing communications, defined as contact via electronic means for purpose of harassing, molesting, threatening, or intimidating a person: misdemeanor, 16-11-39.1	Each school board required to create anti-bullying policy; Dept. of Educ. must make model policy, 20-2-751.4(b)	Cyberbullying specifically included in bullying definition, 20-2-751.4(a)	Hazing as condition of gaining acceptance into school, college, or university organization: misdemeanor of high and aggravated nature, 16-5-61

Table 38: Bullying—Continued

State	Code Section	Criminalized Specifically	State Policy	Cyber Recognized Specifically	Hazing
HAWAII	711-1006; Admin. R. § 8-19-1 to 8-19-21	No; bullying is class B school offense subject to disciplinary action, Admin. R. § 8-19-6; definition of harassment includes insults, taunts, or challenges as well as repeated attempts at communication and is a petty misdemeanor, 711-1106	Disciplinary action required against K-12 student who bullies during school year, Admin. R. § 8-19-6; expulsion from summer program, Admin. R. § 8-19-13; teacher or school official required to report any incident to principal, Admin. R. § 8-19-19	Specifically defined in Admin R. § 8-19-2; definition of harassment in 711-1106 includes "electronic communication"	No
IDAHO	18-917 to 18-917A; 33-512(6)	Student violating 18-917A on school grounds or at school activity may be guilty of infraction	School boards have power and duty to make discipline rules, including rules on bullying, to be included in a district discipline code adopted by the board of trustees and summary provided in writing at beginning of each school year to teachers and students in district, 33-512(6)	No; "An act of harassment, intimidation or bullying may also be committed through the use of a landline, car phone or wireless telephone or through the use of data or computer software that is accessed through a computer, computer system, or computer network," 18-917A(2)	No
ILLINOIS	Bullying Prevention: 105 § 5/27-23.7; 720 §§ 5/26.5-3; 5/26.5-5;	Bullying: no; harassment through electronic communications: criminal offense, 720 § 5/26.5-5	Each school district and other non-sectarian schools required to create and implement policy on bullying, to be filed with the State Bd. of Educ. and to be reviewed every 2 yrs., 105 § 5/27-23.7(d)	Specifically included in bullying definition, 105 § 5/27-23.7(b); "Harassment through electronic communications": class B misdemeanor; 2nd offense: class A misdemeanor; 3rd offense and other circumstances: class 4 felony, 720 § 5/26.5-5	Class A misdemeanor; if great bodily harm or death: class 4 felony, 720 § 5/12C-50; failure of school official to report: class B misdemeanor; if serious bodily harm or death: class A misdemeanor, 720 § 5/12C-50.1

Table 38: Bullying—Continued

State	Code Section	Criminalized Specifically	State Policy	Cyber Recognized Specifically	Hazing
INDIANA	20-33-8-0.2; 20-33-8-12; 20-33-8-13.5; 35-31.5-2-151; 35-45-10.2	No; harassment is offense under 35-45-10-2 and 35-45-2-2	School governing bodies required to adopt discipline rules that must address bullying, 20-33-8-12; 20-33-8-13.5	No; rules against bullying include bullying through use of data or computer software accessed through a computer, computer system, or computer network, 20-33-8-13.5; harassment defined in part as use of computer network or other form of electronic communication to communicate with person or transmit obscene message or indecent or profane words to person: class B misdemeanor, 35-45-2-2	Class B misdemeanor; if serious bodily injury: level 6 felony; if by means of deadly weapon: level 5 felony

Table 38: Bullying—Continued

State	Code Section	Criminalized Specifically	State Policy	Cyber Recognized Specifically	Hazing
IOWA	280.12; 280.28; 708.7; 708.10	No; harassment includes communication with intent to intimidate and is misdemeanor of varying degrees, 708.7	Each school board and authorities in charge of each accredited nonpublic school required to adopt anti-harassment and anti-bullying policy including a statement declaring harassment and bullying to be against state and school policy and setting forth consequences, reporting and investigation procedures, and plan for publicizing the policy; districts and schools are also encouraged to establish programs designed to eliminate harassment and bullying in schools; policy to be integrated into comprehensive school improvement plan required under 256.7(21), 280.28; each school board and nonpublic school authorities required to appoint school improvement advisory committee and utilize its recommendations when determining anti-harassment and anti-bullying prevention policies, 280.12	No; definition of bullying includes electronic communication, 280.28	Simple misdemeanor; if serious bodily injury: serious misdemeanor, 708.10

Table 38: Bullying—Continued

State	Code Section	Criminalized Specifically	State Policy	Cyber Recognized Specifically	Hazing
KANSAS	21-6206; 21-5418; 72-8256	No; harassment by telecommunications device: class A nonperson misdemeanor, 21-6206	Each school board required to adopt policy prohibiting bullying and adopt and implement plan for addressing bullying, including provisions for training and education of staff members and students, 72-8256	Cyberbullying included in bullying definition and also specifically defined as use of any electronic communication device through means including email, instant messaging, text messages, blogs, mobile phones, pagers, online games, and websites, 72-8256	Class B nonperson misdemeanor, 21-5418
KENTUCKY	2.227, 158.148; 164.375;	No	Each school board required to adopt code of acceptable behavior and discipline specifically prohibiting and addressing bullying, 158.148; October declared Anti-Bullying Month by the General Assembly, 2.227	No	Each state college and university, including U. of Kentucky and U. of Louisville, required to adopt anti-hazing policy statement, including penalties for individuals and organizations; penalties are in addition to any pursuant to penal law or those of any other chapter to which violator or organization may be subject, 164.37

Table 38: Bullying—Continued

State	Code Section	Criminalized Specifically	State Policy	Cyber Recognized Specifically	Hazing
LOUISIANA	14:40.7; 14:285; 17:183; 17:416.13; 17:1801	No; harassment by telephone communication that embarrasses or offends another: criminal offense punishable by imprisonment up to 6 mos. and/or fine up to $500; 2nd or subsequent offense: imprisonment with or without hard labor up to 2 yrs. and/or fine up to $5,000	Governing authority of each public elementary or secondary school required to adopt policy to prohibit student on student bullying, including procedures for identifying, reporting, employee training, and disciplinary measures, 17:416.13	Cyberbullying defined as "the transmission of any electronic textual, visual, written, or oral communication with the malicious and willful intent to coerce, abuse, torment, or intimidate a person under the age of eighteen": criminal offense punishable by imprisonment up to 6 mos. and/ or fine up to $500; if offender is under 17 yrs., matter governed by provisions of Title VII of Children's Code, 14:40.7	Prohibited in public elementary and secondary schools; each local board required to develop and enforce anti-hazing policy, including procedures for reporting, investigation, and penalties, 17:183; prohibited in any college or university supported wholly or in part by public funds and punishable by imprisonment 10-30 days and/ or fine $10 to $100 and also expelled from institution for entirety of term, 17:1801
MAINE	Ch. 20-A, §§ 1001; 6553; 6554; 10004	No	School boards required to adopt student code of conduct that includes policies and procedures to address bullying, Tit. 20, §§ 1001(15)(H); 6554; education commissioner required to develop model policy for use by school administrative units in developing local policies, Tit. 20, § 254(11-A)	Cyberbullying defined separately and included in definition on bullying, Tit. 20-A, § 6554	School boards required to adopt anti-hazing policies; trustees of post-secondary institutions required to adopt anti-hazing rules; penalties are similar for both, including ejection from property if not associated with institution, suspension or expulsion, or rescission of permission to operate as student organization, in addition to any other civil or criminal penalties, Tit. 20-A, §§ 6553; 10004

Table 38: Bullying—Continued

State	Code Section	Criminalized Specifically	State Policy	Cyber Recognized Specifically	Hazing
MARYLAND	Crim. Law §§ 3-803; 3-805; 3-807; Educ. §§ 424.1; 424.3	No; harassment without legal purpose after receiving reasonable warning to stop: misdemeanor with varying penalties, Crim. Law. §§ 3-803; 3-805	State Board required to develop model anti-bullying policy for use by schools; each county board and nonpublic school required to establish a policy prohibiting bullying, harassment, or intimidation at school based on the model policy; county boards also required to develop educational bullying prevention programs and instruction for staff on implementation of policy, Educ. §§ 7-424; 7-424.1; 7-424.3	No; definition of bullying includes electronic communication and social media communication, Educ. § 7-424.1; malicious use of electronic communication to alarm or annoy another person with legal purpose after receiving reasonable warning to stop: misdemeanor punishable by imprisonment up to 1 yr. and/or fine up to $500	Hazing at school, college, or university: misdemeanor punishable by imprisonment up to 6 mos. and/or fine up to $500, Crim. Law. § 3-607
MASSACHUSETTS	Ch. 71, § 37o; Ch. 265, § 43A; Ch. 269, §§ 14A; 17; 18	No; harassment and "annoying . . . electronic communication" are criminal offenses that include bullying-like actions, Ch. 265, § 43A; Ch. 269, § 14A	Each school district, charter school, approved private day or residential school, and collaborative school required to provide age-appropriate instruction on bullying prevention in curriculum and to develop and adhere to anti-bullying plan, Ch. 71, § 37o	Cyberbullying specifically defined, Tit. 71, § 37o	Hazing punishable by imprisonment up to 1 yr. and/or fine up to $3,000, Ch. 269, § 17; failure to report: fine up to $1,000

Table 38: Bullying—Continued

State	Code Section	Criminalized Specifically	State Policy	Cyber Recognized Specifically	Hazing
MICHIGAN	The Matt Epling Safe School Law: 380.1310b; 750.411t	No	Each school board required to adopt and implement anti-bullying policy, including procedures for reporting, investigation, education, and staff training, 380.1310b	Cyberbullying specifically included, 380.1310b	If physical injury: misdemeanor punishable by imprisonment up to 93 days and/or fine up to $1,000; if serious impairment of body function: felony punishable by imprisonment up to 5 yrs. and/or fine up to $2,500; if death: felony punishable by imprisonment up to 15 yrs. and/or fine up to $10,000, 750.411t
MINNESOTA	121A.03; 121A.031; 135A.155; 609.748	No; definition of harassment includes "intrusive words that have substantial effect on safety of another," 609.748	Education commission required to maintain and make available to schools a sexual, religious, and racial harassment and violence model policy, 121A.03; districts and schools required to adopt, implement, and post anti-bullying policy; schools that do not develop their own policy must implement and may supplement the state model policy, 121A.031	Cyberbullying specifically defined as part of prohibited conduct, 121A.031	Each school board required to adopt written policy governing student or staff hazing, including reporting procedures and disciplinary consequences for violating policy, 121A.69; Board of Trustees of Minn. State Colleges and Universities required, and Univ. of Minn. requested, to adopt written policy, including reporting procedures and disciplinary actions against individual violators and organizations; eligible private postsecondary institutions also required to adopt policy, 135A.155; no statutory criminal sanction

Table 38: Bullying—Continued

State	Code Section	Criminalized Specifically	State Policy	Cyber Recognized Specifically	Hazing
MISSISSIPPI	37-11-20; 37-11-67; 37-11-69; 97-3-105; 97-29-45	No; intimidating student for purpose of interfering with student right to attend classes or otherwise causing student to not attend classes: misdemeanor punishable by imprisonment up to 6 mos. and/or fine up to $500; if violator is under age 17: jurisdiction of youth court, 37-11-20	Each school district required to adopt anti-bullying policies, including procedures for reporting, investigating and addressing behavior. Policies must recognize fundamental right of every student to take reasonable actions to defend self from attack by another student, 37-11-69; 37-11-67	No; definition of bullying includes "electronic communications," 37-11-67;	1st degree hazing if substantial risk of physical injury: misdemeanor punishable by fine up to $1,000; 2nd degree hazing if injury occurs: misdemeanor punishable by imprisonment in county jail up to 6 mos. and/or fine up to $2,000, in addition to any other criminal charges, 97-3-105
MISSOURI	160.775; 192.2400-505; 565.090; 578.365	No; acts with purpose to cause emotional distress to another person even if distress does not occur: 2nd degree harassment: class A misdemeanor, 565.091; if distress does occur: class E felony, 565.090	Every district required to adopt anti-bullying policy, including procedures for reporting, investigation, and consequences, 160.775	Cyberbullying specifically defined and addressed in policy provisions, 160.775	Class A misdemeanor; if substantial risk to life of student or prospective member: class D felony; each public and private university required to adopt written policy prohibiting hazing by any organization operating under sanction of institution, 578.365
MONTANA	Bully-Free Montana Act: 20-5-207 to 20-5-210	No	No	No; definition of bullying includes "electronic communications," 20-5-208	No; definition of bullying includes hazing but does not mention or define hazing beyond that, 20-5-208

Table 38: Bullying—Continued

State	Code Section	Criminalized Specifically	State Policy	Cyber Recognized Specifically	Hazing
NEBRASKA	28-311.02; 28-311.06; 79-267; 79-2,137	No; definition of harassment includes threatening or intimidating conduct, 28-311.02; intimidation by telephone call includes telephone contact with intent to intimidate, harass, annoy, or offend, 28-1310	Each school district required to develop and adopt bullying prevention and education policy, 79-2,137	No; definition of bullying includes "electronic abuse," 2-2,137	Class III misdemeanor; if committed for purpose of initiation, admission, affiliation, or continued membership with organization of student members operating under sanction of postsecondary educational institution and committed by members of organization: fine to organization up to $10,000, 28-311.06
NEVADA	200.605; 200.900 388.122 to 388.137	Knowing and willful use by minor of an electronic communication device to transmit or distribute image of bullying committed against minor to another person with intent to encourage, further, or promote bullying and to cause harm to the minor: child in need of supervision, not delinquent; 2nd offense: delinquent act, and court may order detention of minor in same manner as if minor had committed act that would have been misdemeanor if committed by an adult	Each school district required to provide safe and respectful learning environment free of bullying and cyberbullying, 388.1321; Dept. of Educ. must prescribe by regulation policy for all school districts and public schools to provide that environment, 388.133; school boards required to adopt the Dept. of Educ. policy or expanded policy if it complies with Department's policy, 388.134	Cyberbullying defined as bullying through electronic communication, 388.123; 388.124	Misdemeanor; if substantial bodily harm: gross misdemeanor, 200.605

Table 38: Bullying—Continued

State	Code Section	Criminalized Specifically	State Policy	Cyber Recognized Specifically	Hazing
NEW HAMPSHIRE	Pupil Safety and Violence Prevention Act of 2000: 193-F:1 TO 193-F:10; 631:7; 644:4	No; harassment: misdemeanor, 644:4	Each school district and charter school required to adopt written policy prohibiting bullying and cyberbullying, including procedures for identification, reporting, communication, and disciplinary consequences; Dept. of Educ. may develop model policy that may be used by districts as basis for local policy, 193-F:4	Cyberbullying defined as bullying undertaken through use of electronic devices, 193-F:3	Hazing or failure to report hazing at secondary or postsecondary institution: Class B misdemeanor; if institution knowingly permits or condones hazing or fails to prevent or report hazing, it is also guilty of misdemeanor, 631:7
NEW JERSEY	2C:33-4; 2C:33-4.1; 2C:40-3; Anti-Bullying Bill of Rights Act: 18A:37-13 to 18A:37-32.1	No; harassment: petty disorderly persons offense, 2C:33-4; cyberharassment: Crime of 4th degree; if person is 21 or older and impersonates minor for purpose of cyberharassing a minor: crime of 3rd degree, 2C:33-4.1	Each school district required to adopt policy prohibiting bullying, including statement of expected behavior, procedures for reporting, consequences, investigation, and publicizing; Commissioner of Education shall develop model policy for use by districts and amend as necessary, 18A:37-15	Cyberharassment: Crime of 4th degree; if person is 21 or older and impersonates minor for purpose of cyberharassing a minor: crime of 3rd degree, 2C:33-4.1	Hazing: Disorderly persons offense; if serious bodily injury: aggravated hazing, a crime of 4th degree, 2C:40-3
NEW MEXICO	22-2-21; 30-3A-2; Carlos Vigil Memorial Act: 32A-25-1 to 32A-25-5	No; harassment: misdemeanor	Dept. of Education to establish guidelines for anti-bullying policies to be adopted by local school boards; each local school board and charter school required to adopt anti-bullying policy and anti-cyberbullying policy, including reporting, employee training to recognize cyberbullying, and disciplinary action, 22-2-21	Cyberbullying defined and school boards required to adopt anti-cyberbullying policy, 22-2-21	No

Table 38: Bullying—Continued

State	Code Section	Criminalized Specifically	State Policy	Cyber Recognized Specifically	Hazing
NEW YORK	Educ. §§ 10 to 18; Penal §§ 120.16; 120.17; 240.25; 240.26	No; 1st degree harassment: class B misdemeanor, Penal § 240.26; 2nd degree harassment: violation, Penal § 240.25; penalties are escalated if against protected class, Penal §§ 240.30; 240.31	Every school district required to create anti-bullying policy, including procedures for reporting, identification, investigation, bullying prevention strategy, employee training, and disciplinary and education guidelines, Educ. § 13	Cyberbullying defined as bullying through means of electronic communication, Educ. § 11(8)	Hazing in 2nd degree: violation, Penal § 120.17; if personal injury, hazing in 1st degree: class A misdemeanor, Penal § 120.16
NORTH CAROLINA	14-35; 14-196; 1115C-407.15 to 1115C-407.18	Yes: Cyberbullying, 14-458.1; anonymous or threatening letters, 14-394; and using indecent language over telephone, 14-196, criminalize bullying-like behavior	Each school required to adopt anti-bullying policy, including expected behavior, consequences, procedures for reporting and investigation, 115C-407.16	Cyberbullying: class 2 misdemeanor, 14-458.1; cyberbullying of school employee by student: class 2 misdemeanor, 14-458.2; student who does this must be transferred to another school, 115C-366.4	Class 2 misdemeanor, 14-35
NORTH DAKOTA	12.1-10-07; 12.1-17-10; 15.1-19-17 to 15.1-19-22	No; harassment definition includes conduct that threatens or is repeated with no legal purpose: class B misdemeanor, if threat: class A misdemeanor, 12.1-17-07	Each school district required to adopt policy prohibiting bullying, including procedures for reporting, investigating, disciplinary measures, and strategies to protect victim, 15.1-19-18	No; definition of bullying includes the use of technology or other electronic media, 15.1-19-17	Class B misdemeanor; if physical injury, class A misdemeanor, 12.1-17-10

Table 38: Bullying—Continued

State	Code Section	Criminalized Specifically	State Policy	Cyber Recognized Specifically	Hazing
OHIO	5.2296; 2903.31; 2917.21; 3313.666	No; harassment by telecommunication: 1st degree misdemeanor; 2nd and subsequent offenses: 4th degree felony, 2917.21	September is designated as School Bullying Prevention Awareness Month to highlight policies against bullying, 5.2296; school boards required to adopt policy prohibiting harassment, intimidation, or bullying, including procedures for documenting, investigation, disciplinary action, and strategies for protection of victim, 3313.666	No; "electronic acts" are included in bullying definition, 3313.666	Hazing: 4th degree misdemeanor

Table 38: Bullying—Continued

State	Code Section	Criminalized Specifically	State Policy	Cyber Recognized Specifically	Hazing
OKLAHOMA	Tit. 21, §§ 1172, 1190; School Safety and Bullying Prevention Act: Tit. 70, §§ 24-100.2 to 24-100.5	No; use of electronic communication to make lewd or "filthy" comment: misdemeanor; 2nd and subsequent offense: felony, Tit. 21, § 1172	Each district board of education required to adopt policy, including expected standards of conduct and discipline options, procedures for reporting, investigation, publicity, training, and education, and referral, Tit. 70, § 24-100.4; each school to appoint Safe School Committee each year to study and make recommendations regarding bullying, review the school anti-bullying policy, and review anti-bullying programs of other states or school districts; Dept. of Educ. to develop model anti-bullying policy and training materials on components to be included in school policies and provide and publicize a list of research-based programs appropriate for prevention of bullying of students; if school district implements commercial bullying prevention program, it must be one listed by Dept. of Educ., Tit. 70 § 100.5	No; definition of bullying includes electronic communication Tit. 70, § 24-100.3; Bullying by electronic communication specifically mentioned to be addressed in school policy, Tit. 70, § 24-100.4	Every public or private school or institution of higher education to distribute anti-hazing policy to each enrolled student and shall be deemed to be part of the bylaws of all organizations operating at the public school or institution of higher education. Penalty to individual: misdemeanor punishable by imprisonment up to 90 days in county jail and/or fine up to $500; organization: misdemeanor punishable by fine up to $1,500 and forfeit of all rights and privileges as organization at school for at least 1 yr., Tit. 24, § 1190

Table 38: Bullying—Continued

State	Code Section	Criminalized Specifically	State Policy	Cyber Recognized Specifically	Hazing
OREGON	163.197; 166.065; 166.090; 339.351 to 339.364	No; harassment and harassment by telephone: class B misdemeanor, 166.065; 166.090	Each school district required to adopt policy prohibiting harassment, intimidation or bullying and prohibiting cyberbullying, including procedures for reporting, investigation, review, and consequences, 339.356	Cyberbullying specifically defined, 339.351 and specifically to be part of anti-bullying policies of schools, 339.356	Violation by student organization: class A misdemeanor; violation by student member of organization: class B misdemeanor, 163.197
PENNSYLVANIA	Tit. 18 Ann., § 2709; Tit. 24, §§ 13-1301.1-A; Antihazing Law, §§ 5351 to 5354	No; harassment by lewd, threatening, or obscene communication: 3rd degree misdemeanor, Tit. 18 Ann., § 2709	Each school entity required to adopt anti-bullying policy delineating disciplinary consequences for bullying; policy may provide for prevention, intervention, and education programs, Tit. 24, § 13-1301.1-A	Definition of bullying includes by electronic means, Tit. 24, § 13-1301.1-A(e); Cyberharassment of child: 3rd degree misdemeanor, Tit. 18 Ann., § 2709	Each institution and secondary school required to adopt written antihazing policy and rules prohibiting students or other persons associated with sanctioned or recognized organizations from engaging in activity that can be described as hazing; hazing is 3rd degree misdemeanor, other penalties may include imposition of fines, withholding of diplomas or transcripts, suspension, dismissal or expulsion; penalties to organization may include revision of permission for organization to operate on campus or school property, Tit. 24, §§ 5353; 5354

Table 38: Bullying—Continued

State	Code Section	Criminalized Specifically	State Policy	Cyber Recognized Specifically	Hazing
RHODE ISLAND	11-21-1 to 11-21-3; 11-52-4.2; 16-21-33; 16-21-34	No; cyberharassment: misdemeanor punishable by imprisonment up to 1 yr. and/or fine up to $500, 11-52-4.2	Dept. of Education required to prescribe by regulation a statewide bullying policy, ensuring consistent and unified statewide approach to prohibition of bullying at school; all school districts, charter schools, career and technical schools, approved private day or residential schools, and collaborative schools must adopt statewide bullying policy, 16-21-34	Cyberbullying specifically defined, 16-21-33(2); cyberharassment: misdemeanor; 2nd and subsequent offenses: felony, 11-52-4.2	Individual: Misdemeanor punishable by imprisonment 30 days to 1 yr. and/or fine up to $500, 11-21-1; any school official who knowingly permits hazing: misdemeanor punishable by fine $10 to $100, 11-21-2; permanent disfigurement or tattooing another person: crime of the degree of mayhem punishable by imprisonment 1 to 10 yrs., 11-21-3
SOUTH CAROLINA	16-17-430; 16-3-510 to 16-3-549; Safe School Climate Act: 59-63-110 to 59-63-150	No; vulgar and immoral message using electronic communications: misdemeanor 16-17-430	Each school district required to adopt anti-bullying policy; State Bd. of Educ. will develop model K-12 policy and teacher training standards to assist schools, 59-63-140	No; electronic communication included in bullying definition, 59-63-120	Hazing or failure to report: misdemeanor punishable by imprisonment up to 12 mos. and/or fine up to $500, 16-3-540
SOUTH DAKOTA	13-32-14 to 13-32-19; 22-19A-4	No; harassment is defined as conduct which annoys with no legitimate purpose, 22-19A-4	Schools may develop own anti-bullying policies; if they do not, by default the model bullying policy outlined in 13-32-19 applies, 13-32-14	No; definition of bullying includes use of data or computer software, 13-32-15	No

Table 38: Bullying—Continued

State	Code Section	Criminalized Specifically	State Policy	Cyber Recognized Specifically	Hazing
TENNESSEE	39-17-308; 49-2-120; 49-6-4503 to 49-6-45; 49-7-123	No; harassment: class A misdemeanor	Each school district required to adopt policy prohibiting bullying or cyberbullying, including description of expected behavior, consequences, procedures for reporting, investigation, response, and counseling and support services, 45-6-4503	Cyberbullying specifically defined, 49-6-4502; specifically included in directives for school policies, 45-6-4503	Governing body of each Local Education Agency (LEA) and each higher education institution must adopt written policy prohibiting hazing by any student or organization sanctioned by LEA or the institution; policy must be distributed or made available to each student at beginning of year and time set aside to specifically discuss policy and ramifications as criminal offense and institutional penalties that may be imposed by LEA or higher education institution, 49-2-120; 49-7-123

Table 38: Bullying—Continued

State	Code Section	Criminalized Specifically	State Policy	Cyber Recognized Specifically	Hazing
TEXAS	Educ. §§ 37.0832; 37.151 to 37.157; 37.218; Penal § 42.07	No; harassment: class B misdemeanor; 2nd and subsequent offense: class A misdemeanor, Penal § 42.07	Each school board required to adopt policy prohibiting bullying, Educ. § 37.0832	Cyberbullying specifically defined as use of any electronic communication device to engage in bullying or intimidation, Educ. § 37.218; definition of bullying in Educ. § 37.0832 includes expression through electronic means	Hazing or failure to report by individual: class B misdemeanor; if serious bodily injury, class A misdemeanor; if death, state jail felony, Educ. § 37.152; if organization condones or encourages hazing or if officers or members, or alumni commit or assist in commission of hazing: misdemeanor punishable by fine $5,000 to $10,000; if personal injury, property damage, or other loss: fine $5,000 to double amount lost or expenses incurred, Educ. § 37.153; educational institution may also enforce its own penalties, Educ. § 37.156

Table 38: Bullying—Continued

State	Code Section	Criminalized Specifically	State Policy	Cyber Recognized Specifically	Hazing
UTAH	Bullying and Hazing: 53A-11a-101 to 53A-11a-402; 76-5-107.5; 79-9-201		Each school board required to adopt bullying, cyber-bullying, harassment, hazing, and retaliation policy, 53A-11a-301; Bd. of Educ. must produce model policy and post on Bd. of Educ. website, 53A-11a-302	Cyberbullying specifically defined, 53A-11a-102; cyberbullying specifically prohibited, 53A-11a-201; Bd. of Educ. model policy must include cyberbullying, 53A-11a-302	School board anti-bullying policies and Bd. of Educ. model policy specifically include hazing, 53A-11a-301; criminal violations include: hazing: class B misdemeanor; if act involves operation of motor vehicle, consumption of alcohol or drugs: class A misdemeanor; if dangerous weapon or serious bodily injury: 3rd degree felony; if dangerous weapon and serious bodily injury: 2nd degree felony, in addition to any other charges, 76-5-107.5

Table 38: Bullying—Continued

State	Code Section	Criminalized Specifically	State Policy	Cyber Recognized Specifically	Hazing
VERMONT	Tit. 13, § 1027; Tit. 16, §§ 11(a)(32); 570 to 570L		It is Vermont policy that all Vermont educational institutions provide safe, orderly, civil, and positive learning environments. Harassment, hazing, and bullying have no place and will not be tolerated in Vermont schools; no Vermont student should feel threatened or be discriminated against while enrolled in a Vermont school; each school board must adopt, enforce, and make available harassment, hazing, and bullying prevention policies at least as stringent as model policy developed by Educ. Secretary; if board fails to adopt policy, most current model policy is in effect by default, Tit. 16, § 570	No; definition of bullying includes act conducted by electronic means, Tit. 16, § 11(a)(32)	Civil penalty for hazing: Fine up to $5,000; no statutory criminal penalty; educational institution may impose its own penalties, Tit. 16, §§ 570j to 570L

Table 38: Bullying—Continued

State	Code Section	Criminalized Specifically	State Policy	Cyber Recognized Specifically	Hazing
VIRGINIA	18.2-56; 18.2-152.7:1; 22.1-276.01; 22.1-279.6; 22.1-291.4	No; harassment by computer: class 1 misdemeanor, 18.2-152.7:1	Bd. of Educ. to establish model codes for student conduct, including policy on bullying, to aid local school boards; local boards required to adopt policies at least as stringent as model policy, 22.1-279.6; each school board required to implement education procedures for school board employees about bullying, as defined in § 22.1-276.01, and need to create bully-free environment, 22.1-291.4	Definition of bullying specifically includes cyberbullying, 22.1-476.01	Class 1 misdemeanor; any person receiving bodily injury by hazing has right to sue, civilly, guilty person(s); presiding official of publicly funded school, college, or university shall sanction and discipline student according to school policy and report hazing causing bodily injury to county or city attorney, 18.2-56

Table 38: Bullying—Continued

State	Code Section	Criminalized Specifically	State Policy	Cyber Recognized Specifically	Hazing
WASHINGTON	9.61.260; 28A.300.285; 28B.10.900 to 28B.10.901	No	Each school district is required to adopt policy to prohibit bullying that at minimum incorporates the state model policy, 28A.300.285	Advisory committee of state school directors' association to develop model policy prohibiting cyberbullying, including educational materials on seriousness of cyberbullying and responsible and safe internet use, 28A.300.285; cyberstalking, defined as using lewd or obscene words with intent to harass or embarrass: gross misdemeanor, 9.61.260	Hazing: misdemeanor; groups that knowingly permit hazing are strictly liable and directors of group may be individually liable for damages, 288.10.901 Any organization, association, or student living group that knowingly permits hazing is strictly liable for harm caused to persons or property resulting from hazing. If the organization, association, or student living group is a corporation whether for profit or nonprofit, the individual directors of the corporation may be held individually liable for damages.
WEST VIRGINIA	18-2C-1 through 18-2C-6; 18-16-2 to 18-16-3; 61-8-16	No	Each county board is required to adopt policy prohibiting bullying; the board has control over content if it contains requirements listed in statute, 18-2C-3	No; definition of bullying includes electronic communication or transmission, 18-2C-2	Misdemeanor punishable by imprisonment in county or regional jail for up to 9 mos. and/or fine $100 to $1,000, unless act would otherwise be felony, 18-16-3

Table 38: Bullying—Continued

State	Code Section	Criminalized Specifically	State Policy	Cyber Recognized Specifically	Hazing
WISCONSIN	118.02; 118.46; 947.0125; 947.013; 948.51	No; conduct that repeatedly harasses or intimidates another and has no legitimate purpose: class B forfeiture, 947.013; sending harassing electronic communication: class B misdemeanor, 947.0125	Dept. of Instruction shall develop a model policy prohibiting bullying; each school board is required to adopt anti-bullying policy and may elect to adopt the state's model policy, 118.46; the Legislature has declared Wednesday of the 4th week in September to be Bullying Awareness Day, 118.02	No	Class A misdemeanor; if great bodily harm: class H felony; if death: class G felony, 948.51
WYOMING	Safe School Climate Act: 21-4-311 to 21-4-315	No	Each school district is required to adopt policy prohibiting bullying, including consequences, procedures for reporting, documentation, and investigation; Dept. of Educ. to provide model K-12 to assist school districts in developing policies, 21-4-314	No; definition of "harassment, intimidation, or bullying" includes electronic communication, 21-4-312	No

39. CIVIL RIGHTS

Civil rights laws are among the most volatile and controversial in the American legal system. The force behind these laws is that certain groups of individuals in our society need protection from infringement on certain basic rights that are recognized under our legal system and are inherent in our form of government.

Civil rights are considered fundamental to all citizens under the Constitution of the United States. These rights include freedom of speech and association, freedom to seek employment, and freedom from discrimination on the basis of religious belief, race, or national origin. When certain groups have historically been denied any of these civil rights, the government has stepped in to make it illegal to interfere in that group's exercise of their rights. For example, African Americans historically have been excluded from certain types of activities in pursuit of their livelihoods. Thus civil rights laws have been enacted at both the federal and state levels to both guarantee African Americans their rights to freely seek employment in the workplace and to obtain an education in the institution of their choice without fear of discrimination on the basis of race and also to provide a legal remedy for individuals who are discriminated against. Under civil rights law, acts by certain classes of people that deny others their civil rights can be either criminal in nature or actionable in civil court.

Interestingly, over the last three years since this book was last updated, nearly every state has amended or proposed amendments to its civil rights laws to include sexual orientation to the list of protected persons. Several other states have updated their statutes to include various handicaps and accommodations, such as need for service animals.

Federal civil rights laws may be enforced by the Justice Department. Usually, violations of the laws are punished by fines and/or injunctions. They may also serve as the basis for private lawsuits by individuals. Civil rights laws usually specify limits to the amount of recovery available in lawsuits filed under them. Also, they often require that a civil rights suit be filed under the available statute rather than under general common law. This is called the doctrine of preemption, where civil rights laws preempt ordinary tort actions. Preemption is important because it caps the amount of damages for which a defendant may be liable.

Many states have gone even further than the federal laws in protecting civil rights. In those states that have established their own civil rights laws, most have authorized either the creation of new state agencies or have authorized existing agencies to handle the enforcement, administration, and/or investigation of violations of the laws. In some cases, the jurisdiction of the agencies is preemptive. For example, if a worker is fired because of his or her age, the firing may violate civil rights laws against age discrimination. If the state laws preempt private actions, the employee may only bring the complaint against the employer through the state agency or under the state law. In this case, the employee is bound by any restrictions regarding the type or size of the remedy. If the state law is not preemptive, or if the state law permits separate rights of action by the employee, the employee will be free to pursue his or her own course of action against the employer in court. The potential recovery for individual acts of discrimination or other civil rights infringements can be virtually limitless.

In many states, civil rights laws may be very specifically divided in coverage and in agencies within state government. Housing and employment are the most frequent specific types of discrimination covered by state laws.

Table 39: Civil Rights

State	Code Section	Agency	Administrative Preemption
ALABAMA	Age: 25-1-20 to 25-1-29; Housing: 24-8-1 to 24-8-15	Age: Alabama Dept. of Economic and Community Affairs	No
ALASKA	Generally: 18.80.200 to 18.80.295; Education: 14.18.010	Commission for Human Rights; Bd. of Regents	No
ARIZONA	41-1401 to 41-1493.04	Civil Rights Advisory Bd.	No
ARKANSAS	Generally: 16-123-107 to 16-123-348; Age; Public Employment: 21-3-201 to 206; Credit: 4-87-101 to 4-87-105; Employment: 11-4-601	Employment: Dept. of Labor	No
CALIFORNIA	Public Accommodations: Civ. §§ 51 to 53.7; Housing & Employment: Gov't §§ 12940 to 12956.2	Civ. Code: None; Gov't Code: Dept. of Fair Employment and Housing	No
COLORADO	24-34-301 to 24-34-804	Civil Rights Commission.	Yes, with exception
CONNECTICUT	46a-51 to 46a-125	Comm. on Human Rights and Opportunities	Yes
DELAWARE	Housing: Tit. 6, §§ 4601 to 4620; Employment: Tit. 19, §§ 710 to 728; Public Accommodations: Tit. 6, §§ 4500 to 4513	Housing & Pub. Accomm.: Human Relations Comm.; Employment: Dept. of Labor	Yes
DISTRICT OF COLUMBIA	Generally: 2-1401.01 to 2-1404,04; Handicapped: 7-1001 to 7-1009	Generally: Commission. on Human Rights; Handicapped: None	No
FLORIDA	760.01 to 760.854	Commission on Human Relations	Yes
GEORGIA	Credit: 7-6-1 to 7-6-2; Housing: 8-3-200 to 8-3-223; Age: 34-1-2; Public Employment: 45-19-20 to 45-19-46	Public Employment and Housing: Commission on Equal Opportunities	No
HAWAII	Employment: 378-1 to 378-6; Public Accommodations: 489-1 to 489-23; Housing: 515-1 to 515-20	Civil Rights Commission	Yes
IDAHO	67-5901 to 67-5912	Commission on Human Rights	No
ILLINOIS	775 §§ 5/1-101 to 5/10-104	Human Rights Commission and Dept. of Human Rights	Yes
INDIANA	22-9-1-1 to 22-9-10-15	Civil Rights Commission	No
IOWA	Generally: 216.1 to 216.21; Fair Employment: 729.4	Generally: Civil Rights Commission; Fair Employment: None	Generally: Yes; Fair Employment: No
KANSAS	44-1001 to 44-1138	Human Rights Commission	Yes
KENTUCKY	344.010 to 344.990	Commission on Human Rights	Yes
LOUISIANA	Employment: 23:301 to 23:369; Handicapped: 46:2251 to 46:2256; Housing: 51:2601 to 51:2614	Handicapped: None; Housing: Louisiana Dept. of Justice; Employment: None	Handicapped: No; Housing: No; Employment: No
MAINE	Tit. 5, §§ 4551 to 4634	Human Rights Commission	Yes
MARYLAND	State Gov't §§ 20-101 to 20-1203	Commission on Human Relations	Yes
MASSACHUSETTS	Generally: Ch. 151B, §§ 1 to 10; Public Accommodations: Ch. 272, §§ 98 to 98B	Generally: Commission Against Discrimination; Public Accommodations: None	Generally: Yes; Public Accommodations: No

Private Action Permitted	Attorney Fees	Statute of Limitations
Yes	Age: Yes; Housing: Discretionary	Age: 300 days; Housing: 180 days with agency; private actions: 1 yr.
Yes	Discretionary	Not specified
Yes	Yes	2 yrs.; 180 days through the Civil Rights Div.
Public Employment: No; Credit: Yes; Employment: Yes; Generally: Yes	Credit: Yes; Employment: Yes; Generally: Discretionary	Credit: 1 yr.; Employment: 2 yrs.; Generally: 1 yr.
Yes	Yes	Civ. Code: 3 yrs.; Gov't Code: 1 yr./agency
Yes	Yes	Variable
Yes	Yes	180 days, 30 days if violation of § 46a-80a
Housing: Yes; Employment: Yes; Public Accomm.: No	Housing: Yes; Employment: Yes; Public Accomm.: No	Employment: 90/120 days; Housing: 1 yr.; Public Accomm..: 90 days
Generally: Yes; Handicapped: No	Generally: Yes; Handicapped: No	Generally: 1 yr.; Handicapped: Not specified
Yes, after exhaustion	Yes	365 days/agency
Credit: Yes; Age: No; Public Employment: No; Housing: Yes	Credit: No; Age: No; Public Employment: Discretionary; Housing: Yes	Public Employment: 180 days/agency Housing: 1 yr./agency; 2 yrs./private
Employment: No; Housing: Yes, with exceptions; Public Accommodations: Yes	Employment: Yes; Housing: Yes; Public Accommodations: Yes	Employment: 90 days; Housing: 1 yr.; Public Accommodations: Not specified
Yes	No	1 yr.
Yes, for temporary relief	Yes	180 days
Yes	No	Not specified
Generally: Yes; Fair Employment: No	Generally: Yes; Fair Employment: No	Generally: 180 days; Fair Employment: Not specified
Generally: No; Housing: Yes	No	Generally: 6 mos.; Housing: 1 yr.; Employment and Age: 300 days
Yes	Yes	180 days
Handicapped: Yes; Housing: Yes; Employment: Yes	Handicapped: Yes; Housing: Yes; Employment: Yes	Handicapped: 80 days to 1 yr.; Housing: 1 yr./agency, 2 yrs./private action; Employment: Not specified
Yes	Yes, with conditions	6 mos.
Yes	Discretionary	6 mos.
Generally: No; Public Accommodations: Yes	Generally: Yes; Public Accommodations: No	Generally: 300 days; Civil Rights Actions: 3 yrs., Ch. 260, § 5B

Table 39: Civil Rights—Continued

State	Code Section	Agency	Administrative Preemption
MICHIGAN	37.2101 to 37.2803	Civil Rights Commission	No
MINNESOTA	363A.01 to 363A.44	Dept. of Human Rights	No
MISSISSIPPI	State Service Employment: 25-9-149; Government Housing: 43-33-723 to 43-33-727	Government Housing: Home Corporation Oversight Committee; State Service Employment: None	Government Housing: Yes; State Service Employment: Yes
MISSOURI	Generally: 213.010 to 213.137; Credit: 408.550	Generally: Commission on Human Rights; Credit: None	Generally: Yes; Credit: No
MONTANA	49-1-101 to 49-4-215	Commission for Human Rights	Yes
NEBRASKA	Generally: 20-126 to 20-170; Housing: 20-301 to 20-344; Employment: 48-1101 to 48-1126	Equal Opportunity Commission	Generally: No; Employment: Yes
NEVADA	Credit: 598B.010 to 598B.180; Employment: 613.310 to 613.435; Public Accommodations: 651.050 to 651.120	Employment: Equal Rights Commission; Public Accommodations: Equal Rights Commission; Credit: Banking Division	Employment: Yes; Public Accommodations: No; Credit: No
NEW HAMPSHIRE	354-A:1 to 354-A:26	Commission for Human Rights	Yes
NEW JERSEY	10:5-1 to 10:5-49	Division on Civil Rights	No
NEW MEXICO	28-1-1 to 28-23-6	Human Rights Commission	No
NEW YORK	Civ. Rights §§ 1 to 84; Exec. §§ 290 to 301	Generally: Division of Human Rights; Public Housing: State Human Rights Appeal Board	No
NORTH CAROLINA	Housing: 41A-1 to 41A-10; Employment: 143-422.1 to 143-422.3	Human Relations Commission	No
NORTH DAKOTA	14-02.4-01 to 14-02.5-46	Division of Human Rights	No
OHIO	4112.01 to 4112.99	Civil Rights Commission	No
OKLAHOMA	Tit. 25, §§ 1101 to 1706	Human Rights Commission	Yes
OREGON	659A.001 to 659A.990	Bureau of Labor and Industries	No
PENNSYLVANIA	Tit. 43, §§ 951 to 963	Human Relations Commission	Yes
RHODE ISLAND	Employment: 28-5-1 to 28-5-42 ; Housing: 34-37-1 to 34-37-11; Handicapped: 42-87-1 to 42-87-5	Handicapped, Housing: Commission for Human Rights; Employment: Commission Against Discrimination	Handicapped, Housing: No; Employment: Yes
SOUTH CAROLINA	Employment: 1-13-10 to 1-13-110; Housing: 31-21-10 to 31-21-150	Human Affairs Commission	Employment: Yes; Housing: No
SOUTH DAKOTA	Generally: 20-13-1 to 20-13-56; Sex: 60-12-15 to 60-12-21	Generally: Commission of Human Rights	Generally: Yes; Sex: No
TENNESSEE	4-21-101 to 4-21-1004	Human Rights Commission	No
TEXAS	Disabled: Hum. Res. §§ 121.001 to 121.011; Employment: Lab. §§ 21.001 to 22.004; Housing: Prop. §§ 301.001 to 301.17	Disabled: None; Other: Human Rights Commission	No

Private Action Permitted	Attorney Fees	Statute of Limitations
Yes	Yes	3 yrs.
Yes	Yes	1 yr.
Government Housing: No; State Service Employment: No	Government Housing: No; State Service Employment: No	Government Housing: Not specified; State Service Employment: Not specified
Generally: Yes; Credit: Yes	Yes	Generally: 180 days with commission; 2 yrs. civil action; Credit: Not specified.
Yes	Yes	180 days with certain exceptions
Yes	Yes	300 days
Yes	Employment: Yes; Public Accommodations: Yes; Credit: No	Employment: 180 days; Public Accommodations: 1 yr.; Credit: 1 yr.
No	Discretionary	180 days
Yes	Yes	180 days/agency; 2 yrs./private action
Yes	Yes	180 days with commission; 30 days for de novo appeal
Yes	No	Variable
Employment: No; Housing: Yes	Employment: No; Housing: Yes	Employment: None; Housing: 1 yr.
Yes	Yes	Housing: 180 days; Employment: 300 days
Yes	Discretionary	1 yr.
No	Yes	180 days
Yes	Yes	1 yr.
Yes	Discretionary	180 days/agency; 2 yrs./private action
Yes	Yes	Housing: 1 yr./agency; 2 yrs./private action; Employment: 1 yr.; Handicapped: Not specified
Employment: No; Housing: Yes	Employment: No; Housing: Yes	Employment: 180 days; Housing: 180 days/agency; 1 yr./private action
Generally: Yes; Sex: Yes	Generally: Yes; Sex: Yes	Generally: 180 days; Sex: 2 yrs.
Yes	Yes	180 days/agency; 1 yr./private action
Yes	No	Disabled: Not specified; Employment: 180 days/agency, 2 yrs./private action; Housing: 1 yr./agency, 2 yrs./private

Table 39: Civil Rights—Continued

State	Code Section	Agency	Administrative Preemption
UTAH	Public Accommodations: 13-7-1 to 13-7-4; Employment: 34A-5-101 to 34A-5-108; Housing: 57-21-1 to 57-21-14	Public Accommodations: None; Employment: Antidiscrimination Division; Housing: Labor Commission	Public Accommodations: No; Employment: Yes; Housing: No
VERMONT	Public Accommodations; Tit. 9, §§ 4500 to 4507; Employment: Tit. 21, §§ 495 to 496A	Public Accommodations Human Rights Commission; Employment: None	No
VIRGINIA	Generally: 2.2-3900 to 2.2-3903; Housing: 36-96.1 to 36-96.23; Equal Pay: 40.1-28.6	Generally: Human Rights Council; Housing: Fair Housing Board and Real Estate Board; Equal Pay: None;	No
WASHINGTON	49.60.010 to 49.60.505	Human Rights Commission	No
WEST VIRGINIA	5-11-1 to 5-11B-7	Human Rights Commission	No
WISCONSIN	Housing & Public Places: 106.50 to 106.58; Employment: 111.31 to 111.397	Housing & Public Places; Employment: Dept. of Workfare Development	Housing & Public Places: No; Employment: Yes
WYOMING	Employment: 27-9-101 to 27-9-106	Dept. of Employment	Yes

Private Action Permitted	Attorney Fees	Statute of Limitations
Public Accommodations: Yes; Employment: No; Housing: Yes	Public Accommodations: Not specified; Employment: Yes; Housing: Yes	Public Accommodations: 3 yrs., 78-12-26; Employment: 180 days; Housing: 180 days/ agency; 2 yrs./private
Yes	Yes	Public Accommodations: Not specified; Employment: 6 yrs., Tit. 12, § 511
Yes	Generally: Yes; Housing: Yes; Equal Pay: Yes	Generally: 180 days; Housing: 1 yr./agency, 2 yr./private
Yes	Yes	6 mos.; real estate: 1 yr.
Yes	Yes	1 yr./agency; 2 yrs./private action
Housing & Public Places: Yes; Employment: Yes	Housing & Public Places: Yes; Employment: No	Housing & Public Places: 1 yr./private action; 1 yr./agency; Employment: 300 days
No	No	6 mos.

40. CIVIL SHOPLIFTING

Acts of shoplifting cost retailers billions of dollars each year. In an effort to reduce the frequency and economic impact of this type of theft, all 50 states and the District of Columbia have enacted civil shoplifting statutes. These statutes, which operate independently of and in addition to the respective state's criminal statutes, provide retailers a special civil remedy against individuals who shoplift from their stores. Most civil shoplifting statutes permit a retailer to recover from the shoplifter not only the actual damages suffered as a result of the incident of shoplifting, but also a substantial civil penalty. In Mississippi, for instance, a retailer is entitled to recover actual damages incurred (e.g., the cost of replacing the item stolen), plus a civil penalty of three times the value of the item, or up to $200, whichever is greater. The additional civil penalty is meant to reimburse the retailer for general overhead costs associated with its loss prevention program. The theory is that the shoplifter, as opposed to the retailer or its paying customers, should bear responsibility for the costs associated with shoplifting.

With the adoption of these statutes, many states sought to decriminalize shoplifting by providing retailers an alternative to criminal prosecution as a means to restitution. In practice, however, most large retailers pursue criminal charges and a civil remedy.

Retailers rarely file suit to collect under the civil shoplifting statute, but instead rely on the statute as authority for demanding money from shoplifters through a series of demand letters. Often, these letters are sent while the criminal charges are pending, leading many recipients to believe payment will result in the charges being dismissed, which it will not.

Many merchants engage the services of independent collection firms to harvest civil penalties from those accused of shoplifting. One such firm, which represents several large retailers, reported sending over 1 million civil demand letters a year. While civil shoplifting statutes have developed into lucrative profit centers for retailers and collection firms, there is little evidence to indicate they have had any positive impact on reducing incidents of shoplifting, stabilizing the price of consumer goods, or decriminalizing acts of petty theft.

Critics argue the statutes unfairly subject shoplifters to two penalties for the same offense: a criminal penalty paid to the state, and a second penalty paid to the retailer. Others have scrutinized the proportionality of the amount demanded compared to the actual direct damage incurred. In most states, a stolen candy bar can result in a civil penalty of over $100, in addition to any criminal penalty imposed by the state. Furthering this criticism is the fact that many states allow for a substantial civil penalty even when the item is immediately returned to the shelf in merchantable condition. Some scholars have also expressed concern that the statutes unfavorably impact the poor.

Although a number of common themes can be identified among state civil shoplifting statutes, no two statutes are the same. This chapter provides and compares the significant components of each state's statute, specifically as it pertains to 1) actual damages recoverable, 2) additional penalties, 3) attorney's fees, 4) pre-suit demand letters, and 5) the impact of a conviction on a retailer's ability to recover a civil remedy under the statute. The following sections highlight significant themes and anomalies among the state statutes.

Actual Damages

Every state's civil shoplifting statute allows for the recovery of actual damages (or at least includes actual damages in the calculation of compensatory damages). Most states limit actual damages if the merchandise is recovered in a merchantable condition. Some states, however, provide no limits on actual damages. Nine states' statutes expressly provide that actual damages may include incidental or consequential damages. Of those states, four exclude from incidental damages lost time or wages, while two specifically permit recovery of those particular expenses.

Additional Penalties

Every state except Nebraska and Maryland grants retailers authority to collect penalties in addition to direct damage sustained from the incident. Most statutes set forth the maximum penalty recoverable:

- Three states have a maximum penalty of $50.

- Eight states have a maximum penalty between $100 and $200.
- Nine states have a maximum penalty between $250 and $300.
- Eight states have a maximum penalty between $350 and $500.
- Seven states have a maximum penalty between $550 and $1000.
- Two states have a maximum penalty in excess of $1000.

Of the states that do not provide a specific dollar limit on civil penalties, most fix the penalty as a multiple of an unlimited retail value of the stolen merchandise, or an unlimited retail value of the stolen merchandise in addition to a specified penalty. Three states require civil penalties be reduced by the amount of court-ordered restitution received by the retailer. Only four states reduce the amount recoverable based on whether the merchandise was recovered or the condition of the merchandise recovered. Oklahoma allows for the performance of community service in lieu of paying the additional penalty.

Attorney's Fees

A majority of states' statutes specifically provide for the recovery of a reasonable attorney's fee. Only three states put a monetary cap on attorney's fees recoverable, and only seven specifically require that the retailer be the prevailing party to recover reasonable attorney's fees. Two states expressly require suit be filed (after all statutory demand letter procedures are followed) in order to recover reasonable attorney's fees. In Maryland, if the alleged shoplifter prevails in the civil action, he or she is entitled to an award of attorney's fees.

Pre-Suit Demand Letters

Most states' statutes expressly authorize, condone, or require retailers to send civil demand letters to alleged shoplifters prior to, or instead of, filing suit. Nineteen states explicitly reserve a statutory right for retailers to send a civil demand letter to an alleged shoplifter. Eleven states list the sending of a demand letter as a condition precedent to maintaining a civil action under the state's civil shoplifting statute. The remaining twenty states and the District of Columbia make no mention of a demand letter in their civil shoplifting statutes.

Only two states require a copy of the civil shoplifting statute be sent with a demand letter. Nine states specify how much time a recipient shall have to pay the demand in order to avoid a civil action—ranging from 15 to 30 days.

Criminal Conviction

Interestingly, most state statutes specifically permit collection of shoplifting civil penalties even where no criminal conviction was obtained. In fact, thirty-three states provide that no conviction is required, seventeen are silent on the issue, and only one state requires a conviction in order to impose the civil penalty. In two states, although a conviction is not required, efforts to obtain civil recovery must be stayed during the pendency of any criminal action. In South Carolina, if the retailer pursues the civil remedy, it is prohibited from filing criminal charges.

---

*This chapter was authored by Ryan P. Sullivan, Assistant Professor of Law with the University of Nebraska College of Law.

Table 40: Civil Shoplifting

State	Code Section	Actual Damages	Additional Penalties
ALABAMA	6-5-270 to 6-5-275	Full retail value of merchandise if not recovered in merchantable condition	$200 for expenses in recovery of merchandise
ALASKA	09.68.110	Actual damages recoverable (not defined in statute)	Lesser of retail value or $1,000 plus additional penalty $100 to $200
ARIZONA	12-691 to 12-694	Actual damages recoverable (not defined in statute)	Retail value of merchandise, plus additional minimum penalty of $250
ARKANSAS	16-122-101 to 16-122-103	Full retail value of merchandise if not recovered in merchantable condition	$200 collectable with demand letter or up to $1,000 in civil penalties if civil action
CALIFORNIA	Penal § 490.5	Full retail value of merchandise if not recovered in merchantable condition	$50 to $500
COLORADO	§ 13-21-107.5	Actual damages recoverable (not defined in statute)	$100 to $250; $100 if theft of shopping cart
CONNECTICUT	52-564A; 52-572	Full retail value of merchandise if not recovered in merchantable condition	Up to $300
DELAWARE	Tit. 10, § 8143	Full retail value of merchandise if not recovered in merchantable condition	Greater of retail value or $150
DISTRICT OF COLUMBIA	27-102	Greater of full retail value of merchandise if not recovered, loss of value of merchandise if recovered, or $50	Treble amount of actual damages
FLORIDA	772.11; 772.104	Actual damages recoverable (not defined in statute)	Greater of treble actual damages or $200
GEORGIA	51-10-6	Actual damages, including value of property and "any other loss sustained as a result of the willful damage or theft offense"	Greater of treble actual damages or $300 if actual damages are less than $5,000
HAWAII	663A-2	Actual damages recoverable (not defined in statute)	$75 collectable with demand letter; additional civil penalty of $50 to $500 may be awarded by court
IDAHO	48-701 to 48-702	Full retail value of merchandise	$100 to $250
ILLINOIS	720 § 5/16-27	Full retail value of merchandise	$100 to $1,000
INDIANA	34-24-3-1 to 34-24-4	Actual damages with irrebuttable presumption of at least $100 loss if value is less or merchandise is recovered, plus actual expenses for loss of time and wages in recovery	Up to treble amount of actual damages

Attorney Fees	Pre-Suit Demand Letter	Criminal Conviction
Reasonable attorney fees and court costs up to $1,000 recoverable in civil action	Statutory right to demand letter; letter must be sent at least 30 days before filing of action; statute requires certain contents in demand letter	Conviction not condition precedent to maintaining action
Prevailing party entitled to reasonable attorney fees	Demand letter must be sent at least 15 days before filing of action unless individual is charged or convicted	
	Conviction not condition precedent to maintaining action; person convicted for shoplifting precluded from denying essential allegations of the offense in any civil recovery action under this article	
Reasonable attorney fees and court costs recoverable in civil action	Demand letter must be sent at least 30 days before filing of action	Conviction not condition precedent to maintaining action
		Conviction not condition precedent to maintaining action
Reasonable attorney fees and court costs		Conviction not condition precedent to maintaining action
Reasonable attorney fees recoverable with no apparent requirement that suit must be filed	Statutory right to demand letter; letter may be sent at least 20 days before filing of action; no civil action may be maintained if demand letter is complied with within 20 days	Conviction not condition precedent to maintaining action
Reasonable attorney fees and court costs recoverable in civil action	Demand letter is condition precedent to maintaining an action; statute requires certain contents in demand letter	
Reasonable attorney fees and court costs if statutory demand letter procedures are followed before filing action	Demand letter is condition precedent to maintaining an action; statute requires certain contents in demand letter	
	Statutory right to demand letter; lack of demand letter reduces amount recoverable for civil penalty	Conviction not necessary to bring action
Reasonable attorney fees and costs recoverable		
Reasonable attorney fees and court costs		Conviction not condition precedent to maintaining action
Reasonable attorney fees and court costs recoverable in civil action		Conviction not condition precedent to maintaining action; lack of conviction bars recovery of punitive damages

Table 40: Civil Shoplifting—Continued

State	Code Section	Actual Damages	Additional Penalties
IOWA	645.3; 613.16	Full retail value of merchandise if not recovered; actual damages of any decrease in value of recovered merchandise	Greater of $50 or actual costs up to $200; damages reduced by amount received by owner pursuant to court-ordered restitution; parent(s) of unemancipated minor child under 18 liable for any judgment against the child, subject to limits established in § 613.16
KANSAS	60-3331	Retail cost of merchandise	If not recovered in merchantable condition: greater of $50 or double retail value up to $500; if recovered in merchantable condition: greater of $50 or half of retail value up to $350; parents of unemancipated minor liable in amount of civil penalty or $50 if property recovered in merchantable condition
KENTUCKY	411.095	Actual damages recoverable (not defined in statute)	Retail value of merchandise up to $500 plus additional penalty $100 to $250
LOUISIANA	9:2799.1	Full retail value of merchandise if not recovered in merchantable condition	$50 to $500; damages reduced by amount recovered from offender as court-ordered restitution
MAINE	Tit. 14, § 8302	Full retail value of merchandise if not recovered in merchantable condition	Treble amount of retail value ($50 to $500)
MARYLAND	Cts. & Jud. Proc. § 3-1301 to 3-1309	Full retail value of merchandise if not recovered in merchantable condition plus actual damages, not including loss of time or wages incurred in connection with apprehension or prosecution of shoplifter	Additional penalties not permitted
MASSACHUSETTS	Ch. 231, §§ 85R ½; 85G	Actual damages recoverable (not defined in statute)	If retail value $50 to $250: up to $50; if retail value $250 to $500: up to $500
MICHIGAN	600.2953	Full retail value of merchandise if not recovered in merchantable condition	10 times retail value ($50 to $200)
MINNESOTA	540.18; 604.14	Full retail value of merchandise at time of theft; no apparent limitation on whether it is recovered	Greater of $50 or full retail value; conspicuous notice of civil liability prerequisite to recovery
MISSISSIPPI	97-23-96	Actual damages recoverable (not defined in statute); statute specifically provides that recovery of stolen goods regardless of condition shall not affect the right to the minimum recovery	Greater of $200 or treble actual damages; "In no event shall punitive damages be awarded under this section"
MISSOURI	570.087	Full retail value of merchandise (no apparent limitation on whether it is recovered); plus any incidental costs to owner up to $100	$100 to $250

Attorney Fees	Pre-Suit Demand Letter	Criminal Conviction
Reasonable attorney fees may be awarded in civil action	Demand letter required; If demand includes threat of criminal prosecution, retailer is precluded from civil recovery	Conviction not condition precedent to maintaining action
	Statutory right to demand letter	Conviction not condition precedent to maintaining action
	Statutory right to demand letter; demand letter must include copy of civil recovery statute	Conviction not condition precedent to maintaining action
Reasonable attorney fees may be awarded to prevailing party in a civil action	Demand letter is condition precedent to maintaining an action; demand letter must be prepared by lawyer admitted to practice law in State of Maryland; 1st demand letter must be sent at least 15 days before filing of action; 2nd demand letter must be sent at least 10 days before filing of action; statute requires certain contents in demand letter	Conviction not condition precedent to maintaining action; any restitution shall be reduced by any civil damages paid
	Statutory right to demand letter; statute requires certain contents in demand letter	
Reasonable attorney fees and court costs recoverable with no apparent requirement that suit must be filed	Statutory right to demand letter; statute requires certain contents in demand letter	
	Statutory right to demand letter; statute requires certain contents in demand letter; demand letter must include copy of civil recovery statute	Conviction not condition precedent to maintaining action
Reasonable attorney fees and court costs recoverable in civil action	Demand letter is condition precedent to maintaining an action; letter must be sent at least 30 days before filing of action; statute requires certain contents in demand letter	
Reasonable attorney fees and court costs recoverable with no apparent requirement that suit must be filed		Conviction not condition precedent to maintaining action

Table 40: Civil Shoplifting—Continued

State	Code Section	Actual Damages	Additional Penalties
MONTANA	27-1-718	Actual damages recoverable (not defined in statute)	Greater of $100 or retail value up to $1,000
NEBRASKA	25-21,194	Actual property damage or loss sustained as direct result of shoplifting: full retail value; cost of repair; cost of replacement	Additional penalties not permitted
NEVADA	597.860; 597.870	Full retail value of merchandise (no apparent limitation on whether it is recovered)	$100 to $250
NEW HAMPSHIRE	507:8-f; 544-C:1	Full retail value of merchandise if not recovered in merchantable condition	Up to $400
NEW JERSEY	2A:61C-1	Value of merchandise up to $500 if merchandise not recovered in merchantable condition plus additional damages arising from incident, not to include any loss of time or wages incurred	Up to $150
NEW MEXICO	30-16-21	Full retail value of merchandise if not recovered in merchantable condition	$100 to $250
NEW YORK	Gen. Oblig. § 11-105	Full retail value of merchandise up to $1500 if not recovered in merchantable condition	Greater of $75 or five times retail value up to $500
NORTH CAROLINA	1-538.2	Full retail value of merchandise if not recovered; loss of value of merchandise if not recovered in merchantable condition; plus consequential damages including lost wages in recovery	$150 to $1,000
NORTH DAKOTA	51-21-05	Full retail value of merchandise (no apparent limitation on whether it is recovered)	Up to $250 in exemplary damages
OHIO	2307.60; 2307.61; 3109.09	Full retail value of property considered in calculation of additional penalties	May elect to recover either: retail value of merchandise plus liquidated damages of $50 if at time of theft value of property was $50 or less; $100 if value $50 to $100; $150 if value over $100; or: liquidated damages of the greater of $200 or three times the retail value of the merchandise
OKLAHOMA	Tit. 21, § 1731.1	Full retail value of merchandise if not recovered or loss of value of merchandise if not recovered in merchantable condition	Exemplary damages or community service
OREGON	30.875	Actual damages recoverable (not defined in statute)	Retail value up to $500 plus $100 to $250

Attorney Fees	Pre-Suit Demand Letter	Criminal Conviction
		Conviction not condition precedent to maintaining action
Reasonable attorney fees and court costs recoverable in civil action if claim is not in Small Claims Court	Statutory right to demand letter	
Reasonable attorney fees and costs recoverable with no apparent requirement that suit must be filed		Conviction not condition precedent to maintaining action
Reasonable attorney fees may be awarded to prevailing party in a civil action	Demand letter is condition precedent to maintaining an action; letter must be sent at least 20 days before filing of action	Conviction not condition precedent to maintaining action
Reasonable attorney fees and costs recoverable with no apparent requirement that suit must be filed		Conviction of shoplifting under 30-16-20 is prerequisite to civil liability
	Statutory right to demand letter	Conviction not condition precedent to maintaining action
Reasonable attorney fees recoverable in civil action	Statutory right to demand letter; statute requires certain contents in demand letter	Conviction not condition precedent to maintaining action
Reasonable attorney fees and costs recoverable with no apparent requirement that suit must be filed		Conviction not condition precedent to maintaining action; if criminal theft charge is filed, merchant may not pursue civil damages until completion of criminal action
Reasonable attorney fees and court costs recoverable in civil action if statutory demand letter procedures are followed	Statutory right to demand letter; lack of demand letter precludes recovery of reasonable administrative costs, reasonable attorney fees and court costs; not prerequisite to suit but prerequisite to recover reasonable administrative costs, costs of maintaining the civil action and reasonable attorney fees; letter must be sent at least 30 days before filing of action; statute requires certain contents in demand letter	
Reasonable attorney fees and court costs recoverable in civil action		
	Statutory right to demand letter	Conviction not condition precedent to maintaining action

Table 40: Civil Shoplifting—Continued

State	Code Section	Actual Damages	Additional Penalties
PENNSYLVANIA	Tit. 42, § 8308	Full retail value of merchandise if not recovered; loss of value of merchandise if not recovered in merchantable condition; plus additional damages arising from incident, not to include any loss of time or wages incurred	Retail value plus $150
RHODE ISLAND	11-41-28	Full retail value of merchandise if not recovered in merchantable condition	Up to $100
SOUTH CAROLINA	15-75-40	Full retail value of merchandise if not recovered in merchantable condition up to $1,500	Greater of $150 or treble retail value, up to $500
SOUTH DAKOTA	22-30A-19.1	Full retail value of merchandise whether it is recovered in merchantable condition or not	Greater of $100 or four times retail value
TENNESSEE	39-14-144	Full retail value of property considered in calculation of compensatory damages	If merchandise is not recovered: greater of $100 or treble retail value; merchandise recovered not in merchantable condition: greater of $100 or treble loss in retail value; merchandise recovered in same condition: greater of $100 or double retail value; no civil remedy if listed retail value greater than $500
TEXAS	Civ. Prac. & Rem. §§ 134.001 to 134.005	Actual damages recoverable (not defined in statute)	Up to $1,000
UTAH	78B-3-108	Actual damages recoverable (not defined in statute)	Retail value up to $1,000 plus additional penalty of $100 to $500
VERMONT	Tit. 13, § 2579	Full retail value of merchandise if not recovered in merchantable condition	Greater of $25 or double retail value up to $300
VIRGINIA	8.01-44.4; 18.2-103; 18.2-104.1	Full retail value of property considered in calculation of additional penalty	Merchandise recovered in merchantable condition: up to $350; merchandise not recovered in merchantable condition: greater of $50 or double retail value
WASHINGTON	4.24.230	Actual damages recoverable (not defined in statute)	Retail value up to $2,850 plus additional penalty of $100 to $650
WEST VIRGINIA	61-3A-5	Full retail value of merchandise if not recovered in merchantable condition plus additional damages arising from incident, not to include any loss of time or wages incurred	Greater of $50 or double retail value

Attorney Fees	Pre-Suit Demand Letter	Criminal Conviction
Reasonable attorney fees and court costs recoverable in civil action	Demand letter is condition precedent to maintaining an action; letter must be sent at least 20 days before filing of action	Conviction not condition precedent to maintaining action
Court costs recoverable with no apparent requirement that suit must be filed	Statutory right to demand letter	Conviction not condition precedent to maintaining action
	Statutory right to demand letter; statute requires certain contents in demand letter	Conviction not condition precedent to maintaining action; retailer who utilizes civil remedy prohibited from filing criminal charges
	Statutory right to demand letter; lack of demand letter requires notice to and consent of attorney general to seek civil recovery under this statute	Conviction not condition precedent to maintaining action
Reasonable and necessary attorney fees may be awarded to prevailing party in a civil action		
Reasonable attorney fees and court costs recoverable in civil action	Demand letter condition precedent to maintaining an action; statute requires certain contents in demand letter	Conviction not condition precedent to maintaining action
	Statutory right to demand letter	Conviction not condition precedent to maintaining action
Reasonable and necessary attorney fees up to $150 may be awarded to prevailing party in a civil action	Statutory right to demand letter	Conviction not condition precedent to maintaining action; pendency of criminal prosecution based on same facts precludes civil action
Reasonable attorney fees and costs expended are recoverable with no apparent requirement that suit must be filed	Demand letter is condition precedent to maintaining an action; statute requires certain contents in demand letter	Conviction not condition precedent to maintaining action
Reasonable attorney fees may be awarded to prevailing party in a civil action	Statutory right to demand letter	Conviction not condition precedent to maintaining action

Table 40: Civil Shoplifting—Continued

State	Code Section	Actual Damages	Additional Penalties
WISCONSIN	943.51	Full retail value of merchandise if not recovered in merchantable condition	Up to treble amount of retail value; recovery barred if merchandise recovered undamaged and unused; recovery reduced by amount recovered from court-ordered restitution involving the same theft
WYOMING	1-1-127	Full retail value of merchandise if not recovered in merchantable condition	Double retail value of $50 to $1,000

Attorney Fees	Pre-Suit Demand Letter	Criminal Conviction
Reasonable attorney fees and costs recoverable with no apparent requirement that suit must be filed; total exemplary and reasonable attorney's fees must not exceed $300		Conviction not condition precedent to maintaining action
Reasonable attorney fees and costs recoverable with no apparent requirement that suit must be filed	Notice to law enforcement officials prerequisite to civil recovery	Conviction not condition precedent to maintaining action

41. CIVIL STATUTES OF LIMITATIONS

The idea behind statutes of limitations is mainly one of general practicability and fairness. It is never fair to let a legal matter hang unfinished over someone's head indefinitely. There needs to be a distinct end to each legal conflict in order to let the parties involved move on with their lives. Particular legal matters may cause parties to cease certain business transactions or personal activity as they await the outcome.

A similar dynamic is at work with respect to statutes of limitations. The offending party in any legal dispute knows that he or she committed or may be accused of committing some wrong against the other party. In such a case, the wronged party must decide whether to press a lawsuit in order to recover for his or her wrong. The law will not tolerate a procrastinative plaintiff, a plaintiff who delays for effect, or one who is negligent or forgetful. After a period of time has passed, the chance to sue disappears.

How Long?

The lengths of time for statutes of limitations correspond roughly to the amount of notice that both parties have regarding the underlying injury or wrong. The more notice both parties have that there is a problem and the more likely it is that the injured party will sue, the longer the statute of limitations. The less likely it is that the offending party will be aware of his wrong or the more inconsequential it is likely to be, the shorter the statute of limitations.

The longest statutes of limitations are generally those regarding the recovery of judgments after a lawsuit. Obviously, the parties are clearly on notice in this situation. If the losing party refuses to pay his judgment, it should come as no surprise that he will be sued, even if it is as many as ten years later. On the other hand, if one person is physically injured by another person but does not sue within a year or two, it is reasonable to expect that the plaintiff either forgot about the injury or it was not as serious as originally suspected. In this case, the potential defendant is protected from a lawsuit that he may not even be aware is pending, especially more than a year or two after the accident that caused the injury occurred.

Where no statute is listed on the following chart, it is probable that there is simply not a specific statute governing the situation. In these cases, a general civil statute of limitations most likely applies. For example, in cases of medical malpractice, the statute of limitations may just as easily be covered by the statute governing personal injury.

From When to When?

There are many interesting controversies about when statutes of limitations begin and end. In many cases, the injured party may not even know he was wronged until a great while after the wrong was committed. This is often true in the case of breach of contract or fraud, and it often arises, perhaps surprisingly, in cases of personal injury or medical malpractice. In the case of certain surgical procedures, the party may not know that, for example, a sponge was left in his abdomen or something else was done improperly—until years later. There has also been much controversy, now largely settled by statute, about whether the statute should begin to run when the wrong was committed or when it was discovered. Court decisions have largely gone in favor of the injured party, allowing the statute to start running upon discovery of the injury or when the injury or act of negligence should "reasonably have been discovered."

Most states "toll" or stop the statute of limitations upon the incapacity of the injured party. But there are a number of ways a person can be incapacitated. If the person has been committed to a mental hospital or is out of the country, these may toll the statute of limitations until they either regain their mental facilities or return from abroad.

Overall, the statutes of limitations are fair and reasonable limitations of potentially disruptive and always distracting legal action between parties. Dramatic stories about lawyers rushing to file papers before the statute runs out are almost always due to the injured party's (or the party's attorney's) procrastination or negligence.

Table 41: Civil Statutes of Limitations

State	Injury to Person	Libel/Slander	Fraud	Injury to Personal Property
ALABAMA	Under contract: 6 yrs., 6-2-34(9); in general: 2 yrs., 6-2-38(l)	2 yrs., 6-2-38(k)	2 yrs. from discovery, 6-2-3	6 yrs., 6-2-34(2)
ALASKA	2 yrs., 09.10.070; actions for certain felony sexual offenses may be brought at any time. Other sexual offenses: 3 yrs. 09.10.065	2 yrs., 09.10.070	Medical assistance payment fraud: 6 yrs. after act committed, or 3 yrs. after discovery, whichever is later. Not to exceed 10 yrs. 09.10.075	2 yrs., 09.10.070
ARIZONA	False imprisonment: 1 yr., 12-541; if not: 2 yrs., 12-542	1 yr., 12-541	3 yrs., 12-543(3)	2 yrs., 15-542
ARKANSAS	1 yr., 16-56-104	Libel: 3 yrs., 16-56-105; slander: 1 yr., 16-56-104	Common law fraud; fraud; deceit: 3 yrs., 16-56-105	3 yrs., 16-56-105
CALIFORNIA	False imprisonment: 1 yr., Civ. Proc. § 340(c); others 2 yrs. § 335.1	1 yr., Civ. Proc. § 340(c)	3 yrs., Civ. Proc. § 338(d)	3 yrs., Civ. Proc. §§ 338(b); 338(c)
COLORADO	1 yr., 13-80-103(1)(a); use or operation of motor vehicle: 3 yrs., 13-80-101(n); domestic violence: 6 yrs. 13-80-103.6; sexual assault, or sexual abuse against a child: 6 yrs. 13-80-103.7	1 yr., 13-80-103(1)(a)	3 yrs., 13-80-101(1)(c)	3 yrs. if from use or operation of a motor vehicle, 13-80-101(n)
CONNECTICUT	3 yrs., 52-577; injury caused by negligence: 2 yrs. 52-584	2 yrs., 52-597	3 yrs., 52-577	2 yrs. from discovery, max. 3 yrs. from act, 52-584

Professional Malpractice	Trespass	Collection of Rents	Contracts	Collection of Debt on Account	Judgments
Medical: 2 yrs., 6-5-482	6 yrs., 6-2-34(1); 6-2-34(2)	6 yrs., 6-2-34(5)	Written: 10 yrs. if under seal, 6-2-33 (1); 6 yrs. if not. 6-2-34 (4); oral: 6 yrs., 6-2-34(9)	6 yrs. stated liquidated account. 6-2-34(5); 3 yrs. open unliquidated account. 6-2-37	20 yrs., 6-2-32
2 yrs., 09.10.070	6 yrs., 09.10.05	10 yrs., 09.10.100	3 yrs., 09.10.053	10 yrs., 09.10.100; the running of time within which an action may be commenced starts from the time the last payment is made, 09.10.210	10 yrs., 09.10.040
Medical: 2 yrs., 12-542	2 yrs., 12-542(3)		Written: 6 yrs., 12-548; Oral (for indebtedness): 3 yrs., 12-543(1)	Oral debt: 3 yrs., 12-543(2); Written: 6 yrs.; credit card 6 yrs., 12-548	Foreign judgment: 4 yrs., 12-544(3)
Legal: 3 yrs., 16-56-105; medical: 2 yrs., 16-114-203	3 yrs., 16-56-105	3 yrs., 16-56-105	Written: 5 yrs., 16-56-111; oral: 3 yrs., 16-56-105	Not written or under seal: 3 yrs., 16-56-105; written: 5 yrs., 1-3-118	10 yrs., 16-56-114
Legal: 1 yr. from discovery, max. of 4 yrs. from the wrong, Civ. Proc. § 340.6; medical: 1 yr. from discovery, 3 yrs. if injury known, Civ. Proc. § 340.5; veterinary: 1 yr. for injury or death of animal, Civ. Proc. § 340(c)	3 yrs., Civ. Proc. § 338(b)	4 yrs., Civ. Proc. § 337.2	Written: 4 yrs., Civ. Proc. § 337; oral: 2 yrs., Civ. Proc. § 339	Book and stated accounts: 4 yrs., Civ. Proc. § 337	10 yrs., Civ. Proc. § 337.5
Veterinary: 2 yrs., 13-80-102(1)(c); medical: 2 yrs. from discovery, 13-80-102.5	2 yrs., 13-80-102	6 yrs., 13-80-103.5(1)(b)	3 yrs., 13-80-101; 2 yrs. if tort action for tortious breach of contract, 13-80-102	Contract: 6 yrs. if contract, 13-80-103.5	
2 yrs. from discovery, max. 3 yrs. from act, 52-584	3 yrs., 52-577		Written: 6 yrs., 52-576 ; oral: 3 yrs., 52-581	6 yrs., 52-576	20 yrs.; variations for small claims judgments, 52-598

Table 41: Civil Statutes of Limitations—Continued

State	Injury to Person	Libel/Slander	Fraud	Injury to Personal Property
DELAWARE	2 yrs., Tit. 10, § 8119; cause of action based upon sexual abuse of a minor by an adult may be filed at any time. Tit. 10, § 8145	2 yrs., Tit. 10, § 8119	2 yrs., Tit. 10, § 8119	2 yrs., Tit. 10, § 8107
DISTRICT OF COLUMBIA	1 yr., 12-301(4)	1 yr., 12-301(4)	3 yrs., 12-301(8)	3 yrs., 12-301(2); 12-301(3)
FLORIDA	4 yrs., 95.11(3)(o)	2 yrs., 95.11(4)(g)	4 yrs., 95.11(3)(j)	4 yrs., 95.11(3)(h)
GEORGIA	2 yrs., 9-3-33	1 yr., 9-3-33	2 yrs., 9-3-33	4 yrs., 9-3-32
HAWAII	2 yrs., 657-7	2 yrs., 657-4	2 yrs., 657-7	2 yrs., 657-7
IDAHO	2 yrs., 5-219(4); 5-219(5),	2 yrs., 5-219(5)	3 yrs., 5-218(4)	3 yrs., 5-218(3)
ILLINOIS	2 yrs., 735 § 5/13-202	1 yr., 735 § 5/13-201	Concealment of a cause of action: 5 yrs., 735 § 5/13-215; 735 § 5/13-220	5 yrs., 735 § 5/13-205
INDIANA	2 yrs., 34-11-2-4(1)	2 yrs., 34-11-2-4(1)	6 yrs., 34-11-2-7(4)	2 yrs., 34-11-2-4(2)
IOWA	2 yrs., 614.1(2)	2 yrs., 614.1(2)	5 yrs., 614.1(4)	5 yrs., 614.1(4)

Professional Malpractice	Trespass	Collection of Rents	Contracts	Collection of Debt on Account	Judgments
2 yrs., Tit. 10, § 8128	3 yrs., Tit. 10, § 8106		3 yrs., Tit. 10, § 8106	3 yrs., Tit. 10, § 8106	5 yrs., Tit. 10, § 5072
3 yrs., 12-301(8)	3 yrs., 12-301(3)	3 yrs., 12-301(8)	Written: Sale contract: 4 yrs.; simple contract: 3 yrs., 28:2-725; 12-301(7)	3 yrs., 12-301(8)	12 yrs., 15-101; foreign judgments according to law of foreign jurisdiction, 12-307
2 yrs.; medical: 2 yrs. from act or discovery, max. 4 yrs., 95.11(4)(a); 95.11(4)(b)	4 yrs., 95.11(3)(g)		Written: 5 yrs., 95.11(2)(b); specific performance: 1 yr., 95.11(5)(a); oral: 4 yrs., 95.11(3) (k)	5 yrs., 95.11(2)	Domestic: 20 yrs., 95.11(1) ; foreign: 5 yrs., 95.11(2)(a)
Medical: 2 yrs., max. 6 yrs. from act, 9-3-71	4 yrs., 9-3-30		Written: 6 yrs., 9-3-24 ; oral: 4 yrs., 9-3-26	4 yrs. , 9-3-25	Foreign judgment: 5 yrs., 9-3-20
Medical: 2 yrs. from reasonable discovery, max. 6 yrs., 657-7.3	2 yrs., 657-7	6 yrs., 657-1	6 yrs., 657-1	6 yrs., 657-1	Court of record: 10 yrs.; court not of record: 6 yrs.
2 yrs., 5-219(4)	3 yrs., 5-218(2)	20 yrs., 5-204	Written: 5 yrs., 5-216; oral: 4 yrs., 5-217		6 yrs., 5-215(1)
Medical: 2 yrs.-4 yrs., 735 § 5/13-212; legal: 2 yrs. from discovery, max. 6 yrs., 735 § 5/13-214.3	5 yrs., 735 § 5/13-205		Written: 10 yrs., 735 § 5/13-206; oral: 5 yrs., 735 § 5/13-205	10 yrs., 735 § 5/13-206; credit card 5 yrs., 735 § 5/13-205	Judgment may be revived within 20 yrs., 735 § 5/13-218
2 yrs., 34-11-2-3	2 yrs., 34-11-2-4	6 yrs., 34-11-2-7	Written: 10 yrs., 34-11-2-11; contract for payment of money: 6 yrs., 34-11-2-9; oral: 6 yrs.; employment agreements: 2 yrs., 4-11-2-7; 34-11-2-1	6 yrs., 34-11-2-7	20 yrs., 34-11-2-12
Medical: 2 yrs. from reasonable discovery, max. 6 yrs. from act, 614.1(9)	5 yrs., 614.1(4)	5 yrs., 614.1(4); 614.1(5)(b)	Written: 10 yrs.; claims for rent: 5 yrs., 614.1(5); oral: 5 yrs., 614.1(4)	10 yrs., 614.1(5)(a)	Court of record: 20 yrs., none for child or spousal support or distribution of marital assets, 614.1(6); court not of record: 10 yrs., claims for rent: 5 yrs., 614.1(5)

Table 41: Civil Statutes of Limitations—Continued

State	Injury to Person	Libel/Slander	Fraud	Injury to Personal Property
KANSAS	1 yr., 60-514(b)	1 yr., 60-514(a)	2 yrs. from discovery, 60-513 (a)(3)	2 yrs., 60-513 (a)(2)
KENTUCKY	1 yr., 413.140 (1)(a)	1 yr., 413.140 (1)(d)	5 yrs., 413.120(11)	2 yrs., 413.125
LOUISIANA	1 yr., Civ. Code Art. 3492	1 yr., Civ. Code Art. 3492	1 yr., Civ. Code Art. 3492	1 yr., Civ. Code Art. 3492
MAINE	2 yrs., Tit. 14, § 753; sexual acts towards minors may be commenced at any time, Tit. 14, § 752-C	2 yrs., Tit. 14, § 753	6 yrs., Tit. 14, § 859	All civil acts must commence within 6 yrs., Title 14, § 752
MARYLAND	1 yr., Cts. & Jud. Proc. § 5-105	1 yr., Cts. & Jud. Proc. § 5-105	3 yrs. general limit, Cts. & Jud. Proc. § 5-101	3 yrs. general limit, Cts. & Jud. Proc. § 5-101
MASSACHUSETTS	3 yrs., Ch. 260, § 4	3 yrs., Ch. 260, § 4	3 yrs., Ch. 260, § 2A	3 yrs., Ch. 260, § 4
MICHIGAN	2 yrs., 600.5805 (3); 5 yrs. for assault/ battery in a dating relationship, 600.5805 (5); 10 yrs. for criminal sexual conduct 600.5805 (6)	1 yr., 600.5805 (11)	6 yrs., 600.5813	3 yrs., 600.5805 (2)
MINNESOTA	2 yrs., 541.07(1)	2 yrs., 541.07(1)	6 yrs., 541.05(6)	6 yrs., 541.05(4)
MISSISSIPPI	1 yr., 15-1-35	1 yr., 15-1-35	3 yrs., 15-1-49	3 yrs., 15-1-59
MISSOURI	2 yrs., 516.140	2 yrs., 516.140	10 yrs., 516.120(5)	5 yrs.; 516.120(4)

Professional Malpractice	Trespass	Collection of Rents	Contracts	Collection of Debt on Account	Judgments
2 yrs. from reasonable discovery, 4 yrs. max., 60-513(a)(7); 60-513(c)	2 yrs., 60-513(a)(1)	Pursuant to express or implied contract: 3 yrs., 60-512	Written: 5 yrs., 60-511(1); oral: 3 yrs., 60-512(1)	Pursuant to express or implied contract: 3 yrs., 60-512	Real estate: 5 yrs., 60-511(3)
Professional service: 1 yr., 413.245; Medical: 1 yr., 413.140(e)	5 yrs., 413.120(4)	Written contract: 15 yrs., 413.090	Written: 15 yrs., 413.090(2); oral: 5 yrs., 413.120(1)	5 yrs., 413.120	15 yrs., 413.090(1)
1 yr., Civ. Code Art. 3492; medical: 1 yr. from discovery, max. 3 yrs. from act, 9:5628	1 yr., Civ. Code Art. 3492	3 yrs., Civ. Code Art. 3494(3)	10 yrs., Civ. Code Art. 3499	3 yrs., Civ. Code Art. 3494(4)	Monetary judgments: 10 yrs., Civ. Code Art. 3501
Architects/Engineers: 4 yrs. to 10 max., Attorneys: 2 yrs., Tit. 14, §§ 752-A; 753-B; Medical: 3 yrs., Tit. 24, § 2902	All civil acts must commence within 6 yrs., Title 14, § 752	All civil acts must commence within 6 yrs., Title 14, § 752	Written: 20 yrs. if under seal, Tit. 14, § 751	All civil acts must commence within 6 yrs., Title 14, § 752	20 yrs., Tit. 14, § 864
Medical: 5 yrs. from injury or 3 yrs. from discovery, whichever is shorter, max. 7 yrs., Cts. & Jud. Proc. § 5-109	3 yrs. general limit, Cts. & Jud. Proc. § 5-101	3 yrs. general limit, Cts. & Jud. Proc. § 5-101	Written: 3 yrs.; 12 yrs. if under seal, Cts. & Jud. Proc. §§ 5-101; 5-102(a)(5)	3 yrs. general limit, Cts. & Jud. Proc. § 5-101	12 yrs., Cts. & Jud. Proc. § 5-102 (a)(3)
3 yrs., max. 7 yrs. (personal injury), Ch. 260, § 4	3 yrs., Ch. 260, § 2A	3 yrs., Ch. 260, § 2A	Written: 6 yrs.; 20 yrs. if under seal; oral: 6 yrs., Ch. 260, §§ 1; 2	6 yrs., Ch. 260, § 2	6 yrs., Ch. 260, § 2
2 yrs., 600.5805 (8)	6 yrs., 600.5813	6 yrs., 600.5813	6 yrs., 600.5807 (9)	6 yrs., 600.5813	10 yrs. court of record; 6 yrs. court not of record, 600.5809 (3)
Medical and veterinary: 2 yrs., 541.07(1)	6 yrs., 541.05 (3)		6 yrs., 541.05(1)		10 yrs., 541.04
2 yrs. from act or discovery, 15-1-36	3 yrs., 15-1-49	3 yrs., 15-1-49	Oral: 3 yrs.; unwritten contract based on employment: 1 yr., 15-1-29	3 yrs., 15-1-29	7 yrs. domestic and foreign judgments, 15-1-43; 15-1-45
Medical: 2 yrs. from discovery, max. 10 yrs., 516.105	5 yrs., 516.120(3)	10 yrs., 516.110(3)	Written: 5 yrs.; payment of money or property: 10 yrs., 516.120(1); 516.110; oral: 5 yrs., 516.120(1)	10 yrs. if in writing, 516.110(1)	10 yrs. , 516.350

Table 41: Civil Statutes of Limitations—Continued

State	Injury to Person	Libel/Slander	Fraud	Injury to Personal Property
MONTANA	Assault & battery: 2 yrs., 27-2-204(3); wrongful death: 3 yrs., 7-2-204(2); childhood sexual abuse: 3 yrs. after discovery 27-2-216	2 yrs., 27-2-204(3)	2 yrs., 27-2-203	2 yrs., 27-2-207(2)
NEBRASKA	1 yr., 25-208	1 yr., 25-208	4 yrs., 25-207(4)	4 yrs., 25-207(2)
NEVADA	2 yrs., 11.190-(4)(c)	2 yrs., 11.190-(4)(c)	3 yrs., 11.190-(3)(d)	3 yrs., 11.190-(3)(c)
NEW HAMPSHIRE	3 yrs., 508:4; actions based on sexual assault and related offenses: 12 yrs. after person's 18th birthday or 3 years after plaintiff discovers the injury, whichever is later. 509:4-g	3 yrs., 508:4	3 yrs., 508:4	3 yrs., 508:4
NEW JERSEY	2 yrs., 2A:14-2	1 yr., 2A:14-3	6 yrs., 2A:14-1	6 yrs., 2A:14-1
NEW MEXICO	3 yrs., 37-1-8; childhood sexual abuse: person's 24th birthday or 3 yrs. from the date of disclosure to a licensed medical/ mental health care provider, whichever is later. 37-1-30	3 yrs., 37-1-8	4 yrs., 37-1-4	4 yrs., 37-1-4
NEW YORK	1 yr., C.P.L.R. § 215; 3 yrs., C.P.L.R. § 214	1 yr., C.P.L.R. § 215	6 yrs., C.P.L.R. § 213	3 yrs., C.P.L.R. § 214

Professional Malpractice	Trespass	Collection of Rents	Contracts	Collection of Debt on Account	Judgments
Legal: 3 yrs. from discovery, max. 10 yrs., 27-2-206; Medical: 2 yrs., max. 5 yrs., 27-2-205	2 yrs., 27-2-207(1)	3 yrs. obligation or liability other than contract not in writing, 27-2-202(3)	Written: 8 yrs., 27-2-202(1); oral: 5 yrs., 27-2-202(2)	Obligation or liability other than contract not in writing: 3 yrs., 27-2-202(3)	10 yrs., 27-2-201(2)
2 yrs. or 1 yr. from discovery, 25-222; 2 yrs., 25-208	4 yrs., 25-207(1)	4 yrs., 25-212	Written: 5 yrs., 25-205; Oral: 4 yrs., 25-206	4 yrs., 25-212	5 yrs. (foreign), 25-205
Accountant, 11.2075; Attorney, Veterinarian: 4 yrs., 11.207; Medical: 2 yrs. after discovery or 4 yrs. after act, 41A.097	3 yrs., 11.190 (3)(b)	4 yrs., 11.220	Written: 6 yrs., 11.190 (1)(b); oral: 4 yrs., 11.190-(2)(c)	4 yrs., 11.190-(2)(a)	6 yrs., 11.190(1)(a)
3 yrs., 508:4	2 yrs., 539:8		Written: 20 yrs. under seal, 508:5	20 yrs., 508:5	20 yrs., 508:5
2 yrs., 2A:14-2	6 yrs., 2A:14-1	16 yrs., 2A:14-4	6 yrs., 2A:14-1	6 yrs., 2A:14-1	Court of record: 20 yrs., 2A:14-5
	4 yrs., 37-1-4		Written: 6 yrs., 37-1-3; Oral: 4 yrs., 37-1-4	4 yrs., 37-1-4	6 yrs., 37-1-3
Medical: 2 1/2 yrs., foreign object in body of patient: 1 yr. from discovery, C.P.L.R § 214-A	3 yrs., C.P.L.R. § 214	6 yrs., C.P.L.R. § 213(1)	6 yrs., C.P.L.R. § 213	6 yrs., C.P.L.R. § 213(1)	20 yrs., C.P.L.R. § 211(b)

Table 41: Civil Statutes of Limitations—Continued

State	Injury to Person	Libel/Slander	Fraud	Injury to Personal Property
NORTH CAROLINA	3 yrs., 1-52	1 yr., 1-54	3 yrs., 1-52(9)	3 yrs., 1-52(4)
NORTH DAKOTA	2 yrs., 28-01-18	2 yrs. 28-01-18	6 yrs., 28-01-16	6 yrs., 28-01-16
OHIO	1 yr.; 2 yrs. if bodily injury, 2305.11(A); 2305.10; 2305.111	1 yr., 2305.11(A)	4 yrs., 2305.09(C)	2 yrs., 2305.10
OKLAHOMA	1 yr., Tit. 12, § 95(4)	1 yr., Tit. 12, § 95(4)	2 yrs. from discovery, Tit. 12, § 95(3)	2 yrs., Tit. 12, § 95(3)
OREGON	2 yrs., 12.110	2 yrs., 12.110	2 yrs. from discovery, 12.110	6 yrs., 12.080
PENNSYLVANIA	2 yrs., Tit. 42, § 5524(1)	1 yr., Tit. 42, § 5523(1)	2 yrs., Tit. 42, § 5524(7)	2 yrs., Tit. 42, § 5524(3)
RHODE ISLAND	3 yrs., 9-1-14; actions based on sexual abuse/ exploitation of a child: 7 yrs. after injury or 7 yrs. after discovery, whichever is later 9-1-51	Slander: 1 yr., 9-1-14		
SOUTH CAROLINA	2 yrs., 15-3-550; actions to recover for sexual abuse or incest must be commenced w/in 6 yrs. of the person turning 21 or 3 yrs. from time of discovery, whichever is later 15-3-555	2 yrs., 15-3-550	13 yrs., 15-3-530(7)	3 yrs., 15-3-530(4)

Professional Malpractice	Trespass	Collection of Rents	Contracts	Collection of Debt on Account	Judgments
2 yrs. or more after the occurrence of the last act of the defendant, max. 4 yrs.; damages by reason of a foreign object left in body; 1 yr. upon discovery, max. 10 yrs., 1-15	3 yrs., 1-52(3)	3 yrs., 1-52	3 yrs., 1-52(1)		10 yrs., 1-47
2 yrs.; medical: max. 6 yrs., 28-01-18	6 yrs., 28-01-16	6 yrs., 28-01-16	6 yrs., 28-01-16	6 yrs., 28-01-16	10 yrs., 28-01-15
1 yr., 2305.11(A); medical: 1 yr., certain exceptions apply, 2305.113	4 yrs., 2305.09 (A)		Written: 8 yrs., 2305.06; oral: 6 yrs., 2305.07	6 yrs., 2305.07	10 yrs., 2325.18
2 yrs., Tit. 12, § 95(3)	2 yrs., Tit. 12, § 95(3)	5 yrs., Tit. 12, § 95(12)	Written: 5 yrs., Tit. 12, § 95(1); oral: 3 yrs., Tit. 12, § 95(2)	5 yrs., Tit. 12, § 95(12)	Foreign judgment: 3 yrs., Tit. 12, § 95(2)
Medical: 2 yrs. from act or reasonable discovery, max. 5 yrs., 12.110(4)	6 yrs., 12.080(3)	1 yr., 12.125	6 yrs., 12.080	6 yrs., 12.080(2)	10 yrs., 12.070
2 yrs., Tit. 42, § 5524(7)	2 yrs., Tit. 42, § 5524(4)	21 yrs., Tit. 42, § 5530(a)(2)	Written: 20 yrs. under seal, 4 years other, Tit. 42, §§ 5529(b); 5525(a)(8); oral: 4 yrs., Tit. 42, § 5525(a)(3)	2 yrs., Tit. 42, § 5524	Tit. 42, § 5525(a)(5)
Medical, veterinary, accounting, insurance, real estate: 3 yrs., 9-1-14.1; Legal: 3 yrs., 9-1-14.3			Written: 20 yrs. under seal, 9-1-17; 4 yrs. sale of goods, 6A-2-725; 10 yrs. other, 9-1-13(a)		20 yrs., 9-1-17
Medical: 3 yrs. from act or reasonable discovery (max. 6 yrs.); if foreign object in body: 2 yrs., 15-3-545	3 yrs., 15-3-530(3)	10 yrs., 15-3-350	Written: 20 yrs. under seal or mortgage of real property, 15-3-520; 6 yrs. contract for sale, 36-2-275; 3 yrs. others, 15-3-530; Oral: 3 yrs., 15-3-530(1)	3 yrs., 15-3-530(1)	10 yrs., 15-3-600

Table 41: Civil Statutes of Limitations—Continued

State	Injury to Person	Libel/Slander	Fraud	Injury to Personal Property
SOUTH DAKOTA	2 yrs., 15-2-15(1)	2 yrs., 15-2-15(1)	6 yrs., 15-2-13(6)	6 yrs., 15-2-13(4)
TENNESSEE	1 yr., 28-3-104(a)(1)	Libel: 1 yr., 28-3-104; slander: 6 mos., 28-3-103	3 yrs., 28-3-105	3 yrs., 28-3-105(1)
TEXAS	2 yrs., Civ. Prac. & Rem. § 16.003(a); 5 yrs. for sex crimes, 15 yrs. for sex crimes against children, Civ. Prac. & Rem. § 16.0045	1 yr., Civ. Prac. & Rem. § 16.002(a)	4 yrs., Civ. Prac. & Rem. § 16.004(a)(4)	2 yrs., Civ. Prac. & Rem. § 16.003(a)
UTAH	1 yr., 78b-2-302(4)	1 yr., 78b-2-302(4)	3 yrs., 78b-2-305(3)	3 yrs., 78b-2-305(2)
VERMONT	3 yrs., Tit. 12, § 512; injury caused by skiing: 1 yr., Tit. 12, § 513	3 yrs., Tit. 12, § 512(3)	6 yrs., Tit. 12, § 511	3 yrs., Tit. 12, § 512(5)
VIRGINIA	2 yrs., 8.01-243(A)	2 yrs., 8.01-243(A)	2 yrs., 8.01-243(A)	5 yrs., 8.01-243(B)
WASHINGTON	2 yrs., 4.16.100(1)	2 yrs., 4.16.100(1)	3 yrs., 4.16.080(4)	2 yrs., 4.16.080(2)
WEST VIRGINIA	2 yrs., 55-2-12(b)	1 yr., 55-2-12(c)		2 yrs., 55-2-12(a)
WISCONSIN	3 yrs., 893.57	3 yrs., 893.57	6 yrs., 893.93(1) (b)	6 yrs., 893.52
WYOMING	1 yr., 1-3-105(a)(v)(B)	1 yr., 1-3-105(a)(v)(A)	4 yrs., 1-3-105(a)(iv)(D)	4 yrs., 1-3-105(a)(iv)(B)

Professional Malpractice	Trespass	Collection of Rents	Contracts	Collection of Debt on Account	Judgments
Medical: 2 yrs., 15-2-14.1; Legal: 3 yrs., 15-2-14.2; Accounting: 4 yrs., 15-2-14.4	6 yrs., 15-2-13(3)	20 yrs., 15-3-2	Written: Under seal (except mortgage): 20 yrs., 15-2-6; other: 6 yrs., 15-2-13; oral: 6 yrs., 15-2-13	6 yrs., 15-2-13	Domestic judgment: 20 yrs., 15-2-6; foreign judgment: 10 yrs., 15-2-8
Legal, accounting: 1 yr., 28-3-104	3 yrs., 28-3-105(1); childhood sexual abuse: 3 yrs. from time of discovery, but no more than 7 yrs. after the child turns 18	6 yrs., 28-3-109(a)(1)	Written and oral: 6 yrs., 28-3-109	6 yrs., 28-3-109	10 yrs., 28-3-110(2)
	2 yrs., Civ. Prac. & Rem. § 16.003(a)		Written: 4 yrs. real property, Civ. Prac. & Rem. § 16.004(a)(3)	4 yrs., Civ. Prac. & Rem. § 16.004(a)(3)	
Medical: 2 yrs., max. 4 yrs., 78b-3-404	3 yrs., 78b-2-305(1)	6 yrs., 78b-2-309 6	Written: 6 yrs., 78b-2-309; oral: 4 yrs., 78b-2-307	4 yrs., 78b-2-307(1)	8 yrs., 78b-2-311
Medical: 3 yrs. from act or 2 from reasonable discovery, max. 7 yrs., Tit. 12, § 521	6 yrs., Tit. 12, §511	6 yrs., Tit. 12, §511	Written: 8 yrs. under seal, Tit. 12, § 507; 6 yrs. other, Tit. 12, § 511; 4 yrs. sales, Tit. 9A, § 2-725 ; oral: 6 yrs., Tit. 12, § 511	6 yrs., Tit. 12, § 511	Court of record: 8 yrs., Tit. 12, § 506; court not of record: 6 yrs., Tit. 12, § 511
Medical: 1 to 2 yrs.; 10 yrs. max., 8.01-243	5 yrs., 8.01-243(B)		Written: 5 yrs.; 8.01-246(2); Oral: 3 yrs., 8.01-246(4)		20 yrs., 8.01-251(A); 10 yrs. to enforce lien, 8.01-251(C)
Medical: 3 yrs. from injury or 1 yr. from discovery, max. 8 yrs., 4.16.350(3)	3 yrs., 4.16.080(1)	6 yrs., 4.16.040(2)	Written: 6 yrs.; 4.16.080(3) oral: 3 yrs., 4.16.040(1)	4.16.040(3) 6 yrs.	10 yrs., 4.16.020(2)
2 yrs., 55-2-12(b)	2 yrs., 55-2-12(a)	5 yrs., 55-4-21	Written: 10 yrs.; 55-2-6 oral: 5 yrs., 55-2-6		Foreign judgment: 10 yrs., 55-2-13
Medical: Later of 3 yrs. from incident or 1 yr. from discovery, max. 5 yrs., 893.55(4)	6 yrs., 893.52	6 yrs., 843.13(1)	6 yrs., 893.43		Court of record: 20 yrs., 893.40; court not of record: 6 yrs., 893.42
	4 yrs., 1-3-105(a)(iv)(A)		Written: 10 yrs.; oral: 8 yrs., 1-3-105(a)(i)	5 yrs., 1-3-105(a)(iii)	Foreign judgment: 5 yrs. 1-3-105(a)(iii)

42. FOOD LAWS

Buy Fresh! Buy Local! The "slow foods" movement has been sweeping the civilized world for more than a decade. The interesting irony is that as civilization grew beyond locally produced foods and crafts, one of its hallmarks was the advent of corporate farming and mass marketing of processed foods in supermarkets and restaurants. As the population has become more affluent and unhealthy, mass produced foods have been blamed for a large share of our unhealthful state. The slow foods movement has grown in response by encouraging people to buy and consume locally produced foods in season. The result has been that farmers' markets have sprung up in nearly every community, and there are now countless restaurants and food stores that sell locally produced foods.

As consumer interest in foods has grown, there has been concern over the different ways that "natural" foods are raised, processed for sale, and distributed. These concerns have translated into regulations that seek to protect consumers from unhealthy practices and ensure that what people are buying from slow foods vendors and producers is fresh, unspoiled, and healthful, as well as what it claims to be. Accordingly, there are different rules for small producers and distributors than for large supermarkets, mass-market food manufacturers, and chains of sit-down and fast food restaurants.

For the most part, the rules governing national food producers and providers are set by the federal government from a whole host of federal agencies: U.S. Department of Agriculture, Food and Drug Administration, Federal Trade Commission, and Department of Labor, to name a few. Small food producers who sell to local restaurants, food stores, and at farmers' markets are primarily regulated by state, county, or municipal governments. Regulation at the state and local level is generally confined to issues surrounding health codes, labeling, taxation, and food handling, all of which

are controlled by local health officials. The state rules are the subject of the present chapter. County and municipal rules are not, and federal rules come into play for the purposes of this chapter only when the states have specifically adopted them.

Overall, the rules actually vary little from state to state as they are focused primarily on licensing, taxation, and basic rules regarding packaging and labeling. There are, however, some occasions in which national market forces and controversial health concerns have driven the content of certain rules. For example, the sale of raw milk is very controversial. There are some people who believe that unpasteurized milk is dangerous and treat it as though it is a poison, while others think that pasteurization renders milk impotent as a food product. Still others say large commercial dairies and milk producers have sought to keep pasteurization as a requirement for sale of milk to help secure their hold on the market since pasteurization is an expensive process that generally puts small local dairies at a disadvantage. Some states ban the sale of raw milk outright, while others allow commercial sales through food stores in the general dairy section. A few ironies present themselves when looking at the rules. Wisconsin, "America's Dairyland," bans outright the sale of raw milk. Other states allow the sale of raw milk but ban local dairies from advertising that they sell it. Still other states allow the sale of raw milk only through purchase of a share of a dairy cow, and by extension, its milk.

Sale of homemade canned, baked, and other "non-hazardous" foods is regulated within certain limits surrounding volume of goods produced and often requires completing a food safety class and licensing by a local or state health department. Sales of eggs and foraged wild mushrooms are also covered in this chapter as states find sale of these foods to be potentially dangerous if not handled, packaged, or labeled properly.

Table 42: Food Laws

State	Sale of Raw Milk	Sale of Eggs	Sale of Cottage Foods	Sale of Wild Foraged Mushrooms
ALABAMA	Sale prohibited for human consumption, Ala. Admin. Code, Rule 420-3-16-.12	Producers who sell eggs from own hens and who do not sell eggs received or purchased from other sources not required to grade or obtain permit, 2-12-4; 2-12-6; Ala. Admin. Code, Rule 80-3-14	Baked goods, canned jam or jelly, dried herb or herb mix, or candy for sale at person's home; gross annual income under $20,000; must sell directly to consumers; internet sales prohibited; producer must maintain certification of having attended and passed approved food safety course, 22-20-5.1	Sale allowed at farmers market, Ala. Admin Code, Rule 80-7-1-.01
ALASKA	Sale prohibited; raw milk available through herd share agreement or personal use of own animal, 18 AAC 32.010 to 32.060	Eggs produced in Alaska and sold by producer directly to consumer are exempt from grading and labeling; no permit requirement, 11 AAC 170	Sale must be directly to consumer; internet sale or sale to stores/restaurants prohibited; producer must gross less than $25,000 per year, 18 AAC 31.012	Sale permitted if food establishment ensures mushroom is identified as "not inspected product," 18 AAC 31.060
ARIZONA	Raw milk products may be sold in retail stores; use or sale in food establishments prohibited, 3-606	Producer may sell 25 cases of "nest run" (ungraded) eggs per year; no permit required, 3-715	Food must be made in private kitchen, labeled, and label provided directly to final consumer; food handler's permit and state registration required to produce, 36-136(H)(4)(g)	No sale allowed, Ariz. Admin. Code § 9-8-107
ARKANSAS	Sale up to 500 gal. per month permitted directly to consumer at farm on which produced; advertising allowed; signage and labeling required, 20-59-248	Sale directly to consumer or retailer permitted; producer must own fewer than 200 hens; eggs must be washed and clean, identified as ungraded with name and address of producer; eggs maintained at temperature of 45°F or below; reuse of cartons only if all markings obliterated; no permit required, 20-58-203; invoice for any sale to retailer must be retained for 2 yrs., 20-58-211	Sale directly to consumer from production site, at market, fair, or other special event, 20-57-201	No; must be either cultivated or processed, Admin. Code 007.04.8-3-2

Table 42: Food Laws—Continued

State	Sale of Raw Milk	Sale of Eggs	Sale of Cottage Foods	Sale of Wild Foraged Mushrooms
CALIFORNIA	Milk Products Act of 1947, Food & Agric. §§ 32501 to 39912: May be sold in retail store and on the farm; must meet standards of "market milk" and be graded, Food & Agric. §§ 32510, 35787, 35891; market milk permit required to produce and distribute, Food & Agric. § 33226; milk products plant license may be required, exemption for business that exclusively produces and distributes raw milk from own production, Food & Agric. § 35017	Registration required, Food & Agric. § 27541; no grading required if sold to consumer without advertising and from flock up to 500 hens; may also sell "restricted" eggs directly to consumer from own flock's production, Cal. Code Regs. tit. 3, §§ 1354.2, 1356.2	Direct and indirect sales allowed; gross annual sales up to $50,000 other restrictions apply, Health & Safety §§ 113758, 114365 to 114365.6	
COLORADO	Retail sales not permitted; raw milk may be obtained through herd share agreement, 25-5.5-117	Producer may sell whole eggs from place produced, at farmers' market, or community-supported agricultural association, without permit or grading, if fewer than 250 doz. eggs per month are sold; sale at farmers' market requires labeling, 25-4-1614(2)(b)(II), 35-21-105	Sale must be directly from producer to informed end consumer; sales must be only in Colorado, no interstate commerce; net revenues of less than $10,000 per year; food handler course required; labeling required, 25-4-1614	Must be obtained from sources where each mushroom is individually inspected and found to be safe by approved mushroom identification expert, 6 Colo. Code Regs. § 1010-2:3-306
CONNECTICUT	Retail sale allowed, transfer through cow share agreement allowed, 22-129; producer must register with state if raw milk or cheese is to be used or disposed of away from place of production, 22-173a; may not be served to consumer in any food establishment, 22-193	Producers selling eggs from own hens directly to consumers are exempt from grading and labeling, 22-47; permit required to sell to food service requirement, Conn. Agencies Regs. § 19-13-B42(n)	Only certain foods processed by residential farmer may be sold on farm or at farmer's market, 21a-62a; 21a-24a	May be sold at farmer's market if considered a "farm product," 22-6r

Table 42: Food Laws—Continued

State	Sale of Raw Milk	Sale of Eggs	Sale of Cottage Foods	Sale of Wild Foraged Mushrooms
DELAWARE	Sales prohibited for human consumption, 16 Del. Admin. Code §§ 4458-3-202.14; 4461-2.0; 4000-FOOD-3-202.14	Eggs from producer's own flock are exempt from grading and labeling if not sold at established place of business away from place of production or advertised to public with price, size, or quality designation or any descriptive term, Tit. 3, § 3510	Must be registered, have no more than $25,000 in annual gross sales, and follow several training requirements; not allowed in food establishments, 16 Del. Admin. Code §§ 4458A-1.0 to 4458A-9.0	May be sold if individually inspected and found to be safe by approved identification expert; food establishment may only sell if approved to do so, 16 Del. Admin. Code §§ 4458-3-201.16; 4000-FOOD-3-201.16
DISTRICT OF COLUMBIA	Sale prohibited for human consumption, 25-A DCMR §§ 702.1; 710.2	All egg handlers must maintain sales records; all eggs must be labeled, 25-B DCMR §§ 702; 3601	Cottage food business must register and pass inspection; food must be labeled and stored on premises; no more than $25,000 annual revenue, 7-742.01; 7-742.02	Must be obtained from sources where each mushroom is individually inspected and found to be safe by approved mushroom identification expert, 25-A DCMR § 705
FLORIDA	Sale prohibited for human consumption, 502.091	Nest run eggs (not washed, sized, or graded) may be sold only by producers or processors to other producers or processors; direct sale prohibited to retail outlets, consumers, or public eating places, 583.01; 583.021	Permit required if more than $15,000 in gross annual sales; no sales over internet, mail order, or at wholesale; food must be labeled; food must be stored on premises, 500.80	Must be obtained from sources where each mushroom is individually inspected and found to be safe by approved mushroom identification expert, Fla. Admin. Code R. 61C-1.001
GEORGIA	Sale prohibited for human consumption, 26-2-238; Ga. Comp. R. & Regs. 40-2-1-.01	Sale of eggs from producer's own flock is exempted from licensing; all eggs offered for sale must be graded, 26-2-261; 26-2-264	Must register including list of proposed products, be inspected and licensed; sales only to end consumers; must produce only non-potentially hazardous foods; food must be labeled, Ga. Comp. R. & Regs. 40-7-19.01 to 40-7-19.10	Food establishment may only sell or serve wild mushrooms if it is approved to do so, Ga. Comp. R. & Regs. 40-7-1.09
HAWAII	Sale prohibited for human consumption, HAR § 11-15-46	All shell eggs must be graded and labeled; temporary food permit required for sale directly to consumer on farm or at farmer's market, 147-71 to 147-80; HAR §§ 4-46-1 to 4-46-13	No; narrow permit exemption for in-home production of whole, uncut fruits and vegetables; dry, not ready-to-eat foods; hand-pounded poi sold directly to consumer, HAR § 11-50-3	Must be obtained from sources where each mushroom is individually inspected and found to be safe by approved mushroom identification expert, HAR § 11-50-31

Table 42: Food Laws—Continued

State	Sale of Raw Milk	Sale of Eggs	Sale of Cottage Foods	Sale of Wild Foraged Mushrooms
IDAHO	Sales are legal on the farm and in retail stores; farmers must obtain a Grade A Milk License and a Retail Raw Milk license, IDAPA 02.04.13.001 to 02.04.13.060	Producers with up to 300 hens may sell ungraded eggs; must be marked "ungraded"; exempt from assessment fees if sold at place of production, 37-1523A	Food must be produced in home kitchen of primary residence or another designated kitchen; must be sold directly to consumer and be labeled, IDAPA 16.02.19.01; 16.02.19.010	Food establishment may only sell or serve wild mushrooms if it is approved to do so, IDAPA 16.02.19.300
ILLINOIS	Sale permitted only on farm on which it was produced, 410 § 635/8	Producer may sell nest run eggs without candling or grading, on own premises where eggs are produced, direct to household consumers, for the consumer's personal use and that consumer's non-paying guests; farmer's market eggs must be graded; no license requirement, 410 §§ 615/6; 615/8	Not regulated by department if foods are made for end use only; food to be sold at farmer's market or on farm if main product is grown on farm; gross annual receipts may not exceed $36,000; label and packaging requirements, 410 § 625/4	May only be sold or served if food establishment has been approved to accept them, 77 Ill. Adm. Code 750.5
INDIANA	Sale prohibited for human consumption, no law on herd shares, 15-18-1-20	Farms and other bona fide egg producers who sell and deliver on the premises where flock is produced are exempt from grading and labeling; farmer's market retail permit required, 16-42-11-8; 16-42-11-9,5	Statute does not define "cottage food," however licensing exempt food establishments include those preparing or serving packaged or unpackaged foods that are not potentially hazardous; cannot have more than 10,000 sq. ft. retail space; must sell at farmer's market or roadside stand or directly to consumer, 16-18-2-137; 16-42-5.2-2	Must be obtained from sources where each mushroom is individually inspected and found to be safe by approved mushroom identification expert, 410 IAC 7-24-164
IOWA	Sale prohibited for human consumption, 192.102 to 192.103	Producers who sell eggs exclusively from own flocks directly to handlers or consumers are not required to grade; no licensing requirement, 196.1 to 196.14	Statute does not directly define "cottage food"; food establishment does not include places offering non-potentially hazardous food or home bakeries; no licensing; food must be sold directly to consumer and be labeled, 137F.1	Sale of morel mushrooms allowed if procured by individual who has completed a morel identification course and mushroom is identified as safe by department "approved wild mushroom expert," Iowa Admin. Code 481-31.1(137F)

Table 42: Food Laws—Continued

State	Sale of Raw Milk	Sale of Eggs	Sale of Cottage Foods	Sale of Wild Foraged Mushrooms
KANSAS	Sale allowed only on farm on which produced and only advertised by sign at farm, 65-771; K.A.R. 4-7-6	Producer must own fewer than 250 hens; sales to consumers only; eggs may be ungraded if labeled as such; used packaging must be void of brand markings; no license required, 2-2508	Statute does not directly define "cottage food"; license not required by producer of foods other than "time and temperature" foods for distribution directly to end consumer; person must operate establishment for less than 7 days/yr.; all food must be labeled, K.A.R. 26-39-105	Must be obtained from sources where each mushroom is individually inspected and found to be safe by approved mushroom identification expert, K.A.R. 26-39-105
KENTUCKY	Raw goat milk only sales allowed on farm, upon written recommendation by physician, no law on herd shares, 217C.090; 217C.902; 902 KAR 50:120	No license required for producer who sells up to 60 doz. eggs/wk. directly to consumers; grading not required if carton is labeled as such, 260.550; 260.630	Regulation does not directly define "cottage food"; "home-based" foods must be grown, harvested, and processed by farmer; water must be tested; food must be labeled; no children can be in kitchen when food is produced; no internet or retail sales; license required, 902 KAR 45:090	Must be obtained from sources where each mushroom is individually inspected and found to be safe by approved mushroom identification expert, 902 KAR 45:005
LOUISIANA	Sale prohibited for human consumption, La. Admin. Code tit. 51, pt. VII, § 323	Producers selling eggs from own flock are exempt from grading; no more than 30 doz. eggs can be sold to 1 person at 1 time; no license or assessment fee required if flock is less than 500 hens, LSA-R.S. 3:326; 3:845; La. Admin. Code tit. 7, pt. V, § 931	No license required for "low risk foods" prepared for sale in home kitchen; annual sales must be no more than $20,000; food must be labeled; no retail sales, LSA-R.S. 40:4.9	No, La. Admin. Code tit. 51, pt. XXIII, §§ 101 to 4739
MAINE	Retail sale permitted; sale not permitted in eating establishments, Tit. 7, §§ 2902-B; 2910	Producers selling eggs from own flock directly to consumers not required to grade or label, Tit. 7, § 636	"Home food manufacturing" requires license; food must be labeled and sold directly to consumer, 01-001 CMR Ch. 345, §§ 1-8	Certified persons may harvest, broker, and sell wild mushrooms, Maine Wild Mushroom Harvesting Certification Program: Tit. 22, § 2175
MARYLAND	Sale prohibited for human consumption, 21-434	All eggs must be graded; all sellers must register, Md. Egg Law: 4-301 to 4-312	No license required; producer may sell only prepackaged and labeled food stored on premises; sales only at farmer's market or public event, no internet sales or interstate commerce; annual sales up to $25,000, 21-301; 21-330.1	Must be obtained from sources where each mushroom is individually inspected and found to be safe by approved mushroom identification expert, COMAR 10.15.01.01

Table 42: Food Laws—Continued

State	Sale of Raw Milk	Sale of Eggs	Sale of Cottage Foods	Sale of Wild Foraged Mushrooms
MASSACHUSETTS	Retail sale allowed, 330 CMR 27.01 to 27.21	All eggs must be labeled; grading and sizing not required but if sold without grading, producer may not advertise, display in bulk, or sell to retailer Ch. 94, §§ 90a to 90e; 330 CMR 5.03	Producer must sell directly to consumer; facility must be inspected and licensed; producer must maintain standardized recipe, 105 CMR 590.002; 590.004	Must be obtained from sources where each mushroom is individually inspected and found to be safe by approved mushroom identification expert; must be packaged and labeled with name of harvester, packer and species, 105 CMS 590.004
MICHIGAN	Sale prohibited; raw milk allowed through herd share agreement, 288.538; MDARD Food & Dairy Division Policy 1.40	Producers with fewer than 3,000 hens may sell directly to consumer or first receiver; container must be labeled; exempt from grading; no sales through internet, mail, or consignment, 289.7114	Producer may sell only prepackaged and labeled food made and stored in domestic primary residence; no internet or mail order sales; gross annual sales less than $20,000 ($25,000 after 12/31/2017), 289.4102	Must be obtained from sources where each mushroom is individually inspected and found to be safe by approved mushroom identification expert, 289.6101
MINNESOTA	Generally no; narrow exception for milk occasionally secured or purchased for personal use by consumer at place or farm where milk was produced, 32D.20	All eggs must be graded and labeled; producer who sells eggs only from own flock exempt from licensing but must register with Minn. Dept. of Agric. egg inspection program, 29.21 to 29.27	Food must be sold directly to consumer or at community event or farmer's market; internet sales allowed if product is hand delivered; gross annual sales up to $18,000; registration with commission of agriculture unless gross receipts under $5,000; producer must complete safe food handling course, 28A.152	Wild mushrooms allowed for sale at retail if identified by state approved mushroom expert, Minn. R. 4626.0155 3-201.16
MISSISSIPPI	Sale of raw goat milk allowed directly to consumer on premises where produced and with no more than 9 producing goats; milk may not be advertised for sale, 75-31-65	Producers who sell eggs from own flock directly from place of production or selling fewer than 6 doz. eggs per week are not required to grade or label, 69-7-321	Sales must be directly to end consumer; no mail order, internet, or wholesale sales allowed; goods must be prepackaged with label; annual gross sales must be less than $20,0009, 75-29-951	

Table 42: Food Laws—Continued

State	Sale of Raw Milk	Sale of Eggs	Sale of Cottage Foods	Sale of Wild Foraged Mushrooms
MISSOURI	Sale and delivery allowed directly from farm to consumers for own use, 196.935	No licensing requirement for producers who sell eggs from own flocks, provided they are not sold at established place of business away from producer's premises; all eggs must be labeled and graded, 196.313; 196.323; 196.326	Food produced out of seller's home; sales must be directly to consumer, no internet sales; gross annual sales less than $50,000, 296.298	May be sold if individually inspected and found to be safe by approved mushroom expert as defined in the Missouri Food Code, 19 CFR 20-1.025
MONTANA	Sale prohibited for human consumption, no law on herd shares, ARM 32.8.102; 32.8.103	No license or candling required if major portion of eggs are produced from own flock or in amounts less than an annual average of 25 cases per month, 81-20-201	Producer must register with local health authority and pay fee; products must be labeled and prepackaged; food must be made and stored in registered area of home, sales directly to consumer, 50-50-102; 50-50-116; 50-50-117; ARM 37.110.501 to 37.110.514	Food establishment may sell or serve wild mushrooms if it is approved to do so, ARM 3i7.110.260
NEBRASKA	Sale allowed only at farm where produced directly to consumer and not for resale, 2-3969	No license required if selling from of flock of up to 3,000 hens; eggs must be labeled, 81-2,243.01; 81-2,270.01	Cottage food not specifically defined; license not required for food produced in private home and sold directly to consumer at farmer's market; must be labeled, 81-2,245.01	No, unless food establishment has been approved to accept, 81-2,257.01
NEVADA	Sale allowed by state law; product must be certified by county milk commission in county of production, but no county milk commissions exist, 584.207; 584.208	All eggs must be graded, labeled, and license is required, 583.110 to 583.210	Food items must be made in private kitchen or approved other kitchen and sold directly to consumer, no telephone or internet sales; items must be labeled; producer must register with health authority; annual gross sales up to $35,000, 446.866	Must be obtained from sources where each mushroom is individually inspected and found to be safe by approved mushroom identification expert, NAC 446.129

Table 42: Food Laws—Continued

State	Sale of Raw Milk	Sale of Eggs	Sale of Cottage Foods	Sale of Wild Foraged Mushrooms
NEW HAMPSHIRE	Sale is allowed in retail stores and from producer directly to consumer; producer-distributor license not required if daily amount produced for sale is less than 20 gallons if sold directly to consumer from farm or at farmers' market; product must be labeled, 180:30-a; 184:84	No state license required; if over 3,000 hens, must register under USDA's Egg Products Inspection Act (EPIA); all eggs must be labeled and graded, 428:22 to 428:29	No license required for "homestead" food products sold directly to consumer from home, at farmers' markets, or to retail food stores if annual gross sales are less than $20,000; license required over $20,000 or to sell to restaurants or other food establishments, over internet, by mail order or to wholesalers, brokers, or other food distributors who will resell products; all food products must be labeled, 143-A:5; 143-A:12; N.H. Code Admin. R. He-P 2311.04	
NEW JERSEY	Sale prohibited for human consumption, 24:10-57.17	If flock of fewer than 3,000 hens, restricted eggs; no license or grading required, labeling required, N.J.A.C. 2:70-1.23; 7 CFR 57.100	Food prepared in a private home shall not be used or offered for human consumption in a retail food establishment, N.J.A.C. 8:24-3.2	
NEW MEXICO	Retail sale allowed, 25-8-1	Producer may sell only ungraded eggs from own production from flock of less than 3,000 birds; must notify New Mexico Dept. of Agric. of intent to sell ungraded eggs, 25-6-6; 25-6-7	Production of non-potentially-hazardous foods; foods must be packaged; sale directly to consumer, no internet or retail sales, 7.6.2.15 NMAC	No sale or service by food establishment unless approved to do so, 7.6.2.8 NMAC
NEW YORK	Sale allowed only on farm on which produced, 1 NYCRR 2.3	Grading and labeling not required for sale to consumer of eggs from seller's own flock, Agric. & Mkts. § 160-c	No licensed required for home processed foods, must be non-potentially-hazardous and labeled, processed in private kitchen using "ordinary kitchen facilities; dept. information indicates only direct sales allowed, Agric. & Mkts. §§ 276.3; 276.4	Must be obtained from sources where each mushroom is individually inspected and found to be safe by approved mushroom identification expert, 1 NYCRR 271-2.2

Table 42: Food Laws—Continued

State	Sale of Raw Milk	Sale of Eggs	Sale of Cottage Foods	Sale of Wild Foraged Mushrooms
NORTH CAROLINA	Sale prohibited for human consumption, 106-266.35	No grading required when selling eggs from own production on premises where eggs are produced, processed, or ungraded sales less than 30 doz. per week, labeling required; handlers selling fewer than 500 cases per year exempt from egg promotion tax, 106-245,15; 106-245.18; 106-245.34		Must be obtained from sources where each mushroom is individually inspected and found to be safe by approved mushroom identification expert, 130A-248

Table 42: Food Laws—Continued

State	Sale of Raw Milk	Sale of Eggs	Sale of Cottage Foods	Sale of Wild Foraged Mushrooms
NORTH DAKOTA	Sale prohibited; raw milk available through herd share agreement, 4.1-25-01; 4.1-25-30; 4.1-25-40	All eggs sold to ultimate consumer must be candled, graded, and labeled, 4.1-19-06; NDAC 7-11-01-02	Cottage food product means baked goods, jams, jellies, and other food and drink products produced by a cottage food operator; sale only to informed end consumer and only for home consumption, no internet, phone, mail, or consignment sales; no sale of uninspected products made from meat except those made from poultry unless cottage food operator slaughters no more than 1,000 poultry per year from own flock, does not buy or sell poultry products except those produced from poultry raised by producer, poultry product is not adulterated or misbranded; except for whole, unprocessed fruits or vegetables, no sales or use in food establishment, processing plant, or store; producer must inform end consumer that product is not certified, labeled, licensed, packaged, regulated, or inspected; all products requiring refrigeration must be labeled; producer must label product or post sign or that product is made in home kitchen not inspected by state or local health department, 23-09.5-01; 23-09.5-02	Must be obtained from sources where each mushroom is individually inspected and found to be safe by approved mushroom identification expert, NDAC 33-33-04-03
OHIO	Sale to ultimate consumer prohibited, 917.04	Producers selling only shell eggs of own hens' production on premises where produced or directly to hatcheries not required to grade or label, 925.10	No licensing requirement; food must be produced in home and labeled, 3715.023; Ohio Admin. Code 901:3-20-04	Mushroom species picked in the wild are prohibited for sale or service in a food service operation or retail food establishment, Ohio Admin. Code 3717-1-03.1

Table 42: Food Laws—Continued

State	Sale of Raw Milk	Sale of Eggs	Sale of Cottage Foods	Sale of Wild Foraged Mushrooms
OKLAHOMA	Sale allowed only on farm on which it was produced, 2 § 7-414	Producers selling ungraded eggs from own flock directly to consumer are exempt from labeling and licensing, 2 § 10-78	Home food establishment exempt from licensing if gross annual sales less than $20,000; labeling required, 63 §§ 1440 to 1440.5	Mushroom species picked in the wild prohibited from sale or service by a food establishment, OAC 310:257-5-7
OREGON	Sale allowed directly to consumer on farm where produced; no more than 2 producing dairy cows, 9 producing sheep or 9 producing goats allowed on the premises where milk is produced, 621.012	Producer selling and delivering eggs of own flock directly to consumer exempt from licensing and grading, labeling required, 632.715; 632.771	License not required if food is produced in residence and is sold directly to end consumer; food must be baked goods or confectionary item and non-hazardous; annual gross sales of less than $20,000; everyone involved in preparation of food must complete food handler training program and be certified, 616.723	Sale allowed in food establishments if inspected and identified by trained person; must be conspicuously identified and labeled as an uninspected product, OAR 333-150-0000
PENNSYLVANIA	Retail sale of raw cow's milk allowed, Tit. 31, § 652	Processor exempt from grading if flock of up to 3,200 laying hens, eggs are marketed within 100 mi. radius, within 5 days of laying, and stored at 60 deg. Fahrenheit or less prior to sale; labeling required, Tit. 31, § 300.3	Cottage foods not directly defined; "limited food processor" may produce non-potentially hazardous foods; registration required, Tit. 3, §§ 5721 to 5737; 7 Pa. Code § 46.1141	No sale or service allowed unless food establishment has been approved to accept, 7 Pa. Code § 46.4
RHODE ISLAND	Purchase of raw goat milk directly from producer allowed with prescription from physician, 21-2-2	All eggs must be graded and labeled, 21-17-1	Food must be produced in kitchen on premises of farm and may be sold at farmers' markets, farm stands, or other outlets operated by farmers for purpose of retail sale of farm products; recipes must be maintained in kitchen for review and inspection; product must be labeled; production limited to non-potentially hazardous food and foods that do not require refrigeration; must register annually with dept. of health, 21-27-6.1	Must be obtained from sources where each mushroom is individually inspected and found to be safe by approved mushroom identification expert, R.I. Admin. Code 31-3-11:3-2

Table 42: Food Laws—Continued

State	Sale of Raw Milk	Sale of Eggs	Sale of Cottage Foods	Sale of Wild Foraged Mushrooms
SOUTH CAROLINA	Sale in retail stores allowed, S.C. Code Regs. 61-34	Persons who sell eggs at a roadside stand near the farm on which the eggs were produced exempt from grading and labeling; no license required, 39-39-170	Producer must sell directly to consumer; non-potentially hazardous baked goods and candy only; food must be labeled; exemption from production requirements if annual sales less than $500; producer may apply for exemption from inspection and labeling requirements if annual sales less than $15,000, 44-1-143	Must be obtained from sources where each mushroom is individually inspected and found to be safe by approved mushroom identification expert, S.C. Code Regs. 61-25
SOUTH DAKOTA	Sale allowed directly to consumer at place where produced or by delivery; no sale allowed at farmers' market or farmer-owned retail store not located at place where milk is produced, 39-6-3	Producer selling and delivering eggs from own flock directly to consumer exempt from licensing requirements, 39-11-2	Non-temperature-controlled baked or canned goods exempt from license if produced in seller's primary residence and total annual gross sales are less than $5,000; labeling required, 34-18-35 to 34-18-38	Must be obtained from sources where each mushroom is individually inspected and found to be safe by approved mushroom identification expert, ARSD 44:02:07:16
TENNESSEE	Sales prohibited; raw milk available through herd share agreement, 53-3-119; Tenn. Comp. R. & Regs. 0080-03-02-.11	Producer selling directly to consumer exempt from licensing and grading; labeling required, 53-2-108; 53-2-116	No permit required to sell food from home, at event, or market; food must be designated with sign; producer encourage to complete food safety course, 53-8-117	Must be obtained from sources where each mushroom is individually inspected and found to be safe by approved mushroom identification expert, Tenn. Comp. R. & Regs. 0080-04-09-.03
TEXAS	Sale allowed directly to consumer from farm on which it was produced; permit required, 25 TAC 217.32; 217.91	Producers selling eggs from own flock directly to consumers not required to license, grade, or label, Agric. §§ 132.002; 132.021	Producer must complete basic food safety training; only non-potentially hazardous food; food must be packaged and labeled; must be sold directly to consumer from home, by delivery, or at farmer's market-like event, no internet, wholesale or mail order sales; gross annual income must be less than $50,000, Health & Safety §§ 437.0191 to 437.0196; 25 TAC 229.661	No sale or service unless food establishment has been approved to do so, 25 TAC 228.62

Table 42: Food Laws—Continued

State	Sale of Raw Milk	Sale of Eggs	Sale of Cottage Foods	Sale of Wild Foraged Mushrooms
UTAH	Producer may sell directly to end consumer from farm where produced or at self-owned retail store, permits required, 4-3-503	Small egg producers with up to 3,000 hens are required to label, not required to grade; license required, U.A.C. R70-410	Food must be non-potentially hazardous and produced in home kitchen; registration, valid food handler permit, packaging, and labeling required; 4-5-501; U.A.C. R70-560	Mushroom species picked in wild shall not be offered for sale or service by food establishment, U.A.C. R392-100
VERMONT	Producer selling less than 87.5 gal. per wk. may sell directly to consumer allowed on farm on which produced or by delivery, must be labeled; producer selling more than 87.5 gal. per wk. subject to additional regulations but may also deliver at farmers' markets; 350 gal. per wk. limit for any sale of raw milk, Tit. 6, § 2777	Sale of ungraded eggs as nest run allowed from one dealer to another; all other eggs must be graded and labeled, Tit. 6, §§ 351 to 358; Vt. Admin. Code 2-4-206	No license required for individual manufacturing and selling bakery products from own home kitchen; average gross retail sales must not exceed $125 per wk., Tit. 18, § 4358	Must be obtained from sources where each mushroom is individually inspected and found to be safe by an approved mushroom identification expert, Vt. Admin. Code 12-5-30:5-204
VIRGINIA	Sale of unpasteurized milk for human consumption prohibited; no law on herd shares, 2 VAC § 5-490-70	Producer selling up to 150 doz. eggs per wk. from own flock exempt from labeling, grading, and invoice requirements, 3.2-5305	Private home making low acid food exempt from inspection if sold to consumer from home or at farmers' market, no internet sales; food must be labeled; annual sales limited to $3,000, 3.2-5130	No sale or service by food establishment unless it has been approved to do so, 12 VAC 5-421-320
WASHINGTON	Sale allowed in retail stores, 15.36.151	Dept. of Agric. Director's discretion to limit licensing requirements for sale of eggs by producer with flock of 3,000 or less or selling from own flock directly to consumer; no license required if selling on farm; no labeling required; eggs must be graded unless producer is wholesale shell egg dealer, 69.25.170;	Food must be produced and stored in home kitchen of primary residence and sold directly to consumer, no internet, mail order, or retail sales; successful completion of food safety training program and permit required, only foods permitted may be sold; foods must be non-potentially hazardous; items must be packaged and labeled; annual gross sales up to $25,000, 69.22.010, WAC 16-49-010 to 140	Permit required to harvest; each mushroom must be individually identified in the fresh state; only certain species offered for sale or service, 76.48.031; WAC 246-215-03225

Table 42: Food Laws—Continued

State	Sale of Raw Milk	Sale of Eggs	Sale of Cottage Foods	Sale of Wild Foraged Mushrooms
WEST VIRGINIA	Sale prohibited; raw milk available through herd share agreement, 19-1-7	Producer selling eggs from own flock exempt from invoicing and grading; labeling required, 19-10A-4	Sale allowed only at farmers' market; food must be labeled; registration required, 19-35-2 to 19-35-4; WV Code St. R. 64-101 to 64-102; WVDHHR Farmers Market Vendor Guide	Must be obtained from sources where each mushroom is individually identified and found to be safe by approved mushroom identification expert, 64-17-3
WISCONSIN	Sale allowed only on farm on which produced, 97.24	Producer exempt from licensing and grading if eggs sold are from own flock of less than 150 hens, sales are directly to consumer from place of production, at farmers' market, or on egg sales route; labeling required, 97.28; WI ADC § ATCP 88	Only foods allowed are low-acidic canned foods; sale in person and directly to consumer at farmers' market or other community event; annual sales less than $5,000; labeling and signage required; no license required, 97.29	
WYOMING	Under Food Freedom Act, sale directly to consumer on farm where produced, farmers' market or by delivery, consumer must be informed that product is not certified, labeled, licensed, packaged, regulated, or inspected; herd share also available, Food Freedom Act, 11-49-101 to 11-49-103; WY ADC AGR FSF Ch. 3 § 8	Under Food Freedom Act, sale directly to consumer on farm where produced, farmers' market or by delivery, consumer must be informed that product is not certified, labeled, licensed, packaged, regulated, or inspected, Food Freedom Act: 11-49-101 to 11-49-103; WY ADC AGR FSF Ch. 4 § 7; Ch. 15 § 1	Under Food Freedom Act, sale directly to consumer on farm where produced, farmers' market or by delivery, consumer must be informed that product is not certified, labeled, licensed, packaged, regulated, or inspected, Food Freedom Act: 11-49-101 to 11-49-103; WY ADC AGR FSF Ch. 1 § 8	Must be obtained from sources where each mushroom is individually inspected and found to be safe by an approved mushroom identification expert, WY ADC AGR FSF Ch. 3 § 3

43. FREEDOM OF INFORMATION ACTS

For centuries, the common law has recognized the public's right to access public records. Access to public records has been an important component of participatory democracy and a judiciary accountable for its decisions. Thus have evolved important aspects of our legal system that we presently take for granted, such as our highly elaborate system of publication of judicial opinions and the detailed reporting of the workings of Congress.

However, this important feature of an open government can also run afoul of another important aspect of our democracy: the right to privacy. There are also matters in which the government must have the ability to exercise discretion and some degree of secrecy, both to protect actors in various government activities and to be able to set policy without risking negotiating strategies. But there are also certain matters in which a person's involvement in government matters may be an embarrassment or may unfairly damage a person's reputation or even compromise his or her safety.

Government, generally, tends to prefer a more secretive approach to governing. Not necessarily because it has secret or malicious motives, but because it is always easier to act in an official capacity if fewer people are aware of the myriad details that surround even the most mundane government business, such as negotiating a foreign trade deal or launching an investigation of a corrupt politician. Most persons in government are happy to make public the results of their actions and policies, but are loath to release details of the discussions or negotiations about how the policy came to be made.

In 1966, the United States Congress passed the Freedom of Information Act (FOIA), for the first time creating a statutory right of public access to public records. Since that time, every state has passed its own version of FOIA. State FOIAs may not contravene any federal laws, but since the states are not custodians of any federal records, little danger exists of states allowing access to federal records that the federal government does not want to make public. State FOIAs instead deal with public access to state records.

In situations where a person desires access to public records that a government agency is unwilling to, or for procedural reasons is unable to, release, the person may file a "FOIA request" with the agency or office. Most government agencies are now set up with special procedures and offices devoted to full-time work on fulfilling FOIA requests. In most cases offices that keep public records have forms on which FOIA requests may be made. Individual requests are then granted or denied based on the standards of disclosure required by the statutes.

The following chart details four distinct aspects of state FOIA laws. Most state FOIAs specify that FOIA requests may be made by citizens of the state. They also specify remedies for violations of the acts. Usually, the acts provide for injunctions if an agency denies a request, or damages if an agency gives out records that it shouldn't. State FOIA statutes are also divided on the issue of whether to allow agencies to charge money for the records given up on such a request. Some states permit agencies to charge for the time it takes to search the records and for the cost of making copies. Some states only permit an agency to charge a reasonable amount for the cost of copying them.

The most interesting aspect of the state FOIA laws are the numbers and natures of exemptions specified in the statutes. Of course, there are some states that provide no enumerated exemptions at all. In those situations, presumably, reasonableness will govern when a disclosure has violated a right to privacy. But some states, such as Hawaii, has a broad exemption statute that says that public records need not be disclosed when it would constitute a "clearly unwarranted" invasion of personal privacy. At the other extreme, the state of California's exemption statutes enumerate dozens and dozens of specific exemptions. Every imaginable type of public record kept by every imaginable public and quasi-public agency or entity is covered in California, from records of alcoholic rehabilitation and records of podiatrists to disciplinary records of public officials. Instead of trying to list every exemption found in each state with enumerated exemptions, the chart only lists the statute numbers where the exemptions may be found. Listing all the exemptions—particularly for states like California—is, for all practical purposes, impossible.

---

*This chapter was compiled by Kristin Thornblad, 2007 graduate of the University of Nebraska, College of Law.

Table 43: Freedom of Information Acts

State	Code Section	Who May Request/What Documents
ALABAMA	36-12-40; 36-12-41	Any citizen; any public writing, 36-12-40
ALASKA	40.25.110 to 40.25.125	Any member of the public; all public records, 40.25.110
ARIZONA	39-121.01 to 39-121.03	Any person; any public record, 39-121.01(D)
ARKANSAS	25-19-101 to 25-19-220	Any citizen of Arkansas; all public records, 25-19-105
CALIFORNIA	Gov't §§ 6250 to 6277	Any person; any public record, Gov't § 6253
COLORADO	24-72-201 to 30-10-101	Any person; all public records, 24-72-201
CONNECTICUT	1-200 to 1-215	Every person; all public records, 1-210(a)
DELAWARE	Tit. 29, §§ 10001 to 10112	Any citizen of Delaware; all public records, Tit. 29, § 10003
FLORIDA	119.01 to 119.19	Any person; all public records, 119.01
GEORGIA	50-18-70 to 50-28-103	Any citizen of Georgia; any public record, 50-18-70
HAWAII	92F-3 to 92F-28	Any person; all government records, 92F-11
IDAHO	74-101 to 74-126	Every person; any public record, 9-338
ILLINOIS	5 §§ 140/1 to 140/11.6	Any person; all public records, 5 § 140/3
INDIANA	5-14-3-1 to 5-14-3-10	Any person; public records of any public agency, 5-14-3-3
IOWA	22.1 to 22.16	Every person; public records, 22.2
KANSAS	45-215 to 45-254	Any person; all public records, 45-218
KENTUCKY	61.870 to 61.884	Any person; all public records, 61.872

Enumerated Exemptions	Remedies for Violation of the Act	Fees for Disclosure of Records?
		Fees for copying and certification, 36-12-41
40.25.120	Injunctive relief without exhausting administrative remedies, 40.25.125	Actual costs for production and copying, 40.25.110
	Special action in the superior court, 39-121.02(A)	Reasonable fee for production and actual cost of reproduction, 39-121.03
25-19-105(b)	Immediate appeal to the Pulaski County Circuit or circuit of county of victim's residence, 25-19-107	Copying costs; transmittal or mailing costs; actual, verifiable personnel costs over 2 hrs. for electronic information request, 25-19-105(3)(A); 25-19-109
Gov't §§ 6254; 6254.1 to 6254.25; 6267; 6276.02 to 6276.48	Petition to the superior court in county where the records are situated, Gov't § 6259	Copying costs or statutory fee, Gov't § 6253(b)
24-72-204	Appeal to agency, then appeal to district court where record is found, 24-72-204(5)	Reasonable fee for copying, 24-72-205
1-210; 1-213; 1-214; 2-215		Fees for copying not to exceed actual cost and as set by statute, 1-212
Tit. 29, § 10002(l)	Appeal to Court of Chancery, Tit. 29, § 10005(a)	Reasonable costs for copying, Tit. 29, § 10003
§ 119.071	Appeal as civil action in court, 119.07(1)(g)	Fees for copying not to exceed actual cost, fees for service in certain circumstances, 119.07(4)
50-18-72	Appeal to superior court, 50-18-73	Reasonable costs of production and copying, or as provided by law, 50-18-71
92F-13; 92F-14; 92F-22	Appeal to circuit court, 92F-15	
74-104 to 74-111	Appeal to district court of county where records are located, 74-115	Any statutory fee; no fee 1st 2 hrs. of labor or 1st 100 pgs. copied; fees may be established for over 2 hrs. labor, 100 pgs. copied, or records from which nonpublic information must be deleted; fees may not exceed actual copying or reasonable labor costs; certain exceptions exist, 74-102(10)
5 § 140/7	Appeal to circuit court, 5 § 140/11	Actual costs of reproducing and certifying; no cost for 1st 50 pgs.; fees for voluminous electronic records; labor costs up to $10/hr. for retrieving and/or redacting records, no charge for 1st 8 hrs.; possible retrieval fee from third-party storage facility , 5 § 140/6
5-14-3-4	Appeal to circuit or superior court in county where disclosure denied, 5-14-3-9	Copying fee greater of 10¢/pg. or actual cost; fees for electronic records; any fee established by statute or court, § 5-14-3-8
22.7	Appeal to district court in which custodian of record has principle place of business, 22.10	Reasonable fee for access and/or copying, 22.3
45-221	Appeal to district court of county in which records are located, 45-222	Reasonable fees for access and/or copying, 45-219(c)
61.878	Appeal to Attorney General, then appeal to Circuit Court of county where relevant public agency has its principle place of business, 61.880; 61.882	Reasonable fee for copying, 61.874(3)

Table 43: Freedom of Information Acts—Continued

State	Code Section	Who May Request/What Documents
LOUISIANA	44:31 to 44:41	Any person 18 or older/any public record, 44:31
MAINE	Tit. 1, §§ 400 to 414	Every person; all public records, Tit. 1, §408-A
MARYLAND	Gen. Provis. §§ 4-101 to 4-601	Any person; any public record, Gen. Provis. § 4-103; 4-201
MASSACHUSETTS	Ch. 66, §§ 3 to 17C	Every person; any public record, Ch. 66, § 10
MICHIGAN	15.231 to 15.246	Any person; any public document, 15.233
MINNESOTA	13.03 to 13.99; Ch. 13 Appendix	Any person; all public records; 13.03
MISSISSIPPI	25-61-1 to 25-61-19	Any person; any public record, 25-61-2
MISSOURI	109.180; 610.010 to 610.150	Any citizen of Missouri; all public records, 109.180
MONTANA	2-6-1001 to 2-6-1020	Every person; any public writing, 2-6-1003
NEBRASKA	84-712 to 84-712.09	Any person; all public records, 84-712
NEVADA	239.010– to 239.303	Any person; all public records, 239.010
NEW HAMPSHIRE	91-A:1 to 91-A:9	Every citizen; all public records, 91-A:4
NEW JERSEY	47:1A-1 to 47:1A-13	All citizens of the state; all public records, 47:1A-1
NEW MEXICO	14-2-1 to 14-2-12	Every person; any public records, 14-2-1
NEW YORK	Pub. Off. §§ 84 to 90	All persons; all public records, Pub. Off. § 84
NORTH CAROLINA	132-1 to 132-9	Any person; any public record, 132-6
NORTH DAKOTA	44-04-18 to 44-04-18.28	Any person; all public records, 44-04-18
OHIO	149.43 to 149.45; 2743.75	Any person; all public records, 149.43(B)(1)
OKLAHOMA	Tit. 51, §§ 24A.1 to 24A.31	Any person; all public records, Tit. 51, § 24A.5
OREGON	192.311 to 192.513	Every person; any public record, 192.314

Enumerated Exemptions	Remedies for Violation of the Act	Fees for Disclosure of Records?
44:31.1	Writ of mandamus in district court for the parish in which the document custodian's office is located, 44:35	Reasonable fees for copying, 44:32
Tit. 1, § 402	Denial: appeal to superior court for county where person resides or agency has primary office; illegal action: appeal to any superior court in state, Tit. 1, § 409	Fees for translating and copying, Tit. 1, § 408-A
Gen. Provis. §§ 4-304 to 4-307	Appeal to circuit court where complainant resides or has a principle place of business, or where record is located, Gen. Provis. § 4-362	Reasonable fees for search, preparation, and reproduction, Gen. Provis. 4-206
Ch. 66, §§ 10; 17A	Appeal to superior court, Ch. 66, § 10A	Actual costs for search and preparation, Ch. 66, § 10
15.243	Administrative appeal to public body, then appeal to circuit court, 15.240	Actual costs for search and preparation, 15.234
13.03	Appeal to district court, 13.03	Actual costs for search and retrieval, 13.03
25-61-9; 25-61-11	Appeal to chancery court in court where public record is located, 25-61-13	Actual costs for search and duplication, 25-61-7
610.021; 610.035; 610.100; 610.120; 610.150	Appeal to circuit court of county where relevant public agent has its principal place of business, 610.027	Actual costs for search and duplication, 610.026
2-6-1003; 2-6-1008(4)	Appeal to district court, 2-6-1009	Fees not to exceed actual costs for search and preparation, 2-6-1006
84-712.05	Writ of mandamus in district court, or petition to the Attorney General, 84-712.03	Fees for reproduction not to exceed actual cost, 84-712
239.0115	Appeal to district court in the county in which the public book or record is located, 239.011	Fees as may be prescribed for the service of copying and certifying, 239.030
91-A:5	Petition to the superior court, 91-A:7	Fees, fees for copying, 91-A:4.IV
47:1A-1; 47:1A-1.2; 47:1A-20	Appeal to the superior court, 47:1A-6	Fees for copying as enumerated by law, 47:1A-5
14-2-1	Appeal to district court, 14-2-12	Fees for reproduction and transmittal, 14-2-9
Pub. Off. §§ 87; 89	Appeal to head, chief executive, or governing body of the entity, then to supreme court in county of denial, Pub. Off. § 89	Actual costs of preparation and reproduction, Pub. Off. § 87
132-1.1 to 132-1.5	Petition to superior court of county in which public custodian of record resides, 132-5.1	Actual cost of reproduction, 132-6.2
44-04-18.1 to 44-04-18.14	File a civil action in county where the entity has its principal office, 44-04-21.2	Reasonable fee for making and/or mailing copy, 44-04-18
149.43(A)	A mandamus action in the court of common pleas in the county where denied, 149.43(C); 2743.75	Costs for preparation and postage, 149.43(B)
Tit. 51, §§ 24A.28; 24A.5(1); 24A.7; 24A.9 to 24A.16a; 24A.19 to 24A.24; 24A.26 to 24A.31	Civil suit for injunctive or declarative relief, Tit. 51, § 24A.17	Reasonable direct costs for copying and reproduction, or as otherwise proscribed by law, Tit. 51, § 24A.5(4)
192.345; 192.355; 192.368; 192.398	Petition to the Attorney General, 192.401; 192.411	Reasonable fees for actual costs for compiling and providing copies, 192.324

Table 43: Freedom of Information Acts—Continued

State	Code Section	Who May Request/What Documents
PENNSYLVANIA	Tit. 65, §§ 67.101 to 67.1310	Every citizen of Pennsylvania; every public record, Tit. 65, §§ 67.301 to 67.304
RHODE ISLAND	38-2-1 to 38-2-15	Every person; all public records, 38-2-3
SOUTH CAROLINA	30-4-10 to 30-4-165	Any person; any public record, 30-4-30
SOUTH DAKOTA	1-27-1 to 1-27-48	Any person; any public record, 1-27-1
TENNESSEE	10-7-503 to 10-7-508	Any citizen of Tennessee; any public records, 10-7-503
TEXAS	Gov't §§ 552.001 to 552.353	Any person; all public information, Gov't § 552.001
UTAH	63G-2-101 to 63G-2-405	Every person; all public records, 63G-2-201
VERMONT	Tit. 1, §§ 315 to 320	Any person; any public record, Tit. 1, § 316(a)
VIRGINIA	2.2-3700 to 2.2-3724	Any citizen of the Commonwealth; any public records, 2.2-3704
WASHINGTON	42.56.001 to 42.56.904	Any person; all public records, 42.56.070; 42.56.080
WEST VIRGINIA	29B-1-1 to 29B-1-7	Every person; any public record, 29B-1-3
WISCONSIN	19.21 to 19.39	Any person; any public record, 19.35
WYOMING	16-4-201 to 16-4-205	Any person; all public records, 16-4-202

Enumerated Exemptions	Remedies for Violation of the Act	Fees for Disclosure of Records?
Tit. 65, § 67.708	Appeal with the Office of Open Records, then a petition for review to the Commonwealth Court, Tit. 65, §§ 67.1101; 67.1301	Reasonable fees for duplication, Tit. 65, § 67.1307
38-2-2	Administrative appeal to the agency, then appeal to superior court, 38-2-8 to 38-2-9	Reasonable charges for copying, preparation, and retrieval, 38-2-4
30-4-40	Appeal to circuit court, 30-4-100	Actual cost of searching for and making copies, 30-4-30
1-27-3; 1-27-1.3; 1-27-1.5 to 1-27-1.9	File civil action or appeal to Office of Hearing Examiners, 1-27-38	Fees for preparation and copying; if fee over $50, custodian will provide written estimate, 1-27-35
10-7-504	Appeal to chancery court for the county in which the requested records are located, 10-7-505	County records commission has power to establish and collect charges for reproducing records; 10-7-409
Gov't §§ 552.101 to 552.158	Request for decision by Attorney General, Gov't § 552.301	Reasonable fee for preparation and copying, Gov't § 552.261
63G-2-201(3); 63G-2-302 to 63G-2-304	Administrative appeal to head of agency, appeal to records committee, judicial review in state court, 63G-2-401 to 63G-2-404	Reasonable fee for actual cost of duplication, 63G-2-203
Tit. 1, § 317(c)	Appeal to superior court in which records located or complainant resides or has a principle place of business, or superior court for Washington County, Tit. 1, § 319	Actual cost of preparation and copying, Tit. 1, § 316(b)
2.203705.1 to 2.2-3705.8	Petition of mandamus to general district court or court of record of the county from where the relevant public official was appointed, elected, 2.2-3713	Reasonable charges for actual costs of preparation and production, 2.2-3704
42.56.210	Appeal to Attorney General; appeal to superior court for county in which the record is maintained, 42.56.530	Reasonable charge for copying and access to copying equipment, 42.56.120
29B-1-4	Appeal to circuit court in the county where the public record is kept, 29B-1-5	Actual cost of making reproductions, 29B-1-3
19.36	Action for mandamus in court and/or request the attorney general or district attorney in county where record is found to bring mandamus action, 19.37	Actual, direct cost of reproduction and transcription, 19.35(3)
16-4-203	Appeal to district court of district where the record is found, 16-4-203(f)	Reasonable fees for preparation and copying, 16-4-204

44. GAMBLING

Gambling is an industry that is undergoing tremendous change. It was not too long ago that Nevada was the only state in the union that allowed casino gambling. Today, numerous states either are considering legalizing gambling or have already done so. There are two factors driving the change. First, Native Americans won the right to establish casinos on their lands regardless of the laws of the state in which they are located. The establishment of these casinos softened the general public's attitudes toward casino gambling and has led to the introduction of legislative initiatives that permit it, or to voter referenda on the issue. Often, in each situation, the initiatives have resulted in outcomes favorable to gambling. The other factor leading to legalization of gambling is economic impact. Many of the regions where gambling has been legalized have realized untold economic benefits in terms of such things as taxes, jobs, and development of infrastructure. Despite the economic developments, the idea of legalizing gambling is not without controversy. Many argue that there is also associated tragedy as people who are addicted to gambling have been known to gamble until they have lost everything and have wreaked havoc on their families and personal lives.

Casino gambling is not the only type of gambling that exists, nor is it the only kind of gambling addressed by state laws. As can be seen in this chapter, there are many different ways to gamble. The most common subject of regulation is betting. Pari-mutuel wagering is a betting pool in which those who bet on competitors finishing in the top three positions share the total amount bet, less a percentage for the management. Horse racing, dog racing or betting on sporting events are those most frequently and specifically banned, however regulation of regional events is common.

Alaska lists about ten different events that are allowed, including many that would be unthinkable in the south: Deep Freeze Classic, Snow Machine Classic, and the Ice Classic, to name a few. Florida lists a number of legal gambling activities that relate specifically to the state's large number of retired citizens: penny-ante games with winnings not exceeding $10, including poker, pinochle, bridge, dominos or mahjong conducted by adults within a dwelling. One of the more unusual prohibitions is found in Massachusetts, where gaming is not permitted within one mile of a cattle show or military muster.

In 1992, the Professional and Amateur Sports Protection Act (PASPA), also known as the Bradley Act, was enacted into law. It essentially defined sports betting at the federal level and made betting on sports illegal in all but four states that had permitted sports gaming prior to 1990. A loophole in PASPA seemed to allow the operation of certain hosted-for-profit online fantasy leagues. Over the years, states have enacted many rules in response to that loophole and banned betting on fantasy teams and internet gaming. In 2018, PASPA was ruled unconstitutional by the United States Supreme Court in the case of *Murphy v. NCAA*, 584 U.S. ___ (2018). The court ruled that PASPA violated the Tenth Amendment by interfering with the sovereignty of individual states. As a result, each state may now regulate sports betting as it sees fit, but as of the summer of 2018, no state has yet passed legislation legalizing or regulating sports betting. It is expected, of course, that there will be many laws proposed in the next round of legislative activity.

Overall, the subject of legalized gambling as an industry is far from settled and is likely to change regularly in the coming years.

Table 44: Gambling

State	Code Section	Gambling	Horse Racing/Off-Track Betting
ALABAMA	11-47-111; 11-65-1; 13A-12-20 to 13A-12-92	Staking or risking something of value upon the outcome of a contest of chance or future contingent event not under one's control	Municipalities allowed to determine through referendum whether horse racing will be permitted
ALASKA	05.15.180; 11.66.200 to 11.66.280	Staking or risking something of value upon the outcome of a contest of chance or future contingent event not under one's control or influence, upon an agreement or understanding that person will receive something of value in event of a certain outcome	Prohibited
ARIZONA	5-101 to 5-116; 13-3301 to 13-3312	Risking or giving something of value for opportunity to obtain benefit from game, contest, or future contingent event	Horse and harness racing permitted; off-track betting prohibited
ARKANSAS	5-66-101 to 5-66-120; 23-110-405; 23-111-508	Betting any money or any valuable thing on any game of hazard or skill	Pari-mutuel wagering only
CALIFORNIA	Penal §§ 330 to 337z; Bus. and Prof. §§ 19400 to 19668	Dealing, playing, or conducting, games of faro, monte, roulette, lansquenet, rouge et noir, rondo, tan, fan-tan, seven-and-a-half, twenty-one, hokey pokey, or any banking or percentage game played with cards or dice	Permitted: Horse and harness racing, pari-mutuel betting only; satellite wagering
COLORADO	44-30-101 to 44-30-106; 44-32-101 to 44-32-901; 18-10-101 to 18-10-108	Risking money or any other thing of value for gain contingent in whole or part upon lot, chance, or the happening or outcome of an event over which the person taking a risk has no control	Permitted: horse racing; standard bred harness horse racing with permit; pari-mutuel wagering only; off-track simulcasts
CONNECTICUT	12-571 to 12-578; 17a-713; 53-278a to 53-278g	Risking something of value for gain contingent on lot, chance, or operation of a gambling device	Permitted: daily double; exacta; quinella; trifecta; superfecta; twin trifecta; pick four; pick six; other forms of pari-mutuel betting; off-track betting
DELAWARE	Tit. 3, §§ 10001 to 10061; Tit. 11, §§ 1401 to 1432	Recording or registering bets or wagers, or directly or indirectly betting or wagering, money or anything of value	Permitted: horse and harness racing, pari-mutuel betting only; off-track betting on out-of-state races
DISTRICT OF COLUMBIA	22-1701 to 22-1708	Playing any game of chance for money or property	Prohibited: all wagering on athletic contests, including horse racing
FLORIDA	550.001 to 550.913; 849.01 to 849.46	Playing or engaging in any card game or game of chance, at any place, by any device, for money or another thing of value	Permitted: pari-mutuel wagering on thoroughbred racing, quarter horse racing, or harness racing with permit; off-track and inter-track wagering allowed

Dog Racing/Off-Track Betting	Casinos Allowed?	Other Kinds of Gambling-Related Activities Permitted or Prohibited
Greyhound races permitted	Prohibited: gambling devices; gaming and gambling houses	Pari-mutuel betting permitted in conjunction with horse and dog racing, also with televised horse and dog racing
Dog mushers' contests permitted	Gambling devices prohibited	Permitted: several games of chance and/or skill, including bingo; Canned Salmon Classic; Deep Freeze Classic; Fish Derby, Goose Classic; Ice Classic, King Salmon Classic; Mercury Classic; Mushing Sweepstakes; Race Classic; Rain Classic; Snow Machine Classic; numbers wheels; animal classics; social in-home gambling
Daytime dog racing not permitted on same day as daytime horse or harness races in same county	Permitted: Indian reservation casinos; charitable organizations' casino night fundraisers; Prohibited: casinos run for profit	Permitted: gambling in which prizes are not offered as a lure to separate players from their money; social gambling; raffles
Franchised greyhound racing permitted, pari-mutuel wagering only	Gambling houses and devices prohibited	Prohibited: all wagering on all sports or games; keno; betting on card games can result in a fine of $10 to $25
Not specified	Slot machines prohibited; gaming on Native American land governed by Indian Gaming Regulatory Act	Permitted: bingo for charity; Prohibited: "Razzle dazzle," card, dice games if played for money, credit, check, or anything of value; draw poker in counties of 4 million or more people; illegal to possess any dice with more than 6 faces
Greyhound races prohibited; pari-mutuel wagering on simulcast races permitted if received by in-state simulcast facility	Permitted: Indian reservation casinos; other limited and only in cities of Central City, Black Hawk, and Cripple Creek: slot machines, poker, black jack, craps, and roulette with maximum single bet of $100;	Permitted: gaming for charitable organizations; social gambling; bingo and raffles regulated by secretary of state; Prohibited: election wagers
Permitted: off-track betting; wagering on out-of-state dog races	Pequot and Mohegan tribes permitted to operate casinos per Tribal-State Compact; bingo parlors permitted; gambling devices otherwise prohibited	Permitted: social gambling; pari-mutuel betting on jai alai exhibitions; any person licensed to conduct betting or wagering events must display informational materials for the prevention, treatment, and rehabilitation of compulsive gamblers
Not specified	Gambling devices prohibited	Permitted: lotteries under state control; merchandising plans not considered gambling; Prohibited: gambling in bowling alleys; craps games; election wagering
Prohibited	Gaming houses and devices prohibited	Permitted: bingo; raffles; Monte Carlo night parties organized for educational and charitable purposes; Prohibited: three-card monte; confidence games; bookmaking
Permitted: pari-mutuel wagering on greyhound dog racing with permit; off-track and intertrack wagering	Permitted: tribal gaming pursuant to Indian Gaming Regulatory Act; pari-mutuel-style card rooms; Prohibited: casino-style card rooms; gambling devices	Permitted: Jai-alai; penny-ante games with winnings not exceeding $10, including poker, pinochle, bridge, dominoes, and mahjongg, if conducted by adults in a dwelling; card rooms; bingo; gaming for charitable organizations; Prohibited: chain letters; pyramid schemes

Table 44: Gambling—Continued

State	Code Section	Gambling	Horse Racing/Off-Track Betting
GEORGIA	16-12-20 to 16-12-62	Betting upon the final result of any game or contest, or upon games played with cards, dice, or balls, in order to win money or other things of value	Prohibited
HAWAII	712-1220 to 712-1231	Staking or risking something of value upon outcome of a contest of chance or uncontrollable future contingent event in order to receive something of value	
IDAHO	18-3801 to 18-3810; 54-2501 to 54-2517; 67-429A to 67-429C; 67-7701 to 67-7719; ID Const. art. III, § 20	Risking any money, credit, deposit or other thing of value upon lot, chance, the operation of a gambling device or the happening or outcome of an event, including sporting events	Permitted: live and simulcast horse racing, pari-mutuel betting only
ILLINOIS	230 §§ 5/1 to 40/85; 720 §§ 5/28-1 to 5/28-9	Playing games of chance or skill for money or other thing of value; wagering upon games, contests, or elections; owning or operating gambling devices	Horse racing and pari-mutuel wagering permitted with license
INDIANA	4-31-1-1 to 4-31-13-9; 35-45-5-1 to 35-45-5-13	Risking money or other property for gain, contingent upon lot, chance, or the operation of a gambling device	Horse racing and satellite facilities licensed for pari-mutuel wagering permitted
IOWA	99.1 to 99g.42; 725.5 to 725.19	Participating in a game for anything of value or making any bet	Permitted: horse racing; licensees may simulcast out-of-state races within racetrack for purpose of pari-mutuel wagering
KANSAS	21-6403 to 21-6409; 74-8801 to 74-8842	Making a bet; entering or remaining in a gambling place with intent to bet; playing a gambling device	Nonprofit organizations may apply to state racing commission for license to construct or own racetrack facility and conduct horse races; pari-mutuel wagering only; no off-track betting
KENTUCKY	528.010; 230.210 to 230.990; 238.500 to 238.995	Staking or risking something of value upon the outcome of a contest or game based upon an element of chance	Permitted: horse running, trotting, and pacing races; harness races; off-track interstate wagering; pari-mutuel wagering only
LOUISIANA	14:90 to 14:90.7; 27:201 to 27:286; 27:301 to 27:305; 27:351 to 27:361	Intentional conducting a game or contest in which a person risks the loss of anything of value in order to realize a profit	Permitted: horse racing on licensed racetracks; interstate and international pari-mutuel wagering

Dog Racing/Off-Track Betting	Casinos Allowed?	Other Kinds of Gambling-Related Activities Permitted or Prohibited
Prohibited	Maintenance of gambling places or equipment prohibited	Permitted: raffles and bingo for non-profit organizations; Prohibited: election wagering; commercial gambling; dogfighting; chain letters; pyramid clubs
	Prohibited: gambling aboard ships; possession of gambling devices, e.g. slot machines	Permitted: social gambling, as long as not committed in a hotel, motel, bar, nightclub, or any business establishment or public place; Prohibited: possession of gambling records; promoting gambling; bookmaking
Permitted: Pari-mutuel betting system for simulcast or televised dog races at facilities licensed and authorized prior to January 1, 1996; exhibition-style live dog races if no pari-mutuel betting	Casino operations and possession of modern slot machines prohibited except on tribal land; antique slot machines may be displayed but not operated.	Permitted: bingo, raffles, and duck races for charitable cause; Prohibited: bookmaking; possession of gambling records; pool selling
Not specified	Riverboat gambling permitted on any navigable stream other than Lake Michigan	Permitted: compensation agreements; bona fide contests of skill, speed, strength, or endurance; manufacture of gambling devices; bingo; raffles; possession of antique slot machines; pull tab and jar games; charitable games
Not specified	Riverboat gambling legal in counties contiguous to Lake Michigan, Ohio River, and Patoka Lake	Permitted: gaming for charitable organizations with license; Prohibited: bookmaking; pool-selling; maintenance of slot machines, dice tables, or roulette wheels; conducting banking games
Permitted: dog racing; licensees may simulcast out-of-state races within racetrack for purpose of pari-mutuel wagering	Excursion boat gambling, including coin-operated games permitted; gambling on land prohibited except for on Indian reservations	Permitted: raffles not exceeding $200 in value; bingo; social gambling; any adult may hold an annual game night with a license, if no consideration is involved except goodwill; Prohibited: bookmaking; card counting; pyramid games
Nonprofit organizations may apply to state racing commission for license to construct or own racetrack facility and conduct greyhound races; pari-mutuel wagering only; no off-track betting	Commercial gambling prohibited except in accordance with Indian tribal gaming statutes	Permitted: bona fide business transactions; prizes to winners of bona fide contests of skill, speed, strength, or endurance; bingo operated by bona fide nonprofit organizations
Not specified	Casinos and gambling establishments prohibited	Permitted: charitable gaming; Prohibited: bookmaking; organizing or promoting gambling; possessing gambling records and devices
Dog racing prohibited	Permitted: riverboat gambling; casinos in selected jurisdictions; must be over age 21 to play video poker	Permitted: gambling on international commercial cruise ships sailing to ports in parishes with populations of 475,000 or more; bona fide charitable raffles, bingo and Keno; social gambling; fantasy sports contest upon parish election; Prohibited: gambling via Internet; gambling at a cockfight

Table 44: Gambling—Continued

State	Code Section	Gambling	Horse Racing/Off-Track Betting
MAINE	Tit. 8, §§ 261-A to 302; Tit. 17-A, §§ 951 to 961	Staking or risking something of value upon the outcome of a contest of chance or a future contingent event not under his control or influence, with intent to receive something of value in the event of a certain outcome	Permitted: harness horse racing; off-track betting
MARYLAND	Bus. Reg. §§ 10-502; 11-101 to 11-1312; Crim. Law §§ 12-101 to 12-114; 13-201 to 13-205	Wagering or betting in any manner to receive something of value dependent upon the result of any race, contest or contingency	Permitted: tthoroughbred and harness racing, pari-mutuel betting; intertrack betting; satellite simulcast betting
MASSACHUSETTS	Ch. 23K, §§ 1 to 71; Ch. 128A, §§ 1 to 14e; Ch. 271, §§ 1 to 14E	Gambling: the playing of a game by a patron of a gaming establishment; Game: a banking or percentage game played with cards, dice, tiles, dominoes, or an electronic, electrical, or mechanical device or machine, played for money, property, checks, credit, or any other representative of value which has been approved by the gaming commission	Permitted: licensed horse racing; on-track pari-mutuel or certificate wagering
MICHIGAN	432.201 to 432.226; 750.301 to 750.315a	Accepting money or a valuable thing contingent upon result of contest or happening of uncertain event	Permitted: LI've horse racing at licensed race tracks; on-track simulcasting; on-track pari-mutuel wagering; Prohibited: simulcast horse races on the premises of a casino
MINNESOTA	240.01 to 240.35; 349.11 to 349.61; 609.75 to 609.763	Making a bet; possessing a gambling device without a license; and allowing a structure under one's control to be used as a gambling place	Permitted: licensed on-track pari-mutuel system of wagering on horse races; card club operation at licensed race track
MISSISSIPPI	75-76-1 to 75-76-325; 97-33-1 to 97-33-203	Encouraging any game, other than a dog fight, for money or other valuable thing	Prohibited
MISSOURI	313.001 to 313.850; 572.010 to 572.125	Staking or risking something of value upon the outcome of a contest of chance or future contingent event	Permitted: horse racing; pari-mutuel wagering on international or interstate horse race simulcasts; Prohibited: off-track wagering
MONTANA	23-4-101 to 23-5-810	Risking money or anything of value for a gain contingent upon lot or chance	Permitted: live or simulcast horse races at licensed racetracks or simulcast facilities, pari-mutuel on-track wagering only

Dog Racing/Off-Track Betting	Casinos Allowed?	Other Kinds of Gambling-Related Activities Permitted or Prohibited
Prohibited: greyhound racing; interstate simulcasts of greyhound racing	Gaming allowed	Permitted: bingo clubs for individuals 62 years of age or older; bona fide business contracts; raffles; Prohibited: bookmaking to the extent that a person receives or accepts in any 24-hour period more than 5 bets totaling more than $500; mutuel schemes; promoting gambling; possession of gambling records and/or devices
Not specified	Permitted: slot machines in certain counties. Prohibited: occupying any house, building or vessel on land or water for purpose of gambling	Permitted: games of entertainment, e.g. bingo and raffles, including bona fide political committee raffles and raffles of real property by charitable organizations; games of chance by retail service stations, but not by supplier of motor fuel; Prohibited: bookmaking; pool-making; jai alai
Dog racing prohibited	Permitted: licensed gaming establishments; Prohibited: betting houses	Permitted: charitable organizations may have raffles or bazaars. Illegal: book making and pool making; betting in pool halls or bowling alleys; gaming within one mile of a cattle show, military muster or public gathering; using a telephone to place or accept a bet
	Licensed casinos permitted; gaming on Native American land governed by Indian Gaming Regulatory Act	Permitted: recreational card playing at senior citizen housing facility; league bowling at alleys not exceeding $1,000; redemption games; bingo; millionaire parties; social media internet games; Prohibited: pool selling; registering bets; gambling in stocks, bonds, grain or produce
Prohibited: training a greyhound for racing using live lure or live bait or conducting greyhound race using live lure or bait	Gaming on tribal land governed by Indian Gaming Regulatory Act	Allowed: pull-tabs; bingo; raffles; private social bets; paddlewheels; tip boards; possession of gambling device in one's dwelling for one's own amusement; social skill games with prizes not in excess of $200; charitable organizations may be licensed to hold gambling activities
Not specified	Permitted: licensed casinos; cruise vessels on Mississippi River or waters within any county bordering river in which voters have approved gambling	Permitted: charitable bingo; Prohibited: cockfights; Indian ball play; duels; raffles; gambling devices; yacht races; shooting matches; gaming tables; minors not allowed any gambling privileges
Not specified	Permitted: licensed excursion gambling boats and floating facilities which house games of chance and skill, including poker, craps, blackjack; must be 21 to wager on gambling boats.	Permitted: bingo sponsored by bona fide charitable organizations; Prohibited: bookmaking; possession of gambling records and devices
Permitted: live or simulcast greyhound races at licensed racetracks or simulcast facilities, pari-mutuel on-track wagering only	Video gambling devices legal permitted; gambling devices otherwise prohibited	Permitted: fishing derbies; wagering on natural occurrences; gambling activities sponsored by nonprofit organizations; possession of antique slot machines; shaking dice for a drink or music; Calcutta pools; bingo; Keno and raffles; sports pools and tab games; fantasy sports leagues; Prohibited: bookmaking; pool selling

Table 44: Gambling—Continued

State	Code Section	Gambling	Horse Racing/Off-Track Betting
NEBRASKA	2-1201 to 2-1247; 9-201 to 9-266; 9-283; 28-1101 to 28-1117	Betting something of value upon the outcome of a future event which is determined by an element of chance	Permitted: lincensed horse racing; pari-mutuel wagering; off-track betting (including simulcasting and telephonic wagering); exotic wagering such as daily double, exacta, quinella, trifecta, pick six
NEVADA	463.010 to 463.790; 466.095	Dealing, operating, carrying on, or exposing for play any game, or operating inter-casino linked systems	Licensed horse racing permitted; off-track betting must be conducted at licensed gaming facilities
NEW HAMPSHIRE	284:1 to 287-H:4; 647:2	Risking something of value upon a future contingent not under one's control or influence, upon an agreement or understanding that something of value will be received in the event of a certain outcome	Licensed horse racing and on-track pari-mutuel wagering permitted
NEW JERSEY	2C:37-1 to 2C:37-9; 5:5-22 to 5:5-189	Staking or risking of something of value upon outcome of contest of chance or future contingent event not under actor's control, upon agreement that actor will receive something of value in event of a certain outcome	Licensed horse racing; on-track pari-mutuel wagering; race simulcasts; licensed inter-track wagering; receipt of and wagering upon simulcast horse races held out of state
NEW MEXICO	30-19-1 to 30-19-15; 60-1A-1 to 60-1A-30	Making a bet; entering or remaining in a gambling place with intent to make a bet or play a gambling device	Licensed horse racing; on-track pari-mutuel wagering for live or simulcast horse races if simulcast horse race is televised at a licensed racetrack
NEW YORK	Penal § 225.00 to 225.95; Rac. Pari-Mut. Wag. & Breed. § 101 to 436; 518; 100 to 1018	Staking or risking something of value upon the outcome of a contest of chance or a future contingent event not under person's control, upon an agreement that he/she will receive something of value, given a certain event	Permitted: licensed horse and harness racing; off-track pari-mutuel wagering at licensed facilities; pari-mutuel wagering on simulcast races, including simulcasting of out-of-state or out-of-country races
NORTH CAROLINA	14-289 to 14-309.20	Operating a game of chance and playing at or betting on any game of chance at which money, property or other thing of value is bet, whether the same be in stake or not	Horse racing prohibited
NORTH DAKOTA	12.1-28-01 to 12.1-28-02; 53-06.1-01 to 53.06.2-16	Risking something of value for gain, contingent, wholly or partially, upon lot, chance, operation of gambling apparatus, or happening or outcome of an event, including elections or sporting events, over which person taking risk has no control	Permitted: licensed horse racing; race simulcasts; pari-mutuel wagering, including place, show, quinella, and combination

Dog Racing/Off-Track Betting	Casinos Allowed?	Other Kinds of Gambling-Related Activities Permitted or Prohibited
No lottery game shall be based on the results of a dog race, horse race, or other sporting event	Permitted: tribal gaming legal, pursuant to Indian Gaming Regulatory Act; Prohibited: gambling devices	Permitted: lawful business transactions; playing amusement devices; conducting prize contests; participating in bingo and raffles in accordance with state statutes; Prohibited: promoting gambling, possessing gambling records, or possessing gambling devices
Dog racing prohibited; off-track pari-mutuel wagering permitted	Licensed casino gambling permitted	Permitted: charitable lotteries; private, social gambling; Prohibited: manipulation of gaming equipment; use of unapproved wagering instruments
Simulcast only	Cruise ships equipped with gambling machines whose primary purpose is touring may enter state for 48 hours, provided that all gambling machines are disabled while in state; others prohibited.	Permitted: charitable organizations' raffles, bingo and games of chance; lucky 7; manufacture of gambling machines; fantasy sports contests; Prohibited: gambling on gas station premises; wagering on games or sports
Sled dog racing allowed for agricultural fairs and exhibitions only	Licensed casino operation permitted	Permitted: raffles and bingo for charitable organizations; Permitted: bookmaking; possession of gambling records; unlicensed maintenance of gambling resorts; possession of gambling devices not regulated by Casino Control Act; unlicensed conduct of games of chance on Sundays; promoting gambling
Not specified	Gambling places prohibited, except as pursuant to Indian Gaming Compact	Permitted: manufacturing and exporting of gambling devices; senior citizen bingo; minors not allowed to play bingo; Prohibited: commercial gambling; permitting premises to be used for gambling; dealing in gambling devices; bookmaking; bribery of contest participants; accepting anything of value on the basis of results of a race, contest or game of skill or chance
Not specified	Gambling devices prohibited	Permitted: games of chance sponsored by bona fide charitable organizations; social, private gambling; Prohibited: promoting gambling; possession of gambling records; bookmaking; possession of gambling devices
Greyhound racing prohibited	Permitted: Indian gaming; Prohibited: other gaming	Permitted: bingo games and raffles sponsored by nonprofit organizations; Prohibited: pyramid and chain schemes; allowing gambling in houses of public entertainment; faro banks and tables; possession and operation of punchboards and slot machines
Simulcast only	Prohibited; Indian gaming allowed by compact	Permitted: lawful contests of skill, speed, strength or endurance; lawful business transactions; bingo, twenty-one, pull tabs, poker, calcutta, paddlewheels, punchboards, sports pools, and raffles sponsored by licensed charitable organizations; Prohibited: bogus chips; marked cards; cheating devices; fraudulent schemes

Table 44: Gambling—Continued

State	Code Section	Gambling	Horse Racing/Off-Track Betting
OHIO	2915.02 to 2915.40; 3769.01 to 3769.28	Bookmaking; facilitating schemes or games of chance for profit; betting on schemes or games of chance for one's livelihood; possession of gambling devices; playing craps; roulette or slot machines for money	Permitted: horse racing with permit; on-track pari-mutuel wagering and wagering at fourteen satellite facilities
OKLAHOMA	Tit. 3A, §§ 200 to 427; Tit. 21, §§ 941 to 993	Betting or bargaining that, dependent upon chance, one stands to lose or win something of value specified in an agreement between parties	Permitted: licensed horse racing; pari-mutuel, off-track, interstate wagering
OREGON	167.108 to 167.167; 462.010 to 462.990	Staking or risking something of value upon outcome of a contest of chance or future contingent event not under control of actor, upon agreement that actor would receive something of value in the event of a certain outcome	Permitted: licensed horse racing and pari-mutuel wagering; off-track pari-mutuel wagering
PENNSYLVANIA	Tit. 3, §§ 9301 to 9374; Tit. 18, §§ 5513; 7103; 7516	Elements of gambling: consideration; element of chance; reward	Permitted: licensed horse and harness racing; interstate simulcasts; on- and off-track pari-mutuel wagering
RHODE ISLAND	11-19-1 to 11-19-45; 41-3-1to 41-4-14.1; 41-10-1 to 41-11-4	Directly or indirectly setting up, publicly or privately, any chance, game or device for the purpose of disposing of money, or assisting others in such actions	Permitted: licensed horse and harness racing, on-track pari-mutuel wagering; off-track pari-mutuel betting with license; simulcast races
SOUTH CAROLINA	16-19-40 to 16-19-160; 52-5-10 to 52-5-150	Playing card or dice games, roly-poly, rouge et noir, faro, gaming tables, machines, or devices	Carolina Cup Race and related races permitted, with proceeds benefitting the Kershaw County Memorial Hospital
SOUTH DAKOTA	22-25-1 to 22-25-50; 42-7-47 to 42-7-106	Wagering anything of value upon the outcome of game of chance; maintaining gambling place or equipment	Permitted: licensed horse racing; off-track pari-mutuel wagering at satellite locations more than 50 mi. away from any licensed horse track
TENNESSEE	39-17-501 to 39-17-509	Risking anything of value for a profit whose return is to any degree contingent on chance, not including lawful business transactions	Permitted: licensed horse racing; interstate simulcast wagering

Dog Racing/Off-Track Betting	Casinos Allowed?	Other Kinds of Gambling-Related Activities Permitted or Prohibited
Not specified	Operating a gambling house prohibited except as pursuant to tribal-state compact	Permitted: games of chance, such as bingo, conducted by charitable organizations for four days or less not more than twice a year; private, social gambling; licensed tag fishing tournaments; Prohibited: public gaming; cheating
Racing animals prohibited except by Horse Racing Act	State Tribal Gaming Act governs casino gambling	Permitted: bona fide business contracts; any charity game conducted pursuant to Oklahoma Charity Games Act; prizes offered to participants of public events such as rodeos, fairs, and athletic events; Prohibited: pyramid schemes; dice games; three-card monte
Permitted: licensed dog racing and pari-mutuel wagering; off-track pari-mutuel wagering	Casinos are legal only if gaming occurs on tribal land	Permitted: bona fide business contracts; contest of chance where players win prizes, not money; bingo, lotto, raffles, and Monte Carlo events sponsored by charitable organizations; social games; counties and cities may authorize game playing in private settings; Prohibited: bookmaking; internet gambling; possession of gambling records; possession of gray machines; cheating
Greyhound racing prohibited	Gambling houses and devices prohibited	Permitted: bingo and local option small games of chance sponsored by charitable organizations; antique slot machines; Prohibited: pool selling and bookmaking; punch boards, drawing cards; private wire for gambling information; cockfighting; bullet play
Permitted: licensed dog racing; on-track pari-mutuel wagering, only in cities of Burrillville, Lincoln, and West Greenwich	Operation of gambling places prohibited	Permitted: bingo and raffles in senior citizen housing; bingo sponsored by charitable organizations; frontons; governmental lotteries; Prohibited: bookmaking; unlicensed horse races
Not specified	Gambling devices prohibited	Permitted: games of tiles, cards, or dice where the games are played among club/social organization members in a private residence or clubhouse; Prohibited: card and dice games; lettered gaming tables; roley-poley tables; rouge et noir; faro banks; playing games in one's home on Sunday; betting on elections; pool selling; bookmaking; punchboards; gray machines
Permitted: licensed dog racing; off-track pari-mutuel wagering at satellite locations more than 50 mi. away from any licensed dog track	Permitted: limited card games and slot machines within city of Deadwood; casinos Indian reservations	Permitted: ownership of antique slot machines and bingo sponsored by charitable organizations with no prize in excess of $2,000; Prohibited: travel for sole purpose of gambling; persuading others to visit gambling places; bookmaking; internet gambling
Not specified	Gambling devices prohibited	Permitted: bingo and games of chance conducted by charitable organizations; Prohibited: promoting gambling; pyramid clubs; possessing gambling devices or records; customer referral rebates

Table 44: Gambling—Continued

State	Code Section	Gambling	Horse Racing/Off-Track Betting
TEXAS	Penal §§ 47.01 to 47.10; Texas Racing Act: Tex. Rev. Civ. Stat. Ann. art. 179e	Agreement to win or lose something of value solely or partially by chance	Permitted: licensed horse racing; simulcast races; on-track pari-mutuel wagering
UTAH	Utah Horse Regulation Act: 4-38-101 to 4-38-501; 76-10-1101 to 76-10-1109	Risking anything of value upon the outcome of a contest, game, scheme, or gaming device when the return or outcome is based upon an element of chance and is in accord with an agreement or understanding that someone will receive something of value in the event of a certain outcome	Permitted: licensed horse racing allowed; Prohibited: betting or any form of gambling
VERMONT	Tit. 13, §§ 2133 to 2156; Tit. 31, §§ 601 to 630	Winning or losing money or another valuable thing by play or hazard at any game	Permitted: Licensed horse racing except on Sundays before 1 p.m.; on-track pari-mutuel wagering
VIRGINIA	18.2-325 to 18.2-340; 59.1-364 to 405.1	Making, placing, or receiving bet or wager of money or other thing of value on any game, contest, or event of chance or uncertain outcome	Permitted: horse racing; pari-mutuel wagering; off-track betting at licensed satellite facilities
WASHINGTON	9.46.010 to 9.46.903; 67.16.010 to 67.16.900	Staking or risking something of value upon the outcome of a contest of chance or future contingent event not under the person's control or influence, upon an agreement that someone will receive something of value	Permitted: licensed horse racing; pari-mutuel wagering
WEST VIRGINIA	19-23-1 to 19-23-30.; 29-22A-1 to 29-22A-19.; 61-10-1 to 61-10-23	Betting or wagering money or another thing of value on any game of chance, or knowingly furnishing money or another thing of value on any game of chance	Permitted: Licensed horse racing and pari-mutuel wagering
WISCONSIN	562.01 to 569.06; 945.01 to 945.13	Bargain in which parties agree, dependent upon chance even though accompanied by some skill, one stands to win or lose something of value specified in the agreement	Permitted: licensed horse racing; on-track pari-mutuel and licensed simulcast wagering; Prohibited: off-track betting
WYOMING	6-7-101 to 6-7-104; 11-25-101 to 11-25-113	Risking any property for gain contingent in whole or part upon lot, chance, or outcome of an event, including sporting event, over which person taking a risk has no control	Permitted: licensed horse, harness, cutter, chariot, and chuckwagon racing; pari-mutuel and licensed off-track simulcast wagering

Dog Racing/Off-Track Betting	Casinos Allowed?	Other Kinds of Gambling-Related Activities Permitted or Prohibited
Permitted: limit of three racetrack licenses for greyhound racing; simulcast races; on-track pari-mutuel wagering	Prohibited: keeping a gambling place	Permitted: social gambling; bingo and raffles sponsored by charitable organizations; bona fide contests of skill; Prohibited: promoting gambling; keeping a place of gambling; communicating gambling information; possessing gambling devices with intent to further gambling
Prohibited	Prohibited	Permitted: lawful business transactions; playing amusement devices; Prohibited: gambling fraud; promotion; possessing a gambling device or record; election wagering; possessing gambling records; confidence games
Prohibited	Gaming houses prohibited	Permitted: games of chance sponsored by nonprofit organizations; contests or games of chance, including sweepstakes, provided that persons who enter are not required to venture money or other valuable things; Prohibited: bookmaking; pool selling; touting gambling
Greyhound racing and simulcasting prohibited	Gambling devices and places prohibited	Permitted: bingo, raffles and duck races sponsored by nonprofit organizations; contests of skill or speed between men, animals, fowl or vehicles; games of chance in private residences; Prohibited: winning by fraud
Greyhound racing and simulcasting prohibited	Permitted: tribal gaming pursuant to Indian Gaming Regulatory Act; maintenance of licensed gambling facilities; gambling devices otherwise prohibited.	Permitted: bingo, raffles, and amusement games sponsored by charitable organizations; fishing derbies; sports pools; golfing and bowling sweepstakes; turkey shoots; social card games; promotional contests; Prohibited: bucket shops; bunco steering; bookmaking; professional gambling
Permitted: Licensed dog racing and pari-mutuel wagering	Permitted: video lottery games at pari-mutuel racing facilities: machines cannot use casino themes such as dice, roulette, or baccarat but may simulate classic slot machines	Permitted: bingo, raffles, and games of chance sponsored by charitable organizations; Prohibited: bucket shops; policy or numbers games; gambling at hotels; keeping gaming tables or devices or allowing them on property; keeping a look out for gambling activities
Permitted: licensed dog racing; on-track pari-mutuel and licensed simulcast wagering; Prohibited: off-track betting	Permitted: Indian gaming; Prohibited: commercial (casino) gambling	Permitted: licensed bingo and raffles; snowmobile racing; bona fide business contracts; contests of skill, speed, strength and endurance; Prohibited: bookmaking; dealing in gambling devices
Permitted: simulcast dog racing and pari-mutuel wagering	Structures, boats or vehicles maintained for gambling purposes prohibited	Permitted: bona fide contests of skill, speed, strength, or endurance; bona fide business contracts; raffles, bingo and pulltabs sold by charitable organizations; bona fide social wagering; Calcutta wagering; display or private use of antique devices; Prohibited: professional gambling; possessing gambling devices; gambling record keeping

45. LEGAL AGES

The law only recognizes as legal the acts of persons who possess the capacity to form the proper intent to perform the particular acts. Two aspects of "capacity" are recognized: the mental capacity to form the intent to commit an act, and maturity, or the roughly objective measure of the ability to form a legal intent. It is maintained that when one reaches a certain age his or her capacity to form the proper intent matures. At this point a person can be held accountable for his or her actions.

The age at which every person is considered an adult is known as the "age of majority" and is usually 18 years old. In addition, some states allow minors who are living apart from their parents and supporting themselves to be "emancipated." This means that the minor will be treated as an adult for legal purposes. The minimum age for majority or emancipation is sometimes set out in statutes, but it is frequently determined by the common law.

The variation of age limits for different activities, such as marrying, voting, or consuming alcohol, illustrates the values a society places on certain types of activities and how a society values individual responsibility and accountability. For instance, when a minor intentionally injures another or damages property, he or she may be held liable for the act at age fourteen, and even earlier, in some instances, in certain courts. But he or she may not be allowed to drink or vote until age 18 or 21. An interesting aspect of the laws in many states is that "marrying" itself may be a criteria for reaching the age of majority or being emancipated without specifying a precise age for being able to marry. In those cases, the state relies on general common law principles for recognizing a person's responsibility and maturity to marry.

The limitations on a minor's ability to contract, however, are established to protect innocent third parties and ignorant or immature first parties. If a minor makes a foolish business decision out of immaturity or ignorance, the contract may be voided on the basis of a lack of capacity to contract.

Table 45: Legal Ages

State	Age of Majority	Emancipation	Contracts
ALABAMA	19 yrs., 26-1-1	18 yrs., 26-13-1	Minor 15 or more at nearest birthday may contract for life, health, accident, annuity insurance; however, not bound by any unperformed agreement to pay premium, 27-14-5
ALASKA	18 yrs., 25.20.010	16 yrs., 09.55.590	May receive and give full discharge and acquittance for insurance payments up to $3,000 if 16 or over, 21.42.290
ARIZONA	18 yrs., 1-215	16 yrs., 12-2451	Governed by common law, 47-1103; 16 or over to contract for educational loans, 44-140.01; May make contracts if veteran or married, 44-131
ARKANSAS	18 yrs., 9-25-101	16 yrs., 9-26-104	Rescission by infant 18 or over permitted only upon full restitution; promise made after full age to pay debt contracted during infancy must be in writing, Ark. R. Civ. P. 17
CALIFORNIA	18 yrs., Fam. 6500	14 yrs., Fam. § 7120; or if married, established a domestic partnership, or in military, Fam. § 7002	Yes, Fam. § 6700; minor may not give a delegation of power, make contract relating to real property, or make contract relating personal property not in immediate possession or control of the minor, Fam. § 6701
COLORADO	13-22-101 18 yrs.	*Koltay v. Koltay* 667 P.2d 1374 (Colo. 1983) Occurs upon attainment of majority	13-22-101(1)(a) 18 yrs.
CONNECTICUT	1-1d 18 yrs.	16 yrs., 46b-150	Common law; 15 yrs. for insurance, 38a-284
DELAWARE	18 yrs., Tit. 1, § 701	Not specified	18 yrs., Tit. 6, § 2705
DISTRICT OF COLUMBIA	18 yrs., 46-101	Not specified	Common law; cannot be charged unless promise made in writing after age of majority, 28-3505
FLORIDA	18 yrs., 743.07	If legal marriage occurs, 743.01; upon petition if 16 or older, 743.015	May contract for higher education financing if 16 or over, 743.05; generally if married, 743.01
GEORGIA	18 yrs., 39-1-1	If legal marriage occurs, during the period when a child is on active duty with U.S. armed forces, or upon petition if 16 or older, 15-11-720	Generally voidable; however, if benefits continue after age of majority, contract is valid, 13-3-20
HAWAII	18 yrs., 577-1	Legal marriage, 577-25	Disaffirmance must be made within reasonable time after reaching age of majority, *Kahanu v. Thompson*, 1 Haw. 421 (1856)
IDAHO	18 yrs., 32-101	Marriage, 32-101	Cannot disaffirm otherwise valid contract to purchase necessities, 32-103 et seq.; 15 yrs. or over, may enter into insurance contract, 41-1807
ILLINOIS	18 yrs., 755 5/11-1	Minors between 16 and 18 may apply if no parental objection, 750 30/1 et eq.	Common law: Voidable unless for necessities; executing contract binding only if ratified after age 18; executed contract binding unless disaffirmed within reasonable time after age 18
INDIANA	Common law: 18 yrs.	Not specified	Common law; If under 18, child is not able to contract except for necessities and higher education expenses, 20-3.1; minors 16 or older may contract for life, accident, sickness insurance and annuities, 27-1-12-15

Ability to Sue	Consent to Medical Treatment
May sue through personal representative, next friend, or guardian ad litem; if 14 or over has 30 days to choose guardian ad litem, Ala. R. Civ. P. 17(c); 17(d)	14 yrs., 22-8-4
By representative, guardian ad litem, or next friend, Alaska R. Civ. P. 17(c)	If living apart from parents or if parent of child, minor may give own consent, 25.20.025
By guardian or special administrator, guardian ad litem, next friend, Ariz. R. Civ. P. 17(f)	If homeless, married or emancipated, 44-132 et seq.
Next friend or guardian, Ark. R. Civ. P. 17	Any minor who is married, emancipated, incarcerated, or sufficiently intelligent to understand consequences of consent, 20-9-602
Guardian, Fam. § 6601	Minor may consent if 15 yrs. or older, living apart from parents, and managing own finances, Fam. § 6922
13-22-101(1)(c) 18 yrs.; Colo. R. Civ. .P. 17(c) by guardian or representative	13-22-101(1)(d) 18 yrs.; 13-22-103(1) 15 if living apart from parents and paying own expenses or married
18 yrs. or upon emancipation, 46b-150d	18 yrs. or upon emancipation, 46b-150d
18 yrs., Tit. 10, § 3923	18 yrs. unless married or a parent, Tit. 13, § 707
By representative, 12-302	If connected to pregnancy, substance abuse, psychological disturbance, or sexually transmitted disease, 22 DCMR 600.7
By next friend or court appointed guardian, Fla. R. Civ. P. 1.210(b)	If emergency, 743.064
Through guardian or guardian ad litem, 9-11-17; Suit started by infant alone not void but guardian must be appointed before verdict, 9-2-28	18 for treatment in general; if treatment is for VD, minor may consent; female minor has valid consent for treatment in connection with pregnancy, 31-9-2
Guardian ad litem, next friend, 551-2	Counseling services for alcohol or drug abuse, 577-26; pregnancy, venereal disease or family planning services, 577A-2
Through guardian, conservator, or like fiduciary, or infant may sue through guardian ad litem or next friend appointed by court, I.R.C.P. 17(c)	14 yrs. for treatment of infectious, contagious, communicable diseases, 39-3801
Guardian ad litem must be appointed or can sue within 2 years of turning 18, 735 § 5/13-211	Consent by minor if married, parent, or victim of sexual assault, 410 § 210/1 et seq.
n own name or through next friend, guardian ad litem, or representative, Ind. R. Trial P. 17(c) I	Minors may consent if emancipated, 14 years or older and living apart from parents, married, or in military service, 16-36-1-3

Table 45: Legal Ages—Continued

State	Age of Majority	Emancipation	Contracts
IOWA	18 yrs., 599.1	Marriage, 599.1; 16 yrs. with petition 232C.1	For necessities; for other contracts, minor is bound unless disaffirmed after reasonable time of attaining majority and restoration made of money and property received, 599.2
KANSAS	18 yrs.; 16 if married, 38-101	At discretion of the court, 38-109	Valid for necessities; also for other contracts unless disaffirmed in reasonable time after majority is obtained and money, property restored, 38-102; may consummate insurance contracts but must have consent of parents and cosignature of party over age 18, 40-237
KENTUCKY	18 yrs., 2.015	Not specified	Valid for necessities not otherwise obtainable; otherwise, common law generally governs; exception made for war veterans, 384.090; minor may contract for educational purpose with parental consent, 286.3-385; Minors 15 or older may purchase insurance, 304.14-070
LOUISIANA	18 yrs., CC Art. 29	16 by court order, CC Art. 366; Marriage, CC Art. 367	Contract by minor may be rescinded except for necessities for support or education, or for a purpose related to his business, CC Art. 1923
MAINE	18 yrs., Tit. 1, § 72(11)	May petition court if 16 or over, Tit. 15, § 3506-A	No, unless minor or authorized person ratified it at age of 18; exceptions are necessaries or real estate to which minor has title and retains benefit; contracts of minors re higher education are valid, Tit. 33, § 32
MARYLAND	18 yrs., Gen. Provis. § 1-401	If married; a parent; serving in military; emancipated by court order; living separately from parents and self-supporting, Est. & Trusts § 4-501	Married minor may buy or sell property and to join in deed, mortgage, lease, notes if spouse is of age, Est. & Trusts § 13-503(a); Age 15 to purchase insurance and cannot repudiate on basis of minority, Est. & Trusts § 13-503(c); If in military, can enter into real estate transactions, Est. & Trusts § 13-503(b)
MASSACHUSETTS	18 yrs., Ch. 231, § 85P	Not specified	Common Law No, except for necessaries and education; 16 or over for motor vehicle liability insurance, Ch. 175 § 113K; 15 or over for life insurance, Ch. 175 § 128
MICHIGAN	18 yrs., 722.1(a)	Through marriage, military service, or by judicial petition at age 16, 722.4	18 yrs. or less may be a defense, Common law, 600.1403
MINNESOTA	18 yrs.; 645.45(14)	Not specified	Common law for necessities only; other contracts voidable
MISSISSIPPI	21 yrs., 1-3-27	By petition, no minimum age specified, 93-19-3	18 for personal property; ratification must be signed in writing, 15-3-11

Ability to Sue	Consent to Medical Treatment
By minor's guardian or by next friend; court may substitute at its discretion, Iowa R. Civ. P. § 1.210	Minors may consent for prevention, diagnosis, or treatment of STD or STI, 139A.35
Through infant's representative; if no representative, then through next friend or guardian ad litem, 60-217(c)	Unmarried pregnant minor may consent to hospital, medical, and surgical care, 38-123; any minor over 16 may consent to any care where no parent or guardian is immediately available, 38-123b
May sue by guardian or next friend if unmarried, CR 17.03; if married, may sue on his or her own, CR 17.02	Minors of any age may consent to emergency care or treatment for pregnancy, drug/alcohol abuse, or venereal disease; minors 16 or older may consent to mental health treatment; emancipated minors may consent to any treatment, 222.441
Through tutor or parent, CCP Art. 683	Minor may consent to treatment without parental consent, 40:1079 to 40:1079.3
Through next friend, guardian ad litem, or parent, Maine R. Civ. P. 17 (b)	Minors may consent to any treatment if living separately from parents and independent of parental support; married; emancipated; in the military. Otherwise, minors may consent to treatment for substance abuse, mental health issues, or sexual assault forensic examination. May give blood at age 17. Tit. 22, § 1502 to 1507
By guardian, next friend, or parent, Md. R. Civ. P. 2-202(b)	If married, a parent. emancipated, or seeking help with drug use, alcoholism, VD, sexual assault, pregnancy, contraception, or if seeking consent would be life threatening, Health-Gen. § 20-102; Minor 16 or older can consent to treatment for emotional disorder, Health-Gen. § 20-104
By next friend, representative, or guardian ad litem, Mass. R. Civ. P. 17(b)	If 12 or over and certified to be drug dependent, may consent to appropriate medical care, Ch. 112, § 12E; Minor may also consent to emergency care when: married, widowed, divorced; is a parent; is a member of armed forces; lives separately from parents and manages own financial affairs; has come into contact with dangerous public health disease; is pregnant, Ch. 112, § 12F
By next friend or guardian of estate; if age 14 or over, can select own, MCR 2.201(E)	Pregnancy, 333.9132; HIV or venereal disease treatment, 333.5127; Substance abuse treatment, 333.1264
At 14 by general guardian ad litem appointed by court; otherwise by general guardian, relative, or friend, by default, Minn. R. Civ. P. § 17.02	Minor may consent if living apart from parents and managing own financial affairs; if married or parent; for pregnancy, venereal disease, or substance abuse, 144.341 to 144.347
18 to settle personal injury claims; married minor may file in marital matters; court appoints guardian ad litem, 9-5-89	Any female, regardless of age or marital status, is empowered to give consent for herself in connection with pregnancy or childbirth, 41-41-3

Table 45: Legal Ages—Continued

State	Age of Majority	Emancipation	Contracts
MISSOURI	18 yrs., Common law	Not specified	Any debt contracted by minor must be ratified after turning 18, 431.060 ; Any minor married to an adult who has or claims any interest in real estate shall be deemed of age for the purpose of joining with the adult spouse in the execution of any instrument affecting the spouse's real estate, 442.040; All instruments affecting title to real estate executed by any person under the age of 18 shall be binding unless disaffirmed within 2 yrs. of becoming an adult, 442.080
MONTANA	18 yrs., 41-1-101	Marriage, 40-6-234; judicial petition after reaching age 16, 41-1-501	Student loan for higher education, 41-1-303; certain contracts may be disaffirmed while minor or within certain time thereafter, 41-1-304 to 41-1-306; contracts for necessaries or made by emancipated minor may not be disaffirmed
NEBRASKA	19 yrs., 43-2101	Marriage, 43-2101	Minor 18 and not ward of state may enter into binding contract or lease of whatever kind and be legally responsible therefor, 43-2101; Minor at least 10 may contract for insurance, 44-705
NEVADA	18 yrs., 129.010	By court order if 16; married; living apart from parent or guardian, 129.080; not exclusive to any other method of emancipation provided by statute or common law, 129.140	Emancipated, 129.130; may contract for insurance at age 16, 687B.070
NEW HAMPSHIRE	18 yrs., 21:44; 21-B:1	Not specified; emancipation decree from another state recognized in New Hampshire, 21-B:2	Loans for higher education, 193:26; can join with spouse in release of homestead interests, 460:4
NEW JERSEY	18 yrs., 9:17B-3	Not specified	Loans for higher education, 9:17A-2; may contract for insurance at age 15, 17B:24-2; 17, if minor spouse for sale of property, 37:2-30; 15 for insurance contracts, 17B:24-2
NEW MEXICO	18 yrs., 32A-1-4(B)	16 if married, active duty military, or declaration of emancipation, Emancipation of Minors Act, §§ 32A-21-1 to 32-A-21-7	Emancipated minor may enter into any contract, 32A-21-5; May contract for insurance at age 15, 59A-18-7
NEW YORK	18 yrs., Dom. Rel. § 2	Marriage emancipates person but not property, Dom. Rel. § 84	May purchase life insurance at age 14.5, Ins. § 3207; loans for higher education at age 16, Educ. § 281; married minor may enter into real estate contracts, Gen. Oblig. § 3-101; many contracts may be disaffirmed if done within reasonable time after reaching majority, exceptions listed in this section, Gen. Oblig. § 3-101; performing arts or athletic contracts may not be disaffirmed, Arts & Cult. Aff. § 35.03

Ability to Sue	Consent to Medical Treatment
By guardian, next friend, or court appointed, Mo. R. Civ. P. 52.02	Minor may consent if married; treatment is for pregnancy, excluding abortion; venereal disease, drug or substance abuse, 431.061
Through general guardian or guardian ad litem, 41-1-202	41-1-402 Married; parent; high school graduate; separated from parents and self-supporting; pregnant or afflicted with reportable communicable disease, or drug or substance abuse; needs emergency care
By guardian or next friend, except as provided in Probate Code, 25-307	Sexually transmitted diseases, 71-504; parent may delegate consent to minor at age 18, 30-2604
General guardian or guardian ad litem, 12.050	Living apart from parents, 129.030; married; mother or has borne child; suffering serious health hazard; under influence of or for treatment for controlled substance abuse, 129.050 ; sexually transmitted disease, 129.060; emancipated, 129.130
Next friend; court may appoint guardian ad litem, 498-A:22	14 or older may consent to treatment for sexually transmitted disease, 141-C:18; 12 or older may consent to drug treatment, 318-B:12-a
By guardian or guardian ad litem, 2A:4A-39	Venereal disease, sexual assault, drug or alcohol treatment, 13 for HIV/AIDS, 9:17A-4; 17 to donate blood, 9:17A-6
By guardian, guardian ad litem, or next friend; married minor may sue in action against him/her or spouse without a guardian, NM R. Civ. P. 1-017(c); Emancipated minor may sue on own behalf, 32A-21-5	Married or emancipated, 24-10-1
Through guardian or parent, adult spouse, guardian ad litem appointed by court or by minor if over 14, N.Y. C.P.L.R. § 1201	Married; pregnant; parent of child; or in immediate need of medical care, Pub. Health § 2504

Table 45: Legal Ages—Continued

State	Age of Majority	Emancipation	Contracts
NORTH CAROLINA	18 yrs., 48A-2	By judicial decree at age 16, 7B-3500; military service, 7B-3402; marriage, 7B-3509	Performing arts or athletics contracts may not be disaffirmed if approved by court, 48A-11 to 48A-12; may purchase insurance at age 15, 58-58-100; loans for higher education at age 17, 116-174.1; emancipated minor has same right and obligations as if adult, 7B-3507; minor spouse of veteran may execute any contract, 143B-1248
NORTH DAKOTA	18 yrs., 14-10-01	Marriage, 14-09-20	May make any contract except real property or personal property not in immediate possession or control; may disaffirm contracts upon age of majority or within 1 yr. thereafter; may not disaffirm statutory contracts or contracts for necessaries, 14-10-09 to 14-10-13
OHIO	18 yrs., 3109.01	Not specified	Common law applies: Contracts are voidable; may be disaffirmed at infancy or within reasonable time after age of majority; exception for necessaries
OKLAHOMA	18 yrs., Tit. 15, § 13	Military service; marriage; court order, Tit. 10, §§ 91 to 94	May not contract for real property or personal property not in immediate possession or control; may make any other contract, subject to disaffirmation; may disaffirm contracts during minority or within 1 yr. after age of majority; may not disaffirm contracts for necessaries, Tit. 15, §§ 13 to 21; minors 16 and over may borrow for expenses of higher education, Tit. 15, §§ 31 to 34; may purchase insurance at age 15, Tit. 36 § 3606
OREGON	18 yrs., 109.510	Marriage, 109.520; court decree, 419B.552	Common Law: Valid for necessaries and education; any others voidable upon attaining majority; may contract for housing and utilities if 16 or under 16 if parent or pregnant, 109.697
PENNSYLVANIA	18 yrs., Tit. 23, § 5101	A minor cannot be emancipated before age 16, Tit. 16 § 2175	Voidable except for necessaries until age 18 (common law)
RHODE ISLAND	15-12-1 18 yrs.	Common law applies; *Pardey v. American Ship Windlass Co.* 34 A. 737 (1896)	*Jacobs v. United Elec. Rys. Co.*, 125 A. 286 (1924) Voidable except for necessaries
SOUTH CAROLINA	18 yrs., 15-1-320	Not specified	Cannot be required to pay for debts contracted as minor, except for necessaries, unless debt is ratified in writing and signed after age of majority, 63-5-310; May obtain loans for higher education, 63-5-320

Ability to Sue	Consent to Medical Treatment
By guardian, testamentary guardian, guardian ad litem, N.C. R. Civ. P. 17(b)	Venereal disease; pregnancy; drug or alcohol abuse; emotional disturbance; certain exceptions apply; emancipated minor may consent to any treatment for self or child, 90-21.5
Through guardian ad litem, 14-10-04	Minors 14 or older may consent to treatment for sexually transmitted disease, alcoholism, or drug abuse, 14-10-17; any minor may consent to emergency medical care, 14-10-17.1
Through personal representative or otherwise may sue by next friend or defend by guardian ad litem; minor not represented must have court appoint guardian ad litem, OH R. Civ. P. 17(B)	Treatment following sexual assault, 2907.29; venereal disease, 3709.241; drug or alcohol abuse, 3719.012; imprisoned minor deemed emancipated for purposes of medical treatment, 5120.172
Guardian, next friend, or representative, Tit. 12, § 2017(c)	Minors may consent if married, a parent, emancipated, separated from parents/legal guardian and not supported by them, or for emergencies, substance abuse, communicable diseases, or pregnancy, Tit. 63, § 2602
By conservator, guardian or guardian ad litem, OR R. Civ. P. 27(A)	Any age may consent to venereal disease/HIV treatment, 109.610 ; may consent to any treatment at age 15, 109.640; any age may receive birth control information and services; 16 or older may donate blood, 109.670; 14 or older may consent to mental health or substance abuse treatment, 109.675
By guardian, guardian ad litem, or next friend, PA R. Civ. P. 2028; person 18 or older may sue or be sued as adult, Tit. 23, § 5101	Age 18; high school graduate; married; is or has been pregnant may consent to any treatment; age 14 may consent to mental health treatment; any minor may consent to treatment for pregnancy, venereal disease or other diseases reportable under the Disease Prevention and Control Law of 1955; treatment for emergencies requires no consent, Tit. 35, §§ 10101 to 10104
By next friend, representative, or guardian ad litem, RI R. Civ. P. 17(c)	Minors who are married or 16 years old may consent to any treatment, 23-4.6-1
By representative, next friend, or guardian ad litem, SC R. Civ. P. 17(c)	Married minor or spouse may consent to any treatment, 63-5-330; 16 or over may consent to any treatment, 63-5-340; No consent required for emergencies, 62-5-350

Table 45: Legal Ages—Continued

State	Age of Majority	Emancipation	Contracts
SOUTH DAKOTA	18 yrs., 26-1-1	Married, 25-5-24 ; active military; declaration of emancipation under 25-5-26--over 16; living apart from parents with their consent and self-supporting not from illegal sources	May make contract except for real property or personal property not under immediate possession or control; contracts binding unless minor disaffirms as permitted; may be disaffirmed if minor under 16 before age of majority or within one year afterwards; if 16 or older, can only disaffirm with restoration of consideration plus interest, 26-2-1 to 26-2-7
TENNESSEE	18 yrs., 1-3-105	By judicial petition, no minimum age specified, 29-31-101 to 29-31-105	Common law applies: May disaffirm within reasonable time after attaining age of majority; may also ratify expressly or by failure to disaffirm within reasonable time; may not disaffirm court-approved performance contract, 50-5-207; Minor veterans may contract as adult, 58-3-103
TEXAS	18 yrs., Civ. Prac. & Rem. § 129.001	Military service; marriage; by court order: minor must be resident of state, 17 or 16 and living apart from parent/guardian, self-supporting and managing own financial affairs; emancipation order issued by another state or nation is honored, Fam. § 31.001 to 31.007	Common law: Must disaffirm within reasonable time after reaching age of majority; voidable only at minor's insistence
UTAH	18 yrs., 15-2-1	Marriage, 15-2-1 ; by court order; must be 16, capable of living apart from parent guardian, and capable of managing own affairs, 78A-6-803	Bound for necessaries; otherwise, contracts valid unless disaffirmed within reasonable time after reaching age of majority and restoration of consideration, 15-2-2 ; may not disaffirm if minor misrepresented age when contract was signed, 15-2-3; may contract for insurance at age 16, 31A-21-103; emancipated minor may enter into any contract and is bound as adult, 78A-6-805
VERMONT	18 yrs., Tit. 1, § 173	Marriage; active duty military; by court order: must be 16 or older; living apart from parent/guardian for at least 3 mos.; managing own finances; demonstrating self-sufficiency; high school graduate or passing grades; not under legal guardianship; not under supervision of Dept. of Corrections, Tit. 12, §§ 7151; 7155	Common law: Voidable, subject to making restitution where possible

Ability to Sue	Consent to Medical Treatment
Through a guardian or conservator or by a guardian ad litem, 15-6-17(c)	Minors of any age may consent to treatment for venereal disease, 34-23-16
By representative, guardian ad litem, or next friend, TN R. Civ. P. 17.03	Drug abuse, 63-6-220; No consent required for emergencies, 63-6-222; pregnancy, 63-6-223; minors may receive contraceptives if pregnant, parent, or married, 68-34-107
Guardian, next friend, guardian ad litem, Tex. R. Civ. P. 44	Minors may consent to any treatment if in military or 16 years old and living apart from parents; any minor may consent to treatment for pregnancy, substance abuse, or infectious diseases, Fam. § 32.003
By guardian or guardian ad litem only, Utah R. Civ. P. 17(9b)	May consent to treatment for sexually transmitted disease, 26-6-18; emancipated minor may consent to any treatment, 78A-6-805; any female in connection with pregnancy or childbirth, 78B-3-406
By representative, next friend, or guardian ad litem, VT R. Civ. Pr. 17(b)	Minors 12 or older may consent to treatment for venereal disease or substance abuse, Tit. 18, § 4226

Table 45: Legal Ages—Continued

State	Age of Majority	Emancipation	Contracts
VIRGINIA	18 yrs., 1-204	By judicial petition at age 16: married; active duty military; lives apart from parent/guardian with consent and capable of supporting self and managing finances, 16.1-331 to 16.1-334.1	Common law: Voidable subject to making restitution when possible with various exceptions for necessities; emancipated minor may enter into any binding contract, 16.1-334; Minors 15 and older may purchase life insurance, 38.2-3105
WASHINGTON	18 yrs., 26.28.010	By judicial petition at age 16: must be resident of state; able to manage financial, personal, social, educational, and non financial affairs, 13.64.010 to 13.64.901; marriage to person of age, 26.28.020	Bound for contracts for necessities; other contracts valid unless disaffirmed within reasonable time after reaching age of majority and restitution of consideration where possible; may not disaffirm if misrepresented age or other party had reason to believe minor capable of contracting, 26.28.030; 26.28.040
WEST VIRGINIA	18 yrs., 2-2-10(aa)	Marriage; court order: must be at least 16 and able to show ability to provide for physical and financial well-being and ability to make decisions for self, 49-4-115	Common law governs; no action can be brought unless contract or ratification is in writing and signed by charged party, 55-1-1
WISCONSIN	18 yrs., 990.01(3)	Marriage, 54.46(6)	Common law: Valid only for necessaries; necessaries contracts not valid if no implied or express provision for payment exists; contract made by minor may be ratified by acts or words after reaching age of majority
WYOMING	18 yrs., 14-1-101	Marriage; military service; court order at age 17 if living apart from parents with consent; minor deemed capable of handling financial affairs and income is lawfully derived, 14-1-201 to 14-1-206	Not specified

Ability to Sue	Consent to Medical Treatment
Next friend; defendant minor represented by guardian ad litem, 8.01-8	Minors may consent to treatment for venereal disease; contagious/infectious disease; birth control or pregnancy; substance abuse; mental illness; married minors may consent to any treatment, 54.1-2969(E)
By guardian; if 14 or over may apply himself for court-appointed guardian; if under 14 application must be made to court through relative or friend, 4.08.050	Minor may consent to treatment of sexually transmitted disease, 70.24.110
By next friend or guardian; defends by guardian ad litem, 56-4-9	Minor may consent to treatment for sexually transmitted disease, 16-4-10; minor may consent to treatment for controlled substance abuse, 60A-5-504(e)
By guardian or guardian ad litem, 803.03(3)	May consent at age 12 for alcohol and drug abuse treatment; under 12 if parent with legal custody cannot be found, 51.47
General guardian, committee, conservator; otherwise by next friend or guardian ad litem, Wyo. R. Civ. P. 17(c)	14-1-101 Yes if married; military, guardian can't be located, or living apart and self-supporting or is emancipated

46. LOST, ABANDONED, AND UNCLAIMED PERSONAL PROPERTY

Inevitably, each of us will be either the finder or loser of personal property. Whether at a park, on a bus, in a hotel or at a sporting event, the loss may be traumatic, but looking for the lost article may be merely the beginning of the drama of recovery. If you can't find the thing you are looking for, to whom do you turn for help? Likewise, should you be the finder of property, what are your responsibilities to locate the unfortunate person who lost it? How long must you wait before you can legally claim the property as your own? Moreover, are your responsibilities the same whether you find cash or a pet?

The tables that follow address only a fraction of these issues. A comprehensive treatment of all the issues surrounding lost, found or abandoned property can easily fill its own book. Topics not treated here are those concerning many financial matters, such as interest owed on closed bank deposits or notices of stock dividends to stockholders whose addresses have changed or who have died or otherwise changed their legal status, or the many ways in which automobiles may be abandoned such as in parking garages, repair shops, or on the sides of highways. This chapter also does not treat the issue of lost livestock, as the rules concerning livestock are astonishingly complex and varied. These tables address representative topics that will answer some of the more interesting and more common questions that arise in the field.

The chart addresses whether the state has formally adopted the Uniform Unclaimed Property Act (UUPA). One of the ironies of the UUPA is that despite the word "uniform" in its title, adoption of it in the various states is anything but "uniform." One of the features of the "uniform" acts movement is that each state that adopts a uniform act is free to modify it as much as it sees fit. As a result, for many uniform acts, there are as many variations as there are states. The UUPA is no exception. To date, 47 states have adopted some version of the UUPA, but even states that have not adopted it have adopted something very similar. Common areas of coverage under the UUPA include rules for disposing of abandoned gift certificates, gift cards, traveler's checks, wages, insurance proceeds, utility refunds, etc. For purposes of this chapter, only the fact of a state's adoption of the UUPA is noted.

Table 46: Lost, Abandoned, and Unclaimed Personal Property

State	Finder Responsibilities Criminal Penalties	Finder Responsibilities Cash/Valuables	Abandoned Museum Property
ALABAMA	Misdemeanor theft if takes lost, mislaid or misdelivered property and does not make reasonable efforts to restore it to rightful owner, 13A-8-6; 13A-8-9	Finder is depositary for hire; finder may sell only if perishable or lawful charges amount to 2/3 of value, 35-12-1 to 35-12-5	
ALASKA	Theft if person takes lost, mislaid or misdelivered property and does not make reasonable efforts to restore it to rightful owner with intent to deprive owner of property; reasonable measures include notifying the identified owner or peace officer, 11.46.100; 11.46.160	Lost property delivered to police vests in finder 1 yr. after delivery or in agency if finder cannot be found, 12.36.045	Title acquired after 7 yrs. holding period; notice to lender plus 30 days or published notice at least weekly for 4 wks. plus 45 days after final notice, 14.57.200 ; undocumented property acquired after 7 yrs. holding period; notice at least weekly for 4 wks. plus 45 days after final notice, 14.57.210
ARIZONA	Felony or misdemeanor theft if person takes lost or mislaid property and fails to make reasonable efforts to notify the true owner, 13-1802		Terminated or 7+ yr. expired loan vests in museum after 30 days notice and 2 wks. published notice; undocumented property acquired after 7 yrs.; 2 wks. published notice; 65 days; 2 more wks. published notice, 44-351 to 44-356
ARKANSAS	Felony or misdemeanor theft if person takes lost or mislaid property known to have been lost, mislaid or misdelivered with intent to deprive true owner and fails to take reasonable measures to restore property to owner, 5-36-105		Expired or 10+ yr. old loan vests in museum after 90 days notice by mail or publication, 13-5-1004; undocumented property vests after 7+ yrs. and 4 wks. published notice, 35-5-1005
CALIFORNIA	Grand theft or petty theft if person takes lost property and does not make reasonable efforts to restore it to rightful owner, Penal § 485	Finder must turn in property to police if value is $100 or more; if $250 or more and not claimed in 90 days, property vests to finder after published notice plus 7 days and payment of costs; if less than $250, property vests to finder after 90 days; police may sell if perishable or lawful charges amount to 2/3 of value, Civ. §§ 2080.1 to 2080.5	Loans unclaimed for 7 yrs. disposed under UUPA; notice must be given to owner 6 to 12 mos. before disposal, Civ. § 1899.11

Abandoned Hotel Property	Tenant Property	Miscellaneous	Uniform Unclaimed Property Act?
Innkeeper not liable for any loss whatsoever if property was not delivered into innkeeper's custody, 34-15-13	Landlord must hold property and give 45 days notice before selling or disposing, 35-12A-8	Vehicles and equipment, laundry and dry cleaning: 1 year; appliances: 3 months; all others: 6 months; all disposed of after 10 days notice by mail, advertisement, or posting at courthouse, 35-12-6; animals left at vet abandoned after 10 days notice to owner, 34-29-86	Yes, 35-12-70 to 35-12-96
Baggage left behind or sent in advance: hotel may hold for 4 mos. and then may sell or deliver to storage, 08.56.060	Landlord must give tenant 15 days notice before selling or disposing; tenant must pay storage costs if claimed after 15 days but before disposal, 34.03.260	Abandoned timber property: state can claim after 30 days public notice or 90 days from reporting, 45.50.230 to 45.50.235; animals seized by police given to vet and notify owner to file claim, otherwise reasonable effort must be made to find owner; animal may be destroyed or adopted if not claimed within 10 days or bond posted, 03.55.120; 03.55.130	Yes, 34.45.110 to 34.45.780
Innkeeper not liable for lost articles not delivered into innkeeper's custody, 33-302	Landlord may sell property after 5 days mailed and posted notice plus 14 days; proceeds to tenant; de minimus may be destroyed, 33-1370	Aircraft: may sell at auction after 60 days abandonment; mailed or published notice of intent to sell and 15 days, 28-8243; held by public officer: vests in finder if tangible property remains unclaimed for 30 days after reasonable efforts made to locate owner; if property has value of $150 or more, agency holding property must post or publish notice; after 30 days if finder does not claim, property may be sold and money given to state, 12-941 to 12-945	Yes, 44-301 to 44-339
Innkeeper not liable for lost property not delivered into innkeeper's custody unless loss due to innkeeper negligence, 20-26-302	Abandoned if left by tenant after voluntary or involuntary termination of the lease; lessor may dispose as he sees fit without recourse by lessee, 18-16-108	Mineral proceeds unclaimed for 3 yrs. deemed abandoned and distributed under the UUPA, 18-28-403; dry cleaning and audio/video equipment—6 months; owner may sell and retain proceeds, 18-28-101	Yes, 18-28-201 to 18-28-230
Property received but not delivered to owner is held for 60 days before public sale, Civ. §§ 2081.1 to 2081.6	15 day notice required to tenant; property sold at public sale or if less than $700, owner may keep or dispose, Civ. §§ 1980 to 1991	Property unclaimed 180 days after discharge from hospital may be sold, Civ. § 1862.5; common carriers: held 60 days before sale, Civ. §§ 2081.1 to 2081.6; pets at vet, groomer, or other facility presumed abandoned after 14 days; if unable to place animal with new owner, shelter or other facility within 10 days, animal care facility may euthanize but is not required to do so, Civ. § 1834.5; person who saves animal from harm, neglect, drowning, or starvation must provide humane care and within reasonable time inform owner, if known, Civ. § 2080	Yes, Civ. Proc. §§ 1500 to 1527

Table 46: Lost, Abandoned, and Unclaimed Personal Property—Continued

State	Finder Responsibilities Criminal Penalties	Finder Responsibilities Cash/Valuables	Abandoned Museum Property
COLORADO			No action may be brought for recovery of any loaned property after 7 yrs. or more than 120 days since written notice of termination of loan, 38-14-103
CONNECTICUT	Failure to deliver found property to police is up to $100 fine or up to 30 days imprisonment or both, 50-10, which applies only if municipality has adopted provisions by ordinance; theft if person takes lost, mislaid or misdelivered property and efforts not made to restore it to rightful owner, 53a-119	Value $1 or more: report to police within 48 hrs.; deliver to police within 1 wk.; goods held for 6 mos. unless perishable; given to finder after 6 mos. or sold if not claimed by finder, 50-10 to 50 14, which apply only if municipality has adopted provisions by ordinance	Any property in possession of museum that is not subject to loan agreement presumed abandoned if unclaimed for 5 yrs. and museum has given notice, 11-82
DELAWARE	Theft if person takes lost, mislaid or misdelivered property with intent to deprive owner of property and does not make reasonable efforts to restore it to rightful owner, Tit. 11, §§ 841 to 842		Museum acquires title to loaned items after expiration of loan and notice given without response within 60 days, Tit. 6, § 5005D; to undocumented property after 3 yrs. and notice given with response within 60 days, Tit. 6, § 5006D
DISTRICT OF COLUMBIA		Property found or turned over to police is given to Property Clerk; after 90 days, notice published for 2 wks.; if not claimed within 45 days, property goes to finder or to city to be sold or destroyed, 5-119.01 to 5-119.11	
FLORIDA	Felony or misdemeanor theft if person takes lost or abandoned property for own use; finder must report to police and deposit money with the police to cover storage costs if finder wants to make a claim to property if the true owner cannot be found, 705.102	Lost or abandoned property held by police for 90 days; must post notice for 45 days if value under $100; posted notice plus 2 wks. published notice if value $100+ then sold if no claims, 705.103	Unclaimed loan vests in museum after 90 days notice to known owner or 90 days notice and 2 published notices to unknown owner, 265.565

Abandoned Hotel Property	Tenant Property	Miscellaneous	Uniform Unclaimed Property Act?
Innkeeper not liable for lost property not delivered into their custody except for articles lost in rooms; liability limited to $200, 6-25-108 to 6-25-111		Lottery prizes are unclaimed after 180 days and remain in lottery fund, 24-35-212; personal property of inactive non-profit association disposed of after 3 yrs. of inactivity, 7-30-109; molds abandoned after 3 yrs. and notice given to customer, 38-20-116; property acquired by law enforcement if unclaimed after 6 mos. is sold at public auction, 42-13-101 to 42-13-109	Yes, 38-13-101 to 38-13-134
Innkeeper not liable for lost articles not delivered into their custody unless loss caused by innkeeper negligence; not liable for more than $500, unless guest declared and furnished receipt of property's worth greater than $500, 44-1 to 44-2	Landlord to keep personal property for 30+ days before disposing, 47a-11b	Common carrier: sold after 6 mos. and 4 wks. notice, 50-3; goods left with a person: sold after 6 mos. and 1 mo. notice, 50-1 to 50-2; abandoned refrigerator: class D misdemeanor, 53-215	No; 3-56a to 3-75a are similar
Innkeeper not liable for items not in safe if innkeeper provides a safe and posts notice, Tit. 24, § 1502	Property deemed abandoned 7 days after appeal period has expired; may be disposed of by landlord without notice or liability, Tit. 25, § 5507	Property found on Delaware Turnpike: held for 120 days then sold after notice if worth over $10 or donated, Tit. 2, § 1320; personal property held by Dept. of Nat. Res.: 1 yr. then sold or given to finder, Tit. 29, § 8026; personal property, such as cars, boats, furnishings, motorcycles, left with another for 1 yr. or more is abandoned; title vests in holder after court declaration, Tit. 25, §§ 4001 to 4007; property held by police: 1 yr. then property sold, money given to finder, Tit. 11, § 8307	No; Tit. 12, §§ 1140 to 1224 are similar
Property considered abandoned after 90 days; sold after 15 days notice, 30-103		Common carrier: property unclaimed for 6 mos. may be sold after 3 weeks notice, 35-101; Impounded animals not claimed within 7 days if wearing ID or 5 days if not deemed abandoned and may be adopted or disposed of in humane manner, 8-1805; held by police: horses and other animals not claimed within 20 days may be sold after 10 days public notice, 5-119.12	Yes, 41-101 to 41-142
Innkeeper not liable for lost property unless negligent; liability limited to $500 unless guest inventoried items with innkeeper, then liability limited to $1,000, 509.111	10 days delivered notice or 15 days mailed notice required; $500+ value is sold; tenant has 1 yr. to claim proceeds; if less than $500 landlord may keep, 715.10 to 715.12	Lost on university campus: held for 30 days then sold, 705.18; jewelry: 1 yr.; TV/radio repair: 6 mos., 715.065; dry cleaning: 6 mos., 715.03; animals with vet deemed abandoned if unclaimed after 10 days notice; given to pound for disposal, 705.19	Yes; 717.001 to 717.1401

Table 46: Lost, Abandoned, and Unclaimed Personal Property—Continued

State	Finder Responsibilities Criminal Penalties	Finder Responsibilities Cash/Valuables	Abandoned Museum Property
GEORGIA	Theft if person takes lost or mislaid property known to be lost without taking reasonable measures to restore it to rightful owner, 16-8-6		Property loaned to museum presumed abandoned after no contact for 7 yrs.; 60 days notice, 10-1-529.4
HAWAII	Theft if person takes lost or mislaid property known to have been lost or misdelivered without taking reasonable measures to restore it to rightful owner, 708-830	Finder to deliver property to police; held for 45 days then to finder; sold if not claimed by finder within 30 days, 52D-10; 52D 12; 52D-14	
IDAHO	Theft if person takes lost or mislaid property known to have been lost or misdelivered without taking reasonable measures to restore it to rightful owner who is known or reasonably ascertainable with intent to deprive owner of property, 18-2403	Finder of goods worth $100 or more must give written notice to county clerk within 10 days and within 20 days give 2 wks. published notice; if no claims within 3 mos. from date of notice, finder is owner; finder liable to county for value of goods if finder fails to comply, 55-405	
ILLINOIS	Theft (petty offense) if person takes lost or mislaid, or misdelivered property without taking reasonable measures to restore it to known or reasonably ascertainable owner and with intent to deprive owner of the property; misdemeanor if value up to $10,000; felony if value over $10,000, 720 § 5/16-2	Property value up to $100: finder must advertise at courthouse, vests after 6 mos.; value $100 or over: finder must file affidavit with court within 5 days; court issues order stating value of property; notice by county clerk published for 3 wks.; after 1 yr. property vests in finder, 765 §§ 1020/27; vessels worth less than $15: finder must post notice in neighborhood, ownership vests to finder if no claims after 3 mos., 765 § 1020/29	Museum acquires ownership of loaned property 1 yr. after notice of intent to terminate the loan; if hazardous then no notice required; undocumented property acquired after 7 yrs., 765 §§ 1033/1 to 1033/50
INDIANA			Expired loan requires notice and 60 days before acquisition; if no expiration date or non-permanent loan acquisition acquired after 7 yrs. of no contact, 32-34-5-12; undocumented property acquired after 3 yrs. plus 60 days notice, 32-34-5-13

Abandoned Hotel Property	Tenant Property	Miscellaneous	Uniform Unclaimed Property Act?
Innkeepers liable up to $750 for lost or damaged property entrusted to their custody; 43-21-8 to 43-21-12		Animals abandoned at vet may be disposed of after 10 days, 44-14-491; pecans presumed abandoned except during harvesting season, 44-12-242	Yes, 44-12-190 to 44-12-236
Innkeeper liability limited to $500 for property entrusted to them absent special agreement, 486K-4; 486K-5		Lost at stadium or at airport: held for 45 days then to finder or sold if not claimed within 30 days, 109-8; 261-17.7; lost animal: finder must immediately notify owner or shelter; $500 fine per violation, 142-99	Yes, 523A-1 to 523A-30
Held for 60 days then sold after 15 days notice, 39-1808		Common carrier/RR: held for 4 mos. then sold after 20 days notice and 10 days published notice, §55-1401 to 55-1404; held by police: sold after 6 mos.; bicycles after 90 days, 55-403; value $25 or less after 30 days; finder of animal to give notice to owner, provide care, may be adopted if no owner, 25-3511	Yes, 14-501 to 14-543
Liability limited to $100 regardless of negligence of innkeeper unless contrary agreement; innkeeper may deposit property in warehouse after 10 days, 740 § 90/4		Rafts, timber, planks: same procedure as lost property, 765 § 1020/21; unclaimed bail deposits over $100: considered abandoned after 3 yrs.; published notice then given: vests in state after 5 yrs., 725 § 5/110-17; common carriers/RR: held for 6 mos. then sold after 15 days notice, 770 § 90/1	Yes, 765 §§ 1025/1 to 1025/30
Unclaimed after 3 mos.: sold after notice and 2 wks. publication; proceeds to county after 1 yr., 32-34-2-1; 32-34-2-2	Landlord may deliver property to warehouse after notice to tenant; tenant may claim but must pay warehouse/ storage facility charges; property may be sold after 90 days from notice, 32-31-4-1 to 32-31-4-5	Molds: 3 years vests in molder, 32-34-6-5; silk screens: 3 years vests in maker or destroyed, 32-34-7-5; drifting boats, timber, rafts, logs: sold after 60 day, 32-34-9-2; property held by police: sold after 6 mos. and 2 wks. notice, 10-11-5-3	Yes; 32-34-1-1 to 32-34-1-52

Table 46: Lost, Abandoned, and Unclaimed Personal Property—Continued

State	Finder Responsibilities Criminal Penalties	Finder Responsibilities Cash/Valuables	Abandoned Museum Property
IOWA		Finder must notify police within 5 days; if value is: $5 or more, finder must put notice on courthouse and 3 most public places; $40 or more requires posting and 3 wks. publication; ownership vests in finder after 12 mos.; finder entitled to compensation, 556F.6 to 556F.16; fine of double the value if finder sells, loans, or takes property out of state before title vests; 1/2 to plaintiff, 1/2 to county, 556F.17; $20 fine for noncompliance, 556F.18	Permanent or expired loan: notice and 1 yr. before acquisition; undocumented property: 3 yrs. notice and 7 yrs., 305B.6 to 305B.7
KANSAS	Misdemeanor theft if value less than $1,000 and person takes lost or mislaid property without taking reasonable measures to restore it to rightful owner known to the finder and intends to deprive the owner of the property, 21-5802		Permanent or expired loan requires 90 days notice before acquisition, 58-4005; undocumented property vests after 7 yrs. plus 1 yr. notice, 58-4006
KENTUCKY	Misdemeanor if person takes lost, mislaid, or misdelivered property with intent to deprive the owner and not taking reasonable measures to restore it to owner; $500 to $10,000: class D felony; over $10,000: class C felony if more than, 514.050		Expired or loan over 7 yrs. requires notice and 2 wks. publication; 6 mos. wait before acquisition, 171.836; 171.840
LOUISIANA		Finder must make diligent effort to find owner, after 3 years acquires title, Civ. Code Art. 3419; Finder of treasure in a thing acquires title if no one owns thing, or gets ½ if someone does own the thing, Civ. Code Art. 3420	Held by any state museum: considered abandoned after 10 yrs.; property vests to museum 65 days after 2 wks. published notice, 25:345; 25:379.5; 25:380.4 to 25:380.105

Abandoned Hotel Property	Tenant Property	Miscellaneous	Uniform Unclaimed Property Act?
Hotel holds baggage at risk of owner after 48 hrs., 671.5		Dry cleaning: 4 mos., to be given to nonprofit, 556G.1; deer venison: 2 mos., to be given to nonprofit, 556H.1; dies, molds, forms: 3 yrs. and 90 days notice; vests in molder, 556C.2; pets: considered abandoned at vet after 7 days; 14 days notice then given; after 7 more days animal is destroyed, 162.19; vessels, rafts, logs, lumber with value of $5 or more: must give affidavit to court within 5 days with description of property; court appoints homeowners to appraise, if value up to $20: notice on courthouse and 3 most public places, vests in finder after 6 mos.; value over $20: notice and publication; after 90 days sold; proceeds to county, 556F.1 to 556F.5	Yes, 556.1 to 556.30
Liability limited to $250 unless property delivered to innkeeper or contrary agreement, 36-402	Landlord may sell or dispose after 30 days so long as 15 days published notice given and 7 days notice to tenant; proceeds to landlord, 58-2565	Self-stored property may be sold 45 days after default and notice twice given to occupant; proceeds held for 1 yr., then to state, 58-817	Yes, 58-3934 to 58-3980
Liability limited to $100 for property left behind, 306.030		Property held by police: held for 3 mos. then sold; proceeds to city, 95.435	Yes, 393A.010 to 393A.860
Innkeeper liability limited to $500 if provides a safe and posts notice of the safe unless contrary agreement, Civ. Code Art. 2945		Abandoned at hospital. 30 days notice to patient; 130 days to others before hospital acquires; sold in January, proceeds to hospital for indigent use, 40:2811; unclaimed retirement checks vest in state after 3 yrs., 11:540	Yes, 9:151 to 9:181

Table 46: Lost, Abandoned, and Unclaimed Personal Property—Continued

State	Finder Responsibilities Criminal Penalties	Finder Responsibilities Cash/Valuables	Abandoned Museum Property
MAINE	Felony or misdemeanor if person takes lost, mislaid, or misdelivered property with intent to deprive owner and not taking reasonable measures to restore it to owner, Tit. 17-A, § 356-A	Value $3 or more: written notice to town clerk and notice placed in public place; value $10 or more: written notice to town clerk, notice placed in public place and published notice; city appraises item(s); owner has 6 mos. to claim; finder claims by paying half of value to town; failure to give notice is penalty up to $20 or half of value, Tit. 33 §§ 1051 to 1058	Museum acquires after 3 yrs. if fair market value is less than $100; if $100 or greater, museum must exercise due diligence in contacting owner by mail or email if available, if not then publish notice weekly for 2 wks.; property vests to museum if no claim within 65 days from date of notice, Tit. 27, § 601
MARYLAND	Felony or misdemeanor theft if person takes lost, mislaid, or misdelivered property with intent to deprive owner and not taking reasonable measures to restore it to owner known or reasonably ascertainable to finder, Crim. Law § 7-104		
MASSACHUSETTS		Finder must report to police within 2 days if value of $3 or more; if no police station finder must publish notice or post in 2 public places; vests in finder after 1 yr., Ch. 134, §§ 1; 3; 4	Museum acquires property under indefinite term or expired loan 1 yr. after notice; if owner unknown, after 7 yrs., Ch. 200B, §§ 4; 5
MICHIGAN		Finder to report lost property to police in jurisdiction where found within 48 hrs.; police stores property; notice sent to owner who has 6 mos. to claim; then to finder or sold and proceeds to police, 434.21 to 434.28	Undocumented property vests in museum after 35 yrs.; 2 wks. notice required posted in museum if museum budget $50,000 or less, published if museum budget over $50,000, 399.61

Abandoned Hotel Property	Tenant Property	Miscellaneous	Uniform Unclaimed Property Act?
Innkeeper not liable for property not delivered into their custody, Tit. 30-a, §§ 3851 to 3854	Landlord must place property in storage and issue notice to tenant; if tenant claims property within 7 days, landlord must release and tenant retrieve property within 14 days; if tenant does not respond within 7 days, landlord may condition release of property on tenant's payment of all rental arrearages, damages and costs of storage or sell for reasonable fair market value with net proceeds to Treasurer of State; if no value, landlord may dispose of property, Tit. 14, § 6013	Found or held by police: held for 30 days then notice published; sold at public auction after 5 mos.; proceeds to be donated to non-profit organization or charity or disposed of as waste; if finder turned property over to police then to finder after 6 mos.; if finder cannot be found, property sold at public auction after 6 mos. and 15 days, Tit. 25, §§ 3501 to 3507	Yes, Tit. 33, §§ 1951 to 1980
Innkeeper not liable for items not deposited with the hotel so long as innkeeper not negligent, Bus. Reg. § 15-103		Held by dept for 6 mos., sold after 30 days notice, Nat. Res. § 1-2A-01; lost in state parks: held for 1 yr., then to state, Nat. Res. § 5-213; common carrier: held for 3 mos., sold after 10 days notice, Bus. Reg. § 19-102; finder on university property: held for 1 year by university then to finder or to state if not claimed within 30 days, Educ. § 13-702	Yes, Com. Law §§ 17-301 to 17-326
Innkeeper may sell property at public auction if not claimed within 6 mos.; notice of sale to be posted for 4 wks.; published for 3 wks. and sent to owner by registered mail, Ch. 140, § 14		Found by police: held for 6 mos. then sold after published notice; proceeds to state if not claimed within 2 yrs., Ch. 92, §§ 89 to 92, 94; common carriers: held for 120 days then sold after 5 wks. published notice; proceeds to state, Ch. 135, § 1; RR or vessel: held for 1 yr., then sold after 3 wks. published notice; proceeds to state if not claimed within 3 yrs., Ch. 135, § 6; lost pets: report to police or post notice in 2 places or publish; finder may sell after 3 mos., Ch. 134, §§ 2; 5 to 7	No; Ch. 175, §§ 149A to 149D; Ch. 158, § 17; Ch. 171, § 75 are similar
Liability for items placed in the custody of the hotel is that of depository for hire, 427.101		Found by police: held for 6 mos. then can be sold in public sale after 5 days published notice, 434.181 to 434.184; unclaimed winning tickets: held for 60 days then to licensee, 431.252; unclaimed lottery winnings: held for 1 yr. then to state, 432.33	Yes, 567.221 to 567.265

Table 46: Lost, Abandoned, and Unclaimed Personal Property—Continued

State	Finder Responsibilities Criminal Penalties	Finder Responsibilities Cash/Valuables	Abandoned Museum Property
MINNESOTA	Theft if person finds lost property and, knowing or having reasonable means of ascertaining true owner, appropriates it to own use or that of another not entitled to it without making reasonable effort to find owner and return property, 609.52	Lost on state lands: property may be sold; proceeds to state, 16B.25; unclaimed with business for 1 yr. plus 60 days notice delivered to police; sold after 10 days notice; proceeds to county after 5 yrs., 345.01 to 345.07	Presumed abandoned after no contact 7 yrs. after date of possession or expiration of loan: 60 day notice to owner within 60 days of abandonment before acquisition; public notice if notice to owner returned; non-documented property thought to be on lease: if no one claims in 7 yrs., museum becomes owner; 60 day public notice required to be free of all claims; property found in museum from unknown source presumed to be gift if not claimed within 90 days of discovery, 345.70 to 345.74
MISSISSIPPI			Museum acquires title after actual notice to lender or 2 published notices 60 days apart and 90 day wait, 39-19-1 to 39-19-21
MISSOURI	Finder not guilty of stealing property unless it was found under circumstances which gave finder knowledge or means of inquiry as to true owner; felony or misdemeanor if finder liable under 570.030 for stealing, 570.060	Value $10 or over: file affidavit with judge within 10 days of finding; judge appoints 3 people to appraise; notice posted on courthouse and 4 other public places; if appraisal $20 or over, then after 40 days must publish notice for 3 wks.; after 180 days property vests in finder; owner has 1 yr. to reclaim, 447.010 to 447.060	Loan may be terminated and property acquired after 7 yrs. and 90 days notice, 184.111; undocumented property acquired after 7 years and 90 days notice, 184.112
MONTANA	Imprisonment up to 6 mos. or fine up to $500 if finder knows owner or reasonable method of identifying owner and fails to take reasonable measures to restore property and has intent to deprive owner, 45-6-302	If value $10 or more, finder must use reasonable diligence to notify owner if known; finder gets rights of depository for hire; finder may sell only if perishable or lawful charges amount to 2/3 of value, 70-5-101 to 70-5-201	Loan may be terminated after 7 years, 30 days mailed notice to owner or 3 weeks published notice if owner unknown, 22-3-501 to 22-3-510

Abandoned Hotel Property	Tenant Property	Miscellaneous	Uniform Unclaimed Property Act?
No liability to owner for property not delivered into innkeeper custody unless innkeeper negligent; lost in room liability limited to $1,000; abandoned property may be disposed of or placed in storage after 10 days, 327.71	Landlord may sell or dispose of property later of 28 days after landlord receives actual notice of abandonment or 28 days after reasonably apparent to landlord that tenant has abandoned premises; landlord must make reasonable efforts to notify tenant of sale at least 14 days prior; up to $1,000 damages if tenant not allowed to retake within 24 hrs., 504B.271	Dies, molds vest in molder after 3 year, 345.20; common carriers: store after 60 days; sell after 12 mos., 345.09 to 345.13	Yes, 345.31 to 345.60
If innkeeper provides a safe, innkeeper not liable for items not delivered to them; for delivered items innkeeper is depository for hire, 75-73-5 to 75-73-7		Timber, boats, floatable things of value abandoned in waters may be claimed by finder, 89-17-1; found/held by police: Board of Supervisors shall post notice in 3 public places, property to be sold after 120 days; proceeds to sheriff, 19-3-85; 21-39-21	Yes, 89-12-1 to 89-12-57
No innkeeper liability if provides a safe and gives notice to guest, 419.010 to 419.020	Landlord may presume property abandoned if reasonable belief premises has been vacated and no rent paid for 30 days; may dispose of abandoned property after 10 day notice posted on property and mailed to tenant's last known address; 441.065	Common carrier: held for 60 days then sold after 20 days notice, 447.070 to 447.110	Yes, 447.500 to 447.595
Unclaimed baggage held for 6 mos. then sold after 4 wks. published notice, proceeds to county if not claimed within 1 yr. of sale, 70-9-501 to 70-9-502	Abandoned after 48 hrs.; landlord may sell or otherwise dispose of property 10 days after notice to tenant if no response to notice or tenant does not retrieve property within 7 days of response; proceeds less costs to county after 3 yrs., 70-24-430	Common carrier: property sold after 90 days; 20 days notice of sale to owner and 10 days published notice; surplus proceeds to county after 60 days, 70-9-402 to 70-9-404; laundry/dry cleaning: disposed of after 180 days, 70-9-601	Yes, 70-9-801 to 70-8-829

Table 46: Lost, Abandoned, and Unclaimed Personal Property—Continued

State	Finder Responsibilities Criminal Penalties	Finder Responsibilities Cash/Valuables	Abandoned Museum Property
NEBRASKA	Theft if person takes lost, mislaid, or misdelivered property with intent to deprive owner and not taking reasonable measures to restore it to owner, 28-514		Expired or indefinite loan terminated after 30 days mailed notice to owner or 3 wks. publication to unknown owner and 1 yr. wait, 51-704; undocumented property: held for 7 yrs., vests to museum after 3 yr. waiting period following 3 wks. publication of notice to claim, 51-705
NEVADA	Felony or misdemeanor theft if person takes lost, mislaid, or misdelivered property with intent to deprive owner and not taking reasonable measures to restore it to owner; misdemeanor if value under $650; felony if value $650 or more, 205.0832; 205.0835		Museum acquires property after 3 or more yrs.; 2 wks. published notice required followed by 60 day wait, 381.009
NEW HAMPSHIRE	Felony or misdemeanor theft if person takes lost, mislaid, or misdelivered property with intent to deprive owner and not taking reasonable measures to restore it to owner, 637:6; 637:11		Expired or loan over 5 yrs. requires notice and 2 wks. publication followed by 90 day wait before acquisition, 201-E:4; undocumented property held 5 or more years acquired after notice and 90 days, 201-E:3
NEW JERSEY	Theft if person takes lost, mislaid, or misdelivered property with intent to deprive owner known to finder and not restoring it to owner, 2C:20-6	Finder may claim lost property if not reclaimed within 120 days of commencement of reasonable efforts to find owner and return; owner of premises where property was found may claim title to buried or hidden lost property or lost property found by trespasser; if neither finder nor owner of premises claim, then city clerk may sell under UUPA, 46:30C-1 to 46:30C-5	Expired loan requires no contact for 5 yrs. after expiration, 10 yrs. from acquisition for indefinite loan period followed by notice plus 180 day waiting period; if unable to deliver notice or owner not known, notice must be published twice at least 60 days apart before waiting period begins, 46:30D-1 to 46:30D-11
NEW MEXICO			Museum acquires property 7 yrs. after loan expiration with no written notice of termination from lender or 7 yrs. from acquisition on indefinite loan with no response to notice within 65 day waiting period; notice must be mailed to last known address or published 2 consecutive weeks if no response or owner unknown, 18-10-1 to 18-10-5

Abandoned Hotel Property	Tenant Property	Miscellaneous	Uniform Unclaimed Property Act?
No liability for items not delivered into custody of hotel if safe and notice provided, 41-208	7 days personal notice or 14 days mailed notice must be given to tenant; property less than $250 may be disposed; $250 or more may be sold; proceeds to state, 69-2301 to 69-2314	Held by county sheriff: held for 180 days then sold after 3 wks. published notice; proceeds to county if unclaimed after 2 yrs., 69-1331 to 69-1332	Yes, 69-1301 to 69-1329
Hotel acquires property after 3 or more yrs.; 2 wks. published notice required followed by 60 day wait, 381.009	Landlord stores for 30 days; may dispose after 14 days notice to tenant, 118A.460	Held by university: vests after 1 yr.; money kept, property sold or donated to charity, 396.432; common carrier: held for 60 days; sold after 10 days published notice; proceeds to county, 108.380 to 108.430; safe deposit box: if rental not paid for 90 days, notice to owner; if no payment within 30 days, contents held for 3 years then turned over to State Treasurer, 663.085	Yes, 120A.010 to 120A.750
No liability for items lost in rooms; innkeeper negligence liability limited to $300, 353:1		Repair business: may dispose of property of value less than $500 if left for 60 or more days, 471-D:2; common carrier: held for 1 yr.; sold after 7 days posted notice; published notice if value $100 or more, 377:18 to 377:21; safe deposit box: presumed abandoned after 5 yrs., 471-C:18 ; stock - 3 yrs., 292:31; insurance funds - 6 years, 402-C:47; self-storage property - 30 days plus 20 days notice, 451-C:1 to 451-C:7; animals at vet - 7 days, 437:19	No; 471-C:1 to 471-C:43 are similar
If safe and notice provided then no liability for items not delivered into custody of hotel, 29:2-2	May be sold or disposed of after 30 days notice; if proceeds unclaimed after 10 yrs. then to state, 2A:18-72 to 2A18-84.	Common carrier: sold after 6 mos. and 6 days notice; proceeds to state, 2A:44-14; held by police: may be sold after 6 mos. and 10 days notice, 40A:14-157; held by state institutions: sold after 1 yr.; proceeds to state, 30:4-134	Yes, 46:30B-1 to 46:30B-109
If safe and notice provided then no liability for items not delivered into custody of hotel, 57-6-1		Held by police: property valued at $50 or more held for 90 days then may be sold or destroyed after 2 wks. notice, 29-1-14	Yes, 7-8A-1 to 7-8A-31

Table 46: Lost, Abandoned, and Unclaimed Personal Property—Continued

State	Finder Responsibilities Criminal Penalties	Finder Responsibilities Cash/Valuables	Abandoned Museum Property
NEW YORK	Misdemeanor theft if person refuses or willfully neglects to comply; punishable by imprisonment up to 6 mos. and/or fine up to $100, Pers. Prop. § 252	Value less than $10: finder acquires after reasonable effort to find owner and 1 yr. waiting period; $20 or more: return to owner within 10 days or report and deposit with police, waiting periods: under $100 - 3 mos.; $100 to $500 - 6 mos.; $500 to $5,000 - 1 yr.; $5,000 and over - 3 yrs.; notice must be given 3 mos. before expiration of waiting period if not returned to owner; vests in finder 3 mos. after notice or sold at public auction after 3 mos. and 10 days if not claimed	Expired loan or no contact in 5 yrs. on permanent or indefinite loan requires two 120 day notices; if no response, application to the supreme court to declare museum's right to the property; undocumented property held for 5 or more yrs. requires published notice and 180 days; if no response, application to supreme court to declare museum's right to property, Educ. § 233-a; Parks, Rec. & Hist. Preserv. §§ 19.17 to 19.19
NORTH CAROLINA			Museum acquires property if expired loan and at least 7 yrs. with no contact or indefinite term with at least 7 yrs. with no contact; if no response to notice after 30 days or unknown owner, notice must be published on official website, 180 days if value up to $10,000; 365 days if value over $10,000 followed by 45 day waiting period, 121-52
NORTH DAKOTA	Felony or misdemeanor theft if person takes lost, mislaid, or misdelivered property with intent to deprive owner and not taking reasonable measures to restore it to owner, 12.1-23-04 to 12.1-23-05	Money or property given to police by finder vests after 2 yrs., otherwise finder is depository for hire and must diligently seek to notify owner; finder may sell only if perishable or lawful charges amount to 2/3 of value, 60-01-34; 60-01-39	Vests after 10 yrs. and 2 wks. published notice and 65 day wait, 55-12-01 to 55-12-04
OHIO			Museum acquires property on expired loan or museum has held for at least 7 yrs. on indefinite loan after mailed or published notice and 6 mos. wait, 3385.02 to 3385.03
OKLAHOMA	Felony or misdemeanor theft if person takes lost property with intent to deprive owner known or reasonably ascertainable to finder and not taking measures to restore it to owner, Tit. 21, § 1702	Finder is a bailee for hire and must diligently give notice to owner; finder may sell only if perishable or lawful charges amount to 2/3 of value, Tit. 15, §§ 511 to 518	Museums not subject to UUPA but may avail itself of its provisions, Tit. 60, § 683.2

Abandoned Hotel Property	Tenant Property	Miscellaneous	Uniform Unclaimed Property Act?
Innkeeper not liable for any loss of clothing or other personal property damaged or lost in the lobby, hallway, or room for any sum exceeding $500 unless loss due to negligence of innkeeper, Gen. Bus. § 201		Abandoning animal to die in public place or failure to act within 3 hrs. of notice of disabled animal: misdemeanor punishable by imprisonment up to 1 yr. and/or fine up to $1,000, Agr. & M §§ 355; safe deposit box after 3 years, Aband. Prop. § 300; Miscellaneous Provisions, Aband. Prop. §§ 1300 to 1317	No; Aband. Prop. §§ 101 to 1502 are similar
No innkeeper liable for loss of money or jewels not deposited in their care, 72-3	If less than $500 landlord may throw property away after 5 days; if $750 or less landlord can deliver to nonprofit after posting notice, 42-25.9	Safe deposit boxes: notice given after 90 days unpaid rent; opened after 30 more days; abandoned after 2 yrs.; contents to state, 53C-6-13; 116B-55; repair shop property may be disposed after 60 days and notice given, 66-67.1; common carrier may sell at public auction after 60 days and notice given, 62-209	Yes, 116B-51 to 116B-80
Hotel not liable for loss suffered by any guest unless delivered into custody of hotel in safe; liability limited to $300, 60-01-29	Less than $2,500 may be disposed of without legal process if more than 28 days since tenant vacated, 47-16-30.1	Common carrier may sell at public auction after holding for 6 mos. and notice given, 8-03-09 to 8-03-10	Yes, 47-30.1-01 to 47-30.1-38
Innkeeper not liable for lost property unless guest has delivered it to innkeeper for custody, 4721.01		Dry cleaning disposed of or sold after 180 days and notice, 1333.22; unclaimed lottery prizes transferred to state, 3770.06; animal at vet abandoned after 10 days, send to shelter or pound, 4741.30	No; 169.02 to 169.13 are similar
	Landlord may take possession of nonresidential tenant property after 15 days and giving notice; may be sold if unclaimed, Tit. 41, § 52; residential tenant property is conclusively presumed abandoned after 30 days and landlord may dispose, Tit. 41, § 130	Held by police: may dispose of unclaimed money or personal property held for 90 or more days; if $100 or more notice must be given to last known owner by mail; if $500 or more mailed and published notice must be given; if still unclaimed then property may be sold, auctioned, donated, disposed of, or destroyed; sale proceeds to municipality; municipality may authorize portion of sale proceeds to be paid to finder as finder's fee, police, Tit. 11, § 34-104	Yes, Tit. 60, §§ 651 to 688

Table 46: Lost, Abandoned, and Unclaimed Personal Property—Continued

State	Finder Responsibilities Criminal Penalties	Finder Responsibilities Cash/Valuables	Abandoned Museum Property
OREGON	Felony or misdemeanor theft if person takes lost, mislaid, or misdelivered property with intent to deprive owner and not taking reasonable measures to restore it to owner; liable to county for full value of goods if valued at $250 or more, 164.065; 98.015	If $250 or more, give notice within 10 days of finding; within 20 days must publish notice once a week for 2 wks.; vests in finder 3 mos. after notice to clerk, 98.005	Museum acquires property after 25 yrs. with no contact; property on loan deemed donated after expiration of term and notice plus 7 yrs.; if no response to notice in 30 days, must be published in newspaper for 3 consecutive wks., 358.414 to 358.440
PENNSYLVANIA	Felony or misdemeanor theft if person takes lost, mislaid, or misdelivered property with intent to deprive owner and not taking reasonable measures to restore it to owner, Tit. 18, § 3903; 3924		
RHODE ISLAND		If $50 or more finder must report to police within 2 days and deliver property to police; vests in finder after 90 days; vests in state after 6 mos. if finder does not claim, 33-21.2-1 to 33-21.2-5	Museum acquires after expiration of loan and notice plus 60 days; property without loan agreement and unclaimed for 5 yrs. deemed abandoned 60 days after notice given, 34-44.1-1 to 34.33.1-8
SOUTH CAROLINA			Terminated loans or undocumented property held for 10 or more yrs.; may be claimed 120 days after giving notice by certified mail and 4 wks. publication, 27-45-10 to 27-45-100
SOUTH DAKOTA	Felony or misdemeanor theft if person takes lost, mislaid, or misdelivered property with intent to deprive owner and not taking reasonable measures to restore it to owner, 22-30A-6	Finder as a depository for hire must make diligent efforts to find owner; finder may sell only if perishable or lawful charges amount to 2/3 of value, 43-41-1 to 43 41-10	Property held for 10 or more yrs. with no claim vests in museum after 2 wks. published notice and 65 days, 43-41C-1 to 43-41C-4
TENNESSEE			Property held for 20 or more yrs. with no claim vests in museum after 2 wks. published notice and 65 days, 66-29-202; 66-29-203

Abandoned Hotel Property	Tenant Property	Miscellaneous	Uniform Unclaimed Property Act?
Property left by guest over 60 days: innkeeper may sell 10 days after notice; proceeds to county unless guest demands within 6 mos. of sale, 699.050	Landlord may sell or dispose of property 15 days after notice is given, 90.425	Held by bailee: delivers to justice of the peace to sell after 1 yr. and 60 days notice to owner; notice of sale must be published 18 days prior to sale, 98.110 to 98.240; held by police: sold after 60 days and 10 days notice of sale, 98.170; unclaimed molds after 3 yrs. if no agreement, 98.475; logs, timber abandoned after 30 days; vests in state, 98.642	Yes, 98.302 to 98.436
Innkeeper not liable for lost property unless guest has delivered it to innkeeper for custody and notice posted, Tit. 48, § 1323		Dry cleaning, laundry, shoe repair may dispose after 30 days notice, Tit. 6, § 33.5; unclaimed morgue property disposed after 1 yr., Tit. 16, § 8437	No; Tit. 72, §§ 1301.1 to 1301.28b are similar
Innkeeper not liable for lost property unless guest has delivered it to innkeeper for custody, 5-14-1		Animals deemed abandoned after 10 days if wearing ID, 5 days if not; property held by police: 6 mos., 33-21-1.14.1; safe deposit boxes: 3 yrs. after lease expiration, 33-21.1-16	Yes, 33-21.1-1 to 33-21.1-41
Innkeeper not liable for lost property unless negligence or guest has delivered it to innkeeper for custody or negligence, 45-1-40	Abandoned personal property of $500 or less may be disposed of by landlord; if $500 or more landlord not liable unless grossly negligent, 27-40-730	Common carrier: may sell after giving notice; unclaimed after 60 days; refused property after 30 days, 58-13-610; held by police: sold after 60 days, 27-21-20	Yes, 27-18-10 to 27-18-400
Innkeeper not liable for lost property unless guest has delivered it to innkeeper for custody, 43-40-1 to 43-40-6	Property not exceeding $500 in value may be disposed of 10 days after tenant has left premises; if $500 or more landlord must store for 30 days before disposing, 43-32-25 to 43-32-26	Lost, abandoned or confiscated bicycles held by police donated to nonprofit after 90 days, 43-41-11; intangible property held by business is abandoned after 3 yrs., 43-41B-2; life insurance abandoned after 3 yrs., 43-41B-7	Yes, 43-41B-1 to 43-41B-44
When safe is provided and guest does not use safe, innkeeper not liable for lost property or theft unless innkeeper failed to inform guest or post notice in guest's room in conspicuous manner of safe's purpose for safekeeping property, 62-7-103	Lost after 30 days absence and 10 days notice; landlord may then sell or dispose, 66-28-405	Held by police: disposed of after 90 days, 8-8-501; common carrier: lost and subject to sale after 2 wks. published notice and 30 days, 65-20-102; dry cleaning: lost and sold after 90 days notice and 12 days notice of sale, 66-16-107	Yes, 66-29-101 to 66-29-153

Table 46: Lost, Abandoned, and Unclaimed Personal Property—Continued

State	Finder Responsibilities Criminal Penalties	Finder Responsibilities Cash/Valuables	Abandoned Museum Property
TEXAS	Failure to comply with report, delivery and claims processes: class B misdemeanor, Prop. § 74.710		Property held for 15 or more yrs. vests in museum after 30 days mailed notice or 2 wks. published notice and 65 days; indefinite or loans 7 or more years long may be terminated and claimed by museum after notice and 65 days, Prop. §§ 80.001 to 80.008
UTAH	Felony or misdemeanor theft if person takes lost, mislaid, or misdelivered property and not taking reasonable measures to restore it to owner, 76-6-407		Property vests in collecting institution after 90 days mailed notice and 2 wks. published notice, 9-8-805
VERMONT	Destroying notices of lost property: $7 fine unless property has already been claimed, Tit. 27, § 1102	Value $3 or more: finder must post 2 notices in town within 6 days; $10 or more: also publish notice for 3 wks.; if owner does not claim within 20 days of notice copy of notice recorded by town clerk; after 90 days property sold; proceeds to town, Tit. 27, §§ 1101 to 1108	Museum acquires property after expiration of loan agreement or with no loan agreement after 10 yrs. with no claim; both require notice monthly for 3 mos. plus 180 days waiting period, Tit. 27, §§ 1151 to 1158
VIRGINIA			Undocumented property held for 5 or more yrs. vests in the museum after 2 wks. published notice and 65 days and a second 2 wk. published notice, 55-210.37
WASHINGTON	Felony or misdemeanor theft if person takes lost, mislaid, or misdelivered property with intent to deprive owner of such property or services, 9A.56.020	Finder must get appraisal from qualified person or judge within 7 days; must publish notice for 2 wks. within 30 days; if value is $25 or more then police holds; if less than $25 finder holds for 60 days; vests in finder after 60 days and paying $10 to treasurer plus cost of publication, 63.21.010 to 63.21.080	Terminated loans or unclaimed for 5 or more yrs. vests in museum after mailed or 2 wks. published notice given and 90 days, 63.26.010 to 63.26.050

Abandoned Hotel Property	Tenant Property	Miscellaneous	Uniform Unclaimed Property Act?
Innkeeper holds property delivered into custody as gratuitous bailee; not liable for property not delivered into its custody for greater than $50 unless innkeeper negligent, Occ. §§ 2155.051 to 2155.053	If tenant abandons personal property landlord may dispose, Prop. § 54.044	Aircraft abandoned after 90 days; notice given; hearing to determine ownership and 60 days, Transp. § 22.901; minerals proceeds held for 3+ yrs. presumed abandoned, Prop. § 75.101; common carrier may sell after 3 mos., Transp. § 6.001	No; Prop. Code § 72.001 to 72.103 are similar
Innkeeper not liable for lost property unless the guest has delivered it to innkeeper for custody, 29-1-1	Owner may store and must post notice of abandonment in conspicuous place and mail notice to tenant; after 15 days with no response from tenant owner may sell property and apply to any amount tenant owes owner or donate property to charity, 78B-6-816	Held by police: notice plus 8 days, then to finder or disposed of if finder cannot be located	Yes, 67-4a-101 to 67-4a-902
Innkeeper not liable for lost property unless guest has delivered it to innkeeper for custody or negligence by the innkeeper, Tit. 9, § 3141	Property vests in landlord after 60 days notice following abandonment, Tit. 9, § 4462	Stock or dividends: abandoned after 3 yrs., Tit., 27 § 1242; life insurance: Abandoned after 3 years, Tit. 27, § 1242; Safe deposit box: abandoned after 5 yrs., Tit. 27, § 1243	No; Tit. 27, §§ 1241 to 1270 are similar
Innkeeper not liable for lost property not delivered to innkeeper for custody if notice posted, 35.1-28	May be disposed of by landlord after 7 days notice, 55 248.38:1	Held by educational institution: held for 120 days then may be sold, 23-4.2; held by police: sold after 60 days and notice, 52-11.4; safe deposit box deemed abandoned after 5 yrs., 210.3:3	Yes, 55-201.1 to 55-210.30
		Held by police: sold after 60 days and notice, 63.32.010; dies, molds, forms: molder may destroy or dispose after 3 yrs. and 120 days notice, 63.52.010; held by bailee: after notice given and 60 days bailee may donate to charity if less than $100 or if $100 or more then give to police, 63.24.160	Yes, 63.29.010 to 63.29.906

Table 46: Lost, Abandoned, and Unclaimed Personal Property—Continued

State	Finder Responsibilities Criminal Penalties	Finder Responsibilities Cash/Valuables	Abandoned Museum Property
WEST VIRGINIA			
WISCONSIN		Value $25 to $100: finder must give notice to police of city where found within 5 days; city will post notice in 2 places; $100 or more: notice to police within 15 days and appraise within 2 mos.; vests in finder after 90 days; failure to give notice of finding goods of $3 or more results in liability for full value of goods: ½ to city, ½ to owner, 70.07 to 170.11	Museum acquires property 7 yrs. with no contact after expiration of loan agreement or after acquisition on indefinite loan; 60 days notice required followed by published notice if no response; undocumented property vests in museum after 7 yrs. free from all claims if owner is unknown or unable to contact, 171.32 to 171.33
WYOMING			Loan greater than 90 days and not subject to loan agreement requires museum to give notice by mail or publication of intent to acquire; lender response to notice renews loan for 10 yrs.; property vests in museum if no response to notice; terminated loans must be claimed within 1 yr. of date of notice, 34-23-102 to 34-23-108

Abandoned Hotel Property	Tenant Property	Miscellaneous	Uniform Unclaimed Property Act?
Innkeeper not liable for lost property not delivered into their custody so long as notice posted, 16-6-22	Landlord may dispose of property after 30 days notice given or if value $300 or more after storing for an additional 30 days, 37-6-6	Safe deposit box contents deemed abandoned after 5 yrs., 36-8-3	Yes, 36-8-1 to 36-8-32
Hotelkeeper not liable for lost property unless delivered for safekeeping or caused by negligence, 97.633 to 97.635	Landlord may dispose of abandoned personal property in any manner that landlord deems appropriate; if property left behind is prescription medication or medical equipment, landlord must hold property for 7 days from discovery before disposing of it, 704.05	Held by police: sold after 60 days notice, 171.06; excess disaster relief money: if $25+ given to charity after 6 mos. and notice given, 171.08; property found by official, employee, or state agent held for 90 days then to state if unclaimed, 170.105; any property abandoned on land belonging to state is acquired by state after 60 days, 20.909	Yes, 177.01 to 177.41
Innkeeper not liable for loss of property when notice posted in conspicuous place unless result of innkeeper negligence, 33-17-101	Abandoned 7 days after service of notice and may be retained or disposed of by landlord, 1-21-1210	Safe deposit box contents deemed abandoned after 5 yrs., 34-23-116	Yes, 34-24-101 to 34-24-140

47. MEDICAL RECORDS

Federal, state, and local governments are responsible for protecting and safeguarding the public health and welfare. Accordingly, during terms of various epidemics the state has required the registration of infected persons in order to treat and/or quarantine them and to study the spread of the disease to ultimately control and eradicate it. Thus, although access to medical records is highly guarded, the reporting of diseases is widely practiced at all levels of government. The Center for Disease Control, for example, publishes The Morbidity and Mortality Weekly Report, containing a comprehensive list of all reported illnesses by both state and region that benefits the family practice doctor as well as the epidemiologist. The reports of cases that are reported, from the flu to various venereal diseases to AIDS (acquired immunodeficiency syndrome), are given in confidence, and access to the records is forbidden for most other purposes.

The outbreak of AIDS has sparked controversy over the confidentiality of medical records and diagnoses. Some employers and insurance companies have sought to have individuals tested for the HIV virus, which can lead to AIDS, before hiring in order to prevent considerable expenses in the future as the employee's health fails. Often these same parties argue for access to medical records for background checks as part of the interview process. The great tension regarding the rights of individuals with the HIV virus or AIDS, the public's interest in controlling and fighting the epidemic, and the interest of employers, insurers, and health officials in providing adequate and affordable medical care has created a very dynamic ethical and legal dilemma that will not soon be resolved.

The laws controlling and regulating access to medical records vary greatly from state to state, although the basic protection is always there: a person's medical records are personal and private. As is historically the case, the federal government has gotten increasingly involved in the area of individual rights and has enacted a number of pieces of privacy legislation. For example, the Federal Privacy Act of 1974 requires the release of information in federal files to the subject individual upon request, although some government agencies have established regulations allowing the release of information to a physician chosen by the requesting individual (5 U.S.C. 552a(f)(3)). Federally funded community mental health and mental retardation centers must maintain safeguards to preserve confidentiality and protect the rights of patients (52 U.S.C. 2689(d)(2)), and the Department of Defense may not use for any adverse personnel decision any personal information obtained in interviews with members of the service who are HIV positive (PL 49-661 §705(c)).

The most significant change to these laws regards certain federal laws. In 1996, Congress passed the Health Insurance Portability and Accountability Act, PL 104-191 (HIPAA). In 2006 the Secretary of Health & Human Services adopted rules to enforce provisions in that act. Essentially, the rules clarify penalties and responsibility for investigating violations of privacy laws. Everyone who has been to a doctor in 2005–2006 has, no doubt, been asked to sign HIPAA forms.

This chapter treats all state statutes that could be found concerning privacy and medical records. It must be noted, however, that this emerging field is increasingly subject to revision and new legislative attention. In addition, in certain areas such as AIDS information, the courts may have construed other statutes as protecting or not protecting AIDS victims. In these cases the courts may be awaiting or inviting legislative action. Spaces on the chart that are left blank are those situations where specific laws cannot be found; this does not necessarily mean that an individual is without protection in these areas.

Table 47: Medical Records

State	Who Has Access	Privilege
ALABAMA	Notifiable disease records confidential, 22-11A-2	Medical records may only be used in commitment proceedings without patient's consent, 22-11A-22
ALASKA	Parent or guardian, 25.20.130; Dept. of Social Services for financial records of medical assistance beneficiaries, 47.07.074; patient, 18.23.00); medical review organization, 18.23.010 to 18.23.070; guardian ad litem, 18.15.362	In the case of emergency medical services, records of those treated may be disclosed to EMTs for emergency purposes, 18.08.087
ARIZONA	Communicable disease related information confidential, except if discovered by health department during investigation, 36-662; release of information by consent or according to 36-664(A)(1)-(12)	Physicians and surgeons in most cases, 12-2235
ARKANSAS	Prosecutor entitled to relevant medical records of person charged with committing sex crime or exposing another to a communicable disease, 5-14-202; generally, not open to public, 25-19-105; available to patient, 23-76-129; or through patient's attorney, 16-46-106	Physician or psychotherapist, A.R.Ev. 503; all medical records privileged, 12-2292

Mandatory Reporting	Patient Waiver	Insurance Purposes	AIDS
Tuberculosis, STDs, and notifiable disease cases must be reported to state Board of Health, 22-11A-1; 22-11A-2; 22-11A-9; 22-11A-14	Waiver of medical record of persons infected with sexually transmitted disease by written consent of patient, 22-11A-22		Individual must be notified of positive test result including face-to-face counseling, information on health care services and services related to locating and testing persons who have been in contact with infected individual; otherwise confidentiality must be maintained, 22-11A-53; 22-11A-54
Physicians must report various listed diseases to state medical officer, 18.15.370	Mental health records may be disclosed only with patient or an individual to whom the patient has given written consent, 47.30.845(2)		
Non-accidental injuries, malnourishment, physical neglect, sexual abuse, or other deprivation with intent to cause or allow injury or death of minor child must be reported to peace officer or child protective services; reports are confidential and may be used only in authorized judicial or administrative proceedings, 13-3620; reports and records about abused or incapacitated adult may only be used in authorized judicial or administrative proceedings, 46-454	Health provider may disclose medical records and/or payment records with written authorization by patient, 12-2292		Any release of information must specifically authorize HIV-related information; person with confidential HIV-related information may not be compelled to disclose information by subpoena, search warrant, or other judicial process, but may report if there is an identifiable third party at risk; no prohibition from listing in death certificate, 36-664
Physicians must report cases of HIV, 20-15-904; 20-15-906; Reye's syndrome, 20-15-401; and cancer, 20-15-201	Express consent, 23-76-129; any person filing claim as beneficiary of state's Special Needs Trust shall be deemed to have waived physician-patient privilege as to communications & records regarding claimant's physical, mental or emotional condition, 20-77-706		Reporting required to Arkansas Dept. of Health by physicians and other medical and lab directors, 20-15-906; all information and reporting confidential, 20-15-904

Table 47: Medical Records—Continued

State	Who Has Access	Privilege
CALIFORNIA	May not be disclosed without authorization except for court order, insurance, HMO, Civ. Code §§ 56 to 56.31; The State Ombudsman shall have access to the medical records of patient or resident of long term care facility if patient consents or, if unable to consent, to the extent necessary for the office to carry out its responsibilities, Welfare & Inst. § 9724	Doctors, including psychotherapists and psychiatrists (Ev. §§ 994, 1010); patient must waive doctor-patient confidentiality when plaintiff in civil suit (Ev. §1016)
COLORADO	Dept. of Public Health may inspect without permission and demand access to medical records when officially investigating communicable diseases or epidemics, 25-1-122; patient or designated representative with written authority, except for psychiatric records that would have significant negative psychological impact, in which case patient is entitled to summary, 25-1-801	Physician, nurse, or psychologist, 13-90-107; all materials and records compiled by the Dept. of Public Health are privileged and confidential except as excepted by law, 25-3-605
CONNECTICUT	Patient or patient's designee may see and copy, 4-105; 20-7c; state law limits disclosure of mental health data about patient by name or other identifier, 52-146h; state departments may receive information on patients only to extent necessary to obtain support or payment for care of patient; all information confidential, 17b-225	Information of all sorts gathered by the Dept. of Public Health, its staff or any facility accredited by the department for purposes of reducing morbidity or mortality from any cause is confidential, except as required to further its mission and may be shared with other persons or organizations with the same mission, 19a-25; physician, 52-146o
DELAWARE	All information and records of known or suspected cases of sexually transmitted disease, including HIV infections, shall be strictly confidential; released only under certain circumstances, Tit. 16, § 711	Physicians and psychotherapists, D. R. Ev. 503; immunity from liability for good faith reporting of child abuse, Tit. 16, § 908; personal and medical records shall be treated confidentially and shall not be made public without express consent of patient or resident of sanatoria, rest home, nursing home, boarding home or related institution, except as needed for a patient's transfer to another facility or as required by 3rd party payment contract, Tit. 16, § 1121 (6)
DISTRICT OF COLUMBIA	Medical records generally confidential, but may be transmitted for peer-review or anonymous use in publications, 44-801 to 44-805; public mental health facility must make patient records available to patient's attorney or personal physician upon that person's written authorization, 21-562	Physician; mental health professionals, 14-307; does not apply to child abuse reports or in criminal cases involving serious bodily harm, 7-1911

Mandatory Reporting	Patient Waiver	Insurance Purposes	AIDS
Developmental centers must immediately report incidences of assault, abuse and other enumerated injuries to local law enforcement. (Welfare & Inst. §4427.5)	No privilege for communication about patient's condition if initially tendered by patient or any party claiming rights or beneficiary of patient (Ev. §996); Patient must waive doctor-patient confidentiality when plaintiff in civil suit (Ev. §1016); In general: Civ. Code §56.07;	Insurer may obtain to the extent noted in (Civ. Code §56.10(c)(2)) Information disclosed to the extent necessary to allow responsibility for payment to be determined and made	Blood testing must be anonymous and test results may not disclose identities of persons tested even through subpoena (H&S 120975 and 121025)
Physicians must report venereal disease, tuberculosis, rabies, and HIV to State Dept. of Public Health, 25-4-402; 25-4-404			Confidential counseling and testing preferred; anonymous testing conducted for persons with high risk, 25-4-1405.5
Physician must report tuberculosis to Dept. of Public Health, 19a-262			Results confidential except to exposed health care workers, or to mental health or prison facilities, 19a-583
Sexually transmitted diseases reported to division of Public Health, some reported in number and manner only, Tit. 16, § 702			Strictly confidential with exceptions made under certain circumstances, Tit. 16, § 711
Mayor may issue list of diseases which physicians must report to Commission of Public Health, 7-131			Information and records pertaining to persons with AIDS are confidential, 7-1605

Table 47: Medical Records—Continued

State	Who Has Access	Privilege
FLORIDA	Patient; legal representative; health care provider except for psychological or psychiatric records which may be provided as a report instead of copies of records, 456.057; patient's guardian; curator; or personal representative; anyone authorized in writing, 395.3025	Psychotherapist-patient, 456.059; patient; patient's attorney; guardian or conservator; personal representative has privilege to refuse to disclose and prevent others from disclosing confidential communications or records made for the purpose of diagnosis or treatment of patient's mental or emotional condition, including alcoholism and other drug addiction, including any diagnosis made or advice given in the course of the professional relationship; privilege may also be claimed by psychotherapist, but only on behalf of patient; no privilege exists relevant to issue in proceedings to compel hospitalization of patient for mental illness if there is reasonable cause to believe that patient is in need of hospitalization or if court has ordered evaluation, 90.503
GEORGIA	Patient, his designee or any other person or entity authorized by law may request access to all medical records and custodian of the records must furnish copies within 30 days of request; custodian may refuse access if determined that disclosure may be detrimental to physician or mental health of the patient, in which case records must be provided to patient's designee at patient's request, 31-33-2; does not apply to psychiatric, psychological, or other mental health records, 31-33-4; 31-33-7	Patient and psychiatrist, psychologist or other licensed mental health professional, 24-5-501; physician; pharmacist, 24-12-1
HAWAII	Dept. of Public Health may inspect medical records without permission when investigating communicable diseases or epidemics, 25-1-122; patient or attorney, but doctor may require patient's authorization to make records available to attorney if detrimental to patient's health, 622-57	Physicians; psychologists, 626-1, Rules 504; 504.1
IDAHO	Patient or agent by subpoena, 9-420; custodial or non-custodial parent of minor child, 32-717A; in some civil actions records may be open to discovery, 39-1392e; government medical records exempted from open records law, 74-106	Physician, 9-203(4); psychologist, 9-203(6)

Mandatory Reporting	Patient Waiver	Insurance Purposes	AIDS
Physicians must report cases of tuberculosis and STDs to Dept. of Health, 384.25; 392.53	Medical records not disclosed unless patient gives written authorization except in certain situations, 456.057		Confidential with certain exceptions to nondisclosure, 381.004
Venereal disease; suspected child abuse, 19-7-5; 31-17-2	Written authorization or waiver by patient or parent/ guardian or by subpoena or appropriate court order, 24-12-1		All AIDS information confidential, 24-12-20; may be disclosed to any person, or in case of minor to parents or guardian and with notice; to spouse/partner if physician believes he or she is at risk, 24-12-21
Physician; health care professional; laboratory director must report in writing to dept. of health any incidence of disease or condition declared to be communicable or dangerous to public health, 325-2			Health care provider may release medical records to next of kin relating to a deceased person's AIDS or AIDS-related complex; diagnosis or treatment of a mental illness; participation in substance abuse program, 622-57; all records of AIDS, HIV, or AIDS-related patients strictly confidential; release of information allowable under circumstances relating to public health and for research purposes, 325-101
Child abuse cases within 24 hrs., 16-1605); enumerated venereal diseases including AIDS and HIV, 39-602	Patient or doctor or nurse responsible for entries in hospital record may request protective order to deny or limit access, 9-420; state or local officials may disclose potential or possible victims of exposure to bodily fluids of a patient or deceased who has tested positive for HIV, 39-610		Confidentiality of patient information maintained; use of information restricted to public health requirements and those with a legitimate need to know, 39-609

Table 47: Medical Records—Continued

State	Who Has Access	Privilege
ILLINOIS	Medical records kept strictly confidential, 735 § 5/8-2101)	Physician; surgeon, 735 § 5/8-802
INDIANA	Must be released to patient or patient's designee on reasonable notice and written request, 16-39-1-1 to 16-39-1-9; medical records may be released to appropriate parties for purposes of protecting public health, 16-4-8-1 to 16-41-8-6; hospitals using electronic records system must do so in a manner that records are available only to authorized personnel, 34-43-1-1 to 34-43-1-17	Physicians, 34-46-3-1
IOWA	Medical and psychiatric records held by Dept. of Human Services are confidential and may only be distributed to other agencies in course of official business or researchers so long as identity is not disclosed, 217.30	Physicians; mental health practitioners, 622.10
KANSAS		Doctor-patient, with exceptions, 60-427; psychologist-patient, 74-5323
KENTUCKY	Patient by written request, 422.317	Psychiatrist-patient privilege, K.R.Ev. 507
LOUISIANA	Healthcare providers must provide copies of records upon patient's request, unless injurious to health or welfare of patient or subject to subpoena, 40:1165.1	Healthcare provider-patient; usually waived in cases of child abuse or molestation. La. Code Ev. § 510
MAINE	Patient or authorized representative if hospital or medical practitioner believes release would be detrimental to patient's health, Tit. 22, §§ 1711; 1711-B; attorney general in criminal proceeding; records remain confidential and dissemination is limited, Tit. 5, § 200-E	Doctor-patient; psychologist-patient; both abrogated in child protective activity, Tit. 22, § 4015)
MARYLAND	All medical records confidential and may only be disclosed to patient or representative upon written authorization or when authorized by statute for research or epidemiological purposes, Health-Gen. §§ 4-301 to 4-309	Psychologist/psychiatrist-patient, Cts. & Jud. Proc. § 9-109

Mandatory Reporting	Patient Waiver	Insurance Purposes	AIDS
Child abuse, 325 § 5/4; sexually transmissible diseases, 410 § 325/4	Right to privacy and confidentiality in health care may be waived in writing by patient or patient's physician, 410 § 50/3		AIDS test information must be kept confidential, 410 § 305/1 to 305/16; no disclosure of AIDS test information without consent; court order; or when necessary to inform possibly infected person, 410 § 305/9
Child abuse; HIV; certain communicable diseases, 31-33-5-1; 16-41-2-2	Patient's physician-patient privilege is waived regarding information reported to appropriate authorities for purposes of protecting and investigating public health, 16-41-2-4	Insurance company may obtain records with written consent, 16-39-5-2	All HIV cases must be reported, 16-41-2-3
Confidential reports of venereal disease must be filed; 139A.30; 139A.31; Dept. of Public Health may designate other diseases as reportable, 139A.2			All reports and information related to HIV are strictly confidential medical information; released under certain circumstances, 141A.9
Any physician or lab director with knowledge of AIDS sufferer must report to secretary of health and environment; information confidential and disclosed as per 65-6002 (c)	General waiver provision only; any person may waive any privilege by contract or by knowingly disclosing privileged information, 60-437		Any physician or lab director with knowledge of AIDS sufferer must report to secretary of health and environment; information confidential, 65-6002
Regulations designate diseases which must be reported to Cabinet for Health Services, 214.010	Patient or physician may ask to prohibit or limit use by protective order, 422.315		Test results disclosed only to those listed in 214.181
	Written patient consent required, 40:1165.1		Information related to HIV is confidential; disclosure may be authorized under certain circumstances, 40:1171.4; 40:1171.5
Physicians must report certain communicable diseases, Tit. 22, § 822; malignant tumors, Tit. 22, § 1402			HIV test results confidential with certain exceptions, Tit. 5, § 19203
Physicians must report infectious diseases and HIV/AIDS, Health-Gen § 18-201			Test results confidential, Health-Gen. § 18-334; physician may inform local health officer if individual refuses to notify sexual or needle-sharing partners, Health-Gen. § 18-337

Table 47: Medical Records—Continued

State	Who Has Access	Privilege
MASSACHUSETTS	Patient or authorized representative; psychotherapist may give summary of record if it would adversely affect patient's well-being, Ch. 112, § 12CC; mental health records private except for court order, at patient or attorney request, or if mental health commissioner allows for sake of best interest of patient, Ch. 123, § 36	Patient communication with psychotherapist is privileged, unless psychotherapist determines that there exists an imminent danger to the patient or another person, Ch. 233, § 20B
MICHIGAN	Any review entity, 331.531; Dept. of Health shall protect privileged communications and individual's expectation of privacy with regard to Dept.'s activities, 333.2611	Physician-patient, 600.2157; full extent of statutory privilege in litigation was challenged in *Thomas v. 1156729 Ontario Inc.*, F. Supp. 2d 780 (2013), and was found to be less stringent than HIPPAA, and, therefore, for those purposes is superseded by HIPPAA
MINNESOTA	Patient or authorized representative has access to all medical records upon written request, 144.291 to 144.34; treating physician has access to all patient's prior medical records, including records regarding treatment of mental illness, 253B.0921	Physician, nurse, or psychologist may not disclose confidential information acquired in professional capacity without the consent of the patient, 595.02
MISSISSIPPI	Medical or dental review committee for evaluation of quality of care; patient's identity not divulged, 41-63-1; 41-63-3)	Physician; dentist; nurse; pharmacist; patient, 13-1-21
MISSOURI	Patient or representative upon request, 191.227	Physicians; psychologists; chiropractors; dentists, 491.060
MONTANA	Patient may authorize disclosure of healthcare information, 50-16-526; without patient's authorization, may be released in limited circumstances, 50-16-530; all records of Dept. of Public Health and Human Services are confidential; disclosed according to 41-3-205	Doctor-patient, 26-1-805; psychologist-client, 26-1-807

Mandatory Reporting	Patient Waiver	Insurance Purposes	AIDS
Any injury from discharge of gun or a burn affecting over 5% of the body; rape or sexual assault; victim's name not included in report, Ch. 112, § 12A; physician may report venereal disease to patient's partner if engaged; parents if minor, Ch. 112, § 12			Labs and hospitals that conduct blood tests for AIDS must not disclose results without obtaining written informed consent of patient, Ch. 111, § 70F
Serious communicable diseases, 333.5117	Patient may give authorization for medical provider to release patient information to 3rd party, 333.20201		All reports of HIV infection and AIDS are confidential; release allowed in certain circumstances, 333.5131
Maltreatment of minors, 626.556			Person with actual knowledge that regulated physician/nurse/dentist/dental hygienist is infected with HIV may report, 214.19
Licensing boards may establish reporting requirements for Hepatitis B virus and HIV, 41-34-1 to 41-34-7	Patient waiver of doctor's privilege implied to comply with state and local health departments and for information regarding communicable diseases, 13-1-21		Convicted sex offenders shall be tested for HIV; results reported to victims and spouses, 99-19-203
			All information concerning one's HIV status is confidential, but may be released to public employees for limited purposes (§191.656)
Must report if conduct is such that might expose another to infection, 50-18-106	Patient may authorize in writing disclosure of medical records; does not constitute a waiver of any rights under any other state laws or common law, 50-16-526		Person may not disclose or be compelled to disclose the identity of a subject of an HIV test or results, 50-16-1009; HIV testing, 50-16-1007

Table 47: Medical Records—Continued

State	Who Has Access	Privilege
NEBRASKA	Patient and duly authorized representative by written request; mental health records may be withheld if any treating physician, psychologist, or mental health practitioner determines release would not be in best interest of patient unless release required by court order, 71-8403; counsel for mentally ill patient who has been taken into custody may make request to county attorney for access to records of patient's treatment, 71-949; person who has been treated for mental illness committed to mental health facility may authorize access to records of such treatment or commitment, but if patient is deemed dangerous to himself or others, the records may be released to relevant authorities, 71-961	Physicians, 27-504
NEVADA	Patient or authorized representative by patient's written request; personal representative of estate or trustee of living trust of deceased patient; parent or guardian of deceased minor patient; investigator for Attorney General or grand jury investigating certain violations; authorized representative or investigator of state licensing board in course of any authorized investigation, 629.061; Div. of Public and Behavioral Health facility required upon patient transfer to another facility or licensed physician to forward patient's medical records to the new facility or physician; does not require patient's consent, 433.332	Patient and physician, 49.225
NEW HAMPSHIRE	Records are deemed property of patient, 332-I:1; anyone with durable power of attorney for health care for patient, 137-J:7; patient and one with patient's written consent or with written certification of ombudsman, 161-F:14; no employee may be required to bear cost of any medical exam or furnish any records required by employer as condition of employment, 275:3	Doctor-patient, 329:26
NEW JERSEY	Medical records confidential but may be disclosed to patient on request; upon court order; certain other circumstance, 30:4-24.3	Psychologist-patient, 45:14B-28; physician-patient, 2A:84A-22.1; 2A:84A-22.2

Mandatory Reporting	Patient Waiver	Insurance Purposes	AIDS
At request of Dept. of Health, hospitals, physicians and dentists must make information contained in medical records of patients who have cancer for Cancer Registry, 81-642; brain injuries for Brain Injury Registry, 81.657; all reportable diseases, including sexually transmitted diseases, 71.503.01			
Communicable diseases, 441A.150	If patient or authorized representative voluntarily discloses confidential matters, including medical records, person shall be deemed to have waived the privilege, 49.385		Law enforcement officer may request person be tested for HIV if person exposed officer to risk during officer's official duties, 441A.195
Communicable disease, 141-C:7			All records and information pertaining to person's HIV testing are confidential and protected from unwarranted intrusion, 141-F:8
Child abuse, 9:6-8.30; pertussis vaccine, 26:2N-5; venereal disease, 26:4-41; AIDS, 26:5C-6			All records with identifying information are confidential, 26:5C-7; disclosure per 26:5C-8 to 26:5C-13

Table 47: Medical Records—Continued

State	Who Has Access	Privilege
NEW MEXICO	Office of state long-term care ombudsman for patient/resident/client, 28-17-13; patient, must provide written authorization; authorization not required in certain circumstances, 43-1-19; worker's compensation: worker; employer; employer's insurer; appropriate peer review organization on written request by any party, except only on worker's written authorization for records directly related to injuries or disabilities claimed by worker for which worker is receiving benefits from employer, 52-10-1	Physician/psychologist-patient, N.M.R.A., Rule 11-504
NEW YORK	Medical director of prison in reference to inmate, Correct. § 601; inspector of mental facility, Mental Hyg. § 16.11; physician or hospital must release medical file to another physician or hospital upon written request of parent, guardian, or patient; records concerning venereal disease treatment or abortion for minor may not be released, even to parent, Pub. Health § 17	Physician; dentist; podiatrist; chiropractor; nurse, C.P.L.R. § 4504
NORTH CAROLINA	Patient or authorized representative or by court order, N.C.R.C. Medico-Legal Guideline III; All privileged patient medical records possessed by Dept. of Health or local health department are confidential, 130A-12; pharmacists when necessary to provide services, 90-85.35	Physician, 8-53), except in cases of alleged child abuse, 8-53.1
NORTH DAKOTA	Long term care ombudsman shall have access to all appropriate medical records, 50-10.1-04	Physicians; psychotherapists N.D. R.Ev., Rule 503
OHIO	Employee or designated representative may request records from employer, physician, health care professional, hospital, or lab when tests are required by employer, 4113.23	Doctor-patient, 2317-02(B)
OKLAHOMA	Patient; in case of psychological/psychiatric records, patient has access if consented to by treating physician or court order or upon finding that it is in the best interest of patient, Tit. 76, § 19; health professional may inform parents of treatment needed or provided to minor; such disclosure does not breach right to privacy, Tit. 63, § 2602; Tit. 43A, § 1-109	Physician/psychotherapist-patient, Tit. 12, § 2503

Mandatory Reporting	Patient Waiver	Insurance Purposes	AIDS
Sexually transmitted diseases, 24-1-7	A person who possesses a privilege of confidential information waives the privilege upon voluntary disclosure or consent to disclose significant part of the privileged information, unless the disclosure itself is privileged, 11-511		Performance of test and results are confidential; disclosure subject to 24-2B-6
Any person or official required to report cases of child abuse or maltreatment must report to medical examiner or coroner any suspicions when a child has died as a result of child abuse or maltreatment, Soc. Serv. § 418			All HIV-related information is confidential and may only be disclosed in limited circumstances, Pub. Health § 2782
Physicians; lab directors; local health directors must report communicable diseases; hospitals may report, 130A-134 to 130A-143			All AIDS information and records are confidential; subject to release only according to 130A-143
Child abuse and communicable diseases designated by Dept. of Health, 23-07-01; 50-25.1-01			Information regarding HIV infection is strictly confidential; release subject to 23-07-02.2
Child abuse, 2151.421; occupational diseases, 3701.25; cases of cancer for cancer registry, 3701.262; contagious or infectious diseases, including AIDS, 3701.24			Disclosure of HIV or AIDS-related information subject to 3701.243
Child abuse (physical, sexual and/or neglect), Tit. 10A, § 1-2-101; communicable or venereal disease, Tit. 63, § 1-528(b)			HIV tests or records upon written request of person affected, or in cases of certain crimes, test results released to victim, Tit. 63, § 1-525

Table 47: Medical Records—Continued

State	Who Has Access	Privilege
OREGON	Patient, 192.553	Patient-psychotherapist, 40.230; patient-physician, 40.235
PENNSYLVANIA	Patient or patient's designee, including attorney, Tit. 42, § 6155	Physician privilege limited to civil matters, Tit. 42, § 5929
RHODE ISLAND	Patient, 5-37-22; holders of medical records must keep them confidential; patient's written consent generally required, 5-37.3-4	Health care providers, 9-17-24
SOUTH CAROLINA	Patient or representative, 44-115-30	Mental health provider-patient, 19-11-95
SOUTH DAKOTA	Patient or representative, 36-2-16	Physician; psychotherapist, 19-19-503
TENNESSEE	Patient may see hospital records upon written request or court order, 68-11-304; medical records of patients in state facilities and those whose care is paid for by state funds are confidential, 10-7-504	Psychiatrists, 24-1-207; psychologists, 63-11-213
TEXAS	Medical information identifiable as to individuals is to be kept confidential and information used for studies is privileged, Health & Safety § 161.022	Physician, Occ. § 159.002
UTAH	Patient or patient's representative, 78B-5-618	Doctor-patient, 78B-1-137

Mandatory Reporting	Patient Waiver	Insurance Purposes	AIDS
Physician; physician's assistant; registered nurse who has reasonable cause to suspect patient has had injury with knife, gun, or other deadly weapon by other than accidental means must report to appropriate law enforcement agency by telephone, followed as soon thereafter as possibly by written report, 146.750			HIV test results confidential, 433.075
Communicable diseases, Tit. 35, § 521.4			All HIV-related information confidential; limited disclosure, Tit. 35, § 7607
Occupational diseases, 23-5-5; sexually transmitted and communicable diseases, 23-8-1; 23-11-5	Any agreement purporting to waive the privilege of confidentiality of medical records is against public policy and void, 5-37.3-10	Patient information cannot be released or transferred without patient's written consent, 5-37.3-4	
Sexually transmitted diseases, 44-29-70			Information and records are strictly confidential except in limited circumstances; in minor cases, if attending public school in grades K-5, superintendent and nurse must be notified, 44-29-135; court orders, 44-29-136
Venereal disease, 34-23-2; child abuse or neglect, 26-8A-3		Division of Insurance must keep medical records confidential, 58-4-5	Victims of sexual assault may request testing and receive notification of results, 23A-35B-1 to 23A-35B-13
Communicable diseases, 68-5-101; sexually transmitted diseases, 68-10-101		Insurance companies may not market/sell identifying patient information without patient's written consent, 56-7-124	Law enforcement officer may request arrested person be tested for Hepatitis B or HIV if exposed to blood, 68-10-116; records strictly confidential; released as per 68-10-113
Bullet or gunshot wounds, Health & Safety § 161.041; certain occupational diseases, Health & Safety § 84.003; certain communicable diseases, Health & Safety § 81.041	Hospital may not reveal patient healthcare information without patient's written consent, Health & Safety § 241.152)		Public safety workers may require persons to be tested for HIV if there has been exposure; generally HIV tests are confidential, Health & Safety §§ 81.050 to 81.052
Suspected child abuse, 62A-4a-403; communicable and infectious diseases, including HIV and AIDS, 26-6-3			All reports regarding communicable diseases are confidential and may only be disclosed to authorized healthcare workers or researchers, 26-6-27

Table 47: Medical Records—Continued

State	Who Has Access	Privilege
VERMONT	Medical personnel directly treating patient or monitoring/researching treatment; all others require patient's authorization, Tit. 18 §1852	Physician; chiropractor; dentist; nurse; mental health professional not allowed to disclose information acquired in attending a patient in a professional capacity, Tit. 12, § 1612
VIRGINIA	Patient or attorney upon patient's written request to hospital or health care records except for records when doctor declares release would be injurious to patient's health or well-being, 8.01-413; certified private review agents shall have reasonable access to patient-specific medical records, 32.1-138.13; results of newborn screenings may be disclosed for research or statistical purposes only, but may not disclose identities of infants, 32.1-67.1	Duly licensed practitioner of any branch of the healing arts dealing with patient in professional capacity including clinical psychologist, 8.01-399
WASHINGTON	Patient may authorize disclosure, 70.02.030; without authorization: health care providers; penal institution officials; public health authorities, 70.02.050; representative of deceased patient, 70.02.140	Psychologist, 18.83.110; physician, 5.60.060(4)
WEST VIRGINIA	Patient through written request; summary provided in case of psychiatric or psychological treatment, 16-29-1	
WISCONSIN	Patient may inspect and copy upon submitting statement of informed consent, 146.83; patient health care records confidential; may be released to certain persons or to persons with the informed consent of the patient or authorized representative, 146.82	Physician; registered nurse; chiropractor; psychologist; social worker; marriage and family therapist; professional counselor/patient, 905.04
WYOMING	Physician, 1-12-101	Child abuse; sexually transmitted diseases; communicable disease, 14-3-205; 35-4-130; 35-4-103

Mandatory Reporting	Patient Waiver	Insurance Purposes	AIDS
Infectious venereal diseases, Tit. 18, § 1093	Patient must give written authorization, Tit. 18, § 1852		HIV-related testing and counseling information disclosed upon court order showing compelling need that can't be accommodated by other means; pseudonym substituted if possible, Tit. 12, § 1705
Statistics regarding immunization records, 32.1-46.01		Insurance company must provide medical information to individual or to medical professional designated by individual; must notify individual that information was released at time of disclosure, 38.2-608	All test results are confidential, released only to that person, his legal representative, Dept. of Health; parents of minor; spouse; by court order; and others authorized by law, 32.1-36.1
Child abuse or adult dependent or developmentally disabled, 26.44.030; tuberculosis, 70.28.010	Patient must give written authorization, 70.02.030		
Sexually transmitted diseases, 16-4-6; suspected child abuse, 49-2-803; gunshot and other wounds; burns, 61-2-27; 61-2-27a			Disclosure of identity of person tested for HIV in limited circumstances, 16-3C-3
Sexually transmitted diseases, 252.11; tuberculosis, 252.07; abused or neglected children and abused unborn children; 48.981; communicable diseases; 252.05			AIDS/HIV test results must remain confidential except as released per 252.15 (5)

48. NEGLIGENCE

Negligence is an actionable tort. This means that if one person's carelessness causes another person injury, the injured party may sue to recover damages (money) for his or her injuries. The idea that a person can sue for negligence is a relatively new phenomenon, only about a century old.

The reason for negligence's late recognition is because common law traditionally recognized only intentional torts; that is, it held parties responsible for injuries that were the result of intentional acts. It was irrelevant that the actor did not intend to injure anyone, much less the injured party, but it only needed to be shown that the actor intended the action that caused the injury. In these cases, evidence of who caused what injury was affirmative, direct, and fairly objective.

The concept of permitting someone to recover damages for injuries caused by someone's lack of action or failure to do something was a revolutionary concept. Since its recognition as an action in tort, negligence has become a major source of very large jury awards. It is the root of all product liability cases. When people complain about our legal system and the outrageous verdicts being awarded nowadays, they are speaking about negligence.

Originally, negligence was recognized by the courts as part of the common law. Over time, as causes of action became more numerous and as damages became larger, various efforts were undertaken to limit the appeal of negligence lawsuits.

Contributory Negligence

When contributory negligence first appeared in the repertoire of personal injury lawyers, the standards of proof needed to succeed were quite high and very severe. Originally, under the doctrine of contributory negligence if it were shown that the plaintiff contributed in any way to his injuries, he was barred from any recovery. This has been modified over time to permit the plaintiff to recover even if he contributed to his injuries, as long as his fault is under 50 percent. In these cases, recovery is relative to fault. For instance, if a jury finds a party's injuries worth $100,000 and holds that the party was 25 percent at fault, the party's recovery would be $75,000. On the other hand, if the jury found the party 60 percent at fault, the party would be barred from any recovery.

Comparative Fault

The doctrine of contributory negligence eventually evolved, in some states, into a system of comparative fault that permitted recovery on a completely relative scale. Thus, in an accident one could be 90 percent at fault for one's own personal injury and still sue to recover the 10 percent of the damages suffered that were caused by the other party.

Contribution Among Tortfeasors

In the doctrine of joint and several liability among tortfeasors, when there are multiple tortfeasors ("guilty" parties), all parties are equally liable for the damages caused to the injured party. This doctrine is quite harsh. For example, if the driver of a truck hits a pedestrian at night and the jury holds that the city is 15 percent responsible because it did not properly maintain the lighting at that portion of the road and the truck driver, who is 85 percent at fault, is uninsured, unemployed, and without assets, the city can be made to pay 100 percent of the damages. Under the doctrine of contribution, one tortfeasor may sue a fellow tortfeasor to recover any damages paid in excess of the proportion of fault. In most comparative fault states liability is the proportionate responsibility of each party.

The State of the Law

As can be seen by looking at the table of negligence laws, there is great diversity among the states as to how negligence is handled. As the law of negligence continues to mature and change, courts have led the way in defining the laws and legislatures have in many cases responded with statutes that both recognize the cause of action and often limit it as well.

There have been many attempts over the years to have Congress or state legislatures pass laws that would specifically limit the amount of recovery available to plaintiffs in negligence actions. So far, none has met with much success. Under the general term "tort reform," such acts promise to be proposed in the future.

Table 48: Negligence

State	Code Section	Uniform Act?	Comparative Negligence
ALABAMA	None	No	
ALASKA	23.25.010 (Employer's liability for negligence)	No	Yes.; contributory fault diminishes proportionately the award based on claimant's fault, but does not bar recovery ("pure" comparative negligence), 09.17.060; employee's contributory negligence does not bar recovery against employer if slight and negligence of employer was gross by comparison, 23.25.020
ARIZONA	12-2505	Yes, 12-2501 to 12-2509	No right to comparative negligence if claimant intentionally, wilfully or wantonly caused/contributed to injury or wrongful death, 12025-5(A)
ARKANSAS	16-64-122	Yes, 16-61-201 to 16-61-212	Yes; modified comparative
CALIFORNIA	Civ. § 1714	No	"Pure" form adopted by *Li v. Yellow Cab Co.*, 532 P.2d 1226 (1975).
COLORADO	13-21-111	Yes, 13-50.5-101 to 13.50.5-106	
CONNECTICUT	52-572h		
DELAWARE	Tit. 10, § 8132	Yes, Tit. 10, §§ 6301 to 6308	
DISTRICT OF COLUMBIA	None		No
FLORIDA	768.81	Yes, 768.31	Any contributory fault chargeable to claimant diminishes proportionately the amount awarded as economic or uneconomic damages, 768.31
GEORGIA	51-11-7	No	

Contributory Negligence	Judicial Imposition of Comparative Negligence?	Contribution Among Tortfeasors?
Plaintiff's negligence is a bar to recovery, *Bethea v. Taylor*, 3 Stew 482 (Ala. 1831); contributory negligence is an affirmative defense, ARCP, Rule 8(c); *Jackson v. Waller*, 410 So.2d 98 (1982); *Williams v. Delta Int'l Machinery Corp.*, 619 So.2d 1330 (Ala.1993)	No	No, 7-3-116; *Gobble v. Bradford*, 147 So. 619 (1933); yes if executed instrument with joint payees or endorsers
	"Pure" form adopted and codified herein, *Kaatz v. Alaska*, 540 P.2d 1037 (1975)	Yes, 09.17.080(d)
		Yes, 12-2501, et seq.
If Plaintiff's fault is of less degree than defendant's, he may recover amount diminished in proportion to degree of his own fault; if plaintiff's fault is equal to or greater than defendant, he may not recover at all, 16-64-122		Yes, 16-61-201 to 16-61-212
	Li v. Yellow Cab Co., 532 P.2d 1226 (1975).	Yes; liability of each defendant per non-economic damages shall be several only and not joint, Civ. § 1431.2
Contributory negligence does not bar recovery if claimant's negligence is not greater than defendant's, but any damages allowed is diminished in proportion to claimant's attributed negligence, 13-21-111		Yes, 13-50.5-101 to 13.50.5-106
Contributory negligence does not bar recovery if claimant's negligence is not greater than combined negligence of defendant(s). However, damages are diminished in proportion to attributed negligence, 52-572h		Yes; must be brought within one year, 52-572e; 52-572h
Claimant's contributory negligence does not bar recovery if such negligence is not greater than the defendant's negligence; any award diminished in proportion to claimant's attributed negligence, Tit. 10, § 8132		Yes, Tit. 10, §§ 6301 to 6308
Plaintiff's negligence is a bar to recovery except the liability of common carriers for injuries to employees, when plaintiff's negligence is slight and employer's is gross, 35-302		No
	Hoffman v. Jones, 280 So. 2d 431 (1973)	Yes, 768.31
Claimant's contributory does not bar recovery provided his fault is less than defendant's and that by ordinary care claimant could not have avoided the consequences of defendant's negligence; claimant's damages are diminished by amount in proportion to the amount of his fault, 51-11-7		Yes, 51-12-32

Table 48: Negligence—Continued

State	Code Section	Uniform Act?	Comparative Negligence
HAWAII	663-31	Yes, 663-11 to 663-17	
IDAHO	6-801	No	
ILLINOIS	735 § 5/2-1116	No	
INDIANA	34-51-2-5 to 34-51-2-6	No	
IOWA	668.3; 668.5	No	
KANSAS	60-258a	No	
KENTUCKY	411.182 "effect of release"	No	Failure to put child in safety restraint is statutorily not contributory negligence; percentage of fault of claimant is used to offset recovery by equal measure; "pure comparative negligence," 189.125
LOUISIANA	Civ. Code Art. 2323	No	Percentage of fault of all persons contributing is determined. If person who suffers as a result partly of his own negligence, the amount of damages reduced in proportion to percentage of attributable negligence unless person suffers injury, death, or loss as a result of fault of an intentional tortfeasor
MAINE	Tit. 14, § 156	No	
MARYLAND	None		Failure to use seatbelt is not contributory negligence, Transp. §§ 22-412.3; 22-412.4
MASSACHUSETTS	Ch. 231, § 85	Ch. 231B, §§ 1 to 4	
MICHIGAN	600.2958; 600.2959		For economic damages, award is reduced proportionately to plaintiff's negligence even if greater than 50%; for non-economic damages, negligence greater than 50% bars any recovery, 600.2959

Contributory Negligence	Judicial Imposition of Comparative Negligence?	Contribution Among Tortfeasors?
Contributory negligence or comparative responsibility does not bar recovery if claimant's negligence or comparative responsibility is not as great as defendants, but any damages are diminished in proportion to the negligence or comparative responsibility attributable to claimant, 663-31		Yes, 663-11 to 663-17
Contributory negligence or comparative responsibility does not bar recovery if claimant's negligence or comparative responsibility is not as great as defendants, but any damages are diminished in proportion to the negligence or comparative responsibility attributable to claimant, 6-801		Yes, 6-803
Over 50% plaintiff's contributory fault: recovery barred; under 50%: damages diminished in proportion to plaintiff's percentage of fault		Yes, 740 §§ 100/0.01 to 100/5
Recovery barred if contributory negligence was greater than defendant's negligence, otherwise reduces recovery proportionately		No, 34-51-2-12
Contributory fault does not bar recovery unless claimant's fault is greater than defendant's, but any damages diminished in proportion to attributable fault.		Yes, 668.5
Contributory negligence not a bar to recovery if claimant's negligence is less than causal negligence of defendants, but damages diminished in proportion to the amount of attributable negligence, 60-258a		Adheres to common law rule of no contribution, *Alseike v. Miller*, 196 Kan. 547 (1966)
Employee not guilty of contributory negligence where violation by carrier of state/ federal safety statute contributed to injury or death. In the case were no safety statute has been violated, contributory negligence is not a bar to recovery, but damages diminished in proportion to the amount of attributable negligence. 277.320 If plaintiff's failure to use ordinary care was substantial cause, defendant shall not be liable, 411.320	Contributory negligence as a complete defense in Kentucky should give way to comparative negligence, *Hilen v. Hays*, 673 S.W. 2d 713 (1984)	Yes, 412.030
		No
		No
The mere negligence of want of ordinary caution . . . would not disentitle the plaintiff to recover, unless it were such that, but for such negligence or want of ordinary caution, the misfortune would not have happened; nor, if the defendant might, by the exercise of care on its part, have avoided that consequences of the neglect or carelessness, *Northern C.R. Co. v. State*, 29 Md. 420, 436 (1868)	Leaving it to legislature	Yes, Cts. & Jud. Proc. § 3-1401; *Harrison v. Montgomery County Bd. of Education*, 295 Md. 442, 463 (1983)
Contributory negligence does not bar recovery if claimant's negligence is not greater than defendant's; any damages allowed is diminished in proportion to claimant's attributed negligence		Ch. 231B, §§ 1 to 4
		Yes, 600.2925c

Table 48: Negligence—Continued

State	Code Section	Uniform Act?	Comparative Negligence
MINNESOTA	604.01 to 604.055		
MISSISSIPPI	11-7-15	No	Contributory negligence no bar to recovery, but damages diminished in proportion to the amount of attributable negligence
MISSOURI	None		In products liability cases, comparative fault is an affirmative defense; fault shall diminish damages proportionately but does not bar recovery, 537.765
MONTANA	27-1-702	No	
NEBRASKA	25-21,185.07 to 25-21,185.12	No	
NEVADA	41.141	17.225 to 17.305	
NEW HAMPSHIRE	507:7-D; 507:7-G	No	
NEW JERSEY	2A:15-5.1 to 2A-15-5.8	No	
NEW MEXICO	None	41-3-1 to 41-3-8	"Pure" comparative negligence
NEW YORK	N.Y.C.P.L.R. §§ 1411 to 1413		Contributory negligence does not bar recovery but damages are diminished in proportion to the attributable conduct.
NORTH CAROLINA	None	1B-1 to 1B-6	
NORTH DAKOTA	32-38-02		Liability of railroads for negligence in injury or death to employee: contributory negligence shall not bar recovery but damages shall be diminished in proportion to amount of negligence attributed to such employee, 49-16-03
OHIO		No	
OKLAHOMA	Tit. 23, §§ 13; 14		
OREGON	31.600; 31.605	No	
PENNSYLVANIA	Tit. 42, § 7102	Tit. 42, §§ 8321-8327	

Contributory Negligence	Judicial Imposition of Comparative Negligence?	Contribution Among Tortfeasors?
Plaintiff's negligence reduces recovery proportionately, but if greater than 50%, recovery is barred		No, 604.02
		Yes, 85-5-7
In cases against railroad company, corporation, or lessee, contributory negligence shall not relieve liability, 389.800		Yes, 537.060
Claimant's negligence does not bar recovery if less than that of defendants; damages diminished in proportion to the amount of negligence attributable.		Yes, 27-1-703
Plaintiff's award diminishes proportionally with negligence, but negligence equal to or greater than defendant's is a total bar		No, 25-21,185.10
When claimant's negligence is greater than defendants, no recovery, otherwise proportionate to fault		Yes, 171.225 to 17.305
Contributory negligence does not bar recovery if claimant's negligence is not greater than defendant's; but any damages allowed is diminished in proportion to claimant's attributed negligence		Yes; 507:7-F
Contributory negligence cannot be greater than the negligence of defendants; damages diminished by the percentage sustained of negligence attributable to claimant		Yes, 2A:15-5.3
		Yes, 41-3-1 to 41-3-8
		N.Y.C.P.L.R. §§ 1501 to 1603
Contributory negligence is an affirmative defense which the defendant must plead and prove, *Pruett v. Inman*, 114 S.E.2d 360 (1960)		Yes, 1B-1 to 1B-6
Plaintiff's negligence diminishes recovery in proportion to fault, but if greater then 50%, recovery is completely barred		Yes, 32-38-01 to 32-38-04
Contributory negligence not a bar to recovery if negligence was not greater than combined negligence of persons claimant seeks recovery and all other persons claimant does not seek recovery. Damages diminished in proportion to claimant's fault, 2315.33		Yes, 2307.25
Contributory negligence cannot be greater than negligence of defendants; damages reduced in proportion to such person's contributory negligence		Yes, Tit. 12, § 832
Contributory negligence not a bar if fault attributable claimant is less than combined fault of defendants		Yes, 31.800
Contributory negligence does not bar recovery if claimant's negligence is not greater than the causal negligence of the defendant; any damages allowed is diminished in proportion to claimant's attributed negligence		Yes, Tit. 42, §§ 8321-8327

Table 48: Negligence—Continued

State	Code Section	Uniform Act?	Comparative Negligence
RHODE ISLAND	9-20-4	10-6-1 to 10-6-11	The fact that the claimant was not in the exercise of due care shall not bar recovery, but damages diminished in proportion to the amount of attributable negligence
SOUTH CAROLINA	None	15-38-10 to 15-38-70	
SOUTH DAKOTA	20-9-2	15-8-11 to 15-8-22	
TENNESSEE	None	29-11-101 to 29-11-107	Comparative negligence in reference to reviewing bank statements of accts. 47-4-406
TEXAS	Civ. Prac. & Rem. § 33.001	No	
UTAH	78B-5-818; 78B-5-820	No	
VERMONT	Tit. 12, § 1036		
VIRGINIA		No	In an action against a common carrier, comparative negligence will not bar recovery and if carrier violated a safety code, the injured party won't be found comparatively negligent, 8.01-58
WASHINGTON	4.22.005 to 4.22.025		Contributory fault diminishes proportionately the amount of damages, but does not bar recovery.
WEST VIRGINIA	None	No	Comparative negligence is reference to discovering and reporting unauthorized signature or alteration- bank statements; otherwise not specified, 46-4-406
WISCONSIN	895.045	No	
WYOMING	1-1-109	No	

Contributory Negligence	Judicial Imposition of Comparative Negligence?	Contribution Among Tortfeasors?
		Yes, 10-6-1 to 10-6-11
Contributory negligence not a bar to recovery if equal or less in motor vehicle accident action		Yes, 15-38-10 to 15-38-70
Plaintiff's negligence diminishes recovery proportionately, but if more than "slight," recovery is completely barred, 20-9-2		Yes, 15-8-12
		Yes, 29-11-101 to 29-11-107
Plaintiff's negligence not greater than defendant's; award diminished in proportion to negligence, Civ. Prac. & Rem. § 33.001		Yes, Civ. Prac. & Rem. §33.015
May only recover from a defendant whose fault exceeds their own contributory fault, 78B-5-818		No, 78B-5-820
Contributory negligence not a bar if negligence was not greater that causal total negligence but damages diminished in proportion to the amount of attributable negligence.		No
Comparative negligence is not the law of this Commonwealth; contributory negligence is an absolute bar to recovery, *City of Bedford v. Zimmerman*, 262 Va. 81, 90 (2001)		Contributory negligence may be applied when the wrong results from negligence and involves no moral turpitude, 8.01-34
		Yes, 4.22.040
Not specified	*Bradley v. Appalachian Power Co.*, 256 S.E.2d 879, 885 (1979)	Yes, 55-7-13
Contributory negligence is not a bar if claimant's negligence is not greater than defendants. Damages diminished in proportion to claimant' attributable negligence		Yes; common law right based on equitable principles, *State Farm Mutual Auto Ins. v. Continental Cas. Co.*, 59 N.W. 2d 425
Contributory fault shall not bar recovery if fault is not more than 50% of the total fault of all actors.; damages diminished in proportion to the amount of fault attributable to claimant		No

49. RIGHT TO DIE

Euthanasia laws, living wills, and the durable power of attorney, often referred to as the "Right-to-Die" laws, are concerned with how an individual who has become incapacitated may exert some influence and control over certain decisions that will be made concerning his or her care. Living wills and the durable power of attorney permit individuals to instruct his or her survivors, guardians, or attending physicians to either administer or withhold life support if they are near death and unable to communicate, such as when in a coma.

The moral questions raised by the right-to-die laws are a direct result of developments in modern technology. From the earliest times, the primary goal of doctors has been to cure the sick and comfort the dying. However, modern technology has now allowed them to prolong life beyond the body's natural ability to maintain itself. Machines can artificially breathe for a person; intravenous feeding can artificially supply sustenance. Indeed, technology can keep a patient's body completely alive even when its brain is dead.

A major problem arises in situations such as these when the patient's desires are not known; it is then up to others to decide how long artificial life-sustaining procedures should be administered. Next of kin are nearly always the ones to whom this emotionally difficult decision falls, and the complexity of right-to-die laws reveals just how legally complicated the decision can be as well.

Next of kin are very often the persons most anxious to end their loved one's suffering. On the other hand, physicians, who are trained to prolong life, maintain an ethical and moral, as well as a legal, obligation to sustain life and are loathe to do anything that will end life unless they are protected from all liability stemming from charges of homicide or wrongful death or violations of codes of professional responsibility. In the past, every time the question of "pulling the plug" arose it was "taken care of quietly" or ended up in court, where a judge determined if the doctor should end life support. If the judge ruled that life support could be withheld, the attending physician and the health care provider were completely protected from liability.

Obviously, this was a very inefficient method of dealing with this situation. After one or two high-profile cases, the public generally accepted "pulling the plug" as an option for the terminally ill. Where once medical practitioners and the public looked upon the act as murder, many have come to see it as merciful. This change in attitude has manifested itself, in most states, in a body of rather dark statutes falling into three specific categories, living wills, durable power of attorney, and euthanasia.

Durable Power of Attorney

A durable power of attorney is an instrument that is similar to a living will except that it gives authority to a named individual to decide whether or not to begin or discontinue artificial life support. Any decision the holder of the durable power of attorney makes regarding life support is said to have the exact same legal effect as though the patient had made the decision himself or herself.

Euthanasia

Three states, Washington, Oregon and Vermont, now have laws that allow people to choose to die rather than endure treatment for a terminal illness. None of these states permit physicians to administer the lethal medication, rather, the patient must request from a physician the medication to end his/her life. After the request, and an appropriate waiting period and patient competency evaluation, the patient may be given the drugs which are variously described as "life-ending medication" to be self administered. In the case of Washington state, the statute specifically forbids the use of the terms, "suicide," or "assisted suicide," in describing the practices outlined in the Act; rather, they are specifically to be referred to by the euphemism, "self-administering life-ending medication."

There is considerable diversity among states regarding the handling of the right-to-die issue, but the variance is entirely in the detail. While every state recognizes some form of durable power of attorney or living will, each has added its own character. Many states require state-sanctioned forms, while some allow as little as "some form of communication" to execute or revoke a durable power of attorney or living will.

Living Wills

A living will is a legal instrument that is executed by a person of sound mind and witnessed in much the same manner as a will. A living will expresses the individual's desires regarding life support should he or she become incapacitated as a result of a terminal illness: specifically, whether or not to administer artificial life-sustaining procedures in the event of an incurable or irreversible terminal condition that would otherwise result in death in a short time.

Note: Because laws governing the right to die are fast changing, all users of this book are advised to consult local statutes before acting on any information contained in this chapter.

Table 49a: Right to Die: Durable Power of Attorney

State	Code Section	Specific Powers, Life-Prolonging Acts	Operative Facts
ALABAMA	26-1-2	Agent may authorize withholding or withdrawal of life-sustaining treatment and make all other health care decisions	Must designate person as attorney and state similar language to "this power of attorney shall not be affected by disability, incompetency, or incapacity of the principal"
ALASKA	13.26.645 to 13.26.675	Consent or refusal to consent to medical care or relief for the principal from pain but agent may not authorize the termination of life-sustaining procedures; may include provision indicating whether a living will has been executed	Must be set out in substantially the same form as found at 13.26.645; designate health care decisions to agent
ARIZONA	36-3221to 36-3224	Power to give or refuse consent to all medical, surgical, hospital, and related health care for principal	Adult; in writing; language clearly indicating intent to create a health care power of attorney; dated; signed; witnessed by at least one adult or a notary public who is not related to principal by blood, marriage, or adoption and not entitled to any of principal's estate
ARKANSAS	Arkansas Rights of the Terminally Ill & Permanently Unconscious Act: 20-17-201 to 20-17-218	Any medical procedure or intervention that will serve only to prolong the dying process or to maintain the patient in a condition of permanent unconsciousness	Adult of sound mind; in writing; signed; 2 witnesses; proxy must be 18
CALIFORNIA	Uniform Healthcare Decisions Act: Prob. §§ 4600 to 4743	Decisions on any care, treatment, service, or procedure; same rights as principal except to consent to commitment, convulsive treatment, or psychosurgery, sterilization or abortion disposition of remains	Adult having capacity; in writing; signed; witnessed by 2 adults or notary public; witnesses may not be related to principal or be medical provider; must be in substantially same form as sample at Prob. § 4703
COLORADO	Colorado Patient Autonomy Act: 15-14-503 to 15-14-509	Authority of an agent to act on behalf of principal who lacks decisional capacity in consenting to or refusing medical treatment including artificial nourishment and hydration; may include conditions or limitations of agent's authority	Directive must contain the words, "This power of attorney shall not be affected by disability of the principal"

Revocation/Duration	Reciprocity	Transfer of Patient if Physician Unwilling	Immunity for Attending Physician
Revocable by written revocation, destruction of document, or verbal expression of intent to cancel	Directives prepared in other states are valid if in compliance with Alabama law		Health care providers who rely in good faith on agent's directions are immune from civil and criminal liability
Revocable at any time		A third party shall honor the terms of a properly executed power of attorney; physician may withdraw after services of another physician have been obtained	A third party who relies on reasonable representations of an attorney-in-fact does not incur a liability to the principal or principal's heirs, assigns, or estate
Person may revoke health care directive or disqualify a surrogate by written revocation; orally notifying surrogate or health care provider; making new health care directive; any other act demonstrating specific intent to revoke	Health care directive prepared in another state is valid in this state if it was valid where and at the time it was adopted to the extent it does not conflict with the criminal laws of Arizona		Health care provider making good faith decisions in reliance on apparently genuine health care directive or decision of a surrogate is immune from civil, criminal, and professional discipline for that reliance
Revocable at any time in any manner by the declarant without regard to declarant's mental/physical condition. Effective upon communication to attending physician	A declaration executed in another state in compliance with the laws of that state or Arkansas law is validly executed	Physician shall as promptly as practicable take all reasonable steps to transfer care to another physician	Physician whose actions under this chapter are in accord with reasonable medical standards is not subject to criminal, civil, or professional liability with respect to them
No authority while principal can give informed consent to a health care decision; principal with capacity may at any time revoke the appointment of the attorney-in-fact orally or in writing; revoke the agent's authority by notifying physician orally or in writing; a subsequent durable power of attorney revokes prior one; divorce revokes any designation of former spouse	Enforceable if executed in another state or jurisdiction in compliance with the laws of that state or jurisdiction or California		Subject to limitations, a physician acting in good faith on decision of attorney-in-fact is not subject to criminal, civil, or professional liability except to the same extent that would be the case if the principal made the decision on own behalf under like circumstances
Divorce, dissolution, annulment, or legal separation revokes any designation of former spouse as agent; otherwise can be revoked at any time	A durable power of attorney executed in another state shall be presumed to comply with this law and may, in good faith, be relied on by a health care provider	Physician must provide for prompt transfer; physician must not provide care and comfort pending transfer	No criminal or civil liability or regulatory sanction for complying in good faith with medical treatment decision of agent acting in accordance with advanced medical directive

Table 49a: Right to Die: Durable Power of Attorney—Continued

State	Code Section	Specific Powers, Life-Prolonging Acts	Operative Facts
CONNECTICUT	19a-570 to 19a-580g	Consent, refuse consent, or withdraw consent to any medical treatment other than that designed solely to maintain physical comfort, withdrawal of life support systems, nutrition or hydration; does not apply to pregnant patient	18 or older; signed; dated; in presence of 2 adult witnesses; substantially in form of sample at 19a-575a or 19a-577
DELAWARE	Tit. 16, §2501 to 2518	Grant, refuse, withdraw consent to provision of medical treatment, including right to refuse medical treatment which would extend patient's life; life sustaining procedure may not be withheld or withdrawn if patient is known to be pregnant, if it is probable the fetus will develop to be viable outside the uterus with the continued application of life-sustaining procedure	Adult; in writing; signed; dated; 2 or more adult witnesses not related to declarant, having any interest or claim to estate, or direct financial responsibility for declarant's medical care; effective upon determination by physician that declarant lacks capacity and has qualifying condition
DISTRICT OF COLUMBIA	21-2201 to 21-2213	Grant, refuse, withdraw consent to the provision of any health-care service, treatment, or procedure if principal is incapable of making or communicating decisions himself; cannot consent to abortion, sterilization, or psycho-surgery unless authorized by court	Competent adult; in writing; signed; in presence of 2 adult witnesses; must include language clearly communicating the intent for attorney-in-fact to have authority to make health-care decisions on behalf of the principal with language that power becomes effective upon principal's incapacity; sample form at 21-2207
FLORIDA	Florida Health Care Surrogate Act: 765.201 to 765.205	All decisions regarding principal's health care during principal's incapacity, including life-prolonging procedures; does not include medication or medical procedure to provide comfort care or to alleviate pain; cannot withhold or withdraw life prolonging procedures from pregnant patient prior to viability	Competent adult; in writing; signed; in presence of 2 adult witnesses not appointee or related to principal; effective on determination by physician of principal's lack of capacity or at principal direction; sample form at 765.203

Revocation/Duration	Reciprocity	Transfer of Patient if Physician Unwilling	Immunity for Attending Physician
May be revoked at any time, in any manner; automatically revoked by divorce, legal separation, annulment, or dissolution of marriage if spouse is appointed as health care agent, unless principal specifies otherwise	Health care instructions or appointment of a health care proxy executed under the laws of another state are valid if in compliance with the laws of that state or Connecticut and not contrary to Connecticut public policy	Physician shall act as promptly as practicable and take all reasonable steps to transfer patient to complying physician	Physician withholding, removing life-support system of an incapacitated patient shall not be civilly or criminally liable if decision was based on physician's best medical judgment; physician deems patient in a terminal condition; patient's wishes were considered according to an executed document
Revocable by mentally competent individual at any time by signed writing or in any manner that communicates intent to revoke in presence of 2 competent persons, 1 of whom is health care provider; annulment or divorce revokes designation of spouse as agent unless otherwise specified	Directives of other states in compliance with the laws of that state or of Delaware are valid	Must provide continuing care and not impede the transfer of the patient to another health care provider	Physicians or nurses acting in reliance on properly executed document are presumed to be acting in good faith and there is no civil or criminal liability unless negligent
Revocable at any time by notifying health care provider or attorney-in-fact orally or in writing; divorce automatically revokes designation of former spouse			
Revocable by competent principal at any time by signed, dated writing; destruction of declaration; oral expression of intent to revoke; subsequent directive materially different from the previously directive; divorce revokes any designation of the former spouse as surrogate	An advance directive executed in another state in compliance with the laws of that state or Florida is valid	Physician should make reasonable efforts to transfer to a willing health care provider. Physician unwilling to carry out the patient's wishes because of moral or ethical beliefs must within 7 days transfer the patient and pay the cost of transporting the patient to another health care provider or carry out the wishes of the patient unless provisions of judicial intervention	Health care facility, provider, or other person acting under their direction is not subject to criminal, civil, or professional liability for carrying out health care decision

Table 49a: Right to Die: Durable Power of Attorney—Continued

State	Code Section	Specific Powers, Life-Prolonging Acts	Operative Facts
GEORGIA	Georgia Advanced Directives for Health Care Act: 31-32-1 to 31-32-14	All decisions regarding principal's health care, including withholding or withdrawal of life-sustaining or death-delaying procedures after-death decisions, including autopsy, anatomical gifts, and disposition of remains	In writing; signed by principal; attested and subscribed by 2 or more competent adult witnesses; sample form at §31-32-4
HAWAII	Uniform Health-Care Decisions Act (Modified): 327E-1 to 327E-16	Agent may make any lawful health care decisions that could have been made by principal at time of election; agent may decide that principal's life should not be prolonged through surgery, resuscitation, life-sustaining medicine, or procedures for provision of nutrition or hydration if explicitly authorized by principal	Competent adult or emancipated minor; in writing; signed; dated; in presence of 2 or more adult witnesses or notarized; witnesses may not be health care provider, employee of health care provider, or agent; at least one witness must be neither related to agent by blood, marriage, adoption nor entitled to any portion of the estate of the principal upon the principal's death
IDAHO	The Medical Consent and Natural Death Act: 39-4501 to 39-4515	Health care decisions for principal, meaning consent, refusal of consent, or withdrawal of consent to any care, treatment, services, or procedure to maintain, diagnose, or treat an individual's physical condition, including life-prolonging care decisions	Adult; signed; dated; signed by 2 witnesses; may list alternative holders of power; sample form at 39-4510
ILLINOIS	Powers of Attorney for Health Care Law: 755 § 45/4-1 to 45/4-12	Health care powers may be delegated to an agent and include consent or refusal or withdrawal of any type of health care for individual. May extend beyond principal's death if necessary to permit anatomical gift, autopsy, or disposition of remains	Neither attending physician nor health care provider may act as agent; sample form at 755 § 45/4-10); living will not operative as long as properly authorized agent is available

Revocation/Duration	Reciprocity	Transfer of Patient if Physician Unwilling	Immunity for Attending Physician
Revocable at any time by principal without regard to physical or mental condition by destruction of the document; written revocation signed and dated by the principal; by oral or any other expression of intent to revoke in presence of an adult witness who within 30 days must sign and date in writing confirming the expression of such intent; divorce revokes agency in former spouse		Physician should promptly inform the agent who is responsible to make the transfer; physician will continue to afford consultation and care in connection with the pending transfer	No health care provider subject to any civil, criminal, or professional liability solely for complying with decision of agent
Revocable by signed writing or by personally informing health-care provider. Annulment or divorce revokes previous designation of a spouse unless otherwise specified			
Revocable at any time by the maker without regard to competence by destruction of the document; by written, signed revocation; by verbal expression of intent to revoke		Physician may withdraw without civil or criminal liability provided physician or health care provider makes a good faith effort to assist patient in transferring before his/her withdrawal	No civil or criminal liability for physician acting in accordance with wishes of patient as expressed by statutory procedure
Revocable at any time by principal without regard to mental or physical condition by written revocation signed and dated; oral expression in presence of witness who signs and dates a written confirmation; destruction of power of attorney in manner indicating intent to revoke		Agent responsible for transfer after being promptly informed by attending physician of his refusal or failure to comply; attending physician must afford all reasonably necessary consultation and care in connection with transfer	No civil, criminal, or professional liability if good faith reliance on any decision or direction by agent not clearly contrary to terms of a health care agency

Table 49a: Right to Die: Durable Power of Attorney—Continued

State	Code Section	Specific Powers, Life-Prolonging Acts	Operative Facts
INDIANA	16-36-1-1 to 16-36-1-14	Decisions on any care, treatment, service, or procedure to maintain, diagnose, or treat an individual's physical or mental condition including admission to a health care facility and disclosure of medical records to health care provider; this appointment does not affect individual's authorization regarding such life-prolonging measures as a living will; does not authorize euthanasia	In writing; signed by appointer; witnessed by 1 adult other than representative; may specify conditions and terms of the authority delegated; begins when appointer becomes incapable of consenting; legally separated spouse, an individual subject to a protective order or other court order directing that individual to avoid contact with the principal, or an individual who is subject to a pending criminal charge in which the principal was the victim are not eligible to be appointed as agent
IOWA	144B.1 to 144B.12	Consent, refusal of consent, or withdrawal of consent to health care. Attorney-in-fact has priority over court-appointed guardian to make health care decisions; does not include provision of nutrition or hydration except when required parenterally through intubation	Explicitly authorizes attorney-in-fact to make health care decisions; 2 adult witnesses signing in the presence of each other and the principal; notarized; substantially complies with requirements of sample at 144B.5
KANSAS	58-625 to 58-632	Consent, refuse consent, or withdraw consent to any care, treatment, service, or procedure to maintain, diagnose, or treat a physical or mental condition and make decisions about organ donation, autopsy, and disposition of body; make all necessary arrangements for principal at any hospital/facility and employ health care personnel; request and review and execute any information regarding principal's affairs, including medical and hospital records.	Writing must have words of intent that principal conferred authority to be exercised notwithstanding principal's subsequent incapacity; dated; signed; in presence of 2 adult witnesses or notarized; witnesses must not be related to principal or entitled to any portion of estate, financially responsible for principal's health care; substantially in form of sample at 58-632; appointment effective upon occurrence of principal's disability or incapacity

Revocation/Duration	Reciprocity	Transfer of Patient if Physician Unwilling	Immunity for Attending Physician
Revocable at any time by notifying representative or health care provider orally or in writing			No criminal, civil, or professional liability for a physician acting in good faith in reliance on the agent's direction
May be revoked at any time in any manner by which principal is able to communicate intent to revoke; power revoked in case of divorce where spouse designated durable power of attorney for health care	Similar document executed in another state in compliance with the laws of that state is valid and enforceable in Iowa to the extent the document is consistent with Iowa law	Unwilling physician must make provisions to transfer patient to willing health care provider	Health care provider not subject to civil or criminal liability or professional disciplinary action if acting in good faith on decision of attorney-in-fact
In writing witnessed as required for power of attorney or "set out another manner of revocation, if desired"	Any durable power of attorney for health care decisions executed in another state in compliance with the laws of that state at the time it was signed is valid		Any person who in good faith acts pursuant to the terms of a durable power of attorney for health care decisions without knowledge of its invalidity shall be immune from liability that may be incurred or imposed from such action

Table 49a: Right to Die: Durable Power of Attorney—Continued

State	Code Section	Specific Powers, Life-Prolonging Acts	Operative Facts
KENTUCKY	Kentucky Living Will Directive Act, 311.621 to 311.643	Agent may make all health care decisions in accordance with principal's wishes in consideration of recommendations of attending physician including these decisions include withholding or withdrawal of artificial nutrition or hydration if death is imminent; provision of nutrition cannot be physically assimilated; burden or provision of such nutrition and hydration outweighs benefit; artificial nutrition or hydration not to be withdrawn if needed for comfort or relief of pain; when patient is in permanently unconscious state and advanced directive has authorized withdrawal or withholding of such nutrition and hydration; cannot withhold or withdraw life prolonging procedures from pregnant patient unless procedures will not lead to development and live birth of unborn child, are harmful to patient, or will prolong severe pain that cannot be alleviated by medication	Adult with decisional capacity may designate 1 or more adults as surrogates; if 2 or more, any decisions must be unanimous; in writing, dated and signed by grantor; 2 adult witnesses, signed in presence of grantor and in presence of each other or notarized; surrogate may not make decisions when physician has determined in good faith that grantor has decisional capacity
LOUISIANA	40:1151 to 40:1151.9	Any medical procedure or intervention, including invasive administration of nutrition and hydration which would serve only to prolong the dying process for a person diagnosed as having a terminal and irreversible condition; does not include any measure necessary for comfort care	Declarant may designate another person to make treatment decisions should declarant be diagnosed with terminal or irreversible condition and be comatose, incompetent or otherwise mentally or physically incapable of communication; sample form at 40:1551.2 (c)
MAINE	Uniform Health-Care Decisions Act: Tit. 18-A, §§ 5-801 to 5-818	Consent or withhold consent or approval relating to any medical or other health care treatment of the principal including life-sustaining treatment when principal is in terminal condition or persistent vegetative state; agent authorized to make any health-care decision principal could have made while having capacity	Adult or emancipated minor with capacity; in writing; signed by principal and 2 witnesses in person and not by electronic means; power remains in effect notwithstanding principal's later incapacity and may include individual instructions; unless related to the principal by blood, marriage or adoption, agent may not be owner, operator or employee of a residential long-term health-care institution at which the principal is receiving care

Revocation/Duration	Reciprocity	Transfer of Patient if Physician Unwilling	Immunity for Attending Physician
Grantor with decisional capacity may revoke in whole or in part at any time by signed and dated written statement; oral statement made in presence of 2 adults, 1 of whom is health care provider; destruction of document; effective immediately for attending physician once notified; oral statement by grantor with decisional capacity to revoke overrides previous written directive	Directives made outside the provisions of this act do not restrict health care providers from following such directives if they are consistent with accepted medical practice.	Physician must immediately inform patient and family or guardian and shall not impede transfer to complying physician or health care facility; patient's medical records and information shall be supplied to receiving physician or facility	Unlawful for any health care facility or licensing agency to discriminate against unwilling health care professional as long as he or she complies with notification and transfer provisions of Act; no civil, criminal, or professional liability for withholding or withdrawing life prolonging treatment in accordance with directive unless shown by preponderance of evidence that there was bad faith
Revocable at any time by declarant without regard to mental state or competency by destruction of document; written revocation signed and dated by declarant; oral or nonverbal expression by declarant of intent to revoke; effective upon communication to physician	Declaration properly executed in and under the laws of another state deemed to be validly executed	Physician shall make reasonable effort to transfer patient to another physician	Any health care facility, physician or other person acting under their direction shall not be criminally, civilly, or professionally liable for withholding life-sustaining procedures in accordance with the provisions of this chapter
An individual with capacity may revoke the designation of an agent by signed writing or personally informing the supervising health-care provider	Declaration executed in another state in compliance with laws of that state and Maine is valid	Attending physician or other health care provider who is unwilling shall take all reasonable steps as promptly as practicable to transfer to another physician willing to comply; willful failure to transfer is a class E crime	Physician or other health care provider whose action is in accord with reasonable medical standards and in good faith is not subject to criminal or civil liability or discipline for unprofessional conduct

Table 49a: Right to Die: Durable Power of Attorney—Continued

State	Code Section	Specific Powers, Life-Prolonging Acts	Operative Facts
MARYLAND	Health Care Decisions Act: Health-Gen. §§ 5-601 to 5-618	Make any health care decisions on declarant's behalf, subject to any conditions or limitations listed in directive and based on the wishes of the patient; cannot authorize sterilization or treatment for mental disorder	Competent individual; written or electronic; dated; signed; 2 witnesses, no witness required for electronic declaration if identity of declarant is authenticated; oral directive has same effect if in presence of physician, physician's assistant, or nurse practitioner and 1 witness who sign and make declaration part of declarant's medical records; effective when declarant's attending physician and a 2nd physician certify in writing that patient is incapable of making an informed decision, if patient is unconscious or unable to communicate, 2nd physician not required
MASSACHUSETTS	Ch. 201D, §§ 1 to 17	Any and all health care decisions on principal's behalf that principal could make including decisions about life-sustaining treatment, not including those procedures to provide comfort care or pain alleviation, subject to any express limitations of health care proxy's authority; proxy has priority over other persons, including one with durable power of attorney unless limited by principal or court order	Competent adult; in writing; signed; in presence and subscribed by 2 adult witnesses, that the principal appeared to be 18, of sound mind and under no constraint or undue influence; health care proxy must contain identities of principal and health care agent and indicate principal intends agent to have authority to make health care decisions on his behalf, describe any limitations, and indicate agent's authority effective if it is determined that principal lacks decisional capacity
MICHIGAN	700.5501 to 700.5520	Designation may authorize exercise of one or more powers concerning patient's care, custody, and medical treatment that patient could have exercised on own behalf; may make decision to withhold or withdraw treatment which would allow patient to die only if patient has expressed in clear and convincing manner that advocate is allowed to do so and patient acknowledges that such a decision would allow death	18 or older and of sound mind; written; signed; in presence of and signed by 2 witnesses; proposed patient advocate must sign acceptance; executed voluntarily; made part of patient's medical record before implementation; exercisable only when patient is unable to participate in decisions; cannot be used for pregnant patient

Revocation/Duration	Reciprocity	Transfer of Patient if Physician Unwilling	Immunity for Attending Physician
Revocable at any time by signed and dated writing; oral statement to health care practitioner; execution of subsequent directive	Declaration executed in another state by nonresident is effective if in compliance with the laws of that state or Maryland	Attending physician shall make every reasonable effort to transfer declarant to another healthcare provider; assist in transfer; and pending transfer comply with competent individual or healthcare agent/ surrogate for person incapable of making a decision if failure to comply would likely result in death of individual	Any healthcare provider who withholds or withdraws health care or life-sustaining procedures in accordance with this subtitle and in good faith, is not subject to civil or criminal liability and may not be found to have committed professional misconduct
Revocable by notification of agent or health care provider orally or in writing or by any other act evidencing specific intent to revoke the proxy; execution of subsequent health care proxy; divorce or legal separation revokes designation if spouse was principal's agent under health care proxy	Proxy executed in another state or jurisdiction is valid if in compliance with laws of that state or jurisdiction provided §§14 and 15 of Chap. 201D are not violated	Physician should arrange for transfer of patient to equivalent facility "reasonably accessible" to patient's family; if unable to do so, physician shall seek judicial relief or honor agent's decision	No civil, criminal, or professional liability for carrying out in good faith a health care decision by an agent pursuant to a health care proxy
Revocable at any time and in any manner sufficient to communicate intent by patient to revoke; resignation or removal of patient advocate; subsequent designation that revokes prior designation, either expressly or by inconsistency; divorce revokes designation of patient advocate in former spouse; death of patient; order of probate court; occurrence of provision for revocation contained in designation; any current desires of patient are binding on patient advocate		Physician or health care provider is bound by sound medical practice and instructions of patient advocate if patient advocate complies with law	Person providing, performing, withholding, withdrawing medical treatment reasonably relying on decisions of patient advocate is liable in same manner and to same extent as if patient had made decision on his or her own behalf

Table 49a: Right to Die: Durable Power of Attorney—Continued

State	Code Section	Specific Powers, Life-Prolonging Acts	Operative Facts
MINNESOTA	Health Care Directives, 23-06.5-01 to 23-06.5-19	Power to consent, refuse to consent, or withdraw consent to any care, treatment, procedure or health care decision to maintain, diagnose, or treat mental or physical condition of principal including food and water by artificial means	Signed by principal; dated; signed by 2 adult witnesses or acknowledged by principal before a notary public; when inconsistencies arise between proxy, living will, or agent, most recently executed document takes precedence; sample form at 145C.05
MISSISSIPPI	Uniformed Health-Care Decisions Act: 41-41-201 to 41-41-303	Consent, refuse consent, or withdraw consent to any care, treatment, service, or procedure to maintain, diagnose, or treat an individual's physical or mental condition; may include decisions after death such as anatomical gift, autopsy, and disposition of remains; does not affect health care treatment in an emergency	Durable power of attorney must specifically authorize the attorney-in-fact to make health care decisions; dated; witnessed by 2 individuals or notarized; sample form at 41-41-209
MISSOURI	Durable Power of Attorney- for Health Care Act: 404.800 to 404.872	May make health care decisions, but no agent may authorize withdrawal of artificially supplied nutrition and hydration which the patient may ingest through natural means	Signed; dated; includes provision that durable power shall not terminate if principal becomes disabled or incapacitated; powers generally commence upon certification by 2 licensed physicians that patient is incapacitated
MONTANA	Rights of the Terminally Ill Act: 50-9-101 to 50-9-111	Withholding or withdrawal of life-sustaining treatment, defined as any medical procedure or intervention that will serve only to prolong the dying process; life-sustaining procedures may not be withdrawn when qualified patient is known to be pregnant and when it is likely fetus will result in live birth	18 yrs. and of sound mind; signed by declarant or another at his request; 2 witnesses; communicated to physician and made part of patient's medical record; declared to be terminal and no longer able to make decisions regarding life-sustaining treatment; declarant may designate another individual, 18 yrs. old and of sound mind, to make decisions regarding life-sustaining treatment; sample form at 50-9-103

Revocation/Duration	Reciprocity	Transfer of Patient if Physician Unwilling	Immunity for Attending Physician
Divorce revokes any designation of former spouse as agent to make health care decisions; revocable at any time by destroying; written statement expressing intent to revoke; verbally expressing intent to revoke in presence of 2 witnesses; executing subsequent instrument	Power of attorney document executed in another state in compliance with that state's law is valid and enforceable in Minnesota to the extent it is consistent with Minnesota law	Provider who has legal and actual capability of providing transfer and who is unwilling to provide directed health care may transfer patient to complying provider but must take all reasonable steps to provide directed health care until patient is transferred	Health care provider who relies in good faith on health care decision made by agent not subject to criminal prosecution, civil liability or professional disciplinary action; no criminal, civil, or professional liability for health care provider who administers health care to keep patient alive, despite agent's decision, if all reasonable steps were promptly taken to transfer patient to complying provider
Document effective until revoked by principal unless document provides shorter time; revocable at any time the principal has capacity by notifying the attorney-in-fact in writing. notifying the health care provider in writing, or executing subsequent valid durable power of attorney for health care		Must promptly inform patient of refusal and assist patient in being transferred to another institution	No civil, criminal, or professional responsibility if health care provider relies in good faith on health care decision
Revocable at any time in any manner by which patient is able to communicate the intent to revoke; effective upon communication to agent or to physician		Physician may not impede the attorney-in-fact from transferring patient to another physician or facility	Any third party acting in good faith may rely on the instructions of the attorney-in-fact without liability to the patient or the patient's successors-in-interest
Revocable at any time in any manner without regard to physical or mental condition; effective upon notice	Declaration made in another state in compliance with that state's laws executed in a substantially similar manner to laws of Montana is effective	Unwilling physician shall take all reasonable steps as promptly as practicable to transfer to another who is willing	Individual appointed under this section not criminally or civilly liable for decisions made pursuant to executed declaration; attending physician or health care provider not subject to civil or criminal liability or guilty of unprofessional conduct if acting in accordance with reasonable medical standards and in good faith

Table 49a: Right to Die: Durable Power of Attorney—Continued

State	Code Section	Specific Powers, Life-Prolonging Acts	Operative Facts
NEBRASKA	Health Care Power of Attorney, 30-3401 to 30-3432	Consent, refusal of consent, withdrawal of consent to health care; does not include withdrawal of routine comfort care, withdrawal of usual and typical provision of nutrition and hydration, withdrawal or withholding of life-sustaining procedures or artificially administered nutrition or hydration except if declarant gives that authority; attempted suicide by the principal shall not be construed as indicating the principal's wishes with regard to health care	In writing; dated; identify parties; specifically authorize attorney-in-fact to make decisions when principal is documented to be incapable by physician indicating cause and nature of incapacity; signed and witnessed by 2 adults; not operative when principal is known to be pregnant and live birth is probable; sample form at 30-3408
NEVADA	Durable Power of Attorney for Health Care Decisions, 162a.700 to 162a.860	Attorney-in-fact has power to make health care decisions before or after death for disabled principal including consent, refusal of consent, or withdrawal of consent to any care, treatment, service, or procedure to maintain, diagnose, or treat physical or mental condition except treatment specifically stated: commitment to mental facility, convulsive treatment, psychosurgery, sterilization, or abortion or any other specifically designated treatments.	Signed; notarized or 2 witnesses; sample form: § 449.613 to designate person to make decision re: life-sustaining treatment; sample form t 162A.860 to create durable power of attorney for health care decisions
NEW HAMPSHIRE	Durable Power of Attorney for Health Care, 137-J:1 to 137-J:33	Document delegating health care decisions to agent; includes consent, refusal to consent or withdrawal of consent to any care, treatment, admission to a health care facility, any service or procedure to maintain, diagnose or treat an individual's physical or mental condition; artificial nutrition and hydration may not be withdrawn or withheld unless clear expression of such power in document; does not include power to consent to voluntary admission to state institution, voluntary sterilization or consent to withholding of life-sustaining treatment for pregnant patient unless treatment will not permit continuing development and live birth of unborn child	In writing; 2 subscribing witnesses who affirm that principal appeared to be of sound mind and free from duress and was aware of the nature of the document and signed it voluntarily; include disclosure statement in substantially same form as sample at 137-J:19 prior to execution; document in substantially same form as sample at 137-J:20

Revocation/Duration	Reciprocity	Transfer of Patient if Physician Unwilling	Immunity for Attending Physician
Revocable at any time by competent principal in any manner communicating an intent to revoke; withdrawal at any time by attorney-in-fact; otherwise, effective until death of principal; divorce or legal separation, unless otherwise noted in divorce decree, shall be deemed to revoke power of attorney for health care in spouse	Declaration executed in another state is valid according to its terms if valid under the laws of that state	Unwilling physician shall inform attorney-in-fact and promptly assist in transferring principal to willing physician	No criminal, civil, or professional liability if acting in good faith; does not limit liability for negligence
Divorce revokes designation of former spouse; power of attorney remains valid indefinitely unless principal designates shorter period or it is revoked or another power of attorney is executed subsequently	A power of attorney executed in a jurisdiction outside of Nevada is valid in Nevada if, when the power of attorney was executed, the execution complied with the laws of that jurisdiction or the requirements for a military power of attorney pursuant to 10 U.S.C. § 1044b.		
Revocable by notifying attorney-in-fact or health care provider orally or in writing or in any other way communicating specific intent to revoke; execution of subsequent durable power of attorney; filing of action of divorce if spouse is agent; revocation effective upon notice to health care provider or to attorney-in-fact; person directly interested or related to patient may file action to revoke durable power of attorney on grounds that principal was not of sound mind or under duress, fraud, or undue influence	Documents executed in another state are enforceable if they are in compliance with the law of that state or jurisdiction	Unwilling physician or health care provider must inform attorney-in-fact and allow for transfer of patient to another facility	No person acting in good faith pursuant to durable power of attorney terms shall be subject to criminal or civil liability or unprofessional conduct. No liability for facility which refuses to carry out terms of agent's direction provided they informed agent of their refusal

Table 49a: Right to Die: Durable Power of Attorney—Continued

State	Code Section	Specific Powers, Life-Prolonging Acts	Operative Facts
NEW JERSEY	26:2H-53 to 26:2H-91	Decisions to accept or refuse treatment, service, or procedure used to diagnose, treat, or care for a patient's physical or mental condition including life-sustaining treatment; includes decisions on acceptance or rejection of services of particular physician or health care provider or transfer of care; on the use of any medical device or procedure, artificially provided fluids and nutrition, drugs, surgery or therapy that uses mechanical or other artificial means to sustain, restore, or supplant a vital bodily function and thereby increase the expected life span of a patient; does not include provision of comfort care or alleviation of pain	Competent adult; signed; dated; 2 witnesses who attest that declarant is of sound mind and free of duress and undue influence or acknowledged before notary public or other person authorized to administer oaths; may be supplemented by video or audio tape recording; directive implemented when determination of lack of decision-making capacity is documented and confirmed by physicians
NEW MEXICO	Uniform Health Care Decisions Act: 24-7A-1 to 24-7A-18	Make health care decisions including selection and discharge of health care providers, approval and disapproval of diagnostic tests, surgical procedures, programs of medication, orders not to resuscitate, and directions to provide, withhold or withdraw artificial nutrition and hydration and all others forms of treatment or health care which maintains, diagnoses, or otherwise affects an individual's mental or physical condition	Adult or emancipated minor having capacity; in writing; signed by principal; may include individual instructions; effective upon determination that principal lacks capacity
NEW YORK	Pub. Health § 2980 to 2994	Any decision to consent or refuse consent of any treatment, service, or procedure to diagnose or treat an individual's physical or mental condition	Competent adult; signed; dated; 2 adult witnesses who shall sign proxy and state that principal appeared to execute proxy willingly and free from duress; indicate that principal wants agent to make health care decisions for him; agent's authority begins when it is determined principal lacks capacity to make health care decisions, made by attending physician to a reasonable degree of medical certainty and in writing; in case of decision to withhold or withdraw life-sustaining treatment another physician must confirm determination; sample form at Pub. Health § 298(5)(d)

Revocation/Duration	Reciprocity	Transfer of Patient if Physician Unwilling	Immunity for Attending Physician
Revocable by oral or written notification; execution of subsequent directive; divorce revokes former spouse's designation as representative; patient's clearly expressed wishes take precedent over any patient's decision or proxy directive	Effective if executed in compliance with New Jersey law or the laws of that state; effective if executed in a foreign country in compliance with that country's laws or the laws of New Jersey and not contrary to public policy of New Jersey	Unwilling physician should act as soon as practicable to effect an appropriate, respectful and timely transfer of care and to assure patient is not abandoned or treated disrespectfully	No civil, criminal, or professional liability for any physician acting in good faith and pursuant to this act
Individual with capacity may revoke by signed writing; personally informing supervising health care provider; in any manner that communicates intent to revoke; (filing for divorce or legal separation revokes designation of spouse as agent, revived by remarriage; conflicting earlier health care directive, to the extent of the conflict	Valid if it complies with provisions of Uniform Health Care Decisions Act regardless of where it was executed or communicated	Physician or health care provider who declines to comply with health care decision must inform patient or agent, provide continuing care until a transfer can be effected, and make reasonable efforts to assist in transfer to willing health care provider or physician	No civil or criminal liability or discipline for unprofessional conduct if health care provider acting in good faith and in accordance with generally accepted health care standards in complying with provisions of this Act
Proxy may provide that it expires on a specified date or occurrence of condition, otherwise in effect until revoked; revocable by notifying agent or health care provider orally, in writing, or any other manner evidencing intent to revoke; divorce if former spouse was agent; upon execution of a subsequent health care proxy	Effective if executed in another state in compliance with laws of that state	If agent's health care decision cannot be honored, agent must be informed prior to admission if possible and transferred promptly to another hospital that is reasonably accessible under the circumstances and willing to honor agent's decision; health care provider shall cooperate in facilitating such transfer	No criminal, civil, or professional liability for acting in good faith pursuant to statute

Table 49a: Right to Die: Durable Power of Attorney—Continued

State	Code Section	Specific Powers, Life-Prolonging Acts	Operative Facts
NORTH CAROLINA	Health Care Powers of Attorney, 32A-15 to 32A-27	Decisions regarding life-sustaining procedures, including those which serve to artificially prolong the dying process and may include mechanical ventilation, dialysis, antibiotics, artificial nutrition and hydration and other forms of treatment which sustain, restore, or supplant vital bodily functions but do not include care necessary to provide comfort or alleviate pain	18 yrs. old; understanding and capacity to make and communicate health care decisions; in writing; signed in presence of 2 witnesses and acknowledged before a notary; sample form at 32A-25.1
NORTH DAKOTA	Health Care Directives, 23-06.5-01 to 23-06.5-19	Agent has power to make any health care decisions principal could if not lacking capacity; decisions including consent, refusal to consent or withdrawal of consent or request any care, treatment, service, or procedure to maintain, diagnose, or treat individual's physical or mental condition; does not include admission to mental health facility, psychosurgery, abortion, or sterilization	Signed; 2 witnesses who affirm principal was of sound mind and signed it freely and voluntarily; agent must accept appointment in writing; statutory form of durable power of attorney is preferred format; sample form at 23-06.5-17
OHIO	1337.11 to 1337.17	Medical procedure, treatment, intervention, or other measure that will serve to prolong the process of dying, including right to give informed consent and make other decisions principal could if not lacking capacity	Adult; sound mind; signed; dated; signed in presence of 2 adult witnesses or notarized, including attestation that principal is of sound mind and free from duress
OKLAHOMA	Uniform Durable Power of Attorney Act: Tit. 58, §§ 1071 to 1077	Agent may grant complete or limited authority to make health and medical care decisions but not life-sustaining treatment decisions unless the power complies with requirements for a health care proxy under Oklahoma Rights of Terminally Ill or Persistently Unconscious Act, Tit. 63, §§ 3101 to 3102.3	Signed; 2 adult witnesses who sign in the presence of the principal and each other; sample form at Tit. 58, § 1072.2

Revocation/Duration	Reciprocity	Transfer of Patient if Physician Unwilling	Immunity for Attending Physician
May be revoked at any time by principal capable of making and communicating health care decisions or by death of principal or by execution of a subsequent instrument or written instrument of revocation or any other method where intent to revoke is communicated, effective upon communication; revoked on decree of divorce if spouse is agent, except if alternate has been appointed; if all health care attorneys-in-fact are unwilling or unable to act, the health care power of attorney will cease to be effective	Valid if it appears to have been executed in accordance with the applicable requirements of the jurisdiction in which it was executed or of the requirements of North Carolina		No person acting on the authority of the health care attorney shall be liable for actions taken pursuant to decision of health care attorney; withholding or discontinuing life-sustaining procedures shall not be considered suicide or cause of death for criminal or civil purpose
Revocable by notification of agent orally, in writing, or any other act evidencing specific intent to revoke; execution of subsequent durable power of attorney; divorce where spouse was principal's agent	Effective if executed in another state in compliance with the law of that state	Physician has duty to inform principal or agent and take all reasonable steps to transfer care to another who is willing to honor agent's directive	No civil, criminal, or professional liability if acting in good faith and with ordinary care pursuant to directives of durable power of attorney
Does not expire unless principal specifies an expiration date in the instrument; revocable at any time in any manner; effective when expressed, but if physician had knowledge of the durable power of attorney, revocation is effective on communication to physician; valid durable power of attorney for health care revokes prior instrument	Effective if document complies with the laws of the state where executed and that substantially complies with Ohio law	Physician may not prevent or delay patient's transfer to another physician	No civil, criminal, or professional liability for good faith reliance which is in accordance with reasonable medical standards on agent's health care decisions
Revocable in whole or in part in any manner at any time without regard to declarant's mental or physical condition; effective upon communication to physician	Document executed in another state is effective if it substantially complies with the Uniform Durable Power of Attorney Act	Physician shall take all reasonable steps to arrange for care by another physician	No civil, criminal, or professional liability for carrying out the directives of durable power of attorney in good faith and in accordance with reasonable medical standards

Table 49a: Right to Die: Durable Power of Attorney—Continued

State	Code Section	Specific Powers, Life-Prolonging Acts	Operative Facts
OREGON	Oregon Health Care Decisions Act: 127.505 to 127.660	Power to make health care decisions for principal regarding life-sustaining procedures including any medical procedure or intervention that uses mechanical or other artificial means to sustain, restore, or supplant a vital function only when authorized or when principal is terminally ill and such treatment only serves to artificially prolong the moment of death; does not include procedures to sustain patient cleanliness and comfort	In writing; signed by 2 witnesses who make written declarations; mandatory statutory form at 127.531; agent must accept appointment
PENNSYLVANIA	Health Care Agents and Representatives Act: Tit. 20, §§ 5451 to 5471	Make any health care decision and exercise any right and power regarding the principal's care, custody and health care treatment that the principal could have made and exercised; authority may extend beyond principal's death to make anatomical gifts, dispose of remains and consent to autopsies	18 or older, a high school graduate, married, or an emancipated minor; power of attorney must be dated and signed by principal or other at principal's direction; witnessed by 2 individuals 18 or older who are neither the proxy signer nor health care provider or agent
RHODE ISLAND	Health Care Power of Attorney, 23-4.10-1 to 23-4-12	Any medical procedure or intervention that will only prolong the dying process; does not include intervention necessary to alleviate pain or provide comfort	18 yrs.; resident of Rhode Island; 2 adult witnesses; only in statutory form set forth at 23-4.10-2; no effect or force to document if patient is pregnant and live birth is probable with continued application of treatment
SOUTH CAROLINA	South Carolina Statutory Health Care Power of Attorney Act: 62-5-501 to 62-5-518	Medical procedure or intervention serving only to prolong the dying process, not including medication or treatment for pain alleviation or comfort care; principal should indicate whether provision of nutrition and hydration through surgically implanted tubes is desired	Signed; dated; 2 witnesses; name and address of adult agent; cannot withhold or withdraw life-sustaining procedures during pregnancy
SOUTH DAKOTA	59-7-2.1 to 59-7-9	Any health care decisions for principal which principal could have made with decisional capacity, including rejection or withdrawal of consent for medical procedures, treatment, or intervention; agent may not authorize withholding artificial nutrition and hydration for comfort care or pain relief; artificial nutrition or hydration may be withheld under certain circumstances or if specifically authorized.	Specific intent must be included in document for durable power of attorney to extend even when principal is disabled but life-sustaining treatment must be given to a pregnant woman unless live birth unlikely to a reasonable degree of medical certainty; must be signed by the principal or in the principal's conscious presence and witnessed by two other adults or a notary public

Revocation/Duration	Reciprocity	Transfer of Patient if Physician Unwilling	Immunity for Attending Physician
Agent may withdraw up to time of principal's incapacity; principal may revoke in any manner principal is able to communicate intent to revoke to health care provider or agent; by execution of subsequent durable power of attorney; upon divorce if spouse is agent	Declaration executed in another state in compliance with laws of that state and Oregon is valid	Physician must promptly notify health care representative if unable or unwilling to comply with durable power of attorney and representative shall make a reasonable effort to transfer the principal to a complying physician	Health care provider acting on a durable power of attorney or health care agent in good faith is not liable for criminal, civil, or professional disciplinary actions
Revoke by writing executed in same manner as power of attorney or by personally informing attending physician, health care provider or health care agent	Documents executed in other states valid except to extent they allow agents to make decisions inconsistent with Pennsylvania law		Person acting in good faith reliance on power of attorney shall incur no liability as a result
Revocable at any time in any manner declarant is able to communicate intent to revoke, without regard to physical or mental condition; effective upon communication to physician; controls over living will executed by same person for any inconsistent provisions	Durable power of attorney executed in another state in compliance with laws of that state is valid	Unwilling physician must make necessary arrangements to effect transfer to complying physician	No civil, criminal, or professional liability when acting in accordance with the statute and in accordance with reasonable medical standards
Revocable by written or oral statement or other act constituting notification to agent or health care provider of specific intent to revoke; principal's execution of subsequent health care power of attorney	Effective if executed in compliance with South Carolina law or laws of another state and recorded as required by 62-5-501 (c)	Physician must make reasonable effort to locate a physician who will follow directive and has a duty to transfer patient to that physician	No civil, criminal, or professional liability for relying in good faith on agent's health care decisions
Revocation must be recorded with register of deeds			No civil, criminal, or professional liability for physician acting in good faith on a health care decision by agent or attorney-in-fact

Table 49a: Right to Die: Durable Power of Attorney—Continued

State	Code Section	Specific Powers, Life-Prolonging Acts	Operative Facts
TENNESSEE	34-6-201 to 34-6-218	Any procedure, treatment to diagnose, assess, or treat a disease, illness, or injury, including surgery, drugs, transfusions, mechanical ventilation, dialysis, CPR, artificial nourishment, hydration or other nutrients, radiation; death by starvation or dehydration allowed only if specifically directed with statutory phrase	Signed before 2 witnesses or notary public and specifically authorizes health care decisions
TEXAS	Health & Safety §§ 166.151 to 166.166	Decisions regarding consent to health care, treatment, service, or procedure to maintain, diagnose, or treat individual's physical or mental condition; agent may not consent to voluntary in-patient mental health services, convulsive treatment, psychosurgery, abortion, or neglect of principal through omission of care primarily intended to provide for comfort of principal	Signed; in presence of 2 or more subscribing witnesses; substantially statutory to form at Health & Safety §§ 166.163 and 166.164 and accompanied by disclosure statement; principal may designate alternative agents
UTAH	Advance Health Care Directive Act: 75-2A-101 to 75-2A-125	Any medical procedure or intervention that would serve only to prolong the dying process including artificial nutrition and hydration unless declaration specifically excludes; does not include medication, sustenance, or any procedure to alleviate pain; separate procedure for do not resuscitate directive	May be oral or written; witnessed by disinterested adult; agent must be 18 or older or emancipated minor and may not be health care provider or owner/employee of health care facility at which declarant is receiving care; sample form at 75-2a-117
VERMONT	Tit. 18, §§ 9700 to 9720	To make health care decisions for principal during periods of incapacity as certified in writing by principal's attending physician including withdrawal of consent to any care, treatment, service, or procedure or to maintain, diagnose, or treat an individual's physical or mental condition; does not include consent to sterilization or admission to state institution	Signed; 2 witnesses; signed statement that principal understands a disclosure statement on durable powers of attorney; substantially same form as sample at 9703

Revocation/Duration	Reciprocity	Transfer of Patient if Physician Unwilling	Immunity for Attending Physician
Revocable by notifying the attorney-in-fact orally or in writing; notifying health care giver orally or in writing; executing subsequent durable power of attorney; divorce if former spouse was designated; principal's current wishes supersede durable power of attorney	Effective if document complies with laws of Tennessee or laws of the state of principal's residence	Prompt and orderly transfer required	No criminal, civil, or professional liability for physician acting in good faith
Effective indefinitely upon execution and delivery of document unless revoked; revocable orally or in writing with specific intent to revoke or execution of subsequent power of attorney; divorce if spouse is agent; effective upon receipt and notice to agent and health care provider	Durable power of attorney executed in another state valid if it complies with the law of that state or jurisdiction	Physician must notify agent immediately to arrange for transfer	Agent not liable for health care decision made in good faith; physician not liable for acts or decisions made under durable power of attorney if done in good faith and does not constitute a failure to exercise due care in the provision of health care services
Writing "void" across the document, burning or otherwise destroying document in any manner indicating an intent to revoke or instructing another to do the same; written and signed revocation; oral expression of intent to revoke; decree of annulment, divorce, legal separation revokes spouse as agent; conflict with an earlier directive revokes the earlier	A similar instrument executed in another state is presumed to comply with Utah law and may be relied upon in good faith	Unwilling physician required to transfer patient promptly	No civil, criminal, or professional liability for good faith compliance with directive
Principal's current wishes supersede directives at all times; revocable by notifying agent or health care provider orally or in writing or any other act evidencing specific intent to revoke; executing a subsequent durable power of attorney; divorce, if former spouse was principal's agent	Effective if in compliance with the law of the state in which it was executed	Unwilling physician must inform agent and principal if possible and assist in selecting another physician willing to honor agent's directive	No civil, criminal, or professional liability if physician acts in good faith; no immunity for failure to exercise due care in provision of services

Table 49a: Right to Die: Durable Power of Attorney—Continued

State	Code Section	Specific Powers, Life-Prolonging Acts	Operative Facts
VIRGINIA	Health Care Decisions Act: 54.1-2981 to 54.1-2993	Any medical procedure, treatment, intervention, utilizing mechanical or other artificial means to sustain, restore, or supplant a vital function, or is of a nature to afford patient no reasonable expectation of recovery from a terminal condition and when applied to a patient in terminal condition, would serve only to prolong the dying process. Includes artificially administered hydration and nutrition and CPR by emergency medical services personnel, but does not include any medication or procedure to alleviate pain or provide comfort care	Competent adult; written advance directive; signed in presence of 2 subscribing witnesses; oral declaration in presence of physician and 2 witnesses for those in terminal condition; responsibility of declarant to provide notification of advance directive to attending physician; sample form at 54.1-2984
WASHINGTON	Uniform Power of Attorney Act, 11.125.010 to 11.125.420	Appointed attorney-in-fact may make health care decisions on principal's behalf or provide informed consent	In writing; principal designates another as his attorney-in-fact; must include words showing intent of principal that authority be conferred notwithstanding principal's disability; must be signed, dated, and acknowledged either before a notary or 2 competent adult witnesses who are unrelated to principal
WEST VIRGINIA	Health Care Decisions Act: 16-30-1 to 16-30-25	To affect a patient's decision to accept or reject medical or surgical treatments which prolong the dying process artificially	18 yrs.; in writing; signed by declarant or someone at his or her directive; dated; 2 witnesses; notarized; with words indicating effective upon patient's incapacity; sample form at 16-30A-18
WISCONSIN	155.01 to 155.80	Designation of another for purpose of making informed decisions in the exercise of the right to accept, maintain, discontinue, or refuse any care, treatment, service or procedure to diagnose, maintain, or treat physical or mental condition; feeding tube may be withheld or withdrawn unless it would cause pain; agent may not consent to withholding or withdrawing of orally ingested nutrition or hydration unless provision is medically contra-indicated	18 yrs. and sound mind; in writing; signed; dated; 2 witnesses; voluntarily executed; takes effect upon finding of incapacity by 2 physicians; substantially same form as sample at 155.30; (9) may file with register in probate

Revocation/Duration	Reciprocity	Transfer of Patient if Physician Unwilling	Immunity for Attending Physician
Revocable at any time by signed, dated writing; physical cancellation or destruction; oral expression of intent to revoke; effective upon communication to attending physician	Directive executed in another state valid if in compliance with Virginia law or law of state where executed; such directives shall be construed in accordance with Virginia laws	If physician thinks treatment is medically or ethically inappropriate or is contrary to terms of advanced directive, unwilling physician must make reasonable effort to transfer patient to another physician	No civil, criminal, or professional liability if acting in good faith. It would have to be shown by preponderance of the evidence that the person authorizing life-prolonging procedures acted in bad faith
Continues until revoked or terminated by principal, court-appointed guardian or court order			Anyone acting in good faith and without negligence shall incur no liability
Desires of principal at all times supersede effect of medical power of attorney; revocable at any time by destruction of document; written revocation signed and dated; verbal expression with witness present; divorce if former spouse was designated	Valid if in compliance with laws of West Virginia or state where executed and expressly delegates health care decisions	Unwilling physician shall cause the transfer of principal to a complying physician	No criminal or civil liability for good faith compliance with directions of medical power of attorney or representative
Revocable at any time by canceling or destroying document; revocation in writing signed and dated; verbal revocation in presence of 2 witnesses; executing a subsequent power of attorney; divorce if former spouse was attorney-in-fact		Must make good faith attempt to transfer principal to complying physician	No civil, criminal, or professional liability if acting in good faith

Table 49a: Right to Die: Durable Power of Attorney—Continued

State	Code Section	Specific Powers, Life-Prolonging Acts	Operative Facts
WYOMING	Wyoming Health Care Decisions Act: 35-22-401 to 35-22-416	Consent, refusal of consent, or withdrawal of consent to any medical procedure, care, treatment, intervention, or nourishment by artificial means in the event of a terminal condition except for alleviation of pain and comfort care and consent to convulsive treatment, psychosurgery, or commitment to mental facility; does not affect health care treatment in an emergency	Signed; dated; 2 witnesses; notarized; attorney-in-fact authorized to make health care decisions

Revocation/Duration	Reciprocity	Transfer of Patient if Physician Unwilling	Immunity for Attending Physician
Principal's wishes if able to give informed consent take precedent over durable power of attorney; revocable by notifying attorney-in-fact in writing; notifying health care provider in writing; divorce if former spouse was attorney-in-fact; a subsequent valid durable power of attorney for health care		Must promptly inform the patient, if possible, and any person authorized to make health care decisions, provide continuing life sustaining care until a transfer can be effected, and immediately make all reasonable efforts to assist in the transfer of the patient to another willing provider	No criminal, civil, or professional liability if acting in good faith

Table 49b: Right to Die: Euthanasia

State	Code Section	Mercy Killing Condoned?	Operative Facts
ALABAMA	22-8A-10; 22-8A-9(a)	Not condoned nor authorized; no affirmative act or omission to end life allowed other than to permit natural process of dying	Withholding or withdrawal of life-sustaining procedures in accordance with chapter 22-8A does not constitute assisting suicide
ALASKA	11.41.120(a)(2); 13.52.120	Not authorized or condoned	Intentionally aiding another person to commit suicide: manslaughter
ARIZONA	36-3201 to 36-3297	Not authorized or approved	Authorized surrogate or health care provider complying with provisions of chapter are immune from liability.
ARKANSAS	20-17-210(a); 20-17-210(g)	Not condoned, authorized, or approved	Death resulting from withholding or withdrawal of life-sustaining treatment pursuant to declaration and in accordance with this section does not constitute suicide or homicide
CALIFORNIA	Prob. § 4653; End of Life Option Act: Health & Safety §§ 443 to 443.22	Not condoned, authorized, or approved; no affirmative act or omission to end life permitted other than withholding of health care pursuant to durable power of attorney so as to permit natural process of dying; in making health care decisions under durable power of attorney, attempted suicide shall not be construed to indicate decision that health care treatment be restricted or inhibited	Withholding or withdrawal of life-sustaining procedures or artificially administered nutrition and hydration does not constitute suicide, assisted, homicide or mercy killing; patient may request physician assistance for obtaining and self-administering life-ending medication under End of Life Option Act
COLORADO	15-14-111; 15-18-112; End of Life Options Act, 25-48-101 to 25-48-123	Not condoned, authorized, or approved; no affirmative or deliberate act to end person's life allowed except to permit natural death	Withholding or withdrawal of life sustaining treatment does not for any purpose constitute suicide, assisted suicide, mercy killing, or homicide; patient may request physician assistance for obtaining and self-administering life-ending medication under End of Life Options Act
CONNECTICUT	No statutory provisions		
DELAWARE	Tit. 16, § 2512	Not condoned, authorized, or approved; no affirmative act or omission to end life permitted other than to permit the natural process of dying, Tit. 16, Pt. II, Ch. 25, Refs. & Annos.	Neither execution of advance health care directive nor withholding maintenance medical treatment from patient in accordance with directive shall constitute suicide
DISTRICT OF COLUMBIA	7-628; 7-630; 21-2212; Death with Dignity Act: 7-661.01 to 7-661.16	Not condoned, authorized, or approved; no affirmative or deliberate act or omission to end a human life is allowed other than to permit the natural process of dying	Withholding or withdrawing life-sustaining procedures in accordance with the Natural Death chapter shall not constitute the crime of assisting suicide; patient may request physician assistance for obtaining and self-administering life-ending medication under Death with Dignity Act

Table 49b: Right to Die: Euthanasia—Continued

State	Code Section	Mercy Killing Condoned?	Operative Facts
FLORIDA	765.309	Not condoned, authorized, or approved; no affirmative or deliberate act or omission to end life allowed other than to permit the natural process of dying	Death resulting from withdrawing life-prolonging procedures from patient in accordance with any provision of statute does not for any purpose constitute a suicide
GEORGIA	31-32-14	Not condoned, authorized, or approved; any affirmative or deliberate act or omission permitted to end life other than to permit the process of dying	Making of a living will pursuant to this chapter shall not for any purpose constitute a suicide
HAWAII	3.27E-13; Our Care, Our Choice Act: 327L-1 to 327L-25 (eff. 1/1/19)	Not condoned, authorized, or approved	Death resulting from witholding or withdrawal of life sustaining procedures does not constitute suicide or homicide; patient may request physician assistance for obtaining and self-administering life-ending medication under Our Care, Our Choice Act as of 1/1/19
IDAHO	39-4514	Not condoned; no affirmative or deliberate act or omission to end life allowed other than to allow the natural process of dying	
ILLINOIS	755 §§ 35/9; 45/4-8e	Not condoned; no affirmative or deliberate act or omission to end life allowed other than to permit natural process of dying	Death resulting from withholding or withdrawal of death delaying procedures does not constitute suicide, homicide, or murder
INDIANA	16-36-1-13, 16-36-4-19	Not condoned or authorized; no affirmative or deliberate act or omission to end life allowed other than to permit the natural process of dying, including the withholding or withdrawing of life prolonging procedures	
IOWA	144A.11.6; 144B.12	Not condoned, authorized, or approved; no affirmative or deliberate act or omission to end life allowed other than to permit the natural process of dying	Death resulting from withholding or withdrawal of life-sustaining procedures pursuant to a declaration does not for any purpose constitute suicide or homicide
KANSAS	65-28,108; 65-28,109	Not condoned, authorized, or approved; no affirmative or deliberate act or omission to end life allowed other than to permit the natural process of dying	Acting in accordance with the Natural Death Act shall not for any purpose constitute a suicide or the crime of assisting suicide
KENTUCKY	311.637; 311.639	Not condoned; no affirmative or deliberate act to end life allowed other than to permit natural process of dying	Death resulting from withholding or withdrawal of life prolonging treatment or artificially provided nutrition and hydration shall not constitute suicide
LOUISIANA	40:1151.9	Not condoned, authorized, or approved; no affirmative or deliberate act or omission to end life allowed other than to permit the natural process of dying	Withholding of life-sustaining procedures in accordance with this part shall not for any purpose constitute suicide

Table 49b: Right to Die: Euthanasia—Continued

State	Code Section	Mercy Killing Condoned?	Operative Facts
MAINE	Tit. 18-C, § 5-814	Not authorized; provision, withholding, or withdrawal of health care not authorized to the extent prohibited by other statutes of this state.	Death resulting from withholding or withdrawal of health care in accordance with this statute does not for any purpose constitute a suicide or homicide
MARYLAND	Health-Gen. §§ 5-611; 5-614	Not condoned, authorized, or approved; no affirmative or deliberate act or omission to end life allowed other than to permit the natural process of dying	Withdrawal or withholding of life-sustaining procedures in accordance with provisions of directive shall not for any purpose be considered to be a suicide
MASSACHUSETTS	Ch. 201D § 12	Not condoned, authorized, or approved; no affirmative or deliberate act to end one's own life allowed than to permit the natural process of dying	
MICHIGAN	Michigan Dignified Death Act: 333.5651 to 333.5661; 333.5660	The Michigan Dignified Death Act does not condone, allow, permit, authorize, or approve suicide or homicide	
MINNESOTA	145B.14; 145C:14	Not condoned, authorized or approved	
MISSISSIPPI	Uniform Health-Care Decisions Act: 41-41-201 to 41-41-229; 41-41-227	Not authorized by the Uniform Health-Care Decisions Act, to the extent prohibited by other state statutes	Death resulting from the withholding or withdrawal of health care in accordance with the Uniform Health-Care Decisions Act does not for any purpose constitute a suicide or homicide
MISSOURI	404.845; 459.055	Not condoned; no affirmative or deliberate act or omission to shorten or end life permitted	Death resulting from withholding or withdrawing life-sustaining treatment in accordance with a durable power of attorney does not for any purpose constitute a suicide or homicide
MONTANA	50-9-205; 50-10-104	Not condoned, authorized, or approved	Death resulting from the withholding or withdrawal of life-sustaining procedures pursuant to a valid DNR order does not for any purpose constitute a suicide or homicide
NEBRASKA	20-412; 28-307; 30-3401	Homicide, suicide, or assisted suicide not approved, authorized or condoned; assisting suicide is a class IV felony	Death resulting from withholding or withdrawal of life-sustaining treatment in accordance with the Rights of the Terminally Ill Act shall not for any purpose constitute a homicide or suicide
NEVADA	449.650; 449.670	Not condoned, authorized, or approved	Death resulting from withholding or withdrawal of life-sustaining treatment in accordance with Nevada law does not for any purpose constitute a suicide or homicide

Table 49b: Right to Die: Euthanasia—Continued

State	Code Section	Mercy Killing Condoned?	Operative Facts
NEW HAMPSHIRE	137-J-10	Not condoned or authorized; no affirmative or deliberate act or omission to end life other than to permit the natural process of dying of those in a terminal or permanently unconscious condition	Withdrawing or withholding life-sustaining procedures from a patient according to living will or consistent with directive shall not be construed as suicide for any legal purpose
NEW JERSEY	26:2H-77; 26:2H-54	Active euthanasia not authorized	Withholding or withdrawing of life-sustaining treatment pursuant to an advanced directive when performed in good faith does not constitute homicide, suicide, assisted suicide, or active euthanasia
NEW MEXICO	Uniform Health-Care Decisions Act: 24-7A-1 to 24-7A-18; 24-7A-13	Mercy killing, assisted suicide, euthanasia, or the provision, withholding or withdrawal of health care not authorized by Uniform Health Care Decisions Act to the extent prohibited by other state statutes	Withholding of medical treatment pursuant to Uniform Health-Care Decisions Act does not for any purpose constitute a suicide
NEW YORK	Pub. Health § 2989	Statute not intended to promote or permit suicide, assisted suicide, or euthanasia; nor to be construed to permit agent to consent to any act or omission to which the principal could not consent under law	Any person acting as agent pursuant to health care proxy not subject to criminal or civil liability for making health care decision in good faith
NORTH CAROLINA	32A-24; 90-320(b)	No affirmative or deliberate act or omission to end life authorized other than to permit natural process of dying	Withholding life support not considered a suicide or cause of death for civil or criminal purposes
NORTH DAKOTA	23-06.5-01; 23-06.5-13	Not condoned nor authorized; no other act or omission to end life allowed other than to allow natural process of dying	Death resulting from withholding or withdrawal of life-prolonging treatment does not for any purpose constitute suicide or homicide
OHIO	2133.12	Not condoned or authorized	Death of any patient resulting from withholding life-sustaining treatment does not for any purpose constitute suicide, murder or any homicide offense
OKLAHOMA	Tit. 63, §§ 3101.2; 3101.12	Not condoned or authorized	Death from withdrawing life-sustaining treatment does not constitute homicide or suicide
OREGON	127.570; Oregon Death with Dignity Act, 127.800 to 127.897; 127.805; 127.880	Not condoned, authorized, or approved; no affirmative or deliberate act or omission to end life permitted other than to allow the natural process of dying	Withholding or withdrawal of life-sustaining procedures or artificially administered nutrition and hydration does not constitute suicide, assisted suicide, homicide or mercy killing; patient may request physician assistance for obtaining and self-administering life-ending medication under Death with Dignity Act
PENNSYLVANIA	Tit. 20, §§ 5423; 5426	Not condoned, authorized, or approved; no affirmative or deliberate act or omission to end life permitted, other than defined in Title 20, chapter 54	Death resulting from withholding or withdrawal of life-sustaining treatment in does not constitute suicide or homicide

Table 49b: Right to Die: Euthanasia—Continued

State	Code Section	Mercy Killing Condoned?	Operative Facts
RHODE ISLAND	23-4.10-9; 23-4.11-10	Not condoned or authorized	Death resulting from withdrawal or withholding of life-sustaining procedures does not constitute suicide or homicide
SOUTH CAROLINA	44-77-110; 44-77-130	Not condoned or authorized; no act or omission to end life permitted other than to allow the natural process of dying	Death resulting from withdrawal or withholding of life-sustaining procedures pursuant to declaration does not for any purpose constitute suicide
SOUTH DAKOTA	34-12D-14; 34-12D-20	Not condoned or authorized	Death resulting from withdrawal or withholding of life-sustaining treatment does not constitute suicide or homicide
TENNESSEE	32-11-110; 39-13-216	Assisted suicide is a class D felony	Withdrawal or withholding of medical care in accordance with declaration does not constitute suicide, euthanasia, or homicide
TEXAS	Health & Safety §§ 166.047; 166.050	Not condoned or authorized; no act or omission permitted other than to allow the natural process of dying	Withdrawal or withholding of life-sustaining procedures from qualified patient does not constitute offense of Aiding Suicide
UTAH	75-2A-119; 75-2A-122	Not condoned or authorized; no act or omission or withdrawal to extent prohibited by state law	Death resulting from withholding or withdrawal of life-sustaining procedures does not for any purpose constitute a suicide or homicide
VERMONT	Patient Choice at End of Life Act, Tit. 18, §§ 5281 to 5292	Not authorized	Withholding or withdrawal of life sustaining treatment does not for any purpose constitute suicide, assisted suicide, mercy killing, or homicide; patient may request physician assistance for obtaining and self-administering life-ending medication under Patient Choice at End of Life Act
VIRGINIA	54.1-2990; 54.1-2991	Not condoned, approved, or authorized; no affirmative or deliberate act or omission permitted other than to allow the natural process of dying	Withholding or withdrawing life-prolonging procedures in accordance with provisions of directive do not constitute a suicide
WASHINGTON	Washington Death with Dignity Act, 70.245.010 to 70.245.904; 70.245.180	Not condoned or authorized by Washington law, nor is any act or omission other than to allow the natural process of dying.	Withholding or withdrawal of life sustaining treatment does not for any purpose constitute suicide, assisted suicide, mercy killing, or homicide; patient may request physician assistance for obtaining and self-administering life-ending medication under Death with Dignity Act; statute forbids referring to practices under the Act as suicide or assisted suicide
WEST VIRGINIA	16-30-15	Not condoned or authorized; no act or omission permitted other than to allow the natural process of dying	Withholding or withdrawal of life-prolonging intervention does not constitute assisted suicide or murder

Table 49b: Right to Die: Euthanasia—Continued

State	Code Section	Mercy Killing Condoned?	Operative Facts
WISCONSIN	154.11; 155.70	Not condoned or authorized; no affirmative or deliberate act or omission permitted other than to allow the natural process of dying	Withholding or withdrawal of life-sustaining procedures or feeding tubes does not constitute suicide; execution of declaration does not constitute attempted suicide
WYOMING	35-22-410; 35-22-414(c)	Not condoned or authorized; no affirmative or deliberate act or omission permitted other than to allow the natural process of dying	Withholding or withdrawal of life-sustaining procedures from qualified patient does not constitute a crime

Table 49c: Right to Die: Living Wills

State	Code Section	Specific Powers, Life-Prolonging Acts	Operative Facts
ALABAMA	Natural Death Act: 22-8A	Any medical procedure or intervention serving only to prolong the dying process and where death will occur whether or not such intervention is utilized; does not include medication or any medical procedure deemed necessary to provide comfort care or pain alleviation	Competent adult; in writing; signed by declarant; dated; signed in presence of 2 or more witnesses over 19; declaration should be substantially in statutory format
ALASKA	Health Care Decisions Act: 13.52.010 to 13.52.395	Any medical treatment, procedure, or intervention that when applied to patient would serve only to prolong the dying process or when administered to patient with condition of permanent unconsciousness may keep patient alive but is not expected to restore consciousness; includes assisted ventilation, renal dialysis, surgical procedures, blood transfusions, and administration of drugs including antibiotics, or artificial nutrition and hydration	Adult; oral or written
ARIZONA	36-3251; 36-3261 to 36-3262; 36-3291 to 36-3297	Does not include comfort care or alleviation of pain but may include life-sustaining treatment artificially delaying the moment of death, CPR, drugs, electric shock, artificial breathing, artificially administered food and fluids	Adult; in writing; language clearly indicating intent to create a living will; dated; signed; witnessed by at least one adult or a notary public
ARKANSAS	Arkansas Rights of the Terminally Ill & Permanently Unconscious Act: 20-17-201 to 20-17-218	Any medical procedure or intervention that will serve only to prolong the dying process or to maintain the patient in a condition of permanent unconsciousness	Sound mind; 18 yrs. or older; signed by declarant; witnessed by 2 individuals; no effect if patient is pregnant and it is possible fetus can develop to live birth
CALIFORNIA	Health Care Decisions Law: Prob. §§ 4600 to 4806	Decision made by patient including selection and discharge of health care providers and institutions, approval or disapproval of diagnostic tests, surgical procedures, and programs of medication or directions to provide, withhold, or withdraw artificial nutrition and hydration and all other forms of health care, including cardiopulmonary resuscitation	Adult having capacity; written or oral, written or electronic is satisfied if dated, signed, notarized or 2 witnesses

Revocation/Duration	Reciprocity	Transfer of Patient if Physician Unwilling	Immunity for Attending Physician
Revocable at any time by destruction of document in manner intending to cancel; execution of written revocation by declarant; oral revocation in presence of adult witness over 19	Declaration executed in another state is valid if valid under laws of that state	Physician shall permit patient to be transferred	No criminal, civil, or professional liability for physician acting in good faith pursuant to reasonable medical standards and pursuant to a declaration
Revocable at any time and in any manner that communicates an intent to revoke	Directive made in compliance with laws of another state is valid if it complies with the laws of Alaska	Physician shall inform patient, provide continuing care, and shall transfer patient to another health care institution	Health care provider acting in good faith is not subject to civil or criminal liability or to discipline for unprofessional conduct
Person may revoke health care directive or disqualify a surrogate by written revocation; orally notifying surrogate or health care provider; making new health care directive; any other act demonstrating specific intent to revoke	Health care directive prepared in another state is valid in this state if it was valid where and at the time it was adopted to the extent it does not conflict with the criminal laws of Arizona	Physician must effect prompt transfer to a physician willing to comply	Health care provider making good faith decisions in reliance on apparently genuine health care directive or decision of a surrogate or living will is immune from criminal, civil, and professional discipline for that reliance unless provider is negligent
Revocable at any time, in any manner by declarant without regard to declarant's mental/physical condition; effective upon communication to attending physician	A declaration executed in another state in compliance with the laws of that state or Arkansas law is valid	The provisions of Arkansas Healthcare Decisions Act concerning compliance by health care provider or institution apply to determine whether attending physician or other health care provider may decline to comply with declaration of patient and to any duty to transfer a patient when attending physician or other health care provider declines to comply with declaration, 20-6-109	Physician whose actions under this chapter are in accord with reasonable medical standards is not subject to criminal, civil, or professional liability with respect to them
Revocable at any time in any manner that indicates an intent to revoke	Declaration executed in another state in compliance with the laws of that state or California law is valid	Physician shall take all reasonable steps as promptly as practicable to transfer the patient to a physician who is willing to comply	Physician is not subject to civil, criminal, or professional liability for acting in good faith pursuant to declaration

Table 49c: Right to Die: Living Wills—Continued

State	Code Section	Specific Powers, Life-Prolonging Acts	Operative Facts
COLORADO	Colorado Medical Treatment Decision Act: 15-18-101 to 15-18-113	Any medical procedure or intervention that would serve only to prolong the dying process; it shall not include any medical procedure for nourishment or considered by attending physician to provide comfort or alleviate pain; however, artificial nourishment may be withdrawn pursuant to declaration that artificial nutrition not be provided or continued when it is the only procedure being provided or be continued for a specified period when it is the only procedure being provided	Adult; decisional capacity; before 2 witnesses with decisional capacity; no force if declarant has viable fetus
CONNECTICUT	Removal of Life Support Systems: 19a-570 to 19a-580g	Any medical procedure or intervention serving only to postpone the moment of death or maintain individual in a state of permanent unconsciousness including artificial means of nutrition/hydration, artificial respiration, CPR; comfort care and pain alleviation shall be provided in all cases	Over 18; signed; dated; presence of 2 witnesses; substantially in form of sample at 19a-575a
DELAWARE	Tit. 16, §§ 2501 to 2518	Any medical procedure, treatment, or intervention that utilizes mechanical or other artificial means to sustain, restore, or supplant vital function and is of such a nature to afford a patient no reasonable expectation of recovery from a terminal condition or permanent unconsciousness including assisted ventilation, renal dialysis, surgical procedures, blood transfusions, and the administration of drugs, antibiotics, and artificial nutrition and hydration	Legally adult, competent, of sound mind; written declaration; declarant in terminal condition confirmed in writing by 2 physicians; signed by declarant or another person in declarant's presence and at his express direction; dated; 2 or more adult witnesses who state in writing that they are not prohibited from being a witness; not pregnant
DISTRICT OF COLUMBIA	7-621 to 7-630	Any medical procedure or intervention which would serve only to artificially prolong the dying process and where death will occur whether or not such procedures are utilized; does not include medication or any medical procedure necessary to alleviate pain or provide comfort care	Age 18 or older; in writing; dated; signed; in presence of 2 or more witnesses over 18; declaration should be substantially in form of sample at 6-2422

Revocation/Duration	Reciprocity	Transfer of Patient if Physician Unwilling	Immunity for Attending Physician
Revocable by declarant orally, in writing, or by burning, tearing, cancelling; obliterating, or destroying the declaration	Declaration executed in compliance with laws of another state effective to the extent that such declaration does not violate any laws of Colorado	Physician shall transfer care of declarant to a physician who is willing to comply	No hospital or physician acting under direction of physician and participating in the withholding or withdrawal of life-sustaining procedures in compliance with a declaration shall be subject to any civil or criminal liability or licensing sanction in the absence of revocation, fraud, misrepresentation, or improper execution.
May be revoked at any time in any manner	Instruction under laws of another state in compliance with that state or the laws of Connecticut are deemed valid	Physician shall act as promptly as practicable and take all reasonable steps to transfer patient to complying physician	Physician withholding, removing life-support system of an incapacitated patient shall not be civilly or criminally liable if decision was based on physician's best medical judgment; physician deems patient in a terminal condition; patient's wishes were considered according to an executed document
Revocable by a signed writing in any manner that communicates an intent to revoke done in the presence of 2 witnesses, 1 of whom is a healthcare provider; new declaration with contrary intent; receipt of emergency treatment	Declarations executed in other states are valid if valid in that state	Physician shall not impede a transfer	Physicians or nurses acting in reliance on properly executed document are presumed to be acting in good faith and there is no civil or criminal liability or discipline for unprofessional conduct
Revocable at any time by declarant without regard to declarant's mental state by destruction of documents; written revocation signed and dated; verbal expression of intent to revoke in presence of witness at 18 or older; desires of qualified patient at all times supersede the effect of the declaration		Physician must effect a transfer and failure to do so shall constitute unprofessional conduct	No civil, criminal, professional liability for physician who acts in good faith pursuant to reasonable medical standard and to a declaration made

Table 49c: Right to Die: Living Wills—Continued

State	Code Section	Specific Powers, Life-Prolonging Acts	Operative Facts
FLORIDA	765.101 to 765.404	Any medical procedure, treatment, or intervention which utilizes mechanical or other artificial means to sustain, restore, supplant a spontaneous vital function and serves only to prolong the dying process of a patient in terminal condition; does not include medication or a medical procedure to provide comfort care or to alleviate pain	Competent; adult; signed by principal; in presence of 2 subscribing witnesses, one of whom is neither spouse nor blood relative, suggested form at 765.303
GEORGIA	Advance Directives for Health Care Act: 31-32-1 to 31-32-14	Any medical procedures or interventions which would serve only to prolong the dying process for a patient in a terminal condition, coma, or persistent vegetative state with no reasonable expectation of regaining consciousness or cognitive function; may include provision of nourishment and hydration but shall not include medication or any medical procedure to alleviate pain	Person of sound mind; emancipated or over 18; in writing; signed by declarant; witnessed by 2 or more persons of sound mind over 18
HAWAII	Uniform Health-Care Decisions Act (Modified): 327E-1 to 327E-16	Execute declaration directing provision, continuation, withholding, or withdrawal of any medical procedure or intervention including artificial provisions of fluids, nourishment, medication that when administered to patient will only serve to prolong dying process; does not include procedure necessary for patient comfort or relief	Adult or emancipated minor; oral or written
IDAHO	The Medical Consent and Natural Death Act: 39-4501 to 39-4515	Any medical procedure or intervention which utilizes mechanical means to sustain or supplant a vital function serving only to artificially prolong the moment of death and where death is imminent whether or not procedures are utilized; does not include the administration of medication or a medical procedure to alleviate pain	Competent person; dated and signed; substantially in the form of sample at 39-4510

Revocation/Duration	Reciprocity	Transfer of Patient if Physician Unwilling	Immunity for Attending Physician
Revocable at any time by principal by signed, dated writing; destruction of the declaration; oral expression of intent to revoke; subsequent advance directive materially different from the previously executed advance directive; divorce revokes the designation of former spouse as surrogate; revocation effective when properly communicated	Advanced directive executed in another state is validly executed if in compliance with the laws of that state or Florida	Physician should make reasonable efforts to transfer to a health care provider who will comply with the declaration; a physician unwilling to carry out patient's wishes because of moral or ethical beliefs must within 7 days transfer the patient and pay the cost of transporting the patient to another health care provider or carry out the wishes of the patient unless provisions of judicial intervention apply	Health care facility, provider, or other person who acts under the direction of a health care facility or provider is not subject to criminal prosecution or civil or professional liability for carrying out a health care decision
Revocable at any time by declarant without regard to mental state or competency by destruction of document; declarant signs and dates a written revocation expressing intent to revoke; any verbal or nonverbal expression by declarant of intent to revoke which clearly revokes the living will as opposed to a will relating to the disposition of property after death	Any document executed in another state and valid under the laws of that state shall be honored	Advise promptly the next of kin or guardian and at their election make a good faith attempt to effect transfer or permit next of kin or guardian to obtain complying physician	No physician acting in good faith in accordance with the requirements of this chapter shall be subject to any civil liability, guilty of any criminal act, or unprofessional conduct
Revocable at any time in any manner that indicates an intent to revoke	Directive is valid if it complies with the laws of Hawaii or with the laws of the state where executed	Physician shall without delay make necessary arrangements to transfer patient and medical records to another physician	No physician acting in good faith shall be subject to civil or criminal liability or to discipline for unprofessional conduct
Revocable at any time by declarant without regard to competence by destruction of the document; BY written, signed revocation; by verbal expression of intent to revoke; by any other action indicating intent to revoke	Any document executed in another state that substantially complies with this Act deemed in compliance with Idaho law	Physician may withdraw without civil or criminal liability provided the physician makes a good faith effort to assist the patient in transferring before his/her withdrawal, 39-4513	No civil or criminal liability for a physician acting in accordance with the wishes of the patient as expressed by statutory procedure

Table 49c: Right to Die: Living Wills—Continued

State	Code Section	Specific Powers, Life-Prolonging Acts	Operative Facts
ILLINOIS	Illinois Living Will Act: 755 §§ 35/1 to 35/10	Individual may execute document directing that if he is suffering from a terminal condition and no longer able to participate actively in decisions about himself, then death–delaying procedure shall not be utilized for the prolongation of his life. These procedures include any which serve to postpone the moment of death and specifically include, but are not limited to, assisted ventilation, artificial kidney treatment, intravenous feeding/medication, blood transfusions and tube feedings, but does not include procedures providing for patient's comfort care or alleviation of pain	Sound mind and age of majority or status of emancipated person (sample form at 35/3e); signed by declarant or another at declarant's direction; 2 witnesses over 18; not pregnant or at point where fetus could develop to point of live birth with continued application of death delaying procedures; notify attending physician
INDIANA	16-36-4-1 to 16-36-4-21	Living will declarant may ask that life prolonging procedures that would sustain, restore, or supplant a vital function or that would serve to prolong the dying process not be used in case of terminal diagnosis and incapacity; this does not include any medical procedure or medication necessary to provide comfort care or alleviate pain	Person of sound mind at least 18 yrs. old; voluntary; in writing; dated; signed in presence of 2 adult witnesses; notice to declarant's attending physician; is presumptive evidence of declarant's intent; not enforced if pregnant; witnesses must not be related to declarant; sample form at 16-36-4-10
IOWA	Life-Sustaining Procedures Act: 144A.1 to 144A.12	Declarant may declare desire to not have life-sustaining procedures employed to prolong life; life sustaining procedures are those that utilize mechanical or artificial means to sustain, restore, or supplant a spontaneous vital function and/or when applied to a patient in a terminal condition would only serve to prolong the dying process, does not include provision of nutrition or hydration except when required parenterally or though intubation or the administration of medication or performance of medical procedures which provide comfort care or alleviate pain; declaration shall not be in effect when declarant is pregnant as long as fetus can develop to point of live birth	Competent adult; signed in presence of 2 witnesses and in the presence of each other; at least one witness must not be related to declarant; physician may presume declaration is valid; actual notice of declaration to attending physician; declaration given effect when declarant's condition is terminal and he is unable to make treatment decisions; sample form at 144A.3(5)

Revocation/Duration	Reciprocity	Transfer of Patient if Physician Unwilling	Immunity for Attending Physician
Revocable by declarant at any time without regard to mental or physical condition: in writing signed and dated by declarant or person acting at his/her direction; by oral expression in presence of witness who signs and dates a written confirmation; by destroying declaration in manner indicating intent to cancel; revocation is effective upon communication to attending physician	Declaration executed in another state in compliance with law of that state or Illinois is valid	Patient is responsible to initiate transfer; if patient not able to initiate transfer then attending physician shall without delay notify person with highest priority who is available, able, and willing to make arrangements for transfer for effectuation of patient's declaration	No physician, health care provider, or health care expert who in good faith and pursuant to reasonable medical standards causes or participates in withholding or withdrawal of death delaying procedure from qualified patient per declaration shall be subject to criminal or civil liability or be found to have committed an act of unprofessional conduct
Living will declaration is presumed valid, revocable at any time in writing, signed and dated; by physical destruction by declarant or at declarant's direction; by oral expression of revocation		Physician refusing to comply shall transfer to willing physician unless first physician believes declaration is not validly executed and patient is unable to validate declaration; if not transferred, physician should try to ascertain patient's intent and declaration's validity from persons listed in 16-36-4-13 (g)(1-7)	Act of withdrawing or withholding life-prolonging procedures for qualified patient is lawful; physician not subject to criminal or civil liability or unprofessional conduct if done in good faith and in accordance with reasonable medical standards; violation of any provisions of act subjects physician to disciplinary sanctions by medical licensing board
Revocable at any time in any manner that declarant can communicate intent, without regard to mental or physical condition; physician shall make revocation part of medical records	Similar document executed in another state in compliance with the laws of that state is valid and enforceable in Iowa to extent document is consistent with Iowa law	Physician to take reasonable steps to transfer patient to another physician or facility	Individual or health care provider is not liable civilly or criminally or guilty of unprofessional conduct for complying in good faith with provisions in declaration indicating withholding or withdrawal of life-sustaining procedures.

Table 49c: Right to Die: Living Wills—Continued

State	Code Section	Specific Powers, Life-Prolonging Acts	Operative Facts
KANSAS	Natural Death Act: 65-28,101 to 65-28,109	Any medical procedure or intervention which would serve only to prolong the dying process and where death will occur whether or not such procedure is utilized. Does not include medication or any medical procedures necessary to alleviate pain or provide comfort care Declaration not in effect during declarant's pregnancy.	Any adult; in writing; signed by declarant; dated; in presence of 2 or more adult witnesses not related to declarant or acknowledged before a public notary; no effect during course of pregnancy; responsibility of declarant to notify attending physician; substantially same form as sample at 65-28,103(c)
KENTUCKY	Kentucky Living Will Directive Act: 311.621 to 311.643	Any medical procedure, treatment, or intervention which utilizes mechanical or other artificial means to sustain prolong, restore, or supplant a spontaneous vital function or when administered would only prolong dying process; does not include medication or procedure to alleviate pain.	Adult with decisional capacity; in writing; dated and signed; either witnessed by 2 or more adults in presence of grantor and in presence of each other or acknowledged before notary; in substantially the same form as sample at 311.625(1); no witness can be related to grantor
LOUISIANA	40:1151 to 40:1151.9	Any medical procedure or intervention, including but not limited to invasive administration of nutrition and hydration, which would serve only to prolong the dying process for a person diagnosed as having a terminal and irreversible condition; does not include any measure necessary for comfort care	Any adult; written declaration; signed by declarant; in presence of 2 adult witnesses; oral or nonverbal declaration may be made in presence of 2 adult witnesses by any nonwritten means of communication at any time subsequent to the diagnosis of a terminal and irreversible condition; sample form at 40:1151.2
MAINE	Uniform Health-Care Decisions Act: Tit. 18-C §§ 5-801 to 5-816	Any medical procedure or intervention administered only to prolong process of dying; may include artificially administered nutrition and hydration	Over 18 and of sound mind; in writing and signed by declarant or another at his direction; witnessed by 2 people; communicated to attending physician; effective upon determination that principal lacks capacity physician records terms of declaration and determination of terminal condition

Revocation/Duration	Reciprocity	Transfer of Patient if Physician Unwilling	Immunity for Attending Physician
Revocable at any time by declarant by destruction of document; written revocation signed and dated by principal; verbal expression in presence of adult witnesses who signs and dates a written confirmation; effective upon receipt by physician; desires of patient at all times supersede the declaration		Physician shall effect transfer; failure to do so constitutes unprofessional conduct	No criminal, civil, or professional liability for acting in good faith and pursuant to reasonable medical standards when acting pursuant to a declaration
Revocable by written declaration signed and dated by declarant; oral statement of intent to revoke in presence of 2 adults, one of which is a health care provider; destruction of declaration with intent to revoke; effective immediately for attending physician once revocation received; oral statement by grantor with decisional capacity to revoke overrides previous written directive	Directives made outside the provisions of this act do not restrict health care providers from following such directives if they are consistent with accepted medical practice	Physician must immediately inform patient and family or guardian and shall not impede transfer to complying physician or health care facility; patient's medical records and information shall be supplied to receiving physician or facility	Not subject to criminal prosecution or civil liability or deemed to have engaged in unprofessional conduct as a result of withholding or withdrawing life prolonging treatment in accordance with directive unless shown by preponderance of evidence that there was bad faith
Revocable at any time by declarant without regard to mental state or competency by destruction of document; written revocation signed and dated by declarant; oral or nonverbal expression by the declarant of the intent to revoke; effective upon communication to physician	Declaration properly executed in and under the laws of another state deemed valid	Physician shall make reasonable effort to transfer the patient to another physician	Any health care facility, physician, or other person acting under the direction of a physician shall not be civilly, criminally, or professionally liable for withholding life-sustaining procedures in accordance with the provisions of this Act
Revocable at any time and in any manner without regard to declarant's mental or physical condition; revocation effective upon communication to attending physician or health care provider by declarant or witness to revocation	Declaration executed in another state in compliance with laws of that state and Maine is valid	Attending physician or other health care provider who is unwilling shall take all reasonable steps as promptly as practicable to transfer to another physician willing to comply and provide continuing care until transfer is effected; willful failure to transfer is class E crime	Physician or other health care provider whose action is in accord with reasonable medical standards and in good faith is not subject to criminal or civil liability or discipline for unprofessional conduct

Table 49c: Right to Die: Living Wills—Continued

State	Code Section	Specific Powers, Life-Prolonging Acts	Operative Facts
MARYLAND	Health Care Decisions Act: Health-Gen. § 5-602	Any medical procedure, treatment, or intervention which uses mechanical or other artificial means to maintain, restore a spontaneous vital function or of such a nature as to afford patient no reasonable expectation of recovery from a terminal condition, persistent vegetative state, or end-stage condition; includes artificially administered hydration, nutrition, and CPR; does not include medication or procedure necessary to alleviate pain or provide comfort care; may include an anatomical gift directive	Competent person; dated and in writing or electronic; signed by declarant or at express direction of declarant; subscribed by 2 witnesses; unwitnessed video or electronic declaration valid under certain circumstances; directive effective when attending physician and second physician certify in writing that patient is incapable of making an informed decision on basis of physical examination within 2 hrs. of certification, if patient is unconscious, 2nd physician not required; oral directives must be made in presence of attending physician and one witness; physician must sign and date documentation in patient's medical record; suggested form at Health-Gen. § 5-603; in absence of validly executed or witnessed directive, any authentic expression made by competent individual shall be considered
MASSACHUSETTS	No statutory provisions (But see Health Care Proxies Ch. 201D §§ 1 to 17)		
MICHIGAN	No statutory provisions (But see Uniform Durable Power of Attorney Act 700.496)		
MINNESOTA	Living Will Act; 145B.01 to 145B.17; Health Care Directive 145C.01 to 145C.16	Decisions on whether to administer, withhold, or withdraw medical treatment, services, or procedures to maintain, diagnose, or treat an individual's physical condition when the individual is in a terminal condition must be based on reasonable medical practice including continuation of appropriate care to maintain comfort, hygiene, human dignity, and to alleviate pain; oral administration of food and water to a patient who accepts it, except for clearly documented medical reasons	Competent adult; signed by declarant; signed by 2 witnesses or notary public; must state preference regarding artificial administration of nutrition and hydration or give decision to proxy; must be in substantially the form of sample at 145B.04; effective when delivered to physician or health care provider; not given effect if patient is pregnant and it is possible that fetus could develop to live birth with continued treatment
MISSISSIPPI	Uniform Health-Care Decisions Act: 41-41-201 to 41-41-303	May authorize the withdrawal of life-sustaining mechanisms defined as cessation of use of extraordinary techniques and applications including mechanical devises which prolong life through artificial means	Adult or emancipated minor; oral or written; dated; signed by principal; signed by 2 adult witnesses, at least one of whom is not related to principal; acknowledged by notary public

Revocation/Duration	Reciprocity	Transfer of Patient if Physician Unwilling	Immunity for Attending Physician
Revocable at any time by signed and dated written or electronic document; oral statement to health care practitioner; execution of subsequent directive; destruction of directive	Declaration executed in another state shall be deemed to be validly executed if in compliance with the laws of Maryland or the laws of the state where executed	Attending physician shall make every reasonable effort to transfer declarant to another health care provider, assist in transfer, and pending transfer, comply with competent individual or health care agent/surrogate for person incapable of making a decision if failure to comply would likely result in death of individual	Any health care provider who withholds or withdraws health care or life-sustaining procedures in accordance with this subtitle and in good faith, is not subject to civil or criminal liability and may not be found to have committed professional misconduct
Revocable at any time in any manner in whole or in part by declarant without regard to declarant's physical or mental condition; effective upon communication to physician; divorce revokes any designation of the former spouse as a proxy to make health care decisions	Effective when executed in another state if it substantially complies with Minnesota law	Physician must notify competent declarant of unwillingness but has no duty to transfer; if physician received living will from competent patient and did not notify declarant of unwillingness to comply and declarant subsequently becomes incompetent, physician must take all reasonable steps to transfer to complying physician	Physician acting in good faith and in accordance with applicable standards of care is immune from criminal prosecution, civil liability, or professional disciplinary action
Revocable at any time in any manner that communicates an intent to revoke; designation of agent revoked only by signed writing or by personally informing physician	Directive is valid if it complies with Mississippi law regardless of when or where it is executed	Physician must promptly inform patient; provide continuing care until transfer can be effectuated; make all reasonable efforts to assist in transfer	Physician, acting in good faith and in accordance with provisions of this Act, who causes withdrawal of life-sustaining mechanisms is not guilty of a criminal offense, or civil or professional liability

Table 49c: Right to Die: Living Wills—Continued

State	Code Section	Specific Powers, Life-Prolonging Acts	Operative Facts
MISSOURI	459.010 to 459.055	Any medical procedure or intervention which would serve only to prolong artificially the dying process where death will occur within a short time whether or not such procedure or intervention is utilized. Does not include medication or procedure to provide comfort care or alleviate pain or any procedure to provide nutrition or hydration	Competent person; in writing; signed by declarant; dated; if not wholly in declarant's handwriting, signed in presence of 2 adult witnesses; operative only when declarant's condition is determined to be terminal or declarant is unable to make treatment decisions; declaration shall have no effect during course of declarant's pregnancy; sample form at 459.015(3)
MONTANA	Montana Rights of the Terminally Ill Act: 50-9-101 to 50-9-505	Withholding or withdrawal of life-sustaining treatment, defined as any medical procedure or intervention that will serve only to prolong the dying process.; qualified patient may designate another individual to make decisions governing withholding or withdrawal of life-sustaining treatment; life-sustaining procedures may not be withdrawn when qualified patient is known to be pregnant and when it is likely fetus will result in live birth	18 years or older and of sound mind; signed by declarant or another at declarant's direction; witnessed by 2 individuals; communicated to physician and made part of patient's medical record; declared to be terminal and no longer able to make decisions regarding life-sustaining treatment; absent contrary actual notice, physician or health care provider may presume that declaration is valid; sample form at 50-9-103
NEBRASKA	Rights of the Terminally Ill Act: 20-401 to 20-416	Any medical procedure or intervention that will serve only to prolong the process of dying or maintain the patient in a persistent vegetative act, meaning that to a reasonable degree of medical certainty one has a total and irreversible loss of consciousness and capacity for cognitive interaction with the environment with no reasonable hope of improvement; does not affect physician's responsibility to provide treatment, including nutrition and hydration for patient's comfort care or alleviation of pain; life-sustaining treatment shall be provided if declarant is pregnant and fetus is likely to develop to the point of live birth with continued application of life-sustaining treatment	Adult of sound mind; signed by declarant or another at declarant's direction; witnessed by 2 adults or notary public; communicated to attending physician; patient in terminal condition, persistent vegetative state, or unable to make decisions regarding administration of life-sustaining treatment; physician must notify reasonably available member of declarant's immediate family or guardian of his or her diagnosis and of intent to invoke the patient's declaration; sample form at 20-404

Revocation/Duration	Reciprocity	Transfer of Patient if Physician Unwilling	Immunity for Attending Physician
Revocable at any time in any manner declarant is able to communicate intent to revoke, without regard for mental or physical condition; directions of declarant shall at all times supersede declaration		Physician must take all reasonable steps to effect the transfer of a declarant	No criminal, civil, or professional liability for acting in good faith pursuant to usual and customary medical standards who withholds or withdraws death-prolonging procedures from patient pursuant to a declaration
Revocable at any time in any manner without regard to physical or mental condition; effective upon communication to attending physician or health care provider; health care provider or emergency medical services personnel in receipt of such communication shall act upon revocation an communicate it to attending physician at earliest opportunity; revocation shall become part of declarant's medical record	Declaration made in another state in compliance with that state's laws executed in a substantially similar manner to laws of Montana is valid	Attending physician or health care provider who is unable or unwilling to comply shall take all reasonable steps as promptly as practicable to transfer to another who is willing	Attending physician or health care provider not subject to civil or criminal liability or guilty of unprofessional conduct as long as acting in accordance with reasonable medical standards and in good faith
Revocable at any time in any manner without regard to declarant's mental or physical condition effective upon communication to physician or other health care provider; revocation shall become part of declarant's medical record.	Declaration executed in another state in compliance with that state or Nebraska is valid	Physician shall take all prompt and reasonable steps to transfer to a willing physician	Not subject to civil, criminal, or professional discipline in the absence of knowledge of revocation or whose action under this Act is in accord with reasonable medical standards; unjustifiable violation of patient's directions shall be a civil cause of action maintainable by patient or patient's next officer

Table 49c: Right to Die: Living Wills—Continued

State	Code Section	Specific Powers, Life-Prolonging Acts	Operative Facts
NEVADA	Uniform Act on Rights of the Terminally Ill: 449.535 to 449.690	Any medical procedure that when administered serves only to prolong the process of dying; does not include medication or procedures necessary to alleviate pain; artificial nutrition and hydration by way of gastro-intestinal tract is considered medical procedure or life sustaining treatment and must be withheld unless different desire is expressed in writing or agent has authority to withhold consent.	18 yrs. or older and of sound mind; may designate another to make decisions governing withholding or withdrawing; signed by declarant or another at declarant's direction; 2 witnesses; not operative if patient is known to be pregnant and live birth is probable; declaration part of medical record; sample forms at 449-610 and 449-613
NEW HAMPSHIRE	137-J:1 to 137-J:18	Qualified patient may instruct physician not to use life-sustaining procedures in the event the person is in a terminal condition or is permanently unconscious; there must be a clear expression of one's intent to withdraw or withhold artificial nutrition and hydration.	Person of sound mind, 18 yrs. or older; document signed voluntarily by declarant; witnessed by 2 persons not a spouse or heir at law or by public notary or justice of the peace; upon request, physician shall made document part of medical record; effective if person is permanently incapable of participating in decisions about his care; not permitted when physician has knowledge that patient is pregnant; sample form at 137-J:20
NEW JERSEY	Advanced Directives for Health Care Act: 26:2H-53 to 26:2H-90	Decisions to accept or refuse any treatment, service, or procedure used to diagnose, treat, or care for a patient's physical or mental condition including life-sustaining treatment; includes decisions to accept or refuse services of a particular physician or health care provider or a transfer of care; or use of any medical device or procedure, artificially provided fluids and nutrition drugs, surgery, or therapy that uses mechanical or other artificial means to sustain, restore, or supplant a vital bodily function and thereby increase the expected life span of a patient; does not include providing comfort care or to alleviate pain.	Of sound mind; adult; signed; dated; in presence of 2 witnesses who shall attest that declarant is of sound mind and free of duress and undue influence or in front of a notary public, attorney, or another person authorized to administer oaths; may be supplemented by video or audio tape recording; directive implemented when determination of lack of decision-making capacity is documented and confirmed by physicians
NEW MEXICO	Uniform Health-Care Decisions Act: 24-7A-1 to 24-7A-18	Any medical treatment or procedure without which the individual is likely to die within a short time	Adult or emancipated minor; oral or written; If oral, must be made by personally informing health-care provider; effective when patient no long able to make own healthcare decision; sample form at 24-7A-4

Revocation/Duration	Reciprocity	Transfer of Patient if Physician Unwilling	Immunity for Attending Physician
Revocable at any time and in any manner; effective upon communication to the attending physician or other provider of health care	Declaration executed in another state in compliance with the law of that state or of this state is valid	Physician shall take all reasonable steps as promptly as possible to transfer care of declarant to another physician	Not subject to civil, criminal liability or professional discipline if acted in good faith and in accordance with reasonable medical standards; no liability for failure to follow patient's directions; physician may consider "other factors" in determining whether the circumstances warrant following the directions
Revocable by destroying document; signed and dated written revocation; oral revocation before 2 witnesses; execution of subsequent advance directive; divorce, legal separation, annulment, or protective order where principal and agent are parties, except where alternate agent is designated and alternate agent shall become effective; revocation effective upon communication to attending physician	An advance directive executed in another state and valid according to the laws of that state or New Hampshire is valid	Physician shall make necessary arrangements without delay to effect transfer to chosen physician	Physician or health care professional is immune from civil or criminal liability for good faith actions in keeping with reasonable medical standards pursuant to the living will and in accordance with New Hampshire Law
Revocable by oral or written notification or execution of subsequent directive; divorce revokes former spouse's designation as the health care representative; patient's clearly expressed wishes take precedent over any patient's decision or instruction directive	Effective if executed in compliance with New Jersey law or the laws of that state; effective if executed in a foreign country in compliance with that country's laws or the laws of New Jersey and is not contrary to the public policy of New Jersey	Physician should act as soon as practicable to effect an appropriate, respectful, and timely transfer of care and to assure that patient is not abandoned or treated disrespectfully	No civil, criminal, or professional liability for any physician acting in good faith and pursuant to this Act
Revocable at any time in any way that communicates an intent to revoke	Document uniformly applied and construed among states enacting Uniform Health-Care Decisions Act	Physician must take appropriate steps to transfer the patient to another qualified physician and provide continuing care to patient until transfer	No civil or criminal liability or professional discipline for acting pursuant to statute in good faith

913

Table 49c: Right to Die: Living Wills—Continued

State	Code Section	Specific Powers, Life-Prolonging Acts	Operative Facts
NEW YORK	No statutory provisions (But see Health Care Agents and Proxies, Pub. Health §§ 2980 to 2994)		
NORTH CAROLINA	90-320 to 90-323	Medical procedures or interventions which serve only to postpone artificially the moment of death by sustaining, restoring, or supplanting a vital function. Does not include care necessary to provide comfort or to alleviate pain, 32A-16(4)	Signed in presence of 2 witnesses who believe declarant is of sound mind; dated; notarized or proved before a clerk; sample form at 90-321(d1)
NORTH DAKOTA	23-06.5-01 to 23-06.5-19	Right to refuse any care, treatment, service, or procedure to maintain, diagnose, or treat an individual's physical or mental condition, including: diagnostic tests, surgical procedures, programs of medication, and orders not to resuscitate; directions to provide, withhold, or withdraw artificial nutrition and hydration and all other forms of health care	Directive must be in writing; dated; state principal's name; executed by the principal with capacity to do so or by another person authorized by the principal to sign on his or her behalf; notarized or witnessed as provided in 23-06.5(2); include health care instruction or power of attorney for health care, or both; sample form at 23-06.5-17
OHIO	Modified Uniform Rights of the Terminally Ill Act: 2133.01 to 2133.16	Any medical procedure, treatment, intervention, or other measure that will serve principally to prolong the process of dying; declarant may authorize withholding hydration and nutrition; cannot withdraw or withhold life-sustaining treatment from pregnant patient, unless it is believed to a reasonable degree of certainty, that the fetus would not be born alive	Adult; of sound mind; signed by declarant; dated; in presence of 2 witnesses or notary public who attests that principal is of sound mind and free from duress
OKLAHOMA	Oklahoma Advance Directive Act: Tit. 63, §§ 3101.1 to 3102.4	Any medical procedure or intervention that will serve only to prolong the dying process including artificial administration of nutrition and hydration but only if declarant has specifically authorized its withdrawal; does not include treatment to alleviate pain or the normal consumption of food and water	18 yrs.; of sound mind; signed by declarant; witnessed by 2 adults; in substantially the same form as sample at Tit. 63, § 3101.4(C); operative when communicated to attending physician and when declarant can no longer make decisions regarding the administration of life-sustaining treatment; not operative during course of pregnancy unless patient in her own words specifically authorizes it

Revocation/Duration	Reciprocity	Transfer of Patient if Physician Unwilling	Immunity for Attending Physician
Revocable in any manner by which declarant is able to communicate his intent to revoke without regard for mental or physical state; effective upon communication to physician	Declaration executed in a jurisdiction other than North Carolina shall be valid in this state if executed in accordance with that jurisdiction or North Carolina		Withholding or discontinuing of extraordinary means shall not be considered cause of death for civil or criminal purposes; these provisions may be asserted as a defense to any civil or criminal suits or charges filed against a health care provider
Notification by principal to agent or health care provider orally or in writing, or by any other act evidencing a specific intent to revoke the directive; execution of a subsequent health care directive; divorce if the spouse is the principal's agent. Health care or long-term care services provider shall immediately record the revocation in principal's medical record and notify agent, if any, attending physician, and staff responsible for principal's care of the revocation	Effective if executed in another state or jurisdiction in compliance with the law of that state or jurisdiction. done in good faith and with ordinary care if the act or intentional failure to act is done pursuant to the dictates of a health care directive, the directives of the patient's agent	Physician must notify agent of unwillingness to comply and document notification in principal's medical records; physician must take all reasonable steps to transfer patient as promptly as practical to physician willing to comply with statute and continue to provide continuing care until transfer can be made	No civil, criminal, or professional liability for actions done in good faith and with ordinary care if the act or intentional failure to act is done pursuant to the dictates of a health care directive, the directives of the patient's agent, or authorized by statute
Revocable at any time and in any manner; effective when expressed and communicated to a witness or physician	Effective if executed in another state in compliance with that law or in substantial compliance with Ohio law	Physician may not prevent or unreasonably delay a transfer	No civil, criminal, or professional liability for physician acting in good faith within the scope of their authority
Revocable in whole or in part in any manner at any time without regard to declarant's mental or physical condition; effective upon communication to physician	Effective if complies with Oklahoma law or in compliance with law of that state so long as it does not exceed authorizations allowed under Oklahoma law	Physician shall take all reasonable steps to arrange for care by another physician; must comply with decision until transfer	No civil, criminal, or professional liability for carrying out the advance directive pursuant to statute in good faith and in accord with reasonable medical standards

Table 49c: Right to Die: Living Wills—Continued

State	Code Section	Specific Powers, Life-Prolonging Acts	Operative Facts
OREGON	Oregon Health Care Decisions Act: 127.505 to 127.660	Life-sustaining acts means mechanical or other artificial means to sustain, restore, or supplant a vital function that is used to maintain life of a person suffering from a terminal condition and serves only to prolong artificially the moment of death; does not include procedures to sustain patient cleanliness and comfort	In writing; dated; witnessed and signed by 2 adults or before a public notary
PENNSYLVANIA	Living Will Act: Tit. 20, §§ 5441 to 5447	Any medical procedure or intervention that serves only to prolong the process of dying or maintain the patient in a state of permanent unconsciousness; includes artificially or invasively administered nutrition and hydration if specifically provided for in declaration; does not apply to emergency medical services.	Of sound mind; 18 yrs., graduated from high school, married, or emancipated minor; signed and dated; 2 adult witnesses; operative when declarant determined to be incompetent by attending physician as certified in writing; not operative during pregnancy unless it will not maintain woman so as to permit live birth; sample form at Tit. 20, § 5471
RHODE ISLAND	Rights of Terminally Ill Act: 23-4.11-1 to 23-4.11-15	Any medical procedure or intervention serving only to prolong the dying process; does not include anything necessary to alleviate pain or provide comfort and care; must wear DNR bracelet in order to effectuate "do not resuscitate" order	18 yrs. and competent; signed; in presence of 2 witnesses; given no force or effect as long as live birth is probable for pregnant patient; neither witness related to declarant; sample form at 23-4.11-3(d)
SOUTH CAROLINA	Death with Dignity Act: 44-77-10 to 44-77-160	Medical procedures or intervention serving only to prolong the dying process; does not include treatment for comfort care or pain alleviation; declarant should indicate whether nutrition and hydration through surgically implanted tubes is desired; if declarant fails to do so, nutrition and hydration necessary for comfort care and pain alleviation will be provided	Declaration must set out intent for no life-sustaining procedures; signed; dated; in presence of officer authorized to administer oaths; in presence of 2 witnesses; substantially same as sample at 44-77-50; not effective during course of declarant's pregnancy; terminal condition must be certified by 2 examining physicians and patient must be given active treatment for at least 6 hrs. following diagnosis before physician can give effect to declaration
SOUTH DAKOTA	34-12D-1 to 34-12D-29	Any medical procedure or intervention that will serve only to postpone death or maintain person in state of permanent unconsciousness; does not include comfort care, hygiene and human dignity, oral administration of food and water, or medical procedure to alleviate pain	Competent adult; signed by declarant; witnessed by 2 adults; may be in presence of notary public; not operative for pregnant woman unless live birth unlikely to a reasonable degree of medical certainty; sample form at 34-12D.3

Revocation/Duration	Reciprocity	Transfer of Patient if Physician Unwilling	Immunity for Attending Physician
Directive may be revoked at any time or in any manner by which the principal is able to communicate the intent to revoke; effective upon communication to the attending physician	Valid subject to laws of Oregon if executed in compliance with the laws of the state where principal is located or resides or with the laws of the state of Oregon	Physician shall notify any representative or discharge patient (without abandoning) or make a reasonable effort to locate and transfer to a willing physician	No liability, if in good faith has acted on fully executed directive, for criminal or civil liability or professional disciplinary action
Revocable at any time in any manner without regard to declarant's mental or physical condition; effective upon communication to physician.	Living will executed in another state or jurisdiction in conformity with the laws of that state or jurisdiction is valid in Pennsylvania	Unwilling physician must inform declarant, surrogate, or family, and make every reasonable effort to assist in the transfer of declarant to complying physician	No civil, criminal, or professional liability in following wishes of declarant pursuant to declaration executed according to statute
Revocable at any time in any manner by which declarant is able to communicate the intent to revoke without regard to physical or mental condition; only effective upon communication to physician by declarant or one witnessing the revocation	Declaration executed in another state in compliance with the laws of that state is valid	Physician shall make necessary arrangements to effect a transfer	No civil, criminal, or professional liability for acting in accordance with requirements of the statute and in accordance with reasonable medical standards
Destruction of document when communicated to physician; written revocation signed and dated upon communication to physician; oral expression of intent to revoke when communicated to physician; communication of oral revocation may be made by someone present when revocation made, if communicated within reasonable time and declarant is physically or mentally able to confirm or by designee if declarant is incompetent; execution of subsequent declaration	For patients in terminal condition, document with same intent as this chapter and in compliance with the laws of that state is effective	Physician must make a reasonable effort to locate a physician who will effectuate patient's declaration and has a duty to transfer patient to such physician	No criminal or civil liability for acting in good faith and in accordance with the standards of reasonable medical care pursuant to the statute
Revocable at any time in any manner without regard to declarant's physical or mental condition; effective upon communication to physician or other health care provider	Document is valid if it meets execution requirements of place where executed, place where declarant was a resident, or requirements of the state of South Dakota	Unwilling physician must make a reasonable effort to locate and transfer a patient to a physician who will honor the declaration; must continue treatment or care until transfer is effectuated	No civil, criminal, or professional liability for giving effect to a declaration

Table 49c: Right to Die: Living Wills—Continued

State	Code Section	Specific Powers, Life-Prolonging Acts	Operative Facts
TENNESSEE	Tennessee Right to Natural Death Act: 32-11-101 to 32-11-113	Any procedure, treatment to diagnose, assess, or treat a disease, illness, or injury; includes surgery, drugs, transfusions, mechanical ventilation, dialysis, CPR, artificial nourishment, hydration or other nutrients, radiation; death by starvation or dehydration allowed only if specifically directed by using statutory phrase	Competent adult; in writing and signed; in presence of 2 witnesses or public notary; witnesses must not be related to declarant; substantially in form of sample at 32-11-105
TEXAS	Advance Directives Act: Health & Safety §§ 166.001 to 166.053	Treatment that sustains the life of the patient and without which the patient will die; includes both life-sustaining medications and artificial life support.; does not include administration of medication or performance of procedure to provide comfort to alleviate pain.	Competent adult; 2 witnesses, or if no witnesses, may be notarized; may be oral with 2 witnesses and attending physician; directive shall become a part of medical record of declarant, witnesses must sign medical records if oral); not operative for pregnant patients; sample form at Health & Safety § 166.033
UTAH	Advance Health Care Directive Act: 75-2A-101 to 75-2A-125	Any medical intervention, including procedures, administration of medication, or use of a medical device, that maintains life by sustaining, restoring, or supplanting a vital function; does not include comfort care.	Adult; oral or written; witnessed by a disinterested adult; substantially same form as sample at 75-2a-117; no force during the course of declarant's pregnancy
VERMONT	Tit. 18, §§ 9700 to 9720	Any medical intervention, including nutrition and hydration, intended to extend life and without which the principal would die	Adult with capacity; dated; signed; in presence of 2 or more witnesses over 18

Revocation/Duration	Reciprocity	Transfer of Patient if Physician Unwilling	Immunity for Attending Physician
Revocable at any time by declarant regardless of mental state if effectively communicated to the physician by written revocation dated and signed or oral statement made to physician	Effective if in compliance with Tennessee law or the law of the state of declarant's residence; subsequent declaration revokes prior declarations	Unwilling physician must make every reasonable effort to assist in a transfer	No civil, criminal, or professional liability if acting in accord with reasonable medical standards
Revocable at any time without regard to declarant's mental state or competency; may be revoked by declarant or someone in presence destroying document; by signed and dated written revocation; orally stating intent to revoke. Effective when delivered or mailed to attending physician, or when physician notified of oral revocation; directive effective until revoked; desire of qualified competent patient supersedes directive	An advance directive executed in another state or jurisdiction shall be given the same effect as a directive executed under Texas law	Unwilling physician must make reasonable effort to transfer patient to another physician	Immune from effects of revocation if not adequately notified. No criminal or civil liability for failing to effectuate a directive if there is no knowledge of it. By complying with legal directive, one does not commit act of criminally aiding suicide. No civil, criminal, or professional liability for acting in accordance with this Act unless negligent.
Current wishes of declarant take precedent over any directive; revocable at any time by writing "void" across declaration; signed revocation or destruction of document or oral expression of intent to revoke in presence of adult witness.; effective on receipt by physician	Similar instrument executed in another state is presumed to comply with Utah law and may be relied upon in good faith	Physician must inform the patient of unwillingness to comply; make a good faith attempt to resolve conflict; provide continuing care until a transfer can be made.	No civil, criminal, or professional liability for good faith compliance with a directive
Revocable by signed writing; personally informing the principal's physician; destroying the document; any other act evidencing a specific intent to revoke	An advance directive executed in another state or jurisdiction in compliance with the law of that state or jurisdiction is valid in Vermont	Unwilling physician must actively assist in selecting another physician willing to honor patient's directive	No civil or criminal liability for physician acting pursuant to the terminal care document

Table 49c: Right to Die: Living Wills—Continued

State	Code Section	Specific Powers, Life-Prolonging Acts	Operative Facts
VIRGINIA	Health Care Decisions Act: 54.1-2981 to 54.1-2993	Any medical procedure, treatment, intervention, utilizing mechanical or other artificial means to sustain, restore, or supplant a vital function, or is of a nature to afford a patient no reasonable expectation of recovery from a terminal condition, and when applied to a patient in terminal condition, would serve only to prolong the dying process; includes artificially administered hydration and nutrition and CPR by emergency medical services personnel; does not include any medication or procedure to alleviate pain or provide comfort care.	Competent adult; written advance directive; signed in presence of 2 subscribing witnesses; oral declaration in presence of physician and 2 witnesses for those in terminal condition; responsibility of declarant to provide notification of advanced directive to attending physician; sample form at 54.1-2984
WASHINGTON	Natural Death Act: 70.122.010 to 70.122.925	Withdrawal or withholding of any medical or surgical intervention which utilizes mechanical or other artificial means including artificially provided nutrition and hydration to sustain, restore, or supplant a vital function which would serve only to artificially prolong life; does not include administration of medication to alleviate pain	Any adult; signed by declarant; presence of 2 witnesses not declarant's relative or physician; sample form at 70.122.030
WEST VIRGINIA	West Virginia Health Care Decisions Act: 16-30-1 to 16-30-25	Any medical procedure or intervention which should serve solely to artificially prolong the dying process or maintain the person in a persistent vegetative state; does not include medication or other medical procedure necessary for comfort or to alleviate pain	Competent adult; in writing; executed by declarant or at his direction; dated; in presence of 2 witnesses at least 18; in front of public notary; sample form at 16-30-4
WISCONSIN	154.01 to 154.15	Any medical procedure or intervention that would serve to prolong the dying process but not avert death; includes assistance in respiration, artificial maintenance of blood pressure and heart rate, blood transfusion, kidney dialysis, and similar procedures but does not include pain alleviation or provision of nutrition or hydration	18 yrs. and of sound mind; signed; in presence of 2 witnesses not related to declarant or health care provider; notify physician; no effect during pregnancy; may file with register in probate; sample form at 154.03
WYOMING	Wyoming Health Care Decisions Act: 35-22-401 to 35-22-416		Adult or emancipated minor; oral or written; signed and dated; in presence of 2 or more adult witnesses not related to declarant; no effect during course of qualified patient's pregnancy; terminal condition must be certified in writing by 2 physicians

Revocation/Duration	Reciprocity	Transfer of Patient if Physician Unwilling	Immunity for Attending Physician
Revocable at any time by (1) signed, dated writing; (2) physical cancellation or destruction of declaration; (3) oral expression of intent to revoke. Effective upon communication to attending physician	Directive executed in another state valid if in compliance with Virginia law or law of state where executed. Such directives shall be construed in accordance with Virginia laws.	If physician thinks treatment is medically or ethically inappropriate or contrary to terms of advanced directive, unwilling physician shall make reasonable effort to transfer patient to another physician.	No civil, criminal, or professional liability if acting in good faith.
Revocable at any time without regard to declarer's mental state or competency by defacing or destroying document; written revocation signed and dated and communicated to attending physician; oral revocation to physician by declarant or one acting on behalf of declarant	Valid to the extent permitted by Washington law and federal constitution law	Attending physician must inform patient or agent of any policy that would preclude the honoring of patient's directive; if patient chooses to retain that physician, a written plan is filed showing physician's intended actions should directive become operative	No civil, criminal, or professional liability if acting in good faith unless otherwise negligent
Revocable at any time without regard to declarant's mental state by destruction of document; written revocation effective on delivery; verbal expression in presence of a witness; desires of capable declarant always supersede effect of living will	Valid in West Virginia if executed in compliance with West Virginia law or the law of state where executed	Unwilling physician must effect a transfer to physician willing to honor the living will	No criminal or civil liability if acting in good faith and pursuant to reasonable medical standards
Revocable at any time by destruction of document, written revocation signed and dated, or verbal expression of revocation effective upon notifying physician; desires of qualified patient supersede declaration at all times	Declarations made in other states valid to the extent consistent with the laws of this state	Must make good faith effort to transfer	No criminal, civil, or professional liability when acting in good faith
An individual may revoke a directive at any time and in any manner that communicates an intention to revoke; oral revocations shall as soon as possible be documented in a writing signed and dated by the individual or a witness	Document uniformly applied and construed among states enacting Uniform Health-Care Decisions Act	Unwilling physician must inform the patient, provide continuing care, and immediately make all reasonable efforts to assist in the transfer of the patient	No criminal or civil liability or discipline by a licensing board for unprofessional conduct acting in good faith and pursuant to reasonable medical standards

50. STALKING

Stalking is a relatively new crime now on the books in every state. It is generally defined as the intentional, repeated following of a person for the purpose of harassing the person with express or implied threats of violence or death. The definitions vary only slightly from state to state, with some states adding things like lying in wait, surveillance or warnings from police officers. Stalking statutes have become very important legal devices that, with protective orders, can help shield people from the threatening or harassing behavior of others in a variety of circumstances.

Most notably, celebrities have been the victims of stalking activity, when fans become obsessed with the object of their attention. Stalking may also occur when a jilted lover becomes obsessed with his or her ex-lover or spouse, or even when a person becomes obsessed with a complete stranger or co-worker. The crime can turn everyday life into a nightmare for the victim of this crime. Consequently states have been quick to enact laws that specifically protect victims from harassing or stalking activity, even if the victim has not yet actually been physically injured by the defendant.

Several states have particular requirements in order for enhanced penalties to apply. The enhanced stalking crimes are usually distinguished by their designations as either first and second degree, or felony and misdemeanor stalking. Most often, enhancements are if the victim is below a certain age, or if the defendant has violated a court order or protective order, or if a deadly weapon was used.

Certain notorious cases have given rise in some states to specific legislation aimed at protecting particular persons. This may be the case in Illinois and New Jersey, each of which have provisions that state that incarcerated persons in penal institutions who transmit threats are not barred from prosecution under their stalking legislation.

Minnesota has a very broad stalker statute that exemplifies the variety of situations in which the law is used. Under this law, a person can be found guilty of stalking by harassment, or by intent to injure person, property or rights of another. A stalker may stalk using telephone calls, letters, telegraphs, delivery of packages or engaging in any conduct which interferes or intrudes on another's privacy or liberty. These acts are considered "gross misdemeanors." They are various situations where the crime of stalking in Minnesota is increased to a felony if the harassing activity is based on race, color, religion, sex, sexual orientation, disability or national origin, if stalking is accomplished by falsely impersonating another or using a dangerous weapon, if the victim is under 18 or if stalker is more than 36 months older than the victim. Although Minnesota's state is unusual in terms of the breadth and detailed listing of activities covered, nearly every element contained in it can be found in some form in the provisions of some other state. A few states have added to the stalker's penalties liability for the victim's counseling for emotional trauma caused by the stress of the stalking experience.

Four states have amended their stalking laws to include cyberstalking. First enact about ten years ago by Illinois and Florida, only two states, Rhode Island and Louisiana, have added it to their statutes. With the recent attention to "cyber-bullying" it is likely that there will soon be more provisions that protect people from cyberstalkers and bullies.

Table 50: Stalking

State	Code Section	Defined As
ALABAMA	13A-6-90 to 13A-6-94	Stalking 2nd degree: intentional and repeated following, harassing, telephoning or initiating communication with another, member of other's immediate family or acquaintance, causing material harm to mental or emotional health of person or causing fear of threat to employment, business, or career, after having been informed to cease such conduct; Stalking 1st degree: intentional and repeated following or harassing of another with threat with intent to place person in reasonable fear of death or serious bodily harm; Aggravated stalking 2nd degree: stalking 2nd degree in violation of court order or injunction; Aggravated stalking 1st degree: stalking 1st degree in violation of any court order or injunction
ALASKA	11.41.260; 11.41.270	Stalking 2nd degree: knowingly engaging in course of conduct that recklessly places another person in fear of death or physical injury of self or family member; Stalking 1st degree: Stalking and in violation of order, probation, release before trial, release after conviction, or parole; victim is under 16; in possession of deadly weapon; previous stalking conviction in any jurisdiction; previous conviction of certain other crimes involving same victim
ARIZONA	13-2923	Intentionally or knowingly engaging in course of conduct that is directed toward another and causes fear of personal safety or death of self or immediate family
ARKANSAS	5-71-229; 5-13-301; 5-13-310	Stalking 3rd degree: knowingly committing act that would cause reasonable person emotional distress and fear for safety of self or third person; Stalking 2nd degree: knowingly harassing another and making terroristic threat with intent to place person in imminent fear of death or serious bodily injury to self or immediate family; Stalking 1st degree: stalking 3rd degree and in violation of court order; previous stalking or certain other convictions in any jurisdiction within past 10 yrs.; armed or representing to be armed with deadly weapon
CALIFORNIA	Penal § 646.9	Willful, malicious, and repeated following and harassment of another and credible threat with intent to place person in reasonable fear for own safety or safety of immediate family
COLORADO	18-3-602	Knowingly making credible threat to another and repeatedly following, approaching, contacting or placing under surveillance that person, member of immediate family or someone with whom person has continuing relationship; making credible threat to another and repeatedly communicating with person or listed others, regardless of whether conversation ensues; or repeatedly following, approaching, contacting, placing under surveillance or making any form of communication with person or listed others in a manner that would cause reasonable person to suffer serious emotional distress and does cause such distress

Punishment/Classification	Repeat Offense	Arrest or Restraining Order Specifically Authorized by Statute?	Constitutionally Protected Activities Exempted?
Stalking 2nd degree: class B misdemeanor; Stalking 1st degree: class C felony; Aggravated stalking 2nd degree: class C misdemeanor; Aggravated stalking 1st degree: class B felony			Yes
Stalking 2nd degree: class A misdemeanor; Stalking 1st degree: class C felony	Stalking 1st degree: class C felony		
Class 5 felony; if fear of death: class 3 felony			Yes
Stalking 3rd degree: class A misdemeanor; Stalking 2nd degree: class D felony; Stalking 1st degree: class C felony	Stalking 1st degree if previous 2nd deg. stalking conviction within past 10 yrs.; terroristic threatening; terroristic act; stalking or threats against another person's safety in any other jurisdiction	No contact order to remain in effect during pendency of any appeal of conviction	Yes
Imprisonment up to 1 yr. in county jail or state prison and/or fine up to $1,000; if probation granted or sentenced suspended, counseling required but imposition at court's discretion; if convicted of spouse or child abuse felony or violation of protection order or making terroristic threats: imprisonment up to 1 yr. in county jail and/or fine up to $1,000, or imprisonment for 2, 3, or 5 yrs. in state prison; if in violation of temporary restraining order, injunction or court order: imprisonment in state prison for 2, 3, or 4 yrs.	Second/subsequent violation: imprisonment in state prison for 2, 3 or 5 yrs.	Yes, valid up to 10 yrs.	Constitutionally protected activity is not included within the meaning of "course of conduct"; conduct during labor picketing is also exempt
Class 5 felony; class 4 felony if in violation of restraining or any other court order	Second or subsequent offense: class 4 felony if within 7 yrs. of prior conviction		No

Table 50: Stalking—Continued

State	Code Section	Defined As
CONNECTICUT	53a-181c to 53a-181e	Stalking 3rd Degree: recklessly causing another person to reasonably physical safety by wilfully and repeatedly following or lying in wait for such other person; Stalking 2nd Degree: knowingly engaging in course of conduct directed at another that would cause reasonable person to fear for physical safety or the physical safety of a third person; intentionally, and for no legitimate purpose, engaging in a course of conduct directed at another that would cause reasonable person to fear that employment, business or career is threatened, by telephoning, appearing at or initiating communication at the person's place of employment or business; Stalking 1st Degree: stalking in 2nd degree and previous 2nd degree stalking conviction; in violation of court order; victim is under 16
DELAWARE	Tit. 11, § 1312	Knowingly engaging in course of conduct directed at another that would cause a reasonable person to fear physical injury to self or another person or suffer other significant mental anguish or distress that may, but does not necessarily, require medical or other professional treatment or counseling
DISTRICT OF COLUMBIA	22-3131 to 22-3135	Intentionally engaging in course of conduct directed at another that person knew or should have known would cause victim to fear for his or her safety or the safety of another person, feel seriously alarmed, disturbed, or frightened, or suffer emotional distress
FLORIDA	784.048	Stalking: willful, malicious, and repeated following or harassing of another person; Aggravated stalking: willful, malicious, and repeated following, cyberstalking, or harassing of another person: with credible threats with the intent to place person in reasonable fear of death or bodily injury; who is a minor under 16; after injunction for protection or any court-imposed prohibition of conduct toward the person or the person's property

Punishment/Classification	Repeat Offense	Arrest or Restraining Order Specifically Authorized by Statute?	Constitutionally Protected Activities Exempted?
Stalking 3rd degree: class B misdemeanor; Stalking 2nd degree: class A misdemeanor; Stalking 1st degree: class D felony	Stalking 1st degree: class D felony		Yes
Stalking: class G felony; Stalking and: 21 or older and the victim is under 14; in violation of any order prohibiting contact with the victim; victim is 62 or older; course of conduct includes threat of death or serious physical injury to victim or another person; or person causes physical injury to the victim: Class F felony; if course of conduct includes any act or acts previously prohibited by a then-existing court order or sentence: imprisonment min. 6 mos., first 6 mos. not subject to suspension; Stalking and: possession of deadly weapon; person causes serious physical injury to victim: class C felony	If within 5 yrs. of prior stalking conviction: imprisonment min. 1 yr., first yr. not subject to suspension.	No	No; lawful picketing is an affirmative defense; § 1312 does not apply to conduct that occurs in furtherance of law enforcement activities or to private investigators, security officers or private detectives
Imprisonment up to 12 mos. and/or fine up to $2,500; imprisonment up to 5 yrs. and/or fine up to $12,500 if any of the following: order prohibiting contact was in effect; prior stalking conviction in any jurisdiction within previous 10 yrs.; at time of event, person was at least 4 yrs. older than victim, and victim was less than 18; person caused more than $2,500 in financial injury	Imprisonment up to 5 yrs. and/or fine up to $12,500 if prior conviction for stalking in any jurisdiction within previous 10 yrs.; imprisonment up to 10 yrs. and/or fine up to $25,000 if 2 or more convictions in any jurisdiction for stalking any person, at least one of which was for a jury demandable offense		Yes
Stalking: 1st degree misdemeanor punishable by imprisonment up to 1 yr. and/or fine up to $1,000; Aggravated stalking: 3rd degree felony punishable by imprisonment up to 5 yrs. and/or fine up to $5,000; other penalties may apply; See §§ 775.082 to 775.084		Arrest without warrant if probable cause to believe statute is violated; court may issue restraining order valid up to 10 yrs. as part of sentencing	Yes; includes picketing and organized protests

Table 50: Stalking—Continued

State	Code Section	Defined As
GEORGIA	16-5-90 to 16-5-96	Stalking: following, placing under surveillance or contacting another person without consent for the purpose of harassing and intimidating the other person; knowingly broadcasting or publishing the picture, name, address, or phone number of a person in violation of a court order, condition of pretrial release, probation, or parole without consent of that person and in a manner that causes third persons to harass or intimidate the person; Aggravated stalking; stalking in violation of a court order, condition of pretrial release, probation, or parole
HAWAII	711.1106.4; 711.1106.5	Harassment by stalking: pursuit, surveillance, or nonconsensual contact of another person with intent to harass, annoy, or alarm, or in reckless disregard of risk thereof on more than one occasion without legitimate purpose; Aggravated harassment by stalking: harassment by stalking and previous stalking conviction within the past 5 yrs.
IDAHO	18-7901 to 18-7906	Stalking 2nd degree: knowingly and maliciously engaging in course of conduct that seriously alarms, annoys or harasses another in a manner to cause a reasonable person substantial emotional distress or fear of death or physical injury to self or family or household member; Stalking 1st degree: stalking in violation of restraining or other court order or injunction, parole or probation; victim is under 16; possession of deadly weapon; previous stalking conviction with past 7 yrs.; previous conviction of certain crimes involving the victim within past 7 yrs.
ILLINOIS	Ch. 720 §§ 5/12-7.3 to 5/12-7.5	Stalking: knowing engagement in course of conduct to cause reasonable person to fear for safety of self or third person or suffer emotional distress; knowing and unlawfully unjustified following or surveillance of another on at least 2 separate occasions and with threat of imminent or future harm to person or family member or creates reasonable apprehension of such harm; Aggravated stalking: stalking and causing bodily harm to, confining or restraining victim; in violation of restraining or other court order; person is required to register under Sex Offender Registration Act and stalking is of same victim or family member that prompted registration; Cyberstalking: stalking through the use of electronic communication; incarceration of the person who commits a course of conduct or threat described in this act is not a bar to prosecution
INDIANA	35-45-10-1 to 35-45-10-5	Knowing or intentional conduct with repeated or continuing harassment of another that would cause reasonable person to feel terrorized, frightened or threatened and that actually causes such feelings
IOWA	708.11	Purposefully engages in course of conduct that would cause reasonable person to fear bodily injury or death to himself or immediate family; perpetrator knows or should have known that person would be fearful and course of conduct actually induces fear

Punishment/Classification	Repeat Offense	Arrest or Restraining Order Specifically Authorized by Statute?	Constitutionally Protected Activities Exempted?
Stalking: misdemeanor; Aggravated stalking: felony, punishable by imprisonment 1 to 10 yrs. and fine up to $10,000	Felony: imprisonment 1 to 10 yrs.	Yes; restraining order issued upon filing of petition setting forth probable cause; at time of sentencing, the judge is authorized to issue permanent restraining order against offender to protect the person stalked and the members of person's immediate family	Yes
Harassment by stalking: misdemeanor; Aggravated harassment by stalking: class C felony	Aggravated harassment by stalking: class C felony		
Stalking 2nd degree: imprisonment in county jail up to 1 yr. and/or fine $1,000; Stalking 1st degree: felony punishable by 1 to 5 yrs. imprisonment in state prison and/or fine up to $10,000	Stalking 1st degree		Yes
Stalking: class 4 felony; Aggravated stalking: class 3 felony; Cyberstalking: class 4 felony	Stalking: class 3 felony; Aggravated stalking: class 2 felony; Cyberstalking: class 3 felony		Picketing or exercise of the right of free speech or assembly that is otherwise lawful
Level 6 felony; Level 5 felony if person stalks and makes threat with intent to place victim in reasonable fear; in violation of court order, pretrial release, probation, or parole in any jurisdiction; if criminal complaint of stalking same victim is pending in court; Level 4 felony if use of deadly weapon or previous conviction against same victim	Level 4 felony		Yes
Aggravated misdemeanor; Class D felony if dangerous weapon; in violation of protective or other court order; victim under 18	2nd offense: class D felony; 3rd or subsequent offense: class C felony	Court shall issue arrest warrant upon filing of complaint and finding of probable cause	

Table 50: Stalking—Continued

State	Code Section	Defined As
KANSAS	21-5427	Stalking 1: recklessly engaging in course of conduct targeted at specific person to cause reasonable person to fear for safety of self, immediate family and is actually placed in fear; Stalking 2: engaging in such course of conduct targeted at specific person knowing it will place that person in fear for safety of self or immediate family; Stalking 3: recklessly engaging in such course of conduct in violation of protective order
KENTUCKY	508.130 to 508.155	Stalking: intentional course of conduct directed at specific person that seriously annoys, intimidates, or harasses and which serves no legitimate purpose and would cause person to suffer substantial mental distress; Stalking 2nd degree: stalking with explicit or implicit threat made with intent to place person in fear of sexual contact, injury, or death; Stalking 1st degree: stalking 2nd degree and in violation of protective order for same victim; pending criminal complaint by same person; convicted in previous 5 yrs. of felony or class A misdemeanor against same person; in possession of deadly weapon
LOUISIANA	14:40.2; 14:40.3	Stalking: intentional and repeated following or harassing that would cause a reasonable person to feel alarmed or to suffer emotional distress; Cyberstalking: use in email or other electronic communication of words or language threatening bodily harm of or injury to property of person or family, or for extortion; repeatedly threaten, terrify, or harass person through email or other electronic communication; knowingly make false statement by email or other electronic communication regarding death, injury, illness, disfigurement, or indecent or criminal conduct of a person or person's family with intent to threaten, terrify, or harass
MAINE	Tit. 17-A, § 210-A	Intentionally or knowingly engaging in a course of conduct directed at a specific person that would cause a reasonable person to suffer serious inconvenience or emotional distress, fear bodily injury or death to self or close relation, fear damage or destruction to or tampering with property, or fear injury to or death of an animal owned by or in the possession and control of that person
MARYLAND	Crim. Law §§ 3-802; 3-805	Malicious course of conduct including approaching or pursuing another with intent to place in reasonable fear of serious bodily injury, assault, rape, attempted rape or sexual offense, false imprisonment or death
MASSACHUSETTS	Ch. 265, § 43	Wilfully and maliciously engage in conduct which seriously alarms or annoys specific person and would cause reasonable person to suffer substantial emotional distress; make threat with intent to place person in fear of death or bodily injury

Punishment/Classification	Repeat Offense	Arrest or Restraining Order Specifically Authorized by Statute?	Constitutionally Protected Activities Exempted?
Stalking 1: class A person misdemeanor; Stalking 2: class A person misdemeanor; Stalking 3: severity level 9, person felony	2nd or subsequent conviction: Stalking 1: severity level 7, person felony; Stalking 2: severity level 5, person felony; Stalking 3: severity level 5, person felony		Yes
Stalking 2nd degree: class A misdemeanor; Stalking 1st degree: class D felony	Class D felony	Restraining order valid up to 10 yrs. upon conviction	Yes
Stalking: imprisonment 30 days to 1 yr. and fine $500 to $1,000; if victim under 18: imprisonment 2 to 5 yrs. and/or fine $1,000 to $2,000; if in possession of dangerous weapon or found to have placed victim in reasonable fear of death or injury: imprisonment 1 to 5 yrs. and/or $1,000 fine; if victim under 18: imprisonment 2 to 5 yrs. and/or fine $1,000 to $2,000; if in violation of protective or other court order: imprisonment 90 days to 2 yrs. and/or fine up to $5,000; Cyberstalking: imprisonment up to 1 yr. and/or fine up to $2,000	Stalking: 2nd offense within 7 yrs.: imprisonment 5 to 20 yrs. and/or fine up to $5,000; 3rd or subsequent offense: imprisonment 10 to 40 yrs. and/or fine up to $5,000; Cyberstalking: 2nd offense within 7 yrs.: imprisonment 180 days to 3 yrs. and/or fine up to $5,000; 3rd or subsequent offense within 7 yrs.: imprisonment 2 to 5 yrs. and or fine up to $5,000	Protective order may be granted, can be for indefinite period or for specified period up to 18 mos., 40.21(F)	Yes
Class D crime	If 2 or more prior convictions in any jurisdiction: class C crime		Yes
Misdemeanor: imprisonment up to 5 yrs. and/or fine up to $5,000; if conduct is through electronic mail: imprisonment up to 1 yr. and/or fine up to $500		Police officer may arrest without warrant with probable cause with evidence and reason to believe victim is in imminent danger of bodily harm or death, § 2-205	Yes
Imprisonment up to 5 yrs. in state prison or up to 2.5 yrs. in house of correction and/or fine up to $1,000; in violation of court order: imprisonment 1 to 5 yrs.	Imprisonment 2 to 10 yrs.		

Table 50: Stalking—Continued

State	Code Section	Defined As
MICHIGAN	750.411h; 750.411i; 600.2954	Stalking: willful course of conduct involving repeated or continuing harassment that would cause reasonable person to feel terrorized, frightened, intimidated, threatened, harassed, or molested and that actually causes victim to feel such; Aggravated stalking: stalking in violation of restraining order or injunction; violation of probation, pretrial release or bond release; course of conduct includes 1 or more credible threats against victim, victim's family or an individual living with victim; individual previously convicted of stalking.

Punishment/Classification	Repeat Offense	Arrest or Restraining Order Specifically Authorized by Statute?	Constitutionally Protected Activities Exempted?
Stalking: misdemeanor punishable by imprisonment up to 1 yr. and/or fine up to $1,000; if victim is under 18 and stalker is 5 yrs. older: felony punishable by imprisonment up to 5 yrs. and/or fine up to $10,000; court may order probation up to 5 yrs.; Aggravated stalking: felony punishable by imprisonment up to 5 yrs. and/or fine up to $10,000; if victim is under 18 and stalker is 5 yrs. older: imprisonment up to 10 yrs. and/or fine up to $15,000; court may order probation of at least 5 yrs.; victim may maintain civil action against individual who engages in conduct prohibited under § 411h or 411i of the Michigan penal code for damages incurred by victim as a result of that conduct; victim may also seek and be awarded exemplary damages, costs of action, and reasonable attorney fees in an action brought under this section; civil action may be brought regardless of whether individual who is alleged to have engaged in prohibited conduct has been charged or convicted for the alleged violation	Previous conviction: aggravated stalking		Yes

Table 50: Stalking—Continued

State	Code Section	Defined As
MINNESOTA	609.749	Conduct which the actor knows or has reason to know would cause the victim under the circumstances to feel frightened, threatened, oppressed, persecuted, or intimidated, and causes this reaction
MISSISSIPPI	97-3-107	Stalking: knowing, purposeful following, confronting, contacting by telephone, mail or electronic communication, or making credible threat against another that would cause a reasonable person to fear for safety of self or another or fear damage to property; Aggravated stalking: stalking involving use or display of deadly weapon; any prior stalking conviction in any jurisdiction within past 7 yrs.; registered sex offender and victim under 18

Punishment/Classification	Repeat Offense	Arrest or Restraining Order Specifically Authorized by Statute?	Constitutionally Protected Activities Exempted?
Intent to injure person, property, or rights of another by commission of unlawful act; follows, monitors, or pursues another, in person or through technological or other means; returns to property of another without consent; repeatedly makes phone calls or sends text messages; makes or causes the victim's telephone repeatedly or continuously to ring; repeatedly mails or delivers by any means, letters, telegrams, messages, packages, or other objects; knowingly makes false allegations against peace officer concerning the officer's performance of official duties with intent to influence or tamper with such performance: gross misdemeanor; if based on race, color, religion, sex, sexual orientation, disability, or national origin; falsely impersonating another or with a dangerous weapon; intent to influence or tamper with juror or judicial proceeding to retaliate against judicial officer or attorney; victim is under 18 and actor is more than 36 mos. older: felony, punishable by imprisonment up to 5 yrs. and/or fine up to $10,000; if victim is under 18 and actor is more than 36 mos. older and act is committed with sexual or aggressive intent: felony, punishable by imprisonment up to 10 yrs. and/or fine up to $20,000; extensive regulations regarding possession of firearms after stalking conviction	2nd stalking conviction within 10 yrs. of certain prior domestic violence convictions: felony, punishable by imprisonment up to 5 yrs. and/or fine up to $10,000; Subsequent convictions: felony, punishable by imprisonment up to 10 yrs. and/or fine up to $20,000 if stalking conviction is within 10 yrs. of first of 2 or more certain prior domestic violence convictions; Pattern of stalking conduct: felony, punishable by imprisonment up to 10 yrs. and/or fine up to $20,000	Peace officer may arrest without warrant except in case of false allegations against a peace officer concerning the officer's performance of official duties with intent to influence or tamper with the officer's performance of official duties	Yes, including speech, handbilling, and picketing
Stalking: county jail up to 1 yr. and/or fine up to $1,000; if in violation of restraining or other court order: county jail up to 1 yr. and fine up to $1,500; Aggravated stalking: imprisonment up to 5 yrs. and fine up to $3,000; if at time of offense, perpetrator required to register as sex offender and victim under 18: imprisonment up to 6 yrs. and $4,000 fine	Aggravated stalking: imprisonment up to 5 yrs. and fine up to $3,000	Upon conviction, court shall consider order prohibiting contact with victim	Yes

Table 50: Stalking—Continued

State	Code Section	Defined As
MISSOURI	Stalking: 565.225 to 565.240; Domestic Abuse: 455.010; 455.020; 455.035	Stalking 2nd degree: purposely disturbs or follow with the intent to disturb another person; disturbs: engage in a course of conduct directed at a specific person that serves no legitimate purpose and that would cause a reasonable person under the circumstances to be frightened, intimidated, or emotionally distressed; Stalking 1st degree: purposely disturbs or follows with the intent of disturbing another person and makes threat communicated with intent to cause target to reasonably fear for own safety or that of family, household member, or domestic animals or livestock kept at person's residence or property; in violation of protection order; in violation of probation, parole, pretrial release, or release on bond pending appeal; previously found guilty of domestic assault, violation of protection order, or any other crime where person was victim; knowingly accessing or attempting to access address of victim if victim is participant of address confidentiality program under 589.660 to 589.681; Unlawful posting of certain information over the internet: knowingly post on the internet the name, home address, Social Security number, or telephone number of any person with intent to cause great bodily harm or death or threaten to cause great bodily harm or death to such person
MONTANA	45-5-220	Purposely or knowingly causing another substantial emotional distress or reasonable apprehension of bodily injury or death by repeatedly following the person or harassing, threatening, or intimidating him or her in person or by mail, electronic communication or any other method
NEBRASKA	28-311.02 to 28-311.05	Stalking: willfully harass with intent to injure, terrify, threaten, or intimidate; Harass: engage in knowing and willful course of conduct directed at specific person which seriously terrifies, threatens, or intimidates the person and serves no legitimate purpose
NEVADA	200.575 to 200.601	Willful or malicious conduct that causes reasonable person to feel terrorized, frightened, intimidated, or harassed and actually causes victim to feel such
NEW HAMPSHIRE	633:3-A	Purposely, knowingly, or recklessly engage in course of conduct targeted at specific person which would cause reasonable person to fear for safety or safety of family; violate protective order

Punishment/Classification	Repeat Offense	Arrest or Restraining Order Specifically Authorized by Statute?	Constitutionally Protected Activities Exempted?
Stalking 2nd degree: class A misdemeanor; if previous conviction victim is targeted because he or she is relative within 2nd degree of consanguinity to law enforcement officer: class D felony: class E felony; Stalking 1st degree: class E felony; if previous conviction or victim is targeted because he or she is relative within 2nd degree of consanguinity to law enforcement officer: class D felony; Unlawful posting of certain information over the internet: class C misdemeanor	Stalking 2nd degree: class E felony if previous stalking conviction in any jurisdiction; Stalking 1st degree: class D felony if previous stalking conviction in any jurisdiction	Arrest without warrant allowed if probable cause to believe statute is violated; Domestic cases: judge may issue restraining order issued victim filing petition	Yes, including picketing or other organized protests
Imprisonment in county jail up to 1 yr. and/or fine up to $1,000; if in violation of restraining order: imprisonment in state prison up to 5 yrs. and/or fine up to $10,000; may be sentenced to pay all medical, counseling, and other costs of victim	Imprisonment in state prison up to 5 yrs. and/or fine up to $10,000	Restraining order issued upon presentation of credible evidence	Yes
Class I misdemeanor; if in possession of deadly weapon; victim under 16; previous conviction within past 7 yrs.: class IIIA felony	If prior conviction against same victim within past 7 years: class IIIA felony		Labor picketing
Stalking: misdemeanor; Aggravated stalking: stalking with threats of death or bodily harm: category B felony, punishable by imprisonment 2-15 yrs. and fine up to $5,000; if stalking with use of internet or network site, email, text messaging, or any other similar means to publish, display, or distribute information in manner substantially increasing risk of harm or violence: category C felony, punishable by imprisonment 1-5 yrs. and fine up to $10,000	Stalking subsequent offense: gross misdemeanor	Restraining order issued upon filing of petition	Yes, including picketing; activities of reporters, photographers, and cameramen; free speech and assembly
Class A misdemeanor	If 2nd or subsequent within 7 years: class B felony	May arrest without warrant if has probable cause to believe suspect's acts violate statute within 6 hours; restraining order issued upon filing of petition and proof by preponderance	Yes

Table 50: Stalking—Continued

State	Code Section	Defined As
NEW JERSEY	2C:12-10 to 2C:12-10.2	Purposeful conduct directed at specific person that would cause a reasonable person to fear bodily injury or death to himself or family member and knowingly, recklessly, or negligently places person in reasonable fear of bodily injury or death to himself or family member
NEW MEXICO	30-3A-3 to 30-3A-4	Stalking: knowingly pursuing pattern of conduct that would cause reasonable person to feel frightened, intimidated, or threatened; stalker must intend to cause reasonable apprehension; stalker must follow, surveil, or harass; Aggravated stalking: stalking when it violates restraining order; while possessing a deadly weapon; victim under 16
NEW YORK	Penal §§ 120.45 to 120.60; 240.26; 240.31	Stalking in 4th degree: intentionally and with no legitimate purpose engage in conduct that s/he knows or should reasonably know: will cause reasonable fear of material harm to victim or member of victim's immediate family or causes material harm to mental or emotional health of victim or member of victim's immediate family or causes a reasonable fear that victim's employment or business is threatened; Stalking 3rd degree: stalking 4th degree and 3 or more victims involved or victim has reasonable fear of physical harm or serious bodily injury; Stalking 2nd degree: stalking 3rd degree when a weapon is involved in commission; 2nd conviction within 5 yrs.; victim is 14 or under and actor is 21 or older; Stalking 1st degree: Stalking 3rd or 2nd degree with intentional or reckless physical harm to victim
NORTH CAROLINA	14-196.3; 14-277.3A	Willfully on more than 1 occasion follow or harass without legal purpose and with intent to place victim in reasonable fear of safety of self or family or cause victim to suffer emotional distress by placing victim in fear of death or bodily harm
NORTH DAKOTA	12.1-17-07.1	Intentional conduct directed at specific person that frightens, intimidates, or harasses and serves no legitimate purpose towards a person or person's immediate family; unauthorized tracking or person's movements or location through GPS or other electronic means that would cause reasonable person to be frightened, intimidated, or harassed and serves no legitimate purpose
OHIO	2903.211 to 2903.215	Knowingly causing another fear of physical harm or mental distress
OKLAHOMA	Tit. 21, §§ 1172; 1173	Wilfully, maliciously, and repeatedly follow or harass another in a manner that would cause reasonable person or member of immediate family to feel frightened, intimidated, threatened, harassed, or molested and actually causes person or family member to feel such
OREGON	163.730 to 163.755	Knowingly alarm or coerce another person or person's family member/household by engaging in repeated and unwanted contact that causes victim(s) reasonable apprehension regarding personal safety

Punishment/Classification	Repeat Offense	Arrest or Restraining Order Specifically Authorized by Statute?	Constitutionally Protected Activities Exempted?
Crime of the 4th degree; If court order prohibiting the behavior; if in violation of order prohibiting the behavior or while imprisoned or on parole or probation as result of conviction for any indictable offense in any jurisdiction: crime of the 3rd degree	2nd or subsequent against same victim: crime of the 3rd degree	Stalking conviction acts as application for permanent restraining order	Organized group picketing
Stalking: misdemeanor; must also complete professional counseling; Aggravated stalking: 4th degree felony	2nd or subsequent conviction: 4th degree felony; must also complete professional counseling; Aggravated stalking: 3rd degree felony		Within scope of lawful employment or constitutionally protected activity
Stalking 4th degree: class B misdemeanor; Stalking 3rd degree: class A misdemeanor; Stalking 2nd degree: class E felony; Stalking 1st degree: class D felony	Subsequent conviction within past 10 yrs.: stalking 3rd degree; class A misdemeanor; Subsequent conviction within past 5 yrs.: stalking 2nd degree; class E felony		Yes; harassment does not apply to activities regulated by National Labor Relations Act, Railway Labor Act, or Federal Employment Labor Management Act
Stalking: class A1 misdemeanor; if in violation of court order: class H felony; if conduct is through electronic communication: class 2 misdemeanor	Class F felony		
Stalking: class A misdemeanor; if in violation of court order; previous conviction against same victim of assault, terrorizing, menacing, or harassment; previous stalking conviction: class C felony	Class C felony		Yes
Misdemeanor in 1st degree	Felony of 4th degree	Restraining order allowed	
Stalking: misdemeanor, punishable by imprisonment in county jail up to 1 yr. and/or fine up to $1,000; if in violation of court order, injunction, probation or parole conditions or previous violation within past 10 years: felony, punishable by imprisonment up to 5 yrs. and/or fine up to $2,500; if through use of electronic communications: misdemeanor	2nd offense within 10 yrs.: felony, punishable by imprisonment up to 5 yrs. and/or fine up to $2,500; subsequent offense within 10 yrs.: felony, punishable by imprisonment up to 10 yrs. and/or fine of at least $5,000; subsequent offense through use of electronic communications: felony		Yes
Class A misdemeanor; class C felony if perpetrator has prior conviction for stalking or violates court order	Class C felony	Restraining order may be issues upon citation for stalking	Conduct authorized or protected by labor laws exempt

Table 50: Stalking—Continued

State	Code Section	Defined As
PENNSYLVANIA	Tit. 18, § 2709.1	Course of conduct or repeated acts without authorization with intent to place person in reasonable fear or cause substantial emotional distress
RHODE ISLAND	11-52-4.2; 11-59-1; 11-59-2	Stalking: harassment or willful, malicious and repeated following with intent to place in reasonable fear; Cyberstalking: stalking by computer or other electronic device
SOUTH CAROLINA	16-3-1700 to 16-3-1840	Stalking: pattern of words or conduct that causes fear of death, assault, bodily injury, criminal sexual contact, kidnapping, or property damage to victim or victim's family member; Aggravated stalking: stalking accompanied by an act of violence
SOUTH DAKOTA	22-19A-1 to 22-19A-18	Willful, malicious and repeated following, harassing or making credible threats with intent of placing person in reasonable fear
TENNESSEE	39-17-315	Intentionally and repeatedly follow or harass in a manner that causes fear
TEXAS	Penal § 42.072	Knowingly engage in conduct on more than one occasion against specific person that stalker knows or reasonably believes victim will view as threatening; causes fear; would cause a reasonable person to fear
UTAH	76-5-106.5	Intentionally or knowingly cause a reasonable person to fear for self or a third person or to suffer emotional distress
VERMONT	Tit. 13, §§ 1061 to 1063	Stalking: intentionally follow, lie in wait, or harass and cause fear without legitimate purpose; Aggravated stalking: intentionally stalk in violation of court order; previous conviction of stalking or aggravated stalking; convicted of offense an element of which involves an act of violence against same person; victim under 16

Punishment/Classification	Repeat Offense	Arrest or Restraining Order Specifically Authorized by Statute?	Constitutionally Protected Activities Exempted?
Misdemeanor of the 1st degree; felony of the 3rd degree if previously convicted of crime of violence against victim, family or household member	Felony of the 3rd degree		Labor disputes or any constitutionally protected activity
Stalking: felony, punishable by imprisonment up to 5 yrs. and/or fine up to $10,000; Cyberstalking: misdemeanor, punishable by imprisonment up to 1 yr. an/or fine up to $500	Cyberstalking 2nd offense: felony punishable by imprisonment up to 2 yrs. and/or fine up to $6,000		Yes
Stalking: misdemeanor, punishable by imprisonment up to 1 yr. and/or fine up to $1,000 ; if in violation of injunction or order: imprisonment up to 2 yrs. and/or fine up to $2,000; Aggravated stalking: felony, punishable by imprisonment up to 5 yrs. and fine up to $5,000; if in violation of injunction or order: imprisonment up to 10 yrs. and/or fine up to $7,000; other criminal and civil remedies may be available	Stalking: subsequent offense within past 7 yrs.: felony, punishable by imprisonment up to 5 yrs. and/or fine up to $5,000; Aggravated stalking: subsequent offense within past 7 years: felony, punishable by imprisonment up to 15 yrs. and/or fine up to $10,000	Restraining order authorized; police may arrest someone for violating a restraining order without a warrant	Constitutionally protected activity is not included within the meaning of "course of conduct"
Class 1 misdemeanor; class 6 felony if in violation of protective order or injunction or victim 12 or under	Subsequent offense within past 10 yrs.: class 6 felony; within 7 years and against same victim and involving acts of violence or credible threat: class 5 felony	Restraining order issued upon filing petition	Yes
Class A misdemeanor	Subsequent offense within past 7 years: class E felony; if within past 7 yrs. against same victim: class C felony		Following another during course of a lawful business activity
3rd degree felony	2nd degree felony		
Stalking: class A misdemeanor; if previous conviction of stalking; conviction in another jurisdiction to an offense similar to stalking; convicted of felony offense in which victim or victim's family was victim: 3rd degree felony; if used deadly weapon or other means of force; previously convicted 2 or more times of stalking or offenses similar to stalking in another jurisdiction; convicted 2 or more times of felonies in which victim was also a victim of felonies: 2nd degree felony	2nd and subsequent offenses: 3rd degree felony	Conviction for stalking acts as application for permanent restraining order	
Stalking: imprisonment up to 2 yrs. and/or fine up to $5,000; Aggravated stalking: imprisonment up to 5 yrs. and/or fine up to $25,000	Aggravated stalking: imprisonment up to 5 yrs. and/or fine up to $25,000		Constitutionally protected activity not included within the meaning of "course of conduct"

Table 50: Stalking—Continued

State	Code Section	Defined As
VIRGINIA	18.2-60.3	Intent or knowledge that repeated acts cause reasonable fear
WASHINGTON	9A.46.110	Intentionally and repeatedly harassing or following another person in manner that would cause reasonable person to fear for safety of self or others and person feels such fear; actions must be without lawful authority and under circumstances not amounting to a felony attempt of another crime
WEST VIRGINIA	61-2-9a	Repeatedly follow another knowing or having reason to know that conduct causes person followed to reasonably fear for safety or to suffer significant emotional distress; repeatedly harass or make credible threats against another
WISCONSIN	940.32	Intentionally engage in course of conduct directed at specific person causes person to suffer serious emotional distress or fear of death or bodily injury to self or member of family or household and would cause same response in a reasonable person in same situation; actor knows or should know that at least one of these acts will cause this response
WYOMING	6-2-506	Intentionally engage in course of conduct reasonably likely to harass another person by communicating electronically or otherwise; following; surveilling; otherwise harassing; Harass: engage in course of conduct directed at person that defendant knew or should have known would cause reasonable person to suffer substantial emotional distress; fear for safety of self or another person; fear for destruction of property

Punishment/Classification	Repeat Offense	Arrest or Restraining Order Specifically Authorized by Statute?	Constitutionally Protected Activities Exempted?
Class 1 misdemeanor	Commission of 3rd offense within 5 yrs.: class 6 felony	Restraining order issued upon conviction	
Stalking: gross misdemeanor; subsequent conviction against same victim; in violation of protective order; armed with deadly weapon; victim public officer stalked in retaliation; victim witness stalked in retaliation: class B felony	Class B felony		
Misdemeanor: imprisonment in county or regional jail up to 6 mos. and/or fine up to $1,000; if in violation of court order: imprisonment in county jail 90 days to 1 yr. and/or $2,000 to $5,000 fine; if in violation of protective order for injunctive relief under 48-27-501: felony, punishable by imprisonment 1 to 5 yrs. and/or fine $3,000 to $10,000	Second or subsequent conviction within past 5 yrs.: felony, punishable by imprisonment 1 to 5 yrs. and/or fine $3,000 to $10,000; if also in violation of court order county jail for 6 months to 1 year and/or fine between $2,000 and $5,000	Upon conviction, court may issue restraining order for period not to exceed 10 yrs.	Any labor disputes or other activities protected by the Constitution
Stalking: class I felony; if information about victim is gathered electronically or victim is under 18: class H felony; if stalker uses weapon; act results in bodily injury to victim or family member; previous conviction in past 7 yrs.: Class F felony	Subsequent offense within past 7 yrs.: Class H felony		Freedom of speech and peaceable assembly
Stalking: misdemeanor, punishable by imprisonment up to 1 yr. and/or fine up to $750; if prior conviction within past 5 yrs.; serious bodily harm to victim or another person; in violation of probation, parole, or bail; in violation of protective order: Felony stalking, punishable by imprisonment up to 10 yrs.	Subsequent offense within 5 yrs. of completion of sentence, including all periods of incarceration, parole, and probation: Felony stalking, punishable by imprisonment up to 10 yrs.		Lawful demonstration, assembly or picketing

51. STATE LOTTERIES

State lotteries have become nearly ubiquitous as state government activity. Forty-three states permit lotteries. In virtually all states with lotteries, the stated purpose is to raise revenue. However, there is wide diversity in how the money raised is distributed. Most states (about 17) designate lottery profits for schools and education, about 13 states distribute profit to the general fund, or a fund for economic development, such as highway construction or in support of stadium authorities. A few states designate lottery revenues to fund various general environmental activities.

Many states apply the revenues to more than one purpose. A few states are quite unique. For example, Pennsylvania uses its revenue for programs designed to help the elderly with rent rebates and property tax assistance. Massachusetts uses its revenue in support of the arts. Washington uses substantial portions of its lottery revenue to raise money for sports stadium construction and operation.

A number of states have enacted provisions designed to help problem gamblers. Louisiana, for example, requires all lottery tickets to be printed with a toll-free gambler's assistance hotline phone number. At least four other states also have various provisions designed to assist problem gamblers.

One interesting provision in many state lottery laws provides for the garnishment of prizes to collect various debts, ranging from unpaid taxes to outstanding child support obligations. Usually, only prizes over a certain amount may be garnished. One state specifies that only prizes over $100 may be garnished, another sets the limit at $5,000. Texas permits garnishment of prizes won by persons who have defaulted on guaranteed student loans.

Interestingly, there are some unusual circumstances in various states. Maine, New Hampshire and Vermont each authorize two lotteries: their own and a Tri-State Lotto that is authorized under a tri-state compact. The proceeds are distributed equally among the three states. Finally, it is interesting to note that Nevada does not permit a state lottery. Perhaps this would be seen as competing with one of the state's major industries.

Overall, the matter of state lotteries is only one category, albeit a big one, of the laws relating to gambling. The law of gambling is a very complex and varied area of state regulation. Of late, gambling itself has been subject to many political pressures, both for and against legalization. Although gambling is not treated in this chapter, one interested in the subject may use statute citations provided to locate the general gambling laws for each state.

Table 51: State Lotteries

State	Code Section	Distribution of Revenue	Additional Purpose
ALABAMA	Prohibited: Ala. Const. art. IV, § 65		
ALASKA	05.15.100		Department of Revenue may license municipalities and organizations to conduct lotteries
ARIZONA	5-531 to 5-575	Up to 18.5% sale of lottery tickets and up to 35% from special instant games to state lottery fund for administrative and advertising expenses; 50% payment of prizes; rest to state lottery fund to be used as prescribed by 5-572	
ARKANSAS	Ark. Const. art. 19, § 14	Proceeds to be used to pay operating expenses of lotteries, including prizes, and to fund or provide for scholarships and grants to citizens of the state enrolled in public and private non-profit 2 and 4 year colleges and universities within the state that are certified according to criteria established by the General Assembly	
CALIFORNIA	Govt. §§ 8880 to 8880.72	50% prizes; 34% benefit public education; 16% expenses	For the preservation of the rights, liberties, and welfare of the people to benefit education without additional or increased taxes, money should supplement, not be substituted for, public education funds
COLORADO	24-35-201 to 24-35-222	Of net proceeds: 40% conservation trust fund with 10% going to Division of Parks and Outdoor Recreation for acquisition and development; 50% of total revenue for disbursements of prizes	Acquisition of state correctional facilities
CONNECTICUT	12-568a; 12-800 to 12-834	Of net proceeds, $1,900,000 goes to gamblers' rehabilitation programs	
DELAWARE	Tit. 29, §§ 4801 to 4855	At least 30% to the General Fund of the state from the "State Lottery Fund"; 45% payment of prizes; 20% administration and expenses	To produce the greatest income for the state; for "video lottery"—to provide nonstate supported assistance to the harness and thoroughbred racing industries
DISTRICT OF COLUMBIA	3-1301 to 3-1337	1st pay operation, administration and capital expenses (including payment of prizes); remainder to General Fund of District of Columbia as general purpose revenue funds Lottery and charitable games fund pays for operation	

Prize Subject to Garnishment	Time Limit to Claim Prize/ Disposition	Prohibited Related Activities
On prizes over $600, a set-off is allowed for any debts over $100 owed to the state, including overdue support	180 days/70% to state lottery prize fund and 30% to special advocate fund	Sale to minor; alteration of ticket; sale by unauthorized person; sale at unauthorized price; sale to person using public assistance voucher or EBT card to purchase
		Except as authorized, lotteries and sale of lottery tickets prohibited
	180 days; to benefit public purpose of education	Sales to minors; counterfeit/altered tickets
Offset for those who owe child support debt or arrearages up to full amount of prize	180 days	Sell ticket at greater price; unauthorized sale; sale to minor
		Forgery/counterfeiting tickets; sale to minors; sale of out-of-state lottery tickets; unlicensed sale; at greater price
	1 yr./State Lottery Fund	Sales to minors; at greater price; alteration/forgery
	180 days/General Fund of District of Columbia	Unauthorized sales; forged/counterfeited/altered tickets; sale to minor

Table 51: State Lotteries—Continued

State	Code Section	Distribution of Revenue	Additional Purpose
FLORIDA	FL Const. Art. 10 § 15; 24.101 to 24.124	Proceeds from the constitutionally mandated, Florida Education Lotteries shall be deposited in administrative Trust Fund; remaining revenue to pay administrative expenses of lottery department	To support improvements in public education and not as a substitute for educational funds
GEORGIA	50-27-1 to 50-27-104	45% prize money; 35% of net proceeds to go to Lottery for Education Account (with 10% as a scholarship shortfall reserve account)	To support improvements and enhancements for educational purposes and programs; funds used as supplement, not substitute
HAWAII	712-1220 to 712-1231 Gambling is prohibited		
IDAHO	67-7401 to 67-7452	45% prize expense; 15% administrative costs; 3½% advertising and promotional costs. Of the rest, annually on July 1: 3/8 of net income to permanent building account, 1/4 of net income to the bond levy equalization fund after reserving sufficient moneys to ensure the continuation of the lottery.	To benefit public purposes consonant with the public good
ILLINOIS	20 §§ 1605/1 to 1605/29	Set by department; all revenue to go to State Lottery Fund	To support the state's Common School Fund
INDIANA	4-30-1-1 to 4-30-19-4.2	Administrative trust fund for prizes and expenses; any surplus revenue (where roughly $30 million goes to state teachers' retirement fund and $7.5 million to pension relief fund with remaining surplus to the "Build Indiana Fund" for highway construction, job creation, economic development and state and local capital projects)	To enable the people of Indiana to benefit from significant money for capital improvements
IOWA	99G.1 to 99G.42		To support a variety of programs and services and provide continuing entertainment to the public
KANSAS	74-8701 to 74-8773; 79-4801 to 79-4806	30% lottery operating fund for expenses; 45% prizes; rest to state gaming revenues fund and state general fund for state economic development, correctional institution buildings, county reappraisal fund	
KENTUCKY	154A.010 to 154A.990; Ky. Const. § 226	35% general fund; rest for expenses and prizes	

Prize Subject to Garnishment	Time Limit to Claim Prize/ Disposition	Prohibited Related Activities
On prizes over $600; offset by outstanding obligation to any state agency or owing child support through a court	180 days/added to "pool from which future prizes are awarded or for special prize promotions"	Unlawful assignment/transfer; unauthorized sale as retailer; sale to minor; counterfeited/altered ticket; at greater price; extension offered to purchase ticket
On prizes over $5,000, set-off for all debts over $100 owed to any state agency including taxes, child support, and judgments or liens	180 days/up to $200,000 to Department of Human Resources to treat compulsive gambling disorders with the rest added to a pool for future prizes or special prize promotions	Sale only at set price by authorized retailer; sale to minors; stolen, forged, or counterfeited tickets
Subject to garnishment for unpaid taxes, child or spousal support; or public assistance benefits	180 days/added to future prize pools	Sales to minors; counterfeited, altered, or forged tickets
Withheld for past due support	Set by department/added to prize pool for special drawings	At greater price; to charge a fee to redeem a prize; from unlicensed sales agent; altering ticket; sale to minors
For prizes over $599, (1) if owes outstanding debt to state agency, (2) is on the department of state revenue's most recent tax warrant list; or (3) owes child support paid through a court [if multiple obligations, 1st to child support, 2nd to judgments owed, 3rd to tax liens, and 4th to unsecured debts owed by prize winner]	180 days/added to pool for future prizes or used for special prize promotions	Sale to minors; stolen/counterfeited/altered tickets; at different price; by unauthorized retailer or agent; sale on credit
Prizes over $600 subject to garnishment for claimant agencies	Period deemed appropriate by commissioner/added to future prize pools and given to holders of winning tickets or shares in addition to amounts already allocated	Sale at greater price; sale to minor (under 21); unauthorized sale; forged/altered ticket
	Within period established by rules and regulations/added to prize pools of subsequent lottery games	Forgery; unauthorized sale. Sale at greater price sale to minor (under 18)
Yes	180 days/ added to pool for future prizes or special prize promotions	Sale to minor; alter or forge tickets; attempt to win through fraud or deception or tampering with lottery equipment

Table 51: State Lotteries—Continued

State	Code Section	Distribution of Revenue	Additional Purpose
LOUISIANA	47:9000 to 47:9081	Corporate operating fund for expenses and prizes; with at least 35% to Lottery Proceeds Fund with $500,000 allocated to Compulsive and Problem Gaming Fund	"Enable the people of the state to benefit from the profits"; tickets must include toll-free phone number for mental health services for compulsive arrearages or problem gambling
MAINE	Tit. 8, §§ 371 to 389; "Tri-State Lotto" with New Hampshire and Vermont, Tit. 8, §§ 401 to 422	45% distributed as prizes; rest divided between expenses, General Fund, and Maine Outdoor Heritage Fund	
MARYLAND	State Gov't. §§ 9-101 to 9-125	Pro rata basis for prizes and administrative expenses; for other lotteries, into General Fund of the state	
MASSACHUSETTS	Ch. 10, §§ 22 to 35	45% payment of prizes; 15% administration and operating expenses; balance State Lottery Fund	Authorized to conduct lottery for the benefit of the arts; provide property tax relief and continue services at the local level
MICHIGAN	432.1 to 432.47	After payment of prizes (approximately 45%) and expenses, net revenue to state school aid fun	10% of yearly state lottery advertising budget not to exceed $1 million goes to compulsive gaming prevention fund
MINNESOTA	349A.01 to 349A.20	15% lottery operations; 2.75% advertising; 60% prizes; rest to lottery fund/special revenue fund with 40% of these net proceeds going to Minnesota Environment and Natural Resources Trust Fund	
MISSISSIPPI	Prohibited 97-33-31		
MISSOURI	313.200 to 313.351	After expenses and prizes paid, remaining moneys to general revenue fund; 45% prizes, then expenses, remainder to general revenue fund	
MONTANA	23-7-101	45% prize money; after expenses, net revenue transferred to state lottery fund. Net revenue transferred to state general fund effective 7/1/99	
NEBRASKA	9-801 to 9-841	40% prizes, 25% divided among Education Innovation Fund, Environmental Trust Fund, Compulsive Gambler's Assistance Fund, Nebraska Scholarship Fund	Education Fund to encourage and fund high performance learning innovations, pilot projects, and model programs
NEVADA	Prohibited. Nev. Const. art. 4, § 24		
NEW HAMPSHIRE	287-F:1 to 287-F:19; "Tri-State Lotto" with Maine and Vermont	50% common prize pool; operating costs charged proportionally to each state	For raising additional revenue

Prize Subject to Garnishment	Time Limit to Claim Prize/ Disposition	Prohibited Related Activities
Yes	180 days/ added to pool for future prizes or special prize promotions	Sale to minor; false or altered tickets; influence winning or tampering with lottery equipment; illegal lottery devices; skimming lottery proceeds; bulk sale
Child support purposes	1 yr./transferred to General Fund as undedicated revenue	Sale at greater price; sale to minor; alter or forge tickets
Under appropriate court order, prize may be paid to person other than winner; or any unpaid state or municipal tax	182 days; added to unclaimed prize fund or nondaily/weekly lottery drawing	Sale to minor; forged/altered tickets; unauthorized sale
For past due child support on any prizes over $600	1 yr./allocated in same manner as other lottery revenue	Forged/altered tickets; sale to minor; sale at greater price
For prizes over $1,000, for liabilities to state or support arrearages	1 yr./deposited in state school aid fund and distributed pursuant to law	Sales to minors; sale at greater price; unauthorized sale; forged/altered ticket
For prizes over $600, for delinquent state taxes; child support; court ordered restitution; or amount due any other claimant agency	1 yr. of unclaimed prize money is added to the general fund	Sale to or purchase by minors; sale at greater price; unauthorized sale
Only pursuant to an appropriate judicial order; set-offs for delinquent child support and unpaid debts to city jail	180 days/revert to state lottery fund	Sale to minors; sale at greater price; forged/altered ticket; unauthorized sale
For prizes over $600, those owing child support through state child support enforcement agency	6 mos./paid into state lottery fund	Sale to minor; purchase only with cash or check; no credit
On prizes over $500, any outstanding state tax liability or child or spousal support	Period of time set by regulation/used at discretion of tax commissioner for purposes set out in lottery statutes	Sale to person under 19 years of age; at price other than proscribed; unauthorized sale; alter ticket; no phone; mail or credit sales
Yes	1 yr./credited to prize pool	Sale at greater price; sale to minor; unauthorized sale

Table 51: State Lotteries—Continued

State	Code Section	Distribution of Revenue	Additional Purpose
NEW JERSEY	5:9-1 to 5:9-25	Payment of prizes and expenses with appropriations to state institutions and state aid for education	Entire net proceeds to be used for state institutions and state aid for education including higher education and senior citizen education
NEW MEXICO	6-24-1 to 6-24-34	50% to prizes minus operating expenses with net remaining revenues: to lottery tuition fund	To benefit state residents by funding critical capital outlay needs of public schools and provide tuition assistance to resident undergraduates at New Mexico post-secondary schools
NEW YORK	Tax §§ 1600 to 1620	40–65% for prizes depending on the game; 45–25% to state lottery fund	Supplemental aid to all school children; signs must be posted to assist compulsive gamblers
NORTH CAROLINA	Prohibited. 14-289 to 14-291.2		
NORTH DAKOTA	53-12.1-01 to 53-12.1-13	50% for prizes, payment of expenses, $50,000 to compulsive gambling prevention and treatment fund, remainder to state general fund	
OHIO	3770.01 to 3770.99	50% prize payment less operation expenses; then at least 30% Lottery Profits Education Fund	Lottery Profits Education Fund used to support elementary, secondary, vocational, and special education programs in appropriations made by the general assembly
OKLAHOMA	Oklahoma Education Lottery Act: Tit. 3a, §§ 701 to 735	From gross proceeds: operating expenses; at least 45% of gross proceeds available as prize money; net proceeds of at least 35% of gross to Oklahoma Education Lottery Trust Fund as follows: 45% early childhood education programs and K-12 public education; 45% tuition grants/loans/scholarships to citizens of state to attend colleges or universities within the state, construction of educational facilities, and other programs Tit. 3a § 713(C)(2); 5% School Consolidation and Assistance Fund, 5% Teachers' Retirement System Dedicated Revenue Revolving Fund	Education Lottery Trust Fund
OREGON	461.010 to 461.740; OR Const. art. XV, § 4	50% prizes; 16% expenses; 34% benefit public purpose (state lottery fund for jobs and economic development in Oregon)	To provide additional moneys for public purpose of creating jobs and furthering economic development in Oregon without additional or increased taxes

Prize Subject to Garnishment	Time Limit to Claim Prize/Disposition	Prohibited Related Activities
For arrears of court-ordered child support obligations, and former recipients of Aid to Families with Dependent Children (AFDC), food stamps, or low income home energy assistance who were overpaid	1 yr./allocated in same manner as lottery revenue is allocated by state	Forged/altered tickets; sale above fixed price; unauthorized sale
On prizes over $600, those owing debt to or collected by human services department for child support enforcement	Time period established by authority/paid into prize fund	Sale at greater price; sale to minors; unauthorized sale; no sales on credit; forged/altered tickets; influencing winning of prize through fraud or deception
On prizes over $600, applied against past-due support (including alimony, child or spousal support or maintenance) and against any public assistance benefits given an individual within the last 10 years (not to exceed 50% of prize)	1 yr./retained in lottery prize account to be used for special lotto or supplemental lotto prizes or for promotion purposes to supplement other games on an occasional basis	Sale to minors (under 18)
For prizes over $600, those owing debt to agencies, with priority to child support payments	Set by attorney general, but no more than 1 yr.	Forged/altered tickets; sale to minors; sale above fixed price
On prizes over $5,000, for default of support payment under support order	180 days/returned to state lottery fund in unclaimed lottery prizes fund	Sale at greater price; unauthorized sale; sale to minor; influence lottery sales agent; on Ohio fairgrounds at annual exhibition
	180 days/90 days	Sale at greater price; sale to minor; sale at locations other than listed in retailer's contract
On prizes in excess of $600, garnishment for person in arrears on child support obligation	1 yr./remain property of lottery commission and be allocated to the benefit of the public purpose (may be exempt from 1 year redemption period if in active military service with evidence of possession of winning—then have 1 year after discharge to redeem	Sale at greater price; sale to minors; altered/forged tickets

Table 51: State Lotteries—Continued

State	Code Section	Distribution of Revenue	Additional Purpose
PENNSYLVANIA	Tit. 72, §§ 3761-101 to 3761-2103	40% to pay prizes; after expenses, rest pursuant to "Senior Citizens Property Tax or Rent Rebate and Older Persons Inflation Needs Act"	For purpose of providing property tax relief to the elderly and to provide free or reduced fare transit service for the elderly; also to curb illegal gambling operations in Pennsylvania
RHODE ISLAND	42-61-1 to 42-61.2-15; R.I. Const. art. 6, § 15	45–65% prize fund (keno 45–72%) less expenses; 25% (15% for keno) to general revenue fund (different percentages for video lottery games)	
SOUTH CAROLINA	59-150-10 to 59-15-410; S.C. Const. art. 17, § 7	45% prizes, 15% expenses, remainder in Education Lottery Account only appropriated for educational purposes and programs	
SOUTH DAKOTA	42-7A-1 to 42-7A-64	Expenses and prizes (approx. 50%) from lottery operating fund; net proceeds to state general fund; state corrections facility construction fund, and state capital construction fund (lottery expenses may not exceed amount of net proceeds to these funds) Video lottery income directly deposited in state property tax reduction fund, 42-7A-24	
TENNESSEE	Prohibited. Tenn. Const. art. XI, § 5 Tennessee Constitution		
TEXAS	Govt. §§ 466.001 to 466.453	Payment of prizes, cost and expenses not to exceed 12%; establishment of pooled bond fund, lottery prize reserve fund, unclaimed prize fund, and prize payment account, balance to foundation school fund	
UTAH	Prohibited. Art. VI, § 27 Utah Constitution		
VERMONT	Tit. 31, §§ 651 to 667; and "Tri-State Lotto" with Maine and New Hampshire, Tit. 31, §§ 671 to 678	After payment of prizes and expenses, proceeds go to state lottery fund, which after expenses, goes to general fund to be used solely for capital expenses and debt service; not less than 50% to be paid in prizes	
VIRGINIA	58.1-4000 to 58.1-4027	Operating costs and administration not to exceed 10% (with special reserve fund); rest to general fund solely for purpose of public education	

Prize Subject to Garnishment	Time Limit to Claim Prize/ Disposition	Prohibited Related Activities
Yes	1 yr./ paid to state lottery fund for statutorily prescribed purposes	Sales in excess of fixed price; unauthorized sales; sales to minors
For prizes over $600, set-off for unpaid child support arrearages over $500	1 yr./reverts to lottery fund	Sales above fixed price; sales to minors; altered /forged tickets
For prizes over $500, subject to attachments, garnishments, or executions issued pursuant to law	180 days/reverts to Education Lottery Account	Sales to minors, altered/forged tickets
For prizes in excess of $100, liability setoff program to satisfy debts owed or collected through state agencies (child support payments have priority)	1 yr. or period deemed appropriate by executive director/added to prize pools of subsequent lottery games	Counterfeiting lottery tickets; sale at greater price; sales to minors
Delinquent tax, child support payments, or default in student guaranteed loan shall be deducted	180 days/provides additional money to state lottery account; $20 million for TX Dept. of Health teaching hospital account, $5 million for Health and Human Services Commission for inpatient hospital services, rest to general fund	Sales to minors; sales by phone; stolen, forged or altered tickets; sale at greater price; sale on credit; unauthorized sale; sale for food stamps or with AFDC check; influencing selection of winner; fraud
	After one yr., unclaimed prizes revert to state lottery fund	Sale to minors; sale at greater price; no license to convicted felons.
Unpaid child support obligations and payment of public assistance owed by individual	180 days/paid into Literary Fund (prizes of less than $25 go into state lottery fund)	Sale over fixed price; sales to minors; altered/forged tickets

Table 51: State Lotteries—Continued

State	Code Section	Distribution of Revenue	Additional Purpose
WASHINGTON	67.70.010 to 67.70.906	State lottery fund used for: payment of prizes and lottery administration; deposits to Washington Opportunities Pathways account; distribution to county for payment of baseball stadium bonds (for no more than 20 years)	
WEST VIRGINIA	29-22-1	45% disbursement as prizes; 15% operation and administration expenses; excess is net profit: goes to school building debt service fund (up to $18 million); lottery education fund; school construction fund; lottery senior citizens fund; commerce division of tourism and parks	
WISCONSIN	565.01 to 565.50; Wis. Const. art. IV, § 24	Proceeds deposited into state treasury for property tax relief	
WYOMING	Wyoming Lottery Act: 9-17-101 to 9-17-128	At least 45% of net proceeds shall be made available as prize money. the net proceeds shall be transferred to the treasurer's office and until June 30, 2019, the first $6 million each fiscal year shall be paid to each county, determined by the percentage that net sales taxes collected attributed to vendors in each county	

Prize Subject to Garnishment	Time Limit to Claim Prize/ Disposition	Prohibited Related Activities
On prizes over $600, any debts to state agency or political subdivision may be setoff	180 days/retained in state lottery fund for further use as prizes	Sale to minors; sale at greater price; altered/forged tickets
For delinquent payment of child or spousal support	180 days/reverts to state lottery fund for the purpose of awarding additional prizes	Altered/forged tickets; unauthorized sales; sale at greater price; sales to minors
Prizes over $1,000 are subject to child support payments and spousal support	180 days/used for future prizes	Forging ticket; sales to minors
Past due child support	Unclaimed: 180 days, amount not to exceed $200,000 annually; shall be used for programs for treatment of compulsive gambling disorder and educational programs related to the disorder; may be added to pool for future prizes or special prize promotion	Sale to minors; fraud; alter, forge, or counterfeit tickets

52. WILLS

The purpose of a will is to permit the living to provide for those who come after him or her. By "willing" their estates, individuals can control the way their property is distributed after their deaths. If an individual dies without a will and without heirs or relatives, however, the estate escheats to the state. A will is thus a way to keep the estate in the hands of family and/or loved ones, and out of the hands of the state.

Over the years, the law of wills developed into a very mechanical, strict set of rules generally uniform among states that safeguard against unscrupulous heirs who may forge or tamper with wills for financial gain. Virtually all states require the testator (the person making the will) to be over eighteen or "an adult," the will must be typed or printed, and the only writing permitted on the document is the signature of the testator and witnesses.

Some noteworthy types of wills are nuncupative and holographic. Nuncupative wills are oral testaments with a very special, very limited purpose. Typically, the oral will has the power to dispose of only a limited amount of personal property. The original purpose of this type of will was to permit mortally injured soldiers or sailors to give gifts of personal property to their comrades-in-arms. This provision is still reflected in many of the nuncupative statutes; it permits a dying individual to grant specific bequests to friends who may have cared for him during his last injury. Only 15 states still recognize nuncupative wills, and the number is slowly shrinking.

Holographic wills are testaments that are entirely handwritten instead of being typed or printed. They are generally not as formal as typed wills and are therefore more suspect by law, for a greedy heir may more easily be able to persuade the testator to hastily write out a will without the proper amount of counsel or reflection. It is for these reasons that holographic wills are looked upon with general disfavor, are subject to closer scrutiny, and are less commonly recognized than other wills.

Traditionally, the law of wills has been very slow to change, but even it has begun to feel the impact of the "computer revolution." Nevada, in 2001, added statutes that recognize "electronic wills," apparently becoming the first state in the union to do so.

Table 52: Wills

State	Code Section	Age of Testator	Number of Witnesses
ALABAMA	43-8-130 to 43-8-141	18 or older and of sound mind	Signed by at least 2 persons, each of whom witnessed either the signing or testator's acknowledgment of signature or of will
ALASKA	13.12.501 to 13.12.517	18 or older and of sound mind.	Signed by at least 2 individuals within a reasonable time after witnessing either the signing of the will or the testator's acknowledgment of signature or the will
ARIZONA	14-2501 to 14-2517	18 or older and of sound mind	Signed by at least 2 persons, each of whom signed within a reasonable time after witnessing testator's signature or acknowledgment of signature or will
ARKANSAS	28-25-101 to 28-25-110	18 or older and of sound mind	Signed by 2 or more attesting witnesses at request and in presence of testator, each of whom witnessed signing of will or testator's acknowledgment of signature or will
CALIFORNIA	Prob. §§ 6100 to 6113	18 or older and of sound mind	At least 2 persons present at the same time, witnessing either signing of will or testator's acknowledgment and must understand that it is testator's will
COLORADO	15-11-501 to 15-11-517	18 or older and of sound mind	Signed by at least 2 individuals, either before or after the testator's death, each of whom signed within a reasonable time after witnessing, in the conscious presence of the testator, either the signing or testator's acknowledgment of signature or of will
CONNECTICUT	45a-250 to 45a-251	18 or older and of sound mind	Attested by 2 witnesses, each subscribing in presence of testator
DELAWARE	Tit. 12, §§ 201 to 214	18 or older and of sound and disposing mind and memory	Witnessed in testator's presence by 2 generally competent witnesses
DISTRICT OF COLUMBIA	18-102 to 18-112	18 or older and of sound and disposing mind and capable of executing a valid deed or contract	Attested and subscribed in presence of testator by 2 credible witnesses
FLORIDA	732.501 to 732.518	18 and of sound mind or emancipated minor and of sound mind	Testator must sign will in presence of 2 attesting witnesses; witnesses must sign in presence of each other and testator
GEORGIA	53-4-10 to 53-4-24	14 years and not "laboring under some legal disability arising either from a want of capacity or a want of perfect liberty of action"	Attested and subscribed in testator's presence by 2 or more competent persons, each of whom witnessed either signing or testator's acknowledgment of signature of will
HAWAII	560:2-501 to 560:2-517	18 or older and of sound mind	Signed by at least 2 individuals, each of whom signed within a reasonable time after witnessing either the signing of the will or testator's acknowledgment of that signature or will

Nuncupative (Oral Wills)	Holographic Wills
Not recognized	Not recognized because of statutory requirement that every will must be witnessed and attested by at least 2 people; will in handwriting of testator and attested to by 2 witnesses is not considered holographic will
Not recognized	Recognized as valid if signature and material provisions are in handwriting of testator; does not need to be witnessed
Not recognized	Valid if signature and material provisions are in handwriting of testator; does not need to be witnessed
Not recognized	Valid if entire body and signature is in handwriting of testator and evidence of three credible disinterested witnesses to handwriting
Not recognized	Valid if signature and material provisions are in handwriting of testator; does not need witnesses; must show testamentary intent which can be shown by extrinsic evidence
Not recognized	Valid if signature and material provisions are in handwriting of testator; witnesses not necessary
Not valid if made in CT; valid if made outside the state according to the laws of state or country where made	Not valid if executed in CT; valid if properly made outside the state according to the laws of state or country where executed
Not recognized	Not recognized
Oral will made after 1/1/1902 is not valid except person in actual military or naval service or mariner at sea may dispose of personal property by word of mouth if oral will is proved by at least 2 individuals present at the making and requested by testator to bear witness that the disposition was the last will; and the will is made during time of last illness of deceased; and substance of will is reduced to writing 10 days after it was made	Attested and subscribed in the presence of testator by 2 credible witnesses
Not recognized	Not recognized; properly executed will in testator's handwriting is not considered holographic will
Not recognized	Not recognized
Not recognized	Valid if signature and material provisions are in handwriting of testator; does not need witnesses

Table 52: Wills—Continued

State	Code Section	Age of Testator	Number of Witnesses
IDAHO	15-2-501 to 15-2-513	18 or older or any emancipated minor and of sound mind	Signed by 2 or more persons 18 or older, each of whom witnessed either the signing or testator's acknowledgment of the signature or of the will
ILLINOIS	755 §§ 5/4-1 to 5/4-15	18 or older and of sound mind and memory	Attested in presence of testator by 2 or more credible witnesses; witnesses not required to sign in each other's presence
INDIANA	29-1-5-1 to 29-1-5-9	18 or older and of sound mind or younger and member of the armed forces or U.S. Merchant Marine or allies of the U.S.	Must be signed and acknowledged in presence of 2 or more witnesses; witnesses must sign in presence of testator and each other
IOWA	633.264; 633.279 to 633.284	Any person of full age and sound mind	Must be signed and acknowledged and witnessed by 2 competent persons, at testator's request; witnesses must sign in presence of testator and each other
KANSAS	59-601 to 59-623	Anyone of sound mind and possessing rights of majority	Must be attested and subscribed in presence of testator by 2 or more competent witnesses who saw testator subscribe or heard him acknowledge same
KENTUCKY	394.020 to 394.550	18 or older and of sound mind or younger if in pursuance of power specially given to that effect or if a parent for purpose of appointing a guardian for his or her child	If will is not wholly written by testator, testator must sign or acknowledge in presence of at least 2 credible witnesses; witnesses must sign in presence of testator and each other
LOUISIANA	Civ. Code Art. 1470; 1476; 1477; 1574 to 1582.1	16 and of sound mind; younger to provide for spouse or children; must be able to comprehend generally the nature and consequences of the disposition s/he is making	Signed and acknowledged in presence of notary and two competent witnesses; notary and witnesses must sign in presence of testator and each other
MAINE	Tit. 18-A, §§ 2-501 to 2-514	18 or older and of sound mind	Signed by at least 2 persons, each of whom witnessed either the signing or testator's acknowledgment of signature or of will.
MARYLAND	Est. & Trusts §§ 4-101 to 4-107	18 or older and legally competent	Must be attested and signed in presence of testator by 2 or more credible witnesses.

Nuncupative (Oral Wills)	Holographic Wills
Not recognized	Valid if signature and material provisions are in handwriting of testator; does not need witnesses
Not valid	Valid if attested in the presence of testator by 2 or more credible witnesses
Valid only if made in imminent peril of death and testator dies from such peril; requires 2 disinterested witnesses; 1 of whom is to reduce will to writing within 30 days after declaration; will to probate within 6 mos. after death; disposes of personal property only not exceeding $1,000 in value; persons in active military service in time of war can dispose of personal property not exceeding $10,000 in value; oral will does not revoke existing written will; it is changed only to the extent necessary to give effect to the nuncupative will	No statutory provisions
Not authorized	Valid if witnessed, at testator's request, by 2 competent persons; witnesses must sign in the presence of testator and each other; or if properly made in another state according to the laws of that state
Oral will made in the last sickness shall be valid in respect to personal property, if reduced to writing and subscribed by 2 competent, disinterested witnesses within 30 days after the speaking of the testamentary words	Not recognized
Not recognized	Recognized if wholly written by the testator
Nuncupative wills by public or private article statutes were repealed effective 7/1/1999; Civ. Code Art. 1579 describes notarial procedure for person unable to read	Valid if entirely written, dated, and signed by testator; not subject to any other formality
Not recognized	Valid if signature and material provisions are in handwriting of testator; does not need to be witnessed.
Not valid	Valid if entirely in the handwriting of a testator who is serving in the armed services of the United States and signed by the testator outside of a state of the United States, the District of Columbia, or a territory of the United States; no witnesses are necessary; void 1 yr. after testator is discharged from armed services unless testator has died prior to the expiration of the year or does not then possess testamentary capacity

Table 52: Wills—Continued

State	Code Section	Age of Testator	Number of Witnesses
MASSACHUSETTS	Ch. 190B, §§ 2-501 to 2-517	18 or older and of sound mind	Signed by at least 2 persons, each of whom witnessed either signing or testator's acknowledgement of signature or will
MICHIGAN	700.2501 to 700.2519	18 or older and of sufficient mental capacity	Signed by at least 2 competent persons, each of whom witnessed either the signing or testator's acknowledgment of signature or of will
MINNESOTA	524.2-501 to 524.2-517	18 or older and of sound mind	Signed by at least 2 persons, each of whom signed within a reasonable time after witnessing either the signing or testator's acknowledgment of signature or of will
MISSISSIPPI	91-5-1 to 91-5-35	18 or older and of sound and disposing mind	Attested to by 2 or more credible witnesses in testator's presence
MISSOURI	474.310 to 474.530	18 or older and of sound mind, or any emancipated minor	Must be attested by 2 or more competent witnesses subscribing their names to the will in presence of testator
MONTANA	72-2-521 to 72-2-537	18 or older and of sound mind	Signed by at least 2 individuals, each of whom signed within a reasonable time after having witnessed either the signing or testator's acknowledgment of signature or will
NEBRASKA	30-2326 to 30-2338	18 yrs. or older or not a minor and of sound mind	Signed by at least 2 individuals, each of whom witnessed either the signing or testator's acknowledgment of signature or of the will
NEVADA	133.020 to 133.100; Nevada recognizes electronic wills 133.085	Every person of sound mind over 18	Attested by at least 2 competent witnesses in presence of testator; electronic will does not require witnesses
NEW HAMPSHIRE	551:1 to 551:17	18 or older or younger if married and of sound mind	Signed by 2 credible witnesses at request and in presence of testator
NEW JERSEY	3B:3-1 to 3B:3-12	18 or older and of sound mind	Signed within reasonable time by at least 2 people who witnessed signing or testator's acknowledgment of signature or will
NEW MEXICO	45-2-501 to 45-2-517	18 or older; emancipated minor and of sound mind	Signed by 2 competent witnesses in presence of testator and each other after witnessing signing of will
NEW YORK	Est. Powers & Trusts §§ 3-1.1 to 3-2.2	18 or older and of sound mind and memory	At least 2 witnesses who, within one 30-day period, must attest to testator's signature or acknowledgment thereof and at testator's request sign their names and provide residence addresses at end of will; failure to affix address does not affect validity of will

Nuncupative (Oral Wills)	Holographic Wills
Not recognized	Not recognized
Not recognized	Valid if dated and testator's signature and material provisions are in testator's handwriting; does not need witnesses
Not recognized	Not recognized
Must be made at time of the last illness of the deceased at home or where s/he resided for 10 days prior to death, except when taken sick and s/he dies before returning home.; maximum bequeathed is $100, unless the will can be proved by two witnesses that the testator called on to bear testimony that this was his or her will	Must be testamentary in character, wholly written, dated, and signed by testator
Valid only if made in imminent peril of death and death results; declared to be person's will before 2 disinterested witnesses, reduced to writing by or under direction of 1 of them within 30 days and submitted for probate within 6 mos. of death; can only dispose of personal property of no more than $500; does not change or revoke existing will; may be revoked by another nuncupative will	No statutory provisions
Not recognized	Valid if signature and material provisions are in testator's handwriting; witnesses not required
Not recognized	Valid if signature, material provisions, and indication of date of signing are in handwriting of testator; if not dated, will is valid if date is determinable by contents, extrinsic circumstances, or other evidence or is only such instrument or contains no inconsistency with any like instrument; witnesses not necessary
Not valid	Valid if entirely written, dated, and signed in handwriting of testator; can be made in or out of state; may dispose of all or part of estate, real or personal; witnesses not necessary
Allowed to soldier in actual military service, or a mariner or seaman at sea; may dispose of movables and personal property as s/he would have before	Not recognized
Not recognized	Valid if signature and material provisions are in testator's handwriting; witnesses not necessary
Not recognized	Not recognized
Valid only if made by active member of U.S. Armed Forces or person who serves with or accompanies such armed force during a war or other armed conflict, or mariner at sea; expires 1 yr. following discharge or time person ceases serving with or accompanying armed force; in case of mariner, expires 3 yrs. from time will was made	Same provisions as for nuncupative wills and written entirely in testator's handwriting

Table 52: Wills—Continued

State	Code Section	Age of Testator	Number of Witnesses
NORTH CAROLINA	31-1 to 31-4.2	18 or older and of sound mind	Signed by at least 2 competent persons, each of whom witnessed either the signing or testator's acknowledgment of signature or will; witnesses must sign in presence of testator but need not sign in presence of each other
NORTH DAKOTA	30.1-08-01 to 30.1-08-13	Any adult who is of sound mind	Either signed by at least 2 persons, each of whom signed within reasonable time after witnessing either signing or testator's acknowledgment of signature or will; or acknowledged by testator before notary public or other individual authorized by law to take acknowledgments
OHIO	2107.01 to 2107.06; 2107.60	18 or older, of sound mind and memory, and not under restraint	Attested and subscribed in conscious presence of testator by 2 or more competent witnesses who saw testator subscribe or heard testator acknowledge signature
OKLAHOMA	Tit. 84 §§ 41 to 146	18 or older and of sound mind	Signed at request and in presence of testator by at least two attesting witnesses, each of whom witnessed either the signing or testator's acknowledgment of signature or of will
OREGON	112.225 to 112.435	18 or older, lawfully married, or emancipated minor and of sound mind	At least 2 witnesses who see testator sign will or hear him acknowledge signature and attest by signing their names to it
PENNSYLVANIA	Tit. 20, §§ 2501 to 2521	18 or older and of sound mind	Signed by 2 witnesses in presence of testator; testator must declare instrument to be his will in presence of witnesses.
RHODE ISLAND	33-5-2 to 33-5-12	18 or older and of sane mind	Must be signed or acknowledged by testator in front of 2 or more witnesses present at same time who must attest and subscribe will in presence of testator.
SOUTH CAROLINA	62-2-501 to 62-2-512	18 or older or married or emancipated minor and of sound mind	Signed by at least 2 persons each of whom witnessed either signing or testator's acknowledgment of signature or will.
SOUTH DAKOTA	29A-2-501 to 29A-2-517	18 or older and of sound mind	Signed in conscious presence of testator by 2 or more individuals who witnessed either the signing of the will or the testator's acknowledgment of that signature
TENNESSEE	32-1-101 to 32-1-113	18 or older and of sound mind	Signed by 2 or more attesting witnesses, each of whom witnessed either the signing or testator's acknowledgment of signature or will; witnesses must sign in presence of testator and each other

Nuncupative (Oral Wills)	Holographic Wills
Made by person in his last sickness or in such imminent peril of death and who does not survive such sickness or peril and declared to be his will before 2 competent witnesses simultaneously present and specially requested by him to bear witness thereto.	Written entirely in testator's handwriting, subscribed by testator, and found after testator's death among valuable papers or in safe deposit box or other safe place or in possession or custody of person or firm with whom testator deposited it for safekeeping
Not recognized	Valid if the signature and material portions of the document are in the testator's handwriting; witnesses not necessary
Valid in respect to personal property if made in the last sickness and reduced to writing and subscribed by 2 competent disinterested witnesses within 10 days after the speaking; witnesses must prove that testator was of sound mind and memory, not under restraint, and called upon some person present at time the testamentary words were spoken to bear testimony to disposition as the testator's will; must be offered to probate within 3 mos. after death	Will may be handwritten but must be attested and subscribed in conscious presence of testator by 2 competent persons who saw testator subscribe or heard testator acknowledge signature
Valid with following requirements: Value of estate must not exceed $1,000; will must be proved by 2 witnesses present at making, 1 at testator's request; testator must have been in actual military service in field or duty at sea and in actual contemplation, fear, or peril of death or testator must have been in expectation of immediate death from injury received same day.	Must be entirely written, dated, and signed by testator's hand; need not be witnessed.
Not recognized	Not recognized
Not valid	Not recognized
Not recognized except any soldier or airman in actual military service or any mariner or sailor at sea may dispose of his or her personal estate by will as he or she might heretofore have done	No statutory provision; valid if made outside the state according to the laws of state where made, provided it is in writing and subscribed by testator
Not recognized	Impliedly forbidden by statute unless specifically recognized by valid out-of-state execution or out-of-state probate
Not recognized	Valid if signature and material portions are in testator's handwriting; witnesses not necessary
Made only by person in imminent peril of death and valid only if testator dies as result; must be declared to be will before 2 disinterested witnesses and reduced to writing by or under direction of 1 of the witnesses within 30 days and submitted to probate within 6 mos. after death of testator; valid for personal property not exceeding $1,000 unless person is in active military service in time of war, then $10,000; neither revokes nor changes existing written will.	Signature and material provisions must be in handwriting of testator; handwriting must be proved by 2 witnesses; no witness to will is necessary

Table 52: Wills—Continued

State	Code Section	Age of Testator	Number of Witnesses
TEXAS	Est. §§ 251.001 to 251.107	18 or older; has been married or member of U.S. Armed Forces or auxiliaries or U.S. Maritime Service and of sound mind	Attested by 2 or more credible witnesses above age of 14 subscribing names in presence of testator
UTAH	75-2-501 to 75-2-515	18 or older and of sound mind	Signed by at least 2 individuals, each of whom signed within a reasonable time after witnessing either the testator's signing or acknowledgment of signing or will
VERMONT	Tit. 14, §§ 1 to 11	18 and older or emancipated minor and of sound mind	Attested and subscribed by 2 or more credible witnesses in presence of testator and each other
VIRGINIA	64.2-400 to 64.2-409	18 or older or emancipated minor and of sound mind	Signed by 2 or more competent witnesses each of whom witnessed either signing or testator's acknowledgment of signature or will; must sign in presence of testator and each other
WASHINGTON	11.12.010 to 11.12.265	18 or older and of sound mind	Attested by 2 or more competent witnesses by subscribing their names to the will or by signing an affidavit while in the presence of and at the direction of the testator
WEST VIRGINIA	41-1-1 to 41-1-10	18 or older and of sound mind	Signed by 2 competent witnesses in presence of testator and each other and who either witnessed signing of will or testator's acknowledgment of signature or will
WISCONSIN	853.01 to 853.41	18 or older and of sound mind	Signed by at least 2 witnesses within reasonable time following testator's signing or acknowledgment of signature or will in conscious presence of witness; witnesses need not be present at same time
WYOMING	2-6-101 to 2-6-124	Any person of legal age and sound mind	Witnessed by 2 competent witnesses

Nuncupative (Oral Wills)	Holographic Wills
Not recognized	Will wholly written in handwriting of testator needs no attesting witnesses and may be self-proved by testator attaching affidavit that it is his last will, that testator is of age or otherwise qualified and has not revoked will
Not recognized	Valid if signature and material provisions are in handwriting of testator; witnesses not necessary
Not recognized	Not recognized
Not recognized	A will wholly in the testator's handwriting is valid without further requirements; proof of handwriting must be by at least two disinterested witnesses.
No real estate; personal property not more than $1,000; members of U.S. Armed Forces and persons employed on U.S. Merchant Marine vessels may dispose of wages and personal property; must be made with 2 witnesses present at time of making that testator requested person to bear witness to will and that it was made at time of last sickness; must be reduced to writing, proof offered within 6 mos. of words spoken, and citation issued to widows and heirs-at-law that they might contest	Executed in Washington not admissible but valid if properly made outside the state according to the laws of state where made
Not recognized	Valid if entirely written and signed in hand of testator; need not be witnessed or acknowledged
Not valid	Not recognized except if valid in state where executed
Not recognized	Valid if entirely written and signed in hand of testator; need not be witnessed

VII. REAL ESTATE LAWS

53. ADVERSE POSSESSION

The doctrine of "adverse possession" is one of the most interesting in the field of real property law. The character of the law reflects the pioneer spirit of a growing world in both North America and Europe over the last few centuries.

If a person moves into possession of property, improves it and possesses it in a public manner, then after a certain amount of time he will acquire title to the property even though it is actually owned by someone else. The idea for adverse possession has at its root that land should not lie idle. If it does, it is wasted to the community. Therefore, if someone moves onto the land and makes it productive, that person may earn the right to claim it as his or her own. It is also reflective of the imprecise nature of ancient land sales: a person who believes he owns land, establishes himself on it in public, and is not hindered after a period of time, should be entitled to own the land.

Requirements

The basic requirement for adverse possession is that the claiming party must take exclusive possession of the property. This type of possession is called "open and notorious" or proactive and absolutely not secretive possession. Some states require that the possession be "under color of title," or that the person must believe that he has the right to possess it and has some form of document or is relying on some fact that while not actually conveying title, appears to do so. In addition, many states require concurrent the payment of property taxes for a specified period of time, and a few states also require that improvements be made upon the land. Eventually, the possessor is required to file for title with the county recorder. The actual owner then has a limited amount of time in which to challenge the newcomer's title. Essentially, the owner's only argument is to claim some sort of disability; such as age, mental instability, or imprisonment. The owner is not required to do much in order to stop the possessor from acquiring title; merely sending the possessor a note granting permission to be there will usually suffice. Various rules exist regarding the continuousness of the possession and the ability to "tack" various periods of possession together in order to satisfy the time of possession requirement; see your state codes or the code of the state in which you are interested for more detailed information.

Table 53: Adverse Possession

State	Code Section	Prescriptive Period	Occupation	Time to Challenge	Improvements	Payment of Taxes	Title from Tax Assessor
ALABAMA	6-5-200	20 yrs. (Bradley v. Demos, 599 So.2d 1148 (Ala. 1992))	and Color of Title: 10 yrs. and Payment of Taxes: 10 yrs.			10 yrs. required	
ALASKA	09.45.052		and Color of Title: 7 yrs. or good faith mistaken belief: 10 yrs.				
ARIZONA	12-521 to 12-530	2 yrs. (if occupied with no claim to title)	and Color of Title: 3 yrs. or 5 yrs. if city lot	3 yrs. after cause of action arrives	Taxes plus cultivation: 5 yrs.; Cultivation only: 10 yrs.	5 consecutive yrs. before suit to recover	
ARKANSAS	18-11-101 to 18-11-106; 18-61-101	7 yrs.	Can't eject after 5 yrs.	After disability lifted: 3 yrs.		7 successive years; for wild and unimproved land, 15 consecutive years creates presumption of color of title	
CALIFORNIA	Civ. Proc. §§ 318; 325; 328		and Payment of Taxes: 5 yrs.	With disability: 20 yrs.; After disability lifted: 5 yrs.		5 years required	
COLORADO	38-41-101 to 38-41-119	18 yrs.	and Color of Title/Payment of Taxes: 7 yrs.	After disability lifted: 2 yrs.		7 years	
CONNECTICUT	52-575	15 yrs.		After disability lifted: 5 yrs.			
DELAWARE	Tit. 10, §§ 7901 to 7904	20 yrs.		After disability lifted: 10 yrs.			
DISTRICT OF COLUMBIA	16-1113; 16-3301	15 yrs.		With disability: max. 22 yrs.; After disability lifted: 2 yrs.		Time not specified but considered proof	
FLORIDA	95.16; 95.18; 95.191; 95.192		and Color of Title: 7 yrs. and Payment of Taxes: 7 yrs.		One way to possess land	4 yrs.	4 yrs.

Table 53: Adverse Possession—Continued

State	Code Section	Prescriptive Period	Occupation	Time to Challenge	Improve-ments	Payment of Taxes	Title from Tax Assessor
GEORGIA	44-5-160 to 44-5-177	20 yrs.	and Color of Title: 7 yrs.	Prescriptive period does not run until disability removed			
HAWAII	657-31 to 657-38; 669-1	20 yrs.		After disability lifted: 5 yrs.			
IDAHO	5-203 to 5-213	20 yrs.	and Color of Title: 20 yrs. and Payment of Taxes: 20 yrs.	After disability lifted: 20 yrs.	Taxes plus cultivation 5 years	Required	
ILLINOIS	735 §§ 5/13-101 to 5/13-122	20 yrs.	and Color of Title: 7 yrs. and Payment of Taxes: 7 yrs.	After disability lifted: 2 yrs.			7 yrs.
INDIANA	32-21-7-1 to 32-21-7-2; 34-11-1-2	10 yrs. (15 yrs. if cause of action arose before Sept. 1, 1982)		After disability lifted: 2 yrs.		Required	
IOWA	614.8; 614.17; 560.2	Within 1 year (after 7/1/80)	and Color of Title/Payment of taxes; 5 yrs.	After disability lifted: 1 yr.	With occupancy, one way to possess land		
KANSAS	60-503 to 60-509	15 yrs.		With disability: max. 23 yrs.; After disability lifted: 2 yrs.			
KENTUCKY	413.010; 413.060; 413.020	15 yrs.	and Color of Title: 7 yrs.	After disability lifted: 3 yrs.			
LOUISIANA	Civ. Code Art. 3473 to 3485	10 yrs.	and Color of Title: 10 yrs.				
MAINE	Tit. 14, §§ 801 to 817	20 yrs.	and Color of Title/payment of taxes: 20 years	After disability lifted: 10 yrs. notwithstanding 20 yrs. have expired		Required on uncultivated lands in un-incorporated areas	
MARYLAND	Cts. & Jud. Proc. §§ 5-103; 5-201	20 yrs.		After disability lifted: 3 yrs.			

Table 53: Adverse Possession—Continued

State	Code Section	Prescriptive Period	Occupation	Time to Challenge	Improve-ments	Payment of Taxes	Title from Tax Assessor
MASSACHUSETTS	Ch. 260, § 21	20 yrs.					
MICHIGAN	600.5801; 600.5851	15 yrs.		After disability lifted: 1 yr.			10 years
MINNESOTA	541.02; 541.15	15 yrs.	and payment of taxes for 5 consecutive years	With disability: 5 yrs. (except for infancy); After disability lifted: 1 yr.			
MISSISSIPPI	15-1-7; 15-1-13; 15-1-15	10 yrs.	and Color of Title: 10 years and Payment of Taxes: 2 years	With disability: 31 yrs.; After disability lifted: 10 yrs.		2 yrs.	3 yrs. after 2 yrs. from day of sale by tax collector
MISSOURI	516.010; 516.030	10 yrs.		After disability lifted: 3 yrs., max. 21 yrs.			
MONTANA	70-19-401; 70-19-411; 70-19-413	5 yrs.	and Color of Title: 5 yrs. and Color of Title/Payment of Taxes: 5 yrs.	After disability lifted: 5 yrs.		Required	
NEBRASKA	25-202; 25-213	10 yrs.		With disability: 20 yrs.; After disability lifted: 10 yrs.			
NEVADA	11.070; 11.110; 11.150; 11.180	5 yrs.	and Color of Title: 5 yrs. and Payment of Taxes: 5 yrs.	After disability lifted: 2 yrs.		Required	
NEW HAMPSHIRE	508:2; 508.3	20 yrs.		After disability lifted: 5 yrs.			
NEW JERSEY	2A:14-30 to 2A:14-32; 2A:62-2	30 yrs. or 60 yrs. if woodland	and Color of Title: 30 yrs. and Payment of Taxes: 5 yrs.	After disability lifted: 5 yrs.			
NEW MEXICO	37-1-22	10 yrs.	and Color of Title/Payment of Taxes: 10 yrs.	After disability lifted: 1 yr.		Required	
NEW YORK	Real Prop. Acts. §§ 501 to 551	10 yrs.	and Color of Title: 10 yrs.		One way to possess land		

Table 53: Adverse Possession—Continued

State	Code Section	Prescriptive Period	Occupation	Time to Challenge	Improvements	Payment of Taxes	Title from Tax Assessor
NORTH CAROLINA	1-17; 1-38 to 1-45.1	20 yrs.	and Color of Title: 7 yrs.	After disability lifted: 3 yrs.			
NORTH DAKOTA	28-01-04 to 28-01-14.; 47-06-03	20 yrs.	and Color of Title: 20 yrs. and Color of Title/Payment of Taxes: 10 yrs.	After disability lifted: 10 yrs.	One way to possess land	10 yrs.	
OHIO	2305.04	21 yrs.		With disability: 21 yrs.; After disability lifted: 10 yrs.			
OKLAHOMA	Tit. 12, §§ 93, 94	15 yrs.		After disability lifted: 2 yrs.			5 yrs.
OREGON	12.050; 12.160	10 yrs.		With disability: 5 yrs.; After disability lifted: 1 yr.			
PENNSYLVANIA	Tit. 42, § 5530	21 yrs.					
RHODE ISLAND	34-7-1 to 34-7-9	10 yrs.		After disability lifted: 10 yrs.			
SOUTH CAROLINA	15-67-210 to 15-67-270	10 yrs.	and Color of Title: 10 yrs.		One way to possess land		
SOUTH DAKOTA	15-3-1 to 15-3-19	20 yrs.	and Color of Title: 20 yrs. and Color of Title/Payment of Taxes: 10 yrs.	With disability: 20 yrs.; After disability lifted: 10 yrs.	One way to possess land		
TENNESSEE	28-2-101 to 28-2-111	7 yrs.				20 yrs.	
TEXAS	Civ. Prac. & Rem. §§ 16.021 to 16.037	10 yrs.	and Color of Title: 3 yrs. and Color of Title/Payment of taxes: 5 yrs.	With disability: 25 yrs.	Taxes plus cultivation: 5 yrs.; Cultivation only: 10 yrs.	Required	
UTAH	78B-2-201 to 788-2-226	7 yrs.	and Color of Title/Payment of Taxes: 7 yrs.		Cultivation only: 7 yrs.	Required	
VERMONT	Tit. 12, § 501	15 yrs.					
VIRGINIA	8.01-236; 8.01-237	15 yrs.	and Color of Title: 15 yrs.	With disability: 25 yrs. max.			

Table 53: Adverse Possession—Continued

State	Code Section	Prescriptive Period	Occupation	Time to Challenge	Improve-ments	Payment of Taxes	Title from Tax Assessor
WASHINGTON	7.28.050 to 7.28.320	7 yrs.	and Color of Title: 7 yrs. and Color of Title/Payment of Taxes: 7 yrs.	After disability lifted: 3 yrs.		Required	
WEST VIRGINIA	55-2-1; 55-2-3	10 yrs.		After disability lifted: 5 yrs.			
WISCONSIN	893.16; 893.25 to 893.27	20 yrs.	and Color of Title: 10 yrs. and Color of Title/Payment of Taxes: 7 yrs.	With disability: 5 yrs., except when due to insanity or imprisonment. After disability lifted: 2 yrs.	One way to prove possession.		
WYOMING	1-3-103; 1-3-104	10 yrs.		After disability lifted: 10 yrs.			

54. HOMESTEAD

Homestead laws are designed to protect small individual property owners, such as homeowners, from the everchanging economic climate of the United States. Often when the economy changes, small property owners are unable to meet the demands of their creditors. Homestead laws allow an individual to register a portion of his real and personal property as "homestead," thereby making that portion of the individual's estate off-limits to most creditors. The idea behind these homestead laws is the preservation of the family farm, home, or other assets in the face of severe economic conditions.

The items and amounts of money that can be set aside as a homestead are varied. The rules governing which property can be registered as homestead property seem to adhere to regional patterns. Real property that may be subject to the homestead exemptions vary in value from a $300 exemption from judgments in Pennsylvania to a $500,000 exemption in Massachusetts. They vary in character from the District of Columbia's allowable homestead of $1,625 worth of tools, to Colorado's unlimited acreage or Texas's 200 acres. In each case, the property that may be homesteaded is designed to perpetuate the family's estate and improve its chances for survival in hard times.

Limitations

The homestead is a back-up and a type of insurance against unexpected catastrophe; it will not ordinarily protect you from a bad business deal or from ordinary bankruptcy.

Nonetheless, because an unscrupulous person could manipulate the homestead protections as a shield from living up to his legal obligations, there is much case law on homesteads. Indeed, ordinary business and commercial creditors ordinarily may penetrate property set aside as homestead.

Table 54: Homestead

State	Code Section	Maximum Value of Property	Maximum Acreage (Urban)	Maximum Acreage (Rural)
ALABAMA	6-10-2; Const. art. X, § 205	Constitution: $2,000; Statute: $15,000	Constitution: Lot; Statute: Lot or track	Constitution: 80 acres; Statute: 160 acres
ALASKA	09.38.010	$54,000		
ARIZONA	33-1101	$150,000		
ARKANSAS	16-66-210; Const. art. IX, §§ 4; 5	$2,500. All homesteads less than $1,000 assessed valuation are exempt from all state taxes referred to in art. XVI, § 18 of the Arkansas Constitution. If homestead's value exceeds $1,000, exemption shall apply to first $1,000 of valuation (Const. amend. XXII, § 1)	One acre but not less than 1/4 acre	Cannot exceed 160 acres, will not be reduced to less than 80 acres.
CALIFORNIA	Civ. Proc. §§ 704.710 to 704.850	$175,000 if either spouse is over 65 or disabled and unable to engage in substantial employment; $175,000 if person is 55 or older with gross income of not more than $25,000, or if married, not more than $35,000 and sale is involuntary; $100,000 if debtor or spouse resides in house with at least one member of the family with no interest in the homestead; $75,000 for all others		
COLORADO	38-41-201 to 38-41-212	$60,000 if occupied as home by an owner's family, or $90,000 if homestead is occupied as home by elderly (over 60) or disabled owner, spouse of owner or dependent of owner	No limits to acreage	No limits to acreage
CONNECTICUT	12-81(21)	$10,000 if disabled veteran; only $5,000 exemption if loss the use of one arm or one leg; $3,000 maximum income if unmarried and over 65; $5,000 maximum income if married and over 65; $6,000 maximum income for all others--combined adjusted gross income and tax exempt interest		
DELAWARE	Tit. 10, § 4902 (personal property); Tit. 22, § 1002	$75 trade, business in New Castle, Sussex County; $50 trade, business in Kent County; homestead exemption for persons 65 and older to be determined by local ordinance		
DISTRICT OF COLUMBIA	15-501 (personal property)	$2,575 automobile interest, household items up to $8,625, family pictures not in excess of $400, tools of the trade up to $1,625		
FLORIDA	196.031; Const. art. X, § 4	$25,000 for taxes levied by governing bodies of school districts; $5,000 for all others	1/2 acre	160 acres

Table 54: Homestead—Continued

State	Code Section	Maximum Value of Property	Maximum Acreage (Urban)	Maximum Acreage (Rural)
GEORGIA	44-13-1	$5,000 or $21,500 for real or personal property that is the debtor's primary residence		
HAWAII	651-92	$30,000 if head of family or 65 years old; $20,000 for all others		
IDAHO	55-1001; 55-1003	Lesser of $100,000 or total net value of lands, mobile home, or improvements. Net value means market value minus all liens and encumbrances		
ILLINOIS	735 § 5/12-901	$15,000, if two or more own property, value of each proportional exemption can't exceed a total of $30,000		
INDIANA	34-55-10-2	$15,000 for residential; $8,000 for other real estate or tangible personal property; $300 for intangible personal property		
IOWA	561.1 to 561.26	$500	1/2 acre	40 acres
KANSAS	60-2301; 60-2304	$1,000 in ornaments, $20,000 in transportation, $7,500 in trade tools	1 acre	160 acres
KENTUCKY	427.010; 427.080	$5,000 plus $3,000 in any personal property		
LOUISIANA	Const. art. VII, § 20	$7,500	160 acres	160 acres
MAINE	Tit. 14, § 4422	Aggregate interest not to exceed $47,500 (or $95,000 if have minor dependents) including exemptions for car, clothing, furniture, jewelry, and tools of the trade. $95,000 if debtor or dependent is either 60 or older, disabled, or unable to engage in gainful employment		
MARYLAND	Cts. & Jud. Proc. § 11-504	$6,000 plus an additional $5,000 in a Title 11 bankruptcy in value, in real property, or personal property		
MASSACHUSETTS	Ch. 188, § 1	$500,000 - declared; $125,000 - automatic		
MICHIGAN	600.6023	$3,500 realty, $1,000 trade tools	Lot	40 acres
MINNESOTA	510.01 to 510.09	$390,000, or if primarily agricultural, $975,000		160 acres
MISSISSIPPI	85-3-21	$75,000	160 acres	160 acres
MISSOURI	513.475	$15,000		
MONTANA	70-32-101; 70-32-104	$250,000		
NEBRASKA	77-3502 (taxation); 40-101 (judgments)	$60,000	1 acre; 2 lots	160 acres
NEVADA	115.01	$350,000		
NEW HAMPSHIRE	480:01	$120,000		

Table 54: Homestead—Continued

State	Code Section	Maximum Value of Property	Maximum Acreage (Urban)	Maximum Acreage (Rural)
NEW JERSEY	Homestead Property Tax Credit Act: 54:4-8.57 to 54:4-8.66 and 54:4--8.58a and 54:4-8.66a to 54:4-8.66e; 2A:17-19 personal property	$1,000 personal property; Homeowner, $600 min. rebate if income is less than $125,000; min. is $500 if income is between $125,000 and $200,000; Renter, $150 if income does not exceed $100,000		
NEW MEXICO	42-10-9 to 42-10-10	$60,000 or in lieu thereof, $2,000 in any property		
NEW YORK	Civ. Prac. L. & R. § 5206	$150,000 for counties of Kings, Queens, New York, Bronx, Richmond, Nassau, Suffolk, Rockland, Westchester, and Putnam; $125,000 for counties of Dutchess, Albany, Columbia, Orange, Saratoga, and Ulster; $75,000 for remaining counties		
NORTH CAROLINA	Const. art. X, § 2	$1,000		
NORTH DAKOTA	47-18-01	$100,000		
OHIO	2329.66	$125,000		
OKLAHOMA	Tit. 31, § 2		1 acre	160 acres
OREGON	18.395; 18.402	$40,000 or $50,000 if more than one debtor is subject to liability	1 block	160 acres
PENNSYLVANIA	Tit. 42, § 8123; Tit. 53, §§ 6926.1303 to 6926.1313	$300 monetary exemption from judgment only; for senior citizens, a formula based on a sliding scale of income up to $15,000		
RHODE ISLAND	9-26-4; 9-26-4.1	$2,000 for tools, $9,600 for furniture, $300 for books, $12,000 for motor vehicles; $500,000 in real property		
SOUTH CAROLINA	15-41-30	$50,000 up to a maximum of $100,000 if there are multiple exemptions on same living unit; various kinds of personal property		
SOUTH DAKOTA	43-31-4		1 acre; mineral lands: 1 acre	160 acres; mineral lands: 40 acres placer claim; 5 acres lode mining
TENNESSEE	26-2-301	$5,000 or $7,500 if more than one debtor is subject to liability; $12,500 up to $25,000 if 62 yrs. old		
TEXAS	Const. art. XVI, § 51		10 acres	200 acres
UTAH	78B-5-503	$5,000 if property is not primary personal residence, $30,000 if property is primary personal residence		
VERMONT	Tit. 27, § 101	$125,000		
VIRGINIA	34-4	$5,000 plus if support dependent, then $500 for each dependent		

Table 54: Homestead—Continued

State	Code Section	Maximum Value of Property	Maximum Acreage (Urban)	Maximum Acreage (Rural)
WASHINGTON	6.13.010; 6.13.030	Choice of $125,000 in real property or $15,000 in personal property		
WEST VIRGINIA	38-9-1; Const. art. VI, § 48	$5,000 in real property and $1,000 in personal property		
WISCONSIN	815.20; 990.01(14)	$75,000	Not less than 1/4 acre or more than 40 acres	Same as urban
WYOMING	1-20-101	$20,000		

55. LEASES AND RENTAL AGREEMENTS

When an individual agrees to rent or lease real estate property, the tenant signs either a lease or a rental agreement with the owner of the property outlining the terms of the agreement. The difference between rentals and leases is that the terms of leases are generally for at least one year, though lease payments are usually paid by the month. Terms for rentals are generally month-to-month, although they are occasionally paid on a weekly term. Virtually all states recognize that at the end of a lease, the term converts to a month-to-month rental unless a new lease is signed and the landlord continues to accept monthly payments.

Many states have imposed limits on the size of security deposits safeguarding against damage to the property that may be collected by landlords. However, roughly half the states have lifted the limit altogether. The highest deposit stated in a statute is three months' rent for a furnished property, and one month's rent was the general rule. Roughly half the states do not require interest to be returned with deposits.

All states have statutes limiting discrimination by landlords. Under these statutes, landlords are prohibited from not renting to certain classes of people, for example, those with young children and pets. New classes are also finding their way into the law books. Since 1993 virtually every state has legislated against discrimination on the basis of race, gender, religion or national origin. State legislatures generally ensure equal access to housing to the broadest range of citizens.

Table 55: Leases and Rental Agreements

State	Code Section	Terms of Leases	Deposits	Discrimination	Uniform Residential Landlord & Tenant Act Adopted?
ALABAMA	24-8-4; 24-8-7; 35-9-3	Renting for an unspecified term is presumed to be from December 1 to December 1, unless it is expressly a tenancy at will, then either party may terminate it at will, by 10 days notice in writing		No discrimination on basis of race, color, religion, sex, familial status, national origin; municipal corporations may zone/regulate as to different classes of inhabitants, but not to discriminate against or favor any class of inhabitants; housing for older persons exempted	No
ALASKA	18.80.210; 34.03.020; 34.03.070; 34.03.290	Unless otherwise agreed, rent is payable monthly and the term is month-to-month	Limit of 2 mos. rent (unless rent exceeds $2,000/ mo.), interest on deposit not required; deposit must be returned within 14 days of termination if terminated under §§ 34.03.290, otherwise 30 days	No discrimination on basis of sex, physical/ mental disability, marital status, changes in marital status, pregnancy, parenthood, race, religion, color, national origin	Yes
ARIZONA	9-462.01(A) (11); 33-303; 33-342; 33-1321; 41-1491.14	Lease does not automatically renew but is converted into a tenancy from month-to-month	Limit 1½ mos. rent; interest on deposit not required; deposit must be returned within 14 days of termination	No discrimination on basis of race, color, religion, sex, familial status, national origin; any municipality may establish age-specific community zoning and may restrict residency to head of household or spouse of specific age or older and prohibit minors; housing for older persons exempted	Yes
ARKANSAS	18-16-304 18-16-305; 16-123-310	When rent accepted by a landlord of a holding-over tenant, the term becomes a tenancy from year-to-year (*Jonesboro Trust Co. v. Harbough*, 244 S.W. 455, 456 (Ark. 1922))	Limit of 2 mos. rent; interest on deposit not required; deposit must be returned within 30 days of termination	No discrimination on the basis of race, color, religion, sex, familial status, or national origin.	No

Table 55: Leases and Rental Agreements—Continued

State	Code Section	Terms of Leases	Deposits	Discrimination	Uniform Residential Landlord & Tenant Act Adopted?
CALIFORNIA	Civ. §§ 51.2; 1945; 1950.5; Govt. §§ 12920; 12955	If tenant remains in possession and landlord accepts rent, parties are presumed to have renewed lease on same terms and for same time, not to exceed 1 year	Limit 2 mos. rent for unfurnished, 3 mos. rent for furnished; interest on deposit not required; deposit must be refunded between 21 and 60 days from date of termination	No discrimination based on race, color, religion, sex, sexual orientation, marital status, national origin, ancestry, familial status or disability; special accommodations for senior citizen housing, familial status or disability	No
COLORADO	24-34-502; 24-34-502.2; 38-12-102 to 38-12-104		Interest on deposit not required; damages subtracted must be itemized and balance returned within 1 month of termination unless otherwise agreed, but never over 60 days	No discrimination on basis of age, sex, marital status, familial status, handicap, race, religion, creed, color, national origin, but does not prohibit compliance with local zoning ordinance provisions concerning residential restrictions on marital status	No
CONNECTICUT	46a-64c; 47a-3d; 47a-21	Holdover not evidence of a new lease; converts to month-to-month	Tenant under age of 62: limit 2 mos. rent; tenant over 62: limit 1 mo. rent; interest on deposit required; deposit must be refunded within 30 days or within 15 days of receiving tenant's forwarding address	No discrimination on basis of race, creed, color, national origin, ancestry, sex, marital status, age, lawful source of income, familial status; may refuse to rent to people not blood related who are not married; public or private programs allowed to assist persons over 64 as long as there is no discrimination on basis of age among those eligible	No

Table 55: Leases and Rental Agreements—Continued

State	Code Section	Terms of Leases	Deposits	Discrimination	Uniform Residential Landlord & Tenant Act Adopted?
DELAWARE	Tit. 6, § 4603; Tit. 25, § 5514	If tenant remains in possession and landlord accepts rent, creation of new tenancy from year-to-year is inferred (*Makin v. Mack*, 336 A.2d 230 (1975))	Limit 1 mo. rent; interest on deposit not required; deposit must be returned within 20 days of termination; if deposit not returned within 30 days, tenant entitled to double the amount of security deposit	No discrimination on basis of race, age, marital status, creed, color, sex, handicap, national origin, gender identity	No
DISTRICT OF COLUMBIA	2-1401.01; 42-3502.09; 42-3502.17; 42-3505.05	Receipt of rent for new term or part thereof amounts to waiver of landlord's right to demand possession (*Shapiro v. Christopher*, 195 F.2d 785 (D.C. Cir. 1952); *Byrne v. Morrison*, 25 App. D.C. 72 (1905))	Interest on deposit required at 5% annually on tenancy for 12 mos. or more; deposit returned within 45 days of termination	No discrimination on basis of race, color, religion, national origin, sex, age, marital status, personal appearance, sexual orientation, family responsibilities, gender identity or expression, genetic information, physical handicap, matriculation, political affiliation, source of income, place of residence or business; also illegal to discriminate against elderly or families receiving or eligible to receive Tenant Assistance Program assistance	No

Table 55: Leases and Rental Agreements—Continued

State	Code Section	Terms of Leases	Deposits	Discrimination	Uniform Residential Landlord & Tenant Act Adopted?
FLORIDA	83.01 et seq.; 760.23	Mere payment of rent is not construed as a renewal for the term, but if tenant holding over does so with written consent of landlord, it becomes a tenancy at will; otherwise tenancy at sufferance	No limits on deposits; landlord may elect to (1) put deposit in non-interest bearing account; (2) hold in interest bearing account at either 75% of average rate or 5%; or (3) post a surety bond and pay tenant interest at 5%; landlord must inform tenant of choice in writing within 30 days; must return deposit within 15 days of termination	No discrimination on basis of race, color, national origin, sex, familial status, handicap, or religion; same as Fair Housing Act	Yes
GEORGIA	8-3-201; 8-3-202; 44-7-31	Rent accepted after expiration of 1 year lease implies renewal of lease for another year (*Allen v. Montgomery*, 105 S.E. 33 (1920))	Deposit must be deposited in escrow account and held in trust for tenant; any damages subtracted must be itemized and deposit must be returned within 30 days of termination	No discrimination on basis of race, color, religion, sex, handicap, familial status, or national origin; allowable housing for "older people" included in statutes	No
HAWAII	515-3; 515-4; 521-44; 521-71	Landlord accepting rent in advance after first 60 days of holdover creates a month-to-month tenancy absent contrary agreement; absence of any agreement makes term equal to that at which the rent is computed; notice to quit must give 28 days	Limit 1 mo. rent; no interest on deposit required; deposit must be returned within 14 days of termination	No discrimination on basis of HIV infection, race, sex, color, marital status, parental status, age, sexual orientation, ancestry, handicapped status; section regarding parental status does not apply to housing for older persons as defined in 42 USC § 3607(b)(2)	Yes

Table 55: Leases and Rental Agreements—Continued

State	Code Section	Terms of Leases	Deposits	Discrimination	Uniform Residential Landlord & Tenant Act Adopted?
IDAHO	6-321; 67-5909	Whether landlord waives right to give notice to quit the tenancy is question of intent; intent to waive must clearly appear; each case to be judged on case-by-case basis (*Riverside Dev. Co. v. Ritchie*, 650 P.2d 657, 663 (1982))	No limit on deposit; no interest on deposit required; deposit must be returned within 21 days if no time is fixed by agreement or in any case within 30 days after surrender of possession by tenant	No discrimination on basis of race, color, religion, sex, national origin, with exceptions	No
ILLINOIS	65 §§ 5/11 to 5/11.1-1; 775 §§ 5/3-105; 5/3-106; 765 § 715/1	Tenant holds over and landlord receives rent, presumed that new year-to-year tenancy created, absent express intent otherwise (*Demerath v. Schennum*, 59 N.E.2d 348 (1945))	No limits on deposit; interest required on deposit at minimum deposit passbook savings account interest rate paid by largest commercial bank in the state if held for over 6 mos. and if lessor owns 25 units or more in one building or complex of buildings	No discrimination on basis of race, color, religion, sex, creed, ancestry, national origin, physical/mental handicap; statute repealed prohibiting discrimination against children; provisions for senior citizen housing	No
INDIANA	22-9.5-3-4; 22-9.5-5-1; 32-31-3-1.1 to 32-31-3-19	Holding over from a year tenancy and paying rent creates year-to-year tenancy (*Alleman v. Vink*, 62 N.E. 461 (1902))	No limits on deposit; interest on deposit not required; any damages subtracted must be itemized and returned within 45 days of termination	No discrimination on basis of race, color, religion, sex, familial status, handicap, or national origin; housing for older persons exempted	No
IOWA	216.8; 562A.9(4); 562A.12	Holding over converts to month-to-month tenancy	Limit 2 mos. rent; any interest earned on deposit for first 5 yrs. of tenancy is landlord's property; deposit must be returned within 30 days if given forwarding address	No discrimination on basis of race, color, creed, sex, religion, origin, disability, or family status; housing for older persons exempted	Yes

Table 55: Leases and Rental Agreements—Continued

State	Code Section	Terms of Leases	Deposits	Discrimination	Uniform Residential Landlord & Tenant Act Adopted?
KANSAS	44-1016; 58-2545; 58-2550	Holdover converts to month-to-month tenancy	Limit 1 mo. rent; special rules for pets and furnishings; interest on deposit not required unless renting from municipal housing authority; deposit must be returned within 14 days after determination and written notice of any deductions from deposit except for unpaid rent, but in no event to exceed 30 days after termination	No discrimination on basis of race, religion, color, sex, disability, familial status, national origin or ancestry, or an intention to make any such preference, limitation, specification or discrimination; housing for older persons exempted	Yes
KENTUCKY	344.360; 344.362; 383.565(3); 383.580	Holdover converts to month-to-month tenancy	No limit on deposit; interest on deposit not required; landlord must send notice to last known/determinable address that tenant has a refund due, if tenant does not respond within 60 days, it becomes landlord's property	No discrimination on basis of race, color, religion, national origin, sex, familial status, disability; housing for older persons exempted; landlord may refuse to rent to unmarried couple	Yes
LOUISIANA	9:3251; 51:2602 to 51:2614	Landlord's right to eject is waived when he accepts rent from holdover tenant (*Canal Realty & Improvement Co. v. Pailet*, 46 So.2d 303 (1950))	No limit on deposit; interest on deposit not required; deposit must be returned within 1 mo. of termination along with an itemized statement for any retained amount	No discrimination on basis of race, color, religion, sex, handicap, familial status, national origin; housing for older persons exempted	No

Table 55: Leases and Rental Agreements—Continued

State	Code Section	Terms of Leases	Deposits	Discrimination	Uniform Residential Landlord & Tenant Act Adopted?
MAINE	Tit. 5, § 4552; Tit. 14, §§ 6031 to 6039		Limit 2 mos. rent; interest on deposit not required; if written agreement, deposit must be returned within timeframe of lease not to exceed 30 days or if tenancy at will, within 21 days of termination; landlord must provide written statement for any deductions	No discrimination on basis of race, color, sex, physical or mental disability, religion, sexual orientation, ancestry, national origin, familial status; housing for older persons exempted.	No
MARYLAND	Real Prop. §§ 8-203; 8-402; State Gov't §§ 20-701 to 20-710	Holdover tenancy becomes week-to-week if weekly before and month-to-month in all other cases	Limit 2 mos. rent; interest on deposit required at the U.S. Treasury yield curve rate for 1 yr. as of the 1st business day of each year or 1.5%, whichever is greater; landlord must return deposit within 45 days of termination and provide written notice of any portion withheld to tenant's last known address	No discrimination on basis of race, religion, color, sex, sexual orientation, national origin, marital status, handicap. If owner maintains personal residence in dwelling which has 5 or less units, owner may discriminate on sex or marital status. May rent to elderly exclusively only if dwelling planned specifically for specified age group	No
MASSACHUSETTS	Ch. 151B, § 4; Ch. 186, § 15B	Payment and acceptance of rent create tenancy at will (*Staples v. Collins*, 73 N.E.2d 729 (1947)); certain acts/conduct may negate this presumption (*Corcoran Management Co., Ins. v. Withers*, 513 N.E.2d 218 (1987))	Limit 1 mo. rent; interest on deposit required at 5% from first day of tenancy if landlord has held deposit for 1 yr.; deposit must be returned within 30 days	No discrimination on basis of race, religious creed, color, national origin, sex, sexual orientation, age, ancestry, marital status, member of armed forces, handicapped in any multiple dwelling, contiguously located housing accommodations or publicly assisted dwellings	No

Table 55: Leases and Rental Agreements—Continued

State	Code Section	Terms of Leases	Deposits	Discrimination	Uniform Residential Landlord & Tenant Act Adopted?
MICHIGAN	37.2102; 37.2502; 37.2503; 554.601 to 554.616	Holdover converts to year-to-year tenancy (*Faraci v. Fassulo*, 212 Mich. 216 (1920))	Limit 1½ mos. rent; interest on deposit not required; landlord must supply tenant with checklist of all damages upon termination of lease	No discrimination on basis of religion, race, color, national origin, age, sex, height, weight, familial status, marital status. Housing programs for elderly exempted; children may be restricted to certain areas of complex (*Dept. of Civil Rights v. Beznos Corp.*, 421 Mich. 110 (1984))	No
MINNESOTA	363A.21; 363A.09; 504B.141; 504B.178	Period of the shortest interval between times of payment of rent under expired lease	No limit on deposit; interest on deposit required at 3-4%; deposit must be returned within 3 weeks of termination; landlord must provide a written statement of damages within 3 weeks of termination	No discrimination on basis of race, color, creed, religion, national origin, sex, marital status, disability, sexual orientation, familial status; housing for older persons exempted; landlords may advertise "adults only"	No
MISSISSIPPI	89-8-19; 89-8-21; 43-33-723	Holdover converts to month-to-month tenancy unless tenant pays weekly	No limit on deposit; interest on deposit not required; deposit must be returned within 45 days of termination	No discrimination on basis of race, religious principles, color, sex, national origin, ancestry, handicap; in housing receiving assistance: no discrimination on the basis of age or, in the case of families, because of children, except in housing restricted to persons over 62	No
MISSOURI	213.040; 441.060; 535.300	All tenancies not made in writing and signed by parties shall be held as month-to-month	Limit 2 mos. rent; interest on deposit not required; deposit must be must be returned within 30 days of termination	No discrimination on basis of race, color, religion, national origin, familial status, ancestry, sex, handicap; housing for older persons exempted	No

Table 55: Leases and Rental Agreements—Continued

State	Code Section	Terms of Leases	Deposits	Discrimination	Uniform Residential Landlord & Tenant Act Adopted?
MONTANA	49-2-305; 70-24-201(2); 70-25-201 to 70-25-206	Holdover converts to month-to-month tenancy unless tenant pays weekly, then week-to-week	No limit on deposit; interest on deposit not required; before any damages are subtracted from deposit, landlord must give tenant an itemized list and provide an opportunity for tenant to clean or fix the problem; deposit must be returned within 10 days of termination	No discrimination on basis of sex, marital status, race, creed, religion, age, familial status, physical/ mental handicap, color, national origin; housing for older persons exempted; landlord may discriminate against children in duplex in which owner resides in half	Yes
NEBRASKA	18-1724; 76-1414; 76-1416	Holdover converts to month-to-month tenancy unless tenant pays weekly, then week-to-week	Limit 1 mo. rent plus ¼ of 1 mo. rent pet deposit; deposit must be returned within 14 days after demand and designation of location to be mailed	No discrimination on basis of race, color, creed, religion, age, ancestry, sex, marital status, national origin, familial status, handicap or disability	Yes
NEVADA	118A.242; 118A.470; 207.300	Holdover converts to month-to month tenancy unless tenant pays weekly, then week-to-week	Limit 3 mos. rent; interest on deposit not required; deposit must be returned within 30 days of termination	No discrimination on basis of race, religious creed, color, national origin, disability, ancestry, familial status, sex	No
NEW HAMPSHIRE	354-A:1; 354-A.15; 5540:1; 540-A:6; 540-A:7	Every tenancy shall be deemed to be at will and rent payable on demand absent contrary contract shown	Limit 1 mo. rent or $100, whichever is greater; interest on deposit required and must be returned to tenant if he holds the deposit for 1 yr. or longer; deposit must be returned within 30 days	No discrimination on basis of age, sex, race, creed, color, marital status, physical/mental disability, national origin, familial status; retirement communities exempted	No

Table 55: Leases and Rental Agreements—Continued

State	Code Section	Terms of Leases	Deposits	Discrimination	Uniform Residential Landlord & Tenant Act Adopted?
NEW JERSEY	46:8-10; 46:8-21.1; 46:8-21.2	Holdover converts to month-to-month tenancy absent agreement to the contrary	Limit 1½ mos. rent; interest on deposit required; any damages subtracted from deposit must be itemized and balance of deposit must be returned within 30 days of termination	No discrimination on basis of race, creed, color, national origin, ancestry, age, disability, marital status, affectionate or sexual orientation, familial status, or sex; retirement communities exempted	No
NEW MEXICO	28-1-7(G); 47-8-15; 47-8-18; 47-8-37	Holdover converts to month-to-month tenancy unless tenant pays weekly, then week-to-week	If term is under 1 yr., then limit is 1 mo. rent; interest on deposit required if landlord demands deposit in excess of 1 mo. rent; deposit must be returned within 30 days of termination or departure, whichever is later	No discrimination on basis of race, religion, color, national origin, ancestry, sex, physical or mental handicap, sexual orientation, spousal affiliation or gender identity	Yes
NEW YORK	Real Prop. §§ 232-C; 236-237; Exec. § 296(5)(A); Gen. Oblig. § 7-103; Rent & Evict. Regs. § 2105.5	Holdover converts to month-to-month tenancy absent agreement otherwise	Limit 1 mo. rent; interest on deposit required	No discrimination on basis of race, creed, color, national origin, sex, age, disability, sexual orientation, military status, marital status, familial status; exception for housing accommodations exclusively for those 55 and older or same sex; landlord may discriminate against children in senior citizen housing, 1 or 2 family homes, mobile homes parks for those 55 or older	No

Table 55: Leases and Rental Agreements—Continued

State	Code Section	Terms of Leases	Deposits	Discrimination	Uniform Residential Landlord & Tenant Act Adopted?
NORTH CAROLINA	41A-4; 41A-6(e); 42-50 to 42-56	Landlord may treat tenant as trespasser and eject or may recognize him as tenant with presumption of year-to-year tenancy. (*Murrill v. Palmer*, 80 S.E. 55 (1913)); this presumption is rebuttable and will yield to the actual intention of the parties (*Gurtis v. City of Sanford*, 197 S.E. 2d 584 (1973))	Limits: week-to-week, 2 wks. rent; month-to-month, 1½ mos. rent; over month-to-month, 2 mos. rent; interest on deposits not required; deposit must be returned within 30 days of termination	No discrimination on basis of race, religion, color, sex, national origin, handicap, or familial status; housing for older persons exempted	No
NORTH DAKOTA	14-02.4-01; 47-16-06; 47-16-07.1	Lease renews on holdover for same time and terms as previous one but not exceeding 1 yr.	Limit 1 mo. rent; interest on deposit required unless occupancy less than 9 mos.; deposit must be returned within 30 days	No discrimination on basis of race, color, religion, sex, national origin, age, physical or mental handicap, or status in marriage or public assistance	No
OHIO	4112.02(H); 5321.01 to 5321.19	Presumption that holdover converts to year-to-year term but it is rebuttable (*Bumiller v. Walker*, 116 N.E. 797 (1917))	Interest on deposit required at 5% per yr. if tenant remains in possession 6 mos. or more and deposit is greater than $50 or one month's rent; deposit must be returned within 30 days of termination	No discrimination on basis of race, color, religion, sex, ancestry, handicap, national origin, familial, or military status	Yes
OKLAHOMA	Tit. 41 §§ 35; 115; Tit. 25, § 1452; 1453	Parties presumed to have renewed lease for same terms and time, not exceeding 1 yr.	No limit on deposit; interest on deposit not required; deposit must be returned within 30 days of termination	No discrimination on basis of race, color, religion, gender, national origin, age, familial status, handicap; housing for older persons exempted	No

Table 55: Leases and Rental Agreements—Continued

State	Code Section	Terms of Leases	Deposits	Discrimination	Uniform Residential Landlord & Tenant Act Adopted?
OREGON	90.20; 90.30; 427; 659A.421	Holdover converts to month-to-month tenancy	No limit on deposit; interest on deposit not required; deposit must be returned within 30 days after termination	No discrimination on basis of race, color, sex, marital status, familial status, religion, source of income or national origin; housing for older persons exempted	Yes
PENNSYLVANIA	Tit. 43, § 955(h); Tit. 68, §§ 250.101 to 250.510-b	Holdover converts to same term as original lease if it was for 1 yr. or less	Limit 2 mos. rent; interest on deposit required if deposit held over 2 yrs.	No discrimination on basis of race, color, familial status, age, religious creed, ancestry, sex, national origin, handicap, disability; housing for older persons exempted	No
RHODE ISLAND	34-18-15; 34-18-19; 34-37-2 to 34-37-11	Parties may agree to a term, otherwise month-to-month unless tenant pays weekly, then week-to-week	Limit 1 mo. rent; interest on deposit not required; deposit must be returned within 20 days of termination	No discrimination on basis of race, color, religion, sex, sexual orientation, marital status, ancestral origin, gender identity or expression, handicap, age or familial status; housing specifically for older persons exempted; landlord may discriminate against children in certain circumstances	Yes
SOUTH CAROLINA	27-40-310; 27-40-410; 31-21-40	Holdover converts to month-to-month tenancy unless tenant pays weekly, then week-to-week	No limit on deposit; interest on deposit not required; deposit must be returned within 30 days of termination	No discrimination on basis of race, color, religion, sex, familial status, or national origin; housing for older persons exempted; landlord may discriminate against children in single family dwellings and certain other small unit buildings	Yes

Table 55: Leases and Rental Agreements—Continued

State	Code Section	Terms of Leases	Deposits	Discrimination	Uniform Residential Landlord & Tenant Act Adopted?
SOUTH DAKOTA	20-13-10 to 20-13-21.2; 43-32-6.1; 43-32-14; 43-32-24	Holdover converts to rental on same terms and same time as original lease	Limit 1 mo. rent, unless otherwise agreed because special conditions pose a danger to premises maintenance; interest on deposit not required; deposit must be returned within 2 wks. of termination	No discrimination on basis of race, color, creed, religion, sex, ancestry, disability, familial status or national origin; housing for older persons exempted; landlord may discriminate against children in duplexes where one unit is owner-occupied	No
TENNESSEE	4-21-601; 4-21-602; 66-28-201; 66-28-301; 66-28-512;	Holdover converts to month-to-month tenancy or upon agreement, apportionable day-to-day	No limit on deposit; interest on deposit not required	No discrimination on basis of race, color, creed, religion, sex, handicap, familial status, or national origin; housing for older persons exempted	Yes
TEXAS	Prop. §§ 92.101 to 92.109; 301.001 to 301.171	Holdover implies an agreement between landlord and tenant; normally lease for 1 yr. will be implied absent express or implied contrary agreement (*Barragan v. Munoz*, 525 S.W. 2d 559 (1975))	No limit on deposit; interest on deposit required; deposit must be returned within 30 days of termination	No discrimination on basis of race, color, religion, sex, familial status, national origin; housing for older persons exempted	No
UTAH	57-17-1 to 57-17-1; 57-21-1 to 57-21-14	Holdover tenant is bound to covenants previously agreed to and binding in first term (*Cottonwood Mall Co. v. Sine*, 767 P.2d 499, 503 (1988))	No limit on deposit; interest on deposit not required; deposit must be returned within 30 days of termination	No discrimination on basis of race, color, religion, sex, national origin, familial status, source of income, disability; housing for older persons exempted; no discrimination against children unless in adults-only apartment complex, condo, or other housing not violating federal law	No

Table 55: Leases and Rental Agreements—Continued

State	Code Section	Terms of Leases	Deposits	Discrimination	Uniform Residential Landlord & Tenant Act Adopted?
VERMONT	Tit. 9, §§ 4461; 4503	Holdover may convert into year-to-year tenancy; result of legal consequence of conduct of parties and does not depend on tenant's intention (*Malaitty v. Carroll Co.*, 41 A.2d 144 (Vt. 1945))	No limit on deposit; interest on deposit not required; deposit must be returned within 14 days of termination or landlord forfeits right to withhold any of it	No discrimination on basis of race, sex, sexual orientation, age, marital status, religious creed, color, national origin, handicap, recipient of public assistance, or because person intends to occupy with children; housing for older persons exempted	No
VIRGINIA	36-96.3; 55-248.15:1	Holdover converts to month-to-month or any lesser term	Limit 2 mos. rent; deposit must be returned within 30 days of termination	No discrimination on basis of race, color, religion, national origin, sex, elderliness, or familial status; special provisions for housing for elderly	Yes
WASHINGTON	49.60.010; 59.04.010; 59.04.020; 59.18.260 to 59.18.285	When term of tenancy is indefinite, period becomes that on which rent is payable	No limit on deposit, but no deposit may be collected unless rental agreement is in writing; interest on deposit not required; deposit must be returned within 14 days of termination	No discrimination on basis of race, creed, color, national origin, families with children, sex, marital status, sexual orientation, age, honorably discharged veteran or military status, or the presence of any sensory, mental, or physical disability or the use of a trained dog guide or service animal by a person with a disability	Yes
WEST VIRGINIA	5-11A-5; 37-6-5	Holdover converts to year-to-year tenancy upon terms of original lease (*Allen v. Bartlett*, 20 W. Va. 46 (1882))		No discrimination on basis of race, sex, color, religion, ancestry, familial status, blindness, handicap, or national origin; housing for older persons exempted	No

Table 55: Leases and Rental Agreements—Continued

State	Code Section	Terms of Leases	Deposits	Discrimination	Uniform Residential Landlord & Tenant Act Adopted?
WISCONSIN	106.50; 704.25	Landlord may elect to hold tenant to month-to-month basis on holdover, unless the lease is for weekly or daily rent		No discrimination on basis of race, sex, color, sexual orientation, disability, religion, national origin, marital status, family status, income source (lawful), age, ancestry; housing for older persons exempted	No
WYOMING	1-21-1207; 1-21-1208; 6-9-102; 34-2-128; 34-2-129	Accepting rent on holdover does not imply renewal; constitutes only tenancy by sufferance	No limit on deposit; deposit must be returned within 30 days of termination	No discrimination based on race, color, sex, creed, or national origin	No

VIII. TAX LAWS

56. CONSUMER TAXES

The taxation system in the United States is very complicated due, in part, to the attempt by governing bodies to make taxation, across the board, appear reasonable and invisible.

Overall, there are two types of consumer taxes. Some are meant merely to raise revenues while others are designed to inhibit certain behavior. (In the income tax arena, however, which is significantly in the domain of the federal government, taxes and deductions and exemptions are used to actually promote certain behavior, such as saving money or buying a house.) In many cases, the behavioral control aspect of the tax has outweighed the particular tax's revenue-raising function. Examples are the taxes on tobacco, gasoline and liquor. The taxes vary widely from state to state, often reflecting the loci of the business being taxed. Taxes on tobacco are relatively low in tobacco-producing states.

Market forces also influence consumer taxes. For example, the tax on wines produced in California is low compared to taxes on wines produced in other states. If California taxes were close to the national average, then California wines sold in other states would have artificially inflated prices, thus hurting its marketability.

The taxes treated in this chapter are not exhaustive. Rather, they are representative of the most common and significant consumer taxes levied by states.

Table 56: Consumer Taxes

State	Sales Tax	Use Tax	Cigarette Tax
ALABAMA	4%, 40-23-2	4%, 40-23-61; agricultural machinery: 1.5%, 40-23-63	67.5¢/pack, 40-25-2
ALASKA	None	None	$2/pack, 43.50.090; 43.50.190
ARIZONA	5%, 42-5010	Same as sales for same type of activity, 42-5155	$2/pack, 42-3052
ARKANSAS	6.5%, 26-52-301 to 26-52-302; AR Const. Amend. 91, § 3	6.5%, 26-52-302; 26-53-106; 26-53-107	$1.15/pack, 26-57-208
CALIFORNIA	7.25%, Rev. & Tax §§ 6051 to 6051.4; 6201 to 6201.5; 7203.1; Cal.Const. Art. 13, §§ 35; 36	7.25%, Rev. & Tax §§ 6201 to 6201.4	$2.87/pack, Rev. & Tax. §§ 30101; 30123
COLORADO	2.9%, 39-26-106	2.9%, 39-26-202	84¢/pack, 39-28-103
CONNECTICUT	6.35%, 12-408	6.35%, 12-411	$3.40/pack, 12-316
DELAWARE	No sales tax; $75 annual fee plus .126% gross receipts tax on sales, Tit. 30, § 2702	Tax on lease of tangible personal property and automobiles: 1.9914%, Tit. 30, § 4302	$2.10/pack, Tit. 30, § 5305
DISTRICT OF COLUMBIA	6%, 47-2002	6%, 47-2202	$4.50/pack, 47-2402
FLORIDA	6%, 212.05	6%, 212.05	$1.339/pack, 210.02
GEORGIA	4%, 48-8-30	4%, 48-3-30	37¢/pack, 48-11-2
HAWAII	4%, 237-13	4%, 238-2	$3.20/pack, 245-3
IDAHO	6%, 63-3619	6%, 63-3621	57¢/pack, 63-2506
ILLINOIS	6.25%, 35 § 120/2-10	6.25%, 35 § 105/3-10	$1.98/pack, 35 § 130/2; 135/2
INDIANA	7%, 6-2.5-2-2	7%, 6-2.5-3-3	99.5¢/pack, 6-7-1-12
IOWA	6%, 423.2	5%, 423.5	$1.36/pack, 453A.6
KANSAS	6.5%, 79-3603	6.5%, 79-3703	$1.29/pack, 79-3310
KENTUCKY	6%, 139.200	6%, 139.310	$1.10/pack, 138.140

Gasoline Tax per Gallon	Liquor Tax
16¢, 40-17-325; lubricating oil: 4¢/gal., 40-17-220	Liquor monopoly state: Beer: 5.0¢/12 oz. + 1.625¢/4 oz., 28-3-184; 28-3-190; Wine and spirits: 10% wholesale price + 56%, 28-3-200 to 282-3-205; Table wine <16.5%: 45¢/liter; >16.5%: $2.42/liter, 28-7-16
8¢, 43.40.010	Beer: $1.07/gal.; Wine and spirits: ≤21% alcohol: $2.50/gal.; >21%: $12.80/gal., 43.60.010
18¢, 28-5606	Beer 16¢/gal.; Wine <24% 84¢/gal., >24% 25¢/gal.; Cider: .5-7%: $1.07/gal.; Spirits $3/gal., 42-3052
21.5¢, 26-55-205; 26-55-1002	Beer 24¢/gal.; Light wine .5 to 5% 25¢/gal.; Wine >5% 75¢/gal.; Spirits ≥$2.50/gal.; Premixed spirits $1/gal.; Light spirits .5-5% 50¢/gal., 3-7-104
41.7¢, Rev. & Tax. § 7360	Beer: 20¢/gal.; Wine 20¢/gal.; Sparkling hard cider: 20¢/gal.; Sparkling wine: 30¢/gal.; Spirits ≤100 proof: $3.30/gal.; >100 proof: $6.60/gal., Rev. & Tax §§ 32151; 32201; 32220
22¢, 39-27-102; 39-27-103	Beer 8¢/gal.; Wine 7.33¢/liter; Colorado wines: 12.33¢/liter; Cider: 8¢/gal.; Spirits 60.26¢/liter, 12-47-503
25¢, 12-458	Beer: $7.20/barrel; 24¢/gal; Still wine: ≤21% 72¢/gal.; >21% and sparkling wine $1.58/gal.; Cider: 24¢/gal.; Spirits $5.40/gal., 12-435
23¢, Tit. 30, § 5110	Beer: $4.85/barrel, 16¢/gal.; Wine 97¢/gal.; Spirits <25% $3.64/gal., >25% $5.46/gal., Tit. 4, §§ 581
8% of average wholesale price, 23.5¢/gal. as of 7/2018, 47-2301	Beer: $2.79/barrel, 25-902; Wine: ≤14% 30¢/gal; >14% 40¢/gal.; Sparkling wine: 45¢/gal.; Spirits: $1.50/gal., 25-901
17.4¢ + 1-11¢ at county's discretion, 206.41	Beer 48¢/gal., 563.05; 564.06; Wine <17.259% $2.25/gal., >17.259% $3/gal.; Sparkling wine $3.50/gal.; Spirits 17.259% to 55.78% $6.50/gal., >55.78% $9.53/gal., 565.12
26.8¢, 48-9-3	Beer: $10/barrel, in bottles or cans 4.5¢/12 oz., 3-5-60; counties add tax of $6/barrel or 5¢/12 oz., 3-5-80; Wine: 40¢/liter + 27¢ excise tax on dessert wine, 3-6-50; Spirits: 50¢/liter, 70¢/liter imported, 3-4-60
16¢ + additional county rates or 17-23¢/gal., 243-4; 243-5	Draft beer: 54¢/gal.; Bottle beer: 93¢/gal.; Still wine: $1.38/gal.; Sparkling wine: $2.12/gal.; Spirits: $5.98/gal.; rates adjusted semiannually, 244D-4
33¢, 63-2405; 63-24-2; 41-4909	Liquor monopoly state; Beer: $4.65/barrel, 15¢/gal. 23-1008; Wine: 45¢/gal., 23-1319; alcoholic liquor surcharge, 23-217
19¢, 35 § 505/2	Beer: 23.1¢/gal.; Wine: $1.39/gal.; Spirits: $8.55/gal., 235 § 5/8-1
29¢, 6-6-1.1-201	Beer: 11.5¢/gal., 7.1-4-2-1; Wine: ≤21% 47¢/gal.; >21% $2.68/gal., 7.1-4-4-1; Spirits: $2.68/gal., 7.1-4-3-1
29¢ with ethanol; 30.7¢ without ethanol, 452A.3	Liquor monopoly state; Beer: $5.89/barrel, 123.136; Wine: $1.75/gal.; the Alcoholic Beverages Division of the Iowa Dept. of Commerce is responsible for the regulation and control of alcohol in the state of Iowa, 123.183
24¢, 79-3408; 79-34,141	Beer: 18¢/gal.; Wine: ≤14% 30¢/gal.; >14% 75¢/gal.; Spirits: $2.50/gal., 41-501; additional taxes for on-premises consumption, 79-4101; 79-41a02
9% of average wholesale price; 2018 price: 26¢/gal., 138.210; 138.228	Beer $2.50/barrel; Wine: 50¢/gal.; Spirits: $1.92/gal., 243.720

Table 56: Consumer Taxes—Continued

State	Sales Tax	Use Tax	Cigarette Tax
LOUISIANA	4.45%, 47:302; 47:331	4%, 47:302; 47:331	$1.08/pack, 47:841
MAINE	5.5% Tit. 36, § 1811	5.5%, Tit. 36, § 1861	$3.51/pack, Tit. 36, § 4365
MARYLAND	6%, Tax-Gen. § 11-104	6%, Tax-Gen. § 11-104	$2/pack, Tax-Gen. § 12-105
MASSACHUSETTS	6.25%, Ch. 64H, § 2	6.25%, Ch. 641, § 2	$3.51/pack, Ch. 64C, § 6
MICHIGAN	6%, 205.52	6%, 205.93	$2/pack, 205.427
MINNESOTA	6.875%, 297A.62	6.5%, 297A.63	$3.04/pack, 297F.05
MISSISSIPPI	7%, 27-65-17	Same rate as sales tax: 7%, 27-67-5	68¢/pack, 27-69-13
MISSOURI	4.225%, 144.020; Mo. Const. art. IV, §§ 43(a) and 47(c)	Same rate as sales tax: 4.225%, 144.610	17¢/pack, 149.015
MONTANA	None	None	$1.70/pack, 16-11-111
NEBRASKA	5.5%, 77-2701.02 ; legislature is required to set rate each year, 77-2715.01	5.5%, 77-2701.02; 77-2715.01	64¢/pack, 77-2602
NEVADA	6.85%, 372.105; 374.110; 377.040	6.85%, 372.185; 374.190; 377.040	$1.80/pack, 370.165
NEW HAMPSHIRE	None	None	$1.78/pack, 78:7
NEW JERSEY	7%, 54:32B-3	7%, 54:32B-6	$2.70/pack, 54:40A-8
NEW MEXICO	5.125%, 7-9-4	5.125%, 7-9-7	$1.66/pack, 7-12-3
NEW YORK	4%, Tax § 1105	4%, Tax § 1110	$4.35/pack, Tax § 471
NORTH CAROLINA	4.75%, 105-164.4	4.75%, 105.164.6	45¢/pack, 105-113.5
NORTH DAKOTA	5%, 57-39.2-02.1	5%, 57-40.2-02.1	44¢/pack, 57-36-06
OHIO	5.75%, 5739.025	5.75%., 5741.02	$1.60/pack, 5743.02; 5743.023
OKLAHOMA	4.5%, Tit. 68, § 1354	4.5%, Tit. 68, § 1402	$2.03/pack, Tit. 68, § 302
OREGON	None	None	$1.33/pack, 323.030

Gasoline Tax per Gallon	Liquor Tax
20¢, 47:711; 47:820.1	Beer: $12.50/barrel; Still wine: ≤14% 20¢/liter; 14-24% 35¢/liter; >24% 55¢/liter; Sparkling wine: 55¢/liter; Spirits: 80¢/liter, 26:341; 26:342
29.5¢, Tit. 36, § 2903	Liquor monopoly state, Tit. 28-A, § 1651; Beer: 35¢/gal.; Wine: 60¢/gal.; Sparkling wine: $1.24/gal., Tit. 28-A, § 1652; Spirits: Commission must sell at price that will produce state liquor tax sufficient to pay premium of $1.25/proof gal., Tit. 28-A § 1703
35.3¢, Tax-Gen. § 9-305	Beer: 9¢/gal.; Wine: 40¢/gal.; Spirits: $1.50 gal., Tax-Gen. § 5-105
24¢, Ch. 64A, § 1	Beer: $3.30/barrel; Still wine: 55¢/gal.; Sparkling wine: 70¢/gal.; Spirits: ≤15% $1.10/proof gal.; 15-50% $4.05/proof gal.; >50% $4.05/proof gal., Ch. 138, § 21
26.3¢, 207.1008	Liquor monopoly state: Beer: $6.30/barrel, 436.1409; Wine: ≤16% 13.5¢/liter; >16% 20¢/liter, 436.1301; Spirits: offsale 13.85% of retail selling price; onsale 12% of retail selling price; additional 4% tax on retail selling price, 436.1301; 436.2201
28.5¢, 296A.07	Beer: 3.2% $2.40/barrel, >3.2% $4.60/barrel, 297G.04; Wine: ≤14% 30¢/gal.; 14-21% 95¢/gal.; 21-24% $1.82/gal.; >24% $3.52/gal.; Sparkling wine: $1.82/gal.; Spirits: $5.03/gal., 297G.03
18.4¢, 27-55-11	Liquor monopoly state; Beer, light wine: 42.68¢/gal., 27-71-307; Wine: 35¢/gal.; Sparkling wine: $1/gal.; Spirits: $2.50/gal., 27-71-7
17¢; 19¢ eff. 7/1/19, 142.803	Beer: $1.86/barrel; Wine: 36¢/gal.; Spirits: $2/gal., 311.550; 311.554
31.5¢, 15-70-403	Liquor monopoly state, 16-1-401; 16-1-404; Beer: over 10,000 barrels: $4.30/barrel, 16-1-406; Wine: 27¢/liter, 16-1-411; 16-2-301
28¢, 66-489; 66-4,105; 66-4,144; 66-4,145; 66-4,146	Beer: 31¢/gal.; Wine: 95¢/gal.; Spirits $3.75/gal.; Wine from farm wineries: 6¢/gal., 53-160
24¢, 365.175 365.180; 365.190; 365.192	Beer: 16¢/gal.; Wine ≤14% 70¢/gal.; 14-22% $1.30/gal.; >22% $3.60/gal., 369.330
23.8¢, 260:32	Liquor monopoly state, 177:6; Beer: 30¢/gal., 178:26
41.4¢, 54:39-103	Beer: 12¢/gal.; Wine: 87.5¢/gal.; Spirits: $5.50/gal., 54:43-1
17¢, 7-13-3	Beer: 41¢/gal.; Wine: 45¢/liter; Spirits: $1.60/liter, 7-17-5
25¢, Tax §§ 284 to 284-C	Beer: 14¢/gal.; Still and sparkling wine: 30¢/gal. (natural); Spirits: ≤24% 67¢/liter; other $1.70/liter, Tax § 424
36.2¢ eff. 1/1/19 plus either 3.5¢/gal. or 7% of average wholesale price, 105-449.80	Liquor monopoly state: Beer: 61.71¢/gal.; Wine: 26.34¢/liter unfortified; 19.34¢/liter fortified; Spirits: 30% retail, 105-113.80
23¢, 57-43.1-02	Beer: 8¢/gal. in barrels; 16¢/gal. in bottles; Wine: ≤17% 50¢/gal.; 17-24% 60¢/gal.; Spirits: $2.50/gal., 5-03-07
28¢, 5735.25; 5735.05	Liquor monopoly state; Beer: $5.58/barrel; container ≤12 oz. .014¢/oz.; >12 oz .084¢/6 oz. or fraction thereof, 4301.42; 4305.01; Wine 4-14% 30¢/gal.; 14-21% $98¢/gal.; Vermouth $1.08/gal.; Sparkling wine $1.48/gal.; Mixed beverages $1.20/gal., 4301.43
19¢, Tit. 68, § 500.4	Beer: $12.50/barrel; Wine: 9¢/liter; Sparkling wine: 55¢/liter; Spirits: $1.47/liter, Tit. 37a, § 5-101
34¢, 319.020	Liquor monopoly state, 471.745; Beer: $2.60/barrel; Wine ≤14% 67¢/gal.; 14-21% 77¢/gal., 473.030

Table 56: Consumer Taxes—Continued

State	Sales Tax	Use Tax	Cigarette Tax
PENNSYLVANIA	7%, Tit. 72, § 7202	6%, Tit. 72, §7202	$2.60/pack, Tit. 72, § 8206
RHODE ISLAND	7%, 44-18-18; 44-18-20	7%, 44-18-20	$4.25/pack, 44-20-12
SOUTH CAROLINA	5%, 12-36-910	5%, 12-36-1310	57¢/pack, 12-21-620
SOUTH DAKOTA	4.5%, 10-45-2	Same general rates as sales tax: 4,5%, 10-46-2	$1.53/pack, 10-50-3; 10-50-10
TENNESSEE	7%, 67-6-202	7%, 67-6-203	62¢/pack, 67-4-1004
TEXAS	6.25%, Tax § 151.051	6.25%, Tax § 151.101	$1.41/pack, Tax § 154.021
UTAH	5.95%, includes 1.25% mandatory local add-on, 59-12-103	4.75%, 59-12-103	$1.70/pack, 59-14-204
VERMONT	6%, Tit. 32, § 9771	6%, Tit. 32, § 9773	$2.75/pack, Tit. 32, § 7771
VIRGINIA	5.3%, 58.1-603	5.3%, 58.1-604	30¢/pack, 58.1-1001
WASHINGTON	6.5%, 82.08.020	6.5%, 82.12.020	$3.025/pack, 82.24.020
WEST VIRGINIA	6%, 11-15-3	6%, 11-15A-2	55¢/pack, 11-17-3
WISCONSIN	5%, 77.52	5%, 77.53	$2.52/pack, 139.31(1)
WYOMING	4%, 39-15-104	14¢, 39-16-104	60¢/pack, 39-18-104

Gasoline Tax per Gallon	Liquor Tax
57.6¢, Tit. 75, § 9004	Liquor monopoly state; Beer: $2.48/barrel, Tit. 72, § 9003
33¢, 31-36-7	Made in state: Beer: $3.30/barrel; Still wine: $1.40/gal.; from Rhode Island grapes 30¢/gal.; Sparkling wine: 75¢/gal.; Spirits: $5.40/gal., 3-10-1; variable rates for imported malt beverages, 3-10-17
22¢, 12-28-310	General, 12¢/8 oz., unless measured metrically, 50.7¢/liter, 12-33-230; additional 5% on-premise excise tax, 12-33-245; Beer: 77¢/gal.; Wine: 90¢/gal., 12-21-1020
22¢, 10-47B-4	Beer: $8.50/barrel; Wine: 3.2-14% 93¢/gal.; 14-20% $1.45/gal.; 21-24% (except sparkling) $2.07/gal.; All other: $3.93/gal., 35-5-3; additional 2% imposed on all but malt beverages by wholesaler from distiller, manufacturer, or supplier, 35-5-6.1
25¢; 26¢ eff. 7/1/19, 67-3-201	Beer: $4.29/barrel, 57-5-201; Wine: $1.21/gal.; Spirits: $4.40/gal., 57-3-302
20¢, Tax § 162.102	Beer: $6/barrel, Alco. Bev. § 203.01; Malt liquor: >4% 19.8¢/gal. Alco. Bev. § 201.42; Still wine: ≤14% 20.4¢/gal.; >14% 40.8¢/gal.; Sparkling wine: 51.6¢/gal., Alco. Bev. 6 201.04; Spirits $2.40/gal., Alco. Bev. § 201.03
30¢, 59-13-201	Liquor monopoly state; Beer: $12.80/barrel, 59-15-101
30¢, Tit. 23, §3106	Liquor monopoly state; Beer: ≤6% 26.5¢/gal.; 6-8% 55¢/gal.; Wine: 55¢/gal., Tit. 7, § 421; Spirits and fortified wine: 25% of gross revenues, Tit. 7, § 422
16.2¢/gal., 5.1% of average wholesale price of gallon of gasoline, 58.1-2217	Liquor monopoly state; Beer: 25.65¢/gal./barrel; 2¢/bottle ≤7 oz.; 2.65¢/bottle 7-12 oz.; .222¢/oz./bottle >12 oz., 4.1-236; Wine: 40¢/liter; Farm wine and vermouth: 4% of price charged Spirits: 20% of price charged, 4.1-234
49.4¢, 82.36.025	Beer: Low rate $4.782/barrel; high rate $8.08/barrel, 66.24.290; wine: 87¢/gal.; >14% $1.72/gal., 66.24.210; 82.02.030; spirits: 14.47/gal. plus 20.5% of retail sale, 82.08.150
35.7¢, 11-14C-5	Liquor monopoly state; Nonintoxicating beer: $5.50/barrel, 11-16-13; Intoxicating liquor: 5% of purchase price, 60-3A-21
30.9¢, 78.01; 78.015; 78.017	Beer: $2/barrel, 139.02; Wine: ≤14% 6.605¢/liter; 14-21% 11.89¢/liter; all other 85.86¢/liter; administrative fee on all beverages >21%: 3¢/gal.; Other intoxicating liquor: 85.86¢/liter, 139.03
24¢, 39-17-104	Liquor monopoly state; Beer: .5¢/liter; Wine 75¢/liter; Spirits 25¢/liter, 12-3-101

57. PERSONAL INCOME TAX

If you live in Alaska, Florida, Nevada, South Dakota, Texas, Washington, or Wyoming, you may not be aware that most of the rest of the country has to file two tax returns every April. Every other state, aside from these lucky seven, requires income tax—over and above federal taxes—from its citizens.

The drum that all politicians seem to love to beat on both sides of the aisle is "no new taxes," or "lower taxes," or a variant of the two. Both statements appear to be an impossibility, because virtually no states have joined those mentioned above, and, while virtually every state has tweaked with their tax brackets and rates since the last edition, on the whole nothing has really changed. Rates range from 1.22% on the first $36,000 in North Dakota to 8.8% on income over $1,000,000 in New York. The highest rates are found in Rhode Island and Vermont where the rates are 25% and 24%, respectively, but is applied to the total federal tax liability and are not applied directly to the taxpayer's income. The highest rate on income is in Hawaii where a person must pay 11% on income over $400,000.

Six states (and the District of Columbia) have had their income tax schemes challenged in court: Delaware, Illinois, Michigan, Nebraska, Ohio, and Oklahoma. All of these tax codes have been "certified" constitutional by federal courts.

The chart in this chapter deals only with the general principles of state personal income tax. The tax tables are accurate but are very much consolidated and generalized in order to give the reader a broad basis for comparison. The rates listed are, for the most part, for married couples filing jointly or for heads of households. Where this is not the case, the rate is noted. Slightly different rates and tables will apply in most states for couples filing separately or for single individuals. Also, there are countless deductions and exemptions available to the taxpayer that are similar to those available in the federal income tax code. Included here are only the general deductions and exemptions for determining state taxable income. See your state codes or the code of the state in which you are interested for detailed information.

Table 57: Personal Income Tax

State	Code Section	Who Is Required to File
ALABAMA	40-18-1 to 40-18-24.3	Resident natural persons, fiduciaries, estates and trusts, and nonresidents receiving income from property owned or business transacted in the state
ALASKA	Income tax repealed 1980	Individual may file at his or her option to obtain certain tax credits for political donations or expenses for household and child care necessary for employment; credit allowed only if legislature appropriates money, 43.20.013
ARIZONA	43-1011 to 43-1099	All Arizona residents and nonresidents that derive income from activity or ownership of property within the state; partnerships are not taxable
ARKANSAS	26-51-201 to 26-51-207	Resident individuals, estates and trusts, and nonresidents deriving income from local property or activity; partnerships are not taxable
CALIFORNIA	Rev. & Tax §§ 17041 to 17061.5	Resident persons, including estates and trusts; nonresidents and part-year residents are liable for pro-rata share
COLORADO	39-22-104 to 39-22-129	Every individual, estate, and trust that is required to file federal return; non- and part-year residents are liable for pro-rata share; partnerships are not subject to tax
CONNECTICUT	12-700 to 12-746	Each resident individual, trust, and estate with Connecticut taxable income; nonresident individuals, estates, and trusts on Connecticut income
DELAWARE	Tit. 30 §§ 1102 to 1172	Individuals, estates, and trusts with Delaware taxable income; residents and nonresidents of Wilmington are subject to an additional tax of 1.25% on all wages, salaries, commissions, and net profit
DISTRICT OF COLUMBIA	47-1806.01 to 47-1806.14	Any individual domiciled in the district, any resident of 183 days or more, and estates and trusts
FLORIDA	No personal income tax	
GEORGIA	48-7-1 to 48-7-710	Resident individuals with taxable net income on income tax day, December 31, and every individual who, on income tax day has been residing within the state for 183 days or part days of the immediately preceding 365 days.
HAWAII	235-1 to 235-59	Resident individual, estate or trust, and nonresident individual estates or trusts on income derived from Hawaii sources
IDAHO	63-3001 to 63-3087	Resident individuals, estates and trusts with taxable income and nonresident or part-year resident individuals, estates and trusts from Idaho sources; partnerships are not taxable
ILLINOIS	35 §§ 5/201 to 5/250	Individuals, estates, and trusts; partnerships are not taxable
INDIANA	6-3-2-1	Resident individuals, estates and trusts, and nonresidents on adjusted gross income derived from Indiana sources; Partnerships are not taxable

Rate	Federal Income Tax Deductible?	Federal Income Used as Basis?
Single person: First $500, 2%; Next $2,500, 4%; Over $3,000, 5%. Married person: First $1000, 2%; Next $5000, 4%; Over $6000, 5%.	Yes	Yes
N/A	N/A	N/A
Single person: First $10,000, 2.90%; Next $15,000, 3.30%; Next $25,000, 3.90%; Next $100,000, 4.80%; Over $50,000, 5.17% Married person: First $20,000, 2.90%; Next $30,000, 3.30%; Next $50,000, 3.9%; Next $200,000, 4.80%; Over $300,000, 5.17%	No	Yes
First $4,299, 0.9%; Next $4,100, 2.5%; Next $4,200, 3.5%; Next $8,400, 4.5%; Next $14,100, 6%; $35,100 or over, 7%; general rate for all taxpayers; special reduced rates available for low income	No	Yes
First $3,650,1%; Next $8,650, 2%; Next $13,650 4%; Next $18,950, 6%; Next $23,950, 8%; Over $86,934, 9.3%. Head of a Household: First $7300, 1%; Next $10,000, 2%; Next $5000, 4%; Next $5300, 6%; Next $5000, 8%; Over $32,600, $9.300.	No	Yes
4.63% of federal taxable income; general rate for all taxpayers; alternative rates may apply	No	Yes
Individual: First $10,000, 3%; Next $40,000, 5%; Next $50,000, 5.5%; Next $100,000, 6%; Next $50,000; Next $250,000, 6.9%; Over $500,000, 6.99%. Head of Household: First $16,000, 3%; Next $64,000, 5%; Next $80,000, 5.5%; Next $160,000, 6%; Next $80,000, 6.5%; Next $400,000, 6.9%; Over $800,000, 6.99%.	No. But deductions are available for individuals that file to pay federal taxes.	Yes
First $2,000, 2%; Next $3,000, 3.9%; Next $5,000, 3.9%; Next $10,000, 4.8%; Next $5,000, 5.2% Next $35,000, 5.55%; Over $60,000, 6.6%	No	Yes
First $10,000, 4%; Next $30,000, 6%; Next $20,000, 6.5%; Next $290,000, 8.5%; Next $650,000, 8.75%; Over $1,000,000, 8.95%	No	Yes
Single person: First $750, 1%; Next $1,500, 2%; Next $1,500, 3%; Next $1,500, 4%; Next $1,750, 5%; Over $7,000, 7.5%. Head of Household: $1000, 1%; Next $2000, 2%; Next $2000, 3%; Next $2000, 4%; Next $3000, 5%; Over $10,000, 5.75%.	No	Yes
Individual: $4800, 1.40%; Next $4800, 3.20%; Next $9600, 5.50%; Next $9200, 6.40%; Next $9600, 6.80%; Next $9600, 7.20%; Next $24,000, 7.60%; Next $24,000, 7.90%; Next $204,000, 8.25%; Next $50,000, 9%; Next $50,000, 10%; Over $400,000, 11%. Head of Household: First $3600, 1.40%; Next $3600, 3.20%; Next $14,400, 5.50%; Next $7200, 6.40%; Next $7200, 6.80%; Next $7200, 7.20%; Next $18,000, 7.60%; Next $18,000, 7.9%; Next $153,000, 8.25%; Next $37,500, 9%; Next $37,500, 10%; Over $300,000, 11%.	No	Yes
Individual: First $1504, no tax; Next $1504, 3.125%; Next $1503, 3.625%; Next $1504, 4.625%; Next $1504, 5.625%; Next $3760, 6.25%; Over $11,279, 6.95%. Married: First $3008, no tax; Next $3008, 3.125%; Next $3006, 3.625%; Next $3008, 4.625%; Next $3008, 5.625%; Next $7520, 6.625%; Over $22,558, 6.925%.	No	Yes
4.95% of taxable net income imposed on all taxpayers.	No	Yes
3.23% of adjusted gross income; general rate for all resident taxpayers; additional local taxes may be required	No	Yes

Table 57: Personal Income Tax—Continued

State	Code Section	Who Is Required to File
IOWA	422.5 to 422.31	Residents, part-year residents, nonresidents, estates and trusts
KANSAS	79-32, 110 to 79-32,143a	Resident and nonresidents, estates, trusts and fiduciaries
KENTUCKY	141.010 to 141.990	Residents, nonresidents on net income from businesses, trade, professions or other activities carried on in the state or tangible or intangible property located in the state
LOUISIANA	47:31 to 47:79	Residents and nonresidents on Louisiana income; individuals permanently domiciled in the state are taxed on all income from whatever source; all others are taxed on Louisiana income
MAINE	Title 36, §§ 5111 to 5255-B	Every resident: entire taxable income and nonresidents: adjusted gross income, estates, and trusts: entire taxable income
MARYLAND	Tax-Gen. §§ 10-101 to 10-604	Residents and nonresidents on taxable net income. partnerships are not taxed
MASSACHUSETTS	Ch. 62, §§ 1 to 64	Individuals, including fiduciaries, estates of deceased Massachusetts inhabitants, and nonresidents earning income in Massachusetts
MICHIGAN	206.51	Every individual resident of Michigan.
MINNESOTA	290.01 to 290.9744	Resident and nonresident individuals, estates and trusts
MISSISSIPPI	27-7-5 to 27-7-107	Resident individuals, trusts and estates on entire net income
MISSOURI	143.011 to 143.265	Resident individuals, nonresidents with income derived from Missouri sources, and estates and trusts; partnerships are not taxable; local taxes may be required
MONTANA	15-30-2101 to 15-30-2651	Residents on entire net income; nonresidents on net income from property owned and business carried on in Montana
NEBRASKA	77-2701.1; 77-2714 to 77-27,123	Residents on entire income and nonresidents on income derived from Nebraska sources
NEVADA	No personal income tax	
NEW HAMPSHIRE	77:1 to 77:37	Inhabitants and part-year residents, partnerships, associations and trusts, and fiduciaries with income of more than $2,400 per year
NEW JERSEY	54A:1-1 to 54A:10-12	Individuals, estates and trusts, residents and nonresident taxed on gross income; nonresidents are only taxed on income derived from New Jersey sources; partnerships and associations are not taxable; local taxes may be required
NEW MEXICO	7-2-1 to 7-2-36	Residents on net income and nonresidents deriving income from business, employment, or property in New Mexico, including estates and trusts
NEW YORK	Tax §§ 601 to 699	Individuals, estates and trusts, and nonresidents on income derived from New York sources
NORTH CAROLINA	105-153.1 to 105-159	Every individual on North Carolina taxable income, and income of estates and trusts
NORTH DAKOTA	57-38-02 to 57-38-65	Residents and nonresidents on property owned, employment, or business carried on in North Dakota; individuals, estates, and trusts have optional tax available

Rate	Federal Income Tax Deductible?	Federal Income Used as Basis?
First $1,000, 0.36%; Next $1,000, 0.72%; Next $2,000, 2.43%; Next $5,000, 4.50%; Next $6,000, 6.12%; Next $5,000, 6.48%; Next $10,000, 6.80%; Next $15,000, 7.92%; Over $45,000, 8.98%	Yes	Yes
Individuals: First $15,000, 3.1%; Next $15,000, 5.25%; Over $30,000, 5.7%. Married: First $30,000, 3.1%; Next $30,000, 5.25%; Over $60,000, 5.7%.	No	Yes
Tax is 5% on all net income.	No	Yes
First $12,500, 2%; Next $37,500, 4%; Over $50,000, 6%	No	Yes
Individual: First $21,050, 5.8%; Next $28,950, 6.75%; Over $50,000, 7.15%. Head of Household: First $31,500, 5.8%; Next $43,450, 6.75%; Over $75,000, 7.15%.	No	Yes
First $1,000, 2%; Next $1,000, 3%; Next $1,000, 4%; Next $97,000, 4.75%; Next $25,000, 5%; Next $25,000, 5.25%; Next $100,000, 5.5%; Over $250,000, 5.75%	No	Yes
Interest, dividends, 5.95%; short term capital gains, 12%; all other income, 5.3%	No	Yes
4.25% of taxable income	No	Yes
Single person: First $24,270, 5.35%; Next $55,460, 7.05%; Next $70,270, 7.85%; Over $150,000, 9.85%. Married individuals file joint returns: First $35,480, 5.35%; Next $105,480, 7.05%; Next $109,040, 7.85%; Over $250,000, 9.85%.	No	Yes
First $2000, No tax; Next $3000, 3%; Next $5000, 4%; Over $10,000, 5%.	No	No
First $1,000, 1.5%; Next $1,000, 2%; Next $1,000, 2.5%; Next $1,000, 3%; Next $1,000, 3.5%; Next $1,000, 4%; Next $1,000, 4.5%; Next $1,000, 5%; Next $1,000, 5.5%; Over $9,000, 5.7%	Yes	Yes
First $3000, 1%; Next $2200, 2%; Next $2800, 3%; Next $2800, 4%; Next $3100, 5%; Next $4000, 6%; Over $17,900, 6.9%.	Yes	Yes
Single Taxpayers: First $3150, 2.46%; Next $15,730, 3.51%; Next $11,540, 5.01%; Over $30,420, 6.84%. Head of Household: First $5870, 2.46%; Next $24,340, 3.51%; Next $14,900, 5.01%; Over $45110, 6.84.	No	Yes
5%, limited to interest and dividends	No	No
First $20,000, 1.4%; Next $15,000, 1.75%; Next $5,000, 2.45%; Next $5,000, 3.5%; Next $35,000, 5.525%; Next $425,000, 6.37% Over $500,000, 8.97%	No	No
Single person: First $5,500, 1.7%; Next $5,500, 3.2%; Next $5,000, 4.7%; Over $16,000, 4.9%. Head of Household: First $8000, 1.7%; Next $8000, 3.2%; Next $8000, 4.7%; Over $24,000, 4.9%.	No	Yes
First $17,150, 4%; Next $6450, 4.5%; Next $4300, 5.25%; Next $15,100, 5.9%; Next $118,550, 6.21%; Next $161,650, 6.49%; Next $1,832,150, 6.85%; Over $2,155,350, 8.82%.	No	Yes
Tax of 5.75% on all North Carolina taxable income.	No	Yes
First $37,450, 1.10%; Next $87,000, 2.04%; Next $98,550, 2.27%; Next $222,200, 2.64%; Over $411,500, 2.90%.	Yes	Yes

Table 57: Personal Income Tax—Continued

State	Code Section	Who Is Required to File
OHIO	5747.01 to 5747.99	Every individual and estate residing in or earning or receiving income in Ohio
OKLAHOMA	Title 68, §2351 to 2355.2	Resident and nonresident individuals, estates, and trusts on taxable Oklahoma income
OREGON	316.002 to 316.054	Every Oregon resident on entire taxable income and every nonresident or part-year resident on a prorated amount of their entire taxable income; estates and trusts are taxable; partnerships are not taxable; local taxes may be required
PENNSYLVANIA	Tit. 72, §§ 7301 to 7361	Resident and nonresident individuals, estates, or trusts; nonresidents only pay for portion of income derived from Pennsylvania sources
RHODE ISLAND	44-30-1 to 44-30-100	Resident and nonresident individuals, estates, and trusts on Rhode Island income; partnerships are not taxed
SOUTH CAROLINA	12-6-510 to 12-6-640	Individuals, estates, and trusts; part-year and nonresidents are subject to special tax
SOUTH DAKOTA	No personal income tax	
TENNESSEE	67-2-101 to 67-2-123	Resident persons, partnerships, associations, trusts, estates, and corporations
TEXAS	No personal income tax	
UTAH	59-10-101 to 59-10-136	Resident individuals, estates and trusts, and nonresidents on state taxable income derived from Utah sources
VERMONT	Tit. 32, §§ 5821 to 5830d	Residents, nonresidents, estates, and trusts on Vermont income
VIRGINIA	58.1-300 to 58.1-326	Individuals, estates, and trusts
WASHINGTON	No personal income tax	
WEST VIRGINIA	11-21-1 to 11-21-96	Every individual, estate, and trust; special tax on nonresidents with West Virginia income; partnerships are not taxable
WISCONSIN	71.01 to 71.10	Individuals, fiduciaries (except fiduciaries of nuclear decomposing trust or reserve fund), and trusts on net income; nonresident individuals and trusts on income derived from Wisconsin sources
WYOMING	No personal income tax	

Rate	Federal Income Tax Deductible?	Federal Income Used as Basis?
First $10,500, No tax; Next $5300, 1.980%; Next $5300, 2.47%; Next $21,000, 2.96%; Next $42,100, 3.46%; Next $21,100, 3.96%; Next $105,300, 4.597%; Over $210,600, 4.997%	No	Yes
First $1,000, 0.5%; Next $1,500, 1%; Next $1,250, 2%; Next $1,150, 3%; Next $2,300, 4%; Next $1,500, 5%; Remainder, 5.25%	Yes	Yes
First $3,300, 5%; Next $4,950, 7%; Next $116,750, 9%; Over $125,000, 9.9%	Yes	Yes
3.07%	No	No
25% of federal tax	No	Yes
First $2,220, 2.5%; Next $2,220, 3%; Next $2,220, 4%; Next $2,220, 5%; Next $2,220, 6%; Over $11,100, 7%	No	Yes
2%, limited to interest and dividends, not including ordinary commercial paper, trade acceptances and CD's, and certificates of deposit	No	No
4.95%	No	Yes
First $33,950, 3.55%; Next $48,300, 7%; Next $89,300, 8.25%; Next $201,400, 8.9%; Over $372,950, 9.40%	No	Yes
First $3,000, 2%; Next $2,000, 3%; Next $12,000, 5%; Over $17,000, 5.75%	No	Yes
Tax of 6% is imposed on of the federal income tax.	No	Yes
First $7500, 4.40%; Next $7500, 5.84%; Next $210,000, 6.27%; Over $225,000, 7.65%	No	Yes

APPENDIX
STATUTORY COMPILATIONS USED IN THIS BOOK

The code section numbers used in this book refer to sections within the statutory compilations listed below. In those states where multiple compilations are available, the one preferred by **The Bluebook, A Uniform System of Citation,** 20th ed., 2015 (Harvard Law Review Association: Cambridge, Mass.) is used. As a practical matter, the code always used was the official version, and often there is more than one source to find it. Lexis, Westlaw, official states' websites and CaseMaker were used to access the majority of statutes used in this book.

A caution for those users of this book who are not accustomed to statutory code research: some states do not use a universal system of numeration but separately number individually named codes. For these states the individual code names and the abbreviations used in the book are listed.

Table 58: Statutory Compilations

State	Statutory Compilation	Abbreviation
ALABAMA	Code of Alabama 1975	
ALASKA	Alaska Statutes	
ARIZONA	Arizona Revised Statutes	
ARKANSAS	Arkansas Code of 1987 Annotated	
CALIFORNIA	California Code	
	The following are the named codes in the California codification:	
	Business & Professions	Bus. & Prof.
	Civil	Civ.
	Civil Procedure	Civ. Proc.
	Commercial	Com.
	Corporations	Corp.
	Education	Educ.
	Election	Elec.
	Evidence	Evid.
	Family	Fam.
	Financial	Fin.
	Fish and Game	Fish & Game
	Food and Agricultural	Food & Agric.
	Government	Gov't
	Harbors and Navigation	Harb. & Nav.
	Health and Safety	Health & Safety
	Insurance	Ins.
	Labor	Lab.
	Military and Veterans	Mil. & Vt.
	Penal	Penal

Table 58: Statutory Compilations—Continued

State	Statutory Compilation	Abbreviation
	Probate	Prob.
	Public Contract	Pub. Cont.
	Public Resources	Pub. Res.
	Public Utilities	Pub. Util.
	Revenue and Taxation	Rev. & Tax
	Streets and Highways	Sts. & High.
	Unemployment Insurance	Unemp. Ins.
	Vehicle	Veh.
	Water	Water
	Welfare and Institutions	Welf. & Inst.
COLORADO	Colorado Revised Statutes	
CONNECTICUT	Connecticut General Statutes	
DELAWARE	Delaware Code Annotated	
DISTRICT OF COLUMBIA	District of Columbia Code	
FLORIDA	Florida Statutes	
GEORGIA	Official Code of Georgia Annotated	
HAWAII	Hawaii Revised Statutes	
IDAHO	Idaho Code	
ILLINOIS	Illinois Compiled Statutes	
INDIANA	Indiana Code	
IOWA	Code of Iowa	
KANSAS	Kansas Statutes Annotated	
KENTUCKY	Kentucky Revised Statutes Annotated	
LOUISIANA	Louisiana Statutes	
	Louisiana Children's Code	
	Louisiana Civil Code	
	Louisiana Code of Civil Procedure	
	Louisiana Code of Criminal Procedure	
	Louisiana Code of Evidence	
MAINE	Maine Revised Statutes	
MARYLAND	Code of Maryland	
	The following are the named codes in the Maryland codification:	
	Agriculture	Agric.
	Alcoholic Beverages	Al. Bev.
	Business Occupations and Professions	Bus. Occ. & Prof.
	Business Regulation	Bus. Reg.
	Commercial Law	Com. Law
	Corporations and Associations	Corps. & Ass'ns.
	Correctional Services	Corr. Servs.
	Courts and Judicial Proceedings	Cts. & Jud. Proc.

Table 58: Statutory Compilations—Continued

State	Statutory Compilation	Abbreviation
	Criminal Law	Crim. Law
	Criminal Procedure	Crim. Proc.
	Economic Development	Econ. Dev.
	Education	Educ.
	Election Law	Elec. Law
	Environment	Envir.
	Estates and Trusts	Est. & Trusts
	Family Law	Fam. Law
	Financial Institutions	Fin. Inst.
	General Provisions	Gen. Provis.
	Health-General	Health-Gen. I
	Health Occupations	Health Occ.
	Housing and Community Development	Hous. & Cmty. Dev.
	Human Services	Hum. Servs.
	Insurance	Ins.
	Labor and Employment	Lab. & Empl.
	Land Use	Land Use
	Local Government	Local Gov't
	Natural Resources	Nat. Res.
	Public Safety	Pub. Safety
	Public Utilities	Pub. Util.
	Real Property	Real Prop.
	State Finance and Procurement	State Fin. & Proc.
	State Government	State Gov't
	State Personnel and Pensions	State Pers. & Pens.
	Tax-General	Tax-Gen.
	Tax-Property	Tax-Prop.
	Transportation	Transp.
MASSACHUSETTS	Massachusetts General Laws	
MICHIGAN	Michigan Compiled Laws	
MINNESOTA	Minnesota Statutes	
MISSISSIPPI	Mississippi Code Annotated	
MISSOURI	Missouri Revised Statutes	
MONTANA	Montana Code Annotated	
NEBRASKA	Nebraska Revised Statutes	
NEVADA	Nevada Revised Statutes	
NEW HAMPSHIRE	New Hampshire Revised Statutes Annotated	
NEW JERSEY	New Jersey Statutes	
NEW MEXICO	Michie's New Mexico Statutes Annotated	
NEW YORK	New York Consolidated Laws Service	
	The following are the named codes in the New York codification:	

Table 58: Statutory Compilations—Continued

State	Statutory Compilation	Abbreviation
	Abandoned Property	Aband. Prop.
	Agricultural Conservation and Adjustment	Agric. Conserv. & Adj.
	Agriculture and Markets	Agric. & Mkts
	Alcoholic Beverage Control	Alco. Bev Cont
	Alternative County Government	Alt County Gov't
	Arts and Cultural Government	Arts & Cult. Aff.
	Banking	Banking
	Benevolent Orders	Ben. Ord.
	Business Corporations	Bus. Corp.
	Canal	Canal
	Civil Practice Law and Rules	N.Y. C.P.L.R.
	Civil Rights	Civ. Rights
	Civil Service	Civ. Serv.
	Cooperative Corporations	Coop. Corp.
	Correction	Correct.
	County	County
	Criminal Procedure	Crim. Proc.
	Debtor and Creditor	Debt. & Cred.
	Domestic Relations	Dom. Rel.
	Economic Development	Econ. Dev.
	Education	Educ.
	Elder	Elder
	Election	Elec.
	Eminent Domain Procedure Law	Em. Dom. Proc.
	Employers' Liability	Empl'rs Liab.
	Energy	Energy
	Environmental Conservation	Envtl. Conserv.
	Estates, Powers and Trusts	Est. Powers & Trusts
	Executive	Exec.
	Financial Services	Fin. Serv.
	General Association	Gen. Ass'ns
	General Business	Gen. Bus.
	General City	Gen. City
	General Construction	Gen. Constr.
	General Municipal	Gen. Mun.
	General Obligations	Gen. Oblig.
	Highway	High.
	Indian	Indian
	Insurance	Ins.
	Judiciary	Jud.
	Judiciary Court Acts	Jud. Ct. Acts

Table 58: Statutory Compilations—Continued

State	Statutory Compilation	Abbreviation
	Labor	Lab.
	Legislative	Legis.
	Lien	Lien
	Limited Liability Company	Ltd. Liab. Co.
	Local Finance	Local Fin.
	Mental Hygiene	Mental Hyg.
	Military	Mil.
	Multiple Dwelling	Mult. Dwell.
	Multiple Residence	Mult. Res.
	Municipal Home Rule and Statute of Local Governments	Mun. Home Rule
	Navigation	Nav.
	Not-for-Profit Corporation	Not-for-Profit Corp.
	Optional County Government	Opt. County Govt.
	Parks, Recreation and Historic Preservation	Parks, Rec. & Hist. Preserv.
	Partnership	P'Ship
	Penal	Penal
	Personal Property	Pers. Prop.
	Private Housing Finance	Priv. Hous. Fin.
	Public Authorities	Pub. Auth.
	Public Buildings	Pub. Bldgs.
	Public Health	Pub. Health
	Public Housing	Pub. Hous.
	Public Lands	Pub. Lands
	Public Officers	Pub. Off.
	Public Service	Pub. Serv.
	Racing, Pari-Mutuel Wagering and Breeding	Rac. Pari-Mut. Wag. & Breed.
	Railroad	R.R.
	Rapid Transit	Rapid Trans.
	Real Property	Real Prop.
	Real Property Actions and Proceedings	Real Prop. Acts.
	Real Property Tax	Real Prop. Tax
	Religious Corporations	Relig. Corp.
	Retirement and Social Security	Retire. & Soc. Sec.
	Rural Electric Cooperative	Rural Elec. Coop.
	Second Class Cities	Second Class Cities
	Social Services	Soc. Serv.
	Soil and Water Conservation Districts	Soil & Water Conserv. Dist.
	State	State
	State Administrative Procedure Act	A.P.A.
	State Finance	State Fin.
	State Printing and Public Documents	State Print. & Pub. Doc.

Table 58: Statutory Compilations—Continued

State	Statutory Compilation	Abbreviation
	State Technology	State Tech.
	Statutes	Stat.
	Surrogate's Court Procedure Act	Surr. Ct. Proc. Act
	Tax	Tax
	Town	Town
	Transportation	Transp.
	Transportation Corporations	Transp. Corp.
	Uniform Commercial Code	U.C.C.
	Unconsolidated	Unconsol.
	Vehicle and Traffic	Veh. & Traf.
	Village	Vill.
	Volunteer Ambulance Workers' Benefit	Vol. Ambul. Workers' Ben.
	Volunteer Firefighters' Benefit	Vol. Fire. Ben.
	Workers' Compensation	Workers' Comp.
NORTH CAROLINA	General Statutes of North Carolina	
NORTH DAKOTA	North Dakota Century Code	
OHIO	Ohio Revised Code Annotated	
OKLAHOMA	Oklahoma Statutes	
OREGON	Oregon Revised Statutes	
PENNSYLVANIA	Pennsylvania Consolidated Statutes	
RHODE ISLAND	General Laws of Rhode Island	
SOUTH CAROLINA	Code of Laws of South Carolina 1976 Annotated	
SOUTH DAKOTA	South Dakota Codified Laws	
TENNESSEE	Tennessee Code Annotated	
TEXAS	Vernon's Texas Codes Annotated	
	Vernon's Texas Revised Civil Statutes Annotated	
	The following are the named codes found in the new Texas Code Annotated codification:	
	Agriculture	Agric.
	Alcoholic Beverage	Alco. Bev.
	Business and Commerce	Bus. & Com.
	Business Organizations	Bus. Orgs.
	Civil Practice and Remedies	Civ. Prac. & Rem.
	Education	Educ.
	Election	Elec.
	Estates	Est.
	Family	Fam.
	Finance	Fin.
	Government	Gov't
	Health and Safety	Health & Safety
	Human Resources	Hum. Res.

Table 58: Statutory Compilations—Continued

State	Statutory Compilation	Abbreviation
	Insurance	Ins.
	Labor	Lab.
	Local Government	Loc. Gov't
	Natural Resources	Nat. Res.
	Occupations	Occ.
	Parks and Wildlife	Parks & Wild.
	Penal	Penal
	Property	Prop.
	Special District Local Laws	Spec. Dists
	Tax	Tax
	Transportation	Transp.
	Utilities	Util.
	Water	Water
	Vernon's Texas Revised Civil Statutes Annotated	
	Vernon's Texas Code of Criminal Procedure Annotated	
UTAH	Utah Code Annotated	
VERMONT	Vermont Statutes Annotated	
VIRGINIA	Code of Virginia 1950 Annotated	
WASHINGTON	Revised Code of Washington Annotated	
WEST VIRGINIA	West Virginia Code	
WISCONSIN	Wisconsin Statutes	
WYOMING	Wyoming Statutes Annotated	